The Very Best
Baby Name
Book

Bruce Lansky

Meadowbrook Press
Distributed by Simon & Schuster
New York

Library of Congress Cataloging-in-Publication Data

Lansky, Bruce.
    The very best baby name book in the whole wide world / by Bruce Lansky.
        p. cm.
    ISBN 0-88166-520-7 (Meadowbrook)   ISBN 0-684-04703-9 (Simon & Schuster)
    1. Names, Personal--Dictionaries. I. Title.
    CS2377.L36 2006
    929.4'4--dc22

                            2006026225

Editors: Megan McGinnis, Angela Wiechmann
Editorial Assistants: Alicia Ester, Andrea Patch, Maureen Burns
Production Manager: Paul Woods
Graphic Design Manager: Tamara Peterson
Researcher and Translator: David Rochelero
Researcher: Kelsey Anderson
Cover Art: RubberBall

Published by Meadowbrook Press, 5451 Smetana Drive, Minnetonka, Minnesota 55343

www.meadowbrookpress.com

BOOK TRADE DISTRIBUTION by Simon and Schuster, a division of Simon and Schuster, Inc.,
1230 Avenue of the Americas, New York, New York 10020

09 08 07 06   10 9 8 7 6 5 4 3 2 1

Printed in the United States of America

Contents

Introduction

Searching for just the right name for your baby can be a pleasure if you have just the right book. Let me tell you why I think *The Very Best Baby Name Book* is the right book.

It contains the most names—complete with origins, meanings, variations, fascinating facts, and famous namesakes—of any book in its price range. Here you'll find the most names from major ethnic origins, such as:

- Nearly 7,000 American names, many of which African-American families choose for their children

- Over 5,000 names Hispanic families commonly use

- Over 4,000 French names; 9,000 English names; 6,000 Latin names; 4,000 Irish names; and 6,000 Greek names

- Nearly 6,000 Hebrew names; 2,500 Arabic names; and 4,000 German names

- Thousands of Scottish, Welsh, Italian, Russian, Japanese, Chinese, Scandinavian, Polish, Native American, Hawaiian, African, and Hindi names.

But there's more in *The Very Best Baby Name Book* than just pages and pages of names. Don't miss the step-by-step guide "How to Pick a Name You and Your Baby Will Love." In three simple steps, complete with easy-to-use worksheets, you can select a name that has personal meaning but is also practical. It's the perfect approach for parents who find the idea of reading over 60,000 baby names a bit overwhelming.

"How to Pick a Unique Version of a Popular Name" is an all-new feature you're sure to love. It's filled with helpful tips for parents-to-be who want to infuse a popular name with a unique twist. Also new to this edition are quick and easy instructions for planning a fun Name-the-Baby Shower, brought to you by Becky Long, special-event planner and author of *Themed Baby Showers* (Meadowbrook Press). It's packed with name-themed ideas for everything from invitations to activities to food. Who knows? A Name-the-Baby Shower may just help you pick the perfect name for your baby!

You'll also find over 300 fun, helpful lists that will get you brainstorming names. This includes the latest lists of the top 100 girls' and boys' names. The top 100 lists are now complete with data to help you compare rankings from the previous year's lists, so you can see which names are climbing, which are falling, and which are holding steady. To quickly see what's hot and what's not, check out the Changes in the Top 100. And to find the most popular names in the Girls' Names and Boys' Names sections, look for the special ☙ icon. If you're expecting a double dose of joy, take a look at the lists of the most popular names for twins. Lastly, if you're interested in tracking names over the years or just looking for a timeless name, you'll love the lists of popular names over the last one hundred years, now also complete with comparison rankings from decade to decade.

Want to know what parents in Canada, Australia, Sweden, and Japan are naming their babies? Want to find that perfect name to reflect your heritage? *The Very Best Baby Name Book* features lists of popular names around the world as well as lists of common and interesting names from many different origins. Want to name your baby after your favorite movie star, religious figure, or locale? Check out the lists featuring names inspired by people, places, and things. These lists will get you thinking about names that have special meaning to you. In addition to the 300 fun lists, you'll find features about the names celebrities choose for their babies and for themselves, as well as a helpful Baby Name Legal Guide and hilarious Fascinating Facts about Names.

The Very Best Baby Name Book also has an exclusive new feature to help parents make informed choices about names. Recently, naming trends have been heading in less traditional directions. One such trend is to use traditional boys' names for girls and vice versa. Throughout the Girls' Names and Boys' Names sections, you'll find special icons highlighting names that are shared by both genders. The icons will indicate whether a shared name is used mostly for boys (**B**), used mostly for girls (**G**), or used about evenly by both genders (**BG**). Some parents want androgynous or gender-jumping names, and other parents want names with clear gender identification. Either way, the icons will help you make an informed choice.

As you browse the names with these special icons, you may be surprised to learn that certain names are shared. It's important to keep several factors in mind:

1. The data may include errors. Amanda is listed in the boys' section because records show that 1 out of every 100,000 boys are named Amanda. It's reasonable to think that some boy "Amandas" are simply recording errors, but perhaps some aren't.

2. Names have different roles in different cultures. In the U.S., Andrea is primarily a girls' name, whereas in Italy, it's often used as a boys' name (for example, opera star Andrea Bocelli).

3. This book defines a name by its spelling, not by its pronunciation or meaning. This explains why a name like Julian is listed as a shared name. Julian (pronounced "JOO-lee-en") is a form of Julius, and therefore in the Boys' Names section. Julian (pronounced "Joo-lee-ANN") is a form of Julianne, and therefore in the Girls' Names section. You could argue that these are two different names, but because this book defines a name by its spelling, it treats them as one name.

4. The gender "assignment" of names change—often in surprising ways. For years, Ashley was used often for boys. (Remember Ashley Wilkes in *Gone with the Wind?*) Twenty-five years ago, it was in the top 300 of boys' names. Today it doesn't crack the top 1000, whereas it's the eighth-most-popular name for girls. In 2000, over twice as many boys than girls were named Reese. By 2004, actress Reese Witherspoon had helped those numbers switch places—now nearly twice as many girls than boys are named Reese.

I hope you find this book fun, helpful, and easy to use as you search for just the right name that will help your baby put his or her best foot forward in life.

Bruce Lansky

How to Pick a Name You and Your Baby Will Like

The first edition of *The Best Baby Name Book in the Whole Wide World*, which I wrote back in 1978, had about 10,000 names on 120 pages. So, you could read the introductory material about "15 Things to Consider When You Name Your Baby" and browse all the main listings (and even pause to read the origins, meanings, and variations for names that appealed to you) in a few hours. It's something a couple could even do together.

The Very Best Baby Name Book has more than 60,000 names on 540 pages. I don't know how long it would take you and your partner to browse all the main listings and pause to read more about your favorites, but it could be a daunting task. If you're up to the challenge, go for it. You'll certainly find your favorite names and discover some new names as well.

But if the idea of wading through a sea of 60,000 names sounds overwhelming, I'd like to propose another method. The method I suggest involves generating lists of names you and your partner love and then narrowing down the lists based on how well the names might work for your baby. It's a fun, easy way to come up with a name that has special meaning but is practical as well. Let's get started.

Step 1: Make a List of Names with Special Meaning

Make a list of names to consider by writing down your answers to the following questions. (You each will make your own list.) These questions are based on the lists starting on page 14. Browse those lists to help you answer the questions and to brainstorm other questions specific to your background, preferences, and experiences.

Popular Names (pages 14–19)

What are your favorite names from the most recent Top 100 lists?
What are your favorite names from the lists of most popular names over the past 100 years?
If any of your relatives' names appear in the popularity lists from previous generations, what are your favorites?

Names around the World (pages 30–38)

What country are your parents or grandparents from? What country are you and your partner from?

If any of your relatives' names appear in the international lists, what are your favorites?

What are your favorite names that are currently popular in other countries?

What language(s) do you speak?

Where did you honeymoon?

Where do you like to vacation?

Where did you conceive?

Impressions Names Make (pages 39–44)

What might your baby's personality be like?

How might your baby look physically?

What impression would you like your baby's name to make about him/her?

Names Inspired by People, Places, and Things (pages 45–88)

Who are your favorite literary figures?

Who are your favorite historical figures?

Who are your favorite figures from religion and mythology?

Who are your favorite figures from movies and television?

Who are your favorite musicians? What are your favorite songs?

Who are your favorite sports figures?

What are your favorite natural elements and places?

What are your favorite other ideas for names (last names as first names, old-fashioned names, etc.)?

Once you answer these questions, turn to the Girls' Names and Boys' Names sections to find interesting spellings or variations based on the names from your list. (As you flip through the book, you might stumble across a few new names that capture your attention, too.) That will give you a long list of names to consider for the next step.

Step 2:   Narrow the List Based on What Will Work Best for Your Baby

Now that you've each created a list based on personal considerations, it's time to narrow them down based on practical considerations. This way, you'll choose a name that works well for you and for your baby. You may love a particular name, but if it doesn't hold up to these basic criteria, your baby probably won't love it. It can be unpleasant going through life with a name that for whatever reason doesn't work for you.

Make enough copies of the table on the following page for each name on your list. Have your partner do the same. Rate each name on twelve factors. Example: Consider the popularity of the name Jacob—if you think there might be too many Jacobs in his school, check "too popular." Consider nicknames—if you love Jake, check "appealing." Another example: Consider the way Rafael sounds to you—if it's music to your ears, check "pleasing." Consider its fit with your last name—if you don't think it goes so well with Abramovitz, check "doesn't fit."

When you've completed the table, add up the score by giving three points for every check in the Positive column, two points for every check in the Neutral column, and one point for every check in the Negative column. Scoring each name might help make the subjective process of selecting a name more objective to you.

(Note: If you're pinched for time, mentally complete the table for each name, keeping track of a rough score. The important part is to narrow the list to your top five boys' and girls' names.)

Name:_____

Factors	Positive	Neutral	Negative
1. Spelling	❑ easy	❑ medium	❑ hard
2. Pronunciation	❑ easy	❑ medium	❑ hard
3. Sound	❑ pleasing	❑ okay	❑ unpleasing
4. Last Name	❑ fits well	❑ fits okay	❑ doesn't fit
5. Gender ID	❑ clear	❑ neutral	❑ unclear
6. Nicknames	❑ appealing	❑ okay	❑ unappealing
7. Popularity	❑ not too popular	❑ popular	❑ too popular
8. Uniqueness	❑ not too unique	❑ unique	❑ too unique
9. Impression	❑ positive	❑ okay	❑ negative
10. Namesakes	❑ positive	❑ okay	❑ negative
11. Initials	❑ pleasing	❑ okay	❑ unpleasing
12. Meaning	❑ positive	❑ okay	❑ negative

Final Score:_____

Step 3:   Make the Final Choice

List your top five boys' and girls' names in the chart below, and have your partner do the same. It's now time to share the names. If you have names in common, compare your scores; perhaps average them. If you have different names on your lists, swap names and rate them using the same table as before. In the end, you'll have a handful of names that work well for you, your partner, and your baby. Now all you have to do is make the final decision. Good luck!

Mom's Top Five Names

1._____ Mom's Score: _____ Dad's Score: _____
2._____ Mom's Score: _____ Dad's Score: _____
3._____ Mom's Score: _____ Dad's Score: _____
4._____ Mom's Score: _____ Dad's Score: _____
5._____ Mom's Score: _____ Dad's Score: _____

Dad's Top Five Names

1._____ Dad's Score: _____ Mom's Score: _____
2._____ Dad's Score: _____ Mom's Score: _____
3._____ Dad's Score: _____ Mom's Score: _____
4._____ Dad's Score: _____ Mom's Score: _____
5._____ Dad's Score: _____ Mom's Score: _____

How to Pick a Unique Version of a Popular Name

Every year, expectant parents eagerly await the Social Security Administration's latest top 100 lists for boys' and girls' names in the United States (see pages 15–16). Many parents-to-be like the security and familiarity of popular names. They see them as the "best of the best." After all, Emily and Jacob couldn't become the number one names unless lots of people liked them!

However, it's important to note that the popularity issue cuts two ways: Psychologists say a child with a popular name seems to have better odds of success than a child with an uncommon name, but a child whose name is at the top of the popularity poll may not feel as unique and special as a child whose name is less common. Looking from a child's perspective, nothing contributes quite so much to the feeling that you're not unique as when you share your name with several classmates. Then again, it's one thing for a name to make you feel "unique" and "special," but another thing to make you feel "different" and "odd."

Perhaps a good compromise is to select a unique version of a popular name for your baby. This involves taking a popular name and customizing it with a touch of individuality. Here are some tips to help you do just that:

1. Choose a Variation.

One easy way to select a unique version of a popular name is to look for variations of a top 100 name you like. In the Girls' Names and Boys' Names sections of this book, you can find variations in two ways. One, look for italicized names listed under a main entry. Two, look for bold main entries that have "a form of [root name]" as their meaning. For example, Jake and Kobi are variations you might want to consider for Jacob. If you're worried that William is too popular, you might want to consider less-popular variations Will and Liam. For girls, Emilia and Emmaline are forms of Emily. (It's interesting to point out that Emma is also a variation of Emily. As Emily became more popular, parents viewed Emma as a fresh

variation. But as it turned out, thousands of parents had the same idea, so now this "unique" variation is ironically the number two name in its own right.)

2. Choose a "Name-Book Neighbor."

Go to the Girls' Names or Boys' Names section, find your favorite name from the popularity lists, and scan the names on the page before, the facing page, or the page after. You'll probably come across variations of the name (which we discussed above), but you'll also find "name-book neighbors." These names contain some of the same letters and sounds as the popular name, but they may have different origins and meanings and are often more unique. Sticking with the example of Emily, you'll find the name-book neighbor Emory (a name so good they used it for a top-flight university). For Olivia, you'll find Olinda and Olympia. For fellas, a name-book neighbor of Matthew is Mathias, and a name-book neighbor of Michael is Micah.

3. Change the Spelling.

If you like the sound of a popular name but want to give it a unique treatment, an easy trick is to change the spelling. You can make the change as subtle (Hannah to Hanna) or dramatic (Michael to Mikkel) as you wish. One interesting study in spelling is the name Haley, for which you can mix-and-match *Ha-*, *Hae-*, *Hai-*, and *Hay-* with *-lea*, *-lee*, *-leigh*, *-ley*, *-lie*, *-li*, and *-ly*. As if that weren't enough, you can also double the *l* in any one of these options. The main concern with the spelling approach is that people may not spell or pronounce the name correctly—a daily inconvenience that could frustrate your child. That said, sometimes variant spellings become common names on their own. One example is Aiden, which is ranked only a few notches below the original spelling of Aidan in the boys' top 100. In the girls' top 100, you'll find variant spellings that have surpassed the original spellings in popularity. There's Kaitlyn and Katelyn (but not Caitlin) and Makayla (but not Michaela).

4. Combine Names.

An additional way to put a unique twist on a popular name is to combine it with another name. You can make a double name separated by a space or a hyphen, such as John Paul or Mary-Kate, or you can also make a single name, such as Michaelangelo or Emmalee (which you can pronounce as "Emma Lee" or "Emily"). This technique is especially easy with girls' names, because names like Lyn, Lee, Ann, Tina, Lisa, and Ella blend well with other names. For boys, names like Jay, Bert, and Shawn combine well. If you want to add a personal touch to a combination name, combine your own names or the names of special relatives. If your names are Mary and Lee, combine them to get Marlee. If the grandfathers' names are William and Tony, combine them to get Wilton. The possibilities are endless—but keep in mind that sometimes the results can be quite silly (for example, combining Raymond with Darla can produce Raydar).

5. Add a Prefix or Suffix.

In addition to combining a popular name with another name, you can also add a prefix or suffix to it. This is especially prevalent with names of American origin used by African-African families. Common prefixes are *Da-, De-, Le-, La-, Sha-, Ja-,* and *Ta-*. Common suffixes are *-a, -ia, -ina, -ita, -la, -en, -o, -ta, -te, -us,* and *-y.* When you add these to popular names, you get unique versions of popular names such as Lakayla, Deanthony Sarita, and Josephus. Throughout history, the suffix *-son* has been used to link a father's name to a son's name, as in the case of Jackson and Jameson. These names have since become last names, but they're still commonly used as first names for boys *and* girls. Borrowing from this custom, you can add a twist to a popular name (or perhaps your own name) by adding *-son*.

6. Use an Ethnic Variation.

If you like the name John but find it too popular, consider giving it an ethnic spin: Sean (Irish), Zane (English), Gian (Italian), Hans (Scandinavian) Janne (Finnish), Honza (Czech), Ian (Scottish), Janek (Polish), Jan (Dutch and Slavic), Jean (French), Johann (German), Jens (Danish), Juan (Spanish), or even Keoni (Hawaiian). For girls, Katherine has many interesting ethnic variations, including Ekaterina (Russian), Kasia (Polish), and Kathleen (Irish). You may choose an ethnic variation to reflect your heritage, or perhaps you'll simply choose an ethnic name on its own merits. (Just be careful when you pair the first name with your last name; you might get strange results like Juan Kowalski.)

As you can see, there are several ways to make a unique version of a popular name. With these techniques, you can stray a little or a lot from a popular name, depending on your comfort level and your imagination. In the end, you may come up with a name that's the best of both worlds.

Name-the-Baby Shower

by Becky Long

This baby shower will not only honor the expectant parents, but it also may help them discover just the right name for their bundle of joy.

Invitations

- Buy a package of alphabet letter stencils. (You can find them at any craft or art supply store.) Write shower details on small tag cards, then use decorative thread to tie each to a stencil. Ask guests to come up with favorite boys' and girls' names that begin with the same letter as the stencil, write the names on their stencils, and bring them to the party. Give a prize to the guest whose stencil has the most baby names.

- Burn songs whose titles feature boys' or girls' names onto a CD and make a copy for each guest. See the Name Tunes game on page 11 for a list of suggested songs. Write party particulars on the CD label.

- Print shower specifics on the lower half of a blank note card. Place a decorative alphabet letter sticker on the upper half. Ask guests to bring a list of baby names that begin with their assigned letters to the party.

Decorations

- Use a collection of alphabet-related toys like wooden puzzles, magnetic letters, and blocks to spell various baby names throughout the party space. Present the toys to the mom-to-be at the end of the shower as gifts for baby. Likewise, add large decorative labels to common household objects that can double as potential baby names. The following list can get you started: Matt (on doormat), Crystal (on crystal vase), Rose (on rose in the vase), Art (on artwork), and John (on toilet).

- If the parents-to-be have narrowed the field of names but still need help with the final selection, consider making it a political "party" by decorating in an election motif. Write the list of name "candidates" on a mock ballot; be sure to include room for write-in candidates. Make a copy for each guest. Set up a ballot booth where each guest can vote for a favorite name. Download free clipart of a Democratic donkey and Republican elephant from the Internet. Make several copies and have some of them enlarged. Add a pink hair bow to one symbol, a blue bow tie to the other, and diapers to both. Post them all around the party space.

- Invite guests to become interactive decorations. Before the party, cut alphabet letters from construction paper, then pin one to each guest's back upon arrival. Or present each with a shirt that features an iron-on letter. (These can also serve as party favors.) While wearing the various consonants and vowels, guests mingle and attempt to spell names for the expectant parents' consideration. During the party, award small prizes to guests who collectively spell an original boys' or girls' name with the letters on their shirts.

Games & Activities

- The Name of the Game works as a great icebreaker. Give each guest a blank sheet of paper and a pencil and ask them to write down a favorite first and middle name combination for the baby. After each has completed this step, set a timer for five minutes and see who can create the longest list of additional names using only the letters in the first and middle name combination. Guests earn one point for each baby name that also appears on another guest's list, and they earn two points for each name that appears on only their lists. Present a prize to the person who scores the most points. (Tip: Don't tell guests the goal of the game until after each has first written down a favorite first and middle name combination.)

- Play Name Tunes to test guests' pop music savvy. Before the party, burn a CD of songs whose titles feature boys' or girls' names. To play the game, play snippets of each song and ask guests to write down the name of the artist who made the song famous. Award a gift certificate to a local music store to the guest who provides the most correct answers. The following list can get you started:

> "Roxanne" (The Police)
>
> "Daniel" (Elton John)
>
> "Maria Maria" (Santana)
>
> "A Boy Named Sue" (Johnny Cash)
>
> "Angie" (The Rolling Stones)
>
> "Fernando" (ABBA)
>
> "Beth" (KISS)
>
> "You Can Call Me Al" (Paul Simon)
>
> "Peggy Sue" (Buddy Holly)
>
> "Joey" (Bon Jovi)
>
> "Cecilia" (Simon and Garfunkel)
>
> "Johnny B. Goode" (Chuck Berry)
>
> "Joanna" (Kool & the Gang)
>
> "James Dean" (Eagles)
>
> "Lola" (The Kinks)
>
> "Ben" (Michael Jackson)

(Tip: Use different songs if you plan to use this idea for your invitations so guests won't know the answers before the party.)

- Divide guests into two teams for a game of Namedropper. Before the party, write names from each team's list (see next column) on separate slips of paper and place them in team baskets. To play, have a player from Team A draw a slip from her team's basket. Immediately set a timer for one minute. Using only six one-word clues, that player must try to get her teammates to guess the name on her slip before time's up. She can't say that name or any of its variations. If her team says the name in time, it earns a point. If not, the other team makes one guess, and if correct, earns two points. Alternate play between the teams until all names have been dropped.

Team A	Team B
Bo Peep	George Foreman
Tiger Woods	Oprah Winfrey
Martha Stewart	Albert Einstein
William Shakespeare	Cinderella
Madonna	John Wayne
Benjamin Franklin	Cindy Crawford
Julia Roberts	Elvis Presley
Leonardo da Vinci	Cher
Brooke Shields	Brett Favre
Jimmy Buffett	Minnie Mouse
Wilma Flintstone	Mark Twain
Sylvester Stallone	Vanna White
Mary Poppins	Clark Kent
Shaquille O'Neal	Paris Hilton
Ginger Rogers	Jeff Gordon
Matt Lauer	Carol Burnett
Ariel	Calvin Klein
Bill Cosby	Mary Lou Retton
J. K. Rowling	Charlie Brown
TomKat	Brangelina

- For nametag fun, have guests try translating their names into Hawaiian. Before the party, visit a website like www.alohafriendsluau.com/names.html, then print copies for the guests. This activity may help the expectant parents discover the perfect name for baby!

Gifts

- If the parents-to-be have revealed the sex of the baby, ask guests to bring gifts that correspond to potential baby names. Here are some suggested names and corresponding gifts: Jewel (jewelry box), Jasmine (Disney goodies), Noah (toy ark), or Aaron (tee-ball set).

- As a great group gift, present the mom-to-be with a gift certificate for a personalized bracelet that features her baby's name. Gift certificates to stores that personalize nursery items are also sure to be a hit.

- Play Naming Rights as the mom-to-be opens the presents. Before the party, wrap a small prize. Before the gift opening, quietly tell the guests to pass the package to the right any time the mom-to-be says a guest's name. Keep the activity a secret from the mom-to-be until she opens her last gift. Whoever is holding the prize at that time gets to take it home.

Favors

- Send each guest home with a copy of the CD you made for the Name Tunes game. If you used the songs in the Name Tunes game for your invitations, compile a second volume with other songs.

- Buy personalized note cards for guests or make bookmarks that feature each guest's first name or initial. Include information about the meaning of the name on an attached tag card.

Food

Turn to page 77 for a list of baby names that can also represent food and beverages. There you just might find the perfect name for mom's little "bun in the oven." Following are recipes that salute Brie, a popular name for baby girls, and Kale, a unique option for a baby boy. Both dips happen to taste great with slices of Pita (another name option for a little girl). Create a menu card for your buffet table that features the baby names in pink or blue fancy font. Also include information about the meaning of the name and its variations.

Brie Appetizer

8-ounce round Brie
½ cup peach preserves
½ teaspoon nutmeg
2 tablespoons sliced almonds

Preheat oven to 400°F. Slice top rind from cheese and discard. Place cheese in baking pan. Mix preserves with nutmeg in bowl and spread evenly on top of cheese. Sprinkle with almonds. Bake for 12 minutes until cheese melts slightly. Serve warm.

Kale Pâté

½ bunch kale (2 cups torn and tightly packed)
¼ cup olive oil
1½ teaspoons minced garlic (1 teaspoon reserved)
16-ounce can butter beans, drained
2 cups shredded mozzarella
1 cup sour cream
8-ounce package cream cheese, softened
2 tablespoons butter, softened
1 tablespoon minced onion
1 teaspoon allspice
1 teaspoon pepper
1 teaspoon salt

Wash kale and tear leaves from stems into bite-size pieces. Heat skillet over medium-low heat. Add olive oil and ½ teaspoon minced garlic. Stir in kale leaves. Cover and sauté for two minutes until kale wilts slightly. Remove from heat. Blend reserved garlic and remaining ingredients in food processor. Add kale. Chill and serve. Yield: 4 cups

Name Cake

Prepare your favorite bundt cake or use the following recipe if you know the sex of the baby. When finished, thread small decorative alphabet beads onto thin ribbon. (You can find beads in the jewelry department of a craft store.) Place the beaded ends of the ribbons in the center of the cake and drape the other ends over the sides. (Note: Ice cake with a glaze instead of frosting. Ribbons will get messy in frosting.) Before serving, have each guest pull out a ribbon and suggest a baby's name that starts with the letter on the bead.

Pink Cake*

18.25-ounce box white cake mix
4 eggs
⅔ cup vegetable oil
3-ounce package raspberry gelatin mix
10-ounce package frozen raspberries (thawed)
1 teaspoon vanilla extract

Preheat oven to 325°F. Mix all ingredients together in large mixing bowl until smooth. Pour evenly into greased bundt cake pan. Bake for 45 minutes. Cool for 10 minutes and remove cake from pan. Drizzle with glaze.

Glaze

1 cup powdered sugar
3 tablespoons milk
¼ teaspoon vanilla extract

Pour all ingredients into 16-ounce measuring cup with spout. Stir with spoon until smooth. While cake is still warm, drizzle with glaze.

* If the baby is a boy, turn this pink cake blue by substituting frozen blueberries for the frozen raspberries and blueberry gelatin for the raspberry gelatin.

Becky Long is a special-event planner and author. She has also written *Themed Baby Showers* (Meadowbrook Press), a guide to planning baby showers with fifteen fun, unique themes.

The Most Popular Names
from 1900 to 2005

The popularity of names, like the length of hemlines and the width of ties, is subject to change every year. The changes become even more noticeable when you think about the changes in name "fashions" over long periods.

Think about the names of your grandparents' generation: Margaret, Shirley, George, Harold. Very few of those names are in the current list of top 100 names. Most names from your parents' generation—Susan, Cheryl, Gary, Ronald—don't make the current list of top 100 names either.

It seems that every decade a new group of names rises in popularity and an old group of names declines. So, when choosing a name for your baby, it's wise to consider whether a name's popularity is rising, declining, or holding steady.

To help you assess name popularity trends, we are presenting the latest top 100 names given to baby boys and girls in the United States. The rankings are derived from a survey of new births nationwide conducted by the Social Security Administration. (Alternate spellings of each name are treated as separate names. For example, Sarah and Sara are ranked separately.) You can see from the data how the names have risen or fallen since the previous year's survey. If you're expecting two bundles of joy, don't miss the lists of most popular names for twins in the U.S. In addition, you can track popularity trends over the years with the lists of top 25 names given to girls and boys in each decade since 1900.

For information on how to pick a unique version of a popular name, see pages 8–9.

Top 100 Girls' Names in 2005

2005 Rank	Name	2004 Rank	Rank Change	2005 Rank	Name	2004 Rank	Rank Change	2005 Rank	Name	2004 Rank	Rank Change	2005 Rank	Name	2004 Rank	Rank Change
1	Emily	1	—	26	Hailey	24	−2	51	Faith	53	+2	76	Sara	68	−8
2	Emma	2	—	27	Jessica	21	−6	52	Sofia	69	+17	77	Audrey	80	+3
3	Madison	3	—	28	Victoria	28	—	53	Riley	58	+5	78	Brooklyn	101	+23
4	Abigail	6	+2	29	Jasmine	26	−3	54	Haley	42	−12	79	Vanessa	75	−4
5	Olivia	4	−1	30	Sydney	27	−3	55	Gabrielle	73	+18	80	Amanda	67	−13
6	Isabella	7	+1	31	Julia	32	+1	56	Nicole	46	−1	81	Ariana	79	−2
7	Hannah	5	−2	32	Destiny	39	+7	57	Kylie	49	−8	82	Rebecca	72	−10
8	Samantha	9	+1	33	Morgan	31	−2	58	Katelyn	59	+1	83	Caroline	74	−9
9	Ava	25	+16	34	Kaitlyn	33	−1	59	Zoe	54	−5	84	Amelia	96	+12
10	Ashley	8	−2	35	Savannah	41	+6	60	Paige	51	−9	85	Mariah	113	+28
11	Sophia	15	+4	36	Katherine	35	−1	61	Gabriella	76	+15	86	Jordan	70	−16
12	Elizabeth	10	−2	37	Alexandra	37	—	62	Jenna	56	−6	87	Jocelyn	84	−3
13	Alexis	11	−2	38	Rachel	34	−4	63	Kimberly	61	−2	88	Arianna	86	−2
14	Grace	13	−1	39	Lily	52	+13	64	Stephanie	55	−9	89	Isabel	87	−2
15	Sarah	12	−3	40	Megan	36	−4	65	Alexa	71	+6	90	Marissa	78	−12
16	Alyssa	14	−2	41	Kaylee	50	+9	66	Avery	77	+11	91	Autumn	82	−9
17	Mia	30	+13	42	Jennifer	38	−4	67	Andrea	57	−10	92	Melanie	89	−3
18	Natalie	19	+1	43	Angelina	60	+17	68	Leah	64	−4	93	Aaliyah	94	+1
19	Chloe	23	+4	44	Makayla	47	+3	69	Madeline	62	−7	94	Gracie	114	+20
20	Brianna	17	−3	45	Allison	40	−5	70	Nevaeh	104	+34	95	Claire	98	+3
21	Lauren	16	−5	46	Brooke	44	−2	71	Evelyn	83	+12	96	Isabelle	107	+11
22	Ella	29	+7	47	Maria	45	−2	72	Maya	85	+13	97	Molly	97	—
23	Anna	20	−3	48	Trinity	48	—	73	Mary	63	−10	98	Mya	116	+18
24	Taylor	22	−2	49	Lillian	65	+16	74	Michelle	66	−8	99	Diana	90	−9
25	Kayla	18	−7	50	Mackenzie	43	−7	75	Jada	81	+6	100	Katie	103	+3

Top 100 Boys' Names in 2005

2005 Rank	Name	2004 Rank	Rank Change	2005 Rank	Name	2004 Rank	Rank Change	2005 Rank	Name	2004 Rank	Rank Change	2005 Rank	Name	2004 Rank	Rank Change
1	Jacob	1	—	26	Logan	27	+1	51	Jason	47	−4	76	Carter	87	+11
2	Michael	2	—	27	Brandon	22	−5	52	Cameron	50	−2	77	Hayden	88	+11
3	Joshua	3	—	28	Gabriel	32	+4	53	Hunter	49	−4	78	Jeremiah	78	—
4	Matthew	4	—	29	Zachary	26	−3	54	Jayden	62	+8	79	Cole	75	−4
5	Ethan	5	—	30	Jose	28	−2	55	Juan	54	−1	80	Brayden	107	+27
6	Andrew	6	—	31	Elijah	31	—	56	Charles	56	—	81	Wyatt	90	+9
7	Daniel	7	—	32	Angel	44	+12	57	Aaron	53	−4	82	Chase	80	−2
8	Anthony	11	+3	33	Kevin	34	+1	58	Lucas	67	+9	83	Steven	77	−6
9	Christopher	10	+1	34	Jack	41	+7	59	Luis	57	−2	84	Timothy	79	−5
10	Joseph	9	−1	35	Caleb	33	−2	60	Owen	66	+6	85	Dominic	91	+6
11	William	8	−3	36	Justin	30	−6	61	Landon	86	+25	86	Sebastian	96	+10
12	Alexander	15	+3	37	Austin	35	−2	62	Diego	73	+11	87	Xavier	89	+2
13	Ryan	12	−1	38	Evan	39	+1	63	Brian	59	−4	88	Jaden	83	−5
14	David	14	—	39	Robert	36	−3	64	Adam	58	−6	89	Jesse	94	+5
15	Nicholas	13	−2	40	Thomas	37	−3	65	Adrian	72	+7	90	Devin	81	−9
16	Tyler	16	—	41	Luke	42	+1	66	Kyle	55	−11	91	Seth	82	−9
17	James	17	—	42	Mason	52	+10	67	Eric	61	−6	92	Antonio	93	+1
18	John	18	—	43	Aidan	40	−3	68	Ian	69	+1	93	Richard	92	−1
19	Jonathan	21	+2	44	Jackson	48	+4	69	Nathaniel	68	−1	94	Miguel	97	+3
20	Nathan	20	—	45	Isaiah	45	—	70	Carlos	71	+1	95	Colin	84	−11
21	Samuel	23	+2	46	Jordan	43	−3	71	Alex	63	−8	96	Cody	85	−11
22	Christian	24	+2	47	Gavin	51	+4	72	Bryan	64	−8	97	Alejandro	99	+2
23	Noah	29	+6	48	Connor	38	−10	73	Jesus	70	−3	98	Caden	104	+6
24	Dylan	19	−5	49	Aiden	60	+11	74	Julian	74	—	99	Blake	95	−4
25	Benjamin	25	—	50	Isaac	46	−4	75	Sean	65	−10	100	Carson	101	+1

Changes in Top 100
from 2004 to 2005

Big Gains

Girls		Boys	
Nevaeh	+34	Brayden	+27
Mariah	+28	Landon	+25
Brooklyn	+23	Angel	+12
Gracie	+20	Aiden	+11
Gabrielle	+18	Diego	+11
Mya	+18	Carter	+11
Angelina	+17	Hayden	+11
Sofia	+17	Mason	+10
Ava	+16	Sebastian	+10
Lillian	+16	Lucas	+9

Big Losses

Girls		Boys	
Jordan	−16	Kyle	−11
Amanda	−13	Colin	−11
Haley	−12	Cody	−11
Marissa	−12	Connor	−10
Nicole	−10	Sean	−10
Andrea	−10	Devin	−9
Mary	−10	Seth	−9
Rebecca	−10	Alex	−8
Paige	−9	Bryan	−8
Stephanie	−9	Patrick	−8

Out of Top 100

Girls		Boys	
Leslie	−8	Jake	−4
Amber	−14	Ashton	−31
Danielle	−12	Patrick	−8
Melissa	−4		
Sierra	−13		
Bailey	−9		
Erin	−17		

New to Top 100

Girls		Boys	
Brooklyn	+23	Brayden	+27
Gracie	+20	Caden	+6
Isabelle	+11	Carson	+1
Katie	+3		
Mariah	+28		
Mya	+18		
Nevaeh	+34		

The Most Popular Names
for Twins in 2005

Twin Girls	Twin Boys	Twin Girl & Boy
Faith, Hope	Jacob, Joshua	Taylor, Tyler
Hailey, Hannah	Matthew, Michael	Madison, Mason
Madison, Morgan	Daniel, David	Emma, Ethan
Mackenzie, Madison	Ethan, Evan	Emily, Ethan
Ella, Emma	Isaac, Isaiah	Madison, Matthew
Hannah, Sarah	Joseph, Joshua	Ella, Ethan
Faith, Grace	Nathan, Nicholas	Sophia, Samuel
Emily, Sarah	Alexander, Andrew	Ava, Aidan
Olivia, Sophia	Elijah, Isaiah	Alexis, Alexander
Ashley, Emily	Jordan, Justin	Natalie, Nathan
Elizabeth, Emily	Alexander, Nicholas	Brianna, Brian
Elizabeth, Katherine	Caleb, Joshua	Jada, Jaden
Abigail, Allison	Jonathan, Joshua	
Amy, Emily	Alexander, Benjamin	
Gabriella, Isabella	Andrew, Matthew	
Isabella, Sophia	Benjamin, Samuel	
Megan, Morgan	James, John	
Ava, Olivia	Matthew, Nicholas	
Abigail, Emily	Brandon, Brian	
Anna, Emma	Alexander, Zachary	
Haley, Hannah	Dylan, Tyler	
Reagan, Riley	Christian, Christopher	

The Most Popular Names through the Decades

Most Popular Girls' Names 2000–2005

2000s Rank	Name	1990s Rank	Rank Change
1	Emily	3	+2
2	Madison	29	+27
3	Hannah	11	+8
4	Emma	56	+52
5	Ashley	2	−3
6	Abigail	42	+36
7	Alexis	18	+11
8	Olivia	38	+30
9	Samantha	4	−3
10	Sarah	5	−5
11	Elizabeth	8	−3
12	Alyssa	21	+9
13	Grace	89	+76
14	Isabella	170	+156
15	Lauren	13	−2
16	Jessica	1	−15
17	Taylor	9	−8
18	Brianna	26	+8
19	Kayla	12	−7
20	Anna	35	+15
21	Victoria	19	−2
22	Sophia	132	+110
23	Natalie	52	+29
24	Sydney	59	+35
25	Chloe	123	+98

Most Popular Boys' Names 2000–2005

2000s Rank	Name	1990s Rank	Rank Change
1	Jacob	5	+4
2	Michael	1	−1
3	Joshua	4	+1
4	Matthew	3	−1
5	Andrew	7	+2
6	Christopher	2	−4
7	Joseph	10	+3
8	Daniel	8	—
9	Nicholas	6	−3
10	Ethan	55	+45
11	William	18	+7
12	Anthony	19	+7
13	Ryan	14	+1
14	David	12	−2
15	Tyler	9	−6
16	John	15	−1
17	Alexander	23	+6
18	James	13	−5
19	Brandon	11	−8
20	Zachary	16	−4
21	Jonathan	21	—
22	Dylan	34	+12
23	Christian	32	+9
24	Samuel	33	+9
25	Justin	17	−8

Most Popular Girls' Names 1990–1999

1990s Rank	Name	1980s Rank	Rank Change
1	Ashley	4	+3
2	Jessica	1	−1
3	Emily	24	+21
4	Sarah	5	+1
5	Samantha	26	+21
6	Brittany	20	+14
7	Amanda	3	−4
8	Elizabeth	9	+1
9	Taylor	200	+191
10	Megan	14	+4
11	Stephanie	6	−5
12	Kayla	54	+42
13	Lauren	17	+4
14	Jennifer	2	−12
15	Rachel	15	-
16	Hannah	91	+75
17	Nicole	8	−9
18	Amber	13	−5
19	Alexis	109	+90
20	Courtney	37	+17
21	Victoria	56	+35
22	Danielle	25	+3
23	Alyssa	89	+66
24	Rebecca	22	−2
25	Jasmine	90	+65

Most Popular Boys' Names 1990–1999

1990s Rank	Name	1980s Rank	Rank Change
1	Michael	1	-
2	Christopher	2	-
3	Matthew	3	-
4	Joshua	4	-
5	Jacob	35	+30
6	Andrew	13	+7
7	Daniel	6	−1
8	Nicholas	19	+11
9	Tyler	47	+38
10	Joseph	10	-
11	David	5	−6
12	Brandon	18	+6
13	James	7	−6
14	John	9	−5
15	Ryan	14	−1
16	Zachary	43	+27
17	Justin	12	−5
18	Anthony	20	+2
19	William	15	−4
20	Robert	8	−12
21	Jonathan	17	−4
22	Kyle	30	+8
23	Austin	95	+72
24	Alexander	50	+26
25	Kevin	23	−2

Most Popular Girls' Names 1980–1989

1980s Rank	Name	1970s Rank	Rank Change
1	Jessica	10	+9
2	Jennifer	1	−1
3	Amanda	17	+14
4	Ashley	140	+136
5	Sarah	18	+13
6	Stephanie	9	+3
7	Melissa	3	−4
8	Nicole	12	+4
9	Elizabeth	11	+2
10	Heather	8	−2
11	Tiffany	42	+31
12	Michelle	4	−8
13	Amber	65	+52
14	Megan	89	+75
15	Rachel	33	+18
16	Amy	2	−14
17	Lauren	137	+120
18	Kimberly	5	−13
19	Christina	165	+146
20	Brittany	534	+514
21	Crystal	37	+16
22	Rebecca	13	−9
23	Laura	19	−4
24	Emily	66	+42
25	Danielle	46	+21

Most Popular Boys' Names 1980–1989

1980s Rank	Name	1970s Rank	Rank Change
1	Michael	1	-
2	Christopher	2	-
3	Matthew	10	+7
4	Joshua	25	+21
5	David	4	−1
6	Daniel	11	+5
7	James	5	−2
8	Robert	7	−1
9	John	6	−3
10	Joseph	12	+2
11	Jason	3	−8
12	Justin	38	+26
13	Andrew	28	+15
14	Ryan	26	+12
15	William	9	−6
16	Brian	8	−8
17	Jonathan	32	+15
18	Brandon	51	+33
19	Nicholas	52	+33
20	Anthony	22	+2
21	Eric	14	−7
22	Adam	36	+14
23	Kevin	13	−10
24	Steven	19	−5
25	Thomas	21	−4

Most Popular Girls' Names 1970–1979

1970s Rank	Name	1960s Rank	Rank Change
1	Jennifer	19	+18
2	Amy	35	+33
3	Melissa	33	+30
4	Michelle	9	+5
5	Kimberly	5	-
6	Lisa	1	−5
7	Angela	21	+14
8	Heather	127	+119
9	Stephanie	45	+36
10	Jessica	230	+220
11	Elizabeth	17	+6
12	Nicole	187	+175
13	Rebecca	41	+28
14	Kelly	39	+25
15	Mary	2	−13
16	Christina	72	+56
17	Amanda	199	+182
18	Sarah	90	+72
19	Laura	15	−4
20	Julie	18	−2
21	Shannon	121	+100
22	Christine	27	+5
23	Tammy	14	−9
24	Karen	3	−21
25	Tracy	39	+14

Most Popular Boys' Names 1970–1979

1970s Rank	Name	1960s Rank	Rank Change
1	Michael	1	-
2	Christopher	20	+18
3	Jason	87	+84
4	David	2	−2
5	James	4	−1
6	John	3	−3
7	Robert	5	−2
8	Brian	16	+8
9	William	7	−2
10	Matthew	36	+26
11	Daniel	18	+7
12	Joseph	12	-
13	Kevin	14	+1
14	Eric	111	+97
15	Jeffrey	10	−5
16	Richard	8	−8
17	Scott	15	−2
18	Mark	6	−12
19	Steven	11	−8
20	Timothy	13	−7
21	Thomas	9	−12
22	Anthony	22	-
23	Charles	17	−6
24	Jeremy	365	+341
25	Joshua	327	+302

Most Popular Girls' Names 1960–1969

1960s Rank	Name	1950s Rank	Rank Change
1	Lisa	37	+36
2	Mary	1	−1
3	Karen	8	+5
4	Susan	4	-
5	Kimberly	90	+85
6	Patricia	3	−3
7	Linda	2	−5
8	Donna	10	+2
9	Michelle	93	+84
10	Cynthia	11	+1
11	Sandra	12	+1
12	Deborah	5	−7
13	Pamela	13	-
14	Tammy	140	+126
15	Laura	38	+23
16	Lori	79	+63
17	Elizabeth	20	+3
18	Julie	42	+24
19	Jennifer	98	+79
20	Brenda	18	−2
21	Angela	106	+85
22	Barbara	6	−16
23	Debra	7	−16
24	Sharon	14	−10
25	Teresa	30	+5

Most Popular Boys' Names 1960–1969

1960s Rank	Name	1950s Rank	Rank Change
1	Michael	1	-
2	David	5	+3
3	John	4	+1
4	James	2	−2
5	Robert	3	−2
6	Mark	9	+3
7	William	6	−1
8	Richard	7	−1
9	Thomas	8	−1
10	Jeffrey	24	+14
11	Steven	11	-
12	Joseph	13	+1
13	Timothy	22	+9
14	Kevin	27	+13
15	Scott	36	+21
16	Brian	34	+18
17	Charles	10	−7
18	Daniel	19	+1
19	Paul	17	−2
20	Christopher	47	+27
21	Kenneth	16	−5
22	Anthony	30	+8
23	Gregory	26	+3
24	Ronald	15	−9
25	Donald	14	−11

Most Popular Girls' Names 1950–1959

1950s Rank	Name	1940s Rank	Rank Change
1	Mary	1	-
2	Linda	2	-
3	Patricia	4	+1
4	Susan	10	+6
5	Deborah	68	+63
6	Barbara	3	−3
7	Debra	302	+295
8	Karen	15	+7
9	Nancy	7	−2
10	Donna	16	+6
11	Cynthia	47	+36
12	Sandra	6	−6
13	Pamela	39	+26
14	Sharon	9	−5
15	Kathleen	18	+3
16	Carol	5	−11
17	Diane	22	+5
18	Brenda	26	+8
19	Cheryl	43	+24
20	Elizabeth	23	+3
21	Janet	21	-
22	Kathy	88	+66
23	Margaret	14	−9
24	Janice	24	-
25	Carolyn	12	−13

Most Popular Boys' Names 1950–1959

1950s Rank	Name	1940s Rank	Rank Change
1	Michael	9	+8
2	James	1	−1
3	Robert	2	−1
4	John	3	−1
5	David	6	+1
6	William	4	−2
7	Richard	5	−2
8	Thomas	8	-
9	Mark	54	+45
10	Charles	7	−3
11	Steven	29	+18
12	Gary	14	+2
13	Joseph	13	-
14	Donald	12	−2
15	Ronald	10	−5
16	Kenneth	16	-
17	Paul	17	-
18	Larry	11	−7
19	Daniel	22	+3
20	Stephen	24	+4
21	Dennis	20	−1
22	Timothy	63	+41
23	Edward	18	−5
24	Jeffrey	88	+64
25	George	15	−10

Most Popular Girls' Names 1940–1949

1940s Rank	Name	1930s Rank	Rank Change
1	Mary	1	-
2	Linda	89	+87
3	Barbara	3	-
4	Patricia	5	+1
5	Carol	11	+6
6	Sandra	48	+42
7	Nancy	9	+2
8	Judith	40	+32
9	Sharon	83	+74
10	Susan	117	+107
11	Betty	2	−9
12	Carolyn	29	+17
13	Shirley	4	−9
14	Margaret	8	−6
15	Karen	138	+123
16	Donna	22	+6
17	Judy	112	+95
18	Kathleen	72	+54
19	Joyce	12	−7
20	Dorothy	6	−14
21	Janet	25	+4
22	Diane	115	+93
23	Elizabeth	17	−6
24	Janice	42	+18
25	Joan	7	−18

Most Popular Boys' Names 1940–1949

1940s Rank	Name	1930s Rank	Rank Change
1	James	2	+1
2	Robert	1	−1
3	John	3	-
4	William	4	-
5	Richard	5	-
6	David	11	+5
7	Charles	6	−1
8	Thomas	9	+1
9	Michael	35	+26
10	Ronald	13	+3
11	Larry	30	+19
12	Donald	7	−5
13	Joseph	10	−3
14	Gary	45	+31
15	George	8	−7
16	Kenneth	15	−1
17	Paul	14	−3
18	Edward	12	−6
19	Jerry	23	+4
20	Dennis	70	+50
21	Frank	16	−5
22	Daniel	42	+20
23	Raymond	17	−6
24	Stephen	105	+81
25	Roger	41	+16

Most Popular Girls' Names 1930–1939

1930s Rank	Name	1920s Rank	Rank Change
1	Mary	1	-
2	Betty	4	+2
3	Barbara	18	+15
4	Shirley	17	+13
5	Patricia	29	+24
6	Dorothy	2	−4
7	Joan	60	+53
8	Margaret	5	−3
9	Nancy	62	+53
10	Helen	3	−7
11	Carol	116	+105
12	Joyce	61	+49
13	Doris	8	−5
14	Ruth	6	−8
15	Virginia	7	−8
16	Marilyn	82	+66
17	Elizabeth	10	−7
18	Jean	16	−2
19	Frances	11	−8
20	Dolores	48	+28
21	Beverly	101	+80
22	Donna	104	+82
23	Alice	14	−9
24	Lois	21	−3
25	Janet	112	+87

Most Popular Boys' Names 1930–1939

1930s Rank	Name	1920s Rank	Rank Change
1	Robert	1	-
2	James	3	+1
3	John	2	−1
4	William	4	-
5	Richard	8	+3
6	Charles	5	−1
7	Donald	10	+3
8	George	6	−2
9	Thomas	11	+2
10	Joseph	7	−3
11	David	22	+11
12	Edward	9	−3
13	Ronald	92	+79
14	Paul	13	−1
15	Kenneth	20	+5
16	Frank	12	−4
17	Raymond	16	−1
18	Jack	17	−1
19	Harold	14	−5
20	Billy	48	+28
21	Gerald	44	+23
22	Walter	15	−7
23	Jerry	102	+79
24	Eugene	25	+1
25	Henry	18	−7

Most Popular Girls' Names 1920–1929

1920s Rank	Name	1910s Rank	Rank Change
1	Mary	1	-
2	Dorothy	3	+1
3	Helen	2	−1
4	Betty	37	+33
5	Margaret	4	−1
6	Ruth	5	−1
7	Virginia	12	+5
8	Doris	32	+24
9	Mildred	6	−3
10	Elizabeth	8	−2
11	Frances	9	−2
12	Anna	7	−5
13	Evelyn	11	−2
14	Alice	13	−1
15	Marie	10	−5
16	Jean	45	+29
17	Shirley	129	+112
18	Barbara	76	+58
19	Irene	17	−2
20	Marjorie	39	+19
21	Lois	49	+28
22	Florence	14	−8
23	Rose	15	−8
24	Martha	25	+1
25	Louise	18	−7

Most Popular Boys' Names 1920–1929

1920s Rank	Name	1910s Rank	Rank Change
1	Robert	4	+3
2	John	1	−1
3	James	3	-
4	William	2	−2
5	Charles	7	+2
6	George	6	-
7	Joseph	5	−2
8	Richard	17	+9
9	Edward	8	−1
10	Donald	20	+10
11	Thomas	11	-
12	Frank	9	−3
13	Paul	14	+1
14	Harold	13	−1
15	Walter	10	−5
16	Raymond	15	−1
17	Jack	26	+9
18	Henry	12	−6
19	Arthur	16	−3
20	Kenneth	30	+10
21	Albert	18	−3
22	David	29	+7
23	Harry	19	−4
24	Ralph	21	−3
25	Eugene	39	+14

Most Popular Girls' Names 1910–1919

1910s Rank	Name	1900s Rank	Rank Change
1	Mary	1	-
2	Helen	2	-
3	Dorothy	7	+4
4	Margaret	3	−1
5	Ruth	5	-
6	Mildred	9	+3
7	Anna	4	−3
8	Elizabeth	6	−2
9	Frances	16	+7
10	Marie	8	−2
11	Evelyn	39	+28
12	Virginia	53	+41
13	Alice	10	−3
14	Florence	11	−3
15	Rose	14	−1
16	Lillian	13	−3
17	Irene	21	+4
18	Louise	24	+6
19	Edna	17	−2
20	Gladys	15	−5
21	Catherine	19	−2
22	Ethel	12	−10
23	Josephine	46	+23
24	Ruby	42	+18
25	Martha	38	+13

Most Popular Boys' Names 1910–1919

1910s Rank	Name	1900s Rank	Rank Change
1	John	1	-
2	William	2	-
3	James	3	-
4	Robert	7	+3
5	Joseph	5	-
6	George	4	−2
7	Charles	6	−1
8	Edward	9	+1
9	Frank	8	−1
10	Walter	11	+1
11	Thomas	12	+1
12	Henry	10	−2
13	Harold	15	+2
14	Paul	17	+3
15	Raymond	22	+7
16	Arthur	14	−2
17	Richard	25	+8
18	Albert	16	−2
19	Harry	13	−6
20	Donald	52	+32
21	Ralph	23	+2
22	Louis	21	−1
23	Clarence	18	−5
24	Carl	20	−4
25	Fred	19	−6

Most Popular Girls' Names 1900–1909

1900s Rank	Name	1890s Rank	Rank Change
1	Mary	1	-
2	Helen	4	+2
3	Margaret	3	-
4	Anna	2	−2
5	Ruth	6	+1
6	Elizabeth	5	−1
7	Dorothy	57	+50
8	Marie	10	+2
9	Mildred	42	+33
10	Alice	24	+14
11	Florence	7	−4
12	Ethel	8	−4
13	Lillian	16	+3
14	Rose	22	+8
15	Gladys	43	+28
16	Frances	36	+20
17	Edna	17	-
18	Grace	18	-
19	Catherine	38	+19
20	Hazel	23	+3
21	Irene	44	+23
22	Gertrude	24	+2
23	Clara	11	−12
24	Louise	45	+21
25	Edith	29	+4

Most Popular Boys' Names 1900–1909

1900s Rank	Name	1890s Rank	Rank Change
1	John	1	-
2	William	2	-
3	James	3	-
4	George	4	-
5	Joseph	6	+1
6	Charles	5	−1
7	Robert	8	+1
8	Frank	7	−1
9	Edward	9	-
10	Henry	10	-
11	Walter	13	+2
12	Thomas	12	-
13	Harry	11	−2
14	Arthur	14	-
15	Harold	31	+16
16	Albert	16	-
17	Paul	22	+5
18	Clarence	17	−1
19	Fred	15	−4
20	Carl	23	+3
21	Louis	20	−1
22	Raymond	27	+5
23	Ralph	32	+9
24	Roy	19	−5
25	Richard	26	+1

Names around the World

Want to track popularity trends across the globe? Want to give your baby a name that reflects your heritage, language, or favorite travel destination? The following lists feature names with international flair. You'll learn the latest popular names given to baby girls and boys in several countries. Just as the U.S. popularity lists come from data compiled by the Social Security Administration, these international lists come from records kept by similar organizations across the globe. Beginning on page 34, you'll also discover a sampling of interesting names from particular cultural origins. Use those lists to get you thinking, but don't forget that there are thousands more names in the Girls' Names and Boys' Names sections with the origins you're looking for.

The Most Popular Names around the World

Most Popular Names in Austria in 2004

Girls	Boys
Anna	Lukas
Sarah	Florian
Leonie	Tobias
Julia	David
Lena	Fabian
Laura	Julian
Hannah	Simon
Katharina	Alexander
Lisa	Michael
Sophie	Sebastian

Most Popular Names in Belgium in 2004

Girls	Boys
Emma	Noah
Marie	Thomas
Laura	Lucas
Julie	Milan
Sarah	Nathan
Clara	Louis
Manon	Maxime
Léa	Arthur
Lisa	Robbe
Camille	Hugo
Charlotte	Mohamed
Luna	Nicolas
Louise	Simon

Elise	Romain
Amber	Theo
Chloé	Victor
Lotte	Alexandre
Pauline	Tom
Lara	Seppe
Eva	Wout
Emilie	Rune
Océane	Xander
Britt	Antoine
Amélie	Jelle
Jana	Kobe

Most Popular Names in British Columbia, Canada, in 2005

Girls	Boys
Emma	Ethan
Emily	Joshua
Olivia	Matthew
Hannah	Jacob
Madison	Nathan
Ava	Ryan
Sarah	Alexander
Ella	Liam
Isabella	Nicholas
Grace	Noah
Sophia	Daniel
Samantha	Benjamin

Maya	James
Abigail	William
Jessica	Owen
Hailey	Dylan
Chloe	Logan
Megan	Evan
Julia	Tyler
Lauren	Jack

Most Popular Names in Chile in 2005

Girls	Boys
Constanza	Benjamin
Catalina	Matias
Valentina	Vicente
Javiera	Martin
Martina	Sebastian
Sofia	Diego
Maria	Nicolas
Antonia	Juan
Fernanda	Jose
Francisca	Cristobal
Isidora	Joaquin
Camila	Ignacio
Florencia	Felipe
Josefa	Francisco
Daniela	Bastian
Antonella	Maximiliano
Millaray	Javier

Barbara	Gabriel
Belen	Tomas
Rocio	Luis
Ignacia	Lucas
Krishna	Franco
Monserrat	Daniel
Gabriela	Pablo
Anais	Carlos

Most Popular Names in England/Wales in 2005

Girls	Boys
Jessica	Jack
Emily	Joshua
Sophie	Thomas
Olivia	James
Chloe	Oliver
Ellie	Daniel
Grace	Samuel
Lucy	William
Charlotte	Harry
Katie	Joseph
Ella	Benjamin
Megan	Charlie
Hannah	Luke
Amelia	Matthew
Ruby	Callum
Lily	Jake
Amy	Ethan
Mia	George
Abigail	Lewis
Millie	Alexander
Molly	Jacob
Emma	Alfie
Holly	Mohammed
Leah	Dylan
Isabella	Ryan

Most Popular Names in France in 2004

Girls	Boys
Lea	Enzo
Emma	Lucas
Manon	Theo
Clara	Thomas
Chloe	Hugo
Camille	Mathis
Ines	Nathan
Sarah	Maxime
Oceane	Clement
Marie	Louis
Jade	Alexis
Lucie	Romain
Anais	Leo
Julie	Tom
Laura	Alexandre
Eva	Antoine
Lola	Quentin
Lisa	Matheo
Pauline	Baptiste
Mathilde	Matteo
Romane	Paul
Juliette	Yanis
Celia	Axel
Lena	Arthur
Justine	Nicolas

Most Popular Names in Germany in 2005

Girls	Boys
Marie	Alexander
Sophie/Sofie	Maximilian
Maria	Leon
Anna, Anne	Lukas/Lucas
Leonie	Luca
Lena	Paul
Emily	Jonas
Lea/Leah	Felix

Julia	Tim
Laura	David

Most Popular Names in Hungary in 2005

Girls	Boys
Anna	Bence
Viktória	Máté
Réka	Balázs
Vivien	Dávid
Zsófia	Dániel
Petra	Levente
Dorina	Tamás
Fanni	Ádám
Boglárka	Péter
Eszter	Gergö

Most Popular Names in Ireland in 2004

Girls	Boys
Emma	Sean
Katie	Jack
Sarah	Conor
Amy	Adam
Aoife	James
Ciara	Daniel
Sophie	Cian
Chloe	Luke
Leah	Michael
Niamh	Aaron
Ella	Dylan
Caoimhe	David
Emily	Ryan
Kate	Eoin
Rachel	Darragh
Hannah	Jamie
Lauren	Ben
Ava	Oisin
Megan	Shane
Grace	Thomas

Girls	Boys
Rebecca	John
Lucy	Joshua
Jessica	Matthew
Laura	Patrick
Holly	Evan

Most Popular Names in Japan in 2005

Girls	Boys
Hina	Yuuki
Yui	Haruto
Miyu	Souta
Haruka	Yuuto
Sakura	Haruki
Nanami	Kouki
Ayaka	Kaito
Honoka	Takumi
Mamoka	Hayato
Aoi	Shouta

Most Popular Names in the Netherlands in 2005

Girls	Boys
Sanne	Daan
Emma	Sem
Anna	Thomas
Iris	Tim
Anouk	Lucas
Lisa	Lars
Eva	Thijs
Julia	Milan
Lotte	Jesse
Isa	Bram
Maud	Max
Sophie	Stijn
Fleur	Niels
Lieke	Ruben
Anne	Luuk
Amber	Sven

Noa	Nick
Roos	Jasper
Marit	Daniel
Femke	Tom

Most Popular Names in New South Wales, Australia, in 2005

Girls	Boys
Olivia	Jack
Charlotte	Lachlan
Emily	William
Chloe	Joshua
Ella	Thomas
Jessica	James
Isabella	Ryan
Sophie	Daniel
Mia	Matthew
Emma	Samuel
Grace	Ethan
Sarah	Luke
Hannah	Benjamin
Sienna	Nicholas
Lily	Liam
Amelia	Noah
Georgia	Alexander
Zoe	Jacob
Jasmine	Dylan

Girls	Boys
Ruby	Riley
Hayley	Oliver
Ava	Cooper
Lucy	Jayden
Jade	Harrison
Caitlin	Max

Most Popular Names in Norway in 2005

Girls	Boys
Emma	Markus
Thea	Mathias
Ida	Jonas
Sara	Kristian
Julie	Tobias
Emilie	Alexander
Hanna	Adrian
Nora	Henrik
Malin	Andreas
Ingrid	Martin
Sofie	Magnus
Maria	Kristoffer
Andrea	Emil
Amalie	Daniel
Tuva	Sander
Anna	Sebastian
Mia	Elias
Karoline	Fredrik
Vilde	Oliver
Hedda	Marius
Frida	Benjamin
Marie	Jakob
Maja	Nikolai
Linnea	Sondre
Victoria	Lukas

Most Popular Names in Quebec, Canada, in 2005

Girls	Boys
Lea	Samuel
Jade	William
Sarah	Alexis
Noemie	Gabriel
Rosalie	Felix
Laurence	Nathan
Camille	Antoine

Girls	Boys
Florence	Olivier
Megane	Thomas
Coralie	Xavier
Megan	Justin
Oceane	Jeremy
Ariane	Mathis
Gabrielle	Anthony
Audrey	Raphael
Laurie	Alexandre
Juliette	Zachary
Justine	Jacob
Emilie	Vincent
Elodie	Nicolas
Marianne	Emile
Chloe	Benjamin
Emy	Maxime
Charlotte	Mathieu
Emma	Simon

Most Popular Names in Scotland in 2005

Girls	Boys
Sophie	Lewis
Emma	Jack
Ellie	Callum
Amy	James
Erin	Ryan
Lucy	Cameron
Katie	Kyle
Chloe	Jamie
Rebecca	Daniel
Emily	Matthew
Hannah	Liam
Olivia	Ben
Rachel	Adam
Leah	Dylan
Megan	Connor
Aimee	Andrew

Holly	Alexander
Abbie	Aidan
Jessica	Thomas
Lauren	Aiden
Niamh	Aaron
Sophie	Joshua
Emma	Logan
Ellie	Scott
Amy	Ross

Most Popular Names in Spain in 2004

Girls	Boys
Lucia	Alejandro
Maria	David
Paula	Daniel
Laura	Pablo
Marta	Adrian
Alba	Alvaro
Andrea	Javier
Claudia	Sergio
Sara	Carlos
Nerea	Marcos
Carla	Ivan
Ana	Hugo
Natalia	Mario
Irene	Jorge
Marina	Diego
Cristina	Miguel
Elena	Manuel
Carmen	Raul
Julia	Ruben
Ainhoa	Antonio
Rocio	Juan
Sofia	Alex
Angela	Victor
Nuria	Marc
Alejandra	Alberto

Most Popular Names in Sweden in 2005

Girls	Boys
Emma	Oscar
Maja	William
Julia	Lucas
Alice	Filip
Ida	Isak
Linnéa	Elias
Elin	Alexander
Alva	Emil
Hanna	Hugo
Ella	Viktor
Ebba	Erik
Wilma	Anton
Klara	Simon
Moa	Albin
Amanda	Axel
Matilda	Gustav
Elsa	Linus
Sara	Oliver
Emilia	Jonathan
Filippa	Liam
Isabelle	Max
Felicia	Leo
Tindra	Ludvig
Saga	Adam
Ellen	Carl

Names from around the World

African

Girls	Boys
Afi	Afram
Adia	Axi
Adanna	Bello
Ama	Ekon
Ashanti	Enzi
Batini	Idi
Eshe	Jabari
Fayola	Kayin
Femi	Kitwana
Goma	Kosey
Halla	Kwasi
Imena	Liu
Kameke	Mansa
Kamilah	Moswen
Kia	Mzuzi
Mosi	Nwa
Pita	Nwake
Poni	Ogun
Reta	Ohin
Sharik	Okapi
Siko	Ottah
Tawia	Senwe
Thema	Ulan
Winna	Uzoma
Zina	Zareb

American

Girls	Boys
Abelina	Adarius
Akayla	Buster
Amberlyn	Caden
Betsy	Daevon
Blinda	Dantrell
Coralee	Demarius
Darilynn	Dionte
Doneshia	Jadrien
Emmylou	Jailen
Jaycee	Jamar
Jessalyn	Jareth
Johnessa	Jayce
Karolane	Lashawn
Krystalynn	Lavon
Lakiesha	Montel
Lashana	Mychal
Liza	Reno
Roshawna	Reshawn
Shaniqua	Ryker
Shantel	Tevin
Takayla	Tiger
Tenesha	Treshawn
Teralyn	Tyrees
Trixia	Woody
Tyesha	Ziggy

Arabic

Girls	Boys
Abia	Abdul
Aleah	Ahmad
Cantara	Asad
Emani	Bilal
Fatima	Fadi
Ghada	Fahaad
Habiba	Ferran
Halimah	Ghazi
Imani	Gilad
Jalila	Habib
Kalila	Hadi
Laela	Hakim
Lilith	Hassan
Maja	Imad
Marya	Ismael
Nalia	Jabir
Omaira	Jamaal
Qadira	Mohamed
Rabi	Nadim
Rasha	Omar
Rayya	Rafiq
Samira	Rahul
Shahar	Rashad
Tabina	Samír
Vega	Sayyid

Chinese

Girls	Boys
An	Chen
Bo	Cheung
Chultua	Chi
Hua	Chung
Jun	De
Lee	Dewei
Lian	Fai
Lien	Gan
Lin	Guotin
Ling	Ho
Mani	Hu
Marrim	Jin
Meiying	Keung
Nuwa	Kong
Ping	Lei
Shu	Li
Syá	Liang
Sying	On
Tao	Park
Tu	Po Sin
Ushi	Quon
Xiang	Shing
Xiu Mei	Tung
Yáng	Wing
Yen	Yu

English

Girls	Boys
Addison	Alfie
Ashley	Ashton
Beverly	Baxter
Britany	Blake
Cady	Chip
Chelsea	Cody
Ellen	Dawson
Evelyn	Edward
Hailey	Franklin
Holly	Gordon
Hope	Harry
Janet	Jamison
Jill	Jeffrey
Julie	Jeremy
Leigh	Lane
Maddie	Maxwell
Millicent	Ned
Paige	Parker
Piper	Rodney
Robin	Scott
Sally	Slade
Scarlet	Ted
Shelby	Tucker
Sigourney	Wallace
Twyla	William

French

Girls	Boys
Angelique	Adrien
Annette	Alexandre
Aubrey	Andre
Belle	Antoine
Camille	Christophe
Charlotte	Donatien
Christelle	Edouard
Cosette	François

Girls	Boys
Desiree	Gage
Estelle	Guillaume
Gabrielle	Henri
Genevieve	Jacques
Juliette	Jean
Jolie	Leroy
Lourdes	Luc
Margaux	Marc
Maribel	Marquis
Michelle	Philippe
Monique	Pierre
Nicole	Quincy
Paris	Remy
Raquel	Russel
Salina	Sebastien
Sydney	Stéphane
Yvonne	Sylvian

German

Girls	Boys
Adelaide	Adler
Amelia	Adolf
Christa	Arnold
Edda	Bernard
Elke	Claus
Elsbeth	Conrad
Emma	Derek
Frederica	Dieter
Giselle	Dustin
Gretchen	Frederick
Heidi	Fritz
Hetta	Gerald
Hilda	Harvey
Ida	Johan
Johana	Karl
Katrina	Lance
Klarise	Louis
Lisele	Milo

Lorelei	Philipp
Margret	Roger
Milia	Roland
Monika	Sigmund
Reynalda	Terrell
Velma	Ulrich
Wanda	Walter

Greek

Girls	Boys
Alexandra	Achilles
Amaryllis	Adonis
Anastasia	Alexis
Athena	Christos
Callista	Cristobal
Daphne	Damian
Delia	Darius
Delphine	Demetris
Eleanora	Elias
Eudora	Feoras
Evangelina	Gaylen
Gaea	Georgios
Helena	Julius
Hermione	Krisopher
Ianthe	Leander
Kalliope	Nicholas
Kassandra	Panos
Maia	Paris
Medea	Petros
Oceana	Rhodes
Odelia	Sebastian
Ophelia	Stefanos
Phoebe	Thanos
Rhea	Urian
Selena	Xander

Hebrew

Girls	Boys
Alia	Aaron
Anais	Abel
Becca	Ahab
Beth	Azriel
Cayla	Benjamin
Deborah	Boaz
Dinah	Caleb
Eliane	Coby
Eliza	Daniel
Hannah	Elijah
Ilisha	Emmanuel
Jana	Ira
Judith	Isaak
Kaela	Jacob
Leeza	Jeremiah
Lena	Michael
Mariam	Nathaniel
Mikala	Noah
Naomi	Oren
Rachael	Raphael
Rebecca	Reuben
Ruth	Seth
Sarah	Tobin
Tirza	Zachariah
Yael	Zachary

Irish

Girls	Boys
Aileen	Aidan
Alanna	Brenden
Blaine	Clancy
Breanna	Desmond
Brigit	Donovan
Carlin	Eagan
Colleen	Flynn
Dacia	Garret
Dierdre	Grady
Erin	Keegan
Fallon	Keenan
Ilene	Kevin
Kaitlin	Liam
Keara	Logan
Kelly	Mahon
Kyleigh	Makenzie
Maura	Nevin
Maureen	Nolan
Moira	Owen
Quincy	Phinean
Raleigh	Quinn
Reagan	Reilly
Sinead	Ryan
Sloane	Seamus
Taryn	Sedric

Japanese

Girls	Boys
Aiko	Akemi
Aneko	Akira
Dai	Botan
Hachi	Goro
Hoshi	Hiroshi
Ishi	Isas
Jin	Joben
Keiko	Joji
Kioko	Jum
Kumiko	Kaemon
Leiko	Kentaro
Maeko	Masao
Mai	Michio
Mariko	Minoru
Masago	Naoko
Nari	Raiden
Oki	Rei
Raku	Saburo
Ran	Sen
Ruri	Takeo
Seki	Toru
Tazu	Udo
Yasu	Yasuo
Yei	Yóshi
Yoko	Yuki

Latin

Girls	Boys
Allegra	Amadeus
Aurora	Antony
Beatrice	Austin
Bella	Benedict
Cecily	Bennett
Celeste	Camilo
Deana	Cecil
Felicia	Delfino
Imogene	Dominic
Josalyn	Favian
Karmen	Felix
Laurel	Griffin
Luna	Horacio
Mabel	Hugo
Madonna	Ignatius
Maren	Jerome
Maxine	Jude
Nova	Loren
Olivia	Marius
Paxton	Octavio
Persis	Oliver
Pomona	Quentin
Regina	Roman
Rose	Silas
Sabina	Valentin

Native American

Girls	Boys
Aiyana	Ahanu
Cherokee	Anoki
Dakota	Bly
Dena	Delsin
Halona	Demothi
Heta	Elan
Imala	Elsu
Izusa	Etu
Kachina	Hakan
Kanda	Huslu
Kiona	Inteus
Leotie	Istu
Magena	Iye
Netis	Jolon
Nuna	Knoton
Olathe	Lenno
Oneida	Mingan
Sakuna	Motega
Sora	Muraco
Taima	Neka
Tala	Nodin
Utina	Patwin
Wyanet	Sahale
Wyoming	Songan
Yenene	Wingi

Russian

Girls	Boys
Alena	Alexi
Annika	Christoff
Breasha	Dimitri
Duscha	Egor
Galina	Feliks
Irina	Fyodor
Karina	Gena
Katia	Gyorgy
Lelya	Igor
Liolya	Ilya
Marisha	Iosif
Masha	Ivan
Natasha	Kolya
Natalia	Leonid
Nikita	Maxim
Olena	Michail
Orlenda	Panas
Raisa	Pasha
Sasha	Pavel
Shura	Pyotr
Svetlana	Sacha
Tanya	Sergei
Valera	Valerii
Yekaterina	Viktor
Yelena	Vladimir

Scandinavian

Girls	Boys
Anneka	Anders
Birgitte	Burr
Britta	Frans
Carina	Gustaf
Elga	Hadrian
Freja	Halen
Freya	Hilmar
Gala	Kjell
Gerda	Krister
Gunda	Kristofer
Haldana	Lauris
Ingrid	Lennart
Kalle	Lunt
Karena	Mats
Karin	Mikael
Kolina	Nansen
Lena	Niklas
Lusa	Nils
Maija	Per
Malena	Reinhold
Rika	Rikard
Runa	Rolle
Ulla	Steffan
Unn	Torkel
Valma	Valter

Scottish

Girls	Boys
Aili	Adair
Ailsa	Alastair
Ainsley	Angus
Berkley	Boyd
Blair	Bret
Camden	Caelan
Connor	Cameron
Christal	Dougal
Davonna	Duncan
Eslpeth	Geordan
Greer	Gregor
Isela	Henderson
Jeana	Ian
Jinny	Kennan
Keita	Kenzie
Kelsea	Lennox
Leslie	Leslie
Maisie	Macaulay
Marjie	Malcolm
Mckenzie	Morgan
Mhairie	Perth
Paisley	Ronald
Rhona	Seumas
Roslyn	Stratton
Tavie	Tavish

Spanish		Vietnamese		Welsh	
Girls	**Boys**	**Girls**	**Boys**	**Girls**	**Boys**
Alejandra	Armando	Am	Anh	Bevanne	Bevan
Benita	Carlos	Bian	Antoan	Bronwyn	Bowen
Clarita	Eduardo	Cai	Binh	Carys	Broderick
Esmeralda	Enrique	Cam	Cadao	Deryn	Bryce
Esperanza	Estéban	Hoa	Cham	Enid	Caddock
Felicia	Felipe	Hoai	Duc	Glynnis	Cairn
Gracia	Fernando	Hong	Dinh	Guinevere	Davis
Isabel	Garcia	Huong	Gia	Gwyneth	Dylan
Jacinthe	Gerardo	Kim	Hai	Idelle	Eoin
Juana	Heraldo	Kima	Hieu	Isolde	Gareth
Lola	Jose	Lan	Hoang	Linette	Gavin
Lucia	Jorge	Le	Huy	Mab	Griffith
Madrona	Juan	Mai	Lap	Meghan	Howell
Marisol	Luis	Nu	Minh	Meredith	Jestin
Marquita	Marcos	Nue	Nam	Olwen	Kynan
Nelia	Mateo	Ping	Ngai	Owena	Lewis
Oleda	Pablo	Tam	Nguyen	Rhiannon	Llewellyn
Pilar	Pedro	Tao	Nien	Rhonda	Lloyd
Reina	Rafael	Thanh	Phuok	Ronelle	Maddock
Rosalinda	Ramón	Thao	Pin	Rowena	Price
Rosita	Renaldo	Thi	Tai	Sulwen	Rhett
Salvadora	Salvador	Thuy	Thanh	Teagan	Rhys
Soledad	Santiago	Tuyen	Thian	Vanora	Tristan
Toya	Tobal	Tuyet	Tuan	Wenda	Vaughn
Ynez	Vincinte	Xuan	Tuyen	Wynne	Wren

The Impressions Names Make

Consciously or unconsciously, we all have private pictures associated with certain names. Jackie could be sophisticated and beautiful, like Jackie Kennedy, or fat and funny, like Jackie Gleason. These pictures come from personal experience as well as from images we absorb from the mass media, and thus they may conflict in interesting ways. The name Charlton strikes many people as a sissified, passive, whiny brat—until they think of Charlton Heston. Marilyn may personify voluptuous femininity—until you think of Marilyn, your neighbor with the ratty bathrobe, curlers, and a cigarette dangling out of her mouth.

Over the years, researchers have been fascinated by this question of the "real" meanings of names and their effects. When asked to stereotype names by age, trustworthiness, attractiveness, sociability, kindness, aggressiveness, popularity, masculinity/femininity, degree of activity or passivity, etc., people actually do tend to agree on each name's characteristics.

So if people think of Mallory as cute and likeable, does that influence a girl named Mallory to become cute and likeable? Experts agree that names don't guarantee instant success or condemn people to certain failure, but they do affect self-images, influence relationships with others, and help (or hinder) success in work and school.

Robert Rosenthal's classic experiment identified what he named the Pygmalion effect: randomly selected children who'd been labeled "intellectual bloomers" actually did bloom. Here's how the Pygmalion effect works with names: Researcher S. Gray Garwood conducted a study on sixth graders in New Orleans. He found that students given names popular with teachers scored higher in skills tests, were better adjusted and more consistent in their self-perceptions, were more realistic in their evaluations of themselves, and more frequently expected that they would attain their goals—even though their goals were more ambitious than ones set by their peers. A research study in San Diego suggested that average essays by Davids, Michaels, Karens, and Lisas got better grades than average essays written by Elmers, Huberts, Adelles, and Berthas. The reason? Teachers expected kids with popular names to do better, and thus they assigned those kids higher grades in a self-fulfilling prophecy.

The Sinrod Marketing Group's International Opinion panel surveyed over 100,000 parents to discover their opinions about names. Results of this poll are presented in *The Baby Name Survey Book* by Bruce Lansky and Barry Sinrod. Their book contains the names people most often associate with hundreds of personal attributes such as intelligent, athletic, attractive, and nice (as well as dumb, klutzy, ugly, and nasty). It also contains personality profiles of over 1,700 common and unusual boys' and girls' names and includes real or fictional famous namesakes who may have influenced people's perception of each name.

What the authors found was that most names have very clear images; some even have multiple images. The following are lists of boys' and girls' names that were found to have particular image associations.

Athletic

Girls	Boys
Bailey	Alex
Billie	Ali
Bobbie	Alonso
Casey	Bart
Chris	Brian
Colleen	Buck
Dena	Chuck
Gabriella	Connor
Jackie	Cooper
Jessie	Daniel
Jill	Derek
Jody	Emmitt
Josie	Hakeem
Katie	Houston
Kelsey	Jake
Lindsay	Jock
Lola	Kareem
Martina	Kevin
Mia	Kirby
Morgan	Lynn
Natalia	Marcus
Nora	Riley
Steffi	Rod
Sue	Terry
Tammy	Trey

Beautiful/Handsome

Girls	Boys
Adrienne	Adam
Ariel	Ahmad
Aurora	Alejandro
Bella	Alonzo
Bonita	Austin
Carmen	Beau
Cassandra	Blake
Catherine	Bo
Danielle	Bryant
Ebony	Chaz
Farrah	Christopher
Genevieve	Clint
Jasmine	Damian
Jewel	David
Kendra	Demetrius
Kiera	Denzel
Lydia	Douglas
Marisa	Grant
Maya	Humphrey
Sarah	Joe
Scarlett	Jude
Simone	Kiefer
Tanya	Mitchell
Tessa	Tevin
Whitney	Vance

Blonde

Girls	Boys
Bambie	Aubrey
Barbie	Austin
Bianca	Bjorn
Blanche	Brett
Brigitte	Bud
Bunny	Chance
Candy	Chick
Daisy	Colin
Dolly	Corbin
Heidi	Dalton
Inga	Dane
Jillian	Dennis
Krystal	Dwayne
Lara	Eric
Lorna	Josh
Madonna	Keith
Marcia	Kerry
Marnie	Kipp
Olivia	Kyle
Randi	Lars
Sally	Leif
Shannon	Louis
Sheila	Martin
Tracy	Olaf
Vanna	Sven

Cute

Girls	Boys
Annie	Andrew
Becca	Antoine
Bobbie	Antonio
Cheryl	Barry
Christy	Benjamin
Deanna	Chick
Debbie	Cory
Dee Dee	Danny
Emily	Eric
Jennifer	Francisco
Jody	Franky
Kari	Jon
Lacie	Kipp
Mallory	Linus
Mandy	Louis
Megan	Matthew
Peggy	Mike
Porsha	Nicholas
Randi	Rene
Serena	Robbie
Shannon	Rory
Shirley	Sonny
Stacy	Stevie
Tammy	Timothy
Trudy	Wade

Friendly

Girls	Boys
Bernadette	Allen
Bobbie	Aubrey
Bonnie	Barrett
Carol	Bennie
Christy	Bing
Dorothy	Cal
Elaine	Casper
Gwen	Cole
Joy	Dan
Kathy	Denny
Kenya	Donovan
Kim	Ed
Lila	Fred
Marcie	Gary
Millie	Hakeem
Nancy	Jeff
Nikki	Jerry
Opal	Jim
Patricia	Khalil
Rhoda	Rob
Rose	Russ
Ruby	Sandy
Sandy	Tony
Vivian	Vinny
Wendy	Wally

Funny

Girls	Boys
Dionne	Abbott
Ellen	Ace
Erma	Allen
Fanny	Archie
Gilda	Artie
Gillian	Bennie
Jenny	Bobby
Julie	Carson
Lucille	Chase
Lucy	Diego
Maggie	Dudley
Marge	Eddie
Marsha	Edsel
Maud	Eduardo
Melinda	Fletcher
Mickey	Fraser
Patty	Grady
Paula	Jerome
Rosie	Keenan
Roxanne	Rochester
Sally	Rollie
Stevie	Roscoe
Sunny	Sid
Sydney	Tim
Vivian	Vinny

Hippie

Girls and Boys

Angel
Autumn
Baby
Breezy
Crystal
Dawn
Happy
Harmony
Honey
Indigo
Kharma
Love
Lucky
Meadow
Misty
Moon
Passion
Rainbow
River
Serenity
Skye
Sparkle
Sprout
Star
Sunshine

Intelligent

Girls	Boys
Abigail	Adlai
Agatha	Alexander
Alexis	Barton
Barbara	Brock
Dana	Clifford
Daria	Colin
Diana	Dalton
Eleanor	David
Grace	Donovan
Helen	Edward
Jade	Esteban
Jillian	Fraser
Kate	Jefferson
Kaylyn	Jerome
Laura	John
Leah	Kelsey
Lillian	Kenneth
Mackenzie	Merlin
Marcella	Ned
Meredith	Nelson
Meryl	Roderick
Michaela	Samuel
Shauna	Sebastian
Shelley	Tim
Vanessa	Virgil

Nerdy

Boys
Arnie
Barrett
Bernie
Clarence
Clifford
Creighton
Dexter
Egbert
Khalil
Marvin
Mortimer
Myron
Newt
Norman
Sanford
Seymour
Sheldon
Sinclair
Tracy
Truman
Ulysses
Vern
Vladimir
Waldo
Xavier

Old-Fashioned

Girls	Boys
Abigail	Abe
Adelaide	Amos
Adelle	Arthur
Bea	Bertrand
Charlotte	Clarence
Clementine	Cy
Cora	Cyril
Dinah	Dennis
Edith	Erasmus
Elsie	Erskine
Esther	Ezekiel
Eugenia	Giuseppe
Hattie	Grover
Ida	Herbert
Mamie	Herschel
Martha	Jerome
Maureen	Kermit
Meryl	Lloyd
Mildred	Sanford
Nellie	Silas
Prudence	Spencer
Rosalie	Stanley
Thelma	Sven
Verna	Vic
Wilma	Wilfred

Quiet

Girls	Boys
Bernice	Aaron
Beth	Adrian
Cathleen	Angel
Chloe	Benedict
Diana	Bryce
Donna	Carlo
Faith	Curtis
Fawn	Cy
Fay	Douglas
Grace	Gerald
Jocelyn	Gideon
Leona	Jeremiah
Lisa	Jermaine
Lori	Kiefer
Lydia	Kyle
Moira	Riley
Natalia	Robert
Nina	Robin
Rena	Samson
Sheryl	Spencer
Tessa	Toby
Theresa	Tommy
Ursula	Tucker
Violet	Vaughn
Yoko	Virgil

Rich/Wealthy

Girls	Boys
Alexis	Bartholomew
Amanda	Bradley
Ariel	Brock
Blair	Bryce
Chanel	Burke
Chantal	Cameron
Chastity	Carlos
Chelsea	Chet
Christina	Claybourne
Clara	Clinton
Crystal	Colby
Darlene	Colin
Deandra	Corbin
Jewel	Dane
Larissa	Dante
Madison	Dillon
Marina	Frederick
Meredith	Geoffrey
Moira	Hamilton
Porsha	Harper
Rachel	Montgomery
Taryn	Roosevelt
Tiffany	Sterling
Trisha	Winslow
Zsa Zsa	Winthrop

Sexy

Girls
Alana
Angie
Bambi
Brooke
Caresse
Cari
Carmen
Dani
Desiree
Donna
Honey
Jillian
Kirstie
Kitty
Kyra
Latoya
Leah
Lola
Marilyn
Marlo
Raquel
Sabrina
Sandra
Simone
Zsa Zsa

Southern

Girls	**Boys**
Ada	Ashley
Alma	Beau
Annabel	Bobby
Belle	Cletus
Carolina	Clint
Charlotte	Dale
Clementine	Earl
Dixie	Jackson
Dolly	Jeb
Dottie	Jed
Ellie	Jefferson
Georgeanne	Jesse
Georgia	Jethro
Jolene	Jimmy
LeeAnn	Johnny
Luella	Lee
Mirabel	Luke
Ophelia	Luther
Patsy	Moses
Polly	Otis
Priscilla	Peyton
Rosalind	Rhett
Scarlet	Robert
Tara	Roscoe
Winona	Wade

Strong/Tough

Boys
Amos
Ben
Brandon
Brock
Bronson
Bruce
Bruno
Cain
Christopher
Clint
Cody
Coleman
Colin
Delbert
Demetrius
Duke
Jed
Judd
Kurt
Nick
Sampson
Stefan
Thor
Vince
Zeb

Sweet

Girls
Abby
Alyssa
Angela
Betsy
Candy
Cheryl
Cindy
Dana
Desiree
Elise
Ellie
Esther
Heather
Heidi
Kara
Kristi
Laura
Linda
Marjorie
Melinda
Melissa
Olivia
Rose
Shauna
Sue

Trendy

Girls	Boys
Alexia	Adrian
Alia	Alec
Britney	Angelo
Chanel	Bradley
Char	Carson
Delia	Connor
Destiny	Davis
Gwyneth	Dominic
Hannah	Ellery
India	Garrett
Isabella	Harley
Jen	Harper
Julianna	Jefferson
Keely	Kellan
Lane	Levi
Macy	Liam
Madeleine	Neil
Madison	Olaf
Morgan	Omar
Nadia	Orlando
Natalia	Parker
Olivia	Pierce
Paris	Remington
Ricki	Simon
Taylor	Warren

Weird

Girls	Boys
Abra	Abner
Aida	Barton
Annelise	Boris
Athalie	Cosmo
Belicia	Earl
Calla	Edward
Devonna	Ferris
Dianthe	Gaylord
Elvira	Ira
Garland	Jules
Giselle	Maynard
Happy	Mervin
Hestia	Neville
Keiko	Newt
Kyrene	Nolan
Mahalia	Rod
Modesty	Roscoe
Novia	Seth
Opal	Siegfried
Poppy	Sylvester
Rani	Thaddeus
Sapphire	Tristan
Tierney	Vernon
Twyla	Victor
Velvet	Ward

Wimpy

Boys
Antoine
Archibald
Barton
Bernard
Bradford
Burke
Cecil
Cyril
Dalton
Darren
Duane
Edwin
Gaylord
Homer
Horton
Napoleon
Percival
Prescott
Roosevelt
Rupert
Ulysses
Wesley
Winslow
Winthrop
Yale

Names Inspired by People, Places, and Things

What's in a name? Some parents choose names that carry special meaning. They're sports buffs who name their children after legendary athletes, bookworms who name their children after beloved characters, and nature lovers who name their children after the things they see in their favorite vistas. Then again, some people choose names not because they carry personal significance but simply because they fall in love with them. They may not be sports buffs, bookworms, or nature lovers, but they still choose names like Jordan, Bridget, and Willow.

However you approach it, here are several lists of girls' and boys' names inspired by people, places, and things. (To learn more about choosing names with special meaning, check out the "How to Pick a Name You and Your Baby Will Like" feature on page 3.)

Literature

Authors

Female	Male
Anne (Tyler)	Ambrose (Bierce)
Barbara (Kingsolver)	Bram (Stoker)
Carolyn (Keene)	Cormac (McCarthy)
Charlotte (Brontë)	Dan (Brown)
Doris (Lessing)	Ernest (Hemingway)
Elizabeth (Barrett Browning)	George (Orwell)
Emily (Dickinson)	Henry David (Thoreau)
Harper (Lee)	Homer
Harriet (Beecher Stowe)	J. D. (Salinger)
Jane (Austen)	Jules (Verne)
Joanne Kathleen ("J. K." Rowling)	Leo (Tolstoy)
Judy (Blume)	Lewis (Carroll)
Katherine (Mansfield)	Mario (Puzo)
Louisa (May Alcott)	Mark (Twain)
Lucy Maud (Montgomery)	Nicholas (Sparks)
Madeleine (L'Engle)	Oscar (Wilde)
Margaret (Atwood)	Ray (Bradbury)
Marge (Piercy)	Scott (Fitzgerald)
Mary (Shelley)	Stephen (King)
Maya (Angelou)	Tennessee (Williams)
Paula (Danziger)	Tom (Clancy)
Rebecca (Wells)	Truman (Capote)
Sylvia (Plath)	Virgil
Virginia (Woolf)	Walt (Whitman)
Willa (Cather)	William (Faulkner)

Fictional Characters

Female	Male
Anna (Karenina)	Atticus (Finch)
Anne (Shirley)	Billy (Coleman)
Antonia (Shimerda)	Boo (Radley)
Bridget (Jones)	Cyrus (Trask)
Cosette (Valjean)	Edmond (Dantés)
Daisy (Buchanan)	Ethan (Frome)
Dorothea (Brooke)	Frodo (Baggins)
Edna (Pontellier)	Guy (Montag)
Elizabeth (Bennet)	Harry (Potter)
Emma (Woodhouse)	Heathcliff
Hermione (Granger)	Henry (Fleming)
Hester (Prynne)	Holden (Caulfield)
Isabel (Archer)	Huck (Finn)
Jane (Eyre)	Jake (Barnes)
Josephine (March)	Jay (Gatsby)
Juliet (Capulet)	Jean (Valjean)
Junie (B. Jones)	John (Proctor)
Mary (Lennox)	Odysseus
Meg (Murry)	Owen (Meany)
Ophelia	Pip (Philip Pirrip)
Phoebe (Caulfield)	Rhett (Butler)
Pippi (Longstocking)	Robinson (Crusoe)
Scarlett (O'Hara)	Romer (Montague)
Scout (Finch)	Santiago
Serena (Joy)	Victor (Frankenstein)

Playwrights

Female and Male

Anna (Deavere Smith)
Anton (Chekhov)
Arthur (Miller)
August (Wilson)
Ben (Johnson)
Bertolt (Brecht)
Beth (Henley)
Christopher (Marlowe)
Dario (Fo)
Eugene (O'Neill)
George (Bernard Shaw)
Harold (Pinter)
Henrik (Ibsen)
Jean Baptiste (Poquelin Molière)
Lillian (Hellman)
Neil (Simon)
Noel (Coward)
Oscar (Wilde)
Paula (Vogel)
Samuel (Beckett)
Susan (Glaspell)
Tennessee (Willimas)
Thomas Stearns ("T. S." Eliot)
Thornton (Wilder)
William (Shakespeare)

Dramatic Characters

Female and Male

Abigail (Williams)
Algernon ("Algy" Moncrieff)
Bella (Kurnitz)
Blanche (DuBois)
Christine (Daaé)
Cosette
Edmund (Tyrone)
Eliza (Doolittle)
Emily (Webb)
George (Gibbs)
Gwendolen (Fairfax)
Henry (Higgins)
Jean (Valjean)
Jim (O'Connor)
John (Proctor)
Juliet (Capulet)
Laura (Wingfield)
Linda (Loman)
Mary (Tyrone)
Odysseus
Raoul (de Chagny)
Romeo (Montague)
Stanley (Kowalski)
Vladimir
Willy (Loman)

Shakespearean Characters

Female	Male
Adriana	Angelo
Beatrice	Antony
Cleopatra	Balthasar
Cordelia	Bertram
Emilia	Cicero
Gertrude	Claudio
Helena	Cromwell
Hermia	Duncan
Hero	Edmund
Imogen	Hamlet
Isabella	Iachimo
Juliet	Iago
Katharina	Julius (Caesar)
Lavinia	Lysander
Mariana	Malcolm
Miranda	Oberon
Olivia	Orlando
Ophelia	Othello
Paulina	Paris
Portia	Puck
Regan	Richard
Rosalind	Romeo
Titania	Titus
Ursula	Tybalt
Viola	Vincentio

Poets

Female	Male
Adrienne (Rich)	Alfred (Lord Tennyson)
Amy (Lowell)	Allen (Ginsberg)
Anne (Sexton)	Carl (Sandburg)
Christina (Rossetti)	Czeslaw (Milosz)
Denise (Levertov)	Dante (Alighieri)
Dorothy (Parker)	Dylan (Thomas)
Edna (St. Vincent Millay)	Ezra (Pound)
Elizabeth (Barrett Browning)	James (Dickey)
Emily (Dickinson)	John (Keats)
Gertrude (Stein)	Juan (Ramón Jiménez)
Gwendolyn (Brooks)	Langston (Hughes)
Jamaica (Kincaid)	Louis (Simpson)
Joy (Harjo)	Mark (Strand)
Marianne (Moore)	Matsuo (Basho)
Marilyn (Hacker)	Pablo (Neruda)
Mary (Oliver)	Percy (Bysshe Shelley)
Mary Ann ("George Eliot" Evans)	Philip (Larkin)
Maxine (Kumin)	Robert (Frost)
Maya (Angelou)	Seamus (Heaney)
Muriel (Rukeyser)	Theodore (Roethke)
Rita (Dove)	Thomas (Stearns "T. S." Eliot)
Sarah (Teasdale)	Wallace (Stevens)
Sharon (Olds)	Walt (Whitman)
Sylvia (Plath)	William (Butler Yeats)
Wislawa (Szymborska)	Yusef (Komunyakaa)

Nursery Rhyme Characters

Female and Male

Bo (Peep)
Bobby (Shaftoe)
Bonnie
Elsie (Marley)
Fred
Georgie (Porgie)
Jack
Jerry (Hall)
Jill
John (Jacob Jingleheimer Schmidt)
King Cole
Lou
MacDonald
Margery (Daw)
Mary
Michael
Nancy (Etticoat)
Peter (Piper)
Polly (Flinders)
Robin
Taffy
Tommy (Tittlemouse)
Simon
Solomon (Grundy)
Willie (Winkie)

Picture Book Characters

Female and Male

Alexander
Alice
Arthur
Babar
Cinderella
Clifford
Elmo
Ferdinand
Frances
George
Harold
Horton
Imogene
Lilly
Madeline
Maisy
Max
Olivia
Paddington
Pat
Peter
Ping
Sal
Tikki
Winnie

Comic Strip Characters	Comic Book Superhero Alter Egos	Arthurian Legend Characters	*The Lord of the Rings* Characters
Female and Male	**Female and Male**	**Female and Male**	**Female and Male**
Andy (Capp)	Arthur (Curry, "Aquaman")	Anna	Aragorn
Blondie (Bumstead)	Barbara (Gordon, "Bat Girl")	Arthur	Arwen
Brenda (Starr)	Ben (Grim, "The Thing")	Bors	Bilbo
Calvin	Bruce (Wayne, "Batman")	Ector	Boromir
Cathy	Charles (Xavier, "Professor X")	Emmeline	Celeborn
Charlie (Brown)	Clark (Kent, "Superman")	Gaheris	Denethor
Dennis (Mitchell)	Diana (Prince, "Wonder Woman")	Galahad	Elrond
Dick (Tracy)	Dick (Grayson, "Robin")	Gareth	Eomer
Dolly	Emma (Frost, "White Queen")	Gawain	Eowyn
Elly (Patterson)	Frank (Castle, "The Punisher")	Guinevere	Faramir
Florrie (Capp)	Hal (Jordon, "Green Lantern")	Igraine	Frodo
Garfield	Henry (McCoy, "Beast")	Iseult	Galadriel
George (Wilson)	Jean (Gray, "Phoenix")	Isolde	Gandalf
Hägar (the Horrible)	Logan (Howlett, "Wolverine")	Kay	Gimli
Heathcliff	Matt (Murdock, "Daredevil")	Lancelot	Gollum
Helga	Oliver (Queen, "Green Arrow")	Lot	Grima
Hiram ("Hi" Flagston)	Peter (Parker, "Spider-Man")	Mark	Legolas
Jeffy	Reed (Richards, "Mr. Fantastic")	Merlin	Merry
Lois (Flagston)	Scott (Summers, "Cyclops")	Mordred	Pippin
Luann	Selina (Kyle, "Catwoman")	Morgan (le Fey)	Rosie
Michael (Doonesbury)	Steve (Rogers, "Captain America")	Morgause	Sam
Odie	Susan (Richards, "Invisble Woman")	Nimue	Saruman
Rex (Morgan)	Tony (Stark, "Iron Man")	Percival	Sauron
Sally (Forth)	Wally (West, "Flash")	Tristan	Theoden
Ziggy	Warren (Worthington III, "Archangel")	Uther (Pendragon)	Tom

History

Harry Potter Characters

Female	Male
Alicia (Spinnet)	Albus (Dumbledore)
Angelina (Johnson)	Blaise (Zabini)
Bellatrix (Lestrange)	Cedric (Diggory)
Cho (Chang)	Colin (Creevey)
Dolores (Umbridge)	Dean (Thomas)
Fleur (Delacour)	Draco (Malfoy)
Ginny (Weasley)	Dudley (Dursley)
Hermione (Granger)	Fred (Weasley)
Katie (Bell)	George (Weasley)
Lavender (Brown)	Harry (Potter)
Lily (Potter)	James (Potter)
Luna (Lovegood)	Kingsley (Shacklebolt)
Minerva (McGonagall)	Lucius (Malfoy)
Molly (Weasley)	Neville (Longbottom)
"Moaning" Myrtle	Oliver (Wood)
Narcissa (Malfoy)	Percy (Weasley)
Nymphadora (Tonks)	Peter (Pettigrew)
Padma (Patil)	Remus (Lupin)
Pansy (Parkinson)	Ron (Weasley)
Parvati (Patil)	Rubeus (Hagrid)
Penelope (Clearwater)	Seamus (Finnigan)
Petunia (Dursley)	Severus (Snape)
Poppy (Pomfrey)	Sirius (Black)
Rita (Skeeter)	Tom (Riddle)
Sibyll (Trelawney)	Viktor (Krum)

Presidents

Male

Abraham (Lincoln), Andrew (Jackson), Bill (Clinton), Calvin (Coolidge), Chester (Arthur), Dwight (D. Eisenhower), Franklin (D. Roosevelt), George (Washington), Gerald (Ford), Grover (Cleveland), Harry (S. Truman), Herbert (Hoover), James (Madison), Jimmy (Carter), John (F. Kennedy), Lyndon (B. Johnson), Martin (Van Buren), Millard (Fillmore), Richard (Nixon), Ronald (Reagan), Rutherford (B. Hayes), Thomas (Jefferson), Ulysses (S. Grant), Warren (G. Harding), Woodrow (Wilson)

Members of First Families

Female and Male

Abigail (Adams), Amy (Carter), Barbara (Bush), Benjamin (Pierce), Caroline (Kennedy), Chelsea (Clinton), Dolley (Madison), Eleanor (Roosevelt), Grace (Coolidge), Helen (Taft), Hillary (Rodham Clinton), Jacqueline (Kennedy), Jeb (Bush), Jenna (Bush), John (Fitzgerald Kennedy, Jr.), Julie (Nixon), Kermit (Roosevelt), Laura (Bush), Martha (Washington), Mary (Todd Lincoln), Maureen (Reagan), Nancy (Reagan), Robert (Lincoln), Rosalynn (Carter), Steven (Ford)

50

Democrats	Republicans	Kings	Queens
Female and Male	**Female and Male**	**Male**	**Female**
Al (Gore)	Antonia (Novello)	Albert	Amina
Barbara (Boxer)	Arnold (Schwarzenegger)	Alexander	Anne
Bill (Clinton)	Barry (Goldwater)	Arthur	Beatrix
Bob (Kerrey)	Bob (Dole)	Canute	Candace
Diane (Feinstein)	Condoleeza (Rice)	Charles	Catherine
Dick (Gephardt)	Dan (Quayle)	Cormac	Charlotte
George (McGovern)	Dick (Cheney)	Cyrus	Christina
Geraldine (Ferraro)	Elizabeth (Dole)	David	Cleopatra
Hillary (Rodham Clinton)	George (Bush)	Edgar	Elizabeth
Hubert (Humphrey)	Gerald (Ford)	Edmund	Esther
Jesse (Jackson)	Henry (Kissinger)	Edward	Filippa
Jimmy (Carter)	Jeane (Kirkpatrick)	Ferdinand	Ingrid
John (F. Kennedy)	Laura (Bush)	Frederick	Isabella
Joseph (Lieberman)	Margaret (Chase Smith)	George	Jeanne
Lyndon (B. Johnson)	Mary (Matalin)	Harold	Juliana
Madeleine (Albright)	Nancy (Kassebaum)	Henry	Louise
Michael (Dukakis)	Nelson (Rockefeller)	James	Margaret
Nancy (Pelosi)	Newt (Gingrich)	John	Marie
Paul (Wellstone)	Patrick (Buchanan)	Louis	Mary
Reubin (Askew)	Richard (Nixon)	Magnus	Matilda
Shirley (Chisholm)	Ronald (Reagan)	Malcolm	Silvia
Harry (S. Truman)	Rudy (Giuliani)	Niall	Sofia
Ted (Kennedy)	Rush (Limbaugh)	Phillip	Tamar
Tom (Daschle)	Trent (Lott)	Richard	Victoria
Walter (Mondale)	Wendell (Willkie)	William	Zenobia

50

Members of the British Royal Family	**Military Figures**	**Explorers**	**Activists**
Female and Male	**Female and Male**	**Female and Male**	**Female and Male**
Alexander	Alexander (the Great)	Amelia (Earhart)	Agnes ("Mother Teresa" Gonxha Bojaxhiu)
Alexandra	Andrew (Johnson)	Ann (Bancroft)	Albert (Schweitzer)
Alice	Attila (the Hun)	Amerigo (Vespucci)	Anwar (el-Sadat)
Andrew	Charles (de Gaulle)	Bartolomeu (Dias)	Cesar (Chavez)
Anne	Che (Guevara)	Christopher (Columbus)	Che (Guevara)
Beatrice	Deborah	Eric (The Red)	Desmond (Tutu)
Birgitte	Douglas (MacArthur)	Ferdinand (Magellan)	Dorothy (Day)
Camilla	Dwight (D. Eisenhower)	Francisco (Vásquez de Coronado)	Elizabeth (Cady Stanton)
Charles	Genghis (Khan)	George (Everest)	Frederick (Douglass)
Davina	George (S. Patton)	Gertrude (Bell)	Gloria (Steinem)
Diana	Ivan (Stepanovich Konev)	Harriet (Chalmers Adams)	Harriet (Tubman)
Edward	Jennie (Hodgers)	Henry (Hudson)	Jesse (Jackson)
Elizabeth	Joan (of Arc)	Hernán (Cortés)	Jimmy (Carter)
Eugenie	Julius (Caesar)	Hernando (de Soto)	John (Muir)
Frederick	Moshe (Dayan)	Jacques (Cousteau)	Kim (Dae-jung)
George	Napoleon (Bonaparte)	Juan (Ponce de León)	Lucy (Stone)
Helen	Norman (Schwarzkopf)	James (Cook)	Malcolm (X)
Henry (Harry)	Oliver (Cromwell)	Leif (Ericsson)	Margaret (Sanger)
Louise	Omar (Bradley)	Marco (Polo)	Martin (Luther King)
Michael	Peter (the Great)	Neil (Armstrong)	Mary (Wollstonecraft)
Nicholas	Robert (E. Lee)	Samuel (de Champlain)	Nelson (Mandela)
Peter	Tecumseh	Thor (Heyerdahl)	Rachel (Carson)
Philip	Ulysses (S. Grant)	Walter (Raleigh)	Rosa (Parks)
Richard	William (Wallace)	William (Clark)	Susan (B. Anthony)
William	Winston (Churchill)	Zebulon (Pike)	William ("W. E. B." Du Bois)

Religion and Mythology

Nobel Prize Winners	Old West Figures	Colleges and Universities	Old Testament Figures
Female and Male	**Female and Male**	**Female and Male**	**Male**
Agnes ("Mother Teresa" Gonxha Bojaxhiu)	Annie (Oakley)	Auburn	Abel
Albert (Einstein)	Bat (Masterson)	Berkeley	Abraham
Desmond (Tutu)	Belle (Starr)	Brown	Adam
Elie (Wiesel)	Butch (Cassidy)	Bryn (Mawr)	Cain
Ernest (Hemingway)	Charles ("Black Bart" Boles)	Carleton	Caleb
George (Beadle)	Clay (Allison)	Columbia	Daniel
Godfrey (Hounsfield)	Cole (Younger)	Cornell	David
Günter (Grass)	Daniel (Boone)	Creighton	Eli
Ivan (Pavlov)	Davy (Crockett)	Drake	Esau
Jimmy (Carter)	Doc (Holliday)	Duke	Ezekiel
Kofi (Annan)	Frank (James)	Emerson	Ezra
Marie (Curie)	Harry ("Sundance Kid" Longabaugh)	Emory	Isaac
Martin (Luther King)	Henry (Starr)	Kent	Isaiah
Mikhail (Gorbachev)	James ("Wild Bill" Hickok)	Kenyon	Jacob
Milton (Friedman)	Jesse (James)	Lewis and Clark	Jeremiah
Nadine (Gordimer)	John (Wesley Hardin)	Penn	Job
Nelson (Mandela)	Kit (Carson)	Princeton	Joel
Niels (Bohr)	Martha Jane ("Calamity Jane" Canary)	Regis	Joshua
Octavio (Paz)	Pat (Garrett)	Rhodes	Moses
Pablo (Neruda)	Roy (Bean)	Rice	Nemiah
Pearl (Buck)	Sally (Skull)	Sarah Lawrence	Noah
Samuel (Beckett)	Sam (Houston)	Stanford	Samson
Saul (Bellow)	Tom (Horn)	William and Mary	Samuel
Seamus (Heaney)	William ("Buffalo Bill" Cody)	Xavier	Solomon
Toni (Morrison)	Wyatt (Earp)	Yale	

New Testament Figures	Biblical Women	Saints		Popes
Male	**Female**	**Female**	**Male**	**Male**
Agrippa	Abigail	Agatha	Ambrose	Adrian
Andrew	Bathsheba	Agnes	Andrew	Alexander
Annas	Deborah	Bernadette	Anslem	Benedict
Aquila	Delilah	Bridget	Anthony	Boniface
Gabriel	Dinah	Candida	Augustine	Celestine
Herod	Eden	Catherine	Bartholomew	Clement
James	Elizabeth	Cecilia	Benedict	Constantine
Jesus	Esther	Clare	Christopher	Cornelius
John	Eve	Florence	Felix	Eugene
Joseph	Hagar	Genevieve	Francis	Felix
Judas	Hannah	Hilary	Gregory	Gregory
Jude	Jezebel	Ingrid	Ignatius	Innocent
Luke	Judith	Joan	Jerome	John Paul
Mark	Julia	Julia	John	Julius
Matthew	Leah	Louise	Jude	Leo
Nicolas	Maria	Lucy	Leo	Linus
Paul	Martha	Lydia	Nicholas	Peter
Peter	Mary	Margaret	Patrick	Pius
Philip	Miriam	Maria	Paul	Romanus
Simon	Naomi	Mary	Peter	Sixtus
Stephen	Phoebe	Monica	Sebastian	Stephan
Thomas	Rachel	Regina	Stephen	Theodore
Timothy	Rebekah	Rose	Thomas	Urban
Titus	Ruth	Sylvia	Valentine	Valentine
Zechariah	Sarah	Teresa	Vincent	Zachary

Christmas-Themed Names	Heavenly and Angelic Names	Jewish Figures	Muslim Figures
Female and Male	**Female and Male**	**Female and Male**	**Male**
Angel	Angel	Aaron	Adam
Bell	Angela	Akiva	Al-Yasa
Carol	Angellica	Abraham	Ayub
Claus	Angelo	Daniel	Daud
Ebenezer	Asención	David (Ben Gurion)	Harun
Emmanuel	Beulah	Deborah	Hud
Garland	Celeste	Esther	Ibrahim
Gloria	Divinity	Golda (Meir)	Idris
Holly	Eden	Hillel	Ilyas
Jesus	Faith	Isaac	Isa
Joseph	Gabriel	Jacob	Ishaq
Joy	Gloria	Joseph	Ismail
King	Heaven	Judah (Maccabee)	Lut
Kris	Jannah	Leah	Muhammad
Manger	Lani	Maimonides	Musa
Mary	Michael	Miriam	Nuh
Merry	Nevaeh	Mordechai	Saleh
Nicholas	Paradise	Moses	Shoaib
Noel	Paradiso	Nachimanides	Sulayman
Peace	Raphael	Rachel	Yahya
Rudolf	Seraphim	Rashi	Yaqub
Shepherd	Seraphina	Rebecca	Yunus
Star	Tian	Ruth	Yusuf
Wenceslas	Trinity	Sarah	Zakariya
Yule	Zion	Yochanan (ben Zakkai)	Zulkifl

Hindu Figures	Greek Mythology Figures		Roman Mythology Figures		Egyptian Mythology Figures
Female and Male	**Female**	**Male**	**Female**	**Male**	**Female and Male**
Agni	Aphrodite	Achilles	Aurora	Aeneas	Aker
Arjuna	Artemis	Adonis	Bellona	Aesculapius	Anouke
Bali	Athena	Apollo	Camilla	Amor	Anubis
Brahma	Calliope	Ares	Ceres	Bacchus	Atum
Buddha	Calypso	Atlas	Clementia	Cupid	Bastet
Chandra	Chloe	Dionysus	Concordia	Faunus	Bes
Devi	Daphne	Eros	Decima	Honos	Buto
Dharma	Demeter	Hades	Diana	Inuus	Geb
Indra	Echo	Hector	Fauna	Janus	Hapi
Kali	Electra	Helios	Felicitas	Jove	Hathor
Kama	Europa	Hercules	Flora	Jupiter	Horus
Krishna	Gaea	Hermes	Fortuna	Liber	Isis
Maya	Helen	Icarus	Hippona	Mars	Ma'at
Nala	Hera	Jason	Juno	Mercury	Min
Parvati	Hestia	Midas	Juventus	Neptune	Neith
Rama	Io	Morpheus	Levana	Orcus	Nun
Ravi	Leda	Narcissus	Luna	Pluto	Nunet
Sati	Medusa	Odysseus	Mania	Remus	Osiris
Shiva	Nike	Orion	Minerva	Romulus	Ptah
Sita	Pandora	Pan	Pax	Saturn	Ra
Surya	Penelope	Paris	Roma	Silvanus	Seb
Uma	Persephone	Perseus	Venus	Sol	Seth
Ushas	Phoebe	Poseidon	Veritas	Somnus	Shu
Vishnu	Psyche	Prometheus	Vesta	Ulysses	Sobek
Yama	Rhea	Zeus	Victoria	Vulcan	Thoth

Movies and TV

Norse Mythology Figures	African Mythology	Japanese Mythology	Movie Stars	
Female and Male	**Female and Male**	**Female and Male**	**Female**	**Male**
Aegir	Abuk	Amaterasu	Angelina (Jolie)	Benicio (Del Toro)
Astrild	Agé	Amida	Anjelica (Huston)	Bing (Crosby)
Atla	Aja	Benten	Audrey (Hepburn)	Bruce (Willis)
Balder	Astar	Bishamon	Betty (Grable)	Cary (Grant)
Bragi	Buku	Daikoku	Cameron (Diaz)	Chevy (Chase)
Edda	Deng	Dosojin	Catherine (Zeta-Jones)	Clark (Gable)
Forseti	Edinkira	Ebisu	Cher	Clint (Eastwood)
Freya	Enekpe	Fujin	Drew (Barrymore)	Dustin (Hoffman)
Freyr	Eshu	Gama	Elizabeth (Taylor)	Harrison (Ford)
Frigg	Faro	Gongen	Emma (Thompson)	Jack (Nicholson)
Hel	Gun	Hachiman	Gwyneth (Paltrow)	John (Wayne)
Hermod	Inkosazana	Hiruko	Halle (Berry)	Leonardo (DiCaprio)
Hod	Kuru	Hoderi	Jodie (Foster)	Martin (Sheen)
Idun	Loko	Inari	Julia (Roberts)	Mel (Gibson)
Loki	Mawu	Isora	Katharine (Hepburn)	Mickey (Rooney)
Mimir	Mugasa	Jimmu	Liv (Tyler)	Orlando (Bloom)
Njord	Osawa	Kaminari	Meg (Ryan)	Patrick (Swayze)
Odin	Oshun	Kishijoten	Meryl (Streep)	Robert (De Niro)
Ran	Oya	Marisha-Ten	Michelle (Pfeiffer)	Robin (Williams)
Saga	Shango	Onamuji	Nicole (Kidman)	Rock (Hudson)
Sif	Tamuno	Raiden	Penelope (Cruz)	Russell (Crowe)
Thor	Wele	Sengen	Reese (Witherspoon)	Sean (Connery)
Thrud	Woto	Susanowa	Salma (Hayek)	Spencer (Tracy)
Tyr	Xamaba	Tsuki-Yumi	Sandra (Bullock)	Sylvester (Stallone)
Ull	Yemaja	Uzume	Shirley (Temple)	Tom (Cruise)
Vali				

Oscar Winners

Female	Male
Angelina (Jolie)	Al (Pacino)
Anna (Paquin)	Anthony (Hopkins)
Barbara (Streisand)	Benicio (Del Toro)
Bette (Davis)	Christopher (Walken)
Charlize (Theron)	Cuba (Gooding, Jr.)
Diane (Keaton)	Daniel (Day-Lewis)
Elizabeth (Taylor)	Denzel (Washington)
Goldie (Hawn)	Dustin (Hoffman)
Halle (Berry)	Gene (Hackman)
Hilary (Swank)	Jack (Nicholson)
Jane (Fonda)	James (Stewart)
Jessica (Lange)	Jamie (Foxx)
Jodie (Foster)	Kevin (Spacey)
Julia (Roberts)	Laurence (Olivier)
Julie (Andrews)	Marlon (Brando)
Katharine (Hepburn)	Michael (Caine)
Kathy (Bates)	Morgan (Freeman)
Maggie (Smith)	Philip (Seymour Hoffman)
Marisa (Tomei)	Richard (Dreyfuss)
Meryl (Streep)	Robert (De Niro)
Reese (Witherspoon)	Russell (Crowe)
Sally (Fields)	Sidney (Poitier)
Susan (Sarandon)	Tom (Hanks)
Tatum (O'Neal)	Tommy (Lee Jones)
Whoopi (Goldberg)	Walter (Brennan)

Silver Screen Stars

Female	Male
Audrey (Hepburn)	Bing (Crosby)
Ava (Gardner)	Burt (Lancaster)
Barbara (Stanwyck)	Cary (Grant)
Bette (Davis)	Charlton (Heston)
Carole (Lombard)	Clark (Gable)
Betty (Grable)	Errol (Flynn)
Deborah (Kerr)	Frank (Sinatra)
Ginger (Rogers)	Fred (Astaire)
Grace (Kelly)	Gary (Cooper)
Greta (Garbo)	Gene (Kelly)
Ingrid (Bergman)	Gregory (Peck)
Jean (Harlow)	Henry (Fonda)
Joan (Crawford)	Humphrey (Bogart)
Judy (Garland)	James (Dean)
Katharine (Hepburn)	Jimmy (Stewart)
Lana (Turner)	John (Wayne)
Lauren (Bacall)	Laurence (Olivier)
Loretta (Young)	Marlon (Brando)
Mae (West)	Montgomery (Clift)
Marilyn (Monroe)	Orson (Welles)
Marlene (Dietrich)	Peter (O'Toole)
Natalie (Wood)	Rex (Harrison)
Rita (Hayworth)	Richard (Burton)
Veronica (Lake)	Spencer (Tracy)
Vivien (Leigh)	Walter (Brennan)

Movie Characters

Female	Male
Amélie (Poulain)	Atticus (Finch)
Annie (Hall)	Austin (Powers)
Bonnie (Parker)	Billy (Madison)
Bridget (Jones)	Charles (Foster Kane)
Clarice (Starling)	Forrest (Gump)
Clementine (Kruczynski)	Frodo (Baggins)
Dorothy (Gale)	George (Bailey)
Elaine (Robinson)	Hannibal (Lector)
Eliza (Doolittle)	Harry (Potter)
Ellen (Ripley)	Indiana (Jones)
Erin (Brockovich)	Jack (Sparrow)
Holly (Golightly)	Jacques (Clouseau)
Ilsa (Lund)	James (Bond)
Jean Louise ("Scout" Finch)	Jerry (Maguire)
Lara (Croft)	Judah (Ben-Hur)
Leia (Organa)	Lloyd (Dobler)
Louise (Sawyer)	Luke (Skywalker)
Marge (Gunderson)	Maximus (Decimus Meridius)
Maria (von Trapp)	Napoleon (Dynamite)
Mary (Poppins)	Neo
Norma Rae (Webster)	Norman (Bates)
Sandy (Olsson)	Rhett (Butler)
Scarlett (O'Hara)	Rick (Blaine)
Thelma (Dickerson)	Rocky (Balboa)
Trinity	Vito (Corleone)

Movie Directors

Female and Male

Alfred (Hitchcock)
Clint (Eastwood)
Ethan (Coen)
Francis (Ford Coppola)
Frank (Capra)
George (Lucas)
James (Cameron)
Joel (Coen)
John (Woo)
Martin (Scorsese)
Mel (Brooks)
Michael (Moore)
Oliver (Stone)
Penny (Marshall)
Peter (Jackson)
Quentin (Tarantino)
Roman (Polanski)
Ron (Howard)
Sofia (Coppola)
Spike (Lee)
Stanley (Kubrick)
Steven (Spielberg)
Tim (Burton)
Wes (Craven)
Woody (Allen)

Comedians

Female	**Male**
Carol (Burnett)	Adam (Sandler)
Caroline (Rhea)	Bernie (Mac)
Cheri (Oteri)	Bill (Cosby)
Ellen (DeGeneres)	Bob (Hope)
Fanny (Brice)	Cedric ("The Entertainer" Kyles)
Gilda (Radner)	Chevy (Chase)
Gracie (Allen)	Chris (Rock)
Jane (Curtain)	Dan (Aykroyd)
Janeane (Garofalo)	Dana (Carvey)
Joan (Rivers)	Dave (Chappelle)
Kathy (Griffin)	David (Letterman)
Lily (Tomlin)	Denis (Leary)
Lucille (Ball)	Drew (Carey)
Margaret (Cho)	Eddie (Murphy)
Molly (Shannon)	George (Burns)
Paula (Poundstone)	Jay (Leno)
Phyllis (Diller)	Jerry (Seinfeld)
Rita (Rudner)	Johnny (Carson)
Roseanne (Barr)	Louie (Anderson)
Rosie (O'Donnell)	Mike (Myers)
Sandra (Bernhard)	Ray (Romano)
Tina (Fey)	Rodney (Dangerfield)
Tracey (Ullman)	Steve (Martin)
Wanda (Sykes)	Tim (Allen)
Whoopi (Goldberg)	Will (Ferrell)

TV Characters

Female	**Male**
Abby (Lockhart)	Al (Bundy)
Ally (McBeal)	Alex (P. Keaton)
Buffy (Summers)	Archie (Bunker)
Carmela (Soprano)	Arthur ("Fonzie" Fonzarelli)
Carrie (Bradshaw)	Chandler (Bing)
Claire (Kincaid)	Cliff (Huxtable)
Daphne (Moon Crane)	Cosmo (Kramer)
Darlene (Conner-Healy)	Danny ("Danno" Williams)
Donna (Martin Silver)	Dylan (McKay)
Elaine (Benes)	Fox (Mulder)
Erica (Kane)	Frasier (Crane)
Felicity (Porter)	Gil (Grissom)
Fran (Fine)	Jack (McCoy)
Gabrielle (Solis)	Jean-Luc (Picard)
Grace (Adler)	Jed (Bartlet)
Kelly (Bundy)	Joey (Tribbiani)
Kimberly (Shaw Mancini)	John Ross ("J. R." Ewing, Jr.)
Lucy (Ricardo)	Kevin (Arnold)
Marcia (Brady)	Luka (Kovac)
Margaret ("Hot Lips" Houlihan)	Ricky (Ricardo)
Michelle (Tanner)	Sam (Malone)
Rachel (Green)	Tony (Soprano)
Rebecca (Howe)	Vic (Mackey)
Sydney (Bristow)	Will (Truman)
Vanessa (Huxtable)	Zack (Morris)

TV Personalities

Female

Ann (Curry)
Barbara (Walters)
Brooke (Burke)
Connie (Chung)
Diane (Sawyer)
Ellen (DeGeneres)
Jane (Pauley)
Jenny (Jones)
Joan (Rivers)
Joy (Behar)
Judy ("Judge Judy" Sheindlin)
Kathie (Lee Gifford)
Katie (Couric)
Kelly (Ripa)
Leeza (Gibbons)
Lisa (Ling)
Martha (Stewart)
Meredith (Vieira)
Nancy (O'Dell)
Oprah (Winfrey)
Paige (Davis)
Ricki (Lake)
Sally (Jessy Raphaël)
Star (Jones Reynolds)
Vanna (White)

Male

Ahmad (Rashad)
Al (Roker)
Alex (Trebek)
Bill (O'Reilly)
Bob (Barker)
Carson (Daly)
Conan (O'Brien)
Dan (Rather)
David (Letterman)
Dick (Clark)
Geraldo (Rivera)
Howard (Stern)
Jay (Leno)
Jerry (Springer)
Jim (Lehrer)
Johnny (Carson)
Larry (King)
Matt (Lauer)
Montel (Williams)
Peter (Jennings)
Phil (McGraw)
Regis (Philbin)
Simon (Cowell)
Tom (Brokaw)
Ty (Pennington)

Disney Cartoon Characters

Female

Alice
Ariel
Aurora
Belle
Boo
Cinderella
Daisy (Duck)
Esmeralda
Fauna
Flora
Helen (Parr)
Jane (Porter)
Jasmine
Jessie
Lilo
Marian
Mary (Poppins)
Megara
Minnie
Mulan
Nala
Pocahontas
Ursula
Violet (Parr)
Wendy

Male

Aladdin
Bambi
Bob (Parr)
Buzz (Lightyear)
Chip
Christopher (Robin)
Dale
Dash (Parr)
Dewey
Donald (Duck)
Eric
Gaston
Hercules
Huey
Ichabod (Crane)
Jafar
Louie
Merlin
Mickey
Mufasa
Peter (Pan)
Robin (Hood)
Sebastian
Simba
Timon

Music

Soap Opera Characters

Female and Male
Bo (Brady)
Carly (Corinthos)
Drucilla (Winters)
Eric (Forrester)
Erica (Kane)
Eve (Russell)
Harley (Cooper)
Hope (Brady)
Jack (Deveraux)
Jasper ("Jax" Jacks)
Laura (Spencer)
Lily (Snyder)
Luke (Spencer)
Marlena (Evans)
Nikki (Newman)
Phillip (Spaulding)
Reva (Shane)
Ridge (Forrester)
Sonny (Corinthos)
Tad (Martin)
Taylor (Hayes Forrester)
Theresa (Lopez-Fitzgerald)
Todd (Manning)
Victor (Newman)
Viki (Lord Davidson)

Cartoon Characters

Female
Angelica (Pickles)
April (O'Neil)
Babs (Bunny)
Betty (Rubble)
Blossom
Daisy (Duck)
Daphne (Blake)
Daria (Morgandorffer)
Dora (the Explorer)
Jane (Jetson)
Jerrica ("Jem" Benton)
Judy (Jetson)
Kim (Possible)
Lil (DeVille)
Lisa (Simpson)
Luanne (Platter)
Lucy (Van Pelt)
Maggie (Simpson)
Marge (Simpson)
Peggy (Hill)
Petunia (Pig)
Rainbow (Brite)
Sally (Brown)
Velma (Dinkley)
Wilma (Flintstone)

Male
Arthur
Barney (Rubble)
Bart (Simpson)
Bobby (Hill)
Charlie (Brown)
Donald (Duck)
Elmer (Fudd)
Elroy (Jetson)
Fred (Flintstone)
Garfield
George (Jetson)
Hank (Hill)
Homer (Simpson)
Jimmy (Neutron)
Johnny (Bravo)
Kenny (McCormick)
Linus (Van Pelt)
Marvin (Martian)
Pepe (Le Pew)
Peter (Griffin)
Rocky
Stan (Marsh)
Sylvester
Tommy (Pickles)
Woody (Woodpecker)

Pop Artists

Female
Alanis (Morrisette)
Annie (Lennox)
Avril (Lavigne)
Britney (Spears)
Celine (Dion)
Cher
Christina (Aguilera)
Dido
Fiona (Apple)
Gloria (Estefan)
Gwen (Stefani)
Janet (Jackson)
Jessica (Simpson)
Jewel
Kelly (Clarkson)
Madonna
Mandy (Moore)
Natalie (Imbruglia)
Norah (Jones)
Paula (Abdul)
Pink
Sarah (McLachlan)
Sheryl (Crow)
Tori (Amos)
Vanessa (Carlton)

Male
Adam (Duritz)
Billy (Joel)
Chris (Martin)
Darius (Rucker)
Dave (Matthews)
Edwin (McCain)
Elton (John)
Elvis (Presley)
Enrique (Iglesias)
Eric (Clapton)
George (Michael)
Howie (Day)
Jack (Johnson)
John (Lennon)
Justin (Timberlake)
Marc (Anthony)
Michael (Jackson)
Nick (Lachey)
Paul (McCartney)
Prince
Ricky (Martin)
Ringo (Starr)
Rob (Thomas)
Rod (Stewart)
Sting

Heavy Metal/Hard Rock Artists	Classic Rock Artists	Jazz Artists	Blues Artists
Female and Male	**Female and Male**	**Female and Male**	**Female and Male**
Alice (Cooper)	Bob (Dylan)	Benny (Goodman)	Aaron (Thibeaux "T-Bone" Walker)
Angus (Young)	Brian (Wilson)	Billie (Holiday)	Albert (King)
Axl (Rose)	Carly (Simon)	Cab (Calloway)	B.B. (King)
Bon (Scott)	Carole (King)	Cassandra (Wilson)	Bessie (Smith)
Chris (Cornell)	Don (Henley)	Charlie (Parker)	Billie (Holiday)
Courtney (Love)	George (Harrison)	Chet (Baker)	Bo (Diddley)
David (Lee Roth)	James (Taylor)	Dave (Koz)	Buddy (Guy)
Eddie (Van Halen)	Janis (Joplin)	David (Sanborn)	Chester ("Howlin' Wolf" Burnett)
Gene (Simmons)	Jerry (Garcia)	Diana (Krall)	Dinah (Washington)
James (Hetfield)	Jim (Morrison)	Dizzy (Gillespie)	Elmore (James)
Joe (Perry)	Jimi (Hendrix)	Duke (Ellington)	Eric (Clapton)
Jon (Bon Jovi)	Jimmy (Page)	Grover (Washington, Jr.)	Huddie ("Leadbelly" Ledbetter)
Kurt (Cobain)	Joan (Baez)	Harry (Connick, Jr.)	Jimmy (Rogers)
Layne (Staley)	John (Lennon)	Herbie (Mann)	John (Lee Hooker)
Lita (Ford)	Joni (Mitchell)	John (Coltrane)	Johnny (Lang)
Marilyn (Manson)	Keith (Richards)	Louis (Armstrong)	Kevin ("Keb' Mo'" Moore)
Maynard (James Keenan)	Linda (Ronstadt)	Miles (Davis)	Muddy (Waters)
Ozzy (Osbourne)	Mick (Jagger)	Norah (Jones)	Robert (Cray)
Rob (Halford)	Neil (Young)	Ornette (Coleman)	Robert (Johnson)
Robert (Plant)	Paul (McCartney)	Quincy (Jones)	Ruth (Brown)
Scott (Weiland)	Pete (Townshend)	Ray (Charles)	Sam ("Lightnin'" Hopkins)
Sebastian (Bach)	Ringo (Starr)	Stan (Getz)	Son (House)
Steven (Tyler)	Robert (Plant)	William ("Count" Basie)	Stevie Ray (Vaughn)
Sully (Erna)	Roger (Daltrey)	Wynton (Marsalis)	W. C. (Handy)
Tommy (Lee)	Stevie (Nicks)	Xavier (Cugat)	Willie (Dixon)

Rap/Hip-Hop Artists

Female and Male

Andre ("Dr. Dre" Young)
Anthony ("Tone-Loc" Smith)
Antwan ("Big Boi" Patton)
Calvin ("Snoop Dogg" Broadus)
Carlton ("Chuck D" Ridenhour)
Christopher ("Ludacris" Bridges)
Cornell ("Nelly" Haynes, Jr.)
Curtis ("50 Cent" Jackson)
Dana ("Queen Latifah" Owens)
James ("LL Cool J" Todd Smith)
Jason ("Jam Master Jay" Mizell)
Joseph ("Run" Simmons)
Kimberly ("Lil' Kim" Jones)
Marshall ("Eminem" Mathers)
Melissa ("Missy" Elliot)
Mike ("Mike D" Diamond)
O'Shea ("Ice Cube" Jackson)
Robert ("Vanilla Ice" Van Winkle)
Sean ("P Diddy" Combs)
Shawn ("Jay-Z" Carter)
Stanley ("MC Hammer" Burrell)
Tracy ("Ice-T" Marrow)
Trevor ("Busta Rhymes" Smith, Jr.)
Tupac ("2Pac" Shakur)
William ("Flava Flav" Drayton)

R&B/Soul Artists

Male

Aaron (Neville)
Barry (White)
Bill (Withers)
Brian (McKnight)
Bobby (Brown)
Cedric ("K-Ci" Hailey)
Edwin (Starr)
Freddie (Jackson)
Ike (Turner)
James (Brown)
Joel ("Jo-Jo" Hailey)
Kenneth ("Babyface" Edmonds)
Lionel (Richie)
Lou (Rawls)
Luther (Vandross)
Marvin (Gaye)
Michael ("D'Angelo" Archer)
Otis (Redding)
Percy (Sledge)
Ray (Charles)
Robert ("R. Kelly" Kelly)
Ronnie (DeVoe)
Ruben (Studdard)
Stevie (Wonder)
Usher (Raymond)

Female

Aaliyah
Alicia (Keys)
Aretha (Franklin)
Ashanti
Beyoncé (Knowles)
Brandy (Norwood)
Christina (Milian)
Diana (Ross)
Dionne (Warwick)
Faith (Evans)
Gladys (Knight)
India (Arie)
Jennifer (Lopez)
Kelly (Rowland)
Lauryn (Hill)
Macy (Gray)
Mariah (Carey)
Mary (J. Blige)
Monica (Arnold)
Mya (Harrison)
Patti (LaBelle)
Tina (Turner)
Toni (Braxton)
Vanessa (Williams)
Whitney (Houston)

Country Western Artists

Female

Alison (Krauss)
Carolyn Dawn (Johnson)
Chely (Wright)
Crystal (Gayle)
Cyndi (Thomson)
Dolly (Parton)
Faith (Hill)
Gretchen (Wilson)
Jamie (O'Neal)
Jo Dee (Messina)
Julie (Roberts)
LeAnn (Rimes)
Loretta (Lynn)
Martie (Maguire)
Martina (McBride)
Mary (Chapin Carpenter)
Mindy (McCready)
Natalie (Maines)
Patsy (Cline)
Patty (Loveless)
Reba (McEntire)
Sara (Evans)
Shania (Twain)
Tammy (Wynette)
Terri (Clark)

Male

Alan (Jackson)
Billy Ray (Cyrus)
Brad (Paisley)
Charley (Pride)
Chet (Atkins)
Clint (Black)
Darryl (Worley)
Don (Everly)
Garth (Brooks)
Gene (Autry)
George (Strait)
Hank (Williams)
Joe (Nichols)
Johnny (Cash)
Keith (Urban)
Kenny (Chesney)
Kix (Brooks)
Randy (Travis)
Ronnie (Dunn)
Tim (McGraw)
Toby (Keith)
Trace (Adkins)
Vince (Gill)
Waylon (Jennings)
Willie (Nelson)

Crooners

Female and Male
Al (Jolson)
Andy (Williams)
Artie (Shaw)
Bing (Crosby)
Bobby (Darin)
Cole (Porter)
Dinah (Washington)
Ella (Fitzgerald)
Frank (Sinatra)
Glenn (Miller)
Hoagy (Carmichael)
Jerry (Vale)
Mel (Tormé)
Nat ("King" Cole)
Paul (Anka)
Peggy (Lee)
Perry (Como)
Robert (Goulet)
Rosemary (Clooney)
Sammy (Davis, Jr.)
Sarah (Vaughan)
Thomas ("Fats" Waller)
Tony (Bennett)
Vic (Damone)
William ("Count" Basie)

Classical Composers and Performers

Female and Male
Andrea (Bocelli)
Antonio (Vivaldi)
Camille (Saint-Saëns)
Claude (Debussy)
Felix (Mendelssohn)
Franz (Schubert)
Frédéric (Chopin)
George (Handel)
Giacomo (Puccini)
Giuseppe (Verdi)
Igor (Stravinsky)
Johann (Sebastian Bach)
José (Carreras)
Joseph (Haydn)
Leonard (Bernstein)
Luciano (Pavarotti)
Ludwig (van Beethoven)
Maria (Callas)
Nikolay (Rimsky-Korsakov)
Plácido (Domingo)
Pyotr (Tchaikovsky)
Renata (Scotto)
Richard (Wagner)
Wolfgang (Mozart)
Yo-Yo (Ma)

Musical Terms

Female and Male
Allegro
Aria
Cadence
Canon
Carol
Chante
Clef
Coda
Diva
Fermata
Harmony
Harp
Hymn
Lyric
Major
Medley
Melody
Musika
Opus
Piano
Reed
Rococo
Sonata
Symphony
Viola

Songs with Names in the Titles

Female

"Alison" (Elvis Costello)
"Angie" (The Rolling Stones)
"Annie's Song" (John Denver)
"Beth" (Kiss)
"Billie Jean" (Michael Jackson)
"Come On Eileen" (Dexy's Midnight Runners)
"Georgia on My Mind" (Ray Charles)
"Good Golly Miss Molly" (Little Richard)
"Help Me Rhonda" (The Beach Boys)
"Jack and Diane" (John Mellencamp)
"Janie's Got a Gun" (Aerosmith)
"Jenny from the Block" (Jennifer Lopez)
"Kathy's Song" (Simon & Garfunkel)
"Layla" (Derek and the Dominos)
"Lucy in the Sky with Diamonds" (The Beatles)
"Maggie May" (Rod Stewart)
"Mandy" (Barry Manilow)
"Mary Jane's Last Dance" (Tom Petty and the Heartbreakers)
"Mustang Sally" (Wilson Pickett)
"My Sharona" (The Knack)
"Rosalita (Come Out Tonight)" (Bruce Springsteen)
"Rosanna" (Toto)
"Roxanne" (The Police)
"Sweet Caroline" (Neil Diamond)
"Wake Up Little Susie" (The Everly Brothers)

Male

"Achilles Last Stand" (Led Zeppelin)
"Adam's Song" (blink-182)
"Bad, Bad Leroy Brown" (Jim Croce)
"Bennie and the Jets" (Elton John)
"Billy, Don't Be a Hero" (Paper Lace)
"Buddy Holly" (Weezer)
"Calling Elvis" (Dire Straits)
"Daniel" (Elton John)
"Fernando" (ABBA)
"Galileo" (Indigo Girls)
"Goodbye Earl" (Dixie Chicks)
"Hey Joe" (Jimi Hendrix)
"Hey Jude" (The Beatles)
"James Dean" (The Eagles)
"Jeremy" (Pearl Jam)
"Jessie's Girl" (Rick Springfield)
"Jim Dandy" (Black Oak Arkansas)
"Johnny B. Goode" (Chuck Berry)
"Jumpin' Jack Flash" (The Rolling Stones)
"Louie, Louie" (The Kingsmen)
"Me and Bobby McGee" (Janis Joplin)
"Mickey" (Toni Basil)
"Stan" (Eminem)
"What's the Frequency, Kenneth?" (R.E.M.)
"You Can Call Me Al" (Paul Simon)

Sports and Leisure

Athletes

Female

Anna (Kournikova)
Annika (Sorenstam)
Diana (Taurasi)
Jackie (Joyner-Kersee)
Jennie (Finch)
Kerri (Strug)
Kristi (Yamaguchi)
Florence (Griffith Joyner)
Laila (Ali)
Lisa (Leslie)
Marion (Jones)
Martina (Hingis)
Mary Lou (Retton)
Mia (Hamm)
Monica (Seles)
Nadia (Comaneci)
Babe (Didrikson Zaharias)
Oksana (Baiul)
Picabo (Street)
Rebecca (Lobo)
Sarah (Hughes)
Serena (Williams)
Sheryl (Swoopes)
Steffi (Graf)
Venus (Williams)

Male

Andre (Agassi)
Andy (Roddick)
Babe (Ruth)
Bernie (Williams)
Dale (Earnhardt)
David (Beckham)
Elvis (Stojko)
Hulk (Hogan)
Kasey (Kahne)
Kobe (Bryant)
Lance (Armstrong)
Mark (Spitz)
Michael (Jordan)
Mike (Tyson)
Muhammad (Ali)
Orenthal James ("O. J." Simpson)
Oscar (De La Hoya)
Red (Grange)
Riddick (Bowe)
Rocky (Balboa)
Scott (Hamilton)
Tiger (Woods)
Tony (Hawk)
Wayne (Gretzky)
Yao (Ming)

Basketball Players

Female

Alana (Beard)
Alicia (Thompson)
Chantelle (Anderson)
Coco (Miller)
Dominique (Canty)
Ebony (Hoffman)
Felicia (Ragland)
Giuliana (Mendiola)
Gwen (Jackson)
Jessie (Hicks)
Kaayla (Chones)
Katie (Douglas)
Kiesha (Brown)
Lisa (Leslie)
Lucienne (Berthieu)
Michele (Van Gorp)
Natalie (Williams)
Nykesha (Sales)
Olympia (Scott-Richardson)
Sheryl (Swoopes)
Simone (Edwards)
Tai (Dillard)
Tamicha (Jackson)
Tangela (Smith)
Tari (Phillips)

Male

Alonzo (Mourning)
Anfernee ("Penny" Hardaway)
Bill (Russell)
Carmelo (Anthony)
Dennis (Rodman)
Dwyane (Wade)
Earvin ("Magic" Johnson)
Isiah (Thomas)
Jerry (West)
Julius (Erving)
Kareem (Abdul-Jabbar)
Karl (Malone)
Kevin (Garnett)
Kobe (Bryant)
Larry (Bird)
Latrell (Sprewell)
LeBron (James)
Michael (Jordan)
Moses (Malone)
Patrick (Ewing)
Scottie (Pippen)
Shaquille (O'Neal)
Spud (Webb)
Wilt (Chamberlain)
Yao (Ming)

Baseball Players

Male

Albert (Pujols)
Alex (Rodriguez)
Babe (Ruth)
Barry (Bonds)
Cy (Young)
Derek (Jeter)
Cal (Ripken, Jr.)
Hank (Aaron)
Ichiro (Suzuki)
Jackie (Robinson)
Ken (Griffey, Jr.)
Kirby (Puckett)
Manny (Ramirez)
Mark (McGwire)
Mickey (Mantle)
Nolan (Ryan)
Pete (Rose)
Randy (Johnson)
Roger (Clemens)
Rollie (Fingers)
Sammy (Sosa)
Ted (Williams)
Torii (Hunter)
Wade (Boggs)
Willie (Mays)

Football Players

Male

Barry (Sanders)
Bart (Starr)
Bo (Jackson)
Brett (Favre)
Dan (Marino)
Deion (Sanders)
Donovan (McNabb)
Eli (Manning)
Emmitt (Smith)
Jeremy (Shockey)
Jerry (Rice)
Jim (Brown)
Joe (Montana)
John (Elway)
Johnny (Unitas)
LaDainian (Tomlinson)
Lawrence (Taylor)
Michael (Vick)
Peyton (Manning)
Priest (Holmes)
Randy (Moss)
Ray (Lewis)
Tiki (Barber)
Tom (Brady)
Troy (Aikman)

Golfers

Female

Amy (Alcott)
Annika (Sorenstam)
Babe (Didrikson Zaharias)
Beth (Daniel)
Betsy (King)
Betty (Jameson)
Carol (Mann)
Dinah (Shore)
Donna (Caponi)
Dottie (Pepper)
Hollis (Stacy)
JoAnne (Carner)
Judy (Rankin)
Juli (Inkster)
Karrie (Webb)
Kathy (Whitworth)
Laura (Davies)
Louise (Suggs)
Marlene (Hagge)
Michelle (Wie)
Nancy (Lopez)
Pat (Bradley)
Patty (Berg)
Sandra (Haynie)
Se (Ri Pak)

Male

Arnold (Palmer)
Chi Chi (Rodriguez)
Claude (Harmon)
Craig (Stadler)
Eldrick ("Tiger" Woods)
Ernie (Els)
Gene (Littler)
Greg (Norman)
Hale (Irwin)
Happy (Gilmore)
Harvey (Penick)
Jack (Nicklaus)
Jeff (Maggert)
Jesper (Parnevik)
Ken (Venturi)
Nick (Price)
Payne (Stewart)
Phil (Mickelson)
Raymond (Floyd)
Retief (Goosen)
Sam (Snead)
Sergio (Garcia)
Tommy (Bolt)
Vijay (Singh)
Walter (Hagen)

Hockey Players

Male

Bobby (Orr)
Bret (Hull)
Dominik (Hasek)
Eric (Lindros)
Gordie (Howe)
Grant (Fuhr)
Jacques (Plante)
Jarome (Iginla)
Jaromir (Jagr)
Jeremy (Roenick)
Joe (Sakic)
Mario (Lemieux)
Mark (Messier)
Martin (Brodeur)
Maurice (Richard)
Mike (Modano)
Patrick (Roy)
Paul (Coffey)
Pavel (Bure)
Peter (Forsberg)
Phil (Esposito)
Ray (Bourque)
Sergei (Fedorov)
Steve (Yzerman)
Wayne (Gretzky)

Tennis Players

Female

Amanda (Coetzer)
Amelie (Mauresmo)
Anna (Kournikova)
Anastasia (Myskina)
Billie Jean (King)
Chris (Evert)
Elena (Dementieva)
Gabriela (Sabatini)
Jennifer (Capriati)
Justine (Henin-Hardenne)
Kim (Clijsters)
Lindsay (Davenport)
Maria (Sharapova)
Martina (Navratilova)
Mary (Pierce)
Monica (Seles)
Nadia (Petrova)
Natasha (Zvereva)
Pam (Shriver)
Serena (Williams)
Steffi (Graf)
Svetlana (Kuznetsova)
Tatiana (Golovin)
Tracy (Austin)
Venus (Williams)

Male

Alex (Corretja)
Andre (Agassi)
Andy (Roddick)
Arthur (Ashe)
Bill (Tilden)
Bjorn (Borg)
Boris (Becker)
Carlos (Moya)
Greg (Rusedski)
Guillermo (Coria)
Gustavo (Kuerten)
Ivan (Lendl)
James (Blake)
Jimmy (Connors)
John (McEnroe)
Juan Carlos (Ferrero)
Lleyton (Hewitt)
Mark (Philippoussis)
Michael (Chang)
Pete (Sampras)
Rod (Laver)
Roger (Federer)
Stefan (Edberg)
Todd (Woodbridge)
Tommy (Haas)

Olympians

Female

Amanda (Beard)
Bonnie (Blair)
Dominique (Dawes)
Dorothy (Hamill)
Dot (Richardson)
Florence (Griffith Joyner)
Inge (de Bruijn)
Irina (Slutskaya)
Jackie (Joyner-Kersee)
Janet (Evans)
Janica (Kostelic)
Katarina (Witt)
Kerri (Strug)
Kristi (Yamaguchi)
Larissa (Latynina)
Mary Lou (Retton)
Nadia (Comaneci)
Nancy (Kerrigan)
Oksana (Baiul)
Olga (Korbut)
Peggy (Fleming)
Shannon (Miller)
Summer (Sanders)
Svetlana (Boguinskaya)
Tatyana (Gutsu)

Male

Alberto (Tomba)
Aleksandr (Popov)
Alexei (Yagudin)
Bjørn (Dæhlie)
Brian (Boitano)
Carl (Lewis)
Dan (Jansen)
Dmitri (Bilozerchev)
Elvis (Stojko)
Eric (Heiden)
Gary (Hall, Jr.)
Greg (Louganis)
Hermann (Maier)
Ian (Thorpe)
Ingemar (Stenmark)
Ivar (Ballangrud)
Jonny (Moseley)
Kurt (Browning)
Mark (Spitz)
Matt (Biondi)
Michael (Phelps)
Paul (Hamm)
Scott (Hamilton)
Stephan (Eberharter)
Tamas (Darnyi)

Boxers

Female and Male
Buster (Douglas)
Christy (Martin)
Evander (Holyfield)
Fernando (Vargas)
Floyd (Patterson)
George (Foreman)
Jack (Dempsey)
Jake (LaMotta)
Joe (Louis)
Julio (Cesar Chavez)
Laila (Ali)
Larry (Holmes)
Lennox (Lewis)
Leon (Spinks)
Marvin (Hagler)
Max (Schmeling)
Mike (Tyson)
Muhammad (Ali)
Oscar (De La Hoya)
Riddick (Bowe)
Roberto (Duran)
Rocky (Marciano)
Roy (Jones, Jr.)
Sonny (Liston)
"Sugar" Ray (Leonard)

Soccer Players

Female and Male
Alexi (Lalas)
Brandi (Chastain)
Carlos (Alberto Torres)
Cristiano (Ronaldo)
David (Beckham)
Diego (Maradona)
Edson ("Pele" Arantes do Nascimento)
Filippo (Inzaghi)
Freddy (Adu)
Gabriel (Batistuta)
Heather (Mitts)
Jamie (Carragher)
Joy (Fawcett)
Julie (Foudy)
Kristine (Lilly)
Landon (Donovan)
Mia (Hamm)
Michael (Owen)
Pavel (Nedved)
Raul (Gonzalez Blanco)
Roberto (Baggio)
Ronaldo (Luiz Nazario da Silva)
Ronaldinho (Gaucho)
Shannon (Boxx)
Zinedine (Zidane)

Race Car Drivers

Female and Male
A. J. (Foyt)
Al (Unser, Jr.)
Ashton (Lewis)
Bill (Elliott)
Bobby (Labonte)
Carl (Edwards)
Dale (Earnhardt)
Danica (Patrick)
Darrell (Waltrip)
Jeff (Gordon)
Jimmie (Johnson)
John (Andretti)
Justin (Ashburn)
Kasey (Kahne)
Kenny (Irwin)
Kevin (Harvick)
Kyle (Petty)
Mario (Andretti)
Matt (Kenseth)
Richard (Petty)
Ricky (Rudd)
Rusty (Wallace)
Sterling (Marlin)
Terry (Labonte)
Tony (Stewart)

Coaches

Female and Male
Arnold ("Red" Auerbach)
Bill (Parcells)
Billy (Martin)
Bobby (Knight)
Casey (Stengel)
Dean (Smith)
Don (Shula)
Frank (Robinson)
George (Halas)
Joe (Gibbs)
John (Madden)
Knute (Rockne)
Larry (Brown)
Mike (Krzyzewski)
Ozzie (Guillen)
Pat (Summit)
Paul ("Bear" Bryant)
Pete (Rose)
Phil (Jackson)
Rick (Pitino)
Scotty (Bowman)
Tom (Landry)
Tommy (Lasorda)
Tony (Dungy)
Vince (Lombardi)

Nature and Places

Sportscasters	Flowers	Rocks, Gems, Minerals	Natural Elements	
Female and Male	**Female**	**Female and Male**	**Female**	**Male**
Al (Michaels)	Angelica	Beryl	Amber	Ash
Bob (Uecker)	Calla	Clay	Autumn	Branch
Chick (Hern)	Dahlia	Coal	Breezy	Bud
Chris (Berman)	Daisy	Coral	Blossom	Burr
Dan (Patrick)	Fern	Crystal	Briar	Canyon
Dick (Vitale)	Flora	Diamond	Brook	Cliff
Frank (Gifford)	Flower	Esmerelda	Delta	Crag
Greg (Gumbel)	Holly	Flint	Gale	Dale
Harry (Caray)	Hyacinth	Garnet	Hailey	Eddy
Howard (Cosell)	Iris	Gemma	Heather	Field
Jack (Buck)	Jasmine	Goldie	Ivy	Ford
Jim (Nantz)	Laurel	Jade	Marina	Forest
Joe (Buck)	Lavender	Jasper	Rain	Heath
John (Madden)	Lilac	Jewel	Rainbow	Lake
Keith (Jackson)	Lily	Mercury	Savannah	Marsh
Kenny (Mayne)	Marigold	Mica	Sequoia	Moss
Lesley (Visser)	Pansy	Opal	Sierra	Oakes
Linda (Cohn)	Poppy	Pearl	Skye	Thorne
Marv (Alberts)	Posy	Rock	Star	Ridge
Mel (Allen)	Rose	Ruby	Summer	River
Pat (Summerall)	Sage	Sandy	Sunny	Rye
Peter (Gammons)	Tulip	Sapphire	Terra	Rock
Robin (Roberts)	Verbena	Steele	Tempest	Stone
Terry (Bradshaw)	Vine	Stone	Willow	Storm
Vin (Scully)	Violet	Topaz	Windy	Woody

Celestial Names	Animals	Water-Themed Names	Places	
Female and Male	**Female and Male**	**Female and Male**	**Female**	**Male**
Andromeda	Billy	Bay	Africa	Afton
Antares	Birdie	Brooke	Asia	Austin
Aries	Buck	Chelsea	Brooklyn	Boston
Cassiopeia	Bunny	Delmar	Cheyenne	Chad
Castor	Cat	Delta	China	Cleveland
Cloud	Colt	Dewey	Dakota	Cuba
Corona	Crane	Eddy	Florence	Dakota
Draco	Cricket	Ice	Georgia	Dallas
Étoile	Drake	Lake	Holland	Denver
Leo	Fawn	Marin	India	Diego
Luna	Fox	Marina	Italia	Indiana
Moona	Hawk	Marisol	Jamaica	Israel
Nova	Jaguar	Meri	Kenya	Kent
Orion	Jay	Misty	Lourdes	Laramie
Pollux	Joey	Nile	Madison	London
Rigel	Kitty	Oceana	Montana	Montreal
Saturn	Lark	Rain	Olympia	Nevada
Scorpio	Newt	Rio	Paris	Orlando
Skye	Phoenix	River	Regina	Phoenix
Soleil	Raven	Seabert	Savannah	Reno
Star	Robin	Spring	Siena	Rhodes
Starling	Starling	Storm	Sydney	Rio
Sunny	Tiger	Tempest	Tijuana	Sydney
Ursa	Wolf	Tigris	Victoria	Tennessee
Venus	Wren	Wade	Vienna	Washington

Trades

Trade Names	Leadership Titles	Inventors	Doctors and Nurses
Female and Male	**Female and Male**	**Female and Male**	**Female and Male**
Baker	Baron	Alexander (Graham Bell)	Alexander (Fleming)
Butcher	Bishop	Alfred (Nobel)	Anna (Howard Shaw)
Carver	Caesar	Ann (Tsukamoto)	Barbara (McClintock)
Chandler	Chancellor	Benjamin (Franklin)	Benjamin (Spock)
Cooper	Deacon	Bill (Gates)	Clara (Barton)
Cutler	Duke	Eli (Whitney)	Claude (Bernard)
Draper	Earl	Galileo (Galilei)	Doogie (Howser)
Fletcher	Khan	George (Pullman)	Dorothea (Dix)
Fowler	King	Guglielmo (Marchese Marconi)	Edward (Jenner)
Gardner	Lord	Henry (Ford)	Elizabeth (Blackwell)
Hunter	Major	James (Watt)	Florence (Nightingale)
Marshall	Marquis	Johannes (Gutenberg)	Henry (Jekyll)
Mason	Nagid	Levi (Strauss)	Jack (Kevorkian)
Miller	Oba	Louis (Braille)	James (Kildare)
Painter	Pasha	Nikola (Tesla)	John (Dolittle)
Porter	Pharaoh	Orville (Wright)	Joseph (Lister)
Ranger	Priest	Robert (Fulton)	Leonard (McCoy)
Sawyer	Prince	Ruth (Handler)	Louis (Pasteur)
Scribe	Princess	Samuel (Morse)	Mary (Edwards Walker)
Shepherd	Queen	Steve (Jobs)	Michaela (Quinn)
Slater	Rabbi	Thomas (Edison)	Phil (McGraw)
Smith	Shah	Tim (Berners-Lee)	Sigmund (Freud)
Stockman	Shaman	Virginia (Apgar)	Victor (Frankenstein)
Tailor	Sharif	Wilbur (Wright)	William (Mayo)
Tanner	Sultan	Willis (Carrier)	Yuri (Zhivago)

Scientists and Mathematicians

Female	Male
Alice (Hamilton)	Abraham (Maslow)
Anna (Freud)	Albert (Einstein)
Annie (Jump Cannon)	Alexander (Fleming)
Barbara (McClintock)	Blaise (Pascal)
Caroline (Herschel)	Carl (Jung)
Christine (Ladd-Franklin)	Charles (Darwin)
Dian (Fossey)	Claudius (Ptolemy)
Dorothy (Hodgkin)	Edward (Jenner)
Elizabeth (Blackwell)	Edwin (Hubble)
Emmy (Noether)	Galileo (Galilei)
Gertrude (Elion)	Gregor (Mendel)
Grace (Hopper)	Isaac (Newton)
Hildegard (von Bingen)	Jacques (Cousteau)
Ida (Henrietta Hyde)	James (Joule)
Jane (Goodall)	Jean (Piaget)
Katherine (Blodgett)	Johannes (Kepler)
Lise (Meitner)	Jonas (Salk)
Margaret (Mead)	Louis (Pasteur)
Maria (Agnesi)	Max (Planck)
Marie (Curie)	Michael (Faraday)
Mary (Leakey)	Nicolaus (Copernicus)
Rachel (Carson)	Niels (Bohr)
Rebecca (Cole)	Robert (Oppenheimer)
Sally (Ride)	Sigmund (Freud)
Sophie (Germain)	Stephen (Hawking)

Artists

Male and Female

Andy (Warhol)
Ansel (Adams)
Claude (Monet)
Edgar (Degas)
Edward (Hopper)
Frida (Kahlo)
Henri (Matisse)
Diego (Rivera)
Georgia (O'Keeffe)
Gustav (Klimt)
Jackson (Pollock)
Jasper (Johns)
Leonardo (da Vinci)
Marc (Chagall)
Mary (Cassatt)
Michelangelo (Buonarroti)
Norman (Rockwell)
Pablo (Picasso)
Paul (Cézanne)
Rembrandt (van Rijn)
Robert (Mapplethorpe)
Roy (Lichtenstein)
Salvador (Dali)
Sandro (Botticelli)
Vincent (van Gogh)

Dancers and Choreographers

Female and Male

Agnes (de Mille)
Ann (Miller)
Anna (Pavlova)
Bill ("Bojangles" Robinson)
Bob (Fosse)
Eleanor (Powell)
Fred (Astaire)
Gene (Kelly)
Ginger (Rogers)
Gower (Champion)
Gregory (Hines)
Gwen (Verdon)
Irene (Castle)
José (Greco)
Lew (Christensen)
Margot (Fonteyn)
Michael (Kidd)
Mikhail (Baryshnikov)
Natalia (Makarova)
Ruby (Keeler)
Rudolf (Nureyev)
Susan (Stroman)
Tommy (Tune)
Twyla (Tharp)
Vernon (Castle)

Fashion Designers	Models	Chefs and Cooks
Female and Male	**Female**	**Female and Male**
Betsey (Johnson)	Alek (Wek)	Alain (Ducasse)
Bill (Blass)	Alessandra (Ambrosio)	Alfred (Portale)
Calvin (Klein)	Amber (Valletta)	Alice (Waters)
Catherine (Malandrino)	Bridget (Hall)	Bobby (Flay)
Christian (Dior)	Brooke (Shields)	Charlie (Palmer)
Cynthia (Rowley)	Carolyn (Murphy)	Delia (Smith)
Diane (von Furstenberg)	Cheryl (Tiegs)	Emeril (Lagasse)
Donna (Karan)	Christie (Brinkley)	Eric (Ripert)
Ellen (Tracy)	Christy (Turlington)	Gary (Danko)
Emilio (Pucci)	Cindy (Crawford)	Gordon (Ramsay)
François (Girbaud)	Claudia (Schiffer)	Heston (Blumenthal)
Gianni (Versace)	Elle (MacPherson)	Jacques (Pépin)
Giorgio (Armani)	Elsa (Benitez)	Jamie (Oliver)
Hugo (Boss)	Gisele (Bundchen)	Jean-George (Vongerichten)
Jimmy (Choo)	Heidi (Klum)	Joël (Robuchon)
Kenneth (Cole)	Helena (Christensen)	Josefina (Howard)
Lilly (Pulitzer)	Kate (Moss)	Julia (Child)
Louis (Vuitton)	Laetitia (Casta)	Lidia (Bastianich)
Marc (Jacobs)	Linda (Evangelista)	Mario (Batali)
Michael (Kors)	Naomi (Campbell)	Martin (Yan)
Nicole (Miller)	Niki (Taylor)	Nigella (Lawson)
Oscar (de la Renta)	Rebecca (Romijn)	Nobu (Matsuhisa)
Ralph (Lauren)	Shalom (Harlow)	Rachael (Ray)
Tommy (Hilfiger)	Stephanie (Seymour)	Todd (English)
Vera (Wang)	Tyra (Banks)	Wolfgang (Puck)

Cops, Detectives, and Crime Fighters

Female and Male
Allan (Pinkerton)
Andy (Sipowicz)
Barnaby (Jones)
Barney (Miller)
Chris (Cagney)
Dana (Scully)
Dave (Starsky)
Dick (Tracy)
Elliot (Ness)
Fox (Mulder)
Harry ("Dirty Harry" Callahan)
Hercule (Poirot)
Sonny (Crockett)
Jane ("Miss" Marple)
Jill (Munroe)
Joe (Friday)
John Edgar (Hoover)
Jules (Maigret)
Kelly (Garrett)
Ken ("Hutch" Hutchinson)
Mary Beth (Lacey)
Sabrina (Duncan)
Sam (Spade)
Sherlock (Holmes)
Thomas (Magnum)

Lawyers and Judges

Female and Male
Byron (White)
Charles (Whittaker)
Clarence (Darrow)
Constance (Baker Motley)
David (Kendall)
Francis (Lee Bailey)
Hugo (Black)
Jacques (Vergès)
Jane (Bolin)
Johnnie (Cochran)
Judy (Sheindlin)
Kenneth (Starr)
Lance (Ito)
Marcia (Clark)
Morgan (Chu)
Oliver (Wendell Holmes)
Perry (Mason)
Robert (Shapiro)
Roger (Taney)
Ruth (Ginsburg)
Sandra (Day O'Connor)
Sarah (Weddington)
Thurgood (Marshall)
Warren (Burger)
William (Rehnquist)

Tycoons

Female and Male
Andrew (Carnegie)
Aristotle (Onassis)
Bill (Gates)
Charles (Foster Kane)
Cornelius (Vanderbilt)
Donald (Trump)
Estée (Lauder)
Henry (Ford)
Howard (Hughes)
Hugh (Hefner)
Jay (Gatsby)
John (Rockefeller)
Martha (Stewart)
Michael (Dell)
Oliver ("Daddy" Warbucks)
Oprah (Winfrey)
Ray (Kroc)
Richie (Rich)
Ross (Perot)
Sam (Walton)
Steve (Jobs)
Ted (Turner)
Teresa (Heinz Kerry)
Warren (Buffet)
William (Randolph Hearst)

Pop Culture

Notorious Celebrity Baby Names

Female and Male
Ahmet Emuukha Rodan (son of Frank and Gail Zappa)
Apple Blythe Alison (daughter of Gwyneth Paltrow and Chris Martin)
Audio Science (son of Shannyn Sossamon and Dallas Clayton)
Coco Riley (daughter of Courteney Cox Arquette and David Arquette)
Daisy Boo (daughter of Jamie and Jools Oliver)
Dweezil (son of Frank and Gail Zappa)
Elijah Bob Patricus Guggi Q (son of Bono and Alison Stewart)
Fifi Trixiebelle (daughter of Paula Yates and Bob Geldof)
Hazel Patricia (daughter of Julia Roberts and Danny Moder)
Heavenly Hirani Tiger Lily (daughter of Paula Yates and Michael Hutchence)
Lourdes Maria Ciccone (daughter of Madonna and Carlos Leon)
Moon Unit (daughter of Frank and Gail Zappa)
Moxie CrimeFighter (daughter of Penn and Emily Jillette)
Peaches Honeyblossom (daughter of Paula Yates and Bob Geldof)
Phinnaeus Walter (son of Julia Roberts and Danny Moder)
Pilot Inspektor (son of Jason Lee and Beth Riesgraf)
Pirate Howsmon (son of Jonathan and Deven Davis)
Poppy Honey (daughter of Jamie and Jools Oliver)
Prince Michael (son of Michael Jackson and Debbie Rowe)
Prince Michael II (son of Michael Jackson)
Rocco (son of Madonna and Guy Ritchie)
Rumer Glenn (daughter of Demi Moore and Bruce Willis)
Scout LaRue (daughter of Demi Moore and Bruce Willis)
Seven Sirius (son of Andre 3000 and Erykah Badu)
Tallulah Belle (daughter of Demi Moore and Bruce Willis)

One-Name Wonders

Female and Male
Ann-Margret
Beck
Björk
Bono
Brandy
Cher
Dido
Enya
Fabio
Iman
Jewel
Liberace
Madonna
Moby
Nelly
Pelé
Prince
Roseanne
Sade
Seal
Shakira
Sinbad
Tiffany
Twiggy
Yanni

Famous People Known by Initials

Female and Male
A. A. (Milne)
A. E. (Housman)
A. J. (Foyt)
B. J. (Thomas)
C. S. (Lewis)
D. B. (Cooper)
D. H. (Lawrence)
E. E. (Cummings)
E. M. (Forster)
J. D. (Salinger)
J. K. (Rowling)
J. M. (Barrie)
J. P. (Morgan)
J. R. R. (Tolkien)
L. M. (Montgomery)
O. J. (Simpson)
P. J. (Harvey)
P. J. (O'Rourke)
P. T. (Barnum)
T. S. (Eliot)
V. C. (Andrews)
V. I. (Lennin)
W. C. (Fields)
W. E. B. (DuBois)
Y. A. (Tittle)

Other Ideas for Names

Brand Names	Cars	Food and Beverages	Last Names as First Names
Female and Male	**Female and Male**	**Female and Male**	**Female and Male**
Avis	Audi	Alfredo	Anderson
Chanel	Avalon	Basil	Bradshaw
Delmonte	Bentley	Brandy	Carter
Delta	Camry	Brie	Chavez
Disney	Chevy	Candy	Chen
Espn	Dakota	Chardonnay	Foster
Evian	Diamante	Clementine	Gallagher
Fanta	Ford	Curry	Garcia
Godiva	Infiniti	Dill	Harper
Gucci	Jaguar	Gin	Jackson
Guinness	Jetta	Ginger	Johnson
Harley	Kia	Ham	Keaton
Hennessy	Lexus	Herb	Kennedy
Hyatt	Liberty	Honey	Mackenzie
Ikea	Lincoln	Kale	Madison
Jemima	Lotus	Margarita	Meyer
Levi	Maverick	Midori	Parker
Nike	Maxima	Olive	Patterson
Nivea	Mercedes	Pepper	Ramsey
Oneida	Montero	Pita	Rodriguez
Pepsi	Ram	Rosemary	Sanchez
Shasta	Rover	Rye	Taylor
Stetson	Sedona	Saffron	Tennyson
Timberland	Sienna	Sage	Walker
Velveeta	Wrangler	Sherry	Wang

Double Names		Easily Shortened Names		Names Based on Letters
Female	**Male**	**Female**	**Male**	**Female and Male**
Anne-Marie	Aaronjames	Abigail	Andrew	Ajay
Billie-Jean	Billijo	Angela	Anthony	Alpha
Billie-Jo	Giancarlo	Barbara	Benjamin	Bea
Bobbi-Jo	Gianluca	Caroline	Christopher	Bebe
Bobbi-Lee	Gianpaolo	Christine	Daniel	Bee
Brandy-Lynn	Jaylee	Deborah	Donald	Beta
Brooklyn	Jayquan	Elizabeth	Edward	Cee
Carolanne	Jean-Claude	Gwendolyn	Frederick	Ceejay
Clarabelle	Jean-Luc	Jacqueline	Gregory	Dee
Emmylou	Jean-Paul	Jennifer	Jacob	Dee Dee
Hollyann	Jean-Sebastien	Jessica	Jeffery	Delta
Jody-Ann	Jimmyjo	Jillian	Jonathan	Elle
Julie-Anne	John-Paul	Josephine	Joseph	Em
Katelyn	Joseluis	Katherine	Kenneth	Gigi
Kellyann	Juancarlos	Lillian	Leonardo	Jay
Krystalynn	Kendarius	Margaret	Michael	Jaycee
Leeann	Keyshawn	Nicole	Nicholas	Jaydee
Mary-Kate	Markanthony	Pamela	Peter	Kay
Marylou	Michaelangelo	Rebecca	Richard	Kaycee
Raeann	Miguelangel	Samantha	Robert	Kaydee
Raelynn	Quindarius	Stephanie	Samuel	Ojay
Roseanne	Rayshawn	Suzanne	Thomas	Omega
Ruthann	Tedrick	Valerie	Timothy	Theta
Saralyn	Tyquan	Victoria	Walter	Vijay
Terry-Lynn	Tyshawn	Vivian	William	Zeta

Names Based on Numbers	Virtue Names	Names with Punctuation	Palindrome Names
Female and Male	**Female**	**Female and Male**	**Female and Male**
Decimus	Amity	'Aolani	Ada
Deuce	Blythe	'Aulani	Anna
Dixie	Charity	'Aziz	Ara
Nona	Chastity	A'lexus	Asa
Octavia	Constance	Bre-Anne	Ava
Octavious	Faith	D'andre	Aviva
Osen	Felicity	D'angelo	Aya
Primo	Fidelity	D'Arcy	Aziza
Quartilla	Grace	D'onna	Bob
Quentin	Harmony	D'quan	Davad
Quincy	Honora	Da'shawn	Elle
Quintana	Hope	Da-juan	Emme
Reva	Innocence	Dan'l	Eve
Septima	Joy	Da-Ron	Hallah
Septimus	Justice	Ja'lisa	Hannah
Sextus	Love	Ja'nae	Idi
Tan	Mercy	Ja'von	Iggi
Tertia	Modesty	Jac-E	Lil
Tertius	Passion	Jo-Anna	Nan
Trent	Patience	Mahi'ai	Natan
Trey	Prudence	N'namdi	Nayan
Triana	Purity	O'Shea	Olo
Trinity	Temperance	O'neil	Otto
Una	Unity	Ra'shawn	Pip
Uno	Verity	T'keyah	Viv

Names Used for Both Genders

More for Girls	More for Boys	About Equal
Alexis	Alex	Britt
Ariel	Cameron	Addison
Ashley	Carson	Ashton
Bailey	Chandler	Berwyn
Billie	Chase	Blair
Dominique	Chris	Carey
Guadalupe	Christian	Casey
Holland	Cody	Charley
Jade	Dakota	Derian
Jadyn	Devin	Devyn
Jamie	Drew	Dylan
Kelly	Evan	Gentry
Madison	Hunter	Harley
Morgan	Jaime	Jessie
Payton	Jaylin	Jody
Reagan	Jesse	Kriston
Reese	Jordan	London
Ricki	Logan	Maddox
Robin	Parker	Pat
Shannon	Quinn	Peyton
Shea	Riley	Quincey
Sidney	Ryan	Skylar
Stacy	Skyler	Sunny
Taylor	Terry	Tory
Tegan	Tyler	Tristyn

Anagram Names

Female	Male	Female and Male
Adria, Daria	Alec, Cale	Abe, Bea
Aileen, Elaine	Andrei, Darien	Aden, Edna
Alice, Celia	Andres, Sander	Adlar, Darla
Alli, Lila	Arnold, Ronald	Agni, Gina
Amy, Mya	Blake, Kaleb	Amir, Mira
Anise, Siena	Byron, Robyn	Amos, Soma
Ann, Nan	Chaz, Zach	Belamy, Maybel
April, Pilar	Darnell, Randell	Brady, Darby
Ashanti, Tanisha	Daryn, Randy	Brion, Robin
Ashlee, Sheela	Enzo, Zeno	Clay, Lacy
Blaise, Isabel	Eric, Rice	Daly, Lyda
Dana, Nada	Ernest, Nester	Dashaun, Shaunda
Diana, Nadia	Jason, Jonas	Dylan, Lynda
Easter, Teresa	Kale, Lake	Edwyn, Wendy
Elsa, Sela	Leo, Ole	Etta, Tate
Gem, Meg	Mason, Osman	Hale, Leah
Gina, Inga	Moore, Romeo	Ian, Nia
Hallie, Leilah	Nero, Reno	Jason, Sonja
Lena, Nela	Percy, Pryce	Karl, Lark
Leta, Teal	Roth, Thor	Kory, York
Marta, Tamra	Royce, Corey	Leon, Noel
Mary, Myra	Ryder, Derry	Liam, Mila
Nita, Tina	Santo, Aston	Rico, Cori
Norah, Rhona	Seaton, Easton	Ryker, Kerry
Sita, Tisa	Thane, Ethan	Sayid, Daisy

Rhyming Names

Female	Male	Female and Male
Addison, Madison	Aaron, Darren	Bessie, Jesse
Alyssa, Melissa	Abe, Gabe	Beth, Seth
Ann, Jan	Ace, Chase	Brandy, Randy
Anna, Hannah	Aidan, Jaiden	Cady, Brady
Candy, Mandy	Alvin, Calvin	Cleo, Leo
Carolyn, Marilyn	Barrett, Garrett	Doris, Morris
Celia, Delia	Barry, Larry	Erin, Darren
Chloe, Zoe	Brandon, Landon	Gayle, Dale
Ellen, Helen	Brian, Ryan	Grace, Chase
Erin, Karen	Cade, Jade	Gwen, Ken
Gracie, Stacie	Chance, Lance	Jeanne, Dean
Jane, Elaine	Cody, Brody	Jen, Ben
Jen, Gwen	Craig, Greg	Jodie, Cody
Kailey, Bailey	Devin, Evan	Joy, Roy
Karen, Sharon	Donald, Ronald	Kamie, Jamey
Lori, Tori	Dustin, Justin	Kate, Nate
Mae, Rae	Eric, Derek	Kay, Jay
Maura, Laura	Frank, Hank	Kim, Tim
Molly, Holly	Heath, Keith	Lori, Corey
Rhonda, Shonda	Hogan, Logan	Mandy, Andy
Sara, Kara	Jack, Mack	Mariah, Josiah
Sherry, Carrie	Jake, Blake	Mary, Harry
Stella, Bella	Jason, Mason	Millie, Billy
Valerie, Mallory	Phil, Will	Paige, Gage
Winnie, Minnie	Sean, John	Zoe, Joey

Fun Nicknames

Female	Male
Anka	Binky
Babs	Buddy
Bertie	Chaz
Biddy	Che
Birdie	Chip
Buffy	Danno
Bunny	Deano
Coco	Fonzie
Dodie	Fritz
Fannie	Gino
Fifi	Jimbo
Flo	Jobo
Gigi	Joop
Ginger	Junior
Hattie	Kit
Jas	Lucky
Kiki	Mango
Kitty	Paco
Madge	Paddy
Sissy	Pepe
Steffi	Pinky
Stevie	Rafi
Tottie	Rollo
Trixie	Skip
Xuxa	Ziggy

Old-Fashioned Names
Now Popular

Female	Male
Abigail	Abraham
Alice	Alexander
Anna	Dominic
Ava	Elijah
Caroline	Ethan
Claire	Gabriel
Claudia	Hector
Elizabeth	Isaac
Emily	Isaiah
Emma	Ivan
Evelyn	Jasper
Grace	Julian
Hannah	Maxwell
Hazel	Nathaniel
Isabella	Noah
Katherine	Omar
Leslie	Oscar
Madeline	Owen
Margaret	Samuel
Maria	Sebastian
Olivia	Vernon
Rebecca	Vincent
Sarah	Wesley
Sofia	Xavier
Victoria	Zachary

One-Syllable Names

Female	Male
Ann	Blake
Bea	Chad
Belle	Chen
Brie	Drew
Chai	Gabe
Cher	Hugh
Claire	Jack
Dawn	Jake
Eve	John
Gayle	Juan
Gwen	Lee
Jade	Luke
Jane	Max
Jill	Paul
Kate	Pierce
Lane	Raj
Ling	Ralph
Lynn	Reece
Mae	Sage
Maude	Spence
Paige	Tad
Rose	Tate
Rue	Todd
Skye	Wade
Trish	Will

Two-Syllable Names

Female	Male
Anna	Ashton
Ashley	Brian
Ava	Christian
Carmen	Dante
Carrie	David
Cheyenne	Dylan
Chloe	Eric
Diane	Garrett
Emma	Jacob
Heidi	Jesse
Jada	Jordan
Jasmine	Joseph
Jody	Landon
Juana	Latrell
Kaitlyn	Luis
Kayla	Maddox
Leah	Matthew
Mary	Michael
Maura	Miguel
Megan	Noah
Rachel	Owen
Rosa	Ryan
Sadie	Sanjay
Sydney	William
Zoe	Wyatt

Three-Syllable Names

Female	Male
Aaliyah	Adrian
Andrea	Anthony
Brianna	Benjamin
Claudia	Christopher
Desirae	Deondre
Emily	Diego
Evelyn	Dominic
Gloria	Elijah
Gwendolyn	Francisco
Jacqueline	Gabriel
Kimberly	Gregory
Lakeisha	Isaiah
Mackenzie	Jeremy
Madeline	Jonathan
Madison	Joshua
Makayla	Julian
Olivia	Marcellus
Pamela	Mathias
Rhiannon	Muhammad
Sierra	Nathaniel
Sophia	Nicholas
Stephanie	Orlando
Sylvia	Sebastian
Tabitha	Timothy
Vanessa	Tobias

Four Syllable Names

Female	Male
Alejandra	Alejandro
Amelia	Antonio
Anastasia	Aristotle
Angelina	Bartholomew
Arianna	Benicio
Carolina	Cornelius
Damonica	Deanthony
Dominica	Demetrius
Eleanora	Ebenezer
Elizabeth	Ezekiel
Evangeline	Geronimo
Frederica	Giovanni
Guadalupe	Immanuel
Isabella	Indiana
Josephina	Jebediah
Julianna	Jeremiah
Katarina	Leonardo
Penelope	Macallister
Samuela	Napolean
Serafina	Odysseus
Serenity	Quindarius
Tatiana	Santiago
Valentina	Thelonius
Veronica	Valentino
Victoria	Zachariah

Names of Famous Pairs

Female and Male

Adam and Eve
Amos and Andy
Bert and Ernie
Bill and Ted
Bonnie and Clyde
Brooks and Dunn
Cain and Abel
Castor and Pollux
David and Goliath
Dick and Jane
Ebony and Ivory
Hansel and Gretel
Jack and Jill
Lancelot and Guenevere
Laurel and Hardy
Laverne and Shirley
Lewis and Clark
Mario and Luigi
Milo and Otis
Romeo and Juliet
Romy and Michele
Samson and Delilah
Siegfried and Roy
Sonny and Cher
Thelma and Louise

Names Ending with "A"

Female	Male
Alexandra	Abdula
Amanda	Akiva
Amelia	Aquila
Andrea	Baptista
Brianna	Barretta
Carmela	Bela
Fiona	Bubba
Gabriella	Columbia
Jana	Cuba
Julia	Dakota
Kayla	Dana
Kendra	Daytona
Maria	Elisha
Mia	Ezra
Michaela	Garcia
Pamela	Indiana
Roxanna	Joshua
Sara	Krishna
Selma	Luca
Sonja	Montana
Sophia	Mustafa
Tyra	Nevada
Uma	Santana
Viola	Shea
Wanda	Zacharia

Names Ending with "E"

Female	Male
Angie	Abe
Ashlee	Andre
Bette	Blake
Brooke	Blaze
Chloe	Boone
Claire	Cole
Gabrielle	Dale
Grace	George
Jane	Ike
Jasmine	Jade
Josie	Jake
Julie	Jerome
Juliette	Jesse
Kate	Jose
Kylie	Jude
Belle	Kayne
Marie	Lane
Nicole	Lee
Paige	Louie
Rose	Mike
Sadie	Ozzie
Stephanie	Pierre
Winnie	Reece
Yvonne	Vince
Zoe	Zebedee

Names Ending with "L"

Female	Male
Abigail	Abdul
Angel	Abel
April	Carl
Ariel	Cyrill
Bell	Daniel
Carol	Darrell
Chantal	Denzel
Crystal	Earl
Ethel	Emmanuel
Gail	Gabriel
Hazel	Hershel
Isabel	Jamal
Jewel	Joel
Jill	Lionel
Laurel	Marshall
Mabel	Maxwell
Meryl	Michael
Muriel	Nathaniel
Nell	Neil
Noel	Paul
Pearl	Phil
Rachel	Russell
Sheryl	Samuel
Sybil	Terrell
Val	Will

Names Ending in "N"

Female	Male
Allison	Aidan
Ann	Alan
Ashlyn	Ashton
Autumn	Benjamin
Caitlin	Colin
Carmen	Darren
Ellen	Donovan
Erin	Evan
Fran	Flynn
Gwendolyn	Hayden
Jillian	Holden
Karen	Ian
Kathryn	Jordan
Kirsten	Justin
Lauren	Keenan
Lillian	Kevin
Magdalen	Llewellyn
Megan	Logan
Morgan	Marvin
Reagan	Mason
Rosalyn	Nathan
Shannon	Quentin
Teagan	Steven
Vivian	Tristan
Yasmin	Warren

Names Ending with "O"

Female	Male
Aiko	Alberto
Bayo	Alejandro
Calypso	Alfonzo
Cameo	Angelo
Charo	Antonio
Cleo	Benicio
Clio	Bo
Coco	Bruno
Domino	Carlo
Doro	Cisco
Echo	Eduardo
Flo	Falco
Gerardo	Fredo
Indigo	Georgio
Jo	Leo
Juno	Marco
Kameko	Mario
Koto	Mo
Mariko	Orlando
Marlo	Pablo
Maryjo	Pedro
Orino	Sancho
Ryo	Theo
Tamiko	Waldo
Yoko	Yao

Names Ending with "R"

Female	Male
Amber	Alexander
Blair	Arthur
Briar	Carter
Cedar	Chandler
Cher	Christopher
Easter	Connor
Eleanor	Evander
Ester	Homer
Ginger	Hunter
Harper	Jasper
Heather	Junior
Jennifer	Oliver
Kashmir	Oscar
Kimber	Parker
Lavender	Peter
Pier	River
Pilar	Roger
Piper	Sawyer
September	Spencer
Skyler	Trevor
Star	Tyler
Summer	Victor
Taylor	Walker
Tipper	Walter
Zephyr	Xavier

Names Ending with "Y"

Female	Male
Ashley	Anthony
Audrey	Bailey
Becky	Barry
Bethany	Bradley
Carly	Cody
Courtney	Corey
Dorothy	Darcy
Ebony	Farley
Emily	Gary
Felicity	Gordy
Hailey	Hardy
Jenny	Huey
Josey	Humphrey
Kelsey	Jeffrey
Lily	Jeremey
Mallory	Jerry
Molly	Koby
Polly	Manny
Shelly	Ozzy
Sidney	Randy
Stacy	Riley
Tiffany	Roy
Wendy	Timothy
Whitney	Westley
Zoey	Zachary

Names Inspired by "Ann"	Names Inspired by "Elizabeth"	Names Inspired by "Jacob"	Names Inspired by "Jane"
Female	**Female**	**Male**	**Female**
Ana	Bess	Akiva	Chavon
Anci	Beth	Chago	Ciana
Anezka	Betsy	Coby	Giovanna
Anica	Betty	Diego	Jalena
Anik	Elisa	Giacomo	Jan
Anisha	Elise	Iago	Jana
Anissa	Elizabet	Iakobos	Janae
Anita	Elizaveta	Jack	Janelle
Anja	Elizebeth	Jaco	Janessa
Anka	Elka	Jacobi	Janet
Anna	Elsa	Jacobo	Janica
Annabel	Ilse	Jacobson	Janice
Annah	Libby	Jacorey	Janie
Annaliese	Liese	Jacques	Janiqua
Anne	Liesel	Jaime	Jasa
Anneka	Lisa	Jake	Jasia
Annette	Lisabeth	Jakob	Jean
Annie	Liset	James	Jenine
Annika	Lissie	Jock	Juana
Anya	Liz	Kobe	Maryjane
Hannah	Liza	Kuba	Seana
Nan	Lizabeta	Tiago	Shana
Nancy	Lizbeth	Yakov	Sinead
Nanette	Lizzie	Yasha	Zanna
Nina	Yelisbeta	Yoakim	Zhane

Star Kids
What Celebrities Are Naming Their Kids

Ace Shane
son of Jennie Finch and Casey Daigle

Adelaide Rose
daughter of Rachel Griffiths and Andrew Taylor

Ahmet Emuukha Rodan
son of Frank and Gail Zappa

Aidan Rose
daughter of Faith Daniels

Alabama Luella
daughter of Travis Barker and Shanna Moakler Barker

Alaia
daughter of Stephen and Kenya Baldwin

Alastair Wallace
son of Rod Stewart and Penny Lancaster

Alexandria Zahra Jones
daughter of David Bowie and Iman Abdulmajid

Allegra
daughter of John Leguizamo and Justine Maurer

Allie Colleen
daughter of Garth Brooks and Sandy Mahl

Apple Bythe Alsion
daughter of Gwyneth Paltrow and Chris Martin

Aquinnah Kathleen
daughter of Tracy Pollan and Michael J. Fox

Arpad Flynn
son of Elle Macpherson and Arpad Busson

Atherton Grace
daughter of Don and Kelley Johnson

Atticus
son of Isabella Hoffman and Daniel Baldwin

Audio Science
son of Shannyn Sossamon and Dallas Clayton

August Anna
daughter of Garth Brooks and Sandy Mahl

August Miklos Friedrich
son of Mariska Hargitay and Peter Hermann

Aurora Rose
son of Paul "Triple H" Levesque and Stephanie McMahon Levesque

Aurelius Cy Andre
son of Elle Macpherson and Arpad Busson

Ava Elizabeth
daughter of Reese Witherspoon and Ryan Phillippe

Avery Grace
daughter of Angie Harmon and Jason Sehorn

Bailey
son of Tracey Gold and Roby Marshall

Bailey Jean
daughter of Melissa Etheridge and Julie Cypher

Banjo
son of Rachel Griffiths and Andrew Taylor

Barron William
son of Donald and Melania Trump

Beatrice Milly
daughter of Paul McCartney and Heather Mills

Bechet
daughter of Woody Allen and Soon-Yi Previn

Beckett
son of Conan and Liza O'Brien

Bluebell Madonna
daughter of Geri Halliwell

Bobbi Kristina
daughter of Whitney Houston and Bobby Brown

Braison Chance
son of Billy Ray and Tish Cyrus

Brawley King
son of Nick Nolte and Rebecca Linger

Brooklyn Joseph
son of Victoria "Posh Spice" Adams and David Beckham

Cannon Edward
son of Larry King and Shawn Southwick-King

Carys
daughter of Catherine Zeta-Jones and Michael Douglas

Cash Anthony
son of Saul "Slash" and Perla Hudson

Casper
son of Claudia Schiffer and Matthew Vaughn

Castor
son of James and Francesca Hetfield

Charles Spencer
son of Russell Crowe and Danielle Spencer

Chelsea Belle
daughter of Rosie O'Donnell

Claudia Rose
daughter of Michelle Pfeiffer

Coco Riley
daughter of Courteney Cox Arquette and David Arquette

Connor Antony
son of Nicole Kidman and Tom Cruise

Cruz
son of Victoria "Posh Spice" Adams and David Beckham

Cypress
daughter of Sole

Daisy-Boo
daughter of Jamie and Jools Oliver

Daisy True
daughter of Meg Ryan

Dandelion
daughter of Keith Richards and Anita Pallenberg

Darius
son of James Rubin and Christiane Amanpour

Deacon
son of Reese Witherspoon and Ryan Phillippe

Declyn Wallace
son of Cyndi Lauper and David Thornton

De'jan
daughter of Sole

Delilah Belle
daughter of Harry Hamlin and Lisa Rinna

Denim
son of Toni Braxton and Keri Lewis

Denni Montanta
daughter of Woody Harrelson and Laura Louie

Destry Allyn
daughter of Kate Capshaw and Steven Spielberg

Devo
son of Maynard James Keenan

Dexter Dean
daughter of Diane Keaton

Dhani
son of George and Olivia Harrison

Diezel
son of Toni Braxton and Keri Lewis

Diva Muffin
daughter of Frank and Gail Zappa

Dominik
daughter of Andy and Maria Victoria Garcia

Dream Sarae
daughter of Ginuwine and Sole

Dree Louise
daughter of Mariel Hemingway and Stephen Crisman

Duncan Zowie Heywood
son of David Bowie and Mary Angela Barnett

Dusti Rain
daughter of Rob "Vanilla Ice" and Laura Van Winkle

Dweezil
son of Frank and Gail Zappa

Dylan Frances
daughter of Sean and Robin Wright Penn

Dylan Jagger
son of Pamela Anderson and Tommy Lee

Dylan Paul
son of Bart Conner and Nadia Comaneci

Elijah Bob Patricious Guggi Q
son of Alison Stewart and Bono

Eliot Pauline
son of Sting and Trudie Styler

Emerson Rose
daughter of Teri Hatcher and Jon Tenney

Enzo
son of Patricia Arquette and Paul Rossi

Esme
daughter of Samantha Morton and Charlie Creed-Miles

Fifi Trixiebelle
daughter of Paula Yates and Bob Geldof

Finn
son of Christy Turlington and Ed Burns

Frances Bean
daughter of Kurt Cobain and Courtney Love

Freedom
daughter of Ving Rhames and Deborah Reed

Fushcia Katherine
daughter of Sting and Frances Tomelty

Gaia
daughter of Emma Thompson and Greg Wise

Gianna Maria-Onore
daughter of Kobe and Vanessa Bryant

God'iss Love
daughter of Lil' Mo and Al Stone

Grace Elisabeth
daughter of Elisabeth and Tim Hasselbeck

Gracie Katherine
daughter of Faith Hill and Tim McGraw

Grier Hammond
daughter of Brooke Shields and Chris Henchy

Gulliver Flynn
son of Gary Oldman and Donya Fiorentino

Hazel Patricia
daughter of Julia Roberts and Danny Moder

Heavenly Hirani Tiger Lily
daughter of Paula Yates and Michael Hutchence

Henry Chance
son of Rachel Weisz and Darren Aronofsky

Homer James Jigme
son of Richard Gere and Carey Lowell

Hopper
son of Sean Penn and Robin Wright Penn

Hudson Harden
son of Marcia Gay Harden and Thaddeus Scheel

Indianna August
daughter of Summer Phoenix and Casey Affleck

Indio
son of Deborah Falconer and Robert Downey, Jr.

Ireland Eliesse
daughter of Kim Basinger and Alec Baldwin

Isabella
daughter of Matt and Luciana Damon

Isabella Jane
daughter of Nicole Kidman and Tom Cruise

Jack John Christopher
son of Johnny Depp and Vanessa Paradis

James Padraig
son of Colin Farrell and Kim Bordenave

Jamison Leon
daughter of Billy Baldwin and Chynna Phillips

Jaya
daughter of Ben Harper and Laura Dern

Jelani Asar
son of Wesley and April Snipes

Jennifer Katharine
daughter of Bill and Melinda Gates

Jesse James
son of Jon and Dorothea Bon Jovi

Jett
son of Kelly Preston and John Travolta

Joaquin
son of Kelly Ripa and Mark Consuelos

Johnny
son of Mira Sorvino and Chris Backus

Julian Murray
son of Lisa Kudrow and Michel Stern

Julitta Dee
daughter of Marcia Gay Harden and Thaddeus Scheel

Kaiis Steven
son of Geena Davis and Reza Jarrahy

Karsen
daughter of Ray Liotta and Michelle Grace

Keelee Breeze
daughter of Rob "Vanilla Ice" and Laura Van Winkle

Kian William
son of Geena Davis and Reza Jarrahy

Kingston James McGregor
son of Gwen Stefani and Gavin Rossdale

Kyd Miller
son of David Duchovny and Tea Leoni

Langley Fox
daughter of Mariel Hemingway and Stephen Crisman

Lennon
son of Patsy Kensit and Liam Gallagher

Letesha
daughter of Tracy "Ice-T" and Darlene Morrow

Lily-Rose Melody
daughter of Johnny Depp and Vanessa Paradis

Loewy
son of John Malkovich and Nicoletta Peyran

Lola Rose
daughter of Charlie Sheen and Denise Richards

Lola Simone
daughter of Chris and Malaak Rock

London Emilio
son of Saul "Slash" and Perla Hudson

Lourdes Maria Ciccone
daughter of Madonna and Carlos Leon

Lyric
daughter of Karla De Vito and Robby Benson

Mackenzie Jean Rowling
daughter of J. K. Rowling and Neil Murray

Maddox
son of Angelina Jolie

Madeleine West
daughter of David Duchovny and Tea Leoni

Maggie Elizabeth
daughter of Faith Hill and Tim McGraw

Maggie Rose
daughter of Jon and Tracy Stewart

Magnus Paulin
son of Will Ferrell and Viveca Paulin

Makani Ravello
daughter of Woody Harrelson and Laura Louie

Makena'lei
daughter of Helen Hunt and Matthew Carnahan

Malachy
son of Cillian and Yvonne Murphy

Malu Valentine
daughter of David Byrne and Adelle Lutz

Mandla Kadjaly Carl Stevland Morris
son of Stevie Wonder and Kai Milla

Manzie Tio
daughter of Woody Allen and Soon-Yi Previn

Matalin Mary
daughter of Mary Matalin and James Carville

Matilda Rose
daughter of Heath Ledger and Michelle Williams

Mateo Bravery
son of Benjamin Bratt and Talisa Soto

Mattea Angel
daughter of Mira Sorvino and Chris Backus

McCanna
son of Gary Sinise and Moira Harris

McKenna Lane
daughter of Mary Lou Retton and Shannon Kelly

Me'arah Sanaa
daughter of Shaquille and Shaunie O'Neal

Memphis Eve
daughter of Alison Stewart and Bono

Messiah Lauren
daughter of Allen and Tawanna Iverson

Milo
son of Camryn Manheim

Milo William
son of Liv Tyler and Royston Langdon

Mingus Lucien
son of Helena Christensen and Norman Reedus

Moon Unit
daughter of Frank and Gail Zappa

Moxie CrimeFighter
daughter of Penn and Emily Jillette

Najee
son of James "LL Cool J" and Simone Smith

Nala
daughter of Keenan Ivory Wayans and Daphne Polk

Nana Kwadjo
son of Isaac and Adjowa Hayes

Natashya Lorien
daughter of Tori Amos and Mark Hawley

Nathan Thomas
son of Jon and Tracey Stewart

Nayib
son of Gloria and Emilio Estefan

Neve
daughter of Conan O'Brien and Liza Powell O'Brien

Ocean Alexander
son of Forest Whitaker

Oliver Philip
son of Fred Savage and Jennifer Stone

Owen Isabelle
daughter of Michelle Branch and Teddy Landau:

Paris
son of Blair Underwood and Desiree DeCosta

Paris Michael Katherine
daughter of Michael Jackson and Debbie Rowe

Parker Jaren
son of Rosie O'Donnell

Peaches Honeyblossom
daughter of Paula Yates and Bob Geldof

Pearl
daughter of Maya Rudolph and Paul Thomas Anderson

Phinnaeus Walter
son of Julia Roberts and Danny Moder

Phoenix Chi
daughter of Melanie "Scary Spice" Brown and Jimmy Gulzar

Pilot Inspektor
son of Jason Lee and Beth Riesgraf

Piper Maru
daughter of Gillian Anderson and Clyde Klotz

Pirate Howsmon
son of Jonathan Davis and Deven

Pixie
daughter of Paula Yates and Bob Geldof

Poppy-Honey
daughter of Jamie and Jools Oliver

Praise Mary Ella
daughter of Earl "DMX" and Tishera Simmons

Presley Tanita
daughter of Tanya Tucker and Jerry Laseter

Presley Walker
son of Cindy Crawford and Rande Gerber

Prince Michael
son of Michael Jackson and Debbie Rowe

Prince Michael II
son of Michael Jackson

Puma
daughter of Erykah Badu

Quinlin Dempsey
son of Ben Stiller and Christine Taylor

Rainie
daughter of Andie MacDowell and Paul Qualley

Reignbeau
daughter of Ving Rhames and Deborah Reed

Rio Kelly
son of Sean Young and Robert Lujan

Ripley
daughter of Thandie Newton and Oliver Parker

Roan
son of Sharon Stone and Phil Bronstein

Rocco
son of Madonna and Guy Ritchie

Roman Robert
son of Cate Blanchett and Andrew Upton

Rory
son of Bill Gates and Melinda French

Rowan
daughter of Brooke Shields and Chris Henchy

Rumer Glenn
daughter of Demi Moore and Bruce Willis

Ryan Elizabeth
daughter of Rodney and Holly Robinson Peete

Ryder Russel
son of Kate Husdon and Chris Robinson

Sadie Madison
daughter of Adam Sandler and Jackie Titone Sandler

Saffron Sahara
daughter of Simon Le Bon and Yasmin Parvaneh

Sailor Lee
daughter of Christie Brinkley and Peter Cook

Salome Violetta
daughter of Alex Kingston and Florian Haertel

Samuel Jason
son of Jack Black and Tanya Haden

Sam J.
daughter of Charlie Sheen and Denise Richards

Saoirse Roisin
daughter of Courtney Kennedy and Paul Hill

Satchel Lewis
daughter of Spike Lee and Tonya Linette Lewis

Scarlett Teresa
daughter of Jack White and Karen Elson

Schuyler Frances
daughter of Tracy Pollan and Michael J. Fox

Scout LaRue
daughter of Demi Moore and Bruce Willis

Sean Preston
son of Britney Spears and Kevin Federline

Selah Louise
daughter of Lauryn Hill and Rohan Marley

Seven Sirius
son of Andre 3000 and Erykah Badu

Shepherd Kellen
son of Jerry and Jessica Seinfeld

Shiloh Nouvel
daughter of Angelina Jolie and Brad Pitt

Sindri
son of Bjork and Thor Eldon

Sistine Rose
daughter of Jennifer Flavin and Sylvester Stallone

Slade Lucas Moby
son of David Brenner and Elizabeth Bryan Slater

Solita Liliana
daughter of Geraldo and Erica Rivera

Sonnet Noel
daughter of Forest and Keisha Whitaker

Sosie Ruth
daughter of Kyra Sedgwick and Kevin Bacon

Speck Wildhorse
son of John and Elaine Mellencamp

Stellan
son of Jennifer Connelly and Paul Bettany

Story
daughter of Ginuwine and Sole

Sunny Bebop
daughter of Michael "Flea" Balzary and Frankie Rayder

Suri
daughter of Tom Cruise and Katie Holmes

Sutton Pierce
son of Britney Spears and Kevin Federline

Sy'Rai
daughter of Brandy Norwood and Robert Smith

Tali
daughter of Annie Lennox and Uri Fruchtman

Tallulah Belle
daughter of Demi Moore and Bruce Willis

Taylor Mayne Pearl
daughter of Garth Brooks and Sandy Mahl

Tennyson Spencer
son of Russell Crowe and Danielle Spencer

True
daughter of Forest and Keisha Whitaker

True Harlow
daughter of Joely Fisher and Christopher Duddy

Truman Theodore
son of Rita Wilson and Tom Hanks

Tu Simone Ayer Morrow
daughter of Rob Morrow and Debbon Ayre

Vance Alexander
son of Billy Baldwin and Chyna Phillips

Violet Anne
daughter of Jennifer Garner and Ben Affleck

Violet Maye
daughter of Dave and Jordyn Grohl

Weston
son of Nicolas Cage and Kristina Fulton

Willow
daughter of Will Smith and Jada Pinkett Smith

Wolfgang William
son of Eddie Van Halen and Valerie Bertinelli

Zahara Marley
daughter of Angelina Jolie

Zahra Savannah
daughter of Chris and Malaak Rock

Zelda
daughter of Robin Williams and Marsha Garces Williams

Zephyr
son of Karla De Vito and Robby Benson

Zion David
son of Lauryn Hill and Rohan Marley

Zoe Giordano
daughter of Woody Harrelson and Laura Louie

Zolten Penn
son of Penn and Emily Jillette

The Name Exchange

Historical/Political Figures

Professional Name	Original Name
Johnny Appleseed	John Chapman
Sitting Bull	Tatanka Iyotake
Calamity Jane	Martha Jane Burke
Butch Cassidy	Robert LeRoy Parker
Gerald Ford	Leslie Lynch King, Jr.
Mata Hari	Margareth Geertruide Zelle
Gary Hart	Gary Hartpence
Crazy Horse	Tashuna-Uitco
Sundance Kid	Harry Longbaugh
Nancy Reagan	Anne Frances Robbins
Leon Trotsky	Lev Davydovich Bronstein
Woodrow Wilson	Thomas Woodrow Wilson
Malcolm X	Malcolm Little

Sports Figures

Professional Name	Original Name
Kareem Abdul-Jabbar	Ferdinand Lewis Alcindor, Jr.
Muhammad Ali	Cassius Marcellus Clay
Andre the Giant	Andre Roussinoff
Yogi Berra	Lawrence Peter Berra
Hulk Hogan	Terry Bodello
Magic Johnson	Earvin Johnson
Pelé	Edson Arantes do Nascimento
Ahmad Rashad	Bobby Moore
Tom Seaver	George Thomas Seaver
Gene Tunney	James Joseph Tunney
Tiger Woods	Eldrick Woods
Cy Young	Denton True Young

Literary Figures

Professional Name	Original Name
Maya Angelou	Marguerite Annie Johnson
Pearl Buck	Pearl Comfort Sydenstricker
Truman Capote	Truman Steckfus Pearsons
Lewis Carroll	Charles Lutwidge Dodgeson
Michael Crichton	John Michael Crichton
Agatha Christie	Agatha Mary Clarissa Miller
Isak Dinesen	Baroness Karen Blixen
Victoria Holt	Eleanot Burford Hibbert
Judith Krantz	Judith Tarcher
John le Carre	John Moore Carnwell
Toni Morrison	Chloe Anthony Wofford
George Orwell	Eric Arthur Blair
Satchel Paige	Leroy Robert Paige
Anne Rice	Howard Allen O'Brien
Harold Robbins	Francis Kane
J. K. Rowling	Joanne Kathleen Rowling
Mickey Spillane	Frank Morrison
Danielle Steel	Danielle Schuelein-Steel
R. L. Stine	Robert Lawrence Stine
Dr. Seuss	Theodore Seuss Geisel
J. R. R. Tolkien	John Ronald Reuel Tolkien
Mark Twain	Samuel Clemens
Gore Vidal	Eugene Luther Vidal
Nathaniel West	Nathaniel Wallenstein Weinstein
Tennessee Williams	Thomas Lanier Williams

Entertainment Figures

Professional Name	Original Name
Eddie Albert	Edward Albert Heimberger
Alan Alda	Alphonse D'Abruzzo
Jane Alexander	Jane Quigley
Jason Alexander	Jay Scott Greenspan
Tim Allen	Tim Allen Dick
Woody Allen	Allen Konigsberg
Don Ameche	Dominic Felix Amici
Tori Amos	Myra Ellen Amos
Julie Andrews	Julia Vernon
Ann-Margret	Ann-Margret Olsson
Beatrice Arthur	Bernice Frankel
Ed Asner	Yitzak Edward Asner
Fred Astaire	Frederick Austerlitz
Lauren Bacall	Betty Joan Perske
Anne Bancroft	Anne Italiano
John Barrymore	John Blythe
Warren Beatty	Henry Warren Beaty
Beck	Beck Hansen
Bonnie Bedelia	Bonnie Culkin
Pat Benetar	Patricia Andrejewski
Tony Bennett	Anthony Dominick Benedetto
Jack Benny	Joseph Kubelsky
Robbie Benson	Robert Segal
Ingmar Bergman	Ernst Ingmar Bergman
Milton Berle	Milton Berlinger
Irving Berlin	Israel Baline
Joey Bishop	Joseph Abraham Gottlieb
Bjork	Björk Gudmundsdottir
Robert Blake	Michael James Vijencio Gubitosi
Blondie	Deborah Harry
Michael Bolton	Michael Bolotin
Jon Bon Jovi	John Bonjiovi
Bono	Paul Hewson
Sonny Bono	Salvatore Bono
Pat Boone	Charles Eugene Boone
Victor Borge	Borge Rosenbaum
Bow Wow	Shad Moss

Professional Name	Original Name
David Bowie	David Hayward-Jones
Max Brand	Gerald Kenneth Tierney
Brandy	Brandy Norwood
Beau Bridges	Lloyd Vernet Bridges III
Charles Bronson	Charles Buchinsky
Albert Brooks	Albert Einstein
Garth Brooks	Troyal Garth Brooks
Mel Brooks	Melvin Kaminsky
Yul Brynner	Taidje Kahn, Jr.
George Burns	Nathan Birnbaum
Ellen Burstyn	Edna Rae Gillooly
Richard Burton	Richard Jenkins
Nicolas Cage	Nicholas Coppola
Michael Caine	Maurice Joseph Micklewhite
Maria Callas	Maria Anna Sophia Cecilia Kalogeropoulos
Dyan Cannon	Samile Diane Friesen
Kate Capshaw	Kathleen Sue Nail
Vikki Carr	Florencia Bisenta de Casillas Martinez Cardona
Diahann Carroll	Carol Diahann Johnson
Johnny Cash	J. R. Cash
Stockard Channing	Susan Antonia Williams Stockard
Ray Charles	Ray Charles Robinson
Charo	Maria Rosaria Pilar Martinez Molina Baeza
J. C. Chasez	Joshua Scott Chasez
Chevy Chase	Cornelius Crane Chase
Chubby Checker	Ernest Evans
Cher	Cherilyn Sarkisian LaPierre
Chyna	Joanie Laurer
Eric Clapton	Eric Clapp
Patsy Cline	Virginia Patterson Hensley
Lee J. Cobb	Leo Jacob
Perry Como	Pierino Como
Bert Convy	Bernard Whalen Patrick Convy
Alice Cooper	Vincent Damon Furnier
David Copperfield	David Kotkin
Howard Cosell	Howard William Cohen
Bob Costas	Robert Quinlan Costas

Professional Name	Original Name
Elvis Costello	Declan Patrick McManus
Joan Crawford	Lucille Le Sueur
Bing Crosby	Harry Lillis Crosby
Tom Cruise	Thomas Cruise Mapother IV
Tony Curtis	Bernard Schwartz
Willem Dafoe	William Dafoe
D'Angelo	Michael D'Angelo Archer
Rodney Dangerfield	Jacob Cohen
Dawn	Joyce Elaine Vincent
Doris Day	Doris Kappelhoff
Sandra Dee	Alexandra Zuck
John Denver	Henry John Deutschendorf, Jr.
Bo Derek	Mary Cathleen Collins
Portia de Rossi	Amanda Rogers
Danny DeVito	Daniel Michaeli
Susan Dey	Susan Smith
Marlene Dietrich	Maria von Losch
Phyllis Diller	Phyllis Driver
Kirk Douglas	Issur Danielovitch Demsky
Mike Douglas	Michael Delaney Dowd, Jr.
Patty Duke	Anna Marie Duke
Faye Dunaway	Dorothy Faye Dunaway
Bob Dylan	Robert Zimmerman
Sheena Easton	Sheena Shirley Orr
Buddy Ebsen	Christian Ebsen, Jr.
Barbara Eden	Barbara Huffman
The Edge	David Evans
Carmen Electra	Tara Leigh Patrick
Jenna Elfman	Jenna Butala
Mama Cass Elliot	Ellen Naomi Cohen
Missy Elliott	Melissa Elliott
Elvira	Cassandra Peterson
Eminem	Marshall Mathers III
Werner Erhard	Jack Rosenberg
Dale Evans	Francis Octavia Smith
Chad Everett	Raymond Lee Cramton
Douglas Fairbanks	Julius Ullman

Professional Name	Original Name
Morgan Fairchild	Patsy Ann McClenny
Mia Farrow	Maria de Lourdes Villiers Farrow
Farrah Fawcett	Mary Farrah Fawcett
Will Ferrell	John William Ferrell
Sally Field	Sally Mahoney
W. C. Fields	William Claude Dukenfield
Dame Margot Fonteyn	Margaret Hookham
Glenn Ford	Gwllyn Samuel Newton Ford
John Forsythe	John Freund
Jodie Foster	Alicia Christian Foster
Michael Fox	Michael Andrew Fox
Jamie Foxx	Eric Bishop
Redd Foxx	John Elroy Sanford
Anthony Franciosa	Anthony Papaleo
Connie Francis	Concetta Franconero
Carlton Fredericks	Harold Casper Frederick Kaplan
Greta Garbo	Greta Gustafson
Andy Garcia	Andres Arturo Garcia-Menendez
Judy Garland	Frances Gumm
James Garner	James Baumgarner
Crystal Gayle	Brenda Gail Webb Gatzimos
Boy George	George Alan O'Dowd
Barry Gibb	Douglas Gibb
Kathie Lee Gifford	Kathie Epstein
Goldberg	Bill Goldberg
Whoopi Goldberg	Caryn Johnson
Cary Grant	Archibald Leach
Lee Grant	Lyova Haskell Rosenthal
Peter Graves	Peter Arness
Macy Gray	Natalie McIntyre
Joel Grey	Joel Katz
Charles Grodin	Charles Grodinsky
Robert Guillaume	Robert Williams
Buddy Hackett	Leonard Hacker
Geri Halliwell	Geraldine Estolle Halliwell
Halston	Roy Halston Frowick
Hammer	Stanley Kirk Hacker Burrell

Professional Name	Original Name
Woody Harrelson	Woodrow Tracy Harrelson
Rex Harrison	Reginald Cary
Laurence Harvey	Lavrushka Skikne
Helen Hayes	Helen Brown
Marg Helgenberger	Mary Margaret Helgenberger
Margaux Hemingway	Margot Hemmingway
Audrey Hepburn	Audrey Hepburn-Ruston
Pee Wee Herman	Paul Rubenfeld
Barbara Hershey	Barbara Herzstine
William Holden	William Beedle
Billie Holiday	Eleanora Fagan
Bob Hope	Leslie Townes Hope
Harry Houdini	Ehrich Weiss
Rock Hudson	Roy Scherer, Jr.
D. L. Hughley	Darryl Lynn Hughley
Engelbert Humperdinck	Arnold Dorsey
Mary Beth Hurt	Mary Supinger
Lauren Hutton	Mary Laurence Hutton
Ice Cube	O'Shea Jackson
Billy Idol	William Broad
Don Imus	John Donald Imus, Jr.
Wolfman Jack	Robert Smith
Wyclef Jean	Nelust Wyclef Jean
Jewel	Jewel Kilcher
Elton John	Reginald Kenneth Dwight
Don Johnson	Donald Wayne
Al Jolson	Asa Yoelson
Tom Jones	Thomas Jones Woodward
Louis Jourdan	Louis Gendre
Donna Karan	Donna Faske
Boris Karloff	William Henry Pratt
Danny Kaye	David Kaminsky
Diane Keaton	Diane Hall
Michael Keaton	Michael Douglas
Alicia Keys	Alicia Augello-Cook
Chaka Khan	Yvette Stevens
Kid Rock	Robert James Ritchie

Professional Name	Original Name
Larry King	Larry Zeiger
Ben Kingsley	Krishna Banji
Nastassia Kinski	Nastassja Naksynznki
Calvin Klein	Richard Klein
Ted Knight	Tadeus Wladyslaw Konopka
Johnny Knoxville	Phillip John Clapp
Kreskin	George Joseph Kresge Jr.
Ashton Kutcher	Christopher Ashton Kutcher
Cheryl Ladd	Cheryl Stoppelmoor
Bert Lahr	Irving Lahrheim
Ann Landers	Esther Pauline Lederer
Michael Landon	Eugene Michael Orowitz
Nathan Lane	Joseph Lane
K. D. Lang	Katherine Dawn Lang
Stan Laurel	Arthur Stanley Jefferson Laurel
Ralph Lauren	Ralph Lifshitz
Piper Laurie	Rosetta Jacobs
Jude Law	David Jude Law
Steve Lawrence	Sidney Leibowitz
Heath Ledger	Heathcliff Andrew Ledger
Bruce Lee	Lee Yuen Kam
Gypsy Rose Lee	Louise Hovick
Peggy Lee	Norma Egstrom
Spike Lee	Shelton Jackson Lee
Jay Leno	James Leno
Téa Leoni	Elizabeth Téa Pantaleoni
Huey Lewis	Hugh Cregg
Jerry Lewis	Joseph Levitch
Shari Lewis	Shari Hurwitz
Jet Li	Li Lian Jie
Liberace	Wladziu Valentino Liberace
Hal Linden	Hal Lipshitz
Meat Loaf	Marvin Lee Aday
Jack Lord	J. J. Ryan
Sophia Loren	Sophia Villani Scicolone
Peter Lorre	Laszlo Loewenstein
Courtney Love	Love Michelle Harrison

Professional Name	Original Name
Myrna Loy	Myrna Williams
Bela Lugosi	Bela Ferenc Blasko
Loretta Lynn	Loretta Webb
Bernie Mac	Bernard Jeffery McCullough
Andie MacDowell	Rosalie Anderson MacDowell
Shirley MacLaine	Shirley Beaty
Elle Macpherson	Eleanor Gow
Madonna	Madonna Louise Veronica Ciccone
Lee Majors	Harvey Lee Yeary II
Karl Malden	Mladen Sekulovich
Camryn Manheim	Debra Manheim
Jayne Mansfield	Vera Jane Palmer
Marilyn Manson	Brian Hugh Warner
Fredric March	Frederick Bickel
Penny Marshall	Carole Penny Marshall
Dean Martin	Dino Crocetti
Ricky Martin	Enrique José Martin Morales
Chico Marx	Leonard Marx
Groucho Marx	Julius Henry Marx
Harpo Marx	Arthur Marx
Zeppo Marx	Herbert Marx
Master P	Percy Miller
Walter Matthau	Walter Matuschanskayasky
Ethel Merman	Ethel Zimmermann
Paul McCartney	James Paul McCartney
A. J. McLean	Alexander James McLean
Steve McQueen	Terence Stephen McQueen
George Michael	Georgios Panayiotou
Joni Mitchell	Roberta Joan Anderson Mitchell
Jay Mohr	Jon Ferguson Mohr
Marilyn Monroe	Norma Jean Baker
Yves Montand	Ivo Livi
Demi Moore	Demetria Gene Guynes
Julianne Moore	Julie Anne Smith
Rita Moreno	Rosita Dolores Alverio
Pat Morita	Noriyuki Morita
Van Morrison	George Ivan Morrison

Professional Name	Original Name
Zero Mostel	Samuel Joel Mostel
Ricky Nelson	Eric Hilliard Nelson
Randy Newman	Randall Stuart Newman
Thandie Newton	Thandiwe Newton
Mike Nichols	Michael Igor Peschkowsky
Stevie Nicks	Stephanie Nicks
Chuck Norris	Carlos Ray Norris
Kim Novak	Marilyn Pauline Novak
Hugh O'Brian	Hugh J. Krampe
Tony Orlando	Michael Anthony Orlando Cassavitis
Suze Orman	Suzie Orman
Ozzy Osbourne	John Michael Osbourne
Marie Osmond	Olive Marie Osmond
Peter O'Toole	Seamus O'Toole
Al Pacino	Alfredo James Pacino
Jack Palance	Walter Jack Palanuik
Jane Pauley	Margaret Jane Pauley
Minnie Pearl	Sarah Ophelia Colley Cannon
Gregory Peck	Eldred Gregory Peck
Bernadette Peters	Bernadette Lazzara
Joaquin Phoenix	Joaquin Raphael Bottom
Christopher Pike	Kevin McFadden
Brad Pitt	William Bradley Pitt
Stephanie Powers	Stefania Federkiewicz
Paula Prentiss	Paula Ragusa
Priscilla Presley	Pricilla Wagner Beaulieu
Prince	Prince Rogers Nelson
William Proxmire	Edward William Proxmire
Tony Randall	Leonard Rosenberg
Robert Redford	Charles Robert Rédford
Donna Reed	Donna Belle Mullenger
Della Reese	Delloreese Patricia Early
Judge Reinhold	Edward Ernest Reinhold, Jr.
Lee Remick	Ann Remick
Debbie Reynolds	Mary Frances Reynolds
Busta Rhymes	Trevor Smith
Andy Richter	Paul Andrew Richter

Professional Name	Original Name
Edward G. Robinson	Emanuel Goldenberg
The Rock	Dwayne Douglas Johnson
Ginger Rogers	Virginia McMath
Roy Rogers	Leonard Slye
Mickey Rooney	Joe Yule, Jr.
Diana Ross	Diane Ernestine Ross
Theresa Russell	Theresa Paup
Jeri Ryan	Jeri Lynn Zimmerman
Meg Ryan	Margaret Hyra
Winona Ryder	Winona Laura Horowitz
Buffy Sainte-Marie	Beverly Sainte-Marie
Susan Saint James	Susan Miller
Soupy Sales	Milton Supman
Susan Sarandon	Susan Tomalin
Leo Sayer	Gerald Sayer
John Saxon	Carmen Orrico
Jane Seymour	Joyce Frankenberg
Shaggy	Orville Richard Burrell
Shakira	Shakira Isabel Mebarak Ripoll
Omar Sharif	Michael Shalhouz
Artie Shaw	Arthur Arshowsky
Charlie Sheen	Carlos Irwin Estevez
Martin Sheen	Ramon G. Estevez
Judith Sheindlin	Judy Blum
Brooke Shields	Christa Brooke Shields
Talia Shire	Talia Coppola
Dinah Shore	Frances "Fanny" Rose Shore
Beverly Sills	Belle "Bubbles" Silverman
Neil Simon	Marvin Neil Simon
Sinbad	David Adkins
Sisqo	Mark Andrews
Ione Skye	Ione Skye Leitch
Christian Slater	Christian Hawkins
Snoop Dogg	Calvin Cordozar Broadus
Phoebe Snow	Phoebe Loeb
Leelee Sobieski	Liliane Rudabet Gloria Elsveta Sobieski
Suzanne Somers	Suzanne Mahoney

Professional Name	Original Name
Elke Sommer	Elke Schletz
Ann Sothern	Harriet Lake
Sissy Spacek	Mary Elizabeth Spacek
Robert Stack	Robert Modini
Sylvester Stallone	Michael Sylvester Stallone
Jean Stapleton	Jeanne Murray
Ringo Starr	Richard Starkey
Cat Stevens	(Yusuf Islam) Steven Georgiou
Connie Stevens	Concetta Anne Ingolia
Jon Stewart	Jon Stuart Liebowitz
Sting	Gordon Matthew Sumner
Sly Stone	Sylvester Stone
Meryl Streep	Mary Louise Streep
Barbra Streisand	Barbara Streisand
Donna Summer	LaDonna Gaines
Max von Sydow	Carl Adolph von Sydow
Mr. T	Lawrence Tureaud
Rip Taylor	Charles Elmer, Jr.
Robert Taylor	Spangler Brugh
Danny Thomas	Amos Jacobs
Jonathan Taylor Thomas	Jonathan Weiss
Tiny Tim	Herbert Buckingham Khaury
Lily Tomlin	Mary Jean Tomlin
Rip Torn	Elmore Rual Torn, Jr.
Randy Travis	Randy Traywick
Ted Turner	Robert Edward Turner III
Tina Turner	Anna Mae Bullock
Shania Twain	Eileen Regina Twain
Twiggy	Leslie Hornby
Steven Tyler	Steven Tallarico
Rudolph Valentino	Rudolpho Alphonzo Raffaelo Pierre Filibut Guglielmo di Valentina D'Antonguolla
Rudy Vallee	Hubert Prior Vallée
Abigail Van Buren	Pauline Phillips
Christopher Walken	Ronald Walken
Nancy Walker	Ann Myrtle Swoyer

Professional Name	Original Name
Mike Wallace	Myron Wallace
Andy Warhol	Andrew Warhola
Muddy Waters	McKinley Morganfield
John Wayne	Marion Michael Morrison
Sigourney Weaver	Susan Weaver
Raquel Welch	Raquel Tejada
Tuesday Weld	Susan Kerr Weld
Gene Wilder	Jerome Silberman
Bruce Willis	Walter Bruce Willis
August Wilson	Frederick August Kittel
Flip Wilson	Clerow Wilson
Debra Winger	Mary Debra Winger
Shelley Winters	Shirley Schrift
Reese Witherspoon	Laura Jeanne Reese Witherspoon
Stevie Wonder	Steveland Morris Hardaway
Natalie Wood	Natasha Gurdin
Jane Wyman	Sarah Jane Fulks
Tammy Wynette	Wynette Pugh
Wynonna	Christina Claire Ciminella
Ed Wynn	Isaiah Edwin Leopold
Loretta Young	Gretchen Young
Sean Young	Mary Sean Young

Baby Name Legal Guide

Shortly after your baby is born, someone on the hospital staff will ask you for information to fill out a birth certificate. If your baby is not born in a hospital, either by choice or accident, you still need to file a birth certificate. If you're on your way but don't make it to the hospital in time, the hospital will still take care of filling in the form and presenting it for your signature after you're admitted. If you plan a home birth, you will have to go to the vital statistics office and file a form there—to be certain, find out what your local laws require.

Basic facts about both parents' names, places and dates of birth, and such details about the baby as its sex, weight, length, exact time of arrival, and date of birth will be needed for a birth certificate. Questions regarding other children (if any), their ages, previous miscarriages or children's deaths, the educational levels of both parents, and so on might be asked at this time for records at your local division of vital statistics. They may not appear on the actual birth certificate, though.

The hospital staffer will type up the form and present it for the mother and doctor to sign before sending it to the vital statistics division to be recorded permanently. Once it's recorded you can request copies (needed for things like passports, some jobs, and some legal transactions).

That's what happens in the usual chain of events. But what about the technicalities and specific legal aspects of naming a child? The first thing to know is that laws that govern baby naming vary greatly throughout the country. If your choice of names is in any way unusual (such as giving your baby a hyphenated surname combining the mother's maiden name with the father's name), be sure of the law before you name the baby. And sign the official birth certificate only after it has been filled out to your satisfaction.

A few of the most commonly asked questions concerning legalities are considered here but, since state and territory laws are not uniform, even these answers cannot be definite. Your local municipal health department officials can probably lead you to the proper department or official to handle your particular situation. Contact them if you need more detailed answers to your questions.

Q. Are there any restrictions on the choice of first and middle names for a baby?

A. No, with the possible exception that the baby's names should be composed of letters, not numbers. In 1978 a district court judge refused to allow a young Minneapolis social studies teacher to legally change his name to the number 1069, calling such a change "an offense to human dignity" that would "hasten that day in which we all become lost in faceless numbers."

Freedom in choosing given names is not universal. A spokesperson for the French Consulate in Chicago confirmed that an 1813 French law still governs naming practices in France. It decrees that babies must be named after Catholic saints or "persons known in ancient history."

Q. Is a choice allowed in giving the baby its surname?

A. In former generations a baby's surname was not often considered a matter for personal decision. State regulations dictated that if the parents were married, the baby took on the father's surname. If the parents were not married, the baby's surname was that of its mother.

In the past few decades such state regulations have been changing. For example, in Florida, Hawaii, and North Carolina, federal courts have ruled those three states can no longer determine the choice of a baby's surname, leaving that decision to the parent(s).

Such court rulings represent the trend prevalent in most, if not all, states to leave the choice of babies' surnames to parents. However, to be absolutely certain, be sure to check your state's regulations on this matter.

Q. Must the baby's full name be decided upon before the birth certificate can be registered?

A. In most cases no time limit exists in which given names must be recorded. However, depending on the amount of time since the birth, the evidence required to record the name varies, ranging from a letter signed by the parent to a court order.

Q. How can a baby's name be legally changed after its birth is registered?

A. More than 50,000 Americans ask courts to change their names legally every year. Some of these changes are requested by parents for their children when the names originally chosen no longer suit them.

Changes in a minor child's given names are possible in some states without a court order, with time limits ranging from a few days after birth to any time at all. In some states a simple affidavit signed by the parents or a notarized amendment is sufficient to make a name change. Others require various documents to show proof of an established new name, such as a baptismal certificate, an insurance policy, an immunization record, or the family Bible record. For older children, school records or the school census are usually allowed.

When court procedures are necessary, they involve petitions to a county probate court, a superior court, or a district court, following state laws. Often prior newspaper publication of the intended change is required. The court then issues a "change of name" order or decree. In some states new birth certificates are issued for name changes. In others, certificates are only amended.

Informal name changes can be and often are made simply through the "common law right of choice," which allows individuals to use any names they choose. Such a change is informal, though, and is not legal in official procedures.

Q. What if a mistake is made in the baby's name on the birth certificate?

A. To repeat: the best advice of all is to avoid such an occurrence by being absolutely sure that the completely filled-out certificate is correct in every detail before signing it. If a mistake is made, it is important to handle the matter quickly. Procedures for corrections on certificates vary: sometimes signatures of the parents are sufficient, but in other cases forms must be filled out or documentary evidence supplied.

Q. What are the laws for renaming adopted children?

A. An adoption decree is a court order legally obtained through basically similar procedures in all states and territories. A child's given names are selected by the adoptive parents and the surname is chosen in accordance with whatever state or territory laws exist for surnames of biological children. Then all these names are recorded in the adoption decree. In most places an entirely new birth certificate is drawn up, although the place of birth is not usually changed. Most often, the original birth certificate is sealed with the adoption papers, and the new certificate is filed in place of the original.

Q. How may a child's name be changed by a stepfather, by foster parents, or in the case of legitimization?

A. In the case of a name change by a stepfather or by foster parents, most states require that individuals follow the appropriate procedures for adoption or for legal name change.

Changing a child's surname in the case of legitimization is virtually the same as the adoption procedure in most states and territories. Some require both an affidavit of paternity and a copy of the parents' marriage license, while others do not concern themselves with the marriage of the parents. California has no procedures whatsoever, since illegitimacy is no longer defined in that state.

Fascinating Facts about Names

Ashton Punk'd

It seems like a prank spun up by Ashton Kutcher on *Punk'd*, but the highs and lows of the name Ashton is all too real. Of all the names in the 2004 top 100 list, it saw the biggest gain, rising twenty-five places from 2003. The previous year before that, it had gained a whopping one hundred places. But in 2005, Ashton plummeted thirty-one spots, knocking it out of the top 100 all together.

Jennifer vs. Angelina

Calling to mind a year's worth of juicy tabloid headlines, the number 42 and number 43 names of 2005 are Jennifer and Angelina, respectively. Some gossip mongers may believe this means Jennifer Aniston came out on top in the much-publicized love triangle involving her, Angelina Jolie, and Brad Pitt. But if you look closer, you'll see that the name Jennifer slipped four places from 2004 to 2005, while Angelina was one of 2005's biggest risers, clawing up seventeen places from 2004. While Jennifer may narrowly edge out Angelina, the former is on a decline, while the latter is on a huge upswing. (For the curious, the name Brad gained fifteen places, though it's hardly on the 2005 baby-name radar at number 816. And Vince? It's not even in the top 1000.)

The Rise and Fall of Mariah

The popularity of the name Mariah seems to rise and fall much like the record sales of its most famous namesake. Mariah Carey appeared on the scene in 1990 with her smash self-titled album, and as a result, the name Mariah catapulted from number 259 in 1990 to number 69 in 1991. Mariah (the singer) sustained great success throughout the 90s, as did Mariah (the name). But then in 2001, Mariah experienced a public and professional breakdown, and her first movie, *Glitter*, bombed. By 2002, the name Mariah fell forty-five places in popularity and remained out of the top 100 while the artist struggled with bad record sales and publicity. In 2005, Mariah made a comeback on the power of her hit *The Emancipation of Mimi* album, and it boosted the name back into the top 100 at number 85. Where will the name Mariah and its namesake go from here? Watch the charts!

New Era for Japanese Names

Naming trends change all over the world. One trend seeing a great deal of change is from Japan. Traditionally, the kanji character "ko," meaning *child*, was used as a suffix for nearly all girls' names. Now there are only four names ending in "ko" in the top 100 popular names for girls in Japan. Suffixes such as "ka" and "na" are more popular with the new generation of baby names, accounting for more than 25 percent of the top 100 list.

Mermaids and Murderers

Many names have enjoyed surges in popularity due to movies. Madison, the third-most popular girls' name, didn't appear on the naming scene until Daryl Hannah portrayed the beautiful mermaid Madison in 1984's *Splash*. But sometimes names are inspired by less positive characters. Take Samara, the name of the evil, murderous child in the horror flick *The Ring*. Before the movie premiered in 2002, Samara had barely cracked the top 1000 list. Two years later, the name had tripled in popularity.

Who Is Alan Smithee?

Alan Smithee is a prolific Hollywood director whose name has been attached to dozens of movies and TV shows. He was born in 1969, the same year he directed *Death of a Gunfighter*. How can that be, you ask? "Alan Smithee" is a pseudonym commonly used by directors who feel they have lost creative control of their movies and therefore want to distance themselves from them. (You may also know Alan's "cousin," George Spelvin, whose name appears on many a theater playbill.)

International Anonymity

"John Doe" is an anonymous, generic person in the U.S., but he has many counterparts around the globe. There's Fred Nurk (Australia), Jan Modaal (Holland), Chan Siu Ming (Hong Kong), Gyula Kovacs (Hungary), Jón Jónsson (Iceland), Mario Rossi (Italy), Juan dela Cruz (Philippines), Jan Kowalski (Poland), Juan del Pueblo (Puerto Rico), Jos Bleau (Quebec), Vasya Pupkin (Russia), Janez Novak (Slovenia),

Koos van der Merwe (South Africa), and Joe Bloggs (U.K.).

"They" Said It

When you hear, "They say it's going to be a cold winter" or "They say the crime rate is rising," do you ever wonder who "they" are? Wonder no more: "They" is a good-humored inventor from Branson, Missouri. Andrew Wilson decided he would be the face behind this nameless group when he legally changed his name to They in 2004. His friends tell him, "If anyone but you changed your name to They, they would think he had a problem."

Charlize Craze

As one of Hollywood's most talented and beautiful actresses, Charlize Theron has caused a baby-naming boom in her home country of South Africa. In the U.S., the name Charlize has seen a modest rise in popularity, making it to number 625 on the Social Security Administration list, but the Oscar-winning actress recently discovered that her name is hugely popular back home. She says, "Somebody told me that now every one out of three baby girls born in South Africa is being named Charlize."

Bubba³

Raymond Allen Gray, Jr., of Springfield, Illinois, had gone by "Bubba" his whole life. At age thirty-nine, he decided to fully embrace his nickname, so he legally changed his first name to Bubba. He also changed his middle name to Bubba. And then he changed his last name to—you guessed it—Bubba. Bubba Bubba Bubba is

taking his new moniker in stride, saying, "It's something silly to kind of poke fun with."

It's a Bird, It's a Plane, It's a Baby!

In 2003, tax authorities rejected a Swedish couple's request to name their newborn son Superman. The couple thought Superman was the perfect name because their son was born with one arm pointing upward, which resembled Superman in flight. Authorities did not allow the name, however, saying the child would be subjected to ridicule throughout life. (No telling whether those same authorities would have taken issue with Nicolas Cage's naming his son Kal-El, which is Superman's "birth" name.)

Cyber Names

Technology plays a role in nearly every facet of human life, so it's no surprise that technology would inspire names. Jon Blake Cusack and wife, Jamie, of Holland, Michigan, named their son Jon Blake Cusack Version 2.0, putting a high-tech spin on "Junior." A man in central China tried to name his son "@" but was refused because it cannot be translated into Mandarin, which is a legal requirement. Twenty-three-year-old Karin Robertson of Norfolk, Virginia, changed her name to Goveg.Com, in support of the popular website for vegetarianism. Then there's GoldenPalaceDotCom Silverman, whose parents received $15,000 for auctioning his naming rights to the online casino. As it turns out, GoldenPalaceDotCom is not as uncommon as one may think: The casino also paid $15,199 to Terri Illigan of Tennessee when she changed her name to

GoldenPalace.com as a way to support her five children.

Hangover Names

Two U.K. soccer fans woke up to not only throbbing headaches but also new names the morning after a post-game bender. Jeremy Brown and his friend had legally changed their names to Crazy Horse Invincible and Spaceman Africa, respectively, while in their inebriated states. They decided to keep the names—a decision that caused some hassles: Crazy Horse had trouble booking a plane ticket to Prague because airline officials thought someone with such a name was "up to no good." (Spaceman Africa apparently had no problem booking the same flight.)

Kids Naming Kids

When Jayne and Daniel Peate, from Shropshire, England, announced they were expecting a sixth baby, their youngest felt put-out by the new addition. To ease sibling rivalry, Jayne and Daniel allowed the older children to choose their new sibling's middle name. And so they named their son Rafferty Bob Ash Chewbacca Peate, with middle names inspired by *Bob the Builder,* a *Pokemon* character, and the famous *Star Wars* wookie. (Chewbacca was a substitute for Jar Jar Binks when the family learned that each middle name could be only one word long.) The baby is affectionately known as "Chewy."

Ye Olde Names

If you think today's baby names are a little odd, consider the following names researchers in Cornwall, England, found after reviewing centuries of records: Abraham Thunderwolff, Freke Dorothy Fluck Lane, Boadicea Basher, Philadelphia Bunnyface, Faithful Cock, Susan Booze, Elizabeth Disco, Edward Evil, Fozzitt Bonds, Truth Bullock, Charity Chilly, Gentle Fudge, Obedience Ginger, and Offspring Gurney. They even found a real-life Horatio Hornblower, whose siblings were Azubia, Constantia, Jecoliah, Jedidah, Jerusha, and Erastus. The marriage records included odd pairings such as Nicholas Bone and Priscilla Skin, Charles Swine and Jane Ham, John Mutton and Ann Veale, and Richard Dinner and Mary Cook.

How Many Names Do We Need?
Giving your children first names that start with the same letter is a popular trend. Most families need to think of only two or three such names, but coming up with double-digit number of names can be quite a task if you have a large family. The Cox family in North Carolina gave its eleven children names beginning with "Z": Zadie, Zadoc, Zeber, Zylphia, Zenobia, Zeronial, Zeslie, Zeola, Zero, Zula, and Zelbert. Jim Bob and Michelle Duggar of Arkansas used "J" names for all *sixteen* of their children: Joshua, John David, Janna, Jill, Jessa, Jinger, Joseph, Josiah, Joy-Anna, Jeremiah, Jedidiah, Jason, James, Justin, Jackson, and Johannah.

Hockeytown Baby
Nick and Sarah Arena, from Toledo, Ohio, were having trouble thinking of a baby name. After several hours of fruitless brainstorming, they took a break to watch their favorite hockey team, the Detroit Red Wings. In an instant, they both knew what to name their son. On June 6, 2002, Joe Louis Arena was born, named in homage of the stadium where the Red Wings play.

Put It All Together
On its own, Mary is a harmless, normal, beautiful name. But when combined with a middle and last name, you can get a silly moniker such as Mary Chris Smith. Other unfortunate pairings include Ivan Odor, Shanda Lear (daughter of Bill and Moya Lear of Lear Jets), Tu Morrow (daughter of actor Rob Morrow), and Ima Hogg (who, despite urban legend, did not have a sister named Ura).

Birthrights
In some tribal societies children are not considered born until they are named. Frequently the child's name consists of a statement (that is, rather than having a pool of names as Western culture does, parents in these societies name children with a phrase that describes the circumstances of the child's birth, the family's current activities, and so on). Translated, such names might be "We are glad we moved to Memphis," or "A girl at last," or "Too little rain."

Bible Studies
It's been estimated that the majority of people in the Western hemisphere have names from the Bible. Women outnumber men, yet there are 3,037 male names in the Bible and only 181 female names. The New Testament is a more popular source of names than the Old Testament.

Change of Habit
Popes traditionally choose a new name upon their election by the College of Cardinals. The practice began in 844 A.D. when a priest whose real name was Boca de Porco (Pig's Mouth) was elected. He changed his name to Sergious II.

Saint Who?
Saints' names are a common source of names in the U.S. But saints who are popular in other countries contribute very unusual, even unpronounceable, names for children born in the U.S.—like Tamjesdegerd, Borhedbesheba, and Jafkeranaegzia.

Them Bones
Praise-God Barebones had a brother named If-Christ-Had-Not-Died-For-Thee-Thou-Wouldst-Have-Been-Damned, who was called "Damned Barebones" for short.

Hello, God?
Terril William Clark is listed in the phone book under his new name—God. Now he's looking for someone to publish a book he's written. "Let's face it," he reportedly said. "The last book with my name on it was a blockbuster."

The Status Quo
The most commonly given names in English-speaking countries from about 1750 to the present are drawn from a list with only 179 entries (discounting variations in spelling). Essentially the same practice has been followed in naming children since at least the sixteenth century, though the use of middle names has increased over the years.

It's Mainly Relative

A recent study suggests that about two-thirds of the population of the U.S. is named to honor somebody. Of the people who are namesakes, about 60 percent are named after a relative and 40 percent for someone outside the family.

Once Is Enough

Ann Landers wrote about a couple who had six children, all named Eugene Jerome Dupuis, Junior. The children answered to One, Two, Three, Four, Five, and Six, respectively. Can you imagine what the IRS, the Social Security Administration, and any other institution would do with the Dupuises?

In Sickness and Health

Tonsilitis Jackson has brothers and sisters named Meningitis, Appendicitis, and Peritonitis.

The Old College Try

A couple in Louisiana named their children after colleges: Stanford, Duke, T'Lane, Harvard, Princeton, Auburn, and Cornell. The parents' names? Stanford, Sr., and Loyola.

Peace at All Costs

Harry S. Truman owed his middle name, the initial S, to a compromise his parents worked out. By using only the initial, they were able to please both his grandfathers, whose names were Shippe and Solomon.

Initials Only

A new recruit in the U.S. Army filled out all the forms he was presented with as he always had in school: R. (only) B. (only) Jones. You guessed it—from then on he was, as far as the Army cared about it, Ronly Bonly Jones, and all his records, dogtags, and discharge papers proved the point again and again.

Sticks and Stones May Break My Bones...

The nicknames children make up for each other tend to fall into four patterns: those stemming from the physical appearance of the child, those based on either real or imaginary mental traits (brains or idiocy), those based on social ranking or other relationships, and finally, those based on plays on the child's name. Children who don't conform to the values or looks of their peers are likely to pick up more nicknames than those who do. In these ways nicknames often function as instruments of social control.

The Name's the Game

John Hotvet, of Minnetonka, Minnesota, is—of course—a veterinarian. Sometimes names and occupations get inextricably interwoven. Consider these names and professions:

Dr. Zoltan Ovary, gynecologist

Mr. A. Moron, Commissioner of Education for the Virgin Islands

Reverend Christian Church and Reverend God

Mr. Thomas Crapper of Crapper, Ltd Toilets, in London, who entitled his autobiography "Flushed with Pride"

Assorted physicians named Doctor, Docter, or Doktor

Cardinal Sin, Archbishop of Manila, the Philippines

Mr. Groaner Digger, undertaker in Houston

Mr. I. C. Shivers, iceman

Ms. Justine Tune, chorister in Westminster Choir College, Princeton, New Jersey

Ms. Lavender Sidebottom, masseuse at Elizabeth Arden's in New York City

Mssrs. Lawless and Lynch, attorneys in Jamaica, New York

Major Minor, U.S. Army

Diana Nyad, champion long-distance swimmer

Mssrs. Plummer and Leek, plumbers in Sheringham, Norfolk, England

Mr. Ronald Supena, lawyer

Mrs. Screech, singing teacher in Victoria, British Columbia

Mr. Vroom, motorcycle dealer in Port Elizabeth, South Africa

Mssrs. Wyre and Tapping, detectives in New York City

Ms. A. Forest Burns, professional forester

Dr. McNutt, head of a mental hospital, and Dr. Paul Looney, psychiatrist

Mr. Vice, arrested 820 times and convicted 421 times

Dr. Slaughter, surgeon, Dr. Needles, pediatrician, and Dr. Bonebreak, chiropractor

Time Capsule Names

Celebrities and events often inspire parents in their choices of names for children. Many people are now "dated" by their World War II names, like Pearl (Harbor), Douglas (MacArthur), Dwight (Eisenhower—whose mother named him Dwight David to avoid all nicknames, but whom everyone called Ike!), and Franklin (Roosevelt).

Films and film stars contribute their share of names: Scarlett O'Hara and Rhett Butler have countless namesakes whose parents were swept away by *Gone with the Wind*. Madonna, Elvis, Prince, and virtually all other big stars have their own namesakes as well.

The UN Family

One couple took the time capsule concept to an extreme and named their triplets, born on April 5, 1979, Carter, Begin, and Sadat— to honor U.S. President Jimmy Carter, Israeli Prime Minister Menachem Begin, and Egyptian President Anwar Sadat, the three principle signers of the peace treaty signed in Washington, D.C., on March 1979.

They Add Up

Dick Crouser likes to collect unusual names. Some names tell stories, like Fanny Pistor Bodganoff (although Mr. Crouser admits that he doesn't know what a "bodgan" is); some leave messages, like Hazel Mae Call; some aren't likely to add to their owner's self-esteem, like Seldom Wright and Harley Worthit; some are mere truisms, like Wood Burns; while others announce what you might call philosophies of life, like Daily Goforth and Hazel B. Good.

Truth Stranger than Fiction

Dick Neff, columnist of *Advertising Age*, invited his readers to contribute lists of real names they had encountered that are odd and/or funny, to say the least. Among them were the following: Stanley Zigafoose, Cigar Stubbs, Ladorise Quick, Mad Laughinhouse, Lester Chester Hester, Effie Bong, Dillon C. Quattlebaum, Twila Szwrk, Harry E. Thweatt, Benjamin E. Dymshits, Elmer Ploof, Whipple Filoon, Sweetie Belle Rufus, Peculiar Smith, John Dunwrong, All Dunn, Willie Wunn, H. Whitney Clappsaddle, W. Wesley Muckenfuss, Rudolph J. Ramstack, Sarabelle Scraper Roach, James R. Stufflebeam, Shanda Lear, Arthur Crudder, Mary Crapsey, Memory Lane, Troy Mumpower, Santa Beans, Sividious Stark, Cleveland Biggerstaff, Trinkle Bott, Cleopatra Barksdale, Spring Belch, Fairy Blessing, Royal Fauntleroy Butler, Bozy Ball, Carl W. Gigl, Joy Holy, Peenie Fase, Che Che Creech, J. B. Outhouse, Katz Meow, Stephanie Snatchole, I. O. Silver, Helen Bunpain, Birdie Fawncella Feltis, Elight Starling, Farmer Slusher, Nebraska Minor, Bill Grumbles, Peter Rabbitt, Carbon Petroleum Dubbs, Kick-a-hole-in-the-soup, Wong Bong Fong, Newton Hooton, Sonia Schmeckpeeper, Lewie Wirmelskirchen, Lolita Beanblossom, Liselotte Pook, and Irmgard Quapp.

Popular Names?

In 1979, the Pennsylvania Health Department discovered these two first names among the 159,000 birth certificates issued in the state that year—Pepsi and Cola.

A Boy Named Sue

Researchers have found that boys who had peculiar first names had a higher incidence of mental problems than boys with common ones; no similar correlation was found for girls.

He Who Quacks Last

In a government check of a computer program, researchers turned up a real-life Donald Duck. It seems that programmers used his name to create a bogus G.I. to check out records—and found out he really existed. The Army Engineer won fame and a visit to the Johnny Carson Show as a result of this discovery.

Too-o-o-o Much

Many people dislike their own names. The most common reasons given for this dislike are that the names "sound too ugly," that they're old-fashioned, too hard to pronounce, too common, too uncommon, too long, sound too foreign, are too easy for people to joke about, and that they sound too effeminate (for men) or too masculine (for women).

What Are Parents Thinking?

It may have seemed like a good joke at the time, but did Mr. Homer Frost consider his children's future when he named them Winter Night, Jack White, Snow, Dew, Hail, and Cold (Frost)? And what was Mr. Wind thinking when he named his four children North, South, East, and West (Wind)?

For the Birds

A. Bird was the assistant manager of Britain's Royal Society for the Protection of Birds. Members of his staff were Barbara Buzzard, John Partridge, Celia Peacock, Helen Peacock, and Dorothy Rook.

Historical Irony

On July 30, 1980, *Good Morning America* announced that Richard Nixon arrested Jimmy Carter in Detroit.

Is Nothing Private Anymore?

Mr. & Mrs. Bra, a couple from South Dakota, named their two daughters Iona and Anita (Bra).

The Power of Disney

Walt Disney's popular movie *Aladdin* was released in 1992. Aladdin's love interest was named Princess Jasmine. In 1995, Jasmine is the #21 name for all girls in the U.S., the #12 name for Hispanic-American girls, and the #2 name for African-American girls.

Last But Not Least

Zachary Zzzzra has been listed in the *Guinness Book of World Records* as making "the most determined attempt to be the last personal name in a local telephone directory" in San Francisco. That happened before his place was challenged by one Vladimir Zzzzzzabakov. Zzzzra reports that he called Zzzzzzabakov and demanded to know his real name (Zzzzra's name is really his own, he says). Zzzzzzabakov told him it was none of his...business. At any rate, true to his reputation for determination, Zzzzra changed his name to regain his former—or latter?—position. When the new phone book appeared, he was relieved to find himself comfortably in the last place again, as Zachary Zzzzzzzzzzra. Unknown to him, the contender, Zzzzzzabakov, had disappeared.

The End

One family that was not terribly successful in limiting its expansion has a series of children called, respectively, Finis, Addenda, Appendix, Supplement, and (last but not least) Errata.

Girls

A

A 🅖 (American) an initial used as a first name.

Aaarti (Indian) worship; divine fire in ritual.

Aadab (Indian) hope and need.

Aadarshini (Indian) idealistic.

Aadita (Indian) from the beginning.

Aafreen, Afreen (Indian) encouragement.

Aahana (Indian) first rays of the sun.

Aahna (Indian) exist.

Aakaanksha (Indian) wish, desire.

Aakriti (Indian) shape.

Aaleyah (Hebrew) a form of Aliya.
Aalayah, Aalayaha, Aalea, Aaleah, Aaleaha, Aaleeyah, Aaleyiah, Aaleyyah

Aaliah (Hebrew) a form of Aliya.
Aaliaya, Aaliayah

Aalisha (Greek) a form of Alisha.
Aaleasha, Aaliesha

Aaliyah ❦ 🅖 (Hebrew) a form of Aliya.
Aahliyah, Aailiyah, Aailyah, Aalaiya, Aaleah, Aalia, Aalieyha, Aaliya, Aaliyaha, Aaliyha, Aalliah, Aalliyah, Aalyah, Aalyiah

Aamaal (Indian) hopes, aspirations.

Aanandita (Indian) purveyor of joy.

Aanchal, Anchal (Indian) shelter.

Aani (Chamorro) a form of Ha'ani.

Aaron 🅑 (Hebrew) enlightened. (Arabic) messenger.

Aarushi (Indian) first rays.

Aarzoo (Indian) wish.

Aashi (Indian) smile.

Aashirya (Indian) from the land of God.

Aashiyana (Indian) beautiful home; small dwelling, nest.

Aashna (Indian) beloved; devoted to love.

Aashritha (Indian) somebody who gives shelter.

Aasmaa (Indian) excellent; precious.

Aastha (Indian) faith.

Aathmika (Indian) related to the soul.

Aatmaja, Atmaja (Indian) daughter.

Aayushi (Indian) one with long life.

Abagail (Hebrew) a form of Abigail.
Abagael, Abagaile, Abagale, Abagayle, Abageal, Abagil, Abaigael, Abaigeal

Abani (Indian) earth.

Abbagail (Hebrew) a form of Abigail.
Abbagale, Abbagayle, Abbegail, Abbegale, Abbegayle

Abbey, Abbie, Abby 🅖 (Hebrew) familiar forms of Abigail.
Aabbee, Abbe, Abbea, Abbeigh, Abbi, Abbye, Abeey, Abey, Abi, Abia, Abie, Aby

Abbigail 🅖 (Hebrew) a form of Abigail.

Abbygail (Hebrew) a form of Abigail.
Abbeygale, Abbygale, Abbygayl, Abbygayle

Abegail (Hebrew) a form of Abigail.
Abegale, Abegaile, Abegayle

Abel 🅑 (Hebrew) breath. (Assyrian) meadow. (German) a short form of Abelard (see Boys' Names).

Abelina (American) a combination of Abbey + Lina.
Abilana, Abilene

Abha (Indian) beautiful.

Abhaya, Abhitha (Indian) fearless.

Abhilasha (Indian) wish, desire.

Abia (Arabic) great.
Abbia, Abbiah, Abiah, Abya

Abianne (American) a combination of Abbey + Ann.
Abena, Abeni, Abian, Abinaya

Abida (Arabic) worshiper.
Abedah, Abidah

Abigail ❦ (Hebrew) father's joy. Bible: one of the wives of King David. See also Gail.
Abagail, Abbagail, Abbey, Abbiegail, Abbiegayle, Abbigael, Abbigal, Abbigale, Abbigayl, Abbigayle, Abbygail, Abegail, Abgail, Abgale, Abgayle, Abigael, Abigaile, Abigaill, Abigal, Abigale, Abigayil, Abigayl, Abigayle, Abigel, Abigial, Abugail, Abygail, Avigail

Abigaîl (Spanish) a form of Abigail.

Abinaya (American) a form of Abiann.
Abenaa, Abenaya, Abinaa, Abinaiya, Abinayan

Abira (Hebrew) my strength.
Abbira, Abeer, Abeerah, Abeir, Abera,
Aberah, Abhira, Abiir, Abir

Abishta (Indian) lady of the house.

Ablaa (Indian) perfectly formed.

Aboli (Indian) a kind of flower.

Abra (Hebrew) mother of many nations.
Abree, Abri, Abria

Abria (Hebrew) a form of Abra.
Abréa, Abrea, Abreia, Abriah, Abriéa, Abrya

Abrial (French) open; secure, protected.
Abrail, Abreal, Abreale, Abriale, Abrielle

Abriana (Italian) a form of Abra.
Abbrienna, Abbryana, Abreana, Abreanna,
Abreanne, Abreeana, Abreona, Abreonia,
Abriann, Abrianna, Abriannah, Abrieana,
Abrien, Abrienna, Abrienne, Abrietta, Abrion,
Abrionée, Abrionne, Abriunna, Abryann,
Abryanna, Abryona

Abrielle (French) a form of Abrial.
Aabriella, Abriel, Abriell, Abryell

Abrienda (Spanish) opening.

Abril (French) a form of Abrial.
Abrilla, Abrille

Abundancia (Spanish) a form of Hilda.

Abygail (Hebrew) a form of Abigail.
Abygael, Abygale, Abygayle

Acacia (Greek) thorny. Mythology: the acacia
tree symbolizes immortality and
resurrection. See also Casey.
Acasha, Acatia, Accassia, Acey, Acie, Akacia,
Cacia, Casia, Kasia

Acalia (Latin) adoptive mother of Romulus
and Remus.

Achala (Indian) earth; steady.

Achina (Chuukese) good.

Achla (Indian) constant.

Acmahugo (Chamorro) to be squeezed
together.

Acmaurig (Chamorro) good for each other.

Ada (German) a short form of Adelaide.
(English) prosperous; happy.
Adabelle, Adah, Adan, Adaya, Adda, Auda

Adabella (Spanish) a combination of Ada
and Bella.

Adagi (Chamorro) to guard, protect.

Adah (Hebrew) ornament.
Ada, Addah

Adair G (Greek) a form of Adara.
Adaire

Adalene (Spanish) a form of Adalia.
Adalane, Adalena, Adalin, Adalina, Adaline,
Adalinn, Adalyn, Adalynn, Adalynne, Addalyn,
Addalynn

Adalgisa (German) noble hostage.

Adalia (German, Spanish) noble.
Adal, Adala, Adalea, Adaleah, Adalee,
Adalene, Adali, Adalie, Adaly, Addal, Addala,
Addaly

Adaluz (Spanish) a combination of Ada and
Luz.

Adam B (Phoenician) man; mankind.
(Hebrew) earth; of the red earth.

Adama (Phoenician, Hebrew) a form of
Adam.

Adamma (Ibo) child of beauty.

Adana (Spanish) a form of Adama.

Adanna (Nigerian) her father's daughter.
Adanya

Adara (Greek) beauty. (Arabic) virgin.
Adair, Adaira, Adaora, Adar, Adarah, Adare,
Adaria, Adarra, Adasha, Adauré, Adra

Adaya (American) a form of Ada.
Adaija, Adaijah, Adaja, Adajah, Adayja,
Adayjah, Adejah

Addie (Greek, German) a familiar form of
Adelaide, Adrienne.
Aday, Adde, Addee, Addey, Addi, Addia,
Addy, Ade, Adee, Adei, Adey, Adeye, Adi,
Adie, Ady, Atti, Attie, Atty

Addison BG (English) child of Adam.
Addis, Addisen, Addisson, Adison

Addyson (English) a form of Addison.

Adela (English) a short form of Adelaide.
Adelae, Adelia, Adelista, Adella

Adelaide (German) noble and serene. See
also Ada, Adela, Adeline, Adelle, Ailis, Delia,
Della, Ela, Elke, Heidi.
Adelade, Adelaid, Adelaida, Adelei, Adelheid,
Adeliade, Adelka, Aley, Laidey, Laidy

Adele (English) a form of Adelle.
Adel, Adelie, Adile

Adelfa (Spanish) adelfa flower.

Adelina (English) a form of Adeline.
Adalina, Adeleana, Adelena, Adellyna,
Adeliana, Adellena, Adileena, Adlena

Adeline (English) a form of Adelaide.
Adaline, Adelaine, Adelin, Adelina, Adelind, Adelita, Adeliya, Adelle, Adelyn, Adelynn, Adelynne, Adilene, Adlin, Adline, Adlyn, Adlynn, Aline

Adelle (German, English) a short form of Adelaide, Adeline.
Adele, Adell

Adelma (Teutonic) protector of the needy.

Adena (Hebrew) noble; adorned.
Adeana, Adeen, Adeena, Aden, Adene, Adenia, Adenna, Adina

Adhara (Arabic) name of a star in the Canis constellation.

Adia (Swahili) gift.
Addia, Adéa, Adea, Adiah

Adiani (French) a form of Adrianne.

Adila (Arabic) equal.
Adeala, Adeela, Adela, Adelah, Adeola, Adilah, Adileh, Adilia, Adyla

Adilene (English) a form of Adeline.
Adilen, Adileni, Adilenne, Adlen, Adlene

Adina (Hebrew) a form of Adena. See also Dina.
Adeana, Adiana, Adiena, Adinah, Adine, Adinna, Adyna

Adira (Hebrew) strong.
Ader, Adera, Aderah, Aderra, Adhira, Adirah, Adirana

Adishree (Indian) exalted.

Adison, Adyson (English) forms of Addison, Addyson.
Adis, Adisa, Adisen, Adisynne, Adysen

Aditi (Hindi) unbound. Religion: the mother of the Hindu sun gods.
Adithi, Aditti

Aditri (Indian) highest honor.

Adiya (Indian) God's treasure.

Adleigh (Hebrew) my ornament.
Adla, Adleni

Adlihna (Pohnpeian) a form of Esther.

Adoncia (Spanish) sweet.

Adonia (Spanish) beautiful.
Adonica, Adonis, Adonna, Adonnica, Adonya

Adora (Latin) beloved. See also Dora.
Adore, Adoree, Adoria

Adoración (Latin) action of venerating the magical gods.

Adra (Arabic) virgin.
Adara

Adreana, Adreanna (Latin) forms of Adrienne.
Adrean, Adreanne, Adreauna, Adreeanna, Adreen, Adreena, Adreeyana, Adrena, Adrene, Adrenea, Adréona, Adreonia, Adreonna

Adria (English) a short form of Adriana, Adriene.
Adrea, Adriani, Adrya

Adriadna (Greek) she who is very holy, who doesn't yield.

Adrian B (English) a form of Adriane.

Adriana G (Italian) a form of Adrienne.
Adreiana, Adreinna, Adria

Adriane, Adrianne (English) forms of Adrienne.
Addrian, Adranne, Adria, Adrian, Adreinne, Adriann, Adriayon, Adrion

Adrianna (Italian) a form of Adriana.
Addrianna, Addriyanna, Adriannea, Adriannia, Adrionna

Adrielle (Hebrew) member of God's flock.
Adriel, Adrielli, Adryelle

Adrien, Adriene B (English) forms of Adrienne.

Adrienna (Italian) a form of Adrienne. See also Edrianna.
Adreana, Adrieanna, Adrieaunna, Adriena, Adrienia, Adriennah, Adrieunna

Adrienne G (Greek) rich. (Latin) dark. See also Hadriane.
Addie, Adrien, Adriana, Adriane, Adrianna, Adrianne, Adrie, Adrieanne, Adrien, Adrienna, Adriyanna

Adrika (Indian) celestial.

Adrina (English) a short form of Adriana.
Adrinah, Adrinne

Adriyanna (American) a form of Adrienne.
Adrieyana, Adriyana, Adryan, Adryana, Adryane, Adryanna, Adryanne

Adwita, Adwiteya (Indian) unique.

Adwitiya (Indian) matchless.

Adya (Hindi) Sunday.
Adia

Ae (Korean) distant moon.

Aeoma (Hawaiian) a kind of bird.

Aerial, Aeriel (Hebrew) forms of Ariel.
Aeriale, Aeriela, Aerielle, Aeril, Aerile, Aeryal

Afaf (Indian) chastity.

Afi (African) born on Friday.
Affi, Afia, Efi, Efia

Afra (Hebrew) young doe. (Arabic) earth color. See also Aphra.
Affery, Affrey, Affrie, Afraa

Africa (Latin, Greek) sunny; not cold. Geography: one of the seven continents.
Affrica, Afric, Africah, Africaya, Africia, Africiana, Afrika, Aifric

Afrika (Irish) a form of Africa.
Afrikah

Afrodite, Aphrodite (Greek) Mythology: the goddess of love and beauty.
Afrodita

Afton **G** (English) from Afton, England.
Aftan, Aftine, Aftinn, Aftyn

Agacia (Greek) kind.

Agalia (Spanish) bright, joy.

Agamya (Indian) knowledge, wisdom.

Agapita (Greek) she who is beloved and wanted.

Agar (Hebrew) she who fled.

Agate (English) a semiprecious stone.
Aggie

Agatha (Greek) good, kind. Literature: Agatha Christie was a British writer of more than seventy detective novels. See also Gasha.
Agace, Agaisha, Agasha, Agata, Agatah,

Agathe, Agathi, Agatka, Agetha, Aggie, Ágota, Ágotha, Agueda, Atka

Agathe (Greek) a form of Agatha.

Aggie (Greek) a short form of Agatha, Agnes.
Ag, Aggy, Agi

Aghanashini (Indian) destroyer of sins.

Aglaia (Greek) splendorous one; beautiful; resplendent.

Agmagof (Chamorro) being happy together.

Agñasiña (Chamorro) mighty for each other.

Agnes (Greek) pure. See also Aneesa, Anessa, Anice, Anisha, Ina, Inez, Necha, Nessa, Nessie, Neza, Nyusha, Una, Ynez.
Aganetha, Aggie, Agna, Agne, Agneis, Agnelia, Agnella, Agnés, Agnesa, Agnesca, Agnese, Agnesina, Agness, Agnessa, Agnesse, Agneta, Agneti, Agnetta, Agnies, Agnieszka, Agniya, Agnola, Agnus, Aignéis, Aneska, Anka

Agnishikha (Indian) flames of fire.

Agostina (Spanish) a form of Agustina.
Agostiña

Agot (Chamorro) embrace each other.

Agrata (Indian) leadership.

Agripina (Greek) from the Agripa family.

Agua (Chamorro) milkfish.

Agüeda (Greek) having many virtues.

Águeda (Spanish) a form of Agatha.

Aguilina (Spanish) a form of Justina.

Aguon (Chamorro) food, bread, taro.

Agustina (Latin) a form of Augustine.

Ah (Chinese) from a Chinese character.

Ah Kum (Chinese) treasure.

Ahalya (Indian) wife of Rishi Gautam.

Ahanti (Indian) gift.

Ahava (Hebrew) beloved.
Ahivia

Ahd (Indian) pledge; knowledge.

Ahilya (Indian) wife of a rishi (divinely inspired poet or sage).

Ahladita (Indian) in a happy and nice mood.

Ahlani (Hawaiian) a form of Alani.

Ahliya (Hebrew) a form of Aliya.
Ahlai, Ahlaia, Ahlaya, Ahleah, Ahleeyah, Ahley, Ahleya, Ahlia, Ahliah, Ahliyah

Ahmed **B** (Swahili) praiseworthy.

Ah-Rum (Korean) torch light.

Aida (Latin) helpful. (English) a form of Ada.
Aída, Aidah, Aidan, Aide, Aidee

Aidan, Aiden **B** (Latin) forms of Aida.

Aidia (Spanish) help.

Aiesha (Swahili, Arabic) a form of Aisha.
Aeisha, Aeshia, Aieshia, Aieysha, Aiiesha

Aiisha (Arabic) a form of Aisha.

Aiko (Japanese) beloved.

Ailani (Hawaiian) chief.
Aelani, Ailana

Aileen (Scottish) light bearer. (Irish) a form of Helen. See also Eileen.
Ailean, Aileena, Ailen, Ailene, Aili, Ailina, Ailinn, Aillen

Ailén (Mapuche) ember.

Aili (Scottish) a form of Alice. (Finnish) a form of Helen.
Aila, Ailee, Ailey, Ailie, Aily

Ailín (Mapuche) transparent, very clear.

Ailis (Irish) a form of Adelaide.
Ailesh, Ailish, Ailyse, Eilis

Ailsa (Scottish) island dweller. Geography: Ailsa Craig is an island in Scotland.
Ailsha

Ailya (Hebrew) a form of Aliya.
Ailiyah

Aimee (Latin) a form of Amy. (French) loved.
Aime, Aimée, Aimey, Aimi, Aimia, Aimie, Aimy

Ain (Arabic) eye; the name of an orange star in the constellation of Taurus.

Ainara (Basque) swallow.

Ainhoa (Basque) allusion to the Virgin Mary.

Ainoa (Basque) she who has fertile soil.

Ainsley ☒ (Scottish) my own meadow.
Ainslee, Ainsleigh, Ainslie, Ainsly, Ansley, Aynslee, Aynsley, Aynslie

Airiana (English) a form of Ariana, Arianna.
Airana, Airanna, Aireana, Aireanah, Aireanna, Aireona, Aireonna, Aireyonna, Airianna, Airianne, Airiona, Airriana, Airrion, Airryon, Airyana, Airyanna

Airiél (Hebrew) a form of Ariel.
Aieral, Aierel, Aiiryel, Aire, Aireal, Aireale, Aireel, Airel, Airele, Airelle, Airi, Airial, Airiale, Airrel

Aisha (Swahili) life. (Arabic) woman. See also Asha, Asia, Iesha, Isha, Keisha, Yiesha.
Aaisha, Aaishah, Aesha, Aeshah, Aheesha, Aiasha, Aiesha, Aieshah, Aisa, Aischa, Aish, Aishah, Aisheh, Aishia, Aishiah, Aiysha, Aiyesha, Ayesha, Aysa, Ayse, Aytza

Aishwarya (Indian) wealth, prosperity.

Aislinn, Aislynn (Irish) forms of Ashlyn.
Aishellyn, Aishlinn, Aislee, Aisley, Aislin, Aisling, Aislyn, Aislynne

Aivi (Chuukese) intravenous.

Aiyana (Native American) forever flowering.
Aiyhana, Aiyona, Aiyonia, Ayana

Aiyanna (Hindi) a form of Ayanna.
Aianna, Aiyannah, Aiyonna, Aiyunna

Aja ☒ (Hindi) goat.
Ahjah, Aija, Aijah, Ajá, Ajada, Ajah, Ajara, Ajaran, Ajare, Ajaree, Ajha, Ajia

Ajala (Indian) the Earth.

Ajanae (American) a combination of the letter A + Janae.
Ajahnae, Ajahne, Ajana, Ajanaé, Ajane, Ajané, Ajanee, Ajanique, Ajena, Ajenae, Ajené

Ajanta (Indian) a famous Buddhist cave.

Ajia (Hindi) a form of Aja.
Aijia, Ajhia, Aji, Ajjia

Ajita (Indian) a winner.

Akako (Japanese) red.

Akanisi (Fijian) a form of Agnes.

Akanksha (Indian) wish; desire; hope.

Akasuki (Japanese) bright; helper.

Akata (Fijian) a form of Agueda.

Akayla (American) a combination of the letter A + Kayla.
Akaela, Akaelia, Akaila, Akailah, Akala, Akaylah, Akaylia

Akeisha (American) a combination of the letter A + Keisha.
Akaesha, Akaisha, Akasha, Akasia, Akeecia, Akeesha, Akeishia, Akeshia, Akisha

Akela (Hawaiian) noble.
Ahkayla, Ahkeelah, Akelah, Akelia, Akeliah, Akeya, Akeyla, Akeylah

Akemi (Japanese) the dawn of a beautiful day.

Akeneta (Fijian) a form of Agnes.

Akeria (American) a form of Akira.
Akera, Akerah, Akeri, Akerra, Akerra

Akhila (Indian) complete.

Aki (Japanese) born in autumn.
Akeeye

Akia (American) a combination of the letter A + Kia.
Akaja, Akeia, Akeya, Akiá, Akiah, Akiane, Akiaya, Akiea, Akiya, Akiyah, Akya, Akyan, Akyia, Akyiah

Akiha (Japanese) autumn leaves.

Akiho (Japanese) autumn crops.

Akiko (Japanese) bright light.

Akilah (Arabic) intelligent.
Aikiela, Aikilah, Akeela, Akeelah, Akeila, Akeilah, Akeiyla, Akiela, Akielah, Akila, Akilaih, Akilia, Akilka, Akillah, Akkila, Akyla, Akylah

Akili (Tanzanian) wisdom.

Akimi (Japanese) the truth of autumn.

Akina (Japanese) spring flower.

Akira **G** (American) a combination of the letter A + Kira.
Akeria, Akiera, Akierra, Akirah, Akire, Akiria, Akirrah, Akyra

Akiye (Japanese) glitter; inlet; blessed.

Akiyo (Japanese) bright fourth-born child; life like a poem.

Akriti (Indian) diagram.

Akshadha (Indian) God's blessings.

Akshara (Indian) letter.

Akshata (Indian) rice.

Akshaya (Indian) indestructible.

Akshi (Indian) existence.

Akshita (Indian) wonder girl.

Akuti (Indian) princess.

Alabhya (Indian) unique, difficult to acquire.

Alago (Chamorro) rice soup.

Alai (Chinese) wheat.

Alaina, Alayna (Irish) forms of Alana.
Aalaina, Alainah, Alaine, Alainna, Alainnah,
Alane, Alaynah, Alayne, Alaynna, Aleine, Alleyna, Alleynah, Alleyne

Alair (French) a form of Hilary.
Alaira, Ali, Allaire

Alak, Alaka (Indian) world; beautiful tresses.

Alaknanda (Indian) a river.

Alamea (Hawaiian) ripe; precious.

Alameda (Spanish) poplar tree.

Alan **B** (Irish) beautiful; peaceful.

Alana (Irish) a form of Alan. (Hawaiian) offering. See also Lana.
Alaana, Alaina, Alanae, Alanah, Alane, Alanea, Alani, Alania, Alanis, Alanna, Alawna, Alayna, Allana, Allanah, Allyn, Alonna

Alandra, Alandria (Spanish) forms of Alexandra, Alexandria.
Alandrea, Alantra, Aleandra, Aleandrea

Alani (Hawaiian) orange tree. (Irish) a form of Alana.
Alaini, Alainie, Alania, Alanie, Alaney, Alannie

Alankrita (Indian) decorated lady.

Alanna (Irish) a form of Alana.
Alannah

Alanza (Spanish) noble and eager.

Alas (Chamorro) shell money.

Alasña (Chamorro) her shell money.

Alaysha, Alaysia (American) forms of Alicia.
Alaysh, Alayshia

Alba (Latin) from Alba Longa, an ancient city near Rome, Italy.
Albana, Albani, Albanie, Albany, Albeni, Albina, Albine, Albinia, Albinka

Albert **B** (German, French) noble and bright.

Alberta (German, French) a form of Albert. See also Auberte, Bertha, Elberta.
Albertina, Albertine, Albertyna, Albertyne, Alverta

Albreanna (American) a combination of Alberta + Breanna (see Breana).
Albré, Albrea, Albreona, Albreonna, Albreyon

Alcina (Greek) strong-minded.
Alceena, Alcine, Alcinia, Alseena, Alsinia, Alsyna, Alzina

Alcira (German) adornment of nobility.

Alda (German) old; elder.
Aldina, Aldine

Aldana (Spanish) a combination of Alda and Ana.

Alden **B** (English) old; wise protector.
Aldan, Aldon, Aldyn

Aldina, Aldine (Hebrew) forms of Alda.
Aldeana, Aldene, Aldona, Aldyna, Aldyne

Aldonsa, Aldonza (Spanish) nice.

Alea, Aleah (Arabic) high, exalted. (Persian) God's being.
Aileah, Aleea, Aleeah, Aleia, Aleiah, Allea, Alleah, Alleea, Alleeah

Aleasha, Aleesha (Greek) forms of Alisha.
Aleashae, Aleashea, Aleashia, Aleassa, Aleeshia

Girls A–F

Alec, Alek 🅱 (Greek) short forms of Alexander.

Alecia (Greek) a form of Alicia.
Aalecia, Ahlasia, Aleacia, Aleacya, Aleasia, Alecea, Aleceea, Aleceia, Aleciya, Aleciyah, Alecy, Alecya, Aleeceia, Aleecia, Aleesia, Aleesiya, Aleicia, Alesha, Alesia, Allecia, Alleecia

Aleela (Swahili) she cries.
Aleelah, Alila, Alile

Aleena (Dutch) a form of Aleene.
Ahleena, Aleana, Aleeanna

Aleene (Dutch) alone.
Aleen, Aleena, Alene, Alleen

Aleeya (Hebrew) a form of Aliya.
Alee, Aleea, Aleeyah, Aleiya, Aleiyah

Aleeza (Hebrew) a form of Aliza. See also Leeza.
Aleiza

Alegria (Spanish) cheerful.
Aleggra, Alegra, Alegría, Allegra, Allegria

Aleisha, Alesha (Greek) forms of Alecia, Alisha.
Aleasha, Aleashea, Aleasia, Aleesha, Aleeshah, Aleeshia, Aleeshya, Aleisa, Alesa, Alesah, Aleisha, Aleshia, Aleshya, Alesia, Alessia

Alejandra 🅖 (Spanish) a form of Alexandra.
Aleiandra, Alejanda, Alejandr, Alejandrea, Alejandria, Alejandrina, Alejandro

Alejandro 🅱 (Spanish) a form of Alejandra.

Aleka (Hawaiian) a form of Alice.
Aleeka, Alekah

Alekhya (Indian) that which cannot be written.

Aleksandra (Greek) a form of Alexandra.
Alecsandra, Aleksasha, Aleksandrija, Aleksandriya

Alena (Russian) a form of Helen.
Alenah, Alene, Alenea, Aleni, Alenia, Alenka, Alenna, Alennah, Alenya, Alyna

Alesia, Alessia (Greek) forms of Alice, Alicia, Alisha.
Alessea, Alesya, Allesia

Alessa (Greek) a form of Alice.
Alessi, Allessa

Alessandra (Italian) a form of Alexandra.
Alesandra, Alesandrea, Alissandra, Alissondra, Allesand, Allessandra

Alessandro 🅱 (Italian) a form of Alexander.

Aleta (Greek) a form of Alida. See also Leta.
Aletta, Alletta

Alethea (Greek) truth.
Alathea, Alathia, Aletea, Aletha, Aletheia, Alethia, Aletia, Alithea, Alithia

Alette (Latin) wing.

Alex 🅱 (Greek) a short form of Alexander, Alexandra.
Aleix, Aleks, Alexe, Alexx, Allex, Allexx

Alexa ☝ 🅖 (Greek) a short form of Alexandra.
Aleixa, Alekia, Aleksa, Aleksha, Aleksi, Alexah, Alexsa, Alexssa, Alexxa, Allexa, Alyxa

Alexander 🅱 (Greek) defender of humankind.

Alexandra ☝ 🅖 (Greek) a form of Alexander. History: the last czarina of Russia. See also Lexia, Lexie, Olesia, Ritsa, Sandra, Sandrine, Sasha, Shura, Sondra, Xandra, Zandra.
Alandra, Alaxandra, Aleczandra, Alejandra, Aleksandra, Alessandra, Alex, Alexa, Alexande, Alexandera, Alexandre, Alexas, Alexi, Alexina, Alexine, Alexis, Alexsandra, Alexius, Alexsis, Alexus, Alexxandra, Alexys, Alexzandra, Alix, Alixandra, Aljexi, Alla, Alyx, Alyxandra, Lexandra

Alexandre 🅱 (Greek) a form of Alexandra.

Alexandrea (Greek) a form of Alexandria.
Alexandreana, Alexandreia, Alexandriea, Alexandrieah, Alexanndrea

Alexandria 🅖 (Greek) a form of Alexandra. See also Drinka, Xandra, Zandra.
Alaxandria, Alecsandria, Aleczandria, Alexanderia, Alexanderine, Alexandrea, Alexandrena, Alexandrie, Alexandrina, Alexandrine, Alexanndria, Alexandrya, Alexendria, Alexendrine, Alexia, Alixandrea, Alyxandria

Alexandrine (Greek) a form of Alexandra.
Alexandrina

Alexanne (American) a combination of Alex + Anne.
Alexan, Alexanna, Alexane, Alexann, Alexanna, Alexian, Alexiana

Alexas, Alexes (Greek) short forms of Alexandra.
Alexess

Alexe 🅖 (Greek) a form of Alex.

Alexi, Alexie 🅖 (Greek) short forms of Alexandra.
Aleksey, Aleksi, Alexey, Alexy

Alexia (Greek) a short form of Alexandria. See also Lexia.
Aleksia, Aleska, Alexcia, Alexea, Alexsia, Alexsiya, Allexia, Alyxia

Alexis ♛ G (Greek) a short form of Alexandra.
Aalexis, Ahlexis, Alaxis, Alecsis, Alecxis, Aleexis, Aleksis, Alexcis, Alexias, Alexiou, Alexiss, Alexiz, Alexxis, Alixis, Allexis, Elexis, Lexis

Alexius (Greek) a short form of Alexandra.
Allexius

Alexsandra (Greek) a form of Alexandra.
Alexsandria, Alexsandro, Alixsandra

Alexsis, Alexxis (Greek) short forms of Alexandra.
Alexxiz

Alexus G (Greek) a short form of Alexandra.
Aalexus, Aalexxus, Aelexus, Ahlexus, Alecsus, Alexsus, Alexuss, Alexxus, Alixus, Allexus, Elexus, Lexus

Alexys (Greek) a short form of Alexandra.
Alexsys, Alexyes, Alexyis, Alexyss, Allexys

Alexzandra (Greek) a form of Alexandra.
Alexzand, Alexzandrea, Alexzandriah, Alexzandrya, Alixzandria

Aleya, Aleyah (Hebrew) forms of Aliya.
Alayah, Aleayah, Aleeya, Aléyah, Aleyia, Aleyiah

Alfa (Greek) symbolizes the beginning of all.

Alfie B (English) a familiar form of Alfreda.
Alfi, Alfy

Alfonsa (Spanish) noble.

Alfonsina (German) noble and ready for battle.

Alfreda (English) elf counselor; wise counselor. See also Effie, Elfrida, Freda, Frederica.
Alfie, Alfredda, Alfredia, Alfreeda, Alfreida, Alfrieda

Alhertina (Spanish) noble.

Ali, Aly B (Greek) familiar forms of Alice, Alicia, Alisha, Alison.
Allea, Alli, Allie, Ally

Alia, Aliah (Hebrew) forms of Aliya. See also Aaliyah, Alea.
Aelia, Allia, Alya

Alice G (Greek) truthful. (German) noble. See also Aili, Aleka, Alie, Alisa, Alison, Alli, Alysa, Alyssa, Alysse, Elke.
Adelice, Alecia, Aleece, Alesia, Alicie, Aliece, Alise, Alix, Alize, Alla, Alleece, Allice, Allis, Allise, Allix

Alicia G (English) a form of Alice. See also Elicia, Licia.
Aelicia, Alaysha, Alecea, Alecia, Aleecia, Ali, Alicea, Alicha, Alichia, Aliciah, Alician, Alicja, Alicya, Aliecia, Alisha, Allicea, Allicia, Alycia, Ilysa

Alida (Latin) small and winged. (Spanish) noble. See also Aleta, Lida, Oleda.
Aleda, Aleida, Alidia, Alita, Alleda, Allida, Allidah, Alyda, Alydia, Elida, Elidia

Alie (Greek) a familiar form of Alice.

Aliesha (Greek) a form of Alisha.
Alieshai, Alieshia, Alliesha

Ali'i (Hawaiian) queen, noble, royal.

Alika (Hawaiian) truthful. (Swahili) most beautiful.
Aleka, Alica, Alikah, Alike, Alikee, Aliki

Aliksa (Kosraean) forever.

Alima (Arabic) sea maiden; musical.

Alina, Alyna (Slavic) bright. (Scottish) fair. (English) short forms of Adeline. See also Alena.
Aliana, Alianna, Alinah, Aline, Alinna, Allyna, Alynna, Alyona

Aline (Scottish) a form of Alina.
Alianne, Allene, Alline, Allyn, Allyne, Alyne, Alynne

Alisa (Greek) a form of Alice. See also Elisa, Ilisa.
Aalissah, Aaliysah, Aleessa, Alisah, Alisea, Alisia, Alisza, Alisza, Aliysa, Allissa, Alyssa

Alise, Allise (Greek) forms of Alice.
Alics, Aliese, Alis, Aliss, Alisse, Alisse, Alles, Allesse, Allis, Allisse

Alisha G (Greek) truthful. (German) noble. (English) a form of Alicia. See also Elisha, Ilisha, Lisha.
Aalisha, Aleasha, Aleesha, Aleisha, Alesha, Ali, Aliesha, Aliscia, Alishah, Alishay, Alishaye, Alishia, Alishya, Alitsha, Allisha, Allysha, Alysha

Alishia, Alisia, Alissia (English) forms of Alisha.
Alishea, Alisheia, Alishiana, Alyssaya, Alisea, Alissya, Alisyia, Allissia

Alison G (English) a form of Alice.
Ali, Alicen, Alicyn, Alisan, Alisann, Alisanne, Alisen, Alisenne, Alisin, Alision, Alisonn, Alisson, Alisun

Alissa 🄶 (Greek) a form of Alice. See also Elisa, Ilisa.
Aelicia, Alaysha, Alecea, Alecia, Aleecia, Ali, Alicea, Alicha, Alichia, Aliciah, Alician, Alicja, Alicya, Aliecia, Alisha, Allicea, Allicia, Alycia, Ilysa

Alita (Spanish) a form of Alida.
Allita

Alivia (Latin) a form of Olivia.
Alivah

Alix 🄶 (Greek) a short form of Alexandra, Alice.
Alixe, Alixia, Allix, Alyx

Alixandra, Alixandria (Greek) forms of Alexandria.
Alixandriya, Allixandra, Allixandria, Allixandrya

Aliya (Hebrew) ascender.
Aaleyah, Aaliyah, Aeliyah, Ahliya, Ailya, Alea, Aleya, Alia, Alieya, Alieyah, Aliyah, Aliyiah, Aliyyah, Allia, Alliyah, Aly, Alyah

Aliye (Arabic) noble.
Aliyeh

Aliza (Hebrew) joyful. See also Aleeza, Eliza.
Alieza, Aliezah, Alitza, Aliz, Alizah, Alize, Alizee

Alizabeth (Hebrew) a form of Elizabeth.
Alyzabeth

Alka (Indian) beauty.

Allan 🄱 (Irish) a form of Alan.

Allana, Allanah (Irish) forms of Alana.
Allanie, Allanna, Allauna

Allegra (Latin) cheerful.
Legra

Allen 🄱 (Irish) a form of Alan.

Allena (Irish) a form of Alana.
Alleen, Alleyna, Alleynah

Alli, Ally (Greek) familiar forms of Alice.
Ali, Alley

Allia, Alliah (Hebrew) forms of Aliya.

Allie 🄶 (Greek) familiar forms of Alice.

Allison ☸ 🄶 (English) a form of Alice. See also Lissie.
Alles, Allesse, Alleyson, Allie, Allisson, Allisyn, Allix, Allsun

Allissa (Greek) a form of Alyssa.
Allisa

Alliyah (Hebrew) a form of Aliya.
Alliya, Alliyha, Alliyia, Alliyyah, Allya, Allyah

Allysa, Allyssa (Greek) a form of Alyssa.
Allissa, Allyisa, Allysa, Allysah, Allyssah

Allysha (English) a form of Alisha.
Alishia, Allysia

Allyson, Alyson (English) forms of Alison.
Allysen, Allyson, Allysonn, Allysson, Allysun, Alyson

Alma 🄶 (Arabic) learned. (Latin) soul.
Almah

Almas (Indian) diamond.

Almeda (Arabic) ambitious.
Allmeda, Allmedah, Allmeta, Allmita, Almea, Almedah, Almeta, Almida, Almita

Almira (Arabic) aristocratic, princess; exalted. (Spanish) from Almeíra, Spain. See also Elmira, Mira.
Allmeera, Allmeria, Allmira, Almeera, Almeeria, Almeira, Almeria, Almire

Almudena (Spanish) city.

Almunda (Spanish) refers to the Virgin Mary.

Almundena, Almundina (Spanish) forms of Almunda.

Alo (Chamorro) a form of Alu.

Aloha (Hawaiian) loving, kindhearted, charitable.
Alohi

Alohilani (Hawaiian) bright sky.

Aloisa (German) famous warrior.
Aloisia, Aloysia

Aloki (Indian) brightness.

Alola (Chamorro) a form of Alula.

Aloma (Latin) a short form of Paloma.

Alondra 🄶 (Spanish) a form of Alexandra.
Allandra, Alonda

Alonna (Irish) a form of Alana.
Alona, Alonnah, Alonya, Alonyah

Alonsa (English) eager for battle.

Alonza (English) noble and eager.

Alopa (Indian) faultless.

Alora (American) a combination of the letter A + Lora.
Alorah, Alorha, Alorie, Aloura, Alouria

Alos (Chamorro) a form of Alas.

Alpa (Indian) small.

Alpana (Indian) beautiful.

Alpha (Greek) first-born. Linguistics: the first letter of the Greek alphabet.
Alphia

Alta (Latin) high; tall.
Allta, Altah, Altana, Altanna, Altea, Alto

Altagracia (Spanish) refers to the high grace of the Virgin Mary.

Althea (Greek) wholesome; healer. History: Althea Gibson was the first African American to win a major tennis title. See also Thea.
Altha, Altheda, Altheya, Althia, Elthea, Eltheya, Elthia

Alu (Chamorro) barracuda; shark.

Alula (Chamorro) hurry.

Aluminé (Mapuche) she who shines.

Alva **BG** (Latin, Spanish) white; light skinned. See also Elva.
Alvana, Alvanna, Alvannah

Alvarita, Alvera (Spanish) speaker of truth.

Alvina (English) friend to all; noble friend; friend to elves. See also Elva, Vina.
Alveanea, Alveen, Alveena, Alveenia, Alvenea, Alvie, Alvinae, Alvincia, Alvine, Alvinea, Alvinesha, Alvinia, Alvinna, Alvita, Alvona, Alvyna, Alwin, Alwina, Alwyn

Alyah, Alyiah (Hebrew) forms of Aliya.
Aly, Alya, Aleah, Alyia

Alycia, Alyssia (English) forms of Alicia.
Allyce, Alycea, Alyciah, Alyse, Lycia

Alysa, Alyse (Greek) forms of Alice.
Allys, Allyse, Allyss, Alys, Alyss

Alysha, Alysia (Greek) forms of Alisha.
Allysea, Allyscia, Alysea, Alyshia, Alyssha, Alyssia

Alyssa ⚜ **G** (Greek) rational. Botany: alyssum is a flowering herb. See also Alice, Elissa.
Ahlyssa, Alissa, Allissa, Allyssa, Alyesa, Alyessa, Alyissa, Alysah, Ilyssa, Lyssa, Lyssah

Alysse (Greek) a form of Alice.
Allyce, Allys, Allyse, Allyss, Alys, Alyss

Alyx, Alyxis (Greek) short forms of Alexandra.

Alyxandra, Alyxandria (Greek) forms of Alexandria.
Alyxandrea, Alyxzandrya

Am (Vietnamese) lunar; female.

Ama (African) born on Saturday.

Amabel (Latin) lovable. See also Bel, Mabel.

Amada (Spanish) beloved.
Amadea, Amadi, Amadia, Amadita

Amadis (Latin) great love, the most beloved.

Amai (Chamorro) rain.

Amairani (Greek) a form of Amara.
Amairaine, Amairane, Amairanie, Amairany

Amako (Japanese) child of God.

Amal **G** (Hebrew) worker. (Arabic) hopeful.
Amala

Amaldeepti (Indian) camphor.

Amaleperka (Pohnpeian) royal.

Amalia (German) a form of Amelia.
Ahmalia, Amalea, Amaleah, Amaleta, Amalija, Amalina, Amalisa, Amalita, Amaliya, Amalya, Amalyn

Amalie (German) a form of Amelia.
Amalee, Amali, Amaly

Amalsinda (German) one that God points to.

Amami (Japanese) sky; sea.

Aman, Amani (Arabic) forms of Imani.
Aamani, Ahmani, Amane, Amanee, Amaney, Amanie, Ammanu

Amanada (Latin) a form of Amanda.

Amancái, Amancay (Quechua) voice that gives a name to a beautiful yellow flower streaked with red.

Amanda ⚜ **G** (Latin) lovable. See also Manda.
Amada, Amanada, Amandah, Amandalee, Amandalyn, Amandi, Amandie, Amandine, Amandy

Amandeep **BG** (Punjabi) peaceful light.

Amannie (Arabic) a form of Amani.

Amapola (Arabic) poppy.

Amara (Greek) eternally beautiful. See also Mara.
Amar, Amaira, Amairani, Amarah, Amari, Amaria, Amariah

Amaranta (Spanish) a flower that never fades.

Amarante (Japanese) flower that never fades.

Amari (Greek) a form of Amara.
Amaree, Amarie, Amarii, Amarri

Girls A–F

Amarilia, Amarilla (Greek) she who shines.

Amarinda (Greek) she who shines.

Amaris (Hebrew) promised by God.
Amarissa, Amarys, Maris

Amarú (Quechua) snake, boa.

Amaryllis (Greek) fresh; flower.
Amarillis, Amarylis

Amatullah (Indian) female servant of Allah.

Amaui (Hawaiian) thrush.

Amay (Chamorro) a form of Amai.

Amaya (Japanese) night rain.

Ambalika (Indian) mother.

Ambar Ᏻ (French) a form of Amber.

Amber Ᏻ (French) amber.
*Aamber, Ahmber, Amberia, Amberise,
Amberly, Ambria, Ambur, Ambyr, Ambyre,
Ammber, Ember*

Amberly (American) a familiar form of
Amber.
*Amberle, Amberlea, Amberlee, Amberleigh,
Amberley, Amberli, Amberlie, Amberlly,
Amberlye*

Amberlyn, Amberlynn (American)
combinations of Amber + Lynn.
Amberlin, Amberlina, Amberlyne, Amberlynne

Ambhom (Tai) a form of Jingjing.

Ambria (American) a form of Amber.
Ambrea, Ambra, Ambriah

Ambrosia (Greek) she who is immortal.

Ambu (Indian) water.

Ambuda (Indian) cloud.

Amedia (Spanish) beloved.

Amelia ☙ (German) hard working. (Latin)
a form of Emily. History: Amelia Earhart, an
American aviator, was the first woman to fly
solo across the Atlantic Ocean. See also Ima,
Melia, Millie, Nuela, Yamelia.
*Aemilia, Aimilia, Amalia, Amalie, Amaliya,
Ameila, Ameilia, Amelie, Amelina, Ameline,
Amelisa, Amelita, Amella, Amilia, Amilina,
Amilisa, Amilita, Amilyn, Amylia*

Amélia (Portuguese) a form of Amelia.

Amelie (German) a familiar form of Amelia.
*Amaley, Amalie, Amelee, Ameleigh, Ameley,
Amélie, Amely, Amilie*

Amena (Arabic) a form of Amina.

America (Teutonic) industrious.
América, Americana, Amerika

Ami, Amie (French) forms of Amy.
*Aami, Amiee, Amii, Amiiee, Ammee, Ammie,
Ammiee*

Amihan (Tagalog) abundance.

Amilia, Amilie (Latin, German) forms of
Amelia.
Amilee, Amili, Amillia, Amily, Amilya

Amina (Arabic) trustworthy, faithful. History:
the mother of the prophet Muhammad.
*Aamena, Aamina, Aaminah, Ameena,
Ameenah, Aminah, Aminda, Amindah,
Aminta, Amintah*

Amir Ᏻ (Hebrew) proclaimed. (Punjabi)
wealthy; king's minister. (Arabic) prince.

Amira (Hebrew) speech; utterance. (Arabic)
princess. See also Mira.
Ameera, Ameerah, Amirah

Amisha (Indian) beautiful.

Amishi, Amla (Indian) pure.

Amissa (Hebrew) truth.
Amissah

Amista (Chamorro) fidelity, loyalty.

Amita (Hebrew) truth.
Amitha

Amithi (Indian) unique.

Amitjyoti (Indian) bright.

Amity (Latin) friendship.
Amitie

Amiya (Indian) delightful.

Amlika (Hindi) mother.
Amlikah

Amma (Hindi) god, godlike. Religion:
another name for the Hindu goddess Shakti.

Ammei, Ammey (Chamorro) forms of Amai.

Amoda (Indian) happiness.

Amodini (Indian) pleasurable.

Amog (Chamorro) medicine.

Amolika (Indian) priceless.

Amor (German) a form of Amorie.

Amora (Spanish) a form of Amor.

Amorie (German) industrious leader.

Amorina (Spanish) she who falls in love easily.

Amparo (Spanish) protected.

Amrapali (Indian) disciple of Buddha.

Amrit BG (Sanskrit) nectar.
Amrita

Amritambu (Indian) moon.

Amritkala (Indian) nectarine art.

Amritrashmi (Indian) moonlight.

Amrusha (Indian) sudden.

Amshula, Anshula (Indian) sunny.

Amti (Chamorro) a form of Aorta.

Amuillan (Mapuche) useful, helpful; enthusiastic woman who does all that she can to serve those around her.

Amvi (Indian) a goddess.

Amy G (Latin) beloved. See also Aimee, Emma, Esmé.
Amata, Ame, Amey, Ami, Amia, Amie, Amio, Ammy, Amye, Amylyn

An B (Chinese) peaceful.

Ana (Hawaiian, Spanish) a form of Hannah.
Anai, Anaia

Aña (Chamorro) to overpower; to punish.

Anaan (Indian) clouds.

Anaba (Native American) she returns from battle.

Anabel, Anabelle (English) forms of Annabel.
Anabela, Anabele, Anabell, Anabella

Anaclara (Spanish) a combination of Ana and Clara.

Anacleta (Greek) she who has been called on; the required one.

Anagha (Indian) without sin.

Anahí, Anahid (Guarani) alluding to the flower of the Ceibo plant.

Anahita (Persian) a river and water goddess.
Anahai, Anahi, Anahit, Anahy

Anais (Hebrew) gracious.
Anaise, Anaïse

Anala (Hindi) fine.

Analena (Spanish) a form of Ana.

Analía (Spanish) a combination of Ana and Lía.

Analilia (Indian) full of grace.

Analisa, Analise (English) combinations of Ana + Lisa.
Analice, Analicia, Analis, Analisha, Analisia, Analissa

Anam (Indian) blessing.

Anamaria (English) a combination of Ana + Maria.
Anamarie, Anamary

Anamika (Indian) ring finger.

Anamitra (Indian) the sun.

Anana (Chamorro) she punishes.

Ananda (Hindi) blissful.

Anandamayi (Indian) full of joy.

Anandani, Anandini (Indian) joyful.

Anandi (Indian) joyful; unending.

Anandita (Indian) happy.

Anandmayee (Indian) full of happiness.

Ananti (Indian) gift.

Ananya (Indian) without a second, endless; unique.

Anarghya (Indian) priceless.

Anarosa (English) a form of Ana.

Anasdasia (Pohnpeian) a form of Adela.

Anaseini (Fijian) a combination of Ana + Jane.

Anastacia (Greek) a form of Anastasia.
Anastace, Anastacie

Anastasia (Greek) resurrection. See also Nastasia, Stacey, Stacia, Stasya.
Anastacia, Anastase, Anastascia, Anastasha, Anastashia, Anastasie, Anastasija, Anastassia, Anastassya, Anastasya, Anastatia, Anastaysia, Anastazia, Anastice, Annastasia, Annastasija, Annastaysia, Annastazia, Annstás

Anasua (Indian) one who is not jealous of anyone.

Anatilde (Spanish) a combination of Ana and Matilde.

Anatola (Greek) from the east.

Anatolia (Greek) east.

Anay (Chamorro) when.

Anbar (Indian) perfume.

Ancarla (Spanish) a combination of Ana and Carla.

Girls A–F

Ancelín (Latin) single woman.

Anchita (Indian) honored, worshipped.

Anci (Hungarian) a form of Hannah.
Annus, Annushka

Anda (Japanese) meet at the field.

Andeana (Spanish) leaving.

Andee, Andi, Andie (American) short forms of Andrea, Fernanda.
Ande, Andea, Andy

Andere (Greek) valiant, courageous.

Anderson 🅱 (Swedish) child of Andrew.

Anding (Tagalog) like an eagle.

Andre, André 🅱 (French) forms of Andrew.

Andrea ☙ 🅶 (Greek) strong; courageous.
See also Ondrea.
Aindrea, Andee, Andera, Anderea, Andra, Andrah, Andraia, Andraya, Andreah, Andreaka, Andreana, Andreane, Andree, Andrée, Andreea, Andreia, Andreja, Andreka, Andrel, Andrell, Andrelle, Andreo, Andressa, Andrette, Andreya, Andria, Andriana, Andrieka, Andrietta, Andris, Aundrea

Andréa, Andréia (Portuguese) valiant, courageous.

Andreana, Andreanna (Greek) forms of Andrea.
Ahndrianna, Andreina, Andrena, Andreyana, Andreyonna, Andrina, Andriona, Andrionna

Andreane, Andreanne (Greek) forms of Andrea.
Andrean, Andreeanne, Andree Anne, Andrene, Andrian, Andrienne

Andreas 🅱 (Greek) a form of Andrew.

Andreína (Spanish) a form of Andrea.

Andres 🅱 (Spanish) a form of Andrew.

Andresa (Spanish) a form of Andrea.

Andrew 🅱 (Greek) strong; courageous.

Andria (Greek) a form of Andrea.
Andri, Andriea

Andriana, Andrianna (Greek) forms of Andrea.

Andromaca (Greek) she who battles with a man.

Andromeda (Greek) in Greek mythology, the daughter of Cassiopeia and Cepheus.

Andy 🅱 (American) a form of Andee.

Aneesa, Aneesha (Greek) forms of Agnes.
Ahnesha, Ahnesia, Ahnesshia, Anee, Aneesah, Aneese, Aneeshah, Aneesia, Aneisa, Aneisha, Anessa, Anessia

Aneko (Japanese) older sister.

Anela (Hawaiian) angel.
Anel, Anelle

Anelida, Anelina (Spanish) combinations of Ana and Elida.

Anesin (Chuukese) name derived from the brand name for aspirin.

Anessa (Greek) a form of Agnes.
Anesha, Aneshia, Anesia, Anessia, Annessa

Anetra (American) a form of Annette.
Anitra

Anezka (Czech) a form of Hannah.

Angana (Indian) one with a beautiful body.

Angarika (Indian) flower.

Angel 🅱 (Greek) a short form of Angela.
Angele, Angéle, Angell, Angelle, Angil, Anjel

Angela 🅶 (Greek) angel; messenger.
Angala, Anganita, Angel, Angelanell, Angelanette, Angelee, Angeleigh, Angeles, Angeli, Angelia, Angelica, Angelina, Angelique, Angelita, Angella, Angellita, Angie, Anglea, Anjela, Anjelica

Ángela (Spanish) a form of Angela.

Ángeles (Catalonian) angels.

Angelia (Greek) a form of Angela.
Angelea, Angeleah, Angelie

Angélica (Spanish) a form of Angela.

Angelica, Angelika (Greek) forms of Angela.
Angalic, Angelic, Angelici, Angelicia, Angelike, Angeliki, Angellica, Angilica

Angelina ☙ 🅶 (Russian) a form of Angela.
Angalena, Angalina, Angelena, Angeliana, Angeleana, Angellina, Angelyna, Anhelina, Anjelina

Angeline (Russian) a form of Angela.
Angeleen, Angelene, Angelyn, Angelyna, Angelyne, Angelynn, Angelynne

Angelique (French) a form of Angela.
Angeliqua, Angélique, Angilique, Anjelique

Angéni (Native American) spirit.

Angha (Indian) beauty.

Angie (Greek) a familiar form of Angela.
Ange, Angee, Angey, Angi, Angy

Anginis (Chuukese) a form of Angeles.

Girls A–F

Angkelina (Pohnpeian) a form of Anastasia.

Angoco (Chamorro) trust, rely on.

Angocog, Angog (Chamorro) forms of Angoco.

Angoori (Indian) grape.

Angustias (Latin) she who suffers from grief or sorrow.

Ani (Hawaiian) beautiful.
Aany, Aanye

Ania (Polish) a form of Hannah.
Ahnia, Anaya, Aniah

Anica, Anika (Czech) familiar forms of Anna.
Aanika, Anaka, Aneeky, Aneka, Anekah, Anicka, Anik, Anikah, Anike, Anikka, Anikke, Aniko, Anneka, Annik, Annika, Anouska, Anuska

Anice (English) a form of Agnes.
Anesse, Anis, Anise, Annes, Annice, Annis, Annus

Aniceta (Spanish) she who is invincible because of her great strength.

Anik **G** (Czech) a form of Anica.

Anila (Hindi) Religion: an attendant of the Hindu god Vishnu.
Anilla

Anillang (Mapuche) stable altar; decisive and courageously noble woman.

Anima (Indian) the power of becoming minute.

Anindita (Indian) beautiful.

Anisa, Anisah (Arabic) friendly.
Annissah

Anisha **G** (English) a form of Agnes, Ann.
Aanisha, Aeniesha, Annisha

Anissa (English) a form of Agnes, Ann.
Anis, Anisa, Anissah, Anise, Annisa, Annissa, Anyssa

Anita **G** (Spanish) a form of Ann, Anna. See also Nita.
Aneeta, Aneetah, Aneethah, Anetha, Anitha, Anithah, Anitia, Anitra, Anitte

Anjana, Anjini (Indian) mother of Hanuman.

Anjelica (Greek) a form of Angela.
Anjelika

Anjelita (Spanish) heavenly messenger.

Anjika (Indian) blessed.

Anju (Indian) blessings; unconquerable.

Anjushree, Anjushri (Indian) dear to one's heart.

Anka **G** (Polish) a familiar form of Hannah.
Anke

Ankal (Indian) whole.

Ankita (Indian) distinguished, marked by the Lord; dedicate.

Ann (English) gracious. See also Anne.
Anissa, Anita, Annchen, Annette, Annie, Annik, Annika, Annze, Anouche

Anna ✺ **G** (German, Italian, Czech, Swedish) gracious. Culture: Anna Pavlova was a famous Russian ballerina. See also Anica, Anissa, Nina.
Ahnna, Ana, Anah, Anica, Anita, Annah, Annina, Annora, Anona, Anya, Anyu, Aska

Annabel (English) a combination of Anna + Bel.
Amabel, Anabel, Annabal, Annabelle

Annabelle (English) a form of Annabel.
Anabelle, Annabell, Annabella

Annalie (Finnish) a form of Hannah.
Analee, Annalea, Annaleah, Annalee, Annaleigh, Annaleigha, Annali, Anneli, Annelie

Annalisa, Annalise (English) combinations of Anna + Lisa.
Analisa, Analise, Annaliesa, Annaliese, Annalissa, Annalisse

Annamarie, Annemarie, Annmarie, Anne-Marie (English) combinations of Anne + Marie.
Annamaria, Anna-Maria, Anna-Marie, Annmaria

Annapoorna (Indian) goddess of grains.

Annapurna (Indian) goddess of food.

Anne **G** (English) gracious.

Anneka (Swedish) a form of Hannah.
Annaka, Anneke, Annika, Anniki, Annikki

Annelisa (English) a combination of Ann + Lisa.
Analiese, Anelisa, Anelise, Anneliese, Annelise

Annette (French) a form of Ann. See also Anetra, Nettie.
Anet, Aneta, Anetra, Anett, Anetta, Anette, Anneth, Annett, Annetta

Annie (English) a familiar form of Ann.
Anni, Anny

Annik, Annika (Russian) forms of Ann.
Aneka, Anekah, Annick, Annicka, Annike, Annikka, Anninka, Anouk

Annjanette (American) a combination of Ann + Janette.
Angen, Angenett, Angenette, Anjane, Anjanetta, Anjani

Anokhi (Indian) different.

Anona (English) pineapple.

Anouhea (Hawaiian) cool, soft fragrance.

Anouka (Indian) spirit of God.

Anoushka, Anushka (Indian) a term of endearment.

Anselma (German, Dutch, Italian, Spanish) helmet; protection.

Ansha (Indian) portion.

Anshika (Indian) minute particle.

Anshumali (Indian) sun.

Ansina (Chuukese) a form of Angela.

Ansley �G (Scottish) forms of Ainsley.
Anslea, Anslee, Ansleigh, Anslie

Ansuya (Indian) learned woman.

Antara (Indian) beauty.

Antariksha (Indian) space; sky.

Anthea (Greek) flower.
Antha, Anthe, Anthia, Thia

Anthony ☒ (Latin) praiseworthy. (Greek) flourishing.

Anti (Chamorro) soul.

Antía (Galician) priceless; flourishing; flower.

Antígona (Greek) distinguished by her brothers.

Antione ☒ (French) a form of Anthony.

Antionette (French) a form of Antonia.
Antionet, Antionett, Anntionett

Antoinette (French) a form of Antonia. See also Netti, Toinette, Toni.
Anta, Antanette, Antoinella, Antoinet, Antonella, Antonetta, Antonette, Antonice, Antonieta, Antonietta, Antonique

Antolina (Spanish) flourishing, beautiful as a flower.

Antonia ☒ (Greek) flourishing. (Latin) praiseworthy. See also Toni, Tonya, Tosha.
Ansonia, Ansonya, Antania, Antinia, Antionette, Antoinette, Antona, Antoñía, Antonice, Antonie, Antonina, Antonine, Antoniya, Antonnea, Antonnia, Antonya

Antónia (Portuguese) a form of Antonia.

Antonice (Latin) a form of Antonia.
Antanise, Antanisha, Antonesha, Antoneshia, Antonise, Antonisha

Antoniña (Latin) she who confronts or is the adversary.

Antonio ☒ (Italian) a form of Anthony.

Antti (Chamorro) a form of Anti.

Anubhuti (Indian) feelings.

Anugraha (Indian) divine blessing.

Anugya (Indian) permission.

Anuhea (Hawaiian) sweet fragrance of the rain forest.

Anuhya (Indian) something pleasantly unexpected.

Anuja (Indian) younger sister.

Anukeertana (Indian) praising God's virtues.

Anula (Indian) not wild, agreeable.

Anulata (Indian) one with very slim figure.

Anumati, Anurati (Indian) consent.

Anuncia (Latin) announcer, messenger.

Anunciación (Spanish) annunciation.

Anunciada (Spanish) a form of Anunciación.

Anunciata (Italian) a form of Anunciación.

Anupama (Indian) beautiful.

Anuprabha (Indian) brightness.

Anupriya (Indian) beloved daughter.

Anuradha (Indian) Lord Krishna's consort.

Anuragini (Indian) beloved.

Anusha (Indian) following desires.

Anushri (Indian) pretty; prosperous.

Anusuya (Indian) not jealous.

Anuva (Indian) knowledge.

Anwaar (Indian) rays of light.

Anwesha (Indian) quest.

Anya (Russian) a form of Anna.
Aaniyah, Aniya, Aniyah, Anja

Anyssa (English) a form of Anissa.
Anysa, Anysha

Anzu (Japanese) an apricot.

Aoi (Japanese) hollyhock.

'Aolani (Hawaiian) heavenly cloud.

Aorta (Chamorro) heal.

Aosgi (Chamorro) to resemble one another.

Aosgui (Chamorro) a form of Aosgi.

Apala (Indian) most beautiful.

Aparajita (Indian) undefeated; the name of
a flower.

Aparijita (Indian) a form of Aparajita.

Apeksha, Apekshaa (Indian) expectation.

Aphra (Hebrew) young doe. See also Afra.

Apia (Latin) devout woman.

Apolinaria (Spanish) sun goddess.

Apolinia (Latin) sun goddess.

Apolonia (Greek) devoted to the god, Apollo.

Appa (Chamorro) to place one's hand on
someone's shoulder.

April **G** (Latin) opening. See also Avril.
*Aprele, Aprelle, Apriell, Aprielle, Aprila,
Aprile, Aprilette, Aprili, Aprill, Apryl*

Apryl (Latin) a form of April.
Apryle

Apsara (Indian) angel; the beautiful dancers
of Lord Indra.

Apurba (Indian) never seen before.

Aqilah (Indian) intelligent woman.

Aquene (Native American) peaceful.

Aquilina (Latin) eagle.

Aquilinia (Spanish) eagle.

Ara (Arabic) opinionated.
Ahraya, Aira, Arae, Arah, Araya, Arayah

Arabel (Latin) beautiful altar.

Arabella (Latin) beautiful altar. See also
Belle, Orabella.
Arabela, Arabele, Arabelle

Araceli, Aracely (Latin) heavenly altar.
*Aracele, Aracelia, Aracelli, Araseli, Arasely,
Arcelia, Arceli*

Aracelis (Spanish) altar of heaven.

Aradhana (Indian) prayer.

Arama (Spanish) reference to the Virgin
Mary.

Arán (Catalonian) she is a conflicted virgin.

Aránzazu (Basque) you in the thorn.

Aranzuru (Spanish) a form of Aránzazu.

Arati (Indian) hymns sung in praise of God
with lamp in hand.

Arcadia (Latin) adventurous.

Arcángela (Greek) archangel.

Archa, Archan, Archana (Indian) worship.

Archini, Archisha (Indian) ray of light.

Archita (Indian) one who is worshipped.

Arcilla (Latin) altar of heaven.

Ardelle (Latin) warm; enthusiastic.
Ardelia, Ardelis, Ardella

Arden **G** (English) valley of the eagle.
Literature: in Shakespeare, a romantic place
of refuge.
*Ardeen, Ardeena, Ardena, Ardene, Ardenia,
Ardi, Ardin, Ardina, Ardine*

Ardi (Hebrew) a short form of Arden, Ardice,
Ardith.
Ardie, Arti, Artie

Ardice (Hebrew) a form of Ardith.
Ardis, Artis, Ardiss, Ardyce, Ardys

Ardith (Hebrew) flowering field.
Ardath, Ardi, Ardice, Ardyth

Ardra (Indian) the sixth nakshatra (star
constellation).

Arebela (Latin) beautiful altar.

Areebah (Indian) witty and smart.

Areej (Indian) pleasant smell.

Arejab (Marshallese) a personality like a
lamb or goat.

Areli **G** (American) a form of Oralee.
Areil, Areile, Arelee, Arelis, Arelli, Arellia

Arella (Hebrew) angel; messenger.
Arela, Arelle, Orella, Orelle

Arely (American) a form of Oralee.
Arelly

Ares (Catalonian) virgin of the Pyrenees
mountains.

Aretha (Greek) virtuous. See also Oretha.
*Areatha, Areetha, Areta, Aretina, Aretta,
Arette, Arita, Aritha, Retha, Ritha*

Girls A–F

Aretusa (Greek) Mythology: one of Artemis's companions.

Argelia (Latin) jewelry boxes full of treasures.

Argentina (Latin) she who shines like gold.

Ari 🄶 (Hebrew) a short form of Ariel.

Aria (Hebrew) a short form of Ariel.
Ariah, Ariea, Aryia

Ariadna (Spanish) most holy.

Ariadne (Greek) holy. Mythology: the daughter of King Minos of Crete.

Ariana ❦ 🄶 (Greek) holy.
Aeriana, Ahriana, Airiana, Arieana, Ariona

Ariane, Arianne 🄶 (French, English) forms of Ariana, Arianna.
Aerian, Aeriann, Aerion, Aerionne, Airiann, Ari, Arianie, Ariann, Ariannie, Arieann, Arien, Ariene, Arienne, Arieon, Arionne, Aryane, Aryann, Aryanne

Arianna ❦ (Greek) a form of Ariana.
Aerianna, Aerionna, Ahreanna, Ahrianna, Arionna, Aryonna

Arica (Scandinavian) a form of Erica.
Aerica, Aericka, Aeryka, Aricca, Aricka, Arika, Arike, Arikka

Aricela (Latin) altar of heaven.

Arie (Hebrew) a short form of Ariel.

Ariel 🄶 (Hebrew) lion of God.
Aerial, Aeriale, Aeriel, Aeriela, Aeryal, Ahriel, Aire, Aireal, Airial, Ari, Aria, Arial, Ariale, Arieal, Ariela, Arielle, Arrieal, Arriel, Aryel, Auriel

Arielle (French) a form of Ariel.
Aeriell, Ariella, Arriele, Arriell, Arrielle, Aryelle, Aurielle

Arin (Hebrew) enlightened. (Arabic) messenger. See also Erin.
Aaren, Aerin, Aieron, Aieren, Arinn, Aryn

Arista (Greek) best.
Aris, Arissa, Aristana, Aristen

Arjuni (Indian) dawn; white cow.

Arkita (Indian) plentiful.

Arla (German) a form of Carla.

Arleigh (English) a form of Harley.
Arlea, Arlee, Arley, Arlie, Arly

Arlene (Irish) pledge. See also Lena, Lina.
Airlen, Arlana, Arleen, Arleene, Arlen, Arlena, Arlenis, Arlette, Arleyne, Arliene, Arlina, Arlinda, Arline, Arlis

Arlette (English) a form of Arlene.
Arleta, Arletta, Arletty

Arlynn (American) a combination of Arlene + Lynn.
Arlyn, Arlyne, Arlynne

Armanda (Latin) noble.

Armani 🄱 (Persian) desire, goal.
Armahni, Arman, Armanee, Armanii

Armentaria (Latin) pastor of older livestock.

Armida (Spanish) a form of Arminda.

Arminda (German) warrior.

Armine (Latin) noble. (German) soldier. (French) a form of Herman (see Boys' Names).
Armina

Armonía (Spanish) balance, harmony.

Arna (Indian) dewdrops.

Arnalda (Spanish) strong as an eagle.

Arnelle (German) eagle.
Arnell, Arnella

Arni, Aruna (Indian) sun.

Aroa (German) good person.

Aroma (Indian) fragrance.

Aron, Arron 🄱 (Hebrew) forms of Aaron.

Aroob (Indian) she who is loving to her husband.

Arpana (Indian) offering.

Arpita (Indian) a dedication.

Arshia (Indian) divine.

Arte (Tagalog) north.

Artemia (Greek) Greek goddess of the moon and hunt.

Artemisa (Spanish) Greek goddess of the hunt.

Artemisia (Greek) perfection.

Artha (Hindi) wealthy, prosperous.
Arthi, Arti, Artie

Arthur 🄱 (Irish) noble; lofty hill. (Scottish) bear. (English) rock. (Icelandic) follower of Thor.

Artis (Irish, Scottish, English, Icelandic) a form of Arthur.
Arthea, Arthelia, Arthene, Arthette, Arthurette, Arthurina, Arthurine, Artina, Artice

Artura (Celtic) noble, follower of Thor.

A-Rum (Korean) a form of Ai.

Arundhati (Indian) a small star near the Great Bear constellation.

Aruni (Indian) dawn.

Arunima (Indian) red glow of dawn.

Arwa (Indian) female mountain goat.

Aryahi (Indian) another name for the goddess Durga.

Aryana, Aryanna (Italian) forms of Ariana.
Aryan, Aryanah, Aryannah

Aryn (Hebrew) a form of Arin.
Aerryn, Aeryn, Airyn, Aryne, Arynn, Arynne

Arzo (Turkish) a form of Jingjing.

Asa **B** (Japanese) born in the morning.

Asako (Japanese) child of the morning.

Asalah (Indian) purity.

Asami (Japanese) morning birth.

Asansa (Chuukese) toward the east.

Asawari (Indian) raga in Hindustani classical music.

Asayo (Japanese) morning; flax; generation.

Ascención (Spanish) ascension.

Ascharya (Indian) surprise.

Aseelah (Indian) one belonging to a great heritage and family.

Aseema, Ashima (Indian) limitless.

Asgari (Indian) devotee.

Asha (Arabic, Swahili) a form of Aisha, Ashia.

Ashakiran (Indian) ray of hope.

Ashalata (Indian) hope.

Ashanti **G** (Swahili) from a tribe in West Africa.
Achante, Achanti, Asante, Ashanta, Ashantae, Ashante, Ashanté, Ashantee, Ashantie, Ashaunta, Ashauntae, Ashauntee, Ashaunti, Ashonti, Ashuntae, Ashunti

Ashely (English) form of Ashley.
Ashelee, Ashelei, Asheley, Ashelie, Ashelley, Ashelly

Ashia (Arabic) life.
Asha, Ashya, Ashyah, Ashyia, Ayshia

Ashika (Indian) one without sorrow; mercury.

Ashis (Indian) benediction.

Ashita, Asita (Indian) the Yamuna River.

Ashlee **G** (English) a form of Ashley.
Ashle, Ashlea, Ashleah, Ashleeh

Ashleigh **G** (English) a form of Ashley.
Ahsleigh, Asheleigh, Ashlei, Ashliegh

Ashlesha (Indian) a star.

Ashley 🌟 **G** (English) ash-tree meadow. See also Lee.
Ahslee, Aishlee, Ashala, Ashalee, Ashalei, Ashaley, Ashely, Ashla, Ashlay, Ashleay, Ashlee, Ashleigh, Ashleye, Ashli, Ashlie, Ashly, Ashlye

Ashli, Ashlie, Ashly (English) forms of Ashley.
Ashliee

Ashlin (English) a form of Ashlyn.
Ashlean, Ashliann, Ashlianne, Ashline

Ashlyn, Ashlynn **G** (English) ash-tree pool. (Irish) vision, dream.
Ashlan, Ashleann, Ashleen, Ashleene, Ashlen, Ashlene, Ashlin, Ashling, Ashlyne, Ashlynne

Ashmita (Indian) born of the rock, very hard and strong.

Ashna (Indian) a friend.

Ashten, Ashtin (English) forms of Ashton.
Ashtine

Ashton **BG** (English) ash-tree settlement.
Ashten, Ashtyn

Ashtyn **G** (English) a form of Ashton.
Ashtynne

Ashwina (Indian) child of the star.

Asi (Chamorro) pity.

Asia (Greek) resurrection. (English) eastern sunrise. (Swahili) a form of Aisha.
Ahsia, Aisia, Aisian, Asiah, Asian, Asianae, Asya, Aysia, Aysiah, Aysian, Ayzia

Asin (Chamorro) salt.

Aslesha (Indian) a star.

Asmita, Asmitha (Indian) pride.

Asonn (Chamorro) lie down.

Asonna (Chamorro) she lies down.

Aspasia (Greek) follower of the philosopher Aristotle.

Aspen **G** (English) aspen tree.
Aspin, Aspyn

Assa (Chamorro) a form of Asa.

Assi (Chamorro) a form of Asi.

Asson (Chamorro) a form of Asonn.

Assunção (Portuguese) Assumption.

Aster (English) a form of Astra.
Astera, Asteria, Astyr

Astha (Indian) faith.

Astra (Greek) star.
Asta, Astara, Aster, Astraea, Astrea

Astrid (Scandinavian) divine strength.
Astri, Astrida, Astrik, Astrud, Atti, Estrid

Astriz (German) of the stars.

Astryd (German) beloved one of the gods.

Asuka (Japanese) the scent of tomorrow.

Asunción (Spanish) Assumption.

Asunta (Spanish) to go up, to ascend.

Atagui (Chamorro) alternate.

Atala (Greek) youthful one.

Atalanta (Greek) mighty huntress.
Mythology: an athletic young woman who
refused to marry any man who could not
outrun her in a footrace. See also Lani.
Atalaya, Atlanta, Atlante, Atlee

Atalía (Spanish) guard tower.

Atanasia (Spanish) one who will be reborn;
immortal.

Atara (Hebrew) crown.
Atarah, Ataree

Atasi (Indian) a blue flower.

Atenea (Greek) evokes the figure of Palas
Atenea, goddess protectorate of the
Athenians.

Athana (Mycenaean) promise.

Athena (Greek) wise. Mythology: the goddess
of wisdom.
Athenea, Athene, Athina, Atina

Ati, Atie (Chamorro) forms of Atti.

Ática (Greek) city of Athens.

Atira (Hebrew) prayer.

Atisa (Chamorro) increase; brighten.

Atmikha (Indian) light of God.

Atreyi (Indian) a river.

Atsuko (Japanese) child with profound
emotions.

Atsushi (Japanese) rich.

Attau (Chamorro) hides herself.

Attiya (Indian) gift.

Atula (Indian) incomparable.

Au (Japanese) meeting.

Auberte (French) a form of Alberta.
Auberta, Aubertha, Auberthe, Aubine

Aubree, Aubrie 🅖 (French) forms of Aubrey.
Auberi, Aubre, Aubrei, Aubreigh, Aubri,
Aubrielle

Aubrey 🅖 (German) noble; bearlike.
(French) blond ruler; elf ruler.
Aubary, Aubery, Aubray, Aubrea, Aubreah,
Aubree, Aubrette, Aubria, Aubrie, Aubry,
Aubury, Avery

Aubriana, Aubrianna (English)
combinations of Aubrey + Anna.
Aubreyana, Aubreyanna, Aubreyanne,
Aubreyena, Aubrianne

Auchon (Chamorro) torch.

Audelina (German) nobility, strength.

Audey (English) a familiar form of Audrey.
Aude, Audi, Audie

Audra 🅖 (French) a form of Audrey.
Audria, Audriea

Audreanne (English) a combination of
Audrey + Anne.
Audrea, Audreen, Audrianne, Audrienne

Audree, Audrie (English) forms of Audrey.
Audre, Audri

Audrey ☙ 🅖 (English) noble strength.
Adrey, Audey, Audra, Audray, Audree, Audrie,
Audrin, Audriya, Audry, Audrye

Audriana, Audrianna (English)
combinations of Audrey + Anna.
Audreanna, Audrienna, Audrina

Audris (German) fortunate, wealthy.
Audrys

August 🅑 (Latin) a form of Augusta.

Augusta (Latin) a short form of Augustine.
See also Gusta.
Agusta, August, Auguste, Augustia,
Augustus, Austina

Augustine 🅑 (Latin) majestic. Religion:
Saint Augustine was the first archbishop of
Canterbury. See also Tina.
Augusta, Augustina, Augustyna, Augustyne,
Austin

'Aulani (Hawaiian) royal messenger.
Lani, Lanie

Aulii (Hawaiian) dainty; perfect.

Aundrea (Greek) a form of Andrea.
Aundreah

Aura (Greek) soft breeze. (Latin) golden. See also Ora.

Aurelia (Latin) golden. See also Oralia.
Auralea, Auralia, Aurea, Aureal, Aurel, Aurele, Aurelea, Aureliana, Aurelie, Auria, Aurie, Aurilia, Aurita

Aurelie (Latin) a form of Aurelia.
Auralee, Auralei, Aurelee, Aurelei, Aurelle

Auristela (Latin) golden star.

Aurora (Latin) dawn. Mythology: Aurora was the goddess of dawn.
Aurore, Ora, Ori, Orie, Rora

Austen **B** (Latin) a form of Austin.

Austin (Latin) a short form of Augustine.

Austyn (Latin) a form of Austin.
Austynn

Autumn �ібок **G** (Latin) autumn.
Autum

Ava ✗ (Greek) a form of Eva.
Avada, Avae, Ave, Aveen

Avalon (Latin) island.
Avallon

Avani (Indian) earth.

Avanti (Indian) modest.

Avantika (Indian) the princess of Ujjain.

Avelina (Latin) she who was born in Avella.

Avery ✗ **B** (English) a form of Aubrey.
Aivree, Averi, Averie, Avry

Avinashi (Indian) indestructible.

Avis (Latin) bird.
Avais, Avi, Avia, Aviana, Avianca, Aviance, Avianna

Avishi (Indian) earth; river.

Aviva (Hebrew) springtime. See also Viva.
Aviv, Avivah, Avivi, Avivice, Avni, Avnit, Avri, Avrit, Avy

Avneet **G** (Hebrew) a form of Avner (see Boys' Names).

Avnita (Indian) earth.

Avril (French) a form of April.
Averil, Averyl, Avra, Avri, Avrilia, Avrill, Avrille, Avrillia, Avy

Axelle (Latin) axe. (German) small oak tree; source of life.
Aixa

Aya (Hebrew) bird; fly swiftly.
Aia, Aiah, Aiya, Aiyah

Ayaka (Japanese) she who reminds you of summer.

Ayako (Japanese) damask pattern.

Ayalga (Asturian) treasure.

Ayame (Japanese) iris.

Ayanna (Hindi) innocent.
Ahyana, Aiyanna, Ayan, Ayana, Ayania, Ayannica, Ayna

Ayano (Japanese) twill cloth.

Ayati (Indian) royal.

Ayeh (Indian) sun; distinct.

Ayelen (Mapuche) she who represents joy; smiling.

Ayelén (Araucanian) joy.

Ayesha (Persian) a form of Aisha.
Ayasha, Ayeshah, Ayessa, Ayisha, Ayishah, Aysha, Ayshah, Ayshe, Ayshea, Aysia

Ayig (Chamorro) choose.

Ayinhual (Mapuche) beloved, darling, generous and preferred huala (Great Grebe).

Ayinleo (Mapuche) deep, inextinguishable love.

Ayiqueo (Mapuche) soft-spoken; pleasant.

Ayita (Cherokee) first in the dance.

Ayla (Hebrew) oak tree.
Aylana, Aylee, Ayleen, Aylene, Aylie, Aylin

Aymara (Spanish) people and language of the south Andes.

Ayme (Mapuche) significant.

Ayshalynn (Arabic) a form of Aisha.

Ayumi (Japanese) step; beautiful.

Ayushi (Indian) long life.

Ayushmati (Indian) one who has a long life.

Aza (Arabic) comfort.
Aiza, Aizha, Aizia, Azia

Azaad (Persian) dam to stop the flow.

Azad (Persian) a form of Grace.

Azalea (Latin) desert flower.

Azami (Japanese) defiant.

Azari (Japanese) thistle flower.

Azeeza (Indian) esteemed, precious, cherished.

Azhaar (Indian) flowers; blossoms.

Azima (Arabic) resolute, determined.

Aziza (Swahili) precious.
Azize

Azucena (Arabic) admirable mother.

Azura (Spanish) sky blue.

Azusa (Japanese) the catalpa tree.

Azza (Indian) young female gazelle.

B

B 🅱🅶 (American) an initial used as a first name.

Baasima, Baseema (Indian) smiling.

Baba (African) born on Thursday.
Aba

Babe (Latin) a familiar form of Barbara. (American) a form of Baby.
Babby

Babette (French, German) a familiar form of Barbara.
Babita, Barbette

Babs (American) a familiar form of Barbara.
Bab

Baby (American) baby.
Babby, Babe, Bebe

Bach, Bach Yen (Vietnamese) forms of Kasinda.

Bachtuyet (Vietnamese) white; clear.

Bada (Korean) beautiful.

Badriya (Indian) resembling the full moon.

Bae (Vietnamese) white.

Baek (Korean) a form of Ah-Rum.

Bagya (Indian) lucky.

Baheera (Indian) dazzling, brilliant.

Bahiyaa (Indian) beautiful, radiant.

Bahugandha (Indian) very fragrant; the bud of the champa flower.

Bahula (Indian) cow.

Bai (Chinese) outgoing.

Baijanti (Indian) Lord Vishnu's favorite flower.

Baijayanthi (Indian) garland of Lord Vishnu.

Bailee 🅶 (English) a form of Bailey.
Baelee, Bailea, Bailei, Baillee

Baileigh, Baleigh (English) forms of Bailey.
Baeleigh

Bailey 🅶 (English) bailiff.
Baeley, Bailee, Baileigh, Bailley, Bailly, Baily, Bali, Balley, Baylee, Bayley

Bailie (English) a form of Bailey.
Baeli, Baillie, Bailli

Bairavi (Indian) music, melody.

Baisakhi (Indian) of the month Baishakh.

Baishali (Indian) an ancient city.

Baka (Hindi) crane.

Bakul (Indian) the name of a flower.

Bakula (Hindi) flower.

Balbina (Latin) she who mutters.

Baldomera (Spanish) bold, brave; famous.

Balic (Chamorro) worth, value.

Ballari (Indian) creeper.

Balqis (Indian) the name of the Queen of Sheba.

Baltasalisa, Baltasara, Batasara (Assyrian) forms of Baltazara.

Baltazara (Assyrian) may Baal protect the king.

Bambi (Italian) child.
Bambee, Bambie, Bamby

Bambing (Filipino) baby.

Banamala, Banani (Indian) forests.

Banan (Indian) fingertips.

Bandana (Indian) worship.

Bandhula (Indian) charming.

Bandhura (Indian) pretty.

Bandi BG (Punjabi) prisoner.
Banda, Bandy

Banhi (Indian) fire.

Banhishikha (Indian) flame.

Banita (Indian) woman.

Banmala (Indian) a garland of five types of flowers.

Banni (Indian) maiden.

Bansari (Indian) flute; the instrument played by Lord Krishna.

Bansuri (Indian) flute.

Bao-Jin (Chinese) precious gold.

Bao-Yo (Chinese) jade; pretty.

Baptista (Latin) baptizer.
Baptiste, Batista, Battista, Bautista

Bara, Barra (Hebrew) chosen.
Bára, Bari

Baraa'a (Indian) excelling.

Barb (Latin) a short form of Barbara.
Barba, Barbe

Barbara (Latin) stranger, foreigner. See also Bebe, Varvara, Wava.
Babara, Babb, Babbie, Babe, Babette, Babina, Babs, Barb, Barbara-Ann, Barbarit, Barbarita, Barbary, Barbeeleen, Barbera, Barbie, Barbora, Barborah, Barborka, Barbra, Barbraann, Barbro, Barùska, Basha, Bebe, Bobbi, Bobbie

Bárbara (Greek) a form of Barbara.

Barbie (American) a familiar form of Barbara.
Barbee, Barbey, Barbi, Barby, Baubie

Barbra (American) a form of Barbara.
Barbro

Barisha (Indian) pure.

Barkha, Barsha (Indian) rain.

Barnali (Indian) dispersion of seven colors.

Barrett B (German) strong as a bear.

Barrie (Irish) spear; markswoman.
Bari, Barri, Berri, Berrie, Berry

Barry B (Welsh) child of Harry. (Irish) spear, marksman. (French) gate, fence.

Bartolomea (Spanish) daughter of Talmai.

Baruna (Indian) wife of the lord of the sea.

Basabi (Indian) wife of Lord Indra.

Basanti (Indian) spring.

Basheera (Indian) bringer of good tidings.

Basia (Hebrew) daughter of God.
Basya, Bathia, Batia, Batya, Bitya, Bithia

Basiana (Spanish) having acute judgment.

Basilia (Greek) queen, princess; governor.

Basma (Indian) a smile.

Batbara (Chamorro) a form of Barbara.

Bathsheba (Hebrew) daughter of the oath; seventh daughter. Bible: a wife of King David. See also Sheba.
Bathshua, Batsheva, Bersaba, Bethsabee, Bethsheba

Batilde (German) she who battles.

Batini (Swahili) inner thoughts.

Batool (Indian) ascetic virgin.

Baudilia (Teutonic) audacious and brave.

Bay (Vietnamese) white as snow.

Baye, Be, Bich (Vietnamese) Saturday's child; patient; unique.

Baylee G (English) a form of Bailey.
Bayla, Bayle, Baylea, Bayleah, Baylei, Bayli, Bayliee

Bayleigh, Baylie (English) forms of Bailey.
Bayliegh

Bayley G (English) a form of Bailey.
Bayly

Bayo (Yoruba) joy is found.

Bea, Bee (American) short forms of Beatrice.

Beata (Latin) a short form of Beatrice.
Beatta

Beatrice (Latin) blessed; happy; bringer of joy. See also Trish, Trixie.
Bea, Beata, Beatrica, Béatrice, Beatricia, Beatriks, Beatrisa, Beatrise, Beatrissa, Beatriz, Beattie, Beatty, Bebe, Bee, Trice

Beatriz G (Latin) a form of Beatrice.
Beatris, Beatriss, Beatrix, Beitris

Beau B (French) beautiful.

Bebe BG (Spanish) a form of Barbara, Beatrice.
BB, Beebee, Bibi

Becca (Hebrew) a short form of Rebecca.
Beca, Becka, Bekah, Bekka

Bechekldil (Palauan) a form of Athena.

Becky (American) a familiar form of
Rebecca.
Beckey, Becki, Beckie

Bedebii (Palauan) a form of Athena.

Bedelia (Irish) a form of Bridget.
Bedeelia, Biddy, Bidelia

Beena (Indian) a musical instrument.

Beetna (Korean) sea.

Begoña (Basque) place of the dominant hill.

Begonia (Spanish) begonia flower.

Behsel (Pohnpeian) a form of Antonia.

Bei (Chinese) shellfish.

Bel (Hindi) sacred wood of apple trees. A
short form of Amabel, Belinda, Isabel.

Bela ☒☒ (Czech) white. (Hungarian) bright.
Belah, Biela

Belarmina (Spanish) having beautiful
armor.

Belen ☒ (Greek) arrow. (Spanish)
Bethlehem.
Belina

Belicia (Spanish) dedicated to God.
Beli, Belia, Belica

Belinda (Spanish) beautiful. Literature: a
name coined by English poet Alexander
Pope in *The Rape of the Lock*. See also
Blinda, Linda.
Bel, Belindra, Belle, Belynda

Belisa (Latin) most slender.

Belisaria (Greek) right-handed archer; she
who shoots arrows skillfully.

Bella (Latin) beautiful.
Bellah

Belle (French) beautiful. A short form of
Arabella, Belinda, Isabel. See also Billie.
Belita, Bell, Belli, Bellina

Belva (Latin) beautiful view.
Belvia

Bena (Native American) pheasant. See also
Bina.
Benea

Benazir (Indian) incomparable.

Benecia (Latin) a short form of Benedicta.
*Beneisha, Benicia, Benish, Benisha, Benishia,
Bennicia*

Benedicta (Latin) blessed.
*Bendite, Benecia, Benedetta, Benedicte,
Benedikta, Bengta, Benita, Benna, Benni,
Bennicia, Benoîte, Binney*

Benedicte (Latin) a form of Benedicta.

Benedita (Portuguese) blessed.

Benicio (Spanish) benevolent one.

Benigna (Spanish) kind.

Benilda (German) she who fights with the
bears.

Benilde (Spanish) a form of Benilda.

Benita (Spanish) a form of Benedicta.
Beneta, Benetta, Benitta, Bennita, Neeta

Benjamin ☒ (Hebrew) child of my right
hand.

Benjamina (Spanish) preferred daughter.

Bennett ☒ (Latin) little blessed one.
Bennet, Bennetta

Benni (Latin) a familiar form of Benedicta.
Bennie, Binni, Binnie, Binny

Bente (Latin) blessed.

Berar (Fijian) slow.

Berenice (Greek) a form of Bernice.
Berenise, Berenisse, Bereniz, Berenize

Berget (Irish) a form of Bridget.
Bergette, Bergit

Berit (German) glorious.
Beret, Berette

Berkley (Scottish, English) birch-tree
meadow.
Berkeley, Berkly

Berlynn (English) a combination of Bertha
+ Lynn.
*Berla, Berlin, Berlinda, Berline, Berling,
Berlyn, Berlyne, Berlynne*

Bernabela (Hebrew) child of prophecy.

Bernabella (Spanish) a form of Bernabela.

Bernadette ☒ (French) a form of
Bernadine. See also Nadette.
*Bera, Beradette, Berna, Bernadet, Bernadete,
Bernadett, Bernadetta, Bernarda,
Bernardette, Bernedet, Bernedette, Bernessa,
Berneta*

Bernadine (English, German) brave as a
bear.
*Bernadene, Bernadette, Bernadin, Bernadina,
Bernardina, Bernardine, Berni*

Berneta (French) a short form of Bernadette.
Bernatta, Bernetta, Bernette, Bernita

Berni (English) a familiar form of Bernadine, Bernice.
Bernie, Berny

Bernice (Greek) bringer of victory. See also Bunny, Vernice.
Berenice, Berenike, Bernessa, Berni, Bernicia, Bernise, Nixie

Berta (German) a form of Berit.

Bertha (German) bright; illustrious; brilliant ruler. A short form of Alberta. See also Birdie, Peke.
Barta, Bartha, Berta, Berthe, Bertille, Bertita, Bertrona, Bertus, Birtha

Berti (German, English) a familiar form of Gilberte, Bertina.
Berte, Bertie, Berty

Bertilda (German) she who fights; the distinguished one.

Bertilia (German, Latin) a form of Berta.

Bertille (French) a form of Bertha.

Bertina (English) bright, shining.
Bertine

Beryl (Greek) sea green jewel.
Beryle

Besichel (Palauan) new woman.

Bess, Bessie (Hebrew) familiar forms of Elizabeth.
Bessi, Bessy

Betania (Hebrew) name of a village in ancient Palestine.

Beth (Hebrew, Aramaic) house of God. A short form of Bethany, Elizabeth.
Betha, Bethe, Bethia

Bethani, Bethanie (Aramaic) forms of Bethany.
Bethanee, Bethania, Bethannie, Bethni, Bethnie

Bethann (English) a combination of Beth + Ann.
Beth-Ann, Bethan, Bethane, Bethanne, Beth-Anne

Bethany (Aramaic) house of figs. Bible: the site of Lazarus's resurrection.
Beth, Bethaney, Bethani, Bethanney, Bethanny, Bethena, Betheny, Bethia, Bethina, Bethney, Bethny, Betthany

Betikerarengul (Palauan) let us divide and share.

Betra (Marshallese) love.

Betsabe (Hebrew) daughter of an oath or pact.
Betsabé

Betsy (American) a familiar form of Elizabeth.
Betsey, Betsi, Betsie

Bette (French) a form of Betty.
Beta, Beti, Betka, Bett, Betta

Bettina (American) a combination of Beth + Tina.
Betina, Betine, Betti, Bettine

Betty (Hebrew) consecrated to God. (English) a familiar form of Elizabeth.
Bette, Bettey, Betti, Bettie, Bettye, Bettyjean, Betty-Jean, Bettyjo, Betty-Jo, Bettylou, Betty-Lou, Bety, Boski, Bözsi

Betula (Hebrew) girl, maiden.

Beulah (Hebrew) married. Bible: Beulah is a name for Israel.
Beula, Beulla, Beullah

Bev (English) a short form of Beverly.

Bevanne (Welsh) child of Evan.
Bevan, Bevann, Bevany

Beverly **G** (English) beaver field. See also Buffy.
Bev, Bevalee, Beverle, Beverlee, Beverley, Beverlie, Beverlly, Bevlyn, Bevlynn, Bevlynne, Bevvy, Verly

Beverlyann (American) a combination of Beverly + Ann.
Beverliann, Beverlianne, Beverlyanne

Bhadra (Indian) good.

Bhagirathi (Indian) the Ganges River.

Bhagwanti, Bhagya, Bhagyashri, Bhagyawati (Indian) lucky.

Bhagyalakshmi (Indian) goddess of wealth.

Bhagyashree (Indian) fortunate.

Bhairavi (Indian) musical notes.

Bhakti (Indian) prayer.

Bhamini (Indian) a beautiful, short-tempered lady.

Bhanuja (Indian) the Yamuna River.

Bhanumati (Indian) famous.

Bhanuni (Indian) charming woman.

Bhanupriya (Indian) the sun's beloved.

Bharani (Indian) a star.

Girls A–F

Bharavi (Indian) tulsi plant.

Bhavana (Indian) feelings, sentiments.

Bhavi, Bhavini (Indian) emotional.

Bhavika (Indian) cheerful expression.

Bhavna (Indian) good feelings.

Bhawna (Indian) feelings.

Bhilangana (Indian) a river.

Bhini (Indian) mild.

Bhoomi, Bhoomika, Boomika (Indian) the Earth.

Bhrithi (Indian) strengthened, nourished.

Bhumika (Indian) earth.

Bhuvana (Indian) goddess of Earth.

Bhuvi (Indian) heaven.

Bi, Bik (Chinese) jade.

Bian (Vietnamese) hidden; secretive.

Bianca 🄶 (Italian) white. See also Blanca, Vianca.
Biancca, Biancha, Biancia, Bianco, Bianey, Bianica, Bianka, Biannca, Binney, Bionca, Blanca, Blanche, Byanca

Bianka (Italian) a form of Bianca.
Beyanka, Biannka

Biao (Chinese) example.

Bibi (Latin) a short form of Bibiana. (Arabic) lady. (Spanish) a form of Bebe.

Bibiana (Latin) lively.
Bibi

Biblis (Latin) swallow.

Biddy (Irish) a familiar form of Bedelia.
Biddie

Bienvenida (Spanish) welcome.

Bijal, Bijli (Indian) lightning.

Billi (English) a form of Billie.

Billie 🄶 (English) strong willed. (German, French) a familiar form of Belle, Wilhelmina.
Bilee, Bileigh, Bili, Bilie, Billee, Billi, Billy, Billye

Billie-Jean (American) a combination of Billie + Jean.
Billiejean, Billyjean, Billy-Jean

Billie-Jo (American) a combination of Billie + Jo.
Billiejo, Billyjo, Billy-Jo

Billy 🄱 (English) a form of Billie.
Billye

Bilomena (Pohnpeian) a form of Angelina.

Bilomina (Pohnpeian) a form of Bethel.

Bimala (Indian) pure.

Bimbi (Indian) glorious.

Bin (Chinese) refined and courteous.

Bina (Hebrew) wise; understanding. (Swahili) dancer. (Latin) a short form of Sabina. See also Bena.
Binah, Binney, Binta, Bintah

Binata (Indian) the wife of sage Kashyap.

Bindhu, Bindiya (Indian) a drop.

Bindu (Indian) point.

Bing (Chinese) ice.

Bing Qing (Chinese) clear as ice.

Bing-Qing (Chinese) ice; crystal clear.

Binita (Indian) modest.

Binney (English) a familiar form of Benedicta, Bianca, Bina.
Binnee, Binni, Binnie, Binny

Binodini (Indian) handsome.

Biola (Kosraean) young; clear, pure; request; understand; court.

Bionca (Italian) a form of Bianca.
Beonca, Beyonca, Beyonka, Bioncha, Bionica, Bionka, Bionnca

Bipasha (Indian) a river.

Birdie (English) bird. (German) a familiar form of Bertha.
Bird, Birdee, Birdella, Birdena, Birdey, Birdi, Birdy, Byrd, Byrdey, Byrdie, Byrdy

Birgitte (Swedish) a form of Bridget.
Birgit, Birgita, Birgitta

Birte (German) a form of Bertha.

Bishakha (Indian) star.

Blaine 🄱 (Irish) thin.
Blane, Blayne

Blair 🄱🄶 (Scottish) plains dweller.
Blaire

Blaire (Scottish) a form of Blair.
Blare, Blayre

Blaise **B** (French) one who stammers.
Blaize, Blasha, Blasia, Blaza, Blaze, Blazena

Blake **B** (English) dark.
Blaque, Blayke

Blakely **BG** (English) dark meadow.
Blakelea, Blakelee, Blakeleigh, Blakeley, Blakeli, Blakelyn, Blakelynn, Blakesley, Blakley, Blakli

Blanca **G** (Italian) a form of Bianca.
Bellanca, Blancka, Blanka

Blanche (French) a form of Bianca.
Blanch, Blancha, Blinney

Blandina (Latin) flattering.

Blandinas, Blindina (Chamorro) forms of Blandina.

Blasa (French) stammerer.

Blessy (Indian) blessing.

Blinda (American) a short form of Belinda.
Blynda

Bliss **G** (English) blissful, joyful.
Blisse, Blyss, Blysse

Blodwyn (Welsh) flower. See also Wynne.
Blodwen, Blodwynne, Blodyn

Blondelle (French) blond, fair haired.
Blondell, Blondie

Blondie (American) a familiar form of Blondell.
Blondee, Blondey, Blondy

Blossom (English) flower.

Blum (Yiddish) flower.
Bluma

Blythe **G** (English) happy, cheerful.
Blithe, Blyss, Blyth

Bo **B** (Chinese) precious.

Bo Mee (Korean) white; senior, esteemed.

Boacha (Hebrew) blessed.

Bo-Bae (Korean) shining.

Bobbette (American) a familiar form of Roberta.
Bobbet, Bobbetta

Bobbi, Bobbie **G** (American) familiar forms of Barbara, Roberta.
Baubie, Bobbe, Bobbey, Bobbisue, Bobby, Bobbye, Bobi, Bobie, Bobina, Bobbie-Jean, Bobbie-Lynn, Bobbie-Sue

Bobbi-Ann, Bobbie-Ann (American) combinations of Bobbi + Ann.
Bobbiann, Bobbi-Anne, Bobbianne, Bobbie-Anne, Bobby-Ann, Bobbyann, Bobby-Anne, Bobbyanne

Bobbi-Jo (American) a combination of Bobbi + Jo.
Bobbiejo, Bobbie-Jo, Bobbijo, Bobby-Jo, Bobijo

Bobbi-Lee (American) a combination of Bobbi + Lee.
Bobbie-Lee, Bobbilee, Bobbylee, Bobby-Leigh, Bobile

Bobby **B** (American) a form of Bobbi.

Bomy (Korean) a form of Bomy.

Bon (Korean) treasure; precious.

Bonfila, Bonfilia (Italian) good daughter.

Bong-Cha (Korean) like spring.

Bonifacia (Italian) benefactor.

Bonita (Spanish) pretty.
Bonèsha, Bonetta, Bonnetta, Bonnie, Bonny

Bonnie, Bonny (English, Scottish) beautiful, pretty. (Spanish) familiar forms of Bonita.
Boni, Bonie, Bonne, Bonnee, Bonnell, Bonney, Bonni, Bonnin

Bonnie-Bell (American) a combination of Bonnie + Belle.
Bonnebell, Bonnebelle, Bonnibell, Bonnibelle, Bonniebell, Bonniebelle, Bonnybell, Bonnybelle

Boo (Korean) origin; essential.

Boon (Korean) excellent daughter.

Boram (Korean) sage; help, support; wealth; class; written charm; give, bestow.

Boulej (Marshallese) on the lagoon beach side of the atoll.

Boupha (Vietnamese) baby; doll.

Brad **B** (English) a short form of Bradley.

Braden **B** (English) broad valley.

Bradley **B** (English) broad meadow.
Bradlee, Bradleigh, Bradlie

Brady **B** (Irish) spirited.
Bradee, Bradey, Bradi, Bradie, Braedi, Braidee, Braidi, Braidie, Braidey, Braidy, Braydee

Braeden **B** (English) broad hill.
Bradyn, Bradynn, Braedan, Braedean, Braedyn, Braidan, Braidyn, Braydn

Braelyn (American) a combination of Braeden + Lynn.
Braelee, Braeleigh, Braelin, Braelle, Braelon, Braelynn, Braelynne, Brailee, Brailenn, Brailey, Braili, Brailyn, Braylee, Brayley, Braylin, Braylon, Braylyn, Braylynn

Girls A–F

Braiden 🅱 (English) a form of Braeden.

Branca (Portuguese) white.

Branda (Hebrew) blessing.

Brandan 🅱 (English) a form of Branden.

Brandee (Dutch) a form of Brandy.
Brande, Brandea, Brendee

Branden 🅱 (English) beacon valley.
Brendan, Brandyn, Brennan

Brandi, Brandie 🅶 (Dutch) forms of
Brandy.
Brandei, Brandice, Brandiee, Brandii,
Brandily, Brandin, Brandis, Brandise, Brani,
Branndie, Brendi

Brandon 🅱 (English) a form of Branden.

Brandy 🅶 (Dutch) an after-dinner drink
made from distilled wine.
Brand, Brandace, Brandaise, Brandala,
Brandee, Brandeli, Brandell, Brandi, Brandye,
Brandylee, Brandy-Lee, Brandy-Leigh, Brann,
Branyell, Brendy

Brandy-Lynn (American) a combination of
Brandy + Lynn.
Brandalyn, Brandalynn, Brandelyn,
Brandelynn, Brandelynne, Brandilyn,
Brandilynn, Brandilynne, Brandlin, Brandlyn,
Brandlynn, Brandlynne, Brandolyn,
Brandolynn, Brandolynne, Brandylyn, Brandy-
Lyn, Brandylynne, Brandy-Lynne

Brantley 🅱 (Dutch) a form of Brandy.

Bratati (Indian) creeper.

Braulia (Teutonic) gleaming.

Braxton 🅱 (English) Brock's town.
Braxten, Braxtyn

Brayden 🅱 (English) a form of Braeden.

Braydon (English) a form of Braeden.

Brea, Bria (Irish) short forms of Breana,
Briana.
Breah, Breea, Briah, Brya

Breana (Irish) a form of Briana.
Brea, Breanah, Breanda, Bre-Anna, Breasha,
Breawna, Breila

Breann (Irish) a short form of Briana.
Breane, Bree, Breean, Breelyn, Breeon,
Brieon

Breanna 🅶 (Irish) a form of Briana.
Bre-Anna, Breannah, Breannea, Breannia,
Breeanna

Breanne 🅶 (Irish) a short form of Brianna.
Bre-Anne, Breaunne, Breeann, Breeanne,
Breiann, Breighann, Breyenne, Brieann

Breasha (Russian) a familiar form of
Breana.

Breauna, Breunna, Briauna (Irish) forms
of Briana.
Breaunna, Breeauna, Breuna, Breuna,
Briaunna

Breck 🅱🅶 (Irish) freckled.
Brecken

Bree (English) broth. (Irish) a short form of
Breann. See also Brie.
Breay, Brei, Breigh

Breeana, Breeanna (Irish) forms of Briana.
Breeanah, Breeannah

Breena (Irish) fairy palace. A form of Brina.
Breenea, Breene, Breina, Brina

Breiana, Breianna (Irish) forms of Briana.
Breiane, Breiann, Breianne

Brenda 🅶 (Irish) little raven. (English)
sword.
Brendell, Brendelle, Brendette, Brendie,
Brendyl, Brenna

Brenda-Lee (American) a combination of
Brenda + Lee.
Brendalee, Brendaleigh, Brendali, Brendaly,
Brendalys, Brenlee, Brenley

Brendan 🅱 (Irish) little raven. (English)
sword.

Brenden 🅱 (Irish) a form of Brendan.

Brenna 🅶 (Irish) a form of Brenda.
Bren, Brenie, Brenin, Brenn, Brennah,
Brennaugh, Brenne

Brennan 🅱 (English) a form of Brendan.
Brennea, Brennon, Brennyn

Brennen 🅱 (English) a form of Brennan.

Brenton 🅱 (English) steep hill.

Breon 🅱 (Irish, Scottish) a form of Brian.

Breona, Breonna (Irish) forms of Briana.
Breeona, Breiona, Breionna, Breonah,
Breonia, Breonie, Breonne

Bret 🅱 (Irish) a form of Brett.

Brett 🅱 (Irish) a short form of Britany. See
also Brita.
Bret, Brette, Brettin, Bretton

Breyana, Breyann, Breyanna (Irish) forms
of Briana.
Breyan, Breyane, Breyannah, Breyanne

Breyona, Breyonna (Irish) forms of Briana.
Breyonia

Brian **B** (Irish, Scottish) strong; virtuous; honorable.

Briana **G** (Irish) a form of Brian.
Brana, Brea, Breana, Breauna, Breeana, Breiana, Breona, Breyana, Breyona, Bria, Briahna, Brianah, Briand, Brianda, Brina, Briona, Briyana, Bryona

Brianna ※ **G** (Irish) a form of Brian.
Bhrianna, Breann, Briannah, Brianne, Brianni, Briannon, Brienna, Bryanna

Brianne **G** (Irish) a form of Briana.
Briane, Briann, Brienne, Bryanne

Briar (French) heather.
Brear, Brier, Bryar

Brice **B** (Welsh) alert; ambitious. (English) child of Rice.

Bricia (Spanish) represents strength.

Bridey (Irish) a familiar form of Bridget.
Bridi, Bridie, Brydie

Bridget **G** (Irish) strong. See also Bedelia, Bryga, Gitta.
Berget, Birgitte, Bride, Bridey, Bridger, Bridgete, Bridgett, Bridgette, Bridgid, Bridgot, Brietta, Brigada, Briget, Brigid, Brigida, Brigitte, Brita

Bridgett, Bridgette (Irish) forms of Bridget.
Bridgitte, Brigette, Bridggett, Briggitte, Bridgitt, Brigitta

Brie (French) a type of cheese. Geography: a region in France known for its cheese. See also Bree.
Briea, Brielle, Briena, Brieon, Brietta, Briette

Brieana, Brieanna (American) combinations of Brie + Anna.
Brieannah

Brieann, Brieanne (American) combinations of Brie + Ann. See also Briana.
Brie-Ann, Brie-Anne

Brielle **G** (French) a form of Brie.
Briel, Briele, Briell, Briella

Brienna (Irish) a form of Briana.
Briene, Brieon, Brieona, Brieonna

Brienne (French) a form of Briana.
Brienn

Brigette (French) a form of Bridget.
Briget, Brigett, Brigetta, Brigettee, Brigget

Brígida (Celtic) strong, victorious.

Brigidia (Celtic) strong.

Brigitte (French) a form of Bridget.
Briggitte, Brigit, Brigita

Brina (Latin) a short form of Sabrina. (Irish) a familiar form of Briana.
Brin, Brinan, Brinda, Brindi, Brindy, Briney, Brinia, Brinlee, Brinly, Brinn, Brinna, Brinnan, Briona, Bryn, Bryna

Brindha (Indian) the basil plant.

Briona (Irish) a form of Briana.
Brione, Brionna, Brionne, Briony, Briunna, Bryony

Brisa (Spanish) beloved. Mythology: Briseis was the Greek name of Achilles's beloved.
Breezy, Breza, Brisha, Brishia, Brissa, Bryssa

Briselda (Spanish) a form of Briselda.

Brisia, Briza (Greek) beloved.

Brita (Irish) a form of Bridget. (English) a short form of Britany.
Bretta, Brieta, Brietta, Brit, Britta

Britaney, Brittaney (English) forms of Britany, Brittany.
Britanee, Britanny, Britenee, Briteny, Britianey, British, Britkney, Britley, Britlyn, Britney, Briton

Britani, Brittani, Brittanie (English) forms of Britany.
Brit, Britania, Britanica, Britanie, Britanii, Britanni, Britannia, Britatani, Britia, Britini, Brittane, Brittanee, Brittanni, Brittannia, Brittannie, Brittenie, Brittiani, Brittianni

Britany, Brittany **G** (English) from Britain. See also Brett.
Brita, Britana, Britaney, Britani, Britanna, Britlyn, Britney, Britt, Brittainny, Brittainy, Brittamy, Brittana, Brittaney, Brittani, Brittania, Brittanica, Brittanny, Brittany-Ann, Brittanyne, Brittell, Britteny, Brittiany, Brittini, Brittlin, Brittlynn, Brittnee, Brittony, Bryttany

Britin, Brittin (English) from Britain.
Britann, Brittan, Brittin, Brittina, Brittine, Brittini, Brittiny

Britney, Brittny (English) forms of Britany.
Bittney, Bridnee, Bridney, Britnay, Britne, Britnee, Britnei, Britni, Britny, Britnye, Brittnay, Brittnaye, Brytnea, Brytni

Britni, Brittni, Brittnie (English) forms of Britney, Brittny.
Britnie

Briton (English) a form of Britin.
Britton

Britt, Britta (Latin) short forms of Britany, Brittany. (Swedish) strong.
Brett, Briet, Brit, Brita, Britte

Britteny (English) a form of Britany, Brittany.
Britten, Brittenay, Brittenee, Britteney, Brittenie

Brittini, Brittiny (English) forms of Britany, Brittany.
Brittinee, Brittiney, Brittinie, Brittiny

Brittnee (English) a form of Britany, Brittany.
Brittne, Brittnea, Brittnei, Brittneigh

Brittney 🄶 (English) a form of Britany.

Briyana, Briyanna (Irish) forms of Briana.

Brock 🄱 (English) badger.

Brodie 🄱 (Irish) ditch; canal builder.
Brodee, Brodi

Brody 🄱 (Irish) a form of Brodie.

Bronnie (Welsh) a familiar form of Bronwyn.
Bron, Bronia, Bronney, Bronny, Bronya

Bronwyn 🄶 (Welsh) white breasted.
Bronnie, Bronwen, Bronwin, Bronwynn, Bronwynne

Brook 🄶 (English) brook, stream.
Bhrooke, Brookelle, Brookie, Brooky

Brooke �W 🄶 (English) brook, stream.

Brooklyn �W 🄶 (American) a combination of Brook + Lynn.
Brookellen, Brookelyn, Brookelyne, Brookelynn, Brooklen, Brooklin, Brooklyne, Brooklynne

Brooklynn 🄶 (American) a form of Brooklyn.

Brooks 🄱 (English) a form of Brook.

Bruce 🄱 (French) brushwood thicket; woods.

Bruna (German) a short form of Brunhilda.
Brona

Brunela (Italian) a form of Bruna.

Brunhilda (German) armored warrior.
Brinhilda, Brinhilde, Bruna, Brunhilde, Brünnhilde, Brynhild, Brynhilda, Brynhilde, Hilda

Brunilda (German) line of defense in battle.

Bryan 🄱 (Irish) a form of Brian.

Bryana 🄶 (Irish) a form of Bryan.

Bryanna, Bryanne (Irish) short forms of Bryana.
Bryann, Bryanni

Bryce 🄱 (Welsh) alert; ambitious.

Bryden 🄱 (English) a form of Braden.

Bryga (Polish) a form of Bridget.
Brygid, Brygida, Brygitka

Brylee 🄶 (American) a form of Brylie.

Brylie (American) a combination of the letter B + Riley.
Brylei, Bryley, Bryli

Bryn, Brynn 🄶 (Latin) from the boundary line. (Welsh) mound.
Brinn, Brynee, Brynne

Bryna (Latin, Irish) a form of Brina.
Brynan, Brynna, Brynnan

Bryona, Bryonna (Irish) forms of Briana.
Bryonia, Bryony

Bryson 🄱 (Welsh) child of Brice.
Brysan, Brysen, Brysun, Brysyn

Bryton 🄱 (English) a form of Bryttani.

Bryttani, Bryttany (English) forms of Britany.
Brytani, Brytanie, Brytanny, Brytany, Brytnee, Brytnie, Bryttanee, Bryttanie, Bryttine, Bryttney, Bryttnie, Brytton

Bsibs (Palauan) adornment, decoration.

Bu (Vietnamese) jade.

Bua (Vietnamese) flower girl.

Bubby (Indian) my beloved.

Buena (Spanish) good.

Buenaventura (Castilian) she who wishes good fortune and joy to those around her.

Buffy (American) buffalo; from the plains.
Buffee, Buffey, Buffie, Buffye

Bujen (Marshallese) a form of Petra.

Bulbul (Indian) nightingale.

Bulbuli (Indian) a songbird.

Bum (Korean) duty; fragrance; impetuous.

Bunny (Greek) a familiar form of Bernice. (English) little rabbit. See also Bonnie.
Bunni, Bunnie

Burgundy (French) Geography: a region of France known for its Burgundy wine.
Burgandi, Burgandie, Burgandy, Burgunde

Buthayna (Indian) she who has a beautiful and tender body.

Byung (Korean) worth.

C

C BG (American) an initial used as a first name.

Caca (Chamorro) crack, crevice.

Cacac (Chamorro) type of bird.

Cachet (French) prestigious; desirous.
Cachae, Cache, Cachea, Cachee, Cachée

Cade B (English) a form of Cady.

Caden B (American) a form of Kadin (see Boys' Names).

Cadence (Latin) rhythm.
Cadena, Cadenza, Kadena

Cadhna, Chadna (Indian) love.

Cadmi (Chamorro) calm, no breeze.

Cady (English) a form of Kady.
Cade, Cadee, Cadey, Cadi, Cadie, Cadine, Cadye

Caeley, Cailey, Cayley (American) forms of Kaylee, Kelly.
Caela, Caelee, Caeleigh, Caeley, Caeli, Caelie, Caelly, Caely, Cailee, Caileigh, Caili, Cailie, Cailley, Caillie, Caily, Caylee

Caelin, Caelyn (American) forms of Kaelyn.
Caelan, Caelinn, Caelynn, Cailan, Caylan

Cai (Vietnamese) feminine.
Cae, Cay, Caye

Caija (Chamorro) to take a long time.

Cailida (Spanish) adoring.
Kailida

Cailin, Cailyn (American) forms of Caitlin.
Caileen, Cailene, Cailine, Cailynn, Cailynne, Calen, Cayleen, Caylen, Caylene, Caylin, Cayline, Caylyn, Caylyne, Caylynne

Cais (Vietnamese) fortunate.

Caitlan (Irish) a form of Caitlin.
Caitland, Caitlandt

Caitlin G (Irish) pure. See also Kaitlin, Katalina, Katelin, Katelyn, Kaytlyn.
Caetlin, Cailin, Caitlan, Caitleen, Caitlen, Caitlene, Caitlenn, Caitline, Caitlinn, Caitlon, Caitlyn, Catlee, Catleen, Catleene, Catlin

Caitlyn, Caitlynn (Irish) forms of Caitlin. See also Kaitlyn.
Caitlyne, Caitlynne, Catelyn, Catlyn, Catlynn, Catlynne

Cala (Arabic) castle, fortress. See also Callie, Kala.
Calah, Calan, Calla, Callah

Calachuchi (Tagalog) aunt.

Calandra (Greek) lark.
Calan, Calandrea, Calandria, Caleida, Calendra, Calendre, Kalandra, Kalandria

Calanthe (Greek) beautiful flower.

Caleb B (Hebrew) dog; faithful. (Arabic) bold, brave.

Caledonia (Spanish) native of Caledonia.

Caleigh G (American) a form of Caeley.
Caileigh, Caleah

Caley (American) a form of Caeley.

Calfuray (Mapuche) blue or violet flower.

Cali, Calli (Greek) forms of Callie. See also Kali.
Calee

Calida (Spanish) warm; ardent.
Calina, Calinda, Callida, Callinda, Kalida

Calíope (Greek) a form of Calliope.

Calisto (Spanish, Portuguese) most beautiful.

Callie (Greek, Arabic) a familiar form of Cala, Callista. See also Kalli.
Cal, Cali, Calie, Callee, Calley, Calli, Cally, Caly

Calliope (Greek) beautiful voice. Mythology: the Muse of epic poetry.

Callista (Greek) most beautiful. See also Kallista.
Calesta, Calista, Callie, Calysta

Callum B (Irish) dove.

Caltha (Latin) yellow flower.

Calvina (Latin) bald.
Calvine, Calvinetta, Calvinette

Calypso (Greek) concealer. Botany: a pink orchid native to northern regions. Mythology: the sea nymph who held Odysseus captive for seven years.
Caly, Lypsie, Lypsy

Cam B (Vietnamese) sweet citrus.
Kam

Camara (American) a form of Cameron.
Camera, Cameri, Cameria, Camira, Camry

Camberly (American) a form of Kimberly.
Camber, Camberlee, Camberleigh

Cambria (Latin) from Wales. See also Kambria.
Camberry, Cambreia, Cambie, Cambrea, Cambree, Cambrie, Cambrina, Cambry, Cambrya, Cami

Camden 🅑 (Scottish) winding valley.
Camdyn

Camellia (Italian) Botany: a camellia is an evergreen tree or shrub with fragrant roselike flowers.
Camala, Camalia, Camallia, Camela, Camelia, Camelita, Camella, Camellita, Cami, Kamelia, Kamellia

Cameo (Latin) gem or shell on which a portrait is carved.
Cami, Kameo

Cameron 🅑 (Scottish) crooked nose. See also Kameron, Kamryn.
Camara, Cameran, Cameren, Camira, Camiran, Camiron, Camryn

Cami (French) a short form of Camille. See also Kami.
Camey, Camie, Cammi, Cammie, Cammy, Cammye, Camy

Camila, Camilla (Italian) forms of Camille. See also Kamila, Mila.
Camia, Camilia, Camillia, Camilya, Cammilla, Chamelea, Chamelia, Chamika, Chamila, Chamilia

Camille 🅖 (French) young ceremonial attendant. See also Millie.
Cam, Cami, Camiel, Camielle, Camil, Camila, Camile, Camill, Cammille, Cammillie, Cammilyn, Cammyl, Cammyll, Camylle, Chamelle, Chamille, Kamille

Camisha (American) a combination of Cami + Aisha.
Cameasha, Cameesha, Cameisha, Camesa, Camesha, Cameshaa, Cameshia, Camiesha, Camyeshia

Camri, Camrie (American) short forms of Camryn. See also Kamri.
Camrea, Camree, Camrey, Camry

Camron 🅑 (American) a form of Camryn.

Camryn (American) a form of Cameron. See also Kamryn.
Camri, Camrin, Camron, Camrynn

Camylle (French) a form of Camille.
Camyle, Camyll

Can (Chinese) bright.

Cancia (Spanish) native of the city of Anzio.

Canciana, Cancianila (Spanish) forms of Cancia.

Candace (Greek) glittering white; glowing. History: the title of the queens of ancient Ethiopia. See also Dacey, Kandace.
Cace, Canace, Canda, Candas, Candece, Candelle, Candi, Candiace, Candice, Candyce

Candela (Spanish) candle; fire.

Candelaria (Latin) Candlemas; she who shines brightly.

Candelas (Spanish) a form of Candela.

Candi, Candy (American) familiar forms of Candace, Candice, Candida. See also Kandi.
Candee, Candie

Candice 🅖 (Greek) a form of Candace.
Candise, Candiss

Candida (Latin) bright white.
Candeea, Candi, Candia, Candide, Candita

Cándida (Latin) a form of Candida.

Candis (Greek) a form of Candace.
Candes, Candi, Candias, Candies, Candus

Candra (Latin) glowing. See also Kandra.
Candrea, Candria

Candyce (Greek) a form of Candace.
Candys, Candyse, Cyndyss

Canela (Latin) name of an aromatic plant and the color of its dry bark.

Cang (Chinese) sea blue.

Canh (Vietnamese) fortunate.

Cantara (Arabic) small crossing.
Cantarah

Cantrelle (French) song.
Cantrella

Capitolina (Latin) she who lives with the gods.

Capri (Italian) a short form of Caprice. Geography: an island off the west coast of Italy. See also Kapri.
Capria, Caprie, Capry

Caprice (Italian) fanciful.
Cappi, Caprece, Caprecia, Capresha, Capricia, Capriese, Caprina, Capris, Caprise, Caprisha, Capritta

Cara (Latin) dear. (Irish) friend. See also Karah.
Caira, Caragh, Carah, Caralee, Caranda, Carey, Carra

Caralee (Irish) a form of Cara.
Caralea, Caraleigh, Caralia, Caralie, Carely

Caralyn (English) a form of Caroline.
Caralin, Caraline, Caralynn, Caralynna, Caralynne

Carem (Spanish) a form of Karen.

Caressa (French) a form of Carissa.
Caresa, Carese, Caresse, Carissa, Charessa, Charesse, Karessa

Carey BG (Welsh) a familiar form of Cara, Caroline, Karen, Katherine. See also Carrie, Kari.
Caree, Cari, Carrey, Cary

Cari, Carie (Welsh) forms of Carey, Kari.

Caridad (Latin) she who gives love, affection, and tenderness to those around her.

Carina G (Italian) dear little one. (Swedish) a form of Karen. (Greek) a familiar form of Cora.
Carena, Carinah, Carine, Carinna

Carine (Italian) a form of Carina.
Carin, Carinn, Carinne

Carisa, Carrisa (Greek) forms of Carissa.
Carise, Carisha, Carisia, Charisa

Carissa (Greek) beloved. See also Karissa.
Caressa, Carisa, Carrissa, Charissa

Carita (Latin) charitable.
Caritta, Karita, Karitta

Caritina (Latin) grace, graceful.

Carl B (German, English) a short form of Carlton. A form of Charles. See also Carroll, Kale, Kalle, Karl.

Carla (German) farmer. (English) strong. (Latin) a form of Carol, Caroline.
Carila, Carilla, Carleta, Carlia, Carliqua, Carliyle, Carlonda, Carlyjo, Carlyle, Carlysle

Carlee, Carley G (English) forms of Carly. See also Karlee.
Carle, Carlea, Carleah, Carleh

Carleen, Carlene (English) forms of Caroline. See also Karlene.
Carlaen, Carlaena, Carleena, Carlen, Carlena, Carlenna, Carline, Carlyn, Carlyne

Carleigh (English) a form of Carly.

Carli, Carlie G (English) forms of Carly. See also Karli.

Carlin BG (Irish) little champion. (Latin) a short form of Caroline.
Carlan, Carlana, Carlandra, Carlina, Carlinda, Carline, Carling, Carllan, Carlyn, Carllen, Carrlin

Carlisa (American) a form of Carlissa.
Carilis, Carilise, Carilyse, Carleesia, Carlesia, Carletha, Carlethe, Carlicia, Carlis, Carlise, Carlisha, Carlisia, Carlyse

Carlissa (American) a combination of Carl + Lissa.
Carleeza, Carlisa, Carliss, Carlissah, Carlisse, Carlissia, Carlista

Carlos B (Spanish) a form of Carl, Charles.

Carlotta (Italian) a form of Charlotte.
Carletta, Carlita, Carlota

Carlton B (English) Carl's town.

Carly G (English) a familiar form of Caroline, Charlotte. See also Karli.
Carlye

Carlyn, Carlynn (Irish) forms of Carlin.
Carlyna, Carlynne

Carme (Galician) garden.

Carmela, Carmella (Hebrew) garden; vineyard. Bible: Mount Carmel in Israel is often thought of as paradise. See also Karmel.
Carma, Carmalla, Carmarit, Carmel, Carmeli, Carmelia, Carmelina, Carmelit, Carmelle, Carmellia, Carmellina, Carmesa, Carmesha, Carmi, Carmie, Carmiel, Carmil, Carmila, Carmile, Carmilla, Carmille, Carmisha, Leeta, Lita

Carmelit (Hebrew) a form of Carmela.
Carmaletta, Carmalit, Carmalita, Carmelita, Carmelitha, Carmelitia, Carmellit, Carmellita, Carmellitha, Carmellitia

Carmen G (Latin) song. Religion: Nuestra Señora del Carmen-Our Lady of Mount Carmel-is one of the titles of the Virgin Mary. See also Karmen.
Carma, Carmaine, Carman, Carmelina, Carmencita, Carmene, Carmi, Carmia, Carmin, Carmina, Carmine, Carmita, Carmon, Carmynn, Charmaine

Carmiña (Spanish) a form of Carmen.

Carminda (Spanish) beautiful song.

Carmo (Portuguese) garden.

Carnelian (Latin) precious, red rock.

Carol G (German) farmer. (French) song of joy. (English) strong. See also Charlene, Kalle, Karoll.
Carel, Cariel, Caro, Carola, Carole, Carolenia, Carolinda, Caroline, Caroll, Carrie, Carrol, Carroll, Caryl

Carolane, Carolann, Carolanne
(American) combinations of Carol + Ann.
Forms of Caroline.
Carolan, Carol Ann, Carole-Anne

Carole (English) a form of Carol.
Carolee, Karole, Karrole

Carolina 🄶 (Italian) a form of Caroline. See
also Karolina.
*Carilena, Carlena, Carlina, Caroleena,
Caroleina, Carolena, Carrolena*

Caroline ☙ 🄶 (French) little and strong.
See also Carla, Carleen, Carlin, Karolina.
*Caralin, Caraline, Carileen, Carilene, Carilin,
Cariline, Carling, Carly, Caro, Carolann,
Caroleen, Carolin, Carolina, Carolyn, Carrie,
Carroleen, Carrolene, Carrolin, Carroline,
Cary, Charlene*

Carolyn 🄶 (English) a form of Caroline. See
also Karolyn.
*Carilyn, Carilynn, Carilynne, Carlyn, Carlynn,
Carlynne, Carolyne, Carolynn, Carolynne,
Carrolyn, Carrolynn, Carrolynne*

Caron (Welsh) loving, kindhearted,
charitable.
Caronne, Carron, Carrone

Carona (Spanish) crown.

Carra (Irish) a form of Cara.
Carrah

Carrie 🄶 (English) a familiar form of Carol,
Caroline. See also Carey, Kari, Karri.
Carree, Carrey, Carri, Carria, Carry, Cary

Carrola (French) song of joy.

Carson 🄱 (English) child of Carr.
Carsen, Carsyn

Carter 🄱 (English) cart driver.

Caryl (Latin) a form of Carol.
Caryle, Caryll, Carylle

Caryn (Danish) a form of Karen.
*Caren, Carren, Carrin, Carryn, Caryna, Caryne,
Carynn*

Carys (Welsh) love.
Caris, Caryse, Ceris, Cerys

Casandra (Greek) a form of Cassandra.
*Casandera, Casandre, Casandrea, Casandrey,
Casandri, Casandria, Casanndra, Casaundra,
Casaundre, Casaundri, Casaundria, Casondra,
Casondre, Casondri, Casondria*

Casey 🄱🄶 (Irish) brave. (Greek) a familiar
form of Acacia. See also Kasey.
*Cacy, Cascy, Casie, Casse, Cassee, Cassey,
Cassye, Casy, Cayce, Cayse, Caysee, Caysy*

Casiana (Latin) empty, vain.

Casidy (Irish) a form of Cassidy.
Casidee, Casidi

Casie (Irish) a form of Casey.
*Caci, Caesi, Caisie, Casci, Cascie, Casi, Cayci,
Caysi, Caysie, Cazzi*

Casiel (Latin) mother of the earth.

Casilda (Arabic) virgin carrier of the lance.

Casimira (Polish) predicts peace.

Cass 🄱 (Greek) a short form of Cassandra.

Cassady (Irish) a form of Cassidy.
*Casadee, Casadi, Casadie, Cassaday,
Cassadee, Cassadey, Cassadi, Cassadie,
Cassadina*

Cassandra 🄶 (Greek) helper of men.
Mythology: a prophetess of ancient Greece
whose prophesies were not believed. See also

Kassandra, Sandra, Sandy, Zandra.
*Casandra, Cass, Cassandre, Cassandri,
Cassandry, Cassaundra, Cassie, Cassondra*

Cassaundra (Greek) a form of Cassandra.
*Cassaundre, Cassaundri, Cassundra,
Cassundre, Cassundri, Cassundria*

Cassey, Cassi (Greek) familiar forms of
Cassandra, Catherine.
Cassee, Cassii, Cassy, Casy

Cassia (Greek) a cinnamon-like spice. See
also Kasia.
Casia, Cass, Casya

Cassidy 🄶 (Irish) clever. See also Kassidy.
*Casidy, Cassady, Casseday, Cassiddy,
Cassidee, Cassidi, Cassidie, Cassity*

Cassie 🄶 (Greek) a familiar form of
Cassandra, Catherine. See also Kassie.

Cassiopeia (Greek) clever. Mythology: the wife
of the Ethiopian king Cepheus; the mother of
Andromeda.
Cassio

Cassondra (Greek) a form of Cassandra.
Cassondre, Cassondri, Cassondria

Casta (Greek) pure.

Castalia (Greek) fountain of purity.

Castel (Spanish) to the castle.

Castora (Spanish) brilliant.

Catalina (Spanish) a form of Catherine. See
also Katalina.
*Cataleen, Catalena, Catalene, Catalin,
Catalyn, Catalyna, Cateline*

Girls A–F

Catarina (German) a form of Catherine.
Catarena, Catarin, Catarine, Caterin, Caterina, Caterine

Catelyn (Irish) a form of Caitlin.
Catelin, Cateline, Catelyne, Catelynn

Catharine (Greek) a form of Catherine.
Catharen, Catharin, Catharina, Catharyn

Catherine **G** (Greek) pure. (English) a form of Katherine.
Cat, Catalina, Catarina, Cate, Cathann, Cathanne, Catharine, Cathenne, Catheren, Catherene, Catheria, Catherin, Catherina, Catheryn, Catheryne, Cathi, Cathleen, Cathrine, Cathryn, Cathy, Catlaina, Catreeka, Catrelle, Catrice, Catricia, Catrika, Catrina

Cathi, Cathy (Greek) familiar forms of Catherine, Cathleen. See also Kathy.
Catha, Cathe, Cathee, Cathey, Cathie

Cathleen (Irish) a form of Catherine. See also Caitlin, Kathleen.
Caithlyn, Cathaleen, Cathelin, Cathelina, Cathelyn, Cathi, Cathleana, Cathleene, Cathlene, Cathleyn, Cathlin, Cathline, Cathlyn, Cathlyne, Cathlynn, Cathy

Cathrine (Greek) a form of Catherine.

Cathryn (Greek) a form of Catherine.
Cathryne, Cathrynn, Catryn

Catrina (Slavic) a form of Catherine, Katrina.
Caitriana, Caitriona, Catina, Catreen, Catreena, Catrene, Catrenia, Catrin, Catrine, Catrinia, Catriona, Catroina

Cauvery, Cavery (Indian) the name of a river in India.

Cayetana (Spanish) native of the city of Gaeta.

Cayfutray (Mapuche) noise from the bluish sky; blue thread; crystalline, celestial waterfall from heaven.

Cayla (Hebrew) a form of Kayla.
Caylea, Caylia

Caylee, Caylie (American) forms of Caeley, Cailey, Cayley.
Cayle, Cayleigh, Cayli, Cayly

Ceara (Irish) a form of Ciara.
Ceaira, Ceairah, Ceairra, Cearaa, Cearie, Cearah, Cearra, Cera

Cecelia (Latin) a form of Cecilia. See also Sheila.
Caceli, Cacelia, Cece, Ceceilia, Ceceli, Cecelia, Cecelie, Cecely, Cecelyn, Cecette, Cescelia, Cescelie

Cecil **B** (Latin) a short form of Cecilia.

Cecilia (Latin) blind. See also Cicely, Cissy, Secilia, Selia, Sissy.
Cacilia, Caecilia, Cecelia, Cecil, Cecila, Cecile, Cecilea, Cecilija, Cecilla, Cecille, Cecillia, Cecily, Cecilya, Cecla, Cecylia, Cee, Ceil, Ceila, Ceilagh, Ceileh, Ceileigh, Ceilena, Celia, Cesilia, Cicelia

Cecília (Portuguese) a form of Cecilia.

Cecily (Latin) a form of Cecilia.
Cacilie, Cecilee, Ceciley, Cecilie, Cescily, Cicely, Cilley

Ceferina (German) caresses like a soft wind.

Ceil (Latin) a short form of Cecilia.
Ceel, Ciel

Ceira, Ceirra (Irish) forms of Ciara.
Ceire

Celedonia (German) like the celedonia flower.

Celena (Greek) a form of Selena.
Celeena, Celene, Celenia, Celine, Cena

Celene (Greek) a form of Celena.
Celeen

Celerina (Spanish) quick.

Celeste (Latin) celestial, heavenly.
Cele, Celeeste, Celense, Celes, Celesia, Celesley, Celest, Celesta, Celestia, Celestial, Celestin, Celestina, Celestine, Celestinia, Celestyn, Celestyna, Cellest, Celleste, Selestina

Celia (Latin) a short form of Cecilia.
Ceilia, Celie

Célia (Portuguese) a form of Celia.

Celidonia (Greek) a certain type of herbal medicine.

Celina (Greek) a form of Celena. See also Selina.
Caleena, Calena, Calina, Celena, Celinda, Celinka, Celinna, Celka, Cellina

Celine **G** (Greek) a form of Celena.
Caline, Celeen, Celene, Céline, Cellinn

Celmira (Arabic) brilliant one.

Celsa (Latin) very spiritual.

Cemelia (Punic) she has God present.

Cenobia (Greek) stranger.

Centola (Arabic) light of knowledge.

Cera (French) a short form of Cerise.
Cerea, Ceri, Ceria, Cerra

Cercira (Greek) she who is from the island of Circe.

Cerella (Latin) springtime.
Cerelisa, Ceres

Cerise (French) cherry; cherry red.
Cera, Cerese, Cerice, Cericia, Cerissa, Cerria, Cerrice, Cerrina, Cerrita, Cerryce, Ceryce, Cherise

Cesar 🅑 (Spanish) a form of Caesar (see Boys' Names).

Cesara (Latin) longhaired.

Cesare, Cesaria, Cesarina, Cesira (Latin) she who was forcibly separated from her mother.

Cesilia (Latin) a form of Cecilia.
Cesia, Cesya

Chaaya, Chhaya (Indian) shadow.

Chabe (Chamorro) chop; pepper.

Chabela (Hebrew) a form of Isabel.

Chabi (Indian) picture.

Chablis (French) a dry, white wine. Geography: a region in France where wine grapes are grown.
Chabeli, Chabelly, Chabely, Chablee, Chabley, Chabli

Chaca (Chamorro) mouse.

Chad 🅑 (English) warrior. A short form of Chadwick (see Boys' Names). Geography: a country in north-central Africa.

Chadee (French) from Chad, a country in north-central Africa. See also Sade.
Chaday, Chadday, Chade, Chadea, Chadi

Chadfaulus, Charfaulos (Chamorro) forms of Charfaulus.

Chaguna, Changuna (Indian) a good woman.

Chai (Hebrew) life.
Chae, Chaela, Chaeli, Chaella, Chaena, Chaia

Chairavali (Indian) full moon of Chaitra month.

Chaitalee (Indian) girl born in the Chaitra month.

Chaitali (Indian) a season; born in the Chaitra month.

Chaitaly (Indian) name of an ancient city.

Chaitan (Indian) consciousness.

Chaka (Sanskrit) a form of Chakra. See also Shaka.
Chakai, Chakia, Chakka, Chakkah

Chakori (Indian) alert.

Chakra (Sanskrit) circle of energy.
Chaka, Chakara, Chakaria, Chakena, Chakina, Chakira, Chakrah, Chakria, Chakriya, Chakyra

Chalan (Chamorro) way, path.

Chalana (Chamorro) her way.

Chalice (French) goblet.
Chalace, Chalcie, Chalece, Chalicea, Chalie, Chaliese, Chalis, Chalisa, Chalise, Chalisk, Chalissa, Chalisse, Challa, Challaine, Challis, Challisse, Challysse, Chalsey, Chalyce, Chalyn, Chalyse, Chalyssa, Chalysse

Chalina (Spanish) a form of Rose.
Chaline, Chalini

Chalonna (American) a combination of the prefix Cha + Lona.
Chalon, Chalona, Chalonda, Chalonn, Chalonne, Chalonte, Shalon

Chambray (French) a lightweight fabric.
Chambrae, Chambre, Chambree, Chambrée, Chambrey, Chambria, Chambrie

Chameli (Indian) a flower.

Chamiyu (Chamorro) not enough of you.

Chamorra (Chamorro) a woman of the Chamorro people.

Champa (Indian) a flower.

Champabati (Indian) the capital.

Champakali (Indian) a bud of champa.

Champakmala (Indian) a garland made of champa flowers.

Chan 🅑 (Cambodian) sweet-smelling tree.

Chan Juan, Chang-Juan (Chinese) the moon; graceful, ladylike.

Chana (Hebrew) a form of Hannah.
Chanae, Chanai, Chanay, Chanea, Chanie

Chance 🅑 (English) a short form of Chancey.

Chancey (English) chancellor; church official.
Chance, Chancee, Chancie, Chancy

Chanchala (Indian) unsteady; lightening.

Chanchari (Indian) bird.

Chanda (Sanskrit) short tempered. Religion: the demon defeated by the Hindu goddess Chamunda. See also Shanda.
Chandee, Chandey, Chandi, Chandie, Chandin

Chandana (Indian) sandal.

Chandanika (Indian) diminutive.

Chandelle (French) candle.
Chandal, Chandel, Shandal, Shandel

Chandini, Chandrabha, Chandrajyoti, Chandrakanti (Indian) moonlight.

Chandler ⚟ (Hindi) moon. (Old English) candlemaker.
Chandlar, Chandlier, Chandlor, Chandlyr

Chandni (Indian) moonlit.

Chandra (Sanskrit) moon. Religion: the Hindu god of the moon. See also Shandra.
Chandrae, Chandray, Chandre, Chandrea, Chandrelle, Chandria

Chandrabali (Indian) Krishna's girlfriend.

Chandrabhaga (Indian) the Chenab River.

Chandrakala (Indian) phases of the moon.

Chandraki, Chandrakin (Indian) peacock.

Chandralekha (Indian) the phase of moon two nights after new moon; a moon ray.

Chandraleksha (Indian) a moon ray.

Chandramukhi (Indian) one with a round face.

Chandrani (Indian) wife of the moon.

Chandraprabha (Indian) star; moonlight.

Chandrapushpa (Indian) star.

Chandrika, Chandrima (Indian) moon.

Chanel (English) channel. See also Shanel.
Chanal, Chaneel, Chaneil, Chanele, Chanell, Channal, Channel, Chenelle

Chanell, Chanelle (English) forms of Chanel.
Channell, Shanell

Chang (Chinese) free, uninhibited.

Chang-O (Chinese) moon goddess, keeper of the ambrosia of immortality.

Chanise (American) a form of Shanice.
Chanisse, Chenice, Chenise

Channa (Hindi) chickpea.
Channah

Channary (Vietnamese) one who rejoices.

Chantal ⚟ (French) song.
Chandal, Chantaal, Chantael, Chantala, Chantale, Chantall, Chantalle, Chantara, Chantarai, Chantasia, Chante, Chanteau, Chantel, Chantle, Chantoya, Chantrill, Chauntel

Chante ⚎ (French) a short form of Chantal.
Chanta, Chantae, Chantai, Chantay, Chantaye, Chanté, Chantéa, Chantee, Chanti, Chantia, Chaunte, Chauntea, Chauntéa, Chauntee

Chantel, ⚟ (French) a form of Chantal. See also Shantel.

Chantell, Chantelle (French) forms of Chantel.
Chanteese, Chantela, Chantele, Chantella, Chanter, Chantey, Chantez, Chantrel, Chantrell, Chantrelle, Chatell

Chantilly (French) fine lace. See also Shantille.
Chantiel, Chantielle, Chantil, Chantila, Chantilée, Chantill, Chantille

Chantrea (Cambodian) moon; moonbeam.
Chantra, Chantrey, Chantri, Chantria

Chantrice (French) singer. See also Shantrice.
Chantreese, Chantress

Chao (Chinese) great one.

Chapala (Indian) quick.

Charani (Chamorro) lead, guide.

Chardae, Charde (Punjabi) charitable. (French) short forms of Chardonnay. See also Shardae.
Charda, Chardai, Charday, Chardea, Chardee, Chardée, Chardese, Chardey, Chardie

Chardonnay (French) a dry white wine.
Char, Chardae, Chardnay, Chardney, Chardon, Chardonae, Chardonai, Chardonay, Chardonaye, Chardonee, Chardonna, Chardonnae, Chardonnai, Chardonnee, Chardonnée, Chardonney, Shardonay, Shardonnay

Charfaulus (Chamorro) one with a rough appearance.

Charge (Chamorro) to laugh at.

Chargi, Chargui (Chamorro) forms of Charge.

Charis (Greek) grace; kindness.
Charece, Chareece, Chareeze, Charese, Chari, Charice, Charie, Charish, Charisse

Girls A–F

Charissa, Charisse (Greek) forms of Charity.
Charesa, Charese, Charessa, Charesse, Charis, Charisa, Charise, Charisha, Charissee, Charista, Charyssa

Charitha (Indian) good.

Charity ☙ (Latin) charity, kindness.
Chariety, Charis, Charissa, Charisse, Charista, Charita, Chariti, Charitie, Sharity

Charla (French, English) a short form of Charlene, Charlotte.
Char, Charlea

Charlaine (English) a form of Charlene.
Charlaina, Charlane, Charlanna, Charlayna, Charlayne

Charlee, Charley (German, English) forms of Charlie.
Charle, Charleigh

Charlene (English) a form of Caroline. See also Carol, Karla, Sharlene.
Charla, Charlaine, Charlean, Charleen, Charleene, Charleesa, Charlena, Charlenae, Charlesena, Charline, Charlyn, Charlyne, Charlynn, Charlynne, Charlzina, Charoline

Charles ☙ (German) farmer. (English) strong.

Charlie ☙ (German, English) a familiar form of Charles.
Charlee, Charley, Charli, Charyl, Chatty, Sharli, Sharlie

Charlotte (French) a form of Caroline. Literature: Charlotte Brontë was a British novelist and poet best known for her novel *Jane Eyre*. See also Karlotte, Lotte, Sharlotte, Tottie.
Carlotta, Carly, Chara, Charil, Charl, Charla,

Charlet, Charlett, Charletta, Charlette, Charlisa, Charlita, Charlott, Charlotta, Charlottie, Charlotty, Charolet, Charolette, Charolot, Charolotte

Charmaine (French) a form of Carmen. See also Sharmaine.
Charamy, Charma, Charmae, Charmagne, Charmaigne, Charmain, Chamaine, Charmalique, Charman, Charmane, Charmar, Charmara, Charmayane, Charmayne, Charmeen, Charmeine, Charmene, Charmese, Charmian, Charmin, Charmine, Charmion, Charmisa, Charmon, Charmyn, Charmyne, Charmynne

Charnette (American) a combination of Charo + Annette.
Charnetta, Charnita

Charnika (American) a combination of Charo + Nika.
Charneka, Charniqua, Charnique

Charo (Spanish) a familiar form of Rosa.

Charsaga, Chartsagua (Chamorro) forms of Chatsaga.

Charu, Charuprabha (Indian) beautiful.

Charulata (Indian) beautiful; like a creeper.

Charulekha (Indian) beautiful; like a picture.

Charumati, Charvi (Indian) a beautiful lady.

Charusheela (Indian) beautiful jewel.

Charushila (Indian) a diamond.

Charusmita (Indian) one with a beautiful smile.

Charyanna (American) a combination of Charo + Anna.
Charian, Charyian, Cheryn

Chase ☙ (French) hunter.

Chashmum (Indian) my eyes.

Chasidy, Chassidy (Latin) forms of Chastity.
Chasa Dee, Chasadie, Chasady, Chasidee, Chasidey, Chasidie, Chassedi, Chassidi, Chasydi

Chasity (Latin) a form of Chastity.
Chasiti, Chasitie, Chasitty, Chassey, Chassie, Chassiti, Chassity, Chassy

Chastain (French) chestnut-colored hair.

Chastity (Latin) pure.
Chasidy, Chasity, Chasta, Chastady, Chastidy, Chastin, Chastitie, Chastney, Chasty

Chata (Chamorro) not enough.

Chateria (Vietnamese) scenery.

Chathanum (Chamorro) not enough water.

Chatsaga (Chamorro) not enough to live on, poor.

Chau, Cuc (Vietnamese) moon girl.

Chauncey ☙ (English) chancellor; church official.

Chauntel (French) a form of Chantal.
Chaunta, Chauntae, Chauntay, Chaunte, Chauntell, Chauntelle, Chawntel, Chawntell, Chawntelle, Chontelle

Chava (Hebrew) life. (Yiddish) bird. Religion: the original name of Eve.
Chabah, Chavae, Chavah, Chavalah, Chavarra, Chavarria, Chave, Chavé, Chavette, Chaviva, Chavvis, Hava, Kaòa

Chavela (Spanish) consecrated to God.

Chavella (Spanish) a form of Isabel.
Chavel, Chaveli, Chavell, Chavelle, Chevelle, Chavely, Chevie

Chavi (Gypsy) girl.
Chavali

Chavon (Hebrew) a form of Jane.
Chavona, Chavonda, Chavonn, Chavonne, Shavon

Chavonne (Hebrew) a form of Chavon.
(American) a combination of the prefix Cha
+ Yvonne.
Chavondria, Chavonna, Chevon, Chevonn, Chevonna

Chaya (Hebrew) life; living.
Chaike, Chaye, Chayka, Chayla, Chaylah, Chaylea, Chaylee, Chaylene, Chayra

Chaz **B** (English) a familiar form of
Charles.

Cheboc (Chamorro) fat, plump.

Chein (Chuukese) a form of Jane.

Chela (Spanish) consolation.

Chelci, Chelcie (English) forms of Chelsea.
Chelce, Chelcee, Chelcey, Chelcy

Chelo (Spanish) a form of Consuelo.

Chelsea **G** (English) seaport. See also Kelsi,
Shelsea.
Chelci, Chelese, Chelesia, Chelsa, Chelsae, Chelsah, Chelse, Chelseah, Chelsee, Chelsey, Chelsia, Chelsie, Chesea, Cheslee, Chessea

Chelsee (English) a form of Chelsea.
Chelsei, Chelseigh

Chelsey **G** (English) a form of Chelsea. See
also Kelsey.
Chelsay, Chelssey, Chesley

Chelsie (English) a form of Chelsea.
Chelli, Chellie, Chellise, Chellsie, Chelsi, Chelssie, Cheslie, Chessie

Chelsy (English) a form of Chelsea.
Chelcy, Chelssy, Chelsye

Chen (Chinese) dawn.

Chenelle (English) a form of Chanel.
Chenel, Chenell

Cheng (Chinese) succeed; capable.

Chenoa (Native American) white dove.
Chenee, Chenika, Chenita, Chenna, Chenoah

Cher (French) beloved, dearest. (English) a
short form of Cherilyn.
Chere, Cheri, Cherie, Sher

Cherelle, Cherrelle (French) forms of
Cheryl. See also Sherelle.
Charell, Charelle, Cherell, Cherrel, Cherrell

Cherese (Greek) a form of Cherish.
Chereese, Cheresa, Cheresse, Cherice

Cheri, Cherie (French) familiar forms of
Cher.
Cheree, Chérie, Cheriee, Cherri, Cherrie

Cherilyn (English) a combination of Cheryl
+ Lynn.
Cher, Cheralyn, Chereen, Chereena, Cherilynn, Cherlyn, Cherlynn, Cherralyn, Cherrilyn, Cherrylyn, Cherylene, Cherylin, Cheryline, Cheryl-Lyn, Cheryl-Lynn, Cheryl-Lynne, Cherylyn, Cherylynn, Cherylynne, Sherilyn

Cherise (French) a form of Cherish. See also
Sharice, Sherice.
Charisa, Charise, Cherece, Chereese, Cheresa, Cherice, Cheriss, Cherissa, Cherisse, Cherrise

Cherish (English) dearly held, precious.
Charish, Charisha, Cheerish, Cherise, Cherishe, Cherrish, Sherish

Cherokee **G** (Native American) a tribal
name.
Cherika, Cherkita, Cherrokee, Sherokee

Cherry (Latin) a familiar form of Charity.
(French) cherry; cherry red.
Chere, Cheree, Cherey, Cherida, Cherita, Cherrey, Cherrita, Cherry-Ann, Cherry-Anne, Cherrye, Chery, Cherye

Cheryl (French) beloved. See also Sheryl.
Charel, Charil, Charyl, Cherelle, Cherrelle, Cheryl-Ann, Cheryl-Anne, Cheryle, Cherylee, Cheryll, Cherylle, Cheryl-Lee

Chesarey (American) a form of Desiree.
Chesarae, Chessa

Cheshta (Indian) to try.

Chesna (Slavic) peaceful.
Chesnee, Chesney, Chesnie, Chesny

Chessa (American) a short form of Chesarey.
Chessi, Chessie, Chessy

Chetna (Indian) power of intellect; alert.

Cheyanne (Cheyenne) a form of Cheyenne.
Cheyan, Cheyana, Cheyane, Cheyann, Cheyanna, Cheyeana, Cheyeannna, Cheyeannne

Cheyenne 🅖 (Cheyenne) a tribal name. See also Shaianne, Sheyenne, Shianne, Shyann.
Cheyanne, Cheyeene, Cheyena, Cheyene, Cheyenna, Cheyna, Chi, Chi-Anna, Chie, Chyanne

Cheyla (American) a form of Sheila.
Cheylan, Cheyleigh, Cheylo

Cheyna (American) a short form of Cheyenne.
Chey, Cheye, Cheyne, Cheynee, Cheyney, Cheynna

Chhavi (Indian) reflection.

Chi 🅑🅖 (Chinese) younger generation. (Nigerian) personal guardian angel.

Chia (Chinese) home, family; addition; armor.

Chiaki (Japanese) a thousand autumns.

Chiako (Pohnpeian) a form of Filomena.

Chiara (Italian) a form of Clara.
Cheara, Chiarra

Chiharu (Japanese) a thousand; clear weather.

Chihiro (Japanese) she who is very curious.

Chih-Nii (Chinese) goddess of spinners, weavers, and clouds.

Chiho (Japanese) a thousand plants.

Chika (Japanese) near and dear.
Chikaka, Chikako, Chikara, Chikona

Chiko (Japanese) arrow; pledge.

Chiku (Swahili) chatterer.

Chimayi (Indian) blissful.

Chin (Chinese) a form of Jin.

China 🅖 (Chinese) fine porcelain. Geography: a country in eastern Asia. See also Ciana, Shina.
Chinaetta, Chinah, Chinasa, Chinda, Chinea, Chinesia, Chinita, Chinna, Chinwa, Chyna, Chynna

Chinami (Japanese) cause.

Chinatsu (Japanese) she who is as beautiful as the summer.

Chinira (Swahili) God receives.
Chinara, Chinarah, Chinirah

Chinmayi (Indian) happy, blissful.

Chintana, Chintanika (Indian) meditation.

Chinue (Ibo) God's own blessing.

Chioko (Japanese) child.

Chionen (Chuukese) their companion.

Chiquita (Spanish) little one. See also Shiquita.
Chaqueta, Chaquita, Chica, Chickie, Chicky, Chikata, Chikita, Chiqueta, Chiquila, Chiquite, Chiquitha, Chiquithe, Chiquitia, Chiquitta

Chirika (Chamorro) the name of a bird.

Chisa (Japanese) torch.

Chisako (Japanese) torch child.

Chisa-Rae (Japanese) child of Yutso.

Chisato (Japanese) a thousand; knowledge; village.

Chiti (Indian) love.

Chitkala (Indian) knowledge.

Chitose (Japanese) a thousand years.

Chitra (Indian) drawing.

Chitragandha (Indian) a fragrant material.

Chitralekha (Indian) portrait.

Chitrali (Indian) a line of pictures.

Chitramala (Indian) series of pictures.

Chitrangada (Indian) wife of Arjun.

Chitrani (Indian) the Ganges River.

Chitrarekha (Indian) picture.

Chitrita (Indian) beautiful; decorated.

Chiyako (Japanese) thousand valley child.

Chiye (Japanese) a thousand; knowledge; blessed; branch.

Chiyeko (Japanese) prospering child.

Chiyemi (Japanese) wisdom; blessed; beautiful.

Chiyo (Japanese) eternal.
Chiya

Chiyoko (Japanese) wise child of the world.

Chiyoye (Japanese) a thousand blessed generations.

Chizu, Chizue (Japanese) a thousand storks; longevity.

Chizuko (Japanese) a form of Chizue.

Chloe ❦ 🅖 (Greek) blooming, verdant. Mythology: another name for Demeter, the goddess of agriculture.
Chloé, Chlöe, Chloee, Chloie, Cloe, Kloe

Girls A–F

Chloris (Greek) pale. Mythology: the only daughter of Niobe to escape the vengeful arrows of Apollo and Artemis. See also Loris.
Cloris, Clorissa

Cho (Korean) beautiful.
Choe

Chocholage (Chamorro) eat a little more.

Choda (Chamorro) green banana.

Choko (Japanese) butterfly child.

Cholena (Native American) bird.

Chomay (Chamorro) spill, pour.

Chomma (Chamorro) forbid.

Chong, Cong (Chinese) intelligent, clever.

Chow (Chinese) summer.

Chriki (Swahili) blessing.

Chris **B** (Greek) a short form of Christina. See also Kris.
Chrys, Cris

Chrissa (Greek) a short form of Christina. See also Khrissa.
Chrysa, Chryssa, Crissa, Cryssa

Chrissy (English) a familiar form of Christina.
Chrisie, Chrissee, Chrissie, Crissie, Khrissy

Christa **G** (German) a short form of Christina. History: Christa McAuliffe, an American school teacher, was the first civilian on a U.S. space flight. See also Krista.
Chrysta, Crista, Crysta

Christabel (Latin, French) beautiful Christian.
Christabell, Christabella, Christabelle, Christable, Cristabel, Kristabel

Christain **B** (Greek) a form of Christina.
Christana, Christann, Christanna

Christal (Latin) a form of Crystal. (Scottish) a form of Christina.
Christalene, Christalin, Christaline, Christall, Christalle, Christalyn, Christelle, Christle, Chrystal

Christelle (French) a form of Christal.
Christel, Christele, Christell, Chrystel, Chrystelle

Christen **G** (Greek) a form of Christin. See also Kristen.
Christan, Christyn, Chrystan, Chrysten, Chrystyn, Crestienne

Christena (Greek) a form of Christina.

Christi (Greek) a short form of Christina, Christine. See also Kristi.
Christy, Chrysti, Chrysty

Christian **B** (Greek) a form of Christina.

Christiana, Christianna (Greek) forms of Christina. See also Kristian, Krystian.
Christiane, Christiann, Christi-Ann, Christianne, Christi-Anne, Christianni, Christiaun, Christiean, Christien, Christiena, Christienne, Christinan, Christy-Ann, Christy-Anne, Crystian, Chrystyann, Chrystyanne, Crystiann, Crystianne

Christie **G** (Greek) a short form of Christina, Christine.
Christy, Chrysti, Chrysty

Christin **G** (Greek) a short form of Christina.
Chrystin

Christina **G** (Greek) Christian; anointed. See also Khristina, Kristina, Stina, Tina.
Chris, Chrissa, Chrissy, Christa, Christain, Christal, Christeena, Christella, Christen, Christena, Christi, Christian, Christie, Christin, Christinaa, Christine, Christinea, Christinia, Christinna, Christinnah, Christna, Christy, Christyn, Christyna, Christynna, Chrystina, Chrystyna, Cristeena, Cristena, Cristina, Crystina, Chrystena, Cristena

Christine **G** (French, English) a form of Christina. See also Kirsten, Kristen, Kristine.
Chrisa, Christeen, Christen, Christene, Christi, Christie, Christy, Chrystine, Cristeen, Cristene, Cristine, Crystine

Christophe **B** (Greek) a form of Christopher.

Christopher **B** (Greek) Christ-bearer.

Christy **G** (English) a short form of Christina, Christine.
Cristy

Christyn (Greek) a form of Christina.
Christyne

Chrys (English) a form of Chris.
Krys

Chrystal (Latin) a form of Christal.
Chrystale, Chrystalla, Chrystallina, Chrystallynn

Chu (Chinese) neat.

Chu Hua (Chinese) chrysanthemum.

Chuan (Chinese) river.

Chubasca (Chamorro) storm at sea.

Chul (Korean) law, rule; pattern, model.

Chumani (Lakota) dewdrops.
Chumany

Chun **B** (Burmese) nature's renewal.

Chung (Korean) lotus; lovely.

Chunni (Indian) a star.

Chuo (Chinese) ample.

Chyanne, Chyenne (Cheyenne) forms of Cheyenne.
Chyan, Chyana, Chyane, Chyann, Chyanna, Chyeana, Chyenn, Chyenna, Chyennee

Chyna, Chynna (Chinese) forms of China.

Chyou (Chinese) autumn.

Ci (Chinese) tenderhearted.

Ciana (Chinese) a form of China. (Italian) a form of Jane.
Cian, Ciandra, Ciann, Cianna

Ciara, Ciarra 🅖 (Irish) black. See also Sierra.
Ceara, Chiairah, Ciaara, Ciaera, Ciaira, Ciarah, Ciaria, Ciarrah, Cieara, Ciearra, Ciearria, Ciera, Cierra, Cioria, Cyarra

Cibeles (Greek) mythological goddess.

Cicely (English) a form of Cecilia. See also Sissy.
Cicelia, Cicelie, Ciciley, Cicilia, Cicilie, Cicily, Cile, Cilka, Cilla, Cilli, Cillie, Cilly

Cidney (French) a form of Sydney.
Cidnee, Cidni, Cidnie

Cielo (Latin) she who is celestial.

Ciera, Cierra (Irish) forms of Ciara.
Ceira, Cierah, Ciere, Cieria, Cierrah, Cierre, Cierria, Cierro

Cilji (Indian) lovely girl.

Cinderella (French, English) little cinder girl. Literature: a fairy tale heroine.
Cindella

Cindy 🅖 (Greek) moon. (Latin) a familiar form of Cynthia. See also Sindy.
Cindee, Cindi, Cindie, Cyndi

Cinthia, Cinthya (Greek) forms of Cynthia.
Cinthiya, Cintia

Cíntia (Portuguese) a form of Cynthia.

Cipriana (Greek) from Cyprus.

Ciprina (Spanish) blessed by the goddess of love.

Cira (Spanish) a form of Cyrilla.

Circe (Greek) from Greek mythology.

Cirenia, Cirinea (Greek) native of Cyrene, Libya.

Ciri (Greek) lady-like.

Ciríaca (Spanish) she who is the property of the Lord; belonging to God.

Cirila (Greek) great king or Almighty One.

Cissy (American) a familiar form of Cecelia, Cicely.
Cissey, Cissi, Cissie

Citlali (Nahuatl) star.

Claire ☙ 🅖 (French) a form of Clara.
Clair, Klaire, Klarye

Clairissa (Greek) a form of Clarissa.
Clairisa, Clairisse, Claraissa

Clara 🅖 (Latin) clear; bright. Music: Clara Shumann was a famous nineteenth-century German composer. See also Chiara, Klara.
Claira, Claire, Clarabelle, Clare, Claresta, Clarice, Clarie, Clarina, Clarinda, Clarine, Clarissa, Clarita

Clarabelle (Latin) bright and beautiful.
Clarabella, Claribel, Claribell

Clare 🅑 (English) a form of Clara.

Clarence 🅑 (Latin) clear; victorious.

Clarice (Italian) a form of Clara.
Claris, Clarise, Clarisse, Claryce, Cleriese, Klarice, Klarise

Clarie (Latin) a familiar form of Clara.
Clarey, Clari, Clary

Clarisa (Greek) a form of Clarissa.
Claresa, Clarise, Clarisia

Clarissa 🅖 (Greek) brilliant. (Italian) a form of Clara. See also Klarissa.
Clairissa, Clarecia, Claressa, Claresta, Clarisa, Clarissia, Claritza, Clarizza, Clarrisa, Clarrissa, Clerissa

Clarita (Spanish) a form of Clara.
Clairette, Clareta, Claretta, Clarette, Claritza

Clark 🅑 (French) cleric; scholar.

Claude 🅑 (Latin, French) lame.

Claudette (French) a form of Claudia.
Clauddetta

Claudia (Latin) lame. See also Gladys, Klaudia.
Claudeen, Claudel, Claudelle, Claudette, Claudex, Claudiana, Claudiane, Claudie, Claudie-Anne, Claudina, Claudine

Claudie 🅖 (Latin) a form of Claudia.
Claudee

Claudio 🅑 (Italian) a form of Claude.

Clayton 🅑 (English) town built on clay.

Clea (Greek) a form of Cleo, Clio.

Clementine (Latin) merciful.
Clemence, Clemencia, Clemencie, Clemency,
Clementia, Clementina, Clemenza, Clemette

Clemira (Arabic) illuminated, brilliant
princess.

Clena (Marshallese) to arrive at the burial
ground.

Cleo (Greek) a short form of Cleopatra.
Chleo, Clea

Cleodora (Greek) she who represents the gift
of God.

Cleofe (Greek) she who shows signs of glory.

Cleone (Greek) famous.
Cleonie, Cleonna, Cliona

Cleopatra (Greek) her father's fame. History:
a great Egyptian queen.
Cleo

Cleta (Greek) illustrious.

Clidia (Greek) agitated in the sea.

Clifton **B** (English) cliff town.

Clio (Greek) proclaimer; glorifier. Mythology:
the Muse of history.
Clea

Clío (Greek) a form of Clio.

Clitemestra (Greek) Mythology: a form of
Clytemnestra, the daughter of Tyndareus
and Leda.

Cloe (Greek) a form of Chloe.
Clo, Cloei, Cloey, Cloie

Clorinda (Greek) fresh, healthy-looking, and
vital.

Clotilda (German) heroine.

Clotilde (Teutonic) illustrious warrior full of
wisdom.

Clovis (Teutonic) illustrious warrior full of
wisdom.

Coco **G** (Spanish) coconut. See also Koko.

Codey **B** (English) a form of Codi, Cody.

Codi **BG** (English) cushion. See also Kodi.
Coady, Codee, Codey, Codia, Codie

Codie **B** (English) a form of Codi, Cody.

Cody **B** (English) cushion.

Colby **B** (English) coal town. Geography: a
region in England known for cheese-
making.
Cobi, Cobie, Colbi, Colbie

Cole **B** (Irish) a short form of Colleen.

Coleman **B** (Latin) cabbage farmer.
(English) coal miner.

Coleta (French) victory of the people.

Colette (Greek, French) a familiar form of
Nicole.
Coe, Coetta, Coletta, Collet, Collete, Collett,
Colletta, Collette, Kolette, Kollette

Colin **B** (Irish) young cub. (Greek) a short
form of Nicholas (see Boys' Names).

Colleen (Irish) girl. See also Kolina.
Coe, Coel, Cole, Coleen, Colene, Coley,
Coline, Colleene, Collen, Collene, Collie,
Collina, Colline, Colly

Collin **B** (Scottish) a form of Colin.

Collina (Irish) a form of Colleen.
Colena, Colina, Colinda

Collipal (Mapuche) colored star.

Coloma, Columbia (Spanish) forms of
Colomba.

Colomba (Latin) dove.

Colt **B** (English) young horse; frisky. A short
form of Colton.

Colton **B** (English) coal town.

Comemaulig (Chamorro) getting better.

Concepción (Latin) she who conceives;
related to the virginal miracle of Jesus'
mother.

Concetta (Italian) pure.
Concettina, Conchetta

Conchita (Spanish) conception.
Chita, Conceptia, Concha, Conciana

Concordia (Latin) harmonious. Mythology:
the goddess governing the peace after war.
Con, Cordae, Cordaye

Conejo (Chamorro) what was caught.

Conexo (Chamorro) a form of Conejo.

Conner **B** (Scottish, Irish) a form of
Connor.

Connie **G** (Latin) a familiar form of
Constance.
Con, Connee, Conni, Conny, Konnie, Konny

Connie-Kim (Vietnamese) pearls.

Connor **B** (Scottish) wise. (Irish) praised;
exhalted.
Connar, Conner, Connery, Conor

Conor B (Scottish, Irish) a form of Connor.

Consolación (Latin) consolation.

Constance (Latin) constant; firm. History: Constance Motley was the first African-American woman to be appointed as a U.S. federal judge. See also Konstance, Kosta.
Connie, Constancia, Constancy, Constanta, Constantia, Constantina, Constantine, Constanza, Constynse

Constanza (Spanish) a form of Constance.
Constanz, Constanze

Consuelo (Spanish) consolation. Religion: Nuestra Señora del Consuelo Our Lady of Consolation is a name for the Virgin Mary.
Consolata, Consuela, Consuella, Consula, Conzuelo, Konsuela, Konsuelo

Cooper B (English) barrel maker.

Cora (Greek) maiden. Mythology: Kore is another name for Persephone, the goddess of the underworld. See also Kora.
Corah, Coralee, Coretta, Corissa, Corey, Corra

Corabelle (American) a combination of Cora + Belle.
Corabel, Corabella

Coral (Latin) coral. See also Koral.
Coraal, Corral

Coralee (American) a combination of Cora + Lee.
Coralea, Cora-Lee, Coralena, Coralene, Coraley, Coralie, Coraline, Coraly, Coralyn, Corella, Corilee, Koralie

Coralie (American) a form of Coralee.
Corali, Coralia, Coralina, Coralynn, Coralynne

Corazon (Spanish) heart.

Corbin B (Latin) raven.
Corbe, Corbi, Corby, Corbyn, Corbynn

Cordasha (American) a combination of Cora + Dasha.

Cordelia (Latin) warm-hearted. (Welsh) sea jewel. See also Delia, Della.
Cordae, Cordelie, Cordett, Cordette, Cordi, Cordilia, Cordilla, Cordula, Kordelia, Kordula

Cordi (Welsh) a short form of Cordelia.
Cordey, Cordia, Cordie, Cordy

Coretta (Greek) a familiar form of Cora.
Coreta, Corette, Correta, Corretta, Corrette, Koretta, Korretta

Corey, Cory B (Irish) from the hollow. (Greek) familiar forms of Cora. See also Kori.
Coree, Cori, Correy, Correye, Corry

Cori G (Irish) a form of Corey.

Coriann, Corianne (American) combinations of Cori + Ann, Cori + Anne.
Corian, Coriane, Cori-Ann, Corri, Corrie-Ann, Corrianne, Corrie-Anne

Corie, Corrie (Irish) forms of Corey.

Corina, Corinna (Greek) familiar forms of Corinne. See also Korina.
Coreena, Coriana, Corianna, Corinda, Correna, Corrinna, Coryna

Corinne (Greek) maiden.
Coreen, Coren, Corin, Corina, Corine, Corinee, Corinn, Corinna, Corrina, Coryn, Corynn, Corynne

Corissa (Greek) a familiar form of Cora.
Coresa, Coressa, Corisa, Coryssa, Korissa

Corliss (English) cheerful; goodhearted.
Corlisa, Corlise, Corlissa, Corly, Korliss

Cornelia (Latin) horn colored. See also Kornelia, Nelia, Nellie.
Carna, Carniella, Corneilla, Cornela, Cornelie, Cornella, Cornelle, Cornie, Cornilear, Cornisha, Corny

Cornelius B (Greek) cornel tree. (Latin) horn colored.

Corrina, Corrine (Greek) forms of Corinne.
Correen, Corren, Corrin, Corrinn, Corrinna, Corrinne, Corrinne, Corryn

Cortney G (English) a form of Courtney.
Cortne, Cortnea, Cortnee, Cortneia, Cortni, Cortnie, Cortny, Cortnye, Corttney

Cosette (French) a familiar form of Nicole.
Cosetta, Cossetta, Cossette, Cozette

Coty B (French) slope, hillside.

Courtenay (English) a form of Courtney.
Courtaney, Courtany, Courteney, Courteny

Courtnee, Courtnie (English) forms of Courtney.
Courtne, Courtnée, Courtnei, Courtneigh, Courtni, Courtnii

Courtney G (English) from the court. See also Kortney, Kourtney.
Cortney, Courtena, Courtenay, Courtene, Courtnae, Courtnay, Courtnee, Courtny, Courtonie

Covadonga (Spanish) large cave that is close to Asturias, which is the scene of the Spanish avocation of the Virgin Mary.

Craig B (Irish, Scottish) crag; steep rock.

Crescencia (Spanish) growth.

Crimilda (German) she fights wearing a helmet.

Crisanta (Spanish) golden flower.

Crisbell (American) a combination of Crista + Belle.
Crisbel, Cristabel

Crispina (Latin) having curly locks of hair.

Crista, Crysta (Italian) forms of Christa.
Cristah

Cristal **G** (Latin) a form of Crystal.
Cristalie, Cristalina, Cristalle, Cristel, Cristela, Cristelia, Cristella, Cristelle, Cristhie, Cristle

Cristen, Cristin (Irish) forms of Christen, Christin. See also Kristin.
Cristan, Cristyn, Crystan, Crysten, Crystin, Crystyn

Cristian **B** (Greek) a form of Christian.

Cristiana (Spanish) Christian, follower of Christ.

Cristina, Cristine (Greek) forms of Christina. See also Kristina.
Cristiona, Cristy

Cristy (English) a familiar form of Cristina. A form of Christy. See also Kristy.
Cristey, Cristi, Cristie, Crysti, Crystie, Crysty

Cruz **B** (Portuguese, Spanish) cross.

Cruzita (Spanish) a form of Cruz.

Crystal **G** (Latin) clear, brilliant glass. See also Kristal, Krystal.
Christal, Chrystal, Chrystal-Lynn, Chrystel, Cristal, Crystala, Crystale, Crystalee, Crystalin, Crystall, Crystalle, Crystaly, Crystel,

Crystela, Crystelia, Crystelle, Crysthelle, Crystl, Crystle, Crystol, Crystole, Crystyl

Crystalin (Latin) crystal pool.
Crystal-Ann, Cristalanna, Crystal-Anne, Cristalina, Cristallina, Cristalyn, Crystallynn, Crystallynne, Cristilyn, Crystalina, Crystal-Lee, Crystal-Lynn, Crystalyn, Crystalynn

Crystina (Greek) a form of Christina.
Crystin, Crystine, Crystyn, Crystyna, Crystyne

Cui (Chinese) resplendent.

Cullen **B** (Irish) beautiful.

Curipán (Mapuche) brave lioness; black mountain; valorous soul.

Curran **B** (Irish) heroine.
Cura, Curin, Curina, Curinna

Curtis **B** (Latin) enclosure. (French) courteous.

Custodia (Latin) guardian angel.

Cuyen (Mapuche) moon.

Cybele (Greek) a form of Sybil.
Cybel, Cybil, Cybill, Cybille

Cydney (French) a form of Sydney.
Cydne, Cydnee, Cydnei, Cydni, Cydnie

Cyerra (Irish) a form of Ciara.
Cyera, Cyerria

Cyndi (Greek) a form of Cindy.
Cynda, Cyndal, Cyndale, Cyndall, Cyndee, Cyndel, Cyndia, Cyndie, Cyndle, Cyndy

Cynthia **G** (Greek) moon. Mythology: another name for Artemis, the moon goddess. See also Hyacinth, Kynthia.
Cindy, Cinthia, Cyneria, Cynethia, Cynithia, Cynthea, Cynthiana, Cynthiann, Cynthie,

Cynthria, Cynthy, Cynthya, Cyntia, Cyntreia, Cythia, Synthia

Cyrilla (Greek) noble.
Cerelia, Cerella, Cira, Cirilla, Cyrella, Cyrille

Cyteria (Greek) goddess of love.

Czaee (Indian) name of a flower.

D

D **B** (American) an initial used as a first name.

Da (Chinese) eldest.

Dabria (Latin) name of an angel.

Dacey **G** (Irish) southerner. (Greek) a familiar form of Candace.
Dacee, Dacei, Daci, Dacia, Dacie, Dacy, Daicee, Daici, Daicie, Daicy, Daycee, Daycie, Daycy

Dacia (Irish) a form of Dacey.
Daciah

Dadau (Chamorro) fierce, ferocious.

Daddi (Chamorro) young coconut.

Dae (English) day. See also Dai.

Daeja (French) a form of Déja.
Daejah, Daejia

Daelynn (American) a combination of Dae + Lynn.
Daeleen, Daelena, Daelin, Daelyn, Daelynne

Daeshandra (American) a combination of Dae + Shandra.
Daeshandria, Daeshaundra, Daeshaundria, Daeshawndra, Daeshawndria, Daeshondra, Daeshondria

Daeshawna (American) a combination of Dae + Shawna.
Daeshan, Daeshaun, Daeshauna, Daeshavon, Daeshawn, Daeshawntia, Daeshon, Daeshona

Daeshonda (American) a combination of Dae + Shonda.
Daeshanda, Daeshawnda

Dafny (American) a form of Daphne.
Dafany, Daffany, Daffie, Daffy, Dafna, Dafne, Dafney, Dafnie

Dagmar (German) glorious.
Dagmara

Dagny (Scandinavian) day.
Dagna, Dagnanna, Dagne, Dagney, Dagnie

Dago (Chamorro) a type of plant.

Dahlia (Scandinavian) valley. Botany: a perennial flower. See also Daliah.
Dahliah, Dahlya, Dahlye

Dai 🄶 (Japanese) great. See also Dae.
Day, Daye

Daija, Daijah (French) forms of Déja.
Daijaah, Daijea, Daijha, Daijhah, Dayja

Daila (Latin) beautiful like a flower.

Daisha (American) a form of Dasha.
Daesha, Daishae, Daishia, Daishya, Daisia

Daisy (English) day's eye. Botany: a white and yellow flower.
Daisee, Daisey, Daisi, Daisia, Daisie, Dasey, Dasi, Dasie, Dasy, Daysi, Deisy

Daja, Dajah (French) forms of Déja.
Dajae, Dajai, Daje, Dajha, Dajia

Dakayla (American) a combination of the prefix Da + Kayla.
Dakala, Dakila

Dakira (American) a combination of the prefix Da + Kira.
Dakara, Dakaria, Dakarra, Dakirah, Dakyra

Dakota 🄱 (Native American) a tribal name.
Dakkota, Dakoda, Dakotah, Dakotha, Dakotta, Dekoda, Dekota, Dekotah, Dekotha

Dakotah 🄱 (Native American) a form of Dakota.

Daksha (Indian) the Earth; wife of Lord Shiva.

Dakshata (Indian) skill.

Dalaja (Indian) honey.

Dale 🄱 (English) valley.
Dael, Dahl, Daile, Daleleana, Dalena, Dalina, Dayle

Dalia, Daliah (Hebrew) branch. See also Dahlia.
Daelia, Dailia, Daleah, Daleia, Dalialah, Daliyah

Dalila (Swahili) gentle.
Dalela, Dalida, Dalilah, Dalilia

Dalisha (American) a form of Dallas.
Dalisa, Dalishea, Dalishia, Dalishya, Dalisia, Dalissia

Dallas 🄱 (Irish) wise.
Dalis, Dalise, Dalisha, Dalisse, Dallace, Dallis, Dallise, Dallus, Dallys, Dalyce, Dalys

Dallen 🄱 (English) a form of Dallan (see Boys' Names).

Dallyn 🄱 (English) pride's people.

Dalma (Spanish) a form of Dalmacia.

Dalmacia (Latin) native of Dalmacia.

Dalmira (Teutonic) illustrious; respected for her noble ancestry.

Dalton 🄱 (English) town in the valley.

Damaris 🄶 (Greek) gentle girl. See also Maris.
Dama, Damar, Damara, Damarius, Damary, Damarylis, Damarys, Dameress, Dameris, Damiris, Dammaris, Dammeris, Damris, Demaras, Demaris

Damasia (Spanish) a form of Dalmacia.

Damayanti (Indian) wife of Nala.

Damian 🄱 (Greek) tamer; soother.

Damiana (Greek) a form of Damian.
Daimenia, Daimiona, Damia, Damiann, Damianna, Damianne, Damien, Damienne, Damiona, Damon, Demion

Damica (French) friendly.
Damee, Dameeka, Dameka, Damekah, Damicah, Damicia, Damicka, Damie, Damieka, Damika, Damikah, Damyka, Demeeka, Demeka, Demekah, Demica, Demicah

Damien 🄱 (Greek) a form of Damian.

Damini (Indian) lightning.

Damita (Spanish) small noblewoman.
Damee, Damesha, Dameshia, Damesia,
Dametia, Dametra, Dametrah

Damon B (Greek) a form of Damian.

Damonica (American) a combination of the
prefix Da + Monica.
Damonec, Damoneke, Damonik, Damonika,
Damonique, Diamoniqua, Diamonique

Damyanti (Indian) beautiful.

Dan B (Vietnamese) yes. (Hebrew) a short
form of Daniel.

Dana G (English) from Denmark; bright as
day.
Daina, Dainna, Danah, Danaia, Danan,
Danarra, Dane, Danean, Danna, Dayna

Danae (Greek) Mythology: the mother of
Perseus.
Danaë, Danay, Danayla, Danays, Danai,
Danea, Danee, Dannae, Denae, Denee

Dánae (Greek) a form of Danae.

Danalyn (American) a combination of Dana
+ Lynn.
Danalee, Donaleen

Danas (Spanish) a form of Dana.

D'andre B (French) a form of Deandre.

Dane B   (English) a form of Dana.

Daneil (Hebrew) a form of Danielle.
Daneal, Daneala, Daneale, Daneel, Daneela,
Daneila

Danella (American) a form of Danielle.
Danayla, Danela, Danelia, Danelle, Danna,
Donella, Donnella

Danelle (Hebrew) a form of Danielle.
Danael, Danalle, Danel, Danele, Danell,
Danella, Donelle, Donnelle

Danesha, Danisha (American) forms of
Danessa.
Daneisha, Daneshia, Daniesha, Danishia

Danessa (American) a combination of
Danielle + Vanessa. See also Doneshia.
Danasia, Danesa, Danesha, Danessia,
Daniesa, Danisa, Danissa

Danessia (American) a form of Danessa.
Danesia, Danieshia, Danisia, Danissia

Danette (American) a form of Danielle.
Danetra, Danett, Danetta, Donnita

Dani (Hebrew) a familiar form of Danielle.
Danee, Danie, Danne, Dannee, Danni,
Dannie, Danny, Dannye, Dany

Dania, Danya (Hebrew) short forms of Danielle.
Daniah, Danja, Dannia, Danyae

Danica, Danika G (Slavic) morning star.
(Hebrew) forms of Danielle.
Daneca, Daneeka, Daneekah, Danicah,
Danicka, Danieka, Danikah, Danikla,
Danneeka, Dannica, Dannika, Dannikah,
Danyka, Denica, Donica, Donika, Donnaica,
Donnica, Donnika

Danice (American) a combination of
Danielle + Janice.
Donice

Daniel B (Hebrew, French) God is my
judge.

Daniela (Italian) a form of Danielle.
Daniellah, Dannilla, Danijela

Danielan (Spanish) a form of Danielle.

Daniella (English) a form of Dana.
Danka, Danniella, Danyella

Danielle G (Hebrew, French) a form of
Daniel.
Daneen, Daneil, Daneille, Danelle, Dani,
Danial, Danialle, Danica, Daniel, Daniela,
Danielan, Daniele, Danielka, Daniell,
Daniella, Danilka, Danille, Danit, Dannielle,
Danyel, Donniella

Danille (American) a form of Danielle.
Danila, Danile, Danilla, Dannille

Danit (Hebrew) a form of Danielle.
Danett, Danis, Danisha, Daniss, Danita,
Danitra, Danitrea, Danitria, Danitza, Daniz

Danna (Hebrew) a short form of Danella.
Dannah

Dannielle (Hebrew, French) a form of
Danielle.
Danniel, Danniele, Danniell

Danny B (Hebrew) a form of Dani.

Dante, Danté B (Latin) lasting, enduring.

Dany B (Hebrew) a form of Dani.

Danyel G (American) a form of Danielle.
Daniyel, Danyae, Danyail, Danyaile, Danyal,
Danyale, Danyea, Danyele, Danyiel, Danyle,
Donnyale, Donyale

Danyell, Danyelle (American) forms of
Danyel.
Danyielle, Donnyell, Donyell

Dao (Vietnamese) golden girl.

Daphne (Greek) laurel tree.
Dafny, Daphane, Daphany, Dapheney,
Daphna, Daphnee, Daphnique, Daphnit,
Daphny

Daphnee (Greek) a form of Daphne.
*Daphaney, Daphanie, Daphney, Daphni,
Daphnie*

Dara 🄶 (Hebrew) compassionate.
*Dahra, Daira, Dairah, Darah, Daraka, Daralea,
Daralee, Daraleigh, Daralie, Daravie, Darda,
Darice, Darisa, Darissa, Darja, Darra, Darrah*

Darby 🄶 (Irish) free. (Scandinavian) deer
estate.
*Darb, Darbe, Darbee, Darbi, Darbie, Darbra,
Darbye*

Darcelle (French) a form of Darci.
Darcel, Darcell, Darcella, Darselle

Darci, Darcy 🄶 (Irish) dark. (French)
fortress.
*Darcee, Darcelle, Darcey, Darcie, Darsey,
Darsi, Darsie*

Daria (Greek) wealthy.
Dari, Daría, Dariya, Darria, Darya, Daryia

Darian, Darrian 🄱🄶 (Greek) forms of Daron.
*Dariana, Dariane, Dariann, Darianna,
Darianne, Dariyan, Dariyanne, Darriana,
Darriane, Darriann, Darrianna, Darrianne,
Derrian, Driana*

Darielle (French) a form of Daryl.
Dariel, Dariela, Dariell, Darriel, Darrielle

Darien, Darrien 🄱 (Greek) forms of Daron.
Dariene, Darienne, Darriene

Darika (Indian) maiden.

Darilynn (American) a form of Darlene.
*Daralin, Daralyn, Daralynn, Daralynne,
Darilin, Darilyn, Darilynne, Darlin, Darlyn,
Darlynn, Darlynne, Darylin, Darylyn, Darylynn,
Darylynne*

Darin 🄱 (Irish) a form of Darren.

Darion, Darrion 🄱 (Irish) forms of Daron.
*Dariona, Darione, Darionna, Darionne,
Darriona, Darrionna*

Darius 🄱 (Greek) wealthy.

Darla (English) a short form of Darlene.
*Darlecia, Darli, Darlice, Darlie, Darlis, Darly,
Darlys*

Darlene (French) little darling. See also
Daryl.
*Darilynn, Darla, Darlean, Darlee, Darleen,
Darleene, Darlena, Darlenia, Darlenne,
Darletha, Darlin, Darline, Darling, Darlyn,
Darlynn, Darlynne*

Darnee (Irish) a familiar form of Darnelle.

Darnell 🄱 (English) a form of Darnelle.

Darnelle (English) hidden place.
*Darnee, Darnel, Darnell, Darnella, Darnesha,
Darnetta, Darnette, Darnice, Darniece,
Darnita, Darnyell*

Darnesha, Darnisha (American) forms of
Darnelle.
*Darneisha, Darneishia, Darneshea,
Darneshia, Darnesia, Darniesha, Darnishia,
Darnisia, Darrenisha*

Daron (Irish) great.
*Darian, Darien, Darion, Daronica, Daronice,
Darron, Daryn*

Darpana (Indian) mirror.

Darrell (English, French) a form of Daryl.

Darren 🄱 (Irish) great. (English) small;
rocky hill.

Darryl 🄱 (English, French) a form of Daryl.

Darselle (French) a form of Darcelle.
Darsel, Darsell, Darsella

Darshana (Indian) observation.

Darshwana (Indian) pure of heart.

Daru (Hindi) pine tree.

Daryl 🄱 (English) beloved. (French) a short
form of Darlene.
*Darelle, Darielle, Daril, Darilynn, Darrel,
Darrell, Darrelle, Darreshia, Darryl, Darryll,
Daryll, Darylle*

Daryn (Greek) gifts. (Irish) great.
Daron, Daryan, Daryne, Darynn, Darynne

Dasha, Dasia (Russian) forms of Dorothy.
*Daisha, Dashae, Dashenka, Dashia, Dashiah,
Dasiah, Daysha*

Dashawn 🄱 (American) a form of
Dashawna.

Dashawna (American) a combination of the
prefix Da + Shawna.
*Dashawnna, Dashay, Dashell, Dayshana,
Dayshawnna, Dayshona, Deshawna*

Dashiki (Swahili) loose-fitting shirt worn in
Africa.
Dashi, Dashika, Dashka, Desheka, Deshiki

Dashonda (American) a combination of the
prefix Da + Shonda.
Dashawnda, Dishante

Davalinda (American) a combination of
Davida + Linda.
Davalynda, Davelinda, Davilinda, Davylinda

Davalynda (American) a form of Davalinda.
Davelynda, Davilynda, Davylynda

Davalynn (American) a combination of
Davida + Lynn.
Davalin, Davalyn, Davalynne, Davelin,
Davelyn, Davelynn, Davelynne, Davilin,
Davilyn, Davilynn, Davilynne, Dayleen, Devlyn

Dave B (Hebrew) a short form of David,
Davis.

David B (Hebrew) beloved.

Davida (Hebrew) a form of David. See also
Vida.
Daveta, Davetta, Davette, Davika, Davita

Davin B (Scottish) a form of Davina.

Davina (Scottish) a form of Davida. See also
Vina.
Dava, Davannah, Davean, Davee, Daveen,
Daveena, Davene, Daveon, Davey, Davi,
Daviana, Davie, Davin, Davinder, Davine,
Davineen, Davinia, Davinna, Davonna, Davria,
Devean, Deveen, Devene, Devina

Davion B (Scottish, English) a form of
Davonna.

Davis B (American) a form of Davisha.

Davisha (American) a combination of the
prefix Da + Aisha.
Daveisha, Davesia, Davis, Davisa

Davon B (Scottish, English) a short form of
Davonna.

Davonna (Scottish, English) a form of
Davina, Devonna.
Davion, Daviona, Davionna, Davon, Davona,
Davonda, Davone, Davonia, Davonne,
Davonnia

Davonte B (American) a combination of
Davon + the suffix Te.

Dawn G (English) sunrise, dawn.
Dawana, Dawandrea, Dawanna, Dawin,
Dawna, Dawne, Dawnee, Dawnetta,
Dawnisha, Dawnlynn, Dawnn, Dawnrae

Dawna (English) a form of Dawn.
Dawnna, Dawnya

Dawnisha (American) a form of Dawn.
Dawnesha, Dawni, Dawniell, Dawnielle,
Dawnisia, Dawniss, Dawnita, Dawnnisha,
Dawnysha, Dawnysia

Dawnyelle (American) a combination of
Dawn + Danielle.
Dawnele, Dawnell, Dawnelle, Dawnyel,
Dawnyella

Dawson B (English) child of David.

Da-Xia (Chinese) big hero.

Dayamayee (Indian) kind.

Dayamayi, Dayanita (Indian) merciful.

Dayana (Latin) a form of Diana.
Dayanara, Dayani, Dayanna, Dayanne,
Dayanni, Deyanaira, Dyani, Dyanna, Dyia

Dayanira (Greek) she stirs up great passions.

Dayita (Indian) beloved.

Dayle (English) a form of Dale.
Dayla, Daylan, Daylea, Daylee

Dayna (Scandinavian) a form of Dana.
Daynah, Dayne, Daynna, Deyna

Daysha (American) a form of Dasha.
Daysa, Dayshalie, Daysia, Deisha

Daysi, Deysi (English) forms of Daisy.
Daysee, Daysia, Daysie, Daysy, Deysia, Deysy

Dayton B (English) day town; bright, sunny
town.

Daytona (English) a form of Dayton.
Daytonia

De B (Chinese) virtuous.

Dean B (French) leader. (English) valley.

Deana G (Latin) divine. (English) a form
of Dean.
Deanah, Deane, Deanielle, Deanisha,
Deanna, Deeana, Deeann, Deeanna, Deena

Deandra (American) a combination of Dee
+ Andrea.
Dandrea, Deandre, Deandré, Deandrea,
Deandree, Deandreia, Deandria, Deanndra,
Deaundra, Deaundria, Deeandra, Deyaneira,
Deondra, Diandra, Diandre, Diandrea,
Diondria, Dyandra

Deandre B (American) a form of Deandra,
Deanna.

Deangela (Italian) a combination of the
prefix De + Angela.
Deangala, Deangalique, Deangle

Deanna G (Latin) a form of Deana, Diana.
Deaana, Deahana, Deandra, Deandre,
Déanna, Deannia, Deeanna, Deena

Deanne (Latin) a form of Diane.
Deahanne, Deane, Deann, Déanne, Deeann,
Dee-Ann, Deeanne

Debbie (Hebrew) a short form of Deborah.
Debbee, Debbey, Debbi, Debby, Debee, Debi,
Debie

Débora, Déborah (Hebrew) forms of
Deborah.

Deborah ☰ (Hebrew) bee. Bible: a great Hebrew prophetess.
Deb, Debbie, Debbora, Debborah, Deberah, Debor, Debora, Deboran, Deborha, Deborrah, Debra, Debrena, Debrina, Debroah, Devora, Dobra

Debra (American) a form of Deborah.
Debbra, Debbrah, Debrah, Debrea, Debria

Dedra (American) a form of Deirdre.
Deeddra, Deedra, Deedrea, Deedrie

Dedriana (American) a combination of Dedra + Adriana.
Dedranae

Dee (Welsh) black, dark.
De, Dea, Deah, Dede, Dedie, Deea, Deedee, Dee Dee, Didi

Deeba (Indian) silk.

Deena (American) a form of Deana, Dena, Dinah.

Deepa, Deepal (Indian) light.

Deepabali, Deepamala, Deepavali (Indian) row of lamps.

Deepakala (Indian) evening time; the time to light lamps.

Deepali (Indian) collection of lamps.

Deepanwita (Indian) lit by lamps.

Deepaprabha (Indian) light of lamps.

Deepashikha (Indian) the flame of a lamp.

Deepjyoti (Indian) the light of the lamp.

Deepshika, Deepika, Dipashri (Indian) lamp.

Deepta (Indian) luminous, glowing, bright.

Deepti (Indian) full of light.

Deeptikana (Indian) a beam of light.

Deeptimoyee (Indian) lustrous.

Deidamia (Greek) she who is patient in battle.

Deidra, Deidre (Irish) forms of Deirdre.
Deidrah, Deidrea, Deidrie, Diedra, Diedre, Dierdra

Deina (Spanish) religious holiday.

Deion ☰ (Greek) a form of Dion.

Deirdre (Irish) sorrowful; wanderer.
Dedra, Deerdra, Deerdre, Deidra, Deidre, Deirdree, Didi, Diedra, Dierdre, Diérdre, Dierdrie

Deisy (English) a form of Daisy.
Deisi, Deissy

Deitra (Greek) a short form of Demetria.
Deetra, Detria

Deja ☰ (French) a form of Déja.

Déja (French) before.
Daeja, Daija, Deejay, Dejae, Déjah, Dejai, Dejanae, Dejanelle, Dejon

Dejanae (French) a form of Déja.
Dajahnae, Dajona, Dejana, Dejanah, Dejanae, Dejanai, Dejanay, Dejane, Dejanea, Dejanee, Dejanna, Dejannaye, Dejena, Dejonae

Dejanira (Greek) destroyer of men.

Dejon (French) a form of Déja.
Daijon, Dajan, Dejone, Dejonee, Dejonelle, Dejonna

Deka (Somali) pleasing.
Dekah

Delacy (American) a combination of the prefix De + Lacy.
Delaceya

Delainey (Irish) a form of Delaney.
Delaine, Delainee, Delaini, Delainie, Delainy

Delana (German) noble protector.
Dalanna, Dalayna, Daleena, Dalena, Dalenna, Dalina, Dalinda, Dalinna, Delaina, Delania, Delanya, Delayna, Deleena, Delena, Delenya, Delina, Dellaina

Delaney ☰ (Irish) descendant of the challenger. (English) a form of Adeline.
Dalaney, Dalania, Dalene, Daleney, Daline, Del, Delainey, Delane, Delanee, Delanie, Delany, Delayne, Delayney, Delaynie, Deleani, Déline, Della, Dellaney

Delanie (Irish) a form of Delaney.
Delani

Delfina (Greek) a form of Delphine. (Spanish) dolphin.
Delfeena, Delfine

Delia (Greek) visible; from Delos, Greece. (German, Welsh) a short form of Adelaide, Cordelia. Mythology: a festival of Apollo held in ancient Greece.
Dehlia, Delea, Deli, Deliah, Deliana, Delianne, Delinda, Dellia, Dellya, Delya

Delicia (English) delightful.
Delecia, Delesha, Delice, Delisa, Delise, Delisha, Delishia, Delisiah, Delya, Delys, Delyse, Delysia, Doleesha

Delilah (Hebrew) brooder. Bible: the companion of Samson. See also Lila.
Dalialah, Dalila, Daliliah, Delila, Delilia

Della (English) a short form of Adelaide, Cordelia, Delaney.
Del, Dela, Dell, Delle, Delli, Dellie, Dells

Delma (German) noble protector.

Delmara (Latin) of the sea.

Delmira (Spanish) a form of Dalmira.

Delores (Spanish) a form of Dolores.
Delora, Delore, Deloria, Delories, Deloris, Delorise, Delorita, Delsie

Delphine **G** (Greek) from Delphi, Greece. See also Delfina.
Delpha, Delphe, Delphi, Delphia, Delphina, Delphinia, Delvina

Delsie (English) a familiar form of Delores.
Delsa, Delsey, Delza

Delta (Greek) door. Linguistics: the fourth letter in the Greek alphabet. Geography: a triangular land mass at the mouth of a river.
Delte, Deltora, Deltoria, Deltra

Demetria **G** (Greek) cover of the earth. Mythology: Demeter was the Greek goddess of the harvest.
Deitra, Demeta, Demeteria, Demetra, Demetriana, Demetrianna, Demetrias, Demetrice, Demetriona, Demetris, Demetrish, Demetrius, Demi, Demita, Demitra, Demitria, Dymitra

Demetrius **B** (Greek) a form of Demetria.

Demi (French) half. (Greek) a short form of Demetria.
Demia, Demiah, Demii, Demmi, Demmie, Demy

Demofila (Greek) friend of the village.

Den (Japanese) bequest from ancestors.

Dena (English, Native American) valley. (Hebrew) a form of Dinah. See also Deana.
Deane, Deena, Deeyn, Denae, Denah, Dene, Denea, Deney, Denna, Deonna

Denae (Hebrew) a form of Dena.
Denaé, Denay, Denee, Deneé

Deng (Chinese) light.

Deni (French) a short form of Denise.
Deney, Denie, Denni, Dennie, Denny, Dinnie, Dinny

Denica, Denika (Slavic) forms of Danica.
Denikah, Denikia

Denis **B** (Greek) a form of Dennis.

Denisa (Spanish) god of wine.

Denise **G** (French) Mythology: follower of Dionysus, the god of wine.
Danice, Danise, Denese, Deni, Denice, Denicy, Deniece, Denisha, Denisse, Denize, Dennise, Dennys, Denyce, Denys, Denyse

Denisha (American) a form of Denise.
Deneesha, Deneichia, Deneisha, Deneishea, Denesha, Deneshia, Deniesha, Denishia

Denisse (French) a form of Denise.
Denesse, Denissa

Dennis **B** (Greek) Mythology: a follower of Dionysus, the god of wine.

Denver **B** (English) green valley. Geography: the capital of Colorado.

Denzel **B** (Cornish) a form of Denzell (see Boys' Names).

Deon **B** (English) a short form of Deonna.

Deonilde (German) she who fights.

Deonna (English) a form of Dena.
Deona, Deonah, Deondra, Deonne

Deonte **B** (American) a form of Deontae (see Boys' Names).

Dep (Vietnamese) chrysanthemum.

Derek **B** (German) a short form of Theodoric (see Boys' Names).

Derika (German) ruler of the people.
Dereka, Derekia, Derica, Dericka, Derrica, Derricka, Derrika

Derrick **B** (German) ruler of the people. A form of Derek.

Derry **BG** (Irish) redhead.
Deri, Derie

Deryn (Welsh) bird.
Derien, Derienne, Derion, Derin, Deron, Derren, Derrin, Derrine, Derrion, Derriona, Deryne

Desarae (French) a form of Desiree.
Desara, Desarai, Desaraie, Desaray, Desare, Desaré, Desarea, Desaree, Desarie, Dezarae

Desdemona (Greek) she who is very unfortunate; unhappy one.

Deserae, Desirae (French) forms of Desiree.
Desera, Deserai, Deseray, Desere, Deseree, Deseret, Deseri, Deserie, Deserrae, Deserray, Deserré, Dessirae, Dezeray, Dezere, Dezerea, Dezrae, Dezyrae

Deshawn **B** (American) a form of Deshawna.

Deshawna (American) a combination of the prefix De + Shawna.
Dashawna, Deshan, Deshane, Deshaun, Deshawn, Desheania, Deshona, Deshonna

Deshawnda (American) a combination of the prefix De + Shawnda.
Deshanda, Deshandra, Deshaundra, Deshawndra, Deshonda

Desi (French) a short form of Desiree.
Désir, Desira, Dezi, Dezia, Dezzia, Dezzie

Desideria (French) desired or longed for.

Desiha (Indian) happy; lemon.

Desiree (French) desired, longed for. See also Dessa.
Chesarey, Desarae, Deserae, Desi, Desirae, Desirah, Desirai, Desiray, Desire, Desirea, Desireah, Desirée, Désirée, Desirey, Desiri, Desray, Desree, Dessie, Dessire, Dezarae, Dezirae, Deziree

Dessa (Greek) wanderer. (French) a form of Desiree.

Desta (Ethiopian) happy. (French) a short form of Destiny.
Desti, Destie, Desty

Destany (French) a form of Destiny.
Destanee, Destaney, Destani, Destanie, Destannee, Destannie

Destin 🄑 (French) a form of Destiny.

Destina (Spanish) fate.

Destinee, Destini, Destinie (French) forms of Destiny.
Desteni, Destiana, Destine, Destinée, Destnie

Destiney (French) a form of Destiny.

Destiny ⚘ 🄖 (French) fate.
Desnine, Desta, Destany, Destenee, Destenie, Desteny, Destin, Destinee, Destiney, Destini, Destinie, Destonie, Destynee, Dezstany

Destynee, Destyni (French) forms of Destiny.
Desty, Destyn, Destyne, Destyne, Destynie

Deva (Hindi) divine.
Deeva

Devahuti (Indian) daughter of Manu.

Devaki, Devki (Indian) the mother of Lord Krishna.

Devan 🄑 (Irish) a form of Devin.
Devana, Devane, Devanee, Devaney, Devani, Devanie, Devann, Devanna, Devannae, Devanne, Devany

Devangana (Indian) celestial maiden.

Devangi, Devyani (Indian) like a goddess.

Devanshi (Indian) divine.

Devashri, Devasree (Indian) divine beauty.

Deven 🄑 (Irish) a form of Devin.

Devera (Spanish) task.

Devi (Hindi) goddess. Religion: the Hindu goddess of power and destruction.

Devin 🄑 (Irish) poet.
Devan, Deven, Devena, Devenje, Deveny, Devine, Devinn, Devinne, Devyn

Devishi (Indian) chief of the goddesses.

Devkanya (Indian) divine damsel.

Devmani (Indian) divine gift.

Devon 🄑 (English) a short form of Devonna. (Irish) a form of Devin.
Deaven, Devion, Devione, Devionne, Devone, Devoni, Devonne

Devonna (English) from Devonshire.
Davonna, Devon, Devona, Devonda, Devondra, Devonia

Devonta 🄑 (American) a combination of Devon + the suffix Ta.

Devonte 🄑 (American) a combination of Devon + the suffix Te.

Devora (Hebrew) a form of Deborah.
Deva, Devorah, Devra, Devrah

Devota (Latin) faithful to God.

Devyn 🄑🄖 (Irish) a form of Devin.
Deveyn, Devyne, Devynn, Devynne

Dewi (Indonesian) goddess.

Dextra (Latin) adroit, skillful.
Dekstra, Dextria

Deyanira (Latin) destroyer of men.

Dezarae, Dezirae, Deziree (French) forms of Desiree.
Dezaraee, Dezarai, Dezaray, Dezare, Dezaree, Dezarey, Dezerie, Deziray, Dezirea, Dezirée, Dezorae, Dezra

Dhanishta (Indian) the name of a nakshatra, a star constellation.

Dhanvanti (Indian) holding wealth.

Dhanya (Indian) thankful; lucky.

Dhanyata (Indian) success; fulfillment.

Dharani, Dharitri (Indian) the Earth.

Dharini, Dharti, Dhatri (Indian) earth.

Dhriti (Indian) patience.

Dhruti (Indian) motion.

Dhruvi (Indian) firm.

Dhuha (Indian) forenoon.

Dhvani (Indian) sound, voice.

Dhyana (Indian) meditation.

Di (Latin) a short form of Diana, Diane.
Dy

Dia (Latin) a short form of Diana, Diane.

Diamond **G** (Latin) precious gem.
Diamantina, Diamon, Diamonda, Diamonde, Diamonia, Diamonique, Diamonte, Diamontina, Dyamond

Diamondra (English) diamond. .

Diana 🌟 **G** (Latin) divine. Mythology: the goddess of the hunt, the moon, and fertility. See also Deanna, Deanne, Dyan.
Daiana, Daianna, Dayana, Dayanna, Di, Dia, Dianah, Dianalyn, Dianarose, Dianatris, Dianca, Diandra, Diane, Dianelis, Diania, Dianielle, Dianita, Dianna, Dianys, Didi

Diane, Dianne (Latin) short forms of Diana.
Deane, Deanne, Deeane, Deeanne, Di, Dia, Diahann, Dian, Diani, Dianie, Diann

Dianna (Latin) a form of Diana.
Diahanna, Diannah

Diantha (Greek) divine flower.
Diandre, Dianthe

Dibech (Palauan) one's beloved.

Die (Chinese) butterfly.

Diedra (Irish) a form of Deirdre.
Didra, Diedre

Diega (Spanish) supplanter.

Diella (Latin) she who adores God.

Diep (Vietnamese) peach blossom.

Digna (Latin) worthy.

Di'isha (Arabic) a form of Aisha.

Diksha (Indian) initiation.

Dilan (Indian) son of the sea.

Dilbelau (Palauan) termite.

Dilber (Indian) lover.

Dilchur (Palauan) to create.

Dillan **B** (Irish) loyal, faithful.
Dillon, Dillyn

Dillon **B** (Irish) a form of Dillan.

Dilngas (Palauan) woman of Palau.

Dilshad (Indian) happy.

Dilsubed (Palauan) laughing girl.

Dilys (Welsh) perfect; true.

Dimitri **B** (Russian) a form of Demetrius.

Dimple (Indian) dimples.

Dina (Hebrew) a form of Dinah.
Dinna, Dyna

Dinah (Hebrew) vindicated. Bible: a daughter of Jacob and Leah.
Dina, Dinnah, Dynah

Ding (Chinese) calm, stable.

Dinka (Swahili) people.

Dinora (Hebrew) avenged or vindicated.

Dinorah (Aramic) she who personifies light.

Diomira (Spanish) a form of Teodomira.

Dion **B** (Greek) a form of Dionne.

Dionisa (Greek) divine.

Dionisia (Greek) lover of wine; blessed by God in face of adversity.

Dionna (Greek) a form of Dionne.
Deona, Deondra, Deonia, Deonna, Deonyia, Diona, Diondra, Diondrea

Dionne (Greek) divine queen. Mythology: Dione was the mother of Aphrodite, the goddess of love.
Deonne, Dion, Dione, Dionee, Dionis, Dionna, Dionte

Dior (French) golden.
Diora, Diore, Diorra, Diorre

Dipali (Indian) lamps.

Dipti (Indian) brightness.

Dirngas (Palauan) ironwood woman.

Disha (Indian) direction.

Dishita (Indian) focus.

Dita (Spanish) a form of Edith.
Ditka, Ditta

Diti (Indian) idea.

Diu (Vietnamese) beautiful.

Diva (Latin) divine.

Divija (Indian) born to perform great things.

Divinia (Latin) divine.
Devina, Devinae, Devinia, Devinie, Devinna, Diveena, Divina, Divine, Diviniea, Divya

Divyata (Indian) divine lights.

Dixie (French) tenth. (English) wall; dike. Geography: a nickname for the American South.
Dix, Dixee, Dixi, Dixy

Diza (Hebrew) joyful.
Ditza, Ditzah, Dizah

Doan Vien (Vietnamese) leaves; type of trees that have red flowers.

Dodie (Hebrew) beloved. (Greek) a familiar form of Dorothy.
Doda, Dode, Dodee, Dodi, Dody

Dolly (American) a short form of Dolores, Dorothy.
Dol, Doll, Dollee, Dolley, Dolli, Dollie, Dollina

Dolon (Indian) scent of a beautiful white flower.

Dolores ◪ (Spanish) sorrowful. Religion: Nuestra Señora de los Dolores
Our Lady of Sorrows
is a name for the Virgin Mary. See also Lola.
Delores, Deloria, Dolly, Dolorcitas, Dolorita, Doloritas

Domenic ◪ (Latin) an alternate form of Dominic.

Domicia (Greek) she who loves her house.

Domiciana (Spanish) a form of Domicia.

Dominga (Latin) a form of Dominica.

Dominic ◪ (Latin) belonging to the Lord.

Domínica (Latin) a form of Dominica.

Dominica, Dominika (Latin) a form of Dominic. See also Mika.
Domenica, Domenika, Domineca, Domineka, Domini, Dominick, Dominicka, Dominique, Dominixe, Domino, Dominyika, Domka, Domnicka, Domonica, Domonice, Domonika

Dominick ◪ (Latin) a form of Dominica.

Dominique, Domonique ◪ (French) forms of Dominica, Dominika.
Domanique, Domeneque, Domenique, Domineque, Dominiqua, Domino, Dominoque, Dominque, Dominuque, Domique, Domminique, Domoniqua

Domino (English) a short form of Dominica, Dominique.

Dominque ◪◪ (French) a form of Dominique.

Domítica (Spanish) a form of Dominga.

Domitila (Latin) she who loves her house.

Domoko (Pohnpeian) a form of Filomena.

Don ◪ (Scottish) a short form of Donald (see Boys' Names).

Dona (English) world leader; proud ruler. (Italian) a form of Donna.
Donae, Donah, Donalda, Donaldina, Donelda, Donellia, Doni

Doña (Italian) a form of Donna.
Donail, Donalea, Donalisa, Donay, Doni, Donia, Donie, Donise, Donitrae

Donata (Latin) gift.
Donatha, Donato, Donatta, Donetta, Donette, Donita, Donnette, Donnita, Donte

Dondi (American) a familiar form of Donna.
Dondra, Dondrea, Dondria

Doneshia, Donisha (American) forms of Danessa.
Donasha, Donashay, Doneisha, Doneishia, Donesha, Donisa, Donisha, Donishia, Donneshia, Donnisha

Dong (Chinese) east; winter.

Donina (Latin) gift of God.

Donna (Italian) lady.
Doña, Dondi, Donnae, Donnalee, Donnalen, Donnay, Donne, Donnell, Donni, Donnie, Donnise, Donny, Dontia, Donya

Donnell ◪ (Italian) a form of Donna.

Donnie ◪ (Italian) a familiar form of Donna.

Donniella (American) a form of Danielle.
Donella, Doniele, Doniell, Doniella, Donielle, Donnella, Donnielle, Donnyella, Donyelle

Donosa (Latin) she who has grace and charm.

Donte ◪ (Latin) a form of Donata.

Dontrell ◪ (American) a form of Dantrell (see Boys' Names).

Dora (Greek) gift. A short form of Adora, Eudora, Pandora, Theodora.
Dorah, Doralia, Doralie, Doralisa, Doraly, Doralynn, Doran, Dorchen, Dore, Dorece, Doree, Doreece, Doreen, Dorelia, Dorella, Dorelle, Doresha, Doressa, Doretta, Dori, Dorielle, Dorika, Doriley, Dorilis, Dorinda, Dorion, Dorita, Doro, Dory

Doralynn (English) a combination of Dora + Lynn.
Doralin, Doralyn, Doralynne, Dorlin

Dorana (Spanish) a form of Dorotea.

Dorbeta (Spanish) reference to the Virgin Mary.

Dorcas (Greek) gazelle.

Doreen (Irish) moody, sullen. (French) golden. (Greek) a form of Dora.
Doreena, Dorena, Dorene, Dorina, Dorine

Dores (Portuguese) a form of Dolores.

Doretta (American) a form of Dora, Dorothy.
Doretha, Dorette, Dorettie

Dori, Dory (American) familiar forms of Dora, Doria, Doris, Dorothy.
Dore, Dorey, Dorie, Dorree, Dorri, Dorrie, Dorry

Doria (Greek) a form of Dorian.
Dori

Dorian **B** (Greek) from Doris, Greece.
Dorean, Doriana, Doriane, Doriann, Dorianna, Dorianne, Dorin, Dorina, Dorriane

Dorinda (Spanish) a form of Dora.

Doris (Greek) sea. Mythology: wife of Nereus and mother of the Nereids or sea nymphs.
Dori, Dorice, Dorisa, Dorise, Dorris, Dorrise, Dorrys, Dory, Dorys

Dorotea (Greek) a form of Dorothea.

Doroteia (Spanish) gift of God.

Dorotéia (Portuguese) a form of Doroteia.

Dorothea (Greek) a form of Dorothy. See also Thea.
Dorethea, Doroteya, Dorotha, Dorothia, Dorotthea, Dorthea, Dorthia

Dorothy (Greek) gift of God. See also Dasha, Dodie, Lolotea, Theodora.
Dasya, Do, Doa, Doe, Dolly, Doortje, Dorathy,
Dordei, Dordi, Doretta, Dori, Dorika, Doritha, Dorka, Dorle, Dorlisa, Doro, Dorolice, Dorosia, Dorota, Dorothea, Dorothee, Dorothi, Dorothie, Dorottya, Dorte, Dortha, Dorthy, Dory, Dosi, Dossie, Dosya, Dottie

Dorrit (Greek) dwelling. (Hebrew) generation.
Dorit, Dorita, Doritt

Dottie, Dotty (Greek) familiar forms of Dorothy.
Dot, Dottee

Douglas **B** (Scottish) dark river, dark stream.

Doyel (Indian) a songbird.

Drake **B** (English) dragon; owner of the inn with the dragon trademark.

Draupadi (Indian) the wife of Pandavas.

Draven **B** (American) a combination of the letter D + Raven.

Drew **B** (Greek) courageous; strong. (Latin) a short form of Drusilla.
Dru, Drue

Drinka (Spanish) a form of Alexandria.
Dreena, Drena, Drina

Drishti, Drishya, Dristi (Indian) sight.

Drusi (Latin) a short form of Drusilla.
Drucey, Druci, Drucie, Drucy, Drusey, Drusie, Drusy

Drusihla (Pohnpeian) a form of Chiyako.

Drusilla (Latin) descendant of Drusus, the strong one. See also Drew.
Drewsila, Drucella, Drucill, Drucilla, Druscilla, Druscille, Drusi

Du (Chinese) sincere.

Duan (Chinese) upright, proper.

Duane **B** (Irish) a form of Dwayne.

Duda (Chamorro) doubtful, dubious.

Duk (Korean) third; soldier; protection.

Dulari (Indian) dear.

Dulce (Latin) sweet.
Delcina, Delcine, Douce, Doucie, Dulcea, Dulcey, Dulci, Dulcia, Dulciana, Dulcibel, Dulcibella, Dulcie, Dulcine, Dulcinea, Dulcy, Dulse, Dulsea

Dulcina, Dulcinia (Spanish) sweet.

Dulcinea (Spanish) sweet. Literature: Don Quixote's love interest.

Dung (Vietnamese) tender, gentle; mellow.

Dunia (Hebrew) life.

Duo (Chinese) much, more, many.

Durba, Durva (Indian) sacred grass.

Durga (Indian) a goddess.

Duscha (Russian) soul; sweetheart; term of endearment.
Duschah, Dusha, Dushenka

Dusti (English) a familiar form of Dustine.
Dustee, Dustie

Dustin **B** (German, English) a form of Dustine.

Dustine (German) valiant fighter. (English) brown rock quarry.
Dusteena, Dusti, Dustin, Dustina, Dustyn

Dusty B (English) a familiar form of Dustine.

Duyen (Vietnamese) happy reunion.

Dvita (Indian) existing in two forms; spiritual.

Dwayne B (Irish) dark.

Dwipavati (Indian) river.

Dyamond, Dymond (Latin) forms of Diamond.
Dyamin, Dyamon, Dyamone, Dymin, Dymon, Dymonde, Dymone, Dymonn

Dyana (Latin) a form of Diana. (Native American) deer.
Dyan, Dyane, Dyani, Dyann, Dyanna, Dyanne

Dylan B (Welsh) sea.
Dylaan, Dylaina, Dylana, Dylane, Dylanee, Dylanie, Dylann, Dylanna, Dylen, Dylin, Dyllan, Dylynn

Dyllis (Welsh) sincere.
Dilys, Dylis, Dylys

Dynasty (Latin) powerful ruler.
Dynastee, Dynasti, Dynastie

Dyshawna (American) a combination of the prefix Dy + Shawna.
Dyshanta, Dyshawn, Dyshonda, Dyshonna

Dyumna (Indian) glorious.

Dyuti (Indian) light.

E G (American) an initial used as a first name.

Ealani (Hawaiian) a form of Ewelani.

Earlene (Irish) pledge. (English) noblewoman.
Earla, Earlean, Earlecia, Earleen, Earlena, Earlina, Earlinda, Earline, Erla, Erlana, Erlene, Erlenne, Erlina, Erlinda, Erline, Erlisha

Eartha (English) earthy.
Ertha

Easter (English) Easter time. History: a name for a child born on Easter.
Eastan, Eastlyn, Easton

Ebe (Greek) youthful like a flower.

Ebil (Palauan) announcement, message.

Ebone, Ebonee (Greek) forms of Ebony.
Abonee, Ebanee, Eboné, Ebonea, Ebonne, Ebonnee

Eboni, Ebonie (Greek) forms of Ebony.
Ebanie, Ebeni, Ebonni, Ebonnie

Ebony G (Greek) a hard, dark wood.
Abony, Eban, Ebanie, Ebany, Ebbony, Ebone, Eboney, Eboni, Ebonie, Ebonique, Ebonisha, Ebonye, Ebonyi

Ecchumati (Indian) a river.

Echa (Chamorro) to give blessing.

Echo (Greek) repeated sound. Mythology: the nymph who pined for the love of Narcissus until only her voice remained.
Echoe, Ecko, Ekko, Ekkoe

Eda (Irish, English) a short form of Edana, Edith.

Edana (Irish) ardent; flame.
Eda, Edan, Edanna

Edda (German) a form of Hedda.
Etta

Eddy B (American) a familiar form of Edwina.
Eady, Eddi, Eddie, Edy

Edelia (Greek) remains young.

Edeline (English) noble; kind.
Adeline, Edelyne, Ediline, Edilyne

Edelma, Edelmira (Teutonic) of noble heritage; known for her noble heritage.

Eden G (Babylonian) a plain. (Hebrew) delightful. Bible: the earthly paradise.
Eaden, Ede, Edena, Edene, Edenia, Edin, Edyn

Edén (Hebrew) a form of Eden.

Edgar B (English) successful spearman.

Edgarda (Teutonic) defends her homes and land with a lance.

Edha (Indian) sacred.

Edie (English) a familiar form of Edith.
Eadie, Edi, Edy, Edye, Eyde, Eydie

Edilia, Edilma (Greek) remains young.

Edith (English) rich gift. See also Dita.
Eadith, Eda, Ede, Edetta, Edette, Edie, Edit, Edita, Edite, Editha, Edithe, Editta, Ediva, Edyta, Edyth, Edytha, Edythe

Edna (Hebrew) rejuvenation. Religion: the wife of Enoch, according to the Book of Enoch.
Adna, Adnisha, Ednah, Edneisha, Edneshia, Ednisha, Ednita, Edona

Edrianna (Greek) a form of Adrienne.
Edria, Edriana, Edrina

Eduarda (Teutonic) attentive guardian of her domain.

Eduardo **B** (Spanish) a form of Edward (see Boys' Names).

Edurne (Basque) snow.

Eduviges (Teutonic) fighting woman.

Eduvijis (German) fortunate in battle.

Edwin **B** (English) prosperous friend.

Edwina (English) a form of Edwin. See also Winnie.
Eddy, Edina, Edweena, Edwena, Edwine, Edwyna, Edwynn

Eesha (Indian) purity.

Effia (Ghanaian) born on Friday.

Effie (Greek) spoken well of. (English) a short form of Alfreda, Euphemia.
Effi, Effia, Effy, Ephie

Efigenia (Greek) woman of strong heritage.

Efigênia (Portuguese) a form of Efigenia.

Egda (Greek) shield-bearer.

Egege (Chamorro) cardinal honey-eating bird.

Egeria (Greek) she who gives encouragement.

Egida (Spanish) born or having lived in Elade, Greece.

Egidia (Greek) warrior with a shield of goatskin.

Egigi (Chamorro) a form of Egege.

Ei (Japanese) flourishing; excellent.

Eiga (Japanese) long river.

Eiko (Japanese) flourishing child.

Eila (Indian) the Earth.

Eileen **G** (Irish) a form of Helen. See also Aileen, Ilene.
Eilean, Eileena, Eileene, Eilena, Eilene, Eiley, Eilie, Eilieh, Eilina, Eiline, Eilleen, Eillen, Eilyn, Eleen, Elene

Eira (Scandinavian) goddess-protectorate of health.

Eiravati (Indian) the Ravi River.

Ekaja (Indian) only child.

Ekanta (Indian) devoted girl.

Ekantika (Indian) singly focused.

Ekaparana (Indian) wife of Himalaya.

Ekata, Ekta, Ektaa (Indian) unity.

Ekaterina (Russian) a form of Katherine.
Ekaterine, Ekaterini

Ekavali (Indian) single string.

Ela (Polish) a form of Adelaide.

Eladia (Greek) born or having lived in Elade, Greece.

Elaina (French) a form of Helen.
Elainea, Elainia, Elainna

Elaine (French) a form of Helen. See also Lainey, Laine.
Eilane, Elain, Elaina, Elaini, Elan, Elana, Elane, Elania, Elanie, Elanit, Elauna, Elayna, Ellaine

Elaís (Spanish) a form of Elam.

Elam (Hebrew) highlands.

Elana (Greek) a short form of Eleanor. See also Ilana, Lana.
Elan, Elanee, Elaney, Elani, Elania, Elanie, Elanna, Elanni

Elata (Latin) elevated.

Elavarasi (Indian) princess.

Elayna (French) a form of Elaina.
Elayn, Elaynah, Elayne, Elayni

Elba (Latin) a form of Alba.

Elberta (English) a form of Alberta.
Elbertha, Elberthina, Elberthine, Elbertina, Elbertine

Elbia (Spanish) a form of Elba.

Elcira (Teutonic) noble adornment.

Elda (German) she who battles.

Eldora (Spanish) golden, gilded.
Eldoree, Eldorey, Eldori, Eldoria, Eldorie, Eldory

Eleadora (Spanish) gift of the sun.

Eleanor 🄶 (Greek) light. History: Anna Eleanor Roosevelt was a U.S. delegate to the United Nations, a writer, and the thirty-second First Lady of the United States. See also Elana, Ella, Ellen, Leanore, Lena, Lenore, Leonore, Leora, Nellie, Nora, Noreen.
Elana, Elanor, Elanore, Eleanora, Eleanore, Elena, Eleni, Elenor, Elenorah, Elenore, Eleonor, Eleonore, Elianore, Elinor, Elinore, Elladine, Ellenor, Ellie, Elliner, Ellinor, Ellinore, Elna, Elnore, Elynor, Elynore

Eleanora (Greek) a form of Eleanor. See also Lena.
Elenora, Eleonora, Elianora, Ellenora, Ellenorah, Elnora, Elynora

Electa (Greek) blonde like the sun.

Electra (Greek) shining; brilliant. Mythology: the daughter of Agamemnon, leader of the Greeks in the Trojan War.
Elektra

Elena (Greek) a form of Eleanor. (Italian) a form of Helen.
Eleana, Eleen, Eleena, Elen, Elene, Elenitsa, Elenka, Elenna, Elenoa, Elenola, Ellena, Lena

Eleni (Greek) a familiar form of Eleanor.
Elenie, Eleny

Eleodora (Greek) she who came from the sun.

Eleora (Hebrew) the Lord is my light.
Eliora, Elira, Elora

Eleutería (Spanish) free.

Elevuka (Fijian) from Levuka.

Elexis (Greek) a form of Alexis.
Elexas, Elexes, Elexess, Elexeya, Elexia, Elexiah

Elexus (Greek) a form of Alexius, Alexus.
Elexius, Elexsus, Elexxus, Elexys

Elfrida (German) peaceful. See also Freda.
Elfrea, Elfreda, Elfredda, Elfreeda, Elfreyda, Elfrieda, Elfryda

Elga (Norwegian) pious. (German) a form of Helga.
Elgiva

Eli 🄱 (Hebrew) uplifted. A short form of Elijah, Elisha.

Elia 🄶 (Hebrew) a short form of Eliana.
Eliah

Eliana (Hebrew) my God has answered me. See also Iliana.
Elia, Eliane, Elianna, Ellianna, Liana, Liane

Eliane (Hebrew) a form of Eliana.
Elianne, Elliane, Ellianne

Elicia (Hebrew) a form of Elisha. See also Alicia.
Elecia, Elica, Elicea, Elicet, Elichia, Eliscia, Elisia, Elissia, Ellecia, Ellicia

Elida, Elide (Latin) forms of Alida.
Elidee, Elidia, Elidy

Eligia (Italian, Spanish) chosen one.

Elihna (Pohnpeian) a form of Tomoko.

Elijah 🄱 (Hebrew) a form of Eliyahu (see Boys' Names).

Elina (Greek, Italian) a form of Elena.

Elisa (Spanish, Italian, English) a short form of Elizabeth. See also Alisa, Ilisa.
Elecea, Eleesa, Elesa, Elesia, Elisia, Elisya, Ellisa, Ellisia, Ellissa, Ellissia, Ellissya, Ellisya, Elysa, Elysia, Elyssia, Elyssya, Elysya, Lisa

Elisabete (Portuguese) consecrated to God.

Elisabeth 🄶 (Hebrew) a form of Elizabeth.
Elisabet, Elisabeta, Elisabethe, Elisabetta, Elisabette, Elisabith, Elisebet, Elisheba, Elisheva

Elisapeci, Eliseva (Fijian) forms of Elizabeth.

Elise (French, English) a short form of Elizabeth, Elysia. See also Ilise, Liese, Lisette, Lissie.
Eilis, Eilise, Elese, Élise, Elisee, Elisie, Elisse, Elizé, Ellice, Ellise, Ellyce, Ellyse, Ellyze, Elsey, Elsie, Elsy, Elyce, Elyci, Elyse, Elyze, Lisel, Lisl, Lison

Elisea (Hebrew) God is salvation, protect my health.

Elisha 🄱🄶 (Hebrew) consecrated to God. (Greek) a form of Alisha. See also Ilisha, Lisha.
Eleacia, Eleasha, Eleesha, Eleisha, Elesha, Eleshia, Eleticia, Elicia, Elishah, Elisheva, Elishia, Elishua, Eliska, Ellesha, Ellexia, Ellisha, Elsha, Elysha, Elyshia

Elissa (Greek, English) a form of Elizabeth. A short form of Melissa. See also Alissa, Alyssa, Lissa.
Elissah, Ellissa, Ellyssa, Ilissa, Ilyssa

Elita (Latin, French) chosen. See also Lida, Lita.
Elitia, Elitia, Elitie, Ellita, Ellitia, Ellitie, Ilida, Ilita, Litia

Eliza (Hebrew) a short form of Elizabeth. See also Aliza.
Eliz, Elizaida, Elizalina, Elize, Elizea

Elizabet (Hebrew) a form of Elizabeth.
Elizabete, Elizabette

Elizabeth 🌿 **G** (Hebrew) consecrated to
God. Bible: the mother of John the Baptist.
See also Bess, Beth, Betsy, Betty, Elsa, Ilse,
Libby, Liese, Liesel, Lisa, Lisbeth, Lisette,
Lissa, Lissie, Liz, Liza, Lizabeta, Lizabeth,
Lizbeth, Lizina, Lizzy, Veta, Yelisabeta, Zizi.
*Alizabeth, Eliabeth, Elisa, Elisabeth, Elise,
Elissa, Eliza, Elizabee, Elizabet, Elizaveta,
Elizebeth, Elka, Elsabeth, Elsbeth, Elschen,
Elspeth, Elysabeth, Elzbieta, Elzsébet, Helsa,
Ilizzabet, Lusa*

Elizapet (Pohnpeian) a form of Drusilla.

Elizaveta (Polish, English) a form of
Elizabeth.
*Elisavet, Elisaveta, Elisavetta, Elisveta,
Elizavet, Elizavetta, Elizveta, Elsveta, Elzveta*

Elka (Polish) a form of Elizabeth.
Ilka

Elke (German) a form of Adelaide, Alice.
Elki, Ilki

Ella 🌿 **G** (English) elfin; beautiful fairy-
woman. (Greek) a short form of Eleanor.
Ellah, Ellamae, Ellia, Ellie

Elle (Greek) a short form of Eleanor.
(French) she.
El, Ele, Ell

Ellen (English) a form of Eleanor, Helen.
*Elen, Elenee, Eleny, Elin, Elina, Elinda, Ellan,
Ellena, Ellene, Ellie, Ellin, Ellon, Ellyn, Ellynn,
Ellynne, Elyn*

Ellice (English) a form of Elise.
Ellecia, Ellyce, Elyce

Ellie **G** (English) a short form of Eleanor,
Ella, Ellen.
Ele, Elie, Ellee, Elleigh, Elli

Elliot, Elliott **B** (English) forms of Eli,
Elijah.

Ellis **B** (English) a form of Elias.

Elly (English) a short form of Eleanor, Ella,
Ellen.

Elma (Turkish) sweet fruit.

Elmira (Arabic, Spanish) a form of Almira.
Elmeera, Elmera, Elmeria, Elmyra

Elnohra (Pohnpeian) a form of Elena.

Elnora (American) a combination of Ella +
Nora.

Elodie (American) a form of Melody.
(English) a form of Alodie.
Elodee, Elodia, Elody

Eloísa (German) a form of Louise.

Eloise (French) a form of Louise.
Elois, Eloisa, Eloisia

Elora (American) a short form of Elnora.
Ellora, Elloree, Elorie

Elpidia (Greek) she who waits faithfully, who
lives her life waiting.

Elsa (German) noble. (Hebrew) a short form
of Elizabeth. See also Ilse.
Ellsa, Ellse, Else, Elsia, Elsie, Elsje

Elsbeth (German) a form of Elizabeth.
Elsbet, Elzbet, Elzbieta

Elsie (German) a familiar form of Elsa,
Helsa.
Ellsie, Ellsie, Ellsy, Elsi, Elsy

Elspeth (Scottish) a form of Elizabeth.
Elspet, Elspie

Elva (English) elfin. See also Alva, Alvina.
Elvia, Elvie

Elvina (English) a form of Alvina.
Elvenea, Elvinea, Elvinia, Elvinna

Elvira (Latin) white; blond. (German) closed
up. (Spanish) elfin. Geography: the town in
Spain that hosted a Catholic synod in 300 A.
D.
Elva, Elvera, Elvire, Elwira, Vira

Elvisa (Teutonic) famous warrior.

Elvita (Spanish) truth.

Elyse (Latin) a form of Elysia.
Ellysa, Ellyse, Elyce, Elys, Elysee, Elysse

Elysia (Greek) sweet; blissful. Mythology:
Elysium was the dwelling place of happy
souls.
*Elise, Elishia, Ellicia, Elycia, Elyssa, Ilysha,
Ilysia*

Elyssa (Latin) a form of Elysia.
Ellyssa

Emalee (Latin) a form of Emily.
*Emaili, Emalea, Emaleigh, Emali, Emalia,
Emalie*

Emani (Arabic) a form of Iman.
Eman, Emane, Emaneé, Emanie, Emann

Emanuel **B** (Hebrew) a form of Emanuelle.

Emanuelle (Hebrew) a form of Emmanuelle.
Emanual, Emanuel, Emanuela, Emanuella

Ember (French) a form of Amber.
Emberlee, Emberly

Emelia, Emelie (Latin) forms of Emily.
Emellie

Emelinda (Teutonic) hard-working and kind.

Emely (Latin) a form of Emily.
Emelly

Emerald (French) bright green gemstone.
Emelda, Esmeralda

Emerenciana (Latin) she who will be rewarded.

Emerita (Latin) she who God rewards for her virtues.

Emerson 🅱 (German, English) child of Emery.

Emery 🅱 (German) industrious leader.
Emeri, Emerie

Emesta (Spanish) serious.

Emiko (Japanese) blessed and beautiful child.

Emile 🅱 (English) a form of Emilee.

Emilee, Emilie (English) forms of Emily.
Emile, Emilea, Emileigh, Émilie, Emiliee, Emillee, Emillie, Emmélie, Emmilee, Emylee

Emilia (Italian) a form of Amelia, Emily.
Emalia, Emelia, Emila

Emilio 🅱 (Italian, Spanish) a form of Emil (see Boys' Names).

Emily ☀ 🅶 (Latin) flatterer. (German) industrious. See also Amelia, Emma, Millie.
Eimile, Em, Emaily, Emalee, Emeli, Emelia, Emelie, Emelita, Emely, Emilee, Emiley, Emili, Emilia, Emilie, Émilie, Emilis, Emilka, Emillie, Emilly, Emmaline, Emmaly, Emmélie, Emmey, Emmi, Emmie, Emmilly, Emmily, Emmy, Emmye, Emyle

Emilyann (American) a combination of Emily + Ann.
Emileane, Emileann, Emileanna, Emileanne, Emiliana, Emiliann, Emilianna, Emilianne, Emillyane, Emillyann, Emillyanna, Emillyanne, Emliana, Emliann, Emlianna, Emlianne

Emma ☀ 🅶 (German) a short form of Emily. See also Amy.
Em, Ema, Emmah, Emmy

Emmalee (American) a combination of Emma + Lee. A form of Emily.
Emalea, Emalee, Emilee, Emmalea, Emmalei, Emmaleigh, Emmaley, Emmali, Emmalia, Emmalie, Emmaliese, Emmalyse, Emylee

Emmaline (French) a form of Emily.
Emalina, Emaline, Emelina, Emeline, Emilienne, Emilina, Emiline, Emmalina, Emmalene, Emmeline, Emmiline

Emmalynn (American) a combination of Emma + Lynn.
Emelyn, Emelyne, Emelynne, Emilyn, Emilynn, Emilynne, Emlyn, Emlynn, Emlynne, Emmalyn, Emmalynne

Emmanuel 🅱 (Hebrew) God is with us.

Emmanuela (Hebrew) a form of Emmanuelle.

Emmanuelle 🅶 (Hebrew) a form of Emmanuel.
Emanuelle, Emmanuella

Emmy (German) a familiar form of Emma.
Emi, Emie, Emiy, Emmi, Emmie, Emmye, Emy

Emmylou (American) a combination of Emmy + Lou.
Emlou, Emmalou, Emmelou, Emmilou, Emylou

Emna (Teutonic) hard-working and kind.

Emory 🅱 (German) a form of Emery.

Emperatriz (Latin) she who is the sovereign leader.

En (Chinese) favor, grace.

Ena (Irish) a form of Helen.
Enna

Enakshi (Indian) one with eyes like a deer.

Enara (Basque) name given to a swallow.

Encarna, Encarnita (Spanish) forms of Encarnación.

Encarnación (Latin) alluding to the incarnation of Jesus in his mother, Mary.

Enedina (Greek) warm or indulgent.

Enerika (Pohnpeian) a form of Elizabeth.

Enerita (Chuukese) a form of Hilaria.

Enid (Welsh) life; spirit.

Enisa (Chuukese) a form of Elizabeth.

Enma (Hebrew) a form of Emmanuela.

Enrica (Spanish) a form of Henrietta. See also Rica.
Enrieta, Enrietta, Enrika, Enriqua, Enriqueta, Enriquetta, Enriquette

Epifanía (Spanish) epiphany.

Eppie (English) a familiar form of Euphemia.
Effie, Effy, Eppy

Er (Chinese) jade or pearl earring.

Ercilia (Greek) she who is delicate, tender, kind.

Erendira, Erendiria (Spanish) one with a smile.

Erensia (Chamorro) heritage.

Eria (Indian) cat.

Eriahna (Pohnpeian) a form of Eleanor.

Eric **B** (Scandinavian) ruler of all. (English) brave ruler. (German) a short form of Frederick (see Boys' Names).

Erica **G** (Scandinavian) ruler of all. (English) brave ruler. See also Arica, Rica, Ricki.
Érica, Ericca, Ericha, Ericka, Errica

Ericka (Scandinavian) a form of Erica.
Erickah, Erricka

Erik **B** (Scandinavian) a form of Eric.

Erika **G** (Scandinavian) a form of Erica.
Erikaa, Erikah, Erikka, Errika, Eyka, Erykka, Eyrika

Eriko (Japanese) child with a collar.

Erin **G** (Irish) peace. History: another name for Ireland. See also Arin.
Earin, Earrin, Eran, Eren, Erena, Erene, Ereni, Eri, Erian, , Erine, Erinetta, Erinn, Errin, Eryn

Erina (Irish) a form of Erin.

Erinda (Spanish) a form of Erina.

Erinn (Irish) a form of Erin.
Erinna, Erinne

Erma (Latin) a short form of Ermine, Hermina. See also Irma.
Ermelinda

Ermenilda (German) powerful warrior.

Ermine (Latin) a form of Hermina.
Erma, Ermin, Ermina, Erminda, Erminie

Erminia (Latin) a form of Ermine.

Erna (English) a short form of Ernestine.

Ernestine (English) earnest, sincere.
Erna, Ernaline, Ernesia, Ernesta, Ernestina, Ernesztina

Eryn **G** (Irish) a form of Erin.
Eiryn, Eryne, Erynn, Erynne

Escolástica (Latin) she who knows much and teaches.

Eshana (Indian) search.

Eshe (Swahili) life.
Eisha, Esha

Eshita (Indian) one who desires.

Esisihna (Pohnpeian) a form of Enriqueta.

Esiteri (Fijian) a form of Esther.

Esiuch (Palauan) a form of Dilngas.

Eskolastika (Pohnpeian) a form of Ariana.

Esmé (French) a familiar form of Esmeralda. A form of Amy.
Esma, Esme, Esmëe

Esmerada (Latin) shining, standing out. radiates purity and hope.

Esmeralda (Greek, Spanish) a form of Emerald.
Emelda, Esmé, Esmerelda, Esmerilda, Esmiralda, Ezmerelda, Ezmirilda

Esperanza (Spanish) hope. See also Speranza.

Esparanza, Espe, Esperance, Esperans, Esperansa, Esperanta, Esperanz, Esperenza

Essence (Latin) life; existence.
Essa, Essenc, Essencee, Essences, Essenes, Essense, Essynce

Essie (English) a short form of Estelle, Esther.
Essa, Essey, Essie, Essy

Estaquia (Spanish) possessor of a head of wheat.

Estebana (Spanish) crowned with laurels.

Ested (Chamorro) a form of Esther.

Estee (English) a short form of Estelle, Esther.
Esta, Estée, Esti

Estefani, Estefania, Estefany (Spanish) forms of Stephanie.
Estafania, Estefana, Estefane, Estefanía, Estefanie

Estela (French) a form of Estelle.

Estelinda (Teutonic) she who is noble and protects the village.

Estelle (French) a form of Esther. See also Stella, Trella.
Essie, Estee, Estel, Estele, Esteley, Estelina, Estelita, Estell, Estella, Estellina, Estellita, Esthella

Estephanie (Spanish) a form of Stephanie.
Estephania, Estephani, Estephany

Esterina (Greek) she who is strong and vital.

Esterlaine (Persian) a form of Azad.

Esteva (Greek) crowned with laurels.

Esther (Persian) star. Bible: the Jewish captive whom Ahasuerus made his queen. See also Hester.
Essie, Estee, Ester, Esthur, Eszter, Eszti

Estherlita (Persian) noble.

Esthermae (Persian) a form of Esther.

Estralita (Spanish) a form of Estrella.

Estrella (French) star.
Estrela, Estrelinha, Estrell, Estrelle, Estrellita

Eta (Indian) luminous.

Etel (Spanish) a short form of Etelvina.

Etelinda (German) noble one that protects her village.

Etelvina (German) she who is a loyal and noble friend.

Ethan Ｂ (Hebrew) strong; firm.

Ethana (Hebrew) a form of Ethan.

Ethel (English) noble.
Ethelda, Ethelin, Etheline, Ethelle, Ethelyn, Ethelynn, Ethelynne, Ethyl

Etienne Ｂ (French) a form of Stephen.

Étoile (French) star.

Etor (Palauan) woman.

Etsu (Japanese) delight.

Etsuko (Japanese) blessed child.

Etta (German) little. (English) a short form of Henrietta.
Etka, Etke, Etti, Ettie, Etty, Itke, Itta

Eudocia, Eudosia, Eudoxia (Greek) famous one, very knowledgeable.

Eudora (Greek) honored gift. See also Dora.

Eufrasia (Greek) she who is full of joy.

Eugene Ｂ (Greek) born to nobility.

Eugenia (Greek) a form of Eugene. See also Gina.
Eugenie, Eugenina, Eugina, Evgenia

Eugània (Portuguese) a form of Eugenia.

Eugenie (Greek) a form of Eugenia.
Eugenee, Eugénie

Eulalia (Greek) well spoken. See also Ula.
Eula, Eulalee, Eulalie, Eulalya, Eulia

Eulália (Portuguese) a form of Eulalia.

Eulogia (Greek) she who speaks eloquently.

Eumelia (Greek) she who sings well, the melodious one.

Eun (Korean) silver.

Eunice (Greek) happy; victorious. Bible: the mother of Saint Timothy. See also Unice.
Euna, Eunique, Eunise, Euniss

Eunomia (Greek) good order.

Euphemia (Greek) spoken well of, in good repute. History: a fourth-century Christian martyr.
Effam, Effie, Eppie, Eufemia, Euphan, Euphemie, Euphie

Eurídice (Greek) a form of Eurydice.

Eurydice (Greek) wide, broad. Mythology: the wife of Orpheus.
Euridice, Euridyce, Eurydyce

Eusebia (Greek) respectful, pious.

Eustacia (Greek) productive. (Latin) stable; calm. See also Stacey.
Eustasia

Eustaquia (Greek) well-built.

Eutimia (Spanish) she who is benevolent.

Eva Ｇ (Greek) a short form of Evangelina. (Hebrew) a form of Eve. See also Ava, Chava.
Éva, Evah, Evalea, Evalee, Evike

Evalani, Evalonni, Evelanie (Hawaiian) forms of Ewelani.

Evaline (French) a form of Evelyn.
Evalin, Evalina, Evalyn, Evalynn, Eveleen, Evelene, Evelina, Eveline

Evan Ｂ (Irish) young warrior.

Evangelina (Greek) bearer of good news.
Eva, Evangelene, Evangelia, Evangelica, Evangeline, Evangelique, Evangelyn, Evangelynn

Evangelina Eny (Irish) fire.

Evania (Irish) a form of Evan.
Evana, Evanka, Evann, Evanna, Evanne, Evany, Eveania, Evvanne, Evvunea, Evyan

Evarista (Greek) excellent one.

Eve (Hebrew) life. Bible: the first woman created by God. (French) a short form of Evonne. See also Chava, Hava, Naeva, Vica, Yeva.
Eva, Evie, Evita, Evuska, Evyn, Ewa, Yeva

Evelia (Hebrew) she who generates life.

Evelin (English) a form of Evelyn.
Evelina, Eveline

Girls A–F

Evelyn �018 **G** (English) hazelnut.
Avalyn, Aveline, Evaleen, Evalene, Evaline, Evalyn, Evalynn, Evalynne, Eveleen, Evelin, Evelyna, Evelyne, Evelynn, Evelynne, Evline, Ewalina

Everett **B** (German) courageous as a boar.

Everilda (German) she who fought with the wild boar.

Evette (French) a form of Yvette. A familiar form of Evonne. See also Ivette.
Evett

Evie (Hungarian) a form of Eve.
Evey, Evi, Evicka, Evike, Evka, Evuska, Evvie, Evvy, Evy, Ewa

Evita (Spanish) a form of Eve.

Evline (English) a form of Evelyn.
Evleen, Evlene, Evlin, Evlina, Evlyn, Evlynn, Evlynne

Evodia (Greek) she who always wants others to have a good trip.

Evonne (French) a form of Yvonne. See also Ivonne.
Evanne, Eve, Evenie, Evenne, Eveny, Evette, Evin, Evon, Evona, Evone, Evoni, Evonna, Evonnie, Evony, Evyn, Evynn, Eyona, Eyvone

Ewalani (Hawaiian) a form of Ewelani.

Ewelani (Hawaiian) chief of divine descent.

Exal (Spanish) diminutive form of Exaltación.

Exaltación (Spanish) lifted up.

Ezmeralda (Spanish) emerald.

Ezra **B** (Hebrew) a form of Ezri.

Ezri (Hebrew) helper; strong.
Ezra, Ezria

Faasi (Chamorro) clean.

Faatin, Faatina (Indian) captivating.

Fabia (Latin) bean grower.
Fabiana, Fabienne, Fabiola, Fabra, Fabria

Fabian **B** (Latin) a form of Fabienne.

Fabiana (Latin) a form of Fabia.
Fabyana

Fabienne (Latin) a form of Fabia.
Fabian, Fabiann, Fabianne, Fabiene, Fabreanne

Fabiola, Faviola (Latin) forms of Fabia.
Fabiole, Fabyola, Faviana, Faviolha

Fabricia (Latin) artisan, daughter of artisans.

Fachalang (Chamorro) make a path.

Fachalig (Chamorro) she who laughs a lot; she who pretends to laugh.

Facunda (Latin) eloquent speaker.

Fadheela (Indian) virtue.

Fadwa (Indian) name derived from self-sacrifice.

Faedeng (Chamorro) federico palm.

Faith �018 **G** (English) faithful; fidelity. See also Faye, Fidelity.
Fayth, Faythe

Faizah (Arabic) victorious.

Fajyaz (Indian) artistic.

Falda (Icelandic) folded wings.
Faida, Fayda

Faline (Latin) catlike.
Faleen, Falena, Falene, Falin, Falina, Fallyn, Fallyne, Faylina, Fayline, Faylyn, Faylynn, Faylynne, Felenia, Felina

Fallon **G** (Irish) grandchild of the ruler.
Falan, Falen, Fallan, Fallen, Fallonne, Falon, Falyn, Falynn, Falynne, Phalon

Falviana (Spanish) she who has blonde locks of hair.

Fancy (French) betrothed. (English) whimsical; decorative.
Fanchette, Fanchon, Fanci, Fancia, Fancie

Fang (Chinese) fragrant, sweet smelling.

Fang Yin, Fang-Yin (Chinese) fragrant carpet of grass; the scent of flowers.

Fannie, Fanny (American) familiar forms of Frances.
Fan, Fanette, Fani, Fania, Fannee, Fanney, Fanni, Fannia, Fany, Fanya

Fantasia (Greek) imagination.
Fantasy, Fantasya, Fantaysia, Fantazia, Fiantasi

Farah, Farrah (English) beautiful; pleasant.
Fara, Farra, Fayre

Fareeda (Indian) unique.

Fareeha (Indian) happy, joyful.

Faren, Farren (English) wanderer.
Faran, Fare, Farin, Faron, Farrahn, Farran, Farrand, Farrin, Farron, Farryn, Farye, Faryn, Feran, Ferin, Feron, Ferran, Ferren, Ferrin, Ferron, Ferryn

Farha (Indian) happiness.

Farhana (Indian) beautiful.

Farzana (Indian) intelligence.

Fatangisña (Chamorro) she who cries a lot.

Fátim (Arabic) only daughter of Mahoma.

Fatima (Arabic) daughter of the Prophet. History: the daughter of Muhammad.
Fatema, Fathma, Fatimah, Fatime, Fatma, Fatmah, Fatme, Fattim

Fátima (Arabic) a form of Fatima.

Fausta, Faustina (Latin) fortunate or lucky.

Favia (Latin) she who raises beans.

Fawiza (Indian) successful.

Fawn (French) young deer.
Faun, Fawna, Fawne

Fawna (French) a form of Fawn.
Fauna, Fawnia, Fawnna

Fawziya (Indian) successful; victorious.

Faye (French) fairy; elf. (English) a form of Faith.
Fae, Fay, Fayann, Fayanna, Fayette, Fayina, Fey

Fayola (Nigerian) lucky.
Fayla, Feyla

Fe (Latin) trust or belief.

Febe (Greek) shining one.

Fedra (Greek) splendid one.

Fegorgor (Chamorro) one who gossips a lot.

Fegurgur (Chamorro) a form of Fegorgor.

Felecia (Latin) a form of Felicia.
Flecia

Felecidade (Portuguese) happiness.

Felica (Spanish) a short form of Felicia.
Falisa, Felisa, Felisca, Felissa, Feliza

Felice (Latin) a short form of Felicia.
Felece, Felicie, Felise, Felize, Felyce, Felysse

Felicia (Latin) fortunate; happy. See also Lecia, Phylicia.
Falecia, Faleshia, Falicia, Fela, Felecia, Felica, Felice, Felicidad, Feliciona, Felicity, Felicya, Felisea, Felisha, Felisia, Felisiana, Felissya, Felita, Felixia, Felizia, Felka, Fellcia, Felycia, Felysia, Felyssia, Fleasia, Fleichia, Fleishia, Flichia

Feliciana (Spanish, Italian, Ancient Roman) a form of Felix.

Felicity (English) a form of Felicia.
Falicity, Felicita, Felicitas, Félicité, Feliciti, Felisita, Felisity

Felipe 🅱 (Spanish) a form of Philip.

Felisha (Latin) a form of Felicia.
Faleisha, Falesha, Falisha, Falleshia, Feleasha, Feleisha, Felesha, Felishia, Fellishia, Felysha, Flisha

Felix (Latin) fortunate; happy.

Femi (French) woman. (Nigerian) love me.
Femie, Femmi, Femmie, Femy

Fen (Chinese) fragrant, sweet-smelling.

Feng (Chinese) maple.

Feng-Po-Po (Chinese) goddess of winds.

Feodora (Greek) gift of God.
Fedora, Fedoria

Fermina (Spanish) strong.

Fern (English) fern. (German) a short form of Fernanda.
Ferne, Ferni, Fernlee, Fernleigh, Fernley, Fernly

Fernanda (German) daring, adventurous. See also Andee, Nan.
Ferdie, Ferdinanda, Ferdinande, Fern, Fernande, Fernandette, Fernandina, Nanda

Feronia (Latin) goddess of the forest and fountains.

Fersita (Palauan) pearl.

Fesamay (Chamorro) serious child.

Fetangis (Chamorro) one who cries a lot.

Fhoolwathi (Indian) dedicated as a flower.

Fiala (Czech) violet.

Fidelia (Latin) a form of Fidelity.
Fidela, Fidele, Fidelina

Fidelity (Latin) faithful, true. See also Faith.
Fidelia, Fidelita

Fifi 🅶 (French) a familiar form of Josephine.
Feef, Feefee, Fifine

Figan (Chamorro) red hot.

Fiho, Fihon (Chamorro) forms of Fihu.

Fihu (Chamorro) often.

Filippa (Italian) a form of Philippa.
Felipa, Filipa, Filippina, Filpina

Filis (Greek) adorned with leaves.

Filomena (Italian) a form of Philomena.
Fila, Filah, Filemon

Filotea (Greek) she who loves God.

Filza (Indian) light.

Fiona (Irish) fair, white.
Fionna

Fionnula (Irish) white shouldered. See also Nola, Nuala.
Fenella, Fenula, Finella, Finola, Finula

Fiorel (Latin) a form of Flor.

Fiorela (Italian) small flower.

Fiorella (Spanish) a form of Fiorela.

Firdoos (Indian) paradise.

Firoza, Phiroza (Indian) turquoise.

Fiza (Indian) breeze.

Fizza (Indian) nature.

Flair (English) style; verve.
Flaire, Flare

Flaminia (Latin) alluding to one who belongs to a religious order.

Flannery (Irish) redhead. Literature: Flannery O'Connor was a renowned American writer.
Flan, Flann, Flanna

Flavia (Latin) blond, golden haired.
Flavere, Flaviar, Flavie, Flavien, Flavienne, Flaviere, Flavio, Flavyere, Fulvia

Flávia (Portuguese) a form of Flavia.

Flavie (Latin) a form of Flavia.
Flavi

Fleur (French) flower.
Fleure, Fleuree, Fleurette

Flo (American) a short form of Florence.

Flor (Latin) a short form of Flora.

Flora (Latin) flower. A short form of Florence. See also Lore.
Fiora, Fiore, Fiorenza, Florann, Florella, Florelle, Floren, Floria, Floriana, Florianna, Florica, Florimel

Floramaría (Spanish) flower of Mary.

Florehna (Pohnpeian) a form of Efigenia.

Florence (Latin) blooming; flowery; prosperous. History: Florence Nightingale, a British nurse, is considered the founder of modern nursing. See also Florida.
Fiorenza, Flo, Flora, Florance, Florencia, Florency, Florendra, Florentia, Florentina, Florentyna, Florenza, Floretta, Florette, Florie, Florina, Florine, Floris, Flossie

Floria (Basque) a form of Flora.
Flori, Florria

Florida (Spanish) a form of Florence.
Floridia, Florinda, Florita

Florie (English) a familiar form of Florence.
Flore, Flori, Florri, Florrie, Florry, Flory

Florinia (Latin) blooming or flowering.

Floris (English) a form of Florence.
Florisa, Florise

Florisel (Spanish) a form of Flora.

Flossie (English) a familiar form of Florence.
Floss, Flossi, Flossy

Floyd **B** (English) a form of Lloyd.

Fo (Chinese) Buddhist.

Fola (Yoruba) honorable.

Fonda (Latin) foundation. (Spanish) inn.
Fondea, Fonta

Fontanna (French) fountain.
Fontaine, Fontana, Fontane, Fontanne, Fontayne

Foolan, Phoolan (Indian) flowering.

Foolwati, Phoolwati (Indian) delicate as a flower.

Foram, Forum (Indian) fragrance.

Forest **B** (French) a form of Forrest.

Forrest **B** (French) forest; woodsman.

Fortuna (Latin) fortune; fortunate.
Fortoona, Fortune

Fortunata (Latin) fortunate one.

Fran **G** (Latin) a short form of Frances.
Frain, Frann

Frances **G** (Latin) a form of Francis. See also Paquita.
Fanny, Fran, Franca, France, Francee, Francena, Francesca, Francess, Francesta, Franceta, Francetta, Francette, Francine, Francisca, Françoise, Frankie, Frannie, Franny

Francesca **G** (Italian) a form of Frances.
Franceska, Francessca, Francesta, Franchesca, Franzetta

Franchesca (Italian) a form of Francesca.
Cheka, Chekka, Chesca, Cheska, Francheca, Francheka, Franchelle, Franchesa, Francheska, Franchessca, Franchesska

Franci (Hungarian) a familiar form of Francine.
Francey, Francie, Francy

Francine (French) a form of Frances.
Franceen, Franceine, Franceline, Francene, Francenia, Franci, Francin, Francina, Francyne

Francis 🅱 (Latin) free; from France.
Francise, Franncia, Francys

Francisca (Italian) a form of Frances.
Franciska, Franciszka, Frantiska, Franziska

Françoise (French) a form of Frances.

Frankie 🅱 (American) a familiar form of Frances.
Francka, Francki, Franka, Frankey, Franki, Frankia, Franky, Frankye

Franklin 🅱 (English) free landowner.

Frannie, Franny (English) familiar forms of Frances.
Frani, Frania, Franney, Franni, Frany

Fraser 🅱 (French) strawberry. (English) curly haired.

Freda, Freida, Frida (German) short forms of Alfreda, Elfrida, Frederica, Sigfreda.
Frayda, Fredda, Fredella, Fredia, Fredra, Freeda, Freeha, Freia, Frida, Frideborg, Frieda

Freddi (English) familiar forms of Frederica, Winifred.
Fredda, Freddy, Fredi, Fredia, Fredy, Frici

Freddie 🅱 (English) a form of Freddi.

Fredel (Nahuatl) forever you.

Frederica (German) peaceful ruler. See also Alfreda, Rica, Ricki.
Farica, Federica, Freda, Fredalena, Fredaline, Freddi, Freddie, Frederickina, Frederika, Frederike, Frederina, Frederine, Frederique, Fredith, Fredora, Fredreca, Fredrica, Fredricah, Fredricia, Freida, Fritzi, Fryderica

Frederika (German) a form of Frederica.
Fredericka, Fredreka, Fredricka, Fredrika, Fryderyka

Frederike (German) a form of Frederica.
Fredericke, Friederike

Frederique 🅶 (French) a form of Frederica.
Frédérique, Rike

Fredrick 🅱 (German) a form of Frederick (see Boys' Names).

Freja (Scandinavian) a form of Freya.

Frescura (Spanish) freshness.

Freya (Scandinavian) noblewoman. Mythology: the Norse goddess of love.
Fraya, Freya

Freyra (Slavic) goddess of love.

Frine (Spanish) female toad.

Fritzi (German) a familiar form of Frederica.
Friezi, Fritze, Fritzie, Fritzinn, Fritzline, Fritzy

Fronde (Latin) leafy branch.

Fructuosa (Spanish) fruitful.

Fu (Chinese) lotus.

Fu'una (Chamorro) her place.

Fuasyo (Japanese) whole; room; generation.

Fuji (Japanese) wisteria.

Fujiko (Japanese) wisteria child.

Fujita (Japanese) field.

Fujiye (Japanese) wisteria branch.

Fuka (Japanese) she who stays beautiful even in difficult times.

Fukiko (Japanese) wealthy; precious child.

Fukuko (Japanese) child of good fortune.

Fukuyo (Japanese) a lifetime of good fortune.

Fulgencia (Spanish) she who excels because of her great kindness.

Fulki (Indian) spark.

Fullan (Indian) blooming.

Fullara (Indian) wife of Kalketu.

Fulmala (Indian) garland.

Fumi (Japanese) beautiful helper; writings, letter.

Fumie (Kosraean) a form of Alexa.

Fumii (Japanese) that one is a chronicle.

Fumiko (Japanese) beautiful, wealthy child; born to be a writer.

Fumiye (Japanese) born to be a writer; she who chronicles through painting.

Fumiyo (Japanese) she who writes for a lifetime.

Fusa (Japanese) tassel; cluster; room.

Fusae (Japanese) wealthy; clever.

Fusako (Japanese) lotus; gaze; help; child.

Fuyu (Japanese) born in winter.

Fuyuko (Japanese) child of reason.

Fuyumi (Japanese) beautiful winter.

G

G **B** (American) an initial used as a first name.

Gabina (Latin) she who is a native of Gabio, an ancient city close to Rome where Romulus was raised.

Gabriel **B** (French) devoted to God.

Gabriela **G** (Italian) a form of Gabrielle.
Gabriala, Gabrielia, Gabrila

Gabriele (French) forms of Gabrielle.
Gabbriel, Gabbryel, Gabreal, Gabreale, Gabreil, Gabrial, Gabryel

Gabriella 👑 **G** (Italian) a form of Gabrielle.
Gabrialla, Gabriellia, Gabrilla, Gabryella

Gabrielle 👑 **G** (French) a form of Gabriel.
Gabbrielle, Gabielle, Gabrealle, Gabriana, Gabriel, Gabriela, Gabriele, Gabriell, Gabriella, Gabrille, Gabrina, Gabriylle, Gabryell, Gabryelle, Gaby, Gavriella

Gabryel **B** (French) a form of Gabriel.

Gaby (French) a familiar form of Gabrielle.
Gabbey, Gabbi, Gabbie, Gabby, Gabey, Gabi, Gabie, Gavi, Gavy

Gada (Hebrew) lucky.
Gadah

Gaea (Greek) planet Earth. Mythology: the Greek goddess of Earth.
Gaia, Gaiea, Gaya

Gaetana (Italian) from Gaeta. Geography: Gaeta is a city in southern Italy.
Gaetan, Gaétane, Gaetanne

Gafahongoc (Chamorro) cutting off coconuts.

Gafo (Chamorro) coconut.

Gaga (Chamorro) a type of fish.

Gagandeep **B** (Sikh) sky's light.
Gagandip, Gagnadeep, Gagndeep

Gage **B** (French) pledge.

Gago (Chamorro) lazy; ironwood tree.

Gaho (Chamorro) bamboo joint.

Gail (Hebrew) a short form of Abigail. (English) merry, lively.
Gael, Gaela, Gaelle, Gaila, Gaile, Gale, Gayla, Gayle

Gajagamini (Indian) majestic.

Gajara (Indian) garland of flowers.

Gajra (Indian) flowers.

Gala (Norwegian) singer.
Galla

Galatea (Greek) she with skin as white as milk.

Galen **B** (Greek) healer; calm. (Irish) little and lively.
Gaelen, Gaellen, Galyn, Gaylaine, Gayleen, Gaylen, Gaylene, Gaylyn

Galena (Greek) healer; calm.

Galenia (Greek) healer.

Gali (Hebrew) hill; fountain; spring.
Galice, Galie

Galilah (Hebrew) important, exalted.

Galina (Russian) a form of Helen.
Gailya, Galayna, Galenka, Galia, Galiana, Galiena, Galinka, Galochka, Galya, Galyna

Gamami (Chamorro) we love.

Gamomo (Chamorro) she who loves a battle.

Gamumu (Chamorro) a form of Gamomo.

Gamumus (Chamorro) a form of Gamomo.

Gan (Chinese) sweet.

Gandhali (Indian) sweet scent.

Ganesa (Hindi) fortunate. Religion: Ganesha was the Hindu god of wisdom.

Ganga (Indian) sacred river.

Gangika (Indian) river.

Gangotri (Indian) sacred river of India.

Ganika (Indian) flower.

Ganjan (Indian) exceeding.

Ganya **BG** (Hebrew) garden of the Lord. (Zulu) clever.
Gana, Gani, Gania, Ganice, Ganit

Gao (Chinese) tall.

Garabina, Garabine (Spanish) purification.

Garaitz (Basque) victory.

Garati (Indian) virtuous woman.

Garbina, Garbine (Spanish) purification.

García (Latin) she who demonstrates her charm and grace.

Gardenia (English) Botany: a sweet-smelling flower.
Deeni, Denia, Gardena, Gardinia

Garett B (Irish) a form of Garrett.

Gargi (Indian) wise woman.

Garima (Indian) warmth.

Garland B (French) wreath of flowers.

Garnet (English) dark red gem.
Garnetta, Garnette

Garoa (Basque) fern.

Garrett B (Irish) brave spear carrier.

Garrison B (French) troops stationed at a fort; garrison.

Gary B (German) mighty spear carrier. (English) a familiar form of Gerald.

Garyn (English) spear carrier.
Garan, Garen, Garra, Garryn

Gasha (Russian) a familiar form of Agatha.
Gashka

Gaspara (Spanish) treasurer.

Gatita (Indian) a river.

Gaudencia (Spanish) happy, content.

Gauhar (Indian) a pearl.

Gaurika (Indian) pretty young girl.

Gautami (Indian) the Guava River.

Gavin B (Welsh) white hawk.

Gavriella (Hebrew) a form of Gabrielle.
Gavila, Gavilla, Gavrid, Gavrieela, Gavriela, Gavrielle, Gavrila, Gavrilla

Gay (French) merry.
Gae, Gai, Gaye

Gayle (English) a form of Gail.
Gayla

Gayna (English) a familiar form of Guinevere.
Gaynah, Gayner, Gaynor

Gazala (Indian) a deer.

Ge (Chinese) pattern.

Gea (Greek) old name given to the earth.

Gechina (Basque) grace.

Geela (Hebrew) joyful.
Gela, Gila

Geena (American) a form of Gena.
Geania, Geeana, Geeanna

Geeta (Indian) holy book of the Hindus.

Geeti (Indian) melody.

Geetika (Indian) a little song.

Gehna (Indian) ornament.

Gelya (Russian) angelic.

Gema, Gemma (Latin, Italian) jewel, precious stone. See also Jemma.
Gem, Gemmey, Gemmie, Gemmy

Gemini (Greek) twin.
Gemelle, Gemima, Gemina, Geminine, Gemmina

Gen (Japanese) spring. A short form of names beginning with "Gen."

Gena G (French) a form of Gina. A short form of Geneva, Genevieve, Iphigenia.
Geanna, Geena, Geenah, Gen, Genae, Genah, Genai, Genea, Geneja, Geni, Genia, Genie

Gene (Chamorro) a type of plant.

Geneen (Scottish) a form of Jeanine.
Geanine, Geannine, Gen, Genene, Genine, Gineen, Ginene

Genell (American) a form of Jenelle.

Generosa (Spanish) generous.

Genesis G (Latin) origin; birth.
Genes, Genese, Genesha, Genesia, Genesiss, Genessa, Genesse, Genessie, Genessis, Genicis, Genises, Genysis, Yenesis

Geneva (French) juniper tree. A short form of Genevieve. Geography: a city in Switzerland.
Geena, Gen, Gena, Geneieve, Geneiva, Geneive, Geneve, Ginneva, Janeva, Jeaneva, Jeneva

Genevieve G (German, French) a form of Guinevere. See also Gwendolyn.
Gen, Genaveeve, Genaveve, Genavie, Genavieve, Genavive, Geneva, Geneveve, Genevie, Geneviéve, Genevievre, Genevive, Genovieve, Genvieve, Ginette, Gineveve, Ginevieve, Ginevive, Guinevieve, Guinivive, Gwenevieve, Gwenivive, Jennavieve

Genevra (French, Welsh) a form of Guinevere.
Gen, Genever, Genevera, Ginevra

Geng (Chinese) honest.

Genice (American) a form of Janice.
Gen, Genece, Geneice, Genesa, Genesee, Genessia, Genis, Genise

Genita (American) a form of Janita.
Gen, Genet, Geneta

Genji (Chinese) gold.

Genna (English) a form of Jenna.
Gen, Gennae, Gennay, Genni, Gennie, Genny

Gennifer (American) a form of Jennifer.
Gen, Genifer, Ginnifer

Genovieve (French) a form of Genevieve.
Genoveva, Genoveve, Genovive

Georgeanna (English) a combination of Georgia + Anna.
Georgana, Georganna, Georgeana, Georgiana, Georgianna, Georgyanna, Giorgianna

Georgeanne (English) a combination of Georgia + Anne.
Georgann, Georganne, Georgean, Georgeann, Georgie, Georgyann, Georgyanne

Georgene (English) a familiar form of Georgia.
Georgeena, Georgeina, Georgena, Georgenia, Georgiena, Georgienne, Georgina, Georgine

Georgette (French) a form of Georgia.
Georgeta, Georgett, Georgetta, Georjetta

Georgia **G** (Greek) farmer. Art: Georgia O'Keeffe was an American painter known especially for her paintings of flowers. Geography: a southern American state; a country in Eastern Europe. See also Jirina, Jorja.
Georgene, Georgette, Georgie, Giorgia

Georgianna (English) a form of Georgeanna.
Georgiana, Georgiann, Georgianne, Georgie, Georgieann, Georgionna

Georgie (English) a familiar form of Georgeanne, Georgia, Georgianna.
Georgi, Georgy, Giorgi

Georgina (English) a form of Georgia.
Georgena, Georgene, Georgine, Giorgina, Jorgina

Gerald **B** (German) mighty spear carrier.

Geraldine (German) a form of Gerald. See also Dena, Jeraldine.
Geralda, Geraldina, Geraldyna, Geraldyne, Gerhardine, Geri, Gerianna, Gerianne, Gerrilee, Giralda

Geralyn (American) a combination of Geraldine + Lynn.
Geralisha, Geralynn, Gerilyn, Gerrilyn

Geranio (Greek) she is as beautiful as a geranium.

Gerardo **B** (English) brave with a spear.
Gerardine

Gerda (Norwegian) protector. (German) a familiar form of Gertrude.
Gerta

Geri (American) a familiar form of Geraldine. See also Jeri.
Gerri, Gerrie, Gerry

Germaine (French) from Germany. See also Jermaine.
Germain, Germana, Germanee, Germani, Germanie, Germaya, Germine

Gertie (German) a familiar form of Gertrude.
Gert, Gertey, Gerti, Gerty

Gertrude (German) beloved warrior. See also Trudy.
Gerda, Gerta, Gertie, Gertina, Gertraud, Gertrud, Gertruda

Gertrudes, Gertrudis (Spanish) beloved warrior.

Gervaise **BG** (French) skilled with a spear.

Gervasi (Spanish) having to do with spears.

Gessica (Italian) a form of Jessica.
Gesica, Gesika, Gess, Gesse, Gessy

Geva (Hebrew) hill.
Gevah

Gezana, Gezane (Spanish) reference to the Incarnation.

Ghaada (Indian) beautiful.

Ghaaliya (Indian) fragrant.

Ghada (Arabic) young; tender.
Gada

Ghaydaa (Indian) young and delicate.

Ghita (Italian) pearly.
Gita

Ghusoon (Indian) branches.

Giang (Vietnamese) brave, courageous.

Gianira (Greek) nymph from the sea.

Gianna (Italian) a short form of Giovanna. See also Jianna, Johana.
Geona, Geonna, Giana, Gianella, Gianetta, Gianina, Gianinna, Gianne, Giannee, Giannella, Giannetta, Gianni, Giannie, Giannina, Gianny, Gianoula

Giao (Vietnamese) charm and grace.

Gigi (French) a familiar form of Gilberte.
Geegee, G. G., Giggi

Gilana (Hebrew) joyful.
Gila, Gilah

Gilberte (German) brilliant; pledge;
trustworthy. See also Berti.
Gigi, Gilberta, Gilbertina, Gilbertine, Gill

Gilda (English) covered with gold.
Gilde, Gildi, Gildie, Gildy

Gill (Latin, German) a short form of Gilberte,
Gillian.
Gili, Gilli, Gillie, Gilly

Gillian 🄶 (Latin) a form of Jillian.
*Gila, Gilana, Gilenia, Gili, Gilian, Gill, Gilliana,
Gilliane, Gilliann, Gillianna, Gillianne, Gillie,
Gilly, Gillyan, Gillyane, Gillyann, Gillyanne,
Gyllian, Lian*

Gin (Japanese) silver. A short form of names
beginning with "Gin."

Gina (Italian) a short form of Angelina,
Eugenia, Regina, Virginia. See also Jina.
Gena, Gin, Ginah, Ginai, Ginna

Giña (Chamorro) silversides fish.

Ginebra (Celtic) white as foam.

Gines (Greek) she who engenders life.

Ginette (English) a form of Genevieve.
*Gin, Ginata, Ginett, Ginetta, Ginnetta,
Ginnette*

Ging Ging (Tagalog) one who puts on an act
to be noticed.

Ginger (Latin) flower; spice. A familiar form
of Virginia.
Gin, Ginja, Ginjer, Ginny

Ginia (Latin) a familiar form of Virginia.
Gin

Ginnifer (English) white; smooth; soft.
(Welsh) a form of Jennifer.
Gin, Ginifer

Ginny (English) a familiar form of Ginger,
Virginia. See also Jin, Jinny.
*Gin, Gini, Ginney, Ginni, Ginnie, Giny, Gionni,
Gionny*

Gioconda (Latin) she who engenders life.

Giordana (Italian) a form of Jordana.

Giorgianna (English) a form of Georgeanna.
Giorgina

Giovanna (Italian) a form of Jane.
*Geovana, Geovanna, Geovonna, Giavanna,
Giavonna, Giovana, Giovanne, Giovannica,
Giovonna, Givonnie, Jeveny*

Giovanni 🄱 (Italian) a form of Giovanna.

Gira (Indian) language.

Girija (Indian) daughter of the mountain.

Gisa (Hebrew) carved stone.
Gazit, Gissa

Gisela (German) a form of Giselle.
Gisella, Gissela, Gissella

Giselda (German, Teutonic) arrow; ray;
token of happiness.

Giselle 🄶 (German) pledge; hostage. See
also Jizelle.
*Ghisele, Gisel, Gisela, Gisele, Geséle, Giseli,
Gisell, Gissell, Gisselle, Gizela, Gysell*

Gissel, Gisselle (German) forms of Giselle.
Gissell

Gita (Yiddish) good. (Polish) a short form of
Margaret.
Gitka, Gitta, Gituska

Gitali (Indian) melodious.

Gitana (Spanish) gypsy; wanderer.

Gitanjali (Indian) melodious tribute.

Gitika (Indian) a small song.

Gitta (Irish) a short form of Bridget.
Getta

Giulia (Italian) a form of Julia.
*Giulana, Giuliana, Giulianna, Giulliana, Guila,
Guiliana, Guilietta*

Giunia (Latin) she who was born in June.

Gizela (Czech) a form of Giselle.
*Gizel, Gizele, Gizella, Gizelle, Gizi, Giziki,
Gizus*

Gladis (Irish) a form of Gladys.
Gladi, Gladiz

Gladys (Latin) small sword. (Irish) princess.
(Welsh) a form of Claudia.
*Glad, Gladis, Gladness, Gladwys, Glady,
Gwladys*

Glaucia (Portuguese) brave gift.

Glen 🄱 (Irish) a form of Glenn.

Glenda (Welsh) a form of Glenna.
Glanda, Glennda, Glynda

Glenn 🄱 (Irish) valley, glen.

Glenna (Irish) a form of Glenn. See also
Glynnis.
*Glenda, Glenetta, Glenina, Glenine, Glenne,
Glennesha, Glennia, Glennie, Glenora, Gleny,
Glyn*

Glennesha (American) a form of Glenna.
Glenesha, Glenisha, Glennisha, Glennishia

Gloria **G** (Latin) glory. History: Gloria
Steinem, a leading American feminist,
founded Ms. magazine.
*Gloresha, Gloriah, Gloribel, Gloriela, Gloriella,
Glorielle, Gloris, Glorisha, Glorvina, Glory*

Glorianne (American) a combination of
Gloria + Anne.
Gloriana, Gloriane, Gloriann, Glorianna

Glory (Latin) a form of Gloria.

Glynnis (Welsh) a form of Glenna.
*Glenice, Glenis, Glenise, Glenyse, Glennis,
Glennys, Glenwys, Glenys, Glenyss, Glinnis,
Glinys, Glynesha, Glynice, Glynis, Glynisha,
Glyniss, Glynitra, Glynys, Glynyss*

Godalupe (Spanish) reference to the Virgin
Mary.

Godavari (Indian) the Godavari River.

Godavri (Indian) a river.

Godongña (Chamorro) she is entrapped.

Gofaras (Chamorro) a lot of shell money.

Gofhenum (Chamorro) lots of water.

Gofmatanmiyu (Chamorro) your face.

Gofnaam (Chamorro) very great name.

Gofsaina (Chamorro) very supreme, godlike.

Goftalu (Chamorro) very central.

Goftaotao (Chamorro) many people.

Gogo (Chamorro) a form of Gogui.

Gogui (Chamorro) protect; save, rescue.

Golda (English) gold. History: Golda Meir
was a Russian-born politician who served as
prime minister of Israel.
Goldarina, Golden, Goldie, Goldina

Goldie (English) a familiar form of Golda.
Goldi, Goldy

Goma (Swahili) joyful dance.

Gomathi, Gomti (Indian) a river.

Gomati (Indian) the Gomati River.

Gong (Chinese) respectful.

Gool (Indian) a flower.

Gopa (Indian) wife of Gautama.

Gopi (Indian) milkmaid friends of Lord
Krishna.

Gopika (Indian) cowherd girls.

Goptoña (Chamorro) his or her party.

Gourangi (Indian) fair complexion.

Govindi (Indian) a devotee of Lord Krishna.

Graça (Portuguese) a form of Grace.

Grace 👑 (Latin) graceful.
*Engracia, Graca, Gracia, Gracie, Graciela,
Graciella, Gracinha, Graice, Grata, Gratia,
Gray, Grayce, Grecia*

Graceanne (English) a combination of
Grace + Anne.
*Graceann, Graceanna, Gracen, Graciana,
Gracianna, Gracin, Gratiana*

Gracia (Spanish) a form of Grace.
Gracea, Grecia

Gracie 👑 (English) a familiar form of
Grace.
*Gracee, Gracey, Graci, Gracy, Graecie,
Graysie*

Graham **B** (English) grand home.

Grant **B** (English) great; giving.

Granthana (Indian) book.

Grayson **B** (English) bailiff's child.
Graison, Graisyn, Grasien, Grasyn, Graysen

Grazia (Latin) a form of Grace.
Graziella, Grazielle, Graziosa, Grazyna

Greashma (Indian) summer.

Grecia (Latin) a form of Grace.

Greer (Scottish) vigilant.
Grear, Grier

Gregoria (Spanish) vigilant watchman.

Gregoriana (Spanish) a form of Gregoria.

Gregorina (Latin) watches over her group of
people.

Gregory **B** (Latin) vigilant watch guard.

Greta (German) a short form of Gretchen,
Margaret.
*Greatal, Greatel, Greeta, Gretal, Grete, Gretel,
Gretha, Grethal, Grethe, Grethel, Gretta, Grette,
Grieta, Gryta, Grytta*

Gretchen (German) a form of Margaret.
Greta, Gretchin, Gretchyn

Gricelda (German) a form of Griselda.
Gricelle

Griffin **B** (Latin) hooked nose.

Grisel (German) a short form of Griselda.
Grisell, Griselle, Grissel, Grissele, Grissell, Grizel

Grisela (Spanish) a form of Griselda.

Griselda (German) gray woman warrior. See also Selda, Zelda.
Gricelda, Grisel, Griseldis, Griseldys, Griselys, Grishilda, Grishilde, Grisselda, Grissely, Grizelda

Grishma (Indian) warmth.

Gu (Chinese) valley.

Guadalupe G (Arabic) river of black stones. See also Lupe.
Guadalup, Guadelupe, Guadlupe, Guadulupe, Gudalupe

Guan (Chinese) the best.

Guang (Chinese) light, brightness.

Guan-yin (Chinese) the goddess of mercy.

Gudrun (Scandinavian) battler. See also Runa.
Gudren, Gudrin, Gudrinn, Gudruna

Gui (Chinese) precious.

Guía (Spanish) guide.

Guillelmina (Italian, Spanish) resolute protector.

Guillerma (Spanish) a short form of Guillermina.
Guilla, Guillermina

Guinevere (French, Welsh) white wave; white phantom. Literature: the wife of King Arthur. See also Gayna, Genevieve, Genevra, Jennifer, Winifred, Wynne.
Generva, Genn, Ginette, Guenevere, Guenna,

Guinivere, Guinna, Gwen, Gwenevere, Gwenivere, Gwynnevere

Guioma (Spanish) a form of Giuomar.

Guiomar (German) famous in combat.

Gulika (Indian) a pearl.

Gunavati, Gunita, Gunwanti (Indian) virtuous.

Gunda (Norwegian) female warrior.
Gundala, Gunta

Gundelina (Teutonic) she who helps in battle.

Gundelinda (German) pious one in the battle.

Gundenia (German) fighter.

Guneet (Indian) full of talent.

Gunjana (Indian) buzzing of a bee.

Gunjita (Indian) the humming of bee.

Gunnika (Indian) garland.

Guo (Chinese) result.

Gurbani (Indian) Sikh's religious prayer.

Gurit (Hebrew) innocent baby.

Gurjot BG (Sikh) light of the guru.

Gurleen (Sikh) follower of the guru.

Gurpreet BG (Punjabi) religion.
Gurprit

Gurvir B (Sikh) guru's warrior.

Gusta (Latin) a short form of Augusta.
Gus, Gussi, Gussie, Gussy, Gusti, Gustie, Gusty

Gustava (Scandinavian) staff of the Goths.

Guy B (Hebrew) valley. (German) warrior. (French) guide.

Gwen (Welsh) a short form of Guinevere, Gwendolyn.
Gwenesha, Gweness, Gweneta, Gwenetta, Gwenette, Gweni, Gwenisha, Gwenita, Gwenn, Gwenna, Gwennie, Gwenny

Gwenda (Welsh) a familiar form of Gwendolyn.
Gwinda, Gwynda, Gwynedd

Gwendolyn (Welsh) white wave; white browed; new moon. Literature: Gwendoloena was the wife of Merlin, the magician. See also Genevieve, Gwyneth, Wendy.
Guendolen, Gwen, Gwendalin, Gwenda, Gwendalee, Gwendaline, Gwendalyn, Gwendalynn, Gwendela, Gwendelyn, Gwendelynn, Gwendilyn, Gwendolen, Gwendolene, Gwendolin, Gwendoline, Gwendolyne, Gwendolynn, Gwendolynne, Gwendylan, Gwyndolyn, Gwynndolen

Gwyn G (Welsh) a short form of Gwyneth.
Gwinn, Gwinne, Gwynn, Gwynne

Gwyneth (Welsh) a form of Gwendolyn. See also Winnie, Wynne.
Gweneth, Gwenith, Gwenneth, Gwennyth, Gwenyth, Gwyn, Gwynneth

Gypsy (English) wanderer.
Gipsy, Gypsie, Jipsi

H **G** (American) an initial used as a first name.

Ha (Vietnamese) river.

Ha'ane, Haane, Haani (Chamorro) forms of Ha'ani.

Ha'ani (Chamorro) day.

Haadiya (Indian) guide to righteousness.

Haala (Indian) aureole.

Habiba (Arabic) beloved.
Habibah, Habibeh

Hachi (Japanese) eight; good luck.
Hachiko, Hachiyo

Hada (Hebrew) she who radiates joy.

Hadara (Hebrew) adorned with beauty.
Hadarah

Hadasa (Hebrew) myrtle.

Hadassah (Hebrew) myrtle tree.
Hadas, Hadasah, Hadassa, Haddasa, Haddasah

Hadiya (Swahili) gift.
Hadaya, Hadia, Hadiyah, Hadiyyah

Hadley **G** (English) field of heather.
Hadlea, Hadlee, Hadleigh, Hadli, Hadlie, Hadly

Hadriane (Greek, Latin) a form of Adrienne.
Hadriana, Hadrianna, Hadrianne, Hadriene, Hadrienne

Haeley (English) a form of Hailey.
Haelee, Haeleigh, Haeli, Haelie, Haelleigh, Haelli, Haellie, Haely

Hafiza (Indian) protected.

Hagar (Hebrew) forsaken; stranger. Bible: Sarah's handmaiden, the mother of Ishmael.
Haggar

Hai (Vietnamese) happy; kiss of life.

Haidee (Greek) modest.
Hady, Haide, Haidi, Haidy, Haydee, Haydy

Haiden **B** (English) heather-covered hill.
Haden, Hadyn, Haeden, Haidn, Haidyn

Hailee (English) a form of Hayley.
Haile, Hailei, Haileigh, Haillee

Hailey ☀ **G** (English) a form of Hayley.
Haeley, Haiely, Hailea, Hailley, Hailly, Haily

Haili, Hailie (English) forms of Hayley.
Haille, Hailli, Haillie

Haima (Indian) snow.

Haimavati (Indian) Parvati, a consort of Lord Shiva.

Haimi (Indian) golden.

Haisha (Arabic) a form of Aisha.

Hakeem **B** (Arabic) a form of Hakim (see Boys' Names).

Haldana (Norwegian) half-Danish.

Halee **G** (English) a form of Haley.
Hale, Halea, Haleah, Haleh, Halei

Haleigh (English) a form of Haley.

Haley ☀ **G** (Scandinavian) heroine. See also Hailey, Hayley.
Halee, Haleigh, Hali, Halley, Hallie, Haly, Halye

Hali **G** (English) a form of Haley.

Halia (Hawaiian) in loving memory.

Halie (English) a form of Haley.
Haliegh

Halimah (Arabic) gentle; patient.
Halima, Halime

Halina (Hawaiian) likeness. (Russian) a form of Helen.
Haleen, Haleena, Halena, Halinka

Halla (African) unexpected gift.
Hala, Hallah, Halle

Halley **G** (English) a form of Haley.
Hally, Hallye

Hallie **G** (Scandinavian) a form of Haley.
Hallee, Hallei, Halleigh, Halli

Halona (Native American) fortunate.
Halonah, Haloona, Haona

Halsey **G** (English) Hall's island.
Halsea, Halsie

Hama (Japanese) shore.

Hamako (Japanese) a form of Hama.

Hameeda (Indian) praiseworthy.

Hamsini (Indian) one who rides a swan.

Han (Vietnamese) good.

Hana, Hanah (Japanese) flower. (Arabic) happiness. (Slavic) forms of Hannah.
Hanae, Hanan, Haneen, Hanicka, Hanin, Hanita, Hanka

Hanako (Japanese) flower child.

Hang (Vietnamese) old name for shoe.

Hang Man (Korean) iron, firm; wise, knowing.

Hanh (Vietnamese) moral.

Hanh Phuc (Vietnamese) moon.

Hania (Hebrew) resting place.
Haniya, Hanja, Hannia, Hanniah, Hanya

Hanima (Indian) a wave.

Hanna ◪ (Hebrew) a form of Hannah.

Hannah ☝ ◪ (Hebrew) gracious. Bible: the mother of Samuel. See also Anci, Anezka, Ania, Anka, Ann, Anna, Annalie, Anneka, Chana, Nina, Nusi.
Hana, Hanna, Hanneke, Hannele, Hanni, Hannon, Honna

Hanni (Hebrew) a familiar form of Hannah.
Hani, Hanne, Hannie, Hanny

Hano (Hawaiian) glorious, honored, dignified.

Hansa, Hansika (Indian) swan.

Hansamala (Indian) a line of swans.

Hansini (Indian) swan; very pretty lady.

Hansuja (Indian) another name for Laxmi, goddess of wealth.

Hanumta (Chamorro) our water.

Hao (Vietnamese) moral.

Happy (English) happy.
Happi

Hara ◪ (Hindi) tawny. Religion: another name for the Hindu god Shiva, the destroyer.

Harathi (Indian) divine fire in the puja ritual.

Haribala (Indian) daughter of Lord Vishnu.

Harimanti, Hemanti (Indian) born in the Hemant season.

Harinakshi (Indian) one with eyes like a deer.

Harini (Indian) a deer.

Harita (Indian) green.

Harlee, Harleigh, Harlie (English) forms of Harley.
Harlei, Harli

Harley ◪◪ (English) meadow of the hare. See also Arleigh.
Harlee, Harleey, Harly

Harleyann (English) a combination of Harley + Ann.
Harlann, Harlanna, Harlanne, Harleen, Harlene, Harleyanna, Harleyanne, Harliann, Harlianna, Harlianne, Harlina, Harline

Harmony (Latin) harmonious.
Harmene, Harmeni, Harmon, Harmonee, Harmonei, Harmoni, Harmonia, Harmonie

Harpreet ◪ (Punjabi) devoted to God.
Harprit

Harriet (French) ruler of the household. (English) a form of Henrietta. Literature: Harriet Beecher Stowe was an American writer noted for her novel *Uncle Tom's Cabin*.
Harri, Harrie, Harriett, Harrietta, Harriette, Harriot, Harriott, Hattie

Harrison ◪ (English) child of Harry.

Harshada (Indian) giver of joy.

Harshi, Harshini (Indian) joyous.

Harsika (Indian) laugh.

Haru (Japanese) spring.

Harue (Japanese) springtime bay.

Haruka (Japanese) distant fragrance.

Haruna (Japanese) she who blossoms in the spring.

Haruye (Japanese) blessed spring season.

Haruyo (Japanese) healing generation.

Harvir ◪ (Sikh) God's warrior.

Hasana (Swahili) she arrived first. Culture: a name used for the first-born female twin. See also Huseina.
Hasanna, Hasna, Hassana, Hassna, Hassona

Hasina (Swahili) good.
Haseena, Hasena, Hassina

Hasita (Indian) full of laughter.

Hassuyi (Chamorro) to remember.

Hasumati (Indian) happy.

Hateya (Moquelumnan) footprints.

Hatsu (Japanese) first born.

Hatsuko (Japanese) first daughter.

Hatsumi (Japanese) beautiful beginning.

Hatsuye (Japanese) blessed beginning.

Hattie (English) familiar forms of Harriet, Henrietta.
Hatti, Hatty, Hetti, Hettie, Hetty

Haulani (Hawaiian) royal ruler.

Hauoli (Hawaiian) joy, happiness.

Hausu (Moquelumnan) like a bear yawning upon awakening.

Hava (Hebrew) a form of Chava. See also Eve.
Havah, Havvah

Haven **G** (English) a form of Heaven.
Havan, Havana, Havanna, Havannah, Havyn

Haviva (Hebrew) beloved.
Havalee, Havelah, Havi, Hayah

Hayaam (Indian) deliriously in love.

Hayato (Japanese) prompt person.

Hayden **B** (English) a form of Haiden.
Hayde, Haydin, Haydn, Haydon

Hayfa (Arabic) shapely.

Haylee, Hayleigh, Haylie (English) forms of Hayley.
Hayle, Haylea, Haylei, Hayli, Haylle, Hayllie

Hayley **G** (English) hay meadow. See also Hailey, Haley.
Hailee, Haili, Haylee, Hayly

Hazel (English) hazelnut tree; commanding authority.
Hazal, Hazaline, Haze, Hazeline, Hazell, Hazelle, Hazen, Hazyl

Hazuki (Japanese) the eighth lunar month.

He (Chinese) harmony.

Hea (Korean) virtue, goodness; power.

Heath **B** (English) a form of Heather.

Heather **G** (English) flowering heather.
Heatherlee, Heatherly

Heaven **G** (English) place of beauty and happiness. Bible: where God and angels are said to dwell.
Haven, Heavan, Heavenly, Heavin, Heavon, Heavyn, Hevean, Heven, Hevin

Hebe (Greek) youthful like a flower.

Hecuba (Greek) wife of Priam, king of Troy.

Hedda (German) battler. See also Edda, Hedy.
Heda, Hedaya, Hedia, Hedvick, Hedvig, Hedvika, Hedwig, Hedwiga, Heida, Hetta

Hedy (Greek) delightful; sweet. (German) a familiar form of Hedda.
Heddey, Heddi, Heddie, Heddy, Hede, Hedi

Heera (Indian) diamond.

Heerkani, Hirkani (Indian) small diamond.

Hei (Korean) harbor.

Heidi, Heidy (German) short forms of Adelaide.
Heida, Heide, Heidee, Heidie, Heydy, Hidee, Hidi, Hidie, Hidy, Hiede, Hiedi, Hydi

Heija (Korean) grace.

Helda (German) she who battles.

Helen **G** (Greek) light. See also Aileen, Aili, Alena, Eileen, Elaina, Elaine, Eleanor, Ellen, Galina, Ila, Ilene, Ilona, Jelena, Leanore, Leena, Lelya, Lenci, Lene, Liolya, Nellie, Nitsa, Olena, Onella, Yalena, Yelena.
Elana, Ena, Halina, Hela, Hele, Helena, Helene, Helle, Hellen, Helli, Hellin, Hellon, Hellyn, Helon

Helena (Greek) a form of Helen. See also Ilena.
Halena, Halina, Helaina, Helana, Helania, Helayna, Heleana, Heleena, Helenia, Helenka, Helenna, Helina, Hellanna, Hellena, Hellenna, Helona, Helonna

Helene (French) a form of Helen.
Helaine, Helanie, Helayne, Heleen, Heleine, Héléne, Helenor, Heline, Hellenor

Helga (German) pious. (Scandinavian) a form of Olga. See also Elga.

Heli (Spanish) a form of Heliana.

Helia (Greek) as if she were the sun.

Heliana (Greek) she who offers herself to God.

Heliena (Greek) sun.

Helki **BG** (Native American) touched.
Helkey, Helkie, Helky

Helma (German) a short form of Wilhelmina.
Halma, Helme, Helmi, Helmine, Hilma

Heloísa (German) a form of Eloísa.

Heloise (French) a form of Louise.
Héloïse, Hlois

Helsa (Danish) a form of Elizabeth.
Helse, Helsey, Helsi, Helsie, Helsy

Heltu (Moquelumnan) like a bear reaching out.

Helvecia (Latin) member of the Helvetians, ancient inhabitants of Switzerland; happy friend.

Helvia (Latin) she who has blonde locks of hair.

Helya (Chuukese) a form of Helia.

Hema (Indian) gold.

Hemakshi (Indian) golden eyes.

Hemalata (Indian) golden creeper.

Hemali (Indian) to bring wealth.

Hemangi (Indian) golden body.

Hemangini (Indian) girl with a golden body.

Hemaprabha (Indian) golden light.

Hemashri (Indian) one with a golden body.

Hemkanta (Indian) golden girl.

Hemlata (Indian) golden flower.

Heng (Chinese) constant.

Henna (English) a familiar form of Henrietta.
Hena, Henaa, Henah, Heni, Henia, Henny, Henya

Henrietta (English) ruler of the household. See also Enrica, Etta, Yetta.
Harriet, Hattie, Hatty, Hendrika, Heneretta, Henka, Henna, Hennrietta, Hennriette, Henretta, Henrica, Henrie, Henrieta, Henriete, Henriette, Henrika, Henrique, Henriquetta, Henryetta, Hetta, Hettie

Hera (Greek) queen; jealous. Mythology: the queen of heaven and the wife of Zeus.

Hercilia, Hersilia (Greek) she who is delicate, tender, kind.

Hermelinda (German) she who is the shield of strength.

Hermenegilda (Spanish) she who offers sacrifices to God.

Hermia (Greek) messenger.

Hermilda (German) battle of force.

Hermina (Latin) noble. (German) soldier. See also Erma, Ermine, Irma.
Herma, Hermenia, Hermia, Herminna

Herminda (Greek) announcer.

Hermínia (Portuguese) a form of Hermina.

Hermione (Greek) earthy.
Hermalina, Hermia, Hermina, Hermine, Herminia

Hermosa (Spanish) beautiful.

Hernanda (Spanish) bold voyager.

Hertha (English) child of the earth.
Heartha, Hirtha

Herundina (Latin) like a swallow.

Hessa (Indian) destiny.

Hester (Dutch) a form of Esther.
Hessi, Hessie, Hessye, Hesther, Hettie

Hestia (Persian) star. Mythology: the Greek goddess of the hearth and home.
Hestea, Hesti, Hestie, Hesty

Heta (Native American) racer.

Heti (Indian) sunray.

Hetta (German) a form of Hedda. (English) a familiar form of Henrietta.

Hettie (German) a familiar form of Henrietta, Hester.
Hetti, Hetty

Hia (Korean) grace.

Hiah (Korean) bright.

Hidako (Japanese) beautiful child.

Hide (Japanese) excellent.

Hideko (Japanese) excellent child.

Hidemi (Japanese) beautiful; excellent.

Hideyo (Japanese) superior generations.

Hien (Vietnamese) blessing from above.

Higa (Japanese) evil.

Highly (Chuukese) high.

Higinia (Greek) she who has and enjoys good health.

Hikaru (Japanese) generation of excellence.

Hilary, Hillary ☙ (Greek) cheerful, merry. See also Alair.
Hilaree, Hilari, Hilaria, Hilarie, Hilery, Hiliary, Hillaree, Hillari, Hillarie, Hilleary, Hilleree, Hilleri, Hillerie, Hillery, Hillianne, Hilliary, Hillory

Hilda (German) a short form of Brunhilda, Hildegarde.
Helle, Hilde, Hildey, Hildie, Hildur, Hildy, Hulda, Hylda

Hildegarda (German) she who hopes to fight.

Hildegarde (German) fortress.
Hilda, Hildagard, Hildagarde, Hildegard, Hildred

Hildegunda (German) heroic fighter.

Hili (Indian) dancer.

Hilla (Indian) timid.

Hima (Indian) snow.

Himani (Indian) cold.

Himeko (Japanese) princess child.

Hina (Indian) a shrub.

Hinako (Japanese) child named for the sun.

Hind (Indian) proper name.

Hinda (Hebrew) hind; doe.
Hindey, Hindie, Hindy, Hynda

Hipatia (Greek) best.

Hipólita (Greek) she who unties her horse and readies herself for battle.

Hiral (Indian) wealthy.

Hiranmayi (Indian) like a deer.

Hiro (Japanese) broad.

Hiroe (Japanese) large branch.

Hiromi (Japanese) the beautiful ocean.

Hisa (Japanese) long lasting.
Hisae, Hisako, Hisay

Hisano (Japanese) open plain.

Hita (Indian) lovable.

Hitaishi (Indian) well wisher.

Hitee (Indian) love and care.

Hiti (Eskimo) hyena.
Hitty

Hiya (Indian) heart; happiness.

Hoa (Vietnamese) flower; peace.
Ho, Hoai

Hogolina (Teutonic) having clear thoughts and great intelligence.

Hokulani (Hawaiian) star of the heavens.

Hola (Hopi) seed-filled club.

Holden **B** (English) hollow in the valley.

Holley (English) a form of Holly.
Holleah, Hollee

Holli (English) a form of Holly.

Hollie **G** (English) a form of Holly.
Holeigh, Holleigh

Hollis **BG** (English) near the holly bushes.
Hollise, Hollyce, Holyce

Holly **G** (English) holly tree.
Holley, Hollye

Hollyann (English) a combination of Holly + Ann.
Holliann, Hollianna, Hollianne, Hollyanne, Hollyn

Hollyn (English) a short form of Hollyann.
Holin, Holeena, Hollina, Hollynn

Holo (Hawaiian) fleet.

Honami (Japanese) sail; a type of red apple; beautiful.

Honey (English) sweet. (Latin) a familiar form of Honora.
Honalee, Hunney, Hunny

Hong (Vietnamese) pink.

Hong Hoa (Vietnamese) perfect.

Hong Yen (Vietnamese) meek and gentle.

Hongminh (Vietnamese) rose.

Honnesha (Indian) rich person.

Honora (Latin) honorable. See also Nora, Onora.
Honey, Honner, Honnor, Honnour, Honor, Honorah, Honorata, Honore, Honoree, Honoria, Honorina, Honorine, Honour, Honoure

Honoratas (Spanish) honor.

Hoon (Korean) bright.

Hoor (Indian) celestial.

Hooriya (Indian) angel.

Hop (Vietnamese) pink swallow bird.

Hope **G** (English) hope.
Hopey, Hopi, Hopie

Hopoe (Hawaiian) in full bloom.

Hortense (Latin) gardener. See also Ortensia.
Hortencia, Hortensia

Hoshi (Japanese) star.
Hoshie, Hoshiko, Hoshiyo

Hoshimi (Japanese) beautiful, shining star.

Houston 🅱 (English) hill town. Geography: a city in Texas.

Hradini (Indian) lightening.

Hridyesha (Indian) heart.

Hsia (Chinese) summer.

Hsiang (Chinese) incense; village; enjoy; image.

Hsiao (Chinese) dawn; tiny; smile.

Hsiu (Chinese) pretty.

Hsun (Chinese) to teach.

Hu (Chinese) lake.

Hua (Chinese) flower.

Huai (Chinese) bosom.

Huan (Chinese) happiness.

Huan Yue, Huan-Yue (Chinese) joyful, happy.

Huang (Chinese) yellow.

Huanquyi (Mapuche) announcer; she who has a loud voice, shouted.

Huata (Moquelumnan) basket carrier.

Hudaña (Chamorro) she is mute.

Hue (Vietnamese) bright red.

Hugo 🅱 (Latin) a form of Hugh (see Boys' Names).

Hugolina (Teutonic) having clear thoughts and great intelligence.

Hui (Chinese) orchid.

Hui Ying, Hui-Ying (Chinese) bright, intelligent.

Huilen, Huillen, Hullen (Araucanian) spring.

Huma (Indian) bird of paradise.

Humaila (Indian) golden necklace.

Humiko (Palauan) large red ant.

Humildad (Latin) humility.

Hung (Vietnamese) consistent.

Hunter 🅱 (English) hunter.
Hunta, Huntar, Huntter

Huo (Chinese) fire.

Huong (Vietnamese) flower.

Huseina (Swahili) a form of Hasana.

Husn, Husna (Indian) beauty.

Hu-Tu (Chinese) female deity that represents Earth.

Huyen (Vietnamese) lily flower; intelligence, mental brilliance.

Hwan (Korean) a form of Heija.

Hy (Korean) instruct.

Hya (Korean) joyful; ring.

Hyacinth (Greek) Botany: a plant with colorful, fragrant flowers. See also Cynthia, Jacinda.
Giacinta, Hyacintha, Hyacinthe, Hyacinthia, Hyacinthie, Hycinth, Hycynth

Hyang (Korean) a form of Heija.

Hydi, Hydeia (German) forms of Heidi.
Hyde, Hydea, Hydee, Hydia, Hydie, Hydiea

Hye (Korean) graceful.

Hyun (Korean) bright.

Hyun Ah (Korean) fragrance, incense; village; enjoy.

Hyun Mee (Korean) worth; wise; dark; subtle; bowstring, musical string.

Hyun Mi (Korean) she who has wisdom.

Hyung (Korean) a form of Hyun Mi.

Hyunh (Vietnamese) pink rose.

Hyunsook (Korean) unpolished; rice.

I Wei (Chinese) a form of Iwei.

Iaesha, Ieeshia (Arabic) forms of Aisha.

Ian 🅱 (Hebrew) God is gracious.
Iaian, Iain, Iana, Iann, Ianna, Iannel, Iyana

Ianthe (Greek) violet flower.
Iantha, Ianthia, Ianthina

Iara (Tupi) she is a lady.

Iberia (Latin) she who is a native of Iberia or comes from the Iberian peninsula.

Ibtihaaj (Indian) joy.

Ibtisam (Arabic) smiling.

Ibuuch (Palauan) a form of Evarista.

Icess (Egyptian) a form of Isis.
Ices, Icesis, Icesse, Icey, Icia, Icis, Icy

Ichieko (Chuukese) a form of Ichiko.

Ichiko (Japanese) first daughter.

Ida (German) hard working. (English) prosperous.
Idah, Idaia, Idalia, Idalis, Idaly, Idamae, Idania, Idarina, Idarine, Idaya, Ide, Idelle, Idette, Idys

Idalina (English) a combination of Ida + Lina.
Idaleena, Idaleene, Idalena, Idalene, Idaline

Idalis (English) a form of Ida.
Idalesse, Idalise, Idalíz, Idallas, Idallis, Idelis, Idelys, Idialis

Idara (Latin) well-organized woman.

Ideashia (American) a combination of Ida + Iesha.
Idasha, Idaysha, Ideesha, Idesha

Idelgunda (German) combative when fighting.

Idelia, Idelina (German) she who is noble.

Idelle (Welsh) a form of Ida.
Idell, Idella, Idil

Idha (Indian) insight.

Idika (Indian) the Earth.

Iditri (Indian) complimentary.

Idoia (Spanish) reference to the Virgin Mary.

Idoshi (Kosraean) a form of Violeta.

Idoya (Spanish) pond, an important place of worship of the Virgin Mary.

Idub (Palauan) a form of Yumiko.

Idumea (Latin) red.

Idurre (Spanish) reference to the Virgin Mary.

Ieko (Japanese) house child.

Iesha (American) a form of Aisha.
Ieachia, Ieaisha, Ieasha, Ieashe, Ieesha, Ieeshia, Ieisha, Ieishia, Iescha, Ieshah, Ieshea, Iesheia, Ieshia, Iiesha, Iisha

Ifigenia (Greek) having great strength and vitality; woman of strong, vital roots.

Ifiginia (Spanish) a form of Ifigenia.

Ignacia (Latin) fiery, ardent.
Ignacie, Ignasha, Ignashia, Ignatia, Ignatzia

Iha (Indian) wish.

Ihina (Indian) enthusiasm.

Ihita (Indian) desire.

Ijaya (Indian) sacrifice.

Ikia (Hebrew) God is my salvation. (Hawaiian) a form of Isaiah.
Ikaisha, Ikea, Ikeea, Ikeia, Ikeisha, Ikeishi, Ikeishia, Ikesha, Ikeshia, Ikeya, Ikeyia, Ikiea, Ikiia

Ikraam (Indian) honor; hospitality, generosity.

Iksha (Indian) sight.

Ikshita (Indian) visible.

Ikshula (Indian) holy river.

Iku (Japanese) nourishing.

Ikuko (Japanese) flourishing child.

Ikuku (Japanese) perfume child.

Ikumi (Japanese) drinking well.

Ikuye (Japanese) blessed cultural flourishing.

Ila (Hungarian) a form of Helen.

Ilana (Hebrew) tree.
Ilaina, Ilane, Ilani, Ilania, Ilainie, Illana, Illane, Illani, Ilania, Illanie, Ilanit

Ilchahueque (Mapuche) young, virginal woman.

Ilda (German) heroine in battle.

Ildegunda (German) she who knows how to fight.

Ileana (Hebrew) a form of Iliana.
Ilea, Ileah, Ileane, Ileanna, Ileanne, Illeana

Ilebed (Palauan) betel nut.

Ilena (Greek) a form of Helena.
Ileana, Ileena, Ileina, Ilina, Ilyna

Ilene (Irish) a form of Helen. See also Aileen, Eileen.
Ileen, Ileene, Iline, Ilyne

Ileseva (Fijian) a form of Elizabeth.

Ilhaam (Indian) intuition.

Iliana (Greek) from Troy.
Ileana, Ili, Ilia, Iliani, Illiana, Illiani, Illianna, Illyana, Illyanna

Ilima (Hawaiian) flower of Oahu.

Ilisa (Scottish, English) a form of Alisa, Elisa.
Ilicia, Ilissa, Iliza, Illisa, Illissa, Illysa, Ilycia, Ilysa, Ilysia, Ilyssa, Ilyza

Ilisapeci (Fijian) a form of Elizabeth.

Ilise (German) a form of Elise.
Ilese, Illytse, Ilyce, Ilyse

Ilisha (Hebrew) a form of Alisha, Elisha. See also Lisha.
Ileshia, Ilishia, Ilysha, Ilyshia

Ilka (Hungarian) a familiar form of Ilona.
Ilke, Milka, Milke

Ilona (Hungarian) a form of Helen.
Ilka, Illona, Illonia, Illonya, Ilonka, Ilyona

Ilse (German) a form of Elizabeth. See also Elsa.
Ilsa, Ilsey, Ilsie, Ilsy

Iluminada (Spanish) illuminated.

Iluochel (Palauan) something used to kill fish.

Im (Korean) wise and virtuous woman.

Ima (Japanese) presently. (German) a familiar form of Amelia.

Imaculada (Portuguese) immaculate.

Imala (Native American) strong-minded.

Iman 🄶 (Arabic) believer.
Aman, Imana, Imane, Imani

Imani 🄶 (Arabic) a form of Iman.
Amani, Emani, Imahni, Imanie, Imanii, Imonee, Imoni

Imelda (German) warrior.
Imalda, Irmhilde, Melda

Imena (African) dream.
Imee, Imene

Imogene (Latin) image, likeness.
Emogen, Emogene, Imogen, Imogenia, Imojean, Imojeen, Innogen, Innogene

Imperia (Latin) imperial.

Imperio (Latin) head of state, ruler.

Imtithal (Indian) obedience.

In (Korean) two; different; finished.

Ina (Irish) a form of Agnes.
Ena, Inanna, Inanne

Inaam (Indian) act of kindness, bestowal.

Inagangta (Chamorro) our noise.

Inaganta (Chamorro) a form of Inagangta.

Inah (Chamorro) a form of Ina.

Inara, Inaria (Chuukese) forms of Hilaria.

Inaya (Indian) concern.

Inayat (Indian) kindness.

Inayic (Chamorro) choice.

Indali (Indian) powerful.

Indamira, Indemira (Arabic) guest of the princess.

India (Hindi) from India.
Indea, Indeah, Indee, Indeia, Indeya, Indi, Indiah, Indian, Indiana, Indianna, Indie, Indieya, Indiya, Indy, Indya

Indigo (Latin) dark blue color.
Indiga, Indygo

Indira (Hindi) splendid. History: Indira Nehru Gandhi was an Indian politician and prime minister.
Indiara, Indra, Indre, Indria

Indrakshi (Indian) one having beautiful eyes.

Indrani (Indian) wife of Indra.

Indrayani (Indian) a holy river.

Indu, Induleksh (Indian) the moon.

Induja (Indian) the moon's daughter.

Indukala (Indian) phases of the moon.

Indulala (Indian) moonlight.

Indulekha (Indian) moon.

Induma (Indian) moon.

Indumati (Indian) full moon.

Indumukhi (Indian) one with a face like the moon.

Induprabha (Indian) moon rays.

Ine (Japanese) rice plant; clothes; sound.

Inàs (Portuguese) a form of Ines.

Ines, Inés, Inez (Spanish) forms of Agnes. See also Ynez.
Inesa, Inesita, Inésita, Inessa

Inga (Scandinavian) a short form of Ingrid.
Ingaberg, Ingaborg, Inge, Ingeberg, Ingeborg, Ingela

Ingrid (Scandinavian) hero's daughter; beautiful daughter.
Inga, Inger

Inika (Indian) small earth.

Inina (Chuukese) a glimmer of light.

Inmaculada (Latin) she who is pure and clean, without blemishes.

Inoa (Hawaiian) name.

Inocencia, Inoceneia, Inocenta (Spanish) innocence.

Inseng (Tagalog) the plumeria flower.

Insinani (Kosraean) a form of Fumii.

Intisaar (Indian) triumph.

Inu (Indian) attractive.

Invención (Latin) invention.

Ioana (Romanian) a form of Joan.
Ioani, Ioanna

Iola (Greek) dawn; violet colored. (Welsh) worthy of the Lord.
Iole, Iolee, Iolia

Iolana (Hawaiian) soaring like a hawk.

Iolani (Hawaiian) royal hawk.

Iolanthe (English) a form of Yolanda. See also Jolanda.
Iolanda, Iolande

Iona (Greek) violet flower.
Ione, Ioney, Ioni, Ionia, Iyona, Iyonna

Iosefa (Fijian) a form of Josefa.

Iphigenia (Greek) sacrifice. Mythology: the daughter of the Greek leader Agamemnon. See also Gena.

Ipi (Mapuche) harvester; careful.

Ipo (Hawaiian) sweetheart lover.

Ipsa (Indian) ambition; desire.

Ipsita (Indian) desire.

Iraja (Indian) wind's daughter.

Iratze (Basque) reference to the Virgin Mary.

Iravati (Indian) the Ravi River.

Irene **G** (Greek) peaceful. Mythology: the goddess of peace. See also Orina, Rena, Rene, Yarina.
Irén, Irien, Irina, Jereni

Iridia (Latin) belonging to Iris.

Iriel (Hebrew) a form of Uriel.

Irimia (Spanish) name of the place where the Miño river starts.

Irina (Russian) a form of Irene.
Eirena, Erena, Ira, Irana, Iranda, Iranna, Irena, Irenea, Irenka, Iriana, Irin, Irinia, Irinka, Irona, Ironka, Irusya, Iryna, Irynka, Rina

Iris **G** (Greek) rainbow. Mythology: the goddess of the rainbow and messenger of the gods.
Irisa, Irisha, Irissa, Irita, Irys, Iryssa

Irma (Latin) a form of Erma.
Irmina, Irminia

Irmã (Portuguese) a form of Irma.

Irma de la Paz (Spanish) peaceful Irma.

Irta (Greek) pearl.

Irune (Basque) reference to the holy trinity.

Irupe (Guarani) like the flower of the same name.

Irupé (Guarani) refers to the aquatic plant of the same name.

Isabeau (French) a form of Isabel.

Isabel 🌱 **G** (Spanish) consecrated to God. See also Bel, Belle, Chavella, Ysabel.
Isabal, Isabeau, Isabeli, Isabelita, Isabella,
Isabelle, Ishbel, Isobel, Issie, Izabel, Izabele,
Izabella

Isabelina (Hebrew) she who loves God.

Isabella 🌱 **G** (Italian) a form of Isabel.
Isabela, Isabelia, Isabello

Isabelle 🌱 **G** (French) a form of Isabel.
Isabele, Isabell

Isadora (Latin) gift of Isis.
Isidora

Isaiah **B** (Hebrew) God is my salvation.

Isako (Japanese) helpful child.

Isaldina (German) powerful warrior, she who controls harshly.

Isamar **G** (Hebrew) a form of Itamar.

Isamu (Japanese) rock.

Isano (Japanese) helpful.

Isapela (Fijian) a form of Isabel.

Isaura (Greek) native of Isauria, ancient region in Asia Minor.

Isaye (Japanese) help; branch; inlet.

Isberga (German) she who protects, sword in hand.

Isela (Scottish) a form of Isla.
Isel

Iselda (German) she who remains faithful.

Iseult (Welsh) fair lady. Literature: Also known as Isolde, a princess in the Arthurian legends; a heroine in the medieval romance *Tristan and Isolde.* See also Yseult.

Isha (American) a form of Aisha.
Ishae, Ishana, Ishanaa, Ishanda, Ishanee, Ishaney, Ishani, Ishanna, Ishaun, Ishawna, Ishaya, Ishenda, Ishia, Iysha

Ishi (Japanese) rock.
Ishiko, Ishiyo, Shiko, Shiyo

Ishie (Japanese) a form of Ishi.

Ishika (Indian) paintbrush.

Ishita (Indian) superior.

Ishwari (Indian) goddess.

Ishwarya (Indian) wealth, prosperity.

Ishya (Indian) spring.

Isis (Egyptian) supreme goddess. Mythology: the goddess of nature and fertility.
Icess, Issis, Isys

Isla (Scottish) Geography: the River Isla is in Scotland.
Isela

Isleta (Spanish) small island.

Ismelda (German) she who uses the sword in battle.

Ismenia (Greek) she who words anxiously.

Isobel (Spanish) a form of Isabel.
Isobell, Isobella, Isobelle

Isoka (Benin) gift from god.
Soka

Isoko (Japanese) child of the beach.

Isolde (Welsh) fair lady. Literature: Also known as Iseult, a princess in the Arthurian legends; a heroine in the medieval romance *Tristan*

and Isolde. See also Yseult.
Isolda, Isolt, Izolde

Isolina (German) powerful warrior, she who controls harshly.

Isono (Japanese) shore; field, plain.

Issie (Spanish) a familiar form of Isabel.
Isa, Issi, Issy, Iza

Ister (Persian) a form of Esther.

Ita (Irish) thirsty.

Italia (Italian) from Italy.
Itali, Italie, Italy, Italya

Italina (Italian) native of the land between two seas.

Itamar (Hebrew) palm island.
Isamar, Isamari, Isamaria, Ithamar, Ittamar

Itatay (Guarani) hand bell.

Itati (Guarani) refers to the dedication of the virgin of Itatí.

Itatí (Guarani) white rock; refers to the dedication of the virgin of Itatí.

Itkila (Indian) fragrant.

Ito (Japanese) thread.

Itsaso (Basque) sea.

Itsuko (Japanese) fifth daughter.

Itzel (Spanish) protected.
Itcel, Itchel, Itesel, Itsel, Itssel, Itza, Itzallana, Itzayana, Itzell, Ixchel

Iva (Slavic) a short form of Ivana.
Ivah

Ivalani (Hawaiian) a form of Ewelani.

Ivan 🅱 (Russian) a form of John.

Ivana (Slavic) God is gracious. See also Yvanna.
Iva, Ivanah, Ivania, Ivanka, Ivanna, Ivannia, Ivany

Iverem (Tiv) good fortune; blessing.

Iverna (Latin) from Ireland.
Ivernah

Ivette (French) a form of Yvette. See also Evette.
Ivet, Ivete, Iveth, Ivetha, Ivett, Ivetta

Ivey 🅖 (English) a form of Ivy.

Ivón (Spanish) a form of Ivonne.

Ivonne (French) a form of Yvonne. See also Evonne.
Ivon, Ivona, Ivone, Ivonna, Iwona, Iwonka, Iwonna, Iwonne

Ivory (Latin) made of ivory.
Ivoory, Ivori, Ivorie, Ivorine, Ivree

Ivria (Hebrew) from the land of Abraham.
Ivriah, Ivrit

Ivy 🅖 (English) ivy tree.
Ivey, Ivie

Iwa (Japanese) rock.

Iwalani (Hawaiian) heavenly frigate bird.

Iwei (Chinese) consider, think.

Iyabo (Yoruba) mother has returned.

Iyana, Iyanna (Hebrew) forms of Ian.
Iyanah, Iyannah, Iyannia

Izabella (Spanish) a form of Isabel.
Izabela, Izabell, Izabellah, Izabelle, Izobella

Izanami (Japanese) she who invites you to enter.

Izar (Basque) star.

Izarbe (Aragonese) Virgin Mary of the Pyrenees mountains.

Izarra, Izarre (Basque) star.

Izazkun (Basque) reference to the Virgin Mary.

Izdihaar (Indian) flourishing, blossoming.

Izna (Indian) light.

Izora (Arabic) dawn.

Izusa (Native American) white stone.

J **B** (American) an initial used as a first name.

Jaba (Indian) hibiscus.

Jabeen (Indian) forehead.

Jabel (Hebrew) flowing stream.

Jabrea, Jabria (American) combinations of the prefix Ja + Brea.
Jabreal, Jabree, Jabreea, Jabreena, Jabrelle, Jabreona, Jabri, Jabriah, Jabriana, Jabrie, Jabriel, Jabrielle, Jabrienna, Jabrina

Jacalyn (American) a form of Jacqueline.
Jacalynn, Jacolyn, Jacolyne, Jacolynn

Jace **B** (Greek) a form of Jacey.

Jacelyn (American) a form of Jocelyn.
Jaceline, Jacelyne, Jacelynn, Jacilyn, Jacilyne, Jacilynn, Jacylyn, Jacylyne, Jacylynn

Jacey **G** (Greek) a familiar form of Jacinda. (American) a combination of the initials J. + C.

Jaci, Jacie (Greek) forms of Jacey.
Jacci, Jacia, Jacie, Jaciel, Jaici, Jaicie

Jacinda, Jacinta (Greek) beautiful, attractive. (Spanish) forms of Hyacinth.
Jacenda, Jacenta, Jacey, Jacinthe, Jacintia, Jacynthe, Jakinda, Jaxine

Jacinthe (Spanish) a form of Jacinda.
Jacinte, Jacinth, Jacintha

Jackalyn (American) a form of Jacqueline.
Jackalene, Jackalin, Jackaline, Jackalynn, Jackalynne, Jackelin, Jackeline, Jackelyn, Jackelynn, Jackelynne, Jackilin, Jackilyn, Jackilynn, Jackilynne, Jackolin, Jackoline, Jackolyn, Jackolynn, Jackolynne

Jackeline, Jackelyn (American) forms of Jacqueline.
Jackelin, Jackelline, Jackellyn, Jockeline

Jacki (American) a familiar form of Jacqueline.

Jackie **BG** (American) a familiar form of Jacqueline.
Jackee, Jackey, Jackia, Jackielee, Jacky, Jackye

Jacklyn (American) a form of Jacqueline.
Jacklin, Jackline, Jacklyne, Jacklynn, Jacklynne

Jackquel (French) a short form of Jacqueline.
Jackqueline, Jackquetta, Jackquiline, Jackquilyn, Jackquilynn, Jackquilynne

Jackson **B** (English) child of Jack.

Jaclyn **G** (American) a short form of Jacqueline.
Jacleen, Jaclin, Jacline, Jaclyne, Jaclynn

Jacob **B** (Hebrew) supplanter, substitute.

Jacobi (Hebrew) a form of Jacob.
Coby, Jacoba, Jacobee, Jacobette, Jacobia, Jacobina, Jacoby, Jacolbi, Jacolbia, Jacolby

Jacoby **B** (Hebrew) a form of Jacobi.

Jacqualine (French) a form of Jacqueline.
Jacqualin, Jacqualine, Jacqualyn, Jacqualyne, Jacqualynn

Jacquelin (French) a form of Jacqueline.
Jacquelina

Jacqueline (French) supplanter, substitute; little Jacqui.
Jacalyn, Jackalyn, Jackeline, Jacki, Jacklyn, Jackquel, Jaclyn, Jacqueena, Jacqueine, Jacquel, Jacqueleen, Jacquelene, Jacquelin, Jacquelyn, Jacquelynn, Jacquena, Jacquene, Jacquenetta, Jacquenette, Jacqui, Jacquiline, Jacquine, Jakelin, Jaquelin, Jaqueline, Jaquelyn, Jocqueline

Jacquelyn, Jacquelynn (French) forms of Jacqueline.
Jackquelyn, Jackquelynn, Jacquelyne, Jacquelynne

Jacques **B** (French) a form of Jacob, James.

Jacqui (French) a short form of Jacqueline.
Jacquay, Jacqué, Jacquee, Jacqueta, Jacquete, Jacquetta, Jacquette, Jacquie, Jacquise, Jacquita, Jaquay, Jaqui, Jaquie, Jaquiese, Jaquina, Jaquita

Jacquiline (French) a form of Jacqueline.
Jacquil, Jacquilin, Jacquilyn, Jacquilyne, Jacquilynn

Jacqulin, Jacqulyn (American) forms of Jacqueline.
Jackquilin, Jacqul, Jacqulin, Jacqulyne, Jacqulynn, Jacqulynne, Jacquoline

Jacy (Greek) a familiar form of Jacinda. (American) a combination of the initials J. + C.
Jace, Jac-E, Jacee, Jaci, Jacie, Jacylin, Jaice, Jaicee

Jacynthe (Spanish) a form of Jacinda.
Jacynda, Jacynta, Jacynth, Jacyntha

Jada ❦ **G** (Spanish) a form of Jade.
Jadah, Jadda, Jadae, Jadzia, Jadziah, Jaeda, Jaedra, Jayda

Jade **G** (Spanish) jade.
Jadea, Jadeann, Jadee, Jaden, Jadera, Jadi, Jadie, Jadienne, Jady, Jadyn, Jaedra, Jaida, Jaide, Jaiden, Jayde, Jayden

Jadelyn (American) a combination of Jade + Lynn.
Jadalyn, Jadelaine, Jadeline, Jadelyne, Jadelynn, Jadielyn

Jaden **B** (Spanish) a form of Jade.
Jadeen, Jadena, Jadene, Jadeyn, Jadin, Jadine, Jaeden, Jaedine

Jadyn **G** (Spanish) a form of Jade.
Jadynn, Jaedyn, Jaedynn

Jae (Latin) jaybird. (French) a familiar form of Jacqueline.
Jaea, Jaey, Jaya

Jael **G** (Hebrew) mountain goat; climber. See also Yael.
Jaela, Jaelee, Jaeli, Jaelie, Jaelle, Jahla, Jahlea

Jaelyn, Jaelynn (American) combinations of Jae + Lynn.
Jaeleen, Jaelin, Jaelinn, Jaelyn, Jailyn, Jalyn, Jalynn, Jayleen, Jaylyn, Jaylynn, Jaylynne

Jaffa (Hebrew) a form of Yaffa.
Jaffice, Jaffit, Jafit, Jafra

Jagadamba, Jagamata (Indian) mother of the world.

Jagamohini (Indian) one who attracts the world.

Jagrati (Indian) awakening.

Jagravi (Indian) king.

Jagriti (Indian) vigilance.

Jagruti (Indian) awareness.

Jagvi (Indian) worldly.

Jaha (Swahili) dignified.
Jahaida, Jahaira, Jaharra, Jahayra, Jahida, Jahira, Jahitza

Jahanara (Indian) queen of the world.

Jahnavi, Janhavi (Indian) the Ganga River.

Jai **B** (Tai) heart. (Latin) a form of Jaye.

Jaida, Jaide (Spanish) forms of Jade.
Jaidah, Jaidan

Jaiden **B** (Spanish) a form of Jade.
Jaidey, Jaidi, Jaidin, Jaidon

Jaidyn (Spanish) a form of Jade.

Jailyn (American) a form of Jaelyn.
Jaileen, Jailen, Jailene, Jailin, Jailine

Jaime **B** (French) I love.
Jaima, Jaimee, Jaimey, Jaimie, Jaimini, Jaimme, Jaimy, Jamee

Jaimee **G** (French) a form of Jaime.

Jaimie **G** (French) a form of Jaime.
Jaimi, Jaimmie

Jaira (Spanish) Jehovah teaches.
Jairah, Jairy

Jaishree (Indian) honor of victory.

Jaisudha (Indian) nectar of victory.

Jaiwanthi, Jaiwanti (Indian) victory.

Jakeisha (American) a combination of Jakki + Aisha.
Jakeisia, Jakesha, Jakisha

Jakelin (American) a form of Jacqueline.
Jakeline, Jakelyn, Jakelynn, Jakelynne

Jakki (American) a form of Jacki.
Jakala, Jakea, Jakeela, Jakeida, Jakeita, Jakela, Jakelia, Jakell, Jakena, Jaketta, Jakevia, Jaki, Jakia, Jakiah, Jakira, Jakita, Jakiya, Jakiyah, Jakke, Jakkia

Jalabala (Indian) a river.

Jalaja (Indian) goddess of wealth; lotus.

Jalbala (Indian) lotus flower.

Jaleel **B** (Hindi) a form of Jalil (see Boys' Names).

Jaleesa (American) a form of Jalisa.
Jaleasa, Jalece, Jalecea, Jaleesah, Jaleese, Jaleesia, Jaleisa, Jaleisha, Jaleisya

Jalen **B** (American) a form of Jalena.

Jalena (American) a combination of Jane + Lena.
Jalaina, Jalana, Jalani, Jalanie, Jalayna, Jalean, Jaleen, Jaleena, Jaleene, Jalen, Jalene, Jalina, Jaline, Jallena, Jalyna, Jelayna, Jelena, Jelina, Jelyna

Jalesa, Jalessa (American) forms of Jalisa.
Jalese, Jalesha, Jaleshia, Jalesia

Jalia, Jalea (American) combinations of Jae + Leah.
Jaleah, Jalee, Jaleea, Jaleeya, Jaleia, Jalitza

Jalila (Arabic) great.
Jalile

Jalisa, Jalissa (American) combinations of Jae + Lisa.
Jaleesa, Jalesa, Jalise, Jalisha, Jalisia, Jalysa

Jalsa (Indian) celebration.

Jalyn, Jalynn (American) combinations of Jae + Lynn. See also Jaylyn.
Jaelin, Jaeline, Jaelyn, Jaelyne, Jaelynn, Jaelynne, Jalin, Jaline, Jalyne, Jalynne

Jalysa (American) a form of Jalisa.
Jalyse, Jalyssa, Jalyssia

Jamaal **B** (Arabic) a form of Jamal.

Jamaica (Spanish) Geography: an island in the Caribbean.
Jameca, Jamecia, Jameica, Jameika, Jameka, Jamica, Jamika, Jamoka, Jemaica, Jemika, Jemyka

Jamal **B** (Arabic) beautiful.

Jamani (American) a form of Jami.
Jamana

Jamar **B** (American) a form of Jamaria.

Jamarcus **B** (American) a combination of the prefix Ja + Marcus.

Jamaria (American) combinations of Jae + Maria.
Jamar, Jamara, Jamarea, Jamaree, Jamari, Jamarie, Jameira, Jamerial, Jamira

Jamecia (Spanish) a form of Jamaica.

Jamee (French) a form of Jaime.

Jameerah (Indian) beautiful one.

Jameika, Jameka (Spanish) forms of Jamaica.
Jamaika, Jamaka, Jamecka, Jamekia, Jamekka

James **B** (Hebrew) supplanter, substitute. (English) a form of Jacob.

Jamesha (American) a form of Jami.
Jameisha, Jamese, Jameshia, Jameshyia, Jamesia, Jamesica, Jamesika, Jamesina, Jamessa, Jameta, Jametta, Jamiesha, Jamisha, Jammesha, Jammisha

Jameson **B** (English) son of James.

Jamey (English) a form of Jami, Jamie.

Jami, Jamie **G** (Hebrew, English) supplanter, substitute.
Jama, Jamani, Jamay, Jamesha, Jamey, Jamia, Jamii, Jamis, Jamise, Jammie, Jamy, Jamye, Jayme, Jaymee, Jaymie

Jamia (English) a form of Jami, Jamie.
Jamea, Jamiah, Jamiea, Jamiya, Jamiyah, Jamya, Jamyah

Jamica (Spanish) a form of Jamaica.
Jamika

Jamil **B** (Arabic) a form of Jamal.

Jamila (Arabic) beautiful. See also Yamila.
Jahmela, Jahmelia, Jahmil, Jahmilla, Jameela, Jameelah, Jameeliah, Jameila, Jamela, Jamelia, Jameliah, Jamell, Jamella, Jamelle, Jamely, Jamelya, Jamiela, Jamielee, Jamilah, Jamilee, Jamilia, Jamiliah, Jamilla, Jamillah, Jamille, Jamillia, Jamilya, Jamyla, Jemeela, Jemelia, Jemila, Jemilla

Jamilam (Arabic) a form of Jamilah.

Jamilynn (English) a combination of Jami + Lynn.
Jamielin, Jamieline, Jamielyn, Jamielyne, Jamielynn, Jamielynne, Jamilin, Jamiline, Jamilyn, Jamilyne, Jamilynne

Jamini (Indian) night.

Jaminie (Indian) flower.

Jamison **B** (English) child of James.

Jammie (American) a form of Jami.
Jammi, Jammice, Jammise

Jamonica (American) a combination of Jami + Monica.
Jamoni

Jamuna (Indian) holy river.

Jamylin (American) a form of Jamilynn.
Jamylin, Jamyline, Jamylyn, Jamylyne, Jamylynn, Jamylynne, Jaymylin, Jaymyline, Jaymylyn, Jaymylyne, Jaymylynn, Jaymylynne

Girls G–L

Jan ⬛ (Dutch, Slavic) a form of John. (English) a short form of Jane, Janet, Janice.
Jania, Jandy

Jana 🄶 (Hebrew) gracious, merciful. (Slavic) a form of Jane. See also Yana.
Janalee, Janalisa, Janna, Janne

Janaan (Indian) heart; soul.

Janae 🄶 (American) a form of Jane.
Janaé, Janaea, Janaeh, Janah, Janai, Janea, Janee, Janée, Jannae, Jenae, Jennae

Janai (American) a form of Janae.
Janaiah, Janaira, Janaiya

Janaknandini (Indian) daughter of King Janak.

Janalynn (American) a combination of Jana + Lynn.
Janalin, Janaline, Janalyn, Janalyne, Janalynne

Janan (Arabic) heart; soul.
Jananee, Janani, Jananie, Janann, Jananni

Janay (American) a form of Jane.
Janaya, Janaye, Jannay, Jenay, Jenaya, Jennay, Jennaya, Jennaye

Jane 🄶 (Hebrew) God is gracious. See also Chavon, Jean, Joan, Juanita, Seana, Shana, Shawna, Sheena, Shona, Shunta, Sinead, Zaneta, Zanna, Zhana.
Jaine, Jan, Jana, Janae, Janay, Janelle, Janessa, Janet, Jania, Janice, Janie, Janika, Janine, Janis, Janka, Jannie, Jasia, Jayna, Jayne, Jenica

Janel (French) a form of Janelle.
Janiel, Jannel, Jaynel

Janell 🄶 (French) a form of Janelle.
Jannell, Janyll, Jaynell

Janelle 🄶 (French) a form of Jane.
Janel, Janela, Janele, Janelis, Janell, Janella, Janelli, Janellie, Janelly, Janely, Janelys, Janielle, Janille, Jannelle, Jannellies, Jaynelle

Janesha (American) a form of Janessa.
Janeisha, Janeshia, Janiesha, Janisha, Janishia, Jannesha, Jannisha, Janysha, Jenesha, Jenisha, Jennisha

Janessa 🄶 (American) a form of Jane.
Janeesa, Janesa, Janesea, Janesha, Janesia, Janeska, Janessi, Janessia, Janiesa, Janissa, Jannesa, Jannessa, Jannisa, Jannissa, Janyssa, Jenesa, Jenessa, Jenissa, Jennisa, Jennissa

Janet (English) a form of Jane. See also Jessie, Yanet.
Jan, Janeta, Janete, Janeth, Janett, Janette, Jannet, Janot, Jante, Janyte

Janeth (English) a form of Janet.
Janetha, Janith, Janneth

Janette 🄶 (French) a form of Janet.
Janett, Janetta

Janice (Hebrew) God is gracious. (English) a familiar form of Jane. See also Genice.
Jan, Janece, Janecia, Janeice, Janiece, Janizzette, Jannice, Janniece, Janyce, Jenice, Jhanice, Jynice

Janie (English) a familiar form of Jane.
Janey, Jani, Janiyh, Jannie, Janny, Jany

Janika (Slavic) a form of Jane.
Janaca, Janeca, Janecka, Janeika, Janeka, Janica, Janick, Janicka, Janieka, Janikka, Janikke, Janique, Janka, Jankia, Jannica, Jannick, Jannika, Janyca, Jenica, Jenicka, Jenika, Jeniqua, Jenique, Jennica, Jennika, Jonika

Janine 🄶 (French) a form of Jane.
Janean, Janeann, Janeanne, Janeen, Janenan, Janene, Janina, Jannen, Jannina, Jannine, Jannyne, Janyne, Jeannine, Jeneen, Jenine

Janis 🄶 (English) a form of Jane.
Janees, Janese, Janesey, Janess, Janesse, Janise, Jannis, Jannise, Janys, Jenesse, Jenis, Jennise, Jennisse

Janita (American) a form of Juanita. See also Genita.
Janitra, Janitza, Janneta, Jaynita, Jenita, Jennita

Janna (Arabic) harvest of fruit. (Hebrew) a short form of Johana.
Janaya, Janaye, Jannae, Jannah, Jannai

Jannette (French) a form of Janet.
Jannett, Jannetta

Jannie (English) a familiar form of Jan, Jane.
Janney, Janny

Januja (Indian) female offspring.

Jaquan ⬛ (American) a combination of the prefix Ja + Quan (see Boys' Names).

Jaquana (American) a combination of Jacqueline + Anna.
Jaqua, Jaquai, Jaquanda, Jaquania, Jaquanna

Jaquelen (American) a form of Jacqueline.
Jaquala, Jaquera, Jaqulene, Jaquonna

Jaquelin, Jaqueline (French) forms of Jacqueline.
Jaqualin, Jaqualine, Jaquelina, Jaquline, Jaquella

Jaquelyn (French) a form of Jacqueline.
Jaquelyne, Jaquelynn, Jaquelynne

Jardena (Hebrew) a form of Jordan. (French, Spanish) garden.
Jardan, Jardana, Jardane, Jarden, Jardenia, Jardin, Jardine, Jardyn, Jardyne

Jared B (Hebrew) a form of Jordan.

Jarian (American) a combination of Jane + Marian.

Jarita (Arabic) earthen water jug.
Jara, Jaretta, Jari, Jaria, Jarica, Jarida, Jarietta, Jarika, Jarina, Jaritta, Jaritza, Jarixa, Jarnita, Jarrika, Jarrine

Jarod B (Hebrew) a form of Jared.

Jarred B (Hebrew) a form of Jared.

Jarrett B (English) a form of Garrett, Jared.

Jarul (Indian) flower queen.

Jas BG (American) a short form of Jasmine.
Jase, Jass, Jaz, Jazz, Jazze, Jazzi

Jasia (Polish) a form of Jane.
Jaisha, Jasa, Jasea, Jasha, Jashae, Jashala, Jashona, Jashonte, Jasie, Jassie, Jaysa

Jaskaran B (Sikh) sings praises to the Lord.

Jaskarn B (Sikh) a form of Jaskaran.

Jasleen G (Latin) a form of Jocelyn.
Jaslene, Jaslien, Jaslin, Jasline

Jaslyn (Latin) a form of Jocelyn.
Jaslynn, Jaslynne

Jasmain (Persian) a short form of Jasmine.
Jasmaine, Jasmane, Jassmain, Jassmaine

Jasmarie (American) a combination of Jasmine + Marie.
Jasmari

Jasmeet BG (Persian) a form of Jasmine.

Jasmin G (Persian) a form of Jasmine.
Jasimin, Jasman, Jasmeen, Jasmen, Jasmon, Jassmin, Jassminn

Jasmine ❀ G (Persian) jasmine flower.
See also Jessamine, Yasmin.
Jas, Jasma, Jasmain, Jasme, Jasmeet, Jasmene, Jasmin, Jasmina, Jasminne, Jasmira, Jasmit, Jasmyn, Jassma, Jassmin, Jassmine, Jassmit, Jassmon, Jassmyn, Jazmin, Jazmyn, Jazzmin

Jasmyn, Jasmyne (Persian) forms of Jasmine.
Jasmynn, Jasmynne, Jassmyn

Jasoda (Indian) mother of Lord Krishna.

Jasodhara (Indian) mother of Lord Buddha.

Jasone (Basque) assumption.

Jasper B (Punjabi) a form of Jaspreet.

Jaspreet BG (Punjabi) virtuous.
Jaspar, Jasparit, Jasparita, Jasper, Jasprit, Jasprita, Jasprite

Jasum (Indian) hibiscus.

Jasweer (Indian) victorious.

Jatara (American) a combination of Jane + Tara.
Jataria, Jatarra, Jatori, Jatoria

Jauria (Arabic) jewel, gem.

Javana (Malayan) from Java.
Javán, Javanna, Javanne, Javona, Javonna, Jawana, Jawanna, Jawn

Javiera (Spanish) owner of a new house. See also Xaviera.
Javeera, Viera

Javon B (Malayan) a form of Javona.

Javona, Javonna (Malayan) forms of Javana.
Javon, Javonda, Javone, Javoni, Javonne, Javonni, Javonya

Javonte B (American) a form of Javan (see Boys' Names).

Jay B (French) blue jay.

Jaya (Hindi) victory.
Jaea, Jaia

Jayalakshmi, Jayashri (Indian) the goddess of victory.

Jayamala (Indian) a garland of flowers given to the one who wins.

Jayani (Indian) a Shakti (consort) of Ganesha.

Jayaprabha (Indian) the light of victory.

Jayaprada (Indian) one who gives victory.

Jayashree (Indian) victorious woman.

Jayasudha (Indian) the nectar of victory.

Jayati, Jayavanti, Jayita (Indian) victorious.

Jayavardhini (Indian) goddess who increases victory.

Jaycee (American) a combination of the initials J. + C.
Jacee, Jacey, Jaci, Jacie, Jacy, Jayce, Jaycey, Jayci, Jaycie, Jaycy

Girls G–L

Jayda (Spanish) a form of Jada.
Jaydah, Jeyda

Jayde 🅖 (Spanish) a form of Jade.
Jayd

Jaydee (American) a combination of the initials J. + D.
Jadee, Jadey, Jadi, Jadie, Jady, Jaydey, Jaydi, Jaydie, Jaydy

Jayden 🅑 (Spanish) a form of Jade.
Jaydeen, Jaydene, Jaydin, Jaydn, Jaydon

Jaye (Latin) jaybird.
Jae, Jay

Jayla 🅖 (American) a short form of Jaylene.
Jaylaa, Jaylah, Jayli, Jaylia, Jayliah, Jaylie

Jaylen 🅑 (American) a form of Jaylene.

Jaylene (American) forms of Jaylyn.
Jayelene, Jayla, Jaylan, Jayleana, Jaylee, Jayleen, Jayleene, Jaylen, Jaylenne

Jaylin 🅑 (American) a form of Jaylyn.
Jayline, Jaylinn

Jaylon 🅑 (American) a form of Jaylen.

Jaylyn 🅑🅖 (American) a combination of Jaye + Lynn. See also Jalyn.
Jaylene, Jaylin, Jaylyne

Jaylynn (American) a form of Jaylyn.
Jaylynne

Jayme 🅖 (English) a form of Jami.

Jaymee, Jaymi (English) forms of Jami.

Jaymie (English) a form of Jami.
Jaymi, Jaymia, Jaymine, Jaymini

Jayna (Hebrew) a form of Jane.
Jaynae, Jaynah, Jaynna

Jayne (Hindi) victorious. (English) a form of Jane.
Jayn, Jaynie, Jaynne

Jaynie (English) a familiar form of Jayne.
Jaynee, Jayni

Jazlyn (American) a combination of Jazmin + Lynn.
Jasleen, Jazaline, Jazalyn, Jazleen, Jazlene, Jazlin, Jazline, Jazlon, Jazlynn, Jazlynne, Jazzalyn, Jazzleen, Jazzlene, Jazzlin, Jazzline, Jazzlyn, Jazzlynn, Jazzlynne

Jazmin (Persian) a form of Jasmine.
Jazmaine, Jazman, Jazmen, Jazmín, Jazminn, Jazmon, Jazzmit

Jazmine 🅖 (Persian) a form of Jasmine.

Jazmyn, Jazmyne (Persian) forms of Jasmine.
Jazmynn, Jazmynne, Jazzmyn, Jazzmyne

Jazzmin, Jazzmine (Persian) forms of Jasmine.
Jazzman, Jazzmeen, Jazzmen, Jazzmene, Jazzmenn, Jazzmon

Jean 🅑 (Scottish) a form of Jeanne.

Jeana, Jeanna (Scottish) forms of Jean.
Jeanae, Jeannae, Jeannia

Jeanette 🅖 (French) a form of Jean.
Jeanet, Jeanete, Jeanett, Jeanetta, Jeanita, Jenet, Jenett, Jenette, Jinetta, Jinette

Jeanie, Jeannie (Scottish) familiar forms of Jean.
Jeannee, Jeanney, Jeani, Jeanny, Jeany

Jeanine, Jenine (Scottish) forms of Jean. See also Geneen.
Jeaneane, Jeaneen, Jeanene, Jeanina, Jeannina, Jeannine, Jennine

Jeanne (Scottish) God is gracious. See also Kini.
Jeana, Jeanann, Jeancie, Jeane, Jeaneia, Jeanette, Jeaneva, Jeanice, Jeanie, Jeanine, Jeanmaria, Jeanmarie, Jeanna, Jeanné, Jeannie, Jeannita, Jeannot, Jeantelle

Jeannett (French) a form of Jean.
Jeannete, Jeannetta, Jeannette, Jeannita, Jennet, Jennett, Jennetta, Jennette, Jennita

Jedidiah 🅑 (Hebrew) friend of God, beloved of God.

Jeeval (Indian) full of life.

Jeevana (Indian) life.

Jeevankala (Indian) art of life.

Jeevika (Indian) water.

Jefferson 🅑 (English) child of Jeff.

Jeffery 🅑 (English) a form of Jeffrey.

Jeffrey 🅑 (English) divinely peaceful.

Jehannaz (Indian) pride of the universe.

Jelena (Russian) a form of Helen. See also Yelena.
Jalaine, Jalane, Jalani, Jalanna, Jalayna, Jalayne, Jaleen, Jaleena, Jaleene, Jalena, Jalene, Jelaina, Jelaine, Jelana, Jelane, Jelani, Jelanni, Jelayna, Jelayne, Jelean, Jeleana, Jeleen, Jeleena, Jelene

Jelisa (American) a combination of Jean + Lisa.
Jalissa, Jelesha, Jelessa, Jelise, Jelissa, Jellese, Jellice, Jelysa, Jelyssa, Jillisa, Jillissa, Julissa

Jem **G** (Hebrew) a short form of Jemima.
Gem, Jemi, Jemia, Jemiah, Jemie, Jemm, Jemmi, Jemmy

Jemima (Hebrew) dove.
Jamim, Jamima, Jem, Jemimah, Jemma

Jemina, Jenima (Hebrew) dove.

Jemma (Hebrew) a short form of Jemima. (English) a form of Gemma.
Jemmia, Jemmiah, Jemmie, Jemmy

Jena, Jenae (Arabic) forms of Jenna.
Jenah, Jenai, Jenal, Jenay, Jenaya, Jenea

Jenara (Latin) dedicated to the god, Janus.

Jendaya (Zimbabwean) thankful.
Daya, Jenda, Jendayah

Jenelle (American) a combination of Jenny + Nelle.
Genell, Jeanell, Jeanelle, Jenall, Jenalle, Jenel, Jenela, Jenele, Jenell, Jenella, Jenille, Jennel, Jennell, Jennella, Jennelle, Jennielle, Jennille, Jinelle, Jinnell

Jenessa (American) a form of Jenisa.
Jenesa, Jenese, Jenesia, Jenessia, Jennesa, Jennese, Jennessa, Jinessa

Jenica (Romanian) a form of Jane.
Jeneca, Jenika, Jenikka, Jennica, Jennika

Jenifer, Jeniffer (Welsh) forms of Jennifer.
Jenefer

Jenilee (American) a combination of Jennifer + Lee.
Jenalea, Jenalee, Jenaleigh, Jenaly, Jenelea, Jenelee, Jeneleigh, Jenely, Jenelly, Jenileigh, Jenily, Jennalee, Jennely, Jennielee, Jennilea, Jennilee, Jennilie

Jenisa (American) a combination of Jennifer + Nisa.
Jenessa, Jenisha, Jenissa, Jenisse, Jennisa, Jennise, Jennisha, Jennissa, Jennisse, Jennysa, Jennyssa, Jenysa, Jenyse, Jenyssa, Jenysse

Jenka (Czech) a form of Jane.

Jenna ❀ **G** (Arabic) small bird. (Welsh) a short form of Jennifer. See also Gen.
Jena, Jennae, Jennah, Jennai, Jennat, Jennay, Jennaya, Jennaye, Jhenna

Jenni, Jennie (Welsh) familiar forms of Jennifer.
Jeni, Jenne, Jenné, Jennee, Jenney, Jennia, Jennier, Jennita, Jennora, Jensine

Jennifer ❀ **G** (Welsh) white wave; white phantom. A form of Guinevere. See also Gennifer, Ginnifer, Yenifer.
Jen, Jenifer, Jeniffer, Jenipher, Jenna, Jennafer, Jenni, Jenniferanne, Jenniferlee, Jenniffe, Jenniffer, Jenniffier, Jennifier, Jennilee, Jenniphe, Jennipher, Jenny, Jennyfer

Jennilee (American) a combination of Jenny + Lee.
Jennalea, Jennalee, Jennielee, Jennilea, Jennilie, Jinnalee

Jennilyn, Jennilynn (American) combinations of Jenni + Lynn.
Jennalin, Jennaline, Jennalyn, Jenalynann, Jenelyn, Jenilyn, Jennalyne, Jennalynn, Jennalynne, Jennilin, Jenniline, Jennilyne, Jennilynne

Jenny **G** (Welsh) a familiar form of Jennifer.
Jenney, Jenni, Jennie, Jeny, Jinny

Jennyfer (Welsh) a form of Jennifer.
Jenyfer

Jeraldine (English) a form of Geraldine.
Jeraldeen, Jeraldene, Jeraldina, Jeraldyne, Jeralee, Jeri

Jeremiah **B** (Hebrew) God will uplift.

Jeremy **B** (English) a form of Jeremiah.

Jereni (Russian) a form of Irene.
Jerena, Jerenae, Jerina

Jeri, Jerri, Jerrie (American) short forms of Jeraldine. See also Geri.
Jera, Jerae, JeRae, Jeree, Jeriel, Jerilee, Jerinda, Jerra, Jerrah, Jerrece, Jerree, Jerriann, Jerrilee, Jerrine, Jerry, Jerrylee, Jerryne, Jerzy

Jerica (American) a combination of Jeri + Erica.
Jereca, Jerecka, Jerice, Jericka, Jerika, Jerrica, Jerrice, Jeryka

Jerilyn (American) a combination of Jeri + Lynn.
Jeralin, Jeraline, Jeralyn, Jeralyne, Jeralynn, Jeralynne, Jerelin, Jereline, Jerelyn, Jerelyne, Jerelynn, Jerelynne, Jerilin, Jeriline, Jerilyne, Jerilynn, Jerilynne, Jerrilin, Jerriline, Jerrilyn, Jerrilyne, Jerrilynn, Jerrilynne, Jerrylea

Jermaine **B** (French) a form of Germaine.
Jermain, Jerman, Jermanay, Jermanaye, Jermane, Jermanee, Jermani, Jermanique, Jermany, Jermayne, Jermecia, Jermia, Jermice, Jermicia, Jermika, Jermila

Jerónima (Greek) she who has a sacred name.

Jerrica (American) a form of Jerica.
Jerreka, Jerricah, Jerricca, Jerricha, Jerricka, Jerrieka, Jerrika

Jerry B (American) a form of Jeri.

Jerusalén (Hebrew) vision of peace.

Jerusha (Hebrew) inheritance.
Jerushah, Yerusha

Jesabel (Hebrew) God's oath.

Jesenia, Jessenia G (Arabic) flower.
Jescenia, Jessennia, Jessenya

Jeshna (Indian) victory.

Jésica (Slavic) a form of Jessica.

Jesica, Jesika (Hebrew) forms of Jessica.
Jesicca, Jesikah, Jesikkah

Jess B (Hebrew) a short form of Jessie.

Jessa (American) a short form of Jessalyn, Jessamine, Jessica.
Jesa, Jesha, Jessah

Jessalyn (American) a combination of Jessica + Lynn.
Jesalin, Jesaline, Jesalyn, Jesalyne, Jesalynn, Jesalynne, Jesilin, Jesiline, Jesilyn, Jesilyne, Jesilynn, Jesilynne, Jessa, Jessalin, Jessaline, Jessalyne, Jessalynn, Jessalynne, Jesselin, Jesseline, Jesselyn, Jesselyne, Jesselynn, Jesselynne, Jesslyn

Jessamine (French) a form of Jasmine.
Jessa, Jessamin, Jessamon, Jessamy, Jessamyn, Jessemin, Jessemine, Jessimin, Jessimine, Jessmin, Jessmine, Jessmon, Jessmy, Jessmyn

Jesse B (Hebrew) a form of Jessie.
Jese, Jesi, Jesie

Jesseca (Hebrew) a form of Jessica.

Jessi G (Hebrew) a form of Jessie.

Jessica ❀ G (Hebrew) wealthy. Literature: a name perhaps invented by Shakespeare for a character in his play *The Merchant of Venice*. See also Gessica, Yessica.
Jesica, Jesika, Jessa, Jessaca, Jessca, Jesscia, Jesseca, Jessia, Jessicah, Jessicca, Jessicia, Jessicka, Jessika, Jessiqua, Jessy, Jessyca, Jessyka, Jezeca, Jezica, Jezika, Jezyca

Jessie BG (Hebrew) a short form of Jessica. (Scottish) a form of Janet.
Jescie, Jesey, Jessé, Jessee, Jessey, Jessi, Jessia, Jessiya, Jessye

Jessika G (Hebrew) a form of Jessica.
Jessieka

Jesslyn (American) a short form of Jessalyn.
Jessilyn, Jessilynn, Jesslin, Jesslynn, Jesslynne

Jessy B (Hebrew, Scottish) a form of Jessie.

Jessyca, Jessyka (Hebrew) forms of Jessica.

Jesus B (Hebrew) a form of Joshua.

Jesusa (Spanish) Jehovah is salvation.

Jésusa (Hebrew, Spanish) God is my salvation.

Jetta (English) jet black mineral. (American) a familiar form of Jevette.
Jeta, Jetia, Jetje, Jette, Jettie

Jevette (American) a combination of Jean + Yvette.
Jetta, Jeva, Jeveta, Jevetta

Jewel (French) precious gem.
Jewelann, Jewelia, Jeweliana, Jeweliann, Jewelie, Jewell, Jewelle, Jewellee, Jewellene, Jewellie, Juel, Jule

Jezebel (Hebrew) unexalted; impure. Bible: the wife of King Ahab.
Jesibel, Jessabel, Jessebel, Jez, Jezabel, Jezabella, Jezabelle, Jezebell, Jezebella, Jezebelle

Jhalak (Indian) glimpse; spark.

Jharna (Indian) a spring.

Jheel (Indian) lake.

Jhilmil (Indian) sparkling.

Jhinuk (Indian) oyster.

Ji (Chinese) lucky.

Ji Hye (Korean) the ninth of the ten heavenly stems; official.

Ji Won (Korean) mankind; to lead; cause; enduring; tiger; bride.

Jia (Chinese) beautiful.

Jia Hui (Chinese) excellent flower.

Jia Li (Chinese) good and beautiful.

Jian (Chinese) strong.

Jiang (Chinese) river.

Jiang Li, Jiang-Li (Chinese) beautiful river.

Jianna (Italian) a form of Giana.
Jiana, Jianina, Jianine, Jianni, Jiannini

Jiao (Chinese) beautiful, handsome, lovely; tender; charming.

Jibon (Hindi) life.

Jie (Chinese) pure.

Jigisha (Indian) superior.

Jigna, Jignasa (Indian) intellectual curiosity.

Jigya, Jigyasa (Indian) curiosity.

Jill G (English) a short form of Jillian.
Jil, Jilli, Jillie, Jilly

Jillaine (Latin) a form of Jillian.
Jilaine, Jilane, Jilayne, Jillana, Jillane, Jillann, Jillanne, Jillayne

Jilleen (Irish) a form of Jillian.
Jileen, Jilene, Jiline, Jillene, Jillenne, Jilline, Jillyn

Jillian G (Latin) youthful. See also Gillian.
Jilian, Jiliana, Jiliann, Jilianna, Jilianne, Jilienna, Jilienne, Jill, Jillaine, Jilliana, Jilliane, Jilliann, Jillianne, Jileen, Jillien, Jillienne, Jillion, Jilliyn

Jilpa (Indian) life-giving.

Jimi (Hebrew) supplanter, substitute.
Jimae, Jimaria, Jimee, Jimella, Jimena, Jimia, Jimiah, Jimie, Jimiyah, Jimmeka, Jimmet, Jimmi, Jimmia, Jimmie

Jimisha (American) a combination of Jimi + Aisha.
Jimica, Jimicia, Jimmicia, Jimysha

Jimmie B (Hebrew) a form of Jimi.

Jimmy B (English) a familiar form of Jim (see Boys' Names).

Jin B (Japanese) tender. (American) a short form of Ginny, Jinny.

Jina (Swahili) baby with a name. (Italian) a form of Gina.
Jena, Jinae, Jinan, Jinda, Jinna, Jinnae

Jing (Chinese) crystal; sparkly.

Jingjing (Tagalog) a form of Jingjing.

Jinky (Tagalog) term of respect for an elder sister.

Jinny (Scottish) a familiar form of Jenny. (American) a familiar form of Virginia. See also Ginny.
Jin, Jinnee, Jinney, Jinni, Jinnie

Jiong (Chinese) shining.

Jirina (Czech) a form of Georgia.
Jirah, Jireh

Jivantika (Indian) one who gives life.

Jiyoung (Korean) wisdom, intelligence.

Jizelle (American) a form of Giselle.
Jessel, Jezel, Jezell, Jezella, Jezelle, Jisel, Jisela, Jisell, Jisella, Jiselle, Jissel, Jissell, Jissella, Jisselle, Jizel, Jizella, Joselle

Jlu (Chinese) for a long time.

Jo G (American) a short form of Joanna, Jolene, Josephine.
Joangie, Joetta, Joette, Joey

Joan (Hebrew) God is gracious. History: Joan of Arc was a fifteenth-century heroine and resistance fighter. See also Ioana, Jean, Juanita, Siobhan.
Joane, Joaneil, Joanel, Joanelle, Joanie, Joanmarie, Joann, Joannanette, Joanne, Joannel, Joanny, Jonni

Joana (English) a form of Joanna.

Joanie, Joannie (Hebrew) familiar forms of Joan.
Joanee, Joani, Joanni, Joenie, Johanie, Johnnie, Joni

Joanna G (English) a form of Joan. See also Yoanna.
Janka, Jhoana, Jo, Jo-Ana, Joandra, Joanka, Joananna, Jo-Anie, Joanka, Jo-Anna, Joannah, Jo-Annie, Joeana, Joeanna, Johana, Johanna, Johannah

Joanne (English) a form of Joan.
Joanann, Joananne, Joann, Jo-Ann, Jo-Anne, Joayn, Joeann, Joeanne

Joanny (Hebrew) a familiar form of Joan.
Joany

Joaquina (Hebrew) God will establish.
Joaquine

Jobeth (English) a combination of Jo + Beth.

Joby B (Hebrew) afflicted. (English) a familiar form of Jobeth.
Jobey, Jobi, Jobie, Jobina, Jobita, Jobrina, Jobye, Jobyna

Jocacia (American) a combination of Joy + Acacia.

Jocelín (Latin) a form of Jocelin.

Jocelin, Joceline (Latin) forms of Jocelyn.
Jocelina, Jocelinn

Jocelyn ✺ G (Latin) joyous. See also Yocelin, Yoselin.
Jacelyn, Jasleen, Jocelin, Jocelle, Jocelyne, Jocelynn, Joci, Jocia, Jocilyn, Jocilynn, Jocinta, Joclyn, Joclynn, Josalyn, Joscelin, Joselin, Joselyn, Joshlyn, Josilin, Jossalin, Josselyn, Joycelyn

Jocelyne (Latin) a form of Jocelyn.
Joceline, Jocelynne, Joclynne

Jocosa, Jocose (Latin) jubilant.

Jodi, Jodie G (American) familiar forms of Judith.

Jodiann (American) a combination of Jodi + Ann.
Jodene, Jodi-Ann, Jodianna, Jodi-Anna, Jodianne, Jodi-Anne, Jodine, Jodyann, Jody-Ann, Jodyanna, Jody-Anna, Jodyanne, Jody-Anne, Jodyne

Jody BG (American) a familiar form of Judith.
Jodee, Jodele, Jodell, Jodelle, Jodevea, Jodey, Jodia, Jodiee, Jodilee, Jodi-Lee, Jodilynn, Jodi-Lynn, Joedi, Joedy

Joe B (Latin) a form of Joy.

Joel B (Hebrew) God is willing.

Joelle BG (Hebrew) a form of Joel.
Joela, Joele, Joelee, Joeli, Joelia, Joelie, Joell, Joella, Joëlle, Joelli, Joelly, Joely, Joyelle

Joelynn (American) a combination of Joelle + Lynn.
Joeleen, Joelene, Joeline, Joellen, Joellyn, Joelyn, Joelyne

Joey B (French) a familiar form of Josephine. (American) a form of Jo.

Johana, Johanna, Johannah (German) forms of Joana.
Janna, Joahna, Johanah, Johanka, Johanne, Johnna, Johonna, Jonna, Joyhanna, Joyhannah

Johanie, Johannie (Hebrew) forms of Joanie.
Johani, Johanni, Johanny, Johany

John B (Hebrew) God is gracious.

Johnna, Jonna (American) forms of Johana, Joanna.
Jahna, Jahnaya, Jhona, Jhonna, Johna, Johnda, Johnnielynn, Johnnie-Lynn, Johnnquia, Joncie, Jonda, Jondrea, Jontel, Jutta

Johnnessa (American) a combination of Johnna + Nessa.
Jahnessa, Johneatha, Johnecia, Johnesha, Johnetra, Johnisha, Johnishi, Johnnise, Jonyssa

Johnnie B (Hebrew) a form of Joanie.
Johni, Johnie, Johnni, Johnny

Johnny B (Hebrew) a form of Johnnie.

Joi G (Latin) a form of Joy.
Joia, Joie

Jojiana (Fijian) a form of Georgia.

Jokla (Swahili) beautiful robe.

Jolanda (Greek) a form of Yolanda. See also Iolanthe.
Jola, Jolan, Jolán, Jolande, Jolander, Jolanka, Jolánta, Jolantha, Jolanthe

Joleen, Joline (English) forms of Jolene.
Joleena, Joleene, Jolleen, Jollene

Jolene G (Hebrew) God will add, God will increase. (English) a form of Josephine.
Jo, Jolaine, Jolana, Jolane, Jolanna, Jolanne, Jolanta, Jolayne, Jole, Jolean, Joleane, Joleen, Jolena, Joléne, Jolenna, Jolin, Jolina, Jolinda, Joline, Jolinn, Jolinna, Jolleane, Jolleen, Jolline

Jolie (French) pretty.
Jole, Jolea, Jolee, Joleigh, Joley, Joli, Jolibeth, Jollee, Jollie, Jolly, Joly, Jolye

Jolisa (American) a combination of Jo + Lisa.
Joleesa, Joleisha, Joleishia, Jolieasa, Jolise, Jolisha, Jolisia, Jolissa, Jolysa, Jolyssa, Julissa

Jolynn (American) a combination of Jo + Lynn.
Jolyn, Jolyne, Jolynne

Jon B (Hebrew) a form of John. A short form of Jonathan.

Jonah B (Hebrew) dove.

Jonatan B (Hebrew) a form of Jonathan.

Jonatha (Hebrew) gift of God.
Johnasha, Johnasia, Jonesha, Jonisha

Jonathan B (Hebrew) gift of God.

Jonelle (American) a combination of Joan + Elle.
Jahnel, Jahnell, Jahnelle, Johnel, Johnell, Johnella, Johnelle, Jonel, Jonell, Jonella, Jonyelle, Jynell, Jynelle

Jonesha, Jonisha (American) forms of Jonatha.
Joneisha, Jonesa, Joneshia, Jonessa, Jonisa, Jonishia, Jonneisha, Jonnesha, Jonnessia

Jong (Tagalog) little girl.

Joni (American) a familiar form of Joan.
Jona, Jonae, Jonai, Jonann, Jonati, Joncey, Jonci, Joncie, Jonice, Jonie, Jonilee, Joni-lee, Jonis, Jony

Jonika (American) a form of Janika.
Johnica, Johnique, Johnquia, Johnnica, Johnnika, Joneeka, Joneika, Jonica, Joniqua, Jonique

Jonina (Hebrew) dove. See also Yonina.
Jona, Jonita, Jonnina

Jonita (Hebrew) a form of Jonina. See also Yonita.
Johnetta, Johnette, Johnita, Johnittia, Jonati, Jonetia, Jonetta, Jonette, Jonit, Jonnita, Jonta, Jontae, Jontaé, Jontaya

Jonni, Jonnie (American) familiar forms of Joan.
Jonny

Jonquil (Latin, English) Botany: an ornamental plant with fragrant yellow flowers.
Jonquelle, Jonquie, Jonquill, Jonquille

Jontel (American) a form of Johnna.
Jontaya, Jontell, Jontelle, Jontia, Jontila, Jontrice

Joo (Korean) aspiring; volunteering.

Joo-Eun (Korean) wisdom and courage.

Joon (Korean) master, ruler; red; eternity; daytime; boat; tree trunk; pillar.

Jora **G** (Hebrew) autumn rain.
Jorah

Jordan ✵ **B** (Hebrew) descending. See also Jardena.
Jordain, Jordaine, Jordana, Jordane, Jordann, Jordanna, Jordanne, Jordany, Jordea, Jordee, Jorden, Jordi, Jordian, Jordie, Jordin, Jordon, Jordyn, Jori, Jorie, Jourdan

Jordana, Jordanna (Hebrew) forms of Jordan. See also Giordana, Yordana.
Jordannah, Jordina, Jordonna, Jourdana, Jourdanna

Jorden **B** (Hebrew) a form of Jordan.
Jordenne

Jordin (Hebrew) a form of Jordan.
Jordine

Jordon **B** (Hebrew) a form of Jordan.

Jordyn **G** (Hebrew) a form of Jordan.
Jordyne, Jordynn, Jordynne

Jorge **B** (Spanish) a form of George (see Boys' Names).

Jorgelina (Greek) she who works well in the countryside.

Jori, Jorie (Hebrew) familiar forms of Jordan.
Jorai, Jorea, Joree, Jorée, Jorey, Jorian, Jorin, Jorina, Jorine, Jorita, Jorre, Jorrey, Jorri, Jorrian, Jorrie, Jorry, Jory

Joriann (American) a combination of Jori + Ann.
Jori-Ann, Jorianna, Jori-Anna, Jorianne, Jori-Anne, Jorriann, Jorrianna, Jorrianne, Jorryann, Jorryanna, Jorryanne, Joryann, Joryanna, Joryanne

Jorja (American) a form of Georgia.
Jeorgi, Jeorgia, Jorgana, Jorgi, Jorgia, Jorgina, Jorjana, Jorji

Josalyn (Latin) a form of Jocelyn.
Josalene, Josalin, Josalind, Josaline, Josalynn, Joshalyne

Joscelin, Joscelyn (Latin) forms of Jocelyn.
Josceline, Joscelyne, Joscelynn, Joscelynne, Joselin, Joseline, Joselyn, Joselyne, Joselynn, Joselynne, Joshlyn

Jose **B** (Spanish) a form of Joseph.

Josee **G** (American) a familiar form of Josephine.
Joesee, Josey, Josi, Josina, Josy, Jozee

Josée (American) a familiar form of Josephine.

Josefina (Spanish) a form of Josephine.
Josefa, Josefena, Joseffa, Josefine

Joselín (Latin) a form of Joselin.

Joselin, Joseline (Latin) forms of Jocelyn.
Joselina, Joselinne, Josielina

Joselle (American) a form of Jizelle.
Joesell, Jozelle

Joselyn, Joslyn (Latin) forms of Jocelyn.
Joselene, Joselyne, Joselynn, Joshely, Josiline, Josilyn

Joseph **B** (Hebrew) God will add, God will increase.

Josephine **G** (French) a form of Joseph. See also Fifi, Pepita, Yosepha.
Fina, Jo, Joey, Josee, Josée, Josefina, Josepha, Josephe, Josephene, Josephin, Josephina, Josephyna, Josephyne, Josette, Josey, Josie, Jozephine, Jozie, Sefa

Josette (French) a familiar form of Josephine.
Joesette, Josetta, Joshetta, Jozette

Josevini (Fijian) a form of Josephine.

Josey (Hebrew) a familiar form of Josephine.
Josi, Josse, Jossee, Jossie, Josy, Josye

Joshann (American) a combination of Joshlyn + Ann.
Joshana, Joshanna, Joshanne

Girls G–L

Joshika (Indian) young maiden.

Joshita, Joshitha (Indian) pleased.

Joshlyn (Latin) a form of Jocelyn. (Hebrew) God is my salvation.
Joshalin, Joshalyn, Joshalynn, Joshalynne, Joshelle, Joshleen, Joshlene, Joshlin, Joshline, Joshlyne, Joshlynn, Joshlynne

Joshua 🅱 (Hebrew) God is my salvation.

Josiah 🅱 (Hebrew) fire of the Lord.

Josiane, Josianne (American) combinations of Josie + Anne.
Josian, Josie-Ann, Josieann

Josie (Hebrew) a familiar form of Josephine.

Josilin, Joslin (Latin) forms of Jocelyn.
Josielina, Josiline, Josilyn, Josilyne, Josilynn, Josilynne, Joslin, Josline, Joslyn, Joslyne, Joslynn, Joslynne

Josivini (Fijian) a form of Josefa.

Jossalin (Latin) a form of Jocelyn.
Jossaline, Jossalyn, Jossalynn, Jossalynne, Josselyn, Josslin, Jossline

Josselyn (Latin) a form of Jocelyn.
Josselen, Josselin, Josseline, Jossellen, Jossellin, Jossellyn, Josselyne, Josselynn, Josselynne, Josslyn, Josslyne, Josslynn, Josslynne

Josune (Spanish) named for Jesus.

Jourdan (Hebrew) a form of Jordan.
Jourdain, Jourdann, Jourdanne, Jourden, Jourdian, Jourdon, Jourdyn

Jovana (Latin) a form of Jovanna.
Jeovana, Jouvan, Jovan, Jovanah, Jovena, Jovian, Jowan, Jowana

Jovani 🅱 (Italian) a form of Jovannie.

Jovanna (Latin) majestic. (Italian) a form of Giovanna. Mythology: Jove, also known as Jupiter, was the supreme Roman god.
Jeovanna, Jovado, Joval, Jovana, Jovann, Jovannie, Jovena, Jovina, Jovon, Jovonda, Jovonia, Jovonna, Jovonnah, Jovonne, Jowanna

Jovanni 🅱 (Italian) a form of Jovannie.

Jovannie (Italian) a familiar form of Jovanna.
Jovanee, Jovani, Jovanie, Jovanne, Jovanni, Jovanny, Jovonnie

Jovita (Latin) jovial.
Joveda, Joveta, Jovetta, Jovida, Jovitta

Jowaki (Indian) a firefly.

Joy 🅶 (Latin) joyous.
Joya, Joye, Joyeeta, Joyella, Joyia, Joyous, Joyvina

Joyanne (American) a combination of Joy + Anne.
Joyan, Joyann, Joyanna

Joyce (Latin) joyous. A short form of Joycelyn.
Joice, Joycey, Joycie, Joyous, Joysel

Joycelyn (American) a form of Jocelyn.
Joycelin, Joyceline, Joycelyne, Joycelynn, Joycelynne

Joyceta (Spanish) a form of Joyce.

Joylyn (American) a combination of Joy + Lynn.
Joyleen, Joylene, Joylin, Joyline, Joylyne, Joylynn, Joy-Lynn, Joylynne

Jozie (Hebrew) a familiar form of Josephine.
Jozee, Jozée, Jozi, Jozy

Ju (Chinese) chrysanthemum.

Juan (Chinese) beautiful.

Juana (Spanish) a short form of Juanita.
Juanell, Juaney, Juanika, Juanit, Juanna, Juannia

Juana del Pilar (Spanish) a form of Juana.

Juandalyn (Spanish) a form of Juanita.
Jualinn, Juandalin, Juandaline, Juandalyne, Juandalynn, Juandalynne

Juaneta (Spanish) God is gracious.

Juanita (Spanish) a form of Jane, Joan. See also Kwanita, Nita, Waneta, Wanika.
Juana, Juandalyn, Juaneice, Juanequa, Juanesha, Juanice, Juanicia, Juaniqua, Juanisha, Juanishia

Juci (Hungarian) a form of Judy.
Jucika

Judith (Hebrew) praised. Mythology: the slayer of Holofernes, according to ancient Jewish legend. See also Yehudit, Yudita.
Giuditta, Ioudith, Jodi, Jodie, Jody, Jude, Judine, Judit, Judita, Judite, Juditha, Judithe, Judy, Judyta, Jutka

Judy 🅶 (Hebrew) a familiar form of Judith.
Juci, Judi, Judie, Judye

Judyann (American) a combination of Judy + Ann.
Judana, Judiann, Judianna, Judianne, Judyanna, Judyanne

Jue (Chinese) two pieces of jade.

Juhi, Jui (Indian) flower.

Juichi (Japanese) long-lived first-born.

Juily (Indian) a flower.

Jui-Ying (Chinese) beautiful flower; lucky flower.

Jula (Polish) a form of Julia.
Julca, Julcia, Juliska, Julka

Julene (Basque) a form of Julia. See also Yulene.
Julena, Julina, Juline, Julinka, Juliska, Julleen, Jullena, Jullene, Julyne

Julia ✤ **G** (Latin) youthful. See also Giulia, Jill, Jillian, Sulia, Yulia.
Iulia, Jula, Julea, Juleah, Julene, Juliah, Juliana, Juliann, Julica, Julie, Juliea, Juliet, Julija, Julina, Juline, Julisa, Julissa, Julita, Juliya, Julka, Julyssa

Julian **B** (English) a form of Juliann.

Juliana (Czech, Spanish, Hungarian) a form of Julia.
Julieana, Juliena, Julliana, Julyana, Yuliana

Juliann (English) a form of Julia.
Julean, Julian, Juliane, Julien, Juliene, Jullian

Julianna **G** (Czech, Spanish, Hungarian) a form of Julia.
Julieanna, Jullianna, Julyanna

Julianne **G** (English) a form of Julia.
Juleann, Julieann, Julie-Ann, Julieanne, Julie-Anne, Julienn, Julienne

Julie **G** (English) a form of Julia.
Juel, Jule, Julee, Juli, Julie-Lynn, Julie-Mae, Julle, Jullee, Jullie, Jully, July

Julien **B** (English) a form of Juliann.

Juliet **G** (French) a form of Julia.
Julet, Julieta, Jullet, Julliet

Juliette (French) a form of Julia.
Juliett, Julietta, Jullietta

Julio **B** (Hispanic) a form of Julius.

Julisa, Julissa (Latin) forms of Julia.
Julis, Julisha, Julysa, Julyssa

Julita (Spanish) a form of Julia.
Julitta, Julyta

Julius **B** (Greek, Latin) youthful, downy bearded.

Jum (Korean) silver pearl.

Jumaana (Indian) silver pearl.

Jumaris (American) a combination of Julie + Maris.

Jun **B** (Chinese) truthful.

June (Latin) born in the sixth month.
Juna, Junea, Junel, Junell, Junella, Junelle, Junette, Juney, Junia, Junie, Juniet, Junieta, Junietta, Juniette, Junina, Junita

Jung Sook (Korean) true; heroic; handsome; obey, honor.

Junko (Japanese) obedient.

Juno (Latin) queen. Mythology: the supreme Roman goddess.

Juong (Korean) foretell.

Juri (Japanese) scarlet; hometown.

Justa (Latin) she who lives for and according to the law of God.

Justice **G** (Latin) just, righteous.
Justis, Justise, Justiss, Justisse, Justus, Justyce, Justys

Justin **B** (Latin) just, righteous.

Justina **G** (Italian) a form of Justine.
Jestena, Jestina, Justinna, Justyna

Justine **G** (Latin) just, righteous.
Giustina, Jestine, Juste, Justi, Justice, Justie, Justina, Justinn, Justy, Justyn, Justyne, Justynn, Justynne

Justiniana (Spanish) just, fair.

Justyn **B** (Latin) a form of Justine.

Juvencia, Juventina (Latin) youth.

Juwan **B** (American) a form of Jajuan (see Boys' Names).

Jwala (Indian) flame.

Jyeshtha (Indian) biggest.

Jyothi, Jyotika (Indian) light.

Jyoti (Indian) light; brilliant.

Jyotibala (Indian) splendor.

Jyotirmoyee (Indian) lustrous.

Jyotishmati (Indian) luminous, bright, glowing.

K

K **G** (American) an initial used as a first name.

Ka (Korean) chaste, virtuous; quiet, silent.

Kaamla (Indian) perfect.

Kaapuni (Hawaiian) to travel; a hula step.

Kaasni (Indian) flower.

Kacey, Kacy 🄶 (Irish) brave. (American) forms of Casey. Combinations of the initials K. + C.
K. C., Kace, Kacee, Kaci, Kacie, Kaicee, Kaicey, Kasey, Kasie, Kaycee, Kayci, Kaycie

Kachina (Native American) sacred dancer.
Kachine

Kaci, Kacie 🄶 (American) forms of Kacey, Kacy.
Kasci, Kaycie, Kaysie

Kacia (Greek) a short form of Acacia.
Kaycia, Kaysia

Kadalina (Pohnpeian) a form of Flora.

Kadambari (Indian) novel; nightingale bird.

Kadambhari (Indian) goddess.

Kadambini (Indian) clouds.

Kade 🄱 (Scottish) wetlands. (American) a combination of the initials K. + D.

Kadedra (American) a combination of Kady + Dedra.
Kadeadra, Kadedrah, Kadedria, Kadeedra, Kadeidra, Kadeidre, Kadeidria

Kadeem 🄱 (Arabic) servant.

Kadejah (Arabic) a form of Kadijah.
Kadeija, Kadeijah, Kadejá, Kadejia

Kadelyn (American) a combination of Kady + Lynn.

Kaden 🄱 (Arabic) a form of Kadin (see Boys' Names).

Kadesha (American) a combination of Kady + Aisha.
Kadeesha, Kadeeshia, Kadeesia, Kadeesiah, Kadeezia, Kadesa, Kadesheia, Kadeshia, Kadesia, Kadessa, Kadezia

Kadie (English) a form of Kady.
Kadi, Kadia, Kadiah

Kadijah (Arabic) trustworthy.
Kadajah, Kadeeja, Kadeejah, Kadija

Kadisha (American) a form of Kadesha.
Kadiesha, Kadieshia, Kadishia, Kadisia, Kadysha, Kadyshia

Kady (English) a form of Katy. A combination of the initials K. + D. See also Cady.
K. D., Kade, Kadee, Kadey, Kadie, Kadya, Kadyn, Kaidi, Kaidy, Kayde, Kaydee, Kaydey, Kaydi, Kaydie, Kaydy

Kae (Greek, Teutonic, Latin) a form of Kay.

Kaede (Japanese) maple leaf.

Kaedé (Japanese) maple leaf.

Kaela (Hebrew, Arabic) beloved, sweetheart. A short form of Kalila, Kelila.
Kaelah, Kaelea, Kaeleah, Kaelee, Kaeli, Kayla

Kaelee, Kaeli (American) forms of Kaela.
Kaelei, Kaeleigh, Kaeley, Kaelia, Kaelie, Kaelii, Kaelly, Kaely, Kaelye

Kaelin (American) a form of Kaelyn.
Kaeleen, Kaelene, Kaelina, Kaelinn, Kalan

Kaelyn 🄶 (American) a combination of Kae + Lynn. See also Caelin, Kaylyn.
Kaelan, Kaelen, Kaelin, Kaelynn, Kaelynne

Kaetlyn (Irish) a form of Kaitlin.
Kaetlin, Kaetlynn

Kagami (Japanese) mirror.

Kahawi (Hawaiian) river.

Kahekili (Hawaiian) thunder.

Kahkashan (Indian) stars.

Kahlil 🄱 (Arabic) a form of Khalíl (see Boys' Names).

Kaho (Japanese) fragrance; sail.

Kahsha (Native American) fur robe.
Kasha, Kashae, Kashia

Kai 🄱 (Hawaiian) sea. (Hopi, Navajo) willow tree.
Kae, Kaie

Kaia (Greek) earth. Mythology: Gaea was the earth goddess.
Kaiah, Kaija

Kaida (Japanese) little dragon.

Kaila (Hebrew) laurel; crown.
Kailah, Kailea, Kaileah, Kailee, Kailey, Kayla

Kailee, Kailey (American) familiar forms of Kaila. Forms of Kaylee.
Kaile, Kaileh, Kaileigh, Kaili, Kailia, Kailie, Kailli, Kaillie, Kaily, Kailya

Kailyn 🄶 (American) a form of Kaitlin.
Kailan, Kaileen, Kaileena, Kailen, Kailena, Kailene, Kaileyne, Kailin, Kailina, Kailon

Kailynn (American) a form of Kailyn.
Kailynne

Kaiolohia (Hawaiian) calm sea; peace of mind.

Kaipo (Hawaiian) the sweetheart.

Kairos (Greek) last, final, complete.
Mythology: the last goddess born to Jupiter.
Kaira, Kairra

Kaishawn (American) a combination of Kai
+ Shawna.
Kaeshun, Kaisha, Kaishala, Kaishon

Kaitlin **G** (Irish) pure. See also Katelin.
*Kaetlyn, Kailyn, Kailynn, Kaitlan, Kaitland,
Kaitleen, Kaitlen, Kaitlind, Kaitlinn, Kaitlinne,
Kaitlon, Kaytlin*

Kaitlyn �౿ (Irish) a form of Caitlyn.

Kaitlynn (Irish) a form of Caitlyn.
Kaitelynne, Kaitlynne

Kaiulani (Hawaiian) the zenith, the highest
point of the heavens.

Kaiya (Japanese) forgiveness.
Kaiyah, Kaiyia

Kaiyo (Japanese) forgiveness.

Kajal, Kajjali (Indian) eyeliner.

Kajri (Indian) light as a cloud.

Kakali (Indian) the chirping of birds.

Kako (Japanese) summer; rainbow.

Kala **G** (Arabic) a short form of Kalila. A
form of Cala.
Kalah, Kalla, Kallah

Kalama **BG** (Hawaiian) torch.

Kalani **G** (Hawaiian) chieftain; sky.
Kailani, Kalanie, Kaloni

Kalapi (Indian) peacock; nightingale.

Kalapini (Indian) peacock; night.

Kalare (Latin, Basque) bright; clear.

Kalavati (Indian) artist.

Kalea (Hawaiian) bright; clear.
*Kahlea, Kahleah, Kailea, Kaileah, Kaleah,
Kaleeia, Kaleia, Kalia, Kallea, Kalleah,
Kaylea, Kayleah, Khalea, Khaleah*

Kaleb **B** (Hebrew) a form of Caleb.

Kalee, Kalie (American) forms of Caley,
Kaylee.
Kalei

Kalei (Hawaiian) flower wreath.
Kahlei, Kailei, Kallei, Kaylei, Khalei

Kaleigh, Kaley **G** (American) forms of
Caley, Kaylee.
Kalley, Kalleigh, Kally, Kaly

Kaleinani (Hawaiian) the beautiful lei.

Kaleipunani (Hawaiian) the leis of beautiful
flowers.

Kalena (Hawaiian) pure. See also Kalina.
Kaleen, Kaleena, Kalene, Kalenea, Kalenna

Kalere (Swahili) short woman.
Kaleer

Kali **G** (Hindi) the black one. (Hawaiian)
hesitating. Religion: a form of the Hindu
goddess Devi. See also Cali.
*Kalee, Kaleigh, Kaley, Kalie, Kallee, Kalley,
Kalli, Kallie, Kally, Kallye, Kaly*

Kalia (Hawaiian) a form of Kalea.
Kaliah, Kaliea, Kalieya

Kalifa (Somali) chaste; holy.

Kalila (Arabic) beloved, sweetheart. See also
Kaela.
*Kahlila, Kala, Kaleela, Kalilla, Kaylil, Kaylila,
Kelila, Khalila, Khalilah, Khalillah, Kylila,
Kylilah, Kylillah*

Kalima (Indian) blackish.

Kalina (Slavic) flower. (Hawaiian) a form of
Karen. See also Kalena.
Kalin, Kalinna, Kalyna, Kalynah, Kalynna

Kalinda (Hindi) sun.
Kaleenda, Kalindi, Kalynda, Kalyndi

Kalini (Indian) flower.

Kalisa (American) a combination of Kate +
Lisa.
Kalise, Kalissa, Kalysa, Kalyssa

Kalisha (American) a combination of Kate +
Aisha.
Kaleesha, Kaleisha, Kalishia

Kaliska (Moquelumnan) coyote chasing
deer.

Kallan (Slavic) stream, river.
Kalahn, Kalan, Kalen, Kallen, Kallon, Kalon

Kalle **BG** (Finnish) a form of Carol.
Kaille, Kaylle

Kalli, Kallie (Greek) forms of Callie.
Familiar forms of Kalliope, Kallista,
Kalliyan.
Kalle, Kallee, Kalley, Kallita, Kally

Kalliope (Greek) a form of Calliope.
Kalli, Kallie, Kallyope

Kallista (Greek) a form of Callista.
*Kalesta, Kalista, Kallesta, Kalli, Kallie,
Kallysta, Kaysta*

Kalliyan (Cambodian) best.
Kalli, Kallie

Kallol (Indian) large waves; gurgling of water.

Kalpana (Indian) imagination.

Kalpita (Indian) imaginary.

Kaltha (English) marigold, yellow flower.

Kaluwa (Swahili) forgotten one.
Kalua

Kalyani (Indian) fortunate.

Kalyca (Greek) rosebud.
Kalica, Kalika, Kaly

Kalyn 🄖 (American) a form of Kaylyn.
Kalin, Kallen, Kallin, Kallon, Kallyn, Kalyne

Kalynn 🄖 (American) a forms of Kalyn.
Kalynne

Kama (Sanskrit) loved one. Religion: the Hindu god of love.

Kamaka (Hawaiian) the favorite one.

Kamako (Japanese) kettle child; cattail child; scythe child.

Kamala (Hindi) lotus.
Kamalah, Kammala

Kamalakshi (Indian) one with eyes like a lotus.

Kamali (Mahona) spirit guide; protector.
Kamalie

Kamalika, Kamalini (Indian) lotus.

Kamalkali (Indian) the bud of a lotus.

Kamana (Indian) desire.

Kamaria (Swahili) moonlight.
Kamar, Kamara, Kamarae, Kamaree, Kamari, Kamariah, Kamarie, Kamariya, Kamariyah, Kamarya

Kamata (Moquelumnan) gambler.

Kambria (Latin) a form of Cambria.
Kambra, Kambrie, Kambriea, Kambry

Kamea (Hawaiian) one and only; precious.
Kameah, Kameo, Kamiya

Kamehameha (Hawaiian) the solitary.

Kameke (Swahili) blind.

Kameko (Japanese) turtle child. Mythology: the turtle symbolizes longevity.

Kameron 🄱 (American) a form of Cameron.
Kameran, Kamri

Kameyo (Japanese) generations of the tortoise.

Kami 🄖 (Japanese) divine aura. (Italian, North African) a short form of Kamila, Kamilah. See also Cami.
Kamie, Kammi, Kammie, Kammy, Kammye, Kamy

Kamil 🄱 (Arabic) a form of Kamal (see Boys' Names).

Kamila (Slavic) a form of Camila. See also Millie.
Kameela, Kamela, Kamelia, Kamella, Kami, Kamilah, Kamilia, Kamilka, Kamilla, Kamille, Kamma, Kammilla, Kamyla

Kamilah (North African) perfect.
Kameela, Kameelah, Kami, Kamillah, Kammilah

Kamini (Indian) beautiful woman.

Kamiya (Hawaiian) a form of Kamea.
Kamia, Kamiah, Kamiyah

Kamna (Indian) wish.

Kamri (American) a short form of Kameron. See also Camri.
Kamree, Kamrey, Kamrie, Kamry, Kamrye

Kamryn (American) a short form of Kameron. See also Camryn.
Kameryn, Kamren, Kamrin, Kamron, Kamrynn

Kanaka, Kanchana (Indian) gold.

Kanakabati (Indian) a fairytale.

Kanaklata (Indian) gold climber plant.

Kanakpriya (Indian) one who loves gold.

Kananbala (Indian) daughter of the forest.

Kanani (Hawaiian) beautiful.
Kana, Kanae, Kanan

Kanchanprabha (Indian) golden light.

Kanchi (Indian) a waistband.

Kanda (Native American) magical power.

Kandace, Kandice 🄖 (Greek) glittering white; glowing. (American) forms of Candace, Candice.
Kandas, Kandess, Kandi, Kandis, Kandise, Kandiss, Kandus, Kandyce, Kandys, Kandyse

Kandi (American) a familiar form of Kandace, Kandice. See also Candi.
Kandhi, Kandia, Kandie, Kandy, Kendi, Kendie, Kendy, Kenndi, Kenndie, Kenndy

Kandra (American) a form of Kendra. See also Candra.
Kandrea, Kandree, Kandria

Kane B (Japanese) two right hands.

Kaneisha, Kanisha (American) forms of Keneisha.
Kaneasha, Kanecia, Kaneesha, Kanesah, Kanesha, Kaneshea, Kaneshia, Kanessa, Kaneysha, Kaniece, Kanishia

Kanene (Swahili) a little important thing.

Kaneru (Japanese) bronze.

Kang (Chinese) fervent; generous.

Kani (Hawaiian) sound.

Kanika (Mwera) black cloth.
Kanica, Kanicka

Kanira (Indian) grain.

Kanista (Chuukese) a form of Calista.

Kanjri (Indian) bird.

Kankana (Indian) a bracelet.

Kannitha (Cambodian) angel.

Kanoa B (Hawaiian) free.

Kanoe (Hawaiian) mist.

Kanon (Japanese) flower; sound.

Kanta (Indian) beauty.

Kanthi (Indian) luster; loveliness.

Kanti (Indian) light.

Kanya (Hindi) virgin. (Tai) young lady. Religion: a form of the Hindu goddess Devi.
Kanea, Kania, Kaniya, Kanyia

Kaohinani (Hawaiian) gatherer of beauty.

Kaopua (Hawaiian) the rain clouds.

Kaori (Japanese) strong.

Kaoru (Japanese) fragrant.

Kapelani (Hawaiian) a form of Kapiolani.

Kapila (Indian) sacred cow.

Kapiolani (Hawaiian) sacred arch of heaven.

Kapotakshi (Indian) one with eyes like a dove.

Kapri (American) a form of Capri.
Kapre, Kapree, Kapria, Kaprice, Kapricia, Kaprisha, Kaprisia

Kapua (Hawaiian) blossom.

Kapuki (Swahili) first-born daughter.

Kara G (Greek, Danish) pure.
Kaira, Kairah, Karah, Karalea, Karaleah, Karalee, Karalie, Kari, Karra

Karabi (Indian) flower.

Karah (Greek, Danish) a form of Kara. (Irish, Italian) a form of Cara.
Karrah

Karalaini (Fijian) a form of Caroline.

Karalynn (English) a combination of Kara + Lynn.
Karalin, Karaline, Karalyn, Karalyne, Karalynne

Kareem B (Arabic) noble; distinguished.

Karel BG (American) a form of Karelle.

Karelle (American) a form of Carol.
Karel, Kareli, Karell, Karely

Karen G (Greek) pure. See also Carey, Carina, Caryn.
Kaaren, Kalina, Karaina, Karan, Karena, Karin, Karina, Karine, Karna, Karon, Karren, Karron, Karyn, Kerron, Koren

Karena (Scandinavian) a form of Karen.
Kareen, Kareena, Kareina, Karenah, Karene, Karreen, Karreena, Karrena, Karrene

Karessa (French) a form of Caressa.

Kari G (Greek) pure. (Danish) a form of Caroline, Katherine. See also Carey, Cari, Carrie.
Karee, Karey, Karia, Kariah, Karie, Karrey, Karri, Karrie, Karry, Kary

Kariane, Karianne (American) combinations of Kari + Ann.
Karian, Kariana, Kariann, Karianna

Karida (Arabic) untouched, pure.
Kareeda, Karita

Karilynn (American) a combination of Kari + Lynn.
Kareelin, Kareeline, Kareelinn, Kareelyn, Kareelyne, Kareelynn, Kareelynne, Karilin, Kariline, Karilinn, Karilyn, Karilyne, Karilynne, Karylin, Karyline, Karylinn, Karylyn, Karylyne, Karylynn, Karylynne

Karimah (Arabic) generous.
Kareema, Kareemah, Karima, Karime

Karin (Scandinavian) a form of Karen.
Kaarin, Kareen, Karina, Karine, Karinne, Karrin, Kerrin

Karina G (Russian) a form of Karen.
Kaarina, Karinna, Karrina, Karryna, Karyna, Karynna

Karine (Russian) a form of Karen.
Karrine, Karryne, Karyne

Karis (Greek) graceful.
Karess, Karice, Karise, Karisse, Karris, Karys, Karyss

Karissa (Greek) a form of Carissa.
Karese, Karesse, Karisa, Karisha, Karishma, Karisma, Karissimia, Kariza, Karrisa, Karrissa, Karysa, Karyssa, Kerisa

Karla 🅖 (German) a form of Carla. (Slavic) a short form of Karoline.
Karila, Karilla, Karle, Karlene, Karlicka, Karlinka, Karlisha, Karlisia, Karlitha, Karlla, Karlon, Karlyn

Karlee, Karleigh (American) forms of Karley, Karly. See also Carlee.
Karlea, Karleah, Karlei

Karlene, Karlyn (American) forms of Karla. See also Carleen.
Karleen, Karlen, Karlena, Karlign, Karlin, Karlina, Karlinna, Karlyan, Karlynn, Karlynne

Karley, Karly 🅖 (Latin) little and strong. (American) forms of Carly.
Karlee, Karley, Karlie, Karlyan, Karlye

Karli, Karlie (American) forms of Karley, Karly. See also Carli.

Karlotte (American) a form of Charlotte.
Karlita, Karletta, Karlette, Karlotta

Karma (Hindi) fate, destiny; action.

Karmel 🅑🅖 (Hebrew) a form of Carmela.
Karmeita, Karmela, Karmelina, Karmella, Karmelle, Karmiella, Karmielle, Karmyla

Karmen (Latin) song.
Karman, Karmencita, Karmin, Karmina, Karmine, Karmita, Karmon, Karmyn, Karmyne

Karolane (American) a combination of Karoll + Anne.
Karolan, Karolann, Karolanne, Karol-Anne

Karolina, Karoline (Slavic) forms of Caroline. See also Carolina.
Karaleen, Karalena, Karalene, Karalin, Karáline, Karileen, Karilena, Karilene, Karilin, Karilina, Kariline, Karleen, Karlen, Karlena, Karlene, Karling, Karoleena, Karolena, Karolinka, Karroleen, Karrolena, Karrolene, Karrolin, Karroline

Karoll (Slavic) a form of Carol.
Karel, Karilla, Karily, Karol, Karola, Karole, Karoly, Karrol, Karyl, Kerril

Karolyn (American) a form of Carolyn.
Karalyn, Karalyna, Karalynn, Karalynne, Karilyn, Karilyna, Karilynn, Karilynne, Karlyn, Karlynn, Karlynne, Karolyna, Karolynn, Karolynne, Karrolyn, Karrolyna, Karrolynn, Karrolynne

Karri, Karrie (American) forms of Carrie.
Kari, Karie, Karry, Kary

Karsen, Karsyn (English) child of Kar. Forms of Carson.
Karson

Karuka (Indian) heavenly piece of art.

Karuli (Indian) innocent.

Karuna (Hindi) merciful.

Karunamayee (Indian) full of pity for others.

Karunamayi (Indian) merciful.

Karunya (Indian) compassionate.

Karyn (American) a form of Karen.
Karyne, Karynn, Karynna, Kerrynn, Kerrynne

Kasa (Hopi) fur robe.

Kasandra (Greek) a form of Kassandra.
Kasander, Kasandria, Kasandra, Kasaundra, Kasondra, Kasoundra

Kasanita (Fijian) strike wood together to make fire.

Kasey, Kasie 🅖 (Irish) brave. (American) forms of Casey, Kacey.
Kaisee, Kaisie, Kasci, Kascy, Kasee, Kasi, Kassee, Kassey, Kasy, Kasya, Kaysci, Kaysea, Kaysee, Kaysey, Kaysi, Kaysie, Kaysy

Kashawna (American) a combination of Kate + Shawna.
Kasha, Kashae, Kashana, Kashanna, Kashauna, Kashawn, Kasheana, Kasheanna, Kasheena, Kashena, Kashonda, Kashonna

Kashika (Indian) the shiny one.

Kashmir (Sanskrit) Geography: a region located between India and Pakistan.
Cashmere, Kashmear, Kashmere, Kashmia, Kashmira, Kasmir, Kasmira, Kazmir, Kazmira

Kashvi (Indian) shining.

Kashyapi (Indian) earth.

Kasi (Hindi) from the holy city.

Kasia (Polish) a form of Katherine. See also Cassia.
Kashia, Kasiah, Kasian, Kasienka, Kasja, Kaska, Kassa, Kassia, Kassya, Kasya

Kasind (Umbundu) sky.

Kasinda (Umbundu) our last baby.

Kasinta (Umbundu) wish.

Kassandra **G** (Greek) a form of Cassandra.
Kassandr, Kassandre, Kassandré,
Kassaundra, Kassi, Kassondra, Kassondria,
Kassundra, Kazandra, Khrisandra, Krisandra,
Krissandra

Kassi, Kassie (American) familiar forms of
Kassandra, Kassidy. See also Cassie.
Kassey, Kassia, Kassy

Kassidy **G** (Irish) clever. (American) a form
of Cassidy.
Kassadee, Kassadi, Kassadie, Kassadina,
Kassady, Kasseday, Kassedee, Kassi,
Kassiddy, Kassidee, Kassidi, Kassidie,
Kassity, Kassydi

Kasturi (Indian) scented.

Kasuga (Japanese) a child of spring.

Kat'min (Chamorro) a form of Carmen.

Katalina (Irish) a form of Caitlin. See also
Catalina.
Kataleen, Kataleena, Katalena, Katalin,
Katalyn, Katalynn

Katarina (Czech) a form of Katherine.
Kata, Katareena, Katarena, Katarin, Katarine,
Katarinna, Katarinne, Katarrina, Kataryna,
Katarzyna, Katinka, Katrika, Katrinka

Kate **G** (Greek) pure. (English) a short form
of Katherine.
Kait, Kata, Katee, Kati, Katica, Katie, Katka,
Katy, Katya

Katee, Katey (English) familiar forms of
Kate, Katherine.

Katelin (Irish) a form of Caitlin. See also
Kaitlin.
Kaetlin, Katalin, Katelan, Kateland, Kateleen,
Katelen, Katelene, Katelind, Kateline,
Katelinn, Katelun, Kaytlin

Katelyn 🌱 **G** (Irish) a form of Caitlin.
Kaetlyn, Katelyne, Kaytlyn

Katelynn (Irish) a forms of Katelyn.
Kaetlynn, Kaetlynne, Katelynne, Kaytlynn,
Kaytlynne

Katerina **G** (Slavic) a form of Katherine.
Katenka, Katerine, Katerini, Katerinka

Katharine (Greek) a form of Katherine.
Katharaine, Katharin, Katharina, Katharyn

Katherine 🌱 **G** (Greek) pure. See also
Carey, Catherine, Ekaterina, Kara, Karen,
Kari, Kasia, Katerina, Yekaterina.
Ekaterina, Ekatrinna, Kasienka, Kasin, Kat,
Katarina, Katchen, Kate, Katee, Kathann,
Kathanne, Katharine, Kathereen, Katheren,
Katherene, Katherenne, Katherin, Katherina,
Katheryn, Katheryne, Kathi, Kathleen, Kathrine,
Kathryn, Kathy, Kathyrine, Katia, Katina,
Katlaina, Katoka, Katreeka, Katrina, Kay, Kitty

Kathi (English) a form of Kathy. See also
Cathi.

Kathleen (Irish) a form of Katherine. See
also Cathleen.
Katheleen, Kathelene, Kathi, Kathileen,
Kathlean, Kathleena, Kathleene, Kathlene,
Kathlin, Kathlina, Kathlyn, Kathlyne, Kathlynn,
Kathy, Katleen

Kathrine **G** (Greek) a form of Katherine.
Kathreen, Kathreena, Kathrene, Kathrin,
Kathrina

Kathryn **G** (English) a form of Katherine.
Kathren, Kathryne, Kathrynn, Kathrynne

Kathy **G** (English) familiar forms of
Katherine, Kathleen. See also Cathi.
Kaethe, Katha, Kathe, Kathee, Kathey,
Kathie, Katka, Katla, Kató

Kati (Estonian) a familiar form of Kate.
Katja, Katya, Katye

Katia **G** (Russian) a form of Katherine.
Cattiah, Katiya, Kattia, Kattiah

Katie 🌱 (English) a familiar form of Kate.
Katee, Kati, Kātia, Katti, Kattie, Katy, Kayte,
Kaytee, Kaytie

Katilyn (Irish) a form of Katlyn.
Katilin, Katilynn

Katlin **G** (Irish) a form of Katlyn.
Katlina, Katline

Katlyn (Greek) pure. (Irish) a form of Katelin.
Kaatlain, Katilyn, Katland, Katlin, Katlynd,
Katlyne, Katlynn, Katlynne

Katriel (Hebrew) God is my crown.
Katrelle, Katri, Katrie, Katry, Katryel

Katrina (German) a form of Katherine. See
also Catrina, Trina.
Katreen, Katreena, Katrene, Katri, Katrice,
Katricia, Katrien, Katrin, Katrine, Katrinia,
Katriona, Katryn, Katryna, Kattrina, Kattryna,
Katus, Katuska

Katsu (Japanese) victorious.

Katsuki (Japanese) season of victory.

Katsuko (Japanese) fragrant harbor child.

Katsuye (Japanese) blessed victory.

Katy (English) a familiar form of Kate. See
also Cady.
Kady, Katey, Katty, Kayte

Katya (Russian) a form of Katia
Katyah

Kaud (Palauan) ensnared.

Kaulana (Hawaiian) famous.
Kaula, Kauna, Kahuna

Kaulani, Kauleen (Hawaiian) forms of Kaulana.

Kaumudi (Indian) full moon.

Kauser, Kawthar (Indian) a river in paradise.

Kaushalya (Indian) Lord Ram's mother.

Kaushey (Indian) silken.

Kaveri (Hindi) Geography: a sacred river in India.

Kavika (Indian) poetess.

Kavindra (Hindi) poet.

Kawa (Japanese) river.

Kawehi (Hawaiian) the ornament.

Kawena (Hawaiian) glow.
Kawana, Kawona

Kawkab (Indian) satellite.

Kay 🅖 (Greek) rejoicer. (Teutonic) a fortified place. (Latin) merry. A short form of Katherine.
Caye, Kae, Kai, Kaye, Kayla

Kaya (Hopi) wise child. (Japanese) resting place.
Kaja, Kayah, Kayia

Kayani (Persian) a form of Esther.

Kaycee 🅖 (American) a combination of the initials K. + C.
Kayce, Kaysee, Kaysey, Kaysi, Kaysie, Kaysii

Kaydee (American) a combination of the initials K. + D.
Kayda, Kayde, Kayden, Kaydi, Kaydie

Kayden 🅱 (American) a form of Kaydee.

Kayla ❦ 🅖 (Arabic, Hebrew) laurel; crown. A form of Kaela, Kaila. See also Cayla.
Kaylah, Kaylea, Kaylee, Kayleen, Kaylene, Kaylia, Keila, Keyla

Kaylah (Arabic, Hebrew) a form of Kayla.
Kayleah, Kaylia, Keylah

Kaylan 🅖 (Hebrew) a form of Kayleen.
Kaylana, Kayland, Kaylani, Kaylann

Kaylee ❦ 🅖 (American) a form of Kayla. See also Caeley, Kalee.
Kailee, Kayle, Kayleigh, Kayley, Kayli, Kaylie

Kayleen, Kaylene (Hebrew) beloved, sweetheart. Forms of Kayla.
Kaylan, Kayleena, Kayleene, Kaylen, Kaylena

Kayleigh (American) a form of Kaylee.
Kaylei

Kaylen (Hebrew) a form of Kayleen.
Kaylean, Kayleana, Kayleanna, Kaylenn

Kayley, Kayli, Kaylie (American) forms of Kaylee.

Kaylin 🅖 (American) a form of Kaylyn.
Kaylon 🅱 (American) a form of Kaylin.

Kaylyn 🅖 (American) a combination of Kay + Lynn. See also Kaelyn.
Kalyn, Kayleen, Kaylene, Kaylin, Kaylyna, Kaylyne

Kaylynn (American) a combination of Kay + Lynn.
Kalynn, Kaylynne

Kaytlin, Kaytlyn (Irish) forms of Kaitlin.
Kaytlan, Kaytlann, Kaytlen, Kaytlyne, Kaytlynn, Kaytlynne

Kazahi (Japanese) hair ornament.

Kazu (Japanese) first; obedient.

Kazuki (Japanese) the fragrance of the moon.

Kazuko (Japanese) a form of Kazu.

Kazuno (Japanese) to bring peace.

Kazuye (Japanese) blessed, peaceful first daughter.

Ke (Chinese) a jade-like stone.

Ke'ala (Hawaiian) a form of Keala.

Keahi (Hawaiian) the fire.

Keaira (Irish) a form of Keara.
Keair, Keairah, Keairra, Keairre, Keairrea

Keala (Hawaiian) path.

Keana, Keanna 🅖 (German) bold; sharp. (Irish) beautiful.
Keanah, Keanne, Keanu, Keenan, Keeyana, Keeyanah, Keeyanna, Keeyona, Keeyonna, Keiana, Keianna, Keona, Keonna

Keandra, Keondra (American) forms of Kenda.
Keandrah, Keandre, Keandrea, Keandria, Kedeana, Kedia, Keonda, Keondre, Keondria

Keanu 🅱 (German, Irish) a form of Keana.

Keara (Irish) dark; black. Religion: an Irish saint.
Keaira, Kearah, Kearia, Kearra, Keera, Keerra, Keiara, Keiarah, Keiarra, Keira, Kera

Kearsten, Keirsten (Greek) forms of Kirstin.
Kearstin, Kearston, Kearstyn, Keirstan, Keirstein, Keirstin, Keirston, Keirstyn, Keirstynne

Keaton **B** (English) where hawks fly.

Keegan **B** (Irish) little; fiery.

Keeley, Keely **G** (Irish) forms of Kelly.
Kealee, Kealey, Keali, Kealie, Keallie, Kealy, Keela, Keelan, Keele, Keelee, Keeleigh, Keeli, Keelia, Keelie, Keellie, Keelye, Keighla, Keilee, Keileigh, Keiley, Keilly, Kiela, Kiele, Kieley, Kielly, Kiely

Keelyn (Irish) a form of Kellyn.
Kealyn, Keelin, Keilan, Kielyn

Keena (Irish) brave.
Keenya, Kina

Keenan **B** (German, Irish) a form of Keana.

Keertana (Indian) song.

Keerthana (Indian) devotional song.

Keesha (American) a form of Keisha.
Keesa, Keeshae, Keeshana, Keeshanne, Keeshawna, Keeshonna, Keeshya, Keiosha

Kehau (Hawaiian) the dew.

Kehaulani (Hawaiian) the dew of heaven.

Kei (Japanese) reverent.

Keiana, Keianna (Irish) forms of Keana.
(American) forms of Kiana.
Keiann, Keiannah, Keionna

Keiki (Hawaiian) child.
Keikana, Keikann, Keikanna, Keikanne

Keikilani (Hawaiian) the child of heaven.

Keiko (Japanese) happy child.

Keila (Arabic, Hebrew) a form of Kayla.
Keilah, Kela, Kelah

Keilani (Hawaiian) glorious chief.
Kaylani, Keilan, Keilana, Keilany, Kelana, Kelanah, Kelane, Kelani, Kelanie

Keilanylyn (Hawaiian) a form of Keilani.

Keira (Irish) a form of Keara.
Keiara, Keiarra, Keirra, Keirrah, Kera, Keyeira

Keisha (American) a short form of Keneisha.
Keasha, Keashia, Keesha, Keishaun, Keishauna, Keishawn, Kesha, Keysha, Kiesha, Kisha, Kishanda

Keita (Scottish) woods; enclosed place.
Keiti

Keiyona (Indian) morning star.

Kekoe (Hawaiian) the courageous soldier.

Kekona (Hawaiian) second-born child.

Kelcey, Kelci, Kelcie (Scottish) forms of Kelsey.
Kelse, Kelcee, Kelcy

Kelila (Hebrew) crown, laurel. See also Kaela, Kayla, Kalila.
Kelilah, Kelula

Kellen **B** (Irish) a form of Kellyn.

Kelley **G** (Irish) a form of Kelly.

Kelli, Kellie **G** (Irish) familiar forms of Kelly.
Keleigh, Keli, Kelia, Keliah, Kelie, Kellee, Kelleigh, Kellia, Kellisa

Kelly **G** (Irish) brave warrior. See also Caeley.
Keeley, Keely, Kelley, Kelley, Kelli, Kellie, Kellye

Kellyanne (Irish) a combination of Kelly + Anne.
Kelliann, Kellianne, Kellyann

Kellyn (Irish) a combination of Kelly + Lynn.
Keelyn, Kelleen, Kellen, Kellene, Kellina, Kelline, Kellynn, Kellynne

Kelsea **G** (Scottish) a form of Kelsey.
Kelcea, Kelcia, Kelsa, Kelsae, Kelsay, Kelse

Kelsey **G** (Scandinavian, Scottish) ship island. (English) a form of Chelsea.
Kelcey, Kelda, Kellsee, Kellsei, Kellsey, Kellsie, Kellsy, Kelsea, Kelsei, Kelsey, Kelsi, Kelsie, Kelsy, Kelsye

Kelsi, Kelsie, Kelsy **G** (Scottish) forms of Chelsea.
Kalsie, Kelci, Kelcie, Kellsi

Kelton **B** (English) keel town; port.

Kelvin **B** (Irish, English) narrow river. Geography: a river in Scotland.

Ken (Chinese) earnestly, sincerely.

Kenda (English) water baby. (Dakota) magical power.
Keandra, Kendra, Kennda

Kendal **G** (English) a form of Kendall.
Kendahl, Kendale, Kendalie, Kendalin, Kendalyn, Kendalynn, Kendel, Kendele, Kendil, Kindal

Kendall **G** (English) ruler of the valley.
Kendal, Kendalla, Kendalle, Kendell, Kendelle, Kendera, Kendia, Kendyl, Kinda, Kindall, Kindi, Kindle, Kynda, Kyndal, Kyndall, Kyndel

Kendra **G** (English) a form of Kenda.
Kandra, Kendrah, Kendre, Kendrea, Kendreah, Kendria, Kenndra, Kentra, Kentrae, Kindra, Kyndra

Kendrick B (Irish) child of Henry. (Scottish) royal chieftain.

Kendyl (English) a form of Kendall.
Kendyle, Kendyll

Keneisha (American) a combination of the prefix Ken + Aisha.
Kaneisha, Keisha, Keneesha, Kenesha, Keneshia, Kenisha, Kenneisha, Kennesha, Kenneshia, Keosha, Kineisha

Kenenza (English) a form of Kennice.
Kenza

Kenia G (Hebrew) a form of Kenya.
Keniya, Kennia

Kenisha (American) a form of Keneisha.
Kenisa, Kenise, Kenishia, Kenissa, Kennisa, Kennisha, Kennysha

Kenna G (Irish) a short form of Kennice.

Kennedy G (Irish) helmeted chief. History: John F. Kennedy was the thirty-fifth U.S. president.
Kenedee, Kenedey, Kenedi, Kenedie, Kenedy, Kenidee, Kenidi, Kenidie, Kenidy, Kennadee, Kennadi, Kennadie, Kennady, Kennedee, Kennedey, Kennedi, Kennedie, Kennidee, Kennidi, Kennidy, Kynnedi

Kenneth B (Irish) beautiful. (English) royal oath.

Kennice (English) beautiful.
Kanice, Keneese, Kenenza, Kenese, Kennise

Kenny B (Scottish) a familiar form of Kenneth.

Kent B (Welsh) white; bright. Geography: a region in England.

Kentrell B (English) king's estate.

Kenya G (Hebrew) animal horn. Geography: a country in Africa.
Keenya, Kenia, Kenja, Kenyah, Kenyana, Kenyatta, Kenyia

Kenyatta (American) a form of Kenya.
Kenyata, Kenyatah, Kenyatte, Kenyattia, Kenyatta, Kenyette

Kenzie G (Scottish) light skinned. (Irish) a short form of Mackenzie.
Kenzea, Kenzee, Kenzey, Kenzi, Kenzia, Kenzy, Kinzie

Keoki, Keokia (Hawaiian) forms of Georgia.

Keon B (Irish) a form of Ewan (see Boys' Names).

Keona, Keonna (Irish) forms of Keana.
Keiona, Keionna, Keoana, Keoni, Keonia, Keonnah, Keonni, Keonnia

Keosha (American) a short form of Keneisha.
Keoshae, Keoshi, Keoshia, Keosia

Kerani (Hindi) sacred bells. See also Rani.
Kera, Kerah, Keran, Kerana

Keren (Hebrew) animal's horn.
Kerrin, Keryn

Kerensa (Cornish) a form of Karenza.
Karensa, Karenza, Kerenza

Keri, Kerri, Kerrie G (Irish) forms of Kerry.
Keriann, Kerianne, Kerriann, Kerrianne

Kerry G (Irish) dark haired. Geography: a county in Ireland.
Keary, Keiry, Keree, Kerey, Keri, Kerri, Kerrie, Kerryann, Kerryanne, Kery, Kiera, Kierra

Kerstin (Scandinavian) a form of Kirsten.
Kerstan, Kerste, Kerstein, Kersten, Kerstie, Kerstien, Kerston, Kerstyn, Kerstynn

Kesare (Latin) long haired. (Russian) a form of Caesar (see Boys' Names).

Kesari (Indian) saffron; a lion.

Kesha (American) a form of Keisha.
Keshah, Keshal, Keshala, Keshan, Keshana, Keshara, Keshawn, Keshawna, Keshawnna

Keshi, Keshika (Indian) a woman with beautiful hair.

Keshia (American) a form of Keisha. A short form of Keneisha.
Kecia, Keishia, Keschia, Keshea, Kesia, Kesiah, Kessia, Kessiah

Keshini (Indian) one with beautiful hair.

Kesi (Swahili) born during difficult times.

Kesse G (Ashanti) a form of Kessie.

Kessie (Ashanti) chubby baby.
Kess, Kessa, Kessey, Kessi

Ket Nien (Vietnamese) jet black.

Ketaki (Indian) a cream-colored flower.

Ketana, Kethana (Indian) home.

Ketki (Indian) flower.

Keven B (Irish) a form of Kevyn.

Kevin B (Irish) beautiful.

Kevon B (Irish) a form of Kevyn.

Kevyn B (Irish) beautiful.
Keva, Kevan, Keven, Kevia, Keviana, Kevinna, Kevina, Kevion, Kevionna, Kevon, Kevona, Kevone, Kevonia, Kevonna, Kevonne, Kevonya, Kevynn

Keyana **G** (American) a form of Kiana.
Keya, Keyanah, Keyanda, Keyandra

Keyanna (American) a form of Kiana.
Keyannah

Keyara (Irish) a form of Kiara.
Keyarah, Keyari, Keyarra, Keyera, Keyerah, Keyerra

Keyona (American) a form of Kiana.
Keyonda, Keyondra

Keyonna **G** (American) a form of Kiana.
Keyonnia, Keyonnie

Keysha (American) a form of Keisha.
Keyosha, Keyoshia, Keyshana, Keyshanna, Keyshawn, Keyshawna, Keyshia, Keyshla, Keyshona, Keyshonna

Keyuri (Indian) armlet.

Keziah (Hebrew) cinnamon-like spice. Bible: one of the daughters of Job.
Kazia, Kaziah, Ketzi, Ketzia, Ketziah, Kezi, Kezia, Kizzy

Khadijah **G** (Arabic) trustworthy. History: Muhammed's first wife.
Khadaja, Khadajah, Khadeeja, Khadeejah, Khadeja, Khadejah, Khadejha, Khadija, Khadije, Khadijia, Khadijiah

Khairiya (Indian) charitable.

Khalida (Arabic) immortal, everlasting.
Khali, Khalia, Khaliah, Khalidda, Khalita

Khanh (Vietnamese) yellow.

Khawlah (Indian) proper name.

Khrissa (American) a form of Chrissa. (Czech) a form of Krista.
Khrishia, Khryssa, Krisha, Krisia, Krissa, Krysha, Kryssa

Khristina (Russian, Scandinavian) a form of Kristina, Christina.
Khristeen, Khristen, Khristin, Khristine, Khyristya, Khristyana, Khristyna, Khrystyne

Khulood (Indian) immortality.

Khushboo (Indian) fragrance.

Khushi, Khusi (Indian) happiness.

Khuyen (Vietnamese) year of unity.

Khyati (Indian) fame.

Ki (Korean) arisen.

Kia **G** (African) season's beginning. (American) a short form of Kiana.
Kiah

Kiana **G** (American) a combination of the prefix Ki + Ana.
Keanna, Keiana, Keyana, Keyona, Khiana, Khianah, Khianna, Ki, Kiahna, Kiane, Kiani, Kiania, Kianna, Kiandra, Kiandria, Kiauna, Kiaundra, Kiyana, Kyana

Kianna (American) a form of Kiana.
Kiannah, Kianne, Kianni

Kiara **G** (Irish) little and dark.
Keyara, Kiarra, Kieara, Kiearah, Kiearra, Kyara

Kiaria, Kiarra, Kichi (Japanese) fortunate.

Kiele **G** (Hawaiian) gardenia; fragrant blossom.
Kiela, Kieley, Kieli, Kielli, Kielly

Kiera, Kierra (Irish) forms of Kerry.
Kierana, Kieranna, Kierea

Kieran **B** (Irish) little and dark; little Keir.

Kiersten **G** (Scandinavian) a form of Kirsten.
Keirstan, Kerstin, Kierstan, Kierston, Kierstyn, Kierstynn

Kierstin (Scandinavian) a form of Kirsten.

Kieu (Vietnamese) precious stone.

Kik (Japanese) chrysanthemum.

Kiki **G** (Spanish) a familiar form of names ending in "queta."

Kiku (Japanese) chrysanthemum.
Kiko

Kikue (Japanese) chrysanthemum branch.

Kikuko (Japanese) chrysanthemum child.

Kikuno (Japanese) chrysanthemum field.

Kikuye (Japanese) she who ushers in a long period of joy.

Kikuyo (Japanese) long period of joy.

Kilani (Hawaiian) a form of Kalani.

Kiley **G** (Irish) attractive; from the straits.
Kilea, Kilee, Kileigh, Kili, Kilie, Kylee, Kyli, Kylie

Kim **G** (Vietnamese) needle. (English) a short form of Kimberly.
Kima, Kimette, Kym

Kim Cuc (Vietnamese) advise.

Kimana (Shoshone) butterfly.
Kiman, Kimani

Kimaya (Indian) divine.

Kimber (English) a short form of Kimberly.
Kimbra

Kimberlee, Kimberley (English) forms of Kimberly.
Kimbalee, Kimberlea, Kimberlei, Kimberleigh, Kimbley

Kimberly ☙ 🄶 (English) chief, ruler.
Cymberly, Cymbre, Kim, Kimba, Kimbely, Kimber, Kimbereley, Kimberely, Kimberlee, Kimberli, Kimberlie, Kimberlyn, Kimbery, Kimbria, Kimbrie, Kimbry, Kimmie, Kymberly

Kimberlyn (English) a form of Kimberly.
Kimberlin, Kimberlynn

Kimi (Japanese) righteous.
Kimia, Kimika, Kimiko, Kimiyo, Kimmi, Kimmie, Kimmy

Kimiye (Japanese) she who is a blessed and beautiful delight.

Kim-Ly (Vietnamese) graceful; beloved; legend name.

Kimmie (English) a familiar form of Kimberly.
Kimee, Kimme, Kimmee, Kimmi, Kimmy, Kimy

Kin (Japanese) golden.

Kina (Hawaiian) from China.

Kinaari (Indian) shore.

Kineisha (American) a form of Keneisha.
Kineesha, Kinesha, Kineshia, Kinisha, Kinishia

Kineta (Greek) energetic.
Kinetta

Kini 🄶 (Hawaiian) a form of Jean.
Kina

Kinjal (Indian) river bank.

Kinnari (Indian) musical instrument.

Kinsey 🄶 (English) offspring; relative.
Kinsee, Kinsley, Kinza, Kinze, Kinzee, Kinzey, Kinzi, Kinzie, Kinzy

Kinsley (American) a form of Kinsey.
Kinslee, Kinslie, Kinslyn

Kintuben (Indian) a beautiful athlete.

Kinu (Japanese) silk cloth.

Kinuye (Japanese) blessed silk.

Kioko (Japanese) happy child.
Kiyo, Kiyoko

Kiona (Native American) brown hills.
Kionah, Kioni, Kionna

Kioshi (Japanese) clear, bright.

Kira 🄶 (Persian) sun. (Latin) light.
Kirah, Kiri, Kiria, Kiro, Kirra, Kirrah, Kirri

Kiran 🄶 (Hindi) ray of light.

Kiranmala (Indian) garland.

Kirby 🄱 (Scandinavian) church village. (English) cottage by the water.
Kirbee, Kirbi

Kirima (Eskimo) hill.

Kirsi (Hindi) amaranth blossoms.
Kirsie

Kirsta (Scandinavian) a form of Kirsten.

Kirsten 🄶 (Greek) Christian; anointed. (Scandinavian) a form of Christine.
Karsten, Kearsten, Keirstan, Kerstin, Kiersten, Kirsteni, Kirsta, Kirstan, Kirstene, Kirstie, Kirstin, Kirston, Kirsty, Kirstyn, Kjersten, Kursten, Kyersten, Kyrsten, Kyrstin

Kirstie, Kirsty (Scandinavian) familiar forms of Kirsten.
Kerstie, Kirsta, Kirste, Kirstee, Kirstey, Kirsti, Kjersti, Kyrsty

Kirstin (Scandinavian) a form of Kirsten.
Karstin, Kirsteen, Kirstien, Kirstine

Kirstyn (Greek) a form of Kirsten.
Kirstynn

Kirtana (Indian) hymn, a song sung in praise of God.

Kisa (Russian) kitten.
Kisha, Kiska, Kissa, Kiza

Kishi (Japanese) long and happy life.

Kishori (Indian) young damsel.

Kissa (Ugandan) born after twins.

Kita (Japanese) north.

Kitra (Hebrew) crowned.

Kitty (Greek) a familiar form of Katherine.
Ketter, Ketti, Ketty, Kit, Kittee, Kitteen, Kittey, Kitti, Kittie

Kiwa (Japanese) borderline.

Kiyana (American) a form of Kiana.
Kiya, Kiyah, Kiyan, Kiyani, Kiyanna, Kiyenna

Kiyomi (Japanese) precious and beautiful girl.

Kiyono (Japanese) clean and clear field.

Kiyoshi (Japanese) quiet child.

Kiyoye (Japanese) blessedly clean girl.

Kizzy (American) a familiar form of Keziah.
Kezi, Kissie, Kizzi, Kizzie

Klara (Hungarian) a form of Clara.
Klára, Klari, Klarika

Klarise (German) a form of Klarissa.
Klarice, Kláris, Klaryce

Klarissa (German) clear, bright. (Italian) a
form of Clarissa.
*Klarisa, Klarise, Klarrisa, Klarrissa, Klarrissia,
Klarisza, Klarysa, Klaryssa, Kleresa*

Klaudia (American) a form of Claudia.
Klaudija

Kloe (American) a form of Chloe.
Khloe, Kloee, Kloey, Klohe, Kloie

Ko (Japanese) filial piety.

Kodi **BG** (American) a form of Codi.
Kodee, Kodey, Kodie, Kody, Kodye, Koedi

Kody **B** (American) a form of Kodi.

Koffi (Swahili) born on Friday.
Kaffe, Kaffi, Koffe, Koffie

Kohana (Japanese) little flower.

Kokila (Indian) a singer.

Koko (Japanese) stork. See also Coco.

Kolby **B** (American) a form of Colby.
Kobie, Koby, Kolbee, Kolbey, Kolbi, Kolbie

Kolina (Swedish) a form of Katherine. See
also Colleen.
*Koleen, Koleena, Kolena, Kolene, Koli,
Kolleen, Kollena, Kollene, Kolyn, Kolyna*

Koma (Japanese) filly.

Komali (Indian) tender.

Kome (Japanese) rice.

Kona **B** (Hawaiian) lady. (Hindi) angular.
Koni, Konia

Konami (Japanese) she who makes things
happen.

Kong (Chinese) glorious.

Konomi (Japanese) nuts.

Konstance (Latin) a form of Constance.
*Konstantina, Konstantine, Konstanza,
Konstanze*

Kora (Greek) a form of Cora.
Korah, Kore, Koren, Koressa, Koretta, Korra

Koral (American) a form of Coral.
*Korel, Korele, Korella, Korilla, Korral, Korrel,
Korrell, Korrelle*

Korey **B** (American) a form of Kori.

Kori **G** (American) a short form of Korina.
See also Corey, Cori.
*Koree, Korey, Koria, Korie, Korri, Korrie, Korry,
Kory*

Korina (Greek) a form of Corina.
*Koreena, Korena, Koriana, Korianna, Korine,
Korinna, Korreena, Korrina, Korrinna, Koryna,
Korynna*

Korine (Greek) a form of Korina.
*Koreen, Korene, Koriane, Korianne, Korin,
Korinn, Korinne, Korrin, Korrine, Korrinne,
Korryn, Korrynne, Koryn, Koryne, Korynn*

Kornelia (Latin) a form of Cornelia.
*Karniela, Karniella, Karnis, Kornelija,
Kornelis, Kornelya, Korny*

Kortney **G** (English) a form of Courtney.
Kortnay, Kortnee, Kortni, Kortnie, Kortny

Kory **B** (American) a form of Kori.

Kosha (Indian) origin; the name of a river.

Kosma (Greek) order; universe.
Cosma

Kosta (Latin) a short form of Constance.
Kostia, Kostusha, Kostya

Koto (Japanese) harp.

Kotone (Japanese) the sound of the koto.

Kotose (Japanese) star.

Kotoyo (Japanese) she who plays the koto for
a lifetime.

Koume (Japanese) little plum.

Kourtney **G** (American) a form of Courtney.
*Kourtnay, Kourtne, Kourtnee, Kourtnei,
Kourtneigh, Kourtni, Kourtny, Kourtynie*

Kouther (Indian) a river in paradise.

Koyel (Indian) the cuckoo.

Koyuki (Japanese) small snowfall.

Kozakura (Japanese) little cherry tree.

Kozue (Japanese) tree branches.

Kozuye (Japanese) twig.

Krandasi (Indian) the sky and the earth.

Kranti (Indian) revolution.

Krasia (Palauan) whimsical.

Kripa (Indian) compassion.

Girls G–L

Kripi (Indian) beautiful.

Kris 🅱 (American) a short form of Kristine. A form of Chris.
Khris, Krissy

Krisha (Indian) divine.

Krishnakali (Indian) a flower.

Krissy (American) a familiar form of Kris.
Krissey, Krissi, Krissie

Krista 🄶 (Czech) a form of Christina. See also Christa.
Khrissa, Khrista, Khryssa, Khrysta, Krissa, Kryssa, Krysta

Kristal (Latin) a form of Crystal.
Kristale, Kristall, Kristill, Kristl, Kristle, Kristy

Kristan (Greek) a form of Kristen.
Kristana, Kristanna, Kristanne, Kriston, Krystan, Krystane

Kristen 🄶 (Greek) Christian; anointed. (Scandinavian) a form of Christine.
Christen, Kristan, Kristene, Kristien, Kristin, Kristyn, Krysten

Kristi, Kristie (Scandinavian) short forms of Kristine.
Christi

Kristian 🅱 (Greek) Christian; anointed. Forms of Christian.
Khristian, Kristian, Kristiane, Kristiann, Kristi-Ann, Kristianna, Kristianne, Kristi-Anne, Kristienne, Kristyan, Kristyana, Kristy-Ann, Kristy-Anne

Kristiana (Greek) a form of Kristian.

Kristin 🄶 (Scandinavian) a form of Kristen. See also Cristen.
Kristiin, Krystin

Kristina 🄶 (Greek) Christian; anointed. (Scandinavian) a form of Christina. See also Cristina.
Khristina, Kristena, Kristeena, Kristina, Kristinka, Krystina

Kristine 🄶 (Scandinavian) a form of Christine.
Kris, Kristeen, Kristene, Kristi, Kristie, Kristy, Krystine, Krystyne

Kristopher 🅱 (Greek) a form of Christopher.

Kristy 🄶 (American) a familiar form of Kristine, Krystal. See also Cristy.
Kristi, Kristia, Kristie, Krysia, Krysti

Kristyn 🄶 (Greek) a form of Kristen.
Kristyne, Kristynn

Kriti (Indian) work of art.

Krittika (Indian) the third nakshatra (star constellation).

Krupa (Indian) God's forgiveness.

Krupali (Indian) she who always forgives.

Kruthika (Indian) name of a star.

Kruti (Indian) creation.

Krysta (Polish) a form of Krista.
Krystah, Krystka

Krystal 🄶 (American) clear, brilliant glass.
Kristabel, Kristal, Krystalann, Krystalanne, Krystale, Krystall, Krystalle, Krystel, Krystil, Krystle, Krystol

Krystalee (American) a combination of Krystal + Lee.
Kristalea, Kristaleah, Kristalee, Krystalea, Krystaleah, Krystlea, Krystleah, Krystlee, Krystlelea, Krystleleah, Krystlelee

Krystalynn (American) a combination of Krystal + Lynn.
Kristaline, Kristalyn, Kristalynn, Kristilyn, Kristilynn, Kristlyn, Krystaleen, Krystalene, Krystalin, Krystalina, Krystallyn, Krystalyn, Krystalynne

Krystel (Latin) a form of Krystal.
Kristel, Kristell, Kristelle, Krystelle

Krysten (Greek) a form of Kristen.
Krystene, Krystyn, Krystyne

Krystian 🅱🄶 (Greek) a form of Christian.
Krystianne, Krysty-Ann, Krystyan, Krystyanne, Krysty-Anne, Krystyen

Krystiana (Greek) a form of Krystian.
Krystiana, Krystianna, Kristyana, Krystyanna

Krystin (Czech) a form of Kristin.

Krystina (Greek) a form of Kristina.
Krysteena, Krystena, Krystyna, Krystynka

Krystle (American) a form of Krystal.
Krystl, Krystyl

Kshama (Indian) forgiveness, mercy.

Kshamya, Kshiti (Indian) earth.

Kshanaprabha, Kshanika (Indian) lightning.

Kshipa (Indian) night.

Kshipra (Indian) the name of a river in India.

Kshipva (Indian) elasticized.

Kshirin (Indian) flower.

Kuan (Chinese) happy.

Kuan-Yin (Chinese) Buddhist deity of mercy.

Kudio (Swahili) born on Monday.

Kuhu (Indian) the sweet note of the bird.

Kui (Chinese) sunflower.

Kulthoom (Indian) daughter of the prophet Mohammed.

Kuma (Japanese) bear. (Tongan) mouse.

Kumiko (Japanese) girl with braids.
Kumi

Kumkum (Indian) sacred powder.

Kumud, Kumudini (Indian) lotus.

Kumuda (Sanskrit) lotus flower.

Kun (Chinese) female.

Kundanika (Indian) flower.

Kuni (Japanese) born in the country.

Kuniko (Japanese) child from the country.

Kuniye (Japanese) country, nation; branch.

Kunjal (Indian) cuckoo; nightingale.

Kunjalata (Indian) wild climber plant.

Kunjana (Indian) forest girl.

Kunshi (Indian) shining.

Kuntala (Indian) one with beautiful hair.

Kunti (Indian) mother of the five brothers, the Pandavas.

Kunto (Twi) third-born.

Kura (Japanese) treasure house.

Kurangi (Indian) deer.

Kuri (Japanese) chestnut.

Kurva (Japanese) mulberry tree.

Kusa (Hindi) God's grass.

Kushala (Indian) safe; happy; expert.

Kusum, Kusuma (Indian) flower.

Kusumanjali (Indian) flower offering.

Kusumavati (Indian) flowering.

Kusumita (Indian) flowers in bloom.

Kusumlata (Indian) flowering creeper.

Kuvira (Indian) courageous woman.

Kwanita (Zuni) a form of Juanita.

Kwashi (Swahili) born on Sunday.

Kwau (Swahili) born on Thursday.

Kyana (American) a form of Kiana.
Kyanah, Kyani, Kyann, Kyanna, Kyanne, Kyanni, Kyeana, Kyeanna

Kyara (Irish) a form of Kiara.
Kiyara, Kiyera, Kiyerra, Kyarah, Kyaria, Kyarie, Kyarra, Kyera, Kyerra

Kyla **G** (Irish) attractive. (Yiddish) crown; laurel.
Khyla, Kylah, Kylea, Kyleah, Kylia

Kyle **B** (Irish) attractive.
Kial, Kiele, Kylee, Kyleigh, Kylene, Kylie

Kylee **G** (Irish) a familiar form of Kyle.
Kylea, Kyleah, Kylie, Kyliee

Kyleigh (Irish) a form of Kyle.
Kyliegh

Kylene (Irish) a form of Kyle.
Kyleen, Kylen, Kylyn, Kylynn

Kyler **B** (English) a form of Kyle.

Kylie ⚜ **G** (West Australian Aboriginal) curled stick; boomerang. (Irish) a familiar form of Kyle.
Keiley, Keilley, Keilly, Keily, Kiley, Kye, Kylee, Kyley, Kyli, Kyllie

Kym **G** (English, Vietnamese) a form of Kim.

Kymberly (English) a form of Kimberly.
Kymber, Kymberlee, Kymberleigh, Kymberley, Kymberli, Kymberlie, Kymberlyn, Kymberlynn, Kymberlynne

Kyndal (English) a form of Kendall.
Kyndahl, Kyndel, Kyndle, Kyndol

Kyndall **G** (English) a form of Kendall.
Kyndalle, Kyndell, Kyndelle

Kynthia (Greek) a form of Cynthia.
Kyndi

Kyoko (Japanese) mirror.

Kyon (Korean) increase; important.

Kyra (Greek) ladylike. A form of Cyrilla.
Keera, Keira, Kira, Kyrah, Kyrene, Kyria, Kyriah, Kyriann, Kyrie

L

L 🅱🅶 (American) an initial used as a first name.

Laabha (Indian) profit.

Laalamani (Indian) ruby.

Laasya (Indian) name of a dance.

Labangalata (Indian) a flowering creeper.

Laboni (Indian) graceful.

Labuki (Indian) musical instrument.

Lacey, Lacy 🅶 (Latin) cheerful. (Greek) familiar forms of Larissa.
Lacee, Laci, Lacie, Lacye

Lachandra (American) a combination of the prefix La + Chandra.
Lachanda, Lachandice

Laci, Lacie (Latin) forms of Lacey.
Lacia, Laciann, Lacianne

Lacrecia (Latin) a form of Lucretia.
Lacrasha, Lacreash, Lacreasha, Lacreashia, Lacreisha, Lacresha, Lacreshia, Lacresia, Lacretia, Lacricia, Lacriesha, Lacrisah, Lacrisha, Lacrishia, Lacrissa

Lada (Russian) Mythology: the Slavic goddess of beauty.

Ladasha (American) a combination of the prefix La + Dasha.
Ladaesha, Ladaisa, Ladaisha, Ladaishea, Ladaishia, Ladashiah, Ladaseha, Ladashia, Ladasia, Ladassa, Ladaysha, Ladesha, Ladisha, Ladosha

Ladeidra (American) a combination of the prefix La + Deidra.
Ladedra, Ladiedra

Ladli (Indian) loved one.

Ladonna (American) a combination of the prefix La + Donna.
Ladan, Ladana, Ladon, Ladona, Ladonne, Ladonya

Laela (Arabic, Hebrew) a form of Leila.
Lael, Laelle

Laelia (Latin) she who is talkative.

Laghuvi (Indian) tender.

Lahela (Hawaiian) a form of Rachel.

Lai (Chinese) arrive.

Laiba (Indian) female of the haven.

Laica (Greek) pure, secular.

Laila (Arabic) a form of Leila.
Lailah, Laili, Lailie

Laine, Layne 🅱 (French) short forms of Elaine.
Lain, Laina, Lainah, Lainee, Lainna, Layna

Lainey, Layney (French) familiar forms of Elaine.
Laini, Lainie, Laynee, Layni, Laynie

Lajila (Hindi) shy, coy.

Lajita, Lajwati (Indian) modest.

Lajja (Indian) modesty.

Lajjawati (Indian) a sensitive plant; modest woman.

Lajuana (American) a combination of the prefix La + Juana.
Lajuanna, Lawana, Lawanna, Lawanza, Lawanze, Laweania

Lajvanti (Indian) the touch-me-not plant.

Lajvati (Indian) shy.

Lajwanti (Indian) modest, humble.

Laka (Hawaiian) attractive; seductive; tame. Mythology: the goddess of the hula.

Lakayla (American) a combination of the prefix La + Kayla.
Lakala, Lakaya, Lakeila, Lakela, Lakella

Lakeisha (American) a combination of the prefix La + Keisha. See also Lekasha.
Lakaiesha, Lakaisha, Lakasha, Lakashia, Lakaysha, Lakaysia, Lakeasha, Lakecia, Lakeesh, Lakeesha, Lakeeshia, Lakesha, Lakeshia, Lakeysha, Lakezia, Lakicia, Lakieshia, Lakisha

Laken 🅶 (American) a short form of Lakendra.
Lakena

Lakendra (American) a combination of the prefix La + Kendra.
Lakanda, Lakedra, Laken, Lakenda

Lakenya (American) a combination of the prefix La + Kenya.
Lakeena, Lakeenna, Lakeenya, Lakena, Lakenia, Lakinja, Lakinya, Lakwanya, Lekenia, Lekenya

Lakesha, Lakeshia, Lakisha (American) forms of Lakeisha.
Lakecia, Lakeesha, Lakesa, Lakese, Lakeseia, Lakeshya, Lakesi, Lakesia, Lakeyshia, Lakiesha

Laketa (American) a combination of the prefix La + Keita.
Lakeeta, Lakeetah, Lakeita, Lakeitha, Lakeithia, Laketha, Laketia, Laketta, Lakieta, Lakietha, Lakita, Lakitia, Lakitra, Lakitri, Lakitta

Lakia (Arabic) found treasure.
Lakiea, Lakkia

Lakin, Lakyn (American) short forms of Lakendra.
Lakyna, Lakynn

Lakota **BG** (Dakota) a tribal name.
Lakoda, Lakohta, Lakotah

Lakresha (American) a form of Lucretia.
Lacresha, Lacreshia, Lacresia, Lacretia, Lacrisha, Lakreshia, Lakrisha, Lekresha, Lekresia

Laksha, Lakshya (Indian) aim.

Lakshaki (Indian) another name for the goddess Sita.

Lakshana (Indian) one with auspicious signs on her.

Lakshanya (Indian) one who achieves.

Lakshita (Indian) distinguished.

Lakshmi (Indian) the goddess of wealth.

Lakshmishree (Indian) fortunate.

Lakya (Hindi) born on Thursday.
Lakeya, Lakeyah, Lakieya, Lakiya, Lakyia

Lala (Slavic) tulip.
Lalah, Lalla

Lalan (Indian) nurturing.

Lalana (Indian) a girl.

Lalasa (Hindi) love.

Laleh (Persian) tulip.
Lalah

Lali (Spanish) a form of Lulani.
Lalia, Lalli, Lally

Lalima (Indian) beauty.

Lalita (Greek) talkative. (Sanskrit) charming; candid.

Lalitamohana (Indian) attractive, beautiful.

Lalitha (Indian) elegant; beautiful.

Lallie (English) babbler.
Lalli, Lally

Lam (Chinese) jungle or dense forest.

Lamar **B** (German) famous throughout the land. (French) sea, ocean.

Lamesha (American) a combination of the prefix La + Mesha.
Lamees, Lameesha, Lameise, Lameisha, Lameshia, Lamisha, Lamishia, Lemisha

Lamia (German) bright land.
Lama, Lamiah

Lamis (Arabic) soft to the touch.
Lamese, Lamise

Lamonica (American) a combination of the prefix La + Monica.
Lamoni, Lamonika

Lamont **B** (Scandinavian) lawyer.

Lamya (Arabic) dark lipped.
Lama

Lan (Vietnamese) flower.

Lana (Latin) woolly. (Irish) attractive, peaceful. A short form of Alana, Elana. (Hawaiian) floating; bouyant.
Lanae, Lanai, Lanata, Lanay, Laneah, Laneetra, Lanette, Lanna, Lannah

Lanca (Latin) blessed, fortunate one.

Lance **B** (German) a short form of Lancelot (see Boys' Names).

Landa (Basque) another name for the Virgin Mary.

Landin **B** (English) a form of Landon.

Landon **B** (English) open, grassy meadow.
Landan, Landen, Landin, Landyn, Landynne

Landra (German, Spanish) counselor.
Landrea

Landrada (Spanish) counselor.

Lane **B** (English) narrow road.
Laina, Laney, Layne

Laneisha (American) a combination of the prefix La + Keneisha.
Laneasha, Lanecia, Laneesha, Laneise, Laneishia, Lanesha, Laneshe, Laneshea, Laneshia, Lanesia, Lanessa, Lanesse, Lanisha, Lanishia

Laney (English) a familiar form of Lane.
Lanie, Lanni, Lanny, Lany

Lang (Vietnamese) yellow chrysanthemum.

Langging (Tagalog) a form of Jingjing.

Lanh (Vietnamese) golden lion.

Lani **G** (Hawaiian) sky; heaven. A short form of Atalanta, 'Aulani, Leilani.
Lanee, Lanei, Lania, Lanie, Lanita, Lanney, Lanni, Lannie

Girls G–L

Laporsha (American) a combination of the prefix La + Porsha.
Laporcha, Laporche, Laporscha, Laporsche, Laporschia, Laporshe, Laporshia, Laportia

Laqueena (American) a combination of the prefix La + Queenie.
Laqueen, Laquena, Laquenetta, Laquinna

Laquinta (American) a combination of the prefix La + Quintana.
Laquanta, Laqueinta, Laquenda, Laquenta, Laquinda

Laquisha (American) a combination of the prefix La + Queisha.
Laquasha, Laquaysha, Laqueisha, Laquesha, Laquiesha

Laquita (American) a combination of the prefix La + Queta.
Laqeita, Laqueta, Laquetta, Laquia, Laquiata, Laquieta, Laquitta, Lequita

Lara 🄶 (Greek) cheerful. (Latin) shining; famous. Mythology: a Roman nymph. A short form of Laraine, Larissa, Laura.
Larae, Larah, Laretta, Larette

Laraine (Latin) a form of Lorraine.
Lara, Laraene, Larain, Larane, Larayn, Larayne, Laraynna, Larein, Lareina, Lareine, Laren, Larenn, Larenya, Lauraine, Laurraine

Laranya (Indian) graceful.

Larina (Greek) seagull.
Larena, Larine

Larisa (Greek) a form of Larissa.
Lareesa, Lareese, Laresa, Laris, Larise, Larisha, Larrisa, Larysa, Laurisa

Larissa (Greek) cheerful. See also Lacey.
Lara, Laressa, Larisa, Larissah, Larrissa, Larryssa, Laryssa, Laurissa, Laurissah

Lark (English) skylark.

Larry 🄱 (Latin) a familiar form of Lawrence.

Lashae, Lashay (American) combinations of the prefix La + Shay.
Lasha, Lashai, Lashaia, Lashaya, Lashaye, Lashea

Lashana (American) a combination of the prefix La + Shana.
Lashanay, Lashane, Lashanna, Lashannon, Lashona, Lashonna

Lashanda (American) a combination of the prefix La + Shanda.
Lashandra, Lashanta, Lashante

Lashawna (American) a combination of the prefix La + Shawna.
Lashaun, Lashauna, Lashaune, Lashaunna, Lashaunta, Lashawn, Lashawnd, Lashawnda, Lashawndra, Lashawne, Lashawnia, Leshawn, Leshawna

Lashonda (American) a combination of the prefix La + Shonda.
Lachonda, Lashaunda, Lashaundra, Lashon, Lashond, Lashonde, Lashondia, Lashondra, Lashonta, Lashunda, Lashundra, Lashunta, Lashunte, Leshande, Leshandra, Leshondra, Leshundra

Lata (Indian) creeper.

Latakara (Indian) mass of creepers.

Latangi (Indian) slim girl.

Latanya (American) a combination of the prefix La + Tanya.
Latana, Latandra, Latania, Latanja, Latanna, Latanua, Latonshia

Latara (American) a combination of the prefix La + Tara.

Latasha (American) a combination of the prefix La + Tasha.
Latacha, Latacia, Latai, Lataisha, Latashia, Latasia, Lataysha, Letasha, Letashia, Letasiah

Latavia (American) a combination of the prefix La + Tavia.

Lateefah (Arabic) pleasant. (Hebrew) pat, caress.
Lateefa, Latifa, Latifah, Latipha

Latesha (American) a form of Leticia.
Lataeasha, Lateasha, Lateashia, Latecia, Lateicia, Lateisha, Latesa, Lateshia, Latessa, Lateysha, Latisa, Latissa, Leteisha, Leteshia

Latha (Indian) a creeper.

Latia (American) a combination of the prefix La + Tia.
Latea, Lateia, Lateka

Latika (Hindi) elegant.
Lateeka, Lateka

Latisha (Latin) joy. (American) a combination of the prefix La + Tisha.
Laetitia, Laetizia, Latashia, Lateasha, Lateashia, Latecia, Lateesha, Lateicia, Lateisha, Latice, Laticia, Latiesha, Latishia, Latishya, Latissha, Latitia, Latysha

Latona (Latin) Mythology: the powerful goddess who bore Apollo and Diana.
Latonna, Latonnah

Latonya (American) a combination of the prefix La + Tonya. (Latin) a form of Latona.
Latoni, Latonia

Latoria (American) a combination of the prefix La + Tori.
Latoira, Latorio, Latorja, Latorray, Latorreia, Latory, Latorya, Latoyra, Latoyria

Latosha (American) a combination of the prefix La + Tosha.
Latoshia, Latoshya, Latosia

Latoya (American) a combination of the prefix La + Toya.
Latoia, Latoiya, LaToya, Latoye, Latoyia, Latoyita, Latoyo

Latrice (American) a combination of the prefix La + Trice.
Latrece, Latreece, Latreese, Latresa, Latrese, Latressa, Letreece, Letrice

Latricia (American) a combination of the prefix La + Tricia.
Latrecia, Latresh, Latresha, Latreshia, Latrica, Latrisha, Latrishia

Laura **G** (Latin) crowned with laurel.
Lara, Laurah, Lauralee, Laurelen, Laurella, Lauren, Lauricia, Laurie, Laurka, Laury, Lauryn, Lavra, Lolly, Lora, Loretta, Lori, Lorinda, Lorna, Loura

Laurel (Latin) laurel tree.
Laural, Laurell, Laurelle, Lorel, Lorelle

Lauren 🌺 **G** (English) a form of Laura.
Lauran, Laureen, Laurena, Laurene, Laurien, Laurin, Laurine, Lawren, Loren, Lorena

Laurence **G** (Latin) crowned with laurel.
Laurencia, Laurens, Laurent, Laurentana, Laurentina, Lawrencia

Laurianna (English) a combination of Laurie + Anna.
Laurana, Laurann, Laureana, Laureanne, Laureen, Laureena, Laurian, Lauriana,

Lauriane, Laurianna, Laurie Ann, Laurie Anne, Laurina

Laurie **G** (English) a familiar form of Laura.
Lari, Larilia, Laure, Lauré, Lauri, Lawrie

Laurinda, Laurita (Spanish) crowned with laurels.

Laury **G** (English) a familiar form of Laura.

Lauryn (English) a familiar form of Laura.
Laurynn

Lavali (Indian) clove.

Laveda (Latin) cleansed, purified.
Lavare, Lavetta, Lavette

Lavelle (Latin) cleansing.
Lavella

Lavena (Irish, French) joy. (Latin) a form of Lavina.

Laverne (Latin) springtime. (French) grove of alder trees. See also Verna.
Laverine, Lavern, Laverna, La Verne

Laviana (Latin) native of Rome.

Lavina (Latin) purified; woman of Rome. See also Vina.
Lavena, Lavenia, Lavinia, Lavinie, Levenia, Levinia, Livinia, Louvinia, Lovina, Lovinia

Lavonna (American) a combination of the prefix La + Yvonne.
Lavon, Lavonda, Lavonder, Lavondria, Lavone, Lavonia, Lavonica, Lavonn, Lavonne, Lavonnie, Lavonya

Lawan (Tai) pretty.
Lawanne

Lawanda (American) a combination of the prefix La + Wanda.
Lawonda, Lawynda

Lawrence **B** (Latin) crowned with laurel.

Laxmi (Indian) goddess of wealth.

Layce (American) a form of Lacey.
Laycee, Layci, Laycia, Laycie, Laysa, Laysea, Laysie

Layla (Hebrew, Arabic) a form of Leila.
Laylah, Layli, Laylie

Layton **B** (English) a form of Leighton (see Boys' Names).

Le (Vietnamese) pearl.

Lea (Hawaiian) Mythology: the goddess of canoe makers. (Hebrew) a form of Leah.

Leah 🌺 **G** (Hebrew) weary. Bible: the first wife of Jacob. See also Lia.
Lea, Léa, Lee, Leea, Leeah, Leia

Leala (French) faithful, loyal.
Lealia, Lealie, Leial

Lean, Leann (English) forms of Leeann, Lian.
Leane

Leandra (Latin) like a lioness.
Leanda, Leandre, Leandrea, Leandria, Leeanda, Leeandra

Leanna, Leeanna (English) forms of Liana.
Leana, Leeana, Leianna

Leanne **G** (English) a form of Leeann, Lian.

Leanore (Greek) a form of Eleanor. (English) a form of Helen.
Leanora, Lanore

Lecia (Latin) a short form of Felecia.
Leasia, Leecia, Leesha, Leesia, Lesha, Leshia, Lesia

Leda (Greek) lady. Mythology: the queen of Sparta and the mother of Helen of Troy.
Ledah, Lyda, Lydah

Ledicia (Latin) great joy.

Lee 🅱 (Chinese) plum. (Irish) poetic. (English) meadow. A short form of Ashley, Leah.
Lea, Leigh

Leeann, Leeanne (English) combinations of Lee + Ann. Forms of Lian.
Leane, Leean, Leian, Leiann, Leianne

Leelamayee (Indian) playful.

Leena (Estonian) a form of Helen. (Greek, Latin, Arabic) a form of Lina.

Leeza (Hebrew) a short form of Aleeza. (English) a form of Lisa, Liza.
Leesa

Lefitray (Mapuche) sound, the speed of sound, rapid sound.

Leflay (Mapuche) lethargic woman without energies, lacking in curiosity.

Lei 🅱🅶 (Hawaiian) a familiar form of Leilani.

Leigh 🅶 (English) a form of Leah.
Leighann, Leighanne

Leigha (English) a form of Leigh.
Leighanna

Leiko (Japanese) arrogant.

Leila (Hebrew) dark beauty; night. (Arabic) born at night. See also Laela, Layla, Lila.
Laila, Leela, Leelah, Leilah, Leilia, Lela, Lelah, Leland, Lelia, Leyla

Leilani (Hawaiian) heavenly flower; heavenly child.
Lailanee, Lailani, Lailanie, Lailany, Lailoni, Lani, Lei, Leilany, Leiloni, Leilony, Lelani, Lelania

Leira (Basque) reference to the Virgin Mary.

Lekasha (American) a form of Lakeisha.
Lekeesha, Lekeisha, Lekesha, Lekeshia, Lekesia, Lekicia, Lekisha

Lekha (Indian) writing.

Leland 🅱 (Hebrew) a form of Leila.

Leli (Swiss) a form of Magdalen.
Lelie

Lelia (Greek) fair speech. (Hebrew, Arabic) a form of Leila.
Leliah, Lelika, Lelita, Lellia

Lelica (Latin) talkative.

Lelya (Russian) a form of Helen.

Lemmie (Indian) devoted to the Lord.

Lena (Hebrew) dwelling or lodging. (Latin) temptress. (Norwegian) illustrious. (Greek) a short form of Eleanor. Music: Lena Horne, a well-known African American singer and actress.
Lenah, Lene, Lenee, Leni, Lenka, Lenna, Lennah, Lina, Linah

Lenci (Hungarian) a form of Helen.
Lency

Lene (German) a form of Helen.
Leni, Line

Leneisha (American) a combination of the prefix Le + Keneisha.
Lenece, Lenesha, Leniesha, Lenieshia, Leniesia, Leniessia, Lenisa, Lenise, Lenisha, Lennise, Lennisha, Lynesha

Lenia (German) a form of Leona.
Lenayah, Lenda, Lenea, Leneen, Lenna, Lennah, Lennea, Leny

Lenis (Latin) half, soft, silky.

Lenita (Latin) gentle.
Leneta, Lenette, Lennette

Lenore (Greek, Russian) a form of Eleanor.
Lenni, Lenor, Lenora, Lenorah

Leocadia (Greek) she who shines because of her whiteness.

Leocricia (Greek) she who judges her village well.

Leona (German) brave as a lioness. See also Lona.
Lenia, Leoine, Leola, Leolah, Leonae, Leonah, Leondra, Leone, Leonelle, Leonia, Leonice, Leonicia, Leonie, Leonissa, Leonna, Leonne, Liona

Leonarda, Leoncia Leonela (Latin) strong and fierce as a lion.

Leonie (German) a familiar form of Leona.
Leoni, Léonie, Leony

Leonilda (German) fighter.

Leonore (Greek) a form of Eleanor. See also Nora.
Leonor, Leonora, Leonorah, Léonore

Leontina (German) strong as a lion.

Leontine (Latin) like a lioness.
Leona, Leonine, Leontyne, Léontyne

Leopolda (German) princess of the village.

Leopoldina (Spanish) a form of Leopoldo.

Leopoldo (Italian) a form of Leopold (see Boys' Names).

Leora (Hebrew) light. (Greek) a familiar form of Eleanor. See also Liora.
Leorah, Leorit

Leotie (Native American) prairie flower.

Lera (Russian) a short form of Valera.
Lerka

Lesbia (Greek) native of the Greek island of Lesbos.

Lesley **G** (Scottish) gray fortress.
Leslea, Leslee, Leslie, Lesly, Lezlee, Lezley

Leslie **G** (Scottish) a form of Lesley.
Leslei, Lesleigh, Lesli, Lesslie, Lezli

Lesly **G** (Scottish) a form of Lesley.
Leslye, Lessly, Lezly

Lester **B** (Latin) chosen camp. (English) from Leicester, England.

Leta (Latin) glad. (Swahili) bringer. (Greek) a short form of Aleta.
Lita, Lyta

Leticia (Latin) joy. See also Latisha, Tisha.
Laticia, Leisha, Leshia, Let, Leta, Letesa, Letesha, Leteshia, Letha, Lethia, Letice, Letichia, Letisha, Letishia, Letisia, Letissa, Letita, Letitia, Letiticia, Letiza, Letizia, Letty, Letycia, Loutitia

Letty (English) a familiar form of Leticia.
Letta, Letti, Lettie

Levana (Hebrew) moon; white. (Latin) risen. Mythology: the goddess of newborn babies.
Lévana, Levania, Levanna, Levenia, Lewana, Livana

Levani (Fijian) anointed with oil.

Levi **B** (Hebrew) a form of Levia.

Levia (Hebrew) joined, attached.
Leevya, Levi, Levie

Levina (Latin) flash of lightning.
Levene

Levona (Hebrew) spice; incense.
Leavonia, Levonat, Levonna, Levonne, Livona

Lewana (Hebrew) a form of Levana.
Lebhanah, Lewanna

Lewis **B** (Welsh) a form of Llewellyn. (English) a form of Louis (see Boys' Names).

Lexandra (Greek) a short form of Alexandra.
Lisandra

Lexi (Greek) a familiar form of Alexandra.

Lexia (Greek) a familiar form of Alexandra.
Leska, Lesya, Lexa, Lexane, Lexina, Lexine

Lexie **G** (Greek) a familiar form of Alexandra.
Leksi, Lexey, Lexy

Lexis (Greek) a short form of Alexius, Alexus.
Laexis, Lexius, Lexsis, Lexxis

Lexus **G** (Greek) a short form of Alexis.
Lexuss, Lexxus, Lexyss

Leya (Spanish) loyal. (Tamil) the constellation Leo.
Leyah, Leyla

Li (Chinese) strength; beautiful.

Li Hua (Chinese) pear blossom.

Li Mei (Chinese) beautiful plum blossom.

Li Ming (Chinese) beautiful and bright.

Li Na (Chinese) beautiful and graceful.

Li Qin, Li-Qin (Chinese) beautiful stringed musical instrument.

Li Wei (Chinese) beautiful rose.

Lia **G** (Greek) bringer of good news. (Hebrew, Dutch, Italian) dependent. See also Leah.
Lía, Liah

Liam **B** (Irish) a form of William.

Lian (Chinese) graceful willow. (Latin) a short form of Gillian, Lillian.
Lean, Leeann, Liane, Liann, Lianne

Liana, Lianna **G** (Latin) youth. (French) bound, wrapped up; tree covered with vines. (English) meadow. (Hebrew) short forms of Eliana.
Leanna

Liane, Lianne (Hebrew) short forms of Eliane. (English) forms of Lian.
Leeanne

Liang (Chinese) good.

Liao (Chinese) faraway, vast.

Liban **B** (Hawaiian) a form of Laban (see Boys' Names).

w) a familiar form of Elizabeth.
...bee, Libbey, Libbie

Libera, Libera (Latin) she who bestows abundance.

Liberada (Latin) liberated.

Liberata (Latin) she who loves liberty.

Liberia, Liberta (Spanish) freedom.

Libertad (Latin) she who has the skills to act in good faith.

Liberty (Latin) free.
Liberti, Libertie

Libia (Latin) comes from the desert.

Libitina (Latin) she who is wanted.

Libna (Latin) whiteness.

Libni, Lipi (Indian) manuscripts of God.

Liboria (Latin) she who was born in Libor, the name of several ancient cities in Spain and Portugal.

Librada (Latin) liberated.

Lican (Mapuche) flint stone.

Licia (Greek) a short form of Alicia.
Licha, Lishia, Lisia, Lycia

Lida (Greek) happy. (Slavic) loved by people. (Latin) a short form of Alida, Elita.
Leeda, Lidah, Lidochka, Lyda

Lide (Latin, Basque) life.

Lidia (Greek) a form of Lydia.
Lidea, Lidi, Lidija, Lidiya, Lidka, Lidya

Lídia (Portuguese) a form of Lidia.

Lien (Chinese) lotus.
Lienne

Liesabet (German) a short form of Elizabeth.
Liesbeth, Lisbete

Liese (German) a familiar form of Elise, Elizabeth.
Liesa, Lieschen, Lise

Liesel (German) a familiar form of Elizabeth.
Leesel, Leesl, Leezel, Leezl, Liesl, Liezel, Liezl, Lisel

Lieu (Vietnamese) sweet potato.

Ligia (Greek) Mythology: name of a mermaid.

Lígia (Portuguese) a form of Ligia.

Likhitha (Indian) writing.

Lila (Arabic) night. (Hindi) free will of God. (Persian) lilac. A short form of Dalila, Delilah, Lillian.
Lilah, Lilia, Lyla, Lylah

Lilac (Sanskrit) lilac; blue purple.

Lilia (Persian) a form of Lila.
Lili

Lilian (Latin) a form of Lillian.
Liliane, Liliann, Lilianne

Lilián (Spanish) a form of Lilian.

Lílian (Portuguese) a form of Lilian.

Liliana (Latin) a form of Lillian.
Lileana, Lilliana, Lilianna, Lilliana, Lillianna

Lilibeth (English) a combination of Lily + Beth.
Lilibet, Lillibeth, Lillybeth, Lilybet, Lilybeth

Lilith (Arabic) of the night; night demon. Mythology: the first wife of Adam, according to ancient Jewish legends.
Lillis, Lily

Lillian ☙ (Latin) lily flower.
Lian, Lil, Lila, Lilas, Lileane, Lilia, Lilian, Liliana, Lilias, Liliha, Lilja, Lilla, Lilli, Lillia, Lilliane, Lilliann, Lillianne, Lillyann, Lis, Liuka

Lillyann (English) a combination of Lily + Ann. (Latin) a form of Lillian.
Lillyan, Lillyanne, Lily, Lilyan, Lilyana, Lilyann, Lilyanna, Lilyanne

Lilvina (Latin, German) friend of the Iris.

Lily ☙ (Latin, Arabic) a familiar form of Lilith, Lillian, Lillyann.
Lil, Líle, Lili, Lilie, Lilijana, Lilika, Lilike, Liliosa, Lilium, Lilka, Lille, Lilli, Lillie, Lilly

Lim (Chinese) a form of Lin.

Limber (Tiv) joyful.

Lin 🄶 (Chinese) beautiful jade. (English) a form of Lynn.
Linh, Linn

Lin Yao (Chinese) beautiful jade treasure.

Lina (Greek) light. (Arabic) tender. (Latin) a form of Lena.

Lincoln 🄱 (English) settlement by the pool.

Linda 🄶 (Spanish) pretty.
Lind, Lindy, Linita, Lynda

Lindsay 🄶 (English) a form of Lindsey.
Lindsi, Linsay, Lyndsay

Lindsey **G** (English) linden tree island; camp near the stream.
Lind, Lindsea, Lindsee, Lindsi, Linsey, Lyndsey, Lynsey

Lindsi (American) a familiar form of Lindsay, Lindsey.
Lindsie, Lindsy, Lindze, Lindzee, Lindzey, Lindzy

Lindy (Spanish) a familiar form of Linda.
Linde, Lindee, Lindey, Lindi, Lindie

Linette (Welsh) idol. (French) bird.
Lanette, Linet, Linnet, Linnetta, Linnette, Lyannette, Lynette

Ling (Chinese) delicate, dainty.

Lin-Lin (Chinese) beauty of a tinkling bell.

Linnea (Scandinavian) lime tree. Botany: the national flower of Sweden.
Lin, Linae, Linea, Linnae, Linnaea, Linneah, Lynea, Lynnea

Linsey (English) a form of Lindsey.
Linsea, Linsee, Linsi, Linsie, Linsy, Linzee, Linzey, Linzi, Linzie, Linzy, Linzzi, Lynsey

Liolya (Russian) a form of Helen.

Lionela (Greek) little lion.

Liora (Hebrew) light. See also Leora.

Lipika (Indian) alphabets.

Lirit (Hebrew) poetic; lyrical, musical.

Liron **BG** (Hebrew) my song.
Leron, Lerone, Lirone

Li-Rong (Chinese) beautiful lotus.

Lisa **G** (Hebrew) consecrated to God. (English) a short form of Elizabeth.
Leeza, Liesa, Liisa, Lise, Lisenka, Lisette, Liszka, Litsa, Lysa

Lisbeth (English) a short form of Elizabeth.
Lisbet

Lise **G** (German) a form of Lisa.

Lisette **G** (French) a form of Lisa. (English) a familiar form of Elise, Elizabeth.
Liset, Liseta, Lisete, Liseth, Lisett, Lisetta, Lisettina, Lizet, Lizette, Lysette

Lisha (Arabic) darkness before midnight. (Hebrew) a short form of Alisha, Elisha, Ilisha.
Lishe

Lissa (Greek) honey bee. A short form of Elissa, Elizabeth, Melissa, Millicent.
Lyssa

Lissette (French) a form of Lisa. (English) a familiar form of Elise, Elizabeth.
Lisset, Lissete, Lissett

Lissie (American) a familiar form of Allison, Elise, Elizabeth.
Lissee, Lissey, Lissi, Lissy, Lissye

Lita (Latin) a familiar form of names ending in "lita."
Leta, Litah, Litta

Litonya (Moquelumnan) darting hummingbird.

Liu (Chinese) willow.

Liv (Latin) a short form of Livia, Olivia.

Livana (Hebrew) a form of Levana.
Livna, Livnat

Livia (Hebrew) crown. A familiar form of Olivia. (Latin) olive.
Levia, Liv, Livie, Livy, Livya, Livye

Liviya (Hebrew) brave lioness; royal crown.
Leviya, Levya, Livya

Livona (Hebrew) a form of Levona.

Lixue (Chinese) pretty snow.

Liz (English) a short form of Elizabeth.

Liza (American) a short form of Elizabeth.
Leeza, Lizela, Lizka, Lyza

Lizabeta (Russian) a form of Elizabeth.
Lizabetah, Lizaveta, Lizonka

Lizabeth (English) a short form of Elizabeth.
Lisabet, Lisabeth, Lisabette, Lizabette

Lizbeth **G** (English) a short form of Elizabeth.
Lizbet, Lizbett

Lizet, Lizette (French) forms of Lisette.
Lizet, Lizete, Lizeth, Lizett, Lizzet, Lizzeth, Lizzette

Lizina (Latvian) a familiar form of Elizabeth.

Lizzy (American) a familiar form of Elizabeth.
Lizzie, Lizy

Llanquipan (Mapuche) fallen branch; solitary lioness; retiring soul; lady who distances herself from the noise of the world.

Llanquiray (Mapuche) flowered pearl; fallen flower, fallen petals.

Llesenia (Spanish) gypsy female lead in a 1970s soap opera.

Lloyd **B** (Welsh) gray haired; holy.

...rain.

...eye.

Logan ⬛ (Irish) meadow.
Logann, Loganne, Logen, Loghan, Logun, Logyn, Logynn

Lohini (Indian) red skinned.

Loida, Loída (Greek) example of faith and piousness.

Lois (German) famous warrior.

Lok (Chinese) happy.

Lola (Spanish) a familiar form of Carlotta, Dolores, Louise.
Lolah, Lolita

Lolida (Pohnpeian) a form of Jacinta.

Lolita (Spanish) sorrowful. A familiar form of Lola.
Lita, Lulita

Lolly (English) sweet; candy. A familiar form of Laura.

Lolotea (Zuni) a form of Dorothy.

Lomasi (Native American) pretty flower.

Lona (Latin) lioness. (English) solitary. (German) a short form of Leona.
Loni, Lonna

London 🅱🅶 (English) fortress of the moon. Geography: the capital of the United Kingdom.
Landyn, Londen, Londun, Londyn

Loni (American) a form of Lona.
Lonee, Lonie, Lonni, Lonnie

Lonoris (Chuukese) a form of Dolores.

Lopa (Indian) learned.

Lopamudra (Indian) learned woman.

Lora (Latin) crowned with laurel. (American) a form of Laura.
Lorah, Lorane, Lorann, Lorra, Lorrah, Lorrane

Lorda (Spanish) shrine of the Virgin Mary.

Lore (Basque) flower. (Latin) a short form of Flora.
Lor

Lorelei (German) alluring. Mythology: the siren of the Rhine River who lured sailors to their deaths. See also Lurleen.
Loralee, Loralei, Lorali, Loralie, Loralyn, Loreal, Lorelea, Loreley, Loreli, Lorilee, Lorilyn

Lorelle (American) a form of Laurel.

Loren 🅶 (American) a form of Lauren.
Loreen, Lorena, Lorin, Lorne, Lorren, Lorrin, Lorryn, Loryn, Lorynn, Lorynne

Lorena 🅶 (English) a form of Lauren.
Lorene, Lorenea, Lorenia, Lorenna, Lorina, Lorrina, Lorrine, Lurana

Lorenza (Latin) a form of Laura.
Laurencia, Laurentia, Laurentina

Loreta (Spanish) a form of Loreto.

Loreto (Italian) a form of Loretta.

Loretta (English) a familiar form of Laura.
Larretta, Lauretta, Laurette, Loretah, Lorette, Lorita, Lorretta, Lorrette

Lori 🅶 (Latin) crowned with laurel. (French) a short form of Lorraine. (American) a familiar form of Laura.
Loree, Lorey, Loria, Lorianna, Lorianne, Lorie, Lorree, Lorri, Lorrie, Lory

Lorin (American) a form of Loren.
Lorine

Lorinda (Spanish) a form of Laura.

Loris 🅱🅶 (Latin) thong. (Dutch) clown. (Greek) a short form of Chloris.
Laurice, Laurys, Lorice

Lorna (Latin) crowned with laurel. Literature: probably coined by Richard Blackmore in his novel *Lorna Doone*.
Lorrna

Lorraine (Latin) sorrowful. (French) from Lorraine, a former province of France. See also Rayna.
Laraine, Lorain, Loraine, Lorayne, Lorein, Loreine, Lori, Lorine, Lorrain, Lorraina, Lorrayne, Lorreine

Lo-Shen (Chinese) goddess of rivers.

Lotte (German) a short form of Charlotte.
Lotie, Lotta, Lottchen, Lottey, Lottie, Lotty, Loty

Lotus (Greek) lotus.

Lou 🅱 (American) a short form of Louise, Luella.
Lu

Louam (Ethiopian) sleep well.

Louisa (English) a familiar form of Louise. Literature: Louisa May Alcott was an American writer and reformer best known for her novel *Little Women*.
Aloisa, Eloisa, Heloisa, Lou, Louisian, Louisane, Louisina, Louiza, Lovisa, Luisa, Luiza, Lujza, Lujzika

Louise G (German) famous warrior. See also Alison, Eloise, Heloise, Lois, Lola, Ludovica, Luella, Lulu.
Loise, Lou, Louisa, Louisette, Louisiane, Louisine, Lowise, Loyce, Loyise, Luise

Lourdes G (French) from Lourdes, France. Religion: a place where the Virgin Mary was said to have appeared.

Louredes (Spanish) shrine of the Virgin Mary.

Love (English) love, kindness, charity.
Lovely, Lovewell, Lovey, Lovie, Lovy, Luv, Luvvy

Lovisa (German) a form of Louisa.

Lúa (Latin) moon.

Luann (Hebrew, German) graceful woman warrior. (Hawaiian) happy; relaxed. (American) a combination of Louise + Ann.
Louann, Louanne, Lu, Lua, Luan, Luane, Luanna, Luanne, Luanni, Luannie

Luanna (German) a form of Luann.
Lewanna, Louanna, Luana, Luwana

Lubaaba (Indian) the innermost essence.

Lubov (Russian) love.
Luba, Lubna, Lubochka, Lyuba, Lyubov

Luca B (Latin) a form of Lucy.

Lucas B (German, Irish, Danish, Dutch) a form of Lucius (see Boys' Names).

Lucelia (Spanish) a combination of Luz and Celia.

Lucena (Spanish) bringer of light.

Lucerne (Latin) lamp; circle of light. Geography: the Lake of Lucerne is in Switzerland.
Lucerna, Lucero

Lucero (Latin) a form of Lucerne.

Lucetta (English) a familiar form of Lucy.
Lucette

Lucia (Italian, Spanish) a form of Lucy.
Lúcia, Lucía, Luciana, Lucianna

Lucie (French) a familiar form of Lucy.

Lucille (English) a familiar form of Lucy.
Lucila, Lucile, Lucilla

Lucinda (Latin) a form of Lucy. See also Cindy.

Lucine (Arabic) moon. (Basque) a form of Lucy.
Lucienne, Lucina, Lucyna, Lukene, Lusine, Luzine

Lucita (Spanish) a form of Lucy.
Lusita

Lucretia (Latin) rich; rewarded.
Lacrecia, Lucrece, Lucréce, Lucrecia, Lucreecia, Lucresha, Lucreshia, Lucrezia, Lucrisha, Lucrishia

Lucrezia (Italian) a form of Lucretia. History: Lucrezia Borgia was the Duchess of Ferrara and a patron of learning and the arts.

Lucy (Latin) light; bringer of light.
Luca, Luce, Lucetta, Luci, Lucia, Lucida, Lucie, Lucija, Lucika, Lucille, Lucinda, Lucine, Lucita, Luciya, Lucya, Luzca, Luzi

Ludmilla (Slavic) loved by the people. See also Mila.
Ludie, Ludka, Ludmila, Lyuba, Lyudmila

Ludovica (German) a form of Louise.
Ludovika, Ludwiga

Luella (English) elf. (German) a familiar form of Louise.
Loella, Lou, Louella, Ludella, Luelle, Lula, Lulu

Luis B (Spanish) a form of Louis (see Boys' Names).

Luisa G (Spanish) a form of Louisa.

Luisina (Teutonic) celebrated warrior; celebrated; very well known.

Luke B (Latin) a form of Lucius (see Boys' Names).

Lulani BG (Polynesian) highest point of heaven.

Lulu (Arabic) pearl. (English) soothing, comforting. (Native American) hare. (German) a familiar form of Louise, Luella.
Loulou, Lula, Lulie

Luna (Latin) moon.
Lunetta, Lunette, Lunneta, Lunnete

Luo (Chinese) name of a river.

Lupa (Latin) wolf.

Lupe (Latin) wolf. (Spanish) a short form of Guadalupe.
Lupi, Lupita, Luppi

Lupita (Latin) a form of Lupe.

Lurdes (Portuguese, Spanish) a form of Lourdes.

Lurleen, Lurlene (Scandinavian) war horn. (German) forms of Lorelei.
Lura, Lurette, Lurline

Lusa (Finnish) a form of Elizabeth.

Lusela (Moquelumnan) like a bear swinging its foot when licking it.

Lutgarda (German) she who protects her village.

Luvena (Latin, English) little; beloved.
Lovena, Lovina, Luvenia, Luvina

Luyu BG (Moquelumnan) like a pecking bird.

Luz G (Spanish) light. Religion: Nuestra Señora de Luz—Our Lady of the Light—is another name for the Virgin Mary.
Luzi, Luzija

Luzia (Portuguese) a form of Lucia.

Lycoris (Greek) twilight.

Lyda (Greek) a short form of Lidia, Lydia.

Lydia G (Greek) from Lydia, an ancient land in Asia. (Arabic) strife.
Lidia, Lidija, Lidiya, Lyda, Lydie, Lydië

Lyla (French) island. (English) a form of Lyle (see Boys' Names). (Arabic, Hindi, Persian) a form of Lila.
Lila, Lilah

Lynda (Spanish) pretty. (American) a form of Linda.
Lyndah, Lynde, Lyndi, Lynnda

Lyndell (English) a form of Lynelle.
Lyndall, Lyndel, Lyndella

Lyndi (Spanish) a familiar form of Lynda.
Lyndee, Lindie, Lyndy, Lynndie, Lynndy

Lyndsay G (American) a form of Lindsay.
Lyndsaye

Lyndsey (English) linden tree island; camp near the stream. (American) a form of Lindsey.
Lyndsea, Lyndsee, Lyndsi, Lyndsie, Lyndsy, Lyndzee, Lyndzey, Lyndzi, Lyndzie, Lynndsie

Lynelle (English) pretty.
Linel, Linell, Linnell, Lyndell, Lynel, Lynell, Lynella, Lynnell

Lynette (Welsh) idol. (English) a form of Linette.
Lynett, Lynetta, Lynnet, Lynnette

Lynn, Lynne G (English) waterfall; pool below a waterfall.
Lin, Lina, Linley, Linn, Lyn, Lynlee, Lynley, Lynna, Lynnae, Lynnea

Lynnell (English) a form of Lynelle.
Linnell, Lynnelle

Lynsey (American) a form of Lyndsey.
Lynnsey, Lynnzey, Lynsie, Lynsy, Lynzee, Lynzey, Lynzi, Lynzie, Lynzy

Lyra (Greek) lyre player.
Lyre, Lyric, Lyrica, Lyrie, Lyris

Lysandra (Greek) liberator.
Lisandra, Lysandre, Lytle

Lysanne (American) a combination of Lysandra + Anne.
Lisanne, Lizanne

M

M G (American) an initial used as a first name.

Ma (Chinese) agate.

Maanasa (Indian) mind.

Maanika (Indian) ruby.

Mab (Irish) joyous. (Welsh) baby. Literature: queen of the fairies.
Mabry

Mabel (Latin) lovable. A short form of Amabel.
Mabelle, Mable, Mabyn, Maible, Maybel, Maybeline, Maybelle, Maybull

Macarena (Spanish) she who carries the sword; name for the Virgin Mary.

Macaria (Greek) having a long life.

Macawi (Dakota) generous; motherly.

Macayla (American) a form of Michaela.
Macaela, Macaila, Macala, Macalah, Macaylah, Macayle, Macayli, Mackayla

Macey (Polish) a familiar form of Macia.
Macee

Machaela (Hebrew) a form of Michaela.
Machael, Machaelah, Machaelie, Machaila, Machala, Macheala

Machiko (Japanese) fortunate child.
Machi

Macia (Polish) a form of Miriam.
Macelia, Macey, Machia, Macie, Macy, Masha, Mashia

Macie, Macy G (Polish) familiar forms of Macia.
Maci, Macye

Maciela (Latin) very slender, skeletal.

Mackenna (American) a form of Mackenzie.
Mackena, Makenna, Mckenna

Mackenzie ✺ **G** (Irish) child of the wise leader. See also Kenzie.
Macenzie, Mackenna, Mackensi, Mackensie, Mackenze, Mackenzee, Mackenzey, Mackenzi, Mackenzia, Mackenzy, Mackenzye, Mackinsey, Mackynze, Makenzie, McKenzie, Mckinzie, Mekenzie, Mykenzie

Mackinsey (Irish) a form of Mackenzie.
Mackinsie, Mackinze, Mackinzee, Mackinzey, Mackinzi, Mackinzie

Macra (Greek) she who grows.

Mada (English) a short form of Madaline, Magdalen.
Madda, Mahda

Madaline (English) a form of Madeline.
Mada, Madailéin, Madaleen, Madaleine, Madalene, Madalin, Madaline

Madalyn (Greek) a form of Madeline.
Madalyne, Madalynn, Madalynne

Maddie (English) a familiar form of Madeline.
Maddi, Maddy, Mady, Maidie, Maydey

Maddison **G** (English) a form of Madison.
Maddisan, Maddisen, Maddisson, Maddisyn, Maddyson

Madeeha (Indian) praiseworthy.

Madelaine (French) a form of Madeline.
Madelane, Madelayne

Madeleine (French) a form of Madeline.
Madalaine, Madalayne, Madelaine, Madelein, Madeliene

Madelena (English) a form of Madeline.
Madalaina, Madalena, Madalina, Maddalena, Madelaina, Madeleina, Madelina, Madelyna

Madeline ✺ **G** (Greek) high tower. See also Lena, Lina, Maud.
Madaline, Madalyn, Maddie, Madel, Madelaine, Madeleine, Madelena, Madelene, Madelia, Madella, Madelle, Madelon, Madelyn, Madge, Madilyn, Madlen, Madlin, Madline, Madlyn, Madolyn, Maida

Madelón (Spanish) a form of Magdalen.

Madelyn (Greek) a form of Madeline.
Madelyne, Madelynn, Madelynne, Madilyn, Madlyn, Madolyn

Madena, Madia, Madina (Greek) from the high tower.

Madge (Greek) a familiar form of Madeline, Margaret.
Madgi, Madgie, Mady

Madhavi (Indian) honey.

Madhavilata (Indian) a flowering creeper.

Madhuchanda (Indian) pleasing composition.

Madhuksara (Indian) one who showers honey.

Madhul, Madhura, Madhuri (Indian) sweet.

Madhulata (Indian) lovely creeper.

Madhulekha (Indian) beautiful.

Madhulika (Indian) nectar.

Madhumalati (Indian) flowering creeper.

Madhumathi (Indian) delight; moon.

Madhumati, Mahabhadra (Indian) the Ganga River.

Madhumita (Indian) sweet girl.

Madhumitha (Indian) sweet person.

Madhunisha (Indian) pleasant night.

Madhurima (Indian) charming.

Madhusha (Indian) beauty.

Madhushri (Indian) beauty of the spring season.

Madhuvanthi (Indian) one who is sweet like honey.

Madilyn (Greek) a form of Madeline.
Madilen, Madiline, Madilyne, Madilynn

Madirakshi (Indian) woman with intoxicating eyes.

Madisen **G** (English) a form of Madison.
Madisan, Madisin, Madissen, Madisun

Madison ✺ **G** (English) good; child of Maud.
Maddison, Madisen, Madisson, Madisyn, Madyson, Mattison

Madisyn (English) a form of Madison.
Madissyn, Madisynn, Madisynne

Madolyn (Greek) a form of Madeline.
Madoline, Madolyne, Madolynn, Madolynne

Madonna (Latin) my lady.
Madona

Madrona (Spanish) mother.
Madre, Madrena

Madyson (English) a form of Madison.
Madysen, Madysun

Mae (English) a form of May. History: Mae Jemison was the first African American woman in space.
Maelea, Maeleah, Maelen, Maelle, Maeona

Maegan (Irish) a form of Megan.
Maegen, Maeghan, Maegin

Maeko (Japanese) honest child.
Mae, Maemi

Maeve (Irish) joyous. Mythology: a legendary Celtic queen. See also Mavis.
Maevi, Maevy, Maive, Mayve

Mafalda (Spanish) a form of Matilde.

Magadhi (Indian) flower.

Magalí (French) a form of Magali.

Magali, Magaly (Hebrew) from the high tower.
Magalie, Magally

Magan, Magen (Greek) forms of Megan.
Maggen, Maggin

Magda (Czech, Polish, Russian) a form of Magdalen.
Mahda, Makda

Magdalen (Greek) high tower. Bible: Magdala was the home of Saint Mary Magdalen. See also Madeline, Malena, Marlene.
Mada, Magda, Magdala, Magdaleen, Magdalena, Magdalene, Magdaline, Magdalyn, Magdalynn, Magdelane, Magdelene, Magdeline, Magdelyn, Magdlen, Magdolna, Maggie, Magola, Maighdlin, Mala, Malaine

Magdalena (Greek) a form of Magdalen.
Magdalina, Magdelana, Magdelena, Magdelina

Magena (Native American) coming moon.

Maggie (Greek) pearl. (English) a familiar form of Magdalen, Margaret.
Mag, Magge, Maggee, Maggi, Maggia, Maggie, Maggiemae, Maggy, Magi, Magie, Mags

Maggy, Meggy (English) forms of Maggie.
Maggey, Magy

Magnolia (Latin) flowering tree. See also Nollie.
Nola

Mahajabeen (Indian) beautiful.

Mahakanta, Mahika (Indian) earth.

Mahal (Filipino) love.

Mahala (Arabic) fat; marrow; tender. (Native American) powerful woman.
Mahalah, Mahalar, Mahalla, Mahela, Mahila, Mahlah, Mahlaha, Mehala, Mehalah

Mahalia (American) a form of Mahala.
Mahaley, Mahaliah, Mahalie, Mahayla, Mahaylah, Mahaylia, Mahelea, Maheleah, Mahelia, Mahilia, Mehalia

Maharene (Ethiopian) forgive us.

Mahati (Indian) great.

Mahek (Indian) smell.

Mahendi (Indian) leaves.

Mahesa (Hindi) great lord. Religion: a name for the Hindu god Shiva.
Maheesa, Mahisa

Mahi (Indian) the world.

Mahijuba (Indian) a hostess.

Mahila (Sanskrit) woman.

Mahima (Indian) glorious.

Mahina (Hawaiian) moon glow.

Mahira (Hebrew) energetic.
Mahri

Mahiya (Indian) joy.

Maho (Japanese) truth; sail.

Mahogony (Spanish) rich; strong.
Mahagony, Mahoganey, Mahogani, Mahoganie, Mahogany, Mahogney, Mahogny, Mohogany, Mohogony

Mahua (Indian) an intoxicating flower.

Mahuya (Indian) the name of a beautiful flower.

Mai (Japanese) brightness. (Vietnamese) flower. (Navajo) coyote.

Maia (Greek) mother; nurse. (English) kinswoman; maiden. Mythology: the loveliest of the Pleiades, the seven daughters of Atlas, and the mother of Hermes. See also Maya.
Maiah, Maie, Maiya

Maiara (Tupi) wise.

Maida (English) maiden. (Greek) a short form of Madeline.
Maidel, Mayda, Maydena

Maija (Finnish) a form of Mary.
Maiji, Maikki

Maika (Hebrew) a familiar form of Michaela.
Maikala, Maikka, Maiko

Maimoona (Indian) auspicious; blessed.

Maina (Indian) a bird.

Maira **G** (Irish) a form of Mary.
Maairah, Mair, Mairi, Mairim, Mairin, Mairona, Mairwen

Maire (Irish) a form of Mary.

Maisie (Scottish) familiar forms of Margaret.
Maisa, Maise, Maisey, Maisi, Maisy, Maizie, Maycee, Maysie, Mayzie, Mazey, Mazie, Mazy, Mazzy, Mysie, Myzie

Maita (Spanish) a form of Martha.
Maitia

Maite (Spanish) a form of Maita.

Maitea (Spanish) dearly loved.

Maiten (Spanish) a form of Malen.

Maitena (Spanish) a form of Maite.

Maitlyn (American) a combination of Maita + Lynn.
Maitlan, Maitland, Maitlynn, Mattilyn

Maitreyi (Indian) a wise woman.

Maitri (Indian) friendship.

Maiya (Greek) a form of Maia.
Maiyah

Maja (Arabic) a short form of Majidah.
Majal, Majalisa, Majalyn, Majalynn

Majeeda (Indian) glorious.

Majesta (Latin) majesty.

Majidah (Arabic) splendid.
Maja, Majida

Makaarim (Indian) of good and honorable character.

Makaela, Makaila (American) forms of Michaela.
Makaelah, Makaelee, Makaella, Makaely, Makail, Makailah, Makailee, Makailla, Makaillah, Makealah, Makell

Makala (Hawaiian) myrtle. (Hebrew) a form of Michaela.
Makalae, Makalah, Makalai, Makalea, Makalee, Makaleh, Makaleigh, Makaley, Makalia, Makalie, Makalya, Makela, Makelah, Makell, Makella

Makana (Hawaiian) gift, present.

Makani **B** (Hawaiian) wind.

Makara (Hindi) Astrology: another name for the zodiac sign Capricorn.

Makayla ❀ (American) a form of Michaela.
Macayla, Makaylah, Makaylee, Makayleigh, Makayli, Makaylia, Makaylla, Makell, Makyla, Makylah, Mckayla, Mekayla, Mikayla

Makell **G** (American) a short form of Makaela, Makala, Makayla.
Makele, Makelle, Mckell, Mekel

Makenna **G** (American) a form of Mackenna.
Makena, Makennah, Mikenna

Makenzie **G** (Irish) a form of Mackenzie.
Makense, Makensey, Makensie, Makenze, Makenzee, Makenzey, Makenzi, Makenzy, Makenzye, Makinzey, Makynzey, Mekenzie, Mykenzie

Maki (Japanese) she who prays for the truth.

Makiko (Japanese) child of Maki.

Makshi (Indian) honeybee.

Ma-Ku (Chinese) goddess of springtime.

Mala (Greek) a short form of Magdalen.
Malana, Malee, Mali

Malana (Hawaiian) bouyant, light.

Malarvizhi (Indian) cute eyes.

Malashree (Indian) an early evening melody.

Malati (Indian) jasmine; moonlight.

Malavika (Indian) princess of the kingdom of Malava.

Malaya (Filipino) free.
Malayaa, Malayah, Malayna, Malea, Maleah

Malen (Swedish) a form of Malena.

Malena (Swedish) a familiar form of Magdalen.
Malenna, Malin, Malina, Maline, Malini, Malinna

Malha (Hebrew) queen.
Maliah, Malkah, Malkia, Malkiah, Malkie, Malkiya, Malkiyah, Miliah

Mali (Tai) jasmine flower. (Tongan) sweet. (Hungarian) a short form of Malika.
Malea, Malee, Maley

Malia (Hawaiian, Zuni) a form of Mary. (Spanish) a form of Maria.
Malea, Maleah, Maleeya, Maleeyah, Maleia, Maliah, Maliasha, Malie, Maliea, Maliya, Maliyah, Malli, Mally

Malik **B** (Hungarian, Arabic) a form of Malika.

Malika (Hungarian) industrious. (Arabic) queen.
Malak, Maleeka, Maleka, Mali, Maliaka, Malik, Malikah, Malikee, Maliki, Malikia, Malky

Girls M–R

Malina (Hebrew) tower. (Native American) soothing. (Russian) raspberry.
Malin, Maline, Malina, Malinna, Mallie

Malinda (Greek) a form of Melinda.
Malinde, Malinna, Malynda

Malini (Hindi) gardener.
Maliny

Malissa (Greek) a form of Melissa.
Malisa, Malisah, Malyssa

Maljumana (Indian) beautiful.

Mallalai (Pashto) beautiful.

Malley (American) a familiar form of Mallory.
Mallee, Malli, Mallie, Mally, Maly

Mallika (Indian) queen; a creeper plant.

Mallorie (French) a form of Mallory.
Malerie, Mallari, Mallerie, Malloreigh, Mallori

Mallory 🄶 (German) army counselor. (French) unlucky.
Maliri, Mallary, Mallauri, Mallery, Malley, Malloree, Mallorey, Mallorie, Malorie, Malory, Malorym, Malree, Malrie, Mellory

Malorie, Malory (German) forms of Mallory.
Malarie, Maloree, Malori, Melorie, Melory

Malti (Indian) moonlight.

Malva (English) a form of Melba.
Malvi, Malvy

Malvina (Scottish) a form of Melvina. Literature: a name created by the eighteenth-century Romantic poet James Macpherson.
Malvane, Malvi

Mamata (Indian) love, affection.

Mamie (American) a familiar form of Margaret.
Mame, Mamee, Mami, Mammie, Mamy, Mamye

Mamiko (Japanese) child of Mami.

Mamo 🄱🄶 (Hawaiian) saffron flower; yellow bird.

Mamta (Indian) motherly love.

Man (Chinese) trailing plant.

Mana (Hawaiian) psychic; sensitive.
Manal, Manali, Manna, Mannah

Manaal (Indian) attainment, achievement.

Manaar (Indian) guiding light.

Manami (Japanese) beautiful love and affection.

Manana (Indian) meditation.

Manar (Arabic) guiding light.
Manayra

Manchu (Chinese) pure.

Manda (Spanish) woman warrior. (Latin) a short form of Amanda.
Mandy

Mandakini (Indian) a river.

Mandakranta (Indian) a Sanskrit meter.

Mandara (Hindi) calm.

Mandaraa (Indian) coral tree.

Mandarmalika (Indian) a garland of celestial.

Mandavi (Indian) wife of Bharat.

Mandeep 🄱🄶 (Punjabi) enlightened.

Mandira (Indian) melody.

Mandisa (Xhosa) sweet.

Mandodari (Indian) one with narrow abdomen.

Mandy 🄶 (Latin) lovable. A familiar form of Amanda, Manda, Melinda.
Mandee, Mandi, Mandie

Manela (Catalonian) a form of Manuela.

Manette (French) a form of Mary.

Mang (Chinese) rays of light.

Mangala (Indian) auspicious; bliss.

Mangena (Hebrew) song, melody.
Mangina

Mangla (Indian) auspicious.

Mani (Chinese) a mantra repeated in Tibetan Buddhist prayer to impart understanding.
Manee

Manideepa (Indian) a lamp of precious stones.

Manika (Indian) jewel.

Manikuntala (Indian) one whose hair is like gems.

Manila (Latin) woman with small hands.

Manimala (Indian) a string of pearls.

Manimekhala (Indian) a girdle of gems.

Manini (Indian) self-respected.

Maniratna (Indian) diamond.

Manishika (Indian) intelligence.

Manjari (Indian) bud of a mango tree.

Manjira (Indian) ankle bells.

Manjistha (Indian) extremely.

Manjot BG (Indian) light of the mind.

Manju (Indian) pleasant.

Manjubala (Indian) beautiful girl.

Manjula (Indian) lovely, charming.

Manjulika (Indian) a sweet girl.

Manjusha (Indian) lady with a sweet voice.

Manka (Polish, Russian) a form of Mary.

Manmayi (Indian) jealous.

Manoela (Hebrew) God is with us.

Manola (Spanish) a form of Manuela.

Manon (French) a familiar form of Marie.
   Mannon

Manón (Spanish) a form of Manon.

Manorama (Indian) beautiful.

Manoranjana (Indian) entertaining;
   pleasing.

Manpreet G (Punjabi) mind full of love.
   Manprit

Manque (Mapuche) condor; the main
   woman; woman of unyielding character.

Mansha (Indian) wish.

Mansi (Hopi) plucked flower.
   *Mancey, Manci, Mancie, Mansey, Mansie,
   Mansy*

Manuela (Spanish) a form of Emmanuelle.
   Manuala, Manuelita, Manuella, Manuelle

Manya (Russian) a form of Mary.

Mao (Chinese) luxuriant.

Mar (Spanish) sea.

Mara (Hebrew) melody. (Greek) a short form
   of Amara. (Slavic) a form of Mary.
   *Mahra, Marae, Marah, Maralina, Maraline,
   Marra*

Maraam (Indian) aspiration.

Marabel (English) a form of Mirabel.
   Marabella, Marabelle

Marala (Indian) swan.

Maranda (Latin) a form of Miranda.

Maraya (Hebrew) a form of Mariah.
   Mareya

Marcel B (French) a form of Marcellus
   (see Boys' Names).

Marcela (Latin) a form of Marcella.
   *Marcele, Marcelen, Marcelia, Marcelina,
   Marceline, Maricela*

Marcelen (English) a form of Marcella.
   *Marcelen, Marcelin, Marcelina, Marceline,
   Marcellin, Marcellina, Marcelline, Marcelyn,
   Marcilen*

Marceliana (Latin) a form of Marcela.

Marcella (Latin) martial, warlike.
   Mythology: Mars was the god of war.
   Mairsil, Marca, Marce, Marceil, Marcela,

Marcelen, Marcell, Marcelle, Marcello,
   *Marcena, Marchella, Marchelle, Marci,
   Marcia, Marcie, Marciella, Marcile, Marcilla,
   Marcille, Marella, Marsella, Marselle,
   Marsiella*

Marcena (Latin) a form of Marcella, Marcia.
   *Maracena, Marceen, Marcene, Marcenia,
   Marceyne, Marcina*

Marci, Marcie (English) familiar forms of
   Marcella, Marcia.
   *Marca, Marcee, Marcita, Marcy, Marsi,
   Marsie*

Marcia (Latin) martial, warlike. See also
   Marquita.
   *Marcena, Marchia, Marci, Marciale, Marcie,
   Marcsa, Marsha, Martia*

Márcia (Portuguese) a form of Marcia.

Marciann (American) a combination of
   Marci + Ann.
   *Marciane, Marcianna, Marcianne, Marcyane,
   Marcyanna, Marcyanne*

Marcilynn (American) a combination of
   Marci + Lynn.
   *Marcilen, Marcilin, Marciline, Marcilyn,
   Marcilyne, Marcilynne, Marcylen, Marcylin,
   Marcyline, Marcylyn, Marcylyne, Marcylynn,
   Marcylynne*

Marco B (Italian) a form of Marcus.

Marcus B (Latin) martial, warlike.

Marcy (English) a form of Marci.
   Marsey, Marsy

Mardi (French) born on Tuesday. (Aramaic)
   a familiar form of Martha.

Mare (Irish) a form of Mary.
   Mair, Maire

Girls M–R

Marelda (German) renowned warrior.
Marella, Marilda

Maren 🄶 (Latin) sea. (Aramaic) a form of Mary. See also Marina.
Marin, Marine, Marinn, Miren

Maresa, Maressa (Latin) forms of Marisa.
Maresha, Meresa

Maretta (English) a familiar form of Margaret.
Maret, Marette

Margaret 🄶 (Greek) pearl. History: Margaret Hilda Thatcher served as British prime minister. See also Gita, Greta, Gretchen, Marjorie, Markita, Meg, Megan, Peggy, Reet, Rita.
Madge, Maergrethe, Maggie, Maisie, Mamie, Maretta, Marga, Margalo, Marganit, Margara, Maretha, Margarett, Margarette, Margarida, Margarit, Margarita, Margaro, Margaux, Marge, Margeret, Margeretta, Margerette, Margery, Margetta, Margiad, Margie, Margisia, Margit, Margo, Margot, Margret, Marguerite, Meta

Margarit (Greek) a form of Margaret.
Margalide, Margalit, Margalith, Margarid, Margaritt, Margerit

Margarita (Italian, Spanish) a form of Margaret.
Margareta, Margaretta, Margarida, Margaritis, Margaritta, Margeretta, Margharita, Margherita, Margrieta, Margrita, Marguarita, Marguerita, Margurita

Margaux (French) a form of Margaret.
Margeaux

Marge (English) a short form of Margaret, Marjorie.
Margie

Margery (English) a form of Margaret.
Margerie, Margorie

Margie (English) a familiar form of Marge, Margaret.
Margey, Margi, Margy

Margit (Hungarian) a form of Margaret.
Marget, Margette, Margita

Margo, Margot (French) forms of Margaret.
Mago, Margaro

Margret (German) a form of Margaret.
Margreta, Margrete, Margreth, Margrett, Margretta, Margrette, Margrieta, Margrita

Marguerite (French) a form of Margaret.
Margarete, Margaretha, Margarethe, Margarite, Margerite, Marguaretta, Marguarette, Marguarite, Marguerette, Margurite

Mari (Japanese) ball. (Spanish) a form of Mary.

Maria ☙ 🄶 (Hebrew) bitter; sea of bitterness. (Italian, Spanish) a form of Mary.
Maie, Malia, Marea, Mareah, Mariabella, Mariae, Mariesa, Mariessa, Mariha, Marija, Mariya, Mariyah, Marja, Marya

María (Hebrew) a form of Maria.

María de la Concepción (Spanish) Mary of the conception.

María de la Paz (Spanish) Mary of peace.

María de las Nieves (Spanish) Mary of the snows.

María de las Victorias (Spanish) victorious Mary.

María de los Angeles (Spanish) angelic Mary.

María de los Milagros (Spanish) miraculous Mary.

María del Mar (Spanish) Mary of the sea.

María Inmaculada (Spanish) immaculate Mary.

María José (Latin) name composed of María and José.

María Noel (Latin) name composed of María and Noel.

Mariah ☙ 🄶 (Hebrew) a form of Mary. See also Moriah.
Maraia, Maraya, Mariyah, Marriah, Meriah

Mariam 🄶 (Hebrew) a form of Miriam.
Mariama, Mariame, Mariem, Meryam

Marian 🄶 (English) a form of Maryann.
Mariana, Mariane, Mariann, Marianne, Mariene, Marion, Marrian, Marriann

Marián (Spanish) a short form of Mariana.

Mariana, Marianna (Spanish) forms of Marian.
Marriana, Marrianna, Maryana, Maryanna

Mariane, Marianne 🄶 (English) forms of Marian.
Marrianne, Maryanne

Marianela (Spanish) a combination of Mariana and Estela.

Mariángeles (Spanish) a combination of María and Ángeles.

Maribel (French) beautiful. (English) a combination of Maria + Bell.
Marabel, Marbelle, Mariabella, Maribella,

Maribelle, Maridel, Marybel, Marybella,
Marybelle

Marice (Italian) a form of Mary. See also
Maris.
Marica, Marise, Marisse

Maricela (Latin) a form of Marcella.
Maricel, Mariceli, Maricelia, Maricella,
Maricely

Marichi (Indian) name of a star.

Marichika (Indian) mirage; ray.

Maricruz (Spanish) a combination of María
and Cruz.

Maridel (English) a form of Maribel.

Marie **G** (French) a form of Mary.
Maree, Marietta, Marrie

Mariel, Marielle (German, Dutch) forms of
Mary.
Marial, Marieke, Marielana, Mariele, Marieli,
Marielie, Marieline, Mariell, Mariellen,
Marielsie, Mariely, Marielys

Mariela, Mariella (German, Dutch) forms
of Mary.

Marieta (Hebrew) a form of María.

Marietta (Italian) a familiar form of Marie.
Maretta, Marette, Mariet, Mariette,
Marrietta

Marieve (American) a combination of Mary
+ Eve.

Marigold (English) Mary's gold. Botany: a
plant with yellow or orange flowers.
Marygold

Marika (Dutch, Slavic) a form of Mary.
Marica, Marieke, Marija, Marijke, Marikah,
Marike, Marikia, Marikka, Mariska, Mariske,
Marrika, Maryk, Maryka, Merica, Merika

Mariko (Japanese) circle.

Marilee (American) a combination of Mary
+ Lee.
Marili, Marilie, Marily, Marrilee, Marylea,
Marylee, Merrilee, Merrili, Merrily

Marilena (Spanish) a combination of María
and Elena.

Marilina (Latin) a combination of María
and Elina.

Marilla (Hebrew, German) a form of Mary.
Marella, Marelle

Marilou (American) a form of Marylou.
Marilu, Mariluz

Marilú (Spanish) a combination of María
and Luz.

Marilyn (Hebrew) Mary's line of descendants.
See also Merilyn.
Maralin, Maralyn, Maralyne, Maralynn,
Maralynne, Marelyn, Marilin, Marillyn,
Marilyne, Marilynn, Marilynne, Marlyn,
Marolyn, Marralynn, Marrilin, Marrilyn,
Marrilynn, Marrilynne, Marylin, Marylinn,
Marylyn, Marylyne, Marylynn, Marylynne

Marina **G** (Latin) sea. See also Maren.
Mareena, Marena, Marenka, Marinae,
Marinah, Marinda, Marindi, Marinka,
Marinna, Marrina, Maryna, Merina, Mirena

Mariña (Latin) a form of Marina.

Marinés (Spanish) a combination of María
and Inés.

Marini (Swahili) healthy; pretty.

Mario **B** (Italian) a form of Marino (see
Boys' Names).

Mariola (Italian) a form of María.

Marion **G** (French) a form of Mary.
Marrian, Marrion, Maryon, Maryonn

Marión (Spanish) a form of María.

Maris (Latin) sea. (Greek) a short form of
Amaris, Damaris. See also Marice.
Maries, Marise, Marris, Marys, Maryse,
Meris

Marisa (Latin) sea.
Maresa, Mariesa, Mariessa, Marisela,
Marissa, Marita, Mariza, Marrisa, Marrissa,
Marysa, Maryse, Maryssa, Merisa

Marisabel (Spanish) a combination of
María and Isabel.

Marisabela (Spanish) a form of Marisabel.

Marisel (Spanish) a combination of María
and Isabel.

Marisela **G** (Latin) a form of Marisa.
Mariseli, Marisella, Marishelle, Marissela

Marisha (Russian) a familiar form of Mary.
Mareshah, Marishenka, Marishka, Mariska

Marisol (Spanish) sunny sea.
Marise, Marizol, Marysol

Marissa ✺ **G** (Latin) a form of Maris,
Marisa.
Maressa, Marisa, Marisha, Marissah,
Marisse, Marizza, Marrissa, Marrissia,
Maryssa, Merissa, Morissa

Marit (Aramaic) lady.
Marita, Marite

Marita (Spanish) a form of Marisa.
(Aramaic) a form of Marit.
Marité, Maritha

Maritza (Arabic) blessed.
Maritsa, Maritssa

Mariyan (Arabic) purity.
Mariya, Mariyah, Mariyana, Mariyanna

Marja (Finnish) a form of Mary.
Marjae, Marjatta, Marjie

Marjan (Persian) coral. (Polish) a form of
Mary.
Marjaneh, Marjanna

Marjie (Scottish) a familiar form of Marjorie.
Marje, Marjey, Marji, Marjy

Marjolaine 🄶 (French) marjoram.

Marjorie (Greek) a familiar form of
Margaret. (Scottish) a form of Mary.
*Majorie, Marge, Margeree, Margerey,
Margerie, Margery, Margorie, Margory,
Marjarie, Marjary, Marjerie, Marjery, Marjie,
Marjorey, Marjori, Marjory*

Mark 🄱 (Latin) a form of Marcus.

Markayla (American) a combination or
Mary + Kayla.
*Marka, Markaiah, Markaya, Markayel,
Markeela, Markel*

Markeisha (English) a combination of Mary
+ Keisha.
*Markasha, Markeisa, Markeisia, Markesha,
Markeshia, Markesia, Markiesha, Markisha,
Markishia, Marquesha*

Markell 🄱 (Latin) a form of Mark.

Markita (Czech) a form of Margaret.
*Marka, Markeah, Markeda, Markee,
Markeeta, Marketa, Marketta, Marki, Markia,
Markie, Markieta, Markita, Markitha,
Markketta, Merkate*

Marla (English) a short form of Marlena,
Marlene.
Marlah, Marlea, Marleah

Marlana (English) a form of Marlena.
*Marlaena, Marlaina, Marlainna, Marlania,
Marlanna, Marlayna, Marleana*

Marlee (English) a form of Marlene.
Marlea, Marleah, Marleigh

Marlen 🄶 (Greek, Slavic) a form of
Marlene.

Marlena (German) a form of Marlene.
*Marla, Marlaina, Marlana, Marlanna,
Marleena, Marlina, Marlinda, Marlyna,
Marna*

Marlene (Greek) high tower. (Slavic) a form
of Magdalen.
*Marla, Marlaine, Marlane, Marlayne, Marlee,
Marleen, Marleene, Marlen, Marlena,
Marlenne, Marley, Marlin, Marline, Marlyne*

Marley 🄶 (English) a familiar form of
Marlene.
Marlee, Marli, Marlie, Marly

Marlis (English) a combination of Maria +
Lisa.
*Marles, Marlisa, Marlise, Marlys, Marlyse,
Marlyssa*

Marlo (English) a form of Mary.
Marlow, Marlowe

Marlon 🄱 (English) a form of Marlo.

Marlyn 🄶 (Hebrew) a short form of Marilyn.
(Greek, Slavic) a form of Marlene.
Marlynn, Marlynne

Marmara (Greek) sparkling, shining.
Marmee

Marni (Hebrew) a form of Marnie.
Marnia, Marnique

Marnie (Hebrew) a short form of Marnina.
*Marna, Marnay, Marne, Marnee, Marney,
Marni, Marnisha, Marnja, Marny, Marnya,
Marnye*

Marnina (Hebrew) rejoice.

Maro (Japanese) myself.

Maromisa (Japanese) a combination of
Maro+ Misa.

Maroula (Greek) a form of Mary.

Marquesa (Spanish) she who works with a
hammer.

Marquez 🄱 (Portuguese) a form of
Marques (see Boys' Names).

Marquilla (Spanish) bitter.

Marquis 🄱 (French) a form of Marquise.

Marquise 🄱 (French) noblewoman.
*Markese, Marquees, Marquese, Marquice,
Marquies, Marquiese, Marquis, Marquisa,
Marquisee, Marquisha, Marquisse,
Marquiste*

Marquisha (American) a form of Marquise.
Marquiesha, Marquisia

Marquita (Spanish) a form of Marcia.
*Marquatte, Marqueda, Marquedia, Marquee,
Marqueita, Marquet, Marqueta, Marquetta,*

Marquette, Marquia, Marquida, Marquietta, Marquitra, Marquitia, Marquitta

Marrim (Chinese) tribal name in Manpur state.

Marsala (Italian) from Marseilles, France.
Marsali, Marseilles

Marsha (English) a form of Marcia.
Marcha, Marshae, Marshay, Marshel, Marshele, Marshell, Marshia, Marshiela

Marshall **B** (French) caretaker of the horses; military title.

Marta (English) a short form of Martha, Martina.
Martá, Martä, Marte, Martia, Marttaha, Merta

Martha (Aramaic) lady; sorrowful. Bible: a friend of Jesus. See also Mardi.
Maita, Marta, Martaha, Marth, Marthan, Marthe, Marthy, Marti, Marticka, Martita, Mattie, Matty, Martus, Martuska, Masia

Marti **G** (English) a familiar form of Martha, Martina.
Martie, Marty

Martin **B** (Latin, French) a form of Martinus (see Boys' Names).

Martina **G** (Latin) martial, warlike. See also Tina.
Marta, Martel, Martella, Martelle, Martene, Marthena, Marthina, Marthine, Marti, Martine, Martinia, Martino, Martisha, Martosia, Martoya, Martricia, Martrina, Martyna, Martyne, Martynne

Martine **G** (Latin) a form of Martina.

Martiniana (Latin) she who was consecrated to the god Mars; born in May.

Martirio (Spanish) martyrdom.

Martiza (Arabic) blessed.

Maru (Japanese) round.

Maruca (Spanish) a form of Mary.
Maruja, Maruska

Marvella (French) marvelous.
Marva, Marvel, Marvela, Marvele, Marvelle, Marvely, Marvetta, Marvette, Marvia, Marvina

Mary ✤ **G** (Hebrew) bitter; sea of bitterness. Bible: the mother of Jesus. See also Maija, Malia, Maren, Mariah, Marjorie, Maura, Maureen, Miriam, Mitzi, Moira, Mollie, Muriel.
Maira, Maire, Manette, Manka, Manon, Manya, Mara, Mare, Maree, Maren, Marella, Marelle, Mari, Maria, Maricara, Marice, Marie, Mariel, Mariela, Marika, Marilla, Marilyn, Marion, Mariquilla, Mariquita, Marisha, Marja, Marjan, Marlo, Maroula, Maruca, Marye, Maryla, Marynia, Masha, Mavra, Mendi, Mérane, Meridel, Mhairie, Mirja, Molara, Morag, Moya

Marya (Arabic) purity; bright whiteness.
Maryah

Maryam (Hebrew) a form of Miriam.
Maryama

Maryann, Maryanne (English) combinations of Mary + Ann.
Marian, Marryann, Maryan, Meryem

Marybeth (American) a combination of Mary + Beth.
Maribeth, Maribette

Maryellen (American) a combination of Mary + Ellen.
Mariellen

Maryjane (American) a combination of Mary + Jane.

Maryjo (American) a combination of Mary + Jo.
Marijo, Maryjoe

Marykate (American) a combination of Mary + Kate.
Mary-Kate

Marylou (American) a combination of Mary + Lou.
Marilou, Marylu

Maryssa (Latin) a form of Marissa.
Maryse, Marysia

Masa (Japanese) good and straight-forward.

Masago (Japanese) sands of time.

Masako (Japanese) justice.

Masani (Luganda) gap toothed.

Masaye (Japanese) blessedly proper.

Masayo (Japanese) she who thrives for a lifetime.

Masha (Russian) a form of Mary.
Mashka, Mashenka

Mashika (Swahili) born during the rainy season.
Masika

Mason **B** (French) stone worker.

Massimo **B** (Italian) greatest.

Masu (Japanese) increase.

Masumi (Indian) innocence.

Matana (Hebrew) gift.
Matat

Mat-Chinoi (Chinese) serpent goddess, mother of the Chinese.

Mathena (Hebrew) gift of God.

Mathew B (Hebrew) a form of Matthew.

Mathieu B (French) a form of Matthew.

Mathilde (German) a form of Matilda.
Mathilda

Matilda (German) powerful battler. See also Maud, Tilda, Tillie.
Máda, Mahaut, Maitilde, Malkin, Mat, Matelda, Mathilde, , Mattie, Matty, Matusha, Matylda

Matilde (German) a form of Matilda.

Matrika (Hindi) mother. Religion: a name for the Hindu goddess Shakti in the form of the letters of the alphabet.
Matrica

Matsuko (Japanese) pine tree.

Matsuyo (Japanese) she who is as strong as a pine tree.

Mattea (Hebrew) gift of God.
Matea, Mathea, Mathia, Matia, Matte, Matthea, Matthia, Mattia, Matya

Matthew B (Hebrew) gift of God.

Mattie, Matty (English) familiar forms of Martha, Matilda.
Matte, Mattey, Matti, Mattye

Matusha (Spanish) a form of Matilda.
Matuja, Matuxa

Maud, Maude (English) short forms of Madeline, Matilda. See also Madison.
Maudie, Maudine, Maudlin

Maura (Irish) dark. A form of Mary, Maureen. See also Moira.
Maurah, Maure, Maurette, Mauricette, Maurita

Maureen (French) dark. (Irish) a form of Mary.
Maura, Maurene, Maurine, Mo, Moreen, Morena, Morene, Morine, Morreen, Moureen

Maurelle (French) dark; elfin.
Mauriel, Mauriell, Maurielle

Mauricia (Spanish) a form of Mauro.

Mauricio B (Spanish) a form of Maurice (see Boys' Names).

Maurise (French) dark skinned; moor; marshland.
Maurisa, Maurissa, Maurita, Maurizia

Mauro (Latin) a short form of Maurice (see Boys' Names).

Mausam (Indian) season.

Mausami (Indian) seasonal.

Maushmi (Indian) monsoon wind.

Mausi (Native American) plucked flower.

Mausumi (Indian) beauty; monsoon wind.

Mauve (French) violet colored.

Maverick B (American) independent.

Mavis (French) thrush, songbird. See also Maeve.
Mavies, Mavin, Mavine, Mavon, Mavra

Max B (Latin) a short form of Maxine.

Maxie (English) a familiar form of Maxine.
Maxi, Maxy

Máxima (Latin) great one.

Maxime B (Latin) a form of Maxine.

Maximiana (Spanish) a form of Máxima.

Maximiliana (Latin) eldest of all.

Maxine G (Latin) greatest.
Max, Maxa, Maxeen, Maxena, Maxene, Maxie, Maxima, Maxime, Maximiliane, Maxina, Maxna, Maxyne

Maxwell B (English) great spring.

May (Latin) great. (Arabic) discerning. (English) flower; month of May. See also Mae, Maia.
Maj, Mayberry, Maybeth, Mayday, Maydee, Maydena, Maye, Mayela, Mayella, Mayetta, Mayrene

Maya ❧ (Hindi) God's creative power. (Greek) mother; grandmother. (Latin) great. A form of Maia.
Mayam, Mya

Mayako (Japanese) child of Maya.

Maybeline (Latin) a familiar form of Mabel.

Maygan, Maygen (Irish) forms of Megan.
Mayghan, Maygon

Maylyn (American) a combination of May + Lynn.
Mayelene, Mayleen, Maylen, Maylene, Maylin, Maylon, Maylynn, Maylynne

Mayoko (Japanese) child of Mayo.

Mayoree (Tai) beautiful.
Mayra, Mayree, Mayariya

Mayra (Tai) a form of Mayoree.

Maysa (Arabic) walks with a proud stride.

Maysaa, Mayyada (Indian) to walk with a swinging gait.

Maysoon (Indian) of beautiful face and body.

Maysun (Arabic) beautiful.

Mayte (Spanish) a combination of María and Teresa.

Mayu (Japanese) she who possesses truth and reason.

Mayuka, Mayukhi (Indian) peahen.

Mayuko (Japanese) child of Mayu.

Mayumi (Japanese) beautiful truth.

Mayura (Indian) illusion.

Mayurakhsi (Indian) eye of the peacock.

Mayuri (Indian) peahen.

Mayurika (Indian) baby peahen.

Mazel (Hebrew) lucky.
Mazal, Mazala, Mazella

Mc Kenna **G** (American) a form of Mackenna.

Mc Kenzie **G** (Irish) a form of Mackenzie.

Mckay **B** (Scottish) child of Kay.

Mckayla **G** (American) a form of Makayla.
Mckaela, Mckaila, Mckala, Mckaylah,

Mckayle, Mckaylee, Mckayleh, Mckayleigh, Mckayli, Mckaylia, Mckaylie

Mckell **G** (American) a form of Makell.
Mckelle

Mckenna **G** (American) a form of Mackenna.
Mckena, Mckennah, Mckinna, Mckinnah

Mckenzie **G** (Scottish) a form of Mackenzie.
Mckennzie, Mckensee, Mckensey, McKensi, Mckensi, Mckensie, Mckensy, Mckenze, Mckenzee, Mckenzey, Mckenzi, Mckenzy, Mckenzye, Mekensie, Mekenzi, Mekenzie

Mckinley **B** (Irish) daughter of the learned ruler.
Mckinlee, Mckinleigh, Mckinlie, Mckinnley

Mckinzie (American) a form of Mackenzie.
Mckinsey, Mckinze, Mckinzea, Mckinzee, Mckinzi, Mckinzy, Mckynze, Mckynzie

Me (Japanese) triple branch.

Mead, Meade **B** (Greek) honey wine.

Meagan (Irish) a form of Megan.
Maegan, Meagain, Meagann, Meagen, Meagin, Meagnah, Meagon

Meaghan **G** (Welsh) a form of Megan.
Maeghan, Meaghann, Meaghen, Meahgan

Meara (Irish) mirthful.

Mecha (Latin) a form of Mercedes.

Meda (Native American) prophet; priestess.

Medea (Greek) ruling. (Latin) middle. Mythology: a sorceress who helped Jason get the Golden Fleece.
Medeia

Medha (Indian) wisdom, intellect.

Medina (Arabic) History: the site of Muhammed's tomb.
Medinah

Medini (Indian) earth.

Medora (Greek) mother's gift. Literature: a character in Lord Byron's poem *The Corsair*.

Mee (Chinese) beautiful.

Meena (Hindi) blue semiprecious stone; bird. (Greek, German, Dutch) a form of Mena.

Meenakshi (Indian) eye.

Meenal (Indian) precious gem.

Meg (English) a short form of Margaret, Megan.

Megan ✿ **G** (Greek) pearl; great. (Irish) a form of Margaret.
Maegan, Magan, Magen, Meagan, Meaghan, Magen, Maygan, Maygen, Meg, Megane, Megann, Megean, Megen, Meggan, Meggen, Meggie, Meghan, Megyn, Meygan

Megane (Irish) a form of Megan.
Magana, Meganna, Meganne

Megara (Greek) first. Mythology: Heracles's first wife.

Meggie (English) a familiar form of Margaret, Megan.
Meggi, Meggy

Meghamala (Indian) an array of clouds.

Meghan **G** (Welsh) a form of Megan.
Meeghan, Meehan, Megha, Meghana, Meghane, Meghann, Meghanne, Meghean, Meghen, Mehgan, Mehgen

Meghna (Indian) the Ganges River.

Megumi (Japanese) blessing; merry; charity.

Meha (Indian) intelligent; rain.

Mehadi (Hindi) flower.

Mehak (Indian) sweet smell, fragrance.

Mehbooba (Indian) beloved.

Meher (Indian) grace.

Mehira (Hebrew) speedy; energetic.
Mahira

Mehitabel (Hebrew) benefited by trusting God.
Mehetabel, Mehitabelle, Hetty, Hitty

Mehri (Persian) kind; lovable; sunny.

Mehrunissa (Indian) benevolent.

Mei (Hawaiian) great. (Chinese) a short form of Meiying.
Meiko

Meira (Hebrew) light.
Meera

Meit (Burmese) affectionate.

Meiying (Chinese) beautiful flower.
Mei

Meka G (Hebrew) a familiar form of Michaela.

Mekayla (American) a form of Michaela.
Mekaela, Mekaila, Mekayela, Mekaylia

Mekhala (Indian) girdle.

Mel BG (Portuguese, Spanish) sweet as honey.

Mela (Hindi) religious service. (Polish) a form of Melanie.

Melana (Russian) a form of Melanie.
Melanna, Melashka, Melenka, Milana

Melanie �W G (Greek) dark skinned.
Malania, Malanie, Meila, Meilani, Meilin, Melaine, Melainie, Melana, Melane, Melanee, Melaney, Melani, Melania, Mélanie, Melanka, Melanney, Melannie, Melany, Melanya, Melasya, Melayne, Melenia, Mella, Mellanie, Melonie, Melya, Milena, Milya

Melantha (Greek) dark flower.

Melba (Greek) soft; slender. (Latin) mallow flower.
Malva, Melva

Mele (Hawaiian) song; poem.

Melesse (Ethiopian) eternal.
Mellesse

Melia (German) a short form of Amelia.
Melcia, Melea, Meleah, Meleia, Meleisha, Meli, Meliah, Melida, Melika, Mema

Melina (Latin) canary yellow. (Greek) a short form of Melinda.
Melaina, Meleana, Meleena, Melena, Meline, Melinia, Melinna, Melynna

Melinda (Greek) honey. See also Linda, Melina, Mindy.
Maillie, Malinda, Melinde, Melinder, Mellinda, Melynda, Melyne, Milinda, Milynda, Mylenda, Mylinda, Mylynda

Meliora (Latin) better.
Melior, Meliori, Mellear, Melyor, Melyora

Melisa (Greek) a form of Melissa.
Melesa, Mélisa, Melise, Melisha, Melishia, Melisia, Meliza, Melizah, Mellisa, Melosa, Milisa, Mylisa, Mylisia

Melisande (French) a form of Melissa, Millicent.
Lisandra, Malisande, Malissande, Malyssandre, Melesande, Melisandra, Melisandre, Mélisandré, Melisenda, Melissande, Melissandre, Mellisande, Melond, Melysande, Melyssandre

Melissa G (Greek) honey bee. See also Elissa, Lissa, Melisande, Millicent.
Malissa, Mallissa, Melessa, Meleta, Melisa, Mélissa, Melisse, Melissia, Mellie, Mellissa, Melly, Melyssa, Milissa, Millie, Milly, Missy, Molissia, Mollissa, Mylissa, Mylissia

Melita (Greek) a form of Melissa. (Spanish) a short form of Carmelita (see Carmelit).
Malita, Meleeta, Melitta, Melitza, Melletta, Molita

Melitona (Greek) she who was born in Malta.

Melly (American) a familiar form of names beginning with "Mel." See also Millie.
Meli, Melie, Melli, Mellie

Melody (Greek) melody. See also Elodie.
Meladia, Melodee, Melodey, Melodi, Melodia, Melodie, Melodyann, Melodye

Melonie (American) a form of Melanie.
Melloney, Mellonie, Mellony, Melonee, Meloney, Meloni, Melonie, Melonnie, Melony

Melosa (Spanish) sweet; tender.

Melosia (Spanish) sweet.

Melusina (Greek) she who is sweet as honey.

Melvina (Irish) armored chief. See also Malvina.
Melevine, Melva, Melveen, Melvena, Melvene, Melvonna

Melyne (Greek) a short form of Melinda.
Melyn, Melynn, Melynne

Melyssa (Greek) a form of Melissa.

Mena (German, Dutch) strong. (Greek) a short form of Philomena. History: Menes is believed to be the first king of Egypt.
Menah

Menaha (Indian) celestial damsel.

Menaka (Indian) celestial damsel; heavenly beauty.

Mendi (Basque) a form of Mary.
Menda, Mendy

Meng (Chinese) dream.

Meranda (Latin) a form of Miranda.
Merana, Merandah, Merandia, Merannda

Mérane (French) a form of Mary.
Meraine, Merrane

Mercé (Spanish) a form of Mercedes.

Mercedes (Latin) reward, payment. (Spanish) merciful.
Mercades, Mercadez, Mercadie, Meceades, Merced, Mercede, Mercedees, Mercedeez, Mercedez, Mercedies, Mercedis, Mersade, Mersades

Merces (Latin) favors, graces; skills.

Mercia (English) a form of Marcia. History: an ancient British kingdom.

Mercy (English) compassionate, merciful. See also Merry.
Mercey, Merci, Mercie, Mercille, Mersey

Meredith **G** (Welsh) protector of the sea.
Meredeth, Meredithe, Meredy, Meredyth, Meredythe, Meridath, Merideth, Meridie, Meridith, Merridie, Merridith, Merry

Meri (Finnish) sea. (Irish) a short form of Meriel.

Meriel (Irish) shining sea.
Meri, Merial, Meriol, Meryl

Merilyn (English) a combination of Merry + Lynn. See also Marilyn.
Merelyn, Merlyn, Merralyn, Merrelyn, Merrilyn

Merissa (Latin) a form of Marissa.
Merisa, Merisha

Merle **B** (Latin, French) blackbird.
Merl, Merla, Merlina, Merline, Merola, Murle, Myrle, Myrleen, Myrlene, Myrline

Merry (English) cheerful, happy. A familiar form of Mercy, Meredith.
Merie, Merree, Merri, Merrie, Merrielle, Merrilee, Merrili, Merrilyn, Merris, Merrita

Meryl (German) famous. (Irish) shining sea. A form of Meriel, Muriel.
Meral, Merel, Merrall, Merrell, Merril, Merrile, Merrill, Merryl, Meryle, Meryll

Mesha (Hindi) another name for the zodiac sign Aries.
Meshal

Meta (German) a short form of Margaret.
Metta, Mette, Metti

Mhairie (Scottish) a form of Mary.
Mhaire, Mhairi, Mhari, Mhary

Mi, Mye (Chinese) obsessive.

Mia ❀ (Italian) mine. A familiar form of Michaela, Michelle.
Mea, Meah, Miah

Miaka (Japanese) influential.

Mian (Chinese) continuous, unbroken.

Miao (Chinese) wonderful.

Micaela (Hebrew) a form of Michaela.
Macaela, Micaella, Micaila, Micala, Miceala

Micah **B** (Hebrew) a short form of Michael. Bible: one of the Old Testament prophets.
Meecah, Mica, Micha, Mika, Myca, Mycah

Micayla, Michayla (Hebrew) forms of Michaela.
Micayle, Micaylee, Michaylah

Michael **B** (Hebrew) who is like God?

Michaela **G** (Hebrew) a form of Michael.
Machaela, Maika, Makaela, Makaila, Makala, Makayla, Mia, Micaela, Micayla, Michael, Michaelann, Michala, Michayla, Michealia, Michaelina, Michaeline, Michaell, Michaella, Michaelyn, Michaila, Michal, Michala, Micheal, Micheala, Michelia, Michelina, Michelle, Michely, Michelyn, Micheyla, Micheline, Micki, Miguela, Mikaela, Mikala, Misha, Mycala, Mychael, Mychal

Michal **B** (Hebrew) a form of Michaela, Michele.

Michala (Hebrew) a form of Michaela.
Michalann, Michale, Michalene, Michalin, Mchalina, Michalisha, Michalla, Michalle, Michayla, Michayle, Michela

Micheal **B** (Hebrew) a form of Michael.

Michel 🅱 (French) a form of Michelle.

Michele 🅶 (Italian) a form of Michaela.
Michaelle, Michal, Michela

Michelle ♛ 🅶 (French) a form of
Michael. See also Shelley.
*Machealle, Machele, Machell, Machella,
Machelle, Mechelle, Meichelle, Meschell,
Meshell, Meshelle, Mia, Michel, Michéle,
Michell, Michella, Michellene, Michellyn,
Mischel, Mischelle, Mishael, Mishaela,
Mishayla, Mishell, Mishelle, Mitchele,
Mitchelle*

Michi (Japanese) righteous way.
Miche, Michee, Michiko

Michiye (Japanese) beautiful, blessed
knowledge.

Michiyo (Japanese) a lifetime of beautiful
wisdom.

Mickael 🅱 (Hebrew) a form of Mikaela.

Micki (American) a familiar form of
Michaela.
*Mickee, Mickeeya, Mickia, Mickie, Micky,
Mickya, Miquia*

Micol (Hebrew) she who is queen.

Midori (Japanese) green.

Mieko (Japanese) prosperous.
Mieke

Mielikki (Finnish) pleasing.

Miette (French) small; sweet.

Migina (Omaha) new moon.

Mignon (French) dainty, petite; graceful.
*Mignonette, Minnionette, Minnonette,
Minyonette, Minyonne*

Miguel 🅱 (Portuguese, Spanish) a form of
Michael.

Miguela (Spanish) a form of Michaela.
*Micquel, Miguelina, Miguelita, Miquel,
Miquela, Miquella*

Mihika (Indian) dewdrop.

Miho (Japanese) beautiful; keep; step.

Mihoko (Japanese) child of Mihoko.

Mika 🅶 (Japanese) new moon. (Russian)
God's child. (Native American) wise racoon.
(Hebrew) a form of Micah. (Latin) a form of
Dominica.
Mikah, Mikka

Mikael 🅱 (Hebrew) a form of Mikaela.

Mikaela (Hebrew) a form of Michaela.
*Mekaela, Mekala, Mickael, Mickaela,
Mickala, Mickalla, Mickeel, Mickell,
Mickelle, Mikael, Mikail, Mikaila, Mikal,
Mikalene, Mikalovna, Mikalyn, Mikayla,
Mikea, Mikeisha, Mikeita, Mikel, Mikela,
Mikele, Mikell, Mikella, Mikesha, Mikeya,
Mikhaela, Mikie, Mikiela, Mikkel, Mikyla,
Mykaela*

Mikako (Japanese) beautiful girl.

Mikala (Hebrew) a form of Michaela.
*Mickala, Mikalah, Mikale, Mikalea, Mikalee,
Mikaleh*

Mikayla (American) a form of Mikaela.
Mekayla, Mickayla, Mikala, Mikayle, Mikyla

Mikayo (Japanese) a lifetime of beauty.

Mikazuki (Japanese) moon of the third
night.

Mikel 🅱 (Hebrew) a form of Mikaela.

Mikhaela (American) a form of Mikaela.
*Mikhail, Mikhaila, Mikhala, Mikhalea,
Mikhayla, Mikhelle*

Miki 🅶 (Japanese) flower stem.
*Mikia, Mikiala, Mikie, Mikita, Mikiyo, Mikki,
Mikkie, Mikkiya, Mikko, Miko*

Mikiko (Japanese) beautiful and precious
child.

Mikino (Japanese) a beautiful beginning.

Mila (Russian) dear one. (Italian, Slavic) a
short form of Camila, Ludmilla.
Milah, Milla

Milada (Czech) my love.
Mila, Milady

Milagres (Latin) wonder, miracle; prodigy.

Milagros (Spanish) miracle.
Mila, Milagritos, Milagro, Milagrosa, Mirari

Milana (Italian) from Milan, Italy. (Russian)
a form of Melana.
*Milan, Milane, Milani, Milanka, Milanna,
Milanne*

Milba, Milburga (German) kind protector.

Milca, Milcal (Hebrew) queen.

Mildereda (German) she who speaks soft,
kind words.

Mildred (English) gentle counselor.
Mil, Mila, Mildrene, Mildrid, Millie, Milly

Mildreda (German) counselor.

Milena (Greek, Hebrew, Russian) a form of
Ludmilla, Magdalen, Melanie.
Mila, Milène, Milenia, Milenny, Milini, Millini

Mileta (German) generous, merciful.

Milia (German) industrious. A short form of
Amelia, Emily.
Mila, Milka, Milla, Milya

Miliani (Hawaiian) caress.
Milanni, Miliany

Mililani **BG** (Hawaiian) heavenly caress.
Milliani

Milissa (Greek) a form of Melissa.
Milessa, Milisa, Millisa, Millissa

Milka (Czech) a form of Amelia.
Milica, Milika

Millaray (Mapuche) golden or silver flower;
fragrant, pleasant flower; subtle essence of
fragrance.

Millicent (English) industrious. (Greek) a
form of Melissa. See also Lissa, Melisande.
*Melicent, Meliscent, Mellicent, Mellisent,
Melly, Milicent, Milisent, Millie, Milliestone,
Millisent, Milly, Milzie, Missy*

Millie, Milly (English) familiar forms of
Amelia, Camille, Emily, Kamila, Melissa,
Mildred, Millicent.
Mili, Milla, Millee, Milley, Millie, Mylie

Milva (German) kind protector.

Mima (Burmese) woman.
Mimma

Mimi (French) a familiar form of Miriam.

Mina **G** (German) love. (Persian) blue sky.
(Arabic) harbor. (Japanese) south. A short
form of names ending in "mina."
Meena, Mena, Min

Minako (Japanese) child of Mina.

Minakshi (Indian) fish eyes.

Minal (Native American) fruit.

Minati (Indian) prayer.

Minda (Hindi) knowledge.

Mindy (Greek) a familiar form of Melinda.
*Mindee, Mindi, Mindie, Mindyanne,
Mindylee, Myndy*

Mine (Japanese) peak; mountain range.
Mineko

Minerva (Latin) wise. Mythology: the goddess
of wisdom.
Merva, Minivera, Minnie, Myna

Minette (French) faithful defender.
Minnette, Minnita

Mineyo (Japanese) she who reaches the
summit.

Ming (Chinese) shiny; hope of tomorrow.

Ming Ue, Ming Yue, Ming-Yue (Chinese)
bright moon.

Mingmei (Chinese) smart; beautiful.

Minia (German) great, strong.

Miniami (Japanese) a form of Mina.

Minka (Polish) a short form of Wilhelmina.

Minna (German) a short form of
Wilhelmina.
Mina, Minka, Minnie, Minta

Minnie (American) a familiar form of Mina,
Minerva, Minna, Wilhelmina.
Mini, Minie, Minne, Minni, Minny

Minori (Japanese) truth; pear.

Minowa (Native American) singer.
Minowah

Minta (English) Literature: originally coined
by playwright Sir John Vanbrugh in his
comedy *The Confederacy*.
Minty

Minu (Indian) a gem, precious stone.

Minya (Osage) older sister.

Mio (Japanese) three times as strong.

Mira (Latin) wonderful. (Spanish) look,
gaze. A short form of Almira, Amira,
Marabel, Mirabel, Miranda.
Mirae, Mirra, Mirah

Mirabel (Latin) beautiful.
Mira, Mirabell, Mirabella, Mirabelle, Mirable

Miracle **G** (Latin) wonder, marvel.

Mirai (Japanese) future.

Mirana (Spanish) a form of Miranda.

Miranda **G** (Latin) strange; wonderful;
admirable. Literature: the heroine of
Shakespeare's *The Tempest*. See also Randi.
*Maranda, Marenda, Meranda, Mira, Miran,
Miranada, Mirandia, Mirinda, Mirindé,
Mironda, Mirranda, Muranda, Myranda*

Miraya (Indian) Lord Krishna's devotee.

Mireille (Hebrew) God spoke. (Latin)
wonderful.
*Mireil, Mirel, Mirella, Mirelle, Mirelys,
Mireya, Mireyda, Mirielle, Mirilla, Myrella,
Myrilla*

Mireya (Hebrew) a form of Mireille.
Mireea, Miriah, Miryah

Girls M–R

Girls M–R

Miri (Gypsy) a short form of Miriam.
Miria, Miriah

Miriam 🅖 (Hebrew) bitter; sea of bitterness.
Bible: the original form of Mary. See also
Macia, Mimi, Mitzi.
*Mairwen, Mariam, Maryam, Miram, Mirham,
Miri, Miriain, Miriama, Miriame, Mirian,
Mirit, Mirjam, Mirjana, Mirriam, Mirrian,
Miryam, Miryan, Myriam*

Mirium (Indian) wished-for child.

Mirta, Mirtha (Greek) crown of myrtle.

Mirya (French) she who has earned
everyone's admiration.

Misa, Misaye (Japanese) beautiful helper.

Misael 🅑 (Hebrew) a form of Michael.

Misaki (Japanese) she who blooms
beautifully.

Misako (Japanese) child of Misa.

Misao (Japanese) fidelity.

Misayo (Japanese) a lifelong beauty.

Misha 🅖 (Russian) a form of Michaela.
Mischa, Mishae

Mishka (Indian) gift of love.

Mishti (Indian) sweet person.

Misora (Japanese) beautiful sky.

Misri (Indian) sweet.

Missy (English) a familiar form of Melissa,
Millicent.
Missi, Missie

Misty 🅖 (English) shrouded by mist.
*Missty, Mistee, Mistey, Misti, Mistie, Mistin,
Mistina, Mistral, Mistylynn, Mystee, Mysti,
Mystie*

Mitali (Indian) friendly.

Mitchell 🅑 (English) a form of Michael.

Mitra (Hindi) Religion: god of daylight.
(Persian) angel.
Mita

Mitsu (Japanese) shine, reflect.

Mitsuki (Japanese) beautiful month.

Mitsuko (Japanese) child of Mitsu.

Mitsuye (Japanese) blessed beauty.

Mitsuyo (Japanese) beautiful third daughter.

Mituna (Moquelumnan) like a fish wrapped
up in leaves.

Mitzi (German) a form of Mary, Miriam.
Mieze, Mitzee, Mitzie, Mitzy

Miwa (Japanese) wise eyes.
Miwako

Miya (Japanese) temple.
Miyah, Miyana, Miyanna

Miyabi (Japanese) elegant.

Miyako (Japanese) she who is a beautiful
girl.

Miye (Japanese) beautiful inlet.

Miyeko (Japanese) beautiful and blessed girl.

Miyo (Japanese) beautiful generation.
Miyoko, Miyuko

Miyuki (Japanese) snow.

Moana (Hawaiian) ocean; fragrance.

Mocha (Arabic) chocolate-flavored coffee.
Moka

Modesty (Latin) modest.
*Modesta, Modeste, Modestia, Modestie,
Modestina, Modestine, Modestus*

Moe (Japanese) bud, sprout.

Moeka (Japanese) sprouting flower.

Moema (Tupi) sweet.

Moena (Japanese) bud; vegetable.

Moesha (American) a short form of
Monisha.
Myesha

Mohala (Hawaiian) flowers in bloom.
Moala

Mohamed 🅑 (Arabic) a form of
Muhammad (see Boys' Names).

Mohana (Indian) attractive; charming.

Moira (Irish) great. A form of Mary. See also
Maura.
*Moirae, Moirah, Moire, Moya, Moyra,
Moyrah*

Molara (Basque) a form of Mary.

Mollie (Irish) a form of Molly.
Moli, Molie, Molli

Molly ❦ 🅖 (Irish) a familiar form of Mary.
Moll, Mollee, Molley, Mollissa

Momiji (Japanese) a Japanese maple tree.

Momo (Japanese) peaches.

Momoka (Japanese) the scent of a peach.

Momoko (Japanese) child of Momo.

Momone (Japanese) she whose life is made of many great deeds.

Momose (Japanese) one hundred stars.

Momoye (Japanese) a hundred blessings.

Momoyo (Japanese) one hundred; world; lifetime.

Mon (Japanese) gate.

Mona **G** (Irish) noble. (Greek) a short form of Monica, Ramona, Rimona.
Moina, Monah, Mone, Monea, Monna, Moyna

Monal (Indian) bird.

Monalisa (Indian) noble.

Monet (French) Art: Claude Monet was a leading French impressionist remembered for his paintings of water lilies.
Monae, Monay, Monee

Monica **G** (Greek) solitary. (Latin) advisor.
Mona, Monca, Monee, Monia, Monic, Mónica, Monice, Monicia, Monicka, Monika, Monique, Monise, Monn, Monnica, Monnie, Monya

Monifa (Yoruba) I have my luck.

Monika (German) a form of Monica.
Moneka, Monieka, Monike, Monnika

Monique (French) a form of Monica.
Moneeke, Moneik, Moniqua, Moniquea, Moniquie, Munique

Monisha (American) a combination of Monica + Aisha.
Moesha, Moneisha, Monishia

Monita (Spanish) noble.

Montana **G** (Spanish) mountain.
Geography: a U.S. state.
Montanna

Montrell **B** (French) a form of Montreal (see Boys' Names).

Moon (Korean) beautiful; song; able; family; professional; add.

Mora (Spanish) blueberry.
Morae, Morea, Moria, Morita

Morela (Polish) apricot.
Morelia, Morelle

Morena (Irish) a form of Maureen.

Morgan ✿ **G** (Welsh) seashore. Literature: Morgan le Fay was the half-sister of King Arthur.
Morgance, Morgane, Morganetta, Morganette, Morganica, Morgann, Morganne, Morgen, Morghan, Morgyn, Morrigan

Morgana (Welsh) a form of Morgan.
Morganna

Morganda (Spanish) a form of Morgana.

Morghan (Welsh) a form of Morgan.
Morghen, Morghin, Morghyn

Moriah **G** (Hebrew) God is my teacher. (French) dark skinned. Bible: the mountain on which the Temple of Solomon was built. See also Mariah.
Moria, Moriel, Morit, Morria, Morriah

Morie (Japanese) bay.

Morowa (Akan) queen.

Morrisa (Latin) dark skinned; moor; marshland.
Morisa, Morissa, Morrissa

Moselle (Hebrew) drawn from the water. (French) a white wine.
Mozelle

Moses **B** (Hebrew) drawn out of the water. (Egyptian) child.

Mosi **B** (Swahili) first-born.

Moswen **BG** (Tswana) white.

Motoko (Japanese) beginning child.

Motoye (Japanese) origin; branch.

Motoyo (Japanese) the beginning of a new generation.

Moubani (Indian) a flower.

Mouna (Arabic) wish, desire.
Moona, Moonia, Mounia, Muna, Munia

Mrena (Slavic) white eyes.
Mren

Mridu (Indian) gentle.

Mridula (Indian) an ideal woman.

Mrigakshi, Mriganayani (Indian) one with beautiful eyes.

Mrinali (Indian) lotus.

Mrinalika (Indian) stem of the lotus.

Mrinalini (Indian) lotus.

Mrinmayee (Indian) a deer's eye.

Mrinmayi (Indian) of the earth.

Mritsa (Indian) the good earth.

Mrittika (Indian) Mother Earth.

Mrunali (Indian) lotus stalk.

Mu (Chinese) wood.

Mubarak (Indian) blessed.

Mudra (Indian) healing hand movement.

Mudrika (Indian) ring.

Mufeeda (Indian) useful.

Mugdha (Indian) innocent young girl.

Muhja (Indian) heart's blood; soul.

Mukta (Indian) pearl.

Mukti (Indian) liberation.

Mukula, Mukulita (Indian) bud.

Mulan (Chinese) magnolia blossom.

Mumtaz (Arabic) distinguished.

Muneera (Indian) illuminating; shedding light.

Munira (Arabic) she who is the source of light.

Muniya (Indian) name of a bird.

Mura (Japanese) village.

Muracaki (Japanese) purple.

Muriel (Arabic) myrrh. (Irish) shining sea. A form of Mary. See also Meryl.
Merial, Meriel, Meriol, Merrial, Merriel, Muire, Murial, Muriell, Murielle

Musetta (French) little bagpipe.
Musette

Musheera (Indian) giving counsel.

Muskaan (Indian) smile; happiness.

Muslimah (Arabic) devout believer.

Musu (Indian) beautiful.

Mutsuko (Japanese) child of Mutsu.

Mya ❦ 🄶 (Burmese) emerald. (Italian) a form of Mia.
My, Myah, Myia, Myiah

My-duyen (Vietnamese) gentle.

Myesha (American) a form of Moesha.
Myeisha, Myeshia, Myiesha, Myisha

Mykaela, Mykayla (American) forms of Mikaela.
Mykael, Mykaila, Mykal, Mykala, Mykaleen, Mykel, Mykela, Mykyla

Myla (English) merciful.

Mylene (Greek) dark.
Mylaine, Mylana, Mylee, Myleen

Myles 🄱 (Latin) soldier. (German) a form of Miles (see Boys' Names).

Myra (Latin) fragrant ointment.
Mayra, Myrena, Myria

Myranda (Latin) a form of Miranda.
Myrandah, Myrandia, Myrannda

Myriam 🄶 (American) a form of Miriam.
Myriame, Myryam

Myrna (Irish) beloved.
Merna, Mirna, Morna, Muirna

Myrtle (Greek) dark green shrub.
Mertis, Mertle, Mirtle, Myrta, Myrtia, Myrtias, Myrtice, Myrtie, Myrtilla, Myrtis

Mythili (Indian) another name for the goddess Sita.

Mythri (Indian) friendship.

N

N 🄱 (American) an initial used as a first name.

Na (Chinese) graceful.

Naaz (Indian) pride.

Nabeeha (Indian) intelligent.

Nabila (Arabic) born to nobility.
Nabeela, Nabiha, Nabilah

Nachni (Indian) dancer; suggestive look.

Nadal (Catalonian) a form of Natividad.

Nadda (Arabic) generous; dewy.
Nada

Nadeeda (Indian) equal to another person; rival.

Nadette (French) a short form of Bernadette.

Nadia (French, Slavic) hopeful.
Nadea, Nadenka, Nadezhda, Nadiah, Nadie, Nadija, Nadijah, Nadine, Nadiya, Nadiyah, Nadja, Nadjae, Nadjah, Nadka, Nadusha, Nady, Nadya

Nadine 🄶 (French, Slavic) a form of Nadia.
Nadean, Nadeana, Nadeen, Nadena, Nadene, Nadien, Nadin, Nadina, Nadyne, Naidene, Naidine

Nadira (Arabic) rare, precious.
Naadirah, Nadirah

Nadwa (Indian) council.

Naeema (Indian) blessing; living an enjoyable life.

Naeva (French) a form of Eve.
Nahvon

Nafuna (Luganda) born feet first.

Nagida (Hebrew) noble; prosperous.
Nagda, Nageeda

Nagina (Indian) jewel.

Nagisa (Japanese) from the shore.

Nahid (Persian) Mythology: another name for Venus, the goddess of love and beauty.

Nahimana (Dakota) mystic.

Nahla (Indian) a drink of water.

Naho (Japanese) a type of red apple; shore.

Nahoko (Japanese) child of Naho.

Naiara (Spanish) reference to the Virgin Mary.

Naida (Greek) water nymph.
Naiad, Naiya, Nayad, Nyad

Naigisa (Japanese) beach, shore.

Naija (Indian) daughter of wisdom.

Naila (Arabic) successful.
Nailah

Naina (Indian) eyes.

Nairi (Armenian) land of rivers. History: a name for ancient Armenia.
Naira, Naire, Nayra

Naís (Spanish) a form of Inés.

Naisha (Indian) special.

Naishadha (Indian) poetry.

Naiya (Greek) a form of Naida.
Naia, Naiyana, Naja, Najah, Naya

Najaah (Indian) success.

Najam (Arabic) star.
Naja, Najma

Najat (Indian) safety.

Najeeba (Indian) of noble birth.

Najila (Arabic) brilliant eyes.
Naja, Najah, Najia, Najja, Najla

Najiya (Indian) safe.

Najwa (Indian) confidential talk, secret conversation.

Najya (Indian) victorious.

Nakeisha (American) a combination of the prefix Na + Keisha.
Nakeesha, Nakesha, Nakeshea, Nakeshia, Nakeysha, Nakiesha, Nakisha, Nekeisha

Nakeita (American) a form of Nikita.
Nakeeta, Nakeitha, Nakeithra, Nakeitra, Nakeitress, Nakeitta, Nakeittia, Naketta, Nakieta, Nakitha, Nakitia, Nakitta, Nakyta

Nakia **G** (Arabic) pure.
Nakea, Nakeia, Nakeya, Nakeyah, Nakeyia, Nakiah, Nakiaya, Nakiea, Nakiya, Nakiyah, Nekia

Nakita (American) a form of Nikita.
Nakkita, Naquita

Nakula (Indian) another name for the goddess Parvati.

Nalani (Hawaiian) calm as the heavens.
Nalanie, Nalany

Nalika (Indian) lotus.

Nalini (Indian) lotus; sweet nectar.

Nam Ha (Vietnamese) willow tree.

Namaha (Indian) respect; pray.

Ñambi (Guarani) curative herb.

Nami (Japanese) wave.
Namika, Namiko

Namita (Indian) humble.

Namrata (Indian) politeness.

Namya (Indian) worthy of honor.

Nan (German) a short form of Fernanda. (English) a form of Ann.
Nana, Nanice, Nanine, Nanna, Nanon

Nana (Hawaiian) spring.

Naná (Greek) she who is very young.

Nanako (Japanese) child of Nana.

Nanami (Japanese) beautiful vegetable.

Nanase (Japanese) seven stars.

Nanci (English) a form of Nancy.
Nancie, Nancsi, Nansi

Nancy 🄶 (English) gracious. A familiar
form of Nan.
*Nainsi, Nance, Nancee, Nancey, Nanci,
Nancine, Nancye, Nanette, Nanice, Nanncey,
Nanncy, Nanouk, Nansee, Nansey, Nanuk*

Nandika (Indian) water vessel made of clay.

Nandita (Indian) cheerful.

Nanette (French) a form of Nancy.
*Nan, Nanete, Nannette, Nettie, Nineta,
Ninete, Ninetta, Ninette, Nini, Ninita,
Ninnetta, Ninnette, Nynette*

Nani (Greek) charming. (Hawaiian)
beautiful.
Nanni, Nannie, Nanny

Nantilde (German) daring in combat.

Nao (Japanese) truthful; pleasing.

Naoki (Japanese) straight tree.

Naoko (Japanese) child of Nao.

Naolin (Spanish) sun god of the Mexican
people.

Naomi (Hebrew) pleasant, beautiful. Bible:
Ruth's mother-in-law.
*Naoma, Naomia, Naomie, Naomy, Navit,
Neoma, Neomi, Noami, Noemi, Noma, Nomi,
Nyomi*

Naomí (Hebrew) a form of Naomi.

Naomie (Hebrew) a form of Naomi.
Naome, Naomee, Noemie

Napea (Latin) from the valleys.

Nara (Greek) happy. (English) north.
(Japanese) oak.
Narah

Narcissa (Greek) daffodil. Mythology:
Narcissus was the youth who fell in love
with his own reflection.
*Narcessa, Narcisa, Narcisse, Narcyssa,
Narissa, Narkissa*

Narda (Latin) fervently devoted.

Narelle (Australian) woman from the sea.
Narel

Nari (Japanese) thunder.
Narie, Nariko

Narmada (Hindi) pleasure giver.

Naroa (Basque) tranquil, peaceful.

Narois (Indian) flower.

Narpendyah (Indian) queen.

Naseen (Indian) cool breeze.

Nashawna (American) a combination of the
prefix Na + Shawna.
*Nashan, Nashana, Nashanda, Nashaun,
Nashauna, Nashaunda, Nashauwna,
Nashawn, Nasheena, Nashounda, Nashuana*

Nashida (Indian) student.

Nashita (Indian) energetic and full of life.

Nashota (Native American) double; second-
born twin.

Nasiha (Indian) one who gives valuable
advice.

Nasira (Indian) victorious; helper.

Nastasia (Greek) a form of Anastasia.
*Nastasha, Nastashia, Nastasja, Nastassa,
Nastassia, Nastassiya, Nastassja, Nastassya,
Nastasya, Nastazia, Nastisija, Nastka,
Nastusya, Nastya*

Nasya (Hebrew) miracle.
Nasia, Nasyah

Nata (Sanskrit) dancer. (Latin) swimmer.
(Native American) speaker; creator. (Polish,
Russian) a form of Natalie. See also Nadia.
Natia, Natka, Natya

Natacha (Russian) a form of Natasha.
Natachia, Natacia, Naticha

Natalee, Natali (Latin) forms of Natalie.
Natale, Nataleh, Nataleigh, Nattlee

Natalí (Spanish) a form of Natalia.

Natalia (Russian) a form of Natalie. See also
Talia.
*Nacia, Natala, Natalea, Nataliia, Natalija,
Natalina, Nataliya, Nataliyah, Natalja,
Natalka, Natallea, Natallia, Natalya,
Nathalia, Natka*

Natália (Hungarian, Portuguese) a form of
Natalie.

Natalie ✹ 🄶 (Latin) born on Christmas
day. See also Nata, Natasha, Noel, Talia.
*Nat, Natalee, Natali, Natalia, Nataliee,
Nataline, Natalle, Natallie, Nataly, Natelie,
Nathalie, Nathaly, Natie, Natilie, Natlie,
Nattalie, Nattilie*

Nataline (Latin) a form of Natalie.
Natalene, Nataléne, Natalyn

Natalle (French) a form of Natalie.
Natale

Nataly (Latin) a form of Natalie.
Nathaly, Natally, Natallye

Natane (Arapaho) daughter.
Natanne

Natania (Hebrew) gift of God.
Natanya, Natée, Nathania, Nathenia, Netania, Nethania

Natara (Arabic) sacrifice.
Natori, Natoria

Natasha **G** (Russian) a form of Natalie. See also Stacey, Tasha.
Nahtasha, Natacha, Natasa, Natascha, Natashah, Natashea, Natashenka, Natashia, Natashiea, Natashja, Natashka, Natasia, Natassia, Natassija, Natassja, Natasza, Natausha, Natawsha, Natesha, Nateshia, Nathasha, Nathassha, Natisha, Natishia, Natosha, Netasha, Notosha

Natesa (Hindi) cosmic dancer. Religion: another name for the Hindu god Shiva.
Natisa, Natissa

Nathália (Portuguese) a form of Natalie.

Nathalie, Nathaly (Latin) forms of Natalie.
Nathalee, Nathali, Nathalia, Nathalya

Nathan **B** (Hebrew) a short form of Nathaniel.

Nathaniel **B** (Hebrew) gift of God.

Natie (English) a familiar form of Natalie.
Nati, Natti, Nattie, Natty

Natividad (Spanish) nativity.

Natori **G** (Arabic) a form of Natara.

Natosha (Russian) a form of Natasha.
Natoshia, Natoshya, Netosha, Notosha

Natsu, Natsuyo (Japanese) summer's child.

Natsuki (Japanese) vegetable month.

Natsuko (Japanese) summer child.

Natsumi (Japanese) she who is like the sea in summer.

Natsuye (Japanese) summer harbor.

Natun, Navami, Navashree, Navdha, Naveta (Indian) new.

Nauka (Indian) boat.

Nava (Hebrew) beautiful; pleasant.
Navah, Naveh, Navit

Navaneeta (Indian) butter.

Navdeep **BG** (Sikh) new light.

Navneeta (Indian) like butter.

Navya (Indian) young.

Nawar (Indian) flower.

Nayana (Indian) one with attractive eyes.

Nayantara (Indian) star of the eyes.

Nayara (Basque) swallow.

Nayeli (Zapotec) I love you.

Nayely (Irish) a form of Neila.
Naeyli, Nayelia, Nayelli, Nayelly, Nayla

Nayoko (Japanese) child of Nayo.

Nazaaha (Indian) purity; righteousness; honesty.

Nazarena (Hebrew) native of Nazareth.

Nazarha (Indian) a sight.

Nazaria (Spanish) dedicated to God.

Nazeeha (Indian) honest.

Nazeera (Indian) like; equal; matching.

Nazeeya (Indian) optimistic and full of hope.

Nazima (Indian) song.

Neala (Irish) a form of Neila.
Nayela, Naylea, Naylia, Nealia, Neela, Neelia, Neila

Necha (Spanish) a form of Agnes.
Necho

Neci **BG** (Hungarian) fiery, intense.
Necia, Necie

Neda (Slavic) born on Sunday.
Nedah, Nedi, Nedia, Neida

Nedda (English) prosperous guardian.
Neddi, Neddie, Neddy

Neeharika, Neharika (Indian) dewdrops.

Neelabja (Indian) blue lotus.

Neelaja (Indian) river starting from the blue mountain.

Neelakshi (Indian) blue-eyed girl.

Neelanjana (Indian) blue.

Neelima (Indian) blue sky.

Neely (Irish) a familiar form of Neila, Nelia.
Nealee, Nealie, Nealy, Neelee, Neeley, Neeli, Neelie, Neili, Neilie

Neema (Swahili) born during prosperous times.

Neena (Spanish) a form of Nina.
Neenah, Nena

Neepa (Indian) a flower.

Neeraja (Indian) lotus.

Girls M–R

Neeru (Indian) light.

Neeti (Indian) good behavior.

Neftali (Hebrew) she who fights and ends up victorious.

Nehal (Indian) rainy; beautiful.

Neila (Irish) champion. See also Neala, Neely.
Nayely, Neilah, Neile, Neilia, Neilla, Neille

Nekeisha (American) a form of Nakeisha.
Nechesa, Neikeishia, Nekesha, Nekeshia, Nekiesha, Nekisha, Nekysha

Nekia (Arabic) a form of Nakia.
Nekeya, Nekiya, Nekiyah, Nekya, Nekiya

Nelia (Spanish) yellow. (Latin) a familiar form of Cornelia.
Neelia, Neely, Neelya, Nela, Neli, Nelka, Nila

Nélida (Greek) compassionate, merciful.

Nelle (Greek) stone.

Nellie, Nelly 🄶 (English) familiar forms of Cornelia, Eleanor, Helen, Prunella.
Nel, Neli, Nell, Nella, Nelley, Nelli, Nellianne, Nellice, Nellis, Nelma

Nelson 🄱 (English) child of Neil (see Boys' Names).

Nemesia (Greek) she who administers justice.

Nene (Japanese) she who is peaceful and tranquil.

Nenet (Egyptian) born near the sea. Mythology: Nunet was the goddess of the sea.

Neng (Chinese) ability.

Neola (Greek) youthful.
Neolla

Neona (Greek) new moon.

Nereida (Greek) a form of Nerine.
Nereyda, Nereyida, Nerida

Nerine (Greek) sea nymph.
Nereida, Nerina, Nerita, Nerline

Nerissa (Greek) sea nymph. See also Rissa.
Narice, Narissa, Nerice, Nerisa, Nerisse, Nerrisa, Nerys, Neryssa

Nesayem (Indian) flower.

Nesipa (Fijian) a form of Elizabeth.

Nessa (Scandinavian) promontory. (Greek) a short form of Agnes. See also Nessie.
Nesa, Nesha, Neshia, Nesiah, Nessia, Nesta, Nevsa, Neysa, Neysha, Neyshia

Nessie (Greek) a familiar form of Agnes, Nessa, Vanessa.
Nese, Neshie, Nesho, Nesi, Ness, Nessi, Nessy, Nest, Neys

Nestor 🄱 (Greek) traveler; wise.

Neta (Hebrew) plant, shrub. See also Nettie.
Netia, Netta, Nettia

Netis (Native American) trustworthy.

Netra (Indian) eyes.

Netravati (Indian) one with beautiful eyes.

Nettie (French) a familiar form of Annette, Nanette, Antoinette.
Neti, Netie, Netta, Netti, Netty, Nety

Neva (Spanish) snow. (English) new. Geography: a river in Russia.
Neiva, Neve, Nevia, Neyva, Nieve, Niva, Nivea, Nivia

Nevada 🄶 (Spanish) snow. Geography: a western U.S. state.
Neiva, Neva

Nevaeh � (American) the word *heaven* spelled backward.

Neves (Portuguese) a form of Nieves.

Nevina (Irish) worshipper of the saint.
Neveen, Nevein, Nevena, Neveyan, Nevin, Nivena

Neylan (Turkish) fulfilled wish.
Neya, Neyla

Neza (Slavic) a form of Agnes.

Ngoc 🄶 (Vietnamese) jade.

Ngoc Bich (Vietnamese) beautiful, pretty.

Ngu (Vietnamese) the South River.

Nguyet (Vietnamese) sapphire jade.

Nhi (Vietnamese) stupid; to sleep; fisherman; fifth number; written language.

Nhu (Vietnamese) moon child.

Nhung (Vietnamese) little one.

Ni, Niu (Chinese) girl.

Nia 🄶 (Irish) a familiar form of Neila. Mythology: Nia Ben Aur was a legendary Welsh woman.
Neya, Niah, Niajia, Niya, Nya

Niabi (Osage) fawn.

Nian (Chinese) a period of life.

Nibaal (Indian) arrows.

Nicanora (Spanish) victorious army.

Niceta (Spanish) victorious one.

Nichelle (American) a combination of Nicole + Michelle. Culture: Nichelle Nichols was the first African American woman featured in a television drama (*Star Trek*). *Nichele, Nichell, Nishelle*

Nichole (French) a form of Nicole. *Nichol, Nichola, Nicholle*

Nicki (French) a familiar form of Nicole. *Nicci, Nickey, Nickeya, Nickia, Nickie, Nickiya, Nicky, Niki*

Nickolas **B** (Greek) a form of Nicholas (see Boys' Names).

Nickole (French) a form of Nicole. *Nickol*

Nico **B** (Greek) a short form of Nicholas (see Boys' Names).

Nicola **G** (Italian) a form of Nicole. *Nacola, Necola, Nichola, Nickola, Nicolea, Nicolla, Nikkola, Nikola, Nikolia, Nykola*

Nicolas **B** (Italian) a form of Nicholas (see Boys' Names).

Nicolasa (Spanish) victorious people.

Nicole ✼ **G** (French) a form of Nicholas (see Boys' Names). See also Colette, Cosette, Nikita. *Nacole, Necole, Nica, Nichole, Nicia, Nicki, Nickole, Nicol, Nicola, Nicolette, Nicoli, Nicolie, Nicoline, Nicolle, Nikayla, Nikelle, Nikki, Niquole, Nocole, Nycole*

Nicoleta (Greek) winner over all.

Nicolette **G** (French) a form of Nicole. *Nicholette, Nicoletta, Nicollete, Nicollette, Nikkolette, Nikoleta, Nikoletta, Nikolette*

Nicoline (French) a familiar form of Nicole. *Nicholine, Nicholyn, Nicoleen, Nicolene, Nicolina, Nicolyn, Nicolyne, Nicolynn, Nicolynne, Nikolene, Nikolina, Nikoline*

Nicolle (French) a form of Nicole. *Nicholle*

Nida (Omaha) Mythology: an elflike creature. *Nidda*

Nidhi (Indian) wealth.

Nidia (Latin) nest. *Nidi, Nidya*

Nidra (Indian) sleep.

Niesha (American) pure. (Scandinavian) a form of Nissa. *Neisha, Neishia, Neissia, Nesha, Neshia, Nesia, Nessia, Niessia, Nisha, Nyesha*

Nieves (Latin) refers to the blessed Virgin Mary.

Nige (Latin) dark night. *Nigea, Nigela, Nija, Nijae, Nijah*

Nigel **B** (Latin) dark night.

Niharika (Indian) nebula.

Nika (Russian) belonging to God. *Nikka*

Nikayla, Nikelle (American) forms of Nicole. *Nikeille, Nikel, Nikela, Nikelie*

Nike **BG** (Greek) victorious. Mythology: the goddess of victory.

Nikhita (Indian) sharp; earth.

Niki **G** (Russian) a short form of Nikita. (American) a familiar form of Nicole. *Nikia, Nikiah*

Nikita **G** (Russian) victorious people. *Nakeita, Nakata, Niki, Nikitah, Nikitia, Nikitta, Nikki, Nikkita, Niquita, Niquitta*

Nikki **G** (American) a familiar form of Nicole, Nikita. *Nicki, Nikia, Nikkea, Nikkey, Nikkia, Nikkiah, Nikkie, Nikko, Nikky*

Nikko **B** (American) a form of Nikki.

Niko **B** (Hungarian) a form of Nicholas (see Boys' Names).

Nikola **B** (French) a form of Nikole. (Italian) a form of Nicola.

Nikole (French) a form of Nicole. *Nikkole, Nikkolie, Nikola, Nikole, Nikolena, Nicolia, Nikolina, Nikolle*

Nila **G** (Latin) Geography: the Nile River is in Africa. (Irish) a form of Neila. *Nilah, Nilesia, Nyla*

Nilakshi (Indian) blue eyed.

Nilambari (Indian) clothed in blue.

Nilanjana (Indian) one with blue eyes.

Nilasha (Indian) blueness.

Nilaya (Indian) abode, house.

Nilda (Spanish) a short form of Brunilda.

Nileen, Nivedita (Indian) surrendered.

Nili (Hebrew) Botany: a pea plant that yields indigo.

Nilima (Indian) blue.

Girls M–R

Niloufer (Indian) celestial.

Nilutha (Indian) providing water.

Nima (Hebrew) thread. (Arabic) blessing.
Nema, Niama, Nimali

Nimaat (Indian) blessings; loans.

Nimia (Latin) she who has a lot of ambition.

Nimisha (Indian) momentary.

Nina 🄖 (Hebrew) a familiar form of
Hannah. (Spanish) girl. (Native American)
mighty.
*Neena, Ninah, Ninacska, Ninja, Ninna,
Ninon, Ninosca, Ninoshka*

Ninarika (Indian) misty.

Ninfa (Greek) young wife.

Ning (Chinese) peace, rest, tranquility.

Ninon (French) a form of Nina.

Niobe (Greek) she who rejuvenates.

Nipa (Indian) one who watches over.

Niral (Indian) calm.

Niramayee (Indian) pure, clean, spotless.

Nirel (Hebrew) light of God.
Nirali, Nirelle

Nirmala (Indian) clean.

Nirmayi (Indian) without blemish.

Nirosha (Indian) pious.

Nirupa (Indian) a decree.

Nirupama (Indian) matchless.

Nirveli (Hindi) water child.

Nisa (Arabic) woman.

Nisha (American) a form of Niesha, Nissa.
Niasha, Nishay

Nishi (Japanese) west.

Nishita (Indian) alert.

Nishithini (Indian) night.

Nishka (Indian) honest.

Nishtha (Indian) faith.

Nissa (Hebrew) sign, emblem.
(Scandinavian) friendly elf; brownie. See
also Nyssa.
Nisha, Nisse, Nissie, Nissy

Nita (Hebrew) planter. (Choctaw) bear.
(Spanish) a short form of Anita, Juanita.
Nitai, Nitha, Nithai, Nitika

Nitara (Hindi) deeply rooted.

Nitasha (American) a form of Natasha.
Nitasia, Niteisha, Nitisha, Nitishia

Niti (Indian) ethics.

Nitsa (Greek) a form of Helen.

Nituna (Native American) daughter.

Nitya (Indian) eternal.

Nityapriya (Indian) ever-pleasing.

Nitza (Hebrew) flower bud.
Nitzah, Nitzana, Nitzanit, Niza, Nizah

Niveditha (Indian) offered to God.

Nivriti (Indian) bliss.

Nivritti (Indian) nonattachment.

Nixie (German) water sprite.

Niya (Irish) a form of Nia.
Niyah, Niyana, Niyia, Nyia

Niyati (Indian) destiny.

Nizana (Hebrew) a form of Nitza.
Nitzana, Nitzania, Zana

Noah 🄱 (Hebrew) peaceful, restful.

Nobuko (Japanese) the girl who reaches out
to others.

Nobuye (Japanese) blessed belief.

Noe 🄱 (Czech, French) a form of Noah.

Noel 🄱 (Latin) Christmas. See also Natalie.
*Noël, Noela, Noelani, Noele, Noeleen,
Noelene, Noelia, Noeline, Noelle, Noelyn,
Noelynn, Nohely, Noleen, Novelenn, Novelia,
Nowel, Noweleen, Nowell*

Noelani (Hawaiian) beautiful one from
heaven.
Noela

Noelle (French) Christmas.
Noell, Noella, Noelleen, Noelly, Noellyn

Noemi (Hebrew) a form of Naomi.
Noam, Noemie, Noemy, Nohemi, Nomi

Noemí (Hebrew) a form of Noemi.

Noemie (Hebrew) a form of Noemi.

Noemy (Hebrew) a form of Noemi.
Noamy

Noga (Hebrew) morning light.

Nohely (Latin) a form of Noel.
Noeli, Noelie, Noely, Nohal, Noheli

Nokomis (Dakota) moon daughter.

Nola (Latin) small bell. (Irish) famous; noble. A short form of Fionnula.
Nuala

Nolan **B** (Irish) famous; noble.

Noleta (Latin) unwilling.
Nolita

Nollie **B** (English) a familiar form of Magnolia.
Nolia, Nolle, Nolley, Nolli, Nolly

Noma (Hawaiian) a form of Norma.

Nominanda (Latin) she who will be elected.

Nona (Latin) ninth.
Nonah, Noni, Nonia, Nonie, Nonna, Nonnah, Nonya

Noopur, Nupoor, Nupura (Indian) anklet.

Noor (Aramaic) a form of Nura.
Noorie, Nour, Nur

Noorjehan (Indian) light of the world.

Nora **G** (Greek) light. A familiar form of Eleanor, Honora, Leonore.
Norah, Noreen

Noreen (Irish) a form of Eleanor, Nora. (Latin) a familiar form of Norma.
Noorin, Noreena, Noreene, Noren, Norena, Norene, Norina, Norine, Nureen

Norell (Scandinavian) from the north.
Narell, Narelle, Norela, Norelle, Norely

Nori (Japanese) law, tradition.
Noria, Norico, Noriko, Norita

Norika, Norike (Japanese) athletic.

Norma (Latin) rule, precept.
Noma, Noreen, Normi, Normie

Norman **B** (French) Norseman.

Nouf (Indian) highest point on a mountain.

Nova (Latin) new. A short form of Novella, Novia. (Hopi) butterfly chaser. Astronomy: a star that releases bright bursts of energy.

Novella (Latin) newcomer.
Nova, Novela

Novia (Spanish) sweetheart.
Nova, Novka, Nuvia

Nozomi (Japanese) hope.

Nu (Burmese) tender. (Vietnamese) girl.
Nue

Nuala (Irish) a short form of Fionnula.
Nola, Nula

Nuan (Chinese) genial.

Nubia (Latin) cloud.

Nudhar (Indian) gold.

Nuela (Spanish) a form of Amelia.

Nuha (Indian) intelligence; mind.

Numa, Numas (Greek) she who lays down rules and establishes laws.

Numeria (Latin) she who elaborates, who enumerates.

Nuna (Native American) land.

Nuncia (Latin) she who leaves messages, who informs.

Nunciata (Latin) messenger.
Nunzia

Nunila (Spanish) ninth daughter.

Nunu (Vietnamese) gentle, peaceful.

Nuo (Chinese) graceful.

Nura (Aramaic) light.
Noor, Noora, Noorah, Noura, Nurah

Nuria (Aramaic) the Lord's light.
Nuri, Nuriel, Nurin

Nurita (Hebrew) Botany: a flower with red and yellow blossoms.
Nurit

Nuru **BG** (Swahili) daylight.

Nusayba (Indian) proper name.

Nusi (Hungarian) a form of Hannah.

Nusrat (Indian) help.

Nutan (Indian) new; fresh.

Nuwa (Chinese) mother goddess. Mythology: another name for Nü-gua, the creator of mankind.

Nuzha (Indian) pleasure trip; excursion spot.

Nya (Irish) a form of Nia.
Nyaa, Nyah, Nyia

Nycole (French) a form of Nicole.
Nychelle, Nycolette, Nycolle

Nydia (Latin) nest.
Nyda

Nyesha (American) a form of Niesha.
Nyeisha, Nyeshia

Nyla (Latin, Irish) a form of Nila.
Nylah

Nyoko (Japanese) gem, treasure.

Nyomi (Hebrew) a form of Naomi.
Nyome, Nyomee, Nyomie

Nyree (Maori) sea.
Nyra, Nyrie

Nyssa (Greek) beginning. See also Nissa.
Nisha, Nissi, Nissy, Nyasia, Nysa

Nyusha (Russian) a form of Agnes.
Nyushenka, Nyushka

Oba 🅱🅶 (Yoruba) chief, ruler.

Obdulia (Latin) she who takes away sadness and pain.

Obelia (Greek) needle.

Oceana (Greek) ocean. Mythology: Oceanus was the god of the ocean.
Ocean, Oceananna, Oceane, Oceania, Oceanna, Oceanne, Oceaonna, Oceon

Octavia 🅶 (Latin) eighth. See also Tavia.
Octabia, Octaviah, Octaviais, Octavice, Octavie, Octavienne, Octavio, Octavious, Octavise, Octavya, Octivia, Otavia, Ottavia

Octaviana (Spanish) a form of Octavia.

Octavio 🅱 (Latin) a form of Octavia.

Odalis, Odalys (Spanish) a form of Odilia.

Odeda (Hebrew) strong; courageous.

Odele (Greek) melody, song.
Odelet, Odelette, Odell, Odelle

Odelia (Greek) ode; melodic. (Hebrew) I will praise God. (French) wealthy. See also Odetta.
Oda, Odeelia, Odeleya, Odelina, Odelinda, Odelyn, Odila, Odile

Odella (English) wood hill.
Odela, Odelle, Odelyn

Odera (Hebrew) plough.

Odessa (Greek) odyssey, long voyage.
Adesha, Adeshia, Adessa, Adessia, Odessia

Odetta (German, French) a form of Odelia.
Oddetta, Odette

Odilia (Greek, Hebrew, French) a form of Odelia.

Odina (Algonquin) mountain.

Oditi (Indian) dawn.

Ofelia (Greek) a form of Ophelia.
Ofeelia, Ofilia

Ofélia (Portuguese) a form of Ophelia.

Ofira (Hebrew) gold.
Ofarrah, Ophira

Ofra (Hebrew) a form of Aphra.
Ofrat

Ogin (Native American) wild rose.

Oh, Ohara (Japanese) meditative.

Ohanna (Hebrew) God's gracious gift.

Oja (Indian) vitality.

Ojal (Indian) vision.

Ojasvi (Indian) bright.

Ojaswini (Indian) lustrous.

Oka (Japanese) flowering cherry blossom.

Okalani (Hawaiian) heaven.
Okilani

Okei (Japanese) from Oki; ocean.

Oki (Japanese) middle of the ocean.
Okie

Oksana (Latin) a form of Osanna.
Oksanna

Ola 🅶 (Greek) a short form of Olesia. (Scandinavian) ancestor.

Olalla (Spanish) well-spoken one.

Olathe (Native American) beautiful.
Olathia

Olaya (Greek) she who speaks well.

Oleda (Spanish) a form of Alida. See also Leda.
Oleta, Olida, Olita

Olena (Russian) a form of Helen.
Oleena, Olenka, Olenna, Olenya, Olya

Olesia (Greek) a form of Alexandra.
Cesya, Ola, Olecia, Oleesha, Oleishia, Olesha, Olesya, Olexa, Olice, Olicia, Olisha, Olishia, Ollicia

Oletha (Scandinavian) nimble.
Oleta, Yaletha

Olethea (Latin) truthful. See also Alethea.
Oleta

Olga (Scandinavian) holy. See also Helga, Olivia.
Olenka, Olia, Olja, Ollya, Olva, Olya

Oliana (Polynesian) oleander.

Olina (Hawaiian) filled with happiness.

Olinda (Latin) scented. (Spanish) protector of property. (Greek) a form of Yolanda.

Olisa (Ibo) God.

Olive (Latin) olive tree.
Oliff, Oliffe, Olivet, Olivette

Oliver **B** (Latin) olive tree. (Scandinavian) kind; affectionate.

Oliveria (Latin) affectionate.

Olivia ✿ **G** (Latin) a form of Olive. (English) a form of Olga. See also Liv, Livia.
Alivia, Alyvia, Olevia, Oliva, Olivea, Oliveia, Olivetta, Olivi, Olivianne, Olivya, Oliwia, Ollie, Olva, Olyvia

Olívia (Portuguese) a form of Olivia.

Olivier **B** (French) a form of Oliver.

Ollie **BG** (English) a familiar form of Olivia.
Olla, Olly, Ollye

Olwen (Welsh) white footprint.
Olwenn, Olwin, Olwyn, Olwyne, Olwynne

Olympia (Greek) heavenly.
Olimpia, Olympe, Olympie

Olyvia (Latin) a form of Olivia.

Oma (Hebrew) reverent. (German) grandmother. (Arabic) highest.

Omaira (Arabic) red.
Omar, Omara, Omarah, Omari, Omaria, Omarra

Omaja (Indian) result of spiritual unity.

Omana (Indian) a woman.

Omar **B** (Arabic) a form of Omaira.

Omega (Greek) last, final, end. Linguistics: the last letter in the Greek alphabet.

Omisha (Indian) goddess of birth and death.

Ona (Latin, Irish) a form of Oona, Una. (English) river.

Onatah (Iroquois) daughter of the earth and the corn spirit.

Onawa (Native American) wide awake.
Onaja, Onajah

Ondine (Latin) a form of Undine.
Ondene, Ondina, Ondyne

Ondrea (Czech) a form of Andrea.
Ohndrea, Ohndreea, Ohndreya, Ohndria, Ondraya, Ondreana, Ondreea, Ondreya, Ondria, Ondrianna, Ondriea

Oneida (Native American) eagerly awaited.
Onida, Onyda

Onella (Hungarian) a form of Helen.

Onesha (American) a combination of Ondrea + Aisha.
Oneshia, Onesia, Onessa, Onessia, Onethia, Oniesha, Onisha

Oni (Yoruba) born on holy ground.
Onnie

Onora (Latin) a form of Honora.
Onoria, Onorine, Ornora

Oona (Latin, Irish) a form of Una.
Ona, Onna, Onnie, Oonagh, Oonie

Oorja (Indian) energy.

Opa (Choctaw) owl. (German) grandfather.

Opal (Hindi) precious stone.
Opale, Opalina, Opaline

Ophelia (Greek) helper. Literature: Hamlet's love interest in the Shakespearean play *Hamlet*.
Filia, Ofelia, Ophélie, Ophilia, Phelia

Oprah (Hebrew) a form of Orpah.
Ophra, Ophrah, Opra

Ora (Latin) prayer. (Spanish) gold. (English) seacoast. (Greek) a form of Aura.
Orah, Orlice, Orra

Orabella (Latin) a form of Arabella.
Orabel, Orabela, Orabelle

Oraida (Arabic) eloquent; she who speaks well.

Oralee (Hebrew) the Lord is my light. See also Yareli.
Areli, Orali, Oralit, Orelie, Orlee, Orli, Orly

Oralia (French) a form of Aurelia. See also Oriana.
Oralis, Oriel, Orielda, Orielle, Oriena, Orlena, Orlene

Orea (Greek) mountains.
Oreal, Oria, Oriah

Orela (Latin) announcement from the gods; oracle.
Oreal, Orella, Orelle, Oriel, Orielle

Orenda (Iroquois) magical power.

Oretha (Greek) a form of Aretha.
Oreta, Oretta, Orette

Orfilia (German) female wolf.

Oriana (Latin) dawn, sunrise. (Irish) golden.
Orane, Orania, Orelda, Orelle, Ori, Oria, Orian, Oriane, Orianna, Orieana, Oryan

Orieta (Spanish) a form of Oriana.

Orina (Russian) a form of Irene.
Orya, Oryna

Orinda (Hebrew) pine tree. (Irish) light skinned, white.
Orenda

Orino (Japanese) worker's field.
Ori

Oriole (Latin) golden; black-and-orange bird.
Auriel, Oriel, Oriell, Oriella, Oriola

Orion **B** (Greek) child of fire. Mythology: a giant hunter who was killed by Artemis.

Orisha (Greek) a form of Aura.

Orla (Irish) golden woman.
Orlagh, Orlie, Orly

Orlanda (German) famous throughout the land.
Orlandia, Orlantha, Orlenda, Orlinda

Orlenda (Russian) eagle.

Orli (Hebrew) light.
Orlice, Orlie, Orly

Ormanda (Latin) noble. (German) mariner.
Orma

Ornella (Latin) she who is like a flowery ash tree.

Ornice (Hebrew) cedar tree. (Irish) pale; olive colored.
Orna, Ornah, Ornat, Ornette, Ornit

Orpah (Hebrew) runaway. See also Oprah.
Orpa, Orpha, Orphie

Orquidea (Spanish) orchid.
Orquidia

Orquídea (Italian) a form of Orquidea.

Orsa (Latin) a short form of Orseline. See also Ursa.
Orsaline, Orse, Orsel, Orselina, Orseline, Orsola

Ortensia (Italian) a form of Hortense.

Orva (French) golden; worthy. (English) brave friend.

Osaka (Japanese) a commercial and cultural city center.

Osanna (Latin) praise the Lord.
Oksana, Osana

Oscar **B** (Scandinavian) divine spear carrier.

Osen (Japanese) one thousand.

Oseye (Benin) merry.

Oshma (Indian) summer season.

Osma (English) divine protector.
Ozma

Otilde (Spanish) a form of Otilia.

Otilia (Czech) a form of Otilie.

Otilie (Czech) lucky heroine.
Otila, Otka, Ottili, Otylia

Ova (Latin) egg.

Ovia (Latin, Danish) egg.

Ovidia (German) she who takes care of the sheep.

Owen **B** (Irish) born to nobility; young warrior. (Welsh) a form of Evan.

Owena (Welsh) a form of Owen.

Oya **B** (Moquelumnan) called forth.

Oz **BG** (Hebrew) strength.

Ozara (Hebrew) treasure, wealth.

P

P **BG** (American) an initial used as a first name.

Pa (Chinese) flower.

Paasi (Chamorro) a form of Faasi.

Pabla (Spanish) little.

Paca (Spanish) a short form of Pancha. See also Paka.

Pacífica (Spanish) derived from the name of the Pacific Ocean.

Padget **BG** (French) a form of Page.
Padgett, Paget, Pagett

Padma (Hindi) lotus.

Padmakali (Indian) lotus bud.

Padmakshi (Indian) one with eyes like lotuses.

Padmal, Padnuni (Indian) lotus.

Padmalaya (Indian) lake of lotuses.

Padmalochana (Indian) lotus-eyed.

Padmavasa (Indian) one who resided in a lotus.

Padmini (Indian) lotus flower.

Page **G** (French) young assistant.
Pagen, Pagi, Payge

Pahal (Indian) the start.

Paige 🖐 **G** (English) young child.
Payge

Paisley (Scottish) patterned fabric first made in Paisley, Scotland.
Paislay, Paislee, Paisleyann, Paisleyanne, Paizlei, Paizleigh, Paizley, Pasley, Pazley

Paiton (English) warrior's town.
Paiten, Paityn, Paityne, Paiyton, Paten, Patton

Paka (Swahili) kitten. See also Paca.

Pakhi, Pakshi (Indian) bird.

Pakuna (Moquelumnan) deer bounding while running downhill.

Palaciada, Palaciata (Greek) she who has a sumptuous mansion.

Paladia (Spanish) a form of Pallas.

Palas (Greek) goddess of wisdom and war.

Palba (Basque) blond.

Palila (Polynesian) bird.

Palixena (Greek) she who returns from the foreign land.

Pallas (Greek) wise. Mythology: another name for Athena, the goddess of wisdom.

Pallavi (Indian) bud.

Pallavini (Indian) with new leaves.

Palma (Latin) palm tree.
Pallma, Palmira

Palmera (Spanish) palm tree.

Palmira (Spanish) a form of Palma.
Pallmirah, Pallmyra, Palmer, Palmyra

Paloma **G** (Spanish) dove. See also Aloma.
Palloma, Palometa, Palomita, Paluma, Peloma

Pamela (Greek) honey.
Pam, Pama, Pamala, Pamalla, Pamelia, Pamelina, Pamella, Pamila, Pamilla, Pammela, Pammi, Pammie, Pammy, Pamula

Pampa (Indian) river.

Panambi (Guarani) butterfly.

Pancha (Spanish) free; from France.
Paca, Panchita

Pancracia (Greek) she who has all the power.

Pandita (Hindi) scholar.

Pandora (Greek) all-gifted. Mythology: a woman who opened a box out of curiosity and released evil into the world. See also Dora.
Pandi, Pandorah, Pandorra, Pandorrah, Pandy, Panndora, Panndorah, Panndorra, Panndorrah

Pang (Chinese) innovative.

Pankaja (Indian) lotus.

Pankhadi (Indian) petal.

Pankti (Indian) sentence.

Pansy (Greek) flower; fragrant. (French) thoughtful.
Pansey, Pansie

Panthea (Greek) all the gods.
Pantheia, Pantheya

Panya (Swahili) mouse; tiny baby. (Russian) a familiar form of Stephanie.
Panyia

Panyin (Fante) older twin.

Paola **G** (Italian) a form of Paula.
Paoli, Paolina

Papiha (Indian) a sweet singing bird.

Papina (Moquelumnan) vine growing on an oak tree.

Paquita (Spanish) a form of Frances.
Paqua

Parama (Indian) the best.

Paravi, Parnavi (Indian) bird.

Parbarti (Indian) surrender.

Pardeep **B** (Sikh) mystic light.

Pari (Persian) fairy eagle.

Paridhi (Indian) limit.

Parinita (Indian) complete.

Paris 🅖 (French) Geography: the capital of France. Mythology: the Trojan prince who started the Trojan War by abducting Helen.
Parice, Paries, Parisa, Parise, Parish, Parisha, Pariss, Parissa, Parisse, Parris, Parys, Parysse

Parishi (Indian) like a fairy.

Pariyat (Indian) flower.

Parker 🅑 (English) park keeper.
Park, Parke

Parmenia (Greek) constant, faithful.

Parmenias (Spanish) a form of Parmenia.

Parmita (Indian) wisdom.

Parnal, Parni (Indian) leafy.

Parnashri (Indian) leafy beauty.

Parnik (Indian) creeper.

Parnika (Indian) a small leaf.

Parris (French) a form of Paris.
Parrise, Parrish, Parrisha, Parrys, Parrysh

Partenia (Greek) she who is as pure as a virgin.

Parthenia (Greek) virginal.
Partheenia, Parthenie, Parthinia, Pathina

Parthivi (Indian) another name for the goddess Sita.

Parul (Indian) graceful; flow of water.

Parvani (Indian) full moon; a festival or a special day.

Parveneh (Persian) butterfly.

Pascal 🅑 (French) born on Easter or Passover.
Pascalette, Pascaline, Pascalle, Paschale, Paskel

Pascale 🅖 (French) a form of Pascal.

Pascua, Pascualina (Hebrew) she who was born during the Easter festivities.

Pascuala (Spanish) born during the Easter season.

Pascuas (Hebrew) sacrificed for the good of the village.

Pasha 🅑🅖 (Greek) sea.
Palasha, Pascha, Pasche, Pashae, Pashe, Pashel, Pashka, Pasia, Passia

Passion (Latin) passion.
Pashion, Pashonne, Pasion, Passionaé, Passionate, Passionette

Pastora (German) shepherdess.

Pasua (Swahili) born by cesarean section.

Pat 🅑🅖 (Latin) a short form of Patricia, Patsy.

Pati (Moquelumnan) fish baskets made of willow branches.

Patia (Gypsy, Spanish) leaf. (Latin, English) a familiar form of Patience, Patricia.

Patience (English) patient.
Paciencia, Patia, Patiance, Patient, Patince, Patishia

Patra (Greek, Latin) a form of Petra.

Patralekha (Indian) a name from ancient epics.

Patrice 🅖 (French) a form of Patricia.
Patrease, Patrece, Patreece, Patreese, Patreice, Patriece, Patryce, Pattrice

Patricia 🅖 (Latin) noblewoman. See also Payton, Peyton, Tricia, Trisha, Trissa.
Pat, Patia, Patresa, Patrica, Patrice, Patricea, Patriceia, Patrichea, Patriciana, Patricianna, Patricja, Patricka, Patrickia, Patrisha, Patrishia, Patrisia, Patrissa, Patrizia, Patrizzia, Patrycia, Patrycja, Patsy, Patty

Patrick 🅑 (Latin) noble. Religion: the patron saint of Ireland.

Patsy (Latin) a familiar form of Patricia.
Pat, Patsey, Patsi

Patty (English) a familiar form of Patricia.
Patte, Pattee, Patti, Pattie

Paul 🅑 (Latin) small.

Paula (Latin) a form of Paul. See also Pavla, Polly.
Paliki, Paola, Paulane, Paulann, Paule, Paulette, Paulina, Pauline, Paulla, Pavia

Paulette (Latin) a familiar form of Paula.
Paulet, Paulett, Pauletta, Paulita, Paullett, Paulletta, Paullette

Paulina (Slavic) a form of Paula.
Paulena, Paulene, Paulenia, Pauliana, Paulianne, Paullena, Paulyna, Pawlina, Polena, Polina, Polinia

Pauline (French) a form of Paula.
Pauleen, Paulene, Paulien, Paulin, Paulyne, Paulynn, Pouline

Pausha (Hindi) lunar month of Capricorn.

Pavana (Indian) sacred.

Paveena (Indian) freshness, purity.

Pavla (Czech, Russian) a form of Paula.
Pavlina, Pavlinka

Paxton 🅑🅖 (Latin) peaceful town.
Paxtin, Paxtynn

Payge (English) a form of Paige.

Payoja (Indian) lotus.

Payton **G** (Irish) a form of Patricia.
Paydon, Paytan, Payten, Paytin, Paytn, Paytton

Paz **G** (Spanish) peace.

Pazi (Ponca) yellow bird.

Pazia (Hebrew) golden.
Paza, Pazice, Pazit

Peace (English) peaceful.

Pearl (Latin) jewel.
Pearle, Pearleen, Pearlena, Pearlene, Pearlette, Pearlina, Pearline, Pearlisha, Pearlyn, Perl, Perla, Perle, Perlette, Perlie, Perline, Perlline

Pedra (Portuguese) rock.

Peggy (Greek) a familiar form of Margaret.
Peg, Pegeen, Pegg, Peggey, Peggi, Peggie, Pegi

Pei (Chinese) abundant.

Peke (Hawaiian) a form of Bertha.

Pela (Polish) a short form of Penelope.
Pele

Pelagia (Greek) sea.
Pelage, Pelageia, Pelagie, Pelga, Pelgia, Pellagia

Pelipa (Zuni) a form of Philippa.

Pemba (Bambara) the power that controls all life.

Penda (Swahili) loved.

Penelope (Greek) weaver. Mythology: the clever and loyal wife of Odysseus, a Greek hero.
Pela, Pen, Penelopa, Penna, Pennelope, Penny, Pinelopi

Penélope (Greek) a form of Penelope.

Peng (Chinese) friend.

Peni (Carrier) mind.

Peninah (Hebrew) pearl.
Penina, Peninit, Peninnah, Penny

Penny (Greek) a familiar form of Penelope, Peninah.
Penee, Peni, Penney, Penni, Pennie

Peony (Greek) flower.
Peonie

Pepita (Spanish) a familiar form of Josephine.
Pepa, Pepi, Peppy, Peta

Pepper (Latin) condiment from the pepper plant.

Perah (Hebrew) flower.

Perdita (Latin) lost. Literature: a character in Shakespeare's play *The Winter's Tale.*
Perdida, Perdy

Peregrina (Latin) pilgrim, traveler.

Perfecta (Spanish) flawless.

Peri (Greek) mountain dweller. (Persian) fairy or elf.
Perita

Perla (Latin) a form of Pearl.
Pearla

Perlie (Latin) a familiar form of Pearl.
Pearley, Pearlie, Pearly, Perley, Perli, Perly, Purley, Purly

Perlita (Spanish) a form of Perla.

Pernella (Greek, French) rock. (Latin) a short form of Petronella.
Parnella, Pernel, Pernell, Pernelle

Pernita (Indian) answered prayer.

Perpetua (Spanish) continuous.

Perri (Greek, Latin) small rock; traveler. (French) pear tree. (Welsh) child of Harry.
Perre, Perrey, Perriann, Perrie, Perrin, Perrine, Perry

Perry **B** (Greek, French, Welsh) a form of Perri.

Persephone (Greek) Mythology: the goddess of the underworld.
Persephanie, Persephany, Persephonie

Perseveranda (Latin) she who perseveres on the good road.

Persis (Latin) from Persia.
Perssis, Persy

Peta (Blackfoot) golden eagle.

Peter **B** (Greek, Latin) small rock.

Petra (Greek, Latin) small rock. A short form of Petronella.
Patra, Pet, Peta, Petena, Peterina, Petraann, Petrice, Petrina, Petrine, Petrova, Petrovna, Pier, Pierce, Pietra

Petronella (Greek) small rock. (Latin) of the Roman clan Petronius.
Pernella, Peternella, Petra, Petrona, Petronela, Petronella, Petronelle, Petronia, Petronija, Petronilla, Petronille

Petula (Latin) seeker.
Petulah

Petunia (Native American) flower.

Peyeche (Mapuche) unforgettable woman, remembered; popular, sought-after.

Peyton BG (Irish) a form of Patricia.
Peyden, Peydon, Peyten, Peytyn

Phaedra (Greek) bright.
Faydra, Phae, Phaidra, Phe, Phedre

Phallon (Irish) a form of Fallon.
Phalaine, Phalen, Phallan, Phallie, Phalon, Phalyn

Pheakkley (Vietnamese) velvet.

Phebe (Greek) a form of Phoebe.
Pheba, Pheby

Pheodora (Greek, Russian) a form of Feodora.
Phedora, Phedorah, Pheodorah, Pheydora, Pheydorah

Philana (Greek) lover of mankind.
Phila, Philanna, Philene, Philiane, Philina, Philine

Philantha (Greek) lover of flowers.

Philicia (Latin) a form of Phylicia.
Philecia, Philesha, Philica, Philicha, Philycia

Philip B (Greek) lover of horses.

Philippa (Greek) a form of Philip. See also Filippa.
Phil, Philipa, Philippe, Phillipina, Phillippine, Phillie, Philly, Pippa, Pippy

Philomena (Greek) love song; loved one. Bible: a first-century saint. See also Filomena, Mena.
Philoméne, Philomina

Phoebe (Greek) shining.
Phaebe, Phebe, Pheobe, Phoebey

Phuong (Vietnamese) friendly.

Phylicia (Latin) fortunate; happy. (Greek) a form of Felicia.
Philicia, Phylecia, Phylesha, Phylesia, Phylica, Phylisha, Phylisia, Phylissa, Phyllecia, Phyllicia, Phyllisha, Phyllisia, Phyllissa, Phyllyza

Phyllida (Greek) a form of Phyllis.
Fillida, Philida, Phillida, Phillyda

Phyllis (Greek) green bough.
Filise, Fillys, Fyllis, Philis, Phillis, Philliss, Philys, Philyss, Phylis, Phyllida, Phyllis, Phylliss, Phyllys

Pi (Chinese) stringed musical instrument.

Pia (Latin, Italian) devout.
Pía

Piedad (Spanish) devoted; pious.

Pier (French) a form of Petra.
Pierette, Pierrette, Pierra, Pierre

Pierce B (English) a form of Petra.

Pierre B (French) a form of Pier.

Piki (Indian) cuckoo.

Pilar (Spanish) pillar, column.
Peelar, Pilár, Pillar

Pili (Spanish) a form of Pilar.

Pilmayquen (Araucanian) swallow.

Pimpinela (Latin) fickle one.

Ping (Chinese) duckweed. (Vietnamese) peaceful.

Pinga (Eskimo) Mythology: the goddess of game and the hunt.

Piper (English) pipe player.

Pippa (English) a short form of Phillipa.

Pippi (French) rosy cheeked.
Pippen, Pippie, Pippin, Pippy

Piro (Mapuche) snows.

Pita (African) fourth daughter.

Pitrel (Mapuche) very small woman.

Pival, Piyali (Indian) a tree.

Plácida (Latin) she who is gentle and peaceful.

Placidia (Latin) serene.
Placida

Pleasance (French) pleasant.
Pleasence

Plorine (Pohnpeian) a form of Catalina.

Polimnia (Greek) a form of Polyhymnia, one of the nine Muses; she who inspires hymns.

Polixena (Greek) welcoming one.

Polla (Arabic) poppy.
Pola

Polly (Latin) a familiar form of Paula.
Paili, Pali, Pauli, Paulie, Pauly, Poll, Pollee, Polley, Polli, Pollie

Pollyam (Hindi) goddess of the plague. Religion: the Hindu name invoked to ward off bad spirits.

Pollyanna (English) a combination of Polly + Anna. Literature: an overly optimistic heroine created by Eleanor Porter.

Poloma (Choctaw) bow.

Pomona (Latin) apple. Mythology: the goddess of fruit and fruit trees.

Poni (African) second daughter.

Poorbi (Indian) eastern.

Poornima, Purnima (Indian) full moon.

Poorva (Indian) earlier one, elder; east.

Poorvaganga (Indian) the Narmada River.

Poorvaja (Indian) elder sister.

Poorvi (Indian) a classical melody.

Popea (Greek) venerable mother.

Poppy (Latin) poppy flower.
Popi, Poppey, Poppi, Poppie

Pora, Poria (Hebrew) fruitful.

Porcha (Latin) a form of Portia.
Porchae, Porchai, Porche, Porchia, Porcia

Porscha, Porsche (German) forms of Portia.
Porcsha, Porcshe, Porschah, Porsché, Porschea, Porschia, Pourche

Porsha (Latin) a form of Portia.
Porshai, Porshay, Porshe, Porshea, Porshia

Portia (Latin) offering. Literature: the heroine of Shakespeare's play *The Merchant of Venice*.
Porcha, Porscha, Porsche, Porsha, Portiea

Poulomi (Indian) Indra's second wife.

Poushali (Indian) of the month Poush.

Prabha (Indian) light.

Prabhada (Indian) lady.

Prabhati (Indian) of the morning.

Prabhavati (Indian) wife of Sun.

Prabhjot **B** (Sikh) the light of God.

Pracheeta, Prasheetha (Indian) origin, starting point.

Prachi (Indian) east.

Pradeepta (Indian) glowing.

Pradnya, Pragya, Pramiti (Indian) wisdom.

Prafula (Indian) in bloom.

Pragati (Indian) progress.

Pragyaparamita (Indian) wise.

Pragyawati (Indian) a wise woman.

Prajakta (Indian) fragrant flower.

Prakriti (Indian) nature; beautiful.

Prakruthi (Indian) weather.

Prakruti (Indian) nature.

Prama (Indian) knowledge of truth.

Pramada (Indian) beautiful lady.

Pramila (Indian) sleep.

Pranali (Indian) organization.

Pranati (Indian) greeting elders with respect.

Pranjal (Indian) honest and dignified.

Prapti (Indian) advantage.

Prarthana (Indian) prayer.

Prashanti (Indian) complete peace.

Prasheila (Indian) ancient time.

Pratibha (Indian) splendor; intelligence.

Pratichi (Indian) west.

Pratigya (Indian) pledge, vow.

Pratima (Indian) idol.

Pratishtha (Indian) preeminence.

Pratiti (Indian) faith.

Pratyusha (Indian) early morning.

Praveena (Indian) skilled.

Praxedes (Greek) she who has firm intentions.

Práxedes (Greek) a form of Praxedes.

Prayerna (Indian) worship.

Preciosa (Latin) she who possesses great valor and is invaluable.

Precious (French) precious; dear.
Pracious, Preciouse, Precisha, Prescious, Preshious, Presious

Preeti (Indian) happiness.

Preksha (Indian) viewing.

Premala (Indian) loving.

Prerana, Prerna (Indian) inspiration.

Presencia (Spanish) presence.

Presentación (Latin) she who expresses herself.

Presley **G** (English) priest's meadow.
Preslea, Preslee, Preslei, Presli, Preslie, Presly, Preslye, Pressley, Presslie, Pressly

Presta (Spanish) hurry, quick.

Preston 🅱 (English) priest's estate.

Preyasi (Indian) beloved.

Prianka (Indian) favorite.

Prima (Latin) first, beginning; first child.
Prema, Primalia, Primetta, Primina, Priminia

Primavera (Italian, Spanish) spring.

Primitiva (Latin) first of all.

Primrose (English) primrose flower.
Primula

Prina (Indian) content.

Princess (English) daughter of royalty.
Princcess, Princes, Princesa, Princessa, Princetta, Princie, Princilla

Priscilla (Latin) ancient.
Cilla, Piri, Precila, Precilla, Prescilla, Presilla, Pressilia, Pricila, Pricilla, Pris, Prisca, Priscela, Priscella, Priscila, Priscilia, Priscill, Priscille, Priscillia, Prisella, Prisila, Prisilla, Prissila, Prissilla, Prissy, Pryscylla, Prysilla

Prisha (Indian) beloved; God's gift.

Prissy (Latin) a familiar form of Priscilla.
Prisi, Priss, Prissi, Prissie

Prita (Indian) dear one.

Prital, Pritika (Indian) loved one.

Prithika (Indian) flower.

Prithuloma (Indian) fish.

Priti (Indian) love.

Pritikana (Indian) an atom of love.

Pritilata (Indian) a creeper of love.

Priya (Hindi) beloved; sweet natured.
Pria

Priyadarshini (Indian) dear.

Priyadutta (Indian) earth.

Priyal (Indian) beloved.

Priyamvada (Indian) one who speaks with love.

Priyanvada (Indian) one who speaks nicely.

Procopia (Latin) declared leader.

Promise (Latin) promise, pledge.
Promis, Promiss, Promys, Promyse

Proserpina (Greek) she who wants to annihilate.

Próspera (Greek) prosperous.

Pru (Latin) a short form of Prudence.
Prue

Prudence (Latin) cautious; discreet.
Pru, Prudencia, Prudens, Prudy

Prudenciana (Spanish) modest and honest.

Prudy (Latin) a familiar form of Prudence.
Prudee, Prudi, Prudie

Prunella (Latin) brown; little plum. See also Nellie.
Prunela

Psyche (Greek) soul. Mythology: a beautiful mortal loved by Eros, the Greek god of love.

Pu (Chinese) uncut jade.

Pua (Hawaiian) flower.

Pualani (Hawaiian) heavenly flower.
Puni

Puebla (Spanish) taken from the name of the Mexican city.

Puji (Indian) gentle.

Pujita (Indian) worshipped.

Pulak (Indian) a gem; smile.

Puloma (Indian) wife of the sage Bhrigu.

Punarnava (Indian) a star.

Punita (Indian) holy.

Punthali (Indian) doll.

Punya (Indian) virtuous.

Pura (English) a form of Purity.

Purificación (Spanish) a form of Pura.

Purity (English) purity.
Pureza, Purisima

Purva (Indian) elder; breeze.

Purvaja (Indian) elder sister.

Purvi (Indian) from the east.

Pusha (Indian) nourishing.

Pushpa (Indian) flower.

Pushpagandha (Indian) juhi flower.

Pushpalata (Indian) flower creeper.

Pushpanjali (Indian) flower offering.

Pushpita, Pushpitha (Indian) decorated with flowers.

Pusti (Indian) nourishment.

Putul (Indian) doll.

Pyralis (Greek) fire. Pyrene.

Qadira (Arabic) powerful.
Kadira

Qamra (Arabic) moon.
Kamra

Qi (Chinese) fine jade; outstanding; distinguished.

Qian (Chinese) courteous.

Qiao (Chinese) handsome; pretty.

Qin (Chinese) celery.

Qing (Chinese) greenish blue.

Qing Yuan, Qing-Yuan (Chinese) clear spring.

Qiong (Chinese) fine jade.

Qitarah (Arabic) fragrant.

Qiu (Chinese) autumn.

Qu (Chinese) delight.

Quaashie **BG** (Ewe) born on Sunday.

Quadeisha (American) a combination of Qadira + Aisha.
Qudaisha, Quadaishia, Quadajah, Quadasha, Quadasia, Quadayshia, Quadaza, Quadejah, Quadesha, Quadeshia, Quadiasha, Quaesha

Quan (Chinese) goddess of compassion.

Quaneisha (American) a combination of the prefix Qu + Niesha.
Quaneasa, Quanece, Quanecia, Quaneice, Quanesha, Quanisha, Quansha, Quarnisha, Queisha, Qwanisha, Qynisha

Quanesha (American) a form of Quaneisha.
Quamesha, Quaneesha, Quaneshia, Quanesia, Quanessa, Quanessia, Quannesha, Quannneshia, Quannezia, Quayneshia, Quinesha

Quanika (American) a combination of the prefix Qu + Nika.
Quanikka, Quanikki, Quaniqua, Quanique, Quantenique, Quawanica, Queenika, Queenique

Quanisha (American) a form of Quaneisha.
Quaniesha, Quanishia, Quaynisha, Queenisha, Quenisha, Quenishia

Quarrtulain (Indian) God's mercy.

Quartilla (Latin) fourth.
Quantilla

Quasar (Indian) meteor.

Qubilah (Arabic) agreeable.

Que (Chinese) true; reliable.

Queagon (Chamorro) striving for food.

Queen (English) queen. See also Quinn.
Queena, Queenie, Quenna

Queenie (English) a form of Queen.
Queenation, Queeneste, Queeny

Queisha (American) a short form of Quaneisha.
Qeysha, Queshia, Queysha

Quenby **BG** (Scandinavian) feminine.

Quenisha (American) a combination of Queen + Aisha.
Queneesha, Quenesha, Quennisha, Quensha, Quinesha, Quinisha

Quenna (English) a form of Queen.
Quenell, Quenessa

Quentin **B** (Latin) fifth. (English) queen's town.

Querida (Spanish) dear; beloved.

Querima, Querina (Arabic) generous one.

Quesara (Latin) youthful.

Questa (French) searcher.

Queta (Spanish) a short form of names ending in "queta" or "quetta."
Quenetta, Quetta

Quetaca (Chamorro) striving to achieve, attain.

Quetogua (Chamorro) striving to conquer or strike down.

Quetromán (Mapuche) mute condor; restrained soul; prudence.

Quiana (American) a combination of the prefix Qu + Anna.
Quian, Quianah, Quianda, Quiane, Quiani, Quianita, Quianna, Quianne, Quionna

Quíbele (Turkish) goddess mother.

Quidilis (Chamorro) striving to surpass.

Quiliana (Spanish) substantial; productive.

Quillen (Spanish) woman of the heights.

Quimey (Mapuche) beautiful.

Quinby (Scandinavian) queen's estate.

Quincy 🅑 (Irish) fifth.
Quincee, Quincey, Quinci, Quincia, Quincie

Quinella (Latin) a form of Quintana.

Quinesburga (Anglo-Saxon) royal strength.

Quinesha, Quinisha (American) forms of Quenisha.
Quineshia, Quinessa, Quinessia, Quinisa, Quinishia, Quinnesha, Quinneshia, Quinnisha, Quneasha, Quonesha, Quonisha, Quonnisha

Quinetta (Latin) a form of Quintana.
Queenetta, Queenette, Quinette, Quinita, Quinnette

Quinn 🅑 (German, English) queen. See also Queen.
Quin, Quinna, Quinne, Quynn

Quinshawna (American) a combination of Quinn + Shauna.
Quinshea

Quintana (Latin) fifth. (English) queen's lawn. See also Quinella, Quinetta.
Quinntina, Quinta, Quintanna, Quintara, Quintarah, Quintia, Quintila, Quintilla, Quintina, Quintona, Quintonice

Quintessa (Latin) essence. See also Tess.
Quintaysha, Quintesa, Quintesha, Quintessia, Quintice, Quinticia, Quintisha, Quintosha

Quintiliana (Spanish) born in the fifth month of the year.

Quinton 🅑 (Latin) a form of Quentin.

Quintrell (American) a combination of Quinn + Trella.
Quintela, Quintella, Quintrelle

Quintruy (Mapuche) investigator; woman of initiative and curiosity; leader.

Quintuqueo (Mapuche) she who searches for wisdom; woman of experience, having the gifts of knowledge, counseling, and perfection.

Quinturay (Mapuche) she who has a flower; she whose goal is to find the nectar and the essence of the flower.

Quionia (Greek) she who is fertile.

Quipuha (Chamorro) striving to capsize.

Quirina (Latin) she who carries the lance.

Quirita (Latin) citizen.

Quiterie (Latin, French) tranquil.
Quita

Qun (Chinese) the masses.

Quon (Chinese) bright.

Quy (Vietnamese) faithful.

Quyen (Vietnamese) destiny, direction.

Quynh (Vietnamese) precious.

Qwanisha (American) a form of Quaneisha.
Qwanechia, Qwanesha, Qwanessia, Qwantasha

R 🅑🅖 (American) an initial used as a first name.

Raaida (Indian) leader.

Raawiya (Indian) transmitter of ancient Arabic poetry.

Rabab (Indian) white cloud.

Rabani (Indian) divine.

Rabecca (Hebrew) a form of Rebecca.
Rabecka, Rabeca, Rabekah

Rabeea (Indian) garden.

Rabhya (Indian) worshipped.

Rabi 🅑🅖 (Arabic) breeze.
Rabia, Rabiah

Rachael (Hebrew) a form of Rachel.
Rachaele, Rachaell, Rachail, Rachalle

Rachana, Rachna (Indian) creation.

Racheal (Hebrew) a form of Rachel.

Rachel �015 🅖 (Hebrew) female sheep. Bible: the second wife of Jacob. See also Lahela, Rae, Rochelle.
Racha, Rachael, Rachal, Racheal, Rachela, Rachelann, Rachele, Rachelle, Racquel, Raechel, Rahel, Rahela, Rahil, Raiche, Raquel, Rashel, Rashelle, Ray, Raycene, Raychel, Raychelle, Rey, Ruchel

Rachelle (French) a form of Rachel. See also Shelley.
Rachalle, Rachell, Rachella, Raechell, Raechelle, Raeshelle, Rashel, Rashele, Rashell, Rashelle, Raychell, Rayshell, Ruchelle

Rachita (Indian) created.

Racquel (French) a form of Rachel.
Rackel, Racquell, Racquella, Racquelle

Radegunda (German) she who counsels regarding battling.

Radella (German) counselor.

Radeyah (Arabic) content, satisfied.
Radeeyah, Radhiya, Radiah, Radiyah

Radha (Indian) Lord Krishna's lover.

Radhiyaa (Indian) content, satisfied.

Radhwa (Indian) the name of a mountain in Medina.

Radinka (Slavic) full of life; happy, glad.

Radmilla (Slavic) worker for the people.

Rae (English) doe. (Hebrew) a short form of Rachel.
Raeh, Raeneice, Raeneisha, Raesha, Ray, Raye, Rayetta, Rayette, Rayma, Rey

Raeann (American) a combination of Rae + Ann. See also Rayanne.
Raea, Raean, Raeanna, Raeannah, Raeona, Reanna, Raeanne

Raechel (Hebrew) a form of Rachel.
Raechael, Raechal, Raechele, Raechell, Raechyl

Raeden (Japanese) Mythology: Raiden was the god of thunder and lightning.
Raeda, Raedeen

Raegan **G** (Irish) a form of Reagan.
Raegen, Raegene, Raegine, Raegyn

Raelene (American) a combination of Rae + Lee.
Rael, Raela, Raelani, Raele, Raeleah, Raelee, Raeleen, Raeleia, Raeleigh, Raeleigha, Raelein, Raelene, Raelennia, Raelesha, Raelin, Raelina, Raelle, Raelyn, Raelynn

Raelyn, Raelynn (American) forms of Raelene.
Raelynda, Raelyne, Raelynne

Raena (German) a form of Raina.
Raenah, Raenia, Raenie, Raenna, Raeonna, Raeyauna, Raeyn, Raeyonna

Raeven (English) a form of Raven.
Raevin, Raevion, Raevon, Raevonna, Raevyn, Raevynne, Raewyn, Raewynne, Raivan, Raiven, Raivin, Raivyn

Rafa (Arabic) happy; prosperous.

Rafael **B** (Spanish) a form of Raphael.

Rafaela (Hebrew) a form of Raphaela.
Rafaelia, Rafaella

Ragan (Irish) a form of Reagan.
Ragean, Rageane, Rageen, Ragen, Ragene, Rageni, Ragenna, Raggan, Raygan, Raygen, Raygene, Rayghan, Raygin

Raghd (Indian) pleasant.

Ragi (Indian) loving.

Ragine (English) a form of Regina.
Raegina, Ragin, Ragina, Raginee

Ragini (Indian) melody.

Ragnild (Scandinavian) battle counsel.
Ragna, Ragnell, Ragnhild, Rainell, Renilda, Renilde

Rahat (Indian) relief.

Raheem **B** (Punjabi) compassionate God.
Raheema, Rahima

Ráidah (Arabic) leader.

Raimunda (Spanish) wise defender.

Raina (German) mighty. (English) a short form of Regina. See also Rayna.
Raeinna, Raena, Raheena, Rain, Rainah, Rainai, Raine, Rainea, Rainna, Reanna

Rainbow (English) rainbow.
Rainbeau, Rainbeaux, Rainbo, Raynbow

Raine **G** (Latin) a short form of Regina. A form of Raina, Rane.
Rainee, Rainey, Raini, Rainie, Rainy, Reyne

Raingarda (German) prudent defender.

Raisa (Russian) a form of Rose.
Raisah, Raissa, Raiza, Raysa, Rayza, Razia

Raizel (Yiddish) a form of Rose.
Rayzil, Razil, Reizel, Resel

Raja (Arabic) hopeful.
Raia, Rajaah, Rajae, Rajah, Rajai

Rajanigandha (Indian) scented flower.

Rajashri (Indian) king's pride; ornament.

Rajasi (Indian) worthy of a king.

Rajata (Indian) silver.

Rajeshri (Indian) queen.

Rajeshwari (Indian) the goddess of a state.

Rajhans (Indian) swan.

Raji (Indian) shining.

Rajika (Indian) lamp.

Rajkumari, Rajnandhini, Rajnandini (Indian) princess.

Rajni (Indian) night.

Rajrita (Indian) prince of living.

Rajshri (Indian) sage-like king.

Rajul (Indian) brilliant.

Raka (Indian) full moon.

Rakhi (Indian) bond of protection.

Rakti (Indian) pleasing.

Raku (Japanese) pleasure.

Raleigh B (Irish) a form of Riley.
Ralea, Raleiah, Raley

Ralph B (English) wolf counselor.

Rama (Hebrew) lofty, exalted. (Hindi) godlike. Religion: an incarnation of the Hindu god Vishnu.
Ramah

Raman G (Spanish) a form of Ramona.

Ramandeep (Sikh) covered by the light of the Lord's love.

Ramani (Indian) a beautiful girl.

Rambha (Indian) name of an apsaras (female spirit).

Ramira (Spanish) judicious.

Ramita (Indian) pleasing.

Ramla (Swahili) fortuneteller.
Ramlah

Ramona (Spanish) mighty; wise protector. See also Mona.
Raman, Ramonda, Raymona, Romona, Romonda

Ramra (Indian) splendor.

Ramsey B (English) ram's island.
Ramsha, Ramsi, Ramsie, Ramza

Ran (Japanese) water lily. (Scandinavian) destroyer. Mythology: the Norse sea goddess who destroys.

Rana (Sanskrit) royal. (Arabic) gaze, look.
Rahna, Rahni, Rani

Ranait (Irish) graceful; prosperous.
Rane, Renny

Rand (Indian) tree of good scent.

Randall B (English) protected.
Randa, Randah, Randal, Randalee, Randel, Randell, Randelle, Randi, Randilee, Randilynn, Randlyn, Randy, Randyl

Randi G (English) a familiar form of Miranda, Randall.
Rande, Randee, Randeen, Randene, Randey, Randie, Randii

Randy B (English) a form of Randi.

Rane (Scandinavian) queen.
Raine

Rangana (Indian) happy.

Ranhita (Indian) quick.

Rani G (Sanskrit) queen. (Hebrew) joyful. A short form of Kerani.
Rahni, Ranee, Raney, Rania, Ranie, Ranice, Ranique, Ranni, Rannie

Ranita (Hebrew) song; joyful.
Ranata, Ranice, Ranit, Ranite, Ranitta, Ronita

Raniyah (Arabic) gazing.
Ranya, Ranyah

Ranjana (Indian) pleasing; exciting.

Ranjini (Indian) pleasing.

Ranjita (Indian) amusing; decorated.

Rapa (Hawaiian) moonbeam.

Raphael B (Hebrew) God has healed.

Raphaela (Hebrew) healed by God.
Rafaella, Raphaella, Raphaelle

Raphaelle (French) a form of Raphaela.
Rafaelle, Raphael, Raphaele

Raquel G (French) a form of Rachel.
Rakel, Rakhil, Rakhila, Raqueal, Raquela, Raquella, Raquelle, Rickelle, Rickquel, Ricquel, Ricquelle, Rikell, Rikelle, Rockell

Raquildis (German) fighting princess.

Rasha (Arabic) young gazelle.
Rahshea, Rahshia, Rashae, Rashai, Rashea, Rashi, Rashia

Rashawn B (American) a form of Rashawna.

Rashawna (American) a combination of the prefix Ra + Shawna.
Rashana, Rashanae, Rashanah, Rashanda, Rashane, Rashani, Rashanna, Rashanta, Rashaun, Rashauna, Rashaunda, Rashaundra, Rashaune, Rashawn, Rashawnda, Rashawnna, Rashon, Rashona, Rashonda, Rashunda

Rasheed B (Arabic) a form of Rashad (see Boys' Names).

Rashel, Rashelle (American) forms of Rachel.
Rashele, Rashell, Rashella

Rashida G (Swahili, Turkish) righteous.
Rahshea, Rahsheda, Rahsheita, Rashdah, Rasheda, Rashedah, Rasheeda, Rasheedah, Rasheeta, Rasheida, Rashidah, Rashidi

Rashieka (Arabic) descended from royalty.
Rasheeka, Rasheika, Rasheka, Rashika, Rasika

Rashmika (Indian) a ray of light.

Rasia (Greek) rose.

Rasna (Indian) ray.

Ratana (Tai) crystal.
Ratania, Ratanya, Ratna, Rattan, Rattana

Ratanjali (Indian) red sandalwood.

Rathna (Indian) pearl.

Rati (Indian) joy.

Ratnabala (Indian) jeweled.

Ratnabali (Indian) string of pearls.

Ratnajyoti (Indian) light from a jewel.

Ratnajyouti (Indian) lustrous jewel.

Ratnalekha (Indian) beauty of jewels.

Ratnali (Indian) a jewel.

Ratnamala (Indian) a jeweled necklace.

Ratnangi (Indian) whole body adorned with jewels.

Ratnaprabha (Indian) earth; light from a jewel.

Ratnapriya (Indian) one who likes jewels.

Ratnavali (Indian) a bunch of gems; earth.

Ratri (Hindi) night. Religion: the goddess of the night.

Ratrudis (German) faithful counselor.

Raula (French) wolf counselor.
Raoula, Raulla, Raulle

Raven **G** (English) blackbird.
Raeven, Raveen, Raveena, Raveenn, Ravena, Ravene, Ravenn, Ravenna, Ravennah, Ravenne, Raveon, Ravin, Ravon, Ravyn, Rayven, Revena

Ravin (English) a form of Raven.
Ravi, Ravina, Ravine, Ravinne, Ravion

Raviprabha (Indian) light of the sun.

Ravyn (English) a form of Raven.
Ravynn

Rawdha (Indian) garden.

Rawnie (Gypsy) fine lady.
Rawan, Rawna, Rhawnie

Ray **B** (Hebrew) a short form of Raya.

Raya (Hebrew) friend.
Raia, Raiah, Raiya, Ray, Rayah

Rayanne (American) a form of Raeann.
Rayane, Ray-Ann, Rayan, Rayana, Rayann, Rayanna, Rayeanna, Rayona, Rayonna, Reyan, Reyana, Reyann, Reyanna, Reyanne

Raychel, Raychelle (Hebrew) forms of Rachel.
Raychael, Raychele, Raychell, Raychil

Rayén (Araucanian, Mapuche) flower.

Raylene (American) forms of Raylyn.
Ralina, Rayel, Rayele, Rayelle, Rayleana, Raylee, Rayleen, Rayleigh, Raylena, Raylin, Raylinn, Raylona, Raylyn, Raylynn, Raylynne

Raymonde (German) wise protector.
Rayma, Raymae, Raymie

Rayna (Scandinavian) mighty. (Yiddish) pure, clean. (English) king's advisor. (French) a familiar form of Lorraine. See also Raina.
Raynah, Rayne, Raynell, Raynelle, Raynette, Rayona, Rayonna, Reyna

Rayven (English) a form of Raven.
Rayvan, Rayvana, Rayvein, Rayvenne, Rayveona, Rayvin, Rayvon, Rayvonia

Rayya (Arabic) thirsty no longer.

Razi **B** (Aramaic) secretive.
Rayzil, Rayzilee, Raz, Razia, Raziah, Raziela, Razilee, Razili

Raziya (Swahili) agreeable.

Rea (Greek) poppy flower.
Reah

Reagan **G** (Irish) little ruler.
Reagen, Reaghan, Reagine

Reanna (German, English) a form of Raina. (American) a form of Raeann.
Reannah

Reanne (American) a form of Raeann, Reanna.
Reana, Reane, Reann, Reannan, Reanne, Reannen, Reannon, Reeana

Reba (Hebrew) fourth-born child. A short form of Rebecca. See also Reva, Riva.
Rabah, Reeba, Rheba

Rebeca (Hebrew) an alternate form of Rebecca.
Rebbeca, Rebecah

Girls M–R

Rebecca ₩ **G** (Hebrew) tied, bound. Bible:
the wife of Isaac. See also Becca, Becky.
*Rabecca, Reba, Rebbecca, Rebeca,
Rebeccah, Rebeccea, Rebeccka, Rebecha,
Rebecka, Rebeckah, Rebeckia, Rebecky,
Rebekah, Rebeque, Rebi, Reveca, Riva, Rivka*

Rebekah **G** (Hebrew) a form of Rebecca.
*Rebeka, Rebekha, Rebekka, Rebekkah,
Rebekke, Revecca, Reveka, Revekka, Rifka*

Rebha (Indian) sings praises.

Rebi (Hebrew) a familiar form of Rebecca.
Rebbie, Rebe, Rebie, Reby, Ree, Reebie

Reece **B** (Welsh) a form of Rhys.

Reed **B** (English) a form of Reid.

Reena (Greek) peaceful. (English) a form of
Rina. (Hebrew) a form of Rinah.
Reen, Reenie, Rena, Reyna

Reese **G** (Welsh) a form of Reece.

Reet (Estonian) a form of Margaret.
Reatha, Reta, Retha

Regan **G** (Irish) a form of Reagan.
Regane, Reghan

Reganne (Irish) a form of Reagan.
Raegan, Ragan, Reagan, Regin

Reggie **B** (English) a familiar form of
Regina.
Reggi, Reggy, Regi, Regia, Regie

Regina (Latin) queen. (English) king's
advisor. Geography: the capital of
Saskatchewan. See also Gina.
*Ragine, Raina, Raine, Rega, Regena,
Regennia, Reggie, Regiena, Regine, Reginia,
Regis, Reina, Rena*

Reginald **B** (English) king's advisor.

Regine (Latin) a form of Regina.
Regin

Rehana (Indian) sweet-smelling plant.

Rei **G** (Japanese) polite, well behaved.
Reiko

Reia (Spanish) a form of Reina.

Reid **B** (English) redhead.

Reika (Japanese) summit; scent.

Reilly **B** (Irish) a form of Riley.
Reilee, Reileigh, Reiley, Reili, Reilley, Reily

Reina (Spanish) a short form of Regina. See
also Reyna.
*Reinah, Reine, Reinette, Reinie, Reinna,
Reiny, Reiona, Renia, Rina*

Rekha (Hindi) thin line.
Reka, Rekia, Rekiah, Rekiya

Relinda (German) kind-hearted princess.

Remedios (Spanish) remedy.

Remi **B** (French) from Rheims, France.
Raymi, Remee, Remie, Remy

Remington **B** (English) raven estate.
Remmington

Ren (Japanese) arranger; water lily; lotus.

Rena (Hebrew) song; joy. A familiar form of
Irene, Regina, Renata, Sabrina, Serena.
Reena, Rina, Rinna, Rinnah

Renae (French) a form of Renée.
Renay

Renata (French) a form of Renée.
*Ranata, Rena, Renada, Renatta, Renita,
Rennie, Renyatta, Rinada, Rinata*

Rene **B** (Greek) a short form of Irene,
Renée.
Reen, Reenie, Reney, Rennie

Renee **G** (French) a form of René.

Renée (French) born again.
*Renae, Renata, Renay, Rene, Renea, Reneigh,
Renell, Renelle, Renne*

Renita (French) a form of Renata.
Reneeta, Renetta, Renitza

Rennie (English) a familiar form of Renata.
Reni, Renie, Renni

Renu (Indian) particle, grain; sand.

Reseda (Spanish) fragrant mignonette
blossom.

Resha (Indian) line.

Resham (Indian) silk.

Reshawna (American) a combination of the
prefix Re + Shawna.
*Resaunna, Reshana, Reshaunda, Reshawnda,
Reshawnna, Reshonda, Reshonn, Reshonta*

Reshma (Indian) silky.

Reshmi (Indian) silken.

Resi (German) a familiar form of Theresa.
*Resia, Ressa, Resse, Ressie, Reza, Rezka,
Rezi*

Reta (African) shaken.
Reeta, Retta, Rheta, Rhetta

Reubena (Hebrew) behold a child.
Reubina, Reuvena, Rubena, Rubenia, Rubina, Rubine, Rubyna

Reva (Latin) revived. (Hebrew) rain; one-fourth. A form of Reba, Riva.
Ree, Reeva, Revia, Revida

Revati (Indian) prosperity.

Reveca, Reveka (Slavic) forms of Rebecca, Rebekah.
Reve, Revecca, Revekka, Rivka

Rewa (Indian) swift.

Rexanne (American) queen.
Rexan, Rexana, Rexann, Rexanna

Reya (Spanish) a form of Reina.

Reyes (Spanish) a form of Reyna.

Reyhan **B** (Turkish) sweet-smelling flower.

Reyna (Greek) peaceful. (English) a form of Reina.
Reyana, Reyanna, Reyni, Reynna

Reynalda (German) king's advisor.

Réz **BG** (Latin, Hungarian) copper-colored hair.

Reza (Czech) a form of Theresa.
Rezi, Rezka

Rhea (Greek) brook, stream. Mythology: the mother of Zeus.
Rheá, Rhéa, Rhealyn, Rheanna, Rhia, Rhianna

Rheanna, Rhianna (Greek) forms of Rhea.
Rheana, Rheann, Rheanne, Rhiana, Rhiauna

Rhett **B** (Welsh) a form of Rhys.

Rhian (Welsh) a short form of Rhiannon.
Rhianne, Rhyan, Rhyann, Rhyanne, Rian, Riane, Riann, Rianne, Riayn

Rhiannon (Welsh) witch; nymph; goddess.
Rheannan, Rheannin, Rheannon, Rheanon, Rhian, Rhianen, Rhianna, Rhiannan, Rhiannen, Rhianon, Rhianwen, Rhinnon, Rhyanna, Riana, Riannon, Rianon

Rhoda (Greek) from Rhodes, Greece.
Rhode, Rhodeia, Rhodie, Rhody, Roda, Rodi, Rodie, Rodina

Rhona (Scottish) powerful, mighty. (English) king's advisor.
Rhonae, Rhonnie

Rhonda (Welsh) grand.
Rhondene, Rhondiesha, Ronda, Ronelle, Ronnette

Rhys **B** (Welsh) enthusiastic; stream.

Ria (Spanish) river.
Riah

Riana, Rianna (Irish) short forms of Briana. (Arabic) forms of Rihana.
Reana, Reanna, Rhianna, Rhyanna, Riana, Rianah

Rica (Spanish) a short form of Erica, Frederica, Ricarda. See also Enrica, Sandrica, Terrica, Ulrica.
Ricca, Rieca, Riecka, Rieka, Rikka, Riqua, Rycca

Ricarda (Spanish) rich and powerful ruler.
Rica, Richanda, Richarda, Richi, Ricki

Ricardo **B** (Portuguese, Spanish) a form of Richard.

Richael (Irish) saint.

Richard **B** (English) a form of Richart (see Boys' Names).

Richelle (German, French) a form of Ricarda.
Richel, Richela, Richele, Richell, Richella, Richia

Rickelle (American) a form of Raquel.
Rickel, Rickela, Rickell

Rickey **B** (English) a familiar form of Richard.

Ricki, Rikki **G** (American) familiar forms of Erica, Frederica, Ricarda.
Rica, Ricci, Riccy, Rici, Rickee, Rickia, Rickie, Rickilee, Rickina, Rickita, Ricky, Ricquie, Riki, Rikia, Rikita, Rikka, Rikke, Rikkia, Rikkie, Rikky, Riko

Ricky **B** (American) a form of Ricki.

Rico **B** (Spanish) a familiar form of Richard. (Italian) a short form of Enrico (see Boys' Names).

Ricquel (American) a form of Raquel.
Rickquell, Ricquelle, Rikell, Rikelle

Rida **BG** (Arabic) favored by God.

Riddhi (Indian) fortunate.

Rieko (Japanese) child of Rie.

Rigel (Spanish) most brilliant star in the sky.

Rihana (Arabic) sweet basil.
Rhiana, Rhianna, Riana, Rianna

Riju (Indian) innocent.

Rijuta (Indian) innocence.

Rika (Swedish) ruler.
Ricka

Rikako (Japanese) child of Rika.

Riku (Japanese) land.

Rilee (Irish) a form of Riley.
Rielee, Rielle

Riley ☗ **B** (Irish) valiant.
*Raleigh, Reilly, Rieley, Rielly, Riely, Rilee,
Rileigh, Rilie*

Rilla (German) small brook.

Rima (Arabic) white antelope.
*Reem, Reema, Reemah, Rema, Remah,
Rhymia, Rim, Ryma*

Rimona (Hebrew) pomegranate. See also
Mona.

Rimpy (Indian) pretty.

Rin (Japanese) park. Geography: a Japanese
village.
Rini, Rynn

Rina (English) a short form of names ending
in "rina." (Hebrew) a form of Rena, Rinah.
Reena, Rena

Rinah (Hebrew) joyful.
Rina

Rinako (Japanese) child of Rina.

Río (Spanish) river.

Riona (Irish) saint.

Risa (Latin) laughter.
Reesa, Resa

Risako (Japanese) child of Risa.

Risha (Hindi) born during the lunar month
of Taurus.
Rishah, Rishay

Rishika (Indian) saintly.

Rishima (Indian) moonbeam.

Rishita (Indian) the best.

Rishona (Hebrew) first.
Rishina, Rishon

Rissa (Greek) a short form of Nerissa.
Risa, Rissah, Ryssa, Ryssah

Rita (Sanskrit) brave; honest. (Greek) a short
form of Margarita.
*Reatha, Reda, Reeta, Reida, Reitha, Rheta,
Riet, Ritah, Ritamae, Ritamarie*

Riti (Indian) memory; well being.

Ritika (Indian) movement.

Ritsa (Greek) a familiar form of Alexandra.
Ritsah, Ritsi, Ritsie, Ritsy

Ritsuko (Japanese) child of Ritsu.

Ritu (Indian) season.

Riva (French) river bank. (Hebrew) a short
form of Rebecca. See also Reba, Reva.
Rivalee, Rivi, Rivvy

River **B** (Latin, French) stream, water.
Rivana, Rivanna, Rivers, Riviane

Rivka (Hebrew) a short form of Rebecca.
Rivca, Rivcah, Rivkah

Riya (Indian) flower.

Riye (Japanese) blessed truth.

Riyeko (Japanese) flourishing child of
reason.

Riza (Greek) a form of Theresa.
Riesa, Rizus, Rizza

Roanna (American) a form of Rosanna.
Ranna, Roana, Roanda, Roanne

Robbi (English) a familiar form of Roberta.
Robby, Robbye, Robey, Robi, Robia, Roby

Robbie **B** (English) a form of Robbi.

Robert **B** (English) famous brilliance.

Roberta (English) a form of Robert.
*Roba, Robbi, Robbie, Robena, Robertena,
Robertina*

Roberto **B** (Italian, Portuguese, Spanish) a
form of Robert.

Robin **G** (English) robin. A form of Roberta.
*Robann, Robbin, Robeen, Roben, Robena,
Robian, Robina, Robine, Robinette, Robinia,
Robinn, Robinta, Robyn*

Robinette (English) a familiar form of
Robin.
Robernetta, Robinet, Robinett, Robinita

Robyn **G** (English) a form of Robin.
Robbyn, Robbynn, Robyne, Robynn, Robynne

Rochelle **G** (French) large stone. (Hebrew)
a form of Rachel. See also Shelley.
*Reshelle, Roch, Rocheal, Rochealle, Rochel,
Rochele, Rochell, Rochella, Rochette,
Rockelle, Roshele, Roshell, Roshelle*

Rochely (Latin) goddess of the earth.

Rochi (Indian) light.

Rocio (Spanish) dewdrops.
Rocío

Roderica (German) famous ruler.
*Rica, Rika, Rodericka, Roderika, Rodreicka,
Rodricka, Rodrika*

Roderiga (Spanish) notable leader.

Rodnae (English) island clearing.
Rodna, Rodnetta, Rodnicka

Rodneisha (American) a combination of
Rodnae + Aisha.
*Rodesha, Rodisha, Rodishah, Rodnecia,
Rodnesha, Rodneshia, Rodneycia, Rodneysha,
Rodnisha*

Rodney **B** (English) island clearing.

Rogelia (Teutonic) beautiful one.

Rogelio **B** (Spanish) famous warrior.

Rohana (Hindi) sandalwood. (American) a
combination of Rose + Hannah.
Rochana, Rohena

Rohini (Hindi) woman.

Rohita (Indian) Brahma's daughter.

Roja (Spanish) red.

Roku (Japanese) emolument.

Rolanda (German) a form of Rolando.
*Ralna, Rolande, Rolando, Rolaunda,
Roleesha, Rolene, Rolinda, Rollande, Rolonda*

Rolando **B** (German) famous throughout
the land.

Rolene (German) a form of Rolanda.
Rolaine, Rolena, Rolleen, Rollene

Roma (Latin) from Rome.
*Romai, Rome, Romeise, Romeka, Romelle,
Romesha, Rometta, Romia, Romilda, Romilla,
Romina, Romini, Romma, Romonia*

Romaine (French) from Rome.
*Romana, Romanda, Romanelle, Romania,
Romanique, Romany, Romayne, Romona,
Romy*

Romanela (Latin) native of Rome.

Romelia (Hebrew) God's beloved or preferred
one.

Romola (Latin) Roman woman.

Rómula (Spanish) possessor of great strength.

Romy **G** (French) a familiar form of
Romaine. (English) a familiar form of
Rosemary.
Romi, Romie

Rona (Scandinavian) a short form of
Ronalda.
*Rhona, Roana, Ronalda, Ronna, Ronnae,
Ronnay, Ronne, Ronni, Ronsy*

Ronaele (Greek) the name Eleanor spelled
backwards.
Ronalee, Ronni, Ronnie, Ronny

Ronald **B** (Scottish) a form of Reginald.

Ronda (Welsh) a form of Rhonda.
*Rondai, Rondesia, Rondi, Rondie, Ronelle,
Ronnette, Ronni, Ronnie, Ronny*

Rondelle (French) short poem.
Rhondelle, Rondel, Ronndelle

Roneisha (American) a combination of
Rhonda + Aisha.
*Roneasha, Ronecia, Ronee, Roneeka,
Roneesha, Roneice, Ronese, Ronesha,
Roneshia, Ronesia, Ronessa, Ronessia,
Ronichia, Ronicia, Roniesha, Ronisha,
Ronneisha, Ronnesa, Ronnesha, Ronneshia,
Ronni, Ronnie, Ronniesha, Ronny*

Ronelle (Welsh) a form of Rhonda, Ronda.
*Ranell, Ranelle, Ronel, Ronella, Ronielle,
Ronnella, Ronnelle*

Rong (Chinese) lotus; beautiful; elegant.

Ronisha (American) a form of Roneisha.
Ronise, Ronnise, Ronnisha, Ronnishia

Ronli (Hebrew) joyful.
*Ronia, Ronice, Ronit, Ronlee, Ronlie, Ronni,
Ronnie, Ronny*

Ronnette (Welsh) a familiar form of
Rhonda, Ronda.
*Ronetta, Ronette, Ronit, Ronita, Ronnetta,
Ronni, Ronnie, Ronny*

Ronni (American) a familiar form of
Veronica and names beginning with "Ron."
Rone, Ronee, Roni, Ronnee, Ronney

Ronnie, Ronny **B** (American) forms of
Ronni.

Roopa (Indian) blessed with beauty.

Roquelina (Latin) strong as a rock.

Rori (Irish) famous brilliance; famous ruler.
Rorie

Rory **B** (Irish) a form of Rori.

Ros, Roz (English) short forms of Rosalind,
Rosalyn.
Rozz, Rozzey, Rozzi, Rozzie, Rozzy

Rosa **G** (Italian, Spanish) a form of Rose.
History: Rosa Parks inspired the American
Civil Rights movement by refusing to give
up her bus seat to a white man in
Montgomery, Alabama. See also Charo,
Roza.

Rosa de Lima (Spanish) a form of Rosa.

Rosabel (French) beautiful rose.
Rosabelia, Rosabella, Rosabelle, Rosebelle

Rosalba (Latin) white rose.
Rosalva, Roselba

Rosalía (Spanish) a combination of Rosa and Lía.

Rosalie (English) a form of Rosalind.
Rosalea, Rosalee, Rosaleen, Rosaleigh, Rosalene, Rosalia, Rosealee, Rosealie, Roselee, Roseli, Roselia, Roselie, Roseley, Rosely, Rosilee, Rosli, Rozali, Rozália, Rozalie, Rozele

Rosalín, Roselín (Spanish) a combination of Rosa and Linda.

Rosalind (Spanish) fair rose.
Ros, Rosalie, Rosalinda, Rosalinde, Rosalyn, Rosalynd, Rosalynde, Roselind, Roselyn, Rosie, Roz, Rozalind, Rozland

Rosalinda (Spanish) a form of Rosalind.
Rosalina

Rosalyn (Spanish) a form of Rosalind.
Ros, Rosaleen, Rosalin, Rosaline, Rosalyne, Rosalynn, Rosalynne, Rosilyn, Roslin, Roslyn, Roslyne, Roslynn, Roz, Rozalyn, Rozlyn

Rosamond (German) famous guardian.
Rosamund, Rosamunda, Rosemonde, Rozamond

Rosanna, Roseanna (English) combinations of Rose + Anna.
Ranna, Roanna, Rosana, Rosannah, Roseana, Roseannah, Rosehanah, Rosehannah, Rosie, Rossana, Rossanna, Rozana, Rozanna

Rosanne, Roseanne (English) combinations of Rose + Ann.
Roanne, Rosan, Rosann, Roseann, Rose Ann, Rose Anne, Rossann, Rossanne, Rozann, Rozanne

Rosario 🄶 (Filipino, Spanish) rosary.
Rosarah, Rosaria, Rosarie, Rosary, Rosaura

Rose (Latin) rose. See also Chalina, Raisa, Raizel, Roza.
Rada, Rasia, Rasine, Rois, Róise, Rosa, Rosea, Rosella, Roselle, Roses, Rosetta, Rosie, Rosina, Rosita, Rosse

Roselani (Hawaiian) heavenly rose.

Roselyn (Spanish) a form of Rosalind.
Roseleen, Roselene, Roselin, Roseline, Roselyne, Roselynn, Roselynne

Rosemarie (English) a combination of Rose + Marie.
Rosamaria, Rosamarie, Rosemari, Rosemaria, Rose Marie

Rosemary (English) a combination of Rose + Mary.
Romi, Romy

Rosenda (German) excellent lady.

Rosetta (Italian) a form of Rose.
Roseta, Rosette

Roshan (Sanskrit) shining light.

Roshawna (American) a combination of Rose + Shawna.
Roshan, Roshana, Roshanda, Roshani, Roshann, Roshanna, Roshanta, Roshaun, Roshauna, Roshaunda, Roshawn, Roshawnda, Roshawnna, Roshona, Roshonda, Roshowna, Roshunda

Rosie (English) a familiar form of Rosalind, Rosanna, Rose.
Rosey, Rosi, Rosio, Rosse, Rosy, Rozsi, Rozy

Rosilda (German) horse-riding warrior.

Rosina (English) a familiar form of Rose.
Rosena, Rosenah, Rosene, Rosheen, Rozena, Rozina

Rosinda (Teutonic) famous warrior.

Rosine (Latin) little rose.

Rosita (Spanish) a familiar form of Rose.
Roseeta, Roseta, Rozeta, Rozita, Rozyte

Roslyn (Scottish) a form of Rossalyn.
Roslin, Roslynn, Rosslyn, Rosslynn

Rosmarí (Spanish) a combination of Rosa and María.

Rosmira (German) celebrated horse-riding warrior.

Ross 🄱 (Latin) rose. (Scottish) peninsula. (French) red.

Rossalyn (Scottish) cape; promontory.
Roslyn, Rosselyn, Rosylin, Roszaliyn

Rosura (Latin) golden rose.

Rou (Chinese) soft; tender.

Rouble (Indian) money.

Rowan 🄶 (English) tree with red berries. (Welsh) a form of Rowena.
Rowana

Rowena (Welsh) fair-haired. (English) famous friend. Literature: Ivanhoe's love interest in Sir Walter Scott's novel *Ivanhoe*.
Ranna, Ronni, Row, Rowan, Rowe, Roweena, Rowen, Rowina

Roxana, Roxanna (Persian) forms of Roxann.
Rocsana, Roxannah

Roxann, Roxanne (Persian) sunrise. Literature: Roxanne is the heroine of Edmond Rostand's play *Cyrano de Bergerac*.
Rocxann, Roxan, Roxana, Roxane, Roxanna, Roxianne, Roxy

Roxy (Persian) a familiar form of Roxann.
Roxi, Roxie

Royale (English) royal.
Royal, Royalene, Royalle, Roylee, Roylene, Ryal, Ryale

Royanna (English) queenly, royal.
Roya

Royce **B** (English) child of Roy.

Roza (Slavic) a form of Rosa.
Roz, Rozalia, Roze, Rozel, Rozele, Rozell, Rozella, Rozelli, Rozia, Rozsa, Rozsi, Rozyte, Rozza, Rozzie

Rozene (Native American) rose blossom.
Rozena, Rozina, Rozine, Ruzena

Rozmin (Indian) rose.

Ruana (Hindi) stringed musical instrument.
Ruan, Ruon

Rubaina (Indian) bright.

Ruben **BG** (Hebrew) a form of Reuben (see Boys' Names).

Rubena (Hebrew) a form of Reubena.
Rubenia, Rubina, Rubine, Rubinia, Rubyn, Rubyna

Rubi (French) a form of Ruby.
Ruba, Rubbie, Rubee, Rubí, Rubia, Rubie

Ruby **G** (French) precious stone.
Rubby, Rubetta, Rubette, Rubey, Rubi, Rubiann, Rubyann, Rubye

Ruchi (Hindi) one who wishes to please.

Ruchika (Indian) shining; beautiful; desirous.

Ruchira (Indian) saffron; tasty.

Ruchita (Indian) splendorous.

Rudecinda (Spanish) a form of Rosenda.

Rudee (German) famous wolf.
Rudeline, Rudell, Rudella, Rudi, Rudie, Rudina, Rudy

Rudra (Hindi) seeds of the rudraksha plant.

Rudrapriya (Indian) beloved of Rudra.

Rudy **B** (German) a form of Rudee.

Rue (German) famous. (French) street. (English) regretful; strong-scented herbs.
Ru, Ruey

Rufa (Latin) red-haired.

Ruffina (Italian) redhead.
Rufeena, Rufeine, Rufina, Ruphyna

Ruhani (Indian) spiritual; sacred, divine.

Ruhi (Indian) soul.

Ruhin (Indian) spiritual.

Rui (Japanese) affectionate.

Rujula (Indian) she who endows wealth; soft.

Rujuta (Indian) polite.

Ruka (Japanese) flower.

Rukan (Arabic) steady; confident.

Rukma (Indian) gold.

Rukmini (Indian) wife of Krishna.

Ruksana (Indian) brilliant.

Rula (Latin, English) ruler.

Rumi (Japanese) beautiful perch.

Rumiko (Japanese) child of Rumi.

Run (Chinese) moist; smooth, sleek.

Run zhun (Indian) sweet sound.

Runa (Norwegian) secret; flowing.
Runna

Ruo (Chinese) to seem like.

Rupa (Indian) silver.

Rupal (Indian) made of silver.

Rupali (Indian) beautiful, pretty.

Rupashi (Indian) beautiful.

Rupasi (Indian) beautiful lady.

Ruperta (Spanish) a form of Roberta.

Rupeshwari (Indian) the goddess of beauty.

Rupi (Indian) beauty.

Rupika (Indian) gold coin.

Rupinder **G** (Sanskrit) beautiful.

Ruqaya (Indian) name of the prophet's daughter.

Rure, Rurrie, Ruru (Japanese) emerald.

Ruri (Japanese) emerald.
Ruriko

Rusalka (Czech) wood nymph. (Russian) mermaid.

Rusham (Indian) peaceful.

Russhell (French) redhead; fox colored.
Rushell, Rushelle, Russellynn, Russhelle

Rusti (English) redhead.
Russet, Rustie, Rusty

Rute (Portuguese) a form of Ruth.

Ruth (Hebrew) friendship. Bible: daughter-in-law of Naomi.
Rutha, Ruthalma, Ruthe, Ruthella, Ruthetta, Ruthie, Ruthven

Ruthann (American) a combination of Ruth + Ann.
Ruthan, Ruthanna, Ruthannah, Ruthanne, Ruthina, Ruthine

Ruthie (Hebrew) a familiar form of Ruth.
Ruthey, Ruthi, Ruthy

Rutilda (German) strong because of her fame.

Rutuja (Indian) the queen of seasons.

Rutva (Indian) speech.

Ruwayda (Indian) walking gently.

Ruza (Czech) rose.
Ruzena, Ruzenka, Ruzha, Ruzsa

Ryan 🅱 (Irish) little ruler.
Raiann, Raianne, Rhyann, Riana, Riane, Ryana, Ryane, Ryanna, Ryanne, Rye, Ryen, Ryenne

Ryann 🅖 (Irish) a form of Ryan.

Ryba (Czech) fish.

Rylan 🅱 (English) land where rye is grown.

Rylee 🅖 (Irish) valiant.
Rye, Ryelee, Rylea, Ryleigh, Ryley, Rylie, Rylina, Rylyn

Ryleigh, Rylie (Irish) forms of Rylee.
Ryelie, Ryli, Rylleigh, Ryllie

Ryley 🅱 (Irish) a form of Rylee.
Ryeley, Rylly, Ryly

Ryo (Japanese) dragon.
Ryoko

S 🅖 (American) an initial used as a first name.

Saabira (Indian) patient.

Saachee (Indian) beloved.

Saachi (Indian) truth.

Saaliha (Indian) good; useful.

Saalima (Indian) safe.

Saamiya (Indian) elevated.

Saarah (Arabic) princess.

Saashi (Indian) moon.

Saatvika (Indian) calm.

Saba (Arabic) morning. (Greek) a form of Sheba.
Sabaah, Sabah, Sabba, Sabbah

Sabana (Latin) from the open plain.

Sabelia (Spanish) a form of Sabina.

Sabi (Arabic) young girl.

Sabiha (Indian) beautiful.

Sabina (Latin) History: the Sabine were a tribe in ancient Italy. See also Bina.
Sabeen, Sabena, Sabienne, Sabin, Sabine, Sabinka, Sabinna, Sabiny, Saby, Sabyne, Savina, Sebina, Sebinah

Sabiya (Arabic) morning; eastern wind.
Saba, Sabaya, Sabiyah

Sable (English) sable; sleek.
Sabel, Sabela, Sabella

Sabra (Hebrew) thorny cactus fruit. (Arabic) resting. History: a name for native-born Israelis, who were said to be hard on the outside and soft and sweet on the inside.
Sabera, Sabira, Sabrah, Sabre, Sabrea, Sabreah, Sabree, Sabreea, Sabri, Sabria, Sabriah, Sabriya, Sebra

Sabreena (English) a form of Sabrina.
Sabreen, Sabrena, Sabrene

Sabrina 🅖 (Latin) boundary line. (English) princess. (Hebrew) a familiar form of Sabra. See also Bree, Brina, Rena, Zabrina.
Sabre, Sabreena, Sabrinas, Sabrinah, Sabrine, Sabrinia, Sabrinna, Sabryna, Sebree, Sebrina, Subrina

Sabryna (English) a form of Sabrina.
Sabrynna

Sacha 🅱🅖 (Russian) a form of Sasha.
Sache, Sachia

Sachee, Sachey, Sachy, Shashie (Japanese) girl.

Sachi (Japanese) blessed; lucky.
Saatchi, Sachie, Sachiko

Sachita (Indian) wise.

Sachiye (Japanese) blessed happiness.

Sachiyo (Japanese) she who possesses happiness and knowledge for a lifetime.

Sacnite (Mayan) white flower.

Sada (Japanese) chaste. (English) a form of Sadie.
Sadá, Sadah, Sadako

Sadayo (Japanese) she who is decisive throughout her life.

Sade G (Hebrew) a form of Chadee, Sarah, Shardae, Sharday.
Sáde, Sadé, Sadea, Sadee, Shaday

Sadella (American) a combination of Sade + Ella.
Sadelle, Sydel, Sydell, Sydella, Sydelle

Sadgata (Indian) she who moves in the right direction.

Sadgati (Indian) liberation.

Sadguna (Indian) good virtues.

Sadhan (Indian) fulfillment.

Sadhana (Hindi) devoted.

Sadhna (Indian) worship.

Sadhvi (Indian) virtuous woman.

Sadie (Hebrew) a familiar form of Sarah. See also Sada.
Saddie, Sadee, Sadey, Sadi, Sadiey, Sady, Sadye, Saide, Saidee, Saidey, Saidi, Saidia, Saidie, Saidy, Sayde, Saydee, Seidy

Sadiqua (Indian) kindly.

Sadira (Persian) lotus tree. (Arabic) star.
Sadra

Sadiya (Arabic) lucky, fortunate.
Sadi, Sadia, Sadiah, Sadiyah, Sadiyyah, Sadya

Sadvita (Indian) combination.

Sadzi (Carrier) sunny disposition.

Saee (Indian) female friend.

Saeeda (Indian) priestly.

Saeko (Japanese) child of Sae.

Saffron (English) Botany: a plant with purple or white flowers whose orange stigmas are used as a spice.
Safron

Safiya (Arabic) pure; serene; best friend.
Safa, Safeya, Saffa, Safia, Safiyah

Safo (Greek) she who sees with clarity.

Sagara (Hindi) ocean.

Sagarika (Indian) wave.

Sage BG (English) wise. Botany: an herb used as a seasoning.
Sagia, Saige, Salvia

Saguna (Indian) virtuous.

Sahana (Indian) patience.

Sahara (Arabic) desert; wilderness.
Sahar, Saharah, Sahari, Saheer, Saher, Sahira, Sahra, Sahrah

Saheli (Indian) friend.

Sahiba (Indian) the lady.

Sahila (Indian) guide.

Sahima (Indian) snowed.

Sahithi (Indian) literature.

Sahla (Indian) smooth; soft ground; fluent.

Sahoj (Indian) strong.

Sai (Japanese) talented.
Saiko

Saida (Hebrew) a form of Sarah. (Arabic) happy; fortunate.
Saidah

Saige (English) a form of Sage.

Saima (Indian) the mother of flowers.

Saira (Hebrew) a form of Sara.
Sairah, Sairi

Saisha (Indian) God.

Sajala (Indian) cloud.

Sajani (Indian) beloved, well loved.

Sajili (Indian) decorated.

Sajni (Indian) beloved.

Sakae (Japanese) prosperity.

Sakaë (Japanese) prosperous.

Sakari (Hindi) sweet.
Sakkara

Sakaye (Japanese) prosper, flourish.

Sakeena (Indian) tranquility inspired by God.

Sakhi (Indian) friend.

Saki (Japanese) cloak; rice wine.

Sakiko (Japanese) child of Saki.

Girls S–Z

Sakshi (Indian) witness.

Sakti (Hindi) energy, power.

Saku (Japanese) remembrance of the Lord.

Sakuko (Japanese) child of Saku.

Sakuna (Native American) bird.

Sakura (Japanese) cherry blossom; wealthy; prosperous.

Sakurako (Japanese) child of Sakura.

Sala (Hindi) sala tree. Religion: the sacred tree under which Buddha died.

Salaberga (German) she who defends the sacrifice.

Salali (Cherokee) squirrel.

Salama (Arabic) peaceful. See also Zulima.

Salbatora (Spanish) savior.

Salena (French) a form of Salina.
Saleana, Saleen, Saleena, Salene, Salenna, Sallene

Saleta (French) location in the French Alps where there was a sighting of the Virgin Mary.

Salila (Indian) water.

Salima (Arabic) safe and sound; healthy.
Saleema, Salema, Salim, Salimah, Salma

Salina (French) solemn, dignified.
Salena, Salin, Salinah, Salinda, Saline

Salliann (English) a combination of Sally + Ann.
Sallian, Sallianne, Sallyann, Sally-Ann, Sallyanne, Sally-Anne

Sally 🄶 (English) princess. History: Sally Ride, an American astronaut, became the first U.S. woman in space.
Sal, Salaid, Sallee, Salletta, Sallette, Salley, Salli, Sallie

Salome (Hebrew) peaceful. History: Salome Alexandra was a ruler of ancient Judea. Bible: the niece of King Herod.
Saloma, Salomé, Salomey, Salomi

Saloni (Indian) beautiful.

Salud (Spanish) health.

Salvadora (Spanish) savior.

Salvatora (Italian) savior.

Salvia (Spanish) healthy; saved. (Latin) a form of Sage.
Sallvia, Salviana, Salviane, Salvina, Salvine

Salwa (Indian) quail; solace.

Sam 🄱 (Aramaic, Hebrew) a short form of Samantha.

Samaah (Indian) generosity.

Samala (Hebrew) asked of God.
Samale, Sammala

Samali (Indian) bouquet.

Samanta (Hebrew) a form of Samantha.
Samantah, Smanta

Samantha ❣ 🄶 (Aramaic) listener. (Hebrew) told by God.
Sam, Samana, Samanath, Samanatha, Samanitha, Samanithia, Samanta, Samanth, Samanthe, Samanthi, Samanthia, Samatha, Sami, Sammanth, Sammantha, Semantha, Simantha, Smantha, Symantha

Samapti, Sampatti (Indian) wealth.

Samara (Latin) elm-tree seed.
Saimara, Samaira, Samar, Samarah, Samari, Samaria, Samariah, Samarie, Samarra, Samarrea, Samary, Samera, Sameria, Samira, Sammar, Sammara, Samora

Samata (Indian) equality.

Samatha (Hebrew) a form of Samantha.
Sammatha

Sameeha (Indian) generous.

Sameeksha (Indian) abstract.

Sameena (Indian) happy.

Sameh (Hebrew) listener. (Arabic) forgiving.
Samaiya, Samaya

Samhita (Indian) a Vedic composition.

Sami 🄱 (Arabic) praised. (Hebrew) a short form of Samantha, Samuela.
Samia, Samiah, Samiha, Samina, Sammey, Sammi, Sammie, Sammijo, Sammy, Sammyjo, Samya, Samye

Samidha (Indian) an offering for a sacred fire.

Samika (Indian) peaceful.

Samiksha (Indian) close inspection, analysis.

Samira (Arabic) entertaining.
Samirah, Samire, Samiria, Samirra, Samyra

Samita (Indian) collected.

Sammy 🄱 (Arabic, Hebrew) a form of Sami.

Samone (Hebrew) a form of Simone.
Samoan, Samoane, Samon, Samona, Samoné, Samonia

Sampada (Indian) blessing.

Sampriti (Indian) attachment.

Samuel **B** (Hebrew) heard God; asked of God.

Samuela (Hebrew) a form of Samuel.
Samala, Samelia, Samella, Sami, Samielle, Samille, Sammile, Samuelle

Samuelle **G** (Hebrew) a form of Samuela.
Samuella

Samyuktheswari (Indian) a princess.

San (Chinese) three.

Sana (Arabic) mountaintop; splendid; brilliant.
Sanaa, Sanáa, Sanaah, Sane, Sanah

Sanako (Japanese) child of Sana.

Sananda (Indian) pleasure.

Sanaya (Indian) eminent.

Sanaye (Japanese) girl who grows quickly.

Sanchala (Indian) Sanskrit synonym for water.

Sanchali (Indian) movement.

Sanchaya, Sanchita, Sandhaya (Indian) collection.

Sancia (Spanish) holy, sacred.
Sanceska, Sancha, Sancharia, Sanchia, Sancie, Santsia, Sanzia

Sandeep **B** (Punjabi) enlightened.
Sandip

Sandhya (Indian) dusk; perfection.

Sandi (Greek) a familiar form of Sandra.
Sandee, Sandia, Sandie, Sandiey, Sandine, Sanndie

Sandra (Greek) defender of mankind. A short form of Cassandra. History: Sandra Day O'Connor was the first woman appointed to the U.S. Supreme Court. See also Zandra.
Sahndra, Sandi, Sandira, Sandrea, Sandria, Sandrica, Sandy, Sanndra, Saundra

Sandrea (Greek) a form of Sandra.
Sandreea, Sandreia, Sandrell, Sandria, Sanndria

Sandrica (Greek) a form of Sandra. See also Rica.
Sandricka, Sandrika

Sandrine (Greek) a form of Alexandra.
Sandreana, Sandrene, Sandrenna, Sandrianna, Sandrina

Sandy **G** (Greek) a familiar form of Cassandra, Sandra.
Sandya, Sandye

Sanemi (Indian) perfect.

Sang (Vietnamese) bird.

Sangeeta, Sangita (Indian) musical.

Sangeetha (Indian) music.

Sangria (Indian) music.

Sani (Indian) gift.

Sanika (Indian) flute.

Saniya (Indian) wisdom.

Sanjana (Indian) in harmony.

Sanjeevani, Sanjivani (Indian) immortality.

Sanjita (Indian) triumphant.

Sanjoli (Indian) period of twilight.

Sanjukta (Indian) connection.

Sanjula, Sanjushree (Indian) beautiful.

Sanne (Hebrew, Dutch) lily.
Sanea, Saneh, Sanna, Sanneen

Sannidhi (Indian) nearness.

Sanoja (Indian) eternal.

Sansita (Indian) praise.

Sanskriti (Indian) heritage.

Sanskruti (Indian) culture.

Santana **G** (Spanish) Saint Anne.
Santa, Santaniata, Santanna, Santanne, Santena, Santenna, Shantana

Santawana (Indian) consolation.

Santayani (Indian) of the evening.

Santina (Spanish) little saint.
Santinia

Santoshi (Indian) the name of a goddess.

Santushti (Indian) complete satisfaction.

Sanura (Swahili) kitten.
Sanora

Sanuye (Moquelumnan) red clouds at sunset.

Sanvali, Sanwari (Indian) dusky.

Sanya (Sanskrit) born on Saturday.
Sañeiya, Sania, Sanyia

Sanyakta (Indian) joined, united.

Sanyu 🆁🅶 (Luganda) happiness.

Sanyukta (Indian) union.

Saparna (Indian) leafy.

Sapata (Native American) dancing bear.

Saphala (Indian) successful.

Sapna (Indian) dream.

Sapphira (Hebrew) a form of Sapphire.
Safira, Sapheria, Saphira, Saphyra, Sephira

Sapphire (Greek) blue gemstone.
Saffire, Saphire, Saphyre, Sapphira

Saqui (Mapuche) preferred one, chosen one; kind soul.

Sara ⚚ 🅶 (Hebrew) a form of Sarah.
Saira, Sarae, Saralee, Sarra, Sera

Sarah ⚚ 🅶 (Hebrew) princess. Bible: the wife of Abraham and mother of Isaac. See also Sadie, Saida, Sally, Saree, Sharai, Shari, Zara, Zarita.
Sahra, Sara, Saraha, Sarahann, Sarahi, Sarai, Sarann, Saray, Sarha, Sariah, Sarina, Sarita, Sarolta, Sarotte, Sarrah, Sasa, Sayra, Sorcha

Sarai, Saray (Hebrew) forms of Sarah.
Saraya

Sarakshi (Indian) good sight.

Sarala (Indian) simple, black tulsi (a plant).

Saralyn (American) a combination of Sarah + Lynn.
Saralena, Saraly, Saralynn

Sarama (Indian) wife of Bibhisan.

Saranya (Indian) surrendered.

Sarasa (Indian) swan.

Sarasi (Indian) jolly, happy.

Sarasvati, Saraswati (Indian) the goddess of learning.

Saravati (Indian) a river.

Sarayu (Indian) wind.

Saree (Arabic) noble. (Hebrew) a familiar form of Sarah.
Sareeka, Sareka, Sari, Sarika, Sarka, Sarri, Sarrie, Sary

Sariah (Hebrew) forms of Sarah.
Saria, Sarie

Sarila (Turkish) waterfall.

Sarina (Hebrew) a familiar form of Sarah.
Sareen, Sareena, Saren, Sarena, Sarene, Sarenna, Sarin, Sarine, Sarinna, Sarinne

Sarita (Hebrew) a familiar form of Sarah.
Saretta, Sarette, Sarit, Saritia, Saritta

Sarjana (Indian) creative.

Sarla (Indian) straight-forward.

Saroj, Saroja (Indian) lotus.

Sarojini (Indian) in the lotus.

Sarolta (Hungarian) a form of Sarah.

Sarotte (French) a form of Sarah.

Sarrah (Hebrew) a form of Sarah.
Sarra

Saruchi (Indian) wonderful.

Sarupa (Indian) beautiful.

Saruprani (Indian) beautiful woman.

Saryu (Indian) the Sharayu River.

Sasa (Japanese) assistant. (Hungarian) a form of Sarah, Sasha.

Sasha 🅶 (Russian) defender of mankind. See also Zasha.
Sacha, Sahsha, Sasa, Sascha, Saschae, Sashae, Sashah, Sashai, Sashana, Sashay, Sashea, Sashel, Sashenka, Sashey, Sashi, Sashia, Sashira, Sashsha, Sashya, Sasjara, Sauscha, Sausha, Shasha, Shashi, Shashia

Sasmita (Indian) always laughing.

Sasquia (Teutonic) she who carries a knife.

Sass (Irish) Saxon.
Sassie, Sassoon, Sassy

Satara (American) a combination of Sarah + Tara.
Sataria, Satarra, Sateriaa, Saterra, Saterria

Sati (Indian) wife of Shiva.

Satin (French) smooth, shiny.
Satinder

Satinka (Native American) sacred dancer.

Sato (Japanese) sugar.
Satu

Satoko (Japanese) child of Sato.

Satomi (Japanese) wise and beautiful girl.

Satoyo (Japanese) she who stays in her hometown for a lifetime.

Satsuki (Japanese) the fifth month.

Saturia (Latin) she who has it all.

Saturnina (Spanish) gift of Saturn.

Satvari (Indian) night.

Satvi (Indian) existence.

Satyaki (Indian) one who is truthful.

Satyarupa (Indian) truth.

Satyavati (Indian) one who speaks the truth.

Saudamini (Indian) lightning.

Saul **B** (Hebrew) asked for, borrowed.

Saumyi (Indian) moonlight.

Saundra (English) a form of Sandra, Sondra.
Saundee, Saundi, Saundie, Saundy

Saura (Hindi) sun worshiper.

Savana, Savanna (Spanish) forms of
Savannah.
*Saveena, Savhana, Savhanna, Savina,
Savine, Savona, Savonna*

Savanah (Spanish) a form of Savannah.
Savhannah

Savannah �֎ **G** (Spanish) treeless plain.
*Sahvannah, Savana, Savanah, Savanha,
Savanna, Savannha, Savauna, Savonnah,
Savonne, Sevan, Sevanah, Sevanh, Sevann,
Sevanna, Svannah*

Savarna (Indian) daughter of the ocean; wife
of the sun.

Saveria (Teutonic) from the new house.

Savita (Indian) sun.

Savitashri (Indian) luster of the sun.

Savitri (Indian) mother.

Savon **B** (Spanish) a treeless plain.

Sawa (Japanese) swamp. (Moquelumnan)
stone.

Sawda (Indian) proper name.

Sawini (Indian) a river.

Sawyer **B** (English) wood worker.
Sawyar, Sawyor

Sayantini (Indian) evening.

Sayde, Saydee (Hebrew) forms of Sadie.
Saydi, Saydia, Saydie, Saydy

Sayeeda (Indian) leader.

Sayeko (Japanese) blessed and helpful child.

Sayén (Mapuche) sweet, lovable, warm;
openhearted woman.

Sayo (Japanese) born at night.

Sayoko (Japanese) child of Sayo.

Sayra (Hebrew) a form of Sarah.
Sayrah, Sayre, Sayri

Sayuri (Japanese) small; quick; lily.

Scarlett (English) bright red. Literature:
Scarlett O'Hara is the heroine of Margaret
Mitchell's novel *Gone with the Wind*.
Scarlet, Scarlette, Scarlotte, Skarlette

Schyler **G** (Dutch) sheltering.
Schuyla, Schuyler, Schuylia, Schylar

Scott **B** (English) from Scotland.

Scotti (Scottish) from Scotland.
Scota, Scotia, Scottie, Scotty

Se (Chinese) a musical instrument.

Sean **B** (Irish) a form of John.

Seana, Seanna (Irish) forms of Sean. See
also Shauna, Shawna.
*Seaana, Sean, Seane, Seann, Seannae,
Seannah, Seannalisa, Seanté, Sianna, Sina*

Sebastian **B** (Greek) venerable. (Latin)
revered. (French) a form of Sebastian.

Sebastiane (Greek, Latin, French) a form of
Sebastian.
*Sebastene, Sebastia, Sebastian, Sebastiana,
Sebastien, Sebastienne*

Sebastien **B** (Greek, Latin, French) a form
of Sebastian.

Seble (Ethiopian) autumn.

Sebrina (English) a form of Sabrina.
Sebrena, Sebrenna, Sebria, Sebriana

Secilia (Latin) a form of Cecilia.
Saselia, Sasilia, Sesilia, Sileas

Secunda (Latin) second.

Secundina (Latin) family's second daughter.

Seda (Armenian) forest voices.

Sedna (Eskimo) well-fed. Mythology: the
goddess of sea animals.

Seelia (English) a form of Sheila.

Seema (Greek) sprout. (Afghan) sky; profile.
Seemah, Sima, Simah

Seemanti (Indian) parting line.

Seemantini (Indian) woman.

Seerat (Indian) inner beauty; fame.

Sefa (Swiss) a familiar form of Josefina.

Séfora (Hebrew) like a small bird.

Girls S–Z

Segismunda (German) victorious protector.

Segunda (Spanish) second-born.

Sei, Seiko (Japanese) force; truth.

Seika (Japanese) she who is famous for her songs.

Seiki (Japanese) star; beginning.

Seina (Basque) innocent.

Seirra (Irish) a form of Sierra.
Seiara, Seiarra, Seira, Seirria

Seki (Japanese) wonderful.
Seka

Sela (English) a short form of Selena.
Seeley, Selah

Selam (Ethiopian) peaceful.

Selda (German) a short form of Griselda. (Yiddish) a form of Zelda.
Seldah, Selde, Sellda, Selldah

Selena ▣ (Greek) moon. Mythology: Selene was the goddess of the moon. See also Celena.
Saleena, Sela, Selana, Seleana, Seleena, Selen, Selenah, Selene, Séléné, Selenia, Selenna, Selina, Sena, Syleena, Sylena

Selene (Greek) a form of Selena.
Seleni, Selenie, Seleny

Selia (Latin) a short form of Cecilia.
Seel, Seil, Sela, Silia

Selima (Hebrew) peaceful.
Selema, Selemah, Selimah

Selina (Greek) a form of Celina, Selena.
Selie, Selin, Selinda, Seline, Selinia, Selinka, Sellina, Selyna, Selyne, Selynne, Sylina

Selma (German) divine protector. (Irish) fair, just. (Scandinavian) divinely protected. (Arabic) secure. See also Zelma.
Sellma, Sellmah, Selmah

Selva (Latin) she who was born in the jungle.

Selvi (Indian) happy, prosperous daughter.

Sema (Turkish) heaven; divine omen.
Semaj

Semanti (Indian) a white rose.

Semele (Latin) once.

Seminaris, Semíramis (Assyrian) she who lives harmoniously with the doves.

Sempronia (Spanish) prudent and measured.

Sen ▣ (Japanese) Mythology: a magical forest elf that lives for thousands of years.

Senalda (Spanish) sign.
Sena, Senda, Senna

Seneca (Iroquois) a tribal name.
Senaka, Seneka, Senequa, Senequae, Senequai, Seneque

Seni (Fijian) a form of Jane.

Senona (Spanish) lively.

Septima (Latin) seventh.

Sequoia (Cherokee) giant redwood tree.
Seqoiyia, Seqouyia, Seqoya, Sequoi, Sequoiah, Sequora, Sequoya, Sequoyah, Sikoya

Serafina (Hebrew) burning; ardent. Bible: seraphim are an order of angels.
Sarafina, Serafine, Seraphe, Seraphin,
Seraphina, Seraphine, Seraphita, Serapia, Serofina

Serena (Latin) peaceful. See also Rena.
Sarina, Saryna, Seraina, Serana, Sereen, Sereina, Seren, Serenah, Serene, Serenea, Serenia, Serenna, Serina, Serreana, Serrena, Serrenna

Serenela (Spanish) a form of Serena.

Serenity (Latin) peaceful.
Serenidy, Serenitee, Serenitey, Sereniti, Serenitiy, Serinity, Serrennity

Sergia (Greek) attendant.

Serilda (Greek) armed warrior woman.

Serina (Latin) a form of Serena.
Sereena, Serin, Serine, Serreena, Serrin, Serrina, Seryna

Servanda (Latin) she who must be saved and protected.

Servia (Latin) daughter of those who serve the Lord.

Seth ▣ (Hebrew) appointed.

Setsu (Japanese) fidelity.

Setsuko (Japanese) a form of Setsu.

Seva (Indian) worship.

Sevanda (Latin) she who deserves to be saved and guarded.

Sevati (Indian) white rose.

Severa (Spanish) severe.

Severina (Italian, Portuguese, Croatian, German, Ancient Roman) severe.

Sevilla (Spanish) from Seville.
Seville

Sevita (Indian) cherished.

Sha (Chinese) a type of grass.

Shaadiya (Indian) singer.

Shaba (Spanish) rose.
Shabana, Shabina

Shabab (Indian) beauty.

Shabalini (Indian) mossy.

Shabari (Indian) a tribal devotee of Lord Rama.

Shabnam, Shabnum (Indian) dew.

Shachi (Indian) intelligence.

Shada (Native American) pelican.
Shadae, Shadea, Shadeana, Shadee, Shadi, Shadia, Shadiah, Shadie, Shadiya, Shaida

Shaday (American) a form of Sade.
Shadai, Shadaia, Shadaya, Shadayna, Shadei, Shadeziah, Shaiday

Shadrika (American) a combination of the prefix Sha + Rika.
Shadreeka, Shadreka, Shadrica, Shadricka, Shadrieka

Shae **G** (Irish) a form of Shea.
Shaenel, Shaeya, Shai, Shaia

Shaelee (Irish) a form of Shea.
Shaeleigh, Shaeley, Shaelie, Shaely

Shaelyn (Irish) a form of Shea.
Shael, Shaelaine, Shaelan, Shaelanie, Shaelanna, Shaeleen, Shaelene, Shaelin, Shaeline, Shaelyne, Shaelynn, Shae-Lynn, Shaelynne

Shafira (Swahili) distinguished.
Shaffira

Shagufta (Indian) flowering.

Shagun (Indian) auspicious moment.

Shahar (Arabic) moonlit.
Shahara

Shaheda (Indian) whiteness.

Shahina (Arabic) falcon.
Shaheen, Shaheena, Shahi, Shahin

Shahla (Afghani) beautiful eyes.
Shaila, Shailah, Shalah

Shahzeela (Indian) beautiful.

Shaianne (Cheyenne) a form of Cheyenne.
Shaeen, Shaeine, Shaian, Shaiana, Shaiandra, Shaiane, Shaiann, Shaianna

Shaila (Latin) a form of Sheila.
Shaela, Shaelea, Shaeyla, Shailah, Shailee, Shailey, Shaili, Shailie, Shailla, Shaily, Shailyn, Shailynn

Shaiming (Chinese) sunshine.

Shaina **G** (Yiddish) beautiful.
Shaena, Shainah, Shaine, Shainna, Shajna, Shanie, Shayna, Shayndel, Sheina, Sheindel

Shaista (Indian) well behaved.

Shaivi (Indian) prosperity.

Shajuana (American) a combination of the prefix Sha + Juanita. See also Shawanna.
Shajuan, Shajuanda, Shajuanita, Shajuanna, Shajuanza

Shaka **B** (Hindi) a form of Shakti. A short form of names beginning with "Shak." See also Chaka.
Shakah, Shakha

Shakarah (American) a combination of the prefix Sha + Kara.
Shacara, Shacari, Shaccara, Shaka, Shakari, Shakkara, Shikara

Shakayla (Arabic) a form of Shakila.
Shakaela, Shakail, Shakaila, Shakala

Shakeel (Indian) handsome.

Shakeena (American) a combination of the prefix Sha + Keena.
Shaka, Shakeina, Shakeyna, Shakina, Shakyna

Shakeita (American) a combination of the prefix Sha + Keita. See also Shaqueita.
Shaka, Shakeeta, Shakeitha, Shakeithia, Shaketa, Shaketha, Shakethia, Shaketia, Shakita, Shakitra, Sheketa, Shekita, Shikita, Shikitha

Shakera (Arabic) a form of Shakira.
Chakeria, Shakeira, Shakeirra, Shakerah, Shakeria, Shakeriah, Shakeriay, Shakerra, Shakerri, Shakerria, Shakerya, Shakeryia, Shakeyra

Shakia (American) a combination of the prefix Sha + Kia.
Shakeeia, Shakeeyah, Shakeia, Shakeya, Shakiya, Shekeia, Shekia, Shekiah, Shikia

Shakila (Arabic) pretty.
Chakila, Shaka, Shakayla, Shakeela, Shakeena, Shakela, Shakelah, Shakilah, Shakyla, Shekila, Shekilla, Shikeela

Girls S–Z

Shakira (Arabic) thankful.
Shaakira, Shacora, Shaka, Shakeera, Shakeerah, Shakeeria, Shakera, Shakiera, Shakierra, Shakir, Shakirah, Shakirat, Shakirea, Shakirra, Shakora, Shakuria, Shakyra, Shaquira, Shekiera, Shekira, Shikira

Shakti (Hindi) energy, power. Religion: a form of the Hindu goddess Devi.
Sakti, Shaka, Sita

Shakuntala (Indian) the wife of Dushyant.

Shakyra (Arabic) a form of Shakira.
Shakyria

Shalaka (Indian) another name for the goddess Parvati.

Shalalu (Indian) perfume.

Shalana (American) a combination of the prefix Sha + Lana.
Shalaana, Shalain, Shalaina, Shalaine, Shaland, Shalanda, Shalane, Shalann, Shalaun, Shalauna, Shalayna, Shalayne, Shalaynna, Shallan, Shelan, Shelanda

Shaleah (American) a combination of the prefix Sha + Leah.
Shalea, Shalee, Shaleea, Shalia, Shaliah

Shaleisha (American) a combination of the prefix Sha + Aisha.
Shalesha, Shalesia, Shalicia, Shalisha

Shalena (American) a combination of the prefix Sha + Lena.
Shaleana, Shaleen, Shaleena, Shalen, Shálena, Shalene, Shalené, Shalenna, Shalina, Shalinda, Shaline, Shalini, Shalinna, Shelayna, Shelayne, Shelena

Shalika (Indian) flute.

Shalisa (American) a combination of the prefix Sha + Lisa.
Shalesa, Shalese, Shalessa, Shalice, Shalicia, Shaliece, Shalise, Shalisha, Shalishea, Shalisia, Shalissa, Shalisse, Shalyce, Shalys, Shalyse

Shalita (American) a combination of the prefix Sha + Lita.
Shaleta, Shaletta, Shalida, Shalitta

Shalona (American) a combination of the prefix Sha + Lona.
Shalon, Shalone, Shálonna, Shalonne

Shalonda (American) a combination of the prefix Sha + Ondine.
Shalonde, Shalondine, Shalondra, Shalondria

Shalyn (American) a combination of the prefix Sha + Lynn.
Shalin, Shalina, Shalinda, Shaline, Shalyna, Shalynda, Shalyne, Shalynn, Shalynne

Shamara (Arabic) ready for battle.
Shamar, Shamarah, Shamare, Shamarea, Shamaree, Shamari, Shamaria, Shamariah, Shamarra, Shamarri, Shammara, Shamora, Shamori, Shamorra, Shamorria, Shamorriah

Shambari (Indian) illusion.

Shambhukanta (Indian) wife of Shambhu.

Shameena (Indian) beautiful.

Shameka (American) a combination of the prefix Sha + Meka.
Shameaka, Shameakah, Shameca, Shamecca, Shamecha, Shamecia, Shameika, Shameke, Shamekia

Shamika (American) a combination of the prefix Sha + Mika.
Shameeca, Shameeka, Shamica, Shamicia, Shamicka, Shamieka, Shamikia

Shamim (Indian) fire.

Shamira (Hebrew) precious stone.
Shamir, Shamiran, Shamiria, Shamyra

Shamita (Indian) peacemaker.

Shamitha (Indian) she who is calm and disciplined.

Shamiya (American) a combination of the prefix Sha + Mia.
Shamea, Shamia, Shamiah, Shamiyah, Shamyia, Shamyiah, Shamyne

Shampa (Indian) lightning.

Shana (Hebrew) a form of Shane. (Irish) a form of Jane.
Shaana, Shan, Shanae, Shanda, Shandi, Shane, Shania, Shanna, Shannah, Shauna, Shawna

Shanae (Irish) a form of Shana.
Shanay, Shanea

Shanda (American) a form of Chanda, Shana.
Shandae, Shandah, Shandra, Shannda

Shandi (English) a familiar form of Shana.
Shandee, Shandeigh, Shandey, Shandice, Shandie

Shandra (American) a form of Shanda. See also Chandra.
Shandrea, Shandreka, Shandri, Shandria, Shandriah, Shandrice, Shandrie, Shandry

Shane 🅱 (Irish) God is gracious.
Shanea, Shaneah, Shanee, Shanée, Shanie

Shaneisha (American) a combination of the prefix Sha + Aisha.
Shanesha, Shaneshia, Shanessa, Shanisha, Shanissha

Shaneka (American) a form of Shanika.
Shanecka, Shaneeka, Shaneekah,
Shaneequa, Shaneeque, Shaneika,
Shaneikah, Shanekia, Shanequa, Shaneyka,
Shonneka

Shanel, Shanell, Shanelle (American)
forms of Chanel.
Schanel, Schanell, Shanella, Shanelly,
Shannel, Shannell, Shannelle, Shenel,
Shenela, Shenell, Shenelle, Shenelly,
Shinelle, Shonelle, Shynelle

Shaneta (American) a combination of the
prefix Sha + Neta.
Seanette, Shaneeta, Shanetha, Shanethis,
Shanetta, Shanette, Shineta, Shonetta

Shang (Chinese) esteem.

Shani (Swahili) a form of Shany.

Shania (American) a form of Shana.
Shanasia, Shanaya, Shaniah, Shaniya,
Shanya, Shenia

Shanice (American) a form of Janice. See
also Chanise.
Chenise, Shanece, Shaneese, Shaneice,
Shanese, Shanicea, Shaniece, Shanise,
Shanneice, Shannice, Shanyce, Sheneice

Shanida (American) a combination of the
prefix Sha + Ida.
Shaneeda, Shannida

Shanika (American) a combination of the
prefix Sha + Nika.
Shaneka, Shanica, Shanicca, Shanicka,
Shanieka, Shanike, Shanikia, Shanikka,
Shanikqua, Shanikwa, Shaniqua, Shenika,
Shineeca, Shonnika

Shaniqua (American) a form of Shanika.
Shaniqa, Shaniquah, Shanique, Shaniquia,

Shaniquwa, Shaniqwa, Shenequa, Sheniqua,
Shinequa, Shiniqua

Shanise (American) a form of Shanice.
Shanisa, Shanisha, Shanisia, Shanissa,
Shanisse, Shineese

Shanita (American) a combination of the
prefix Sha + Nita.
Shanitha, Shanitra, Shanitta, Shinita

Shankari (Indian) the wife of Lord Shiva.

Shankhamala (Indian) a fairytale princess.

Shanley **G** (Irish) hero's child.
Shanlee, Shanleigh, Shanlie, Shanly

Shanna (Irish) a form of Shana, Shannon.
Shanea, Shannah, Shannea

Shannen (Irish) a form of Shannon.
Shanen, Shanena, Shanene

Shannon **G** (Irish) small and wise.
Shanan, Shanadoah, Shann, Shanna,
Shannan, Shanneen, Shannen, Shannie,
Shannin, Shannyn, Shanon

Shansa (Indian) praise.

Shanta, Shante (French) forms of Chantal.
Shantai, Shantay, Shantaya, Shantaye,
Shanté, Shantea, Shantee, Shantée, Shanteia

Shantae **G** (French) a form of Chantal.

Shantal (American) a form of Shantel.
Shantall, Shontal

Shantana (American) a form of Santana.
Shantan, Shantanae, Shantanell,
Shantanickia, Shantanika, Shantanna

Shantara (American) a combination of the
prefix Sha + Tara.
Shantaria, Shantarra, Shantera, Shanteria,
Shanterra, Shantira, Shontara, Shuntara

Shanteca (American) a combination of the
prefix Sha + Teca.
Shantecca, Shanteka, Shantika, Shantikia

Shantel, Shantell **G** (American) song.
Seantelle, Shanntell, Shanta, Shantal,
Shantae, Shantale, Shante, Shanteal,
Shanteil, Shantele, Shantella, Shantelle,
Shantrell, Shantyl, Shantyle, Shauntel,
Shauntell, Shauntelle, Shauntrel, Shauntrell,
Shauntrella, Shentel, Shentelle, Shontal,
Shontalla, Shontalle, Shontel, Shontelle

Shanteria (American) a form of Shantara.
Shanterica, Shanterria, Shanterrie,
Shantieria, Shantirea, Shonteria

Shantesa (American) a combination of the
prefix Sha + Tess.
Shantese, Shantice, Shantise, Shantisha,
Shontecia, Shontessia

Shantia (American) a combination of the
prefix Sha + Tia.
Shanteya, Shanti, Shantida, Shantie,
Shaunteya, Shauntia, Shontia

Shantille (American) a form of Chantilly.
Shanteil, Shantil, Shantilli, Shantillie,
Shantilly, Shantyl, Shantyle

Shantina (American) a combination of the
prefix Sha + Tina.
Shanteena, Shontina

Shantora (American) a combination of the
prefix Sha + Tory.
Shantoia, Shantori, Shantoria, Shantory,
Shantorya, Shantoya, Shanttoria

Shantrice (American) a combination of the prefix Sha + Trice. See also Chantrice.
Shantrece, Shantrecia, Shantreece, Shantreese, Shantrese, Shantress, Shantrezia, Shantricia, Shantriece, Shantris, Shantrisse, Shontrice

Shany (Swahili) marvelous, wonderful.
Shaney, Shannai, Shannea, Shanni, Shannia, Shannie, Shanny, Shanya

Shao (Chinese) beautiful springtime.

Shappa (Native American) red thunder.

Shaquanda (American) a combination of the prefix Sha + Wanda.
Shaquan, Shaquana, Shaquand, Shaquandey, Shaquandra, Shaquandria, Shaquanera, Shaquani, Shaquania, Shaquanna, Shaquanta, Shaquantae, Shaquantay, Shaquante, Shaquantia, Shaquona, Shaquonda, Shaquondra, Shaquondria

Shaqueita, Shaquita (American) forms of Shakeita.
Shaqueta, Shaquetta, Shaquette, Shaquitta, Shequida, Shequita, Shequittia

Shaquila, Shaquilla (American) forms of Shakila.
Shaquail, Shaquia, Shaquil, Shaquilah, Shaquile, Shaquill, Shaquillah, Shaquille, Shaquillia, Shequela, Shequele, Shequila, Shquiyla

Shaquille 🄱 (American) a form of Shaquila.

Shaquira (American) a form of Shakira.
Shaquirah, Shaquire, Shaquirra, Shaqura, Shaqurah, Shaquri

Shara (Hebrew) a short form of Sharon.
Shaara, Sharah, Sharal, Sharala, Sharalee, Sharlyn, Sharlynn, Sharra, Sharrah

Sharadini (Indian) autumn.

Sharai (Hebrew) princess. See also Sharon.
Sharae, Sharaé, Sharah, Sharaiah, Sharay, Sharaya, Sharayah

Sharan (Hindi) protector.
Sharaine, Sharanda, Sharanjeet

Shardae, Sharday (Punjabi) charity. (Yoruba) honored by royalty. (Arabic) runaway. A form of Chardae.
Sade, Shadae, Sharda, Shar-Dae, Shardai, Shar-Day, Sharde, Shardea, Shardee, Shardée, Shardei, Shardeia, Shardey

Sharee (English) a form of Shari.
Shareen, Shareena, Sharine

Shareefa (Indian) noble.

Shari (French) beloved, dearest. (Hungarian) a form of Sarah. See also Sharita, Sheree, Sherry.
Shara, Share, Sharee, Sharia, Shariah, Sharian, Shariann, Sharianne, Sharie, Sharra, Sharree, Sharri, Sharrie, Sharry, Shary

Sharice (French) a form of Cherice.
Shareese, Sharesse, Sharese, Sharica, Sharicka, Shariece, Sharis, Sharise, Sharish, Shariss, Sharissa, Sharisse, Sharyse

Sharik (African) child of God.

Sharini (Indian) earth.

Sharissa (American) a form of Sharice.
Sharesa, Sharessia, Sharisa, Sharisha, Shereeza, Shericia, Sherisa, Sherissa

Sharita (French) a familiar form of Shari. (American) a form of Charity. See also Sherita.
Shareeta, Sharrita

Sharla (French) a short form of Sharlene, Sharlotte.

Sharlene (French) little and strong.
Scharlane, Scharlene, Shar, Sharla, Sharlaina, Sharlaine, Sharlane, Sharlanna, Sharlee, Sharleen, Sharleine, Sharlena, Sharleyne, Sharline, Sharlyn, Sharlyne, Sharlynn, Sharlynne, Sherlean, Sherleen, Sherlene, Sherline

Sharlotte (American) a form of Charlotte.
Sharlet, Sharlett, Sharlott, Sharlotta

Sharma (American) a short form of Sharmaine.
Sharmae, Sharme

Sharmaine (American) a form of Charmaine.
Sharma, Sharmain, Sharman, Sharmane, Sharmanta, Sharmayne, Sharmeen, Sharmene, Sharmese, Sharmin, Sharmine, Sharmon, Sharmyn

Sharmila (Indian) shy.

Sharmistha (Indian) wife of Yayati.

Sharna (Hebrew) a form of Sharon.
Sharnae, Sharnay, Sharne, Sharnea, Sharnease, Sharnee, Sharneese, Sharnell, Sharnelle, Sharnese, Sharnett, Sharnetta, Sharnise

Sharon 🄶 (Hebrew) desert plain. A form of Sharai.
Shaaron, Shara, Sharai, Sharan, Shareen, Sharen, Shari, Sharin, Sharna, Sharonda, Sharone, Sharran, Sharren, Sharrin, Sharron, Sharrona, Sharyn, Sharyon, Sheren, Sheron, Sherryn

Sharonda (Hebrew) a form of Sharon.
Sharronda, Sheronda, Sherrhonda

Sharrona (Hebrew) a form of Sharon.
Sharona, Sharone, Sharonia, Sharonna,
Sharony, Sharronne, Sheron, Sherona,
Sheronna, Sherron, Sherronna, Sherronne,
Shirona

Sharvari (Indian) twilight.

Shashibala (Indian) a girl with a round
face.

Shashikala (Indian) phases of the moon.

Shashini (Indian) moon.

Shashiprabha (Indian) moonlight.

Shashirekha (Indian) moon ray.

Shaswati (Indian) eternal.

Shatara (Hindi) umbrella. (Arabic) good;
industrious. (American) a combination of
Sharon + Tara.
Shatarea, Shatari, Shataria, Shatarra,
Shataura, Shateira, Shatera, Shaterah,
Shateria, Shaterra, Shaterri, Shaterria,
Shatherian, Shatierra, Shatiria

Shatha (Indian) aromatic.

Shatoria (American) a combination of the
prefix Sha + Tory.
Shatora, Shatorea, Shatori, Shatorri,
Shatorria, Shatory, Shatorya, Shatoya

Shaun **B** (Hebrew, Irish) God is gracious.

Shauna (Hebrew) a form of Shaun. (Irish) a
form of Shana. See also Seana, Shona.
Shaun, Shaunah, Shaunda, Shaune, Shaunee,
Shauneen, Shaunelle, Shaunette, Shauni,
Shaunice, Shaunicy, Shaunie, Shaunika,

Shaunisha, Shaunna, Shaunnea, Shaunta,
Shaunua, Shaunya

Shaunda (Irish) a form of Shauna. See also
Shanda, Shawnda, Shonda.
Shaundal, Shaundala, Shaundel, Shaundela,
Shaundell, Shaundelle, Shaundra, Shaundrea,
Shaundree, Shaundria, Shaundrice

Shaunta (Irish) a form of Shauna. See also
Shawnta, Shonta.
Schunta, Shauntae, Shauntay, Shaunte,
Shauntea, Shauntee, Shauntée, Shaunteena,
Shauntei, Shauntia, Shauntier, Shauntrel,
Shauntrell, Shauntrella

Shavon **G** (American) a form of Shavonne.
Schavon, Schevon, Shavan, Shavana,
Shavaun, Shavona, Shavonda, Shavone,
Shavonia, Shivon

Shavonne (American) a combination of the
prefix Sha + Yvonne. See also Siobhan.
Shavanna, Shavon, Shavondra, Shavonn,
Shavonna, Shavonni, Shavonnia, Shavonnie,
Shavontae, Shavonte, Shavonté, Shavoun,
Shivaun, Shivawn, Shivonne, Shyvon,
Shyvonne

Shawanna (American) a combination of the
prefix Sha + Wanda. See also Shajuana,
Shawna.
Shawan, Shawana, Shawanda, Shawante,
Shiwani

Shawn **B** (Hebrew, Irish) God is gracious.

Shawna (Hebrew) a form of Shawn. (Irish)
a form of Jane. A form of Shana, Shauna.
See also Seana, Shona.
Sawna, Shaw, Shawn, Shawnae, Shawnai,
Shawnea, Shawnee, Shawneen, Shawneena,
Shawnell, Shawnette, Shawnna, Shawnra,
Shawnta, Sheona, Siân, Siana, Sianna

Shawnda (Irish) a form of Shawna. See also
Shanda, Shaunda, Shonda.
Shawndal, Shawndala, Shawndan,
Shawndel, Shawndra, Shawndrea,
Shawndree, Shawndreel, Shawndrell,
Shawndria

Shawnee (Irish) a form of Shawna.
Shawne, Shawneea, Shawney, Shawni,
Shawnie

Shawnika (American) a combination of
Shawna + Nika.
Shawnaka, Shawnequa, Shawneika,
Shawnicka

Shawnta **G** (Irish) a form of Shawna. See
also Shaunta, Shonta.
Shawntae, Shawntay, Shawnte, Shawnté,
Shawntee, Shawntell, Shawntelle,
Shawnteria, Shawntia, Shawntil, Shawntile,
Shawntill, Shawntille, Shawntina,
Shawntish, Shawntrese, Shawntriece

Shay **BG** (Irish) a form of Shea.
Shaya, Shayah, Shayda, Shayha, Shayia,
Shayla, Shey, Sheye

Shaye (Irish) a form of Shay.

Shayla (Irish) a form of Shay.
Shaylagh, Shaylah, Shaylain, Shaylan,
Shaylea, Shayleah, Shaylla, Shaylyn, Sheyla

Shaylee (Irish) a form of Shea.
Shaylei, Shayleigh, Shayley, Shayli, Shaylie,
Shayly, Shealy

Shaylyn (Irish) a form of Shea.
Shaylin, Shaylina, Shaylinn, Shaylynn,
Shaylynne, Shealyn, Sheylyn

Shayna (Hebrew) beautiful.
Shaynae, Shaynah, Shayne, Shaynee, Shayney, Shayni, Shaynie, Shaynna, Shaynne, Shayny, Sheana, Sheanna

Shayne ☗ (Hebrew) a form of Shayna.

Shea ☗ (Irish) fairy palace.
Shae, Shay, Shaylee, Shaylyn, Shealy, Shaelee, Shaelyn, Shealyn, Sheann, Sheannon, Sheanta, Sheaon, Shearra, Sheatara, Sheaunna, Sheavon

Sheba (Hebrew) a short form of Bathsheba. Geography: an ancient country of south Arabia.
Saba, Sabah, Shebah, Sheeba

Sheena (Hebrew) God is gracious. (Irish) a form of Jane.
Sheenagh, Sheenah, Sheenan, Sheeneal, Sheenika, Sheenna, Sheina, Shena, Shiona

Sheetal (Indian) cool.

Shefali (Indian) fragrant.

Shefalika (Indian) a flower.

Shehla (Indian) dark brown, almost black.

Sheila (Latin) blind. (Irish) a form of Cecelia. See also Cheyla, Zelizi.
Seelia, Seila, Selia, Shaila, Sheela, Sheelagh, Sheelah, Sheilagh, Sheilah, Sheileen, Sheiletta, Sheilia, Sheillynn, Sheilya, Shela, Shelagh, Shelah, Shelia, Shiela, Shila, Shilah, Shilea, Shyla

Shejali (Indian) a fruit.

Shelbi, Shelbie (English) forms of Shelby.
Shelbbie, Shellbi, Shellbie

Shelby ☗ (English) ledge estate.
Chelby, Schelby, Shel, Shelbe, Shelbee, Shelbey, Shelbi, Shelbie, Shelbye, Shellby

Sheldon ☗ (English) farm on the ledge.
Sheldina, Sheldine, Sheldrina, Sheldyn, Shelton

Shelee (English) a form of Shelley.
Shelee, Sheleen, Shelena, Sheley, Sheli, Shelia, Shelina, Shelinda, Shelita

Shelisa (American) a combination of Shelley + Lisa.
Sheleza, Shelica, Shelicia, Shelise, Shelisse, Sheliza

Shelley, Shelly ☗ (English) meadow on the ledge. (French) familiar forms of Michelle. See also Rochelle.
Shelee, Shell, Shella, Shellaine, Shellana, Shellany, Shellee, Shellene, Shelli, Shellian, Shelliann, Shellie, Shellina

Shelsea (American) a form of Chelsea.
Shellsea, Shellsey, Shelsey, Shelsie, Shelsy

Shelton ☗ (English) a form of Sheldon.

Shen (Chinese) spiritual, deep-thinking.

Shena (Irish) a form of Sheena.
Shenada, Shenae, Shenah, Shenay, Shenda, Shene, Shenea, Sheneda, Shenee, Sheneena, Shenica, Shenika, Shenina, Sheniqua, Shenita, Shenna, Shennae, Shennah, Shenoa

Sheng (Chinese) holy, sage.

Shera (Aramaic) light.
Sheera, Sheerah, Sherae, Sherah, Sheralee, Sheralle, Sheralyn, Sheralynn, Sheralynne, Sheray, Sheraya

Sheree (French) beloved, dearest.
Scherie, Sheeree, Shere, Shereé, Sherrelle, Shereen, Shereena

Sherelle (French) a form of Cherelle, Sheryl.
Sherel, Sherell, Sheriel, Sherrel, Sherrell, Sherrelle, Shirelle

Sheri, Sherri (French) forms of Sherry.
Sheria, Sheriah, Sherie, Sherrie

Sherian (American) a combination of Sheri + Ann.
Sherianne, Sherrina

Sherice (French) a form of Cherice.
Scherise, Sherece, Shereece, Sherees, Shereese, Sherese, Shericia, Sherise, Sherisse, Sherrish, Sherryse, Sheryce

Sheridan ☗ (Irish) wild.
Sherida, Sheridane, Sherideen, Sheriden, Sheridian, Sheridon, Sherridan, Sherridon

Sherika (Punjabi) relative. (Arabic) easterner.
Shereka, Sherica, Shericka, Sherrica, Sherricka, Sherrika

Sherissa (French) a form of Sherry, Sheryl.
Shereeza, Sheresa, Shericia, Sherrish

Sherita (French) a form of Sherry, Sheryl. See also Sharita.
Shereta, Sheretta, Sherette, Sherrita

Sherleen (French, English) a form of Sheryl, Shirley.
Sherileen, Sherlene, Sherlin, Sherlina, Sherline, Sherlyn, Sherlyne, Sherlynne, Shirlena, Shirlene, Shirlina, Shirlyn

Sherry ☗ (French) beloved, dearest. A familiar form of Sheryl. See also Sheree.
Sherey, Sheri, Sherissa, Sherrey, Sherri, Sherria, Sherriah, Sherrie, Sherye, Sheryy

Sheryl (French) beloved. A familiar form of Shirley. See also Sherry.
Sharel, Sharil, Sharilyn, Sharyl, Sharyll, Sheral, Sherell, Sheriel, Sheril, Sherill, Sherily, Sherilyn, Sherissa, Sherita, Sherleen, Sherral, Sherrelle, Sherril, Sherrill, Sherryl, Sherylly

Sherylyn (American) a combination of Sheryl + Lynn. See also Cherilyn.
Sharolin, Sharolyn, Sharyl-Lynn, Sheralyn, Sherilyn, Sherilynn, Sherilynne, Sherralyn, Sherralynn, Sherrilyn, Sherrilynn, Sherrilynne, Sherrylyn, Sherryn, Sherylanne

Shevalini (Indian) a river.

Shevanti (Indian) a flower.

Shevonne (American) a combination of the prefix She + Yvonne.
Shevaun, Shevon, Shevonda, Shevone

Sheyenne (Cheyenne) a form of Cheyenne. See also Shyann, Shyanne.
Shayhan, Sheyan, Sheyane, Sheyann, Sheyanna, Sheyannah, Sheyanne, Sheyen, Sheyene, Shiante, Shyanne

Shezreen (Indian) particle of gold.

Shianne (Cheyenne) a form of Cheyenne.
She, Shian, Shiana, Shianah, Shianda, Shiane, Shiann, Shianna, Shiannah, Shiany, Shieana, Shieann, Shieanne, Shiena, Shiene, Shienna

Shichi (Indian) glow.

Shielawatti (Indian) river.

Shiesta (Indian) modest; disciplined; cultured.

Shifa (Indian) friend; truthful.

Shifra (Hebrew) beautiful.
Schifra, Shifrah

Shigeko (Japanese) luxuriant child.

Shigemi (Japanese) luxuriant truth.

Shiho (Japanese) to maintain original intention.

Shihobu (Japanese) perseverance.

Shika (Japanese) gentle deer.
Shi, Shikah, Shikha

Shikhi (Indian) peacock; flame.

Shilavati (Indian) a river.

Shilo (Hebrew) God's gift. Bible: a sanctuary for the Israelites where the Ark of the Covenant was kept.
Shiloh

Shilpita (Indian) well proportioned.

Shin (Korean) brightness.

Shina (Japanese) virtuous, good; wealthy. (Chinese) a form of China.
Shinae, Shinay, Shine, Shinna

Shing (Chinese) victory.

Shinjini (Indian) ankle bells.

Shin-Mu (Chinese) mother of perfect intelligence; China's holy virgin.

Shino (Japanese) bamboo stalk.

Shiomi (Japanese) the beautiful tide.

Shione (Japanese) the noise made by the tide.

Shiori (Japanese) she who guides through poetry.

Shipra (Indian) the name of a river.

Shiquita (American) a form of Chiquita.
Shiquata, Shiquitta

Shira (Hebrew) song.
Shirah, Shiray, Shire, Shiree, Shiri, Shirit, Shyra

Shirina, Shrina (Indian) night.

Shirlene (English) a form of Shirley.
Shirleen, Shirline, Shirlynn

Shirley (English) bright meadow. See also Sheryl.
Sherlee, Sherleen, Sherley, Sherli, Sherlie, Shir, Shirl, Shirlee, Shirlie, Shirly, Shirlly, Shurlee, Shurley

Shishirkana (Indian) particles of dew.

Shiuli (Indian) flower.

Shivangi (Indian) beautiful.

Shivani (Hindi) life and death.
Shiva, Shivana, Shivanie, Shivanna

Shivapriya (Indian) liked by Shiva.

Shivasundari (Indian) the goddess Durga.

Shivika (Indian) a palanquin.

Shizu (Japanese) silent.
Shizue, Shizuka, Shizuko, Shizuyo

Shizuye (Japanese) blessed and ambitious girl.

Shobhita (Indian) splendid.

Shobhna (Indian) ornamental; shining; beautiful.

Shoka (Japanese) fly up; beautiful.

Shoko (Japanese) child of Sho.

Shona (Irish) a form of Jane. A form of Shana, Shauna, Shawna.
Shiona, Shonagh, Shonah, Shonalee, Shonda, Shone, Shonee, Shonette, Shoni, Shonie, Shonna, Shonnah, Shonta

Shonda (Irish) a form of Shona. See also Shanda, Shaunda, Shawnda.
Shondalette, Shondalyn, Shondel, Shondelle, Shondi, Shondia, Shondie, Shondra, Shondreka, Shounda

Shonima (Indian) redness.

Shonta (Irish) a form of Shona. See also Shaunta, Shawnta.
Shontá, Shontae, Shontai, Shontalea, Shontasia, Shontavia, Shontaviea, Shontay, Shontaya, Shonte, Shonté, Shontedra, Shontee, Shonteral, Shonti, Shontol, Shontoy, Shontrail, Shountáe

Shorashi (Indian) young woman.

Shoshana (Hebrew) a form of Susan.
Shosha, Shoshan, Shoshanah, Shoshane, Shoshanha, Shoshann, Shoshanna, Shoshannah, Shoshauna, Shoshaunah, Shoshawna, Shoshona, Shoshone, Shoshonee, Shoshoney, Shoshoni, Shoushan, Shushana, Sosha, Soshana

Shou (Chinese) teacher.

Shoumo (Indian) the quiet one; the learned one.

Shrabana, Shravana (Indian) the name of a star.

Shraddha (Indian) faith; very attentive person.

Shradhdha (Indian) faith.

Shramidhi (Indian) girl who likes to work hard and earn.

Shravani (Indian) full moon of Shravan month.

Shravanti (Indian) a name in Buddhist literature.

Shravasti (Indian) an ancient city.

Shravya (Indian) musical tone.

Shreedevi (Indian) goddess.

Shreela, Shrila (Indian) beautiful.

Shreema (Indian) prosperous.

Shreemayi, Shrimati, Shrimayi (Indian) fortunate.

Shreeparna (Indian) a tree adorned with leaves.

Shresta (Indian) foremost.

Shreyashi (Indian) good.

Shreyasi (Indian) one who is most beautiful.

Shri (Indian) luster.

Shridevi (Indian) the goddess of wealth.

Shridula, Shridulla (Indian) blessing.

Shrijani (Indian) creative.

Shrika (Indian) fortune.

Shrikirti (Indian) lustrous fame.

Shrikumari (Indian) lustrous.

Shrilata (Indian) lustrous creeper.

Shristhi (Indian) creation; remembrance.

Shriya (Indian) prosperity.

Shriyadita (Indian) sun.

Shrusti (Indian) world.

Shruti (Indian) knowledge of the Vedas; musical pitch.

Shu (Chinese) kind, gentle.

Shu Fang, Shu-Fang (Chinese) gentle and sweet.

Shuang (Chinese) bright; openhearted.

Shubha (Indian) lucky for everybody.

Shubhada (Indian) one who brings goodness.

Shubhangi (Indian) beautiful.

Shubhi (Indian) good luck.

Shubhra (Indian) white; the Ganga River in mountain stage.

Shuchi (Indian) pure.

Shuchismita (Indian) one who has a pure smile.

Shuchita (Indian) purity.

Shug (American) a short form of Sugar.

Shui (Chinese) water.

Shukti (Indian) pearl oyster.

Shula (Arabic) flaming, bright.
Shulah

Shulamith (Hebrew) peaceful. See also Sula.
Shulamit, Sulamith

Shun (Chinese) smooth.

Shunka (Japanese) high; flower.

Shunta (Irish) a form of Shonta.
Shuntae, Shunté, Shuntel, Shuntell, Shuntelle, Shuntia

Shuo (Chinese) twinkle.

Shura (Russian) a form of Alexandra.
Schura, Shurah, Shuree, Shureen, Shurelle, Shuritta, Shurka, Shurlana

Shushma (Indian) fragrant.

Shveni, Shveta, Shweta, Shwetha (Indian) white.

Shwiti (Indian) fairness.

Shyamali, Shyamalika, Shyamalima, Shyamari, Shyamasri (Indian) dusky.

Shyamangi (Indian) dark complexioned.

Shyamlata (Indian) a creeper with dusky leaves.

Shyann, Shyanne (Cheyenne) forms of Cheyenne. See also Sheyenne.
Shyan, Shyana, Shyandra, Shyane, Shynee, Shyanna, Shyannah, Shye, Shyene, Shyenna, Shyenne

Shyla **G** (English) a form of Sheila.
Shya, Shyah, Shylah, Shylan, Shylayah, Shylana, Shylane, Shyle, Shyleah, Shylee, Shyley, Shyli, Shylia, Shylie, Shylo, Shyloe, Shyloh, Shylon, Shylyn

Shyma (Indian) sister of the prophet Mohammed.

Shyra (Hebrew) a form of Shira.
Shyrae, Shyrah, Shyrai, Shyrie, Shyro

Si (Chinese) silk.

Sianna (Irish) a form of Seana.
Sian, Siana, Sianae, Sianai, Sianey, Siannah, Sianne, Sianni, Sianny, Siany

Siara (Irish) a form of Sierra.
Siarah, Siarra, Siarrah, Sieara

Sibeta (Moquelumnan) finding a fish under a rock.

Sibila (Greek) she who prophesizes.

Sibley (English) sibling; friendly. (Greek) a form of Sybil.
Sybley

Siddhangana (Indian) accomplished; female saint; divine.

Siddhani (Indian) blessed.

Siddheshwari (Indian) Lord Shiva.

Siddhi, Siddhima (Indian) achievement.

Sidney **G** (French) a form of Sydney.
Sidne, Sidnee, Sidnei, Sidneya, Sidni, Sidnie, Sidny, Sidnye

Sidonia (Hebrew) enticing.
Sydania, Syndonia

Sidonie (French) from Saint-Denis, France. See also Sydney.
Sedona, Sidaine, Sidanni, Sidelle, Sidoine, Sidona, Sidonae, Sidonia, Sidony

Sidra (Latin) star child.
Sidrah, Sidras

Sienna (American) a form of Ciana.
Seini, Siena

Siera (Irish) a form of Sierra.
Sierah, Sieria

Sierra **G** (Irish) black. (Spanish) saw toothed. Geography: any rugged range of mountains that, when viewed from a distance, has a jagged profile. See also Ciara.
Seara, Searria, Seera, Seirra, Siara, Siearra, Siera, Sierrah, Sierre, Sierrea, Sierriah, Syerra

Sigfreda (German) victorious peace. See also Freda.
Sigfreida, Sigfrida, Sigfrieda, Sigfryda

Sigmunda (German) victorious protector.
Sigmonda

Signe (Latin) sign, signal. (Scandinavian) a short form of Sigourney.
Sig, Signa, Signy, Singna, Singne

Sigourney (English) victorious conquerer.
Signe, Sigournee, Sigourny

Sigrid (Scandinavian) victorious counselor.
Siegrid, Siegrida, Sigritt

Sihaam (Indian) arrows.

Sihu (Native American) flower; bush.

Sikata (Indian) sand.

Siko (African) crying baby.

Sikta (Indian) wet.

Silas **B** (Latin) a short form of Silvan (see Boys' Names).

Silvana (Latin) a form of Sylvana.
Silvaine, Silvanna, Silviane

Silveria (Spanish) she who was born in the jungle.

Silvia (Latin) a form of Sylvia.
Silivia, Silva, Silvya

Girls S–Z

Silvina (Spanish) a form of Silvana.

Simbala (Indian) pond.

Simcha Ⓑ (Hebrew) joyful.

Simi (Indian) limit.

Simon Ⓑ (Hebrew) he heard. Bible: one of the Twelve Disciples.

Simone Ⓖ (Hebrew, French) a form of Simon.
Samone, Siminie, Simmi, Simmie, Simmona, Simmone, Simoane, Simona, Simonetta, Simonette, Simonia, Simonina, Simonne, Somone, Symone

Simran Ⓖ (Sikh) absorbed in God.
Simren, Simrin, Simrun

Simrit (Indian) remembered.

Sina (Irish) a form of Seana.
Seena, Sinai, Sinaia, Sinan, Sinay

Sinclaire (French) prayer.
Sinclair

Sinclética (Greek) she who is invited.

Sindy (American) a form of Cindy.
Sinda, Sindal, Sindee, Sindi, Sindia, Sindie, Sinnedy, Synda, Syndal, Syndee, Syndey, Syndi, Syndia, Syndie, Syndy

Sinead (Irish) a form of Jane.
Seonaid, Sine, Sinéad

Sinforosa (Latin) full of misfortunes.

Sinjini (Indian) the sound of an anklet.

Sinsapa (Indian) ashok tree.

Sintiques (Greek) she who arrives on a special occasion.

Siobhan Ⓖ (Irish) a form of Joan. See also Shavonne.
Shibahn, Shibani, Shibhan, Shioban, Shobana, Shobha, Shobhana, Siobahn, Siobhana, Siobhann, Siobhon, Siovaun, Siovhan

Sira (Latin) she who comes from Syria.

Sirena (Greek) enchanter. Mythology: Sirens were sea nymphs whose singing enchanted sailors and made them crash their ships into nearby rocks.
Sireena, Sirene, Sirine, Syrena, Syrenia, Syrenna, Syrina

Siria (Persian) brilliant as the sun.

Sisika (Native American) songbird.

Sissy (American) a familiar form of Cecelia.
Sisi, Sisie, Sissey, Sissie

Sita (Hindi) a form of Shakti.
Sitah, Sitarah, Sitha, Sithara

Siteri (Fijian) a form of Esther.

Siti (Swahili) respected woman.

Skye Ⓖ (Arabic) water giver. (Dutch) a short form of Skyler. Geography: an island in the Hebrides, Scotland.
Ski, Skie, Skii, Skky, Sky, Skya, Skyy

Skylar ⒷⒼ (Dutch) a form of Skyler.
Skyela, Skyelar, Skyla, Skylair, Skyylar

Skyler Ⓑ (Dutch) sheltering.
Skila, Skilah, Skye, Skyeler, Skyelur, Skyla, Skylar, Skylee, Skylena, Skyli, Skylia, Skylie, Skylin, Skyllar, Skylor, Skylyn, Skylynn, Skylyr, Skyra

Sloane (Irish) warrior.
Sloan, Sloanne

Socorro (Spanish) helper.

Sofia ♛ Ⓖ (Greek) a form of Sophia. See also Zofia, Zsofia.
Sofeea, Sofeeia, Soffi, Sofi, Soficita, Sofie, Sofija, Sofiya, Sofka, Sofya

Sofía (Greek) a form of Sofia.

Sol (Latin) she who possesses brightness.

Solada (Tai) listener.

Solana (Spanish) sunshine.
Solande, Solanna, Soleil, Solena, Soley, Solina, Solinda

Solange (French) dignified.

Soledad (Spanish) solitary.
Sole, Soleda

Soledada (Spanish) solitary.

Solenne (French) solemn, dignified.
Solaine, Solene, Soléne, Solenna, Solina, Soline, Solonez, Souline, Soulle

Solita (Latin) solitary.

Solomon Ⓑ (Hebrew) peaceful.

Soma (Hindi) lunar.

Sommer (English) summer; summoner. (Arabic) black. See also Summer.
Somara, Somer, Sommar, Sommara, Sommers

Somoche (Mapuche) distinguished woman, woman of her word.

Sondra (Greek) defender of mankind.
Saundra, Sondre, Sonndra, Sonndre

Song (Chinese) independent.

Sonia (Russian, Slavic) a form of Sonya.
Sonica, Sonida, Sonita, Sonna, Sonni, Sonnia, Sonnie, Sonny

Sonja (Scandinavian) a form of Sonya.
Sonjae, Sonjia

Sonny **B** (Russian, Slavic) a form of Sonia.

Sonoko (Japanese) child of the garden.

Sonora (Spanish) pleasant sounding.

Sonya **G** (Greek) wise. (Russian, Slavic) a form of Sophia.
Sonia, Sonja, Sonnya, Sonyae, Sunya

Soo (Korean) letters.

Sook (Korean) pure.

Soon-Vi (Chinese) delightful.

Sopheary (Cambodian) beautiful girl.

Sophia ✿ **G** (Greek) wise. See also Sonya, Zofia.
Sofia, Sophie

Sophie **G** (Greek) a familiar form of Sophia. See also Zocha.
Sophey, Sophi, Sophy

Sophronia (Greek) wise; sensible.
Soffrona, Sofronia

Sora (Native American) chirping songbird.

Sorami (Japanese) a form of Sorano.

Sorano (Japanese) space; truth.

Soraya (Persian) princess.
Suraya

Sorrel **G** (French) reddish brown. Botany: a plant whose leaves are used as salad greens.

Sorya (Spanish) she who is eloquent.

Sosefina (Chuukese) a form of Josefa.

Soso (Native American) tree squirrel dining on pine nuts; chubby-cheeked baby.

Souzan (Persian) burning fire.
Sousan, Souzanne

Spencer **B** (English) dispenser of provisions.
Spenser

Speranza (Italian) a form of Esperanza.
Speranca

Spica (Latin) star's name.

Spring (English) springtime.
Spryng

Stacey, Stacy **G** (Greek) resurrection. (Irish) a short form of Anastasia, Eustacia, Natasha.
Stace, Stacee, Staceyan, Staceyann, Staicy, Stasey, Stasya, Stayce, Staycee, Staci, Steacy

Staci, Stacie (Greek) forms of Stacey.
Stacci, Stacia, Stayci

Stacia (English) a short form of Anastasia.
Stasia, Staysha

Stanley **B** (English) stony meadow.

Starla (English) a form of Starr.
Starrla

Starleen (English) a form of Starr.
Starleena, Starlena, Starlene, Starlin, Starlyn, Starlynn, Starrlen

Starley (English) a familiar form of Starr.
Starle, Starlee, Staly

Starling **BG** (English) bird.

Starr **G** (English) star.
Star, Staria, Starisha, Starla, Starleen, Starlet, Starlette, Starley, Starlight, Starre, Starri, Starria, Starrika, Starrsha, Starsha, Starshanna, Startish

Stasya (Greek) a familiar form of Anastasia. (Russian) a form of Stacey.
Stasa, Stasha, Stashia, Stasia, Stasja, Staska

Stefani, Steffani (Greek) forms of Stephanie.
Stafani, Stefanni, Steffane, Steffanee, Stefini, Stefoni

Stefania (Greek) a form of Stefanie.

Stefanie (Greek) a form of Stephanie.
Stafanie, Staffany, Stefane, Stefanee, Stefaney, Stefania, Stefanié, Stefanija, Stefannie, Stefcia, Stefenie, Steffanie, Steffi, Stefinie, Stefka

Stefany, Steffany (Greek) forms of Stephanie.
Stefanny, Stefanya, Steffaney

Steffi (Greek) a familiar form of Stefanie, Stephanie.
Stefa, Stefcia, Steffee, Steffie, Steffy, Stefi, Stefka, Stefy, Stepha, Stephi, Stephie, Stephy

Stella **G** (Latin) star. (French) a familiar form of Estelle.
Steile, Stellina

Stepania (Russian) a form of Stephanie.
Stepa, Stepahny, Stepanida, Stepanie, Stepanyda, Stepfanie, Stephana

Stephane **B** (Greek) a form of Stephanie.

Stephani (Greek) a form of Stephanie.
Stephania, Stephanni

Stephanie ❦ 🅖 (Greek) a form of
Stephen. See also Estefani, Estephanie,
Panya, Stevie, Zephania.
*Stamatios, Stefani, Stefanie, Stefany, Steffie,
Stepania, Stephaija, Stephaine, Stephanas,
Stephane, Stephanee, Stephani, Stephanida,
Stéphanie, Stephanine, Stephann,
Stephannie, Stephany, Stephene, Stephenie,
Stephianie, Stephney, Stesha, Steshka,
Stevanee*

Stephany 🅖 (Greek) a form of Stephanie.
Stephaney, Stephanye

Stephen 🅑 (Greek) crowned.

Stephene (Greek) a form of Stephanie.
Stephina, Stephine, Stephyne

Stephenie (Greek) a form of Stephanie.
*Stephena, Stephenee, Stepheney, Stepheni,
Stephenny, Stepheny, Stephine, Stephinie*

Stephney (Greek) a form of Stephanie.
Stephne, Stephni, Stephnie, Stephny

Sterling 🅑 (English) valuable; silver penny.

Stetson 🅑 (Danish) stepchild.

Steven 🅑 (Greek) a form of Stephen.

Stevie 🅖 (Greek) a familiar form of
Stephanie.
*Steva, Stevana, Stevanee, Stevee, Stevena,
Stevey, Stevi, Stevy, Stevye*

Stewart 🅑 (English) a form of Stuart.

Stina (German) a short form of Christina.
Steena, Stena, Stine, Stinna

Stockard (English) stockyard.

Storm 🅑 (English) a short form of Stormy.

Stormie (English) a form of Stormy.
Stormee, Stormi, Stormii

Stormy 🅖 (English) impetuous by nature.
Storm, Storme, Stormey, Stormie, Stormm

Stuart 🅑 (English) caretaker, steward.

Suchin (Tai) beautiful thought.

Sue (Hebrew) a short form of Susan,
Susanna.

Sueann, Sueanna (American) combinations
of Sue + Ann, Sue + Anna.
Suann, Suanna, Suannah, Suanne, Sueanne

Suela (Spanish) consolation.
Suelita

Sugako (Japanese) of the sky.

Sugar (American) sweet as sugar.
Shug

Sugi (Japanese) cedar tree.

Sui (Chinese) peaceful.

Suke (Hawaiian) a form of Susan.

Sukey (Hawaiian) a familiar form of Susan.
Suka, Sukee, Suki, Sukie, Suky

Sukhdeep 🅖 (Sikh) light of peace and bliss.
Sukhdip

Suki (Japanese) loved one. (Moquelumnan)
eagle-eyed.
Sukie

Sula (Icelandic) large sea bird. (Greek,
Hebrew) a short form of Shulamith, Ursula.

Sulamita (Hebrew) gentle, peaceful woman.

Suletu (Moquelumnan) soaring bird.

Suli (Fijian) a form of Julia.

Sulia (Latin) a form of Julia.
Suliana

Sulwen (Welsh) bright as the sun.

Sumalee (Tai) beautiful flower.

Sumati (Hindi) unity.

Sumaya (American) a combination of Sue +
Maya.
Sumayah, Sumayya, Sumayyah

Sumi (Japanese) elegant, refined.
Sumiko

Sumiye (Japanese) child who knows how to
give thanks to others.

Summer 🅖 (English) summertime. See also
Sommer.
*Sumer, Summar, Summerann, Summerbreeze,
Summerhaze, Summerine, Summerlee,
Summerlin, Summerlyn, Summerlynn,
Summers, Sumrah, Summyr, Sumyr*

Sun (Korean) obedient.
*Suncance, Sundee, Sundeep, Sundi, Sundip,
Sundrenea, Sunta, Sunya*

Suna (Korean) belief.

Sunee (Tai) good.
Suni

Sun-Hi (Korean) good; joyful.

Suni (Zuni) native; member of our tribe.
*Sunita, Sunitha, Suniti, Sunne, Sunni, Sunnie,
Sunnilei*

Sunki (Hopi) swift.
Sunkia

Sunny BG (English) bright, cheerful.
Sunni, Sunnie

Sunshine (English) sunshine.
Sunshyn, Sunshyne

Suong (Vietnamese) looking or behaving like people of the upper classes.

Surata (Pakistani) blessed joy.

Suri (Todas) pointy nose.
Suree, Surena, Surenia

Surya (Sanskrit) Mythology: a sun god.
Suria, Suriya, Surra

Susammi (French) a combination of Susan + Aimee.
Suzami, Suzamie, Suzamy

Susan G (Hebrew) lily. See also Shoshana, Sukey, Zsa Zsa, Zusa.
Sawsan, Siusan, Sosan, Sosana, Sue, Suesan, Sueva, Suisan, Suke, Susana, Susann, Susanna, Suse, Susen, Susette, Susie, Suson, Suzan, Suzanna, Suzannah, Suzanne, Suzette

Susana G (Hebrew) a form of Susan.
Susanah, Susane

Susanita (Spanish) a form of Susana.

Susanna, Susannah (Hebrew) forms of Susan. See also Xuxa, Zanna, Zsuzsanna.
Sonel, Sosana, Sue, Suesanna, Susana, Susanah, Susanka, Susette, Susie, Suzanna

Suse (Hawaiian) a form of Susan.

Susette (French) a familiar form of Susan, Susanna.
Susetta

Susie, Suzie (American) familiar forms of Susan, Susanna.
Suse, Susey, Susi, Sussi, Sussy, Susy, Suze, Suzi, Suzy, Suzzie

Sute (Japanese) blessed purity.

Suzanna, Suzannah (Hebrew) forms of Susan.
Suzana, Suzenna, Suzzanna

Suzanne G (English) a form of Susan.
Susanne, Suszanne, Suzane, Suzann, Suzzane, Suzzann, Suzzanne

Suzette (French) a form of Susan.
Suzetta, Suzzette

Suzu (Japanese) little bell.
Suzue, Suzuko

Suzuha (Japanese) orphan.

Suzuki (Japanese) bell tree.

Svetlana (Russian) bright light.
Sveta, Svetochka

Syá (Chinese) summer.

Sybella (English) a form of Sybil.
Sebila, Sibbella, Sibeal, Sibel, Sibell, Sibella, Sibelle, Sibilla, Sibylla, Sybel, Sybelle, Sybila, Sybilla

Sybil (Greek) prophet. Mythology: sibyls were oracles who relayed the messages of the gods. See also Cybele, Sibley.
Sib, Sibbel, Sibbie, Sibbill, Sibby, Sibeal, Sibel, Sibyl, Sibylle, Sibylline, Sybella, Sybille, Syble

Sydnee G (French) a form of Sydney.
Sydne, Sydnea, Sydnei

Sydney ✿ G (French) from Saint-Denis, France. See also Sidonie.
Cidney, Cydney, Sidney, Sy, Syd, Sydel, Sydelle, Sydna, Sydnee, Sydni, Sydnie, Sydny, Sydnye, Syndona, Syndonah

Sydni, Sydnie (French) forms of Sydney.

Syed B (Arabic) happy.

Sying BG (Chinese) star.

Sylvana (Latin) forest.
Sylva, Sylvaine, Sylvanah, Sylvania, Sylvanna, Sylvie, Sylvina, Sylvinnia, Sylvonah, Sylvonia, Sylvonna

Sylvia (Latin) forest. Literature: Sylvia Plath was a well-known American poet. See also Silvia, Xylia.
Sylvette, Sylvie, Sylwia

Sylvianne (American) a combination of Sylvia + Anne.
Sylvian

Sylvie (Latin) a familiar form of Sylvia.
Silvi, Silvie, Silvy, Sylvi

Symone (Hebrew) a form of Simone.
Symmeon, Symmone, Symona, Symoné, Symonne

Symphony (Greek) symphony, harmonious sound.
Symfoni, Symphanie, Symphany, Symphánée, Symphoni, Symphoni

Syreeta (Hindi) good traditions. (Arabic) companion.
Syretta, Syrrita

T 🄱🄶 (American) an initial used as a first name.

Tabatha 🄶 (Greek, Aramaic) a form of Tabitha.
Tabathe, Tabathia, Tabbatha

Tabby (English) a familiar form of Tabitha.
Tabbi

Tabetha (Greek, Aramaic) a form of Tabitha.

Tabia (Swahili) talented.
Tabea

Tabina (Arabic) follower of Muhammad.

Tabitha (Greek, Aramaic) gazelle.
Tabatha, Tabbee, Tabbetha, Tabbey, Tabbi, Tabbie, Tabbitha, Tabby, Tabetha, Tabiatha, Tabita, Tabithia, Tabotha, Tabtha, Tabytha

Tabora (Arabic) plays a small drum.

Tabytha (Greek, Aramaic) a form of Tabitha.
Tabbytha

Tacey (English) a familiar form of Tacita.
Tace, Tacee, Taci, Tacy, Tacye

Taci (Zuni) washtub. (English) a form of Tacey.
Tacia, Taciana, Tacie

Tacita (Latin) silent.
Tacey

Tadako (Japanese) bell; leaf.

Tadita (Omaha) runner.
Tadeta, Tadra

Taelor (English) a form of Taylor.
Taelar, Taeler, Taellor, Taelore, Taelyr

Taesha (Latin) a form of Tisha. (American) a combination of the prefix Ta + Aisha.
Tadasha, Taeshayla, Taeshia, Taheisha, Tahisha, Taiesha, Taisha, Taishae, Teasha, Teashia, Teisha, Tesha

Taffy 🄶 (Welsh) beloved.
Taffia, Taffine, Taffye, Tafia, Tafisa, Tafoya

Tahira (Arabic) virginal, pure.
Taheera, Taheerah, Tahera, Tahere, Taheria, Taherri, Tahiara, Tahirah, Tahireh

Tahlia (Greek, Hebrew) a form of Talia.
Tahleah, Tahleia

Tailor (English) a form of Taylor.
Tailar, Tailer, Taillor, Tailyr

Taima 🄶 (Native American) clash of thunder.
Taimi, Taimia, Taimy

Taipa (Moquelumnan) flying quail.

Tais (Greek) she who is beautiful.

Taite (English) cheerful.
Tate, Tayte, Tayten

Taja (Hindi) crown.
Taiajára, Taija, Tajae, Tajah, Tahai, Tehya, Teja, Tejah, Tejal

Taji (Japanese) child of Tada.

Taka (Japanese) honored.

Takako (Japanese) silver and yellow color.

Takala (Hopi) corn tassel.

Takara (Japanese) treasure.
Takarah, Takaria, Takarra, Takra

Takayla (American) a combination of the prefix Ta + Kayla.
Takayler, Takeyli

Take (Japanese) child of Taka.

Takeisha (American) a combination of the prefix Ta + Keisha.
Takecia, Takesha, Takeshia, Takesia, Takisha, Takishea, Takishia, Tekeesha, Tekeisha, Tekeshi, Tekeysia, Tekisha, Tikesha, Tikisha, Tokesia, Tykeisha

Takeko (Japanese) bamboo.

Takenya (Hebrew) animal horn. (Moquelumnan) falcon. (American) a combination of the prefix Ta + Kenya.
Takenia, Takenja

Takeria (American) a form of Takira.
Takera, Takeri, Takerian, Takerra, Takerria, Takierria, Takoria

Taki (Japanese) waterfall.
Tiki

Takia (Arabic) worshiper.
Takeia, Takeiyah, Takeya, Takeyah, Takhiya, Takiah, Takija, Takiya, Takiyah, Takkia, Takya, Takyah, Takyia, Taqiyya, Taquaia, Taquaya, Taquiia, Tekeiya, Tekeiyah, Tekeyia, Tekiya, Tekiyah, Tikia, Tykeia, Tykia

Takiko (Japanese) child of the bamboo.

Takila (American) a form of Tequila.
Takayla, Takeila, Takela, Takelia, Takella, Takeyla, Takiela, Takilah, Takilla, Takilya, Takyla, Takylia, Tatakyla, Tehilla, Tekeila, Tekela, Tekelia, Tekilaa, Tekilia, Tekilla, Tekilyah, Tekla

Takira (American) a combination of the prefix Ta + Kira.
Takara, Takarra, Takeara, Takeera, Takeira, Takeirah, Takera, Takiara, Takiera, Takierah, Takierra, Takirah, Takiria, Takirra, Takora, Takyra, Takyrra, Taquera, Taquira, Tekeria, Tikara, Tikira, Tykera

Tala (Native American) stalking wolf.

Talasi (Hopi) corn tassel.
Talasea, Talasia

Taleah (American) a form of Talia.
Talaya, Talayah, Talayia, Talea, Taleana, Taleea, Taleéi, Talei, Taleia, Taleiya, Tylea, Tyleah, Tylee

Taleisha (American) a combination of Talia + Aisha.
Taileisha, Taleise, Talesha, Talicia, Taliesha, Talisa, Talisha, Talysha, Telisha, Tilisha, Tyleasha, Tyleisha, Tylicia, Tylisha, Tylishia

Talena (American) a combination of the prefix Ta + Lena.
Talayna, Talihna, Taline, Tallenia, Talná, Tilena, Tilene, Tylena

Talesha (American) a form of Taleisha.
Taleesha, Talesa, Talese, Taleshia, Talesia, Tallese, Tallesia, Tylesha, Tyleshia, Tylesia

Talia (Greek) blooming. (Hebrew) dew from heaven. (Latin, French) birthday. A short form of Natalie. See also Thalia.
Tahlia, Taleah, Taliah, Taliatha, Taliea, Taliyah, Talley, Tallia, Tallya, Talya, Tylia

Talía (Greek) a form of Talia.

Talina (American) a combination of Talia + Lina.
Talin, Talinda, Taline, Tallyn, Talyn, Talynn, Tylina, Tyline

Talisa (English) a form of Tallis.
Talisha, Talishia, Talisia, Talissa, Talysa, Talysha, Talysia, Talyssa

Talitha (Arabic) young girl.
Taleetha, Taletha, Talethia, Taliatha, Talita, Talithia, Taliya, Telita, Tiletha

Taliyah (Greek) a form of Talia.
Taleya, Taleyah, Talieya, Talliyah, Talya, Talyah, Talyia

Talley (French) a familiar form of Talia.
Tali, Talle, Tallie, Tally, Taly, Talye

Tallis (French, English) forest.
Talice, Talisa, Talise, Tallys

Tallulah (Choctaw) leaping water.
Tallou, Talula

Talon **B** (French, English) claw, nail.

Tam **B** (Vietnamese) heart.

Tama (Japanese) jewel.
Tamaa, Tamah, Tamaiah, Tamala, Tema

Tamae (Japanese) very noble child.

Tamaka (Japanese) bracelet.
Tamaki, Tamako, Timaka

Tamar **G** (Hebrew) a short form of Tamara. (Russian) History: a twelfth-century Georgian queen. (Hebrew) a short form of Tamara.
Tamer, Tamor, Tamour

Tamara (Hebrew) palm tree. See also Tammy.
Tamar, Tamará, Tamarae, Tamarah, Tamaria, Tamarin, Tamarla, Tamarra, Tamarria, Tamarrian, Tamarsha, Tamary, Tamera, Tamira, Tamma, Tammara, Tamora, Tamoya, Tamra, Tamura, Tamyra, Temara, Temarian,

Thama, Thamar, Thamara, Thamarra, Timara, Tomara, Tymara

Tamassa (Hebrew) a form of Thomasina.
Tamasin, Tamasine, Tamsen, Tamsin, Tamzen, Tamzin

Tamaya (Quechua) in the center.

Tamayo (Japanese) ball; bell.

Tame (Japanese) a form of Tamaki.

Tameea (Japanese) unselfish.

Tameka (Aramaic) twin.
Tameca, Tamecia, Tamecka, Tameeka, Tamekia, Tamiecka, Tamieka, Temeka, Timeeka, Timeka, Tomeka, Tomekia, Trameika, Tymeka, Tymmeeka, Tymmeka

Tamera (Hebrew) a form of Tamara.
Tamer, Tamerai, Tameran, Tameria, Tamerra, Tammera, Thamer, Timera

Tamesha (American) a combination of the prefix Ta + Mesha.
Tameesha, Tameisha, Tameshia, Tameshkia, Tameshya, Tamisha, Tamishia, Tamnesha, Temisha, Timesha, Timisha, Tomesha, Tomiese, Tomise, Tomisha, Tramesha, Tramisha, Tymesha

Tamico (Japanese) little gem.

Tamika (Japanese) a form of Tamiko.
Tamica, Tamieka, Tamikah, Tamikia, Tamikka, Tammika, Tamyka, Timika, Timikia, Tomika, Tymika, Tymmicka

Tamiko (Japanese) child of the people.
Tami, Tamika, Tamike, Tamiqua, Tamiyo, Tammiko

Girls S–Z

Tamila (American) a combination of the prefix Ta + Mila.
Tamala, Tamela, Tamelia, Tamilla, Tamille, Tamillia, Tamilya

Tamira (Hebrew) a form of Tamara.
Tamir, Tamirae, Tamirah, Tamiria, Tamirra, Tamyra, Tamyria, Tamyrra

Tammi, Tammie (English) forms of Tammy.
Tameia, Tami, Tamia, Tamiah, Tamie, Tamijo, Tamiya

Tammy 🄶 (English) twin. (Hebrew) a familiar form of Tamara.
Tamilyn, Tamlyn, Tammee, Tammey, Tammi, Tammie, Tamy, Tamya

Tamra (Hebrew) a short form of Tamara.
Tammra, Tamrah

Tamsin (English) a short form of Thomasina.

Tan (Vietnamese) lotus flower.

Tana (Slavic) a short form of Tanya.
Taina, Tanae, Tanaeah, Tanah, Tanairi, Tanairy, Tanalia, Tanara, Tanavia, Tanaya, Tanaz, Tanna, Tannah

Tanak (Japanese) the people's child.

Tanaka (Japanese) a form of Tamika.

Tandy (English) team.
Tanda, Tandalaya, Tandi, Tandie, Tandis, Tandra, Tandrea, Tandria

Tane (Japanese) dweller.

Taneisha (American) a combination of the prefix Ta + Nesha.
Tahniesha, Taineshia, Tanasha, Tanashia, Tanaysia, Tanniecia, Tanniesha, Tantashea

Tanesha 🄶 (American) a combination of the prefix Ta + Nesha.
Taneshea, Taneshia, Taneshya, Tanesia, Tanesian, Tanessa, Tanessia, Taniesha, Tannesha, Tanneshia, Tantashea

Taneya (Russian, Slavic) a form of Tanya.
Tanea, Taneah, Tanee, Taneé, Taneia

Tang (Chinese) stately, dignified.

Tangia (American) a combination of the prefix Ta + Angela.
Tangela, Tangi, Tangie, Tanja, Tanji, Tanjia, Tanjie

Tani 🄶 (Japanese) valley. (Slavic) stand of glory. A familiar form of Tania.
Tahnee, Tahni, Tahnie, Tanee, Taney, Tanie, Tany

Tania (Russian, Slavic) fairy queen.
Taneea, Tani, Taniah, Tanija, Tanika, Tanis, Taniya, Tannia, Tannis, Tanniya, Tannya, Tarnia

Taniel (American) a combination of Tania + Danielle.
Taniele, Tanielle, Teniel, Teniele, Tenielle

Tanika (American) a form of Tania.
Tanikka, Tanikqua, Taniqua, Tanique, Tannica, Tianeka, Tianika

Tanis 🄶 (Slavic) a form of Tania, Tanya.
Tanas, Tanese, Taniese, Tanise, Tanisia, Tanka, Tenice, Tenise, Tenyse, Tiannis, Tonise, Tranice, Tranise, Tynice, Tyniece, Tyniese, Tynise

Tanisha (American) a combination of the prefix Ta + Nisha.
Tahniscia, Tahnisha, Tanasha, Tanashea, Tanicha, Taniesha, Tanish, Tanishah, Tanishia, Tanitia, Tannicia, Tannisha, Tenisha, Tenishka, Tinisha, Tonisha, Tonnisha, Tynisha

Tanissa (American) a combination of the prefix Tania + Nissa.
Tanesa, Tanisa, Tannesa, Tannisa, Tennessa, Tranissa

Tanita (American) a combination of the prefix Ta + Nita.
Taneta, Tanetta, Tanitra, Tanitta, Teneta, Tenetta, Tenita, Tenitta, Tyneta, Tynetta, Tynette, Tynita, Tynitra, Tynitta

Tanith (Phoenician) Mythology: Tanit is the goddess of love.
Tanitha

Tanner 🄱 (English) leather worker, tanner.
Tannor

Tannis (Slavic) a form of Tania, Tanya.
Tannese, Tanniece, Tanniese, Tannis, Tannise, Tannus, Tannyce, Tiannis

Tansy (Greek) immortal. (Latin) tenacious, persistent.
Tancy, Tansee, Tansey, Tanshay, Tanzey

Tanya (Russian, Slavic) fairy queen.
Tahnee, Tahnya, Tana, Tanaya, Taneya, Tania, Tanis, Taniya, Tanka, Tannis, Tannya, Tanoya, Tany, Tanyia, Taunya, Tawnya, Thanya

Tao (Chinese, Vietnamese) peach.

Tara 🄶 (Aramaic) throw; carry. (Irish) rocky hill. (Arabic) a measurement.
Taira, Tairra, Taraea, Tarah, Taráh, Tarai, Taralee, Tarali, Tarasa, Tarasha, Taraya, Tarha, Tari, Tarra, Taryn, Tayra, Tehra

Taraneh (Persian) melody.

Taree (Japanese) arching branch.
Tarea, Tareya, Tari, Taria

Tari (Irish) a familiar form of Tara.
Taria, Tarika, Tarila, Tarilyn, Tarin, Tarina, Tarita

Tarissa (American) a combination of Tara + Rissa.
Taris, Tarisa, Tarise, Tarisha

Tarra (Irish) a form of Tara.
Tarrah

Tarsicia (Greek) valiant.

Tarsilia (Greek) basket weaver.

Taru (Japanese) dweller.

Taryn **G** (Irish) a form of Tara.
Taran, Tareen, Tareena, Taren, Tarene, Tarin, Tarina, Tarren, Tarrena, Tarrin, Tarrina, Tarron, Tarryn, Taryna

Tasarla (Gypsy) dawn.

Tasha **G** (Greek) born on Christmas day. (Russian) a short form of Natasha. See also Tashi, Tosha.
Tacha, Tachiana, Tahsha, Tasenka, Tashae, Tashana, Tashay, Tashe, Tashee, Tasheka, Tashka, Tasia, Taska, Taysha, Thasha, Tiaisha, Tysha

Tashana (American) a combination of the prefix Ta + Shana.
Tashan, Tashanda, Tashani, Tashanika, Tashanna, Tashiana, Tashianna, Tashina, Tishana, Tishani, Tishanna, Tishanne, Toshanna, Toshanti, Tyshana

Tashara (American) a combination of the prefix Ta + Shara.
Tashar, Tasharah, Tasharia, Tasharna, Tasharra, Tashera, Tasherey, Tasheri, Tasherra, Tashira, Tashirah

Tashawna (American) a combination of the prefix Ta + Shawna.
Tashauna, Tashauni, Tashaunie, Tashaunna, Tashawanna, Tashawn, Tashawnda, Tashawnna, Tashawnnia, Tashonda, Tashondra, Tiashauna, Tishawn, Tishunda, Tishunta, Toshauna, Toshawna, Tyshauna, Tyshawna

Tasheena (American) a combination of the prefix Ta + Sheena.
Tasheana, Tasheeana, Tasheeni, Tashena, Tashenna, Tashennia, Tasheona, Tashina, Tisheena, Tosheena, Tysheana, Tysheena, Tyshyna

Tashelle (American) a combination of the prefix Ta + Shelley.
Tachell, Tashell, Techell, Techelle, Teshell, Teshelle, Tochell, Tochelle, Toshelle, Tychell, Tychelle, Tyshell, Tyshelle

Tashi (Hausa) a bird in flight. (Slavic) a form of Tasha.
Tashia, Tashie, Tashika, Tashima, Tashiya

Tasia (Slavic) a familiar form of Tasha.
Tachia, Tashea, Tasiya, Tassi, Tassia, Tassiana, Tassie, Tasya

Tassos (Greek) a form of Theresa.

Tata (Russian) a familiar form of Tatiana.
Tatia

Tate **B** (English) a short form of Tatum. A form of Taite, Tata.

Tatiana (Slavic) fairy queen. See also Tanya, Tiana.
Tata, Tatania, Tatanya, Tateana, Tati, Tatia, Tatianna, Tatie, Tatihana, Tatiyana, Tatjana, Tatyana, Tiatiana

Tatianna (Slavic) a form of Tatiana.
Taitiann, Taitianna, Tateanna, Tateonna, Tationna

Tatiyana (Slavic) a form of Tatiana.
Tateyana, Tatiayana, Tatiyanna, Tatiyona, Tatiyonna

Tatsu (Japanese) seed.

Tatum **G** (English) cheerful.
Tate, Tatumn

Tatyana (Slavic) a form of Tatiana.
Tatyanah, Tatyani, Tatyanna, Tatyannah, Tatyona, Tatyonna

Taura (Latin) bull. Astrology: Taurus is a sign of the zodiac.
Taurae, Tauria, Taurina

Tauri (English) a form of Tory.
Taure, Taurie, Taury

Tavia (Latin) a short form of Octavia. See also Tawia.
Taiva, Tauvia, Tava, Tavah, Tavita

Tavie (Scottish) twin.
Tavey, Tavi

Tawanna (American) a combination of the prefix Ta + Wanda.
Taiwana, Taiwanna, Taquana, Taquanna, Tawan, Tawana, Tawanda, Tawanne, Tequana, Tequanna, Tequawna, Tewanna, Tewauna, Tiquana, Tiwanna, Tiwena, Towanda, Towanna, Tywania, Tywanna

Tawia (African) born after twins. (Polish) a form of Tavia.

Tawni (English) a form of Tawny.
Tauni, Taunia, Tawnia, Tawnie, Tawnnie, Tiawni

Tawny (Gypsy) little one. (English) brownish yellow, tan.
Tahnee, Tany, Tauna, Tauné, Taunisha, Tawnee, Tawnesha, Tawney, Tawni, Tawnyell, Tiawna

Tawnya (American) a combination of Tawny + Tonya.
Tawna

Taya, Taye (English) short forms of Taylor.
Tay, Tayah, Tayana, Tayiah, Tayna, Tayra, Taysha, Taysia, Tayva, Tayvonne, Teya, Teyanna, Teyona, Teyuna, Tiaya, Tiya, Tiyah, Tiyana, Tye

Tayla (English) a short form of Taylor.
Taylah, Tayleah, Taylee, Tayleigh, Taylie, Teila

Taylar (English) a form of Taylor.
Talar, Tayla, Taylah, Taylare, Tayllar

Tayler ☐ (English) a form of Taylor.
Tayller

Taylor ☝ ☐ (English) tailor.
Taelor, Tailor, Taiylor, Talor, Talora, Taya, Taye, Tayla, Taylar, Tayler, Tayllor, Tayllore, Tayloir, Taylorann, Taylore, Taylorr, Taylour, Taylur, Teylor

Tazu (Japanese) stork; longevity.
Taz, Tazi, Tazia

Te (Chinese) special.

Tea (Spanish) a short form of Dorothy.

Teagan ☐ (Welsh) beautiful, attractive.
Taegen, Teage, Teagen, Teaghan, Teaghanne, Teaghen, Teagin, Teague, Teegan, Teeghan, Tegan, Tegwen, Teigan, Tejan, Tiegan, Tigan, Tijan, Tijana

Teaira (Latin) a form of Tiara.
Teairra, Teairre, Teairria, Teara, Tearah, Teareya, Teari, Tearia, Teariea, Tearra, Tearria

Teal (English) river duck; blue green.
Teala, Teale, Tealia, Tealisha

Teanna (American) a combination of the prefix Te + Anna. A form of Tiana.
Tean, Teana, Teanah, Teann, Teannah, Teanne, Teaunna, Teena, Teuana

Teca (Hungarian) a form of Theresa.
Techa, Teka, Tica, Tika

Tecla (Greek) God's fame.
Tekla, Theckla

Teddi (Greek) a familiar form of Theodora.
Tedde, Teddey, Teddie, Teddy, Tedi, Tediah, Tedy

Tedra (Greek) a short form of Theodora.
Teddra, Teddreya, Tedera, Teedra, Teidra

Tegan ☐ (Welsh) a form of Teagan.
Tega, Tegen, Teggan, Teghan, Tegin, Tegyn, Teigen

Telisha (American) a form of Taleisha.
Teleesha, Teleisia, Telesa, Telesha, Teleshia, Telesia, Telicia, Telisa, Telishia, Telisia, Telissa, Telisse, Tellisa, Tellisha, Telsa, Telysa

Telma (Spanish) will.

Telmao (Greek) loving with her fellow people.

Temira (Hebrew) tall.
Temora, Timora

Temis (Greek) she who establishes order and justice.

Tempest ☐ (French) stormy.
Tempesta, Tempeste, Tempestt, Tempist, Tempistt, Tempress, Tempteste

Tenesha, Tenisha (American) combinations of the prefix Te + Niesha.
Tenecia, Teneesha, Teneisha, Teneshia, Tenesia, Tenessa, Teneusa, Teniesha, Tenishia

Tennille (American) a combination of the prefix Te + Nellie.
Taniel, Tanille, Teneal, Teneil, Teneille, Teniel, Tenille, Tenneal, Tenneill, Tenneille, Tennia, Tennie, Tennielle, Tennile, Tineal, Tiniel, Tonielle, Tonille

Teodelina, Teodolinda (German) she who is loving with the people in her village; she loves her village.

Teodequilda (German) warrior of her village.

Teodomira (Spanish) an important woman in the village.

Teodora (Czech) a form of Theodora.
Teadora

Teofania, Teofanía (Greek) manifestation of God.

Teofila, Teófila (Greek) friend of God, loved by God.

Teolinda (German) a form of Teodelina.

Teona, Teonna (Greek) forms of Tiana, Tianna.
Teon, Teoni, Teonia, Teonie, Teonney, Teonnia, Teonnie

Tequila (Spanish) a kind of liquor. See also Takila.
Taquela, Taquella, Taquila, Taquilla, Tequilia, Tequilla, Tiquila, Tiquilia

Tera, Terra **G** (Latin) earth. (Japanese) swift arrow. (American) forms of Tara.
Terah, Terai, Teria, Terrae, Terrah, Terria, Tierra

Teralyn (American) a combination of Terri + Lynn.
Taralyn, Teralyn, Teralynn, Terralin, Terralyn

Tercera (Spanish) third-born.

Terence **B** (Latin) a form of Terrence (see Boys' Names).

Teresa (Greek) a form of Theresa. See also Tressa.
Taresa, Taressa, Tarissa, Terasa, Tercza, Tereasa, Tereatha, Terese, Teresea, Teresha, Teresia, Teresina, Teresita, Tereska, Tereson, Teressa, Teretha, Tereza, Terezia, Terezie, Terezilya, Terezinha, Terezka, Terezsa, Terisa, Terisha, Teriza, Terrasa, Terresa, Terresha, Terresia, Terressa, Terrosina, Tersa, Tersea, Teruska, Terza, Teté, Tyresa, Tyresia

Terese (Greek) a form of Teresa.
Tarese, Taress, Taris, Tarise, Tereece, Tereese, Teress, Terez, Teris, Terrise

Teresinha (Portuguese) a form of Theresa.

Teri **G** (Greek) reaper. A familiar form of Theresa.
Terie

Terpsícore (Greek) she who enjoys dancing.

Terrance **B** (Latin) a form of Terrence (see Boys' Names).

Terrell **B** (Greek) a form of Terrelle.

Terrelle (Greek) a form of Theresa.
Tarrell, Teral, Terall, Terel, Terell, Teriel, Terral, Terrall, Terrell, Terrella, Terriel, Terriell, Terrielle, Terrill, Terryelle, Terryl, Terryll, Terrylle, Teryl, Tyrell, Tyrelle

Terrene (Latin) smooth.
Tareena, Tarena, Teran, Teranee, Tereena, Terena, Terencia, Terene, Terenia, Terentia, Terina, Terran, Terren, Terrena, Terrin, Terrina, Terron, Terrosina, Terryn, Terun, Teryn, Teryna, Terynn, Tyreen, Tyrene

Terri **G** (Greek) reaper. A familiar form of Theresa.
Terree, Terria, Terrie

Terriann (American) a combination of Terri + Ann.
Teran, Terian, Teriann, Terianne, Teriyan, Terria, Terrian, Terrianne, Terryann

Terrianna (American) a combination of Terri + Anna.
Teriana, Terrianna, Terriana, Terriauna, Terrina, Terriona, Terrionna, Terriyana, Terriyanna, Terryana, Terryauna, Tyrina

Terrica (American) a combination of Terri + Erica. See also Rica.
Tereka, Terica, Tericka, Terika, Terreka, Terricka, Terrika, Tyrica, Tyricka, Tyrika, Tyrikka, Tyronica

Terry **B** (Greek) a short form of Theresa.
Tere, Teree, Terelle, Terene, Teri, Terie, Terrey, Terri, Terrie, Terrye, Tery

Terry-Lynn (American) a combination of Terry + Lynn.
Terelyn, Terelynn, Terri-Lynn, Terrilynn, Terrylynn

Tertia (Latin) third.
Tercia, Tercina, Tercine, Terecena, Tersia, Terza

Teruko (Japanese) barrel.

Tesira (Greek) founder.

Tess **G** (Greek) a short form of Quintessa, Theresa.
Tes, Tese

Tessa **G** (Greek) reaper.
Tesa, Tesah, Teshá, Tesia, Tessah, Tessia, Tezia

Tessie (Greek) a familiar form of Theresa.
Tesi, Tessey, Tessi, Tessy, Tezi

Tetis (Greek) wet nurse; nursemaid.

Tetsu (Japanese) strong as iron.

Tetty (English) a familiar form of Elizabeth.

Tevin **B** (American) a combination of the prefix Te + Kevin.

Tevy (Cambodian) angel.
Teva

Teylor (English) a form of Taylor.
Teighlor, Teylar

Thaddea (Greek) courageous. (Latin) praiser.
Thada, Thadda

Thalassa (Greek) sea, ocean.

Thalia (Greek) a form of Talia. Mythology. the Muse of comedy.
Thaleia, Thalie, Thalya

Tham (Vietnamese) fog.

Than (Vietnamese) new.

Thana (Arabic) happy occasion.
Thaina, Thania, Thanie

Thanh (Vietnamese) bright blue. (Punjabi) good place.
Thantra, Thanya

Thanh Ha (Vietnamese) discreet grace.

Thao (Vietnamese) respectful of parents.

The (Vietnamese) death; brilliant.

Thea (Greek) goddess. A short form of Althea.
Theo

Thelma (Greek) willful.
Thelmalina

Thema (African) queen.

Thena (Mycenaean) a form of Glenna.

Theodora (Greek) a form of Theodore. See also Dora, Dorothy, Feodora.
Taedra, Teddi, Tedra, Teodora, Teodory, Teodosia, Theda, Thedorsha, Thedrica, Theo, Theodore, Theodoria, Theodorian, Theodosia, Theodra

Theodore 🅱 (Greek) gift of God.

Theone (Greek) a form of Theodore.
Theondra, Theoni, Theonie

Theophania (Greek) God's appearance. See also Tiffany.
Theo, Theophanie

Theophila (Greek) loved by God.
Theo

Theresa 🅶 (Greek) reaper. See also Resi, Reza, Riza, Tassos, Teca, Terrelle, Tracey, Tracy, Zilya.
Teresa, Teri, Terri, Terry, Tersea, Tess, Tessa, Tessie, Theresia, Theresina, Theresita,

Theressa, Thereza, Therisa, Therissie, Thersa, Thersea, Tresha, Tressa, Trice

Therese (Greek) a form of Theresa.
Terese, Thérése, Theresia, Theressa, Therra, Therressa, Thersa

Theta (Greek) Linguistics: a letter in the Greek alphabet.

Thetis (Greek) disposed. Mythology: the mother of Achilles.

Thi (Vietnamese) poem.
Thia, Thy, Thya

Thirza (Hebrew) pleasant.
Therza, Thirsa, Thirzah, Thursa, Thurza, Thyrza, Tirshka, Tirza

Thom (Vietnamese) teal river.

Thomas 🅱 (Greek, Aramaic) twin.

Thomasina (Hebrew) twin. See also Tamassa.
Tamsin, Thomasa, Thomasia, Thomasin, Thomasine, Thomazine, Thomencia, Thomethia, Thomisha, Thomsina, Toma, Tomasa, Tomasina, Tomasine, Tomina, Tommie, Tommina

Thora (Scandinavian) thunder.
Thordia, Thordis, Thorri, Thyra, Tyra

Thuong (Vietnamese) pledged.

Thuy (Vietnamese) gentle.

Tia (Greek) princess. (Spanish) aunt.
Téa, Teah, Teeya, Teia, Ti, Tiakeisha, Tialeigh, Tiamarie, Tianda, Tiandria, Tiante, Tiia, Tiye, Tyja

Tiana, Tianna (Greek) princess. (Latin) short forms of Tatiana.
Teana, Teanna, Tiahna, Tianah, Tiane, Tianea,

Tianee, Tiani, Tiann, Tiannah, Tianne, Tianni, Tiaon, Tiauna, Tiena, Tiona, Tionna, Tiyana

Tiara (Latin) crowned.
Teair, Teaira, Teara, Téare, Tearia, Tearria, Teearia, Teira, Teirra, Tiaira, Tiare, Tiarea, Tiareah, Tiari, Tiaria, Tiarra, Tiera, Tierra, Tyara

Tiarra 🅶 (Latin) a form of Tiara.
Tiairra, Tiarrah, Tyarra

Tiauna (Greek) a form of Tiana.
Tiaunah, Tiaunia, Tiaunna

Tiberia (Latin) Geography: the Tiber River in Italy.
Tib, Tibbie, Tibby

Tiburcia (Spanish) born in the place of pleasures.

Tichina (American) a combination of the prefix Ti + China.
Tichian, Tichin, Tichinia

Ticiana (Latin) valiant defender.

Tida (Tai) daughter.

Tien (Vietnamese) sweet smelling; pineapple.

Tien-Hou (Chinese) protector of sailors and others in times of danger.

Tien-Mu (Chinese) goddess of lightning.

Tiera, Tierra (Latin) forms of Tiara.
Tieara, Tiéra, Tierah, Tierre, Tierrea, Tierria

Tierney 🅶 (Irish) noble.
Tieranae, Tierani, Tieranie, Tieranni, Tierany, Tiernan, Tiernee, Tierny

Tiff (Latin) a short form of Tiffani, Tiffanie, Tiffany.

Tiffani, Tiffanie (Latin) forms of Tiffany.
Tephanie, Tifanee, Tifani, Tifanie, Tiff,
Tiffanee, Tiffayne, Tiffeni, Tiffenie, Tiffennie,
Tiffiani, Tiffianie, Tiffine, Tiffini, Tiffinie, Tiffni,
Tiffy, Tiffynie, Tifni

Tiffany **G** (Latin) trinity. (Greek) a short
form of Theophania. See also Tyfany.
Taffanay, Taffany, Tifaney, Tifany, Tiff,
Tiffaney, Tiffani, Tiffanie, Tiffanny, Tiffeney,
Tiffany, Tiffiney, Tiffiny, Tiffnay, Tiffney, Tiffny,
Tiffy, Tiphanie, Triffany

Tiffy (Latin) a familiar form of Tiffani, Tiffany.
Tiffey, Tiffi, Tiffie

Tijuana (Spanish) Geography: a border town
in Mexico.
Tajuana, Tajuanna, Thejuana, Tiajuana,
Tiajuanna, Tiawanna

Tilda (German) a short form of Matilda.
Tilde, Tildie, Tildy, Tylda, Tyldy

Tillie (German) a familiar form of Matilda.
Tilia, Tilley, Tilli, Tillia, Tilly, Tillye

Timi (English) a familiar form of Timothea.
Timia, Timie, Timmi, Timmie

Timotea (Greek) she who honors and praises
God.

Timothea (English) honoring God.
Thea, Timi

Timothy **B** (Greek) honoring God.

Tina **G** (Spanish, American) a short form of
Augustine, Martina, Christina, Valentina.
Teanna, Teena, Teina, Tena, Tenae, Tinai,
Tine, Tinea, Tinia, Tiniah, Tinna, Tinnia, Tyna,
Tynka

Tinble (English) sound bells make.
Tynble

Tinesha (American) a combination of the
prefix Ti + Niesha.
Timnesha, Tinecia, Tineisha, Tinesa, Tineshia,
Tinessa, Tinisha, Tinsia

Ting, Ting-Ting (Chinese) slim and graceful.

Tinisha (American) a form of Tenisha.
Tiniesha, Tinieshia, Tinishia, Tinishya

Tiona, Tionna (American) forms of Tiana.
Teona, Teonna, Tionda, Tiondra, Tiondre,
Tioné, Tionette, Tioni, Tionia, Tionie, Tionja,
Tionnah, Tionne, Tionya, Tyonna

Tiphanie (Latin) a form of Tiffany.
Tiphanee, Tiphani, Tiphany

Tiponya (Native American) great horned owl.
Tipper

Tipper (Irish) water pourer. (Native
American) a short form of Tiponya.

Tira (Hindi) arrow.
Tirah, Tirea, Tirena

Tirtha (Hindi) ford.

Tirza (Hebrew) pleasant.
Thersa, Thirza, Tierza, Tirsa, Tirzah, Tirzha,
Tyrzah

Tisa (Swahili) ninth-born.
Tisah, Tysa, Tyssa

Tish (Latin) a short form of Tisha.

Tisha **G** (Latin) joy. A short form of Leticia.
Taesha, Tesha, Teisha, Tiesha, Tieshia, Tish,
Tishal, Tishia, Tysha, Tyshia

Tita (Greek) giant. (Spanish) a short form of
names ending in "tita. "

Titania (Greek) giant. Mythology: the Titans
were a race of giants.

Tania, Teata, Titanna, Titanya, Titiana, Tiziana,
Tytan, Tytania, Tytiana

Titiana (Greek) a form of Titania.
Titianay, Titiania, Titianna, Titiayana, Titionia,
Titiyana, Titiyanna, Tityana

Tivona (Hebrew) nature lover.

Tiwa (Zuni) onion.

Tiyana (Greek) a form of Tiana.
Tiyan, Tiyani, Tiyania, Tiyanna, Tiyonna

Toan (Vietnamese) love tenderly; in pursuit.

Tobi **G** (Hebrew) God is good.
Tobe, Tobee, Tobey, Tobie, Tobit, Toby, Tobye,
Tova, Tovah, Tove, Tovi, Tybi, Tybie

Toby **B** (Hebrew) a form of Tobi.

Tocarra (American) a combination of the
prefix To + Cara.
Tocara, Toccara

Todd **B** (English) fox.

Toinette (French) a short form of Antoinette.
Toinetta, Tola, Tonetta, Tonette, Toni,
Toniette, Twanette

Toki (Japanese) hopeful.
Toko, Tokoya, Tokyo

Tokiko (Japanese) dragon.

Tokiwa (Japanese) the girl who shines.

Tola (Polish) a form of Toinette.
Tolsia

Tomi **G** (Japanese) rich.
Tomie, Tomiju

Tommie 🅱 (Hebrew) a short form of Thomasina.
Tomme, Tommi, Tommia, Tommy

Tommy 🅱 (Hebrew) a form of Tommie.

Tomo (Japanese) intelligent.
Tomoko

Tomomi (Japanese) child of Toki.

Tonesha (American) a combination of the prefix To + Niesha.
Toneisha, Toneisheia, Tonesha, Tonesia, Toniece, Tonisha, Tonneshia

Tong (Chinese) phoenix tree.

Toni 🅶 (Greek) flourishing. (Latin) praiseworthy.
Tonee, Toney, Tonia, Tonie, Toniee, Tonni, Tonnie, Tony, Tonye

Tonia (Latin, Slavic) a form of Toni, Tonya.
Tonea, Toniah, Toniea, Tonja, Tonje, Tonna, Tonni, Tonnia, Tonnie, Tonnja

Tonisha (American) a form of Toneisha.
Toniesha, Tonisa, Tonise, Tonisia, Tonnisha

Tony 🅱 (Greek, Latin) a form of Toni.

Tonya (Slavic) fairy queen.
Tonia, Tonnya, Tonyea, Tonyetta, Tonyia

Tooka (Japanese) steady.

Topaz (Latin) golden yellow gem.

Topsy (English) on top. Literature: a slave in Harriet Beecher Stowe's novel *Uncle Tom's Cabin*.
Toppsy, Topsey, Topsie

Tora (Japanese) tiger.

Tori 🅶 (Japanese) bird. (English) a form of Tory.
Toria, Toriana, Torie, Torri, Torrie, Torrita

Toria (English) a form of Tori, Tory.
Toriah, Torria

Toriana (English) a form of Tori.
Torian, Toriane, Toriann, Torianna, Torianne, Toriauna, Torin, Torina, Torine, Torinne, Torion, Torionna, Torionne, Toriyanna, Torrina

Toribia (Latin) she who moves on to another life.

Torie, Torrie (English) forms of Tori.
Tore, Toree, Torei, Torre, Torree

Torilyn (English) a combination of Tori + Lynn.
Torilynn, Torrilyn, Torrilynn

Torri (English) a form of Tori.

Tory 🅶 (English) victorious. (Latin) a short form of Victoria.
Tauri, Torey, Tori, Torrey, Torreya, Torry, Torrye, Torya, Torye, Toya

Tosca (Latin) native of Toscana, Italy.

Toscana (Latin) she who was born in Etruria, Tuscany.

Tosha (Punjabi) armaments. (Polish) a familiar form of Antonia. (Russian) a form of Tasha.
Toshea, Toshia, Toshiea, Toshke, Tosia, Toska

Toshi (Japanese) mirror image.
Toshie, Toshiko, Toshikyo

Toshio (Japanese) she who is a beautiful companion.

Toski (Hopi) squashed bug.

Totsi (Hopi) moccasins.

Tottie (English) a familiar form of Charlotte.
Tota, Totti, Totty

Tou-Mou (Chinese) goddess of the polestar.

Tovah (Hebrew) good.
Tova, Tovia

Toya (Spanish) a form of Tory.
Toia, Toyanika, Toyanna, Toyea, Toylea, Toyleah, Toylenn, Toylin, Toylyn

Toyo (Japanese) ten days.

Tracey 🅶 (Greek) a familiar form of Theresa. (Latin) warrior.
Trace, Tracee, Tracell, Traci, Tracie, Tracy, Traice, Trasey, Treesy

Traci, Tracie 🅶 (Latin) forms of Tracey.
Tracia, Tracilee, Tracilyn, Tracilynn, Tracina, Traeci

Tracy 🅶 (Greek) a familiar form of Theresa. (Latin) warrior.
Treacy

Tralena (Latin) a combination of Tracy + Lena.
Traleen, Tralene, Tralin, Tralinda, Tralyn, Tralynn, Tralynne

Tranesha (American) a combination of the prefix Tra + Niesha.
Traneice, Traneis, Traneise, Traneisha, Tranese, Traneshia, Tranice, Traniece, Traniesha, Tranisha, Tranishia

Tranquila (Spanish) calm, tranquil.

Tránsito (Latin) she who moves on to another life.

Trashawn **B** (American) a combination of the prefix Tra + Shawn.
Trashan, Trashana, Trashauna, Trashon, Trayshauna

Trava (Czech) spring grasses.

Travis **B** (English) a form of Travers (see Boys' Names).

Travon **B** (American) a form of Trevon.

Treasure (Latin) treasure, wealth; valuable.
Treasa, Treasur, Treasuré, Treasury

Trella (Spanish) a familiar form of Estelle.

Tremaine **B** (Scottish) house of stone.

Trent **B** (Latin) torrent, rapid stream. (French) thirty. Geography: a city in northern Italy.

Tresha (Greek) a form of Theresa.
Trescha, Trescia, Treshana, Treshia

Tressa (Greek) a short form of Theresa. See also Teresa.
Treaser, Tresa, Tresca, Trese, Treska, Tressia, Tressie, Trez, Treza, Trisa

Trevina (Irish) prudent. (Welsh) homestead.
Treva, Trevanna, Trevena, Trevenia, Treveon, Trevia, Treviana, Trevien, Trevin, Trevona

Trevon **B** (Irish) a form of Trevona.

Trevona (Irish) a form of Trevina.
Trevion, Trevon, Trevonia, Trevonna, Trevonne, Trevonye

Trevor **B** (Irish) prudent. (Welsh) homestead.

Triana (Latin) third. (Greek) a form of Trina.
Tria, Triann, Trianna, Trianne

Trice (Greek) a short form of Theresa.
Treece

Tricia (Latin) a form of Trisha.
Trica, Tricha, Trichelle, Tricina, Trickia

Trilby (English) soft hat.
Tribi, Trilbie, Trillby

Trina **G** (Greek) pure.
Treena, Treina, Trenna, Triana, Trinia, Trinchen, Trind, Trinda, Trine, Trinette, Trini, Trinica, Trinice, Triniece, Trinika, Trinique, Trinisa, Tryna

Trinh (Vietnamese) fairy; spirit; angel.

Trini (Greek) a form of Trina.
Trinia, Trinie

Trinidad (Latin) three people in one God.

Trinity 🌿 **G** (Latin) triad. Religion: the Father, the Son, and the Holy Spirit.
Trinita, Trinite, Trinitee, Triniti, Trinnette, Trinty

Tripaileo (Mapuche) explosion of flames, explosive bomb; explosive, impulsive, passionate, and vehement woman.

Trish (Latin) a short form of Beatrice, Trisha.
Trishell, Trishelle

Trisha (Latin) noblewoman. (Hindi) thirsty. See also Tricia.
Treasha, Trish, Trishann, Trishanna, Trishanne, Trishara, Trishia, Trishna, Trissha, Trycia

Trissa (Latin) a familiar form of Patricia.
Trisa, Trisanne, Trisia, Trisina, Trissi, Trissie, Trissy, Tryssa

Trista (Latin) a short form of Tristen.
Trisatal, Tristess, Tristia, Trysta, Trystia

Tristan **B** (Latin) bold.
Trista, Tristane, Tristanni, Tristany, Tristen, Tristian, Tristiana, Tristin, Triston, Trystan, Trystyn

Tristana (Latin) she who carries sadness with her.

Tristen **B** (Latin) a form of Tristan.
Tristene, Trysten

Tristin **B** (Latin) a form of Tristan.
Tristina, Tristine, Tristinye, Tristn, Trystin

Triston **B** (Latin) a form of Tristan.
Tristony

Trixie (American) a familiar form of Beatrice.
Tris, Trissie, Trissina, Trix, Trixi, Trixy

Troy **B** (Irish) foot soldier.

Troya (Irish) a form of Troy.
Troi, Troia, Troiana, Troiya

Truc (Vietnamese) safe, secure.

Trudel (Dutch) a form of Trudy.

Trudy (German) a familiar form of Gertrude.
Truda, Trude, Trudel, Trudessa, Trudey, Trudi, Trudie

Trung (Vietnamese) pure.

Trycia (Latin) a form of Trisha.

Tryna (Greek) a form of Trina.
Tryane, Tryanna, Trynee

Tryne (Dutch) pure.
Trine

Trystyn (Latin) a form of Tristan.

Tsigana (Hungarian) a form of Zigana.
Tsigane, Tzigana, Tzigane

Tsi-Ku (Chinese) goddess of the outhouse.

Tsuhgi (Japanese) a one-year-old child.

Tsukiko (Japanese) plentiful.

Tsukina (Japanese) second daughter.

Tsuna (Japanese) moon child.

Tsuneko (Japanese) moon; a type of red apple.

Tsuru (Japanese) bond.

Tsuyu (Japanese) a child forever.

Tu ⓑ (Chinese) jade.

Tuan (Chinese) round, circular.

Tucker ⓑ (English) fuller, tucker of cloth.

Tuesday (English) born on the third day of the week.
Tuesdae, Tuesdea, Tuesdee, Tuesdey, Tusdai

Tuki (Japanese) stork; hope for long life.

Tula (Hindi) born in the lunar month of Capricorn.
Tulah, Tulla, Tullah, Tuula

Tullia (Irish) peaceful, quiet.
Tulia, Tulliah

Tulsi (Hindi) basil, a sacred Hindi herb.
Tulsia

Tuo (Chinese) proper, appropriate.

Turner ⓑ (Latin) lathe worker; wood worker.

Turquoise (French) blue-green semi-precious stone.
Turkois, Turkoise, Turkoys, Turkoyse

Tusa (Zuni) prairie dog.

Tusnelda (German) she who fights giants.

Tuyen (Vietnamese) angel.

Tuyet (Vietnamese) snow.

Twyla (English) woven of double thread.
Twila, Twilla

Ty ⓑ (English) a short form of Tyler, Tyson.

Tyanna (American) a combination of the prefix Ty + Anna.
Tya, Tyana, Tyann, Tyannah, Tyanne, Tyannia

Tyeisha (American) a form of Tyesha.
Tyeesha, Tyeishia, Tyieishia, Tyisha, Tyishea, Tyishia

Tyesha (American) a combination of Ty + Aisha.
Tyasha, Tyashia, Tyasia, Tyasiah, Tyeisha, Tyeshia, Tyeyshia, Tyisha

Tyfany (American) a short form of Tiffany.
Tyfani, Tyfanny, Tyffani, Tyffanni, Tyffany, Tyffini, Typhanie, Typhany

Tykeisha (American) a form of Takeisha.
Tkeesha, Tykeisa, Tykeishia, Tykesha, Tykeshia, Tykeysha, Tykeza, Tykisha

Tykera (American) a form of Takira.
Tykeira, Tykeirah, Tykereiah, Tykeria, Tykeriah, Tykerria, Tykiera, Tykierra, Tykira, Tykiria, Tykirra

Tyler ⓑ (English) tailor.
Tyller, Tylor

Tylor ⓑ (English) a form of Tyler.

Tyna (Czech) a short form of Kristina.
Tynae, Tynea, Tynia

Tyne (English) river.
Tine, Tyna, Tynelle, Tynessa, Tynetta

Tynesha (American) a combination of Ty + Niesha.
Tynaise, Tynece, Tyneicia, Tynesa, Tynesha, Tyneshia, Tynessia, Tyniesha, Tynisha, Tyseisha

Tynisha (American) a form of Tynesha.
Tyneisha, Tyneisia, Tynisa, Tynise, Tynishi

Tyra ⓖ (Scandinavian) battler. Mythology: Tyr was the god of war. A form of Thora. (Hindi) a form of Tira.
Tyraa, Tyrah, Tyran, Tyree, Tyria

Tyree ⓑ (Scandinavian) a form of Tyra.

Tyrell ⓑ (Greek) a form of Terrelle.

Tyshanna (American) a combination of Ty + Shawna.
Tyshana, Tyshanae, Tyshane, Tyshaun, Tyshaunda, Tyshawn, Tyshawna, Tyshawnah, Tyshawnda, Tyshawnna, Tysheann, Tysheanna, Tyshonia, Tyshonna, Tyshonya

Tyson ⓑ (French) child of Ty.

Tytiana (Greek) a form of Titania.
Tytana, Tytanna, Tyteana, Tyteanna, Tytianna, Tytianni, Tytionna, Tytiyana, Tytiyanna, Tytyana, Tytyauna

U (Korean) gentle.

Ubaldina (Teutonic) audacious, daring; intelligent.

Udele (English) prosperous.
Uda, Udella, Udelle, Yudelle

Ukara (Japanese) morning dew.

Uki (Japanese) moon.

Ula (Irish) sea jewel. (Scandinavian) wealthy. (Spanish) a short form of Eulalia.
Uli, Ulla

Ulani (Polynesian) cheerful.
Ulana, Ulane

Ulima (Arabic) astute; wise.
Ullima

Ulla (German, Swedish) willful. (Latin) a short form of Ursula.
Ulli

Ulrica (German) wolf ruler; ruler of all. See also Rica.
Ulka, Ullrica, Ullricka, Ullrika, Ulrika, Ulrike

Ultima (Latin) last, endmost, farthest.

Ululani (Hawaiian) heavenly inspiration.

Ulva (German) wolf.

Uma (Hindi) mother. Religion: another name for the Hindu goddess Devi.

Umay (Turkish) hopeful.
Umai

Umbelina (Latin) she who gives protective shade.

Umeko (Japanese) plum-blossom child; patient.
Ume, Umeyo

Umeno (Japanese) beautiful and serene.

Una (Latin) one; united. (Hopi) good memory. (Irish) a form of Agnes. See also Oona.
Unna, Uny

Undine (Latin) little wave. Mythology: the undines were water spirits. See also Ondine.
Undeen, Undene

Unice (English) a form of Eunice.

Unika **G** (American) a form of Unique.
Unica, Unicka, Unik, Unikqua, Unikue

Unique **G** (Latin) only one.
Unika, Uniqia, Uniqua, Uniquia

Unity (English) unity.
Uinita, Unita, Unitee

Unn (Norwegian) she who is loved.

Unna (German) woman.

Uoc (Vietnamese) bamboo; wish.

Urania (Greek) heavenly. Mythology: the Muse of astronomy.
Urainia, Uranie, Uraniya, Uranya

Urano (Japanese) air; hope, pray.

Urbana (Latin) city dweller.
Urbanah, Urbanna

Uriel **B** (Hebrew) God is my light.

Urika (Omaha) useful to everyone.
Ureka

Urit (Hebrew) bright.
Urice

Urraca (German) magpie.

Ursa (Greek) a short form of Ursula. (Latin) a form of Orsa.
Ursey, Ursi, Ursie, Ursy

Ursina (Latin) little bear.

Ursula (Greek) little bear. See also Sula, Ulla, Vorsila.
Irsaline, Ursa, Ursala, Ursel, Ursela, Ursella, Ursely, Ursilla, Ursillane, Ursola, Ursule, Ursulina, Ursuline, Urszula, Urszuli, Urzula

Úrsula (Portuguese) a form of Ursula.

Usagi (Japanese) plum tree field.

Usha (Hindi) sunrise.

Ushi (Chinese) ox. Astrology: a sign of the Chinese zodiac.

Uta (German) rich. (Japanese) poem.
Utako

Utina (Native American) woman of my country.
Utahna, Utona, Utonna

V **G** (American) an initial used as a first name.

Vail **B** (English) valley.
Vale, Vayle

Val **B** (Latin) a short form of Valentina, Valerie.

Vala (German) singled out.
Valla

Valarie (Latin) a form of Valerie.
Valarae, Valaree, Valarey, Valari, Valaria, Vallarie

Valburga (German) she who defends on the battlefield.

Valda (German) famous ruler.
Valida, Velda

Valdrada (German) she who gives advice.

Valencia (Spanish) strong. Geography: a region in eastern Spain.
Valecia, Valence, Valenica, Valentia, Valenzia

Valene (Latin) a short form of Valentina.
Valaine, Valean, Valeda, Valeen, Valen, Valena, Valeney, Valien, Valina, Valine, Vallan, Vallen

Valentina (Latin) strong. History: Valentina Tereshkova, a Soviet cosmonaut, was the first woman in space. See also Tina, Valene, Valli.
Val, Valantina, Vale, Valenteen, Valentena, Valentijn, Valentin, Valentine, Valiaka, Valtina, Valyn, Valynn

Valera (Russian) a form of Valerie. See also Lera.

Valeria (Latin) a form of Valerie.
Valaria, Valeriana, Valeriane, Veleria

Valéria (Hungarian, Portuguese) a form of Valerie.

Valerie 🄶 (Latin) strong.
Vairy, Val, Valarie, Vale, Valera, Valeree, Valeri, Valeria, Valérie, Valery, Valka, Valleree, Valleri, Vallerie, Valli, Vallirie, Valora, Valorie, Valry, Valya, Velerie, Waleria

Valery (Latin) a form of Valerie.
Valerye, Vallary, Vallery

Valeska (Slavic) glorious ruler.
Valesca, Valese, Valeshia, Valeshka, Valezka, Valisha

Valli (Latin) a familiar form of Valentina, Valerie. Botany: a plant native to India.
Vallie, Vally

Valma (Finnish) loyal defender.

Valonia (Latin) shadow valley.
Vallon, Valona

Valora (Latin) a form of Valerie.
Valoria, Valorya, Velora

Valorie (Latin) a form of Valerie.
Vallori, Vallory, Valori, Valory

Vance 🄱 (English) thresher.

Vanda 🄶 (German) a form of Wanda.
Vandana, Vandella, Vandetta, Vandi, Vannda

Vanesa (Greek) a form of Vanessa.
Vanesha, Vaneshah, Vanesia, Vanisa

Vanessa ☙ 🄶 (Greek) butterfly. Literature: a name invented by Jonathan Swift as a nickname for Esther Vanhomrigh. See also Nessie.
Van, Vanassa, Vanesa, Vaneshia, Vanesse, Vanessia, Vanessica, Vanetta, Vaneza, Vaniece, Vaniessa, Vanija, Vanika, Vanissa, Vanita, Vanna, Vannesa, Vannessa, Vanni, Vannie, Vanny, Varnessa, Venessa

Vanetta (English) a form of Vanessa.
Vaneta, Vanita, Vanneta, Vannetta, Vannita, Venetta

Vania, Vanya (Russian) familiar forms of Anna.
Vanija, Vanina, Vaniya, Vanja, Vanka, Vannia

Vanity (English) vain.
Vaniti, Vanitty

Vanna (Cambodian) golden. (Greek) a short form of Vanessa.
Vana, Vanae, Vanelly, Vannah, Vannalee, Vannaleigh, Vannie, Vanny

Vannesa, Vannessa (Greek) forms of Vanessa.
Vannesha, Vanneza

Vanora (Welsh) white wave.
Vannora

Vantrice (American) a combination of the prefix Van + Trice.
Vantrece, Vantricia, Vantrisa, Vantrissa

Varda (Hebrew) rose.
Vadit, Vardia, Vardice, Vardina, Vardis, Vardit

Varinia (Ancient Roman, Spanish) versatile.

Varvara (Slavic) a form of Barbara.
Vara, Varenka, Varina, Varinka, Varya, Varyusha, Vava, Vavka

Vashti (Persian) lovely. Bible: the wife of Ahasuerus, king of Persia.
Vashtee, Vashtie, Vashty

Vaughn 🄱 (Welsh) small.

Veanna (American) a combination of the prefix Ve + Anna.
Veeana, Veena, Veenaya, Veeona

Veda (Sanskrit) sacred lore; knowledge. Religion: the Vedas are the sacred writings of Hinduism.
Vedad, Vedis, Veeda, Veida, Veleda, Vida

Vedette (Italian) sentry; scout. (French) movie star.
Vedetta

Vega (Arabic) falling star.

Velda (German) a form of Valda.

Velika (Slavic) great, wondrous.

Velma (German) a familiar form of Vilhelmina.
Valma, Vellma, Vilma, Vilna

Velvet (English) velvety.

Venancia (Latin) hunter; she likes to hunt deer.

Venecia (Italian) from Venice, Italy.
Vanecia, Vanetia, Veneise, Venesa, Venesha, Venesher, Venesse, Venessia, Venetia, Venette, Venezia, Venice, Venicia, Veniece, Veniesa, Venise, Venisha, Venishia, Venita, Venitia, Venize, Vennesa, Vennice, Vennisa, Vennise, Vonitia, Vonizia

Venessa (Latin) a form of Vanessa.
Veneese, Venesa, Venese, Veneshia, Venesia, Venisa, Venissa, Vennessa

Ventana (Spanish) window.

Ventura (Spanish) good fortune.

Venus (Latin) love. Mythology: the goddess of love and beauty.
Venis, Venusa, Venusina, Vinny

Vera (Latin) true. (Slavic) faith. A short form of Elvera, Veronica. See also Verena, Wera.
Vara, Veera, Veira, Veradis, Verasha, Vere, Verka, Verla, Viera, Vira

Verbena (Latin) sacred plants.
Verbeena, Verbina

Verda (Latin) young, fresh.
Verdi, Verdie, Viridiana, Viridis

Verdad (Spanish) truthful.

Veredigna (Latin) she who has earned great honors for her dignity.

Verena (Latin) truthful. A familiar form of Vera, Verna.
Verene, Verenis, Vereniz, Verina, Verine, Verinka, Veroshka, Verunka, Verusya, Virna

Verenice (Latin) a form of Veronica.
Verenis, Verenise, Vereniz

Verity (Latin) truthful.
Verita, Veritie

Verlene (Latin) a combination of Veronica + Lena.
Verleen, Verlena, Verlin, Verlina, Verlinda, Verline, Verlyn

Verna (Latin) springtime. (French) a familiar form of Laverne. See also Verena, Wera.
Verasha, Verla, Verne, Vernetia, Vernetta, Vernette, Vernia, Vernice, Vernita, Verusya, Viera, Virida, Virna, Virnell

Vernice (Latin) a form of Bernice, Verna.
Vernese, Vernesha, Verneshia, Vernessa, Vernica, Vernicca, Verniece, Vernika, Vernique, Vernis, Vernise, Vernisha, Vernisheia, Vernissia

Veronica (Latin) true image. See also Ronni, Weronika.
Varonica, Vera, Veranique, Verenice, Verhonica, Verinica, Verohnica, Veron, Verona, Verone, Veronic, Véronic, Veronice, Veronika, Veronique, Véronique, Veronne, Veronnica, Veruszhka, Vironica, Vron, Vronica

Verónica (Spanish) a form of Veronica.

Verônica (Portuguese) a form of Veronica.

Veronika (Latin) a form of Veronica.
Varonika, Veronick, Véronick, Veronik, Veronike, Veronka, Veronkia, Veruka

Veronique, Véronique (French) forms of Veronica.

Vespera (Latin) evening star.

Vesta (Latin) keeper of the house. Mythology: the goddess of the home.
Vessy, Vest, Vesteria

Veta (Slavic) a familiar form of Elizabeth.
Veeta, Vita

Vi (Latin, French) a short form of Viola, Violet.
Vye

Vianca (Spanish) a form of Bianca.
Vianeca, Vianica

Vianey (American) a familiar form of Vianna.
Vianney, Viany

Vianna (American) a combination of Vi + Anna.
Viana, Vianey, Viann, Vianne

Vica (Hungarian) a form of Eve.

Vicente B (Spanish) a form of Vincent.

Vicki, Vickie (Latin) familiar forms of Victoria.
Vic, Vicci, Vicke, Vickee, Vickiana, Vickilyn, Vickki, Vicky, Vika, Viki, Vikie, Vikki, Vikky

Vicky G (Latin) a familiar form of Victoria.
Viccy, Vickey, Viky, Vikkey, Vikky

Victoria ✺ **G** (Latin) victorious. See also Tory, Wicktoria, Wisia.
Vicki, Vicky, Victoire, Victoriana, Victorianna, Victorie, Victorina, Victorine, Victoriya, Victorria, Victorriah, Victory, Victorya, Viktoria, Vitoria, Vyctoria

Vida (Sanskrit) a form of Veda. (Hebrew) a short form of Davida.
Vidamarie

Vidonia (Portuguese) branch of a vine.
Vedonia, Vidonya

Vienna (Latin) Geography: the capital of Austria.
Veena, Vena, Venna, Vienette, Vienne, Vina

Viktoria (Latin) a form of Victoria.
Viktorie, Viktorija, Viktorina, Viktorine, Viktorka

Vilhelmina (German) a form of Wilhelmina.
Velma, Vilhelmine, Vilma

Villette (French) small town.
Vietta

Vilma (German) a short form of Vilhemina.

Vina (Hindi) Religion: a musical instrument played by the Hindu goddess of wisdom. (Spanish) vineyard. (Hebrew) a short form of Davina. (English) a short form of Alvina. See also Lavina.
Veena, Vena, Viña, Vinesha, Vinessa, Vinia, Viniece, Vinique, Vinisha, Viñita, Vinna, Vinni, Vinnie, Vinny, Vinora, Vyna

Vincent **B** (Latin) victor, conqueror.

Vincentia (Latin) a form of Vincent.
Vicenta, Vincenta, Vincentena, Vincentina, Vincentine, Vincenza, Vincy, Vinnie

Viñita (Spanish) a form of Vina.
Viñeet, Viñeeta, Viñetta, Viñette, Viñitha, Viñta, Viñti, Viñtia, Vyñetta, Vyñette

Viola (Latin) violet; stringed instrument in the violin family. Literature: the heroine of Shakespeare's play *Twelfth Night*.
Vi, Violaine, Violanta, Violante, Viole, Violeine

Violet (French) Botany: a plant with purplish blue flowers.
Vi, Violeta, Violette, Vyolet, Vyoletta, Vyolette

Violeta (French) a form of Violet.
Violetta

Virgilia (Latin) rod bearer, staff bearer.
Virgillia

Virginia (Latin) pure, virginal. Literature: Virginia Woolf was a well-known British writer. See also Gina, Ginger, Ginny, Jinny.
Verginia, Verginya, Virge, Virgen, Virgenia, Virgenya, Virgie, Virgine, Virginie, Virginië, Virginio, Virginnia, Virgy, Virjeana

Virginie (French) a form of Virginia.

Viridiana (Latin) a form of Viridis.

Viridis (Latin) green.
Virdis, Virida, Viridia, Viridiana

Virtudes (Latin) blessed spirit.

Virtue (Latin) virtuous.

Visitación (Latin) refers to the Virgin Mary visiting Saint Isabel, who was her cousin.

Vita (Latin) life.
Veeta, Veta, Vitaliana, Vitalina, Vitel, Vitella, Vitia, Vitka, Vitke

Vitalia (Latin) she who is full of life.

Vitoria (Spanish) a form of Victoria.
Vittoria

Vitória (Portuguese) a form of Victoria.

Viv (Latin) a short form of Vivian.

Viva (Latin) a short form of Aviva, Vivian.
Vica, Vivan, Vivva

Viveca (Scandinavian) a form of Vivian.
Viv, Vivecca, Vivecka, Viveka, Vivica, Vivieca, Vyveca

Vivian **G** (Latin) full of life.
Vevay, Vevey, Viv, Viva, Viveca, Vivee, Vivi, Vivia, Viviana, Viviane, Viviann, Vivianne, Vivie, Vivien, Vivienne, Vivina, Vivion, Vivyan, Vivyann, Vivyanne, Vyvyan, Vyvyann, Vyvyanne

Viviana (Latin) a form of Vivian.
Viv, Vivianna, Vivyana, Vyvyana

Vondra (Czech) loving woman.
Vonda, Vondrea

Voneisha (American) a combination of Yvonne + Aisha.
Voneishia, Vonesha, Voneshia

Vonna (French) a form of Yvonne.
Vona

Vonny (French) a familiar form of Yvonne.
Vonney, Vonni, Vonnie

Vontricia (American) a combination of Yvonne + Tricia.
Vontrece, Vontrese, Vontrice, Vontriece

Vorsila (Greek) a form of Ursula.
Vorsilla, Vorsula, Vorsulla, Vorsyla

Vui (Vietnamese) medium; loyalty.

W **B** (American) an initial used as a first name.

Wadd (Arabic) beloved.

Waheeda (Arabic) one and only.

Wainani (Hawaiian) beautiful water.

Wakaba (Japanese) coast.

Wakako (Japanese) rabbit.

Wakana (Japanese) plant.

Wakanda (Dakota) magical power.
Wakenda

Wakeisha (American) a combination of the prefix Wa + Keisha.
Wakeishia, Wakesha, Wakeshia, Wakesia

Walad (Arabic) newborn.
Waladah, Walidah

Walda (German) powerful; famous.
Waldina, Waldine, Walida, Wallda, Welda

Waleria (Polish) a form of Valerie.
Wala

Walker **B** (English) cloth; walker.
Wallker

Wallis (English) from Wales.
Wallie, Walliss, Wally, Wallys

Wan (Chinese) gentle; gracious.

Wanda (German) wanderer. See also Wendy.
Vanda, Wahnda, Wandah, Wandely, Wandie, Wandis, Wandja, Wandzia, Wannda, Wonda, Wonnda

Wandie (German) a familiar form of Wanda.
Wandi, Wandy

Waneta (Native American) charger. See also Juanita.
Waneeta, Wanita, Wanite, Wanneta, Waunita, Wonita, Wonnita, Wynita

Wanetta (English) pale face.
Wanette, Wannetta, Wannette

Wang (Chinese) flourishing.

Wang-Mu (Chinese) highest goddess of ancient China.

Wanida (Pohnpeian) a form of Dolores.

Wanika (Hawaiian) a form of Juanita.
Wanicka

Wanya **B** (Russian) a form of Vania.

Warda (German) guardian.
Wardah, Wardeh, Wardena, Wardenia, Wardia, Wardine

Washi (Japanese) eagle.

Wattan (Japanese) homeland.

Wauna (Moquelumnan) snow geese honking.
Waunakee

Wava (Slavic) a form of Barbara.

Waverly **G** (English) quaking aspen-tree meadow.
Waverley, Waverli, Wavierlee

Wayna (Quechua) young.

Waynesha (American) a combination of Waynette + Niesha.
Wayneesha, Wayneisha, Waynie, Waynisha

Waynette (English) wagon maker.
Waynel, Waynelle, Waynetta, Waynlyn

Weeko (Dakota) pretty girl.

Wehilani (Hawaiian) heavenly adornment.

Wei (Chinese) valuable.

Wen (Chinese) cultured, refined.

Wenda (Welsh) a form of Wendy.
Wendaine, Wendayne

Wendelle (English) wanderer.
Wendaline, Wendall, Wendalyn, Wendeline, Wendella, Wendelline, Wendelly

Wendi (Welsh) a form of Wendy.
Wendie

Wendy (Welsh) white; light skinned. A familiar form of Gwendolyn, Wanda.
Wenda, Wende, Wendee, Wendey, Wendi, Wendye, Wuendy

Wera (Polish) a form of Vera. See also Verna.
Wiera, Wiercia, Wierka

Weronika (Polish) a form of Veronica.
Weronikra

Wesisa (Musoga) foolish.

Weslee (English) western meadow.
Weslea, Wesleigh, Weslene, Wesley, Wesli, Weslia, Weslie, Weslyn

Wesley **B** (English) a form of Weslee.

Weston **B** (English) western town.

Whitley 🄶 (English) white field.
*Whitely, Whitlee, Whitleigh, Whitlie,
Whittley*

Whitney 🄶 (English) white island.
*Whiteney, Whitne, Whitné, Whitnee,
Whitneigh, Whitnie, Whitny, Whitnye,
Whytne, Whytney, Witney*

Whitnie (English) a form of Whitney.
Whitani, Whitnei, Whitni, Whytni, Whytnie

Whittney (English) a form of Whitney.
*Whittaney, Whittanie, Whittany, Whitteny,
Whittnay, Whittnee, Whittney, Whittni,
Whittnie*

Whoopi (English) happy; excited.
Whoopie, Whoopy

Wicktoria (Polish) a form of Victoria.
Wicktorja, Wiktoria, Wiktorja

Wilda (German) untamed. (English) willow.
Willda, Wylda

Wileen (English) a short form of
Wilhelmina.
Wilene, Willeen, Willene

Wilhelmina (German) a form of Wilhelm
(see Boys' Names). See also Billie,
Guillerma, Helma, Minka, Minna, Minnie.
*Vilhelmina, Wileen, Wilhelmine, Willa,
Willamina, Willamine, Willemina, Willette,
Williamina, Willie, Willmina, Willmine,
Wilma, Wimina*

Wilikinia (Hawaiian) a form of Virginia.

Willa (German) a short form of Wilhelmina.
Willabella, Willette, Williabelle

Willette (English) a familiar form of
Wilhelmina, Willa.
Wiletta, Wilette, Willetta, Williette

William 🄱 (English) a form of Wilhelm
(see Boys' Names).

Willie 🄱 (English) a familiar form of
Wilhelmina.
Willi, Willina, Willisha, Willishia, Willy

Willow (English) willow tree.
Willough

Wilma (German) a short form of Wilhelmina.
*Williemae, Wilmanie, Wilmayra, Wilmetta,
Wilmette, Wilmina, Wilmyne, Wylma*

Wilona (English) desired.
Willona, Willone, Wilone

Wilson 🄱 (English) child of Will.

Win 🄱 (German) a short form of Winifred.
See also Edwina.
Wyn

Winda (Swahili) hunter.

Windy (English) windy.
*Windee, Windey, Windi, Windie, Wyndee,
Wyndy*

Winema (Moquelumnan) woman chief.

Winifred (German) peaceful friend. (Welsh)
a form of Guinevere. See also Freddi, Una,
Winnie.
*Win, Winafred, Winefred, Winefride,
Winfreda, Winfrieda, Winiefrida, Winifrid,
Winifryd, Winnafred, Winnefred, Winniefred,
Winnifred, Winnifrid, Wynafred, Wynifred,
Wynnifred*

Winna (African) friend.
Winnah

Winnie (English) a familiar form of Edwina,
Gwyneth, Winnifred, Winona, Wynne.
History: Winnie Mandela kept the anti-

apartheid movement alive in South Africa
while her then-husband, Nelson Mandela,
was imprisoned. Literature: the lovable bear
in A. A. Milne's children's story *Winnie-the-
Pooh.*
Wina, Winne, Winney, Winni, Winny, Wynnie

Winola (German) charming friend.
Wynola

Winona (Lakota) oldest daughter.
*Wanona, Wenona, Wenonah, Winnie,
Winonah, Wynonna*

Winter 🄶 (English) winter.
Wintr, Wynter

Wira (Polish) a form of Elvira.
Wiria, Wirke

Wisia (Polish) a form of Victoria.
Wicia, Wikta

Wo (Chinese) fertile.

Wren (English) wren, songbird.

Wu (Chinese) a parasol.

Wyanet (Native American) legendary beauty.
Wyaneta, Wyanita, Wynette

Wyatt 🄱 (French) little warrior.

Wynne (Welsh) white, light skinned. A short
form of Blodwyn, Guinivere, Gwyneth.
Winnie, Wyn, Wynn

Wynonna (Lakota) a form of Winona.
Wynnona, Wynona

Wynter (English) a form of Winter.
Wynteria

Wyoming (Native American) Geography: a
western U.S. state.
Wy, Wye, Wyoh, Wyomia

Xandra (Greek) a form of Zandra. (Spanish) a short form of Alexandra.
Xander, Xandrea, Xandria

Xanthe (Greek) yellow, blond. See also Zanthe.
Xanne, Xantha, Xanthia, Xanthippe

Xanthippe (Greek) a form of Xanthe. History: Socrates's wife.
Xantippie

Xavier **B** (Arabic) bright. (Basque) owner of the new house.

Xaviera (Arabic, Basque) a form of Xavier. See also Javiera, Zaviera.
Xavia, Xaviére, Xavyera, Xiveria

Xela (Quiché) my mountain home.

Xena (Greek) a form of Xenia.

Xenia (Greek) hospitable. See also Zena, Zina.
Xeenia, Xena, Xenea, Xenya, Xinia

Xi (Chinese) rare, uncommon.

Xia (Chinese) glow of the sunrise or sunset.

Xia He, Xia-He (Chinese) summer lotus; pure and elegant.

Xian (Chinese) refined, elegant.

Xiang (Chinese) fragrant.

Xiao (Chinese) dawn.

Xiao Hong, Xiao-Hong (Chinese) morning rainbow.

Xiao-Chen, Xiao Chen (Chinese) early morning.

Xie (Chinese) harmonious.

Xin (Chinese) star.

Xin Qian, Xin-Qian (Chinese) happy and beautiful.

Xing (Chinese) apricot; almond.

Xiomara (Teutonic) glorious forest.
Xiomaris, Xiomayra

Xiu (Chinese) elegant; beautiful.

Xiu Juan, Xiu-Juan (Chinese) elegant, graceful.

Xiu Mei (Chinese) beautiful plum.

Xochitl (Aztec) place of many flowers.
Xochil, Xochilt, Xochilth, Xochiti

Xu (Chinese) brilliance of the rising sun.

Xuan (Vietnamese) spring.

Xue (Chinese) snow.

Xue Fang, Xue-Fang (Chinese) snow; fragrant.

Xun (Chinese) swift.

Xuxa (Portuguese) a familiar form of Susanna.

Xylia (Greek) a form of Sylvia.
Xylina, Xylona

Ya (Chinese) proper, correct.

Yachi (Japanese) young leaf.

Yachiko (Japanese) peaceful and beautiful child.

Yachiyo (Japanese) eight thousand.

Yachne (Hebrew) hospitable.

Yadira **G** (Hebrew) friend.
Yadirah, Yadirha, Yadyra

Yael **G** (Hebrew) strength of God. See also Jael.
Yaeli, Yaella, Yeala

Yaffa (Hebrew) beautiful. See also Jaffa.
Yafeal, Yaffit, Yafit

Yahaira (Hebrew) a form of Yakira.
Yahara, Yahayra, Yahira

Yaíza (Guanche) rainbow.

Yajaira (Hebrew) a form of Yakira.
Yahaira, Yajara, Yajayra, Yajhaira

Yaki, Yama (Japanese) forms of Yachi.

Yakira (Hebrew) precious; dear.
Yahaira, Yajaira

Yalanda (Greek) a form of Yolanda.
Yalando, Yalonda, Ylana, Ylanda

Yalena (Greek, Russian) a form of Helen. See also Lena, Yelena.

Yaletha (American) a form of Oletha.
Yelitsa

Yamary (American) a combination of the
prefix Ya + Mary.
Yamairy, Yamarie, Yamaris, Yamayra

Yamelia (American) a form of Amelia.
Yameily, Yamelya, Yamelys

Yamila (Arabic) a form of Jamila.
*Yamela, Yamely, Yamil, Yamile, Yamilet,
Yamiley, Yamilla, Yamille*

Yaminah (Arabic) right, proper.
Yamina, Yamini, Yemina, Yeminah, Yemini

Yamka (Hopi) blossom.

Yamuna (Hindi) sacred river.

Yan (Chinese) bright red.

Yan Yan, Yan-Yan (Chinese) two swallow
birds; elegant.

Yana (Slavic) a form of Jana.
*Yanae, Yanah, Yanay, Yanaye, Yanesi, Yanet,
Yaneth, Yaney, Yani, Yanik, Yanina, Yanis,
Yanisha, Yanitza, Yanixia, Yanna, Yannah,
Yanni, Yannica, Yannick, Yannina*

Yanaba (Navajo) brave.

Yanamaría (Slavic) bitter grace.

Yaneli (American) a combination of the
prefix Ya + Nellie.
*Yanela, Yanelis, Yaneliz, Yanelle, Yanelli,
Yanely, Yanelys*

Yanet (American) a form of Janet.
*Yanete, Yaneth, Yanethe, Yanette, Yannet,
Yanneth, Yannette*

Yang (Chinese) ocean.

Yáng (Chinese) sun.

Yao (Chinese) gentle and graceful.

Yara (Tupi) she is a lady.

Yareli (American) a form of Oralee.
Yarely, Yaresly

Yarina (Slavic) a form of Irene.
Yaryna

Yaritza (American) a combination of Yana +
Ritsa.
Yaritsa, Yaritza

Yarkona (Hebrew) green.

Yarmilla (Slavic) market trader.

Yashira (Afghan) humble; takes it easy.
(Arabic) wealthy.

Yasinda (Pohnpeian) a form of Flora.

Yasmeen (Persian) a form of Yasmin.
*Yasemeen, Yasemin, Yasmeena, Yasmen,
Yasmene, Yasmeni, Yasmenne, Yassmeen,
Yassmen*

Yasmín (Persian) a form of Yasmin.

Yasmin, Yasmine (Persian) jasmine flower.
*Yashmine, Yasiman, Yasimine, Yasma,
Yasmain, Yasmaine, Yasmina, Yasminda,
Yasmon, Yasmyn, Yazmin, Yesmean,
Yesmeen, Yesmin, Yesmina, Yesmine,
Yesmyn*

Yasu (Japanese) resting, calm.
Yasuko, Yasuyo

Yazmin (Persian) a form of Yasmin.
*Yazmeen, Yazmen, Yazmene, Yazmina,
Yazmine, Yazmyn, Yazmyne, Yazzmien,
Yazzmine, Yazzmmine, Yazzmyn*

Ye (Chinese) leaf.

Yecenia (Arabic) a form of Yesenia.

Yehudit (Hebrew) a form of Judith.
Yudit, Yudita, Yuta

Yei (Japanese) flourishing.

Yeira (Hebrew) light.

Yekaterina (Russian) a form of Katherine.

Yelena (Russian) a form of Helen, Jelena. See
also Lena, Yalena.
*Yeleana, Yelen, Yelenna, Yelenne, Yelina,
Ylena, Ylenia, Ylenna*

Yelisabeta (Russian) a form of Elizabeth.
Yelizaveta

Yemena (Arabic) from Yemen.
Yemina

Yen (Chinese) yearning; desirous.
Yeni, Yenih, Yenny

Yenay (Chino) she who loves.

Yenene (Native American) shaman.

Yenifer (Welsh) a form of Jennifer.
Yenefer, Yennifer

Yeo (Korean) mild.
Yee

Yepa (Native American) snow girl.

Yeruti (Guarani) turtledove.

Yesenia (Arabic) flower.
Yasenya, Yecenia, Yesinia, Yesnia, Yessenia

Yesica (Hebrew) a form of Jessica.
Yesika, Yesiko

Yésica (Hebrew) a form of Yesica.

Yessenia (Arabic) a form of Yesenia.
Yessena, Yessenya, Yissenia

Yessica (Hebrew) a form of Jessica.
Yessika, Yesyka

Yetta (English) a short form of Henrietta.
Yette, Yitta, Yitty

Yeva (Ukrainian) a form of Eve.

Yhlda (Pohnpeian) a form of Juana.

Yi Jie, Yi-Jie (Chinese) happy and pure.

Yi Min, Yi-Min (Chinese) happy and smart.

Yi Ze, Yi-Ze (Chinese) happy and shiny like a pearl.

Yiesha (Arabic, Swahili) a form of Aisha.
Yiasha

Yin (Chinese) silver; polite; sound.

Yín (Chinese) silver.

Ying (Chinese) cherry.

Ynaganta (Chamorro) a form of Inagangta.

Ynez (Spanish) a form of Agnes. See also Inez.
Ynes, Ynesita

Yoanna (Hebrew) a form of Joanna.
Yoana, Yohana, Yohanka, Yohanna, Yohannah

Yocasta (Greek) violet.

Yocelin, Yocelyn (Latin) forms of Jocelyn.
Yoceline, Yocelyne, Yuceli

Yoconda (Italian) happy and jovial.

Yoi (Japanese) born in the evening.

Yoki (Hopi) bluebird.
Yokie

Yoko (Japanese) good girl.
Yo

Yokoh (Japanese) mountain.

Yolanda (Greek) violet flower. See also Iolanthe, Jolanda, Olinda.
Yalanda, Yolie, Yolaine, Yolana, Yoland, Yolande, Yolane, Yolanna, Yolantha, Yolanthe, Yolette, Yolonda, Yorlanda, Youlanda, Yulanda, Yulonda

Yole, Yone (Greek) beautiful as a violet.

Yolie (Greek) a familiar form of Yolanda.
Yola, Yoley, Yoli, Yoly

Yoluta (Native American) summer flower.

Yomara (American) a combination of Yolanda + Tamara.
Yomaira, Yomarie, Yomira

Yon (Burmese) rabbit. (Korean) lotus blossom.
Yona, Yonna

Yoné (Japanese) wealth; rice.

Yong (Chinese) elegant and poised.

Yonina (Hebrew) a form of Jonina.
Yona, Yonah

Yonita (Hebrew) a form of Jonita.
Yonat, Yonati, Yonit

Yonn (Korean) a long life.

Yoomee (Coos) star.
Yoome

Yordana (Basque) descendant. See also Jordana.

Yoree (Japanese) the scent of the sun.

Yorey (Japanese) good; striving.

Yori (Japanese) reliable.
Yoriko, Yoriyo

Yorie, Yory (Japanese) dependable.

Yoselin **G** (Latin) a form of Jocelyn.
Yoseline, Yoselyn, Yosselin, Yosseline, Yosselyn

Yosepha (Hebrew) a form of Josephine.
Yosefa, Yosifa, Yuseffa

Yoshe, Yoshimi (Japanese) dependable.

Yoshi (Japanese) good; respectful.
Yoshie, Yoshiko, Yoshiyo

Yoshino (Japanese) beauty.

You (Chinese) excellence.

Young (Korean) obedient girl.

Yovela (Hebrew) joyful heart; rejoicer.

Ysa (Chamorro) a form of Isa.

Ysabel (Spanish) a form of Isabel.
Ysabell, Ysabella, Ysabelle, Ysbel, Ysbella, Ysobel

Ysanne (American) a combination of Ysabel + Ann.
Ysande, Ysann, Ysanna

Yseult (German) ice rule. (Irish) fair; light skinned. (Welsh) a form of Isolde.
Yseulte, Ysolt

Yu Jie (Chinese) pure beautiful jade.

Yuana (Spanish) a form of Juana.
Yuan, Yuanna

Yudelle (English) a form of Udele.
Yudela, Yudell, Yudella

Yudita (Russian) a form of Judith.
Yudit, Yudith, Yuditt

Yue Wan, Yue-Wan (Chinese) happy and gentle.

Yue Yan, Yue-Yan (Chinese) happy and beautiful.

Yue Ying, Yue-Ying (Chinese) happy and smart; kind.

Yue You, Yue-You (Chinese) happy and friendly.

Yui (Japanese) she who is a fine and beautiful girl.

Yu-Jie (Chinese) jade; pure.

Yuka (Japanese) respectful.

Yukako (Japanese) she who wears her clothing well.

Yukari (Japanese) she who is as beautiful as a flower.

Yuki BG (Japanese) snow.
Yukie, Yukiko, Yukiyo

Yukino, Yumiko (Japanese) child of Yuka.

Yuko (Japanese) beautiful and truthful friend.

Yulene (Basque) a form of Julia.
Yuleen

Yulia (Russian) a form of Julia.
Yula, Yulenka, Yulinka, Yulka, Yulya

Yuliana (Spanish) a form of Juliana.
Yulenia, Yuliani

Yumako (Japanese) snow.

Yumi (Japanese) gracious child.

Yun (Chinese) clouds.

Yuna (Japanese) beauty.

Yuri G (Japanese) lily.
Yuree, Yuriko, Yuriyo

Yuriye (Japanese) arrow child.

Yustina (Pohnpeian) a form of Jacinta.

Yutsuko (Japanese) gentle as a red apple.

Yuzuki (Japanese) she who paints for the benefit of others.

Yvanna (Slavic) a form of Ivana.
Yvan, Yvana, Yvannia

Yvette (French) a familiar form of Yvonne. See also Evette, Ivette.
Yavette, Yevett, Yevette, Yevetta, Yvet, Yveta, Yvett, Yvetta

Yvonne G (French) young archer. (Scandinavian) yew wood; bow wood. See also Evonne, Ivonne, Vonna, Vonny, Yvette.
Yavanda, Yavanna, Yavanne, Yavonda, Yavonna, Yavonne, Yveline, Yvon, Yvone, Yvonna, Yvonnah, Yvonnia, Yvonnie, Yvonny

Z

Z B (American) an initial used as a first name.

Zaba (Hebrew) she who offers a sacrifice to God.

Zabrina (American) a form of Sabrina.
Zabreena, Zabrinia, Zabrinna, Zabryna

Zachariah B (Hebrew) God remembered.

Zacharie B (Hebrew) God remembered.
Zacari, Zacceaus, Zacchaea, Zachary, Zachoia, Zackaria, Zackeisha, Zackeria, Zakaria, Zakaya, Zakeshia, Zakiah, Zakiria, Zakiya, Zakiyah, Zechari

Zachary B (Hebrew) a form of Zacharie.
Zackery, Zakary

Zada (Arabic) fortunate, prosperous.
Zaida, Zayda, Zayeda

Zafina (Arabic) victorious.

Zafirah (Arabic) successful; victorious.

Zahar (Hebrew) daybreak; dawn.
Zahara, Zaharra, Zahera, Zahira, Zahirah, Zeeherah

Zahavah (Hebrew) golden.
Zachava, Zachavah, Zechava, Zechavah, Zehava, Zehavi, Zehavit, Zeheva, Zehuva

Zahra (Swahili) flower. (Arabic) white.
Zahara, Zahraa, Zahrah, Zahreh, Zahria

Zai (Chinese) to be living.

Zaira (Hebrew) a form of Zara.
Zaire, Zairea, Zirrea

Zakia BG (Swahili) smart. (Arabic) chaste.
Zakea, Zakeia, Zakiah, Zakiya

Zakira (Hebrew) a form of Zacharie.
Zaakira, Zakiera, Zakierra, Zakir, Zakirah, Zakiria, Zakiriya, Zykarah, Zykera, Zykeria, Zykerria, Zykira, Zykuria

Zakiya (Arabic) a form of Zakia.
Zakeya, Zakeyia, Zakiyaa, Zakiyah, Zakiyya, Zakiyyah, Zakkiyya, Zakkiyyah, Zakkyyah

Zalika (Swahili) born to royalty.
Zuleika

Zaltana (Native American) high mountain.

Zan (Chinese) praise; support.

Zana **G** (Spanish) a form of Zanna.

Zandra (Greek) a form of Sandra.
Zahndra, Zandrea, Zandria, Zandy, Zanndra, Zondra

Zane **B** (English) a form of John.

Zaneta (Spanish) a form of Jane.
Zanita, Zanitra

Zanna (Spanish) a form of Jane. (English) a short form of Susanna.
Zaina, Zainah, Zainna, Zana, Zanae, Zanah, Zanella, Zanette, Zannah, Zannette, Zannia, Zannie

Zanthe (Greek) a form of Xanthe.
Zanth, Zantha

Zara (Hebrew) a form of Sarah, Zora.
Zaira, Zarah, Zarea, Zaree, Zareea, Zareen, Zareena, Zareh, Zareya, Zari, Zaria, Zariya, Zarria

Zarifa (Arabic) successful.

Zarina (Slavic) empress.

Zarita (Spanish) a form of Sarah.

Zasha (Russian) a form of Sasha.
Zascha, Zashenka, Zashka, Zasho

Zaviera (Spanish) a form of Xaviera.
Zavera, Zavirah

Zawati (Swahili) gift.

Zayit **BG** (Hebrew) olive.

Zaynah (Arabic) beautiful.
Zayn, Zayna

Ze (Chinese) moist, glossy.

Zea (Latin) grain.

Zechariah **B** (Hebrew) a form of Zachariah.

Zelda (Yiddish) gray haired. (German) a short form of Griselda. See also Selda.
Zelde, Zella, Zellda

Zelene (English) sunshine.
Zeleen, Zelena, Zeline

Zelia (Spanish) sunshine.
Zele, Zelene, Zelie, Zélie, Zelina

Zelizi (Basque) a form of Sheila.

Zelma (German) a form of Selma.

Zelmira (Arabic) brilliant one.

Zemirah (Hebrew) song of joy.

Zena (Greek) a form of Xenia. (Ethiopian) news. (Persian) woman. See also Zina.
Zanae, Zanah, Zeena, Zeenat, Zeenet, Zeenia, Zeenya, Zein, Zeina, Zenah, Zenana, Zenea, Zenia, Zenna, Zennah, Zennia, Zenya

Zenadia (Greek) she who is dedicated to God.

Zenaida (Greek) white-winged dove.
Zenaide, Zenaïde, Zenayda, Zenochka

Zenda **G** (Persian) sacred; feminine.

Zeng (Chinese) increase, gain.

Zenobia (Greek) sign, symbol. History: a queen who ruled the city of Palmyra in ancient Syria.
Zeba, Zeeba, Zenobie, Zenovia

Zephania, Zephanie (Greek) forms of Stephanie.
Zepania, Zephanas, Zephany

Zephyr **BG** (Greek) west wind.
Zefiryn, Zephra, Zephria, Zephyer, Zephyrine

Zera (Hebrew) seeds.
Zerah, Zeriah

Zerdali (Turkish) wild apricot.

Zerlina (Latin, Spanish) beautiful dawn. Music: a character in Mozart's opera *Don Giovanni*.
Zerla, Zerlinda

Zerrin (Turkish) golden.
Zerren

Zeta (English) rose. Linguistics: a letter in the Greek alphabet.
Zayit, Zetana, Zetta

Zetta (Portuguese) rose.

Zhan (Chinese) spread the wings.

Zhana (Slavic) a form of Zhane.
Zhanay, Zhanaya, Zhaniah, Zhanna

Zhane **G** (Slavic) a form of Jane.
Zhanae, Zhané, Zhanea, Zhanee, Zhaney, Zhani

Zhao (Chinese) spirit, vigor.

Zhen (Chinese) chaste.

Zhen Juan, Zhen-Juan (Chinese) precious and beautiful.

Zheng (Chinese) honest.

Zhi (Chinese) irises; orchids; noble character; true friendship.

Zho (Chinese) character.

Zhong (Chinese) honorable.

Zhu (Chinese) pearl, jewel.

Zhuan (Chinese) expert.

Zhuang (Chinese) serious, grave.

Zhuo (Chinese) smart; wonderful.

Zia 🄶 (Latin) grain. (Arabic) light.
Zea

Zidanelia (Greek) she who is God's judge; bluish lotus flower.

Zigana (Hungarian) gypsy girl. See also Tsigana.
Zigane

Zihna (Hopi) one who spins tops.

Zilla (Hebrew) shadow.
Zila, Zillah, Zylla

Zilpah (Hebrew) dignified. Bible: Jacob's wife.
Zilpha, Zylpha

Zilya (Russian) a form of Theresa.

Zimra (Hebrew) song of praise.
Zamora, Zemira, Zemora, Zimria

Zina (African) secret spirit. (English) hospitable. (Greek) a form of Zena.
Zinah, Zine

Zinnia (Latin) Botany: a plant with beautiful, rayed, colorful flowers.
Zinia, Zinny, Zinnya, Zinya

Zipporah (Hebrew) bird. Bible: Moses' wife.
Zipora, Ziporah, Zipporia, Ziproh

Zita (Spanish) rose. (Arabic) mistress. A short form of names ending in "sita" or "zita."
Zeeta, Zyta, Zytka

Ziva (Hebrew) bright; radiant.
Zeeva, Ziv, Zivanka, Zivi, Zivit

Zizi (Hungarian) a familiar form of Elizabeth.
Zsi Zsi

Zobeida (Arabic) pleasant as cream.

Zocha (Polish) a form of Sophie.

Zoe ☙ 🄶 (Greek) life.
Zoé, Zoë, Zoee, Zoelie, Zoeline, Zoelle, Zoey, Zoi, Zoie, Zowe, Zowey, Zowie, Zoya

Zoey 🄶 (Greek) a form of Zoe.
Zooey

Zofia (Slavic) a form of Sophia. See also Sofia.
Zofka, Zsofia

Zohar 🄱 (Hebrew) shining, brilliant.
Zoheret

Zohra (Hebrew) blossom.

Zohreh (Persian) happy.
Zahreh, Zohrah

Zola (Italian) piece of earth.
Zoela, Zoila

Zona (Latin) belt, sash.
Zonia

Zondra (Greek) a form of Zandra.
Zohndra

Zong (Chinese) palm.

Zora (Slavic) aurora; dawn. See also Zara.
Zorah, Zorana, Zoreen, Zoreena, Zorna, Zorra, Zorrah, Zorya

Zoraida (Arabic) she who is eloquent.

Zorina (Slavic) golden.
Zorana, Zori, Zorie, Zorine, Zorna, Zory

Zoya (Slavic) a form of Zoe.
Zoia, Zoyara, Zoyechka, Zoyenka, Zoyya

Zsa Zsa (Hungarian) a familiar form of Susan.
Zhazha

Zsofia (Hungarian) a form of Sofia.
Zofia, Zsofi, Zsofika

Zsuzsanna (Hungarian) a form of Susanna.
Zsuska, Zsuzsa, Zsuzsi, Zsuzsika, Zsuzska

Zu (Chinese) earliest ancestor.

Zudora (Sanskrit) laborer.

Zuleica (Arabic) beautiful and plump.

Zuleika (Arabic) brilliant.
Zeleeka, Zul, Zulay, Zulekha, Zuleyka

Zulima (Arabic) a form of Salama.
Zuleima, Zulema, Zulemah, Zulimah

Zulma (Arabic) healthy and vigorous woman.

Zulmara (Spanish) a form of Zulma.

Zuo (Chinese) smart; wonderful.

Zurafa (Arabic) lovely.
Ziraf, Zuruf

Zuri (Basque) white; light skinned. (Swahili) beautiful.
Zuria, Zurie, Zurisha, Zury

Zurina, Zurine (Basque) white.

Zurisaday (Arabic) over the earth.

Zusa (Czech, Polish) a form of Susan.
Zuzana, Zuzanka, Zuzia, Zuzka, Zuzu

Zuwena (Swahili) good.
Zwena

Zyanya (Zapotec) always.

Zytka (Polish) rose.

Boys

A

A 🄶 (American) an initial used as a first name.

Aakash (Hindi) a form of Akash.

Aaliyah 🄶 (Hebrew) a form of Aliya (see Girls' Names).

Aaron ☙ 🄱 (Hebrew) enlightened. (Arabic) messenger. Bible: the brother of Moses and the first high priest. See also Ron.
Aahron, Aaran, Aaren, Aareon, Aarin, Aaronn, Aarron, Aarronn, Aaryn, Aarynn, Aeron, Aharon, Ahran, Ahren, Aranne, Arek, Aren, Ari, Arin, Aron, Aronek, Aronne, Aronos, Arran, Arron

Aaronjames (American) a combination of Aaron + James.
Aaron James, Aaron-James

Aarronn (Hebrew) enlightened. (Arabic) messenger.
Aarynn

Aasiña (Chamorro) each other's mercy.

Abad (Hebrew) unique man.

Abag (Chamorro) lost.

Aban (Persian) Mythology: a figure associated with water and the arts.

Abaramo (Fijian) a form of Abram.

Abasi (Swahili) stern.
Abasee, Abasey, Abasie, Abasy

Abay (Arabic) descendant.

Abban (Latin) white.
Abben, Abbin, Abbine, Abbon

Abbas (Arabic) lion.

Abbau (Chamorro) to clear land.

Abbertus (Spanish) a form of Alberto.

Abbey 🄶 (Hebrew) a familiar form of Abe.
Abbee, Abbie, Abby, Abey, Aby

Abbie 🄶 (Hebrew) a form of Abbey.

Abbigail 🄶 (Hebrew) a form of Abigail (see Girls' Names).

Abbott (Hebrew) father; abbot.
Ab, Abba, Abbah, Abbán, Abbé, Abboid, Abbot, Abot, Abott

Abbu (Arabic) a form of Abu.

Abbud (Arabic) devoted.

Abby 🄶 (Hebrew) a form of Abbey.

Abdi (African) my servant.

Abdías (Hebrew) God's servant.

Abdirahman (Arabic) a form of Abdulrahman.
Abdirehman

Abdón (Hebrew) servant of God; the very helpful man.

Abdul (Arabic) servant.
Abdal, Abdeel, Abdel, Abdoul, Abdual, Abdull, Abul

Abdulaziz (Arabic) servant of the Mighty.
Abdelazim, Abdelaziz, Abdulazaz, Abdulazeez

Abdullah (Arabic) servant of Allah.
Abdala, Abdalah, Abdalla, Abdallah, Abdela, Abduala, Abdualla, Abduallah, Abdula, Abdulah, Abdulahi, Abdulha, Abdulla, Abdullahi

Abdulmalik (Arabic) servant of the Master.

Abdulrahman (Arabic) servant of the Merciful.
Abdelrahim, Abdelrahman, Abdirahman, Abdolrahem, Abdularahman, Abdurrahman, Abdurram

Abe (Hebrew) a short form of Abel, Abraham.
Abb, Abbe

Abel 🄱 (Hebrew) breath. (Assyrian) meadow. (German) a short form of Abelard. Bible: Adam and Eve's second son.
Abe, Abele, Abell, Able, Adal, Avel

Abelard (German) noble; resolute.
Ab, Abalard, Abel, Abelarde, Abelardo, Abelhard, Abilard, Adalard, Adelard

Abelino (Spanish) a form of Avelino.

Abercio (Greek) first son.

Abernethy (Scottish) river's beginning.
Abernathie, Abernethi

Abet (Chamorro) a form of Javier.

Abhinash (Sanskrit) indestructible.

Abi (Turkish) older brother.
Abee, Abbi

Abiah (Hebrew) God is my father.
Abia, Abiel, Abija, Abijah, Abisha, Abishai, Aviya, Aviyah

Abid (Arabic) one who worships God.

Abidan (Hebrew) father of judgment.
Abiden, Abidin, Abidon, Abydan, Abyden, Abydin, Abydon, Abydyn

Boys A-F

Abie (Hebrew) a familiar form of Abraham.

Abiel (Hebrew) a form of Abiah.

Abiner (Pohnpeian) a form of Abner.

Abir (Hebrew) strong.
Abyr

Abisha (Hebrew) gift of God.
Abijah, Abishai, Abishal, Abysha, Abyshah

Abner (Hebrew) father of light. Bible: the commander of Saul's army.
Ab, Avner, Ebner

Abo (Hebrew) father.

Abraham (Hebrew) father of many nations. Bible: the first Hebrew patriarch. See also Avram, Bram, Ibrahim.
Abarran, Abe, Aberham, Abey, Abhiram, Abie, Abrahaim, Abrahame, Abrahamo, Abrahan, Abrahán, Abraheem, Abrahem, Abrahim, Abrahm, Abram, Abramo, Abrán, Abrao, Arram, Avram

Abrahan (Spanish) a form of Abraham.
Abrahin, Abrahon

Abram (Hebrew) a short form of Abraham. See also Bram.
Abrama, Abramo, Abrams, Avram

Absalom (Hebrew) father of peace. Bible: the rebellious third son of King David. See also Avshalom, Axel.
Absalaam, Absalon, Abselon, Absolam, Absolom, Absolum

Absalón (Hebrew) a form of Absalom.

Abu (Arabic) father.

Abug (Chamorro) friend.

Abundancio (Latin) rich, affluent.

Abundio (Latin) he who has a lot of property.

Acab (Hebrew) uncle.

Acacio (Greek) is not evil and is honorable.

Acañir (Mapuche) liberated fox.

Acapana (Quechua) lightning; small hurricane.

Acar (Turkish) bright.

Ace (Latin) unity.
Acer, Acey, Acie

Acfaye (Chamorro) wise together.

Achachic (Aymara) ancestor; grandfather.

Achaigua (Chamorro) similar, a likeness.

Achei (Chamorro) chin.

Achic (Quechua) luminous; resplendent.

Achilles (Greek) Mythology: a hero of the Trojan War. Literature: the hero of Homer's epic poem *Iliad*.
Achil, Achill, Achille, Achillea, Achilleus, Achillios, Achyl, Achyll, Achylle, Achylleus, Akil, Akili, Akilles

Achina (Sanskrit) free from worry.

Achudan (Sanskrit) the hunt, the chase.

Achuga (Chamorro) end together; to give pleasure to each other.

Acisclo (Latin) a pick used to work on rocks.

Ackerley (English) meadow of oak trees.
Accerlee, Accerleigh, Accerley, Ackerlea, Ackerlee, Ackerleigh, Ackerli, Ackerlie, Ackersley, Acklea, Ackleigh, Ackley, Acklie,

Akerlea, Akerlee, Akerleigh, Akerley, Akerli, Akerlie, Akerly

Acklee (English) a short form of Ackerley.
Ackli, Ackly

Aconcauac (Quechua) stone sentinel.

Actassi (Chamorro) share the sea.

Acton (English) oak-tree settlement.
Actan, Acten, Actin, Actun, Actyn

Acursio (Latin) he who heads towards God.

Adahy (Cherokee) in the woods.
Adahi

Adai (Chamorro) friend.

Adair **G** (Scottish) oak-tree ford.
Adaire, Adare, Adayr, Adayre, Addair, Addaire, Addar, Addare, Addayr, Addyre

Adalbaro (Greek) combatant of nobility.

Adalberto (Germanic) belonging to nobility.

Adalgiso, Adalvino (Greek) lance of nobility.

Adalrico (Greek) noble chief of his lineage.

Adam ☽ **B** (Phoenician) man; mankind. (Hebrew) earth; man of the red earth. Bible: the first man created by God. See also Adamson, Addison, Damek, Keddy, Macadam.
Ad, Adama, Adamec, Adamo, Adão, Adas, Addam, Addams, Addis, Addy, Adem, Adham, Adhamh, Adim, Adné, Adok, Adomas, Adym

Adamec (Czech) a form of Adam.
Adamek, Adamik, Adamka, Adamko, Adamok

Adamson (Hebrew) son of Adam.
Adams, Adamsson, Addamson

Boys A–F

Adan (Irish) a form of Aidan.
Aden, Adian, Adin, Adun

Adán (Hebrew) a form of Adam.

Adao (Chamorro) the sun.

Adaoña (Chamorro) his sun.

Adar (Syrian) ruler; prince. (Hebrew) noble; exalted.
Addar

Adarius (American) a combination of Adam + Darius.
Adareus, Adarias, Adarrius, Adarro, Adarruis, Adaruis, Adauris

Adaucto (Latin) increase.

Addel (German) a short form of Adelard.
Adell

Addison 🅱🅶 (English) son of Adam.
Addis, Addisen, Addisun, Addoson, Addyson, Adison, Adisson, Adyson

Addy (Hebrew) a familiar form of Adam, Adlai. (German) a familiar form of Adelard.
Addey, Addi, Addie, Ade, Adi

Ade (Yoruba) royal.

Adelard (German) noble; courageous.
Adal, Adalar, Adalard, Adalarde, Addy, Adel, Adél, Adelar, Adelarde, Adelhard

Adelardo, Adelino (Greek) daring prince.

Adelbai (Palauan) the men's community house.

Adelfo (Greek) male friend.

Adelio (Germanic) father of the noble prince.

Adelmaro (Greek) distinguished because of his lineage.

Adelmo (Germanic) noble protector.

Adelric (German) noble ruler.
Adalric, Adelrich, Adelrick, Adelrik, Adelryc, Adelryck, Adelryk

Ademar, Ademaro, Adhemar, Adimar (German) he whose battles have made him distinguished; celebrated and famous combatant.

Aden (Arabic) Geography: a region in southern Yemen. (Irish) a form of Aidan, Aiden.

Ader (Palauan) the remainder.

Adham (Arabic) black.

Adhelmar (Greek) ennobled by his battles.

Adiel (Hebrew) he was adorned by God.

Adil (Arabic) just; wise.
Adeel, Adeele, Adill, Adyl, Adyll

Adin (Hebrew) pleasant.
Addin, Addyn, Adyn

Adir (Hebrew) majestic; noble.
Adeer

Adirán (Latin) from the Adriatic Sea.

Aditya (Hindi) sun.

Adiv (Hebrew) pleasant; gentle.
Adeev, Adev

Adlai (Hebrew) my ornament.
Ad, Addlai, Addlay, Addy, Adlay, Adley

Adler (German) eagle.
Ad, Addlar, Addler, Adlar

Adli (Turkish) just; wise.
Adlea, Adlee, Adleigh, Adlie, Adly

Admon (Hebrew) peony.

Adnan (Arabic) pleasant.
Adnaan, Adnane

Adney (English) noble's island.
Adnee, Adni, Adnie, Adny

Adolf (German) noble wolf. History: Adolf Hitler's German army was defeated in World War II. See also Dolf.
Ad, Addof, Addoff, Adof, Adolfo, Adolfus, Adolph

Adolfo (Spanish) a form of Adolf.
Addofo, Adolffo, Adolpho, Andolffo, Andolfo, Andolpho

Adolph (German) a form of Adolf.
Adolphe, Adolpho, Adolphus, Adulphus

Adolphus (French) a form of Adolf.
Adolphius

Adom (Akan) help from God.

Adon (Hebrew) Lord. (Greek) a short form of Adonis.

Adonai (Hebrew) my Lord.

Adonías (Hebrew) God is my Lord.

Adonis (Greek) highly attractive. Mythology: the attractive youth loved by Aphrodite.
Adon, Adonise, Adonnis, Adonys, Adonyse

Adren (Spanish) a form of Adriano.

Adri (Indo-Pakistani) rock.
Adree, Adrey, Adrie, Adry

Adrian ❦ **B** (Greek) rich. (Latin) dark. (Swedish) a short form of Hadrian.
Adarian, Ade, Adorjan, Adrain, Adreian, Adreyan, Adri, Adriaan, Adriane, Adriann, Adrianne, Adriano, Adrianus, Adriean, Adrien, Adrik, Adrin, Adrion, Adrionn, Adrionne, Adron, Adryan, Adryn, Adryon

Adrián (Latin) a form of Adrian.

Adriana, Adrianna **G** (Italian) forms of Adrienne.

Adriano (Italian) a form of Adrian.
Adrianno

Adriel (Hebrew) member of God's flock.
Adrial, Adriall, Adriell, Adryel, Adryell

Adrien **B** (French) a form of Adrian.
Adriene, Adrienne, Adryen

Adrienne **G** (French) a form of Adrien.

Adrik (Russian) a form of Adrian.
Adric

Adulfo (Germanic) of noble heritage.

Adwin (Ghanian) creative.
Adwyn

Aeneas (Greek) praised. (Scottish) a form of Angus. Literature: the Trojan hero of Vergil's epic poem *Aeneid*. See also Eneas.

Afaisin (Chamorro) asking each other.

Afi (Chamorro) fire.

Afif (Arabic) chaste, modest.

Afram (African) Geography: a river in Ghana, Africa.

Afton **G** (English) from Afton, England.
Affton, Aftan, Aften, Aftin, Aftyn

Afzal (Arabic) the best.

Aga (Chamorro) a kind of bird, the Marianas crow.

Agada, Agga (Chamorro) forms of Aga.

Agagan (Chamorro) redness.

Agamemnon (Greek) resolute. Mythology: the king of Mycenae who led the Greeks in the Trojan War.

Agamenón (Greek) he who moves slowly down the path.

Agapito (Hebrew) beloved one.

Agar (Hebrew) he who escaped.

Agaton (Greek) good.

Agatón (Greek) victor; good.

Age (Danish) ancestor.

Agenor (Greek) strong man.

Ageo (Hebrew) having a festive character.

Agesislao (Greek) leader of villages.

Agila (Teutonic) he who possesses combat support.

Agnasina (Chamorro) mighty.

Agnelo (Latin) reference to the lamb of God.

Agni (Hindi) Religion: the Hindu fire god.

Agon (Chamorro) a form of Aguon.

Agostine (Italian) a form of Augustine.
Agostyne

Agostiño (Latin) a form of Augusto.

Agrippa (Latin) born feet first. History: the commander of the Roman fleet that defeated Mark Antony and Cleopatra at Actium.
Agripa, Agripah, Agrippah, Agrypa, Agrypah, Agryppa, Agryppah

Agtano (Chamorro) land.

Agu (Ibo) leopard.

Agua (Chamorro) milkfish.

Aguaguat (Chamorro) stubborn; mischievous.

Agua'lin (Chamorro) a form of Aguarin.

Aguan (Chamorro) a form of Aguon.

Aguarin (Chamorro) one who overdresses.

Aguas (Chamorro) baby mullet fish.

Agui (Chamorro) ghost crab.

Aguigan (Chamorro) fish.

Aguon (Chamorro) food, bread.

Agupa (Chamorro) tomorrow.

Agús (Spanish) a form of Agustín.

Agusteen (Latin) a form of Augustine.
Agustyne

Agustin (Latin) a form of Augustine.
Agostino, Agoston, Aguistin, Agustein, Agusteyne, Agustine, Agustis, Agusto, Agustus, Agustyn

Agustín (Latin) a form of Augustine.

Ah (Chinese) from a Chinese character.

Ahab (Hebrew) father's brother. Literature: the captain of the Pequod in Herman Melville's novel *Moby-Dick*.

Ahanu (Native American) laughter.

Ahdik (Native American) caribou; reindeer.
Ahdic, Ahdick, Ahdyc, Ahdyck, Ahdyk

Ahearn (Scottish) lord of the horses. (English) heron.
Ahearne, Aherin, Ahern, Aherne, Aheron, Aheryn, Hearn

Ahgao (Chamorro) a kind of tree.

Ahir (Turkish) last.

Ahkeem (Hebrew) a form of Akeem.
Ahkiem, Ahkyem, Ahkyeme

Ahmad (Arabic) most highly praised. See also Muhammad.
Achmad, Achmed, Ahamad, Ahamada, Ahamed, Ahmaad, Ahmaud, Amad, Amahd, Amed

Ahmed 🅱 (Swahili) praiseworthy.

Ahpel (Pohnpeian) a form of Abel.

Ahsan (Arabic) charitable.

Ai (Japanese) love.

Aian (Chuukese) an exclamation of surprise.

Aichi (Japanese) love; wisdom.

Aichy (Chuukese) a form of Aichi.

Aidan 🏆 🅱 (Irish) fiery.
Adan, Aden, Aiden, Aidun, Aydan, Ayden, Aydin

Aidano (Teutonic) he who distinguishes himself.

Aiden 🏆 🅱 (Irish) a form of Aidan.
Aden, Aidon, Aidwin, Aidwyn, Aidyn

Aiichiro (Japanese) favorite; first son.

Aiken (English) made of oak.
Aicken, Aikin, Ayken, Aykin

Ailwan (English) noble friends.
Ailwen, Ailwin

Aimery (French) a form of Emery.
Aime, Aimeree, Aimerey, Aimeri, Aimeric, Aimerie, Amerey, Aymeric, Aymery

Aimon (French) house. (Irish) a form of Eamon.

Aindrea (Irish) a form of Andrew.
Aindreas

Ainsley 🅶 (Scottish) my own meadow.
Ainslea, Ainslee, Ainslei, Ainsleigh, Ainsli, Ainslie, Ainsly, Ansley, Aynslee, Aynsley, Aynslie

Aisake (Fijian) a form of Isaac.

Aisea (Fijian) a form of Isaias.

Aisek (Pohnpeian) a form of Isaac.

Aisen (Chuukese) my cry.

Aito (Japanese) he who is very affectionate.

Aiyaz (Turkish) frosty winter night.

Aiyub (Arabic) a form of Ayub.

Aizik (Russian) a form of Isaac.

Aja 🅶 (Punjabi) a form of Ajay.

Ajala (Yoruba) potter.
Ajalah

Ajay (Punjabi) victorious; undefeatable. (American) a combination of the initials A. + J.
Aj, Aja, Ajae, Ajai, Ajaye, Ajaz, Ajé, Ajee, Ajit

Ajesh (Sanskrit) lord of illusion.

Ajit (Sanskrit) unconquerable.
Ajeet, Ajith

Akako (Japanese) red; a charm to cure disease.

Akar (Turkish) flowing stream.
Akara, Akare

Akash (Hindi) sky.
Aakash, Akasha, Akshay

Akbar (Arabic) great.
Akbara, Akbare

Akecheta (Sioux) warrior.
Akechetah

Akeem, Akim (Hebrew) short forms of Joachim.
Achim, Achym, Ackeem, Ackim, Ackime, Ackym, Ackyme, Ahkieme, Akeam, Akee, Akiem, Akima, Akym, Arkeem

Akeke (Marshallese) having a stomachache from eating too much.

Akemi (Japanese) dawn.
Akemee, Akemie, Akemy

Akeno (Japanese) in the morning; bright, shining field.

Akhtar (Persian) star, constellation; good omen.

Akifumi (Japanese) he who writes clear, historical chronicles.

Akihiko (Japanese) bright boy.

Akihiro (Japanese) glittering expansiveness.

Akiki (Chuukese) tickle.

Akil (Arabic) intelligent. (Greek) a form of Achilles.
Ahkeel, Akeel, Akeil, Akeyla, Akhil, Akiel, Akila, Akilah, Akile, Akili, Akyl, Akyle

Akimichi (Japanese) clear duty; bright and clear.

Akimitsu (Japanese) glittering adornment.

Akinino (Pohnpeian) a form of Joaquin.

Akinobu (Japanese) distinct beliefs.

Akinori (Japanese) clear ruling.

Akinory (Japanese) a form of Akinori.

Akins (Yoruba) brave.
Akin, Akyn, Akyns

Akioshi (Japanese) large, complete art.

Akioshy (Chuukese) a form of Akioshi.

Akir (Japanese) intelligent.

Akira **G** (Japanese) intelligent.
Akihito, Akio, Akirah, Akiyo, Akyra, Akyrah

Akito (Japanese) luxuriant result.

Akiva (Hebrew) a form of Jacob.
Akiba, Kiva

Akiwo (Kosraean) a form of Akio.

Akiyama (Japanese) autumn; mountain.

Akiyoshi (Japanese) clear justice.

Akiyuki (Japanese) this spirit; famous journey.

Aklea (English) a short form of Ackerley.
Aklee, Akleigh, Akley, Akli, Aklie, Akly

Aklesh (Sanskrit) swift lord.

Akmal (Arabic) perfect.
Ackmal

Akram (Arabic) most generous.

Aksel (Norwegian) father of peace.
Aksell

Akshat (Sanskrit) uninjurable.

Akshay (American) a form of Akash.
Akshaj, Akshaya

Aktar (Persian) a form of Akhtar.

Akuila (Fijian) a form of Aquila.

Akule (Native American) he looks up.
Akul

Akuo (Chuukese) a form of Akio.

Akyo (Japanese) bright.

Al (Irish) a short form of Alan, Albert, Alexander.

Aladdin (Arabic) height of faith. Literature: the hero of a story in the *Arabian Nights*.
Ala, Alaa, Alaaddin, Aladan, Aladdan, Aladden, Aladdyn, Aladean, Aladen, Aladin, Aladino, Aladyn

Alain (French) a form of Alan.
Alaen, Alaine, Alainn, Alayn, Alein, Aleine, Aleyn, Aleyne, Allain, Allayn

Alaire (French) joyful.
Alayr, Alayre

Alam (Arabic) universe.
Alame

Alan **B** (Irish) handsome; peaceful.
Ailan, Ailin, Al, Alaan, Alain, Alair, Aland, Alande, Alando, Alane, Alani, Alann, Alano, Alanson, Alante, Alao, Allan, Allen, Alon, Alun, Alune, Alyn, Alyne

Alanso (Chuukese) a form of Alfonso.

Alardo (Greek) courageous prince.

Alaric (German) ruler of all. See also Ulrich.
Alarich, Alarick, Alarico, Alarik, Alaryc, Alaryck, Alaryk, Aleric, Allaric, Allarick, Alric, Alrick, Alrik

Alastair (Scottish) a form of Alexander.
Alaisdair, Alaistair, Alaister, Alasdair, Alasteir, Alaster, Alastor, Aleister, Alester, Alistair, Allaistar, Allastair, Allaster, Allastir, Allysdair, Alystair

Alba (Latin) town on the white hill.

Alban (Latin) from Alba, Italy.
Albain, Albany, Albean, Albein, Alby, Auban, Auben

Albano (Germanic) belonging to the house of Alba.

Alberic (German) smart; wise ruler.
Alberich, Alberick, Alberyc, Alberyck, Alberyk

Albern (German) noble; courageous.
Alberne, Alburn, Alburne

Albert **B** (German, French) noble and bright. See also Elbert, Ulbrecht.
Adelbert, Ailbert, Al, Albertik, Alberto, Alberts, Albertus, Albie, Albrecht, Albret, Alby, Albyrt, Albyrte, Alvertos, Aubert

Alberto (Italian) a form of Albert.
Albertino, Berto

Albet (Chamorro) a form of Alberto.

Albie, Alby (German, French) familiar forms of Albert.
Albee, Albey, Albi

Albin (Latin) a form of Alvin.
Alben, Albeno, Albinek, Albino, Albins, Albinson, Albun, Alby, Albyn, Auben

Albion (Latin) white cliffs. Geography: a reference to the white cliffs in Dover, England.
Albon, Albyon, Allbion, Allbyon

Alcandor (Greek) manly; strong.

Alceo (Greek) man of great strength and vigor.

Alcibiades (Greek) generous and violent.

Alcibíades (Greek) strong and valiant man.

Alcides (Greek) strong and vigorous.

Alcott (English) old cottage.
Alcot, Alkot, Alkott, Allcot, Allcott, Allkot, Allkott

Alcuino (Teutonic) friend of sacred places, friend of the temple.

Aldair (German, English) a form of Alder.
Aldahir, Aldayr

Aldano, Aldino (Celtic) noble; experienced man.

Alden ☗ (English) old; wise protector.
Aldan, Aldean, Aldin, Aldous, Aldyn, Elden

Alder (German, English) alder tree.
Aldair, Aldar, Aldare, Aldyr

Alderidge (English) alder ridge.
Alderige, Aldrydge, Aldryge

Aldise (English) old house. (German) a form of Aldous.
Aldiss, Aldys

Aldo (Italian) old; elder. (German) a short form of Aldous.
Alda

Aldous (German) a form of Alden.
Aldis, Aldo, Aldon, Aldos, Aldus, Elden

Aldred (English) old; wise counselor.
Alldred, Eldred

Aldrich (English) wise.
Aldric, Aldrick, Aldridge, Aldrige, Aldritch, Aldryc, Aldryck, Aldryk, Alldric, Alldrich, Alldrick, Alldridge, Eldridge

Aldrin (English) old.

Aldwin (English) old friend.
Aldwan, Aldwen, Aldwon, Aldwyn, Eldwin

Alec, Alek ☗ (Greek) short forms of Alexander.
Aleck, Aleik, Alekko, Aleko, Elek

Aleczander (Greek) a form of Alexander.
Alecander, Aleckxander, Alecsander, Alecxander

Aleem (Arabic) learned, wise.

Alejandra ☗ (Spanish) a form of Alexandra.

Alejandrino (Greek) he is the protector and defender of men.

Alejandro ☗ ☗ (Spanish) a form of Alexander.

Alejándro (Spanish) a form of Alexander.
Alejándra, Aléjo, Alexjandro, Alexjándro

Alejo (Greek) he who protects and defends.

Aleksandar, Aleksander (Greek) forms of Alexander.
Aleksandor, Aleksandr, Aleksandras, Aleksandur

Aleksei (Russian) a short form of Alexander.
Aleks, Aleksey, Aleksi, Aleksis, Aleksy, Alexei, Alexey

Alekzander, Alexzander (Greek) forms of Alexander.
Alekxander, Alekxzander, Alexkzandr, Alexzandr, Alexzandyr

Alem (Arabic) wise.

Aleric (German) a form of Alaric.
Alerick, Alerik, Alleric, Allerick, Alleryc, Alleryck, Alleryk

Aleron (Latin) winged.
Aleronn

Alesio (Italian) a form of Alejo.

Alessandro ☗ (Italian) a form of Alexander.
Alessand, Alessander, Alessandre, Allessandro

Alex ☗ ☗ (Greek) a short form of Alexander.
Alax, Alexx, Allax, Allex, Allyx, Allyxx, Alyx, Elek

Alexa ☗ (Greek) a short form of Alexandra.

Alexander ☗ ☗ (Greek) defender of mankind. History: Alexander the Great was the conqueror of the civilized world. See also Alastair, Alistair, Iskander, Jando, Leks, Lex, Lexus, Macallister, Oleksandr, Olés, Sander, Sándor, Sandro, Sandy, Sasha, Xan, Xander, Zander, Zindel.
Al, Alec, Alecsandar, Alejándro, Alek, Alekos, Aleksandar, Aleksander, Aleksei, Alekzander,

Alessandro, Alex, Alexandar, Alexandor,
Alexandr, Alexandre, Alexandro, Alexandros,
Alexi, Alexis, Alexxander, Alexzander, Alic,
Alick, Alisander, Alixander

Alexandra **G** (Greek) defender of
humankind.

Alexandre **B** (French) a form of Alexander.

Alexandria **G** (Greek) a form of Alexandra.

Alexandro (Greek) a form of Alexander.
Alexandras, Alexandros, Alexandru

Alexe **G** (Russian) a form of Alexi. (Greek)
a form of Alex.

Alexi **G** (Russian) a form of Aleksei.
(Greek) a short form of Alexander.
Alexe, Alexee, Alexey, Alexie, Alexio, Alexy,
Alezio

Alexie **G** (Russian, Greek) a form of Alexi.

Alexis **G** (Greek) a short form of Alexander.
Alexei, Alexes, Alexey, Alexios, Alexius,
Alexiz, Alexsis, Alexsus, Alexus, Alexys

Alexsander (Greek) a form of Alexander.

Alexus **G** (Greek) a form of Alexis.

Aleydis (Teutonic) born into a noble family.

Alfie **B** (English) a familiar form of Alfred.
Alfy

Alfio (Greek) he who has a white
complexion.

Alfonso (Italian, Spanish) a form of
Alphonse.
Affonso, Alfons, Alfonse, Alfonsus, Alfonza,
Alfonzo, Alfonzus

Alford (English) old river ford.
Allford

Alfred (English) elf counselor; wise
counselor. See also Fred.
Ailfrid, Ailfryd, Alf, Alfeo, Alfie, Alfredo,
Alfredus, Alfrid, Alfried, Alfryd, Alured

Alfredo (Italian, Spanish) a form of Alfred.
Alfrido

Alger (German) noble spearman. (English)
a short form of Algernon. See also Elger.
Aelfar, Algar, Algor, Allgar

Algernon (English) bearded, wearing a
moustache.
Aelgernon, Algenon, Alger, Algie, Algin,
Algon

Algie (English) a familiar form of Algernon.
Algee, Algia, Algy

Algis (German) spear.
Algiss

Algiso (Greek) lance of nobility.

Ali **B** (Arabic) greatest. (Swahili) exalted.
Aly

Alí (Arabic) a form of Ali.

Alic (Greek) a short form of Alexander.
Alick, Aliek, Alik, Aliko, Alyc, Alyck, Alyk,
Alyko

Alice **G** (Greek) truthful. (German) noble.

Alicia **G** (English) a form of Alice.

Aligao (Chamorro) to search for.

Alijah (Hebrew) a form of Elijah.

Alilim (Chamorro) cateye shell.

Alim (Arabic) scholar. (Arabic) a form of
Alem.
Alym

Alipate (Fijian) a form of Alberto.

Alipio (Greek) he who is not affected by
suffering.

Alisander (Greek) a form of Alexander.
Alisandre, Alisaunder, Alissander, Alissandre,
Alsandair, Alsandare, Alsander

Alisha **G** (Greek) truthful. (German) noble.
(English) a form of Alicia.

Alison, Allison **G** (English) Alice's son.
Allisan, Allisen, Allisun, Allisyn, Allysan,
Allysen, Allysin, Allyson, Allysun, Allysyn

Alissa **G** (Greek) a form of Alice.

Alistair (English) a form of Alexander.
Alisdair, Alistaire, Alistar, Alister, Allistair,
Allistar, Allister, Allistir, Alstair, Alystayr,
Alystyre

Alivereti (Fijian) a form of Alfredo.

Alix **G** (Greek) a short form of Alex.
Alixx, Allix, Allixx, Allyx, Allyxx

Alixander (Greek) a form of Alexander.
Alixandre, Alixandru, Alixsander, Alixxander,
Alixxzander, Alixzander, Alyxxander,
Alyxxsander, Alyxxzander, Alyxzander

Allah (Arabic) God.

Allambee (Australian) quiet place.
Alambee, Alambey, Alambi, Alambie,
Alamby, Allambey, Allambi, Allambie,
Allamby

Allan **B** (Irish) a form of Alan.
Allane, Allayne

Boys A–F

Allante, Allanté (Spanish) forms of Alan.

Allard (English) noble, brave.
Alard, Ellard

Allen 🅱 (Irish) a form of Alan.
Alen, Allene, Alley, Alleyn, Alleyne, Allie, Allin, Alline, Allon, Allyn, Allyne

Allie 🅖 (Irish) a form of Allen.

Alma 🅖 (Arabic) learned. (Latin) soul.

Almeric (German) powerful ruler.
Almauric, Amaurick, Amaurik, Amauryc, Amauryck, Amauryk, Americk, Amerik, Ameryc, Ameryck, Ameryk

Almon (Hebrew) widower.
Alman, Almen, Almin, Almyn

Alo (Chamorro) a form of Alu.

Alois (German) a short form of Aloysius.
Aloys

Aloisio (Spanish) a form of Louis.

Alok (Sanskrit) victorious cry.

Alon (Hebrew) oak.
Alonn

Alondra 🅖 (Spanish) a form of Alexandra.

Alonso, Alonzo (Spanish) forms of Alphonse.
Alano, Alanzo, Alon, Alonz, Alonza, Alonze, Allonza, Allonzo, Elonzo, Lon, Lonnie, Lonso, Lonzo

Aloysius (German) a form of Louis.
Alaois, Alois, Aloisius, Aloisio

Alpert (Pohnpeian) a form of Alberto.

Alphonse (German) noble and eager.
Alf, Alfie, Alfonso, Alonzo, Alphons, Alphonsa, Alphonso, Alphonsus, Alphonza, Alphonzus, Fonzie

Alphonso (Italian) a form of Alphonse.
Alphanso, Alphonzo, Fonso

Alpin (Irish) attractive.
Alpine, Alpyn, Alpyne

Alpino (Pohnpeian) a form of Albino.

Alroy (Spanish) king.
Alroi

Alsantry (Pohnpeian) a form of Alejandro.

Alston (English) noble's settlement.
Allston, Alstan, Alsten, Alstin, Alstun, Alstyn

Altair (Greek) star. (Arabic) flying.
Altayr, Altayre

Alterio (Greek) like a starry night.

Altman (German) old man.
Altmann, Altmen, Atman

Alton (English) old town.
Alten

Alu (Chamorro) barracuda; shark.

Alucio (Latin) he is lucid and illustrious.

Alula (Latin) winged; swift.

Alva 🅱🅖 (Hebrew) sublime.
Alvah

Alvan (German) a form of Alvin.
Alvand, Alvun

Alvar (English) army of elves.
Alvara

Alvaro (Spanish) just; wise.

Alvern (Latin) spring.
Alverne, Elvern

Alvero (Germanic) completely prudent.

Alvin (Latin) white; light skinned. (German) friend to all; noble friend; friend of elves. See also Albin, Elvin.
Aloin, Aluin, Aluino, Alvan, Alven, Alvie, Alvino, Alvon, Alvy, Alvyn, Alwin, Elwin

Alvis (Scandinavian) all-knowing.

Alwin (German) a form of Alvin.
Ailwyn, Alwan, Alwen, Alwon, Alwun, Alwyn, Alwynn, Aylwin

Alyssa 🅖 (Greek) rational. Botany: alyssum is a flowering herb.

Ama, Amay (Chamorro) forms of Amai.

Amactus (Chamorro) breaking off.

Amadeo (Italian) a form of Amadeus.

Amadeus (Latin) loves God. Music: Wolfgang Amadeus Mozart was a famous eighteenth-century Austrian composer.
Amad, Amadeaus, Amadée, Amadeo, Amadei, Amadio, Amadis, Amado, Amador, Amadou, Amando, Amedeo, Amodaos

Amai (Chamorro) rain.

Amal 🅖 (Hebrew) worker. (Arabic) hopeful.
Amahl

Amalio (Greek) a man who is carefree.

Amam (Chamorro) flattering.

Aman (Hebrew) magnificent one.

Amancio (Latin) he who loves God.

Amanda G (Latin) lovable.

Amandeep BG (Punjabi) light of peace.
Amandip, Amanjit, Amanjot, Amanpreet

Amando (French) a form of Amadeus.
Amand, Amandio, Amaniel, Amato

Amani (Arabic) believer. (Yoruba) strength;
builder.
Amanee

Amar (Punjabi) immortal. (Arabic) builder.
*Amare, Amaree, Amari, Amario, Amaris,
Amarjit, Amaro, Amarpreet, Amarri, Ammar,
Ammer*

Amaranto (Greek) he who does not slow
down.

Amaruquispe (Quechua) free, like the
sacred Amaru.

Amarutopac (Quechua) glorious, majestic
Amaru.

Amaruyupanqui (Quechua) he who honors
Amaru; memorable Amaru.

Amato (French) loved.
Amat, Amatto

Ambar G (Sanskrit) sky.

Amber G (French) amber.

Ambrois (French) a form of Ambrose.

Ambrose (Greek) immortal.
*Ambie, Ambrogio, Ambroise, Ambroisius,
Ambros, Ambrosi, Ambrosio, Ambrosios,
Ambrosius, Ambrossye, Ambrosye, Ambrotos,
Ambroz, Ambrus, Amby*

Ameen (Hebrew, Arabic, Hindi) a form of
Amin.

Ameer (Hebrew) a form of Amir.
Ameir, Amer, Amere

Amelio (Teutonic) very hard worker,
energetic.

Americ (French) a form of Emery.

Américo (Germanic) prince in action.

Amerigo (Teutonic) industrious. History:
Amerigo Vespucci was the Italian explorer
for whom America is named.
Americo, Americus, Amerygo

Amérigo (Italian) a form of Amerigo.

Ames (French) friend.
Amess

Ami (Hebrew) builder.

Amicus (English, Latin) beloved friend.
*Amic, Amick, Amicko, Amico, Amik, Amiko,
Amyc, Amyck, Amycko, Amyk, Amyko*

Amid (Arabic) academic dean.

Amida (Japanese) the name of a Buddha.

Amiel (Hebrew) God of my people.
Amiell, Ammiel, Amyel, Amyell

Amílcar (Punic) he who governs the city.

Amin (Hebrew, Arabic) trustworthy; honest.
(Hindi) faithful.
*Amen, Amine, Ammen, Ammin, Ammyn,
Amyn, Amynn*

Amín (Arabic) a form of Amin.

Aminiasi (Fijian) a kind of tree.

Amintor (Greek) protector.

Amir G (Hebrew) proclaimed. (Punjabi)
wealthy; king's minister. (Arabic) prince.
Aamer, Aamir, Ameer, Amire, Amiri, Amyr

Amish (Sanskrit) honest.

Amit (Punjabi) unfriendly. (Arabic) highly
praised.
Amita, Amitan, Amreet

Ammei, Ammey (Chamorro) forms of Amai.

Ammon (Egyptian) hidden. Mythology: the
ancient god associated with reproduction.
Amman

Amol (Hindi) priceless, valuable.
Amul

Amoldo (Spanish) power of an eagle.

Amon (Hebrew) trustworthy; faithful.
Amun

Amón (Hebrew) a form of Amon.

Amory (German) a form of Emory.
*Ameree, Ameri, Amerie, Amery, Ammeree,
Ammerey, Ammeri, Ammerie, Ammery,
Ammoree, Ammorey, Ammori, Ammorie,
Ammory, Amor, Amoree, Amorey, Amori, Amorie*

Amos (Hebrew) burdened, troubled. Bible: an
Old Testament prophet.
Amose, Amous

Amós (Hebrew) a form of Amos.

Amotho (Chamorro) medicine.

Ampelio (Greek) he who makes wine from
his own grapes.

Ampelo (Greek) son of a satyr and a nymph,
who died while trying to pick grapes from a
grapevine.

Amram (Hebrew) mighty nation.
Amarien, Amran, Amren, Amryn

Amrat (Arabic) handsome.

Amrit 🅱🅶 (Sanskrit) nectar. (Punjabi,
Arabic) a form of Amit.
Amryt

Amritpal (Sikh) protector of the Lord's nectar.

Amuillan (Mapuche) movement from the
altar; he who warmly serves others.

Amy 🅶 (Latin) beloved.

An 🅱 (Chinese, Vietnamese) peaceful.
Ana

Aña (Chamorro) to overpower; to punish.

Anacario (Greek) not without grace.

Anacleto (Greek) he who was called upon.

Añaho (Chamorro) I punish; I overcome.

Anaías (Hebrew) Lord answers.

Anand (Hindi) blissful.
Ananda, Anant, Ananth

Anandan (Sanskrit) a form of Anand.

Ananías (Hebrew) he who has the grace of
God.

Añao (Chamorro) to conquer.

Anastasius (Greek) resurrection.
*Anas, Anastacio, Anastacios, Anastagio,
Anastas, Anastase, Anastasi, Anastasio,
Anastasios, Anastatius, Anastice, Anastisis,
Anaztáz, Athanasius*

Anatole (Greek) east.
Anatol, Anatoley, Anatoli, Anatolie,

*Anatolijus, Anatolio, Anatolis, Anatoliy,
Anatoly, Anitoly, Antoly*

Anbesa (Spanish) a Saracen governor of
Spain.

Anca (Quechua) eagle; black eagle.

Ancasmayu (Quechua) blue like the river.

Ancaspoma, Ancaspuma (Quechua)
bluish puma.

Ancavil (Mapuche) identical mythological
being.

Ancavilo (Mapuche) snake's body; a body
that is half snake.

Anchali (Taos) painter.
Anchalee, Anchaley, Anchalie, Anchaly

Ancuguiyca (Quechua) having sacred
resistance.

Andero (Pohnpeian) a form of Andres.

Anders (Swedish) a form of Andrew.
Andar, Ander

Anderson 🅱 (Swedish) son of Andrew.
Andersen

Andolin (Pohnpeian) a form of Antonio.

Andon (Chuukese) a form of Antonio.

Andonios (Greek) a form of Anthony.
Andoni, Andonis, Andonny

Andor (Hungarian) a form of Andrew.

András (Hungarian) a form of Andrew.
*Andraes, Andri, Andris, Andrius, Andriy,
Aundras, Aundreas*

Andre, André 🅱 (French) forms of Andrew.
*Andra, Andrae, Andrecito, Andree, Andrei,
Aundre, Aundré*

Andrea 🅶 (Greek) a form of Andrew.
Andrean, Andreani, Andrian

Andreas 🅱 (Greek) a form of Andrew.
Andres, Andries

Andrei (Bulgarian, Romanian, Russian) a
form of Andrew.
*Andreian, Andrej, Andrey, Andreyan, Andrie,
Aundrei*

Andreo (Greek) manly.

Andres 🅱 (Spanish) a form of Andrew.
Andras, Andrés, Andrez

Andrew ♛ 🅱 (Greek) strong; manly;
courageous. Bible: one of the Twelve
Apostles. See also Bandi, Drew, Endre,
Evangelos, Kendrew, Ondro.
*Aindrea, Anders, Andery, Andonis, Andor,
András, Andre, André, Andrea, Andreas,
Andrei, Andres, Andrews, Andru, Andrue,
Andrus, Andy, Anker, Anndra, Antal, Audrew*

Andrike (Marshallese) something disliked.

Androcles (Greek) man covered with glory.

Andrónico (German) victorious man.

Andros (Polish) sea. Mythology: the god of
the sea.
Andris, Andrius, Andrus

Andrzej (Polish) a form of Andrew.

Andy 🅱 (Greek) a short form of Andrew.
*Ande, Andee, Andey, Andi, Andie, Andino,
Andis, Andje*

Aneurin (Welsh) honorable; gold. See also Nye.
Aneirin

Anfernee (Greek) a form of Anthony.
Anferney, Anfernie, Anferny, Anfranee, Anfrene, Anfrenee, Anpherne

Anfión (Greek) mythological son of Antiope and Jupiter.

Anfonee (Greek) a form of Anthony.
Anfoney, Anfoni, Anfonie, Anfony

Ang (Chinese) high spirited.

Angel ✻ **B** (Greek) angel. (Latin) messenger. See also Gotzon.
Ange, Angell, Angelo, Angie, Angy, Anjel, Anjell

Ángel (Greek) a form of Angel.

Angela **G** (Greek) angel; messenger.

Angelina **G** (Russian) forms of Angela.

Angeline (Russian) forms of Angela.

Angelino (Latin) messenger.

Angelo (Italian) a form of Angel.
Angeleo, Angelito, Angello, Angelos, Angelous, Angiolo, Anglo, Anjello, Anjelo

Anghet (Chamorro) angel.

Angilberto (Teutonic) he who shines with the power of God. A combination of Ángel and Alberto.

Angit (Chamorro) a form of Anghet.

Angkel (Pohnpeian) a form of Angel.

Angoco (Chamorro) to trust, to rely on.

Angocog, Angog (Chamorro) forms of Angoco.

Angus (Scottish) exceptional; outstanding. Mythology: Angus Og was the Celtic god of youth, love, and beauty. See also Ennis, Gus.
Aeneas, Aonghas

Anh (Vietnamese) peace; safety.

Anh Dung (Vietnamese) heroism; strength.

Aniano (Greek) he who is sad and upset.

Anías (Hebrew) God answers.

Anibal (Phoenician) a form of Hannibal.

Aníbal (Punic) he who has the grace of God.

Anicet, Aniceto (Greek) invincible man of great strength.

Anidreb (Marshallese) juggling ball made of pandanus fiber.

Anik **G** (Czech) a form of Anica (see Girls' Names).

Anil (Hindi) wind god.
Aneal, Aneel, Anel, Aniel, Aniello, Anielo, Anyl, Anyll

Anisha **G** (English) a form of Agnes (see Girls' Names).

Anita (Sanskrit) free.

Anitti (Chamorro) spirit.

Anjua (Marshallese) proud.

Anka **G** (Turkish) phoenix.

Anker (Danish) a form of Andrew.
Ankor, Ankur

Anna **G** (Greek) a form of Annas.

Annan (Scottish) brook. (Swahili) fourth-born son.
Annen, Annin, Annon, Annun, Annyn

Annas (Greek) gift from God.
Anis, Anish, Anna, Annais

Anne **G** (English) gracious.

Anno (German) a familiar form of Johann.
Ano

Anoki (Native American) actor.
Anokee, Anokey, Anokie, Anoky

Anoop (Sikh) beauty.

Ansaldo (German) he who represents God; God is with him.

Ansel (French) follower of a nobleman.
Ancell, Ansa, Anselino, Ansell, Ansellus, Anselyno, Ansyl

Anselm (German) divine protector. See also Elmo.
Anse, Anselme, Anselmi, Anselmo

Ansis (Latvian) a form of Janis.

Ansley **G** (Scottish) a form of Ainsley.
Anslea, Anslee, Ansleigh, Ansli, Anslie, Ansly, Ansy

Anson (German) divine. (English) Anne's son.
Ansan, Ansen, Ansin, Ansun, Ansyn

Answer (English) a response.

Anta, Antay (Quechua) copper, copperish.

Antal (Hungarian) a form of Anthony.
Antek, Anti, Antos

Antares (Greek) giant, red star. Astronomy: the brightest star in the constellation Scorpio.
Antar, Antario, Antarious, Antarius, Antarr, Antarus

Antauaya (Quechua) copper-colored meadow; copper-colored grass.

Antavas (Lithuanian) a form of Anthony.
Antae, Antaeus, Antavious, Antavius, Ante, Anteo

Antelmo (Germanic) protector of the homeland.

Antenor (Greek) he who is a fighter.

Anthany (Latin, Greek) a form of Anthony.
Antanas, Antanee, Antanie, Antenee, Anthan, Antheny, Anthine, Anthney

Anthonie (Latin, Greek) a form of Anthony.
Anthone, Anthonee, Anthoni, Anthonia

Anthony ✇ **B** (Latin) praiseworthy. (Greek) flourishing. See also Tony.
Anathony, Andonios, Andor, András, Anothony, Antal, Antavas, Anfernee, Anthany, Anthawn, Anthey, Anthian, Anthino, Anthone, Anthoney, Anthonie, Anthonio, Anthonu, Anthonysha, Anthoy, Anthyoine, Anthyonny, Antione, Antjuan, Antoine, Anton, Antonio, Antony, Antwan, Antwon

Antígono (Greek) he who stands out amongst all of his fellow men.

Antilaf (Mapuche) happy day, joyous day.

Antininan (Quechua) copperish like fire.

Antioco (Greek) he who commands the chariot in the fight against the enemy.

Antione **B** (French) a form of Anthony.
Antion, Antionio, Antionne, Antiono

Antipan (Mapuche) sunny branch of a clear brown color.

Antipas (Greek) he is the enemy of all, in opposition to everyone.

Antivil (Mapuche) sunny snake.

Antjuan (Spanish) a form of Anthony.
Antajuan, Anthjuan, Antuan, Antuane

Antoan (Vietnamese) safe, secure.

An-Toan (Vietnamese) safe, secure.

Antoine (French) a form of Anthony.
Anntoin, Anthoine, Antoiné, Antoinne, Atoine

Antolín (Greek) flourishing, beautiful like a flower.

Anton (Slavic) a form of Anthony.
Anthon, Antone, Antonn, Antonne, Antons, Antos

Antón (Spanish) a form of Antonio.

Antonia **G** (Greek) flourishing. (Latin) praiseworthy.

Antonio ✇ **B** (Italian) a form of Anthony. See also Tino, Tonio.
Anthonio, Antinio, Antoinio, Antoino, Antonello, Antoneo, Antonin, Antonín, Antonino, Antonnio, Antonios, Antonius, Antonyia, Antonyio, Antonyo

Antony (Latin) a form of Anthony.
Antin, Antini, Antius, Antonee, Antoney, Antoni, Antonie, Antonin, Antonios, Antonius, Antonyia, Antonyio, Antonyo, Anty

Antreas (Pohnpeian) a form of Andrés.

Antti (Finnish) manly.
Anthey, Anthi, Anthie, Anthy, Anti, Antty

Antu (Indigenous) salt.

Antwan (Arabic) a form of Anthony.
Antaw, Antawan, Antawn, Anthawn, Antowan, Antowaun, Antowine, Antowne, Antowyn, Antuwan, Antwain, Antwaina, Antwaine, Antwainn, Antwaion, Antwane, Antwann, Antwanne, Antwarn, Antwaun, Antwen, Antwian, Antwine, Antwuan, Antwun, Antwyné

Antwon (Arabic) a form of Anthony.
Antown, Antuwon, Antwion, Antwione, Antwoan, Antwoin, Antwoine, Antwone, Antwonn, Antwonne, Antwoun, Antwyon, Antwyone, Antyon, Antyonne, Antywon

Anukal (Chuukese) alone.

Anukul (Sanskrit) suitable.

Anwar (Arabic) luminous.
Anour, Anouar, Anwi

Anyaypoma, Anyaypuma (Quechua) he who roars and becomes angry like the puma.

Aparama (Fijian) a form of Abraham.

Aparicio (Latin) he who refers to the appearances of the Virgin in different stages.

Apeles (Greek) he who is in a sacred place.

Apenisa (Fijian) a form of Ebenezer.

Api (Indonesian) fire.

Apiatan (Kiowa) wooden lance.

Apiner (Pohnpeian) a form of Abner.

Apisai (Fijian) a form of Abishai.

Boys A–F

Apisalome (Fijian) a form of Apisalome.

Apo' (Chamorro) to lean against.

Apo, Apu (Quechua) chief, Lord God; he who moves forward.

Apólito (Latin) dedicated to the god Apollo.

Apollo (Greek) manly. Mythology: the god of prophecy, healing, music, poetry, and light. See also Polo.
Apolinar, Apolinario, Apollos, Apolo, Apolonio, Appollo, Appolo, Appolonio

Apolodoro (Griego) skill of Apollo.

Apono (Chuukese) a form of Apollo.

Appa (Chamorro) to place one's hand on someone's shoulder.

April **G** (Latin) opening.

Apucachi (Quechua) lord of salt, salty.

Apucatequil, Apucatiquil (Quechua) god of lightning.

Apumaita (Quechua) where are you, master?

Apurimac (Quechua) eloquent master.

Apuyurac (Quechua) white chief.

Aquila (Latin, Spanish) eagle.
Acquilla, Aquil, Aquilas, Aquileo, Aquiles, Aquilino, Aquill, Aquilla, Aquille, Aquillino, Aquyl, Aquyla, Aquyll, Aquylla

Arafat (Arabic) mountain of recognition. History: Yasir Arafat led Al Fatah, an Arab guerilla group, and the Palestine Liberation Organization, advocating an independent Palestinian state.

Araldo (Spanish) a form of Harold.
Aralodo, Aralt, Aroldo, Arry

Aram (Syrian) high, exalted.
Ara, Aramia, Arem, Arim, Arra, Arram, Arum, Arym

Aramis (French) Literature: one of the title characters in Alexandre Dumas's novel *The Three Musketeers*.
Airamis, Aramith, Aramys

Aran (Tai) forest. (Danish) a form of Aren. (Hebrew, Scottish) a form of Arran.
Arane

Arata (Japanese) new.

Arbedul (Palauan) the leaders.

Arcángel (Greek) prince of all angels.

Archer (English) bowman.
Archar, Archie, Archor

Archibald (German) bold. See also Arkady.
Arch, Archaimbaud, Archambault, Archibaldes, Archibaldo, Archibold, Archie, Archybald, Archybalde, Archybaldes, Archybauld, Archybaulde

Archie (German, English) a familiar form of Archer, Archibald.
Arche, Archee, Archey, Archi, Archy

Ardal (Irish) a form of Arnold.
Ardale, Ardall

Ardell (Latin) eager; industrious.
Ardel

Arden **G** (Latin) ardent; fiery.
Ard, Ardan, Ardene, Ardent, Ardian, Ardie, Ardin, Ardint, Ardn, Arduino, Ardyn, Ardynt

Ardley (English) ardent meadow.
Ardlea, Ardlee, Ardleigh, Ardli, Ardlie, Ardly

Ardon (Hebrew) bronzed.
Ardun

Ardur (Chuukese) a form of Arthur.

Areli **G** (American) a form of Oralee (see Girls' names).

Aren (Danish) eagle; ruler. (Hebrew, Arabic) a form of Aaron.

Aretas (Arabic) metal forger.

Aretino (Greek, Italian) victorious.
Aretin, Aretine, Artyn, Artyno

Argenis (Greek) he who has a great whiteness.

Argentino, Argento (Latin) shines like silver.

Argimiro (Greek) careful; vigilant.

Argus (Danish) watchful, vigilant.
Agos, Arguss

Argyle (Irish) from Ireland.
Argile, Argiles, Argyles

Ari **G** (Hebrew) a short form of Ariel. (Greek) a short form of Aristotle.
Aree, Arey, Arias, Arie, Arieh, Arih, Arij, Ario, Arri, Ary, Arye

Aria (Hebrew) a form of Ariel.

Arian (Greek) a form of Arion.
Ariann, Arrian, Aryan

Ariana **G** (Greek) a form of Arian.

Ariane **G** (Greek) a form of Arian.

Boys A–F

Arianne 🄶 (Greek) a form of Arian.

Aric (German) a form of Richard. (Scandinavian) a form of Eric.
Aaric, Aarick, Aarik, Arec, Areck, Arich, Arick, Ariek, Arik, Arrek, Arric, Arrick, Arrik, Aryc, Aryck, Aryk

Ariel 🄶 (Hebrew) lion of God. Bible: another name for Jerusalem. Literature: the name of a sprite in the Shakespearean play *The Tempest*.
Airal, Airel, Arel, Areli, Ari, Ariele, Ariell, Arielle, Ariya, Ariyel, Arrial, Arriel, Aryel, Aryell, Aryl, Aryll, Arylle

Aries (Latin) ram. Astrology: the first sign of the zodiac.
Arees, Ares, Arie, Ariez, Aryes

Arif (Arabic) knowledgeable.
Areef, Aryf

Arion (Greek) enchanted. (Hebrew) melodious.
Arian, Arien, Ario, Arione, Aryon

Aristarco (Greek) best of the princes.

Aristeo (Greek) outstanding one.

Aristides (Greek) son of the best.
Aris, Aristede, Aristedes, Aristeed, Aristide, Aristidis, Aristidis, Arystides, Arystydes

Arístides (Greek) a form of Aristides.

Aristóbulo (Greek) greatest and best counselor; he who gives very good advice.

Aristofanes (Greek) best, the optimum.

Aristóteles (Greek) best; the most renowned; the most optimistic; he who has noble intentions.

Aristotle (Greek) best; wise. History: a third-century b.c. philosopher who tutored Alexander the Great.
Ari, Aris, Aristito, Aristo, Aristokles, Aristotal, Aristotel, Aristotelis, Aristotol, Aristott, Aristotyl, Arystotle

Arjun (Hindi) white; milk colored.
Arjen, Arjin, Arju, Arjuna, Arjune

Arkady (Russian) a form of Archibald.
Arcadio, Arkadee, Arkadey, Arkadi, Arkadie, Arkadij, Arkadiy

Arkin (Norwegian) son of the eternal king.
Aricin, Arkeen, Arkyn

Arledge (English) lake with the hares.
Arlege, Arlidge, Arlledge, Arllege

Arlen (Irish) pledge.
Arlan, Arland, Arlend, Arlin, Arlinn, Arlon, Arlyn, Arlynn

Arley (English) a short form of Harley.
Arleigh, Arlie, Arly

Arlo (Spanish) barberry. (English) fortified hill. A form of Harlow. (German) a form of Charles.
Arlow

Arman (Persian) desire, goal.
Armaan, Armahn, Armaine

Armand (Latin, German) a form of Herman. See also Mandek.
Armad, Arman, Armanda, Armando, Armands, Armanno, Armaude, Armenta, Armond

Armando (Spanish) a form of Armand.
Armondo

Armani 🄱 (Hungarian) sly. (Hebrew) a form of Armon.
Arman, Armanee, Armaney, Armanie, Armann, Armany, Armoni, Armonie, Armonio, Armonni, Armony

Armentario (Greek) herder of livestock.

Armon (Hebrew) high fortress, stronghold.
Armani, Armen, Armin, Armino, Armonn, Armons, Armyn

Armstrong (English) strong arm. History: astronaut Neil Armstrong was the commander of Apollo 11 and the first person to walk on the moon.
Armstron, Armstronge

Arnaud (French) a form of Arnold.
Arnaude, Arnauld, Arnault, Arnoll

Arne (German) a form of Arnold.
Arna, Arnay, Arnel, Arnele, Arnell, Arnelle

Arnette (English) little eagle.
Arnat, Arnatt, Arnet, Arnett, Arnetta, Arnot, Arnott

Arnie (German) a familiar form of Arnold.
Arnee, Arney, Arni, Arnny, Arny

Arno (German) a short form of Arnold. (Czech) a short form of Ernest.
Arnou, Arnoux

Arnold (German) eagle ruler.
Ardal, Arnald, Arnaldo, Arnaud, Arndt, Arne, Arnhold, Arnie, Arno, Arnol, Arnoldas, Arnolde, Arnoldo, Arnoll, Arnolt, Arnoud, Arnulfo, Arnyld

Arnon (Hebrew) rushing river.
Arnan, Arnen, Arnin, Arnyn

Arnulfo (German) a form of Arnold.

Boys A–F

Aron, Arron **B** (Hebrew) forms of Aaron. (Danish) forms of Aren.
Arrion

Aroon (Tai) dawn.
Aroone

Arquelao (Greek) governor of his village.

Arquimedes (Greek) he who has profound thoughts.

Arquímedes (Greek) deep thinker.

Arquipo (Greek) horse breaker.

Arran (Scottish) island dweller. Geography: an island off the west coast of Scotland. (Hebrew) a form of Aaron.
Aeran, Arren, Arrin, Arryn, Aryn

Arrigo (Italian) a form of Harry.
Alrigo, Arrighetto

Arrio (Spanish) warlike.
Ario, Arrow, Arryo, Aryo

Arsenio (Greek) masculine; virile. History: Saint Arsenius was a teacher in the Roman Empire.
Arsen, Arsène, Arseneo, Arsenius, Arseny, Arsenyo, Arsinio, Arsinyo, Arsynio, Arsynyo

Arsha (Persian) venerable.
Arshah

Art (English) a short form of Arthur.

Artemus (Greek) gift of Artemis. Mythology: Artemis was the goddess of the hunt and the moon.
Artemas, Artemio, Artemis, Artimas, Artimis, Artimus

Arthur **B** (Irish) noble; lofty hill. (Scottish) bear. (English) rock. (Icelandic) follower of Thor. See also Turi.
Art, Artair, Artek, Arth, Arther, Arthor, Arthyr, Artie, Artor, Arturo, Artus, Aurthar, Aurther, Aurthur

Artie (English) a familiar form of Arthur.
Arte, Artee, Artian, Artis, Arty, Atty

Artjuni (Sanskrit) white; silvery.

Arturo (Italian) a form of Arthur.
Arthuro, Artur

Arun (Cambodian, Hindi) sun.
Aruns

Arundel (English) eagle valley.

Arurang (Palauan) he who is timid or ashamed.

Arve (Norwegian) heir, inheritor.

Arvel (Welsh) wept over.
Arval, Arvell, Arvelle, Arvil, Arvol, Arvyn

Arvid (Hebrew) wanderer. (Norwegian) eagle tree. See also Ravid.
Arv, Arvad, Arve, Arvie, Arvind, Arvinder, Arvyd, Arvydas

Arvin (German) friend of the people; friend of the army.
Arv, Arvan, Arven, Arvie, Arvind, Arvinder, Arvon, Arvy, Arvyn, Arwan, Arwen, Arwin, Arwon, Arwyn

Arya (Hebrew) a form of Aria.

Aryeh (Hebrew) lion.

Asa **B** (Hebrew) physician, healer. (Yoruba) falcon.
Asaa, Asah, Ase

Asád (Arabic) lion.
Asaad, Asad, Asid, Assad, Azad

Asadel (Arabic) prosperous.
Asadour, Asadul, Asadyl, Asael

Asaf (Hebrew) one chosen by God.

Asaichi (Japanese) first dawn.

Asao (Japanese) morning man.

Ascensión (Spanish) mystical name that alludes to the ascension of Jesus Christ to heaven.

Ascot (English) eastern cottage; style of necktie. Geography: a village near London and the site of the Royal Ascot horseraces.
Ascott

Asdrúbal (Punic) he who is protected by God.

Asgar (Arabic) the smallest; repetitions of names and praises.

Asgard (Scandinavian) court of the gods.

Ash (Hebrew) ash tree.
Ashby

Ashad (Arabic) most vehement.

Ashanti **G** (Swahili) from a tribe in West Africa.
Ashan, Ashani, Ashante, Ashantee, Ashaunte

Ashburn (English) from the ash-tree stream.
Ashbern, Ashberne, Ashbirn, Ashbirne, Ashborn, Ashborne, Ashbourn, Ashbourne, Ashburne, Ashbyrn, Ashbyrne

Ashby (Scandinavian) ash-tree farm. (Hebrew) a form of Ash.
Ashbee, Ashbey, Ashbi, Ashbie

Asher (Hebrew) happy; blessed.
Ashar, Ashir, Ashor, Ashur, Ashyr

Ashford (English) ash-tree ford.
Ash, Ashforde, Ashtin

Ashlee G (English) a form of Ashley.

Ashleigh G (English) a form of Ashley.

Ashley G (English) ash-tree meadow.
Ash, Asheley, Ashelie, Ashely, Ashlan,
Ashlea, Ashlen, Ashli, Ashlie, Ashlin, Ashling,
Ashlinn, Ashlone, Ashly, Ashlynn, Aslan

Ashlyn G (English) a form of Ashley.

Ashon (Swahili) seventh-born son.

Ashraf (Arabic) most honorable.

Ashton BG (English) ash-tree settlement.
Ashtan, Ashten, Ashtian, Ashtin, Ashtion,
Ashtonn, Ashtown, Ashtun

Ashtyn G (English) a form of Ashton.

Ashur (Swahili) Mythology: the principal
Assyrian deity.

Ashwani (Hindi) first. Religion: the first of
the twenty-seven galaxies revolving around
the moon.
Ashwan

Ashwin (Hindi) star.
Ashwen, Ashwon, Ashwyn

Asi (Chamorro) pity.

Asiel (Hebrew) created by God.
Asyel

Asif (Arabic) forgiveness.

Asker (Turkish) soldier.

Aslam (Arabic) safer; freer.

Asou (Chuukese) further out; awaited.

Aspen G (English) aspen tree.

Asraf (Arabic) a form of Ashraf.

Assi (Chamorro) a form of Asi.

Asterio (Greek) mythical figure that was
thrown into the sea because of his escape
from Zeus.

Astley (Greek) starry field.
Asterlea, Asterlee, Asterleigh, Asterley,
Asterli, Asterlie, Asterly, Astlea, Astlee,
Astleigh, Astli, Astlie, Astly

Asto, Astu (Quechua) bird of the Andes.

Astolfo (Greek) he who helps with his lance.

Aston (English) eastern town.
Astan, Asten, Astin, Astown, Astyn

Astuguaraca (Quechua) he who hunts astus
with a sling.

Asuka (Japanese) flying bird.

Aswad (Arabic) dark skinned, black.
Aswald

Ata (Fante) twin.
Atah

Atahualpa (Quechua) bird of fortune.

Atake (Chuukese) farming; gardening.

Atalig (Chamorro) staring.

Atanasio (Greek) immortal.

Atao (Chamorro) sun.

Atau (Quechua) fortunate.

Atauaipa (Quechua) bird of fortune; creator
of fortune.

Atauanca (Quechua) fortunate eagle.

Atauchi (Quechua) he who makes us good
fortunes.

Atchiro (Kosraean) a form of Ichiro.

Atek (Polish) a form of Tanek.

Atenodoro (Greek) gift of wisdom.

Athan (Greek) immortal.
Athen, Athens, Athin, Athon, Athons, Athyn,
Athyns

Atherton (English) town by a spring.
Atharton, Athorton

Athol (Scottish) from Ireland.
Affol, Athal, Athel, Athil, Atholton, Athyl

Atid (Tai) sun.
Atyd

Atif (Arabic) caring.
Ateef, Atef, Atyf

Atik (Chuukese) the name of a fish.

Atila (Gothic) a form of Attila.

Atilano (Spanish) a form of Atila.

Atiniui (Chuukese) man of the sea.

Atirek (Sanskrit) surpassing.

Atish (Sanskrit) great ruler.

Atkins (English) from the home of the
relatives.
Atkin, Atkyn, Atkyns

Atlas (Greek) lifted; carried. Mythology: Atlas
was forced by Zeus to carry the heavens on
his shoulders as a punishment for his share
of the war of the Titans.

Atley (English) meadow.
Atlea, Atlee, Atleigh, Atli, Atlie, Atly, Attlea, Attlee, Attleigh, Attley, Attli, Attlie, Attly

Atma (Sanskrit) the soul.

Ato (Japanese) myself; gift; copper.

Atoc, Atuc (Quechua) sly as a fox; wolf.

Atocuaman (Quechua) he who possesses the strength of a falcon and the shrewdness of a fox.

Atogor, Atogot (Chamorro) forms of Atugud.

Atong (Chuukese) pity.

Atsuhiro (Japanese) developing kindliness.

Atsuo (Japanese) affectionate man.

Atsuyoshi (Japanese) virtuous intentions; affectionate and rare.

Atti (Chamorro) a form of Atti.

Atticus (Latin) from Attica, a region outside Athens.

Attila (Gothic) little father. History: the Hun leader who invaded the Roman Empire.
Atalik, Atila, Atilio, Atilla, Atiya, Attal, Attilah, Attilio, Attyla, Attylah

Atugud (Chamorro) to prop up each other.

Atuguit, Atugus, Atugut (Chamorro) forms of Atugud.

Atwater (English) at the water's edge.
Attwater

Atwell (English) at the well.
Attwel, Atwel

Atwood (English) at the forest.
Attwood

Atworth (English) at the farmstead.
Attworth

Auberon (German) a form of Oberon.
Auberron, Aubrey

Auberto (French) a form of Alberto.

Aubree G (German, French) a form of Aubrey.

Aubrey G (German) noble; bearlike. (French) a familiar form of Auberon.
Aubary, Aube, Aubery, Aubie, Aubré, Aubreii, Aubri, Aubry, Aubury

Aubrie G (German, French) a form of Aubrey.

Auburn (Latin) reddish brown.
Abern, Aberne, Abirn, Abirne, Aburn, Aburne, Abyrn, Abyrne, Aubern, Auberne, Aubin, Aubirn, Aubirne, Aubun, Auburne, Aubyrn, Aubyrne

Auden (English) old friend.
Audan, Audin, Audyn

Audie (German) noble; strong. (English) a familiar form of Edward.
Audee, Audey, Audi, Audiel, Audley, Audy

Audomaro (Greek) famous because of his riches.

Audon (French) old; rich.
Audelon

Audra G (English) a form of Audrey.

Audrey G (English) noble strength.
Audre, Audrea, Audri, Audrius, Audry

Audric (English) wise ruler.
Audrick, Audrik, Audryc, Audryck, Audryk

Audun (Scandinavian) deserted, desolate.

Augie (Latin) a familiar form of August.
Auggie, Augy

August B (Latin) a short form of Augustine, Augustus.
Agosto, Augie, Auguste, Augusto

Augustín (Spanish) a form of Augustine.

Augustine B (Latin) majestic. Religion: Saint Augustine was the first archbishop of Canterbury. See also Austin, Gus, Tino.
Agustin, August, Augusteen, Augustein, Augusteyn, Augusteyne, Augustin, Augustinas, Augustino, Augustyn, Augustyne, Austen, Austin, Auston, Austyn

Augusto (Latin) a form of August.

Augustus (Latin) majestic; venerable. History: an honorary title given to the first Roman emperor, Octavius Caesar.
Agustas, Agustys, August

Aukai (Hawaiian) seafarer.
Aukay

Aundre (Greek) a form of Andre.
Aundrae, Aundray, Aundrea, Aundrey, Aundry

Auqui (Quechua) master; prince.

Auquipuma (Quechua) a prince who is as strong as a puma.

Auquitupac (Quechua) glorious prince.

Auquiyupanqui (Quechua) he who honors his masters.

Aurek (Polish) golden haired.
Aurec

Boys A–F

Aurelia (Latin) gold.

Aurelio (Latin) a short form of Aurelius.
Aurel, Aurele, Aureli, Aurellio

Aurelius (Latin) golden. History: Marcus Aurelius was a second-century A.D. philosopher and emperor of Rome.
Arelian, Areliano, Aurèle, Aureliano, Aurelien, Aurélien, Aurelio, Aurelyus, Aurey, Auriel, Aury

Aurick (German) protecting ruler.
Auric, Aurik, Auryc, Auryck, Auryk

Auseto (Chuukese) come to me.

Austen, Auston, Austyn ⓑ (Latin) short forms of Augustine.
Austan, Austun, Austyne

Austin ♛ ⓑ (Latin) a short form of Augustine.
Astin, Austine, Oistin, Ostin

Austín (Spanish) a form of Augustín.

Autumn ⓖ (Latin) autumn.

Auxilio (Latin) he who saves, who brings help.

Avel (Greek) breath.
Avell

Avelino (Latin) he who was born in Avella, Italy.

Avent (French) born during Advent.
Advent, Aventin, Aventino, Aventyno

Averill (French) born in April.
Ave, Averal, Averall, Averel, Averell, Averiel, Averil, Averyl, Averyll, Avrel, Avrell, Avrill, Avryll

Avery ⓑ (English) a form of Aubrey.
Avary, Aveary, Avere, Averee, Averey, Averi, Averie, Avrey, Avry

Avi (Hebrew) God is my father.
Avian, Avidan, Avidor, Avie, Aviel, Avion, Avy

Avito (Latin) he who is from the grandfather.

Aviv (Hebrew) youth; springtime.

Avneet ⓖ (Hebrew) a form of Avner.

Avner (Hebrew) a form of Abner.
Avniel

Avram (Hebrew) a form of Abraham, Abram.
Arram, Avraam, Avraham, Avrohom, Avrohom, Avrom, Avrum

Avshalom (Hebrew) father of peace. See also Absalom.
Avsalom

Awan (Native American) somebody.

Awes (Chuukese) to call over; finish, end.

Awesh (Sanskrit) excitement.

Axel (Latin) axe. (German) small oak tree; source of life. (Scandinavian) a form of Absalom.
Aksel, Ax, Axe, Axell, Axil, Axill, Axl, Axle, Axyle

Ayar (Quechua) wild quinoa.

Ayden (Irish) a form of Aidan.
Aydean

Aydin (Turkish) intelligent.

Ayers (English) heir to a fortune.

Ayhi (Chamorro) a form of Ayuhi.

Ayig (Chamorro) to choose.

Ayinde (Yoruba) we gave praise and he came.

Aylmer (English) a form of Elmer.
Aillmer, Ailmer, Allmer, Ayllmer

Aymil (Greek) a form of Emil.
Aimil, Aimyl

Aymon (French) a form of Raymond.
Aiman, Aimen, Aimin, Aimyn

Ayo (Yoruba) happiness.

Ayu (Chamorro) that one.

Ayumi (Japanese) walk, step.

Ayumu (Japanese) step, walk; dream.

Ayuyu (Chamorro) coconut crab.

Azaad (Persian) a form of Azad.

Azad (Turkish) free.

Azam (Arabic) the greatest.

Azanías (Hebrew) God hears him.

Azarias (Hebrew) Lord sustains me; divine salvation; God is my soul.

Azarías (Hebrew) Lord sustains and guides me.

Azariel (Hebrew) he who has control over the waters.

Azeem (Arabic) a form of Azim.
Aseem, Asim

Azi (Nigerian) youth.

Azim (Arabic) defender.
Azeem

Aziz (Arabic) strong.

Azizi (Swahili) precious.

Azriel (Hebrew) God is my aid.

Azuriah (Hebrew) aided by God.
Azaria, Azariah, Azuria

Azusa (Japanese) catalpa tree.

B **BG** (American) an initial used as a first name.

Baal (Chaldean) he who dominates a territory; owner and lord.

Babang (Chamorro) butterfly.

Babao (Chamorro) battle flag.

Babaoña (Chamorro) his battle flag.

Babaota (Chamorro) our battle flag.

Babela (Chamorro) moth.

Babeldaob (Palauan) the upper sea; the big island of Palau.

Babul (Sanskrit) relative of the bride.

Bacar (Chamorro) a type of spiny tree.

Bach (Vietnamese) white; clear.

Baco (Greek) he who creates disturbances.

Bada (Korean) sea.

Badahur (Persian) courage, valor; heroism.

Baden (German) bather.
Baeden, Bayden, Baydon

Baek (Korean) white; senior; esteemed; one.

Bahadur (Arabic) brave, bold.

Bahir (Arabic) brilliant, dazzling.

Bahram (Persian) ancient king.

Baiei (Palauan) guest house.

Bailee **G** (French) a form of Bailey.

Bailey **G** (French) bailiff, steward.
Bail, Bailie, Bailio, Baillie, Baily, Bailye, Baley, Bayley

Bain (Irish) a short form of Bainbridge.
Baine, Bayne, Baynn

Bainbridge (Irish) fair bridge.
Bain, Baynbridge, Bayne, Baynebridge

Baird (Irish) traveling minstrel, bard; poet.
Bairde, Bard

Bakar (Arabic) a young camel.

Bakari (Swahili) noble promise.
Bacari, Baccari, Bakarie

Baker (English) baker. See also Baxter.
Bakir, Bakory, Bakr

Bakin, Bakusui (Japanese) literary figures.

Baklai (Maranao) a form of Baklay.

Baklay (Maranao) walking, strolling; traveling.

Bal (Sanskrit) child born with lots of hair.

Balasi (Basque) flat footed.

Balbino (Latin) he who mumbles, who speaks in a stammering manner.

Balbo (Latin) stammerer.
Bailby, Balbi, Ballbo

Baldemar (German) bold; famous.
Baldemer, Baldomero, Baumar, Baumer

Balder (Scandinavian) bald. Mythology: the Norse god of light, summer, purity, and innocence.
Baldier, Baldur, Baudier

Baldesar (Pohnpeian) a form of Baltazar.

Baldovín (Spanish) a form of Balduino.

Baldric (German) brave ruler.
Baldrick, Baudric

Balduino (Germanic) valiant friend.

Baldwin (German) bold friend.
Bald, Baldovino, Balduin, Baldwinn, Baldwyn, Baldwynn, Balldwin, Baudoin

Balfour (Scottish) pastureland.
Balfor, Balfore

Balin (Hindi) mighty soldier.
Bali, Baylen, Baylin, Baylon, Valin

Ballard (German) brave; strong.
Balard

Balraj (Hindi) strongest.

Baltazar (Greek) a form of Balthasar.
Baltasar

Balthasar (Greek) God save the king. Bible: one of the three wise men who bore gifts for the infant Jesus.
Badassare, Baldassare, Baltazar, Balthasaar, Balthazar, Balthazzar, Baltsaros, Belshazar, Belshazzar, Boldizsár

Balu (Sanskrit) child, baby; boy; strength.

Bancroft (English) bean field.
Ban, Bancrofft, Bank, Bankroft, Banky, Binky

Bandemar (Chuukese) a form of Baldemar.

Bandi 🅱🅶 (Hungarian) a form of Andrew.
Bandit

Bandrik (Marshallese) too small to do it.

Bane (Hawaiian) a form of Bartholomew.

Bang (Chinese) nation; state.

Bangoña (Chamorro) he wakes up.

Banner (Scottish, English) flag bearer.
Bannor, Banny

Banning (Irish) small and fair.
Bannie, Banny

Baplo (Chuukese) a form of Pablo.

Barak (Hebrew) lightning bolt. Bible: the valiant warrior who helped Deborah.
Barrak

Baran (Russian) ram.
Baren

Barasa (Kikuyu) meeting place.

Barclay (Scottish, English) birch-tree meadow.
Bar, Barcley, Barklay, Barkley, Barklie, Barrclay, Berkeley

Bard (Irish) a form of Baird.
Bar, Barde, Bardia, Bardiya, Barr

Bardolf (German) bright wolf.
Bardo, Bardolph, Bardou, Bardoul, Bardulf, Bardulph

Bardrick (Teutonic) axe ruler.
Bardric, Bardrik

Baris (Turkish) peaceful.

Barkat (Persian) blessing; abundance; prosperity.

Barker (English) lumberjack; advertiser at a carnival.

Barlow (English) bare hillside.
Barlowe, Barrlow, Barrlowe

Barnabas (Greek, Hebrew, Aramaic, Latin) son of the missionary. Bible: Christian apostle and companion of Paul on his first missionary journey.
Bane, Barna, Barnaba, Barnabus, Barnaby, Barnebas, Barnebus, Barney

Barnaby (English) a form of Barnabas.
Barnabe, Barnabé, Barnabee, Barnabey, Barnabi, Barnabie, Bernabé, Burnaby

Barnard (French) a form of Bernard.
Barn, Barnard, Barnhard, Barnhardo

Barnes (English) bear; son of Barnett.

Barnett (English) nobleman; leader.
Barn, Barnet, Barney, Baronet, Baronett, Barrie, Barron, Barry

Barney (English) a familiar form of Barnabas, Barnett.
Barnie, Barny

Barnum (German) barn; storage place. (English) baron's home.
Barnham

Baron (German, English) nobleman, baron.
Baaron, Barion, Baronie, Barrin, Barrion, Barron, Baryn, Bayron, Berron

Barrett 🅱 (German) strong as a bear.
Bar, Baret, Barrat, Barret, Barretta, Barrette, Barry, Berrett, Berrit

Barric (English) grain farm.
Barrick, Beric, Berric, Berrick, Berrik

Barrington (English) fenced town.
Geography: a town in England.

Barry 🅱 (Welsh) son of Harry. (Irish) spear, marksman. (French) gate, fence.
Baris, Barri, Barrie, Barris, Bary

Bart (Hebrew) a short form of Bartholomew, Barton.
Barrt, Bartel, Bartie, Barty

Bartholomew (Hebrew) son of Talmaí.
Bible: one of the Twelve Apostles. See also Jerney, Parlan, Parthalán.
Balta, Bane, Bart, Bartek, Barth, Barthel, Barthelemy, Barthélemy, Barthélmy, Bartho, Bartholo, Bartholomaus, Bartholome, Bartholomeo, Bartholomeus, Bartholómieu, Bartimous, Bartlet, Barto, Bartolome, Bartolomé, Bartolomeo, Bartolomeð, Bartolommeo, Bartome, Bartz, Bat

Bartlet (English) a form of Bartholomew.
Bartlett, Bartley

Barto (Spanish) a form of Bartholomew.
Bardo, Bardol, Bartol, Bartoli, Bartolo, Bartos

Barton (English) barley town; Bart's town.
Barrton, Bart

Bartram (English) a form of Bertram.
Barthram

Baruc (Hebrew) he who is blessed by God.

Baruch (Hebrew) blessed.
Boruch

Basaant (Sanskrit) spring; garland of yellow flowers.

Basam (Arabic) smiling.
Basem, Basim, Bassam

Basho (Japanese) literary figure.

Basil (Greek, Latin) royal, kingly. Religion: a saint and founder of monasteries. Botany: an herb often used in cooking. See also Vasilis, Wasili.
Bas, Basal, Base, Baseal, Basel, Basle, Basile, Basilio, Basilios, Basilius, Bassel, Bazek, Bazel, Bazil, Bazyli

Basir (Turkish) intelligent, discerning.
Bashar, Basheer, Bashir, Bashiyr, Bechir, Bhasheer

Bassett (English) little person.
Basett, Basit, Basset, Bassit

Bastien (German) a short form of Sebastian.
Baste, Bastiaan, Bastian, Bastion

Basudeo (Sanskrit) lord of the earth.

Bat (English) a short form of Bartholomew.

Baudilio (Teutonic) he who is brave and valiant.

Baul (Gypsy) snail.

Baulis (Tagalog) one with the power of the evil eye.

Bautista (Greek) he who baptizes.

Bavol (Gypsy) wind; air.

Baxter (English) a form of Baker.
Bax, Baxie, Baxty, Baxy

Bay (Vietnamese) seventh son. (French) chestnut brown color; evergreen tree. (English) howler.

Bayani (Tagalog) hero.

Bayard (English) reddish brown hair.
Baiardo, Bay, Bayardo, Bayerd, Bayrd

Baylee **G** (French) a form of Bayley.

Bayley **G** (French) a form of Bailey.
Bayleigh, Baylie, Bayly

Beacan (Irish) small.
Beacán, Becan

Beacher (English) beech trees.
Beach, Beachy, Beech, Beecher, Beechy

Beagan (Irish) small.
Beagen, Beagin

Beale (French) a form of Beau.
Beal, Beall, Bealle, Beals

Beaman (English) beekeeper.
Beamann, Beamen, Beeman, Beman

Beamer (English) trumpet player.

Beasley (English) field of peas.

Beatriz **G** (Latin) a form of Beatrice (see Girls' Names).

Beattie (Latin) blessed; happy; bringer of joy.
Beatie, Beatty, Beaty

Beau **B** (French) handsome.
Beale, Beaux, Bo

Beaufort (French) beautiful fort.

Beaumont (French) beautiful mountain.

Beauregard (French) handsome; beautiful; well regarded.

Beaver (English) beaver.
Beav, Beavo, Beve, Bevo

Bebe **BG** (Spanish) baby.

Beches (Palauan) new, clean; straight.

Beck (English, Scandinavian) brook.
Beckett

Beda (Teutonic) he who orders and provides for.

Bede (English) prayer. Religion: the patron saint of lectors.

Bedinin (Marshallese) to stay on this island.

Bedro (Pohnpeian) a form of Pedro.

Bei (Chinese) north.

Bekebekmad (Palauan) one who is pleasing to the eye.

Beketaut (Palauan) good at shooting.

Bela **BG** (Czech) white. (Hungarian) bright.
Béla, Belaal, Belal, Belall, Belay, Bellal

Belarmino (Germanic) having beautiful armor.

Belau (Palauan) the island of Palau.

Belden (French, English) pretty valley.
Beldin, Beldon, Bellden, Belldon

Belechel (Palauan) good with a slingshot.

Belen **G** (Greek) arrow.

Belengel (Palauan) middle.

Belisario (Greek) he who shoots arrows skillfully.

Bell (French) handsome. (English) bell ringer.

Bellamy (French) beautiful friend.
Belamy, Bell, Bellamey, Bellamie

Bello (African) helper or promoter of Islam.

Belmiro (Portuguese) good-looking; attractive.

Bem (Tiv) peace.
Behm

Ben (Hebrew) a short form of Benjamin.
Behn, Benio, Benn, Benne, Benno

Ben Zion (Hebrew) son of Zion.
Benson, Benzi

Ben-ami (Hebrew) son of my people.
Baram, Barami

Bendicion, Benedicion (Chamorro) forms of Bendision.

Bendision (Chamorro) blessed.

Benedict (Latin) blessed. See also Venedictos, Venya.
Benci, Bendick, Bendict, Bendino, Bendix, Bendrick, Benedetto, Benedick, Benedicto, Benedictus, Benedikt, Bengt, Benito, Benoit

Benedikt (German, Slavic) a form of Benedict.
Bendek, Bendik, Benedek, Benedik

Bengt (Scandinavian) a form of Benedict.
Beng, Benke, Bent

Beniam (Ethiopian) a form of Benjamin.
Beneyam, Beniamin, Beniamino

Benicio (Latin) riding friend.

Benido (Pohnpeian) a form of Bonito.

Benigno (Latin) prodigal son; he who does good deeds.

Benijamini (Fijian) a form of Benjamin.

Benildo (Teutonic) fights against bears.

Benito (Italian) a form of Benedict. History: Benito Mussolini led Italy during World War II.
Benedo, Benino, Benno, Beno, Betto, Beto

Benjamen (Hebrew) a form of Benjamin.
Benejamen, Benjermen, Benjjmen

Benjamin ☙ **B** (Hebrew) son of my right hand. See also Peniamina, Veniamin.
Behnjamin, Bejamin, Bemjiman, Ben, Benejaminas, Bengamin, Beniam, Benja, Benjahmin, Benjaim, Benjam, Benjamaim, Benjaman, Benjamen, Benjamine, Benjaminn, Benjamino, Benjamon, Benjamyn, Benjamynn, Benjemin, Benjermain, Benjermin, Benji, Benjie, Benjiman, Benjy, Benkamin, Bennjamin, Benny, Benyamin, Benyamino, Binyamin, Mincho

Benjamín (Hebrew) a form of Benjamin.

Benjiman (Hebrew) a form of Benjamin.
Benjimen, Benjimin, Benjimon, Benjmain

Benjir (Japanese) peaceful, to enjoy peace.

Benjiro (Japanese) enjoys peace.

Bennett **B** (Latin) little blessed one.
Benet, Benett, Bennet, Benette, Bennete, Bennette

Benny (Hebrew) a familiar form of Benjamin.
Bennie

Beno (Hebrew) son. (Mwera) band member.

Benoit (French) a form of Benedict.
Benott

Benoni (Hebrew) son of my sorrow. Bible: Ben-oni was the son of Jacob and Rachel.
Ben-Oni

Benson (Hebrew) son of Ben. A short form of Ben Zion.
Bensan, Bensen, Benssen, Bensson

Bentley (English) moor; coarse grass meadow.
Bent, Bentlea, Bentlee, Bentlie, Lee

Benton (English) Ben's town; town on the moors.
Bent

Benzi (Hebrew) a familiar form of Ben Zion.

Beouch (Palauan) title of chiefs in Ngardmau.

Beppe (Italian) a form of Joseph.
Beppy

Ber (English) boundary. (Yiddish) bear.

Berardo (Germanic) a form of Bernard.

Bercy (Pohnpeian) a form of Percy.

Beredei (Russian) a form of Hubert.
Berdry, Berdy, Beredej, Beredy

Berenguer (Teutonic) bear that is prepared for battle.

Berg (German) mountain.
Berdj, Berge, Bergh, Berje

Bergen (German, Scandinavian) hill dweller.
Bergin, Birgin

Berger (French) shepherd.

Bergren (Scandinavian) mountain stream.
Berg

Berk (Turkish) solid, rugged.

Berkeley (English) a form of Barclay.
Berk, Berkely, Berkie, Berkley, Berklie, Berkly, Berky

Berl (German) a form of Burl.
Berle, Berlie, Berlin, Berlyn

Berlyn (German) boundary line. See also Burl.
Berlin, Burlin

Bern (German) a short form of Bernard.
Berne

Bernadette **G** (French) a form of Bernadine (see Girls' Names).

Bernal (German) strong as a bear.
Bernald, Bernaldo, Bernel, Bernhald, Bernhold, Bernold

Bernaldino (German) strong bear.

Bernard (German) brave as a bear. See also Bjorn.
Barnard, Bear, Bearnard, Benek, Ber, Berend, Bern, Bernabé, Bernadas, Bernardel, Bernardin, Bernardo, Bernardus, Bernardyn, Bernarr, Bernat, Bernek, Bernal, Bernel, Bernerd, Berngards, Bernhard, Bernhards, Bernhardt, Bernie, Bjorn, Burnard

Bernardo (Spanish) a form of Bernard.
Barnardino, Barnardo, Barnhardo, Benardo, Bernardino, Bernhardo, Berno, Burnardo, Nardo

Bernie (German) a familiar form of Bernard.
Berney, Berni, Berny, Birney, Birnie, Birny, Burney

Berry (English) berry; grape.
Berrie

Bersh (Gypsy) one year.

Bert (German, English) bright, shining. A short form of Berthold, Berton, Bertram, Bertrand, Egbert, Filbert.
Bertie, Bertus, Birt, Burt

Berthold (German) bright; illustrious; brilliant ruler.
Bert, Berthoud, Bertold, Bertolde

Bertie (English) a familiar form of Bert, Egbert.
Berty, Birt, Birtie, Birty

Bertín (Spanish) distinguished friend.
Berti

Berto (Spanish) a short form of Alberto.

Bertoldo (Germanic) splendid boss.

Berton (English) bright settlement; fortified town.
Bert

Bertram (German) bright; illustrious. (English) bright raven. See also Bartram.
Beltran, Beltrán, Beltrano, Bert, Berton, Bertrae, Bertraim, Bertraum, Bertron

Bertrand (German) bright shield.
Bert, Bertran, Bertrando, Bertranno

Bertulfo (Teutonic) warrior who shines.

Berwyn (Welsh) white head.
Berwin, Berwynn, Berwynne

Besarión (Greek) walker.

Besebes (Palauan) vine used for tying and binding.

Betsabé (Hebrew) oath of God.

Bevan (Welsh) son of Evan.
Beavan, Beaven, Beavin, Bev, Beve, Beven, Bevin, Bevo, Bevon

Beverly **G** (English) beaver meadow.
Beverlea, Beverleigh, Beverley, Beverlie

Bevis (French) from Beauvais, France; bull.
Beauvais, Bevys

Bhag (Sanskrit) fate, divine power; glory.

Bhagwandas (Hindi) servant of God.

Bhagwanjee (Sanskrit) God; fortunate, prosperous.

Bhagwanji (Sanskrit) a form of Bhagwanjee.

Bhai (Sanskrit) brother, kinsman.

Bhan (Sanskrit) brightness; sun; master; planet.

Bharkat (Persian) a form of Barkat.

Bhisham (Sanskrit) valiant; superlative.

Bhup (Sanskrit) earth guardian.

Bi (Chinese) green jade.

Bian (Chinese) discriminating.

Bianca **G** (Italian) white.

Biao (Chinese) young tiger.

Bibi (Fijian) heavy.

Bibiano (Spanish) small man.

Bich (Vietnamese) a jewel.

Bickford (English) axe-man's ford.

Boys A–F

Bien (Vietnamese) ocean, sea.

Bienvenido (Filipino) welcome.

Bijan (Persian) ancient hero.
Bihjan, Bijann, Bijhan, Bijhon, Bijon

Bilal (Arabic) chosen.
Bila, Bilaal, Bilale, Bile, Bilel, Billaal, Billal

Bill (German) a short form of William.
Bil, Billee, Billijo, Billye, Byll, Will

Billie 🄶 (German) a form of Billy.

Billiem (Pohnpeian) a form of William.

Billy 🄱 (German) a familiar form of Bill, William.
Bille, Billey, Billie, Billy, Bily, Willie

Binah (Hebrew) understanding; wise.
Bina

Bing (German) kettle-shaped hollow.

Bingo (Chamorro) to bud.

Bing-Qing (Chinese) ice; crystal clear.

Binh (Vietnamese) peaceful.

Binkentios (Greek) a form of Vincent.

Binky (English) a familiar form of Bancroft, Vincent.
Bink, Binkentios, Binkie

Birch (English) white; shining; birch tree.
Birk, Burch

Birger (Norwegian) rescued.

Birkey (English) island with birch trees.
Birk, Birkie, Birky

Birkitt (English) birch-tree coast.
Birk, Birket, Birkit, Burket, Burkett, Burkitt

Birley (English) meadow with the cow barn.
Birlee, Birlie, Birly

Birney (English) island with a brook.
Birne, Birnie, Birny, Burney, Burnie, Burny

Birtle (English) hill with birds.

Bishamon (Japanese) god of war.

Bishop (Greek) overseer. (English) bishop.
Bish, Bishup

Bitang (Palauan) one half.

Bjorn (Scandinavian) a form of Bernard.
Bjarne

Blacheos (Palauan) a kind of tree in the verbena family.

Blackburn (Scottish) black brook.

Blade (English) knife, sword.
Bladen, Bladon, Bladyn, Blae, Blaed, Blayde

Bladimir (Russian) a form of Vladimir.
Bladimer

Bladimiro (Slavic) prince of peace.

Blaine 🄱 (Irish) thin, lean. (English) river source.
Blain, Blane, Blayne

Blair 🄱🄶 (Irish) plain, field. (Welsh) place.
Blaire, Blare, Blayr, Blayre

Blaise, Blaize 🄱 (French) forms of Blaze.
Ballas, Balyse, Blais, Blaisot, Blas, Blase, Blasi, Blasien, Blasius, Blass, Blaz, Blaze, Blayz, Blayze, Blayzz

Blake 🌱 🄱 (English) attractive; dark.
Blaik, Blaike, Blakely, Blakeman, Blakey, Blayke

Blakely 🄱🄶 (English) dark meadow.
Blakelee, Blakeleigh, Blakeley, Blakelie, Blakelin, Blakelyn, Blakeny, Blakley, Blakney

Blanca 🄶 (Italian) a form of Bianca.

Blanco (Spanish) light skinned; white; blond.

Blandino (Latin) he who is flattered.

Blane (Irish) a form of Blaine.
Blaney, Blanne

Blasco (Latin) of a pale color.

Blayne (Irish) a form of Blaine.
Blayn, Blayney

Blaze (Latin) stammerer. (English) flame; trail mark made on a tree.
Balázs, Biaggio, Biagio, Blaise, Blaize, Blazen, Blazer

Blekeu (Palauan) courage.

Bliss 🄶 (English) blissful; joyful.

Blodk (Palauan) cut, slit.

Blosech (Palauan) unusual, strange.

Bloyang (Palauan) he who has been split or cracked.

Blu (Chuukese) blue.

Bly (Native American) high.

Blythe 🄶 (English) carefree; merry, joyful.
Blithe, Blyth

Bo 🄱 (English) a form of Beau, Beauregard. (German) a form of Bogart.
Boe

Boaz (Hebrew) swift; strong.
Bo, Boas, Booz, Bos, Boz

Bob (English) a short form of Robert.
Bobb, Bobby, Bobek, Rob

Bobbi, Bobbie **G** (English) a form of Bobby.

Bobby **B** (English) a familiar form of Bob, Robert.
Bobbey, Bobbie, Bobbye, Boby

Bobek (Czech) a form of Bob, Robert.

Bobi (English) a form of Bobby.

Bobong, Bong (Tagalog) forms of Bongbong.

Bobot, Boboy (Tagalog) forms of Bongbong.

Boden (Scandinavian) sheltered. (French) messenger, herald.
Bodie, Bodin, Bodine, Bodyne, Boe

Bodie (Scandinavian) a familiar form of Boden.
Boddie, Bode, Bodee, Bodey, Bodhi, Bodi, Boedee, Boedi, Boedy

Bodil (Norwegian) mighty ruler.

Bodua (Akan) animal's tail.

Boecio (Greek) he who helps; the defender, who goes into battle ready.

Bogart (German) strong as a bow. (Irish, Welsh) bog, marshland.
Bo, Bogey, Bogie, Bogy

Bohdan (Ukrainian) a form of Donald.
Bogdan, Bogdashka, Bogdon, Bohden, Bohdon

Bokusui, Bokuyo (Japanese) literary figures.

Boleslao (Slavic) most glorious of the glorious.

Bonaro (Italian, Spanish) friend.
Bona, Bonar

Bonaventure (Italian) good luck.

Bond (English) tiller of the soil.
Bondie, Bondon, Bonds, Bondy

Bongbong (Tagalog) boy; junior.

Bon-Hwa (Korean) glorious.

Bonie (Tagalog) a form of Bongbong.

Boniface (Latin) do-gooder.
Bonifacio, Bonifacius, Bonifacy

Boo (Korean) help, support; father; wealth.

Booker (English) bookmaker; book lover; Bible lover.
Bookie, Books, Booky

Boone (Latin, French) good. History: Daniel Boone was an American pioneer.
Bon, Bone, Bonne, Boonie, Boony

Booth (English) hut. (Scandinavian) temporary dwelling.
Boot, Boote, Boothe

Borak (Arabic) lightning. Mythology: the horse that carried Muhammad to seventh heaven.

Boram (Korean) worth.

Borden (French) cottage. (English) valley of the boar; boar's den.
Bord, Bordie, Bordy

Boreas (Greek) north wind.

Borg (Scandinavian) castle.

Boris (Slavic) battler, warrior. Religion: the patron saint of Moscow, princes, and Russia.
Boriss, Borja, Borris, Borya, Boryenka, Borys

Borka (Russian) fighter.
Borkinka

Boromeo (Italian) a good Roman.

Boseda (Tiv) born on Saturday.

Bosley (English) grove of trees.

Botan (Japanese) blossom, bud.

Bourey (Cambodian) country.

Bourne (Latin, French) boundary. (English) brook, stream.

Boutros (Arabic) a form of Peter.

Bowen (Welsh) son of Owen.
Bow, Bowe, Bowie

Bowie (Irish) yellow haired. History: James Bowie was an American-born Mexican colonist who died during the defense of the Alamo.
Bow, Bowen

Boyce (French) woods, forest.
Boice, Boise, Boy, Boycey, Boycie

Boyd (Scottish) yellow haired.
Boid, Boyde

Brad **B** (English) a short form of Bradford, Bradley.
Bradd, Brade

Bradburn (English) broad stream.

Braden **B** (English) broad valley.
Bradan, Bradden, Bradeon, Bradin, Bradine, Bradyn, Braeden, Braiden, Brayden, Bredan, Bredon

Bradford (English) broad river crossing.
Brad, Braddford, Ford

Bradlee (English) a form of Bradley.
Bradlea, Bradleigh, Bradlie

Bradley B (English) broad meadow.
*Brad, Braddly, Bradlay, Bradlee, Bradly,
Bradlyn, Bradney*

Bradly (English) a form of Bradley.

Bradon (English) broad hill.
Braedon, Braidon, Braydon

Bradshaw (English) broad forest.

Brady B (Irish) spirited. (English) broad
island.
Bradey, Bradi, Bradie, Bradye, Braidy

Bradyn (English) a form of Braden.
Bradynne, Breidyn

Braedan (English) a form of Braeden.

Braeden, Braiden B (English) forms of
Braden.
Braedin, Braedyn, Braidyn

Braedon (English) a form of Bradon.
Breadon

Bragi (Scandinavian) poet. Mythology: the
god of poetry, eloquence, and song.
Brage

Braham (Hindi) creator.
Braheem, Braheim, Brahiem, Brahima, Brahm

Brainard (English) bold raven; prince.
Brainerd

Bram (Scottish) bramble, brushwood.
(Hebrew) a short form of Abraham, Abram.
Brame, Bramm, Bramdon

Bramwell (English) bramble spring.
Brammel, Brammell, Bramwel, Bramwyll

Branch (Latin) paw; claw; tree branch.

Brand (English) firebrand; sword. A short
form of Brandon.
*Brandall, Brande, Brandel, Brandell, Brander,
Brandley, Brandol, Brandt, Brandy, Brann*

Brandan B (English) a form of Brandon.

Brandeis (Czech) dweller on a burned
clearing.
Brandis

Branden (English) beacon valley.
*Brandden, Brandene, Brandin, Brandine,
Brandyn, Breandan*

Brandi G (Dutch, English) a form of
Brandy.

Brandon W B (English) beacon hill.
*Bran, Brand, Branddon, Brandone, Brandonn,
Brandyn, Branndan, Branndon, Brannon,
Breandon, Brendon*

Brandt (English) a form of Brant.

Brandy G (Dutch) brandy. (English) a
familiar form of Brand.
Branddy, Brandey, Brandi, Brandie

Brandyn (English) a form of Branden,
Brandon.
Brandynn

Brannon (Irish) a form of Brandon.
Branen, Brannan, Brannen, Branon

Branson (English) son of Brandon, Brant. A
form of Bronson.
Bransen, Bransin, Brantson

Brant (English) proud.
Brandt, Brannt, Brante, Brantley, Branton

Brantley B (English) a form of Brant.
Brantlie, Brantly, Brentlee, Brentley, Brently

Braulio (Italian) a form of Brawley.
Brauli, Brauliuo

Brawley (English) meadow on the hillside.
Braulio, Brawlee, Brawly

Braxton B (English) Brock's town.
*Brax, Braxdon, Braxston, Braxten, Braxtin,
Braxxton*

Brayan (Irish, Scottish) a form of Brian.
Brayn, Brayon

Brayden W B (English) a form of Braden.
*Braydan, Braydn, Bradyn, Breydan, Breyden,
Brydan, Bryden*

Braydon B (English) a form of Bradon.
Braydoon, Brydon, Breydon

Breana, Breanna G (Irish) forms of
Briana.

Breann, Breanne G (Irish) short forms of
Briana.

Breck BG (Irish) freckled.
*Brec, Breckan, Brecken, Breckie, Breckin,
Breckke, Breckyn, Brek, Brexton*

Brede (Scandinavian) iceberg, glacier.

Brencis (Latvian) a form of Lawrence.
Brence

Brenda G (Irish) little raven. (English)
sword.

Brendan B (Irish) little raven. (English) sword.
Breandan, Bren, Brenden, Brendis, Brendon, Brendyn, Brenn, Brennan, Brennen, Brenndan, Brenyan, Bryn

Brenden B (Irish) a form of Brendan.
Bren, Brendene, Brendin, Brendine, Brennden

Brendon (English) a form of Brandon. (Irish, English) a form of Brendan.
Brenndon

Brenna G (English, Irish) a form of Brennan.

Brennan, Brennen B (English, Irish) forms of Brendan.
Bren, Brenan, Brenen, Brenin, Brenn, Brennann, Brenner, Brennin, Brennon, Brennor, Brennyn, Brenon

Brent (English) a short form of Brenton.
Brendt, Brente, Brentson, Brentt

Brenton B (English) steep hill.
Brent, Brentan, Brenten, Brentin, Brentten, Brentton, Brentyn

Breogán (Spanish) indicative of family or origin.

Breon B (Irish, Scottish) a form of Brian.

Bret, Brett B (Scottish) from Great Britain. See also Britton.
Bhrett, Braten, Braton, Brayton, Bretin, Bretley, Bretlin, Breton, Brettan, Brette, Bretten, Bretton, Brit, Britt

Brewster (English) brewer.
Brew, Brewer, Bruwster

Breyon (Irish, Scottish) a form of Brian.
Breyan

Brian �轨 B (Irish, Scottish) strong; virtuous; honorable. History: Brian Boru was an eleventh-century Irish king and national hero. See also Palaina.
Brayan, Breyon, Briann, Briano, Briant, Briante, Briaun, Briayan, Brien, Brience, Brient, Brin, Briny, Brion, Bryan, Bryen

Briana G (Irish, Scottish) a form of Brian.

Brianna G (Irish, Scottish) a form of Brian.

Brianne G (Irish, Scottish) a form of Brian.

Briar (French) heather.
Brier, Brierly, Bryar, Bryer, Bryor

Brice B (Welsh) alert; ambitious. (English) son of Rice.
Bricen, Briceton, Bryce

Bricio (Celtic) represents strength.

Brick (English) bridge.
Bricker, Bricklen, Brickman, Brik

Bridger (English) bridge builder.
Bridd, Bridge, Bridgeley, Bridgely

Bridget G (Irish) strong.

Brielle G (French) a form of Brie (see Girls' Names).

Brigham (English) covered bridge. (French) troops, brigade.
Brig, Brigg, Briggs, Brighton

Brighton (English) bright town.
Breighton, Bright, Brightin, Bryton

Brigido (Celtic) the high one; strength.

Brij (Sanskrit) cattle shed.

Brion (Irish, Scottish) a form of Brian.
Brieon, Brione, Brionn, Brionne

Brit, Britt (Scottish) forms of Bret, Brett. See also Britton.
Brit, Brityce

Britany, Brittany G (English) from Britain.

Britney, Brittney, Brittny G (English) forms of Britany.

Britton (Scottish) from Great Britain. See also Bret, Brett, Brit, Britt.
Britain, Briten, Britian, Britin, Briton, Brittain, Brittan, Britten, Brittian, Brittin, Britton

Brock B (English) badger.
Broc, Brocke, Brockett, Brockie, Brockley, Brockton, Brocky, Brok, Broque

Brod (English) a short form of Broderick.
Brode, Broden

Broderick (Welsh) son of the famous ruler. (English) broad ridge. See also Roderick.
Brod, Broddie, Brodderick, Brodderrick, Broddy, Broderic, Broderrick, Brodrick

Brodie B (Irish) a form of Brody.
Brodi, Broedi

Brodrick (Welsh, English) a form of Broderick.
Broddrick, Brodric, Brodryck

Brody B (Irish) ditch; canal builder.
Brodee, Broden, Brodey, Brodie, Broedy

Brogan (Irish) a heavy work shoe.
Brogen, Broghan, Broghen

Bromley (English) brushwood meadow.

Bron (Afrikaans) source.

Bronislaw (Polish) weapon of glory.

Boys A–F

Bronson (English) son of Brown.
Bransen, Bransin, Branson, Bron, Bronnie, Bronnson, Bronny, Bronsan, Bronsen, Bronsin, Bronsonn, Bronsson, Bronsun, Bronsyn, Brunson

Bronwyn G (Welsh) white breasted.

Brook G (English) brook, stream.
Brooker, Brookin

Brooke G (English) a form of Brook.

Brooklyn, Brooklynn G (American) combinations of Brook + Lynn.

Brooks B (English) son of Brook.
Brookes, Broox

Brown (English) brown; bear.

Bruce B (French) brushwood thicket; woods.
Brucey, Brucy, Brue, Bruis

Bruno (German, Italian) brown haired; brown skinned.
Brunon, Bruns

Bryan W (Irish) a form of Brian.
Brayan, Bryann, Bryant, Bryen

Bryana, Bryanna G (Irish) forms of Bryan.

Bryanne (Irish) a form of Bryan.

Bryant (Irish) a form of Bryan.
Bryent

Bryce B (Welsh) a form of Brice.
Brycen, Bryceton, Bryson, Bryston

Bryden B (English) a form of Brayden.

Brylee G (American) a combination of the letter B + Riley.

Brynn G (German) a form of Bryon.

Bryon (German) cottage. (English) bear.
Bryeon, Bryn, Bryne, Brynne, Bryone

Bryson B (Welsh) child of Brice.

Bryton B (English) a form of Brighton.
Brayten, Brayton, Breyton, Bryeton, Brytan, Bryten, Brytin, Brytten, Brytton

Bu (Vietnamese) leader.

Bubba (German) a boy.
Babba, Babe, Bebba

Buck (German, English) male deer.
Buckie, Buckley, Buckner, Bucko, Bucky

Buckley (English) deer meadow.
Bucklea, Bucklee

Buckminster (English) preacher.

Bud (English) herald, messenger.
Budd, Buddy

Buddy (American) a familiar form of Bud.
Budde, Buddey, Buddie

Buell (German) hill dweller. (English) bull.

Buenaventura (Latin) he who predicts happiness.

Buford (English) ford near the castle.
Burford

Bujen (Marshallese) promise.

Bum (Korean) law, rule; pattern, model.

Burcardo (Germanic) daring protector; the defender of the fortress.

Burgess (English) town dweller; shopkeeper.
Burg, Burges, Burgh, Burgiss, Burr

Burian (Ukrainian) lives near weeds.

Burke (German, French) fortress, castle.
Berk, Berke, Birk, Bourke, Burk, Burkley

Burl (English) cup bearer; wine servant; knot in a tree. (German) a short form of Berlyn.
Berl, Burley, Burlie, Byrle

Burleigh (English) meadow with knotted tree trunks.
Burlee, Burley, Burlie, Byrleigh, Byrlee

Burne (English) brook.
Beirne, Burn, Burnell, Burnett, Burney, Byrn, Byrne

Burney (English) island with a brook. A familiar form of Rayburn.

Burr (Swedish) youth. (English) prickly plant.

Burris (English) town dweller.

Burt (English) a form of Bert. A short form of Burton.
Burrt, Burtt, Burty

Burton (English) fortified town.
Berton, Burt

Busby (Scottish) village in the thicket; tall military hat made of fur.
Busbee, Buzby, Buzz

Buster (American) hitter, puncher.

Butch (American) a short form of Butcher.

Butcher (English) butcher.
Butch

Buuch (Palauan) betel nut.

Buyugo (Chamorro) coaxing; flattering.

Buzz (Scottish) a short form of Busby.
Buzzy

Bwijtak (Marshallese) school of needlefish.

Byford (English) by the ford.

Byochel (Palauan) to be sifted, winnowed.

Byong (Korean) brilliant.

Byram (English) cattle yard.

Byrd (English) birdlike.
Bird, Birdie, Byrdie

Byrne (English) a form of Burne.
Byrn, Byrnes

Byron (French) cottage. (English) barn.
*Beyren, Beyron, Biren, Biron, Buiron, Byram,
Byran, Byrann, Byren, Byrom, Byrone*

Byung (Korean) third; soldier; protection.

C

C **BG** (American) an initial used as a first
name.

Cable (French, English) rope maker.
Cabell

Caca (Chamorro) crack, crevice.

Cachayauri (Quechua) hard as a shard of
copper; sharp as a spine or needle.

Cadao (Vietnamese) folksong.

Cadassi (Chamorro) to have something of
the sea.

Cadby (English) warrior's settlement.

Caddock (Welsh) eager for war.

Cade **B** (Welsh) a short form of Cadell.
Cady

Cadell (Welsh) battler.
Cade, Cadel, Cedell

Caden 🌱 **B** (American) a form of Kadin.
*Cadan, Caddon, Cadian, Cadien, Cadin,
Cadon, Cadyn, Caeden, Caedon, Caid, Caiden,
Cayden*

Cadeo (Vietnamese) folk song.

Cadmus (Greek) from the east. Mythology: a
Phoenician prince who founded Thebes and
introduced writing to the Greeks.

Caelan (Scottish) a form of Nicholas.
*Cael, Caelon, Caelyn, Cailan, Cailean, Caillan,
Cailun, Cailyn, Calan, Calen, Caleon, Caley,
Calin, Callan, Callon, Callyn, Calon, Calyn,
Caylan, Cayley*

Caesar (Latin) long-haired. History: a title
for Roman emperors. See also Kaiser, Kesar,
Sarito.
*Caesarae, Caesear, Caeser, Caezar, Caseare,
Ceasar, Cesar, Ceseare, Cezar, Cézar, Czar,
Seasar*

Cahil (Turkish) young, naive.

Cai (Welsh) a form of Gaius.
Caio, Caius, Caw

Caifas (Assyrian) man of little energy.

Cain (Hebrew) spear; gatherer. Bible: Adam
and Eve's oldest son. See also Kabil, Kane,
Kayne.
*Cainaen, Cainan, Caine, Cainen, Caineth,
Cayn, Cayne*

Caín (Hebrew) a form of Cain.

Cairn (Welsh) landmark made of a mound of
stones.
Cairne, Carn, Carne

Cairo (Arabic) Geography: the capital of
Egypt.
Kairo

Cais (Vietnamese) one who rejoices.

Caitlin **G** (Irish) pure.

Caiya (Quechua) close, nearby; unique.

Calder (Welsh, English) brook, stream.

Caldwell (English) cold well.

Cale (Hebrew) a short form of Caleb.

Caleb 🌱 **B** (Hebrew) dog; faithful.
(Arabic) bold, brave. Bible: one of the twelve
spies sent by Moses. See also Kaleb, Kayleb.
*Caeleb, Calab, Calabe, Cale, Caley, Calib,
Calieb, Callob, Calob, Calyb, Cayleb, Caylebb,
Caylib, Caylob*

Caleigh **G** (Irish) a form of Caley.

Calen, Calin (Scottish) forms of Caelan.
*Caelen, Caelin, Caellin, Cailen, Cailin, Caillin,
Calean, Callen, Caylin*

Calepodio (Greek) he who has beautiful feet.

Caley (Irish) a familiar form of Caleb.
Calee, Caleigh

Calfumil (Mapuche) glazed ceramic tile;
brilliant blue.

Calhoun (Irish) narrow woods. (Scottish)
warrior.
Colhoun, Colhoune, Colquhoun

Boys A–F

Calígula (Latin) he who wears sandals.

Calimaco (Greek) excellent fighter.

Calímaco (Greek) good fighter.

Calimerio (Greek) he who ushers in a beautiful day.

Calinico (Greek) he who secures a beautiful victory.

Calistenes (Greek) beautiful and strong.

Calisto, Calixto (Greek) best and the most beautiful.

Calistrato (Greek) he who commands a great army.

Calístrato (Greek) chief of a great army.

Callahan (Irish) descendant of Ceallachen.
Calahan, Callaghan

Callum ☐ (Irish) dove.
Callam, Calum, Calym

Calogero (Greek) wise one; the beautiful man; he who is going to age well.

Calvert (English) calf herder.
Cal, Calbert, Calvirt

Calvin (Latin) bald. See also Kalvin, Vinny.
Cal, Calv, Calvien, Calvon, Calvyn

Calvino (Latin) bald.

Calvucura (Mapuche) blue stone.

Cam ☐ (Gypsy) beloved. (Scottish) a short form of Cameron. (Latin, French, Scottish) a short form of Campbell.
Camm, Cammie, Cammy, Camy

Cama (Chamorro) resting place.

Camaron (Scottish) a form of Cameron.
Camar, Camari, Camaran, Camaren

Camden ☐ (Scottish) winding valley.
Kamden

Cameron W ☐ (Scottish) crooked nose. See also Kameron.
Cam, Camaron, Cameran, Cameren, Camerin, Cameroun, Camerron, Camerson, Camerun, Cameryn, Camiren, Camiron, Cammeron, Camron

Camille ☐ (French) young ceremonial attendant.
Camile

Camilo (Latin) child born to freedom; noble.
Camiel, Camillo, Camillus

Campbell (Latin, French) beautiful field. (Scottish) crooked mouth.
Cam, Camp, Campy

Camron ☐ (Scottish) a short form of Cameron.
Camren, Cammrin, Cammron, Camran, Camreon, Camrin, Camryn, Camrynn

Can (Vietnamese) advice, counsel.

Canaan (French) a form of Cannon. History: an ancient region between the Jordan River and the Mediterranean.
Canan, Canen, Caynan

Canaho (Chamorro) I am suspended.

Canai (Chamorro) a form of Cannai.

Cancio (Latin) founder of the city of Anzio.

Candice ☐ (Greek) a form of Candace (see Girls' Names).

Candide (Latin) pure; sincere.
Candid, Candido, Candonino

Cándido (Latin) a form of Candide.

Cang (Chinese) dark green pines.

Canh (Vietnamese) scenery; environment.

Cannai (Chamorro) hand; arm.

Cannon (French) church official; large gun. See also Kannon.
Canaan, Cannan, Cannen, Cannin, Canning, Canon

Canute (Latin) white haired. (Scandinavian) knot. History: a Danish king who became king of England after 1016. See also Knute.
Cnut, Cnute

Canuto (Latin) wise man with abundant white hair.

Cao (Chinese) conduct.

Capac, Capah (Quechua) Lord; rich in kindness; great, powerful, just, correct.

Capacuari (Quechua) kind-hearted master and untamable like the vicuna.

Capaquiupanqui (Quechua) he who honors his master; memorable master.

Cappi (Gypsy) good fortune.

Caquia (Quechua) thunder; bolt of lightning.

Car (Irish) a short form of Carney.

Caraca (Chamorro) a type of shell.

Carey ☐☐ (Greek) pure. (Welsh) castle; rocky island. See also Karey.
Care, Caree, Cari, Carre, Carree, Carrie, Cary

Carim (Arabic) generous.

Carina **G** (Italian) dear little one. (Swedish) a form of Karen. (Greek) a familiar form of Cora (see Girls' Names).

Carl **B** (German, English) a short form of Carlton. A form of Charles. See also Carroll, Kale, Kalle, Karl, Karlen, Karol.
Carle, Carles, Carless, Carlis, Carll, Carlo, Carlos, Carlson, Carlston, Carlus, Carolos

Carlee **G** (English) a form of Carly.

Carley **G** (English) a familiar form of Carlin.

Carli **G** (English) a form of Carly.

Carlie **G** (English) a familiar form of Carlin.

Carlin **BG** (Irish) little champion.
Carlan, Carlen, Carley, Carlie, Carling, Carlino, Carly

Carlisle (English) Carl's island.
Carlyle, Carlysle

Carlito (Spanish) a familiar form of Carlos.
Carlitos

Carlo (Italian) a form of Carl, Charles.
Carolo

Carlomagno (Spanish) Charles the great.

Carlos �465 **B** (Spanish) a form of Carl, Charles.
Carlito

Carlton **B** (English) Carl's town.
Carl, Carleton, Carllton, Carlston, Carltonn, Carltton, Charlton

Carly **G** (English) a familiar form of Carlin.

Carmel (Hebrew) vineyard, garden. See also Carmine.
Carmello, Carmelo, Karmel

Carmen **G** (Latin) a form of Carmine.

Carmichael (Scottish) follower of Michael.

Carmine (Latin) song; crimson. (Italian) a form of Carmel.
Carmain, Carmaine, Carman, Carmen, Carmon

Carnelius (Greek, Latin) a form of Cornelius.
Carnealius, Carneilius, Carnellius, Carnilious

Carnell (English) defender of the castle. (French) a form of Cornell.

Carney (Irish) victorious. (Scottish) fighter. See also Kearney.
Car, Carny, Karney

Carol **G** (Irish, German) a form of Carroll.

Carolina **G** (Italian) a form of Caroline.

Caroline **G** (French) little and strong.

Carolyn **G** (English) a form of Caroline.

Carpo (Greek) valuable fruit.

Carr (Scandinavian) marsh. See also Kerr.
Karr

Carrick (Irish) rock.
Carooq, Carricko

Carrie **G** (Greek, Welsh) a form of Carey.

Carrington (Welsh) rocky town.

Carroll (Irish) champion. (German) a form of Carl.
Carel, Carell, Cariel, Cariell, Carol, Carole, Carolo, Carols, Carollan, Carolus, Carrol, Cary, Caryl

Carson �465 **B** (English) son of Carr.
Carsen, Carsino, Carrson, Karson

Carsten (Greek) a form of Karsten.
Carston

Carter �465 **B** (English) cart driver.
Cart

Cartwright (English) cart builder.

Caruamayu (Quechua) yellow river.

Carvell (French, English) village on the marsh.
Carvel, Carvelle, Carvellius

Carver (English) wood-carver; sculptor.

Cary (Welsh) a form of Carey. (German, Irish) a form of Carroll.
Carray, Carry

Casandro (Greek) hero's brother.

Case (Irish) a short form of Casey. (English) a short form of Casimir.

Casey **BG** (Irish) brave.
Case, Casie, Casy, Cayse, Caysey, Kacey, Kasey

Cash (Latin) vain. (Slavic) a short form of Casimir.
Cashe

Casiano (Latin) he who is equipped with a helmet.

Casildo (Arabic) youth that carries the lance.

Casimir (Slavic) peacemaker.
Cachi, Cas, Case, Cash, Cashemere, Cashi, Cashmeire, Cashmere, Casimere, Casimire, Casimiro, Castimer, Kasimir, Kazio

Casiodoro (Greek) gift from a friend.

Casper (Persian) treasurer. (German) imperial. See also Gaspar, Jasper, Kasper.
Caspar, Cass

Cass 🅱 (Irish, Persian) a short form of Casper, Cassidy.

Cassandra 🅖 (Greek) helper.

Cassidy 🅖 (Irish) clever; curly haired.
Casidy, Cass, Cassady, Cassie, Kassidy

Cassie (Irish) a familiar form of Cassidy.
Casi, Casie, Casio, Cassey, Cassy, Casy

Cassius (Latin, French) box; protective cover.
Cassia, Cassio, Cazzie

Casta (Spanish) pure.

Castle (Latin) castle.
Cassle, Castel

Casto (Greek) pure, honest, clean.

Castor (Greek) beaver. Astrology: one of the twins in the constellation Gemini. Mythology: one of the patron saints of mariners.
Caster, Caston

Cástor (Greek) a form of Castor.

Cataldo (Greek) outstanding in war.

Catari (Aymara) serpent.

Catequil, Catiquil, Catuilla (Quechua) ray of light.

Cater (English) caterer.

Catherine 🅖 (Greek) pure. (English) a form of Katherine.

Catlahi (Chamorro) a form of Chatlahe.

Cato (Latin) knowledgeable, wise.
Caton

Catón (Latin) a form of Cato.
Caton, Catón

Catricura (Mapuche) cut stone.

Catulo (Latin) puppy; soft.

Cátulo (Spanish) a form of Catulo.

Cauac (Quechua) sentinel; he who guards.

Cauachi (Quechua) he who makes us attentive, vigilant.

Cauana (Quechua) he who is in a place where all can be seen.

Cautaro (Araucanian) daring and enterprising.

Cavan (Irish) handsome. See also Kevin.
Caven, Cavin, Cavan, Cawoun

Cayden (American) a form of Caden.
Cayde, Caydin

Cayetano (Latin) he who is from Gaeta, an ancient city in the Lacio region.

Caylan (Scottish) a form of Caelan.
Caylans, Caylen, Caylon

Cayo (Latin) happy and fun.

Cayua (Quechua) he who follows, follower; faithful.

Cazzie (American) a familiar form of Cassius.
Caz, Cazz, Cazzy

Ce (Chinese) to plan, scheme.

Cear (Irish) black.

Ceasar (Latin) a form of Caesar.
Ceaser

Cecil 🅱 (Latin) blind.
Cece, Cecile, Cecilio, Cecilius, Cecill, Celio, Siseal

Cedric (English) battle chieftain. See also Kedrick, Rick.
Cad, Caddaric, Ced, Cederic, Cedrec, Cédric, Cedrick, Cedryche, Sedric

Cedrick (English) a form of Cedric.
Ceddrick, Cederick, Cederrick, Cedirick, Cedrik

Cedro (Spanish) strong gift.

Ceejay (American) a combination of the initials C. + J.
Cejay, C.J.

Ceferino (Greek) he who caresses like the wind.

Celedonio (Latin) he is like the swallow.

Celestino (Latin) resident of the celestial reign.

Celine 🅖 (Greek) a form of Celena (see Girls' Names).

Celso (Latin) tall, elevated; noble.

Cemal (Arabic) attractive.

Cencio (Italian) a form of Vicente.

Cenobio (Latin) he who rejects the strangers; God gives him protection and good health.

Cephas (Latin) small rock. Bible: the term used by Jesus to describe Peter.
Cepheus, Cephus

Cerdic (Welsh) beloved.
Caradoc, Caradog, Ceredig, Ceretic

Cerek (Polish) lordly. (Greek) a form of Cyril.

Cesar **B** (Spanish) a form of Caesar.
Casar, César, Cesare, Cesareo, Cesario, Cesaro, Cessar

Cesáreo (Latin) relating to Caesar.

Cesarión (Latin) Caesar's follower.

Cestmir (Czech) fortress.

Cezar (Slavic) a form of Caesar.
Cézar, Cezary, Cezek, Chezrae, Sezar

Chace (French) a form of Chase.
Chayce

Chad **B** (English) warrior. A short form of Chadwick. Geography: a country in north-central Africa.
Ceadd, Chaad, Chadd, Chaddie, Chaddy, Chade, Chadleigh, Chadler, Chadley, Chadlin, Chadlyn, Chadmen, Chado, Chadron, Chady

Chadfaulus, Charfaulos (Chamorro) forms of Charfaulus.

Chadi (Chamorro) fast, quick.

Chadrick (German) mighty warrior.
Chaddrick, Chaderic, Chaderick, Chadrack, Chadric

Chadwick (English) warrior's town.
Chad, Chaddwick, Chadvic, Chadwyck

Chae (Korean) decorated, ornamented.

Chaggi (Chamorro) to attempt.

Chago (Spanish) a form of Jacob.
Chango, Chanti

Chaguina (Chamorro) his attempt.

Chaicu (Aymara) he who has great strength in order to fling stones, is skillful with the sling.

Cha'ife (Chamorro) not fiery.

Chaim (Hebrew) life. See also Hyman.
Chai, Chaimek, Haim, Khaim

Chaise (French) a form of Chase.
Chais, Chaisen, Chaison

Chal (Gypsy) boy; son.
Chalie, Chalin

Chale (Spanish) strong and youthful.

Chalmers (Scottish) son of the lord.
Chalmer, Chalmr, Chamar, Chamarr

Chalten (Tehuelchean) bluish.

Cham (Vietnamese) hard worker.
Chams

Chambi, Champi (Aymara) halberd, lance; he who brings good news.

Chambigüiyca, Champigüiyca (Aymara) beam of sunlight; sent from the gods.

Chammangro (Chamorro) not enough wind.

Champacco (Chamorro) not burnt enough.

Champaklal (Sanskrit) caress of the champion's fragrant yellow flowers.

Chan **B** (Sanskrit) shining. (English) a form of Chauncey. (Spanish) a form of Juan.
Chann, Chano, Chayo

Chanan (Hebrew) cloud.

Chance **B** (English) a short form of Chancellor, Chauncey.
Chanc, Chancee, Chancey, Chancie, Chancy, Chanse, Chansy, Chants, Chantz, Chanze, Chanz, Chaynce

Chancellor (English) record keeper.
Chance, Chancelar, Chancelen, Chanceleor, Chanceler, Chanceller, Chancelor, Chanselor, Chanslor

Chandar (Sanskrit) a form of Chandra.

Chander (Hindi) moon.
Chand, Chandan, Chandany, Chandara, Chandon

Chandler **B** (English) candle maker.
Chandelar, Chandlan, Chandlar, Chandlier, Chandlor, Chandlyr

Chane (Swahili) dependable.

Chaney (French) oak.
Chayne, Cheaney, Cheney, Cheyn, Cheyne, Cheyney

Chang (Chinese) smooth.

Chankrisna (Cambodian) sweet smelling tree.

Channing (English) wise. (French) canon; church official.
Chane, Chann

Chanse (English) a form of Chance.
Chans, Chansey

Chantal G (French) song.

Chante BG (French) singer.
Chant, Chantha, Chanthar, Chantra, Chantry, Shantae

Chantel G (French) a form of Chantal.

Chao (Chinese) surpassing.

Chapman (English) merchant.
Chap, Chappie, Chappy

Charfaulus (Chamorro) one with a rough appearance.

Chargadi, Chargati (Chamorro) forms of Chatgadi.

Chargiya (Chamorro) a form of Charguiya.

Chargualaf (Chamorro) a form of Chatguaraf.

Charguiya (Chamorro) not enough of him.

Charity G (Latin) charity, kindness.

Charles 🖐 B (German) farmer. (English) strong and manly. See also Carl, Searlas, Tearlach, Xarles.
Arlo, Chareles, Charels, Charlese, Carlo, Carlos, Charl, Charle, Charlen, Charlie, Charlot, Charlz, Charlzell, Chaz, Chick, Chip, Chuck

Charlie B (German, English) a familiar form of Charles.
Charle, Charlee, Charley, Charli, Charly

Charlton (English) a form of Carlton.
Charlesten, Charleston, Charleton, Charlotin

Charro (Spanish) cowboy.

Charsaga, Chartsagua (Chamorro) forms of Chatsaga.

Chase 🖐 B (French) hunter.
Chace, Chaise, Chasen, Chason, Chass, Chasse, Chastan, Chasten, Chastin, Chastinn, Chaston, Chasyn, Chayse

Chaska (Sioux) first-born son.

Chataam (Chamorro) a form of Chataan.

Chataan (Chamorro) rainy season.

Chataga (Chamorro) not enough chopping.

Chatam (Chamorro) choosy.

Chatgadi (Chamorro) not catching enough fish.

Chatgaia (Chamorro) disliked.

Chatguaraf (Chamorro) not enough like a full moon.

Chatguemangro (Chamorro) he who doesn't have enough wind.

Chatguiot (Chamorro) not enough support.

Chatguma (Chamorro) not enough of a house.

Chathigam, Chathigem, Chatigam (Chamorro) forms of Chatigan.

Chathigan (Chamorro) a form of Chatigan.

Chatigan (Chamorro) not enough fish.

Chatlahe (Chamorro) not enough of a man.

Chatongo (Chamorro) not knowing enough.

Chatpagat (Chamorro) not preaching enough.

Chatpangon (Chamorro) not awake enough.

Chatsaga (Chamorro) poor.

Chattai (Chamorro) barely enough.

Chau (Vietnamese) pearl.

Chauar (Quechua) fiber, rope.

Chauncey B (English) chancellor; church official.
Chan, Chance, Chancey, Chaunce, Chauncei, Chauncy, Chaunecy, Chaunesy, Chaunszi

Chaupi (Quechua) he who is in the middle of everything.

Chavey (Portuguese) a form of Chaves.

Chavez (Hispanic) a surname used as a first name.
Chavaz, Chaves, Chaveze, Chavies, Chavis, Chavius, Chevez, Cheveze, Cheviez, Chevious, Chevis, Chivass, Chivez

Chayse (French) a form of Chase.
Chaysea, Chaysen, Chayson, Chaysten

Chayton (Lakota) falcon.

Chaz B (English) a familiar form of Charles.
Chas, Chasz, Chaze, Chazwick, Chazy, Chazz, Chez

Che (Spanish) God will add or multiply.

Ché (Spanish) a familiar form of José.
History: Ernesto "Che" Guevara was a revolutionary who fought at Fidel Castro's side in Cuba.
Chay

Cheban (Chamorro) chop off.

Cheboc (Chamorro) fat, plump.

Checha (Spanish) a familiar form of Jacob.

Cheche (Spanish) a familiar form of Joseph.

Chelsea **G** (English) seaport.

Chelsey **G** (English) a form of Chelsea.

Chelsie **G** (English) a form of Chelsea.

Chen (Chinese) great, tremendous.

Chencho (Spanish) a familiar form of Lawrence.

Cheng (Chinese) accomplished.

Cheng-Gong (Chinese) success.

Chepe (Spanish) a familiar form of Joseph.
Cepito

Cherokee **G** (Cherokee) people of a different speech.
Cherrakee

Cherubin (Italian) little cherub.

Chesmu (Native American) gritty.

Chester (English) a short form of Rochester.
Ches, Cheslav, Cheston, Chet

Chet (English) a short form of Chester.
Chett, Chette

Cheung (Chinese) good luck.

Chevalier (French) horseman, knight.
Chev, Chevy

Chevy (French) a familiar form of Chevalier. Geography: Chevy Chase is a town in Maryland. Culture: a short form of Chevrolet, an American automobile company.
Chev, Chevey, Chevi, Chevie, Chevvy, Chewy

Chew (Chinese) mountain.

Cheyenne **G** (Cheyenne) a tribal name.
Chayann, Chayanne, Cheyeenne, Cheyene, Chyenne, Shayan

Chi **BG** (Chinese) younger generation. (Nigerian) personal guardian angel.

Chia (Chinese) home, family; addition.

Chibocta (Chamorro) our little one.

Chican (Quechua) unique, different from the rest.

Chick (English) a familiar form of Charles.
Chic, Chickie, Chicky

Chico (Spanish) boy.

Chien (Vietnamese) fight, battle, combat.

Chih Cheng (Chinese) one who controls the government.

Chiharu (Japanese) a thousand springtimes.

Chihiro (Japanese) a thousand measures; a thousand fathoms.

Chik (Gypsy) earth.

Chika (Japanese) near, close.

Chikaaki (Japanese) a form of Chika.

Chikafusa (Japanese) a form of Chika.

Chikai (Japanese) a thousand heads of grain.

Chikamusa (Japanese) close; good.

Chikao (Japanese) clever, wise.

Chikara (Japanese) tax; strength; energetic man; a thousand tree trunks.

Chike (Ibo) God's power.

Chiko (Japanese) arrow; pledge.

Chilo (Spanish) a familiar form of Francisco.

Chilton (English) farm by the spring.
Chil, Chill, Chillton, Chilt

Chim (Vietnamese) bird.

Chin (Chinese) a form of Jin.

China **G** (Chinese) fine porcelain. Geography: a country in eastern Asia.

Chinami (Japanese) cause.

Chincolef (Mapuche) swift squad; rapid.

Ching Cheng (Chinese) competition.

Chinh (Vietnamese) correctness; righteousness.

Chin-Hwa (Korean) the wealthiest.

Chin-Mae (Korean) truth.

Chinua (Ibo) God's blessing.
Chino, Chinou

Chioke (Ibo) gift of God.

Chip (English) a familiar form of Charles.
Chipman, Chipper

Chiram (Hebrew) exalted; noble.

Chiro (Chuukese) a form of Ichiro.

Chisato (Japanese) very wise.

Chishin (Japanese) historical figure.

Chitamag (Yapese) my father.

Chitaro (Chuukese) the speed of one thousand legs.

Chitose (Japanese) a thousand years.

Chloe **G** (Greek) blooming, verdant.

Cho (Korean) first; herbs; welcome; likeness; excel; foundation.

Chogua (Chamorro) to work.

Chokichi (Japanese) good fortune.

Chong (Chinese) intelligent, clever.

Chong Duy (Vietnamese) eats like a bird.

Chongwon (Korean) garden.

Choque, Chuqui (Quechua) lance; dancer.

Chorche (Aragonese) a form of George.

Chotaro (Japanese) chief son.

Chow (Chinese) everywhere.

Chris **B** (Greek) a short form of Christian, Christopher. See also Kris.
Chriss, Christ, Chrys, Cris, Crist

Christa **G** (Greek) a form of Christian.

Christain **B** (Greek) a form of Christian.
Christai, Christan, Christane, Christaun, Christein

Christen **G** (Greek) a form of Christian.

Christian ☙ **B** (Greek) follower of Christ; anointed. See also Jaan, Kerstan, Khristian, Kit, Krister, Kristian, Krystian.
Chretien, Chris, Christa, Christain, Christé, Christen, Christensen, Christiaan, Christiana, Christiane, Christiann, Christianna, Christianno, Christiano, Christianos, Christien, Christin, Christino, Christion, Christon, Christos, Christyan, Christyon, Chritian, Chrystian, Cristian, Crystek

Christie **G** (Greek) a short form of Christina, Christine.

Christien (Greek) a form of Christian.
Christienne, Christinne, Chrystien

Christin **G** (Greek) a form of Christian.

Christina **G** (Greek) Christian; anointed.

Christine **G** (French, English) a form of Christina.

Christofer (Greek) a form of Christopher.
Christafer, Christafur, Christefor, Christerfer, Christifer, Christoffer, Christofher, Christofper, Chrystofer

Christoff (Russian) a form of Christopher.
Chrisof, Christif, Christof, Cristofe

Christophe **B** (French) a form of Christopher.
Christoph

Christopher ☙ **B** (Greek) Christ-bearer. Religion: the patron saint of travelers. See also Cristopher, Kester, Kit, Kristopher, Risto, Stoffel, Tobal, Topher.
Chris, Chrisopherson, Christapher, Christepher, Christerpher, Christhoper, Christipher, Christobal, Christofer, Christoff, Christoforo, Christoher, Christopehr, Christoper, Christophe, Christopherr, Christophor, Christophoros, Christophr, Christophre, Christophyer, Christophyr, Christorpher, Christos, Christovao, Christpher, Christphere, Christphor, Christpor, Christrpher, Chrystopher, Cristobal

Christophoros (Greek) a form of Christopher.
Christoforo, Christoforos, Christophor, Christophorus, Christphor, Cristoforo, Cristopher

Christos (Greek) a form of Christopher. See also Khristos.

Christy **G** (English) a short form of Christina, Christine.

Chu (Chinese) the stone base of a column.

Chuan (Chinese) river.

Chuang (Chinese) achieve.

Chucho (Hebrew) a familiar form of Jesus.

Chuck (American) a familiar form of Charles.
Chuckey, Chuckie, Chucky

Chui (Swahili) leopard.

Chu-Jung (Chinese) the god of fire and executions.

Chul (Korean) firm.

Chula (Chamorro) to grasp.

Chul-Moo (Korean) iron weapon.

Chuma (Ibo) having many beads, wealthy. (Swahili) iron.

Chuminga (Spanish) a familiar form of Dominic.
Chumin

Chumo (Spanish) a familiar form of Thomas.

Chun **B** (Chinese) spring.

Chung (Chinese) intelligent.
Chungo, Chuong

Chung-Hee, Chung-Ho (Korean) righteous.

Chungi (Chamorro) gray haired.

Chupaho (Chamorro) my smoke.

Boys A–F

Chuquigüaman (Quechua) dancing falcon; golden falcon.

Chuquigüiyca (Quechua) sacred dance.

Chuquilla (Quechua) ray of light; golden light.

Churchill (English) church on the hill. History: Sir Winston Churchill served as British prime minister and won a Nobel Prize for literature.

Chuscu (Quechua) fourth son.

Chu-Tak (Chinese) ancestor's virtue.

Chuya (Quechua) clear as water, pure.

Cian (Irish) ancient.
Céin, Cianán, Kian

Ciara **G** (Irish) black.

Cibrao (Latin) inhabitant of Cyprus.

Cicero (Latin) chickpea. History: a famous Roman orator, philosopher, and statesman.
Cicerón

Cid (Spanish) lord. History: title for Rodrigo Díaz de Vivar, an eleventh-century Spanish soldier and national hero.
Cyd

Cidro (Spanish) strong gift.

Cindy **G** (Greek) moon. (Latin) a familiar form of Cynthia.

Ciqala (Dakota) little.

Ciríaco (Greek) he who belongs to the Lord.

Cirineo (Greek) native of Cyrene (present-day Libya).

Cirrillo (Italian) a form of Cyril.
Cirilio, Cirillo, Cirilo, Ciro

Cisco (Spanish) a short form of Francisco.

Ciset (Spanish) a form of Narciso.

Citino (Latin) quick to act.

Claire **G** (French) a form of Clara.

Clancy (Irish) redheaded fighter.
Clancey, Claney

Clara **G** (Latin) clear; bright.

Clare **G** (Latin) a short form of Clarence.
Clair, Clarey, Clary

Clarence **B** (Latin) clear; victorious.
Clarance, Clare, Clarrance, Clarrence, Clearence

Clarissa **G** (Greek) brilliant. (Italian) a form of Clara.

Clark **B** (French) cleric; scholar.
Clarke, Clerc, Clerk

Claro (Latin) he who is clean and transparent.

Claude **B** (Latin, French) lame.
Claud, Claudan, Claudel, Claudell, Claudey, Claudi, Claudian, Claudianus, Claudie, Claudien, Claudin, Claudio, Claudis, Claudius, Claudy

Claudie **G** (Latin, French) a form of Claude.

Claudino (Latin) he who belongs to the ancient Roman family Claudios.

Claudio **B** (Italian) a form of Claude.

Claus (German) a short form of Nicholas. See also Klaus.
Claas, Claes, Clause

Clay (English) clay pit. A short form of Clayborne, Clayton.
Klay

Clayborne (English) brook near the clay pit.
Claibern, Claiborn, Claiborne, Claibrone, Clay, Claybon, Clayborn, Claybourn, Claybourne, Clayburn, Clebourn

Clayton **B** (English) town built on clay.
Clay, Clayten, Cleighton, Cleyton, Clyton, Klayton

Cleandro (Greek) glorious man.

Cleary (Irish) learned.

Cleavon (English) cliff.
Clavin, Clavion, Clavon, Clavone, Clayvon, Claywon, Clévon, Clevonn, Clyvon

Clem (Latin) a short form of Clement.
Cleme, Clemmy, Clim

Clement (Latin) merciful. Bible: a coworker of Paul. See also Klement, Menz.
Clem, Clemens, Clément, Clemente, Clementius, Clemmons

Clemente (Italian, Spanish) a form of Clement.
Clemento, Clemenza

Clenn (Marshallese) a form of Glenn.

Cleofas (Greek) he is the glory of his father.

Cleon (Greek) famous.
Kleon

Cleto (Greek) he was chosen to fight.

Cletus (Greek) illustrious. History: a Roman pope and martyr.
Cleatus, Cledis, Cleotis, Clete, Cletis

Cleveland (English) land of cliffs.
Cleaveland, Cleavland, Cleavon, Cleve, Clevelend, Clevelynn, Clevey, Clevie, Clevon

Cliff (English) a short form of Clifford, Clifton.
Clif, Clift, Clive, Clyff, Clyph, Kliff

Clifford (English) cliff at the river crossing.
Cliff, Cliford, Clyfford, Klifford

Clifton 🅑 (English) cliff town.
Cliff, Cliffton, Clift, Cliften, Clyfton

Climaco (Greek) he who climbs the ladder.

Clímaco (Greek) he who ascends.

Clímene (Greek) famous, celebrated.

Clint (English) a short form of Clinton.
Klint

Clinton (English) hill town.
Clenten, Clint, Clinten, Clintion, Clintton, Clynton, Klinton

Clive (English) a form of Cliff.
Cleve, Clivans, Clivens, Clyve, Klyve

Clodio (German) glorious.

Clodoaldo (Teutonic) prince that is the chosen and illustrious captain.

Clodomiro (Germanic) he of illustrious fame.

Clodulfo (Germanic) glory.

Clorindo (Greek) he who is like the grass.

Clotario (Gothic) a form of Lotario.

Cloud (English) cloud.

Clove (Spanish) nail.

Clovis (German) famous soldier. See also Louis.

Cluny (Irish) meadow.

Clyde (Welsh) warm. (Scottish) Geography: a river in Scotland.
Cly, Clywd, Klyde

Coby (Hebrew) a familiar form of Jacob.
Cob, Cobby, Cobe, Cobey, Cobi, Cobia, Cobie

Cochise (Apache) hardwood. History: a famous Chiricahua Apache leader.

Coco 🅖 (French) a familiar form of Jacques.
Coko, Koko

Codey 🅑 (English) a form of Cody.
Coday

Codi 🅑🅖 (English) a form of Cody.

Codie 🅑 (English) a form of Cody.
Coadi, Codea

Cody ❦ 🅑 (English) cushion. History: William "Buffalo Bill" Cody was an American frontier scout who toured America and Europe with his Wild West show. See also Kody.
Coady, Coddy, Code, Codee, Codell, Codey, Codi, Codiak, Codie, Coedy

Coffie (Ewe) born on Friday.

Coique (Quechua) silver.

Coiquiyoc (Quechua) he who is rich with silver.

Coka (Fijian) running stomach.

Cola (Italian) a familiar form of Nicholas, Nicola.
Colas

Colar (French) a form of Nicholas.

Colbert (English) famous seafarer.
Cole, Colt, Colvert, Culbert

Colby 🅑 (English) dark; dark haired.
Colbey, Colbi, Colbie, Colbin, Colebee, Coleby, Collby, Kolby

Cole ❦ 🅑 (Latin) cabbage farmer. (English) a short form of Coleman.
Colet, Coley, Colie, Kole

Coleman 🅑 (Latin) cabbage farmer. (English) coal miner.
Cole, Colemann, Colm, Colman, Koleman

Colin ❦ 🅑 (Irish) young cub. (Greek) a short form of Nicholas.
Cailean, Colan, Cole, Colen, Coleon, Colinn, Collin, Colyn, Kolin

Colla, Culla (Quechua) from the village Colla; eminent, excellent.

Collacapac, Cullacapac (Quechua) Lord Colla, eminent and kind-hearted lord.

Collana, Cullana (Quechua) best; he who excels.

Collatupac, Cullatupac (Quechua) glorious, majestic Colla; royal eminence.

Colley (English) black haired; swarthy.
Colee, Collie, Collis

Collier (English) miner.
Colier, Collayer, Collie, Collyer, Colyer

Collin 🅑 (Scottish) a form of Colin, Collins.
Collan, Collen, Collian, Collon, Collyn

Collins (Greek) son of Colin. (Irish) holly.
Collin, Collis

Colon (Latin) he has the beauty of a dove.

Colson (Greek, English) son of Nicholas.
Colsen, Coulson

Colt **B** (English) young horse; frisky. A short form of Colter, Colton.
Colte

Colten (English) a form of Colton.

Colter (English) herd of colts.
Colt

Colton **B** (English) coal town.
Colt, Coltan, Colten, Coltin, Coltinn, Coltn, Coltrane, Colttan, Coltton, Coltun, Coltyn, Coltyne, Kolton

Columba (Latin) dove.
Coim, Colum, Columbia, Columbus

Colwyn (Welsh) Geography: a river in Wales.
Colwin, Colwinn

Coman (Arabic) noble. (Irish) bent.
Comán

Coñalef (Mapuche) swift youngster; rapid, agile; well meaning.

Conall (Irish) high, mighty.
Conal, Connal, Connel, Connell, Connelly, Connolly

Conan (Irish) praised; exalted. (Scottish) wise.
Conant, Conary, Connen, Connie, Connon, Connor, Conon

Conary (Irish) a form of Conan.
Conaire

Cong (Chinese) intelligent.

Coni (Quechua) warm.

Coniraya (Quechua) heat from the sun; he who has heat from the sun.

Conlan (Irish) hero.
Conlen, Conley, Conlin, Conlyn

Conner **B** (Irish) a form of Connor.
Connar, Connary, Conneer, Connery, Konner

Connie **G** (English, Irish) a familiar form of Conan, Conrad, Constantine, Conway.
Con, Conn, Conney, Conny

Connor ⚜ **B** (Scottish) wise. (Irish) a form of Conan.
Conner, Connoer, Connory, Connyr, Conor, Konner, Konnor

Cono (Mapuche) ringdove.

Conor **B** (Irish) a form of Connor.
Conar, Coner, Conour, Konner

Conrad (German) brave counselor.
Connie, Conrade, Conrado, Corrado, Konrad

Conroy (Irish) wise.
Conry, Roy

Constancio (Latin) perseverant one.

Constant (Latin) a short form of Constantine.

Constantine (Latin) firm, constant. History: Constantine the Great was the Roman emperor who adopted the Christian faith. See also Dinos, Konstantin, Stancio.
Connie, Constadine, Constandine, Constandios, Constanstine, Constant, Constantin, Constantino, Constantinos, Constantios, Costa

Contardo (Teutonic) he who is daring and valiant.

Conun-Huenu (Mapuche) entrance to the sky; elevated hill.

Conway (Irish) hound of the plain.
Connie, Conwy

Cook (English) cook.
Cooke

Cooper **B** (English) barrel maker. See also Keiffer.
Coop, Couper

Corbett (Latin) raven.
Corbbitt, Corbet, Corbette, Corbit, Corbitt

Corbin **B** (Latin) raven.
Corban, Corben, Corbey, Corbie, Corbon, Corby, Corbyn, Korbin

Corcoran (Irish) ruddy.

Cordaro (Spanish) a form of Cordero.
Coradaro, Cordairo, Cordara, Cordarel, Cordarell, Cordarelle, Cordareo, Cordarin, Cordario, Cordarion, Cordarious, Cordarius, Cordarrel, Cordarrell, Cordarris, Cordarrius, Cordarro, Cordarrol, Cordarus, Cordarryl, Cordaryal, Corddarro, Corrdarl

Cordell (French) rope maker.
Cord, Cordae, Cordale, Corday, Cordeal, Cordeil, Cordel, Cordele, Cordelle, Cordie, Cordy, Kordell

Cordero (Spanish) little lamb.
Cordaro, Cordeal, Cordeara, Cordearo, Cordeiro, Cordelro, Corder, Cordera, Corderall, Corderias, Corderious, Corderral, Corderro, Corderryn, Corderun, Corderus, Cordiaro, Cordierre, Cordy, Corrderio

Corey 🅱 (Irish) hollow. See also Korey, Kory.
*Core, Coreaa, Coree, Cori, Corian, Corie,
Corio, Correy, Corria, Corrie, Corry, Corrye,
Cory*

Cori 🅶 (Irish) a form of Corey.

Coriguaman (Quechua) golden falcon.

Coriñaui (Quechua) he who has eyes that are
the color and beauty of gold.

Coripoma (Quechua) golden puma.

Cormac (Irish) raven's son. History: a third-
century king of Ireland who was a great
lawmaker.
Cormack, Cormick

Cornelius 🅱 (Greek) cornel tree. (Latin)
horn colored. See also Kornel, Kornelius,
Nelek.
*Carnelius, Conny, Cornealous, Corneili,
Corneilius, Corneilus, Corneliaus, Cornelious,
Cornelias, Cornelis, Corneliu, Cornell,
Cornellious, Cornellis, Cornellius, Cornelous,
Corneluis, Cornelus, Corney, Cornie,
Cornielius, Corniellus, Corny, Cournelius,
Cournelyous, Nelius, Nellie*

Cornell (French) a form of Cornelius.
*Carnell, Cornall, Corneil, Cornel, Cornelio,
Corney, Cornie, Corny, Nellie*

Cornwallis (English) from Cornwall.

Corona (Latin) crown.

Corrado (Italian) a form of Conrad.
Carrado

Corrigan (Irish) spearman.
*Carrigan, Carrigen, Corrigon, Corrigun,
Korrigan*

Corrin (Irish) spear carrier.
Corin, Corion

Corry (Latin) a form of Corey.

Cort (German) bold. (Scandinavian) short.
(English) a short form of Courtney.
Corte, Cortie, Corty, Kort

Cortez (Spanish) conqueror. History:
Hernando Cortés was a Spanish
conquistador who conquered Aztec Mexico.
*Cartez, Cortes, Cortis, Cortize, Courtes,
Courtez, Curtez, Kortez*

Cortney 🅶 (English) a form of Courtney.

Corwin (English) heart's companion; heart's
delight.
Corwinn, Corwyn, Corwynn, Corwynne

Cory 🅱 (Latin) a form of Corey. (French) a
familiar form of Cornell. (Greek) a short
form of Corydon.
Corye

Corydon (Greek) helmet, crest.
Coridon, Corradino, Cory, Coryden, Coryell

Cosgrove (Irish) victor, champion.

Cosimus (Italian) a form of Cosme.

Cosme (Greek) a form of Cosmo.

Cosmo (Greek) orderly; harmonious;
universe.
Cos, Cosimo, Cosme, Cosmé, Cozmo, Kosmo

Costa (Greek) a short form of Constantine.
Costandinos, Costantinos, Costas, Costes

Coty 🅱 (French) slope, hillside.
Cote, Cotee, Cotey, Coti, Cotie, Cotty, Cotye

Courtland (English) court's land.
Court, Courtlan, Courtlana, Courtlandt,
*Courtlin, Courtlind, Courtlon, Courtlyn,
Kourtland*

Courtney 🅶 (English) court.
*Cort, Cortnay, Cortne, Cortney, Court, Courten,
Courtenay, Courteney, Courtnay, Courtnee,
Curt, Kortney*

Cowan (Irish) hillside hollow.
Coe, Coven, Covin, Cowen, Cowey, Cowie

Coy (English) woods.
Coye, Coyie, Coyt

Coyahue (Mapuche) meeting place for
speaking and debating.

Coyle (Irish) leader in battle.

Coyne (French) modest.
Coyan

Craddock (Welsh) love.
Caradoc, Caradog

Craig 🅱 (Irish, Scottish) crag; steep rock.
*Crag, Craige, Craigen, Craigery, Craigh,
Craigon, Creag, Creg, Cregan, Cregg, Creig,
Creigh, Criag, Kraig*

Crandall (English) crane's valley.
Cran, Crandal, Crandel, Crandell, Crendal

Crandon (English) from the hill of cranes.

Crawford (English) ford where crows fly.
Craw, Crow, Ford

Creed (Latin) belief.
Creedon

Creighton (English) town near the rocks.
*Cray, Crayton, Creighm, Creight, Creighto,
Crichton*

Crepin (French) a form of Crispin.

Crescencio (Latin) he who constantly increases his virtue.

Crescente (Latin) growing.

Cripín, Cripo (Latin) having curly hair.

Crisanto (Greek) golden flower.

Crisipo (Greek) golden horse.

Crisoforo (Greek) he who wears gold.

Crisóforo (Greek) he who gives advice that has value; his word is valuable.

Crisologo (Greek) he who says words that are like gold.

Crisólogo (Greek) he who gives advice that is as good as gold.

Crisostomo (Greek) mouth of gold.

Crisóstomo (Greek) he who gives valuable advice.

Crispin (Latin) curly haired.
Crepin, Cris, Crispian, Crispien, Crispino, Crispo, Krispin

Cristal **G** (Latin) a form of Crystal.

Cristian **B** (Greek) a form of Christian.
Crétien, Cristean, Cristhian, Cristiano, Cristien, Cristino, Cristle, Criston, Cristos, Cristy, Cristyan, Crystek, Crystian

Cristián (Latin) Christian, he who follows Christ.

Cristo (Greek) because of the Messiah.

Cristobal (Greek) a form of Christopher.
Cristóbal, Cristoval, Cristovao

Cristoforo (Italian) a form of Christopher.
Cristofor

Cristopher (Greek) a form of Christopher.
Cristaph, Cristhofer, Cristifer, Cristofer, Cristoph, Cristophe, Crystapher, Crystifer

Cristovo (Greek) Christ's servant.

Crofton (Irish) town with cottages.

Cromwell (English) crooked spring, winding spring.

Crosby (Scandinavian) shrine of the cross.
Crosbey, Crosbie, Cross

Crosley (English) meadow of the cross.
Cross

Crowther (English) fiddler.

Cruz **B** (Portuguese, Spanish) cross.
Cruze, Kruz

Crystal **G** (Latin) clear, brilliant glass.

Crystek (Polish) a form of Christian.

Cuarto (Spanish) born fourth.

Cuasimodo (Latin) he who is child-like.

Cui (Chinese) resplendent.

Cuirpuma (Quechua) golden puma.

Cuiycui (Quechua) silver.

Cullen **B** (Irish) handsome.
Cull, Cullan, Cullie, Cullin

Culley (Irish) woods.
Cullie, Cully

Culver (English) dove.
Colver, Cull, Cullie, Cully

Cuminao (Mapuche) crimson glow, the sun's last twinkle.

Cumya (Quechua) thunder, thundering; luminous.

Cunac (Quechua) he who counsels; counselor.

Cuñi (Quechua) warm.

Cunibaldo (Greek) of noble birth.

Cuniberto (Teutonic) he who stands apart from the other noble gentlemen because of his heritage.

Cuñiraya (Quechua) heat from the sun; he who has heat from the sun.

Cunningham (Irish) village of the milk pail.

Cuntur (Quechua) condor.

Cunturcanqui, Cunturchaua (Quechua) he who has all the virtues of a condor.

Cunturi (Aymara) representative of the gods; sent from the ancestral spirits.

Cunturpoma, Cunturpuma (Quechua) powerful as the puma and the condor.

Cunturuari (Quechua) untamable and savage like the vicuna and the condor.

Cunturumi (Quechua) strong as the stone and the condor.

Cuong (Vietnamese) healthy and prosperous.

Curamil (Mapuche) brilliant stone of gold and silver.

Curi (Quechua) golden.

Curiguaman (Quechua) golden falcon.

Boys A–F

Curileo (Mapuche) black river.

Curiman (Mapuche) black condor.

Curiñaui (Quechua) he who has eyes that are the color and beauty of gold.

Curipan (Mapuche) leafy stinging nettle; furious puma.

Curran 🅱 (Irish) hero.
Curan, Curon, Curr, Curren, Currey, Curri, Currie, Currin, Curry

Currito (Spanish) a form of Curtis.
Curcio

Curro (Spanish) polite or courteous.

Curt (Latin) a short form of Courtney, Curtis. See also Kurt.

Curtis 🅱 (Latin) enclosure. (French) courteous. See also Kurtis.
Curio, Currito, Curt, Curtice, Curtiss, Curtus

Cusi (Quechua) happy, fortunate, prosperous man who is always lucky in all that he does.

Cusiguaman (Quechua) happy falcon.

Cusiguaypa (Quechua) happy rooster; creator of joyous things.

Cusiñaui (Quechua) smiling, with happy eyes.

Cusipoma, Cusipuma (Quechua) happy puma.

Cusirimachi (Quechua) he who fills us with happy words.

Cusiyupanqui (Quechua) honored and fortunate.

Custodio (Latin) guardian spirit, guardian angel.

Cuthbert (English) brilliant.

Cutler (English) knife maker.
Cut, Cuttie, Cutty

Cutmano (Anglo Saxon) man who is famous.

Cuycusi (Quechua) he who moves happily.

Cuyquiyuc (Quechua) he who is rich with silver.

Cuyuc (Quechua) he who moves; restless.

Cuyuchi (Quechua) he who makes us move.

Cy (Persian) a short form of Cyrus.

Cyle (Irish) a form of Kyle.

Cynthia 🅶 (Greek) moon.

Cyprian (Latin) from the island of Cyprus.
Ciprian, Cipriano, Ciprien, Cyprien

Cyrano (Greek) from Cyrene, an ancient city in North Africa. Literature: *Cyrano de Bergerac* is a play by Edmond Rostand about a great guardsman and poet whose large nose prevented him from pursuing the woman he loved.

Cyril (Greek) lordly. See also Kiril.
Cerek, Cerel, Ceril, Ciril, Cirillo, Cirrillo, Cyra, Cyrel, Cyrell, Cyrelle, Cyrill, Cyrille, Cyrillus, Syrell, Syril

Cyrus (Persian) sun. Historical: Cyrus the Great was a king in ancient Persia. See also Kir.
Ciro, Cy, Cyress, Cyris, Cyriss, Cyruss, Syris, Syrus

Czaren, Czarin (Russian) forms of Czar.

Czyz (Polish) greenfinch.

D

D 🅱 (American) an initial used as a first name.

Da (Chinese) attainment.

Dabi (Basque) a form of David.

Dabir (Arabic) tutor.

Dac Kien (Vietnamese) acquired view or knowledge.

Dacey 🅶 (Latin) from Dacia, an area now in Romania. (Irish) southerner.
Dace, Dache, Dacian, Dacias, Dacio, Dacy, Daicey, Daicy

Dachelbai (Palauan) skillful, clever.

Dada (Yoruba) curly haired.
Dadi

Daedalus (Greek) clever worker.

Daegel (English) from Daegel, England.

Daelen (English) a form of Dale.
Daelan, Daelin, Daelon, Daelyn, Daelyne

Daemon (Greek) a form of Damian. (Greek, Latin) a form of Damon.
Daemean, Daemeon, Daemien, Daemin, Daemion, Daemyen

Daequan (American) a form of Daquan.
Daequane, Daequon, Daequone, Daeqwan

Boys A–F

Daeshawn (American) a combination of the prefix Da + Shawn.
Daesean, Daeshaun, Daeshon, Daeshun, Daisean, Daishaun, Daishawn, Daishon, Daishoun

Daevon (American) a form of Davon.
Daevion, Daevohn, Daevonne, Daevonte, Daevontey

Daeyong (Korean) substitution.

Dafi (Chamorro) weak.

Dafydd (Welsh) a form of David.
Dafyd

Dag (Scandinavian) day; bright.
Daeg, Daegan, Dagen, Dagny, Deegan

Dagan (Hebrew) corn; grain.
Daegan, Daegon, Dagen, Dageon, Dagon

Dagfel (Yapese) I am not good.

Dago (Chamorro) a type of plant.

Dagoberto (Germanic) he who shines like the sun.

Dagwood (English) shining forest.

Dahi (Chamorro) friend.

Dai **G** (Japanese) big.

Daichi (Japanese) large; grand.

Daigoro (Japanese) great fifth-born son.

Daijiro (Japanese) great second son.

Daimian (Greek) a form of Damian.
Daiman, Daimean, Daimen, Daimeon, Daimeyon, Daimien, Daimin, Daimion, Daimyan

Daimon (Greek, Latin) a form of Damon.
Daimone

Daiquan (American) a form of Dajuan.
Daekwaun, Daekwon, Daiqone, Daiqua, Daiquane, Daiquawn, Daiquon, Daiqwan, Daiqwon

Daishiro (Japanese) great fourth-born son.

Daisuke (Japanese) big help; voluminous writings.

Daitaro (Japanese) great first-born son.

Daivon (American) a form of Davon.
Daivain, Daivion, Daivonn, Daivonte, Daiwan

Dajon (American) a form of Dajuan.
Dajean, Dajiawn, Dajin, Dajion, Dajn, Dajohn, Dajonae

Dajuan (American) a combination of the prefix Da + Juan. See also Dejuan.
Daejon, Daejuan, Daiquan, Dajon, Da Jon, Da-Juan, Dajwan, Dajwoun, Dakuan, Dakwan, Dawan, Dawaun, Dawawn, Dawon, Dawoyan, Dijuan, Diuan, Dujuan, D'Juan, D'juan, Dwaun

Dakarai (Shona) happy.
Dakairi, Dakar, Dakaraia, Dakari, Dakarri

Dakasy (Pohnpeian) a form of Takashi.

Dak-Ho (Korean) deep lake.

Dakoda (Dakota) a form of Dakota.
Dacoda, Dacodah, Dakodah, Dakodas

Dakota **B** (Dakota) friend; partner; tribal name.
Dac, Dack, Dackota, Dacota, DaCota, Dak, Dakcota, Dakkota, Dakoata, Dakoda, Dakotah, Dakotha, Dakotta, Dekota

Dakotah **B** (Dakota) a form of Dakota.
Dakottah

Daksh (Hindi) efficient.

Dalal (Sanskrit) broker.

Dalbert (English) bright, shining. See also Delbert.

Dale **B** (English) dale, valley.
Dael, Daelen, Dal, Dalen, Daley, Dalibor, Dallan, Dallin, Dallyn, Daly, Dayl, Dayle

Dalen (English) a form of Dale.
Dailin, Dalaan, Dalan, Dalane, Daleon, Dalian, Dalibor, Dalione, Dallan, Dalon, Daylan, Daylen, Daylin, Daylon

Daley (Irish) assembly. (English) a familiar form of Dale.
Daily, Daly, Dawley

Dalip (Yapese) three.

Dallan (English) a form of Dale.
Dallen, Dallon

Dallas **B** (Scottish) valley of the water; resting place. Geography: a town in Scotland; a city in Texas.
Dal, Dalieass, Dall, Dalles, Dallis, Dalys, Dellis

Dallen **B** (English) a form of Dallan.

Dallin, Dallyn **B** (English) pride's people.
Dalin, Dalyn

Dalmacio (Latin) native of Dalmatia, the western part of the Balkans.

Dalmazio (Italian) a form of Dalmacio.

Dalmiro (Germanic) illustrious one because of his heritage.

Dalston (English) Daegel's place.
Dalis, Dallon

Dalton **B** (English) town in the valley.
Dal, Dalaton, Dallton, Dalt, Daltan, Dalten, Daltin, Daltyn, Daulton, Delton

Dalvin (English) a form of Delvin.
Dalven, Dalvon, Dalvyn

Dalziel (Scottish) small field.

Damar (American) a short form of Damarcus, Damario.
Damare, Damari, Damarre, Damauri

Damarcus (American) a combination of the prefix Da + Marcus.
Damacus, Damar, Damarco, Damarcue, Damarick, Damark, Damarkco, Damarkis, Damarko, Damarkus, Damarques, Damarquez, Damarquis, Damarrco

Damario (Greek) gentle. (American) a combination of the prefix Da + Mario.
Damar, Damarea, Damareus, Damaria, Damarie, Damarino, Damarion, Damarious, Damaris, Damarius, Damarrea, Damarrion, Damarrious, Damarrius, Damaryo, Dameris, Damerius

Damaris **G** (Greek, American) a form of Damario.

Damaso (Greek) skillful horse breaker.

Dámaso (Greek) skillful tamer.

Damek (Slavic) a form of Adam.
Damick, Damicke

Dameon (Greek) a form of Damian.
Damein, Dameion, Dameone

Dametrius (Greek) a form of Demetrius.
Dametri, Dametries, Dametrious, Damitri, Damitric, Damitrie, Damitrious, Damitrius

Damian **B** (Greek) tamer; soother.
Daemon, Daimian, Damaiaon, Damaian, Damaien, Damain, Damaine, Damaion, Damani, Damanni, Damaun, Damayon, Dame, Damean, Dameon, Damián, Damiane, Damiann, Damiano, Damianos, Damien, Damion, Damiyan, Damján, Damyan, Daymian, Dema, Demyan

Damien **B** (Greek) a form of Damian. Religion: Father Damien ministered to the leper colony on the Hawaiian island Molokai.
Daemien, Daimien, Damie, Damienne, Damyen

Damion (Greek) a form of Damian.
Damieon, Damiion, Damin, Damine, Damionne, Damiyon, Dammion, Damyon

Damocles (Greek) gives glory to his village.

Damon **B** (Greek) constant, loyal. (Latin) spirit, demon.
Daemen, Daemon, Daemond, Daimon, Daman, Damen, Damond, Damone, Damoni, Damonn, Damonni, Damonta, Damontae, Damonte, Damontez, Damontis, Damyn, Daymon, Daymond

Dan **B** (Vietnamese) yes. (Hebrew) a short form of Daniel.
Dahn, Danh, Danne

Dana **G** (Scandinavian) from Denmark.
Dain, Daina, Dayna

Dandin (Hindi) holy man.

D'andre **B** (French) a form of Deandre.

Dandré (French) a combination of the prefix De + André.
D'André, Dandrae, D'andrea, Dandras, Dandray, Dandre, Dondrea

Dane **B** (English) from Denmark. See also Halden.
Dain, Daine, Danie, Dayne, Dhane

Danek (Polish) a form of Daniel.

Danforth (English) a form of Daniel.

Danglon (Chamorro) cowfish.

Danial (Hebrew) a form of Daniel.
Danal, Daneal, Danieal, Daniyal, Dannial

Danick, Dannick (Slavic) familiar forms of Daniel.
Danek, Danieko, Danik, Danika, Danyck

Daniel **W** **B** (Hebrew) God is my judge. Bible: a Hebrew prophet. See also Danno, Kanaiela.
Dacso, Dainel, Dan, Daneel, Daneil, Danek, Danel, Danforth, Danial, Danick, Dániel, Daniël, Daniele, Danielius, Daniell, Daniels, Danielson, Danilo, Daniyel, Dan'l, Dannel, Dannick, Danniel, Dannil, Danno, Danny, Dano, Danukas, Dany, Danyel, Danyell, Daoud, Dasco, Dayne, Deniel, Doneal, Doniel, Donois, Dusan, Nelo

Daniele (Hebrew) a form of Daniel.
Danile, Danniele

Danielle **G** (Hebrew, French) a form of Daniel

Danika **G** (Slavic) a form of Danick.

Danilo (Slavic) a form of Daniel.
Danielo, Danil, Danila, Danilka, Danylo

Danior (Gypsy) born with teeth.

Danladi (Hausa) born on Sunday.

Danno (Hebrew) a familiar form of Daniel. (Japanese) gathering in the meadow.
Dannon, Dano

Dannon (American) a form of Danno.
Daenan, Daenen, Dainon, Danaan, Danen, Danon

Danny, Dany **B** (Hebrew) familiar forms of Daniel.
Daney, Dani, Dannee, Danney, Danni, Dannie, Dannye

Dano (Czech) a form of Daniel.
Danko, Danno

Dante, Danté **B** (Latin) lasting, enduring.
Danatay, Danaté, Dant, Dantae, Dantay, Dantee, Dauntay, Dauntaye, Daunté, Dauntrae, Deante, Dontae, Donté

Dantel (Latin) enduring.

Dantrell (American) a combination of Dante + Darell.
Dantrel, Dantrey, Dantril, Dantyrell, Dontrell

Danyel **G** (Hebrew) a form of Daniel.
Danya, Danyal, Danyale, Danyele, Danyell, Danyiel, Danyl, Danyle, Danylets, Danylo, Donyell

Dao (Vietnamese) religions.

Daoud (Arabic) a form of David.
Daudi, Daudy, Dauod, Dawud

Daquan (American) a combination of the prefix Da + Quan.
Daequan, Daqon, Daquain, Daquaine, Da'quan, Daquandre, Daquandrey, Daquane, Daquann, Daquantae, Daquante, Daquarius, Daquaun, Daquawn, Daquin, Daquon, Daquone, Daquwon, Daqwain, Daqwan, Daqwane, Daqwann, Daqwon, Daqwone, Dayquan, Dequain, Dequan, Dequann, Dequaun

Dar (Hebrew) pearl.

Dara **G** (Cambodian) stars.

Daran (Irish) a form of Darren.
Darann, Darawn, Darian, Darran, Dayran, Deran

Darby **G** (Irish) free. (English) deer park.
Dar, Darb, Darbee, Darbey, Darbie, Derby

Darcy **G** (Irish) dark. (French) from Arcy, France.
Dar, Daray, D'Aray, Darce, Darcee, Darcel, Darcey, Darcio, D'Arcy, Darsey, Darsy

Dardo (Greek) astute and skillful.

Dareh (Persian) wealthy.

Darell (English) a form of Darrell.
Darall, Daralle, Dareal, Darel, Darelle, Darral, Darrall

Daren (Hausa) born at night. (Irish, English) a form of Darren.
Dare, Dayren, Dheren

Darian, Darrian **BG** (Irish) forms of Darren.
Daryan

Darick (German) a form of Derek.
Darek, Daric, Darico, Darieck, Dariek, Darik, Daryk

Darien, Darrien **B** (Irish) forms of Darren.

Darin **B** (Irish) a form of Darren.
Daryn, Darynn, Dayrin, Dearin, Dharin

Dario (Spanish) affluent.

Darío (Spanish) a form of Dario.

Darion, Darrion **B** (Irish) forms of Darren.
Dairean, Dairion, Darian, Darien, Darion, Darrian, Darrien, Darrione, Darriyun, Daryeon, Daryon, Derrian, Derrion

Darius **B** (Greek) wealthy.
Dairus, Dare, Darieus, Darioush, Dariuse, Dariush, Dariuss, Dariusz, Darrius

Darnell **B** (English) hidden place.
Dar, Darn, Darnall, Darneal, Darneil, Darnel, Darnelle, Darnyell, Darnyll

Daron **B** (Irish) a form of Darren.
Daeron, Dairon, Darone, Daronn, Darroun, Dayron, Dearon, Dharon, Diron

Darrell **B** (French) darling, beloved; grove of oak trees.
Dare, Darel, Darell, Darral, Darrel, Darrill, Darrol, Darryl, Derrell

Darren **B** (Irish) great. (English) small; rocky hill.
Daran, Dare, Daren, Darian, Darien, Darin, Darion, Daron, Darran, Darrian, Darrien, Darrience, Darrin, Darrion, Darron, Darryn, Darun, Daryn, Dearron, Deren, Dereon, Derren, Derron

Darrick (German) a form of Derek.
Darrec, Darrek, Darric, Darrik, Darryk

Darrin (Irish) a form of Darren.

Darrius (Greek) a form of Darius.
Darreus, Darrias, Darrious, Darris, Darriuss, Darrus, Darryus, Derrious, Derris, Derrius

Darron (Irish) a form of Darren.
Darriun, Darroun

Darryl **B** (French) darling, beloved; grove of oak trees. A form of Darrell.
Dahrll, Darryle, Darryll, Daryl, Daryle, Daryll, Derryl

Boys A–F

Darshan (Hindi) god; godlike. Religion: another name for the Hindu god Shiva.
Darshaun, Darshon

Darton (English) deer town.
Dartel, Dartrel

Darwin (English) dear friend. History: Charles Darwin was the British naturalist who established the theory of evolution.
Darvin, Darvon, Darwyn, Derwin, Derwynn, Durwin

Daryl B (French) a form of Darryl.
Darel, Daril, Darl, Darly, Daryell, Daryle, Daryll, Darylle, Daroyl

Dasan (Pomo) leader of the bird clan.
Dassan

Dashawn B (American) a combination of the prefix Da + Shawn.
Dasean, Dashan, Dashane, Dashante, Dashaun, Dashaunte, Dashean, Dashon, Dashonnie, Dashonte, Dashuan, Dashun, Dashwan, Dayshawn

Dativo (Latin) term from Roman law, which is applied to educators.

Dato (Latin) a form of Donato.

Dauid (Swahili) a form of David.

Daulton (English) a form of Dalton.

Davante (American) a form of Davonte.
Davanta, Davantay, Davinte

Davaris (American) a combination of Dave + Darius.
Davario, Davarious, Davarius, Davarrius, Davarus

Dave B (Hebrew) a short form of David, Davis.

Davey (Hebrew) a familiar form of David.
Davee, Davi, Davie, Davy

David ☽ B (Hebrew) beloved. Bible: the second king of Israel. See also Dov, Havika, Kawika, Taaveti, Taffy, Tevel.
Dabi, Daevid, Dafydd, Dai, Daivid, Daoud, Dauid, Dav, Dave, Daved, Daveed, Daven, Davey, Davidde, Davide, Davidek, Davido, Davon, Davoud, Davyd, Dawid, Dawit, Dawud, Dayvid, Dodya, Dov

Davin B (Scandinavian) brilliant Finn.
Daevin, Davion, Davon, Davyn, Dawan, Dawin, Dawine, Dayvon, Deavan, Deaven

Davion B (American) a form of Davin.
Davione, Davionne, Daviyon, Davyon, Deaveon

Davis B (Welsh) son of David.
Dave, Davidson, Davies, Davison

Davon B (American) a form of Davin.
Daevon, Daivon, Davon, Davone, Davonn, Davonne, Deavon, Deavone, Devon

Davonte B (American) a combination of Davon + the suffix Te.
Davante, Davonnte, Davonta, Davontae, Davontah, Davontai, Davontay, Davontaye, Davontea, Davontee, Davonti

Dawan (American) a form of Davin.
Dawann, Dawante, Dawaun, Dawayne, Dawon, Dawone, Dawoon, Dawyne, Dawyun

Dawit (Ethiopian) a form of David.

Dawn G (English) sunrise, dawn.

Dawson B (English) son of David.
Dawsyn

Dax (French, English) water.

Day (English) a form of Daniel.

Daylon (American) a form of Dillon.
Daylan, Daylen, Daylin, Daylun, Daylyn

Daymian (Greek) a form of Damian.
Daymayne, Daymen, Daymeon, Daymiane, Daymien, Daymin, Dayminn, Daymion, Daymn

Dayne (Scandinavian) a form of Dane.
Dayn

Dayquan (American) a form of Daquan.
Dayquain, Dayquawane, Dayquin, Dayqwan

Dayshawn (American) a form of Dashawn.
Daysean, Daysen, Dayshaun, Dayshon, Dayson

Dayton B (English) day town; bright, sunny town.
Daeton, Daiton, Daythan, Daython, Daytona, Daytonn, Deyton

Dayvon (American) a form of Davin.
Dayven, Dayveon, Dayvin, Dayvion, Dayvonn

De B (Chinese) virtuous.

Deacon (Greek) one who serves.
Deke

Dean B (French) leader. (English) valley. See also Dino.
Deane, Deen, Dene, Deyn, Deyne

Deana G (Latin) divine. (English) valley.

Deandre B (French) a combination of the prefix De + André.
D'andre, D'andré, D'André, D'andrea, Deandra, Deandrae, Déandre, Deandré, De André, Deandrea, De Andrea, Deandres, Deandrey, Deaundera, Deaundra, Deaundray, Deaundre, De Aundre, Deaundrey, Deaundry, Deondre, Diandre, Dondre

Boys A–F

Deangelo (Italian) a combination of the prefix De + Angelo.
Dang, Dangelo, D'Angelo, Danglo, Deaengelo, Deangelio, Deangello, Déangelo, De Angelo, Deangilio, Deangleo, Deanglo, Deangulo, Diangelo, Di'angelo

Deanna **G** (Latin) a form of Deana, Diana.

Deante (Latin) a form of Dante.
Deanta, Deantai, Deantay, Deanté, De Anté, Deanteé, Deaunta, Diantae, Diante, Diantey

Deanthony (Italian) a combination of the prefix De + Anthony.
D'anthony, Danton, Dianthony

Dearborn (English) deer brook.
Dearbourn, Dearburne, Deaurburn, Deerborn

Debesol (Palauan) one who is to be cut from the tree, like fruit before it is ripe.

Deborah **G** (Hebrew) bee.

Decarlos (Spanish) a combination of the prefix De + Carlos.
Dacarlos, Decarlo, Di'carlos

Decha (Tai) strong.

Decherong (Palauan) just standing up.

Decimus (Latin) tenth.

Decio (Latin) tenth.

Declan (Irish) man of prayer. Religion: Saint Declan was a fifth-century Irish bishop.
Deklan

Decoroso (Latin) he is well; he is practical.

Dédalo (Greek) industrious and skillful artisan.

Dedrick (German) ruler of the people. See also Derek, Theodoric.
Deadrick, Deddrick, Dederick, Dedrek, Dedreko, Dedric, Dedrix, Dedrrick, Deedrick, Diedrich, Diedrick, Dietrich, Detrick

Deems (English) judge's child.

Deicola (Latin) he who cultivates a relationship with God.

Deion **B** (Greek) a form of Dion.
Deione, Deionta, Deionte

Deja **G** (French) a form of Déja (see Girls' Names).

Dejuan (American) a combination of the prefix De + Juan. See also Dajuan.
Dejan, Dejon, Dejuane, Dejun, Dewan, Dewaun, Dewon, Dijaun, Djuan, D'Juan, Dujuan, Dujuane, D'Won

Dekel (Hebrew, Arabic) palm tree, date tree.

Dekota (Dakota) a form of Dakota.
Decoda, Dekoda, Dekodda, Dekotes

Del (English) a short form of Delbert, Delvin, Delwin.

Delaney **G** (Irish) descendant of the challenger.
Delaine, Delainey, Delainy, Delan, Delane, Delanny, Delany

Delano (French) nut tree. (Irish) dark.
Delanio, Delayno, Dellano

Delbert (English) bright as day. See also Dalbert.
Bert, Del, Dilbert

Delfín (Greek) playful one with a graceful and beautiful form.

Delfino (Latin) dolphin.
Delfine

Déli (Chinese) virtuous.

Dell (English) small valley. A short form of Udell.

Delling (Scandinavian) scintillating.

Delmar (Latin) sea.
Dalmar, Dalmer, Delmare, Delmario, Delmarr, Delmer, Delmor, Delmore

Delon (American) a form of Dillon.
Deloin, Delone, Deloni, Delonne

Delphine **G** (Greek) from Delphi, Greece.

Delroy (French) belonging to the king. See also Elroy, Leroy.
Delray, Delree, Delroi

Delshawn (American) a combination of Del + Shawn.
Delsean, Delshon, Delsin, Delson

Delsin (Native American) he is so.
Delsy

Delton (English) a form of Dalton.
Delten, Deltyn

Delvin (English) proud friend; friend from the valley.
Dalvin, Del, Delavan, Delvian, Delvon, Delvyn, Delwin

Delwin (English) a form of Delvin.
Dalwin, Dalwyn, Del, Dellwin, Dellwyn, Delwyn, Delwynn

Deman (Dutch) man.

Boys A–F

Demarco (Italian) a combination of the prefix De + Marco.
Damarco, Demarcco, Demarceo, Demarcio, Demarkco, Demarkeo, Demarko, Demarquo, D'Marco

Demarcus (American) a combination of the prefix De + Marcus.
Damarcius, Damarcus, Demarces, Demarcis, Demarcius, Demarcos, Demarcuse, Demarkes, Demarkis, Demarkos, Demarkus, Demarqus, D'Marcus

Demario (Italian) a combination of the prefix De + Mario.
Demarea, Demaree, Demareo, Demari, Demaria, Demariea, Demarion, Demarreio, Demariez, Demarious, Demaris, Demariuz, Demarrio, Demerio, Demerrio

Demarius (American) a combination of the prefix De + Marius.

Demarquis (American) a combination of the prefix De + Marquis.
Demarques, Demarquez, Demarqui

Dembe (Luganda) peaceful.
Damba

Demetri, Demitri (Greek) short forms of Demetrius.
Dametri, Damitré, Demeter, Demetre, Demetrea, Demetriel, Demitre, Demitrie, Domotor

Demetria ☷ (Greek) cover of the earth.

Demetris (Greek) a short form of Demetrius.
Demeatric, Demeatrice, Demeatris, Demetres, Demetress, Demetric, Demetrice, Demetrick, Demetrics, Demetricus, Demetrik, Demitrez, Demitries, Demitris

Demetrius ☐ (Greek) lover of the earth. Mythology: a follower of Demeter, the goddess of the harvest. See also Dimitri, Mimis, Mitsos.
Dametrius, Demeitrius, Demeterious, Demetreus, Demetri, Demetrias, Demetrio, Demetrios, Demetrious, Demetris, Demetriu, Demetrium, Demetrois, Demetruis, Demetrus, Demitirus, Demitri, Demitrias, Demitriu, Demitrius, Demitrus, Demtrius, Demtrus, Dimitri, Dimitrios, Dimitrius, Dmetrius, Dymek

Demian (Greek) he who emerged from the village.

Demián (Spanish) a form of Demian.

Demichael (American) a combination of the prefix De + Michael.
Dumichael

Demócrito (Greek) chosen by the villagers to be judge; the arbiter of the village.

Demond (Irish) a short form of Desmond.
Demonde, Demonds, Demone, Dumonde

Demont (French) mountain.
Démont, Demonta, Demontae, Demontay, Demontaz, Demonte, Demontez, Demontre

Demorris (American) a combination of the prefix De + Morris.
Demoris, DeMorris, Demorus

Demos (Greek) people.
Demas, Demosthenes

Demóstenes (Greek) strength of the village.

Demothi (Native American) talks while walking.

Dempsey (Irish) proud.
Demp, Demps, Dempsie, Dempsy

Dempster (English) one who judges.
Demster

Denbei, Denji (Japanese) forms of Den.

Denby (Scandinavian) Geography: a Danish village.
Danby, Den, Denbey, Denney, Dennie, Denny

Deng (Chinese) to ascend.

Dengyo (Japanese) historical figure.

Denham (English) village in the valley.

Denholm (Scottish) Geography: a town in Scotland.

Denis ☐ (Greek) a form of Dennis.
Deniz

Denise ☷ (Greek) a form of Denis.

Denjiro (Japanese) good ancestors.

Denley (English) meadow; valley.
Denlie, Denly

Denman (English) man from the valley.

Dennis ☐ (Greek) Mythology: a follower of Dionysus, the god of wine. See also Dion, Nicho.
Den, Dénes, Denies, Denis, Deniz, Dennes, Dennet, Dennez, Denny, Dennys, Denya, Denys, Deon, Dinis

Dennison (English) son of Dennis. See also Dyson, Tennyson.
Den, Denison, Denisson, Dennyson

Denny (Greek) a familiar form of Dennis.
Den, Denney, Dennie, Deny

Denton (English) happy home.
Dent, Denten, Dentin

Denver **B** (English) green valley.
Geography: the capital of Colorado.

Denzel **B** (Cornish) a form of Denzell.
Danzel, Dennzel, Denzal, Denzale, Denzall,
Denzell, Denzelle, Denzle, Denzsel

Denzell (Cornish) Geography: a location in
Cornwall, England.
Dennzil, Dennzyl, Denzel, Denzial, Denziel,
Denzil, Denzill, Denzyel, Denzyl, Donzell

Deodato (Latin) he who serves God.

Deon **B** (Greek) a form of Dennis. See also
Dion.
Deion, Deone, Deonn, Deonno

Deondre (French) a form of Deandre.
Deiondray, Deiondre, Deondra, Deondrae,
Deondray, Deondré, Deondrea, Deondree,
Deondrei, Deondrey, Diondra, Diondrae,
Diondre, Diondrey

Deontae (American) a combination of the
prefix De + Dontae.
Deonta, Deontai, Deontay, Deontaye, Deonte,
Deonté, Deontea, Deonteya, Deonteye,
Deontia, Dionte

Deonte, Deonté **B** (American) forms of
Deontae.
D'Ante, Deante, Deontée, Deontie

Deontre (American) a form of Deontae.
Deontrae, Deontrais, Deontray, Deontrea,
Deontrey, Deontrez, Deontreze, Deontrus

Dequan (American) a combination of the
prefix De + Quan.
Dequain, Dequane, Dequann, Dequante,
Dequantez, Dequantis, Dequaun, Dequavius,
Dequawn, Dequan, Dequin, Dequine,
Dequinn, Dequion, Dequoin, Dequon,
Deqwan, Deqwon, Deqwone

Dereck, Derick (German) forms of Derek.
Derekk, Dericka, Derico, Deriek, Derique,
Deryck, Deryk, Deryke, Detrek

Derek **B** (German) a short form of
Theodoric. See also Dedrick, Dirk.
Darek, Darick, Darrick, Derak, Dereck,
Derecke, Derele, Deric, Derick, Derik, Derk,
Derke, Derrek, Derrick, Deryek

Deric, Derik (German) forms of Derek.
Deriek, Derikk

Dermot (Irish) free from envy. (English) free.
(Hebrew) a short form of Jeremiah. See also
Kermit.
Der, Dermod, Dermott, Diarmid, Diarmuid

Deron (Hebrew) bird; freedom. (American) a
combination of the prefix De + Ron.
Daaron, Daron, Da-Ron, Darone, Darron,
Dayron, Dereon, Deronn, Deronne, Derrin,
Derrion, Derron, Derronn, Derronne, Derryn,
Diron, Duron, Durron, Dyron

Deror (Hebrew) lover of freedom.
Derori, Derorie

Derrek (German) a form of Derek.
Derrec, Derreck

Derrell (French) a form of Darrell.
Derel, Derele, Derell, Derelle, Derrel, Dérrell,
Derriel, Derril, Derrill, Deryl, Deryll

Derren (Irish, English) a form of Darren.
Deren, Derran, Derraun, Derreon, Derrian,
Derrien, Derrin, Derrion, Derron, Derryn,
Deryan, Deryn, Deryon

Derrick **B** (German) ruler of the people. A
form of Derek.
Derric, Derrik, Derryck, Derryk

Derry **BG** (Irish) redhead. Geography: a city
in Northern Ireland.
Darrie, Darry, Derri, Derrie, Derrye, Dery

Derryl (French) a form of Darryl.
Deryl, Deryll

Derward (English) deer keeper.

Derwin (English) a form of Darwin.
Derwyn

Desean (American) a combination of the
prefix De + Sean.
Dasean, D'Sean, Dusean

Deshane (American) a combination of the
prefix De + Shane.
Deshan, Deshayne

Deshaun (American) a combination of the
prefix De + Shaun.
Deshan, Deshane, Deshann, Deshaon,
Deshaune, D'shaun, D'Shaun, Dushaun

Deshawn **B** (American) a combination of
the prefix De + Shawn.
Dashaun, Dashawn, Deshauwn, Deshawan,
Deshawon, Deshon, D'shawn, D'Shawn,
Dushan, Dushawn

Deshea (American) a combination of the
prefix De + Shea.
Deshay

Deshi (Chinese) moral.

Déshì (Chinese) virtuous.

Deshon (American) a form of Deshawn.
Deshondre, Deshone, Deshonn, Deshonte,
Deshun, Deshunn

Desiderato (Latin) he who is desired.

Desiderio (Spanish) desired.

Desiderius (German) a form of Desiderio.

Desmond (Irish) from south Munster.
Demond, Des, Desi, Desimon, Desman, Desmand, Desmane, Desmen, Desmine, Desmon, Desmound, Desmund, Desmyn, Dezmon, Dezmond

Destin 🅱 (French) destiny, fate.
Destan, Desten, Destine, Deston, Destry, Destyn

Destiny 🅶 (French) fate.

Destry (American) a form of Destin.
Destrey, Destrie

Detrick (German) a form of Dedrick.
Detrek, Detric, Detrich, Detrik, Detrix

Devan 🅱 (Irish) a form of Devin.
Devaan, Devain, Devane, Devann, Devean, Devun, Diwan

Devante (American) a combination of Devan + the suffix Te.
Devanta, Devantae, Devantay, Devanté, Devantée, Devantez, Devanty, Devaughntae, Devaughnte, Devaunte, Deventae, Deventay, Devente, Divante

Devaughn (American) a form of Devin.
Devaugh, Devaun

Devayne (American) a form of Dewayne.
Devain, Devaine, Devan, Devane, Devayn, Devein, Deveion

Deven 🅱 (Hindi) for God. (Irish) a form of Devin.
Deaven, Deiven, Devein, Devenn, Devven, Diven

Devender (Sanskrit) Indra, the greatest god.

Deverell (English) riverbank.

Devin ☙ 🅱 (Irish) poet.
Deavin, Deivin, Dev, Devan, Devaughn, Deven, Devlyn, Devon, Devvin, Devy, Devyn, Dyvon

Devine (Latin) divine. (Irish) ox.
Davon, Devinn, Devon, Devyn, Devyne, Dewine

Devlin (Irish) brave, fierce.
Dev, Devlan, Devland, Devlen, Devlon, Devlyn

Devon 🅱 (Irish) a form of Devin.
Deavon, Deivon, Deivone, Deivonne, Deveon, Deveone, Devion, Devoen, Devohn, Devonae, Devone, Devoni, Devonio, Devonn, Devonne, Devontaine, Devvon, Devvonne, Dewon, Dewone, Divon, Diwon

Devonta 🅱 (American) a combination of Devon + the suffix Ta.
Deveonta, Devonnta, Devonntae, Devontae, Devontai, Devontay, Devontaye

Devonte 🅱 (American) a combination of Devon + the suffix Te.
Deveonte, Devionte, Devonté, Devontea, Devontee, Devonti, Devontia, Devontre

Devyn 🅱🅶 (Irish) a form of Devin.
Devyin, Devynn, Devynne

Dewayne (Irish) a form of Dwayne. (American) a combination of the prefix De + Wayne.
Deuwayne, Devayne, Dewain, Dewaine, Dewan, Dewane, Dewaun, Dewaune, Dewayen, Dewean, Dewon, Dewune

Dewei (Chinese) highly virtuous.

Dewey (Welsh) prized.
Dew, Dewi, Dewie

DeWitt (Flemish) blond.
Dewitt, Dwight, Wit

Dexter (Latin) dexterous, adroit. (English) fabric dyer.
Daxter, Decca, Deck, Decka, Dekka, Dex, Dextar, Dextor, Dextrel, Dextron

Dezmon, Dezmond (Irish) forms of Desmond.
Dezman, Dezmand, Dezmen, Dezmin

Dhani (Sanskrit) a rich person.

Dhanpal (Sanskrit) property; riches.

Dharam (Sanskrit) that which is held fast or kept; law; custom.

Di (Chinese) to enlighten.

Diakelmad (Palauan) never die.

Diamond 🅶 (English) brilliant gem; bright guardian.
Diaman, Diamanta, Diamante, Diamend, Diamenn, Diamont, Diamonta, Diamonte, Diamund, Dimond, Dimonta, Dimontae, Dimonte

Dian (Chinese) model, type.

Diana 🅶 (Latin) divine. Mythology: the goddess of the hunt, the moon, and fertility.

Dick (German) a short form of Frederick, Richard.
Dic, Dicken, Dickens, Dickie, Dickon, Dicky, Dik

Dickran (Armenian) History: an ancient Armenian king.
Dicran, Dikran

Dickson (English) son of Dick.
Dickenson, Dickerson, Dikerson, Diksan

Diderot (Spanish) a form of Desiderio.

Didi (Hebrew) a familiar form of Jedidiah, Yedidyah.

Didier (French) desired, longed for.

Didimo (Greek) twin brother.

Dídimo (Greek) identical twin brother.

Didio (Spanish) given by God.

Diedrich (German) a form of Dedrick, Dietrich.
Didrich, Didrick, Didrik, Diederick

Diego ✵ (Spanish) a form of Jacob, James.
Iago, Diaz, Jago

Dien (Vietnamese) farm, farming.

Dietbald (German) a form of Theobald.
Dietbalt, Dietbolt

Dieter (German) army of the people.
Deiter

Dietrich (German) a form of Dedrick.
Deitrich, Deitrick, Deke, Diedrich, Dietrick, Dierck, Dieter, Dieterich, Dieterick, Dietz

Dieu Hien (Vietnamese) amaryllis.

Digby (Irish) ditch town; dike town.

Dillan **B** (Irish) a form of Dillon.
Dilan, Dillian, Dilun, Dilyan

Dillon **B** (Irish) loyal, faithful. See also Dylan.
Daylon, Delon, Dil, Dill, Dillan, Dillen, Dillie, Dillin, Dillion, Dilly, Dillyn, Dilon, Dilyn, Dilynn

Dilwyn (Welsh) shady place.
Dillwyn

Dima (Russian) a familiar form of Vladimir.
Dimka

Dimas (Greek) loyal comrade; exemplary companion.

Dimitri **B** (Russian) a form of Demetrius.
Dimetra, Dimetri, Dimetric, Dimetrie, Dimitr, Dimitric, Dimitrie, Dimitrik, Dimitris, Dimitry, Dimmy, Dmitri, Dymitr, Dymitry

Dimitrios (Greek) a form of Demetrius.
Dhimitrios, Dimitrius, Dimos, Dmitrios

Dimitrius (Greek) a form of Demetrius.
Dimetrius, Dimitricus, Dimitrius, Dimetrus, Dmitrius

Ding (Chinese) able-bodied man.

Dingbang (Chinese) protector of the country.

Dinh (Vietnamese) calm, peaceful.
Din

Dinh Hoa (Vietnamese) flower at the peak.

Dinís (Greek) devoted to Dionysus.

Dino (German) little sword. (Italian) a form of Dean.
Deano

Dinos (Greek) a familiar form of Constantine, Konstantin.

Dinsmore (Irish) fortified hill.
Dinnie, Dinny, Dinse

Diodoro (Greek) Mythology: the grandson of Hercules who brought to submission many villages.

Diogenes (Greek) honest. History: an ancient philosopher who searched with a lantern in daylight for an honest man.
Diogenese

Diógenes (Greek) a form of Diogenes.

Diómedes (Greek) he who trusts in God's protection.

Dion **B** (Greek) a short form of Dennis, Dionysus.
Deion, Deon, Dio, Dione, Dionigi, Dionis, Dionn, Dionne, Diontae, Dionte, Diontray

Dionisio (Greek) a form of Dionysus.

Dionte (American) a form of Deontae.
Diante, Dionta, Diontae, Diontay, Diontaye, Dionté, Diontea

Dionysus (Greek) celebration. Mythology: the god of wine.
Dion, Dionesios, Dionicio, Dionisio, Dionisios, Dionusios, Dionysios, Dionysius, Dunixi

Dioscoro (Latin) he who is of the Lord.

Dióscoro (Greek) a form of Dioscoro.

Dip (Sanskrit) light.

Diquan (American) a combination of the prefix Di + Quan.
Diqawan, Diqawn, Diquane

Dirk (German) a short form of Derek, Theodoric.
Derk, Dirck, Dirke, Durc, Durk, Dyrk

Dishi (Chinese) man of virtue.

Diven (Sanskrit) a form of Divendra.

Divendra (Sanskrit) divine Indra; most divine.

Dixon (English) son of Dick.
Dickson, Dix

Dmitri (Russian) a form of Dimitri.
Dmetriy, Dmitiri, Dmitri, Dmitrik, Dmitriy

Doami (Japanese) literary figure.

Boys A–F

Doane (English) low, rolling hills.
Doan

Dob (English) a familiar form of Robert.
Dobie

Dobry (Polish) good.

Doherty (Irish) harmful.
Docherty, Dougherty, Douherty

Doho (Japanese) literary figure.

Dohpi (Pohnpeian) a form of Toby.

Dolan (Irish) dark haired.
Dolin, Dolyn

Dolf, Dolph (German) short forms of Adolf, Adolph, Rudolf, Rudolph.
Dolfe, Dolfi, Dolphe, Dolphus

Dolores 🄶 (Spanish) sorrowful.

Dom (Latin) a short form of Dominic.
Dome, Domó

Domenic 🄱 (Latin) an alternate form of Dominic.
Domanick, Domenick

Domenico (Italian) a form of Dominic.
Domenic, Domicio, Dominico, Menico

Domiciano (Spanish) a form of Domicio.

Domicio (Italian) a form of Domenico.

Domigko, Domingko (Chuukese) forms of Domingo.

Domingo (Spanish) born on Sunday. See also Mingo.
Demingo, Domingos

Dominic ☀ 🄱 (Latin) belonging to the Lord. See also Chuminga.
Deco, Demenico, Dom, Domanic, Domeka, Domenic, Domenico, Domini, Dominie, Dominik, Dominique, Dominitric, Dominy, Domminic, Domnenique, Domokos, Domonic, Nick

Dominick 🄱 (Latin) a form of Dominic.
Domiku, Domineck, Dominick, Dominicke, Dominiek, Dominik, Dominnick, Dominyck, Domminick, Dommonick, Domnick, Domokos, Domonick, Donek, Dumin

Dominik (Latin) a form of Dominic.
Domenik, Dominiko, Dominyk, Domonik

Dominique 🄶 (French) a form of Dominic.
Domeniq, Domeniqu, Domenique, Domenque, Dominiqu, Dominque, Dominiqueia, Domnenique, Domnique, Domoniqu, Domonique, Domunique

Dominque 🄱🄶 (French) a form of Dominique.

Domokos (Hungarian) a form of Dominic.
Dedo, Dome, Domek, Domok, Domonkos

Domonique 🄶 (French) a form of Dominique.

Domotom (Chuukese) a form of Domingo.

Don 🄱 (Scottish) a short form of Donald. See also Kona.
Donn

Donado (Pohnpeian) a form of Donato.

Donahue (Irish) dark warrior.
Donohoe, Donohue

Donal (Irish) a form of Donald.

Donald (Scottish) world leader; proud ruler. See also Bohdan, Tauno.
Don, Donal, Dónal, Donaldo, Donall, Donalt, Donát, Donaugh, Donnie

Donardo (Celtic) he who governs boldly.

Donatien (French) gift.
Donathan, Donathon

Donato (Italian) gift.
Dodek, Donatello, Donati, Donatien, Donatus

Donavan (Irish) a form of Donovan.
Donaven, Donavin, Donavon, Donavyn

Dondre (French) a form of Deandre.
Dondra, Dondrae, Dondray, Dondré, Dondrea

Dong (Vietnamese) easterner.
Duong

Dong-Sun (Korean) eastern integrity.

Dong-Yul (Korean) eastern passion.

Donkor (Akan) humble.

Donnell 🄱 (Irish) brave; dark.
Doneal, Donel, Donele, Donell, Donelle, Doniel, Donielle, Donnel, Donnele, Donnelle, Donnelly, Donniel, Donyel, Donyell

Donnelly (Irish) a form of Donnell.
Donelly, Donlee, Donley

Donnie, Donny 🄱 (Irish) familiar forms of Donald.

Donovan (Irish) dark warrior.
Dohnovan, Donavan, Donevan, Donevon, Donivan, Donnivan, Donnovan, Donnoven, Donoven, Donovin, Donovon, Donvan

Dontae, Donté (American) forms of Dante.
Donta, Dontai, Dontao, Dontate, Dontavious,

Dontavius, Dontay, Dontaye, Dontea, Dontee, Dontez

Donte **B** (Latin) a form of Donata (see Girls' Names).

Dontrell **B** (American) a form of Dantrell.
Dontral, Dontrall, Dontray, Dontre, Dontreal, Dontrel, Dontrelle, Dontriel, Dontriell

Donzell (Cornish) a form of Denzell.
Donzeil, Donzel, Donzelle, Donzello

Dooley (Irish) dark hero.
Dooly

Dopi (Pohnpeian) a form of Tobias.

Dopias (Pohnpeian) a form of Tobias.

Dor (Hebrew) generation.

Doran (Greek, Hebrew) gift. (Irish) stranger; exile.
Dore, Dorin, Dorran, Doron, Dorren, Dory

Dorian **B** (Greek) from Doris, Greece. See also Isidore.
Dore, Dorey, Dorie, Dorien, Dorin, Dorion, Dorján, Doron, Dorrian, Dorrien, Dorrin, Dorrion, Dorron, Dorryen, Dory

Doroteo (Greek) gift of God.

Dorrell (Scottish) king's doorkeeper. See also Durell.
Dorrel, Dorrelle

Dositeo (Greek) God's possession.

Dotan (Hebrew) law.
Dothan

Doug (Scottish) a short form of Dougal, Douglas.
Dougie, Dougy, Dugey, Dugie, Dugy

Dougal (Scottish) dark stranger. See also Doyle.
Doug, Dougall, Dugal, Dugald, Dugall, Dughall

Douglas **B** (Scottish) dark river, dark stream. See also Koukalaka.
Doug, Douglass, Dougles, Dugaid, Dughlas

Dov (Yiddish) bear. (Hebrew) a familiar form of David.
Dovid, Dovidas, Dowid

Dovev (Hebrew) whisper.

Dow (Irish) dark haired.

Doyle (Irish) a form of Dougal.
Doy, Doyal, Doyel

Drago (Italian) a form of Drake.

Drake **B** (English) dragon; owner of the inn with the dragon trademark.
Drago

Draper (English) fabric maker.
Dray, Draypr

Draven **B** (American) a combination of the letter D + Raven.
Dravian, Dravin, Dravion, Dravon, Dravone, Dravyn, Drayven, Drevon

Dreng (Norwegian) hired hand; brave.

Dreshawn (American) a combination of Drew + Shawn.
Dreshaun, Dreshon, Dreshown

Drevon (American) a form of Draven.
Drevan, Drevaun, Dreven, Drevin, Drevion, Drevone

Drew **B** (Welsh) wise. (English) a short form of Andrew.
Drewe, Dru

Dru (English) a form of Drew.
Druan, Drud, Drue, Drugi, Drui

Drummond (Scottish) druid's mountain.
Drummund, Drumond, Drumund

Drury (French) loving. Geography: Drury Lane is a street in London's theater district.

Dryden (English) dry valley.
Dry

Du (Vietnamese) play.

Duan (Chinese) upright.

Duane **B** (Irish) a form of Dwayne.
Deune, Duain, Duaine, Duana

Duardo (Spanish) prosperous guardian.

Duarte (Portuguese) rich guard. See also Edward.

Duc (Vietnamese) moral.
Duoc, Duy

Duck-Hwan (Korean) integrity returns.

Duck-Young (Korean) integrity lasts.

Dudd (English) a short form of Dudley.
Dud, Dudde, Duddy

Dudley (English) common field.
Dudd, Dudly

Dudus (Chamorro) flirtatious; handsome.

Due (Vietnamese) virtuous.

Duer (Scottish) heroic.

Boys A–F

Duff (Scottish) dark.
Duffey, Duffie, Duffy

Dugan (Irish) dark.
Doogan, Dougan, Douggan, Duggan

Duilio (Latin) ready to fight.

Duke (French) leader; duke.
Dukey, Dukie, Duky

Dukker (Gypsy) fortuneteller.

Dulani (Nguni) cutting.

Dulcidio (Latin) sweet.

Dumaka (Ibo) helping hand.

Duman (Turkish) misty, smoky.

Duncan (Scottish) brown warrior. Literature: King Duncan was Macbeth's victim in Shakespeare's play *Macbeth*.
Dunc, Dunn

Dung (Vietnamese) bravery.

Dunham (Scottish) brown.

Dunixi (Basque) a form of Dionysus.

Dunley (English) hilly meadow.

Dunlop (Scottish) muddy hill.

Dunmore (Scottish) fortress on the hill.

Dunn (Scottish) a short form of Duncan.
Dun, Dune, Dunne

Dunstan (English) brownstone fortress.
Dun, Dunston

Dunton (English) hill town.

Duo (Chinese) much, many; more.

Dur (Hebrew) stacked up. (English) a short form of Durwin.

Durand (Latin) a form of Durant.

Durant (Latin) enduring.
Duran, Durance, Durand, Durante, Durontae, Durrant

Durell (Scottish, English) king's doorkeeper. See also Dorrell.
Durel, Durial, Durreil, Durrell, Durrelle

Durko (Czech) a form of George.

Durriken (Gypsy) fortuneteller.

Durril (Gypsy) gooseberry.
Durrel, Durrell

Durward (English) gatekeeper.
Dur, Ward

Durwin (English) a form of Darwin.

Dushawn (American) a combination of the prefix Du + Shawn.
Dusan, Dusean, Dushan, Dushane, Dushaun, Dushon, Dushun

Dustin ⬛ (German) valiant fighter. (English) brown rock quarry.
Dust, Dustain, Dustan, Dusten, Dustie, Dustine, Dustion, Duston, Dusty, Dustyn, Dustynn

Dusty ⬛ (English) a familiar form of Dustin.

Dustyn (English) a form of Dustin.

Dutch (Dutch) from the Netherlands; from Germany.

Duval (French) a combination of the prefix Du + Val.
Duvall, Duveuil

Dwaun (American) a form of Dajuan.
Dwan, Dwaunn, Dwawn, Dwon, Dwuann

Dwayne ⬛ (Irish) dark. See also Dewayne.
Dawayne, Dawyne, Duane, Duwain, Duwan, Duwane, Duwayn, Duwayne, Dwain, Dwaine, Dwan, Dwane, Dwyane, Dywan, Dywane, Dywayne, Dywone

Dwight (English) a form of DeWitt.

Dyami (Native American) soaring eagle.

Dyer (English) fabric dyer.

Dyke (English) dike; ditch.
Dike

Dylan ☙ ⬛ (Welsh) sea. See also Dillon.
Dylane, Dylann, Dylen, Dylian, Dylin, Dyllan, Dyllen, Dyllian, Dyllin, Dyllyn, Dylon, Dylyn

Dylon (Welsh) a form of Dylan.
Dyllion, Dyllon

Dyonis (German) a form of Dionisio.

Dyre (Norwegian) dear heart.

Dyson (English) a short form of Dennison.
Dysen, Dysonn

E 🄶 (American) an initial used as a first name.

Ea (Irish) a form of Hugh.

Eachan (Irish) horseman.

Boys A–F

Eadberto (Teutonic) outstanding for his riches.

Eagan (Irish) very mighty.
Egan, Egon

Eamon (Irish) a form of Edmond, Edmund.
Aimon, Eammon, Eamonn

Ean (English) a form of Ian.
Eaen, Eann, Eayon, Eion, Eon, Eyan, Eyon

Earl (Irish) pledge. (English) nobleman.
Airle, Earld, Earle, Earlie, Earlson, Early, Eorl, Erl, Erle, Errol

Earnest (English) a form of Ernest.
Earn, Earnesto, Earnie, Eranest

Easton (English) eastern town.
Eason, Easten, Eastin, Eastton

Eaton (English) estate on the river.
Eatton, Eton, Eyton

Eb (Hebrew) a short form of Ebenezer.
Ebb, Ebbie, Ebby

Eben (Hebrew) rock.
Eban, Ebin, Ebon

Ebenezer (Hebrew) foundation stone. Literature: Ebenezer Scrooge is a miserly character in Charles Dickens's *A Christmas Carol*.
Eb, Ebbaneza, Eben, Ebeneezer, Ebeneser, Ebenezar, Eveneser

Eberhard (German) courageous as a boar. See also Everett.
Eber, Ebere, Eberardo, Eberhardt, Evard, Everard, Everardo, Everhardt, Everhart

Ebisu (Japanese) god of labor and luck.

Ebner (English) a form of Abner.

Ebo (Fante) born on Tuesday.

Ebony G (Greek) a hard, dark wood.

Echa (Chamorro) to give blessing.

Echu (Chamorro) completed.

Ecio (Latin) possessor of great strength.

Eco (Greek) sound, resonance.

Ed (English) a short form of Edgar, Edsel, Edward.
Edd

Edan (Scottish) fire.
Edain

Edbert (English) wealthy; bright.
Ediberto

Edberto (Germanic) he whose blade makes him shine.

Edco (Greek) he who blows with force.

Eddie (English) a familiar form of Edgar, Edsel, Edward.
Eddee, Eddy, Edi, Edie

Eddy B (English) a form of Eddie.
Eddye, Edy

Edel (German) noble.
Adel, Edell, Edelmar, Edelweiss

Edelberto (Teutonic) descendant of nobles.

Edelio (Greek) person who always remains young.

Edelmiro (Germanic) celebrated for the nobility that he represents.

Eden G (Hebrew) delightful. Bible: the garden that was first home to Adam and Eve.
Eaden, Eadin, Edan, Edenson, Edin, Edyn, Eiden

Edeng (Palauan) shark.

Eder (Hebrew) flock.
Ederick, Edir

Edgar B (English) successful spearman. See also Garek, Gerik, Medgar.
Ed, Eddie, Edek, Edgard, Edgardo, Edgars

Edgardo (Spanish) a form of Edgar.

Edigar (Pohnpeian) a form of Edgardo.

Edilio (Greek) he who is like a statue.

Edipo (Greek) he who has swollen feet.

Edison (English) son of Edward.
Eddison, Edisen, Edson

Edmond (English) a form of Edmund.
Eamon, Edmon, Edmonde, Edmondo, Edmondson, Esmond

Edmund (English) prosperous protector.
Eadmund, Eamon, Edmand, Edmáund, Edmond, Edmun, Edmundo, Edmunds

Edmundo (Spanish) a form of Edmund.
Edmando, Mundo

Edo (Czech) a form of Edward.

Edoardo (Italian) a form of Edward.

Edorta (Basque) a form of Edward.

Edouard (French) a form of Edward.
Édoard, Édouard

Edric (English) prosperous ruler.
Eddric, Eddrick, Ederick, Edrek, Edrice, Edrick, Edrico

Edsel (English) rich man's house.
Ed, Eddie, Edsell

Edson (English) a short form of Edison.
Eddson, Edsen

Eduardo 🅱 (Spanish) a form of Edward.
Estuardo, Estvardo

Edur (Basque) snow.

Edward (English) prosperous guardian. See also Audie, Duarte, Ekewaka, Ned, Ted, Teddy.
Ed, Eddie, Edik, Edko, Edo, Edoardo, Edorta, Édouard, Eduard, Eduardo, Edus, Edvard, Edvardo, Edwardo, Edwards, Edwy, Edzio, Ekewaka, Etzio, Ewart

Edwin 🅱 (English) prosperous friend. See also Ned, Ted.
Eadwinn, Edik, Edlin, Eduino, Edwan, Edwen, Edwon, Edwyn

Efrain (Hebrew) fruitful.
Efran, Efrane, Efrayin, Efren, Efrian, Eifraine

Efraín (Hebrew) a form of Efrain.

Efrat (Hebrew) honored.

Efreín, Efrén (Spanish) a form of Efraín.

Efrem (Hebrew) a short form of Ephraim.
Efe, Efraim, Efrim, Efrum

Efren (Hebrew) a form of Efrain, Ephraim.

Egan (Irish) ardent, fiery.
Egann, Egen, Egon

Egbert (English) bright sword. See also Bert, Bertie.

Egerton (English) Edgar's town.
Edgarton, Edgartown, Edgerton, Egeton

Egidio (Greek) he who, in battle, carries the goatskin sword.

Egil (Norwegian) awe inspiring.
Eigil

Eginhard (German) power of the sword.
Eginhardt, Einhard, Einhardt, Enno

Egisto (Greek) raised on goat's milk.

Egon (German) formidable.

Egor (Russian) a form of George. See also Igor, Yegor.

Ehnos (Pohnpeian) a form of Enos.

Ehpel (Pohnpeian) a form of Abel.

Ehren (German) honorable.

Eiichi (Japanese) excellent first son.

Eiji (Japanese) excellent second son.

Eijiro (Japanese) splendid next son.

Eikki (Finnish) ever powerful.

Eileen 🅶 (Irish) a form of Helen.

Einar (Scandinavian) individualist.
Ejnar, Inar

Eion (Irish) a form of Ean, Ian.
Eann, Eian, Ein, Eine, Einn

Eisaku (Japanese) eternal creation; witty creation; flourishing creation.

Eitan (Hebrew) a form of Ethan.
Eita, Eithan, Eiton

Eitaro (Japanese) big, tall man; witty big man; prosperous man.

Eito (Japanese) prosperous person.

Ejau (Ateso) we have received.

Ekewaka (Hawaiian) a form of Edward.

Ekit (Chuukese) a form of Ekitekit.

Ekitekit (Chuukese) to strive for.

Ekon (Nigerian) strong.

Eladio (Greek) he who came from Greece.

Elam (Hebrew) highlands.

Elan (Hebrew) tree. (Native American) friendly.
Elann

Elbert (English) a form of Albert.
Elberto

Elbio (Celtic) he who comes from the mountain.

Elchanan (Hebrew) a form of John.
Elchan, Elchonon, Elhanan, Elhannan

Elden (English) a form of Alden, Aldous.
Eldan, Eldin

Elder (English) dweller near the elder trees.

Eldon (English) holy hill.

Eldred (English) a form of Aldred.
Eldrid

Eldridge (English) a form of Aldrich.
El, Eldred, Eldredge, Eldrege, Eldrid, Eldrige, Elric

Eldwin (English) a form of Aldwin.
Eldwinn, Eldwyn, Eldwynn

Eleanor 🅶 (Greek) light.

Eleazar (Hebrew) God has helped. See also
Lazarus.
*Elazar, Elazaro, Eleasar, Eléazar, Eliazar,
Eliezer*

Eleazaro (Hebrew) God will help me.

Elek (Hungarian) a form of Alec, Alex.
Elec, Elic, Elik

Elenio (Greek) he who shines like the sun.

Eleno (Spanish) bright.

Eleodoro (Greek) he who comes from the
sun.

Eleuterio (Greek) he who enjoys liberty for
being honest.

Elevuka (Fijian) from Levuka.

Elger (German) a form of Alger.
Elger, Ellgar, Ellger

Elgin (English) noble; white.
Elgan, Elgen

Eli **B** (Hebrew) uplifted. A short form of
Elijah, Elisha. Bible: the high priest who
trained the prophet Samuel. See also Elliot.
Elie, Elier, Ellie, Eloi, Eloy, Ely

Elia **G** (Zuni) a short form of Elijah.
Eliah, Elio, Eliya, Elya

Elian (English) a form of Elijah. See also
Trevelyan.
Elion

Elias (Greek) a form of Elijah.
*Elia, Eliasz, Elice, Eliyas, Ellias, Ellice, Ellis,
Elyas, Elyes*

Elías (Hebrew) a form of Elias.

Eliazar (Hebrew) a form of Eleazar.
Eliasar, Eliazer, Elizar, Elizardo

Elido (Greek) native of Elida.

Elie (Hebrew) a form of Eli.

Eliecer (Hebrew) God is his constant aid.

Eliezer (Hebrew) a form of Eleazar.
Elieser

Eligio (Latin) he who has been elected by
God.

Elihu (Hebrew) a short form of Eliyahu.
Elih, Eliu, Ellihu

Elijah 🌿 **B** (Hebrew) a form of Eliyahu.
Bible: a Hebrew prophet. See also Eli, Elisha,
Elliot, Ilias, Ilya.
*El, Elia, Elian, Elias, Elija, Elijha, Elijiah, Elijio,
Elijuah, Elijuo, Elisjsha, Eliya, Eliyah, Ellis*

Elika (Hawaiian) a form of Eric.

Eliki (Fijian) a form of Alejandro.

Elimas (Chuukese) crescent moon.

Elisabeth **G** (Hebrew) a form of Elizabeth.

Elisandro (Greek) liberator of men.

Eliseo (Hebrew) a form of Elisha.
Elisee, Elisée, Elisei, Elisiah, Elisio

Elisha **BG** (Hebrew) God is my salvation.
Bible: a Hebrew prophet, successor to Elijah.
See also Eli, Elijah.
*Elijsha, Eliseo, Elish, Elishah, Elisher, Elishia,
Elishua, Elysha, Lisha*

Eliyahu (Hebrew) the Lord is my God.
Eliyahou, Elihu

Elizabeth **G** (Hebrew) consecrated to God

Elkan (Hebrew) God is jealous.
Elkana, Elkanah, Elkin, Elkins

Elki (Moquelumnan) hanging over the top.

Ella **G** (English) elfin; beautiful. (Greek) a
short form of Eleanor.

Ellard (German) sacred; brave.
Allard, Ellerd

Ellery (English) from a surname derived
from the name Hilary.
Ellary, Ellerey

Ellie **G** (Hebrew) a form of Eli.

Elliot, Elliott **B** (English) forms of Eli,
Elijah.
*Elio, Eliot, Eliott, Eliud, Eliut, Elliotte, Elyot,
Elyott*

Ellis **B** (English) a form of Elias (see Boys'
Names).
Elis

Ellison (English) son of Ellis.
Elison, Ellson, Ellyson, Elson

Ellsworth (English) nobleman's estate.
Ellswerth, Elsworth

Elman (German) like an elm tree.
Elmen

Elmer (English) noble; famous.
Aylmer, Elemér, Ellmer, Elmir, Elmo

Elmo (Greek) lovable, friendly. (Italian)
guardian. (Latin) a familiar form of
Anselm. (English) a form of Elmer.

Elmore (English) moor where the elm trees
grow.

Elong (Palauan) big talker, braggart.

Eloni (Fijian) oak.

Elonzo (Spanish) a form of Alonzo.
Elon, Élon, Elonso

Eloy (Latin) chosen.
Eloi

Elpidio (Greek) he who has hopes.

Elrad (Hebrew) God rules.
Rad, Radd

Elroy (French) a form of Delroy, Leroy.
Elroi

Elsdon (English) nobleman's hill.

Elston (English) noble's town.
Ellston

Elsu (Native American) swooping, soaring falcon.

Elsworth (English) noble's estate.

Elton (English) old town.
Alton, Eldon, Ellton, Elthon, Eltonia

Eluney (Mapuche) gift.

Elvern (Latin) a form of Alvern.
Elver, Elverne

Elvin (English) a form of Alvin.
El, Elvyn, Elwin, Elwyn, Elwynn

Elvio (Spanish) light skinned; blond.

Elvis (Scandinavian) wise.
El, Elviz, Elvys

Elvy (English) elfin warrior.

Elwell (English) old well.

Elwood (English) old forest. See also Wood, Woody.

Ely (Hebrew) a form of Eli. Geography: a region of England with extensive drained fens.
Elya, Elyie

Eman (Czech) a form of Emmanuel.
Emaney, Emani

Emanuel 🅱 (Hebrew) a form of Emmanuel.
Emaniel, Emannual, Emannuel, Emanual, Emanueal, Emanuele, Emanuell, Emanuelle

Emanueli (Fijian) a form of Manuel.

Emerenciano (Latin) to be deserving, to acquire the rights to something.

Emerson 🅱 (German, English) son of Emery.
Emmerson, Emreson

Emery 🅱 (German) industrious leader.
Aimery, Emari, Emarri, Emeri, Emerich, Emerio, Emmerich, Emmerie, Emmery, Emmo, Emory, Emrick, Emry, Inre, Imrich

Emesto (Spanish) serious.

Emeterio (Greek) he who deserves affection.

Emigdio (Greek) he who has brown skin.

Emiir, Emr (Arabic) forms of Amir.

Emil (Latin) flatterer. (German) industrious. See also Milko, Milo.
Aymil, Emiel, Émile, Emilek, Emiliano, Emilio, Emill, Emils, Emilyan, Emlyn

Emile 🅱 (French) a form of Émile.

Émile (French) a form of Emil.
Emiel, Emile, Emille

Emiliano (Italian) a form of Emil.
Emilian, Emilion

Emilien (Latin) friendly; industrious.

Emilio 🅱 (Italian, Spanish) a form of Emil.
Emielio, Emileo, Emilio, Emilios, Emillio, Emilo

Emillen (Latin) hard-working man.

Emily 🅶 (Latin) flatterer. (German) industrious.

Emir (Arabic) chief, commander.

Emlyn (Welsh) waterfall.
Emelen, Emlen, Emlin

Emma 🅶 (German) a short form of Emily.

Emmanuel 🅱 (Hebrew) God is with us. See also Immanuel, Maco, Mango, Manuel.
Eman, Emanuel, Emanuell, Emek, Emmahnuel, Emmanel, Emmaneuol, Emmanle, Emmanual, Emmanueal, Emmanuele, Emmanuell, Emmanuelle, Emmanuil, Enmanuel

Emmanuelle 🅶 (Hebrew) a form of Emmanuel.

Emmett (German) industrious; strong. (English) ant. History: Robert Emmett was an Irish patriot.
Em, Emet, Emett, Emitt, Emmet, Emmette, Emmitt, Emmot, Emmott, Emmy

Emmitt (German, English) a form of Emmett.
Emmit

Emory 🅱 (German) a form of Emery.
Amory, Emmory, Emorye

Emosi (Fijian) a form of Amos.

Emre (Turkish) brother.
Emra, Emrah, Emreson

Emrick (German) a form of Emery.
Emeric, Emerick, Emric, Emrique, Emryk

Emul (Palauan) weeds.

En (Chinese) kindness.

Enap (Chuukese) powerful one.

Enapay (Sioux) brave appearance; he appears.

Endre (Hungarian) a form of Andrew.
Ender

Eneas (Greek) a form of Aeneas.
Eneias, Enné

Eneriko (Pohnpeian) a form of Enrique.

Engelbert (German) bright as an angel. See also Ingelbert.
Bert, Englebert

Engelberto (Germanic) shining of the Anglos.

Enio (Spanish) second divinity of war.

Enlai (Chinese) thankful.

Enli (Dene) that dog over there.

Ennio (Italian) from the area of Enna.

Ennis (Greek) mine. (Scottish) a form of Angus.
Eni, Enni

Enoch (Hebrew) dedicated, consecrated. Bible: the father of Methuselah.
Enoc, Enock, Enok

Enol (Asturian) referring to lake Enol.

Enon (Hebrew) very strong.

Enos (Hebrew) man.
Enosh

Enric (Romanian) a form of Henry.
Enrica

Enrick (Spanish) a form of Henry.
Enricky

Enrico (Italian) a form of Henry.
Enzio, Enzo, Rico

Enrikos (Greek) a form of Henry.

Enrique (Spanish) a form of Henry. See also Quiqui.
Enrigué, Enriqué, Enriquez, Enrrique

Enunaurois (Palauan) facing a mountain.

Enver (Turkish) bright; handsome.

Enyeto (Native American) walks like a bear.

Enzi (Swahili) powerful.

Eoin (Welsh) a form of Evan.

Eparama (Fijian) a form of Abraham.

Epel, Epeli (Chuukese) forms of Abel.

Epenisa (Fijian) a form of Ebenezer.

Ephraim (Hebrew) fruitful. Bible: the second son of Joseph.
Efraim, Efrayim, Efrem, Efren, Ephraen, Ephrain, Ephram, Ephrem, Ephriam

Epicuro (Greek) he who helps.

Epifanio (Greek) he who gives off brilliance because of his form.

Epimachus (Palauan) a form of Epimaco.

Epimaco (Greek) easy to attack, easy to wipe out.

Epineri (Fijian) a form of Abner.

Epipanio (Pohnpeian) a form of Epifanio.

Eponu (Chuukese) a navigator.

Epreim (Pohnpeian) a form of Efren.

Epulef (Mapuche) two races, two quick trips.

Er (Chinese) son.

Eraclio (Spanish) a form of Heraclio.

Eradio (Chuukese) a form of Eladio.

Erardo (Greek) he who is the guest of honor, to whom homage is paid.

Erasmus (Greek) lovable.
Érasme, Erasmo, Rasmus

Erastus (Greek) beloved.
Éraste, Erastious, Ras, Rastus

Erato (Greek) kind, pleasant.

Erbert (German) a short form of Herbert.
Ebert, Erberto

Ercole (Italian) splendid gift.

Erek (Scandinavian) a form of Eric.
Erec

Erhard (German) strong; resolute.
Erhardt, Erhart

Eri (Teutonic) vigilant.

Eriberto (Italian) a form of Herbert.
Erberto, Heriberto

Boys A–F

Eric ❦ **B** (Scandinavian) ruler of all. (English) brave ruler. (German) a short form of Frederick. History: Eric the Red was a Norwegian explorer who founded Greenland's first colony.
Aric, Ehrich, Elika, Erek, Éric, Ericc, Erich, Erick, Erico, Erik, Erikur, Erric, Eryc, Rick

Erica **G** (Scandinavian) a form of Eric.

Erich (Czech, German) a form of Eric.

Erick (English) a form of Eric.
Errick, Eryck

Erickson (English) son of Eric.
Erickzon, Erics, Ericson, Ericsson, Erikson, Erikzzon, Eriqson

Erik **B** (Scandinavian) a form of Eric.
Erek, Erike, Eriks, Erikur, Errick, Errik, Eryk

Erika **G** (Scandanavian) a form of Erica.

Eriki (Fijian) a form of Eric.

Erikur (Icelandic) a form of Eric, Erik.

Erin **G** (Irish) peaceful. History: an ancient name for Ireland.
Erine, Erinn, Erino, Eron, Errin, Eryn, Erynn

Erland (English) nobleman's land.
Erlend

Erling (English) nobleman's son.

Ermanno (Italian) a form of Herman.
Erman

Ermano (Spanish) a form of Herman.
Ermin, Ermine, Erminio, Ermon

Ermelindo (Teutonic) offers sacrifices to God.

Ermino (Spanish) a form of Erminia (see Girls' names).

Erminoldo (Germanic) government of strength.

Ernest (English) earnest, sincere. See also Arno.
Earnest, Ernestino, Ernesto, Ernestus, Ernie, Erno, Ernst

Ernesto (Spanish) a form of Ernest.
Ernester, Neto

Ernie (English) a familiar form of Ernest.
Earnie, Erney, Erny

Erno (Hungarian) a form of Ernest.
Ernö

Ernst (German) a form of Ernest.
Erns

Erol (Turkish) strong, courageous.
Eroll

Eron (Irish) a form of Erin.
Erran, Erren, Errion, Erron

Eros (Greek) love.

Errando (Basque) bold.

Errol (Latin) wanderer. (English) a form of Earl.
Erol, Erold, Erroll, Erryl

Erroman (Basque) from Rome.

Erskine (Scottish) high cliff. (English) from Ireland.
Ersin, Erskin, Kinny

Erungel (Palauan) for good.

Ervin, Erwin (English) sea friend. Forms of Irving, Irwin.
Earvin, Erv, Erven, Ervyn, Erwan, Erwinek, Erwinn, Erwyn, Erwynn

Ervine (English) a form of Irving.
Erv, Ervin, Ervince, Erving, Ervins

Ervino (Germanic) he who is consistent with honors.

Eryn **G** (Irish) a form of Erin.

Esang (Palauan) spider conch; nosy.

Esau (Hebrew) rough; hairy. Bible: Jacob's twin brother.
Esaw

Esaú (Hebrew) a form of Esau.

Escipión (Latin) man who uses a cane.

Escolástico (Latin) man who teaches all that he knows.

Esculapio (Greek) doctor.

Esdanis (Pohnpeian) a form of Estanislao.

Esekaia (Fijian) a form of Hezekiah.

Esequiel (Hebrew) a form of Ezekiel.

Eshkol (Hebrew) grape clusters.

Esi (Chuukese) sliced to make thinner.

Eskiel (Chuukese) a form of Ezequiel.

Eskil (Norwegian) god vessel.

Esleban (Hebrew) bearer of children.

Esmond (English) rich protector.

Esopo (Greek) he who brings good luck.

Espartaco (Greek) he who plants.

Espen (Danish) bear of the gods.

Esprancio (Spanish) hope.

Essien (Ochi) sixth-born son.

Estanislao (Slavic) glory of his village.

Estanislau (Slavic) glory.

Este (Italian) east.
Estes

Esteban (Spanish) crowned.

Estéban (Spanish) a form of Stephen.
*Estabon, Esteben, Estefan, Estefano, Estefen,
Estephan, Estephen*

Estebe (Basque) a form of Stephen.

Estepan (Pohnpeian) a form of Esteban.

Estevan (Spanish) a form of Stephen.
Esteven, Estevon, Estiven

Estevao (Spanish) a form of Stephen.
Estevez

Estraton (Greek) man of the army.

Etcaro (Pohnpeian) a form of Edgardo.

Etelberto (Spanish) a form of Adalberto.

Eterio (Greek) as clean and pure as heaven.

Ethan ✿ **B** (Hebrew) strong; firm.
*Eathan, Eathen, Eathon, Eeathen, Eitan, Etan,
Ethaen, Ethe, Ethen, Ethian*

Etienne **B** (French) a form of Stephen.

Étienne (French) a form of Stephen.
Etian, Etien, Étienn, Ettien

Etmont (Pohnpeian) a form of Edmundo.

Etongo (Chamorro) to search for knowledge.

Etsuo (Japanese) rejoicing man.

Ettore (Italian) steadfast.
Etor, Etore

Etu (Native American) sunny.

Etuate (Fijian) a form of Eduardo.

Eubulo (Greek) good counselor.

Eucario (Greek) gracious, generous.

Eucarpo (Greek) he who bears good fruit.

Euclid (Greek) intelligent. History: the
founder of Euclidean geometry.

Eudoro (Greek) beautiful gift.

Eudoxio (Greek) good thought, he who is
famous.

Eufemio (Greek) he who has a good
reputation.

Eufrasio (Greek) he who uses words well,
who is full of happiness.

Eufronio (Greek) having a good mind; he
who makes others happy, who gives
pleasure.

Eugen (German) a form of Eugene.

Eugene **B** (Greek) born to nobility. See also
Ewan, Gene, Gino, Iukini, Jenö, Yevgenyi,
Zenda.
*Eoghan, Eugen, Eugéne, Eugeni, Eugenio,
Eugenius, Evgeny, Ezven*

Eugenio (Spanish) a form of Eugene.

Eulalio (Greek) good speaker.

Eulises (Latin) a form of Ulysses.

Eulogio (Greek) he who speaks well.

Eumenio (Greek) opportune, favorable; the
kind-hearted one.

Eungel (Palauan) underneath.

Euniciano (Spanish) happy victory.

Euno (Greek) intellect, reason,
understanding.

Eupilo (Greek) warmly welcomed.

Euprepio (Greek) decent, comfortable.

Eupsiquio (Greek) having a good soul;
valiant.

Euquerio (Greek) sure handed.

Eurico (Germanic) prince to whom all pay
homage.

Eusebio (Greek) with good feelings.

Eusiquio (Greek) a form of Eupsiquio.

Eustace (Greek) productive. (Latin) stable,
calm. See also Stacey.
*Eustache, Eustachius, Eustachy, Eustashe,
Eustasius, Eustatius, Eustazio, Eustis, Eustiss*

Eustacio, Eustasio (Greek) healthy and
strong.

Eustaquio (Greek) he who has many heads
of wheat.

Eustoquio (Greek) good marksman; a
skillful man.

Eustorgio (Greek) well-loved.

Eustrato (Greek) good soldier.

Eutiquio (Greek) fortunate.

Eutrapio (Greek) returning; changing,
transforming.

Eva 🅖 (Greek) a short form of Evangelina. (Hebrew) a form of Eve (see Girls' Names).

Evan ☙ 🅑 (Irish) young warrior. (English) a form of John. See also Bevan, Owen.
Eavan, Eoin, Ev, Evaine, Evann, Evans, Even, Evens, Evin, Evon, Evyn, Ewan, Ewen

Evando (Greek) he is considered a good man.

Evangelino (Greek) he who brings glad tidings.

Evangelos (Greek) a form of Andrew.
Evagelos, Evaggelos, Evangelo

Evaristo (Greek) excellent one.

Evelio (Hebrew) he who gives life.

Evelyn 🅖 (English) hazelnut.
Evelin

Evencio (Latin) successful.

Everardo (German) strong as a boar.
Everado

Everett 🅑 (English) a form of Eberhard.
Ev, Evered, Everet, Everette, Everhett, Everit, Everitt, Everrett, Evert, Evrett

Everley (English) boar meadow.
Everlea, Everlee

Everton (English) boar town.

Evgeny (Russian) a form of Eugene. See also Zhek.
Evgeni, Evgenij, Evgenyi

Evin (Irish) a form of Evan.
Evian, Evinn, Evins

Evodio (Greek) he who follows a good road.

Ewald (German) always powerful. (English) a powerful lawman.

Ewan (Scottish) a form of Eugene, Evan. See also Keon.
Euan, Euann, Euen, Ewen, Ewhen

Ewert (English) ewe herder, shepherd.
Ewart

Ewing (English) friend of the law.
Ewin, Ewynn

Exavier (Basque) a form of Xavier.
Exaviar, Exavior, Ezavier

Exequiel (Hebrew) God is my strength.

Expedito (Latin) unencumbered, free of hindrances.

Exuperancio (Latin) he who is outstanding, excellent, superior.

Exuperio (Latin) he who exceeds expectations.

Eyota (Native American) great.

Ezekiel (Hebrew) strength of God. Bible: a Hebrew prophet. See also Haskel, Zeke.
Esequiel, Ezakiel, Ezéchiel, Ezeck, Ezeckiel, Ezeeckel, Ezekeial, Ezekeil, Ezekeyial, Ezekial, Ezekielle, Ezell, Ezequiel, Eziakah, Eziechiele

Ezequias (Hebrew) Yahweh is my strength.

Ezequías (Hebrew) one to whom God gave powers; the one has divine power.

Ezequiel (Hebrew) a form of Ezekiel.
Esequiel, Eziequel

Ezer (Hebrew) a form of Ezra.

Ezio (Latin) he who has a nose like an eagle.

Ezra 🅑 (Hebrew) helper; strong. Bible: a Jewish priest who led the Jews back to Jerusalem.
Esdras, Esra, Ezer, Ezera, Ezrah, Ezri, Ezry

Ezven (Czech) a form of Eugene.
Esven, Esvin, Ezavin, Ezavine

Fa (Chinese) beginning.

Faber (German) a form of Fabian.

Fabian 🅑 (Latin) bean grower.
Fabain, Fabayan, Fabe, Fabein, Fabek, Fabeon, Faber, Fabert, Fabi, Fabiano, Fabien, Fabin, Fabio, Fabion, Fabius, Fabiyan, Fabiyus, Fabyan, Fabyen, Faybian, Faybien

Fabián (Spanish) a form of Fabio.

Fabiano (Italian) a form of Fabian.
Fabianno, Fabio

Fabio (Latin) a form of Fabian. (Italian) a short form of Fabiano.
Fabbio

Fabrizio (Italian) craftsman.
Fabrice, Fabricio, Fabrizius

Fabron (French) little blacksmith; apprentice.
Fabre, Fabroni

Facundo (Latin) he who puts forth arguments that convince people.

Fadey (Ukrainian) a form of Thaddeus.
Faday, Faddei, Faddey, Faddy, Fade, Fadeyka, Fadie, Fady

Fadi (Arabic) redeemer.
Fadhi

Fadil (Arabic) generous.
Fadeel, Fadel

Fadrique (Spanish) a form of Federico.

Fagan (Irish) little fiery one.
Fagin

Fahd (Arabic) lynx.
Fahaad, Fahad

Fai (Chinese) beginning.

Fairfax (English) blond.
Fair, Fax

Faisal (Arabic) decisive.
Faisel, Faisil, Faisl, Faiyaz, Faiz, Faizal, Faize, Faizel, Faizi, Fasel, Fasil, Faysal, Fayzal, Fayzel

Faith **G** (English) faithful; fidelity.

Fakhir (Arabic) excellent.
Fahkry, Fakher

Fakih (Arabic) thinker; reader of the Koran.

Falaninug (Yapese) my thoughts are good.

Falco (Latin) falconer.
Falcon, Falk, Falke, Falken

Falito (Italian) a familiar form of Rafael, Raphael.

Falkner (English) trainer of falcons. See also Falco.
Falconer, Falconner, Faulconer, Faulconner, Faulkner

Fallon **G** (Irish) grandchild of the ruler.

Falthin (Yapese) good word.

Fan (Chinese) sail.

Fanathin (Yapese) silent word, sign language.

Fane (English) joyful, glad.
Fanes, Faniel

Fang (Chinese) wind.

Fantino (Latin) infant-like; innocent.

Fanuel (Hebrew) vision of God.

Faraji (Swahili) consolation.

Faraón (Egyptian) pharaoh; inhabitant of the grand palace.

Farid (Arabic) unique.

Faris (Arabic) horseman.
Faraz, Fares, Farhaz, Farice, Fariez, Farris

Farley (English) bull meadow; sheep meadow. See also Lee.
Fairlay, Fairlee, Fairleigh, Fairley, Fairlie, Far, Farlay, Farlee, Farleigh, Farlie, Farly, Farrleigh, Farrley

Farnell (English) fern-covered hill.
Farnall, Fernald, Fernall, Furnald

Farnham (English) field of ferns.
Farnam, Farnum, Fernham

Farnley (English) fern meadow.
Farnlea, Farnlee, Farnleigh, Farnly, Fernlea, Fernlee, Fernleigh, Fernley

Faro (Spanish) reference to the card game faro.

Faroh (Latin) a form of Pharaoh.

Farold (English) mighty traveler.

Farquhar (Scottish) dear.
Fark, Farq, Farquar, Farquarson, Farque, Farquharson, Farquy, Farqy

Farr (English) traveler.
Faer, Farran, Farren, Farrin, Farrington, Farron

Farrell (Irish) heroic; courageous.
Farrel, Farrill, Farryll, Ferrell

Farrow (English) piglet.

Farruco (Spanish) a form of Francis, Francisco.
Frascuelo

Faruq (Arabic) honest.
Farook, Farooq, Faroque, Farouk, Faruqh

Faste (Norwegian) firm.

Fastino (Kosraean) a form of Faustino.

Fath (Arabic) victor.

Fatin (Arabic) clever.

Fauac (Quechua) he who flies.

Fauacuaipa (Quechua) rooster in flight.

Faust (Latin) lucky, fortunate. History: the sixteenth-century German necromancer who inspired many legends.
Faustino, Faustis, Fausto, Faustus

Faustiniano (Latin) a form of Faustinus.

Faustino (Italian) a form of Faust.

Fausto (Italian) a form of Faust.

Favian (Latin) understanding.
Favain, Favio, Favyen

Faxon (German) long-haired.

Boys A–F

Febe, Febo (Latin) he who shines, who stands out.

Federico (Italian, Spanish) a form of Frederick.
Federic, Federigo, Federoquito

Fedro (Greek) splendid man.

Fegorgor (Chamorro) one who gossips a lot.

Fegurgur (Chamorro) a form of Fegorgor.

Fei (Chinese) striking.

Feivel (Yiddish) God aids.

Feliks (Russian) a form of Felix.

Felipe 🅱 (Spanish) a form of Philip.
Feeleep, Felipino, Felo, Filip, Filippo, Filips, Fillip, Flip

Felippo (Italian) a form of Philip.
Felip, Filippo, Lipp, Lippo, Pip, Pippo

Felis (Chamorro) happy.

Felisardo (Latin) valiant and skillful man.

Felix (Latin) fortunate; happy. See also Pitin.
Fee, Felic, Félice, Feliciano, Felicio, Felike, Feliks, Felo, Félix, Felizio, Phelix

Félix (Latin) a form of Felix.

Felton (English) field town.
Felten, Feltin

Felu (Chamorro) blade.

Feng (Chinese) handsome.

Fenton (English) marshland farm.
Fen, Fennie, Fenny, Fintan, Finton

Feo (Spanish) ugly.

Feodor (Slavic) a form of Theodore.
Dorek, Fedar, Fedinka, Fedor, Fedya, Fyodor

Feoras (Greek) smooth rock.

Ferdinand (German) daring, adventurous. See also Hernando.
Feranado, Ferd, Ferda, Ferdie, Ferdinánd, Ferdy, Ferdynand, Fernando, Nando

Ferenc (Hungarian) a form of Francis.
Feri, Ferke, Ferko

Feres (Chuukese) a form of Fares.

Fereti (Fijian) a form of Fred.

Fergus (Irish) strong; manly.
Fearghas, Fearghus, Feargus, Ferghus, Fergie, Ferguson, Fergusson

Fermin (French, Spanish) firm, strong.
Ferman, Firmin, Furman

Fermín (Spanish) a form of Fermin.

Fernán (Spanish) a form of Fernando.

Fernando (Spanish) a form of Ferdinand.
Ferando, Ferdinando, Ferdnando, Ferdo, Fernand, Fernandez, Fernendo

Feroz (Persian) fortunate.

Ferran (Arabic) baker.
Feran, Feron, Ferrin, Ferron

Ferrand (French) iron gray hair.
Farand, Farrand, Farrant, Ferrant

Ferrell (Irish) a form of Farrell.
Ferrel, Ferrill, Ferryl

Ferris (Irish) a form of Peter.
Fares, Faris, Fariz, Farris, Farrish, Feris, Ferriss

Fesongao (Chamorro) burning a lot.

Feta-plom (Mapuche) high and large plain.

Fiacro (Latin) soldier, combatant.

Fico (Spanish) a familiar form of Frederick.

Fidel (Latin) faithful. History: Fidel Castro was the Cuban revolutionary who overthrew a dictatorship in 1959 and established a communist regime in Cuba.
Fidele, Fidèle, Fidelio, Fidelis, Fidell, Fido

Fidencio (Latin) trusting; fearless, self-assured.

Field (English) a short form of Fielding.
Fields

Fielding (English) field; field worker.
Field

Fife (Scottish) from Fife, Scotland.
Fyfe

Fifi 🅖 (Fante) born on Friday.

Fiir (Yapese) that person.

Fil (Polish) a form of Phil.
Filipek

Filadelfo, Filademo (Greek) man who loves his brothers.

Filbert (English) brilliant. See also Bert.
Filberte, Filberto, Filiberto, Philbert

Fileas (Greek) he who loves deeply.

Fileberto (Yapese) a form of Philbert.

Filelio (Latin) he who is trustworthy.

Filemón (Greek) horse-lover; he who is spirited and friendly.

Filiberto (Spanish) a form of Filbert.

Filip (Greek) a form of Philip.
Filip, Filippo

Fillipp (Russian) a form of Philip.
Filip, Filipe, Filipek, Filips, Fill, Fillip, Filya

Filmore (English) famous.
Fillmore, Filmer, Fyllmer, Fylmer, Philmore

Filón (Greek) philosophical friend.

Filya (Russian) a form of Philip.

Finata (Chuukese) to decide.

Fineas (Irish) a form of Phineas.
Finneas

Fineto (Chuukese) spinning.

Finian (Irish) light skinned; white.
Finnen, Finnian, Fionan, Fionn, Phinean

Finisongsong (Chamorro) language of the village.

Finlay (Irish) blond-haired soldier.
Findlay, Findley, Finlea, Finlee, Finley, Finn, Finnlea, Finnley

Finn (German) from Finland. (Irish) blond haired; light skinned. A short form of Finlay. (Norwegian) from the Lapland.
Fin, Finnie, Finnis, Finny

Finnegan (Irish) light skinned; white.
Finegan

Finoho (Chamorro) my language.

Finoña (Chamorro) his language.

Fiorello (Italian) little flower.
Fiore

Firas (Arabic) persistent.

Firipo (Fijian) a form of Felipe.

Firman (French) firm; strong.
Ferman, Firmin

Firmino (Latin) firm, sure.

Firmo (Latin) morally and physically firm.

Firth (English) woodland.

Fischel (Yiddish) a form of Phillip.

Fiske (English) fisherman.
Fisk

Fitch (English) weasel, ermine.
Fitche

Fitelis (Chuukese) a form of Fidel.

Fito (Spanish) a form of Adolfo.

Fitz (English) son.
Filz

Fitzgerald (English) son of Gerald.

Fitzhugh (English) son of Hugh.
Hugh

Fitzpatrick (English) son of Patrick.

Fitzroy (Irish) son of Roy.

Fiu (Chuukese) a form of Pío.

Fiz (Latin) happy, fertile.

Flaminio (Spanish) Religion: Marcantonio Flaminio coauthored one of the most important texts of the Italian Reformation.

Flann (Irish) redhead.
Flainn, Flannan, Flannery

Flavian (Latin) blond, yellow haired.
Flavel, Flavelle, Flavien, Flavio, Flawiusz

Flaviano (Latin) belonging to the old Roman family, Flavia; one of the blonde ones.

Flavio (Italian) a form of Flavian.
Flabio, Flavious, Flavius

Fleming (English) from Denmark; from Flanders.
Flemming, Flemmyng, Flemyng

Fletcher (English) arrow featherer, arrow maker.
Flecher, Fletch

Flint (English) stream; flint stone.
Flynt

Flip (Spanish) a short form of Felipe. (American) a short form of Philip.

Floreal (Latin) alludes to the eighth month of the French Revolution.

Florencio (Italian) a form of Florent.

Florent (French) flowering.
Florenci, Florencio, Florentin, Florentino, Florentyn, Florentz, Florinio, Florino

Florente (Latin) to bloom.

Florian (Latin) flowering, blooming.
Florien, Florrian, Flory, Floryan

Florián (Latin) a form of Florian.

Floriano (Spanish) a form of Florian.

Florio (Spanish) a form of Florián.

Floyd **B** (English) a form of Lloyd.

Flurry (English) flourishing, blooming.

Flynn (Irish) son of the red-haired man.
Flin, Flinn, Flyn

Fo (Chinese) Buddha.

Focio (Latin) illuminated, shining.

Folke (German) a form of Volker.
Folker

Foluke (Yoruba) given to God.

Foma (Bulgarian, Russian) a form of
Thomas.
Fomka

Fonso (German, Italian) a short form of
Alphonso.
Fonzo

Fontaine (French) fountain.

Fonzie (German) a familiar form of
Alphonse.
Fons, Fonsie, Fonsy, Fonz

Forbes (Irish) prosperous.
Forbe

Ford (English) a short form of names ending
in "ford."

Fordel (Gypsy) forgiving.

Forest ☒ (French) a form of Forrest.
Forestt, Foryst

Forester (English) forest guardian.
Forrester, Forrie, Forry, Forster, Foss, Foster

Formerio (Latin) beauty.

Forrest ☒ (French) forest; woodsman.
*Forest, Forester, Forrestar, Forrester, Forrestt,
Forrie*

Fortino (Italian) fortunate, lucky.

Fortune (French) fortunate, lucky.
Fortun, Fortunato, Fortuné, Fortunio

Foster (Latin) a short form of Forester.

Fowler (English) trapper of wildfowl.

Fran ☒ (Latin) a short form of Francis.
Franh

Frances ☒ (Latin) a form of Francis.

Francesca ☒ (Italian) a form of Frances.

Francesco (Italian) a form of Francis.

Franchot (French) a form of Francis.

Francis ☒ (Latin) free; from France.
Religion: Saint Francis of Assisi was the
founder of the Franciscan order. See also
Farruco, Ferenc.
*Fran, France, Frances, Francesco, Franchot,
Francisco, Franciskus, Franco, François, Frang,
Frank, Frannie, Franny, Frans, Franscis,
Fransis, Franta, Frantisek, Frants, Franus,
Frantisek, Franz, Frencis*

Francisco (Portuguese, Spanish) a form of
Francis. See also Chilo, Cisco, Farruco, Paco,
Pancho.
Franco, Fransisco, Fransysco, Frasco, Frisco

Franco (Latin) a short form of Francis.
Franko

François (French) a form of Francis.
Francoise

Frank (English) a short form of Francis,
Franklin. See also Palani, Pancho.
*Franc, Franck, Franek, Frang, Franio, Franke,
Frankie, Franko*

Frankie ☒ (English) a familiar form of
Frank.
*Francky, Franke, Frankey, Franki, Franky,
Franqui*

Franklin ☒ (English) free landowner.
*Fran, Francklen, Francklin, Francklyn,
Francylen, Frank, Frankin, Franklen, Franklinn,
Franklyn, Franquelin*

Franklyn (English) a form of Franklin.
Franklynn

Frans (Swedish) a form of Francis.
Frants

Frantisek (Czech) a form of Francis.
Franta

Franz (German) a form of Francis.
*Fransz, Frantz, Franzen, Franzie, Franzin,
Franzl, Franzy*

Fraser ☒ (French) strawberry. (English)
curly haired.
Fraizer, Frasier, Fraze, Frazer, Frazier

Fraterno (Latin) relating to the brother.

Frayne (French) dweller at the ash tree.
(English) stranger.
Fraine, Frayn, Frean, Freen, Freyne

Fred (German) a short form of Alfred,
Frederick, Manfred.
Fredd, Fredde, Fredo, Fredson

Freddie ☒ (German) a familiar form of
Frederick.
Freddi, Freddy, Fredi, Fredy

Freddy, Fredy (German) familiar forms of
Frederick.

Frederic (German) a form of Frederick.
Frédéric, Frederich, Frederric, Fredric, Fredrich

Frederick (German) peaceful ruler. See also
Dick, Eric, Fico, Peleke, Rick.
*Federico, Fico, Fred, Fredderick, Freddie,
Freddrick, Freddy, Fredek, Frederic, Frédérick,*

Frédérick, Frederik, Frederique, Frederrick, Fredo, Fredrick, Fredwick, Fredwyck, Fredy, Friedrich, Fritz

Frederico (Spanish) a form of Frederick.
Fredrico, Frederigo

Frederik (German) a form of Frederick.
Frédérik, Frederrik, Fredrik

Frederique G (French) a form of Frederick.

Fredo (Spanish) a form of Fred.

Fredrick B (German) a form of Frederick.
Fredric, Fredricka, Fredricks

Freeborn (English) child of freedom.
Free

Freeman (English) free.
Free, Freedman, Freemin, Freemon, Friedman, Friedmann

Fremont (German) free; noble protector.

Fresco (Spanish) fresh.

Frewin (English) free; noble friend.
Frewen

Frey (English) lord. (Scandinavian) Mythology: the Norse god who dispenses peace and prosperity.

Frick (English) bold.

Fridolf (English) peaceful wolf.
Freydolf, Freydulf, Fridulf

Fridolino (Teutonic) he who loves peace.

Friedrich (German) a form of Frederick.
Friedel, Friedrick, Fridrich, Fridrick, Friedrike, Friedryk, Fryderyk

Frisco (Spanish) a short form of Francisco.

Fritz (German) a familiar form of Frederick.
Fritson, Fritts, Fritzchen, Fritzl

Froberto (Spanish) a form of Roberto.

Frode (Norwegian) wise.

Froilan (Teutonic) rich and beloved young master.

Froilán (Germanic) a form of Froilan.

Fronton (Latin) he who thinks.

Fructuoso (Latin) he who bears much fruit.

Frumencio (Latin) he who provides wheat.

Fu (Chinese) wealthy.

Fudo (Japanese) the god of fire and wisdom.

Fu-Hsi (Chinese) god of happiness, symbolized by a bat.

Fujikawa (Japanese) fruitful earth stream.

Fujita (Japanese) field.

Fukuo (Japanese) blessing hero.

Fukutaro (Japanese) big son blessing.

Fulberto (Germanic) he who shines amongst all in the village.

Fulbright (German) very bright.
Fulbert

Fulco (Spanish) village.

Fulgencio (Latin) he who shines and stands out because of his goodness.

Fuller (English) cloth thickener.

Fulton (English) field near town.

Fulu (Chamorro) to wrestle.

Fulvio (Latin) he who has reddish hair.

Fumihiko, Fumito (Japanese) he who writes or is a historian.

Fumihiro (Japanese) he who writes abundantly.

Fumio (Japanese) a great man about whom much has been written.

Fumitaka (Japanese) dutiful historian.

Fumiya (Japanese) he who will be a writer or historian.

Funsoni (Nguni) requested.

Fusao (Japanese) cluster of men.

Fuyuki (Japanese) winter; noble; precious.

Fyfe (Scottish) a form of Fife.
Fyffe

Fynn (Ghanaian) Geography: another name for the Offin River in Ghana.

Fyodor (Russian) a form of Theodore.

G

G B (American) an initial used as a first name.

Gabby (American) a familiar form of Gabriel.
Gabbi, Gabbie, Gabi, Gabie, Gaby

Gabe (Hebrew) a short form of Gabriel.

Gabibic (Chamorro) a form of Gabibig.

Gabibig (Chamorro) he who likes to whistle.

Gabino (American) a form of Gabriel.
Gabin, Gabrino

Gábor (Hungarian) God is my strength.
Gabbo, Gabko, Gabo

Gabrial (Hebrew) a form of Gabriel.
Gaberial, Gabrael, Gabraiel, Gabrail, Gabreal, Gabriael, Gabrieal, Gabryalle

Gabriel ☝ **B** (Hebrew) devoted to God. Bible: the angel of the Annunciation.
Gab, Gabe, Gabby, Gabino, Gabis, Gábor, Gabreil, Gabrel, Gabrell, Gabrial, Gabriël, Gabriele, Gabriell, Gabrielle, Gabrielli, Gabrile, Gabris, Gabryel, Gabys, Gavril, Gebereal, Ghabriel, Riel

Gabriela, Gabriella **G** (Italian) forms of Gabrielle.

Gabrielle **G** (Hebrew) a form of Gabriel.

Gabrielli (Italian) a form of Gabriel.
Gabriello

Gabrio (Spanish) God is my strength.

Gabryel **B** (Hebrew) a form of Gabriel.

Gachi (Chamorro) ax.

Gadao (Chamorro) the grouper fish.

Gadi (Arabic) God is my fortune.
Gad, Gaddy, Gadiel

Gadiña (Chamorro) he is catching fish at night with palm leaves.

Gaetan (Italian) from Gaeta, a region in southern Italy.
Gaetano, Gaetono

Gagandeep **B** (Sikh) sky's light.

Gage **B** (French) pledge.
Gager, Gaige, Gaje

Gago (Chamorro) lazy; ironwood tree.

Gaige (French) a form of Gage.

Gair (Irish) small.
Gaer, Gearr, Geir

Gaius (Latin) rejoicer. See also Cai.

Gakuto (Japanese) he who is from the mountain.

Galbraith (Irish) Scotsman in Ireland.
Galbrait, Galbreath

Gale (Greek) a short form of Galen.
Gael, Gail, Gaile, Gayle

Galeaso (Latin) he who is protected by the helmet.

Galen **B** (Greek) healer; calm. (Irish) little and lively.
Gaelan, Gaelen, Gaelin, Gaelyn, Gailen, Galan, Gale, Galeno, Galin, Galyn, Gaylen

Galeno (Spanish) illuminated child. (Greek, Irish) a form of Galen.

Galileo (Hebrew) he who comes from Galilee.

Gallagher (Irish) eager helper.

Galloway (Irish) Scotsman in Ireland.
Gallway, Galway

Galo (Latin) native of Galilee.

Galt (Norwegian) high ground.

Galton (English) owner of a rented estate.
Gallton

Galvin (Irish) sparrow.
Gal, Gall, Gallven, Gallvin, Galvan, Galven

Gamal (Arabic) camel. See also Jamal.
Gamall, Gamel, Gamil

Gamaliel (Hebrew) God is your reward.

Gamble (Scandinavian) old.

Gamelberto (Germanic) distinguished because of his advancing age.

Gan (Chinese) daring, adventurous. (Vietnamese) near.

Gaña (Chamorro) to prefer.

Ganchu (Chamorro) hook; gaff.

Gandolfo (Germanic) valiant warrior.

Gang (Chinese) firm; strong.

Ganimedes (Spanish) he was the most beautiful of the mortals.

Gannon (Irish) light skinned, white.
Gannan, Gannen, Gannie, Ganny

Ganya **BG** (Zulu) clever.

Gao (Chinese) tall, high.

Gar (English) a short form of Gareth, Garnett, Garrett, Garvin.
Garr

Garcia (Spanish) mighty with a spear.

García (Spanish) a form of Garcia.

Garcilaso (Spanish) a form of García.

Gardner (English) gardener.
Gard, Gardener, Gardie, Gardiner, Gardy

Garek (Polish) a form of Edgar.

Garen (English) a form of Garry.
Garan, Garen, Garin, Garion, Garon, Garyn, Garyon

Gareth (Welsh) gentle.
Gar, Garith, Garreth, Garrith, Garth, Garyth

Garett **B** (Irish) a form of Garrett.
Gared, Garet, Garette, Garhett, Garit, Garitt, Garritt

Garfield (English) field of spears; battlefield.

Garibaldo (Germanic) he who is bold with a lance.

Garland **B** (French) wreath of flowers; prize. (English) land of spears; battleground.
Garlan, Garlen, Garllan, Garlund, Garlyn

Garman (English) spearman.
Garmann, Garrman

Garner (French) army guard, sentry.
Garnier

Garnett (Latin) pomegranate seed; garnet stone. (English) armed with a spear.
Gar, Garnet, Garnie, Garrnett

Garnock (Welsh) dweller by the alder river.

Garrad (English) a form of Garrett.
Gared, Garrard, Garred, Garrod, Gerred, Gerrid, Gerrod, Garrode, Jared

Garren, Garrin (English) forms of Garry.
Garran, Garrion, Garron, Garyn, Gerren, Gerron, Gerryn

Garret (Irish) a form of Garrett.
Garrit, Garyt, Gerret, Garrid, Gerrit, Gerrot

Garrett **B** (Irish) brave spearman. See also Jarrett.
Gar, Gareth, Garett, Garrad, Garret, Garrette, Gerrett, Gerritt, Gerrott

Garrick (English) oak spear.
Gaerick, Garek, Garick, Garik, Garreck, Garrek, Garric, Garrik, Garryck, Garryk, Gerreck, Gerrick

Garrison **B** (French) troops stationed at a fort; garrison.
Garison, Garisson, Garris

Garroway (English) spear fighter.
Garraway

Garry (English) a form of Gary.
Garen, Garrey, Garri, Garrie, Garren, Garrin

Garson (English) son of Gar.

Garth (Scandinavian) garden, gardener. (Welsh) a short form of Gareth.

Garvey (Irish) rough peace.
Garbhán, Garrvey, Garrvie, Garv, Garvan, Garvie, Garvy

Garvin (English) comrade in battle.
Gar, Garvan, Garven, Garvyn, Garwen, Garwin, Garwyn, Garwynn

Garwood (English) evergreen forest. See also Wood, Woody.
Garrwood

Gary **B** (German) mighty spearman. (English) a familiar form of Gerald. See also Kali.
Gare, Garey, Gari, Garry

Gaspar (French) a form of Casper.
Gáspár, Gaspard, Gaspare, Gaspari, Gasparo, Gasper, Gazsi

Gaston (French) from Gascony, France.
Gascon, Gastaun

Gastón (Germanic) a form of Gaston.

Gaudencio (Latin) he who is happy and content.

Gaudioso (Latin) happy, joyful.

Gausberto (Germanic) Gothic brightness.

Gaute (Norwegian) great.

Gautier (French) a form of Walter.
Galtero, Gaulterio, Gaultier, Gaultiero, Gauthier

Gavin �ધ **B** (Welsh) white hawk.
Gav, Gavan, Gaven, Gavinn, Gavino, Gavn, Gavohn, Gavon, Gavyn, Gavynn, Gawain

Gavriel (Hebrew) man of God.
Gav, Gavi, Gavrel, Gavril, Gavy

Gavril (Russian) a form of Gavriel.
Ganya, Gavrilo, Gavrilushka

Gawain (Welsh) a form of Gavin.
Gawaine, Gawayn, Gawayne, Gawen, Gwayne

Gaylen (Greek) a form of Galen.
Gaylin, Gaylinn, Gaylon, Gaylyn

Gaylord (French) merry lord; jailer.
Gaillard, Gallard, Gay, Gayelord, Gayler, Gaylor

Gaynor (Irish) son of the fair-skinned man.
Gainer, Gainor, Gay, Gayner, Gaynnor

Ge (Chinese) standard; pattern.

Geary (English) variable, changeable.
Gearey, Gery

Gedeon (Bulgarian, French) a form of Gideon.

Gedeón (Hebrew) a form of Gideon.

Geffrey (English) a form of Geoffrey. See also Jeffrey.
Gefery, Geff, Geffery, Geffrard

Gelasio (Greek) cheerful and happy, enjoys having fun.

Gellert (Hungarian) a form of Gerald.

Gemelo (Latin) fraternal twin.

Geminiano (Latin) identical twin.

Gen (Chinese) root; base.

Gena 🄶 (Russian) a short form of Yevgenyi.
Genka, Genya, Gine

Genaro (Latin) consecrated to God.
Genereo, Genero, Gennaro

Gendo, Genji, Genku (Japanese) literary figures.

Gene 🄱 (Greek) a short form of Eugene.
Genek

Genek (Polish) a form of Gene.

Generos, Generoso (Spanish) generous.

Genesis 🄶 (Latin) origin; birth.

Genevieve 🄶 (German, French) a form of Guinevere (see Girls' Names).

Geng (Chinese) honest, just.

Genjiro (Japanese) good source.

Genkei (Japanese) source of reverence.

Genkichi (Japanese) fortunate source.

Genmei (Japanese) historical figure.

Geno (Italian) a form of John. A short form of Genovese.
Genio, Jeno

Genovese (Italian) from Genoa, Italy.
Geno, Genovis

Gent (English) gentleman.
Gentle, Gentry

Genty (Irish, English) snow.

Geoff (English) a short form of Geoffrey.

Geoffery (English) a form of Geoffrey.
Geofery

Geoffrey (English) a form of Jeffrey. See also Giotto, Godfrey, Gottfried, Jeff.
Geffrey, Geoff, Geoffery, Geoffre, Geoffrie, Geoffroi, Geoffroy, Geoffry, Geofrey, Geofri, Gofery

Geordan (Scottish) a form of Gordon.
Geordann, Geordian, Geordin, Geordon

Geordie (Scottish) a form of George.
Geordi, Geordy

Georg (Scandinavian) a form of George.

George (Greek) farmer. See also Durko, Egor, Iorgos, Jerzy, Jiri, Joji, Jörg, Jorge, Jorgen, Joris, Jorrín, Jur, Jurgis, Keoki, Mahiái, Semer, Yegor, Yorgos, Yoyi, Yrjo, Yuri, Zhora.
Geordie, Georg, Georgas, Georges, Georget, Georgi, Georgii, Georgio, Georgios, Georgiy, Georgy, Gevork, Gheorghe, Giorgio, Giorgos, Goerge, Goran, Gordios, Gorge, Gorje, Gorya, Grzegorz, Gyorgy

Georges (French) a form of George.
Geórges

Georgia 🄶 (Greek) a form of George.

Georgio (Italian) a form of George.

Georgios (Greek) a form of George.
Georgious, Georgius

Georgy (Greek) a familiar form of George.
Georgie

Geovanni, Geovanny (Italian) forms of Giovanni.
Geovan, Geovani, Geovanne, Geovannee, Geovannhi, Geovany

Geraint (English) old.

Gerald 🄱 (German) mighty spearman. See also Fitzgerald, Jarell, Jarrell, Jerald, Jerry, Kharald.
Garald, Garold, Garolds, Gary, Gearalt, Gellert, Gérald, Geralde, Geraldo, Gerale, Geraud, Gerek, Gerick, Gerik, Gerold, Gerrald, Gerrell, Gérrick, Gerrild, Gerrin, Gerrit, Gerrold, Gerry, Geryld, Giraldo, Giraud, Girauld

Geraldo (Italian, Spanish) a form of Gerald.

Gerard (English) brave spearman. See also Jerard, Jerry.
Garrard, Garrat, Garratt, Gearard, Gerad, Gerar, Gérard, Gerardo, Geraro, Géraud, Gerd, Gerek, Gerhard, Gerrard, Gerrit, Gerry, Girard

Gerardo 🄱 (Spanish) a form of Gerard.
Gherardo

Gerasimo (Greek) award, recompense.

Géraud (French) a form of Gerard.
Gerrad, Gerraud

Boys G–L

Gerbrando (Germanic) sword.

Gerek (Polish) a form of Gerard.

Geremia (Hebrew) exalted by God. (Italian) a form of Jeremiah.

Geremiah (Italian) a form of Jeremiah.
Geremia, Gerimiah, Geromiah

Gerhard (German) a form of Gerard.
Garhard, Gerhardi, Gerhardt, Gerhart, Gerhort

Gerik (Polish) a form of Edgar.
Geric, Gerick

Germain (French) from Germany. (English) sprout, bud. See also Jermaine.
Germaine, German, Germane, Germano, Germayn, Germayne

Germán (Germanic) male warrior.

Germinal (Latin) he who sprouts.

Geroldo (Germanic) commander of the lance.

Gerome (English) a form of Jerome.

Geronimo (Greek, Italian) a form of Jerome. History: a famous Apache chief.
Geronemo

Gerónimo (Greek) a form of Geronimo.

Gerrit (Dutch) a form of Gerald.

Gerry (English) a familiar form of Gerald, Gerard. See also Jerry.
Geri, Gerre, Gerri, Gerrie, Gerryson

Gershom (Hebrew) exiled. (Yiddish) stranger in exile.
Gersham, Gersho, Gershon, Gerson, Geurson, Gursham, Gurshan

Gerson (English) son of Gar.
Gersan, Gershawn

Gert (German, Danish) fighter.

Gervaise **BG** (French) honorable. See also Jervis.
Garvais, Garvaise, Garvey, Gervais, Gervase, Gervasio, Gervaso, Gervayse, Gervis, Gerwazy

Gerwin (Welsh) fair love.

Gesualdo (Germanic) prisoner of the king.

Gethin (Welsh) dusky.
Geth

Getulio (Latin) he who came from Getulia in the northern region of Africa.

Ghazi (Arabic) conqueror.

Ghilchrist (Irish) servant of Christ. See also Gil.
Gilchrist, Gilcrist, Gilie, Gill, Gilley, Gilly

Ghislain (French) pledge.

Gi (Korean) brave.

Gia (Vietnamese) family.

Giacinto (Portuguese, Spanish) a form of Jacinto.
Giacintho

Giacomo (Italian) a form of Jacob.
Gaimo, Giacamo, Giaco, Giacobbe, Giacobo, Giacopo

Gian (Italian) a form of Giovanni, John.
Gianetto, Giann, Gianne, Giannes, Gianni, Giannis, Giannos, Ghian

Giancarlo (Italian) a combination of John + Charles.
Giancarlos, Gianncarlo

Giang (Vietnamese) river.

Gianluca (Italian) a combination of John + Lucas.

Gianni (Italian) a form of Johnny.
Giani, Gionni

Gianpaolo (Italian) a combination of John + Paul.
Gianpaulo

Giao (Vietnamese) to pass.

Gib (English) a short form of Gilbert.
Gibb, Gibbie, Gibby

Gibor (Hebrew) powerful.

Gibson (English) son of Gilbert.
Gibbon, Gibbons, Gibbs, Gillson, Gilson

Gideon (Hebrew) tree cutter. Bible: the judge who defeated the Midianites.
Gedeon, Gideone, Gidon, Hedeon

Gidon (Hebrew) a form of Gideon.

Gifford (English) bold giver.
Giff, Giffard, Gifferd, Giffie, Giffy

Gig (English) horse-drawn carriage.

Giichi (Japanese) righteous first son.

Gil (Greek) shield bearer. (Hebrew) happy. (English) a short form of Ghilchrist, Gilbert.
Gili, Gill, Gilli, Gillie, Gillis, Gilly

Gilad (Arabic) camel hump; from Giladi, Saudi Arabia.
Giladi, Gilead

Boys G–L

Gilamu (Basque) a form of William.
Gillen

Gilbert (English) brilliant pledge;
trustworthy. See also Gil, Gillett.
*Gib, Gilberto, Gilburt, Giselbert, Giselberto,
Giselbertus, Guilbert*

Gilberto (Spanish) a form of Gilbert.

Gilby (Scandinavian) hostage's estate. (Irish)
blond boy.
Gilbey, Gillbey, Gillbie, Gillby

Gilchrist (Irish) a form of Ghilchrist.

Gildo (Spanish) a form of Hermenegildo.

Gilen (Basque, German) illustrious pledge.

Giles (French) goatskin shield.
Gide, Gilles, Gyles

Gillean (Irish) Bible: Saint John's servant.
Gillan, Gillen, Gillian

Gillermo (Spanish) resolute protector.

Gillespie (Irish) son of the bishop's servant.
Gillis

Gillett (French) young Gilbert.
Gelett, Gelette, Gillette

Gillian ☙ (Irish) a form of Gillean.

Gilmer (English) famous hostage.
Gilmar

Gilmore (Irish) devoted to the Virgin Mary.
Gillmore, Gillmour, Gilmour

Gilon (Hebrew) circle.

Gilroy (Irish) devoted to the king.
Gilderoy, Gildray, Gildroy, Gillroy, Roy

Giltamag (Yapese) my two fathers.

Gines (Greek) he who produces life.

Ginjiro (Japanese) good silver.

Gino (Greek) a familiar form of Eugene.
(Italian) a short form of names ending in
"gene," "gino."
Ghino

Giona (Italian) a form of Jonah.

Giordano (Italian) a form of Jordan.
Giordan, Giordana, Giordin, Guordan

Giorgio (Italian) a form of George.

Giorgos (Greek) a form of George.
Georgos, Giorgios

Giosia (Italian) a form of Joshua.

Giotto (Italian) a form of Geoffrey.

Giovani (Italian) a form of Giovanni.
Giavani, Giovan, Giovane, Giovanie, Giovon

Giovanni ☙ (Italian) a form of John. See
also Jeovanni, Jiovanni.
*Geovanni, Geovanny, Gian, Gianni, Giannino,
Giovani, Giovann, Giovannie, Giovanno,
Giovanny, Giovonathon, Giovonni, Giovonnia,
Giovonnie, Givonni*

Giovanny (Italian) a form of Giovanni.
Giovany

Gipsy (English) wanderer.
Gipson, Gypsy

Girvin (Irish) small; tough.
Girvan, Girven, Girvon

Gisberto (Germanic) he who shines in battle
with his sword.

Giselle ☙ (German) pledge; hostage.

Gitano (Spanish) gypsy.

Giuliano (Italian) a form of Julius.
Giulano, Giulino, Giulliano

Giulio (Italian) a form of Julius.
Guilano

Giuseppe (Italian) a form of Joseph.
*Giuseppi, Giuseppino, Giusseppe, Guiseppe,
Guiseppi, Guiseppie, Guisseppe*

Giustino (Italian) a form of Justin.
Giusto

Givon (Hebrew) hill; heights.
Givan, Givawn, Givyn

Gladwin (English) cheerful. See also Win.
*Glad, Gladdie, Gladdy, Gladwinn, Gladwyn,
Gladwynne*

Glanville (English) village with oak trees.

Glen ☙ (Irish) a form of Glenn.
Glyn

Glendon (Scottish) fortress in the glen.
*Glenden, Glendin, Glenn, Glennden,
Glennton, Glenton*

Glendower (Welsh) from Glyndwr, Wales.

Glenn ☙ (Irish) a short form of Glendon.
*Gleann, Glen, Glennie, Glennis, Glennon,
Glenny, Glynn*

Glentworth (English) from Glenton,
England.

Glenville (Irish) village in the glen.

Gloria ☙ (Latin) glory.

Glyn (Welsh) a form of Glen.
Glin, Glynn

Goana (Fijian) time.

Goddard (German) divinely firm.
Godard, Godart, Goddart, Godhardt, Godhart, Gothart, Gotthard, Gotthardt, Gotthart

Godfredo (Spanish) friend of God.

Godfrey (Irish) God's peace. (German) a form of Jeffrey. See also Geoffrey, Gottfried.
Giotto, Godefroi, Godfree, Godfry, Godofredo, Godoired, Godrey, Goffredo, Gofraidh, Gofredo, Gorry

Godo (Chamorro) entrapped.

Godwin (English) friend of God. See also Win.
Godewyn, Godwinn, Godwyn, Goodwin, Goodwyn, Goodwynn, Goodwynne

Goel (Hebrew) redeemer.

Gofchegi (Chamorro) to try a lot.

Gofgualaf (Chamorro) very round, like a full moon.

Gofhigam, Gofhigen (Chamorro) forms of Gofhigan.

Gofhigan (Chamorro) lots of fish.

Gofhihos (Chamorro) very close.

Goflache (Chamorro) very wrong.

Gofmanglo (Chamorro) very windy.

Gofsagua (Chamorro) rich.

Gogui (Chamorro) to protect, save, or rescue.

Gokomatsu (Japanese) historical figure.

Goldwin (English) golden friend. See also Win.
Golden, Goldewin, Goldewinn, Goldewyn, Goldwyn, Goldwynn

Goliard (Spanish) rebel.

Goliat (Hebrew) he who lives his life making pilgrimages.

Goliath (Hebrew) exiled. Bible: the giant Philistine whom David slew with a slingshot.
Golliath

Gomda (Kiowa) wind.

Gomer (Hebrew) completed, finished. (English) famous battle.

Gong (Chinese) capable.

Gonza (Rutooro) love.

Gonzalo (Spanish) wolf.
Goncalve, Gonsalo, Gonsalve, Gonzales, Gonzelee, Gonzolo

Goptoña (Chamorro) his party.

Gordon (English) triangular-shaped hill.
Geordan, Gord, Gordain, Gordan, Gorden, Gordonn, Gordy

Gordy (English) a familiar form of Gordon.
Gordie

Gore (English) triangular-shaped land; wedge-shaped land.

Gorgonio (Greek) violent one.

Gorman (Irish) small; blue eyed.

Goro (Japanese) fifth.

Gosheven (Native American) great leaper.

Gosvino (Teutonic) friend of God.

Gotardo (Germanic) he who is valiant because of the strength that he receives from God.

Gottfried (German) a form of Geoffrey, Godfrey.
Gotfrid, Gotfrids, Gottfrid

Gotzon (German) a form of Angel.

Govert (Dutch) heavenly peace.

Gower (Welsh) pure.

Gowon (Tiv) rainmaker.
Gowan

Goyo (Spanish) a form of Gérardo.

Gozol (Hebrew) soaring bird.
Gozal

Gracián (Latin) possessor of grace.

Graciano (Latin) one recognized by God; he has love and divine blessing.

Graciliano (Latin) name comes from Gados, the useful martyr from Faleria, Italy.

Grady (Irish) noble; illustrious.
Gradea, Gradee, Gradey, Gradleigh, Graidey, Graidy

Graeme (Scottish) a form of Graham.
Graem

Graham **B** (English) grand home.
Graeham, Graehame, Graehme, Graeme, Grahamme, Grahm, Grahame, Grahme, Gram, Grame, Gramm, Grayeme, Grayham

Granger (French) farmer.
Grainger, Grange

Grant 🅱 (English) a short form of Grantland.
Grand, Grantham, Granthem, Grantley

Grantland (English) great plains.
Grant

Granville (French) large village.
Gran, Granvel, Granvil, Granvile, Granvill, Grenville, Greville

Grato (Latin) one recognized by God; he has love and divine blessing.

Grau (Spanish) a form of Gerardo.

Gray (English) gray haired.
Graye, Grey, Greye

Grayden (English) gray haired.
Graden, Graydan, Graydyn, Greyden

Graydon (English) gray hill.
Gradon, Grayton, Greydon

Grayson 🅱 (English) bailiff's son. See also Sonny.
Graysen, Greyson

Grazián (Spanish) a form of Graciano.

Greeley (English) gray meadow.
Greelea, Greeleigh, Greely

Greenwood (English) green forest.
Green, Greener

Greg, Gregg (Latin) short forms of Gregory.
Graig, Greig, Gregson

Greggory (Latin) a form of Gregory.
Greggery

Gregor (Scottish) a form of Gregory.
Gregoor, Grégor, Gregore

Gregorio (Italian, Portuguese) a form of Gregory.
Gregorios

Gregory 🅱 (Latin) vigilant watchman. See also Jörn, Krikor.
Gergely, Gergo, Greagoir, Greagory, Greer, Greg, Gregary, Greger, Gregery, Greggory, Grégoire, Gregor, Gregorey, Gregori, Grégorie, Gregorio, Gregorius, Gregors, Gregos, Gregrey, Gregroy, Gregry, Greogry, Gries, Grisha, Grzegorz

Gresham (English) village in the pasture.

Greyson (English) a form of Grayson.
Greysen, Greysten, Greyston

Griffin 🅱 (Latin) hooked nose.
Griff, Griffen, Griffie, Griffon, Griffy, Gryphon

Griffith (Welsh) fierce chief; ruddy.
Grifen, Griff, Griffeth, Griffie, Griffy, Griffyn, Griffynn, Gryphon

Grigori (Bulgarian) a form of Gregory.
Grigoi, Grigor, Grigore, Grigorios, Grigorov, Grigory

Grimoaldo (Spanish) confessor.

Grimshaw (English) dark woods.

Grisha (Russian) a form of Gregory.

Griswold (German, French) gray forest.
Gris, Griz, Grizwald

Grosvener (French) big hunter.

Grover (English) grove.
Grove

Gu, Guo (Chinese) resolute.

Guacraya (Quechua) strong and brave like a bull.

Guadalberto (Germanic) he is all-powerful and shines because of it.

Guadalupe 🅶 (Arabic) river of black stones.
Guadalope

Guaina (Quechua) young; friend.

Gualberto (Spanish) a form of Walter.
Gualterio

Gualtar (Spanish) a form of Gerardo.

Gualtiero (Italian) a form of Walter.
Gualterio

Guaman (Quechua) falcon.

Guamanachachi (Quechua) he who has valorous ancestors such as the falcon.

Guamancapac (Quechua) lord falcon.

Guamancaranca (Quechua) he who fights like a thousand falcons.

Guamanchaua (Quechua) cruel as a falcon.

Guamanchuri (Quechua) son of the falcon.

Guamanpuma (Quechua) strong and powerful as a puma and a falcon.

Guamantiupac (Quechua) glorious falcon.

Guamanyana (Quechua) black falcon.

Guamanyurac (Quechua) white falcon.

Guamay (Quechua) young, fresh, new.

Guan (Chinese) champion.

Guanca, Guancar (Quechua) rock; summit; drum.

Guang (Chinese) light.

Guanpú (Aymara) born in a festive time; he who arrives in an opportune moment.

Guari (Quechua) savage, untamable, untiring; wild like the vicuna; protected by the gods.

Guarino (Teutonic) he who defends well.

Guariruna (Quechua) untamed and wild man.

Guarititu, Guartito (Quechua) untamed and difficult to deal with, like the vicuna.

Guascar (Quechua) he of the chain, rope of bindweed.

Guaual (Quechua) myrtle.

Guayasamin (Quechua) happy, white bird in flight.

Guayau (Quechua) royal willow.

Guaynacapac (Quechua) young master.

Guaynarimac (Quechua) young speaker.

Guaynay (Quechua) my youngster; my beloved.

Guaypa, Guaypaya (Quechua) rooster; creator, inventor.

Guayra (Quechua) wind, fast as the wind.

Guayua (Aymara) restless, mischievous; fast as the wind.

Guglielmo (Italian) a form of William.

Gui (Chinese) noble.

Guido (Italian) a form of Guy.

Guilford (English) ford with yellow flowers.
Guildford

Guilherme (Portuguese) a form of William.

Güillac (Quechua) he who warns.

Guillaume (French) a form of William.
Guillaums, Guilleaume, Guilem, Guyllaume

Guillermo (Spanish) a form of William.
Guillerrmo

Güiracocha, Güiracucha (Quechua) sea foam; the sea's vital energy.

Güisa (Quechua) prophet; he is a sorcerer for having been a twin.

Güiuyac (Quechua) brilliant, luminous.

Güiyca (Quechua) sacred.

Güiycauaman (Quechua) sacred falcon.

Gumaña (Chamorro) his house.

Gumaro (Germanic) army of men; disciplined man.

Gumersindo (Germanic) excellent man.

Gundelberto (Teutonic) he who shines in battle.

Gunnar (Scandinavian) a form of Gunther.
Guner, Gunner

Gunther (Scandinavian) battle army; warrior.
Guenter, Guenther, Gun, Gunnar, Guntar, Gunter, Guntero, Gunthar, Günther

Guotin (Chinese) polite; strong leader.

Gurion (Hebrew) young lion.
Gur, Guri, Guriel

Gurjot **BG** (Sikh) light of the guru.

Gurpreet **BG** (Sikh) devoted to the guru; devoted to the Prophet.
Gurjeet, Gurmeet, Guruprit

Gurvir **B** (Sikh) guru's warrior.
Gurveer

Gus (Scandinavian) a short form of Angus, Augustine, Gustave.
Guss, Gussie, Gussy, Gusti, Gustry, Gusty

Gustaf (Swedish) a form of Gustave.
Gustaaf, Gustaff

Gustave (Scandinavian) staff of the Goths. History: Gustavus Adolphus was a king of Sweden. See also Kosti, Tabo, Tavo.
Gus, Gustaf, Gustaff, Gustaof, Gustav, Gustáv, Gustava, Gustaves, Gustavo, Gustavs, Gustavus, Gustik, Gustus, Gusztav

Gustavo (Italian, Spanish) a form of Gustave.
Gustabo

Guthrie (German) war hero. (Irish) windy place.
Guthrey, Guthry

Gutierre (Spanish) a form of Walter.

Guy **B** (Hebrew) valley. (German) warrior. (French) guide. See also Guido.
Guyon

Guyapi (Native American) candid.

Guzman (Gothic) good man; man of God.

Guzmán (Teutonic) a form of Guzman.

Gwayne (Welsh) a form of Gawain.
Gwaine, Gwayn

Gwidon (Polish) life.

Gwilym (Welsh) a form of William.
Gwillym

Gwyn 🄖 (Welsh) fair; blessed.
Gwynn, Gwynne

Gyasi (Akan) marvelous baby.

Gyorgy (Russian) a form of George.
Gyoergy, György, Gyuri, Gyurka

Gyula (Hungarian) youth.
Gyala, Gyuszi

H 🄖 (American) an initial used as a first name.

Ha (Korean) summer; congratulate; river; lotus.

Habib (Arabic) beloved.

Habid (Arabic) appreciated one.

Hacan (Quechua) brilliant, splendorous.

Hacanpoma, Hacanpuma (Quechua) brilliant puma.

Hackett (German, French) little wood cutter.
Hacket, Hackit, Hackitt

Hackman (German, French) wood cutter.

Hadar (Hebrew) glory.

Haddad (Arabic) blacksmith.

Hadden (English) heather-covered hill.
Haddan, Haddon, Haden

Haden (English) a form of Hadden.
Hadin, Hadon, Hadyn, Haeden

Hadi (Arabic) guiding to the right.
Hadee, Hady

Hadley 🄖 (English) heather-covered meadow.
Had, Hadlea, Hadlee, Hadleigh, Hadly, Lee, Leigh

Hadrian (Latin, Swedish) dark.
Adrian, Hadrien

Hadrián (Latin) a form of Hadrian.

Hadulfo (Germanic) combat wolf.

Hadwin (English) friend in a time of war.
Hadwinn, Hadwyn, Hadwynn, Hadwynne

Hae (Korean) sun; sea; boar; release.

Hag'man (Chamorro) eel.

Hagan (German) strong defense.
Haggan

Hagen (Irish) young, youthful.

Hagley (English) enclosed meadow.

Hagos (Ethiopian) happy.

Hahnee (Native American) beggar.

Hai (Vietnamese) sea.

Haidar (Arabic) lion.
Haider

Haiden 🄑 (English) a form of Hayden.
Haidyn

Haig (English) enclosed with hedges.

Hailey 🄖 (Irish) a form of Haley.
Haile, Haille, Haily, Halee

Haji (Swahili) born during the pilgrimage to Mecca.

Hajime (Japanese) first son.

Hajin (Japanese) literary figure.

Hakan (Native American) fiery.

Hakeem 🄑 (Arabic) a form of Hakim.
Hakam, Hakem

Hakik (Persian) truth; genuine, real.

Hakim (Arabic) wise. (Ethiopian) doctor.
Hakeem, Hakiem

Hakon (Scandinavian) of Nordic ancestry.
Haaken, Haakin, Haakon, Haeo, Hak, Hakan, Hako

Hal (English) a short form of Halden, Hall, Harold.

Halbert (English) shining hero.
Bert, Halburt

Halden (Scandinavian) half-Danish. See also Dane.
Hal, Haldan, Haldane, Halfdan, Halvdan

Hale (English) a short form of Haley. (Hawaiian) a form of Harry.
Hayle, Heall

Halee 🄖 (Irish) a form of Hailey.

Halen (Swedish) hall.
Hale, Hallen, Haylan, Haylen

Haley 🄖 (Irish) ingenious.
Hailey, Hale, Haleigh, Halley, Hayleigh, Hayley, Hayli

Halford (English) valley ford.

Hali 🄖 (Greek) sea.

Halian (Zuni) young.

Halil (Turkish) dear friend.
Halill

Halim (Arabic) mild, gentle.
Haleem

Hall (English) manor, hall.
Hal, Halstead, Halsted

Hallam (English) valley.

Hallan (English) dweller at the hall; dweller at the manor.
Halin, Hallene, Hallin

Halley **G** (English) meadow near the hall; holy.

Hallie **G** (English) a form of Halley.

Halliwell (English) holy well.
Hallewell, Hellewell, Helliwell

Hallward (English) hall guard.

Halomtano (Chamorro) jungle; forest.

Halsey **G** (English) Hal's island.

Halstead (English) manor grounds.
Halsted

Halton (English) estate on the hill.

Halvor (Norwegian) rock; protector.
Halvard

Ham (Hebrew) hot. Bible: one of Noah's sons.

Hama (Japanese) shore.

Hamal (Arabic) lamb. Astronomy: a bright star in the constellation of Aries.

Hamar (Scandinavian) hammer.

Hamid (Arabic) praised. See also Muhammad.
Haamid, Hamaad, Hamadi, Hamd, Hamdrem, Hamed, Hamedo, Hameed, Hamidi, Hammad, Hammed, Humayd

Hamill (English) scarred.
Hamel, Hamell, Hammill

Hamilton (English) proud estate.
Hamel, Hamelton, Hamil, Hamill, Tony

Hamish (Scottish) a form of Jacob, James.

Hamisi (Swahili) born on Thursday.

Hamlet (German, French) little village; home. Literature: one of Shakespeare's tragic heroes.

Hamlin (German, French) loves his home.
Hamblin, Hamelen, Hamelin, Hamlen, Hamlyn, Lin

Hammet (English, Scandinavian) village.
Hammett, Hamnet, Hamnett

Hammond (English) village.
Hamond

Hampton (English) Geography: a town in England.
Hamp

Hamza (Arabic) powerful.
Hamzah, Hamze, Hamzeh, Hamzia

Han (Chinese) self-restraint.

Han Min (Korean) the (Korean) people.

Hanale (Hawaiian) a form of Henry.
Haneke

Hanan (Hebrew) grace.
Hananel, Hananiah, Johanan

Hanbal (Arabic) pure. History: Ahmad Ibn Hanbal founded an Islamic school of thought.

Handel (German, English) a form of John. Music: George Frideric Handel was a German composer whose works include *Messiah* and *Water Music.*

Ha-Neul (Korean) sky.

Hanford (English) high ford.

Hang (Korean) constant; bay; navigate.

Hanif (Arabic) true believer.
Haneef, Hanef

Hank (American) a familiar form of Henry.

Hanley (English) high meadow.
Handlea, Handleigh, Handley, Hanlea, Hanlee, Hanleigh, Hanly, Henlea, Henlee, Henleigh, Henley

Hanna, Hannah **G** (German) forms of Hanno.

Hannes (Finnish) a form of John.

Hannibal (Phoenician) grace of God. History: a famous Carthaginian general who fought the Romans.
Anibal

Hanno (German) a short form of Johan.
Hannon, Hannu, Hanon

Hanomtano (Chamorro) water land.

Hans (Scandinavian) a form of John.
Hanschen, Hansel, Hants, Hanz

Hansel (Scandinavian) a form of Hans.
Haensel, Hansell, Hansl, Hanzel

Boys G–L

Hansen (Scandinavian) son of Hans.
Hanson

Hansh (Hindi) god; godlike.

Hanson (Scandinavian) a form of Hansen.
Hansen, Hanssen, Hansson

Hansuke (Japanese) sail; mediation.

Hanus (Czech) a form of John.

Hao (Vietnamese) good; perfect.

Haoa (Hawaiian) a form of Howard.

Hara G (Hindi) seizer. Religion: another
name for the Hindu god Shiva.

Harald (Scandinavian) a form of Harold.
Haraldo, Haralds, Haralpos

Harb (Arabic) warrior.

Harbin (German, French) little bright
warrior.
Harben, Harbyn

Harcourt (French) fortified dwelling.
Court, Harcort

Hardeep (Punjabi) a form of Harpreet.

Harden (English) valley of the hares.
Hardian, Hardin

Harding (English) brave; hardy.
Hardin

Hardwin (English) brave friend.

Hardy (German) bold, daring.
Hardie

Harel (Hebrew) mountain of God.
Harell, Hariel, Harrell

Harford (English) ford of the hares.

Hargrove (English) grove of the hares.
Hargreave, Hargreaves

Hari (Hindi) tawny.
Hariel, Harin

Harith (Arabic) cultivator.

Harjot (Sikh) light of God.
Harjeet, Harjit, Harjodh

Harkin (Irish) dark red.
Harkan, Harken

Harlan (English) hare's land; army land.
*Harland, Harlen, Harlenn, Harlin, Harlon,
Harlyn, Harlynn*

Harland (English) a form of Harlan.
Harlend

Harley BG (English) hare's meadow; army
meadow.
Arley, Harlea, Harlee, Harleigh, Harly

Harlow (English) hare's hill; army hill. See
also Arlo.

Harman, Harmon (English) forms of
Herman.
Harm, Harmen, Harmond, Harms

Harold (Scandinavian) army ruler. See also
Jindra.
*Araldo, Garald, Garold, Hal, Harald, Haraldas,
Haraldo, Haralds, Harry, Heraldo, Herold,
Heronim, Herrick, Herryck*

Haroldo (Germanic) he who dominates the
region with his army.

Haroun (Arabic) lofty; exalted.
Haarun, Harin, Haron, Haroon, Harron, Harun

Harper (English) harp player.
Harp, Harpo

Harpreet G (Punjabi) loves God, devoted to
God.
Hardeep

Harris (English) a short form of Harrison.
Haris, Hariss

Harrison B (English) son of Harry.
Harison, Harreson, Harris, Harrisen, Harrisson

Harrod (Hebrew) hero; conqueror.

Harry (English) a familiar form of Harold.
See also Arrigo, Hale, Parry.
Harm, Harray, Harrey, Harri, Harrie

Hart (English) a short form of Hartley.

Hartley (English) deer meadow.
Hart, Hartlea, Hartlee, Hartleigh, Hartly

Hartman (German) hard; strong.

Hartwell (English) deer well.
Harwell, Harwill

Hartwig (German) strong advisor.

Hartwood (English) deer forest.
Harwood

Haru (Japanese) born in the spring.

Haruakira, Haruchika (Japanese) forms of
Haru.

Harue (Japanese) springtime bay.

Harujiro (Japanese) spring-born second son.

Haruka (Japanese) tranquil.

Haruki (Japanese) shining brightly.

Haruko (Japanese) first born.

Haruto (Japanese) spring.

Harvey (German) army warrior.
Harv, Hervé, Hervey, Hervie, Hervy

Harvir **B** (Sikh) God's warrior.
Harvier

Hasad (Turkish) reaper, harvester.

Hasan (Arabic) a form of Hassan.
Hasaan, Hasain, Hasaun, Hashaan, Hason

Hasani (Swahili) handsome.
Hasan, Hasanni, Hassani, Heseny, Hassen, Hassian, Husani

Hashida (Japanese) from the bridge by the rice field.

Hashim (Arabic) destroyer of evil.
Haashim, Hasham, Hasheem, Hashem

Hasin (Hindi) laughing.
Haseen, Hasen, Hassin, Hazen, Hesen

Haskel (Hebrew) a form of Ezekiel.
Haskell

Haslett (English) hazel-tree land.
Haze, Hazel, Hazlett, Hazlitt

Hasrat (Arabic) grief; longing, desire.

Hassan (Arabic) handsome.
Hasan, Hassen, Hasson

Hassel (German, English) witches' corner.
Hassal, Hassall, Hassell, Hazael, Hazell

Hastin (Hindi) elephant.

Hastings (Latin) spear. (English) house council.
Hastie, Hasty

Hastu (Quechua) bird of the Andes.

Hatim (Arabic) judge.
Hateem, Hatem

Hatuntupac (Quechua) magnificent, great and majestic.

Hauk (Norwegian) hawk.
Haukeye

Havelock (Norwegian) sea battler.

Haven **G** (Dutch, English) harbor, port; safe place.
Haeven, Havin, Hevin, Hevon, Hovan

Havika (Hawaiian) a form of David.

Hawk (English) hawk.
Hawke, Hawkin, Hawkins

Hawley (English) hedged meadow.
Hawleigh, Hawly

Hawthorne (English) hawthorn tree.

Hayato (Japanese) fast person; brave person.

Hayden 🌱 **B** (English) hedged valley.
Haiden, Haydan, Haydenn, Haydn, Haydon

Hayes (English) hedged valley.
Hayse

Hayley **G** (Irish) a form of Haley.

Hayward (English) guardian of the hedged area.
Haward, Heyvard, Heyward

Haywood (English) hedged forest.
Heywood, Woody

Haziel (Hebrew) vision of God.

He (Chinese) river.

Hearn (Scottish, English) a short form of Ahearn.
Hearne, Herin, Hern

Heath **B** (English) heath.
Heathe, Heith

Heathcliff (English) cliff near the heath. Literature: the hero of Emily Brontë's novel *Wuthering Heights*.

Heather **G** (English) flowering heather.

Heaton (English) high place.

Heaven **G** (English) place of beauty and happiness. Bible: where God and angels are said to dwell.

Heber (Hebrew) ally, partner.

Hector (Greek) steadfast. Mythology: the greatest hero of the Trojan War in Homer's epic poem *Iliad*.

Héctor (Greek) a form of Hector.

Hedley (English) heather-filled meadow.
Headley, Headly, Hedly

Hegesipo (Greek) horse rider.

Heiichi (Japanese) peaceful first-born son.

Heinrich (German) a form of Henry.
Heindrick, Heiner, Heinreich, Heinrick, Heinrik, Hinrich

Heinz (German) a familiar form of Henry.

Heladio (Greek) native of Halade, Greece.

Helaku (Native American) sunny day.

Heldrado (Germanic) counselor of warriors.

Helen **G** (Greek) light.

Boys G–L

Helge (Russian) holy.

Heli (Hebrew) he who offers himself to God.

Helio (Spanish) gift of the sun god.

Heliodoro (Greek) gift of god.

Heliogabalo (Syrian) he who adores the sun.

Helki BG (Moquelumnan) touching.

Helmer (German) warrior's wrath.

Helmut (German) courageous.
Helmuth

Helvecio (Latin) ancient inhabitants of present-day Switzerland.

Heman (Hebrew) faithful.

Henderson (Scottish, English) son of Henry.
Hendrie, Hendries, Hendron, Henryson

Hendrick (Dutch) a form of Henry.
Hendricks, Hendrickson, Hendrik, Hendriks, Hendrikus, Hendrix, Henning

Heng (Chinese) eternal.

Heniek (Polish) a form of Henry.
Henier

Henley (English) high meadow.

Henning (German) a form of Hendrick, Henry.

Henoch (Yiddish) initiator.
Enoch, Henock, Henok

Henri (French) a form of Henry.
Henrico, Henrri

Henrick (Dutch) a form of Henry.
Heinrick, Henerik, Henrich, Henrik, Henryk

Henrique (Portuguese) a form of Henry.

Henry (German) ruler of the household. See also Arrigo, Enric, Enrick, Enrico, Enrikos, Enrique, Hanale, Honok, Kiki.
Hagan, Hank, Harro, Harry, Heike, Heinrich, Heinz, Hendrick, Henery, Heniek, Henning, Henraoi, Henri, Henrick, Henrim, Henrique, Henrry, Heromin, Hersz

Hentrick (Pohnpeian) a form of Enrique.

Heracleos, Heraclio (Greek) belonging to Hercules.

Heraclito, Heráclito (Greek) he who is drawn to the sacred.

Heraldo (Spanish) a form of Harold.
Herald, Hiraldo

Herb (German) a short form of Herbert.
Herbie, Herby

Herbert (German) glorious soldier.
Bert, Erbert, Eriberto, Harbert, Hebèrt, Hébert, Heberto, Herb, Heriberto, Hurbert

Herculano (Latin) belonging to Hercules.

Hercules (Latin) glorious gift. Mythology: a Greek hero of fabulous strength, renowned for his twelve labors.
Herakles, Herc, Hercule, Herculie

Hércules (Etruscan) a form of Hercules.

Herfy (Chuukese) a form of Harvey.

Heriberto (Spanish) a form of Herbert.
Heribert

Hermagoras (Greek) disciple of Hermes.

Hermalindo, Hermelindo (German) he who is like a shield of strength.

Herman (Latin) noble. (German) soldier. See also Armand, Ermanno, Ermano, Mandek.
Harmon, Hermaan, Hermann, Hermie, Herminio, Hermino, Hermon, Hermy, Heromin

Hermán (Germanic) a form of Herman.

Hermenegildo (Germanic) he who offers sacrifices to God.

Hermes (Greek) messenger. Mythology: the divine herald of Greek mythology.

Hermógenes (Greek) sent from Hermes.

Hernan (German) peacemaker.

Hernán (Germanic) a form of Herman.

Hernando (Spanish) a form of Ferdinand.
Hernandes, Hernandez

Herodes (Greek) fire dragon.

Herodoto (Greek) sacred talent.

Heródoto (Greek) divine talent; gift.

Herón, Heros (Latin) hero.

Herrick (German) war ruler.
Herrik, Herryck

Herschel (Hebrew) a form of Hershel.
Herchel, Hersch, Herschel, Herschell

Hersh (Hebrew) a short form of Hershel.
Hersch, Hirsch

Hershel (Hebrew) deer.
Herschel, Hersh, Hershal, Hershall, Hershell, Herzl, Hirschel, Hirshel

Hertz (Yiddish) my strife.
Herzel

Herve (Breton) active in combat.

Hervé (French) a form of Harvey.

Hesiquio (Greek) tranquil.

Hesperos (Greek) evening star.
Hespero

Hesutu (Moquelumnan) picking up a yellow jacket's nest.

Heung (Korean) prosperous; fun.

Hew (Welsh) a form of Hugh.
Hewe, Huw

Hewitt (German, French) little smart one.
Hewe, Hewet, Hewett, Hewie, Hewit,
Hewlett, Hewlitt, Hugh

Hewson (English) son of Hugh.

Hezekiah (Hebrew) God gives strength.
Hezekyah, Hazikiah, Hezikyah

Hiamovi (Cheyenne) high chief.

Hibah (Arabic) gift.

Hibiki (Japanese) sound; echo, reverberation.

Hidalgo (Spanish) noble one.

Hidayat (Arabic) guidance, instruction.

Hideak (Japanese) smart, clever.

Hideaki (Japanese) smart, clever.
Hideo

Hideharu (Japanese) excellent peacemaker.

Hidehisa (Japanese) long-lasting excellence.

Hidekazu (Japanese) harmonious beauty.

Hideki (Japanese) excellent foundation.

Hidenori (Japanese) excellent writings.

Hidetaka (Japanese) excellent obedience; prosperous.

Hidetaro (Japanese) witty big son; excellent big son.

Hideto (Japanese) excellent talent.

Hidetsugu (Japanese) gifted second-born; beautiful next-born; life of excellence.

Hideuki (Japanese) a form of Hideyuki.

Hideyuki (Japanese) good fortune; excellent traveling.

Hien (Vietnamese) meek and gentle.

Hiep (Vietnamese) chivalrous.

Hieremias (Greek) God will uplift.

Hieronymos (Greek) a form of Jerome. Art: Hieronymus Bosch was a fifteenth-century Dutch painter.
Hierome, Hieronim, Hieronimo, Hieronimos,
Hieronymo, Hieronymus

Hieu (Vietnamese) respectful.

Higinio (Greek) he who has good health.

Hikaru (Japanese) shine.

Hikokatsu (Japanese) doorway to victory.

Hila'an (Chamorro) a man of words.

Hilario (Spanish) a form of Hilary.

Hilary **G** (Latin) cheerful. See also Ilari.
Hi, Hilair, Hilaire, Hilarie, Hilario, Hilarion,
Hilarius, Hil, Hill, Hillary, Hillery, Hilliary,
Hillie, Hilly

Hildebrand (German) battle sword.
Hildebrando, Hildo

Hildemaro (Germanic) famous in combat.

Hilel (Arabic) new moon.

Hillary **G** (Latin) a form of Hilary.

Hillel (Hebrew) greatly praised. Religion: Rabbi Hillel originated the Talmud.

Hilliard (German) brave warrior.
Hillard, Hiller, Hillier, Hillierd, Hillyard, Hillyer,
Hillyerd

Hilmar (Swedish) famous noble.

Hilton (English) town on a hill.
Hylton

Hineti (Chamorro) to brush against.

Hinto (Dakota) blue.

Hinun (Native American) spirit of the storm.

Hipacio (Spanish) confessor.

Hipócrates (Greek) powerful because of his cavalry.

Hipólito (Greek) a form of Hippolyte.

Hippolyte (Greek) horseman.
Hipolito, Hippolit, Hippolitos, Hippolytus,
Ippolito

Hirabhai (Sanskrit) diamond brother.

Hiram (Hebrew) noblest; exalted.
Hi, Hirom, Huram, Hyrum

Hirao (Chamorro) emotion; attention; caring; heed.

Hiroaki (Japanese) abundant light.

Hirokazu (Japanese) abundant peace.

Hiroki (Japanese) air; space; noble.

Hiromasa (Japanese) fair, just.

Hiromichi (Japanese) wide street.

Hiromitsu (Japanese) extensive light.

Hironobu (Japanese) broad minded.

Hironori (Japanese) extensive writings.

Hiroshi (Japanese) generous.

Hiroto (Japanese) abundant.

Hiroyuki (Japanese) very fortunate.

Hisashi (Japanese) long period of time.

Hisoka (Japanese) secretive, reserved.

Hit (Chamorro) a form of Gil.

Hiteo (Kosraean) a form of Hideo.

Hiu (Hawaiian) a form of Hugh.

Ho (Chinese) good.

Hoa (Vietnamese) flower.

Hoai (Vietnamese) always, eternal.

Hoang (Vietnamese) finished.

Hobart (German) Bart's hill.
Hobard, Hobbie, Hobby, Hobie, Hoebart

Hoben (Chamorro) youthful; vigorous; fresh.

Hobert (German) Bert's hill.
Hobey

Hobson (English) son of Robert.
Hobbs, Hobs

Hoc (Vietnamese) studious.

Hocchocña (Chamorro) no more of him.

Hochoc (Chamorro) no more.

Hochocguafiña (Chamorro) his fire is no more.

Hochochinagu (Chamorro) no more breath.

Hococnineti (Chamorro) no longer sharp like the sword grass.

Hod (Hebrew) a short form of Hodgson.

Hodaka (Japanese) tall plant.

Hodgson (English) son of Roger.
Hod

Hogan (Irish) youth.
Hogin

Holbrook (English) brook in the hollow.
Brook, Holbrooke

Holden 🅑 (English) hollow in the valley.
Holdan, Holdin, Holdon, Holdun, Holdyn

Holic (Czech) barber.

Holland (French) Geography: a former province of the Netherlands.

Holleb (Polish) dove.
Hollub, Holub

Hollie 🅖 (English) a form of Hollis.

Hollis 🅑🅖 (English) grove of holly trees.

Holly 🅖 (English) a form of Hollis.

Holmes (English) river islands.

Holt (English) forest.
Holten, Holton

Homer (Greek) hostage; pledge; security. Literature: a renowned Greek epic poet.
Homar, Homere, Homère, Homero, Homeros, Homerus

Hondo (Shona) warrior.

Honesto (Filipino) honest.

Hong (Chinese) magnificent.

Hongi (Chamorro) to believe, trust.

Hongminh (Vietnamese) bright red.

Honi (Hebrew) gracious.
Choni

Honok (Polish) a form of Henry.

Honon (Moquelumnan) bear.

Honorato (Spanish) honorable.

Honoré (Latin) honored.
Honor, Honoratus, Honoray, Honorio, Honorius

Honovi (Native American) strong.

Honza (Czech) a form of John.

Hoon (Korean) instruct.

Hop (Chinese) agreeable.

Hope 🅖 (English) hope.

Horace (Latin) keeper of the hours. Literature: a famous Roman lyric poet and satirist.
Horacio, Horaz

Horacio (Latin) a form of Horace.

Horado (Spanish) timekeeper.

Horangel (Greek) messenger from the heights or from the mountain.

Horatio (Latin) clan name. See also Orris.
Horatius, Oratio

Horst (German) dense grove; thicket.
Hurst

Hortencio (Latin) he who has a garden and loves it.

Hortensio (Latin) gardener.

Horton (English) garden estate.
Hort, Horten, Orton

Hosa (Arapaho) young crow.

Hosea (Hebrew) salvation. Bible: a Hebrew prophet.
Hose, Hoseia, Hoshea, Hosheah

Hoshi (Japanese) star.

Hospicio (Spanish) he who is accommodating.

Hotah (Lakota) white.

Hototo (Native American) whistler.

Hou (Chinese) nobleman.

Hou-Chi (Chinese) an ancient harvest god.

Houghton (English) settlement on the headland.

Houston **B** (English) hill town. Geography: a city in Texas.
Housten, Houstin, Hustin, Huston

Howard (English) watchman. See also Haoa.
Howie, Ward

Howe (German) high.
Howey, Howie

Howell (Welsh) remarkable.
Howel

Howi (Moquelumnan) turtledove.

Howie (English) a familiar form of Howard, Howland.
Howey

Howin (Chinese) loyal swallow.

Howland (English) hilly land.
Howie, Howlan, Howlen

Hoyoung (Korean) vanity.

Hoyt (Irish) mind; spirit.

Hsia (Chinese) summer.

Hsiang (Chinese) incense; village; enjoy; image.

Hsiao (Chinese) dawn; tiny; smile.

Hsin (Chinese) after an ancient dynasty.

Hsun (Chinese) teach.

Hu (Chinese) tiger.

Hua (Chinese) the best part (the cream).

Huai (Chinese) scholar.

Huaiquilaf (Mapuche) good, straight lance.

Huan (Chinese) happiness.

Huang (Chinese) yellow.

Huan-Yue (Chinese) joyful, happy.

Huapi (Mapuche) island.

Hubbard (German) a form of Hubert.

Hubert (German) bright mind; bright spirit. See also Beredei, Uberto.
Bert, Hobart, Hubbard, Hubbert, Huber, Hubertek, Huberto, Hubertson, Hubie, Huey, Hugh, Hugibert, Huibert, Humberto

Huberto (Spanish) a form of Hubert.
Humberto

Hubie (English) a familiar form of Hubert.
Hube, Hubi

Huc (Korean) earth, ground.

Hucsuncu (Quechua) he who has only one love; faithful.

Hud (Arabic) Religion: a Muslim prophet.

Hudson (English) son of Hud.

Huechacura (Mapuche) sharp rock; peak.

Huenchulaf (Mapuche) healthy man; happy, joyous, festive.

Huenchuleo (Mapuche) brave; handsome river; having grown up near the river.

Huenchuman (Mapuche) proud male condor.

Huenchumilla (Mapuche) ascending light; lucent point.

Huenchuñir (Mapuche) male fox.

Huentemil (Mapuche) light from above, beam of light; possessor of much silver and gold.

Huenuhueque (Mapuche) lamb from heaven.

Huenullan (Mapuche) heavenly altar.

Huenuman (Mapuche) condor from the sky; from heaven.

Huenupan (Mapuche) branch from heaven; lion from heaven.

Huey (English) a familiar form of Hugh.
Hughey, Hughie, Hughy, Hui

Hueypín (Mapuche) broken, odd land.

Hugh (English) a short form of Hubert. See also Ea, Hewitt, Huxley, Maccoy, Ugo.
Fitzhugh, Hew, Hiu, Hue, Huey, Hughes, Hugo, Hugues

Hugo ☐ (Latin) a form of Hugh.
Ugo

Hugolino (Germanic) he who has spirit and intelligence.

Hugua (Chamorro) two.

Huichacura (Mapuche) rock with just one ridge, just one side.

Huichahue (Mapuche) battlefield.

Huichalef (Mapuche) he who runs on just one side; one straight line.

Huichañir (Mapuche) fox from another region.

Huidaleo (Mapuche) branch in the river; the river separates.

Huinculche (Mapuche) people that live on the hill.

Huircalaf (Mapuche) cry of joy; healthy shout.

Huircaleo (Mapuche) whisper of the river, noise from the river.

Hui-Ying (Chinese) brilliant, intelligent.

Hulbert (German) brilliant grace.
Bert, Hulbard, Hulburd, Hulburt, Hull

Hullen (Mapuche) spring.

Humbaldo (Germanic) daring as a lion cub.

Humbert (German) brilliant strength. See also Umberto.
Hum, Humberto

Humberto (Portuguese) a form of Humbert.

Humio (Palauan) a form of Umio.

Humphrey (German) peaceful strength. See also Onofrio, Onufry.
Hum, Humfredo, Humfrey, Humfrid, Humfried, Humfry, Hump, Humph, Humphery, Humphry, Humphrys, Hunfredo

Huna (Chamorro) sand.

Hung (Vietnamese) brave.

Hunt (English) a short form of names beginning with "Hunt."

Hunter �015 ☐ (English) hunter.
Hunt, Huntur

Huntington (English) hunting estate.
Hunt, Huntingdon

Huntley (English) hunter's meadow.
Hunt, Huntlea, Huntlee, Huntleigh, Huntly

Huo (Chinese) fire.

Hurao (Chamorro) a form of Hirao.

Hurley (Irish) sea tide.
Hurlee, Hurleigh

Hurst (English) a form of Horst.
Hearst, Hirst

Husai (Hebrew) hurried one.

Husam (Arabic) sword.

Husamettin (Turkish) sharp sword.

Huslu (Native American) hairy bear.

Hussain (Arabic) a form of Hussein.
Hossain, Husain, Husani, Husayn, Hussan, Hussayn

Hussein (Arabic) little; handsome.
Hossein, Houssein, Houssin, Huissien, Huossein, Husein, Husien, Husain, Hussien

Hussien (Arabic) a form of Hussein.
Husian, Hussin

Husto (Chamorro) just, fair.

Hutchinson (English) son of the hutch dweller.
Hutcheson

Hute (Native American) star.

Hutton (English) house on the jutting ledge.
Hut, Hutt, Huttan

Huu (Vietnamese) very much so; amplifies the meaning of the first name.

Huxley (English) Hugh's meadow.
Hux, Huxlea, Huxlee, Huxleigh, Lee

Huy (Vietnamese) glorious.

Huyen (Vietnamese) black; mysterious; string of a musical instrument.

Huynh (Vietnamese) older brother.

Hwan (Korean) joyful; ring.

Hy (Vietnamese) hopeful. (English) a short form of Hyman.

Hyacinthe (French) hyacinth.

Hyang (Korean) fragrance, incense; village; enjoy.

Hyatt (English) high gate.
Hyat

Hyde (English) cache; measure of land equal to 120 acres; animal hide.

Hyder (English) tanner, preparer of animal hides for tanning.

Hye (Korean) favor, grace; kindness; wisdom, cleverness, wit.

Hyman (English) a form of Chaim.
Haim, Hayim, Hayvim, Hayyim, Hy, Hyam, Hymie

Hyosuke (Japanese) ice; mediation.

Hyota (Japanese) very icy.

Hyun (Korean) worth; wise; dark; subtle; bowstring, musical string.

Hyung (Korean) elder brother; successful; glowworm.

Hyun-Ki (Korean) wise.

Hyun-Shik (Korean) clever.

I (Korean) two; different; finished; extraordinary.

I Wei (Chinese) a form of Iwei.

Iacobus, Iocobus (Pohnpeian) forms of Jacob.

Iago (Spanish, Welsh) a form of Jacob, James. Literature: the villain in Shakespeare's *Othello*.
Jago

Iain (Scottish) a form of Ian.

Iakobos (Greek) a form of Jacob.
Iakov, Iakovos, Iakovs

Ian �td **B** (Scottish) a form of John. See also Ean, Eion.
Iain, Iane, Iann

Ianos (Czech) a form of John.
Iannis

Ib (Phoenician, Danish) oath of Baal.

Iban (Basque) a form of John.

Iber, Ibérico, Iberio, Ibero (Latin) native of Iberia or who comes from the Iberian peninsula.

Ibi (Latin) at another place.

Ibon (Basque) a form of Ivor.

Ibrahim (Hausa) my father is exalted.
Ibrahaim, Ibraham, Ibraheem, Ibrahem, Ibrahiem, Ibrahiim, Ibrahmim

Ichabod (Hebrew) glory is gone. Literature: Ichabod Crane is the main character of Washington Irving's story "The Legend of Sleepy Hollow."

Ichitaro (Japanese) first-born big son.

Idi (Swahili) born during the Idd festival.

Idris (Welsh) eager lord. (Arabic) Religion: a Muslim prophet.
Idrease, Idrees, Idres, Idress, Idreus, Idriece, Idriss, Idrissa, Idriys

Idumeo (Latin) red.

Iens (Pohnpeian) a form of Jens.

Iestyn (Welsh) a form of Justin.

Ietaka (Japanese) literary figure.

Iferemi (Fijian) a form of Efren.

Ifraim, Ifram (Chuukese) forms of Efren.

Igashu (Native American) wanderer; seeker.
Igasho

Igenansio, Igenasio (Fijian) forms of Ignacio.

Iggy (Latin) a familiar form of Ignatius.

Iginas (Chuukese) a form of Ignacio.

Ignacio (Italian) a form of Ignatius.
Ignazio

Ignado (Spanish) fiery or ardent.

Ignathio (Yapese) a form of Ignacio.

Ignatius (Latin) fiery, ardent. Religion: Saint Ignatius of Loyola founded the Jesuit order. See also Inigo, Neci.
Iggie, Iggy, Ignac, Ignác, Ignace, Ignacio, Ignacius, Ignatios, Ignatious, Ignatz, Ignaz, Ignazio

Igor (Russian) a form of Inger, Ingvar. See also Egor, Yegor.
Igoryok

Ihorangi (Maori) rain.

Ihsan (Turkish) compassionate.

Ike (Hebrew) a familiar form of Isaac.
History: the nickname of the thirty-fourth
U.S. president Dwight D. Eisenhower.
Ikee, Ikey

Ikeda (Japanese) from the rice field pool.

Iker (Basque) visitation.

Ikinas (Pohnpeian) a form of Ignacio.

Ikki (Japanese) tree.

Ikrebai (Palauan) in the back of the meeting
house.

Iku (Japanese) nourishing.

Ikuo (Japanese) cultured man; conqueror.

Ikuya (Japanese) he who is cultured.

Il (Korean) one, first; best; sun; leisure.

Ilan (Hebrew) tree. (Basque) youth.

Ilari (Basque) a form of Hilary.
Ilario

Ilengelkei (Palauan) you are stopped from
the side.

Ilias (Greek) a form of Elijah.
Illias, Illyas, Ilyas, Ilyes

Ilidio (Latin) troop.

Ilikena (Fijian) a form of Elkanah.

Illan (Basque, Latin) youth.

Illayuc (Quechua) luminous; fortunate,
touched by the gods.

Ilom (Ibo) my enemies are many.

Ilsan (Korean) first-born child.

Iluminado (Latin) he who receives the
inspiration of God.

Ilya (Russian) a form of Elijah.
Ilia, Ilie, Ilija, Iliya, Ilja, Illia, Illya

Imad (Arabic) supportive; mainstay.

Iman 🄶 (Hebrew) a short form of
Immanuel.

Imani 🄶 (Hebrew) a form of Iman.
Imanni

Imetengel (Palauan) to come down.

Immanuel (Hebrew) a form of Emmanuel.
*Iman, Imanol, Imanuel, Immanual,
Immanuele, Immuneal*

Imran (Arabic) host.
Imraan

Imre (Hungarian) a form of Emery.
Imri

Imrich (Czech) a form of Emery.
Imrus

In (Korean) mankind; lead, guide; humanity;
cause, origin; end.

Inagangta (Chamorro) our noise, our
loudness.

Inaganta (Chamorro) a form of Inagangta.

Inalef (Mapuche) swift reinforcement; he
who follows behind.

Inapo (Chamorro) the wave.

Inario (Chuukese) a form of Hilario.

Inay (Hindi) god; godlike.

Inca (Quechua) king; prince or male-child of
royal heritage.

Incaurco, Incaurcu (Quechua) hill; Incan
god.

Ince (Hungarian) innocent.

Indalecio (Arabic) same as the master.

Inder (Hindi) god; godlike.
*Inderbir, Inderdeep, Inderjeet, Inderjit,
Inderpal, Inderpreet, Inderveer, Indervir, Indra,
Indrajit*

Indiana (American) land of Indians.
Geography: name of a U.S. state.
Indi, Indy

Indíbil (Spanish) he who is very black.

Indro (Spanish) victor.

Inek (Welsh) a form of Irvin.

Ing (Scandinavian) a short form of Ingmar.
Inge

Ingelbert (German) a form of Engelbert.
Inglebert

Inger (Scandinavian) son's army.
Igor, Ingemar, Ingmar

Ingmar (Scandinavian) famous son.
Ing, Ingamar, Ingamur, Ingemar

Ingram (English) angel.
Inglis, Ingra, Ingraham, Ingrim

Ingvar (Scandinavian) Ing's soldier.
Igor, Ingevar

Inigo (Basque) a form of Ignatius.
Iñaki, Iniego, Iñigo

Iniko (Ibo) born during bad times.

Injung (Korean) acknowledged, recognized.

Inkem (Osage) red rabbit.

Innis (Irish) island.
Innes, Inness, Inniss

Innocenzio (Italian) innocent.
Innocenty, Inocenci, Inocencio, Inocente, Inosente

Inoke (Fijian) a form of Enoch.

Inos, Inosi (Fijian) forms of Enos.

Inriann (Chuukese) a form of Henry.

Inteus (Native American) proud; unashamed.

Intiauqui (Quechua) sun prince.

Intichurin (Quechua) child of the sun.

Intiguaman (Quechua) sun falcon.

Intiyafa (Quechua) ray of sunlight.

Inus (Kosraean) a form of Enos.

Ioakim (Russian) a form of Joachim.
Ioachime, Ioakimo, Iov

Ioan (Greek, Bulgarian, Romanian) a form of John.
Ioane, Ioann, Ioannes, Ioannikios, Ioannis, Ionel

Ioanis (Pohnpeian) a form of Johannes.

Iokepa (Hawaiian) a form of Joseph.
Keo

Iolo (Welsh) the Lord is worthy.
Iorwerth

Ionakana (Hawaiian) a form of Jonathan.

Ionis (Pohnpeian) a form of Juan.

Iop (Pohnpeian) a form of Job.

Iorgos (Greek) a form of George.

Iosefa (Fijian) a form of Jose.

Iosif (Greek, Russian) a form of Joseph.

Iosua (Romanian) a form of Joshua.

Iowahn (Pohnpeian) a form of Johannes.

Iowane (Fijian) a form of Johannes.

Iowanes, Iwanis (Chuukese) forms of Johannes.

Ipyana (Nyakyusa) graceful.

Ira (Hebrew) watchful.

Iram (English) bright.

Irasdos (Pohnpeian) a form of Irastos.

Irasema (Fijian) a form of Erasmo.

Irastos (Pohnpeian) a form of Erastus.

Irene **G** (Greek) peaceful.

Ireneo, Irineo (Greek) lover of peace.

Iris **G** (Greek) rainbow.

Irumba (Rutooro) born after twins.

Irv (Irish, Welsh, English) a short form of Irvin, Irving.

Irvin (Irish, Welsh, English) a short form of Irving. See also Ervine.
Inek, Irv, Irven, Irvine, Irvinn, Irvon

Irving (Irish) handsome. (Welsh) white river. (English) sea friend. See also Ervin, Ervine.
Irv, Irvin, Irvington, Irwin, Irwing

Irwin (English) a form of Irving. See also Ervin.
Irwinn, Irwyn

Isa (Arabic) a form of Jesus.
Isaah

Isaac � (Hebrew) he will laugh. Bible: the son of Abraham and Sarah. See also Itzak, Izak, Yitzchak.
Aizik, Icek, Ike, Ikey, Ikie, Isaak, Isaakios, Isac, Isacc, Isacco, Isack, Isaic, Ishaq, Isiac, Isiacc, Issac, Issca, Itzak, Izak, Izzy

Isaak (Hebrew) a form of Isaac.
Isack, Isak, Isik, Issak

Isabel **G** (Spanish) consecrated to God.

Isabella **G** (Italian) a form of Isabel.

Isabelle **G** (French) a form of Isabel.

Isacar (Hebrew) he was given for a favor.

Isadoro (Spanish) gift of Isis.

Isaiah �више **B** (Hebrew) God is my salvation. Bible: a Hebrew prophet.
Isa, Isai, Isaia, Isaias, Isaid, Isaih, Isaish, Ishaq, Isia, Isiah, Isiash, Issia, Issiah, Izaiah, Izaiha, Izaya, Izayah, Izayaih, Izayiah, Izeyah, Izeyha

Isaias (Hebrew) a form of Isaiah.
Isaiahs, Isais, Izayus

Isaías (Hebrew) a form of Isaias.

Isake (Fijian) a form of Isaac.

Isam (Arabic) safeguard.

Isamar **G** (Hebrew) a form of Itamar.

Isaoshi (Japanese) honor.

Boys G–L

Boys G–L

Isaoshy (Chuukese) a form of Isaoshi.

Isas (Japanese) meritorious.

Iscay (Quechua) second child.

Iscaycuari (Quechua) doubly savage and untamable.

Isekemu (Native American) slow-moving creek.

Isham (English) home of the iron one.

Ishan (Hindi) direction.
Ishaan, Ishaun

Ishaq (Arabic) a form of Isaac.
Ishaac, Ishak

Ishi (Japanese) stone.

Ishio (Japanese) a form of Ishi.

Ishmael (Hebrew) God will hear. Literature: the narrator of Herman Melville's novel *Moby-Dick*.
Isamael, Isamail, Ishma, Ishmail, Ishmale, Ishmeal, Ishmeil, Ishmel, Ishmil, Ismael, Ismail

Isidore (Greek) gift of Isis. See also Dorian, Ysidro.
Isador, Isadore, Isadorios, Isidor, Isidro, Issy, Ixidor, Izadore, Izidor, Izidore, Izydor, Izzy

Isidro (Greek) a form of Isidore.
Isidoro, Isidoros

Isikel (Chuukese) a form of Ezequiel.

Isikeli (Fijian) a form of Ezequiel.

Isikia (Fijian) a form of Esekaia.

Isikio (Pohnpeian) a form of Ezequiel.

Isiler (Chuukese) I know them.

Isimeli (Fijian) a form of Ismael.

Isireli (Fijian) a form of Israel.

Iskander (Afghan) a form of Alexander.

Ismael (Arabic) a form of Ishmael.

Ismail (Arabic) a form of Ishmael.
Ismeil, Ismiel

Isocrates (Greek) he who can do as much as the next man.

Isod (Hebrew) God fights and prevails; the angel's antagonist.

Israel (Hebrew) prince of God; wrestled with God. History: the nation of Israel took its name from the name given Jacob after he wrestled with the angel of the Lord. See also Yisrael.
Iser, Isreal, Israhel, Isrell, Isrrael, Isser, Izrael, Izzy, Yisrael

Isreal (Hebrew) a form of Israel.
Isrieal

Issa (Swahili) God is our salvation.

Issac (Hebrew) a form of Isaac.
Issacc, Issaic, Issiac

Issiah (Hebrew) a form of Isaiah.
Issaiah, Issia

Istu (Native American) sugar pine.

István (Hungarian) a form of Stephen.
Isti, Istvan, Pista

Itaete (Guarani) blade.

Italo (Latin) he came from the land that is between the seas.

Itamar, Ittamar (Hebrew) island of palms.

Itchiro (Kosraean) a form of Ichiro.

Ithel (Welsh) generous lord.

Itoshi (Japanese) this thread.

Itsuo (Japanese) fifth son; man of leisure.

Ittu (Kosraean) first, winner.

Itzak (Hebrew) a form of Isaac, Yitzchak.
Itzik

Iuaiu (Palauan) calm, peaceful.

Iukini (Hawaiian) a form of Eugene.
Kini

Iul (Palauan) the freycinetia tree.

Iusful (Chuukese) useful.

Iustin (Bulgarian, Russian) a form of Justin.

Ivan (Russian) a form of John.
Iván, Ivanchik, Ivanichek, Ivann, Ivano, Ivas, Iven, Ivin, Ivon, Ivyn, Vanya

Ivar 🅱 (Scandinavian) a form of Ivor. See also Yves, Yvon.
Iv, Iva

Ives (English) young archer.
Ive, Iven, Ivey, Yves

Ivey 🅶 (English) a form of Ives.

Ivo (German) yew wood; bow wood.
Ibon, Ivar, Ives, Ivon, Ivonnie, Ivor, Yvo

Ivor (Scandinavian) a form of Ivo.
Ibon, Ifor, Ivar, Iver, Ivory, Ivry

Ivy 🅶 (English) ivy tree.

Iwan (Polish) a form of John.

Iwao (Japanese) rock of life; rugged.

Iwei (Chinese) to consider.

Iyafa, Iyapa (Quechua) lightning.

Iyapo (Yoruba) many trials; many obstacles.

Iyapoma, Iyapuma (Quechua) puma of light.

Iyapu (Quechua) lightning.

Iyatecsi, Iyaticsi (Quechua) eternal light; origin of light.

Iye (Native American) smoke.

Izak (Czech) a form of Isaac.
Itzhak, Ixaka, Izaac, Izaak, Izac, Izaic, Izak, Izec, Izeke, Izick, Iżik, Izsak, Izsák, Izzak

Izzy (Hebrew) a familiar form of Isaac, Isidore, Israel.
Issy

J

J **B** (American) an initial used as a first name.
J.

Ja (Korean) attractive, magnetic.

Jaali (Swahili) powerful.

Jaan (Estonian) a form of Christian.

Jaap (Dutch) a form of Jim.

Jabari (Swahili) fearless, brave.
Jabaar, Jabahri, Jabar, Jabarae, Jabare, Jabaree, Jabarei, Jabarie, Jabarri, Jabarrie,

Jabary, Jabbar, Jabbaree, Jabbari, Jaber, Jabiari, Jabier, Jabori, Jaborie

Jabel (Hebrew) like the arrow that flies.

Jabez (Hebrew) born in pain.
Jabe, Jabes, Jabesh

Jabin (Hebrew) God has created.
Jabain, Jabien, Jabon

Jabir (Arabic) consoler, comforter.
Jabiri, Jabori

Jabranne (Arabic) consolation; reward.

Jabril (Arabic) a form of Jibril.
Jabrail, Jabree, Jabreel, Jabrel, Jabrell, Jabrelle, Jabri, Jabrial, Jabrie, Jabriel, Jabrielle, Jabrille

Jabulani (Shona) happy.

Jabuwe (Marshallese) don't get on.

Jacan (Hebrew) trouble.
Jachin

Jacari (American) a form of Jacorey.
Jacarey, Jacaris, Jacarius, Jacarre, Jacarri, Jacarrus, Jacarus, Jacary, Jacaure, Jacauri, Jaccar, Jaccari

Jace **B** (American) a combination of the initials J. + C.
JC, J.C., Jacee, Jacek, Jacey, Jacie, Jaice, Jaicee

Jacen (Greek) a form of Jason.
Jaceon

Jacey **G** (American) a form of Jace.

Jacho (Korean) to bring on oneself.

Jacinto (Portuguese, Spanish) hyacinth. See also Giacinto.
Jacindo, Jacint, Jacinta

Jack ⚜ (American) a familiar form of Jacob, John. See also Keaka.
Jackie, Jacko, Jackub, Jak, Jax, Jock, Jocko

Jackie, Jacky **BG** (American) familiar forms of Jack.
Jackey

Jackson ⚜ **B** (English) son of Jack.
Jacksen, Jacksin, Jacson, Jakson, Jaxon

Jaclyn **G** (American) a short form of Jacqueline (see Girls' Names).

Jaco (Portuguese) a form of Jacob.

Jacob ⚜ **B** (Hebrew) supplanter, substitute. Bible: son of Isaac, brother of Esau. See also Akiva, Chago, Checha, Coby, Diego, Giacomo, Hamish, Iago, Iakobos, James, Kiva, Koby, Kuba, Tiago, Yakov, Yasha, Yoakim.
Jaap, Jachob, Jack, Jackob, Jackub, Jaco, Jacobb, Jacobe, Jacobi, Jacobo, Jacoby, Jacolbi, Jacolby, Jacque, Jacques, Jacub, Jaecob, Jago, Jaicob, Jaime, Jake, Jakob, Jalu, Jasha, Jaycob, Jecis, Jeks, Jeska, Jim, Jocek, Jock, Jocob, Jocobb, Jocoby, Jocolby, Jokubas

Jacobi, Jacoby **B** (Hebrew) forms of Jacob.
Jachobi, Jacobbe, Jacobee, Jacobey, Jacobie, Jacobii, Jacobis

Jacobo (Hebrew) a form of Jacob.

Jacobson (English) son of Jacob.
Jacobs, Jacobsen, Jacobsin, Jacobus

Jacorey (American) a combination of Jacob + Corey.
Jacari, Jacori, Jacoria, Jacorie, Jacoris, Jacorius, Jacorrey, Jacorrien, Jacorry, Jacory, Jacouri, Jacourie, Jakari

Jacque (French) a form of Jacob.
Jacquay, Jacqui, Jocque, Jocqui

Jacques 🅱 (French) a form of Jacob, James. See also Coco.
Jackque, Jackques, Jackquise, Jacot, Jacquan, Jacquees, Jacquese, Jacquess, Jacquet, Jacquett, Jacquez, Jacquis, Jacquise, Jaquez, Jarques, Jarquis

Jacquez, Jaquez (French) forms of Jacques.
Jaques, Jaquese, Jaqueus, Jaqueze, Jaquis, Jaquise, Jaquze, Jocquez

Jacy (Tupi-Guarani) moon.
Jaicy, Jaycee

Jada 🅶 (American) a short form of Jadrien.

Jade 🅶 (Spanish) jade, precious stone.
Jaeid, Jaid, Jaide

Jaden ☙ 🅱 (Hebrew) a form of Jadon.
Jadee, Jadeen, Jadenn, Jadeon, Jadin, Jaeden

Jadon (Hebrew) God has heard.
Jaden, Jadyn, Jaedon, Jaiden, Jaydon

Jadrien (American) a combination of Jay + Adrien.
Jad, Jada, Jadd, Jader, Jadrian

Jadyn 🅶 (Hebrew) a form of Jadon.
Jadyne, Jaedyn

Jae Jik (Korean) to hold office, to be in service.

Jaegar (German) hunter.
Jaager, Jaeger, Jagur

Jae-Hwa (Korean) rich, prosperous.

Jael 🅶 (Hebrew) mountain goat.
Yael

Jaelen (American) a form of Jalen.
Jaelan, Jaelaun, Jaelin, Jaelon, Jaelyn

Ja'far (Sanskrit) little stream.
Jafar, Jafari, Jaffar, Jaffer, Jafur

Jage (Sanskrit) the world.

Jagger (English) carter.
Jagar, Jager, Jaggar

Jago (English) a form of James.

Jaguar (Spanish) jaguar.
Jagguar

Jahi (Swahili) dignified.

Jahlil (Hindi) a form of Jalil.
Jahlal, Jahlee, Jahleel, Jahliel

Jahmar (American) a form of Jamar.
Jahmare, Jahmari, Jahmarr, Jahmer

Jahvon (Hebrew) a form of Javan.
Jahvan, Jahvine, Jahwaan, Jahwon

Jai 🅱 (Tai) heart.
Jaie, Jaii

Jaiden 🅱 (Hebrew) a form of Jadon.
Jaidan, Jaidon, Jaidyn

Jailen (American) a form of Jalen.
Jailan, Jailani, Jaileen, Jailen, Jailon, Jailyn, Jailynn

Jaime 🅱 (Spanish) a form of Jacob, James.
Jaimey, Jaimie, Jaimito, Jaimy, Jayme, Jaymie

Jaimee 🅶 (Spanish) a form of Jaime.

Jaimie 🅶 (English) a form of Jamie. (Spanish) a form of Jaime.

Jair (Spanish) a form of Jairo.

Jairo (Spanish) God enlightens.
Jair, Jairay, Jaire, Jairus, Jarius

Jaison (Greek) a form of Jason.
Jaisan, Jaisen, Jaishon, Jaishun

Jaivon (Hebrew) a form of Javan.
Jaiven, Jaivion, Jaiwon

Jaiya (Sanskrit) a form of Jaya.

Jaja (Ibo) honored.

Jajuan (American) a combination of the prefix Ja + Juan.
Ja Juan, Jauan, Jawaun, Jejuan, Jujuan, Juwan

Jakari (American) a form of Jacorey.
Jakaire, Jakar, Jakaray, Jakarie, Jakarious, Jakarius, Jakarre, Jakarri, Jakarus

Jake (Hebrew) a short form of Jacob.
Jakie, Jayk, Jayke

Jakeem (Arabic) uplifted.

Jakob (Hebrew) a form of Jacob.
Jaekob, Jaikab, Jaikob, Jakab, Jakeb, Jakeob, Jakeub, Jakib, Jakiv, Jakobe, Jakobi, Jakobus, Jakoby, Jakov, Jakovian, Jakub, Jakubek, Jekebs

Jakome (Basque) a form of James.
Xanti

Jal (Gypsy) wanderer.

Jalan (American) a form of Jalen.
Jalaan, Jalaen, Jalain, Jaland, Jalane, Jalani, Jalanie, Jalann, Jalaun, Jalean, Jallan

Jale (Fijian) a form of Charles.

Jaleel **B** (Hindi) a form of Jalil.
Jaleell, Jaleil, Jalel

Jalen **B** (American) a combination of the prefix Ja + Len.
Jaelen, Jailen, Jalan, Jaleen, Jalend, Jalene, Jalin, Jallen, Jalon, Jalyn

Jalil (Hindi) revered.
Jahlil, Jalaal, Jalal

Jalin, Jalyn (American) forms of Jalen.
Jalian, Jaline, Jalynn, Jalynne

Jalisat (Arabic) he who receives little, gives more.

Jalon (American) a form of Jalen.
Jalone, Jaloni, Jalun

Jam (American) a short form of Jamal, Jamar.
Jama

Jamaal **B** (Arabic) a form of Jamal.

Jamaine (Arabic) a form of Germain.

Jamal **B** (Arabic) handsome. See also Gamal.
Jahmal, Jahmall, Jahmalle, Jahmeal, Jahmeel, Jahmeil, Jahmel, Jahmelle, Jahmil, Jahmile, Jaimal, Jam, Jamaal, Jamael, Jamahl, Jamail, Jamaile, Jamala, Jamale, Jamall, Jamalle, Jamar, Jamaul, Jamel, Jamil, Jammal, Jamor, Jamual, Jarmal, Jaumal, Jemal, Jermal, Jomal, Jomall

Jamar **B** (American) a form of Jamal.
Jam, Jamaar, Jamaari, Jamahrae, Jamair, Jamara, Jamaras, Jamaraus, Jamarl, Jamarr, Jamarre, Jamarrea, Jamarree, Jamarri, Jamarvis, Jamaur, Jamir, Jamire, Jamiree, Jammar, Jarmar, Jarmarr, Jaumar, Jemaar, Jemar, Jimar, Jomar

Jamarcus **B** (American) a combination of the prefix Ja + Marcus.
Jamarco, Jamarkus, Jemarcus, Jimarcus

Jamari (American) a form of Jamario.
Jamare, Jamarea, Jamaree, Jamareh, Jamaria, Jamarie, Jamaul

Jamario (American) a combination of the prefix Ja + Mario.
Jamareo, Jamari, Jamariel, Jamarious, Jamaris, Jamarius, Jamariya, Jemario, Jemarus

Jamarquis (American) a combination of the prefix Ja + Marquis.
Jamarkees, Jamarkeus, Jamarkis, Jamarqese, Jamarqueis, Jamarques, Jamarquez, Jamarquios, Jamarqus

Jamel (Arabic) a form of Jamal.
Jameel, Jamele, Jamell, Jamelle, Jammel, Jamuel, Jamul, Jarmel, Jaumal, Jaumell, Je-Mell, Jimell

James ♛ **B** (Hebrew) supplanter, substitute. (English) a form of Jacob. Bible: James the Great and James the Less were two of the Twelve Apostles. See also Diego, Hamish, Iago, Kimo, Santiago, Seamus, Seumas, Yago, Yasha.
Jacques, Jago, Jaime, Jaimes, Jakome, Jamesie, Jamesy, Jamez, Jameze, Jamie, Jamies, Jamse, Jamyes, Jamze, Jas, Jasha, Jay, Jaymes, Jem, Jemes, Jim

Jamesa, Jemesa (Fijian) forms of James.

Jameson **B** (English) son of James.
Jamerson, Jamesian, Jamison, Jaymeson

Jami **G** (English) a form of Jamie.

Jamie **G** (English) a familiar form of James.
Jaime, Jaimey, Jaimie, Jame, Jamee, Jamey, Jameyel, Jami, Jamia, Jamiah, Jamian, Jamme, Jammie, Jamiee, Jammy, Jamy, Jamye, Jayme, Jaymee, Jaymie

Jamil **B** (Arabic) a form of Jamal.
Jamiel, Jamiell, Jamielle, Jamile, Jamill, Jamille, Jamyl, Jarmil

Jamin (Hebrew) favored.
Jamen, Jamian, Jamien, Jamion, Jamionn, Jamon, Jamun, Jamyn, Jarmin, Jarmon, Jaymin

Jamison **B** (English) son of James.
Jamiesen, Jamieson, Jamis, Jamisen, Jamyson, Jaymison

Jamon (Hebrew) a form of Jamin.
Jamohn, Jamone, Jamoni

Jamond (American) a combination of James + Raymond.
Jamod, Jamont, Jamonta, Jamontae, Jamontay, Jamonte, Jarmond

Jamor (American) a form of Jamal.
Jamoree, Jamori, Jamorie, Jamorius, Jamorrio, Jamorris, Jamory, Jamour

Jamsheed (Persian) from Persia.
Jamshaid, Jamshed

Jan **B** (Dutch, Slavic) a form of John.
Jaan, Jana, Janae, Jann, Janne, Jano, Janson, Jenda, Yan

Jana **G** (Dutch, Slavic) a form of Jan.

Janab (Sanskrit) kin, acquaintance.

Janae **G** (Dutch, Slavic) a form of Jan.

Janco (Czech) a form of John.
Jancsi, Janke, Janko

Jando (Spanish) a form of Alexander.
Jandino

Jane **G** (Hebrew) God is gracious.

Janeil (American) a combination of the prefix Ja + Neil.
Janal, Janel, Janell, Janelle, Janiel, Janielle, Janile, Janille, Jarnail, Jarneil, Jarnell

Janek (Polish) a form of John.
Janak, Janik, Janika, Janka, Jankiel, Janko

Janell, Janelle **G** (American) forms of Janeil.

Janessa **G** (American) a form of Jane.

Janette **G** (French) a form of Janet (see Girls' Names).

Jang (Persian) battle, war.

Janine **G** (French) a form of Jane.

Janis **G** (Latvian) a form of John.
Ansis, Jancis, Zanis

Janne (Finnish) a form of John.
Jann, Jannes

János (Hungarian) a form of John.
Jancsi, Jani, Jankia, Jano

Janson (Scandinavian) son of Jan.
Janse, Jansen, Jansin, Janssen, Jansun, Jantzen, Janzen, Jensen, Jenson

Jantzen (Scandinavian) a form of Janson.
Janten, Jantsen, Jantson

Janus (Latin) gate, passageway; born in January. Mythology: the Roman god of beginnings and endings.
Jannese, Jannus, Januario, Janusz

Japheth (Hebrew) handsome. (Arabic) abundant. Bible: a son of Noah. See also Yaphet.
Japeth, Japhet

Jaquan **B** (American) a combination of the prefix Ja + Quan.
Jaequan, Jaiqaun, Jaiquan, Jaqaun, Jaqawan, Jaquaan, Jaquain, Ja'quan, Jaquane, Jaquann, Jaquanne, Jaquavius, Jaquawn, Jaquin, Jaquon, Jaqwan

Jaquarius (American) a combination of Jaquan + Darius.
Jaquari, Jaquarious, Jaquaris

Jaquavius (American) a form of Jaquan.
Jaquavas, Jaquaveis, Jaquaveius, Jaquaveon, Jaquaveous, Jaquavias, Jaquavious, Jaquavis, Jaquavus

Jaquon (American) a form of Jaquan.
Jaequon, Jaqoun, Jaquinn, Jaqune, Jaquoin, Jaquone, Jaqwon

Jarad (Hebrew) a form of Jared.
Jaraad, Jaraed

Jarah (Hebrew) sweet as honey.
Jerah

Jardan (Hebrew) a form of Jordan.
Jarden, Jardin, Jardon

Jareb (Hebrew) contending.
Jarib

Jared **B** (Hebrew) a form of Jordan.
Jahred, Jaired, Jarad, Jaredd, Jareid, Jarid, Jarod, Jarred, Jarrett, Jarrod, Jarryd, Jerad, Jered, Jerod, Jerrad, Jerred, Jerrod, Jerryd, Jordan

Jarek (Slavic) born in January.
Janiuszck, Januarius, Januisz, Jarec, Jarrek, Jarric, Jarrick

Jarell (Scandinavian) a form of Gerald.
Jairell, Jarael, Jareil, Jarel, Jarelle, Jariel, Jarrell, Jarryl, Jayryl, Jerel, Jerell, Jerrell, Jharell

Jaren (Hebrew) a form of Jaron.
Jarian, Jarien, Jarin, Jarion

Jareth (American) a combination of Jared + Gareth.
Jarreth, Jereth, Jarreth

Jarett (English) a form of Jarrett.
Jaret, Jarette

Jarl (Scandinavian) earl, nobleman.

Jarlath (Latin) in control.
Jarl, Jarlen

Jarman (German) from Germany.
Jerman

Jarod **B** (Hebrew) a form of Jared.
Jarodd, Jaroid

Jaron (Hebrew) he will sing; he will cry out.
Jaaron, Jairon, Jaren, Jarone, Jarren, Jarron, Jaryn, Jayron, Jayronn, Je Ronn, J'ron

Jaroslav (Czech) glory of spring.
Jarda

Jarred **B** (Hebrew) a form of Jared.
Ja'red, Jarrad, Jarrayd, Jarrid, Jarrod, Jarryd, Jerrid

Jarrell (English) a form of Gerald.
Jarel, Jarell, Jarrel, Jerall, Jerel, Jerell

Jarren (Hebrew) a form of Jaron.
Jarrain, Jarran, Jarrian, Jarrin

Jarrett **B** (English) a form of Garrett, Jared.
*Jairett, Jareth, Jarett, Jaretté, Jarhett,
Jarratt, Jarret, Jarrette, Jarrot, Jarrott,
Jerrett*

Jarrod (Hebrew) a form of Jared.
Jarod, Jerod, Jerrod

Jarryd (Hebrew) a form of Jared.
Jarrayd, Jaryd

Jarvis (German) skilled with a spear.
*Jaravis, Jarv, Jarvaris, Jarvas, Jarvaska,
Jarvey, Jarvez, Jarvie, Jarvios, Jarvious,
Jarvius, Jarvorice, Jarvoris, Jarvous, Jarvus,
Javaris, Jervey, Jervis*

Jaryn (Hebrew) a form of Jaron.
Jarryn, Jarynn, Jaryon

Jas **BG** (Polish) a form of John. (English) a
familiar form of James.
Jasio

Jasha (Russian) a familiar form of Jacob,
James.
Jascha

Jashawn (American) a combination of the
prefix Ja + Shawn.
Jasean, Jashan, Jashaun, Jashion, Jashon

Jaskaran **B** (Sikh) sings praises to the
Lord.
Jaskaren, Jaskarn, Jaskiran

Jaskarn **B** (Sikh) a form of Jaskaran.

Jasleen **G** (Latin) a form of Jocelyn.

Jasmeet **BG** (Persian) a form of Jasmine.

Jasmin **G** (Persian) jasmine flower.
*Jasman, Jasmanie, Jasmine, Jasmon,
Jasmond*

Jasmine **G** (Persian) a form of Jasmin.

Jason 👑 (Greek) healer. Mythology: the
hero who led the Argonauts in search of the
Golden Fleece.
*Jacen, Jaeson, Jahson, Jaison, Jasan,
Jasaun, Jase, Jasen, Jasin, Jasson, Jasten,
Jasun, Jasyn, Jathan, Jathon, Jay, Jayson*

Jasón (Greek) a form of Jason.

Jaspal (Punjabi) living a virtuous lifestyle.

Jasper **B** (French) brown, red, or yellow
ornamental stone. (English) a form of
Casper. See also Kasper.
Jaspar, Jazper, Jespar, Jesper

Jaspreet **BG** (Punjabi) virtuous.

Jasson (Greek) a form of Jason.
Jassen, Jassin

Jatinra (Hindi) great Brahmin sage.

Javan (Hebrew) Bible: son of Japheth.
*Jaewan, Jahvaughan, Jahvon, Jaivon,
Javante, Javaon, JaVaughn, Javen, Javian,
Javien, Javin, Javine, Javoanta, Javon,
Javona, Javone, Javonte, Jayvin, Jayvion,
Jayvon, Jevan, Jevon*

Javante (American) a form of Javan.
Javantae, Javantai, Javantée, Javanti

Javaris (English) a form of Jarvis.
*Javaor, Javar, Javaras, Javare, Javares,
Javari, Javarias, Javaries, Javario, Javarius,
Javaro, Javaron, Javarous, Javarre,
Javarreis, Javarri, Javarrious, Javarris,
Javarro, Javarte, Javarus, Javorious, Javoris,
Javorius, Javouris*

Javas (Sanskrit) quick, swift.
Jayvas, Jayvis

Javid (Persian) eternal, immortal; perpetual.

Javier (Spanish) owner of a new house. See
also Xavier.
Jabier, Javer, Javere, Javiar

Javiero (Spanish) born in January.

Javon **B** (Hebrew) a form of Javan.
*Jaavon, Jaevin, Jaevon, Jaewon, Javeon,
Javion, Javionne, Javohn, Javona, Javone,
Javoney, Javoni, Javonn, Javonne, Javonni,
Javonnie, Javonnte, Javoun, Jayvon*

Javonte **B** (American) a form of Javan.
*Javona, Javontae, Javontai, Javontay,
Javontaye, Javonté, Javontee, Javonteh,
Javontey*

Jawaun (American) a form of Jajuan.
*Jawaan, Jawan, Jawann, Jawn, Jawon,
Jawuan*

Jawhar (Arabic) jewel; essence.

Jaxon (English) a form of Jackson.
Jaxen, Jaxsen, Jaxson, Jaxsun, Jaxun

Jay **B** (French) blue jay. (English) a short
form of James, Jason.
Jae, Jai, Jave, Jaye, Jeays, Jeyes

Jaya (Sanskrit) victory.

Jayantha (Sanskrit) victorious, triumphant.

Jayce (American) a combination of the
initials J. + C.
JC, J.C., Jayc, Jaycee, Jay Cee, Jaycey, Jecie

Jaycob (Hebrew) a form of Jacob.
Jaycub, Jaykob

Boys
G–L

Jayde 🄶 (American) a combination of the initials J. + D.
JD, J.D., Jayd, Jaydee, Jayden

Jayden ❦ 🄱 (American) a form of Jayde.
Jaydan, Jaydin, Jaydn, Jaydon

Jayla 🄶 (American) a form of Jaylee.

Jaylee (American) a combination of Jay + Lee.
Jayla, Jayle, Jaylen

Jaylen 🄱 (American) a combination of Jay + Len.
Jaylaan, Jaylan, Jayland, Jayleen, Jaylend, Jaylin, Jayln, Jaylon, Jaylun, Jaylund, Jaylyn

Jaylin 🄱 (American) a form of Jaylen.
Jaylian, Jayline

Jaylon 🄱 (American) a form of Jaylen.
Jayleon

Jaylyn 🄱🄶 (American) a form of Jaylen.
Jaylynd, Jaylynn, Jaylynne

Jayme 🄶 (English) a form of Jamie.
Jaymie

Jaymes (English) a form of James.
Jaymis, Jayms, Jaymz

Jayquan (American) a combination of Jay + Quan.
Jaykwan, Jaykwon, Jayqon, Jayquawn, Jayqunn

Jayson (Greek) a form of Jason.
Jaycent, Jaysean, Jaysen, Jayshaun, Jayshawn, Jayshon, Jayshun, Jaysin, Jaysn, Jayssen, Jaysson, Jaysun

Jayvon (American) a form of Javon.
Jayvion, Jayvohn, Jayvone, Jayvonn, Jayvontay, Jayvonte, Jaywan, Jaywaun, Jaywin

Jaywant (Sanskrit) possessing victory.

Jazmine 🄶 (Persian) a form of Jasmine.

Jazz (American) jazz.
Jaz, Jazze, Jazzlee, Jazzman, Jazzmen, Jazzmin, Jazzmon, Jazztin, Jazzton, Jazzy

Jean 🄱 (French) a form of John.
Jéan, Jeane, Jeannah, Jeannie, Jeannot, Jeano, Jeanot, Jeanty, Jene

Jeanette 🄶 (French) a form of Jean.

Jeb (Hebrew) a short form of Jebediah.
Jebb, Jebi, Jeby

Jebediah (Hebrew) a form of Jedidiah.
Jeb, Jebadia, Jebadiah, Jebadieh, Jebidiah

Jed (Hebrew) a short form of Jedidiah. (Arabic) hand.
Jedd, Jeddy, Jedi

Jediah (Hebrew) hand of God.
Jedaia, Jedaiah, Jedeiah, Jedi, Yedaya

Jedidiah 🄱 (Hebrew) friend of God, beloved of God. See also Didi.
Jebediah, Jed, Jedadiah, Jeddediah, Jedediah, Jedediha, Jedidia, Jedidiah, Jedidiyah, Yedidya

Jedrek (Polish) strong; manly.
Jedric, Jedrik, Jedrus

Jeff (English) a short form of Jefferson, Jeffrey. A familiar form of Geoffrey.
Jef, Jefe, Jeffe, Jeffey, Jeffie, Jeffy, Jhef

Jefferson 🄱 (English) son of Jeff. History: Thomas Jefferson was the third U.S. president.
Jeferson, Jeff, Jeffers

Jeffery 🄱 (English) a form of Jeffrey.
Jefery, Jeffari, Jeffary, Jeffeory, Jefferay, Jeffereoy, Jefferey, Jefferie, Jeffory

Jefford (English) Jeff's ford.

Jeffrey 🄱 (English) divinely peaceful. See also Geffrey, Geoffrey, Godfrey.
Jeff, Jefferies, Jeffery, Jeffre, Jeffree, Jeffrery, Jeffrie, Jeffries, Jeffry, Jefre, Jefri, Jefry, Jeoffroi, Joffre, Joffrey

Jeffry (English) a form of Jeffrey.

Jehan (French) a form of John.
Jehann

Jehová (Hebrew) I am what I am.

Jehu (Hebrew) God lives. Bible: a military commander and king of Israel.
Yehu

Jeke (Fijian) a form of Jack.

Jekesoni (Fijian) a form of Jackson.

Jelani (Swahili) mighty.
Jel, Jelan, Jelanie, Jelaun

Jeltanbwij (Marshallese) someone who makes trouble in the family.

Jem 🄶 (English) a short form of James, Jeremiah.
Jemmie, Jemmy

Jemal (Arabic) a form of Jamal.
Jemaal, Jemael, Jemale, Jemel

Jemaluit (Marshallese) rainbow.

Jemel (Arabic) a form of Jemal.
Jemeal, Jemehl, Jemehyl, Jemell, Jemelle, Jemello, Jemeyle, Jemile, Jemmy

Jemond (French) worldly.
Jemon, Jémond, Jemonde, Jemone

Jenaro (Latin) born in January.

Jenkin (Flemish) little John.
Jenkins, Jenkyn, Jenkyns, Jennings

Jenna **G** (Arabic) small bird. (Welsh) a short form of Jennifer.

Jennifer **G** (Welsh) white wave; white phantom. A form of Guinevere (see Girls' Names).

Jenny **G** (Welsh) a familiar form of Jennifer.

Jenō (Hungarian) a form of Eugene.
Jenci, Jency, Jenoe, Jensi, Jensy

Jenofonte (Greek) he who comes from another country and is eloquent.

Jens (Danish) a form of John.
Jense, Jensen, Jenson, Jenssen, Jensy, Jentz

Jeovanni (Italian) a form of Giovanni.
Jeovahny, Jeovan, Jeovani, Jeovany

Jequan (American) a combination of the prefix Je + Quan.
Jeqaun, Jequann, Jequon

Jerad, Jerrad (Hebrew) forms of Jared.
Jeread, Jeredd

Jerahmy (Hebrew) a form of Jeremy.
Jerahmeel, Jerahmeil, Jerahmey

Jerald (English) a form of Gerald.
Jeraldo, Jerold, Jerral, Jerrald, Jerrold, Jerry

Jerall (English) a form of Jarrell.
Jerael, Jerai, Jerail, Jeraile, Jeral, Jerale, Jerall, Jerrail, Jerral, Jerrel, Jerrell, Jerrelle

Jeramie, Jeramy (Hebrew) forms of Jeremy.
Jerame, Jeramee, Jeramey, Jerami, Jerammie

Jerard (French) a form of Gerard.
Jarard, Jarrard, Jerardo, Jeraude, Jerrard

Jere (Hebrew) a short form of Jeremiah, Jeremy.
Jeré, Jeree

Jered, Jerred (Hebrew) forms of Jared.
Jereed, Jerid, Jerryd, Jeryd

Jerel, Jerell, Jerrell (English) forms of Jarell.
Jerelle, Jeriel, Jeril, Jerrail, Jerral, Jerrall, Jerrel, Jerrill, Jerrol, Jerroll, Jerryl, Jerryll, Jeryl, Jeryle

Jeremaia (Fijian) a form of Jeremy.

Jereme, Jeremey (Hebrew) forms of Jeremy.
Jarame

Jeremiah 🐾 **B** (Hebrew) God will uplift. Bible: a Hebrew prophet. See also Dermot, Yeremey, Yirmaya.
Geremiah, Jaramia, Jem, Jemeriah, Jemiah, Jeramiah, Jeramiha, Jere, Jereias, Jeremaya, Jeremi, Jeremia, Jeremial, Jeremias, Jeremija, Jeremy, Jerimiah, Jerimiha, Jerimya, Jermiah, Jermija, Jerry

Jeremías (Hebrew) a form of Jeremiah.

Jeremie, Jérémie (Hebrew) forms of Jeremy.
Jeremi, Jérémie, Jeremii

Jeremy **B** (English) a form of Jeremiah.
Jaremay, Jaremi, Jaremy, Jem, Jemmy, Jerahmy, Jeramie, Jeramy, Jere, Jereamy, Jereme, Jeremee, Jeremey, Jeremie, Jérémie, Jeremry, Jérémy, Jeremye,

Jereomy, Jeriemy, Jerime, Jerimy, Jermey, Jeromy, Jerremy

Jeriah (Hebrew) Jehovah has seen.

Jericho (Arabic) city of the moon. Bible: a city conquered by Joshua.
Jeric, Jerick, Jerico, Jerik, Jerric, Jerrick, Jerrico, Jerricoh, Jerryco

Jermaine **B** (French) a form of Germain. (English) sprout, bud.
Jarman, Jeremaine, Jeremane, Jerimane, Jermain, Jerman, Jermane, Jermanie, Jermanne, Jermany, Jermayn, Jermayne, Jermiane, Jermine, Jer-Mon, Jermone, Jermoney, Jhirmaine

Jermal (Arabic) a form of Jamal.
Jermael, Jermail, Jermall, Jermaul, Jermel, Jermell, Jermil, Jermol, Jermyll

Jermey (English) a form of Jeremy.
Jerme, Jermee, Jermere, Jermery, Jermie, Jermy, Jhermie

Jermiah (Hebrew) a form of Jeremiah.
Jermiha, Jermiya

Jerney (Slavic) a form of Bartholomew.

Jerod, Jerrod (Hebrew) forms of Jarrod.
Jerode, Jeroid

Jerolin (Basque, Latin) holy.

Jerome (Latin) holy. See also Geronimo, Hieronymos.
Gerome, Jere, Jeroen, Jerom, Jérome, Jérôme, Jeromo, Jeromy, Jeron, Jerónimo, Jerrome, Jerromy

Jeromy (Latin) a form of Jerome.
Jeromee, Jeromey, Jeromie

Jeron (English) a form of Jerome.
Jéron, Jerone, Jeronimo, Jerrin, Jerrion, Jerron, Jerrone, J'ron

Jeronimwus (Pohnpeian) a form of Jeronimo.

Jerrett (Hebrew) a form of Jarrett.
Jeret, Jerett, Jeritt, Jerret, Jerrette, Jerriot, Jerritt, Jerrot, Jerrott

Jerrick (American) a combination of Jerry + Derrick.
Jaric, Jarrick, Jerick, Jerrik

Jerry 🅱 (German) mighty spearman. (English) a familiar form of Gerald, Gerard. See also Gerry, Kele.
Jehri, Jere, Jeree, Jeris, Jerison, Jerri, Jerrie, Jery

Jerusalén (Hebrew) peaceful place.

Jervis (English) a form of Gervaise, Jarvis.

Jerzy (Polish) a form of George.
Jersey, Jerzey, Jurek

Jesabel, Jezabel (Hebrew) oath of God.

Jeshua (Hebrew) a form of Joshua.
Jeshuah

Jess 🅱 (Hebrew) a short form of Jesse.

Jesse ☙ 🅱 (Hebrew) wealthy. Bible: the father of David. See also Yishai.
Jese, Jesee, Jesi, Jess, Jessé, Jessee, Jessie, Jessy

Jessenia 🅶 (Arabic) flower.

Jessi 🅶 (Hebrew) a form of Jessie.

Jessica 🅶 (Hebrew) wealthy.

Jessie 🅱🅶 (Hebrew) a form of Jesse.
Jesie

Jessika 🅶 (Hebrew) a form of Jessica.

Jessy 🅱 (Hebrew) a form of Jesse.
Jescey, Jessey, Jessye, Jessyie, Jesy

Jestin (Welsh) a form of Justin.
Jessten, Jesten, Jeston, Jesstin, Jesston

Jesualdo (Germanic) he who takes the lead.

Jesus ☙ 🅱 (Hebrew) a form of Joshua. Bible: son of Mary and Joseph, believed by Christians to be the Son of God. See also Chucho, Isa, Yosu.
Jecho, Jessus, Jesu, Jesús, Josu

Jesús (Hispanic) a form of Jesus.

Jethro (Hebrew) abundant. Bible: the father-in-law of Moses. See also Yitro.
Jeth, Jethroe, Jetro, Jett

Jett (English) hard, black mineral. (Hebrew) a short form of Jethro.
Jet, Jetson, Jetter, Jetty

Jevan (Hebrew) a form of Javan.
Jevaun, Jeven, Jevin

Jevon (Hebrew) a form of Javan.
Jevion, Jevohn, Jevone, Jevonn, Jevonne, Jevonnie

Jevonte (American) a form of Jevon.
Jevonta, Jevontae, Jevontaye, Jevonté

Ji Hye (Korean) wisdom, intelligence.

Jia (Chinese) increase.

Jiang-Li (Chinese) river; beautiful.

Jiao (Chinese) beautiful, handsome.

Jibade (Yoruba) born close to royalty.

Jibben (Gypsy) life.
Jibin

Jibril (Arabic) archangel of Allah.
Jabril, Jibreel, Jibriel

Jie (Chinese) pure.

Jien (Japanese) literary figure.

Jieri (Fijian) a form of Jerry.

Jill 🅶 (English) a short form of Jillian.

Jillian 🅶 (Latin) youthful.

Jilt (Dutch) money.

Jim (Hebrew, English) a short form of James. See also Jaap.
Jimbo, Jimm, Jimmy

Jimbo (American) a familiar form of Jim.
Jimboo

Jimell (Arabic) a form of Jamel.
Jimel, Jimelle, Jimill, Jimmell, Jimmelle, Jimmiel, Jimmil

Jimeno (Spanish) a form of Simeón.

Jimiyu (Abaluhya) born in the dry season.

Jimmie 🅱 (English) a form of Jimmy.
Jimi, Jimie, Jimmee, Jimmi

Jimmy 🅱 (English) a familiar form of Jim.
Jimmey, Jimmie, Jimmye, Jimmyjo, Jimy

Jimoh (Swahili) born on Friday.

Jin 🅱 (Chinese) gold.
Jinn

Jindra (Czech) a form of Harold.

Jing (Chinese) unblemished.

Jing-Quo (Chinese) ruler of the country.

Jioje, Jioji, Joiji (Fijian) forms of George.

Jione (Fijian) a form of John.

Jiong (Chinese) bright, shining.

Jiovanni (Italian) a form of Giovanni.
Jio, Jiovani, Jiovanie, Jiovann, Jiovannie, Jiovanny, Jiovany, Jiovoni, Jivan

Jirair (Armenian) strong; hard working.

Jiri (Czech) a form of George.
Jirka

Jiro (Japanese) second son.

Jivin (Hindi) life giver.
Jivanta

Jiyoung (Korean) wisdom and courage.

Jle (Chinese) wonderful.

Jln (Chinese) golden.

Jlu (Chinese) for a long time.

Jo G (Hebrew, Japanese) a form of Joe.

Joab (Hebrew) God is father. See also Yoav.
Joabe, Joaby

Joachim (Hebrew) God will establish. See also Akeem, Ioakim, Yehoyakem.
Joacheim, Joakim, Joaquim, Joaquín, Jokin, Jov

Joanes (Chuukese) a form of Johannes.

Joanis (Pohnpeian) a form of Johannes.

Joanna G (English) a form of Joan (see Girls' Names).

João (Portuguese) a form of John.

Joaquim (Portuguese) a form of Joachim.

Joaquín (Spanish) a form of Joachim, Yehoyakem.
Jehoichin, Joaquin, Jocquin, Jocquinn, Juaquin

Job (Hebrew) afflicted. Bible: a righteous man whose faith in God survived the test of many afflictions.
Jobe, Jobert, Jobey, Jobie, Joby

Joben (Japanese) enjoys cleanliness.
Joban, Jobin

Jobo (Spanish) a familiar form of Joseph.

Joby B (Hebrew) a familiar form of Job.
Jobie

Jocelyn G (Latin) joyous.

Jock (American) a familiar form of Jacob.
Jocko, Joco, Jocoby, Jocolby

Jocquez (French) a form of Jacquez.
Jocques, Jocquis, Jocquise

Jodan (Hebrew) a combination of Jo + Dan.
Jodahn, Joden, Jodhan, Jodian, Jodin, Jodon, Jodonnis

Jodi, Jodie G (Hebrew) forms of Jody.

Jody BG (Hebrew) a familiar form of Joseph.
Jodey, Jodi, Jodie, Jodiha, Joedy

Joe B (Hebrew) a short form of Joseph.
Jo, Joely, Joey

Joel B (Hebrew) God is willing. Bible: an Old Testament Hebrew prophet.
Jôel, Joël, Joell, Joelle, Joely, Jole, Yoel

Joelle BG (Hebrew) a form of Joel.

Joeseph (Hebrew) a form of Joseph.
Joesph

Joey B (Hebrew) a familiar form of Joe, Joseph.

Johan, Johann (German) forms of John. See also Anno, Hanno, Yoan, Yohan.
Joahan, Joannes, Johahn, Johan, Johanan, Johane, Johannan, Johannes, Johanthan, Johatan, Johathan, Johathon, Johaun, Johon

Johannes (German) a form of Johan, Johann.
Johanes, Johannas, Johannus, Johansen, Johanson, Johonson

John �֎ B (Hebrew) God is gracious. Bible: the name honoring John the Baptist and John the Evangelist. See also Elchanan, Evan, Geno, Gian, Giovanni, Handel, Hannes, Hans, Hanus, Honza, Ian, Ianos, Iban, Ioan, Ivan, Iwan, Keoni, Kwam, Ohannes, Sean, Ugutz, Yan, Yanka, Yanni, Yochanan, Yohance, Zane.
Jack, Jacsi, Jaenda, Jahn, Jan, Janak, Janco, Janek, Janis, Janne, János, Jansen, Jantje, Jantzen, Jas, Jean, Jehan, Jen, Jenkin, Jenkyn, Jens, Jhan, Jhanick, Jhon, Jian, Joáo, João, Jock, Joen, Johan, Johann, Johne, Johnl, Johnlee, Johnnie, Johnny, Johnson, Jon, Jonam, Jonas, Jone, Jones, Jonny, Jonté, Jovan, Juan, Juhana

Johnathan (Hebrew) a form of Jonathan.
Jhonathan, Johathe, Johnatan, Johnathann, Johnathaon, Johnathen, Johnathyne, Johnatten, Johniathin, Johnothan, Johnthan

Johnathon (Hebrew) a form of Jonathon. See also Yanton.
Johnaton

Johnnie B (Hebrew) a familiar form of John.
Johnie, Johnier, Johnni, Johnsie, Jonni, Jonnie

Boys G–L

Johnny 🅱 (Hebrew) a familiar form of John. See also Gianni.
Jantje, Jhonny, Johney, Johnney, Johny, Jonny

Johnson (English) son of John.
Johnston, Jonson

Joi 🄶 (Latin) a form of Joy.

Joji (Japanese) a form of George.

Jojo (Fante) born on Monday.

Jokim (Basque) a form of Joachim.

Joklur (Marshallese) calm landing.

Jolene 🄶 (Hebrew) God will add, God will increase. (English) a form of Josephine.

Jolon (Native American) valley of the dead oaks.
Jolyon

Jomar (American) a form of Jamar.
Jomari, Jomarie, Jomarri

Jomei (Japanese) spreads light.

Jon 🅱 (Hebrew) a form of John. A short form of Jonathan.
J'on, Joni, Jonn, Jonnie, Jonny, Jony

Jonacani (Fijian) a form of Jonathan.

Jonah 🅱 (Hebrew) dove. Bible: an Old Testament prophet who was swallowed by a large fish.
Giona, Jona, Yonah, Yunus

Jonas (Hebrew) he accomplishes. (Lithuanian) a form of John.
Jonahs, Jonass, Jonaus, Jonelis, Jonukas, Jonus, Jonutis, Joonas

Jonás (Hebrew) a form of Jonas.

Jonasa (Fijian) a form of Jona.

Jonatan 🅱 (Hebrew) a form of Jonathan.
Jonatane, Jonate, Jonattan, Jonnattan

Jonathan ♛ 🅱 (Hebrew) gift of God. Bible: the son of King Saul who became a loyal friend of David. See also Ionakana, Yanton, Yonatan.
Janathan, Johnathan, Johnathon, Jon, Jonatan, Jonatha, Jonathen, Jonathin, Jonathon, Jonathun, Jonathyn, Jonethen, Jonnatha, Jonnathan, Jonnathun, Jonothan, Jonthan

Jonathon (Hebrew) a form of Jonathan.
Joanathon, Johnathon, Jonnathon, Jonothon, Jonthon, Jounathon, Yanaton

Jones (Welsh) son of John.
Joenns, Joness, Jonesy

Jonetani (Fijian) a form of Jonathan.

Jonny (Hebrew) a familiar form of John.
Jonhy, Joni, Jonnee, Jony

Jontae (French) a combination of Jon + the suffix Tae.
Johntae, Jontay, Jontea, Jonteau, Jontez

Jontay (American) a form of Jontae.
Johntay, Johnte, Johntez, Jontai, Jonte, Jonté, Jontez

Joo (Korean) jewel; lord, master, ruler; red; universe; eternity.

Joo-Chan (Korean) praise the Lord.

Joop (Dutch) a familiar form of Joseph.
Jopie

Joost (Dutch) just.

Jope (Indonesian) a form of Job.

Joquin (Spanish) a form of Joaquín.
Joquan, Joquawn, Joqunn, Joquon

Jora 🄶 (Hebrew) teacher.
Yora, Jorah

Joram (Hebrew) Jehovah is exalted.
Joran, Jorim

Jordan ♛🅱 (Hebrew) descending. See also Giordano, Yarden.
Jardan, Jared, Jordaan, Jordae, Jordain, Jordaine, Jordane, Jordani, Jordanio, Jordann, Jordanny, Jordano, Jordany, Jordáo, Jordayne, Jorden, Jordian, Jordin, Jordon, Jordun, Jordy, Jordyn, Jorrdan, Jory, Jourdan

Jordán (Hebrew) a form of Jordan.

Jorden 🅱 (Hebrew) a form of Jordan.
Jordenn

Jordon 🅱 (Hebrew) a form of Jordan.
Jeordon, Johordan

Jordy (Hebrew) a familiar form of Jordan.
Jordi, Jordie

Jordyn 🄶 (Hebrew) a form of Jordan.

Jorell (American) he saves. Literature: a name inspired by the fictional character Jor-El, Superman's father.
Jorel, Jor-El, Jorelle, Jorl, Jorrel, Jorrell

Jörg (German) a form of George.
Jeorg, Juergen, Jungen, Jürgen

Jorge 🅱 (Spanish) a form of George.
Jorrín

Jorgen (Danish) a form of George.
Joergen, Jorgan, Jörgen

Joribwij (Marshallese) broken family.

Joris (Dutch) a form of George.

Jorlikej (Marshallese) pillar on the windward side of the atoll.

Jörn (German) a familiar form of Gregory.

Jorrín (Spanish) a form of George.
Jorian, Jorje

Jory (Hebrew) a familiar form of Jordan.
Joar, Joary, Jorey, Jori, Jorie, Jorrie

Josafat (Hebrew) God's judgment.

Josaia (Fijian) a form of Josiah.

Jose � B (Spanish) a form of Joseph.

José (Spanish) a form of Joseph. See also Ché, Pepe.
Josean, Josecito, Josee, Joseito, Joselito, Josey

Josee G (Spanish) a form of José.

Josef (German, Portuguese, Czech, Scandinavian) a form of Joseph.
Joosef, Joseff, Josif, Jozef, József, Juzef

Joseluis (Spanish) a combination of Jose + Luis.

Joseph ☆ B (Hebrew) God will add, God will increase. Bible: in the Old Testament, the son of Jacob who came to rule Egypt; in the New Testament, the husband of Mary. See also Beppe, Cheche, Chepe, Giuseppe, Iokepa, Iosif, Osip, Pepa, Peppe, Pino, Sepp, Yeska, Yosef, Yousef, Youssel, Yusif, Yusuf, Zeusef.
Jazeps, Jo, Jobo, Jody, Joe, Joeseph, Joey, Jojo, Joop, Joos, Joosseppi, Jopie, José, Joseba, Josef, Josep, Josephat, Josephe, Josephie, Josephus, Josheph, Josip, Jóska, Joza, Joze, Jozef, Jozeph, Jozhe, Jozio, Jozka, Jozsi, Jozzepi, Jupp, Juziu

Josephine G (French) a form of Joseph.

Josese (Fijian) a form of Jose.

Joseva (Fijian) a form of Jose.

Josh (Hebrew) a short form of Joshua.
Joshe

Josha (Hindi) satisfied.

Joshi (Swahili) galloping.

Joshua ☆ B (Hebrew) God is my salvation. Bible: led the Israelites into the Promised Land. See also Giosia, Iosua, Jesus, Yehoshua.
Jeshua, Johsua, Johusa, Josh, Joshau, Joshaua, Joshauh, Joshawa, Joshawah, Joshia, Joshu, Joshuaa, Joshuah, Joshuea, Joshuia, Joshula, Joshus, Joshusa, Joshuwa, Joshwa, Josue, Jousha, Jozshua, Jozsua, Jozua, Jushua

Josiah B (Hebrew) fire of the Lord. See also Yoshiyahu.
Joshiah, Josia, Josiahs, Josian, Josias, Josie

Josie G (Hebrew) a form of Josiah.

Joss (Chinese) luck; fate.
Josse, Jossy

Josue (Hebrew) a form of Joshua.
Joshue, Jossue, Josu, Josua, Josuha, Jozus

Josué (Hebrew) a form of Josue.

Jotama (Fijian) a form of Jotham.

Jotham (Hebrew) may God complete. Bible: a king of Judah.

Jourdan (Hebrew) a form of Jordan.
Jourdain, Jourden, Jourdin, Jourdon, Jourdyn

Jovan (Latin) Jove-like, majestic. (Slavic) a form of John. Mythology: Jove, also known as Jupiter, was the supreme Roman deity.
Johvan, Johvon, Jovaan, Jovane, Jovani, Jovanic, Jovann, Jovanni, Jovannis, Jovanny, Jovany, Jovaughn, Jovaun, Joven, Jovenal, Jovenel, Jovi, Jovian, Jovin, Jovito, Jovoan, Jovon, Jovone, Jovonn, Jovonne, Jowan, Jowaun, Yovan, Yovani

Jovani, Jovanni B (Latin) forms of Jovan.
Jovanie, Jovannie, Jovoni, Jovonie, Jovonni

Jovanny, Jovany (Latin) forms of Jovan.
Jovony

Joy G (Latin) joyous.

Jr (Latin) a short form of Junior.
Jr.

Ju (Chinese) to hold up.

Juan ☆ B (Spanish) a form of John. See also Chan.
Juanch, Juanchito, Juane, Juanito, Juann, Juaun

Juancarlos (Spanish) a combination of Juan + Carlos.

Juanelo (Spanish) a form of Juan.

Juanjo (Spanish) a combination of Juan and José.

Juanma (Spanish) a combination of Juan and Manuel.

Juaquin (Spanish) a form of Joaquín.
Juaqin, Juaqine, Juquan, Juaquine

Jubal (Hebrew) ram's horn. Bible: a musician and a descendant of Cain.

Jucundo (Latin) happy, joyous one.

Boys G–L

Judah (Hebrew) praised. Bible: the fourth of Jacob's sons. See also Yehudi.
Juda, Judas, Judd, Jude

Judas (Latin) a form of Judah. Bible: Judas Iscariot was the disciple who betrayed Jesus.
Jude

Judd (Hebrew) a short form of Judah.
Jud, Judson

Jude (Latin) a short form of Judah, Judas. Bible: one of the Twelve Apostles, author of "The Epistle of Jude."

Judson (English) son of Judd.

Judy 💥 (Hebrew) a familiar form of Judith (see Girls' Names).

Juhana (Finnish) a form of John.
Juha, Juho

Juku (Estonian) a form of Richard.
Jukka

Jules (French) a form of Julius.
Joles, Jule

Julia 💥 (Latin) youthful.

Julian 💥 B (Greek, Latin) a form of Julius.
Jolyon, Julean, Juliaan, Julianne, Juliano, Julien, Jullian, Julyan

Julián (Spanish) a form of Julio.

Julianna 💥 (Czech, Spanish, Hungarian) a form of Julia.

Julianne 💥 (Greek, Latin) a form of Julian.

Julie 💥 (Greek, Latin) a familiar form of Julius.

Julien B (Latin) a form of Julian.
Juliene, Julienn, Julienne, Jullien, Jullin

Juliet 💥 (French) a form of Julia.

Julio B (Hispanic) a form of Julius.

Julius B (Greek, Latin) youthful, downy bearded. History: Julius Caesar was a great Roman dictator. See also Giuliano.
Jolyon, Julas, Jule, Jules, Julen, Jules, Julian, Julias, Julie, Julio, Juliusz, Jullius, Juluis

Ju-Long (Chinese) powerful.

Jum (Korean) foretell.

Jumaane (Swahili) born on Tuesday.

Jumah (Arabic, Swahili) born on Friday, a holy day in the Islamic religion.
Jimoh, Juma

Jumoke (Yoruba) loved by everyone.

Jun B (Chinese) truthful. (Japanese) obedient; pure.
Junnie

Jun'ichi (Japanese) first born; purity.

Jung (Korean) righteous.

Junior (Latin) young.
Jr, Junious, Junius, Junor

Junji (Japanese) pure peace; obedient listener.

Juong (Korean) increase; give; important; all; second born.

Júpiter (Latin) origin or source of light. *Jupiter*

Jupp (German) a form of Joseph.

Jur (Czech) a form of George.
Juraz, Jurek, Jurik, Jurko, Juro

Jurgis (Lithuanian) a form of George.
Jurgi, Juri

Juro (Japanese) best wishes; long life.

Jurrien (Dutch) God will uplift.
Jore, Jurian, Jurre

Justen (Latin) a form of Justin.
Jasten

Justice 💥 (Latin) a form of Justis.
Justic, Justiz, Justyc, Justyce

Justin 💥 B (Latin) just, righteous. See also Giustino, Iestyn, Iustin, Tutu, Ustin, Yustyn.
Jastin, Jaston, Jestin, Jobst, Joost, Jost, Jusa, Just, Justain, Justan, Justas, Justek, Justen, Justian, Justinas, Justine, Justinian, Justinius, Justinn, Justino, Justins, Justinus, Justo, Juston, Justton, Justukas, Justun, Justyn

Justina 💥 (Italian) a form of Justine.

Justine 💥 (Latin) a form of Justin.

Justiniano (Spanish) a form of Justino.

Justino (Latin) a form of Justin.

Justis (French) just.
Justice, Justs, Justus, Justyse

Justyn B (Latin) a form of Justin.
Justn, Justyne, Justynn

Juven, Juvencio, Juventino (Latin) he is the one that represents youth.

Juvenal (Latin) young. Literature: a Roman satirist.
Juvon, Juvone

Juwan B (American) a form of Jajuan.
Juvon, Juvone, Juvaun, Juwaan, Juwain,

Juwane, Juwann, Juwaun, Juwon, Juwonn, Juwuan, Juwuane, Juwvan, Jwan, Jwon

K

K **G** (American) an initial used as a first name.

Ka (Korean) beautiful; good; song; able; family; professional.

Kabiito (Rutooro) born while foreigners are visiting.

Kabil (Turkish) a form of Cain.
Kabel

Kabir (Hindi) History: an Indian mystic poet.
Kabar, Kabeer, Kabier

Kabonero (Runyankore) sign.

Kabonesa (Rutooro) difficult birth.

Kabua (Marshallese) uncle.

Kacani (Chuukese) a form of Kasani.

Kacey **G** (Irish) a form of Casey. (American) a combination of the initials K.+ C. See also KC.
Kace, Kacee, Kaci, Kacy, Kaesy, Kase, Kasey, Kasie, Kasy, Kaycee

Kachio (Japanese) victor.

Kachumasa (Chuukese) a form of Katsumasa.

Kachuo (Chuukese) a form of Kachio.

Kachutoshi (Chuukese) a form of Katsutoshi.

Kaci **G** (Irish) a form of Kacey.

Kadar (Arabic) powerful.
Kader

Kadarius (American) a combination of Kade + Darius.
Kadairious, Kadarious, Kadaris, Kadarrius, Kadarus, Kaddarrius, Kaderious, Kaderius

Kade **B** (Scottish) wetlands. (American) a combination of the initials K. + D.
Kadee, Kady, Kaid, Kaide, Kaydee

Kadeem **B** (Arabic) servant.
Kadim, Khadeem

Kaden **B** (Arabic) a form of Kadin.
Kadeen, Kadein, Kaidan, Kaiden

Kadiasang (Palauan) big spear.

Kadin (Arabic) friend, companion.
Caden, Kaden, Kadyn, Kaeden, Kayden

Kadir (Arabic) spring greening.
Kadeer

Kado (Japanese) gateway.

Kaeden (Arabic) a form of Kadin.
Kaedin, Kaedon, Kaedyn

Kaelan, Kaelin (Irish) forms of Kellen.
Kael, Kaelen, Kaelon, Kaelyn

Kaeleb (Hebrew) a form of Kaleb.
Kaelib, Kaelob, Kaelyb, Kailab, Kaileb

Kaelyn **G** (Irish) a form of Kaelan.

Kaemon (Japanese) joyful; right-handed.
Kaeman, Kaemen, Kaemin

Kaenan (Irish) a form of Keenan.
Kaenen, Kaenin, Kaenyn

Ka'eo (Hawaiian) victorious.

Kafele (Nguni) worth dying for.

Kaga (Native American) writer.

Kagan (Irish) a form of Keegan.
Kage, Kagen, Kaghen, Kaigan

Kahale (Hawaiian) home.

Kahil (Turkish) young; inexperienced; naive.
Cahil, Kaheel, Kale, Kayle

Kahlil **B** (Arabic) a form of Khalíl.
Kahleal, Kahlee, Kahleel, Kahleil, Kahli, Kahliel, Kahlill, Kalel, Kalil

Kaholo (Hawaiian) runner.

Kahraman (Turkish) hero.

Kai **B** (Welsh) keeper of the keys. (German) a form of Kay. (Hawaiian) sea.
Kae, Kaie, Kaii

Kaikara (Runyoro) Religion: a Banyoro deity.

Kailen (Irish) a form of Kellen.
Kail, Kailan, Kailey, Kailin, Kailon, Kailyn

Kaili (Hawaiian) Religion: a Hawaiian god.
Kailli

Kailyn **G** (Irish) a form of Kailen.

Kaimu (Japanese) sea; dream.

Kain (Welsh, Irish) a form of Kane.
Kainan, Kaine, Kainen, Kainin, Kainon

Kainoa (Hawaiian) name.

Kaipo (Hawaiian) sweetheart.

Boys G–L

Kairo (Arabic) a form of Cairo.
Kaire, Kairee, Kairi

Kaiser (German) a form of Caesar.
Kaesar, Kaisar, Kaizer

Kaisho (Japanese) to fly to the sea.

Kaitlin �G (Irish) pure.

Kaito (Japanese) sea.

Kaiven (American) a form of Kevin.
Kaivan, Kaiven, Kaivon, Kaiwan

Kaj (Danish) earth.
Kai, Kaje

Kakar (Hindi) grass.

Kala �G (Hindi) black; phase. (Hawaiian)
sun.

Kalama ☷ (Hawaiian) torch.
Kalam

Kalan (Irish) a form of Kalen.
Kalane, Kallan

Kalani �G (Hawaiian) sky; chief.
Kalan

Kale (Arabic) a short form of Kahlil.
(Hawaiian) a familiar form of Carl.
*Kalee, Kalen, Kaleu, Kaley, Kali, Kalin, Kalle,
Kayle*

Kaleb ☐ (Hebrew) a form of Caleb.
*Kaeleb, Kal, Kalab, Kalabe, Kalb, Kale,
Kaleob, Kalev, Kalib, Kalieb, Kallb, Kalleb,
Kalob, Kaloeb, Kalub, Kalyb, Kilab*

Kaleigh ☐ (American) a form of Caley.

Kalen, Kalin (Arabic, Hawaiian) forms of
Kale. (Irish) forms of Kellen.
Kalan

Kalevi (Finnish) hero.

Kaley ☐ (Arabic) a familiar form of Kale.

Kali ☐ (Arabic) a short form of Kalil.
(Hawaiian) a form of Gary.

Kalil (Arabic) a form of Khalíl.
Kaleel, Kalell, Kali, Kaliel, Kaliil

Kaliova (Fijian) a form of Caleb.

Kaliq (Arabic) a form of Khaliq.
Kalic, Kalique

Kalkin (Hindi) tenth. Religion: Kalki is the
final incarnation of the Hindu god Vishnu.
Kalki

Kalle ☷ (Scandinavian) a form of Carl.
(Arabic, Hawaiian) a form of Kale.

Kallen (Irish) a form of Kellen.
Kallan, Kallin, Kallion, Kallon, Kallun, Kalun

Kalon (Irish) forms of Kellen.
Kalone, Kalonn, Kalyen, Kalyne, Kalynn

Kaloosh (Armenian) blessed event.

Kalover (Chuukese) call over.

Kalvin (Latin) a form of Calvin.
*Kal, Kalv, Kalvan, Kalven, Kalvon, Kalvyn,
Vinny*

Kalwin (Pohnpeian) a form of Calvin.

Kalyn ☐ (Irish) a form of Kellen.

Kamaka (Hawaiian) face.

Kamakani (Hawaiian) wind.

Kamal (Hindi) lotus. (Arabic) perfect,
perfection.
Kamaal, Kamel, Kamil

Kamau (Kikuyu) quiet warrior.

Kamden (Scottish) a form of Camden.
Kamdon

Kameron ☐ (Scottish) a form of Cameron.
*Kam, Kamaren, Kamaron, Kameran, Kameren,
Kamerin, Kamerion, Kamerron, Kamerun,
Kameryn, Kamey, Kammeren, Kammeron,
Kammy, Kamoryn, Kamran, Kamron*

Kami ☐ (Hindi) loving.

Kamil ☐ (Arabic) a form of Kamal.
Kameel

Kamlyn (Japanese) a form of Kami.

Kamran, Kamron (Scottish) forms of
Kameron.
*Kammron, Kamrein, Kamren, Kamrin,
Kamrun, Kamryn*

Kamuela (Hawaiian) a form of Samuel.

Kamuhanda (Runyankore) born on the way
to the hospital.

Kamukama (Runyankore) protected by God.

Kamuzu (Nguni) medicine.

Kamya (Luganda) born after twin brothers.

Kana (Japanese) powerful; capable.
(Hawaiian) Mythology: a demigod.

Kanae (Japanese) fragrant seedling.

Kanaiela (Hawaiian) a form of Daniel.
Kana, Kaneii

Kaname (Japanese) main point.

Kanaye (Japanese) zealous one.

Kandace **G** (Greek) glittering white; glowing. (American) a form of Candice.

Kane **B** (Welsh) beautiful. (Irish) tribute. (Japanese) golden. (Hawaiian) eastern sky. (English) a form of Keene. See Kahan, Kain, Kaney, Kayne.

Kange (Lakota) raven. *Kang, Kanga*

Kaniel (Hebrew) stalk, reed. *Kan, Kani, Kannie, Kanny*

Kanji (Japanese) generous second son; thorough administrator.

Kannan (Hindi) Religion: another name for the Hindu god Krishna. *Kanaan, Kanan, Kanen, Kanin, Kanine, Kannen*

Kannon (Polynesian) free. (French) A form of Cannon. *Kanon*

Kano (Japanese) one's masculine power; capability.

Kanoa **B** (Hawaiian) free.

Kantit (Chamorro) cliff.

Kantu (Hindi) happy.

Kanu (Swahili) wildcat.

Kaori (Japanese) strong.

Kap (Korean) first; armor.

Kapila (Hindi) ancient prophet. *Kapil*

Kapono (Hawaiian) righteous. *Kapena*

Kapriel (Pohnpeian) a form of Gabriel.

Kara **G** (Greek, Danish) pure.

Karaistiani (Fijian) a form of Christian.

Karavi (Fijian) poling a boat through mangroves.

Kardal (Arabic) mustard seed. *Karandal, Kardell*

Kare (Norwegian) enormous. *Karee*

Kareem **B** (Arabic) noble; distinguished. *Karee, Karem, Kareme, Karim, Karriem*

Karel **BG** (Czech) a form of Carl. *Karell, Karil, Karrell*

Karen **G** (Greek) pure.

Karey (Greek) a form of Carey. *Karee, Kari, Karry, Kary*

Kari **G** (Greek) a form of Karey.

Karif (Arabic) born in autumn. *Kareef*

Kariisa (Runyankore) herdsman.

Karim (Arabic) a form of Kareem.

Karina **G** (Russian) a form of Karen.

Karl (German) a form of Carl. *Kaarle, Kaarlo, Kale, Kalle, Kalman, Kálmán, Karcsi, Karel, Kari, Karlen, Karlitis, Karlo, Karlos, Karlton, Karlus, Karol, Kjell*

Karla **G** (German) a form of Carla. (Slavic) a short form of Karoline (see Girls' Names).

Karlen (Latvian, Russian) a form of Carl. *Karlan, Karlens, Karlik, Karlin, Karlis, Karlon*

Karly **G** (Latin) little and strong. (American) a form of Carly.

Karmel **BG** (Hebrew) a form of Carmel.

Karney (Irish) a form of Carney.

Karol (Czech, Polish) a form of Carl. *Karal, Karolek, Karolis, Karalos, Károly, Karrel, Karrol*

Karr (Scandinavian) a form of Carr.

Karson (English) a form of Carson. *Karrson, Karsen*

Karsten (Greek) anointed. *Carsten, Karstan, Karston*

Karu (Hindi) cousin. *Karun*

Karutunda (Runyankore) little.

Karwana (Rutooro) born during wartime.

Kasani (Chuukese) you like it.

Kasau (Chuukese) ashamed.

Kaseem (Arabic) divided. *Kasceem, Kaseam, Kaseym, Kasim, Kasseem, Kassem, Kazeem*

Kaseko (Rhodesian) mocked, ridiculed.

Kasem (Tai) happiness.

Kasen (Basque) protected with a helmet. *Kasean, Kasene, Kaseon, Kasin, Kason, Kassen*

Kasey **G** (Irish) a form of Casey. *Kaese, Kaesy, Kasay, Kassey*

Boys G–L

Kashawn (American) a combination of the prefix Ka + Shawn.
Kashain, Kashan, Kashaun, Kashen, Kashon

Kasib (Arabic) fertile.

Kasim (Arabic) a form of Kaseem.
Kassim

Kasimir (Arabic) peace. (Slavic) a form of Casimir.
Kasim, Kazimierz, Kazimir, Kazio, Kazmer, Kazmér, Kázmér

Kasiya (Nguni) separate.

Kasper (Persian) treasurer. (German) a form of Casper.
Jasper, Kaspar, Kaspero

Kass (German) blackbird.
Kaese, Kasch, Kase

Kassandra ◨ (Greek) a form of Cassandra.

Kassidy ◨ (Irish) a form of Cassidy.
Kassady, Kassie, Kassy

Kastino, Kasty (Chuukese) forms of Kasto.

Kasto (Chuukese) pure; chaste.

Kasumi (Japanese) haze, mist.

Kate ◨ (Greek) pure. (English) a short form of Katherine.

Kateb (Arabic) writer.

Katelyn ◨ (Irish) a form of Caitlin.

Katerina ◨ (Slavic) a form of Katherine.

Katherine ◨ (Greek) pure.

Kathrine ◨ (Greek) a form of Katherine.

Kathryn ◨ (English) a form of Katherine.

Kathy ◨ (English) a familiar form of Katherine.

Katia ◨ (Russian) a form of Katherine.

Katie ◨ (English) a familiar form of Kate.

Katlin ◨ (Irish) a form of Katlyn (see Girls' Names).

Kato (Runyankore) second of twins.

Katsumasa (Japanese) flourishing victory; border man; righteous.

Katsumi (Japanese) beautiful winner; patient snake.

Katsunori (Japanese) patient lawmaker.

Katsutoshi (Japanese) kindly victory; victory age.

Katungi (Runyankore) rich.

Kaumerang (Palauan) trust each other.

Kavan (Irish) handsome.
Cavan, Kavanagh, Kavaugn, Kaven, Kavenaugh, Kavin, Kavon, Kayvan

Kaveh (Persian) ancient hero.

Kavi (Hindi) poet.

Kavin, Kavon (Irish) forms of Kavan.
Kaveon, Kavion, Kavone, Kayvon, Kaywon

Kawasio (Chuukese) a form of Jarvis.

Kawika (Hawaiian) a form of David.

Kay ◨ (Greek) rejoicing. (German) fortified place. Literature: one of King Arthur's knights of the Round Table.
Kai, Kaycee, Kaye, Kayson

Kayako (Japanese) miscanthus reed.

Kaycee ◨ (Greek, German) a form of Kay. (American, Irish) a form of Kacey.

Kayden ◧ (Arabic) a form of Kadin.
Kayde, Kaydee, Kaydin, Kaydn, Kaydon

Kayin (Nigerian) celebrated. (Yoruba) long-hoped-for child.

Kayla ◨ (Hebrew, Arabic) a form of Kayle.

Kaylan ◨ (Irish) a form of Kaylen.

Kayle (Hebrew) faithful dog. (Arabic) a short form of Kahlil.
Kayl, Kayla, Kaylee

Kayleb (Hebrew) a form of Caleb.
Kaylib, Kaylob, Kaylub

Kaylee ◨ (Hebrew, Arabic) a form of Kayle.

Kaylen (Irish) a form of Kellen.
Kaylan, Kaylin, Kaylon, Kaylyn, Kaylynn

Kaylin ◨ (Irish) a form of Kaylen.

Kaylon ◧ (Irish) a form of Kaylen.

Kaylyn, Kaylynn ◨ (Irish) forms of Kaylen.

Kayne (Hebrew) a form of Cain.
Kaynan, Kaynen, Kaynon

Kayode (Yoruba) he brought joy.

Kayonga (Runyankore) ash.

Kazio (Polish) a form of Casimir, Kasimir. See also Cassidy.

Kazu (Japanese) first; obedient.

Kazuaki (Japanese) peaceful; brilliant light.

Kazujiro (Japanese) obedient second son.

Kazuki (Japanese) he who prays for peace.

Kazumi (Japanese) fruit of harmony.

Kazuo (Japanese) man of peace.

Kazushige (Japanese) harmonious luxury.

Kazuto (Japanese) harmonious person; the first to ascend.

Kazuyuki (Japanese) harmonious travel.

KC (American) a combination of the initials K. + C. See also Kacey.
Kc, K.C., Kcee, Kcey

Ke (Chinese) able.

Keagan (Irish) a form of Keegan.
Keagean, Keagen, Keaghan, Keagyn

Keahi (Hawaiian) flames.

Keaka (Hawaiian) a form of Jack.

Kealoha (Hawaiian) fragrant.
Ke'ala

Keanan (Irish) a form of Keenan.
Keanen, Keanna, Keannan, Keanon

Keandre (American) a combination of the prefix Ke + Andre.
Keandra, Keandray, Keandré, Keandree, Keandrell, Keondre

Keane (German) bold; sharp. (Irish) handsome. (English) a form of Keene.
Kean

Keanna **G** (Irish) a form of Keanan.

Keanu **B** (Irish) a form of Keenan.
Keaneu, Keani, Keanno, Keano, Keanue, Keeno, Keenu, Kianu

Kearn (Irish) a short form of Kearney.
Kearne

Kearney (Irish) a form of Carney.
Kar, Karney, Karny, Kearn, Kearny

Keary (Irish) a form of Kerry.
Kearie

Keaton **B** (English) where hawks fly.
Keatan, Keaten, Keatin, Keatton, Keatyn, Keeton, Keetun

Keaven (Irish) a form of Kevin.
Keavan, Keavon

Keawe (Hawaiian) strand.

Keb (Egyptian) earth. Mythology: an ancient earth god, also known as Geb.

Kebekol (Palauan) to go sailing together.

Keboech (Palauan) hurl spears together.

Ked (Palauan) hill.

Kedar (Hindi) mountain lord. (Arabic) powerful. Religion: another name for the Hindu god Shiva.
Kadar, Kedaar, Keder

Keddy (Scottish) a form of Adam.
Keddie

Kedem (Hebrew) ancient.

Kedrick (English) a form of Cedric.
Keddrick, Kederick, Kedrek, Kedric, Kiedric, Kiedrick

Keefe (Irish) handsome; loved.

Keegan **B** (Irish) little; fiery.
Kaegan, Kagan, Keagan, Keagen, Keeghan, Keegon, Keegun, Kegan, Keigan

Keelan (Irish) little; slender.
Keelen, Keelin, Keelyn, Keilan, Kelan

Keeley **G** (Irish) handsome.
Kealey, Kealy, Keeli, Keelian, Keelie

Keely **G** (Irish) a form of Keeley.

Keenan **B** (Irish) little Keene.
Kaenan, Keanan, Keanu, Keenen, Keennan, Keenon, Kenan, Keynan, Kienan, Kienon

Keene (German) bold; sharp. (English) smart. See also Kane.
Kaene, Keane, Keen, Keenan

Keenen (Irish) a form of Keenan.
Keenin, Kienen

Kees (Dutch) a form of Kornelius.
Keese, Keesee, Keyes

Keevon (Irish) a form of Kevin.
Keevan, Keeven, Keevin, Keewan, Keewin

Kegan (Irish) a form of Keegan.
Kegen, Keghan, Kegon, Kegun

Kehind (Yoruba) second-born twin.
Kehinde

Keichiro (Chuukese) a form of Kiichiro.

Keiffer (German) a form of Cooper.
Keefer, Keifer, Kiefer

Keigan (Irish) a form of Keegan.
Keighan, Keighen

Keigo (Japanese) corner; self.

Keiji (Japanese) cautious ruler.

Keilan (Irish) a form of Keelan.
Keilen, Keilin, Keillene, Keillyn, Keilon, Keilynn

Keir (Irish) a short form of Kieran.

Keitaro (Japanese) blessed.
Keita

Keith (Welsh) forest. (Scottish) battle place.
See also Kika.
Keath, Keeth, Keithen

Keithen (Welsh, Scottish) a form of Keith.
Keithan, Keitheon, Keithon

Keivan (Irish) a form of Kevin.
Keiven, Keivn, Keivon, Keivone

Keizo (Japanese) respectful third son.

Kekapa (Hawaiian) tapa cloth.

Kekerelchad (Palauan) young man.

Kekipi (Hawaiian) rebel.

Kekoa (Hawaiian) bold, courageous.

Kelby (German) farm by the spring.
Keelby, Kelbee, Kelbey, Kelbi, Kellby

Kele (Hopi) sparrow hawk. (Hawaiian) a
form of Jerry.
Kelle

Kelemen (Hungarian) gentle; kind.
Kellman

Kelevi (Finnish) hero.

Keli (Hawaiian) a form of Terry.

Keli'i (Hawaiian) chief.

Kelile (Ethiopian) protected.

Kell (Scandinavian) spring.

Kellan (Irish) a form of Kellen.
Keillan

Kellen **B** (Irish) mighty warrior.
*Kaelan, Kailen, Kalan, Kalen, Kalin, Kallen,
Kalon, Kalyn, Kaylen, Keelan, Kelden, Kelin,
Kellan, Kelle, Kellin, Kellyn, Kelyn, Kelynn*

Keller (Irish) little companion.

Kelley **G** (Irish) a form of Kelly.

Kelli, Kellie **G** (Irish) forms of Kelly.

Kelly **G** (Irish) warrior.
Kelle, Kellen, Kelley, Kelli, Kellie, Kely

Kelmen (Basque) merciful.
Kelmin

Kelsea **G** (Scandinavian) a form of Kelsey.

Kelsey **G** (Scandinavian) island of ships.
*Kelcy, Kelse, Kelsea, Kelsi, Kelsie, Kelso,
Kelsy, Kesley, Kesly*

Kelsi, Kelsy **G** (Scandinavian) forms of
Kelsey.

Kelton **B** (English) keel town; port.
*Kelden, Keldon, Kelson, Kelston, Kelten,
Keltin, Keltonn, Keltyn*

Kelulau (Palauan) confidential; a whisper.

Kelvin **B** (Irish, English) narrow river.
Geography: a river in Scotland.
*Kelvan, Kelven, Kelvon, Kelvyn, Kelwin,
Kelwyn*

Kemal (Turkish) highest honor.

Kemen (Basque) strong.

Kemp (English) fighter; champion.

Kempton (English) military town.

Ken (Japanese) one's own kind. (Scottish) a
short form of Kendall, Kendrick, Kenneth.
Kena, Kenn, Keno

Ken'ichi (Japanese) healthy first born;
modest first born.

Kenan (Irish) a form of Keenan.

Kenaz (Hebrew) bright.

Kenchy (Chuukese) a form of Ken'ichi.

Kendal **G** (English) a form of Kendall.
Kendale, Kendali, Kendel, Kendul, Kendyl

Kendall **G** (English) valley of the river Kent.
*Ken, Kendal, Kendell, Kendrall, Kendryll,
Kendyll, Kyndall*

Kendarius (American) a combination of Ken
+ Darius.
*Kendarious, Kendarrious, Kendarrius,
Kenderious, Kenderius, Kenderyious*

Kendell (English) a form of Kendall.
Kendelle, Kendrel, Kendrell

Kendra **G** (English) a form of Kenda (see
Girls' Names).

Kendrew (Scottish) a form of Andrew.

Kendrick **B** (Irish) son of Henry. (Scottish)
royal chieftain.
*Ken, Kenderrick, Kendric, Kendrich,
Kenedrick, Kendricks, Kendrik, Kendrix,
Kendryck, Kenndrick, Keondric, Keondrick*

Kenia **G** (Hebrew) a form of Kenya.

Kenjiro (Japanese) second son who sees with
insight.

Kenley (English) royal meadow.
Kenlea, Kenlee, Kenleigh, Kenlie, Kenly

Kenn (Scottish) a form of Ken.

Kenna **G** (Scottich) a form of Kennan.

Kennan (Scottish) little Ken.
Kenna, Kenan, Kenen, Kennen, Kennon

Kennard (Irish) brave chieftain.
Kenner

Kennedy **G** (Irish) helmeted chief. History:
John F. Kennedy was the thirty-fifth U.S.
president.
Kenedy, Kenidy, Kennady, Kennedey

Kenneth **B** (Irish) handsome. (English)
royal oath.
*Ken, Keneth, Kenneith, Kennet, Kennethen,
Kennett, Kennieth, Kennith, Kennth, Kenny,
Kennyth, Kenya*

Kenny **B** (Scottish) a familiar form of
Kenneth.
Keni, Kenney, Kenni, Kennie, Kinnie

Kenrick (English) bold ruler; royal ruler.
Kenric, Kenricks, Kenrik

Kent **B** (Welsh) white; bright. (English) a
short form of Kenton. Geography: a region
in England.

Kenta (Japanese) very healthy.

Kentaro (Japanese) big boy.

Kento (Japanese) he who has good health.

Kenton (English) from Kent, England.
Kent, Kenten, Kentin, Kentonn

Kentrell **B** (English) king's estate.
Kenreal, Kentrel, Kentrelle

Kenward (English) brave; royal guardian.

Kenya **G** (Hebrew) animal horn. (Russian)
a form of Kenneth. Geography: a country in
east-central Africa.
Kenyatta

Kenyatta (American) a form of Kenya.
*Kenyata, Kenyatae, Kenyatee, Kenyatter,
Kenyatti, Kenyotta*

Kenyon (Irish) white haired, blond.
Kenyan, Kenynn, Keonyon

Kenzie **G** (Scottish) wise leader. See also
Mackenzie.
Kensie

Keoki (Hawaiian) a form of George.

Keola (Hawaiian) life.

Keon **B** (Irish) a form of Ewan.
*Keeon, Keion, Keionne, Keondre, Keone,
Keonne, Keonte, Keony, Keyon, Kian, Kion*

Keoni (Hawaiian) a form of John.

Keonte (American) a form of Keon.
*Keonntay, Keonta, Keontae, Keontay,
Keontaye, Keontez, Keontia, Keontis,
Keontrae, Keontre, Keontrey, Keontrye*

Kerbasi (Basque) warrior.

Kerel (Afrikaans) young.
Kerell

Kerem (Turkish) noble; kind.
Kereem

Keremes (Chuukese) a form of Jeremy.

Kerey (Gypsy) homeward bound.
Ker

Keri **G** (Irish) a form of Kerry.

Kerman (Basque) from Germany.

Kermit (Irish) a form of Dermot.
Kermey, Kermie, Kermitt, Kermy

Kern (Irish) a short form of Kieran.
Kearn, Kerne

Kerr (Scandinavian) a form of Carr.
Karr

Kerri (Irish) a form of Kerry.

Kerrick (English) king's rule.

Kerry (Irish) dark; dark haired.
Keary, Keri, Kerrey, Kerri, Kerrie

Kers (Todas) Botany: an Indian plant.

Kersen (Indonesian) cherry.

Kerstan (Dutch) a form of Christian.

Kerwin (Irish) little; dark. (English) friend of
the marshlands.
*Kervin, Kervyn, Kerwinn, Kerwyn, Kerwynn,
Kirwin, Kirwyn*

Kesar (Russian) a form of Caesar.
Kesare

Keshawn (American) a combination of the
prefix Ke + Shawn.
*Keeshaun, Keeshawn, Keeshon, Kesean,
Keshan, Keshane, Keshaun, Keshayne,
Keshion, Keshon, Keshone, Keshun, Kishan*

Kesin (Hindi) long-haired beggar.

Kesse **G** (Ashanti, Fante) chubby baby.
Kessie

Kester (English) a form of Christopher.

Kestrel (English) falcon.
Kes

Keung (Chinese) universe.

Boys G–L

Kevan (Irish) a form of Kevin.
Kavan, Kewan, Kewane, Kewaun, Keyvan, Kiwan, Kiwane

Keven 🅱 (Irish) a form of Kevin.
Keve, Keveen, Kiven

Kevin ☙ 🅱 (Irish) handsome. See also Cavan.
Kaiven, Keaven, Keevon, Keivan, Kev, Kevan, Keven, Keverne, Kevian, Kevien, Kévin, Kevinn, Kevins, Kevis, Kevn, Kevon, Kevvy, Kevyn, Kyven

Kevon 🅱 (Irish) a form of Kevin.
Keveon, Kevion, Kevone, Kevonne, Kevontae, Kevonte, Kevoyn, Kevron, Kewon, Kewone, Keyvon, Kivon

Kevyn 🅱 (Irish) a form of Kevin.
Kevyon

Key (English) key; protected.

Keyana 🅶 (American) a form of Kiana.

Keyon (Irish) a form of Keon.
Keyan, Keyen, Keyin, Keyion

Keyonna 🅶 (American) a form of Kiana.

Keyshawn (American) a combination of Key + Shawn.
Keyshan, Keyshaun, Keyshon, Keyshun

Khachig (Armenian) small cross.
Khachik

Khadijah 🅶 (Arabic) trustworthy.

Khaim (Russian) a form of Chaim.

Khaldun (Arabic) forever.
Khaldoon, Khaldoun

Khalfani (Swahili) born to lead.
Khalfan

Khālid (Arabic) eternal.
Khaled, Khallid, Khalyd

Khalíl (Arabic) friend.
Kahlil, Kaleel, Kalil, Khahlil, Khailil, Khailyl, Khalee, Khaleel, Khaleil, Khali, Khalial, Khaliel, Khalihl, Khalill, Khaliyl

Khaliq (Arabic) creative.
Kaliq, Khalique

Khamisi (Swahili) born on Thursday.
Kham

Khan (Turkish) prince.
Khanh

Kharald (Russian) a form of Gerald.

Khayru (Arabic) benevolent.
Khiri, Khiry, Kiry

Khoury (Arabic) priest.
Khory

Khristian (Greek) a form of Christian, Kristian.
Khris, Khristan, Khristin, Khriston, Khrystian

Khristopher (Greek) a form of Kristopher.
Khristofer, Khristophar, Khrystopher

Khristos (Greek) a form of Christos.
Khris, Khristophe, Kristo, Kristos

Khuyen (Vietnamese) advise.

Kia 🅶 (African) season's beginning. (American) a short form of Kiana.

Kiana 🅶 (American) a combination of the prefix Ki + Anna.

Kiara 🅶 (Irish) little and dark.

Kibo (Uset) worldly; wise.

Kibuuka (Luganda) brave warrior. History: a Ganda warrior deity.

Kidd (English) child; young goat.

Kiefer (German) a form of Keifer.
Kief, Kieffer, Kiefor, Kiffer, Kiiefer

Kiel (Irish) a form of Kyle.
Kiell

Kiele 🅶 (Hawaiian) gardenia.

Kieran 🅱 (Irish) little and dark; little Keir.
Keiran, Keiren, Keiron, Kiaron, Kiarron, Kier, Kieren, Kierian, Kierien, Kierin, Kiernan, Kieron, Kierr, Kierre, Kierron, Kyran

Kiernan (Irish) a form of Kieran.
Kern, Kernan, Kiernen

Kiersten 🅶 (Scandanavian) a form of Kirsten.

Kiet (Tai) honor.

Kifeda (Luo) only boy among girls.

Kiho (Rutoóro) born on a foggy day.

Kiichiro (Japanese) pleasing first son.

Kijika (Native American) quiet walker.

Kika (Hawaiian) a form of Keith.

Kiki 🅶 (Spanish) a form of Henry.

Kile (Irish) a form of Kyle.
Kilee, Kilen, Kiley, Kiyl, Kiyle

Kiley 🅶 (Irish) a form of Kile, Kyle.

Killian (Irish) little Kelly.
Kilean, Kilian, Kilien, Killie, Killien, Killiean, Killion, Killy

Kim G (English) a short form of Kimball.
Kimie, Kimmy

Kimball (Greek) hollow vessel. (English) warrior chief.
Kim, Kimbal, Kimbel, Kimbell, Kimble

Kimberly G (English) chief, ruler.

Kimo (Hawaiian) a form of James.

Kimokeo (Hawaiian) a form of Timothy.

Kimy (Vietnamese) gold.

Kin (Japanese) golden.

Kincaid (Scottish) battle chief.
Kincade, Kinkaid

Kindin (Basque) fifth.

King (English) king. A short form of names beginning with "King."

Kingsley (English) king's meadow.
King, Kings, Kingslea, Kingslie, Kingsly, Kingzlee, Kinslea, Kinslee, Kinsley, Kinslie, Kinsly

Kingston (English) king's estate.
King, Kinston

Kingswell (English) king's well.
King

Kini G (Hawaiian) a short form of Iukini.

Kinjiro (Japanese) golden second son.

Kinnard (Irish) tall slope.

Kinsey G (English) victorious royalty.
Kinze, Kinzie

Kinshiro (Japanese) golden fourth-born son.

Kintaro (Japanese) golden boy.

Kinton (Hindi) crowned.

Kion (Irish) a form of Keon.
Kione, Kionie, Kionne

Kioshi (Japanese) quiet.

Kiosho (Japanese) clear, bright.

Kipp (English) pointed hill.
Kip, Kippar, Kipper, Kippie, Kippy

Kir (Bulgarian) a familiar form of Cyrus.

Kira G (Persian) sun. (Latin) light.

Kiral (Turkish) king; supreme leader.

Kiran G (Sanskrit) beam of light.
Kyran

Kirby B (Scandinavian) church village. (English) cottage by the water.
Kerbey, Kerbie, Kerby, Kirbey, Kirbie, Kirkby

Kiri (Cambodian) mountain.

Kiril (Slavic) a form of Cyril.
Kirill, Kiryl, Kyrillos

Kirios (Greek) supreme being, the Lord.

Kiritan (Hindi) wearing a crown.

Kirk (Scandinavian) church.
Kerk

Kirkland (English) church land.
Kirklin, Kirklind, Kirklynd

Kirkley (English) church meadow.

Kirklin (English) a form of Kirkland.
Kirklan, Kirklen, Kirkline, Kirkloun, Kirklun, Kirklyn, Kirklynn

Kirkwell (English) church well; church spring.

Kirkwood (English) church forest.

Kirsten G (Greek) Christian; anointed. (Scandinavian) a form of Christine.

Kirton (English) church town.

Kishan (American) a form of Keshawn.
Kishaun, Kishawn, Kishen, Kishon, Kyshon, Kyshun

Kishi (Japanese) long and happy life.

Kisho (Japanese) one who knows his own mind.

Kistna (Hindi) sacred, holy. Geography: a sacred river in India.

Kistur (Gypsy) skillful rider.

Kit (Greek) a familiar form of Christian, Christopher, Kristopher.
Kitt, Kitts

Kito (Swahili) jewel; precious child.

Kitwana (Swahili) pledged to live.

Kiva (Hebrew) a short form of Akiva, Jacob.
Kiba, Kivi, Kiwa

Kiyoshi (Japanese) quiet; peaceful.

Kiyoto (Japanese) noble person.

Kizza (Luganda) born after twins.
Kizzy

Kjell (Swedish) a form of Karl.
Kjel

Klaudio (Pohnpeian) a form of Claudio.

Klaus (German) a short form of Nicholas. A form of Claus.
Klaas, Klaes, Klas, Klause

Klay (English) a form of Clay.

Klayton (English) a form of Clayton.

Kleef (Dutch) cliff.

Klement (Czech) a form of Clement.
Klema, Klemenis, Klemens, Klemet, Klemo, Klim, Klimek, Kliment, Klimka

Kleng (Norwegian) claw.

Knight (English) armored knight.
Knightly

Knoton (Native American) a form of Nodin.

Knowles (English) grassy slope.
Knolls, Nowles

Knox (English) hill.

Knute (Scandinavian) a form of Canute.
Knud, Knut

Koby (Polish) a familiar form of Jacob.
Kobby, Kobe, Kobey, Kobi, Kobia, Kobie

Kodi 🅱🅶 (English) a form of Kody.
Kode, Kodee, Kodie

Kody 🅱 (English) a form of Cody.
Kodey, Kodi, Kodye, Koty

Kofi (Twi) born on Friday.

Kohana (Lakota) swift.

Kohei (Japanese) peace.

Koi (Choctaw) panther. (Hawaiian) a form of Troy.

Koichi (Japanese) obedient first son.

Koji (Japanese) successful peacemaker.

Kojo (Akan) born on Monday.

Koka (Hawaiian) Scotsman.

Kokai (Japanese) he who crosses over the sea.

Kokayi (Shona) gathered together.

Koki (Japanese) shine; to be hopeful.

Kolby 🅱 (English) a form of Colby.
Kelby, Koalby, Koelby, Kohlbe, Kohlby, Kolbe, Kolbey, Kolbi, Kolbie, Kolebe, Koleby, Kollby

Kole (English) a form of Cole.
Kohl, Kohle

Koleman (English) a form of Coleman.
Kolemann, Kolemen

Kolin (English) a form of Colin.
Kolen, Kollen, Kollin, Kollyn, Kolyn

Kolton (English) a form of Colton.
Kolt, Koltan, Kolte, Kolten, Koltin, Koltn, Koltyn

Kolya (Russian) a familiar form of Nikolai, Nikolos.
Kola, Kolenka, Kolia, Kolja

Kona 🅱 (Hawaiian) a form of Don.
Konala

Konane (Hawaiian) bright moonlight.

Kondo (Swahili) war.

Kong (Chinese) glorious; sky.

Konner (Irish) a form of Conner, Connor.
Konar, Koner

Konnor (Irish) a form of Connor.
Kohner, Kohnor, Konor

Kono (Moquelumnan) squirrel eating a pine nut.

Konrad (German) a form of Conrad.
Khonrad, Koen, Koenraad, Kon, Konn, Konney, Konni, Konnie, Konny, Konrád, Konrade, Konrado, Kord, Kort, Kunz

Konstantin (German, Russian) a form of Constantine. See also Dinos.
Konstancji, Konstadine, Konstadino, Konstandinos, Konstantinas, Konstantine, Konstantinos, Konstantio, Konstanty, Konstantyn, Konstanz, Konstatino, Kostadino, Kostadinos, Kostandino, Kostandinos, Kostantin, Kostantino, Kostas, Kostenka, Kostya, Kotsos

Kontar (Akan) only child.

Korb (German) basket.

Korbin (English) a form of Corbin.
Korban, Korben, Korbyn

Kordell (English) a form of Cordell.
Kordel

Korey 🅱 (Irish) a form of Corey, Kory.
Kore, Koree, Korei, Korio, Korre, Korria, Korrye

Kori 🅶 (Irish) a form of Kory.

Kornel (Latin) a form of Cornelius, Kornelius.
Kees, Korneil, Kornél, Korneli, Kornelisz, Kornell, Krelis, Soma

Kornelius (Latin) a form of Cornelius. See also Kees, Kornel.
Karnelius, Korneilius, Korneliaus, Kornelious, Kornellius

Korrigan (Irish) a form of Corrigan.
Korigan, Korigan, Korrigon, Korrigun

Kort (German, Dutch) a form of Cort, Kurt.
Kourt

Kortney **G** (English) a form of Courtney.
Kortni, Kourtney

Korudon (Greek) helmeted one.

Kory **B** (Irish) a form of Corey.
Korey, Kori, Korie, Korrey, Korri, Korrie, Korry

Kosei (Japanese) he who navigates through life well.

Kosey (African) lion.
Kosse

Kositatino (Fijian) a form of Constantino.

Kosmo (Greek) a form of Cosmo.
Kosmy, Kozmo

Kostas (Greek) a short form of Konstantin.

Kosti (Finnish) a form of Gustave.

Kosuke (Japanese) inlet; clear; help.

Kosumi (Moquelumnan) spear fisher.

Kota (Japanese) very fortunate.

Koukalaka (Hawaiian) a form of Douglas.

Kourtland (English) a form of Courtland.
Kortlan, Kortland, Kortlend, Kortlon, Kourtlin

Kourtney **G** (American) a form of Courtney.

Kovit (Tai) expert.

Kozue (Japanese) tree branches.

Kraig (Irish, Scottish) a form of Craig.
Kraggie, Kraggy, Krayg, Kreg, Kreig, Kreigh

Krikor (Armenian) a form of Gregory.

Kris **B** (Greek) a form of Chris. A short form of Kristian, Kristofer, Kristopher.
Kriss, Krys

Krischan (German) a form of Christian.
Krishan, Krishaun, Krishawn, Krishon, Krishun

Krishna (Hindi) delightful, pleasurable. Religion: the eighth and principal avatar of the Hindu god Vishnu.
Kistna, Kistnah, Krisha, Krishnah

Krispin (Latin) a form of Crispin.
Krispian, Krispino, Krispo

Krista **G** (Czech) a form of Christina.

Kristen **G** (Greek) a form of Kristian, Kristyn. (French, English) a form of Christine.

Krister (Swedish) a form of Christian.
Krist, Kristar

Kristian **B** (Greek) a form of Christian, Khristian.
Kerstan, Khristos, Kit, Kris, Krischan, Krist, Kristan, Kristar, Kristek, Kristen, Krister, Kristien, Kristin, Kristine, Kristinn, Kristion, Kristjan, Kristo, Kristos, Krists, Krystek, Krystian, Khrystiyan

Kristin **G** (Greek) a form of Kristian.

Kristina **G** (Greek) Christian; anointed. (Scandinavian) a form of Christina.

Kristine **G** (Greek) a form of Kristian.

Kristo (Greek) a short form of Khristos.

Kristofer (Swedish) a form of Kristopher.
Kris, Kristafer, Kristef, Kristifer, Kristoff, Kristoffer, Kristofo, Kristofor, Kristofyr, Kristufer, Kristus, Krystofer

Kristoff (Greek) a short form of Kristofer, Kristopher.
Kristof, Kristóf

Kristophe (French) a form of Kristopher.

Kristopher **B** (Greek) a form of Christopher. See also Topher.
Khristopher, Kit, Kris, Krisstopher, Kristapher, Kristepher, Kristfer, Kristfor, Kristo, Kristofer, Kristoff, Kristoforo, Kristoph, Kristophe, Kristophor, Kristos, Krists, Krisus, Krystopher, Krystupas, Krzysztof

Kristy **G** (American) a familiar form of Kristine, Krystal.

Kristyn **G** (Greek) a form of Kristen.

Kruz (Spanish) a form of Cruz.
Kruise, Kruize, Kruse, Kruze

Krystal **G** (American) clear, brilliant glass.

Krystian **BG** (Polish) a form of Christian.
Krys, Krystek, Krystien, Krystin

Kuan (Chinese) well-off.

Kuan-Ti (Chinese) god of war and fortunetelling.

Kuan-Yin (Chinese) Buddhist deity of mercy.

Kuba (Czech) a form of Jacob.
Kubo, Kubus

Kueng (Chinese) universe.

Kugonza (Rutooro) love.

Kui (Chinese) stalwart.

Kuiril (Basque) lord.

Kulian (Pohnpeian) a form of Julio.

Kuma (Japanese) bear.

Kumar (Sanskrit) prince.

Kumi (Japanese) long, continued beauty.

Boys G–L

Boys G–L

Kun (Chinese) universe; mountain range.

Kunihide (Japanese) beautiful nation.

Kunihiro (Japanese) spacious nation.

Kuniyuki (Japanese) nation full of good fortune.

Kunle (Yoruba) home filled with honors.

Kuper (Yiddish) copper.

Kuri (Japanese) chestnut.

Kurt (Latin, German, French) a short form of Kurtis. A form of Curt.
Kirt, Kort, Kuno, Kurtt

Kurtis (Latin, French) a form of Curtis.
Kirtis, Kirtus, Kurt, Kurtes, Kurtez, Kurtice, Kurties, Kurtiss, Kurtus, Kurtys

Kuruk (Pawnee) bear.

Kustin (Pohnpeian) a form of Justo.

Kustino (Fijian) a form of Justo.

Kuya (Japanese) sky.

Kuzih (Carrier) good speaker.

Kwabena (Akan) born on Tuesday.

Kwacha (Nguni) morning.

Kwako (Akan) born on Wednesday.
Kwaka, Kwaku

Kwam (Zuni) a form of John.

Kwame (Akan) born on Saturday.
Kwamen, Kwami, Kwamin

Kwan (Korean) strong.
Kwane

Kwasi (Akan) born on Sunday. (Swahili) wealthy.
Kwasie, Kwazzi, Kwesi

Kwayera (Nguni) dawn.

Kwende (Nguni) let's go.

Kyele (Irish) a form of Kyle.

Kyla G (Irish) attractive. (Yiddish) crown; laurel.

Kylan (Irish) a form of Kyle.
Kyelen, Kyleen, Kylen, Kylin, Kyline, Kylon, Kylun

Kyle ❦ B (Irish) narrow piece of land; place where cattle graze. (Yiddish) crowned with laurels.
Cyle, Kiel, Kilan, Kile, Kilen, Kiley, Ky, Kye, Kyel, Kyele, Kylan, Kylee, Kyler, Kyley, Kylie, Kyll, Kylle, Kyrell

Kylee G (Irish) a form of Kyle.

Kyler B (English) a form of Kyle.
Kylar, Kylor

Kylie G (West Australian Aboriginal) curled stick; boomerang. (Irish) a familiar form of Kyle.

Kym G (English, Vietnamese) a form of Kim.

Kynan (Welsh) chief.

Kyndall G (English) a form of Kendall.
Kyndal, Kyndel, Kyndell, Kyndle

Kyne (English) royal.

Kyoshi (Japanese) quiet.

Kyran (Sanskrit) a form of Kiran.
Kyren, Kyron, Kyrone

Kyros (Greek) master.

Kyven (American) a form of Kevin.
Kyvan, Kyvaun, Kyvon, Kywon, Kywynn

L

L BG (American) an initial used as a first name.

Laban (Hawaiian) white.
Labon, Lebaan, Leban, Liban

Labaron (American) a combination of the prefix La + Baron.
Labaren, Labarren, Labarron, Labearon, Labron

Labib (Arabic) sensible; intelligent.

Labrentsis (Russian) a form of Lawrence.
Labhras, Labhruinn, Labrencis

Lacey G (Latin) cheerful. (Greek) a familiar form of Larissa.

Lachlan (Scottish) land of lakes.
Lache, Lachlann, Lachunn, Lakelan, Lakeland

Lacy G (Latin) a form of Lacey.

Ladarian (American) a combination of the prefix La + Darian.
Ladarien, Ladarin, Ladarion, Ladarren, Ladarrian, Ladarrien, Ladarrin, Ladarrion, Laderion, Laderrian, Laderrion

Ladarius (American) a combination of the prefix La + Darius.
Ladarious, Ladaris, Ladarrius, Ladauris, Laderius, Ladirus

Ladarrius (American) a form of Ladarius.
Ladarrias, Ladarries, Ladarrious, Laderrious, Laderris

Ladd (English) attendant.
Lad, Laddey, Laddie, Laddy

Laderrick (American) a combination of the prefix La + Derrick.
Ladarrick, Ladereck, Laderic, Laderricks

Ladio (Slavic) he who governs with glory.

Ladislao (Slavic) he who governs with glory.

Ladislav (Czech) a form of Walter.
Laco, Lada, Ladislaus

Lado (Fante) second-born son.

Ladolfo, Landolfo (Germanic) skillful as a wolf in the city.

Laertes (Greek) rock-picker.

Lafayette (French) History: Marquis de Lafayette was a French soldier and politician who aided the American Revolution.
Lafaiete, Lafayett, Lafette, Laffyette

Lahual (Araucanian) larch tree.

Lai (Chinese) future.

Laijia (Fijian) a form of Elias.

Laine **B** (English) a form of Lane.
Lain

Laird (Scottish) wealthy landowner.

Lais (Arabic) lion.

Lajos (Hungarian) famous; holy.
Lajcsi, Laji, Lali

Lake (English) lake.
Lakan, Lakane, Lakee, Laken, Lakin

Laken **G** (English) a form of Lake.

Lakota **BG** (Dakota) a tribal name.
Lakoda

Lal (Hindi) beloved.

Lam (Vietnamese) full understanding, knowledge.

Lamar **B** (German) famous throughout the land. (French) sea, ocean.
Lamair, Lamario, Lamaris, Lamarr, Lamarre, Larmar, Lemar

Lambert (German) bright land.
Bert, Lambard, Lamberto, Lambirt, Lampard, Landbert

Lamond (French) world.
Lammond, Lamon, Lamonde, Lamondo, Lamondre, Lamund, Lemond

Lamont **B** (Scandinavian) lawyer.
Lamaunt, Lamonta, Lamonte, Lamontie, Lamonto, Lamount, Lemont

Lan (Vietnamese) fictitious four-legged animal with a single horn.

Lance **B** (German) a short form of Lancelot.
Lancy, Lantz, Lanz, Launce

Lancelot (French) attendant. Literature: the knight who loved King Arthur's wife, Queen Guinevere.
Lance, Lancelott, Launcelet, Launcelot

Landelino (Teutonic) he who is a friend of the earth.

Landen (English) a form of Landon.
Landenn

Lander (Basque) lion man. (English) landowner.
Landers, Landor

Landerico (Teutonic) powerful in the region; he who exercises power in the region.

Landin **B** (English) a form of Landon.

Lando (Portuguese, Spanish) a short form of Orlando, Rolando.

Landon ✿ **B** (English) open, grassy meadow.
Landan, Landen, Landin, Landyn

Landrada (Teutonic) counselor in his village.

Landry (French, English) ruler.
Landre, Landré, Landrue

Lane **B** (English) narrow road.
Laine, Laney, Lanie, Layne

Lang (Scandinavian) tall man.
Lange

Langdon (English) long hill.
Landon, Langsdon, Langston

Langford (English) long ford.
Lanford, Lankford

Langley (English) long meadow.
Langlea, Langlee, Langleigh, Langly

Langston (English) long, narrow town.
Langsden, Langsdon

Langundo (Native American) peaceful.

Lanh (Vietnamese) quick-minded, smart; street smart.

Lani G (Hawaiian) heaven.

Lanny (American) a familiar form of
Lawrence, Laurence.
Lanney, Lannie, Lennie

Lanu (Moquelumnan) running around the
pole.

Lanz (Italian) a form of Lance.
Lanzo, Lonzo

Lao (Spanish) a short form of Stanislaus.

Lap (Vietnamese) independent.

Lapidos (Hebrew) torches.
Lapidoth

Laquan (American) a combination of the
prefix La + Quan.
*Laquain, Laquann, Laquanta, Laquantae,
Laquante, Laquawn, Laquawne, Laquin,
Laquinn, Laqun, Laquon, Laquone, Laqwan,
Laqwon*

Laquintin (American) a combination of the
prefix La + Quintin.
*Laquentin, Laquenton, Laquintas, Laquinten,
Laquintiss, Laquinton*

Lara G (Greek) cheerful. (Latin) shining;
famous. Mythology: a Roman nymph. A
short form of Laraine, Laura.

Laramie (French) tears of love. Geography: a
town in Wyoming on the Overland Trail.
Larami, Laramy, Laremy

Larenzo (Italian, Spanish) a form of
Lorenzo.
Larenz, Larenza, Larinzo, Laurenzo

Larissa (Greek) cheerful.

Larkin (Irish) rough; fierce.
Larklin

Larnell (American) a combination of Larry +
Darnell.

Laron (French) thief.
*Laran, La'ron, La Ron, Larone, Laronn, Larron,
La Ruan*

Larrimore (French) armorer.
Larimore, Larmer, Larmor

Larry B (Latin) a familiar form of
Lawrence.
Larrie, Lary

Lars (Scandinavian) a form of Lawrence.
*Laris, Larris, Larse, Larsen, Larson, Larsson,
Larz, Lasse, Laurans, Laurits, Lavrans, Lorens*

LaSalle (French) hall.
Lasal, Lasalle, Lascell, Lascelles

Lasarusa (Fijian) a form of Eleazar.

Lash (Gypsy) a form of Louis.
Lashi, Lasho

Lashawn (American) a combination of the
prefix La + Shawn.
*Lasaun, Lasean, Lashajaun, Lashan, Lashane,
Lashaun, Lashon, Lashun*

Lashon (American) a form of Lashawn.
Lashone, Lashonne

Lasse (Finnish) a form of Nicholas.

László (Hungarian) famous ruler.
Laci, Lacko, Laslo, Lazlo

Lateef (Arabic) gentle; pleasant.
Latif, Letif

Latham (Scandinavian) barn. (English) district.
Laith, Lathe, Lay

Lathan (American) a combination of the
prefix La + Nathan.
Lathaniel, Lathen, Lathyn, Leathan

Lathrop (English) barn, farmstead.
Lathe, Lathrope, Lay

Latimer (English) interpreter.
Lat, Latimor, Lattie, Latty, Latymer

Latravis (American) a combination of the
prefix La + Travis.
*Latavious, Latavius, Latraveus, Latraviaus,
Latravious, Latravius, Latrayvious, Latrayvous,
Latrivis*

Latrell (American) a combination of the
prefix La + Kentrell.
*Latreal, Latreil, Latrel, Latrelle, Letreal, Letrel,
Letrell, Letrelle*

Laudalino (Portuguese) praised.
Lino

Laughlin (Irish) servant of Saint Secundinus.
Lanty, Lauchlin, Leachlainn

Laura G (Latin) crowned with laurel.

Laurelino, Laurentino (Latin) winner;
worthy of honors.

Lauren G (Latin) a form of Laurence.

Laurence G (Latin) crowned with laurel. A
form of Lawrence. See also Rance, Raulas,
Raulo, Renzo.
*Lanny, Lauran, Laurance, Laureano,
Laurencho, Laurencio, Laurens, Laurent,
Laurentij, Laurentios, Laurentiu, Laurentius,
Laurentz, Laurentzi, Laurie, Laurin, Lauris,
Laurits, Lauritz, Laurnet, Lauro, Laurus,
Lavrenti, Lurance*

Laurencio (Spanish) a form of Laurence.

Laurens (Dutch) a form of Laurence.
Laurenz

Laurent (French) a form of Laurence.
Laurente

Laurie **G** (English) a familiar form of
Laurence.
Lauri, Laury, Lorry

Lauris (Swedish) a form of Laurence.

Lauro (Filipino) a form of Laurence.

Laury **G** (English) a form of Laurie.

Lautaro (Araucanian) daring and
enterprising.

LaValle (French) valley.
Lavail, Laval, Lavalei, Lavalle, Lavell

Lavan (Hebrew) white.
Lavane, Lavaughan, Laven, Lavon, Levan

Lavaughan (American) a form of Lavan.
Lavaughn, Levaughan, Levaughn

Lave (Italian) lava. (English) lord.

Lavell (French) a form of LaValle.
Lavel, Lavele, Lavelle, Levele, Levell, Levelle

Lavi (Hebrew) lion.

Lavon (American) a form of Lavan.
*Lavion, Lavone, Lavonn, Lavonne, Lavont,
Lavonte*

Lavrenti (Russian) a form of Lawrence.
Larenti, Lavrentij, Lavrusha, Lavrik, Lavro

Lawerence (Latin) a form of Lawrence.
Lawerance

Lawford (English) ford on the hill.
Ford, Law

Lawler (Irish) soft-spoken.
Lawlor, Lollar, Loller

Lawrence **B** (Latin) crowned with laurel.
See also Brencis, Chencho.
*Labrentsis, Laiurenty, Lanny, Lanty, Larance,
Laren, Larian, Larien, Laris, Larka, Larrance,
Larrence, Larry, Lars, Larya, Laurence, Lavrenti,
Law, Lawerence, Lawrance, Lawren, Lawrey,
Lawrie, Lawron, Lawry, Lencho, Lon, Lóránt,
Loreca, Loren, Loretto, Lorenzo, Lorne, Lourenco,
Lowrance*

Lawson (English) son of Lawrence.
Lawsen, Layson

Lawton (English) town on the hill.
Laughton, Law

Layne **B** (English) a form of Lane.
Layn, Laynee

Layton **B** (English) a form of Leighton.
Laydon, Layten, Layth, Laythan, Laython

Lazaro, Lázaro (Italian) forms of Lazarus.
Lazarillo, Lazarito, Lazzaro

Lazarus (Greek) a form of Eleazar. Bible:
Lazarus was raised from the dead by Jesus.
*Lazar, Lázár, Lazare, Lazarius, Lazaro, Lazaros,
Lazorus*

Leah **G** (Hebrew) weary.

Leal (Spanish) loyal and faithful worker.

Leander (Greek) lion-man; brave as a lion.
Ander, Leandro

Leandre (Greek) calm, serene man.

Leandro (Spanish) a form of Leander.
Leandra, Léandre, Leandrew, Leandros

Leanne **G** (English) a form of Leeann, Lian
(see Girls' Names).

Learco (Greek) judge of his village.

Leben (Yiddish) life.
Laben, Lebon

Lebna (Ethiopian) spirit; heart.

Ledarius (American) a combination of the
prefix Le + Darius.
Ledarrious, Ledarrius, Lederious, Lederris

Lee **B** (English) a short form of Farley,
Leonard, and names containing "lee."
Leigh

Leggett (French) one who is sent; delegate.
Legate, Legette, Leggitt, Liggett

Lei **BG** (Chinese) thunder. (Hawaiian) a
form of Ray.

Leib (Yiddish) roaring lion.
Leibel

Leif (Scandinavian) beloved.
Laif, Leife, Lief

Leigh **G** (English) a form of Lee.

Leighton (English) meadow farm.
Lay, Layton, Leigh, Leyton

Leith (Scottish) broad river.

Lek (Tai) small.

Lekeke (Hawaiian) powerful ruler.

Leks (Estonian) a familiar form of Alexander.
Leksik, Lekso

Lel (Gypsy) taker.

Leland 🅱 (English) meadowland; protected land.
Lealand, Lee, Leeland, Leigh, Leighland, Lelan, Lelann, Lelend, Lelund, Leyland

Lelio (Latin) he who is talkative.

Lemar (French) a form of Lamar.
Lemario, Lemarr

Lemuel (Hebrew) devoted to God.
Lem, Lemmie, Lemmy

Len (Hopi) flute. (German) a short form of Leonard.

Lenard (German) a form of Leonard.
Lennard

Lencho (Spanish) a form of Lawrence.
Lenci, Lenzy

Lennart (Swedish) a form of Leonard.
Lennerd

Lenno (Native American) man.

Lennon (Irish) small cloak; cape.
Lenon

Lennor (Gypsy) spring; summer.

Lennox (Scottish) with many elms.
Lennix, Lenox

Lenny (German) a familiar form of Leonard.
Leni, Lennie, Leny

Leo (Latin) lion. (German) a short form of Leon, Leopold.
Lavi, Leão, Lee, Leib, Leibel, Léo, Léocadie, Leos, Leosko, Leosoko, Lev, Lio, Lion, Liutas, Lyon, Nardek

Leobardo (Italian) a form of Leonard.

Leocadio (Greek) he who shines because of his whiteness.

Leodoualdo (Teutonic) he who governs his village.

Leofrido (Teutonic) he who brings peace to his village.

Leon (Greek, German) a short form of Leonard, Napoleon.
Leo, Léon, Leonas, Léonce, Leoncio, Leondris, Leone, Leonek, Leonetti, Leoni, Leonid, Leonidas, Leonirez, Leonizio, Leonon, Leons, Leontes, Leontios, Leontrae, Liutas

León (Latin) a form of Leon.

Leonard (German) brave as a lion.
Leanard, Lee, Len, Lena, Lenard, Lennart, Lenny, Leno, Leobardo, Leon, Léonard, Leonardis, Leonardo, Leonart, Leonerd, Leonhard, Leonidas, Leonnard, Leontes, Lernard, Lienard, Linek, Lnard, Lon, Londard, Lonnard, Lonya, Lynnard

Leonardo (Italian) a form of Leonard.
Leonaldo, Lionardo

Leonel (English) little lion. See also Lionel.
Leonell

Leonelo (Spanish) a form of Leonel.

Leonhard (German) a form of Leonard.
Leonhards

Leonid (Russian) a form of Leonard.
Leonide, Lyonechka, Lyonya

Leonidas (Greek) a form of Leonard.
Leonida, Leonides

Leónidas (Spanish) a form of León.

Leontino (German) strong as a lion.

Leopold (German) brave people.
Leo, Leopoldo, Leorad, Lipót, Lopolda, Luepold, Luitpold, Poldi

Leopoldo (Italian) a form of Leopold.

Leor (Hebrew) my light.
Leory, Lior

Lequinton (American) a combination of the prefix Le + Quinton.
Lequentin, Lequenton, Lequinn

Leron (French) round, circle. (American) a combination of the prefix Le + Ron.
Leeron, Le Ron, Lerone, Liron, Lyron

Leroy (French) king. See also Delroy, Elroy.
Lee, Leeroy, LeeRoy, Leigh, Lerai, Leroi, LeRoi, LeRoy, Roy

Les (Scottish, English) a short form of Leslie, Lester.
Lessie

Lesharo (Pawnee) chief.

Leshawn (American) a combination of the prefix Le + Shawn.
Lashan, Lesean, Leshaun, Leshon, Leshun

Lesley 🅶 (Scottish) a form of Leslie.

Leslie 🅶 (Scottish) gray fortress.
Lee, Leigh, Les, Leslea, Leslee, Lesley, Lesli, Lesly, Lezlie, Lezly

Lesly 🅶 (Scottish) a form of Leslie.

Lesmes (Teutonic) he whose nobility protects him.

Lester 🅱 (Latin) chosen camp. (English) from Leicester, England.
Leicester, Les

Leto (Latin) he who is always happy.

Leuco (Greek) luminous one.

Lev (Hebrew) heart. (Russian) a form of Leo. A short form of Leverett, Levi.
Leb, Leva, Levka, Levko, Levushka

Leverett (French) young hare.
Lev, Leveret, Leverit, Leveritt

Levi **B** (Hebrew) joined in harmony. Bible: the third son of Jacob; Levites are the priestly tribe of the Israelites.
Leavi, Leevi, Leevie, Lev, Levey, Levie, Levin, Levitis, Levy, Lewi, Leyvi

Levin (Hebrew) a form of Levi.
Levine, Levion

Levon (American) a form of Lavon.
Leevon, Levone, Levonn, Levonne, Levonte, Lyvonne

Lew (English) a short form of Lewis.

Lewin (English) beloved friend.

Lewis **B** (Welsh) a form of Llewellyn. (English) a form of Louis.
Lew, Lewes, Lewie, Lewy

Lex (English) a short form of Alexander.
Lexi, Lexin

Lexie **G** (English) a form of Lex.

Lexus **G** (Greek) a short form of Alexander.
Lexis, Lexius, Lexxus

Leyati (Moquelumnan) shape of an abalone shell.

Li (Chinese) strength.

Lí (Chinese) strong.

Lia **G** (Greek) bringer of good news. (Hebrew, Dutch, Italian) dependent.

Liam **B** (Irish) a form of William.
Liem, Lliam, Lyam

Liana **G** (Latin) youth. (French) bound, wrapped up; tree covered with vines. (English) meadow. (Hebrew) short form of Eliana (see Girls' Names).

Liang (Chinese) good, excellent.

Liao (Chinese) faraway; vast.

Liban **B** (Hawaiian) a form of Laban.
Libaan, Lieban

Líbano (Latin) white.

Liber (Latin) he who spreads abundance.

Liberal (Latin) lover of liberty.

Liberato (Latin) liberated one.

Liberio (Portuguese) liberation.
Liberaratore, Liborio

Liberto (Latin) a form of Liberal.

Libiac, Llipiac (Quechua) ray of light; brilliant, glowing.

Libio, Livio (Latin) born in a dry place; comes from the desert.

Licas (Greek) wolf.

Licurgo (Greek) he who frightens off wolves.

Lidio (Greek, Portuguese) ancient.

Lie (Chinese) strong, raging fire.

Ligongo (Yao) who is this?

Likeke (Hawaiian) a form of Richard.

Liko (Chinese) protected by Buddha. (Hawaiian) bud.
Like

Lim (Chinese) a form of Lin.

Lin **G** (Burmese) bright. (English) a short form of Lyndon.
Linh, Linn, Linny, Lyn, Lynn

Linc (English) a short form of Lincoln.
Link

Lincoln **B** (English) settlement by the pool. History: Abraham Lincoln was the sixteenth U.S. president.
Linc, Lincon, Lyncoln

Linda **G** (Spanish) pretty.

Lindberg (German) mountain where linden grow.
Lindbergh, Lindburg, Lindy

Lindell (English) valley of the linden.
Lendall, Lendel, Lendell, Lindall, Lindel, Lyndale, Lyndall, Lyndel, Lyndell

Linden (English) a form of Lyndon.

Lindley (English) linden field.
Lindlea, Lindlee, Lindleigh, Lindly

Lindon (English) a form of Lyndon.
Lin, Lindan

Lindor (Latin) he who seduces, likes to seduce.

Lindsay **G** (English) a form of Lindsey.
Linsay

Lindsey **G** (English) linden-tree island.
Lind, Lindsay, Lindsee, Lindsie, Lindsy, Lindzy, Linsey, Linzie, Linzy, Lyndsay, Lyndsey, Lyndsie, Lynzie

Boys G–L

Linford (English) linden ford.
Lynford

Linfred (German) peaceful, calm.

Ling (Chinese) quick, clever.

Linley (English) flax meadow.
Linlea, Linlee, Linleigh, Linly

Linton (English) flax town.
Lintonn, Lynton, Lyntonn

Linu (Hindi) lily.

Linus (Greek) flaxen haired.
Linas, Linux

Linwood (English) flax wood.

Lio (Hawaiian) a form of Leo.

Lionel (French) lion cub. See also Leonel.
Lional, Lionell, Lionello, Lynel, Lynell, Lyonel

Li-Qin (Chinese) beautiful stringed musical instrument.

Liron **BG** (Hebrew) my song.
Lyron

Lisa **G** (Hebrew) consecrated to God. (English) a short form of Elizabeth.

Lisandro, Lisias (Spanish) liberator.

Lisardo (Hebrew) defender of the faith, fights for God.

Lise **G** (Moquelumnan) salmon's head coming out of the water.

Lisette **G** (French) a form of Lisa. (English) a familiar form of Elise, Elizabeth.

Lisimba (Yao) lion.
Simba

Lisístrato (Greek) he who fights for the liberating army.

Lister (English) dyer.

Litton (English) town on the hill.
Liton

Liu (African) voice.

Liuz (Polish) light.
Lius

Livingston (English) Leif's town.
Livingstone

Liwanu (Moquelumnan) growling bear.

Lizbeth **G** (English) a short form of Elizabeth.

Llacsa (Quechua) he who is the color of bronze.

Llallaua (Aymara) magnificent.

Llancamil (Mapuche) shining stone, gold and silver pearl.

Llancañir (Mapuche) fox that is pearl-colored.

Llanqui (Quechua) potter's clay.

Llarico, Llaricu (Aymara) indomitable; he who does not allow himself to be humiliated nor does he to bow to anyone.

Llashapoma, Llashapuma (Quechua) heavy puma; slow.

Llewellyn (Welsh) lionlike.
Lewis, Llewelin, Llewellen, Llewelleyn, Llewellin, Llewlyn, Llywellyn, Llywellynn, Llywelyn

Lloque, Lluqui (Quechua) left-handed, from the left side.

Lloqueyupanqui, Lluquiyupanqui (Quechua) left-handed, memorable.

Lloyd **B** (Welsh) gray haired; holy. See also Floyd.
Loy, Loyd, Loyde, Loydie

Lobo (Spanish) wolf.

Lochlain (Irish, Scottish) land of lakes.
Laughlin, Lochlan, Lochlann, Lochlin, Locklynn

Locke (English) forest.
Lock, Lockwood

Loe (Hawaiian) a form of Roy.

Logan ☙ **B** (Irish) meadow.
Llogan, Loagan, Loagen, Loagon, Logann, Logen, Loggan, Loghan, Logon, Logn, Logun, Logunn, Logyn

Lok (Chinese) happy.

Lokela (Hawaiian) a form of Roger.

Lokni (Moquelumnan) raining through the roof.

Lomán (Irish) bare. (Slavic) sensitive.

Lombard (Latin) long bearded.
Bard, Barr

Lon (Irish) fierce. (Spanish) a short form of Alonso, Alonzo, Leonard, Lonnie.
Lonn

Lonan (Zuni) cloud.

Lonato (Native American) flint stone.

Loncopan (Mapuche) puma's head; leader of the pumas; principal branch or capitol.

London **BG** (English) fortress of the moon. Geography: the capital of the United Kingdom.
Londen, Londyn, Lunden, Lundon

Long (Chinese) dragon. (Vietnamese) hair.

Lonnie (German, Spanish) a familiar form of Alonso, Alonzo.
Lon, Loni, Lonie, Lonnell, Lonney, Lonni, Lonniel, Lonny

Lono (Hawaiian) Mythology: the god of learning and intellect.

Lonzo (German, Spanish) a short form of Alonso, Alonzo.
Lonso

Lootah (Lakota) red.

Lopaka (Hawaiian) a form of Robert.

Loránd (Hungarian) a form of Roland.

Lóránt (Hungarian) a form of Lawrence.
Lorant

Lorcan (Irish) little; fierce.

Lord (English) noble title.

Loren **G** (Latin) a short form of Lawrence.
Lorin, Lorren, Lorrin, Loryn

Lorena **G** (English) a form of Lauren.

Lorenzo (Italian, Spanish) a form of Lawrence.
Larenzo, Lerenzo, Lewrenzo, Lorenc, Lorence,

Lorenco, Lorencz, Lorens, Lorenso, Lorentz, Lorenz, Lorenza, Loretto, Lorinc, Lörinc, Lorinzo, Loritz, Lorrenzo, Lorrie, Lorry, Lourenza, Lourenzo, Lowrenzo, Renzo, Zo

Loretto (Italian) a form of Lawrence.
Loreto

Lori **G** (English) a form of Lorry.

Lorién (Aragonese) a form of Lorenzo.

Lorimer (Latin) harness maker.
Lorrie, Lorrimer, Lorry

Loring (German) son of the famous warrior.
Lorrie, Lorring, Lorry

Loris **BG** (Dutch) clown.

Loritz (Latin, Danish) laurel.
Lauritz

Lorne (Latin) a short form of Lawrence.
Lorn, Lornie

Lorry (English) a form of Laurie.
Lori, Lorri, Lory

Lot (Hebrew) hidden, covered. Bible: Lot fled from Sodom, but his wife glanced back upon its destruction and was transformed into a pillar of salt.
Lott

Lotario (Germanic) distinguished warrior.

Lothar (German) a form of Luther.
Lotaire, Lotarrio, Lothair, Lothaire, Lothario, Lotharrio

Lou **B** (German) a short form of Louis.

Loudon (German) low valley.
Loudan, Louden, Loudin, Lowden

Louie (German) a familiar form of Louis.

Louis (German) famous warrior. See also Aloisio, Aloysius, Clovis, Luigi.
Lash, Lashi, Lasho, Lewis, Lou, Loudovicus, Louie, Louies, Louise, Lucho, Lude, Ludek, Ludirk, Ludis, Ludko, Ludwig, Lughaidh, Lui, Luigi, Luis, Luiz, Luki, Lutek

Louise **G** (German) famous warrior.

Lourdes **G** (French) from Lourdes, France. Religion: a place where the Virgin Mary was said to have appeared.

Louvain (English) Lou's vanity. Geography: a city in Belgium.
Louvin

Lovell (English) a form of Lowell.
Louvell, Lovel, Lovelle, Lovey

Lowell (French) young wolf. (English) beloved.
Lovell, Lowe, Lowel

Loyal (English) faithful, loyal.
Loy, Loyall, Loye, Lyall, Lyell

Loyola (Latin) has a wolf in his shield.

Lu (Chinese) land.

Luan (Chinese) mountain.

Luano (Latin) fountain.

Lubomir (Polish) lover of peace.

Luboslaw (Polish) lover of glory.
Lubs, Lubz

Luc (French) a form of Luke.
Luce

Luca **B** (Italian) a form of Lucius.
Lucca, Luka

Lucas 💥 **B** (German, Irish, Danish, Dutch) a form of Lucius.
Lucais, Lucassie, Lucaus, Luccas, Luccus, Luckas, Lucus

Lucero (Spanish) bringer of light.

Lucian (Latin) a form of Lucius.
Liuz, Lucan, Lucanus, Luciano, Lucianus, Lucias, Lucjan, Lukianos, Lukyan

Luciano (Italian) a form of Lucian.
Luca, Lucca, Lucino, Lucio

Lucien (French) a form of Lucius.

Lucila (Latin) bringer of light.

Lucio (Italian) a form of Lucius.

Lucius (Latin) light; bringer of light.
Loukas, Luc, Luca, Lucais, Lucanus, Lucas, Luce, Lucian, Lucien, Lucio, Lucious, Lucis, Luke, Lusio

Lucky (American) fortunate.
Luckee, Luckie, Luckson, Lucson

Lucrecio (Latin) twilight of dawn.

Ludlow (English) prince's hill.

Ludovic (German) a form of Ludwig.
Ludovick, Ludovico

Ludwig (German) a form of Louis. Music: Ludwig van Beethoven was a famous nineteenth-century German composer.
Ludovic, Ludvig, Ludvik, Ludwik, Lutz

Lu-Hsing (Chinese) god of pay and employees.

Lui (Hawaiian) a form of Louis.

Luigi (Italian) a form of Louis.
Lui, Luiggi, Luigino, Luigy

Luis 💥 **B** (Spanish) a form of Louis.
Luise

Luís (Spanish) a form of Luis.

Luisa **G** (Spanish) a form of Louisa (see Girls' Names).

Luiz (Spanish) a form of Louis.

Lukas, Lukus (Greek, Czech, Swedish) forms of Luke.
Loukas, Lukais, Lukash, Lukasha, Lukass, Lukasz, Lukaus, Lukkas

Luke 💥 **B** (Latin) a form of Lucius. Bible: companion of Saint Paul and author of the third Gospel of the New Testament.
Luc, Luchok, Luck, Lucky, Luk, Luka, Lúkács, Lukas, Luken, Lukes, Lukus, Lukyan, Lusio

Lukela (Hawaiian) a form of Russel.

Luken (Basque) bringer of light.
Lucan, Lucane, Lucano, Luk

Luki (Basque) famous warrior.

Lukman (Arabic) prophet.
Luqman

Lulani **BG** (Hawaiian) highest point in heaven.

Lumo (Ewe) born facedown.

Lun (Chinese) logic; order.

Lundy (Scottish) grove by the island.

Lunn (Irish) warlike.
Lon, Lonn

Lunt (Swedish) grove.

Luo (Chinese) name of a river.

Luong (Vietnamese) from the land.

Lu-Pan (Chinese) god of carpenters and masons.

Lupercio (Latin) name given to people from Lupercus.

Luperco (Latin) he who frightens off wolves.

Lusila (Hindi) leader.

Lusio (Zuni) a form of Lucius.

Lusorio (Latin) he enjoys games.

Lutalo (Luganda) warrior.

Lutardo (Teutonic) he who is valiant in his village.

Lutfi (Arabic) kind, friendly.

Luther (German) famous warrior. History: Martin Luther was one of the central figures of the Reformation.
Lothar, Lutero, Luthor

Lutherum (Gypsy) slumber.

Luyu **BG** (Moquelumnan) head shaker.

Luz **G** (Spanish) light.

Lyall, Lyell (Scottish) loyal.

Lydia **G** (Greek) from Lydia, an ancient land in Asia. (Arabic) strife.

Lyle (French) island.
Lisle, Ly, Lysle

Lyman (English) meadow.
Leaman, Leeman, Lymon

Lynch (Irish) mariner.
Linch

Lyndal (English) valley of lime trees.
Lyndale, Lyndall, Lyndel, Lyndell

Lyndon (English) linden hill. History: Lyndon B. Johnson was the thirty-sixth U.S. president.
Lin, Linden, Lindon, Lyden, Lydon, Lyn, Lyndan, Lynden, Lynn

Lyndsay **G** (English) a form of Lindsey.

Lynn **G** (English) waterfall; brook.
Lyn, Lynell, Lynette, Lynnard, Lynoll

Lyron (Hebrew) a form of Leron, Liron.

Lysander (Greek) liberator.
Lyzander, Sander

M **G** (American) an initial used as a first name.

Ma (Chinese) agate.

Maalik (Punjabi) a form of Malik.
Maalek, Maaliek

Mac (Scottish) son.
Macs

Macabeo (Hebrew) progressing.

Macadam (Scottish) son of Adam.
MacAdam, McAdam

Macallister (Irish) son of Alistair.
Macalaster, Macalister, MacAlister, McAlister, McAllister

Macario (Spanish) a form of Makarios.

Macarthur (Irish) son of Arthur.
MacArthur, McArthur

Macaulay (Scottish) son of righteousness.
Macaulee, Macauley, Macaully, Macauly, Maccauley, Mackauly, Macualay, McCauley

Macbride (Scottish) son of a follower of Saint Brigid.
Macbryde, Mcbride, McBride

Maccoy (Irish) son of Hugh, Coy.
MacCoy, Mccoy, McCoy

Maccrea (Irish) son of grace.
MacCrae, MacCray, MacCrea, Macrae, Macray, Makray, Mccrea, McCrea

Macdonald (Scottish) son of Donald.
MacDonald, Mcdonald, McDonald, Mcdonna, Mcdonnell, McDonnell

Macdougal (Scottish) son of Dougal.
MacDougal, Mcdougal, McDougal, McDougall, Dougal

Mace (French) club. (English) a short form of Macy, Mason.
Macean, Maceo, Macer, Macey, Macie, Macy

Macedonio (Greek) he who triumphs and grows in stature.

Macerio (Spanish) blessed.

Macgregor (Scottish) son of Gregor.
Macgreggor

Machas (Polish) a form of Michael.

Macías (Hebrew) a form of Matías.

Macie **G** (French, English) a form of Mace.

Maciel (Latin) very slender, skeleton-like.

Mack (Scottish) a short form of names beginning with "Mac" and "Mc."
Macke, Mackey, Mackie, Macklin, Macks, Macky

Mackenzie **G** (Irish) son of Kenzie.
Mackensy, Mackenxo, Mackenze, Mackenzey, Mackenzi, MacKenzie, Mackenzly, Mackenzy, Mackienzie, Mackinsey, Mackinzie, Makenzie, McKenzie, Mickenzie

Mackinnley (Irish) son of the learned ruler.
Mackinley, MacKinnley, Mackinnly, Mckinley

Macklain (Irish) a form of Maclean.
Macklaine, Macklane

Maclean (Irish) son of Leander.
Machlin, Macklain, MacLain, MacLean, Maclin, Maclyn, Makleen, McLaine, McLean

Macmahon (Irish) son of Mahon.
MacMahon, McMahon

Macmurray (Irish) son of Murray.
McMurray

Macnair (Scottish) son of the heir.
Macknair

Maco (Hungarian) a form of Emmanuel.

Macon (German, English) maker.

Macrobio (Greek) he who enjoys a long life.

Macy **G** (French) Matthew's estate.
Mace, Macey

Maddison **G** (English) a form of Madison.

Maddock (Welsh) generous.
Madoc, Madock, Madog

Maddox (Welsh, English) benefactor's son.
Maddux, Madox

Madeline 🅖 (Greek) high tower.

Madhar (Hindi) full of intoxication; relating to spring.

Madisen 🅖 (English) a form of Madison.

Madison 🅖 (English) son of Maude; good son.
Maddie, Maddison, Maddy, Madisen, Madisson, Madisyn, Madsen, Son, Sonny

Madongo (Luganda) uncircumcised.

Madu (Ibo) people.

Mael (Celtic) prince.

Maemi (Japanese) honest child.

Magar (Armenian) groom's attendant.
Magarious

Magee (Irish) son of Hugh.
MacGee, MacGhee, McGee

Magen (Hebrew) protector.

Magín (Latin) he who is imaginative.

Magnar (Norwegian) strong; warrior.
Magne

Magno (Latin) great, of great fame; magnificent.

Magnus (Latin) great.
Maghnus, Magnes, Manius, Mayer

Magomu (Luganda) younger of twins.

Maguire (Irish) son of the beige one.
MacGuire, McGuire, McGwire

Mahammed (Arabic) a form of Muhammad.
Mahamad, Mahamed

Mahdi (Arabic) guided to the right path.
Mahde, Mahdee, Mahdy

Mahesa (Hindi) great lord. Religion: another name for the Hindu god Shiva.

Mahi'ai (Hawaiian) a form of George.

Mahir (Arabic, Hebrew) excellent; industrious.
Maher

Mahkah (Lakota) earth.

Mahmoud (Arabic) a form of Muhammad.
Mahamoud, Mahmmoud, Mahmuod

Mahmúd (Arabic) a form of Muhammad.
Mahmed, Mahmood, Mahmut

Mahoma (Arabic) worthy of being praised.

Mahomet (Arabic) a form of Muhammad.
Mehemet, Mehmet

Mahon (Irish) bear.

Mahpee (Lakota) sky.

Mai (Chinese) to advance with big strides.

Maicu (Quechua) eagle.

Maimun (Arabic) lucky.
Maimon

Maiqui (Quechua) tree.

Maira 🅖 (Irish) a form of Mary.

Mairtin (Irish) a form of Martin.
Martain, Martainn

Maitias (Irish) a form of Mathias.
Maithias

Maitiú (Irish) a form of Matthew.

Maitland (English) meadowland.

Majencio (Latin) he who becomes more and more famous.

Majid (Arabic) great, glorious.
Majd, Majde, Majdi, Majdy, Majed, Majeed

Major (Latin) greater; military rank.
Majar, Maje, Majer, Mayer, Mayor

Makaio (Hawaiian) a form of Matthew.

Makalani (Mwera) writer.

Makani 🅑 (Hawaiian) wind.

Makarios (Greek) happy; blessed.
Macario, Macarios, Maccario, Maccarios

Makell 🅖 (Hebrew) a form of Michael.

Makenna 🅖 (American) a form of Mackenna (see Girls' Names).

Makenzie 🅖 (Irish) a form of Mackenzie.
Makensie, Makenzy

Makin (Arabic) strong.
Makeen

Makis (Greek) a form of Michael.

Makoto (Japanese) sincere.

Maks (Hungarian) a form of Max.
Makszi

Maksim (Russian) a form of Maximilian.
Maksimka, Maksym, Maxim

Maksym (Polish) a form of Maximilian.
Makimus, Maksim, Maksymilian

Makyah (Hopi) eagle hunter.

Mal (Irish) a short form of names beginning with "Mal."

Malachi (Hebrew) angel of God. Bible: the last canonical Hebrew prophet.
Maeleachlainn, Mal, Malachai, Malachia, Malachie, Malachy, Malakai, Malake, Malaki, Malchija, Malechy, Málik

Malachy (Irish) a form of Malachi.

Malajitm (Sanskrit) garland of victory.

Malaquias, Malaquías (Hebrew) my messenger.

Malco, Malcon (Hebrew) he who is like a king.

Malcolm (Scottish) follower of Saint Columba who Christianized North Scotland. (Arabic) dove.
Mal, Malcalm, Malcohm, Malcolum, Malcom, Malkolm

Malcom (Scottish) a form of Malcolm.
Malcome, Malcum, Malkom, Malkum

Malden (English) meeting place in a pasture.
Mal, Maldon

Malek (Arabic) a form of Málik.
Maleak, Maleek, Maleik, Maleka, Maleke, Mallek

Maleko (Hawaiian) a form of Mark.

Malik **B** (Punjabi, Arabic) a form of Málik.

Málik (Punjabi) lord, master. (Arabic) a form of Malachi.
Maalik, Mailik, Malak, Malic, Malick, Malicke, Maliek, Maliik, Malik, Malike, Malikh, Maliq, Malique, Mallik, Malyk, Malyq

Malin (English) strong, little warrior.
Mal, Mallin, Mallon

Mallory **G** (German) army counselor. (French) wild duck.
Lory, Mal, Mallery, Mallori, Mallorie, Malory

Maloney (Irish) church going.
Malone, Malony

Malvern (Welsh) bare hill.
Malverne

Malvin (Irish, English) a form of Melvin.
Mal, Malvinn, Malvyn, Malvynn

Mamani (Aymara) falcon.

Mamertino (Latin) name given to inhabitants of Mesina in Sicily.

Mamerto (Latin) native of Mamertium, an ancient city in the south of Italy.

Mamo **BG** (Hawaiian) yellow flower; yellow bird.

Mamoru (Japanese) earth.

Manabu (Japanese) studious.

Manases (Hebrew) he who forgets everything.

Manchu (Chinese) pure.

Mancio (Latin) he who foretells the future.

Manco (Peruvian) supreme leader. History: a sixteenth-century Incan king.

Mandala (Yao) flowers.
Manda, Mandela

Mandeep **BG** (Punjabi) mind full of light.
Mandieep

Mandek (Polish) a form of Armand, Herman.
Mandie

Mandel (German) almond.
Mandell

Mander (Gypsy) from me.

Mandy **G** (Latin) lovable. A familiar form of Amanda.

Manford (English) small ford.

Manfred (English) man of peace. See also Fred.
Manfret, Manfrid, Manfried, Maniferd, Mannfred, Mannfryd

Manfredo (Germanic) he who has power to safeguard the peace.

Mang (Chinese) brilliant light.

Manger (French) stable.

Mango (Spanish) a familiar form of Emmanuel, Manuel.

Manheim (German) servant's home.

Manipi (Native American) living marvel.

Manius (Scottish) a form of Magnus.
Manus, Manyus

Manjot **BG** (Indian) light of the mind.

Manley (English) hero's meadow.
Manlea, Manleigh, Manly

Manlio (Latin) he who was born in the morning.

Mann (German) man.
Manin

Manning (English) son of the hero.

Mannix (Irish) monk.
Mainchin

Manny (German, Spanish) a familiar form of Manuel.
Mani, Manni, Mannie, Many

Mano (Hawaiian) shark. (Spanish) a short form of Manuel.
Manno, Manolo

Manoj (Sanskrit) cupid.

Manolito (Spanish) God is with us.

Manpreet G (Punjabi) mind full of love.

Manque (Mapuche) condor.

Manquecura (Mapuche) refuge from the condor; two-colored rock.

Manquepan (Mapuche) condor's branch; spotted puma.

Mansa (Swahili) king. History: a fourteenth-century king of Mali.

Mansel (English) manse; house occupied by a clergyman.
Mansell

Mansfield (English) field by the river; hero's field.

Man-Shik (Korean) deeply rooted.

Manso (Latin) delivered, trusted one.

Mansueto (Latin) he who is peaceful, docile.

Mansür (Arabic) divinely aided.
Mansoor, Mansour

Manton (English) man's town; hero's town.
Mannton, Manten

Manu (Hindi) lawmaker. History: the reputed writer of the Hindi compendium of sacred laws and customs. (Hawaiian) bird. (Ghanaian) second-born son.

Manuel (Hebrew) a short form of Emmanuel.
Maco, Mango, Mannuel, Manny, Mano, Manolón, Manual, Manuale, Manue, Manuelli, Manuelo, Manuil, Manyuil, Minel

Manville (French) worker's village. (English) hero's village.
Mandeville, Manvel, Manvil

Man-Young (Korean) ten thousand years of prosperity.

Manzo (Japanese) third son.

Manzur (Arabic) winner, he who defeats all.

Mao (Chinese) hair.

Maona (Winnebago) creator, earth maker.

Mapira (Yao) millet.

Marc (French) a form of Mark.

Marcel B (French) a form of Marcellus.
Marcell, Marsale, Marsel

Marceliano (Spanish) a form of Marcelo.

Marcelino (Italian) a form of Marcellus.
Marceleno, Marcelin, Marcellin, Marcellino

Marcellus (Latin) a familiar form of Marcus.
Marceau, Marcel, Marceles, Marcelias, Marcelino, Marcelis, Marcelius, Marcellas, Marcelleous, Marcellis, Marcellous, Marcelluas, Marcelo, Marcelus, Marcely, Marciano, Marcilka, Marcsseau, Marquel, Marsalis

Marcelo, Marcello (Italian) forms of Marcellus.
Marchello, Marsello, Marselo

March (English) dweller by a boundary.

Marcial (Spanish) a form of Marcio.

Marciano (Italian) a form of Martin.
Marci, Marcio

Marcilka (Hungarian) a form of Marcellus.
Marci, Marcilki

Marcin (Polish) a form of Martin.

Marcio (Italian) a form of Marciano.

Marco B (Italian) a form of Marcus. History: Marco Polo was a thirteenth-century Venetian traveler who explored Asia.
Marcko, Marko

Marcos (Spanish) a form of Marcus.
Marckos, Marcous, Markos, Markose

Marcus B (Latin) martial, warlike.
Marc, Marcas, Marcellus, Marcio, Marckus, Marco, Marcos, Marcous, Marcuss, Marcuus, Marcux, Marek, Mark, Markov, Markus

Mardonio (Persian) male warrior.

Mardoqueo (Hebrew) he who adores the god of war.

Marek (Slavic) a form of Marcus.

Maren G (Basque) sea.

Mareo (Japanese) uncommon.

Margaret G (Greek) pearl.

Maria G (Hebrew) bitter; sea of bitterness. (Italian, Spanish) a form of Mary.

Mariah G (Hebrew) a form of Mary.

Mariam G (Hebrew) a form of Miriam.

Marian G (Polish) a form of Mark.

Marianne G (English) a form of Marian.

Mariano (Italian) a form of Mark.

Marid (Arabic) rebellious.

Marie G (French) a form of Mary.

Marin (French) sailor.
Marine, Mariner, Marino, Marius, Marriner

Marina G (Latin) sea.

Marino (Italian) a form of Marin.
Marinos, Marinus, Mario, Mariono

Mario B (Italian) a form of Marino.
Marios, Marrio

Marion G (French) bitter; sea of bitterness.
Mareon, Mariano

Marise (Japanese) infinite; endless.

Marisela G (Latin) a form of Marisa (see Girls' Names).

Marissa G (Latin) a form of Marisa (see Girls' Names).

Marius (Latin) a form of Marin.
Marious

Marjolaine G (French) marjoram.

Mark B (Latin) a form of Marcus. Bible: author of the second Gospel in the New Testament. See also Maleko.
Marc, Marek, Marian, Mariano, Marke, Markee, Markel, Markell, Markey, Marko,
Markos, Márkus, Markusha, Marque, Martial, Marx

Markanthony (Italian) a combination of Mark + Anthony.

Marke (Polish) a form of Mark.

Markel, Markell B (Latin) forms of Mark.
Markelle, Markelo

Markes (Portuguese) a form of Marques.
Markess, Markest

Markese (French) a form of Marquis.
Markease, Markeece, Markees, Markeese, Markei, Markeice, Markeis, Markeise, Markes, Markez, Markeze, Markice

Markham (English) homestead on the boundary.

Markis (French) a form of Marquis.
Markies, Markiese, Markise, Markiss, Markist

Marko (Latin) a form of Marco, Mark.
Markco

Markus (Latin) a form of Marcus.
Markas, Markcus, Markcuss, Markys, Marqus

Marland (English) lake land.

Marlen G (English) a form of Marlin.

Marley G (English) lake meadow.
Marlea, Marleigh, Marly, Marrley

Marlin (English) deep-sea fish.
Marlion, Marlyn

Marlon B (French) a form of Merlin.

Marlow (English) hill by the lake.
Mar, Marlo, Marlowe

Marlyn G (English) a form of Marlin.

Marmion (French) small.
Marmyon

Marnin (Hebrew) singer; bringer of joy.

Maro (Japanese) myself.

Marón (Arabic) male saint.

Marquan (American) a combination of Mark + Quan.
Marquane, Marquante

Marquel (American) a form of Marcellus.
Marqueal, Marquelis, Marquell, Marquelle, Marquellis, Marquiel, Marquil, Marquiles, Marquill, Marquille, Marquillus, Marqwel, Marqwell

Marques (Portuguese) nobleman.
Markes, Markqes, Markques, Markquese, Marqese, Marqesse, Marqez, Marqeze, Marquees, Marquese, Marquess, Marquesse, Marquest, Markqueus, Marquez, Marqus

Marquez B (Portuguese) a form of Marques.
Marqueze, Marquiez

Marquice (American) a form of Marquis.
Marquaice, Marquece

Marquis, Marquise B (French) nobleman.
Marcquis, Marcuis, Markis, Markquis, Markquise, Markuis, Marqise, Marquee, Marqui, Marquice, Marquie, Marquies, Marquiss, Marquist, Marquiz, Marquize

Marquon (American) a combination of Mark + Quon.
Marquin, Marquinn, Marqwan, Marqwon, Marqwyn

Boys M–R

Marr (Spanish) divine. (Arabic) forbidden.

Mars (Latin) bold warrior. Mythology: the Roman god of war.

Marsalis (Italian) a form of Marcellus.
Marsalius, Marsallis, Marsellis, Marsellius, Marsellus

Marsden (English) marsh valley.
Marsdon

Marsh (English) swamp land. (French) a short form of Marshall.

Marshal (French) a form of Marshall.
Marschal, Marshel

Marshall 🅱 (French) caretaker of the horses; military title.
Marsh, Marshal, Marshell

Marshawn (American) a combination of Mark + Shawn.
Marshaine, Marshaun, Marshauwn, Marshean, Marshon, Marshun

Marston (English) town by the marsh.

Martell (English) hammerer.
Martel, Martele, Martellis

Marten (Dutch) a form of Martin.
Maarten, Martein

Martez (Spanish) a form of Martin.
Martaz, Martaze, Martes, Martese, Marteze, Martice, Martiece, Marties, Martiese, Martiez, Martis, Martise, Martize

Marti 🅶 (Spanish) a form of Martin.
Martee, Martie

Martial (Latin) martial, warlike. (French) a form of Mark.

Martin 🅱 (Latin, French) a form of Martinus. History: Martin Luther King, Jr. led the Civil Rights movement and won the Nobel Peace Prize. See also Tynek.
Maartin, Mairtin, Marciano, Marcin, Marinos, Marius, Mart, Martan, Marten, Martez, Marti, Martijn, Martinas, Martine, Martinez, Martinho, Martiniano, Martinien, Martinka, Martino, Martins, Marto, Marton, Márton, Marts, Marty, Martyn, Mattin, Mertin, Morten, Moss

Martín (Latin) a form of Martin.

Martina 🅶 (Latin) a form of Martin.

Martine 🅶 (Latin, French) a form of Martin.

Martinez (Spanish) a form of Martin.
Martines

Martinho (Portuguese) a form of Martin.

Martino (Italian) a form of Martin.
Martinos

Martiño (Latin) a form of Martin.

Martins (Latvian) a form of Martin.

Martinus (Latin) martial, warlike.
Martin

Martir (Greek) he who gives a testament of faith.

Marty (Latin) a familiar form of Martin.
Martey, Marti, Martie

Marut (Hindi) Religion: the Hindu god of the wind.

Marv (English) a short form of Marvin.
Marve, Marvi, Marvis

Marvin (English) lover of the sea.
Marv, Marvein, Marven, Marvion, Marvn, Marvon, Marvyn, Marwin, Marwynn, Mervin

Marwan (Arabic) history personage.

Marwood (English) forest pond.

Mary 🅶 (Hebrew) bitter; sea of bitterness.

Masa (Japanese) good and straightforward.

Masaaki (Japanese) prosperous; brilliant.

Masaccio (Italian) twin.
Masaki

Masafumi (Japanese) prosperous writer.

Masahide (Japanese) prosperous commander.

Masahiro (Japanese) broad-minded.

Masaji, Masajiro (Japanese) integrity.

Masajun (Japanese) good; obedient.

Masakatsu (Japanese) patient; successful ruler.

Masakazu (Japanese) first son of Masa.

Masamba (Yao) leaves.

Masami (Japanese) beautiful ruler.

Masamitsu (Japanese) feeling.

Masanao (Japanese) good.

Masanobu (Japanese) elegant; trustworthy.

Masao (Japanese) righteous.

Masaru (Japanese) gentleness; intelligence.

Masashi (Japanese) ambitious truth-seeker.

Masataro (Japanese) good boy.

Masato (Japanese) just.

Masayuki (Japanese) problematic.

Mashama (Shona) surprising.

Mashiro (Japanese) broad minded.

Maska (Native American) powerful.
(Russian) mask.

Maslin (French) little Thomas.
Maslen, Masling

Mason ☀ **B** (French) stone worker.
*Mace, Maison, Masson, Masun, Masyn,
Sonny*

Masou (Native American) fire god.

Massey (English) twin.
Massi

Massimo **B** (Italian) greatest.
Massimiliano

Masud (Arabic, Swahili) fortunate.
Masood, Masoud, Mhasood

Masura (Japanese) fated for a good life.

Matai (Basque, Bulgarian) a form of
Matthew.
Máté, Matei

Matalino (Filipino) bright.

Mateo (Spanish) a form of Matthew.
Matías, Matteo

Mateos, Mathías (Hebrew) offered up to
God.

Mateusz (Polish) a form of Matthew.
Matejs, Mateus

Mathe (German) a short form of Matthew.

Mather (English) powerful army.

Matheu (German) a form of Matthew.
Matheau, Matheus, Mathu

Mathew **B** (Hebrew) a form of Matthew.

Mathias, Matthias (German, Swedish)
forms of Matthew.
*Maitias, Mathi, Mathia, Mathis, Matías,
Matthia, Matthieus, Mattia, Mattias, Matus*

Mathieu, Matthieu **B** (French) forms of
Matthew.
*Mathie, Mathieux, Mathiew, Matthiew,
Mattieu, Mattieux*

Matías (Spanish) a form of Mathias.
Mattias

Mato (Native American) brave.

Matope (Rhodesian) our last child.

Matoskah (Lakota) white bear.

Mats (Swedish) a familiar form of Matthew.
Matts, Matz

Matson (Hebrew) son of Matt.
Matison, Matsen, Mattison, Mattson

Matsu (Japanese) pine.

Matt (Hebrew) a short form of Matthew.
Mat

Matteen (Afghan) disciplined; polite.

Matteus (Scandinavian) a form of Matthew.

Matthew ☀ **B** (Hebrew) gift of God. Bible:
author of the first Gospel of the New
Testament.
*Mads, Makaio, Maitiú, Mata, Matai, Matek,
Mateo, Mateusz, Matfei, Mathe, Matheson,
Matheu, Mathew, Mathian, Mathias,
Mathieson, Mathieu, Matro, Mats, Matt,
Matteus, Matthaeus, Matthaios, Matthaus,
Matthäus, Mattheus, Matthews, Mattmias,
Matty, Matvey, Matyas, Mayhew*

Matty (Hebrew) a familiar form of Matthew.
Mattie

Matus (Czech) a form of Mathias.

Matusalén (Hebrew) symbol of longevity.

Matvey (Russian) a form of Matthew.
Matviy, Matviyko, Matyash, Motka, Motya

Matyas (Polish) a form of Matthew.
Mátyás

Mauli (Hawaiian) a form of Maurice.

Maurice (Latin) dark skinned; moor;
marshland. See also Seymour.
*Mauli, Maur, Maurance, Maureo, Mauricio,
Maurids, Mauriece, Maurikas, Maurin,
Maurino, Maurise, Mauritz, Maurius,
Maurizio, Mauro, Maurrel, Maurtel, Maury,
Maurycy, Meurig, Moore, Morice, Moritz,
Morrel, Morrice, Morrie, Morrill, Morris*

Mauricio **B** (Spanish) a form of Maurice.
Mauriccio, Mauriceo, Maurico, Maurisio

Mauritz (German) a form of Maurice.

Maurizio (Italian) a form of Maurice.

Mauro (Latin) a short form of Maurice.
Maur, Maurio

Maury (Latin) a familiar form of Maurice.
Maurey, Maurie, Morrie

Maverick **B** (American) independent.
Maverik, Maveryke, Mavric, Mavrick

Boys M–R

Mawuli (Ewe) there is a God.

Max B (Latin) a short form of Maximilian, Maxwell.
Mac, Mack, Maks, Maxe, Maxx, Maxy, Miksa

Maxfield (English) Mack's field.

Maxi (Czech, Hungarian, Spanish) a familiar form of Maximilian, Máximo.
Makszi, Maxey, Maxie, Maxis, Maxy

Maxim (Russian) a form of Maxime.

Maxime B (French) most excellent.
Maxim, Maxyme

Maximilian (Latin) greatest.
Mac, Mack, Maixim, Maksim, Maksym, Max, Maxamillion, Maxemilian, Maxemilion, Maxi, Maximalian, Maximili, Maximilia, Maximiliano, Maximilianus, Maximilien, Maximillian, Máximo, Maximos, Maxmilian, Maxmillion, Maxon, Maxymilian, Maxymillian, Mayhew, Miksa

Maximiliano (Italian) a form of Maximilian.
Massimiliano, Maximiano, Maximino

Maximillian (Latin) a form of Maximilian.
Maximillan, Maximillano, Maximillien, Maximillion, Maxmillian, Maxximillian, Maxximillion

Máximo (Spanish) a form of Maximilian.
Massimo, Maxi, Maximiano, Maximiliano, Maximino, Máximo

Maximos (Greek) a form of Maximilian.

Maxine G (Latin) greatest.

Maxwell B (English) great spring.
Max, Maxwel, Maxwill, Maxxwell, Maxy

Maxy (English) a familiar form of Max, Maxwell.
Maxi

Mayer (Hebrew) a form of Meir. (Latin) a form of Magnus, Major.
Mahyar, Mayeer, Mayor, Mayur

Mayes (English) field.
Mayo, Mays

Mayhew (English) a form of Matthew.

Maynard (English) powerful; brave. See also Meinhard.
May, Mayne, Maynhard, Maynor, Ménard

Mayo (Irish) yew-tree plain. (English) a form of Mayes. Geography: a county in Ireland.

Mayon (Indian) person of black complexion. Religion: another name for the Indian god Mal.

Mayonga (Luganda) lake sailor.

Mayta (Quechua) where are you?

Maytacuapac (Quechua) oh, Lord, where are you?

Mayua (Quechua) violet, purple.

Mazi (Ibo) sir.
Mazzi

Mazin (Arabic) proper.
Mazen, Mazinn, Mazzin

Mbita (Swahili) born on a cold night.

Mbwana (Swahili) master.

Mc Kenna G (American) a form of Mackenna (see Girls' Names).

Mc Kenzie G (Irish) a form of Mackenzie.

McGeorge (Scottish) son of George.
MacGeorge

Mckade (Scottish) son of Kade.
Mccade

Mckay B (Scottish) son of Kay.
Mackay, MacKay, Mckae, Mckai, McKay

Mckayla G (American) a form of Makayla (see Girls' Names).

Mckell (American) a form of Makell.

Mckenna G (American) a form of Mackenna (see Girls' Names).

McKenzie, Mckenzie G (Irish) forms of Mackenzie.
Mccenzie, Mckennzie, Mckensey, Mckensie, Mckenson, Mckensson, Mckenzi, Mckenzy, Mckinzie

Mckinley B (Irish) a form of Mackinnley.
Mckinely, Mckinnely, Mckinnlee, Mckinnley, McKinnley

Mead B (English) meadow.
Meade, Meed

Meaghan G (Welsh) a form of Megan.

Medardo (Germanic) boldly powerful; he who is worthy of honors.

Medarno (Saxon) he who deserves to be honored, distinguished, awarded.

Medgar (German) a form of Edgar.

Medwin (German) faithful friend.

Megan G (Greek) pearl; great. (Irish) a form of Margaret.

Meghan G (Welsh) a form of Megan.

Meginardo (Teutonic) he who is a strong leader.

Mehetabel (Hebrew) who God benefits.

Mehrdad (Persian) gift of the sun.

Mehtar (Sanskrit) prince.
Mehta

Meinhard (German) strong, firm. See also Maynard.
Meinhardt, Meinke, Meino, Mendar

Meinrad (German) strong counsel.

Meir (Hebrew) one who brightens, shines; enlightener. History: Golda Meir was the prime minister of Israel.
Mayer, Meyer, Muki, Myer

Meka G (Hawaiian) eyes.

Mel BG (English, Irish) a familiar form of Melvin.

Melanie G (Greek) dark skinned.

Melanio (Greek) having black skin.

Melbourne (English) mill stream.
Melborn, Melburn, Melby, Milborn, Milbourn, Milbourne, Milburn, Millburn, Millburne

Melchior (Hebrew) king.
Meilseoir, Melchor, Melker, Melkior

Meldon (English) mill hill.
Melden

Melecio (Greek) careful and attentive.

Melibeo (Greek) he who takes care of the mentally handicapped.

Melissa G (Greek) honey bee.

Meliton, Melitón (Greek) from the island of Malta.

Melivilu (Mapuche) four snakes.

Melquíades (Hebrew) king of God.

Melrone (Irish) servant of Saint Ruadhan.

Melvern (Native American) great chief.

Melville (French) mill town. Literature: Herman Melville was a well-known nineteenth-century American writer.
Milville

Melvin (Irish) armored chief. (English) mill friend; council friend. See also Vinny.
Malvin, Mel, Melvino, Melvon, Melvyn, Melwin, Melwyn, Melwynn

Menachem (Hebrew) comforter.
Menahem, Nachman

Menandro (Greek) he who remains a man.

Menas (Greek) related to the months.

Menassah (Hebrew) cause to forget.
Menashe, Menashi, Menashia, Menashiah, Menashya, Manasseh

Mendel (English) repairman.
Mendeley, Mendell, Mendie, Mendy

Mendo (Spanish) a form of Hermenegildo.

Menelao (Greek) he who goes to the village to fight.

Meng (Chinese) eldest brother.

Mengesha (Ethiopian) kingdom.

Menico (Spanish) a short form of Domenico.

Mensah (Ewe) third son.

Mentor (Greek) teacher.

Menz (German) a short form of Clement.

Mercer (English) storekeeper.
Merce

Mercurio (Latin) he who pays attention to business.

Mered (Hebrew) revolter.

Meredith G (Welsh) guardian from the sea.
Meredyth, Merideth, Meridith, Merry

Merion (Welsh) from Merion, Wales.
Merrion

Merle B (French) a short form of Merlin, Merrill.
Meryl

Merlin (English) falcon. Literature: the magician who served as counselor in King Arthur's court.
Marlon, Merle, Merlen, Merlinn, Merlyn, Merlynn

Merlín (Spanish) a form of Merlin.

Merlino (Spanish) a form of Merlín.

Merrick (English) ruler of the sea.
Merek, Meric, Merick, Merik, Merric, Merrik, Meryk, Meyrick, Myrucj

Merrill (Irish) bright sea. (French) famous.
Meril, Merill, Merle, Merrel, Merrell, Merril, Meryl

Merritt (Latin, Irish) valuable; deserving.
Merit, Meritt, Merrett

Merton (English) sea town.
Murton

Merulo (Latin) he who is fine as a blackbird.

Merv (Irish) a short form of Mervin.

Merville (French) sea village.

Mervin (Irish) a form of Marvin.
Merv, Mervyn, Mervynn, Merwin, Merwinn, Merwyn, Murvin, Murvyn, Myrvyn, Myrvynn, Myrwyn

Meshach (Hebrew) artist. Bible: one of Daniel's three friends who emerged unharmed from the fiery furnace of Babylon.

Mesut (Turkish) happy.

Metikla (Moquelumnan) reaching a hand underwater to catch a fish.

Metrenco (Mapuche) still water, without a current; stagnant.

Metrofanes (Greek) he who resembles his mother.

Mette (Greek, Danish) pearl.
Almeta, Mete

Meulén (Mapuche) whirlwind.

Meurig (Welsh) a form of Maurice.

Meyer (German) farmer.
Mayer, Meier, Myer

Mhina (Swahili) delightful.

Mi (Chinese) overflowing.

Mian (Chinese) continuous.

Miao (Chinese) young plant, seedling.

Micah 🅱 (Hebrew) a form of Michael. Bible: a Hebrew prophet.
Mic, Micaiah, Michiah, Mika, Mikah, Myca, Mycah

Micha (Hebrew) a short form of Michael.
Mica, Micha, Michah

Michael ☘ 🅱 (Hebrew) who is like God? See also Micah, Miguel, Mika, Miles.
Machael, Machas, Mahail, Maichail, Maikal, Makael, Makal, Makel, Makell, Makis, Meikel, Mekal, Mekhail, Mhichael, Micael, Micah, Micahel, Mical, Micha, Michaele, Michaell, Michail, Michak, Michal, Michale, Michalek, Michalel, Michau, Micheal, Micheil, Michel, Michele, Michelet, Michiel, Micho, Michoel, Mick, Mickael, Mickey, Mihail, Mihalje, Mihkel, Mika, Mikael, Mikáele, Mikal, Mike, Mikeal, Mikel, Mikelis, Mikell, Mikhail, Mikkel, Mikko, Miksa, Milko, Miquel, Misael, Misi, Miska, Mitchell, Mychael, Mychajlo, Mychal, Mykal, Mykhas

Michaela 🅖 (Hebrew) who is like God?

Michail (Russian) a form of Michael.
Mihas, Mikail, Mikale, Misha

Michal 🅱 (Polish) a form of Michael.
Michak, Michalek, Michall

Micheal 🅱 (Irish) a form of Michael.

Michel 🅱 (French) a form of Michael.
Michaud, Miche, Michee, Michell, Michelle, Michon

Michelangelo (Italian) a combination of Michael + Angelo. Art: Michelangelo Buonarroti was one of the greatest Renaissance painters.
Michelange, Miguelangelo

Michele 🅖 (Italian) a form of Michael.

Michelle 🅖 (French) a form of Michele.

Michinori (Japanese) he who leads by good example.

Michio (Japanese) man with the strength of three thousand.

Mick (English) a short form of Michael, Mickey.
Mickerson

Mickael 🅱 (English) a form of Michael.
Mickaele, Mickal, Mickale, Mickeal, Mickel, Mickell, Mickelle, Mickle

Mickenzie (Irish) a form of Mackenzie.
Mickenze, Mickenzy, Mikenzie

Mickey (Irish) a familiar form of Michael.
Mick, Micki, Mickie, Micky, Miki, Mique

Micu (Hungarian) a form of Nick.

Midas (Greek) fleeting and admirable business.

Mieko (Japanese) bright.

Miguel ☘ 🅱 (Portuguese, Spanish) a form of Michael.
Migeel, Migel, Miguelly, Migui

Miguelangel (Spanish) a combination of Miguel + Angel.

Mihail (Greek, Bulgarian, Romanian) a form of Michael.
Mihailo, Mihal, Mihalis, Mikail

Mijaíl (Russian) a form of Miguel.

Mika 🅖 (Ponca) raccoon. (Hebrew) a form of Micah. (Russian) a familiar form of Michael.
Miika, Mikah

Mikael **B** (Swedish) a form of Michael.
Mikaeel, Mikaele

Mikáele (Hawaiian) a form of Michael.
Mikele

Mikal (Hebrew) a form of Michael.
Mekal, Mikahl, Mikale

Mikasi (Omaha) coyote.

Mike (Hebrew) a short form of Michael.
Mikey, Myk

Mikeal (Irish) a form of Michael.

Mikel **B** (Basque) a form of Michael.
Mekel, Mikele, Mekell, Mikell, Mikelle

Mikelis (Latvian) a form of Michael.
Mikus, Milkins

Mikhail (Greek, Russian) a form of Michael.
Mekhail, Mihály, Mikhael, Mikhale, Mikhalis, Mikhalka, Mikhall, Mikhel, Mikhial, Mikhos

Miki **G** (Japanese) tree.
Mikio

Mikkel (Norwegian) a form of Michael.
Mikkael, Mikle

Mikko (Finnish) a form of Michael.
Mikk, Mikka, Mikkohl, Mikkol, Miko, Mikol

Mikolaj (Polish) a form of Nicholas.
Mikolai

Mikolas (Greek) a form of Nicholas.
Miklós, Milek

Miksa (Hungarian) a form of Max.
Miks

Milagro (Spanish) miracle.

Milan (Italian) northerner. Geography: a city in northern Italy.
Milaan, Milano, Milen, Millan, Millen, Mylan, Mylen, Mylon, Mylynn

Milap (Native American) giving.

Milborough (English) middle borough.
Milbrough

Milcíades (Greek) he of reddish complexion.

Milek (Polish) a familiar form of Nicholas.

Miles (Greek) millstone. (Latin) soldier. (German) merciful. (English) a short form of Michael.
Milas, Milles, Milo, Milson, Myles

Milford (English) mill by the ford.

Mililani **BG** (Hawaiian) heavenly caress.

Milko (Czech) a form of Michael. (German) a familiar form of Emil.
Milkins

Millán (Latin) belonging to the Emilia family.

Millañir (Mapuche) silver fox.

Millard (Latin) caretaker of the mill.
Mill, Millar, Miller, Millward, Milward, Myller

Miller (English) miller; grain grinder.
Mellar, Millard, Millen

Mills (English) mills.

Milo (German) a form of Miles. A familiar form of Emil.
Millo, Mylo

Milos (Greek, Slavic) pleasant.

Miloslav (Czech) lover of glory.
Milda

Milt (English) a short form of Milton.

Milton (English) mill town.
Milt, Miltie, Milty, Mylton

Mimis (Greek) a familiar form of Demetrius.

Min (Burmese) king.

Mina **G** (Burmese) a form of Min.

Mincho (Spanish) a form of Benjamin.

Minel (Spanish) a form of Manuel.

Mineo, Mineto (Japanese) he who reaches the summit.

Miner (English) miner.

Ming (Chinese) comes from a dynasty.

Ming Yue, Ming-Yue (Chinese) bright moon.

Mingan (Native American) gray wolf.

Mingo (Spanish) a short form of Domingo.

Minh (Vietnamese) bright.
Minhao, Minhduc, Minhkhan, Minhtong, Minhy

Minkah (Akan) just, fair.

Minor (Latin) junior; younger.
Mynor

Minoru (Japanese) fruitful.

Mio (Spanish) mine.

Mique (Spanish) a form of Mickey.
Mequel, Mequelin, Miquel

Miracle ☐ (Latin) wonder, marvel.

Miranda ☐ (Latin) strange; wonderful; admirable.

Mirco (Spanish) he who assures the peace.

Miriam ☐ (Hebrew) bitter; sea of bitterness.

Miron (Polish) peace.

Miroslav (Czech) peace; glory.
Mirek, Miroslaw, Miroslawy

Mirwais (Afghan) noble ruler.

Misael ☐ (Hebrew) a form of Michael.
Mischael, Mishael, Missael

Misha ☐ (Russian) a short form of Michail.
Misa, Mischa, Mishael, Mishal, Mishe, Mishenka, Mishka

Miska (Hungarian) a form of Michael.
Misi, Misik, Misko, Miso

Mister (English) mister.
Mistur

Misty ☐ (English) shrouded by mist.

Misu (Moquelumnan) rippling water.

Mitch (English) a short form of Mitchell.

Mitchel (English) a form of Mitchell.
Mitchael, Mitchal, Mitcheal, Mitchele, Mitchil, Mytchel

Mitchell ☐ (English) a form of Michael.
Mitch, Mitchall, Mitchel, Mitchelle, Mitchem, Mytch, Mytchell

Mitsos (Greek) a familiar form of Demetrius.

Mitsu (Japanese) light.

Mitsuaki (Japanese) he who shines brightly.

Mitsuhiro (Japanese) abundant shining light.

Mitsuho (Japanese) fullness; the blade of a plant.

Mitsunobu (Japanese) trustworthy light giver.

Mitsuo (Japanese) beautiful third son.

Mitsuru (Japanese) full; satisfactory.

Modesto (Latin) modest.

Moe (English) a short form of Moses.
Mo

Moeta (Japanese) sprout; luxury; large.

Mogens (Dutch) powerful.

Mohamad (Arabic) a form of Muhammad.
Mohamid

Mohamed ☐ (Arabic) a form of Muhammad.
Mohamd, Mohameed

Mohamet (Arabic) a form of Muhammad.
Mahomet, Mehemet, Mehmet

Mohammad (Arabic) a form of Muhammad.
Mahammad, Mohammadi, Mohammd, Mohammid, Mohanad, Mohmad

Mohammed (Arabic) a form of Muhammad.
Mahammed, Mahomet, Mohammad, Mohaned, Mouhamed, Muhammad

Mohamud (Arabic) a form of Muhammad.
Mohammud, Mohamoud

Mohan (Hindi) delightful.

Moises (Portuguese, Spanish) a form of Moses.
Moices, Moise, Moisés, Moisey, Moisis

Moishe (Yiddish) a form of Moses.
Moshe

Mojag (Native American) crying baby.

Molimo (Moquelumnan) bear going under shady trees.

Molly ☐ (Irish) a familiar form of Mary.

Momuso (Moquelumnan) yellow jackets crowded in their nests for the winter.

Mona ☐ (Moquelumnan) gathering jimsonweed seed.

Monahan (Irish) monk.
Monaghan, Monoghan

Mongo (Yoruba) famous.

Monica ☐ (Greek) solitary. (Latin) advisor.

Monitor (Latin) he who counsels.

Monroe (Irish) Geography: the mouth of the Roe River.
Monro, Munro, Munroe

Montague (French) pointed mountain.
Montagne, Montagu, Monte

Montana ☐ (Spanish) mountain. Geography: a U.S. state.
Montaine, Montanna

Montaro (Japanese) big boy.
Montario, Monterio, Montero

Monte (Spanish) a short form of Montgomery.
Montae, Montaé, Montay, Montea, Montee, Monti, Montoya, Monty

Montego (Spanish) mountainous.

Montel (American) a form of Montreal.
Montele, Montell, Montelle

Montenegro (Spanish) black mountain.

Montes (Spanish) mountains.

Montez (Spanish) dweller in the mountains.
Monteiz, Monteze, Montezz, Montisze

Montgomery (English) rich man's mountain.
Monte, Montgomerie, Monty

Montre (French) show.
Montra, Montrae, Montray, Montraz, Montres, Montrey, Montrez, Montreze

Montreal (French) royal mountain. Geography: a city in Quebec.
Montel, Monterial, Monterrell, Montrail, Montrale, Montrall, Montreall, Montrell, Montrial

Montrell **B** (French) a form of Montreal.
Montral, Montrel, Montrele, Montrelle

Montsho (Tswana) black.

Monty (English) a familiar form of Montgomery.

Moore (French) dark; moor; marshland.
Moor, Mooro, More

Mordecai (Hebrew) martial, warlike. Mythology: Marduk was the Babylonian god of war. Bible: wise counselor to Queen Esther.
Mord, Mordachai, Mordechai, Mordie, Mordy, Mort

Mordred (Latin) painful. Literature: the bastard son of King Arthur.
Modred

Morel (French) an edible mushroom.
Morrel

Moreland (English) moor; marshland.
Moorland, Morland

Morell (French) dark; from Morocco.
Moor, Moore, Morelle, Morelli, Morill, Morrell, Morrill, Murrel, Murrell

Morey (Greek) a familiar form of Moris. (Latin) a form of Morrie.
Morrey, Morry

Morfeo (Greek) he who makes you see beautiful figures.

Morgan **G** (Scottish) sea warrior.
Morgen, Morghan, Morgin, Morgon, Morgun, Morgunn, Morgwn, Morgyn, Morrgan

Moriah **G** (Hebrew) God is my teacher. (French) dark skinned.

Morio (Japanese) forest.

Moris (Greek) son of the dark one. (English) a form of Morris.
Morey, Morisz, Moriz

Moritz (German) a form of Maurice, Morris.
Morisz

Morley (English) meadow by the moor.
Moorley, Moorly, Morlee, Morleigh, Morlon, Morly, Morlyn, Morrley

Morrie (Latin) a familiar form of Maurice, Morse.
Maury, Morey, Mori, Morie, Morry, Mory, Morye

Morris (Latin) dark skinned; moor; marshland. (English) a form of Maurice.
Moris, Moriss, Moritz, Morrese, Morrise, Morriss, Morry, Moss

Morse (English) son of Maurice.
Morresse, Morrie, Morrison, Morrisson

Mort (French, English) a short form of Morten, Mortimer, Morton.
Morte, Mortey, Mortie, Mortty, Morty

Morten (Norwegian) a form of Martin.
Mort

Mortimer (French) still water.
Mort, Mortymer

Morton (English) town near the moor.
Mort

Morven (Scottish) mariner.
Morvien, Morvin

Mose (Hebrew) a short form of Moses.

Moses **B** (Hebrew) drawn out of the water. (Egyptian) son, child. Bible: the Hebrew lawgiver who brought the Ten Commandments down from Mount Sinai.
Moe, Moise, Moïse, Moisei, Moises, Moishe, Mose, Mosese, Moshe, Mosiah, Mosie, Moss, Mosses, Mosya, Mosze, Moszek, Mousa, Moyses, Moze

Moshe (Hebrew, Polish) a form of Moses.
Mosheh

Mosi **B** (Swahili) first-born.

Moss (Irish) a short form of Maurice, Morris. (English) a short form of Moses.

Moswen **BG** (African) light in color.

Motega (Native American) new arrow.

Mouhamed (Arabic) a form of Muhammad.
Mouhamad, Mouhamadou, Mouhammed,
Mouhamoin

Mousa (Arabic) a form of Moses.
Moussa

Moze (Lithuanian) a form of Moses.
Mozes, Mózes

Mpasa (Nguni) mat.

Mposi (Nyakyusa) blacksmith.

Mpoza (Luganda) tax collector.

Msrah (Akan) sixth-born.

Mtima (Nguni) heart.

Mu (Chinese) wood.

Muata (Moquelumnan) yellow jackets in
their nest.

Mucio (Latin) he who endures silence.

Mugamba (Runyoro) talks too much.

Mugisa (Rutooro) lucky.
Mugisha, Mukisa

Muhammad (Arabic) praised. History: the
founder of the Islamic religion. See also
Ahmad, Hamid, Yasin.
Mahmoud, Mahmúd, Mohamed, Mohamet,
Mohamud, Mohammed, Mouhamed,
Muhamad, Muhamed, Muhamet,
Muhammadali, Muhammed

Muhannad (Arabic) sword.
Muhanad

Muhsin (Arabic) beneficent; charitable.

Muhtadi (Arabic) rightly guided.

Muir (Scottish) moor; marshland.

Mujahid (Arabic) fighter in the way of Allah.

Mukasa (Luganda) God's chief
administrator.

Mukhtar (Arabic) chosen.
Mukhtaar

Mukul (Sanskrit) bud, blossom; soul.

Mullu (Quechua) coral, jewel.

Mulogo (Musoga) wizard.

Mundan (Rhodesian) garden.

Mundo (Spanish) a short form of Edmundo.

Mundy (Irish) from Reamonn.

Mungo (Scottish) amiable.

Mun-Hee (Korean) literate; shiny.

Munir (Arabic) brilliant; shining.

Munny (Cambodian) wise.

Muraco (Native American) white moon.

Murali (Hindi) flute. Religion: the
instrument the Hindu god Krishna is usually
depicted as playing.

Murat (Turkish) wish come true.

Murdock (Scottish) wealthy sailor.
Murdo, Murdoch, Murtagh

Murphy (Irish) sea warrior.
Murfey, Murfy

Murray (Scottish) sailor.
Macmurray, Moray, Murrey, Murry

Murtagh (Irish) a form of Murdock.
Murtaugh

Musa (Swahili) child.

Musád (Arabic) untied camel.

Musoke (Rukonjo) born while a rainbow
was in the sky.

Mustafa (Arabic) chosen; royal.
Mostafa, Mostaffa, Moustafa, Mustafaa,
Mustafah, Mustafe, Mustaffa, Mustafo,
Mustapha, Mustoffa, Mustofo

Mustafá (Turkish) a form of Mustafa.

Mustapha (Arabic) a form of Mustafa.
Mostapha, Moustapha

Muti (Arabic) obedient.

Mwaka (Luganda) born on New Year's Eve.

Mwamba (Nyakyusa) strong.

Mwanje (Luganda) leopard.

Mwinyi (Swahili) king.

Mwita (Swahili) summoner.

Mya ☖ (Burmese) emerald. (Italian) a form
of Mia (see Girls' Names).

Mychajlo (Latvian) a form of Michael.
Mykhaltso, Mykhas

Mychal (American) a form of Michael.
Mychall, Mychalo, Mycheal

Myer (English) a form of Meir.
Myers, Myur

Mykal, Mykel (American) forms of Michael.
Mykael, Mikele, Mykell

Myles **B** (Latin) soldier. (German) a form of Miles.
Myels, Mylez, Mylles, Mylz

Mynor (Latin) a form of Minor.

Myo (Burmese) city.

Myriam **G** (American) a form of Miriam.

Myron (Greek) fragrant ointment.
Mehran, Mehrayan, My, Myran, Myrone, Ron

Myung-Dae (Korean) right; great.

Mzuzi (Swahili) inventive.

N **B** (American) an initial used as a first name.

Na (Chinese) graceful.

Naaman (Hebrew) pleasant.

Nabiha (Arabic) intelligent.

Nabil (Arabic) noble.
Nabeel, Nabiel

Nabor (Hebrew) prophet's light.

Nabucodonosor (Chaldean) God protects my reign.

Nachman (Hebrew) a short form of Menachem.
Nachum, Nahum

Nada (Arabic) generous.

Nadav (Hebrew) generous; noble.
Nadiv

Nadidah (Arabic) equal to anyone else.

Nadim (Arabic) friend.
Nadeem

Nadine **G** (French, Slavic) a form of Nadia (see Girls' Names).

Nadir (Afghan, Arabic) dear, rare.
Nader

Nadisu (Hindi) beautiful river.

Naeem (Arabic) benevolent.
Naem, Naim, Naiym, Nieem

Naftali (Hebrew) wreath.
Naftalie

Nagid (Hebrew) ruler; prince.

Nahele (Hawaiian) forest.

Nahma (Native American) sturgeon.

Nahuel (Araucanian) tiger.

Nai (Chinese) endurance.

Naiara (Spanish) reference to the Virgin Mary.

Nailah (Arabic) successful.

Nairn (Scottish) river with alder trees.
Nairne

Najee (Arabic) a form of Naji.
Najae, Najée, Najei, Najiee

Naji (Arabic) safe.
Najee, Najih

Najíb (Arabic) born to nobility.
Najib, Nejeeb

Najji (Muganda) second child.

Nakia **G** (Arabic) pure.
Nakai, Nakee, Nakeia, Naki, Nakiah, Nakii

Nakos (Arapaho) sage, wise.

Naldo (Spanish) a familiar form of Reginald.

Nalren (Dene) thawed out.

Nam (Vietnamese) scrape off.

Namaka (Hawaiian) eyes.

Namid (Ojibwa) star dancer.

Namir (Hebrew) leopard.
Namer

Namuncura (Mapuche) foot of stone, strong foot.

Nan (Chinese) man.

Ñancuvilu (Mapuche) snake that is the color of lead, off-white.

Nancy **G** (English) gracious. A familiar form of Nan (see Girls' Names).

Nandin (Hindi) Religion: a servant of the Hindu god Shiva.
Nandan

Nando (German) a familiar form of Ferdinand.
Nandor

Nangila (Abaluhya) born while parents traveled.

Nangwaya (Mwera) don't mess with me.

Nansen (Swedish) son of Nancy.

Nantai (Navajo) chief.

Nantan (Apache) spokesman.

Naoki (Japanese) repair; heal; tree.

Naoko (Japanese) straight, honest.

Naolin (Spanish) sun god of the Mexican people.

Naoya (Japanese) he who heals.

Napayshni (Lakota) he does not flee; courageous.

Napier (Spanish) new city.
Neper

Napoleon (Greek) lion of the woodland. (Italian) from Naples, Italy. History: Napoleon Bonaparte was a famous nineteenth-century French emperor.
Leon, Nap, Napolean, Napoléon, Napoleone, Nappie, Nappy

Napoleón (Greek) a form of Napoleon.

Naquan (American) a combination of the prefix Na + Quan.
Naqawn, Naquain, Naquen, Naquon

Narain (Hindi) protector. Religion: another name for the Hindu god Vishnu.
Narayan

Narciso (French) a form of Narcisse.

Narcisse (French) a form of Narcissus.
Narcis, Narciso, Narkis, Narkissos

Narcissus (Greek) daffodil. Mythology: the youth who fell in love with his own reflection.
Narcisse

Nard (Persian) chess player.

Nardo (German) strong, hardy. (Spanish) a short form of Bernardo.

Narno (Latin) he who was born in the Italian city of Narnia.

Narses (Persian) what the two martyrs brought from Persia.

Narve (Dutch) healthy, strong.

Nashashuk (Fox, Sauk) loud thunder.

Nashoba (Choctaw) wolf.

Nasim (Persian) breeze; fresh air.
Naseem, Nassim

Nasser (Arabic) victorious.
Naseer, Naser, Nasier, Nasir, Nasr, Nassir, Nassor

Nat (English) a short form of Nathan, Nathaniel.
Natt, Natty

Natal (Spanish) a form of Noël.
Natale, Natalie, Natalino, Natalio, Nataly

Natalie ☷ (Spanish) a form of Natal.

Natan (Hebrew, Hungarian, Polish, Russian, Spanish) God has given.
Naten

Natanael (Hebrew) a form of Nathaniel.
Natanel, Nataniel

Natasha ☷ (Russian) a form of Natalie.

Nate (Hebrew) a short form of Nathan, Nathaniel.

Natesh (Hindi) destroyer. Religion: another name for the Hindu god Shiva.

Nathan ☙ ℬ (Hebrew) a short form of Nathaniel. Bible: a prophet during the reigns of David and Solomon.
Naethan, Nat, Nate, Nathann, Nathean, Nathen, Nathian, Nathin, Nathon, Nathyn, Natthan, Naythan, Nethan

Nathanael (Hebrew) gift of God. Bible: one of the Twelve Apostles. Also known as Bartholomew.
Nathanae, Nathanal, Nathaneal, Nathaneil, Nathanel, Nathaneol

Nathanial (Hebrew) a form of Nathaniel.
Nathanyal, Nathanual

Nathanie (Hebrew) a familiar form of Nathaniel.
Nathania, Nathanni

Nathaniel ☙ ℬ (Hebrew) gift of God.
Nat, Natanael, Nate, Nathan, Nathanael, Nathanial, Nathanie, Nathanielle, Nathanil, Nathanile, Nathanuel, Nathanyel, Nathanyl, Natheal, Nathel, Nathinel, Nethaniel, Thaniel

Nathen (Hebrew) a form of Nathan.

Natividad (Spanish) nativity.

Natori ☷ (Arabic) a form of Natara (see Girls' Names).

Natsu (Japanese) born in summer.

Natsuhiko (Japanese) summer; boy.

Natsuki (Japanese) summer; tree.

Natsuo (Japanese) summer; birth.

Ñaupac (Quechua) first, principal, first-born; before everyone.

Ñaupari (Quechua) ahead, first.

Ñauque, Ñauqui (Quechua) before everyone.

Nav (Gypsy) name.

Naval (Latin) god of the sailing vessels.

Navarro (Spanish) plains.
Navarre

Navdeep 𝐁𝐆 (Sikh) new light.
Navdip

Navin (Hindi) new, novel.
Naveen, Naven

Nawat (Native American) left-handed.

Nawkaw (Winnebago) wood.

Nayati (Native American) wrestler.

Nayland (English) island dweller.

Nazareno (Hebrew) he who has separated himself from the rest of the people because he feels constricted, because he has decided to be solitary.

Nazareth (Hebrew) born in Nazareth, Israel.
Nazaire, Nazaret, Nazarie, Nazario, Nazerene, Nazerine

Nazih (Arabic) pure, chaste.
Nazeeh, Nazeem, Nazeer, Nazieh, Nazim, Nazir, Nazz

Ndale (Nguni) trick.

Neal (Irish) a form of Neil.
Neale, Neall, Nealle, Nealon, Nealy

Neandro (Greek) young and manly.

Nebrido (Greek) graceful like the fawn.

Neci 𝐁𝐆 (Latin) a familiar form of Ignatius.

Nectario (Greek) he who sweetens life with nectar.

Nectarios (Greek) saint. Religion: a saint in the Greek Orthodox Church.

Neculman (Mapuche) swift condor; swift and rapid flight.

Neculqueo (Mapuche) rapid speaker, good with words.

Ned (English) a familiar form of Edward, Edwin.
Neddie, Neddym, Nedrick

Nehemiah (Hebrew) compassion of Jehovah. Bible: a Jewish leader.
Nahemiah, Nechemya, Nehemias, Nehemie, Nehemyah, Nehimiah, Nehmia, Nehmiah, Nemo, Neyamia

Nehru (Hindi) canal.

Neil (Irish) champion.
Neal, Neel, Neihl, Neile, Neill, Neille, Nels, Niall, Niele, Niels, Nigel, Nil, Niles, Nilo, Nils, Nyle

Neka (Native American) wild goose.

Nelek (Polish) a form of Cornelius.

Nelius (Latin) a short form of Cornelius.

Nellie 𝐆 (English) a familiar form of Cornelius, Cornell, Nelson.
Nell, Nelly

Nelo (Spanish) a form of Daniel.
Nello, Nilo

Nels (Scandinavian) a form of Neil, Nelson.
Nelse, Nelson, Nils

Nelson 𝐁 (English) son of Neil.
Nealson, Neilsen, Neilson, Nellie, Nels, Nelsen, Nilson, Nilsson

Nemesio (Spanish) just.
Nemi

Nemo (Greek) glen, glade. (Hebrew) a short form of Nehemiah.

Nen (Egyptian) ancient waters.

Neng (Chinese) capability.

Neofito (Greek) he who began recently.

Neon (Greek) he who is strong.

Neopolo (Spanish) a form of Napoleón.

Nepomuceno (Slavic) he who gives his help.

Neptune (Latin) sea ruler. Mythology: the Roman god of the sea.

Neptuno (Greek) god of the sea.

Nereo (Greek) he who is the captain at sea.

Nerio (Greek) sea traveler.

Nero (Latin, Spanish) stern. History: a cruel Roman emperor.
Neron, Nerone, Nerron

Nerón (Latin) very strong and intrepid.

Nesbit (English) nose-shaped bend in a river.
Naisbit, Naisbitt, Nesbitt, Nisbet, Nisbett

Nesto (Spanish) serious.

Nestor 𝐁 (Greek) traveler; wise.
Nester

Néstor (Greek) a form of Nestor.

Nestorio (Greek) a form of Nestor.

Nethaniel (Hebrew) a form of Nathaniel.
Netanel, Netania, Netaniah, Netaniel, Netanya, Nethanel, Nethanial, Nethaniel, Nethanyal, Nethanyel

Neto (Spanish) a short form of Ernesto.

Nevada 🄶 (Spanish) covered in snow.
Geography: a U.S. state.
Navada, Nevade

Nevan (Irish) holy.
Nevean

Neville (French) new town.
Nev, Nevil, Nevile, Nevill, Nevyle

Nevin (Irish) worshiper of the saint.
(English) middle; herb.
Nefen, Nev, Nevan, Neven, Nevins, Nevyn, Niven

Newbold (English) new tree.

Newell (English) new hall.
Newall, Newel, Newyle

Newland (English) new land.
Newlan

Newlin (Welsh) new lake.
Newlyn

Newman (English) newcomer.
Neiman, Neimann, Neimon, Neuman, Numan, Numen

Newton (English) new town.
Newt

Ngai (Vietnamese) herb.

Nghia (Vietnamese) forever.

Ngoc 🄶 (Vietnamese) jade.

Ngozi (Ibo) blessing.

Ngu (Vietnamese) sleep.

Nguyen (Vietnamese) a form of Ngu.

Nhat (Vietnamese) long life; number one.

Nhean (Cambodian) self-knowledge.

Nhung (Vietnamese) velvet.

Nia 🄶 (Irish) a familiar form of Neila (see Girls' Names).

Niall (Irish) a form of Neil. History: Niall of the Nine Hostages was a famous Irish king.
Nial, Nialle

Nian (Chinese) year, age.

Nibal (Arabic) arrows.
Nibel

Nibaw (Native American) standing tall.

Nicabar (Gypsy) stealthy.

Nicandro (Greek) he who is victorious amongst men.

Nicasio, Niceto, Nicón (Greek) victorious one.

Níceas (Greek) he of the great victory.

Nicéforo (Greek) he who brings victory.

Nicho (Spanish) a form of Dennis.

Nicholas ❦ (Greek) victorious people.
Religion: Nicholas of Myra is a patron saint of children. See also Caelan, Claus, Cola, Colar, Cole, Colin, Colson, Klaus, Lasse, Mikolaj, Mikolas, Milek.
Niccolas, Nichalas, Nichelas, Nichele, Nichlas, Nichlos, Nichola, Nicholaas, Nicholaes, Nicholase, Nicholaus, Nichole, Nicholias, Nicholl, Nichollas, Nicholos,
Nichols, Nicholus, Nick, Nickalus, Nicklaus, Nickolas, Nicky, Niclas, Niclasse, Nico, Nicola, Nicolai, Nicolas, Nicoles, Nicolis, Nicoll, Nicolo, Nikhil, Niki, Nikili, Nikita, Nikko, Niklas, Niko, Nikolai, Nikolas, Nikolaus, Nikolos, Nils, Nioclás, Niocol, Nycholas

Nicholaus (Greek) a form of Nicholas.
Nichalaus, Nichalous, Nichaolas, Nichlaus, Nichloas, Nichlous, Nicholaos, Nicholous

Nichols, Nicholson (English) son of Nicholas.
Nicholes, Nicholis, Nicolls, Nickelson, Nickoles

Nick (English) a short form of Dominic, Nicholas. See also Micu.
Nic, Nik

Nickalus (Greek) a form of Nicholas.
Nickalas, Nickalis, Nickalos, Nickelas, Nickelus

Nicklaus, Nicklas (Greek) forms of Nicholas.
Nickalaus, Nickalous, Nickelous, Nicklauss, Nicklos, Nicklous, Nicklus, Nickolau, Nickolaus, Nicolaus, Niklaus, Nikolaus

Nickolas 🄱 (Greek) a form of Nicholas.
Nickolaos, Nickolis, Nickolos, Nickolus, Nickolys, Nickoulas

Nicky (Greek) a familiar form of Nicholas.
Nickey, Nicki, Nickie, Niki, Nikki

Nico 🄱 (Greek) a short form of Nicholas.
Nicco

Nicodemus (Greek) conqueror of the people.
Nicodem, Nicodemius, Nikodem, Nikodema, Nikodemious, Nikodim

Nicola G (Italian) a form of Nicholas. See also Cola.
Nicolá, Nikolah

Nicolai (Norwegian, Russian) a form of Nicholas.
Nicholai, Nickolai, Nicolaj, Nicolau, Nicolay, Nicoly, Nikalai

Nicolas B (Italian) a form of Nicholas.
Nico, Nicolaas, Nicolás, Nicolaus, Nicoles, Nicolis, Nicolus

Nicole G (French) a form of Nicholas.

Nicolette G (French) a form of Nicole.

Nicolo (Italian) a form of Nicholas.
Niccolo, Niccolò, Nicol, Nicolao, Nicollo

Nicomedes (Greek) he who prepares the victories.

Nicostrato (Greek) general who leads to victory.

Ñielol (Mapuche) eye of the subterranean cavity, eye of the cave.

Niels (Danish) a form of Neil.
Niel, Nielsen, Nielson, Niles, Nils

Nien (Vietnamese) year.

Nigan (Native American) ahead.
Nigen

Nigel B (Latin) dark night.
Niegel, Nigal, Nigale, Nigele, Nigell, Nigiel, Nigil, Nigle, Nijel, Nye, Nygel, Nyigel, Nyjil

Nika (Yoruba) ferocious.

Nike BG (Greek) victorious.
Nikka

Niki G (Hungarian) a familiar form of Nicholas.
Nikia, Nikiah, Nikki, Nikkie, Nykei, Nykey

Nikita G (Russian) a form of Nicholas.
Nakita, Nakitas, Nikula

Nikiti (Native American) round and smooth like an abalone shell.

Nikki G (Greek) a form of Nicky. (Hungarian) a form of Niki.

Nikko, Niko B (Hungarian) forms of Nicholas.
Nikoe, Nyko

Niklas (Latvian, Swedish) a form of Nicholas.
Niklaas, Niklaus

Nikola B (Greek) a short form of Nicholas.
Nikolao, Nikolay, Nykola

Nikolai (Estonian, Russian) a form of Nicholas.
Kolya, Nikolais, Nikolaj, Nikolajs, Nikolay, Nikoli, Nikolia, Nikula, Nikulas

Nikolas (Greek) a form of Nicholas.
Nicanor, Nikalas, Nikalis, Nikalus, Nikholas, Nikolaas, Nikolaos, Nikolis, Nikolos, Nikos, Nilos, Nykolas, Nykolus

Nikolaus (Greek) a form of Nicholas.
Nikalous, Nikolaos

Nikolos (Greek) a form of Nicholas. See also Kolya.
Niklos, Nikolaos, Nikolò, Nikolous, Nikolus, Nikos, Nilos

Nil (Russian) a form of Neil.
Nilya

Nila G (Hindi) blue.

Niles (English) son of Neil.
Nilesh, Nyles

Nilo (Finnish) a form of Neil.

Nils (Swedish) a short form of Nicholas.

Nimrod (Hebrew) rebel. Bible: a great-grandson of Noah.

Nina G (Hebrew) a familiar form of Hanna. (Native American) mighty.

Ninacolla (Quechua) flame of fire.

Ninacuyuchi (Quechua) he who moves or stokes the fire; restless and lively like fire.

Ninan (Quechua) fire; restless and lively like fire.

Ninauari (Quechua) llama-like animal of fire; he who is uncontrollable like the vicuna.

Ninauíca (Quechua) sacred fire.

Ning (Chinese) peace, tranquility; rest.

Nino (Chaldean) possessor of palaces.

Niño (Spanish) young child.

Niran (Tai) eternal.

Nishan (Armenian) cross, sign, mark.
Nishon

Nissan (Hebrew) sign, omen; miracle.
Nisan, Nissim, Nissin, Nisson

Nitis (Native American) friend.
Netis

Nixon (English) son of Nick.
Nixan, Nixson

Nizam (Arabic) leader.

Nkunda (Runyankore) loves those who hate him.

N'namdi (Ibo) his father's name lives on.

Noach (Hebrew) a form of Noah.

Noah ☀ 🅱 (Hebrew) peaceful, restful. Bible: the patriarch who built the ark to survive the Flood.
Noach, Noak, Noe, Noé, Noi

Noam (Hebrew) sweet; friend.

Noble (Latin) born to nobility.
Nobe, Nobie, Noby

Nodin (Native American) wind.
Knoton, Noton

Noe 🅱 (Czech, French) a form of Noah.

Noé (Hebrew, Spanish) quiet, peaceful. See also Noah.

Noel 🅱 (French) a form of Noël.

Noël (French) day of Christ's birth. See also Natal.
Noel, Noél, Noell, Nole, Noli, Nowel, Nowell

Noelino (Spanish) a form of Natal.

Nohea (Hawaiian) handsome.
Noha, Nohe

Nokonyu (Native American) katydid's nose.
Noko, Nokoni

Nolan 🅱 (Irish) famous; noble.
Noland, Nolande, Nolane, Nolen, Nolin, Nollan, Nolyn

Nolasco (Hebrew) he who departs and forgets about promises.

Nolberto (Teutonic) a form of Norberto.

Nollie 🅱 (Latin, Scandinavian) a familiar form of Oliver.
Noll, Nolly

Nong (Chinese) farming.

Nora 🅶 (Greek) light.

Norbert (Scandinavian) brilliant hero.
Bert, Norberto, Norbie, Norby

Norberto (Spanish) a form of Norbert.

Nori (Japanese) belief.

Noriaki (Japanese) bright ruler.

Norio (Japanese) he who sets a good example as a husband.

Noriyuki (Japanese) he who governs with good fortune.

Norman 🅱 (French) Norseman. History: a name for the Scandinavians who settled in northern France in the tenth century, and who later conquered England in 1066.
Norm, Normand, Normen, Normie, Normy

Normando (Spanish) man from the north.

Norris (French) northerner. (English) Norman's horse.
Norice, Norie, Noris, Norreys, Norrie, Norry, Norrys

Northcliff (English) northern cliff.
Northcliffe, Northclyff, Northclyffe

Northrop (English) north farm.
North, Northup

Norton (English) northern town.

Norville (French, English) northern town.
Norval, Norvel, Norvell, Norvil, Norvill, Norvylle

Norvin (English) northern friend.
Norvyn, Norwin, Norwinn, Norwyn, Norwynn

Norward (English) protector of the north.
Norwerd

Norwood (English) northern woods.

Nostriano (Latin) he who is from our homeland.

Notaku (Moquelumnan) growing bear.

Notelmo (Teutonic) he who protects himself in combat with the helmet.

Nowles (English) a short form of Knowles.

Nsoah (Akan) seventh-born.

Numa (Arabic) pleasant.

Numair (Arabic) panther.

Nuncio (Italian) messenger.
Nunzi, Nunzio

Nuri (Hebrew, Arabic) my fire.
Nery, Noori, Nur, Nuris, Nurism, Nury

Nuriel (Hebrew, Arabic) fire of the Lord.
Nuria, Nuriah, Nuriya

Nuru 🅱🅶 (Swahili) born in daylight.

Nusair (Arabic) bird of prey.

Nwa (Nigerian) son.

Nwake (Nigerian) born on market day.

Nye (English) a familiar form of Aneurin, Nigel.

Nyle (English) island. (Irish) a form of Neil.
Nyal, Nyll

Oakes (English) oak trees.
Oak, Oakie, Oaks, Ochs

Oakley (English) oak-tree field.
Oak, Oakes, Oakie, Oaklee, Oakleigh, Oakly, Oaks

Oalo (Spanish) a form of Paul.

Oba **BG** (Yoruba) king.

Obadele (Yoruba) king arrives at the house.

Obadiah (Hebrew) servant of God.
Obadias, Obed, Obediah, Obie, Ovadiach, Ovadiah, Ovadya

Obdulio (Latin) he who calms in sorrowful moments.

Obed (English) a short form of Obadiah.

Oberon (German) noble; bearlike. Literature: the king of the fairies in the Shakespearean play *A Midsummer Night's Dream.* See also Auberon, Aubrey.
Oberen, Oberron, Oeberon

Obert (German) wealthy; bright.

Oberto (Germanic) a form of Adalberto.

Obie (English) a familiar form of Obadiah.
Obbie, Obe, Obey, Obi, Oby

Ocan (Luo) hard times.

Octavia **G** (Latin) a form of Octavio.

Octavio **B** (Latin) eighth. See also Tavey, Tavian.
Octave, Octavia, Octavian, Octaviano, Octavien, Octavious, Octavius, Octavo, Octavous, Octavus, Ottavio

Octavious, Octavius (Latin) forms of Octavio.
Octavaius, Octaveous, Octaveus, Octavias, Octaviaus, Octavis, Octavous, Octavus

Odakota (Lakota) friendly.
Oda

Odd (Norwegian) point.
Oddvar

Ode (Benin) born along the road. (Irish, English) a short form of Odell.
Odey, Odie, Ody

Odeberto (Teutonic) he who shines because of his possessions.

Oded (Hebrew) encouraging.

Odell (Greek) ode, melody. (Irish) otter. (English) forested hill.
Dell, Odall, Ode

Odilón (Teutonic) owner of a bountiful inheritance.

Odin (Scandinavian) ruler. Mythology: the Norse god of wisdom and war.
Oden, Odín

Odion (Benin) first of twins.

Odo (Norwegian) a form of Otto.
Audo

Odoacro (German) he who watches over his inheritance.

Odolf (German) prosperous wolf.
Odolff

Odom (Ghanaian) oak tree.

Odon (Hungarian) wealthy protector.
Odi

Odón (Latin) a form of Odon.

Odran (Irish) pale green.
Odhrán, Oran, Oren, Orin, Orran, Orren, Orrin

Odysseus (Greek) wrathful. Literature: the hero of Homer's epic poem *Odyssey.*

Ofer (Hebrew) young deer.

Ofir (Hebrew) ferocious.

Og (Aramaic) king. Bible: the king of Basham.

Ogaleesha (Lakota) red shirt.

Ogano (Japanese) wise.

Ogbay (Ethiopian) don't take him from me.

Ogbonna (Ibo) image of his father.
Ogbonnia

Ogden (English) oak valley. Literature: Ogden Nash was a twentieth-century American writer of light verse.
Ogdan, Ogdon

Ogima (Chippewa) chief.

Ogo, Ogu (Chamorro) forms of Hochoc.

Ogun (Nigerian) Mythology: the god of war.
Ogunkeye, Ogunsanwo, Ogunsheye

Ohanko (Native American) restless.

Ohannes (Turkish) a form of John.

Ohanzee (Lakota) comforting shadow.

Ohin (African) chief.
Ohan

Ohitekah (Lakota) brave.

Ohln (Japanese) wanted child.

Oistin (Irish) a form of Austin.
Osten, Ostyn, Ostynn

OJ (American) a combination of the initials
O. + J.
O.J., Ojay

Ojo (Yoruba) difficult delivery.

Okapi (Swahili) an African animal related to
the giraffe but having a short neck.

Oke (Hawaiian) a form of Oscar.

Okechuku (Ibo) God's gift.

Okeke (Ibo) born on market day.
Okorie

Okie (American) from Oklahoma.
Okee, Okey

Oko (Ghanaian) older twin. (Yoruba) god of
war.

Okon (Japanese) from the darkness.

Okorie (Ibo) a form of Okeke.

Okpara (Ibo) first son.

Okuth (Luo) born in a rain shower.

Ola 🄶 (Yoruba) wealthy, rich.

Olaf (Scandinavian) ancestor. History: a
patron saint and king of Norway.
Olaff, Olafur, Olav, Ole, Olef, Olof, Oluf

Olajuwon (Yoruba) wealth and honor are
God's gifts.
*Olajawon, Olajawun, Olajowuan, Olajuan,
Olajuanne, Olajuawon, Olajuwa, Olajuwan,
Olaujawon, Oljuwoun*

Olamina (Yoruba) this is my wealth.

Olatunji (Yoruba) honor reawakens.

Olav (Scandinavian) a form of Olaf.
*Ola, Olave, Olavus, Ole, Olen, Olin, Olle, Olov,
Olyn*

Ole (Scandinavian) a familiar form of Olaf,
Olav.
Olay, Oleh, Olle

Oleg (Latvian, Russian) holy.
Olezka

Olegario (Germanic) he who dominates with
his strength and his lance.

Oleksandr (Russian) a form of Alexander.
Olek, Olesandr, Olesko

Olés (Polish) a familiar form of Alexander.

Olimpo (Greek) party; sky; regarding Mount
Olympus or the Olympus sanctuary.

Olin (English) holly.
Olen, Olney, Olyn

Olindo (Italian) from Olinthos, Greece.

Oliver 🄱 (Latin) olive tree. (Scandinavian)
kind; affectionate.
*Nollie, Oilibhéar, Oliverio, Oliverios, Olivero,
Olivier, Oliviero, Oliwa, Ollie, Olliver, Ollivor,
Olvan*

Olivia 🄶 (Latin) a form of Olive (see Girls'
Names).

Olivier 🄱 (French) a form of Oliver.

Oliwa (Hawaiian) a form of Oliver.

Ollanta (Aymara) warrior who sees
everything from his watchtower.

Ollantay (Quechua) lord Ollanta.

Ollie 🄱🄶 (English) a familiar form of Oliver.
Olie, Olle, Olley, Olly

Olo (Spanish) a short form of Orlando,
Rolando.

Olubayo (Yoruba) highest joy.

Olufemi (Yoruba) wealth and honor favors
me.

Olujimi (Yoruba) God gave me this.

Olushola (Yoruba) God has blessed me.

Omar 🄱 (Arabic) highest; follower of the
Prophet. (Hebrew) reverent.
Omair, Omari, Omarr, Omer, Umar

Omari (Swahili) a form of Omar.
Omare, Omaree, Omarey

Omaro (Spanish) a form of Omar.

Omer (Arabic) a form of Omar.
Omeer, Omero

Omolara (Benin) child born at the right
time.

On (Burmese) coconut. (Chinese) peace.

Onan (Turkish) prosperous.

Onaona (Hawaiian) pleasant fragrance.

Ondro (Czech) a form of Andrew.
Ondra, Ondre, Ondrea, Ondrey

O'neil (Irish) son of Neil.
Oneal, O'neal, Oneil, O'neill, Onel, Oniel, Onil

Onesíforo (Greek) he who bears much fruit.

Onésimo (Greek) he who is useful and worthwhile.

Onkar (Hindi) God in his entirety.

Onofrio (German) a form of Humphrey.
Oinfre, Onfre, Onfrio, Onofre, Onofredo

Onslow (English) enthusiast's hill.
Ounslow

Onufry (Polish) a form of Humphrey.

Onur (Turkish) honor.

Ophir (Hebrew) faithful. Bible: an Old Testament people and country.

Opio (Ateso) first of twin boys.

Optato (Latin) desired.

Oral (Latin) verbal; speaker.

Oran (Irish) green.
Odhran, Odran, Ora, Orane, Orran

Orangel (Greek) messenger from the heights or from the mountain.

Oratio (Latin) a form of Horatio.
Orazio

Orbán (Hungarian) born in the city.

Ordell (Latin) beginning.
Orde

Oren (Hebrew) pine tree. (Irish) light skinned, white.
Oran, Orin, Oris, Orono, Orren, Orrin

Orencio (Greek) examining judge.

Orestes (Greek) mountain man. Mythology: the son of the Greek leader Agamemnon.
Aresty, Oreste

Orfeo (Greek) he who has a good voice.

Ori (Hebrew) my light.
Oree, Orie, Orri, Ory

Orien (Latin) visitor from the east.
Orian, Orie, Orin, Oris, Oron, Orono, Orrin, Oryan

Orígenes (Greek) he who comes from Horus, the god of light; born into caring arms.

Oriol (Latin) golden oriole.

Orion **B** (Greek) son of fire. Mythology: a giant hunter who was killed by Artemis. See also Zorion.

Orión (Greek) a form of Orion.

Orji (Ibo) mighty tree.

Orlando (German) famous throughout the land. (Spanish) a form of Roland.
Lando, Olando, Olo, Orlan, Orland, Orlanda, Orlandas, Orlandes, Orlandis, Orlandos, Orlandus, Orlo, Orlondo, Orlondon

Orleans (Latin) golden.
Orlean, Orlin

Orman (German) mariner, seaman. (Scandinavian) serpent, worm.
Ormand

Ormond (English) bear mountain; spear protector.
Ormande, Ormon, Ormonde

Oro (Spanish) golden.

Oroncio (Persian) runner.

Orono (Latin) a form of Oren.
Oron

Orosco (Greek) he who lives in the mountains.

Orrick (English) old oak tree.
Orric

Orrin (English) river.
Orin, Oryn, Orynn

Orris (Latin) a form of Horatio.
Oris, Orriss

Orry (Latin) from the Orient.
Oarrie, Orrey, Orrie

Orsino (Italian) a form of Orson.

Orson (Latin) bearlike.
Orscino, Orsen, Orsin, Orsini, Orsino, Son, Sonny, Urson

Orton (English) shore town.

Ortzi (Basque) sky.

Orunjan (Yoruba) born under the midday sun.

Orval (English) a form of Orville.
Orvel

Orville (French) golden village. History: Orville Wright and his brother Wilbur were the first men to fly an airplane.
Orv, Orval, Orvell, Orvie, Orvil

Orvin (English) spear friend.
Orwin, Owynn

Osahar (Benin) God hears.

Osakwe (Japanese) good destiny.

Osamu (Japanese) to study; to govern; peace.

Osanmwesr (Japanese) leaving.

Osayaba (Benin) God forgives.

Osaze (Benin) whom God likes.

Osbert (English) divine; bright.

Osborn (Scandinavian) divine bear.
(English) warrior of God.
Osbern, Osbon, Osborne, Osbourn, Osbourne, Osburn, Osburne, Oz, Ozzie

Oscar ▣ (Scandinavian) divine spearman.
Oke, Oskar, Osker, Oszkar

Óscar (Germanic) a form of Oscar.

Ose (Pohnpeian) a form of Jose.

Osea (Fijian) a form of Joshua.

Oseas, Osías, Ozías (Hebrew) Lord sustains me; divine salvation; God is my soul.

Osei (Fante) noble.
Osee

Osgood (English) divinely good.

O'Shea (Irish) son of Shea.
Oshae, Oshai, Oshane, O'Shane, Oshaun, Oshay, Oshaye, Oshe, Oshea, Osheon

Osip (Russian, Ukrainian) a form of Joseph, Yosef. See also Osya.

Osiris (Egyptian) he who possesses a powerful vision.

Oskar (Scandinavian) a form of Oscar.
Osker, Ozker

Osman (Turkish) ruler. (English) servant of God.
Osmanek, Osmen, Osmin, Otthmor, Ottmar

Osmán (Arabic) he who is as docile as a pigeon chick.

Osmar (English) divine; wonderful.

Osmaro (Germanic) he who shines like the glory of God.

Osmond (English) divine protector.
Osmand, Osmonde, Osmont, Osmund, Osmunde, Osmundo

Osorio (Slavic) killer of wolves.

Osric (English) divine ruler.
Osrick

Ostiano (Spanish) confessor.

Ostin (Latin) a form of Austin.
Ostan, Osten, Ostyn

Osvaldo (Spanish) a form of Oswald.
Osbaldo, Osbalto, Osvald, Osvalda

Oswald (English) God's power; God's crest. See also Waldo.
Osvaldo, Oswaldo, Oswall, Oswell, Oswold, Oz, Ozzie

Oswaldo (Spanish) a form of Oswald.

Oswin (English) divine friend.
Osvin, Oswinn, Oswyn, Oswynn

Osya (Russian) a familiar form of Osip.

Ota (Czech) prosperous.
Otik

Otadan (Native American) plentiful.

Otaktay (Lakota) kills many; strikes many.

Otek (Polish) a form of Otto.

Otello (Italian) a form of Othello.

Otelo (Spanish) a form of Otón.

Otem (Luo) born away from home.

Othello (Spanish) a form of Otto. Literature: the title character in the Shakespearean tragedy *Othello*.
Otello

Othman (German) wealthy.
Ottoman

Otilde (Teutonic) owner of a bountiful inheritance.

Otis (Greek) keen of hearing. (German) son of Otto.
Oates, Odis, Otes, Otess, Otez, Otise, Ottis, Otys

Otniel, Otoniel (Hebrew) God is my strength.

Otoronco (Quechua) jaguar; tiger; the bravest.

Ottah (Nigerian) thin baby.

Ottar (Norwegian) point warrior; fright warrior.

Ottmar (Turkish) a form of Osman.
Otomars, Ottomar

Otto (German) rich.
Odo, Otek, Otello, Otfried, Othello, Otho, Othon, Otik, Otilio, Otman, Oto, Otón, Otton, Ottone

Ottokar (German) happy warrior.
Otokars, Ottocar

Otu (Native American) collecting seashells in a basket.

Ouray (Ute) arrow. Astrology: born under the sign of Sagittarius.

Oved (Hebrew) worshiper, follower.

Ovid (Latin) having the shape of an egg.

Ovidio (Latin) he who takes care of sheep.

Owen ✴ **B** (Irish) born to nobility; young warrior. (Welsh) a form of Evan.
Owain, Owens, Owin, Uaine

Owney (Irish) elderly.
Oney

Oxford (English) place where oxen cross the river.
Ford

Oya **B** (Moquelumnan) speaking of the jacksnipe.

Oystein (Norwegian) rock of happiness.
Ostein, Osten, Ostin, _ystein

Oz **BG** (Hebrew) a short form of Osborn, Oswald.

Oziel (Hebrew) he who has divine strength.

Ozora (Japanese) big sky.

Ozturk (Turkish) pure; genuine Turk.

Ozzie (English) a familiar form of Osborn, Oswald.
Ossie, Ossy, Ozee, Ozi, Ozzi, Ozzy

P

P **BG** (American) an initial used as a first name.

Paavo (Finnish) a form of Paul.
Paaveli

Pabel (Russian) a form of Paul.

Pablo (Spanish) a form of Paul.
Pable, Paublo

Pace (English) a form of Pascal.
Payce

Pachacutec, Pachacutic (Quechua) he who changes the world, who helps bring about a new era.

Pacho (Spanish) free.

Paciano (Latin) he who belongs to the peace.

Paciente (Latin) he who knows how to be patient.

Pacifico (Filipino) peaceful.

Pacífico (Latin) he who searches for peace.

Paco (Italian) pack. (Spanish) a familiar form of Francisco. (Native American) bald eagle. See also Quico.
Pacorro, Panchito, Pancho, Paquito

Pacomio (Greek) he who is robust.

Paddy (Irish) a familiar form of Padraic, Patrick.
Paddey, Paddi, Paddie

Paden (English) a form of Patton.

Padget **BG** (English) a form of Page.
Padgett, Paget, Pagett

Padraic (Irish) a form of Patrick.
Paddrick, Paddy, Padhraig, Padrai, Pádraig, Padraigh, Padreic, Padriac, Padric, Padron, Padruig

Pafnucio (Greek) rich in merits.

Page **G** (French) youthful assistant.
Padget, Paggio, Paige, Payge

Paige **G** (English) a form of Page.

Paillalef (Mapuche) return quickly, go back.

Painecura (Mapuche) iridescent stone.

Painevilu (Mapuche) iridescent snake.

Pakelika (Hawaiian) a form of Patrick.

Paki (African) witness.

Pal (Swedish) a form of Paul.

Pál (Hungarian) a form of Paul.
Pali, Palika

Palaina (Hawaiian) a form of Brian.

Palani (Hawaiian) a form of Frank.

Palash (Hindi) flowery tree.

Palatino (Latin) he who comes from Mount Palatine.

Palben (Basque) blond.

Palladin (Native American) fighter.
Pallaton, Palleten

Palmacio (Latin) adorned with bordered palm leaves.

Palmer (English) palm-bearing pilgrim.
Pallmer, Palmar

Paloma **G** (Spanish) dove.

Palti (Hebrew) God liberates.
Palti-el

Pampín (Latin) he who has the vigor of a sprouting plant.

Boys M–R

Pan (Chinese) huge rock.

Panapasa (Fijian) a form of Bernabe.

Panas (Russian) immortal.

Panayiotis (Greek) a form of Peter.
*Panagiotis, Panajotis, Panayioti, Panayoti,
Panayotis*

Pancho (Spanish) a familiar form of
Francisco, Frank.
Panchito

Pancracio (Greek) all-powerful one.

Panfilo (Greek) friend of all.

Pánfilo (Greek) a form of Panfilo.

Pang (Chinese) large.

Panos (Greek) a form of Peter.
Petros

Pantaleón (Greek) he who is all-merciful
and has everything under control.

Panteno (Greek) he who is worthy of all
praise.

Panti (Quechua) species of brush.

Paola 🅖 (Italian) a form of Paula (see
Girls' Names).

Paolo (Italian) a form of Paul.

Papias (Greek) venerable father.

Paquito (Spanish) a familiar form of Paco.

Paramesh (Hindi) greatest. Religion:
another name for the Hindu god Shiva.

Pardeep 🅱 (Sikh) mystic light.
Pardip

Pardulfo (Germanic) brave warrior, armed
with an ax.

Paris 🅖 (Greek) lover. Geography: the
capital of France. Mythology: the prince of
Troy who started the Trojan War by
abducting Helen.
*Paras, Paree, Pares, Parese, Parie, Parris,
Parys*

París (Greek) a form of Paris.

Parisio (Spanish) a form of Paris.

Pariuana (Quechua) Andean flamingo.

Park (Chinese) cypress tree. (English) a short
form of Parker.
Parke, Parkes, Parkey, Parks

Parker 🅱 (English) park keeper.
Park

Parkin (English) little Peter.
Perkin

Parlan (Scottish) a form of Bartholomew. See
also Parthalán.

Parménides (Greek) he who is a constant
presence.

Parmenio (Greek) he who is loyal and offers
his constant presence.

Parnell (French) little Peter. History: Charles
Stewart Parnell was a famous Irish
politician.
Nell, Parle, Parnel, Parrnell, Pernell

Parodio (Greek) he who imitates the singing.

Parr (English) cattle enclosure, barn.

Parrish (English) church district.
Parish, Parrie, Parrisch, Parrysh

Parry (Welsh) son of Harry.
Parrey, Parrie, Pary

Partemio (Greek) having a pure and virginal
appearance.

Parth (Irish) a short form of Parthalán.
Partha, Parthey

Parthalán (Irish) plowman. See also
Bartholomew.
Parlan, Parth

Parthenios (Greek) virgin. Religion: a Greek
Orthodox saint.

Partol (Chuukese) a form of Bartolomé.

Pascal 🅱 (French) born on Easter or
Passover.
*Pace, Pascale, Pascalle, Paschal, Paschalis,
Pascoe, Pascow, Pascual, Pasquale*

Pascale 🅖 (French) a form of Pascal.

Pascasio (Spanish) a form of Pascual.

Pascua (Hebrew) in reference to Easter, to
the sacrifice of the village.

Pascual (Spanish) a form of Pascal.
Pascul

Pasha 🅱🅖 (Russian) a form of Paul.
Pashenka, Pashka

Pasicrates (Greek) he who dominates
everyone.

Pasquale (Italian) a form of Pascal.
Pascuale, Pasqual, Pasquali, Pasquel

Pastor (Latin) spiritual leader.

Pat 🅱🅖 (Native American) fish. (English) a
short form of Patrick.
Pattie, Patty

Patakusu (Moquelumnan) ant biting a person.

Patamon (Native American) raging.

Patek (Polish) a form of Patrick.
Patick

Paterio (Greek) he who was born in Pateria.

Paterno (Latin) belonging to the father.

Patric (Latin) a form of Patrick.

Patrice G (French) a form of Patrick.

Patricia G (Latin) noble.

Patricio (Spanish) a form of Patrick.
Patricius, Patrizio

Patrick B (Latin) nobleman. Religion: the patron saint of Ireland. See also Fitzpatrick, Ticho.
Paddy, Padraic, Pakelika, Pat, Patek, Patric, Patrice, Patricio, Patrickk, Patrik, Patrique, Patrizius, Patryk, Pats, Patsy, Pattrick

Patrido (Latin) noble.

Patrin (Gypsy) leaf trail.

Patrocinio (Latin) patronage, protection.

Patryk (Latin) a form of Patrick.
Patryck

Patterson (Irish) son of Pat.
Patteson

Pattin (Gypsy) leaf.

Patton (English) warrior's town.
Paden, Paten, Patin, Paton, Patten, Pattin, Patty, Payton, Peyton

Patwin (Native American) man.

Patxi (Basque, Teutonic) free.

Paucar (Quechua) very refined, excellent.

Paucartupac (Quechua) majestic and excellent.

Paul B (Latin) small. Bible: Saul, later renamed Paul, was the first to bring the teachings of Christ to the Gentiles.
Oalo, Paavo, Pablo, Pal, Pál, Pall, Paolo, Pasha, Pasko, Pauli, Paulia, Paulin, Paulino, Paulis, Paulo, Pauls, Paulus, Pavel, Pavlos, Pawel, Pol, Poul

Pauli (Latin) a familiar form of Paul.
Pauley, Paulie, Pauly

Paulin (German, Polish) a form of Paul.

Paulino, Pauliño (Spanish) forms of Paul.

Paulo (Portuguese, Swedish, Hawaiian) a form of Paul.

Pausidio (Greek) deliberate, calm man.

Pauyu (Aymara) he who finishes, who brings to a happy ending all work that he undertakes.

Pavel (Russian) a form of Paul.
Paavel, Pasha, Pavils, Pavlik, Pavlo, Pavlusha, Pavlushenka, Pawl

Pavit (Hindi) pious, pure.

Pawel (Polish) a form of Paul.
Pawelek, Pawl

Pax (Latin) peaceful.

Paxton BG (Latin) peaceful town.
Packston, Pax, Paxon, Paxten, Paxtun

Payat (Native American) he is on his way.
Pay, Payatt

Payden (English) a form of Payton.
Paydon

Payne (Latin) from the country.
Paine, Paynn

Paytah (Lakota) fire.
Pay, Payta

Payton G (English) a form of Patton.
Paiton, Pate, Payden, Peaton, Peighton, Peyton

Paz G (Spanish) a form of Pax.

Pearce (English) a form of Pierce.
Pears, Pearse

Pearson (English) son of Peter. See also Pierson.
Pearsson, Pehrson, Peirson, Peterson

Peder (Scandinavian) a form of Peter.
Peadar, Pedey

Pedro (Spanish) a form of Peter.
Pedrin, Pedrín, Petronio

Peers (English) a form of Peter.
Peerus, Piers

Peeter (Estonian) a form of Peter.
Peet

Pegaso (Greek) born next to the fountain.

Pei (Chinese) abundant.

Peirce (English) a form of Peter.
Peirs

Pekelo (Hawaiian) a form of Peter.
Pekka

Pelagio, Pelayo (Greek) excellent sailor.

Peleke (Hawaiian) a form of Frederick.

Pelham (English) tannery town.

Pelí (Latin, Basque) happy.

Pelihpe, Pelipe (Pohnpeian) forms of Felipe.

Pell (English) parchment.
Pall

Pello (Greek, Basque) stone.
Peru, Piarres

Pelope (Greek) having a brown complexion.

Pelton (English) town by a pool.

Pembroke (Welsh) headland. (French) wine dealer. (English) broken fence.
Pembrook

Peng (Chinese) a bright future.

Peniame (Fijian) a form of Benjamin.

Peniamina (Hawaiian) a form of Benjamin.
Peni

Penley (English) enclosed meadow.

Penn (Latin) pen, quill. (English) enclosure. (German) a short form of Penrod.
Pen, Penna, Penney, Pennie, Penny

Penrod (German) famous commander.
Penn, Pennrod, Rod

Pepa (Czech) a familiar form of Joseph.
Pepek, Pepik

Pepe (Spanish) a familiar form of José.
Pepillo, Pepito, Pequin, Pipo

Pepin (German) determined; petitioner. History: Pepin the Short was an eighth-century king of the Franks.
Pepi, Peppie, Peppy

Peppe (Italian) a familiar form of Joseph.
Peppi, Peppo, Pino

Per (Swedish) a form of Peter.

Perben (Greek, Danish) stone.

Percival (French) pierce the valley. Literature: a knight of the Round Table who first appears in Chrétien de Troyes's poem about the quest for the Holy Grail.
Parsafal, Parsefal, Parsifal, Parzival, Perc, Perce, Perceval, Percevall, Percivall, Percy, Peredur, Purcell

Percy (French) a familiar form of Percival.
Pearcey, Pearcy, Percey, Percie, Piercey, Piercy

Perdinant (Pohnpeian) a form of Fernando.

Peregrine (Latin) traveler; pilgrim; falcon.
Peregrin, Peregryne, Perine, Perry

Peregrino (Latin) he who travels.

Perfecto (Latin) upright; errorless, without any defects.

Periandro (Greek) worries about men.

Pericles (Greek) just leader. History: an Athenian statesman.

Perico (Spanish) a form of Peter.
Pequin, Perequin

Perine (Latin) a short form of Peregrine.
Perino, Perion, Perrin, Perryn

Perkin (English) little Peter.
Perka, Perkins, Perkyn, Perrin

Pernell (French) a form of Parnell.
Perren, Perrnall

Perpetuo (Latin) having an unchanging goal, who remains faithful to his faith.

Perry ₿ (English) a familiar form of Peregrine, Peter.
Parry, Perrie, Perrye

Perseo (Greek) destroyer, the destructive one.

Perth (Scottish) thorn-bush thicket. Geography: a burgh in Scotland; a city in Australia.

Pervis (Latin) passage.
Pervez

Pesach (Hebrew) spared. Religion: another name for Passover.
Pessach

Petar (Greek) a form of Peter.

Pete (English) a short form of Peter.
Peat, Peet, Petey, Peti, Petie, Piet, Pit

Peter ₿ (Greek, Latin) small rock. Bible: Simon, renamed Peter, was the leader of the Twelve Apostles. See also Boutros, Ferris, Takis.
Panayiotos, Panos, Peadair, Peder, Pedro, Peers, Peeter, Peirce, Pekelo, Per, Perico, Perion, Perkin, Perry, Petar, Pete, Péter, Peterke, Peterus, Petr, Petras, Petros, Petru, Petruno, Petter, Peyo, Piaras, Pierce, Piero, Pierre, Pieter, Pietrek, Pietro, Piotr, Piter, Piti, Pjeter, Pyotr

Peterson (English) son of Peter.
Peteris, Petersen

Petiri (Shona) where we are.
Petri

Petr (Bulgarian) a form of Peter.

Petras (Lithuanian) a form of Peter.
Petra, Petrelis

Petros (Greek) a form of Peter.
Petro

Petru (Romanian) a form of Peter.
Petrukas, Petrus, Petruso

Petter (Norwegian) a form of Peter.

Peverell (French) piper.
Peverall, Peverel, Peveril

Peyo (Spanish) a form of Peter.

Peyton **BG** (English) a form of Patton,
Payton.
Peyt, Peyten, Peython, Peytonn

Pharaoh (Latin) ruler. History: a title for the
ancient kings of Egypt.
Faroh, Pharo, Pharoah, Pharoh

Pharis (Chuukese) a form of Fares.

Phelan (Irish) wolf.

Phelipe (Spanish) a form of Philip.

Phelix (Latin) a form of Felix.

Phelps (English) son of Phillip.

Phil (Greek) a short form of Philip, Phillip.
Fil, Phill

Philander (Greek) lover of mankind.

Philbert (English) a form of Filbert.
Philibert, Phillbert

Philemon (Greek) kiss.
*Phila, Philamina, Phileman, Philémon,
Philmon*

Philip **B** (Greek) lover of horses. Bible: one
of the Twelve Apostles. See also Felipe,
Felippo, Filip, Fillipp, Filya, Fischel, Flip.
*Phelps, Phelipe, Phil, Philipp, Philippe,
Philippo, Phillip, Phillipos, Phillp, Philly, Philp,
Phylip, Piers, Pilib, Pilipo, Pippo*

Philipp (German) a form of Philip.
Phillipp

Philippe (French) a form of Philip.
*Philipe, Phillepe, Phillipe, Phillippe,
Phillippee, Phyllipe*

Phillip (Greek) a form of Philip.
Phil, Phillipos, Phillipp, Phillips, Philly, Phyllip

Phillipos (Greek) a form of Phillip.

Philly (American) a familiar form of Philip,
Phillip.
Phillie

Philo (Greek) love.

Phinean (Irish) a form of Finian.
Phinian

Phineas (English) a form of Pinchas.
Fineas, Phinehas, Phinny

Phirun (Cambodian) rain.

Phoenix (Latin) phoenix, a legendary bird.
Phenix, Pheonix, Phynix

Phong (Vietnamese) wind.

Phuc (Vietnamese) luck; blessings.

Phuok (Vietnamese) good.
Phuoc

Phuong (Vietnamese) destiny; direction.

Pias (Gypsy) fun.

Pichi (Araucanian) small.

Pichiu (Quechua) baby bird.

Pichulman (Mapuche) condor's feather.

Pichunlaf (Mapuche) lucky feather; virtue
that brings health and happiness.

Pickford (English) ford at the peak.

Pickworth (English) wood cutter's estate.

Pierce **B** (English) a form of Peter.
Pearce, Peerce, Peers, Peirce, Piercy, Piers

Piero (Italian) a form of Peter.
Pero, Pierro

Pierre **B** (French) a form of Peter.
Peirre, Piere, Pierrot

Pierre-Luc (French) a combination of Pierre
+ Luc.
Piere Luc

Piers (English) a form of Philip.

Pierson (English) son of Peter. See also
Pearson.
Pierrson, Piersen, Piersson, Piersun

Pieter (Dutch) a form of Peter.
Pietr

Pietro (Italian) a form of Peter.

Pigmalion (Spanish) sculptor.

Pihdelis (Pohnpeian) a form of Fidel.

Pilar (Spanish) pillar.

Pilato (Latin) soldier armed with a lance.

Pilatos (Latin) he who is armed with a pick.

Pili (Swahili) second born.

Pilipo (Hawaiian) a form of Philip.

Pillan (Native American) supreme essence.
Pilan

Pin (Vietnamese) faithful boy.

Pinchas (Hebrew) oracle. (Egyptian) dark
skinned.
Phineas, Pincas, Pinchos, Pincus, Pinkas,
Pinkus, Pinky

Ping (Chinese) peaceful.

Pinky (American) a familiar form of Pinchas.
Pink

Pino (Italian) a form of Joseph.

Piñon (Tupi-Guarani) Mythology: the hunter
who became the constellation Orion.

Pio, Pío (Latin) pious.

Piotr (Bulgarian) a form of Peter.
Piotrek

Pipino (Latin) he who has a small stature.

Pippin (German) father.

Piquichaqui (Quechua) feet of a bug, light-
footed.

Piran (Irish) prayer. Religion: the patron
saint of miners.
Peran, Pieran

Pirro (Greek, Spanish) flaming hair.

Pista (Hungarian) a familiar form of István.
Pisti

Pitágoras (Greek) he who is like a divine
oracle.

Piti (Spanish) a form of Peter.

Pitin (Spanish) a form of Felix.
Pito

Pitney (English) island of the strong-willed
man.
Pittney

Pitt (English) pit, ditch.

Piyco, Piycu (Quechua) red bird.

Piycomayu, Piycumayu (Quechua) a river
as red as a bright, red bird.

Placido (Spanish) serene.
Placide, Placidus, Placyd, Placydo

Plácido (Latin) a form of Placido.

Plato (Greek) broad shouldered. History: a
famous Greek philosopher.
Platon

Platón (Greek) wide-shouldered.

Platt (French) flatland.
Platte

Plauto, Plotino (Greek) he who has flat feet.

Plinio (Latin) he who has many skills, gifts.

Plubio (Greek) man of the sea.

Plutarco (Greek) rich prince.

Plutón (Greek) owner of many riches.

Po Sin (Chinese) grandfather elephant.

Pol (Swedish) a form of Paul.
Pól, Pola, Poul

Poldi (German) a familiar form of Leopold.
Poldo

Poliano (Greek) he who suffers, the sorrowful
one.

Policarpo (Greek) he who produces
abundant fruit.

Policeto (Greek) he who caused much
sorrow.

Polidoro (Greek) having virtues.

Poliecto (Greek) he who is very desired.

Polifemo (Greek) he who is spoken about a
lot.

Polión (Greek) powerful Lord who protects.

Pollard (German) close-cropped head.
Poll, Pollerd, Pollyrd

Pollock (English) a form of Pollux. Art:
American artist Jackson Pollock was a leader
of abstract expressionism.
Pollack, Polloch

Pollux (Greek) crown. Astronomy: one of the
stars in the constellation Gemini.
Pollock

Polo (Tibetan) brave wanderer. (Greek) a
short form of Apollo. Culture: a game played
on horseback. History: Marco Polo was a
thirteenth-century Venetian explorer who
traveled throughout Asia.

Poma, Pomacana (Quechua) strong and
powerful puma.

Pomacaua (Quechua) he who guards with
the quietness of a puma.

Pomagüiyca (Quechua) sacred like the
puma.

Pomalloque (Quechua) left-handed puma.

Pomauari (Quechua) indomitable as a vicuna and strong as a puma.

Pomayauri (Quechua) copper-colored puma.

Pomeroy (French) apple orchard.
Pommeray, Pommeroy

Pompeyo (Greek) he who heads the procession.

Pomponio (Latin) lover of grandeur and the open plains.

Ponce (Spanish) fifth. History: Juan Ponce de León of Spain searched for the Fountain of Youth in Florida.

Poncio (Greek) having come from the sea.

Ponpey (English) a form of Pompeyo.

Pony (Scottish) small horse.
Poni

Porcio (Latin) he who earns his living raising pigs.

Porfirio (Greek, Spanish) purple stone.
Porphirios, Prophyrios

Porfiro (Greek) purple stone.

Porter (Latin) gatekeeper.
Port, Portie, Porty

Poseidón (Greek) owner of the waters.

Poshita (Sanskrit) cherished.

Posidio (Greek) he who is devoted to Poseidon.

Potenciano (Latin) he who dominates with his empire.

Poul (Danish) a form of Paul.
Poulos, Poulus

Pov (Gypsy) earth.

Powa (Native American) wealthy.

Powell (English) alert.
Powel

Prabhjot **B** (Sikh) the light of God.

Prácido (Latin) tranquil, calm.

Pragnacio (Greek) he who is skillful and practical in business.

Pramad (Hindi) rejoicing.

Pratyush (Indian) sun.

Pravan (Indian) bowed down; modest.

Pravar (Indian) chief.

Pravat (Tai) history.

Praveen (Indian) expert, skilled.

Praveer (Indian) an excellent warrior or king.

Prayadarshi (Indian) one who is liked by all.

Preetam (Indian) beloved; husband.

Preetidutt (Indian) gifted with love.

Preetish (Indian) god of love.

Preetiwardhan (Indian) one who increases love.

Prem (Hindi) love.

Premanand (Indian) joy of love.

Prentice (English) apprentice.
Prent, Prentis, Prentiss, Printes, Printiss

Prescott (English) priest's cottage. See also Scott.
Prescot, Prestcot, Prestcott

Presidio (Latin) he who gives pleasant shelter.

Presley **G** (English) priest's meadow. Music: Elvis Presley was an influential American rock 'n' roll singer.
Presleigh, Presly, Presslee, Pressley, Prestley, Priestley, Priestly

Preston **B** (English) priest's estate.
Prestan, Presten, Prestin, Prestyn

Pretextato (Latin) covered by a toga.

Prewitt (French) brave little one.
Preuet, Prewet, Prewett, Prewit, Pruit, Pruitt

Priamo (Greek) rescued one.

Príamo (Greek) a form of Priamo.

Price (Welsh) son of the ardent one.
Brice, Bryce, Pryce

Pricha (Tai) clever.

Prilidiano (Greek) he who remembers things from the past.

Primeiro (Italian) born first.

Primitivo (Latin) original.

Primo (Italian) first; premier quality.
Preemo, Premo

Prince (Latin) chief; prince.
Prence, Prinz, Prinze

Princeton (English) princely town.
Prenston, Princeston, Princton

Prithu (Indian) broad, spacious.

Prithvijaj (Indian) king of the earth.

Priyadarshan (Indian) nice to look at, handsome.

Priyam, Priyaranjan (Indian) beloved.

Priyanvad (Indian) sweet-talking person.

Probo (Latin) having moral conduct.

Proceso (Latin) he who moves forward.

Procopio (Greek) he who progresses.

Procoro (Greek) he who prospers.

Proctor (Latin) official, administrator.
Prockter, Procter

Proculo (Latin) he who was born far from home.

Prokopios (Greek) declared leader.

Promaco (Greek) he who prepares for battle.

Prometeo (Greek) he who resembles God.

Prosper (Latin) fortunate.
Prospero, Próspero

Protasio (Greek) he who is in front; the preferred one.

Proteo (Greek) lord of the sea's waves.

Proterio (Greek) he who precedes all the rest.

Proto (Greek) first.

Protólico (Greek) preferred one; he who deserves first place.

Prudenciano (Spanish) humble and honest.

Prudencio (Latin) he who works with sensitivity and modesty.

Pryor (Latin) head of the monastery; prior.
Prior, Pry

Pu (Chinese) uncut jade.

Publio (Latin) he who is popular.

Puchac (Quechua) leader; he who leads others down a good path.

Pueblo (Spanish) from the city.

Pujan (Indian) the ceremony of worshiping.

Pulkit (Indian) happy, thrilled, overjoyed.

Pulqueria (Latin) beautiful one.

Pulqui (Araucanian) arrow.

Puma, Pumacana (Quechua) strong and powerful puma.

Pumacaua (Quechua) he who guards with the quietness of a puma.

Pumagüiyca (Quechua) sacred like the puma.

Pumalluqui (Quechua) left-handed puma.

Pumasonjo, Pumasuncu (Quechua) courageous heart; heart of a puma.

Pumauari (Quechua) indomitable as a vicuna and strong as a puma.

Pumayauri (Quechua) copper-colored puma.

Pumeet (Sanskrit) pure.

Pundarik (Indian) white lotus.

Puneeth (Indian) pure.

Pupulo (Latin) little boy.

Purdy (Hindi) recluse.

Puric (Quechua) walker, fond of walking.

Purnendu (Indian) full moon.

Purujit (Indian) conqueror of the city.

Purumitra (Indian) friend of the city.

Purushottam (Indian) best among men.

Purvis (French, English) providing food.
Pervis, Purves, Purviss

Pushkara (Indian) blue lotus; fountain; lake.

Pushpad (Indian) he who gives flowers.

Pushpaj (Indian) born from a flower.

Pushpak (Indian) Kuber's plane taken away by Ravan.

Pushpakar (Indian) the spring season; flower season.

Pushpaketu (Indian) Kamdev, the love god.

Putnam (English) dweller by the pond.
Putnem

Putta (Indian) small baby.

Pyas (Indian) thirsty.

Pyotr (Russian) a form of Peter.
Petenka, Petinka, Petrusha, Petya, Pyatr

Qabil (Arabic) able.

Qadim (Arabic) ancient.

Qadir (Arabic) powerful.
Qaadir, Qadeer, Quaadir, Quadeer, Quadir

Qamar (Arabic) moon.
Quamar, Quamir

Qasim (Arabic) divider.
Quasim

Qatadah (Indian) a hardwood tree.

Qays (Indian) firm.

Qi (Chinese) fine jade; outstanding; distinguished.

Qian (Chinese) thousand.

Qiang (Chinese) powerful.

Qiao (Chinese) pretty, handsome.

Qimat (Hindi) valuable.

Qin (Chinese) industrious.

Qing (Chinese) stainless.

Qing Yuan, Qing-Yuan (Chinese) deep water; clear spring.

Qiong (Chinese) fine jade.

Qiu (Chinese) autumn.

Qu (Chinese) interest, delight.

Quaashie **BG** (Ewe) born on Sunday.

Quadarius (American) a combination of Quan + Darius.
Quadara, Quadarious, Quadaris, Quandarious, Quandarius, Quandarrius, Qudarius, Qudaruis

Quade (Latin) fourth.
Quadell, Quaden, Quadon, Quadre, Quadrie, Quadrine, Quadrion, Quaid, Quayd, Quayde, Qwade

Quamaine (American) a combination of Quan + Jermaine.
Quamain, Quaman, Quamane, Quamayne, Quarmaine

Quan (Comanche) a short form of Quanah.

Quanah (Comanche) fragrant.
Quan

Quandre (American) a combination of Quan + Andre.
Quandrae, Quandré

Quang (Vietnamese) clear; brilliant; good reputation.

Quant (Greek) how much?
Quanta, Quantae, Quantai, Quantas, Quantay, Quante, Quantea, Quantey, Quantez, Quantu

Quantavius (American) a combination of Quan + Octavius.
Quantavian, Quantavin, Quantavion, Quantavious, Quantavis, Quantavous, Quatavious, Quatavius

Quashawn (American) a combination of Quan + Shawn.
Quasean, Quashaan, Quashan, Quashaun, Quashaunn, Quashon, Quashone, Quashun, Queshan, Queshon, Qweshawn, Qyshawn

Qudamah (Arabic) courage.

Que (Chinese) reliable.

Quenby **BG** (Scandinavian) a form of Quimby.

Quennell (French) small oak.
Quenell, Quennel

Quenten (Latin) a form of Quentin.
Quienten

Quenti, Quinti (Quechua) hummingbird; shy, small.

Quentin **B** (Latin) fifth. (English) queen's town.
Qeuntin, Quantin, Quent, Quentan, Quenten, Quentine, Quenton, Quentyn, Quentynn, Quientin, Quinten, Quintin, Quinton, Qwentin

Quenton (Latin) a form of Quentin.
Quienton

Querubín (Hebrew) swift, young bull.

Quespi, Quispe, Quispi (Quechua) free, liberated; jewel, shiny like a diamond.

Queupulicán (Mapuche) white stone with a black stripe.

Queupumil (Mapuche) shining stone; brilliant, precious.

Quichuasamin (Quechua) he who brings fortune and happiness to the village.

Quico (Spanish) a familiar form of many names.
Paco

Quidequeo (Mapuche) brilliant; fiery tongue.

Quigley (Irish) maternal side.
Quigly

Quillan (Irish) cub.
Quill, Quillen, Quillin, Quillon

Quillinchu, Quilliyicu (Quechua) sparrow hawk.

Quimby (Scandinavian) woman's estate.
Quenby, Quinby

Quincy **B** (French) fifth son's estate.
Quenci, Quency, Quince, Quincee, Quincey, Quinci, Quinn, Quinncy, Quinnsy, Quinsey, Quinzy

Quindarius (American) a combination of Quinn + Darius.
Quindarious, Quindarrius, Quinderious, Quinderus, Quindrius

Quiñelef (Mapuche) a rapid trip, quick race.

Quinlan (Irish) strong; well shaped.
Quindlen, Quinlen, Quinlin, Quinn, Quinnlan, Quinnlin

Quinn **B** (Irish) a short form of Quincy, Quinlan, Quinton.
Quin

Quintavius (American) a combination of Quinn + Octavius.
Quintavious, Quintavis, Quintavus, Quintayvious

Quinten (Latin) a form of Quentin.
Quinnten

Quintilian (French) a form of Quintiliano.

Quintiliano (Spanish) a form of Quintilio.

Quintilio (Latin) he who was born in the fifth month.

Quintin (Latin) a form of Quentin.
Quinntin, Quintine, Quintyn

Quintín (Spanish) a form of Quinto.

Quinto (Latin) a form of Quinton.

Quinton **B** (Latin) a form of Quentin.
Quinn, Quinneton, Quinnton, Quint, Quintan, Quintann, Quintin, Quintion, Quintus, Quitin, Quito, Quiton, Qunton, Qwinton

Quintrilpe (Mapuche) place of organization.

Quintuillan (Mapuche) searching for the altar.

Quiqui (Spanish) a familiar form of Enrique.
Quinto, Quiquin

Quirino (Latin) he who carries a lance.

Quispiyupanqui (Quechua) he who honors his liberty.

Quisu (Aymara) he who appreciates the value of things.

Quitin (Latin) a short form of Quinton.
Quiten, Quito, Quiton

Quito (Spanish) a short form of Quinton.

Qun (Chinese) the masses.

Quon (Chinese) bright.

Qutaybah (Indian) irritable, impatient.

Quy (Vietnamese) precious.

R

R **BG** (American) an initial used as a first name.

Raakin (Indian) respectful.

Raamiz (Indian) symbol.

Raanan (Hebrew) fresh; luxuriant.

Raatib (Indian) arranger.

Rabi **BG** (Arabic) breeze.
Rabbi, Rabee, Rabeeh, Rabiah, Rabie, Rabih

Race (English) race.
Racel, Rayce

Racham (Hebrew) compassionate.
Rachaman, Rachamim, Rachim, Rachman, Rachmiel, Rachum, Raham, Rahamim

Rachel **G** (Hebrew) sheep.

Rad (English) advisor. (Slavic) happy.
Raad, Radd, Raddie, Raddy, Rade, Radee, Radell, Radey, Radi

Radbert (English) brilliant advisor.

Radburn (English) red brook; brook with reeds.
Radborn, Radborne, Radbourn, Radbourne, Radburne

Radcliff (English) red cliff; cliff with reeds.
Radcliffe, Radclyffe

Radford (English) red ford; ford with reeds.

Radhakrishnan (Indian) the goddess Radha.

Radley (English) red meadow; meadow of reeds.
Radlea, Radlee, Radleigh, Radly

Radman (Slavic) joyful.
Radmen, Radusha

Radnor (English) red shore; shore with reeds.

Radomil (Slavic) happy peace.

Radoslaw (Polish) happy glory.
Radik, Rado, Radzmir, Slawek

Ra'ed (Indian) leader.

Raegan **G** (Irish) a form of Reagan.

Raekwon (American) a form of Raquan.
Raekwan, Raikwan, Rakwane, Rakwon

Raequan (American) a form of Raquan.
Raequon, Raeqwon, Raiquan, Raiquen, Raiqoun

Raeshawn (American) a form of Rashawn.
Raesean, Raeshaun, Raeshon, Raeshun

Rafael **B** (Spanish) a form of Raphael. See also Falito.
Rafaelle, Rafaello, Rafaelo, Rafal, Rafeal, Rafeé, Rafel, Rafello, Raffael, Raffaelo, Raffeal, Raffel, Raffiel, Rafiel

Rafaele (Italian) a form of Raphael.
Raffaele

Rafal (Polish) a form of Raphael.

Rafe (English) a short form of Rafferty, Ralph.
Raff

Rafee' (Indian) kind friend.

Rafer (Irish) a short form of Rafferty.
Raffer

Rafferty (Irish) rich, prosperous.
Rafe, Rafer, Raferty, Raffarty, Raffer

Rafi (Arabic) exalted. (Hebrew) a familiar form of Raphael.
Raffe, Raffee, Raffi, Raffy, Rafi

Rafiq (Arabic) friend.
Raafiq, Rafeeq, Rafic, Rafique

Rafu (Japanese) a net.

Ragesh (Indian) the man who sings sweet ragas.

Ragheb (Indian) desirous.

Raghib (Arabic) desirous.
Raquib

Raghnall (Irish) wise power.

Ragnar (Norwegian) powerful army.
Ragnor, Rainer, Rainier, Ranieri, Rayner, Raynor, Reinhold

Rago (Hausa) ram.

Raguel (Hebrew) everybody's friend.

Raheem **B** (Punjabi) compassionate God.
Rakeem

Rahim (Arabic) merciful.
Raaheim, Rahaeim, Raheam, Raheim, Rahiem, Rahiim, Rahime, Rahium, Rakim

Rahman (Arabic) compassionate.
Rahmatt, Rahmet

Rahul (Arabic) traveler.

Rai (Spanish) mighty protector.

Raíd (Arabic) leader.

Raiden (Japanese) Mythology: the thunder god.
Raidan, Rayden

Railef (Mapuche) a flower that is bedraggled because of a strong wind.

Raimi (Quechua) party, celebration.

Raimondo (Italian) a form of Raymond.
Raymondo, Reimundo

Raimund (German) a form of Raymond.
Rajmund

Raimundo (Portuguese, Spanish) a form of Raymond.
Mundo, Raimon, Raimond, Raimonds, Raymundo

Raine **G** (English) lord; wise.
Rain, Raines, Rayne

Rainer (German) counselor.
Rainar, Rainey, Rainier, Rainor, Raynier, Reinier

Rainero (Germanic) intelligence that guides.

Rainey (German) a familiar form of Rainer.
Raine, Rainee, Rainie, Rainney, Rainy, Reiny

Raini (Tupi-Guarani) Religion: the god who created the world.

Raishawn (American) a form of Rashawn.
Raishon, Raishun

Rajab (Indian) the seventh month of the Islamic calendar.

Rajabu (Swahili) born in the seventh month of the Islamic calendar.

Rajah (Hindi) prince; chief.
Raj, Raja, Rajaah, Rajae, Rajahe, Rajan, Raje, Rajeh, Raji

Rajak (Hindi) cleansing.

Rajan (Hindi) a form of Rajah.
Rajaahn, Rajain, Rajen, Rajin

Rajaneesh (Indian) the god of night; god of the moon.

Rajani (Indian) night.

Rajanikanta, Rajivlochan, Rajivnayan (Indian) king's sage.

Rajeet (Indian) decorated.

Rajiv (Indian) a blue lotus.

Rajkumar (Indian) prince.

Rajyeshwar (Indian) king.

Rakeem (Punjabi) a form of Raheem.
Rakeeme, Rakeim, Rakem

Rakim (Arabic) a form of Rahim.
Rakiim

Rakin (Arabic) respectable.
Rakeen

Rakishi (Indian) wide load.

Raksha (Indian) the moon; protection.

Rakshak (Indian) rescue.

Raktakamal (Indian) a red lotus.

Raktim (Hindi) bright red.

Raleigh 🅱 (English) a form of Rawleigh.
Ralegh

Ralph 🅱 (English) wolf counselor.
Radolphus, Rafe, Ralf, Ralpheal, Ralphel, Ralphie, Ralston, Raoul, Raul, Rolf

Ralphie (English) a familiar form of Ralph.
Ralphy

Ralston (English) Ralph's settlement.

Ram (Hindi) god; godlike. Religion: another name for the Hindu god Rama. (English) male sheep. A short form of Ramsey.
Rami, Ramie, Ramy

Ramadan (Arabic) ninth month of the Arabic year in the Islamic calendar.
Rama

Ramakant (Indian) husband of Rama.

Ramakrishna (Indian) a combination of Rama + Krishna.

Raman 🅶 (Hindi) a short form of Ramanan.

Ramanan (Hindi) god; godlike.
Raman, Ramandeep, Ramanjit, Ramanjot

Ramanuja (Indian) born after Lord Rama.

Ramavatar (Indian) reincarnation of Lord Rama.

Ramdas (Indian) devotee of Rama.

Ramesh (Indian) the preserver.

Rami (Hindi, English) a form of Ram. (Spanish) a short form of Ramiro.
Rame, Ramee, Ramey, Ramih

Ramiro (Portuguese, Spanish) supreme judge.
Ramario, Rameer, Rameir, Ramere, Rameriz, Ramero, Rami, Ramires, Ramirez, Ramos

Ramón (Spanish) a form of Raymond.
Ramon, Remon, Remone, Romone

Ramone (Dutch) a form of Raymond.
Raemon, Raemonn, Ramond, Ramonte, Remone

Ramsden (English) valley of rams.

Ramsey 🅱 (English) ram's island.
Ram, Ramsay, Ramsee, Ramsie, Ramsy, Ramzee, Ramzey, Ramzi, Ramzy

Ran (Chinese) correct.

Ranajit (Indian) victorious.

Rance (English) a short form of Laurence. (American) a familiar form of Laurence.
Rancel, Rancell, Rances, Rancey, Rancie, Rancy, Ransel, Ransell

Rancul (Araucanian) plant from the grasslands whose leaves are used to make roofs for huts.

Rand (English) shield; warrior.
Randy

Randal (English) a form of Randall.
Randahl, Randale, Randel, Randl, Randle

Randall 🅱 (English) a form of Randolph.
Randal, Randell, Randy, Randyll

Randheer (Indian) one who shows bravery and boldness in war.

Randi 🅶 (English) a form of Randy.

Randolph (English) shield wolf.
Randall, Randol, Randolf, Randolfo, Randolpho, Randy, Ranolph

Randy 🅱 (English) a familiar form of Rand, Randall, Randolph.
Randdy, Randee, Randey, Randi, Randie, Ranndy

Rangan (Indian) a flower.

Ranger (French) forest keeper.
Rainger, Range

Rangle (American) cowboy.
Rangler, Wrangle

Rangsey (Cambodian) seven kinds of colors.

Rani 🅶 (Hebrew) my song; my joy.
Ranen, Ranie, Ranon, Roni

Ranieri (Italian) a form of Ragnar.
Raneir, Ranier, Rannier

Ranjan (Hindi) delighted; gladdened.

Ranjeet (Indian) victor in wars.

Rankin (English) small shield.
Randkin

Ransford (English) raven's ford.

Ransley (English) raven's field.

Ransom (Latin) redeemer. (English) son of
the shield.
Rance, Ransome, Ranson

Ranveer (Indian) winner.

Raoul (French) a form of Ralph, Rudolph.
Raol, Raul, Raúl, Reuel

Raphael **B** (Hebrew) God has healed. Bible:
one of the archangels. Art: a prominent
painter of the Renaissance. See also Falito,
Rafi.
*Rafael, Rafaele, Rafal, Rafel, Raphaél,
Raphale, Raphaello, Rapheal, Raphel,
Raphello, Raphiel, Ray, Rephael*

Rapheal (Hebrew) a form of Raphael.
Rafel, Raphiel

Rapier (French) blade-sharp.

Rapiman (Mapuche) condor's vomit;
indigestion.

Raquan (American) a combination of the
prefix Ra + Quan.
*Raaquan, Rackwon, Racquan, Raekwon,
Raequan, Rahquan, Raquané, Raquon,
Raquwan, Raquwn, Raquwon, Raqwan,
Raqwann*

Raquel **G** (French) a form of Rachel.

Rashaad (Arabic) a form of Rashad.

Rashaan (American) a form of Rashawn.
Rasaan, Rashan, Rashann

Rashad (Arabic) wise counselor.
*Raashad, Rachad, Rachard, Raeshad,
Raishard, Rashaad, Rashadd, Rashade,
Rashaud, Rasheed, Rashid, Rashod, Reshad,
Rhashad, Rishad, Roshad*

Rashard (American) a form of Richard.
Rasharrd

Rashaud (Arabic) a form of Rashad.
Rachaud, Rashaude

Rashaun (American) a form of Rashawn.

Rashawn **B** (American) a combination of
the prefix Ra + Shawn.
*Raashawn, Raashen, Raeshawn, Rahshawn,
Raishawn, Rasaun, Rasawn, Rashaan,
Rashaun, Rashaw, Rashon, Rashun, Raushan,
Raushawn, Rhashan, Rhashaun, Rhashawn*

Rashean (American) a combination of the
prefix Ra + Sean.
*Rahsaan, Rahsean, Rahseen, Rasean,
Rashane, Rasheen, Rashien, Rashiena*

Rasheed **B** (Arabic) a form of Rashad.
Rashead, Rashed, Rasheid, Rhasheed

Rashid (Arabic) a form of Rashad.
*Rasheyd, Rashida, Rashidah, Rashied,
Rashieda, Raushaid*

Rashida **G** (Swahili) righteous.

Rashidi (Swahili) wise counselor.

Rashod (Arabic) a form of Rashad.
*Rashoda, Rashodd, Rashoud, Rayshod,
Rhashod*

Rashon (American) a form of Rashawn.
*Rashion, Rashone, Rashonn, Rashuan,
Rashun, Rashunn*

Rasmus (Greek, Danish) a short form of
Erasmus.

Rasraj (Indian) king of liquid; romance.

Ratan (Indian) gem.

Ratchell (Vietnamese) a form of Ritchell.

Rateesh (Indian) god and husband of Ratee.

Ratnakar (Indian) mine of jewels; sea.

Ratul (Indian) sweet.

Rauel (Hebrew) friend of God.

Raul (French) a form of Ralph.

Raulas (Lithuanian) a form of Laurence.

Raulo (Lithuanian) a form of Laurence.
Raulas

Raunak (Indian) pride, glory.

Raurac (Quechua) burning; ardent.

Raven **G** (English) a short form of Ravenel.
*Ravan, Ravean, Raveen, Ravin, Ravine,
Ravon, Ravyn, Reven, Rhaven*

Ravenel (English) raven.
Raven, Ravenell, Revenel

Ravi (Hindi) sun.
Ravee, Ravijot

Ravid (Hebrew) a form of Arvid.

Boys M–R

Ravikiran (Indian) sun ray.

Ravinandan (Indian) son of the sun.

Ravindra (Indian) sun.

Ravinshu (Indian) Kamdev, the love god.

Raviv (Hebrew) rain, dew.

Ravon (English) a form of Raven.
Raveon, Ravion, Ravone, Ravonn, Ravonne, Rayvon, Revon

Rawdon (English) rough hill.

Rawleigh (English) deer meadow.
Raleigh, Rawle, Rawley, Rawling, Rawly, Rawylyn

Rawlins (French) a form of Roland.
Rawlings, Rawlinson, Rawson

Ray B (French) kingly, royal. (English) a short form of Rayburn, Raymond. See also Lei.
Rae, Raye

Rayan (Irish) a form of Ryan.
Rayaun

Rayburn (English) deer brook.
Burney, Raeborn, Raeborne, Raebourn, Ray, Raybourn, Raybourne, Rayburne

Rayce (English) a form of Race.

Rayden (Japanese) a form of Raiden.
Raidin, Raydun, Rayedon

Rayhan (Arabic) favored by God.
Rayhaan

Rayi (Hebrew) my friend, my companion.

Raymon (English) a form of Raymond.
Rayman, Raymann, Raymen, Raymone, Raymun, Reamonn

Raymond (English) mighty; wise protector. See also Aymon.
Radmond, Raemond, Raimondo, Raimund, Raimundo, Ramón, Ramond, Ramonde, Ramone, Ray, Raymand, Rayment, Raymon, Raymont, Raymund, Raymunde, Raymundo, Redmond, Reymond, Reymundo

Raymundo (Spanish) a form of Raymond.
Raemondo, Raimondo, Raimundo, Raymondo

Raynaldo (Spanish) a form of Reynold.
Raynal, Raynald, Raynold

Raynard (French) a form of Renard, Reynard.
Raynarde

Rayne (English) a form of Raine.
Raynee, Rayno

Raynor (Scandinavian) a form of Ragnar.
Rainer, Rainor, Ranier, Ranieri, Raynar, Rayner

Rayshawn (American) a combination of Ray + Shawn.
Raysean, Rayshaan, Rayshan, Rayshaun, Raysheen, Rayshon, Rayshone, Rayshonn, Rayshun, Rayshunn

Rayshod (American) a form of Rashad.
Raychard, Rayshad, Rayshard, Rayshaud

Rayvon (American) a form of Ravon.
Rayvan, Rayvaun, Rayven, Rayvone, Reyven, Reyvon

Razi B (Aramaic) my secret.
Raz, Raziel, Raziq

Read (English) a form of Reed, Reid.
Raed, Raede, Raeed, Reaad, Reade

Raymon (English) a form of Raymond.

Reading (English) son of the red wanderer.
Redding, Reeding, Reiding

Reagan G (Irish) little king. History: Ronald Wilson Reagan was the fortieth U.S. president.
Raegan, Reagen, Reaghan, Reegan, Reegen, Regan, Reigan, Reighan, Reign, Rheagan

Rebecca G (Hebrew) tied, bound.

Rebekah G (Hebrew) a form of Rebecca.

Rebel (American) rebel.
Reb

Recaredo (Teutonic) counsels his superiors.

Red (American) red, redhead.
Redd

Reda (Arabic) satisfied.
Ridha

Redford (English) red river crossing.
Ford, Radford, Reaford, Red, Redd

Redley (English) red meadow; meadow with reeds.
Radley, Redlea, Redleigh, Redly

Redmond (German) protecting counselor. (English) a form of Raymond.
Radmond, Radmund, Reddin, Redmund

Redpath (English) red path.

Reece B (Welsh) a form of Rhys.
Reace, Rece, Reice, Reyes, Rhys, Rice, Ryese

Reed B (English) a form of Reid.
Raeed, Read, Reyde, Rheed

Reese B (Welsh) a form of Reece.
Rease, Rees, Reis, Reise, Reiss, Riese, Riess

Reeve (English) steward.
Reave, Reaves, Reeves

Reg (English) a short form of Reginald.

Regan **G** (Irish) a form of Reagan.
Regen

Reggie **B** (English) a familiar form of
Reginald.
Regi, Regie

Reginal (English) a form of Reginald.
Reginale, Reginel

Reginald **B** (English) king's advisor. A form
of Reynold. See also Naldo.
*Reg, Reggie, Regginald, Reggis, Reginal,
Reginaldo, Reginalt, Reginauld, Reginault,
Reginold, Reginuld, Regnauld, Ronald*

Regis (Latin) regal.

Regulo, Régulo (Latin) forms of Rex.

Rehema (Swahili) second-born.

Rei **G** (Japanese) rule, law.

Reid **B** (English) redhead.
Read, Reed, Reide, Reyd, Ried

Reidar (Norwegian) nest warrior.

Reiji (Japanese) wise governor.

Reilly **B** (Irish) a form of Riley.
Reiley, Reilley, Reily, Rielly

Reinaldo (Spanish) a form of Reynold.

Reinardo (Teutonic) valiant counselor.

Reinhart (German) a form of Reynard.
*Rainart, Rainhard, Rainhardt, Rainhart,
Reinart, Reinhard, Reinhardt, Renke*

Reinhold (Swedish) a form of Ragnar.
Reinold

Reizo (Japanese) cool, calm; well groomed.

Reku (Finnish) a form of Richard.

Remi, Rémi **B** (French) forms of Remy.
Remie, Remmie

Remigio (Latin) he who mans the oars.

Remington **B** (English) raven estate.
Rem, Reminton, Tony

Remo (Greek) strong one.

Remus (Latin) speedy, quick. Mythology:
Remus and his twin brother, Romulus,
founded Rome.

Remy (French) from Rheims, France.
Ramey, Remee, Remi, Rémi, Remmy

Renaldo (Spanish) a form of Reynold.
Raynaldo, Reynaldo, Rinaldo

Renán (Irish) seal.

Renard (French) a form of Reynard.
Ranard, Raynard, Reinard, Rennard

Renardo (Italian) a form of Reynard.

Renato (Italian) reborn.

Renaud (French) a form of Reynard,
Reynold.
Renauld, Renauldo, Renault, Renould

Rendor (Hungarian) policeman.

Rene **B** (Greek) a short form of Irene,
Renée.

René (French) reborn.
*Renat, Renato, Renatus, Renault, Renay,
Benee, Renny*

Renee **G** (French) a form of René.

Renfred (English) lasting peace.

Renfrew (Welsh) raven woods.

Renjiro (Japanese) virtuous.

Renny (Irish) small but strong. (French) a
familiar form of René.
Ren, Renn, Renne, Rennie

Reno (American) gambler. Geography: a city
in Nevada known for gambling.
Renos, Rino

Renshaw (English) raven woods.
Renishaw

Renton (English) settlement of the roe deer.

Renzo (Latin) a familiar form of Laurence.
(Italian) a short form of Lorenzo.
Renz, Renzy, Renzzo

Repucura (Mapuche) jagged rock; rocky
road.

Reshad (American) a form of Rashad.
*Reshade, Reshard, Resharrd, Reshaud,
Reshawd, Reshead, Reshod*

Reshawn (American) a combination of the
prefix Re + Shawn.
Reshaun, Reshaw, Reshon, Reshun

Reshean (American) a combination of the
prefix Re + Sean.
*Resean, Reshae, Reshane, Reshay, Reshayne,
Reshea, Resheen, Reshey*

Restituto (Latin) he who returns to God.

Reuben (Hebrew) behold a son.
Reuban, Reubin, Reuven, Rheuben, Rhuben, Rube, Ruben, Rubey, Rubin, Ruby, Rueben

Reuven (Hebrew) a form of Reuben.
Reuvin, Rouvin, Ruvim

Rex (Latin) king.
Rexx

Rexford (English) king's ford.

Rexton (English) king's town.

Rey (Spanish) a short form of Reynaldo, Reynard, Reynold.

Reyes (English) a form of Reece.
Reyce

Reyhan 🅱 (Arabic) favored by God.
Reyham

Reymond (English) a form of Raymond.
Reymon, Reymound, Reymund

Reymundo (Spanish) a form of Raymond.
Reimond, Reimonde, Reimundo, Reymon

Reynaldo (Spanish) a form of Reynold.
Renaldo, Rey, Reynauldo

Reynard (French) wise; bold, courageous.
Raynard, Reinhard, Reinhardt, Reinhart, Renard, Renardo, Renaud, Rennard, Rey, Reynardo, Reynaud

Reynold (English) king's advisor. See also Reginald.
Rainault, Rainhold, Ranald, Raynald, Raynaldo, Reinald, Reinaldo, Reinaldos, Reinhart, Reinhold, Reinold, Reinwald, Renald, Renaldi, Renaldo, Renaud, Renauld, Rennold, Renold, Rey, Reynald, Reynaldo, Reynaldos, Reynol, Reynolds, Rinaldo, Ronald

Réz 🅱🅶 (Hungarian) copper; redhead.
Rezsö

Rhett 🅱 (Welsh) a form of Rhys. Literature: Rhett Butler was the hero of Margaret Mitchell's novel *Gone with the Wind.*
Rhet

Rhodes (Greek) where roses grow. Geography: an island of southeast Greece.
Rhoads, Rhodas, Rodas

Rhyan (Irish) a form of Rian.
Rhian

Rhys 🅱 (Welsh) enthusiastic; stream.
Rhett, Rhyce, Rhyse, Rice

Rian (Irish) little king.
Rhyan

Ric (Italian, Spanish) a short form of Rico.
Ricca, Ricci, Ricco

Ricardo 🅱 (Portuguese, Spanish) a form of Richard.
Racardo, Recard, Ricaldo, Ricard, Ricardoe, Ricardos, Riccardo, Riccarrdo, Ricciardo, Richardo

Rice (English) rich, noble. (Welsh) a form of Reece.
Ryce

Rich (English) a short form of Richard.
Ritch

Richard 👑 🅱 (English) a form of Richart. See also Aric, Dick, Juku, Likeke.
Rashard, Reku, Ricardo, Rich, Richar, Richards, Richardson, Richart, Richaud, Richer, Richerd, Richie, Richird, Richshard, Rick, Rickard, Rickert, Rickey, Ricky, Rico, Rihardos, Rihards, Rikard, Riocard, Riócard, Risa, Risardas, Rishard, Ristéard, Ritchard, Rostik, Rye, Rysio, Ryszard

Richart (German) rich and powerful ruler.

Richie (English) a familiar form of Richard.
Richey, Richi, Richy, Rishi, Ritchie

Richman (English) powerful.

Richmond (German) powerful protector.
Richmon, Richmound

Rick (German, English) a short form of Cedric, Frederick, Richard.
Ric, Ricke, Rickey, Ricks, Ricky, Rik, Riki, Rykk

Rickard (Swedish) a form of Richard.

Ricker (English) powerful army.

Rickey 🅱 (English) a familiar form of Richard, Rick, Riqui.

Ricki 🅶 (English) a form of Rickie.

Rickie (English) a form of Ricky.
Rickee, Ricki

Rickward (English) mighty guardian.
Rickwerd, Rickwood

Ricky 🅱 (English) a familiar form of Richard, Rick.
Ricci, Rickie, Riczi, Riki, Rikki, Rikky, Riqui

Rico 🅱 (Spanish) a familiar form of Richard. (Italian) a short form of Enrico.
Ric, Ricco

Rida 🅱🅶 (Arabic) favor.

Riddock (Irish) smooth field.
Riddick

Rider (English) horseman.
Ridder, Ryder

Ridge (English) ridge of a cliff.
Ridgy, Rig, Rigg

Ridgeley (English) meadow near the ridge.
Ridgeleigh, Ridglea, Ridglee, Ridgleigh, Ridgley

Ridgeway (English) path along the ridge.

Ridhwan (Indian) acceptance; good will.

Ridley (English) meadow of reeds.
Rhidley, Riddley, Ridlea, Ridleigh, Ridly

Riel (Spanish) a short form of Gabriel.

Rigby (English) ruler's valley.

Rigel (Arabic) foot. Astronomy: one of the stars in the constellation Orion.

Rigg (English) ridge.
Rigo

Rigoberto (German) splendid; wealthy.
Rigobert

Riichi (Japanese) truthful first son.

Rijul (Indian) innocent.

Rikard (Scandinavian) a form of Richard.
Rikárd

Rikhil (Indian) eternity.

Riki (Estonian) a form of Rick.
Rikkey, Rikki, Riks, Riky

Rikki **G** (English) a form of Ricky.
(Estonian) a form of Riki.

Riku, Rikuto (Japanese) land; shore.

Riley **B** (Irish) valiant.
Reilly, Rhiley, Rhylee, Rhyley, Rieley, Rielly, Riely, Rilee, Rilley, Rily, Rilye, Rylee, Ryley

Rimac (Quechua) speaker, eloquent.

Rimachi (Quechua) he who makes us speak.

Rin (Japanese) park.

Rinaldo (Italian) a form of Reynold.
Rinald, Rinaldi

Ring (English) ring.
Ringo

Ringo (Japanese) apple. (English) a familiar form of Ring.

Rinji (Japanese) peaceful forest.

Rio (Spanish) river. Geography: Rio de Janeiro is a city in Brazil.

Riordan (Irish) bard, royal poet.
Rearden, Reardin, Reardon

Rip (Dutch) ripe; full grown. (English) a short form of Ripley.
Ripp

Ripley (English) meadow near the river.
Rip, Ripleigh, Ripply

Ripudaman (Indian) one who defeats his enemies.

Riqui (Spanish) a form of Rickey.

Rishabh (Indian) superior.

Rishad (American) a form of Rashad.
Rishaad

Rishawn (American) a combination of the prefix Ri + Shawn.
Rishan, Rishaun, Rishon, Rishone

Rishi (Hindi) sage.

Risley (English) meadow with shrubs.
Rislea, Rislee, Risleigh, Risly, Wrisley

Risto (Finnish) a short form of Christopher.

Riston (English) settlement near the shrubs.
Wriston

Ritchard (English) a form of Richard.
Ritcherd, Ritchyrd, Ritshard, Ritsherd

Ritchell (Vietnamese) nasty, gross.

Ritchie (English) a form of Richie.
Ritchy

Rithisak (Cambodian) powerful.

Rithwik (Indian) saint.

Ritter (German) knight; chivalrous.
Rittner

Ritujeet (Indian) conqueror of seasons.

River **B** (English) river; riverbank.
Rivers, Riviera, Rivor

Riyad (Arabic) gardens.
Riad, Riyaad, Riyadh, Riyaz, Riyod

Roald (Norwegian) famous ruler.

Roan (English) a short form of Rowan.
Rhoan

Roano (Spanish) reddish brown skin.

Roar (Norwegian) praised warrior.
Roary

Roarke (Irish) famous ruler.
Roark, Rorke, Rourke, Ruark

Rob (English) a short form of Robert.
Robb, Robe

Robbie **B** (English) a familiar form of Robert.
Robie, Robbi

Robby (English) a familiar form of Robert.
Rhobbie, Robbey, Robhy, Roby

Robert � **B** (English) famous brilliance.
See also Bobek, Dob, Lopaka.
*Bob, Bobby, Rab, Rabbie, Raby, Riobard,
Riobart, Rob, Robars, Robart, Robbie, Robby,
Rober, Roberd, Robers, Roberte, Roberto,
Roberts, Robin, Robinson, Roibeárd, Rosertas,
Rubert, Ruberto, Rudbert, Rupert*

Robertino (Spanish) a form of Roberto.

Roberto **B** (Italian, Portuguese, Spanish) a
form of Robert.

Roberts, Robertson (English) son of Robert.
*Roberson, Robertson, Robeson, Robinson,
Robson*

Robin **G** (English) a short form of Robert.
*Robben, Robbin, Robbins, Robbyn, Roben,
Robinet, Robinn, Robins, Robyn, Roibín*

Robinson (English) a form of Roberts.
*Robbinson, Robens, Robenson, Robson,
Robynson*

Robustiano (Latin) strong as the wood of an
oak tree.

Robyn **G** (English) a form of Robin.

Roca, Ruca (Aymara) principal, chief,
prince; strong.

Rocco (Italian) rock.
Rocca, Rocio, Rocko, Rocky, Roko, Roque

Rochan (Indian) red lotus; bright.

Rochelle **G** (French) large stone. (Hebrew)
a form of Rachel.

Rochester (English) rocky fortress.
Chester, Chet

Rock (English) a short form of Rockwell.
Roch, Rocky

Rockford (English) rocky ford.

Rockland (English) rocky land.

Rockledge (English) rocky ledge.

Rockley (English) rocky field.
Rockle

Rockwell (English) rocky spring. Art:
Norman Rockwell was a well-known
twentieth-century American illustrator.
Rock

Rocky (American) a familiar form of Rocco,
Rock.
Rockey, Rockie

Rod (English) a short form of Penrod,
Roderick, Rodney.
Rodd

Rodas (Greek, Spanish) a form of Rhodes.

Roddy (English) a familiar form of Roderick.
Roddie, Rody

Rode (Greek) pink.

Roden (English) red valley. Art: Auguste
Rodin was an innovative French sculptor.
Rodin

Roderich (German) a form of Roderick.

Roderick (German) famous ruler. See also
Broderick.
*Rhoderick, Rod, Rodderick, Roddy, Roderic,
Roderich, Roderigo, Roderik, Roderrick,
Roderyck, Rodgrick, Rodrick, Rodricki,
Rodrigo, Rodrigue, Rodrugue, Roodney, Rory,
Rurik, Ruy*

Rodger (German) a form of Roger.
Rodge, Rodgy

Rodman (German) famous man, hero.
Rodmond

Rodney **B** (English) island clearing.
*Rhodney, Rod, Rodnee, Rodnei, Rodni,
Rodnie, Rodnne, Rodny*

Rodolfo (Spanish) a form of Rudolph.
Rodolpho, Rodulfo

Rodrick (German) a form of Roderick.
*Roddrick, Rodric, Rodrich, Rodrik, Rodrique,
Rodryck, Rodryk*

Rodrigo (Italian, Spanish) a form of
Roderick.

Rodriguez (Spanish) son of Rodrigo.
Roddrigues, Rodrigues, Rodriquez

Rodrik (German) famous ruler.

Rodriquez (Spanish) a form of Rodriguez.
Rodrigquez, Rodriques, Rodriquiez

Roe (English) roe deer.
Row, Rowe

Rogan (Irish) redhead.
Rogein, Rogen

Rogelio **B** (Spanish) famous warrior.
Rojelio

Roger (German) famous spearman. See also
Lokela.
*Rodger, Rog, Rogelio, Rogerick, Rogerio,
Rogers, Rogiero, Rojelio, Rüdiger, Ruggerio,
Rutger*

Rogerio (Portuguese, Spanish) a form of
Roger.
Rogerios

Rohan (Hindi) sandalwood.

Rohin (Hindi) upward path.

Rohiniraman (Indian) the enchanted lord; Krishna.

Rohit (Hindi) big and beautiful fish.

Rohitashwa (Indian) one with red horse; fire.

Roi (French) a form of Roy.

Roja (Spanish) red.
Rojay

Roka (Japanese) white crest of the wave.

Rolán (Spanish) a form of Rolando.

Roland (German) famous throughout the land.
Loránd, Orlando, Rawlins, Rolan, Rolanda, Rolando, Rolek, Rolland, Rolle, Rollie, Rollin, Rollo, Rowe, Rowland, Ruland

Rolando **B** (Portuguese, Spanish) a form of Roland.
Lando, Olo, Roldan, Roldán, Rolondo

Rolf (German) a form of Ralph. A short form of Rudolph.
Rolfe, Rolle, Rolph, Rolphe

Rolle (Swedish) a familiar form of Roland, Rolf.

Rollie (English) a familiar form of Roland.
Roley, Rolle, Rolli, Rolly

Rollin (English) a form of Roland.
Rolin, Rollins

Rollo (English) a familiar form of Roland.
Rolla, Rolo

Rolon (Spanish) famous wolf.

Romain (French) a form of Roman.
Romaine, Romane, Romanne

Roman, Román (Latin) from Rome, Italy.
Roma, Romain, Romann, Romanos, Romman, Romochka, Romy

Romanos (Greek) a form of Roman.
Romano

Romario (Italian) a form of Romeo.
Romar, Romarius, Romaro, Romarrio

Romel (Latin) a short form of Romulus.
Romele, Romell, Romello, Rommel

Romelio (Hebrew) God's very beloved one.

Romello (Italian) of Romel.
Romelo, Rommello

Romeo (Italian) pilgrim to Rome; Roman. Literature: the title character of the Shakespearean play *Romeo and Juliet.*
Romario, Roméo, Romero

Romero (Latin) a form of Romeo.
Romario, Romeiro, Romer, Romere, Romerio, Romeris, Romeryo

Romildo (Germanic) glorious hero.

Romney (Welsh) winding river.
Romoney

Romualdo (Germanic) glorious king.

Rómulo (Greek) he who is full of strength.

Romulus (Latin) citizen of Rome. Mythology: Romulus and his twin brother, Remus, founded Rome.
Romel, Romolo, Romono, Romulo

Romy **G** (Italian) a familiar form of Roman.
Rommie, Rommy

Ron (Hebrew) a short form of Aaron, Ronald.
Ronn

Ronald **B** (Scottish) a form of Reginald.
Ranald, Ron, Ronal, Ronaldo, Ronnald, Ronney, Ronnie, Ronnold, Ronoldo

Ronaldo (Portuguese) a form of Ronald.

Rónán (Irish) seal.
Renan, Ronan, Ronat

Rondel (French) short poem.
Rondal, Rondale, Rondall, Rondeal, Rondell, Rondey, Rondie, Rondrell, Rondy, Ronel

Ronel (American) a form of Rondel.
Ronell, Ronelle, Ronnel, Ronnell, Ronyell

Rong (Chinese) martial.

Roni (Hebrew) my song; my joy.
Rani, Roneet, Roney, Ronit, Ronli, Rony

Ronin (Japanese) samurai without a master.

Ronnie **B** (Scottish) a familiar form of Ronald.
Roni, Ronie, Ronnie, Ronny

Ronny **B** (Scottish) a form of Ronnie.
Ronney

Ronson (Scottish) son of Ronald.
Ronaldson

Ronté (American) a combination of Ron + the suffix Te.
Rontae, Rontay, Ronte, Rontez

Rooney (Irish) redhead.

Boys M–R

Roosevelt (Dutch) rose field. History: Theodore and Franklin D. Roosevelt were the twenty-sixth and thirty-second U.S. presidents, respectively.
Roosvelt, Rosevelt

Roper (English) rope maker.

Rory 🅑 (German) a familiar form of Roderick. (Irish) red king.
Rorey, Rori, Rorrie, Rorry

Rosa 🅖 (Italian, Spanish) a form of Rose (see Girls' Names).

Rosalio (Spanish) rose.
Rosalino

Rosario 🅖 (Portuguese) rosary.

Roscoe (Scandinavian) deer forest.
Rosco

Rosendo (Germanic) excellent master.

Roshad (American) a form of Rashad.
Roshard

Roshean (American) a combination of the prefix Ro + Sean.
Roshain, Roshan, Roshane, Roshaun, Roshawn, Roshay, Rosheen, Roshene

Rosito (Filipino) rose.

Ross 🅑 (Latin) rose. (Scottish) peninsula. (French) red.
Rosse, Rossell, Rossi, Rossie, Rossy

Rosswell (English) springtime of roses.
Rosvel

Rostislav (Czech) growing glory.
Rosta, Rostya

Roswald (English) field of roses.
Ross, Roswell

Roth (German) redhead.

Rothwell (Scandinavian) red spring.

Rover (English) traveler.

Rowan 🅖 (English) tree with red berries.
Roan, Rowe, Rowen, Rowney, Rowyn

Rowell (English) roe-deer well.

Rowland (English) rough land. (German) a form of Roland.
Rowlando, Rowlands, Rowlandson

Rowley (English) rough meadow.
Rowlea, Rowlee, Rowleigh, Rowly

Rowson (English) son of the redhead.

Roxbury (English) rook's town or fortress.
Roxburghe

Roy (French) king. A short form of Royal, Royce. See also Conroy, Delroy, Fitzroy, Leroy, Loe.
Rey, Roi, Roye, Ruy

Royal (French) kingly, royal.
Roy, Royale, Royall, Royell

Royce 🅑 (English) son of Roy.
Roice, Roy, Royz

Royden (English) rye hill.
Royd, Roydan

Ru (Chinese) scholar.

Ruben 🅑 (Hebrew) a form of Reuben.
Ruban, Rube, Rubean, Rubens, Rubin, Ruby

Rubén (Hebrew) a form of Ruben.

Rubert (Czech) a form of Robert.

Ruby 🅖 (Hebrew) a familiar form of Reuben, Ruben.

Rucahue (Mapuche) place of construction, field that is used for construction.

Rucalaf (Mapuche) sanitarium, resting home; house of joy.

Ruchir (Indian) radiant.

Ruchit (Indian) bright, shining; pleasant.

Ruda (Czech) a form of Rudolph.
Rude, Rudek

Rudd (English) a short form of Rudyard.

Rudecindo (Spanish) a form of Rosendo.

Rudesindo (Teutonic) excellent gentleman.

Rudi (Spanish) a familiar form of Rudolph.
Ruedi

Rudo (Shona) love.

Rudolf (German) a form of Rudolph.
Rodolf, Rodolfo, Rudolfo

Rudolph (German) famous wolf. See also Dolf.
Raoul, Rezsó, Rodolfo, Rodolph, Rodolphe, Rolf, Ruda, Rudek, Rudi, Rudolf, Rudolpho, Rudolphus, Rudy

Rudolpho (Italian) a form of Rudolph.

Rudy 🅑 (English) a familiar form of Rudolph.
Roody, Ruddy, Ruddie, Rudey, Rudi, Rudie

Rudyard (English) red enclosure.
Rudd

Rueben (Hebrew) a form of Reuben.
Rueban, Ruebin

Rufay (Quechua) warm.

Ruff (French) redhead.

Rufin (Polish) redhead.
　Rufino

Rufio (Latin) red-haired.

Ruford (English) red ford; ford with reeds.
　Rufford

Rufus (Latin) redhead.
　Rayfus, Rufe, Ruffis, Ruffus, Rufino, Rufo,
　Rufous

Rugby (English) rook fortress. History: a
　famous British school after which the sport
　of Rugby was named.

Ruggerio (Italian) a form of Roger.
　Rogero, Ruggero, Ruggiero

Ruhakana (Rukiga) argumentative.

Rujul (Indian) simple; honest.

Ruland (German) a form of Roland.
　Rulan, Rulon, Rulondo

Rumford (English) wide river crossing.

Rumi (Quechua) strong and as eternal as a
　rock.

Rumimaqui, Rumiñaui (Quechua) he who
　has strong hands, hands of stone.

Rumisonjo, Rumisuncu (Quechua) hard-
　hearted, heart of stone.

Run (Chinese) sleek.

Runacatu, Runacoto (Quechua) short man,
　small man.

Runako (Shona) handsome.

Rune (German, Swedish) secret.

Runrot (Tai) prosperous.

Runto, Runtu (Quechua) hailstone.

Rupak (Indian) sign, feature; acting.

Rupang (Indian) beautiful.

Rupert (German) a form of Robert.
　Ruperth, Ruperto, Ruprecht

Ruperto (Italian) a form of Rupert.

Rupin (Indian) embodied beauty.

Rupinder **G** (Sanskrit) handsome.

Ruprecht (German) a form of Rupert.

Rush (French) redhead. (English) a short
　form of Russell.
　Rushi

Rushford (English) ford with rushes.

Rusk (Spanish) twisted bread.

Ruskin (French) redhead.
　Rush, Russ

Russ (French) a short form of Russell.

Russel (French) a form of Russell.

Russell (French) redhead; fox colored. See
　also Lukela.
　Roussell, Rush, Russ, Russel, Russelle, Rusty

Rusty (French) a familiar form of Russell.
　Ruste, Rusten, Rustie, Rustin, Ruston, Rustyn

Rutajit (Indian) conqueror of truth.

Rutger (Scandinavian) a form of Roger.
　Ruttger

Rutherford (English) cattle ford.
　Rutherfurd

Ruthvik (Indian) saint.

Rutland (Scandinavian) red land.

Rutledge (English) red ledge.

Rutley (English) red meadow.

Rutujit (Indian) conqueror of seasons.

Rutveg (Indian) can travel in all climatic
　conditions.

Ruy (Spanish) a short form of Roderick.
　Rui

Ruyan (Spanish) little king.

Ryan ☀ **B** (Irish) little king.
　Rayan, Rhyan, Rhyne, Ryane, Ryann, Ryen,
　Ryian, Ryiann, Ryin, Ryne, Ryon, Ryuan, Ryun,
　Ryyan

Ryann **G** (Irish) a form of Ryan.

Rycroft (English) rye field.
　Ryecroft

Ryder (English) a form of Rider.
　Rydder, Rye

Rye (English) a short form of Ryder. A grain
　used in cereal and whiskey. (Gypsy)
　gentleman.
　Ry

Ryen (Irish) a form of Ryan.
　Ryein, Ryien

Ryerson (English) son of Rider, Ryder.

Ryese (English) a form of Reece.
　Reyse, Ryez, Ryse

Ryker (American) a surname used as a first name.
Riker, Ryk

Rylan 🅱 (English) land where rye is grown.
Ryland, Rylean, Rylen, Rylin, Rylon, Rylyn, Rylynn

Ryland (English) a form of Rylan.
Ryeland, Rylund

Ryle (English) rye hill.
Ryal, Ryel

Rylee 🅖 (Irish) a form of Riley.
Ryeleigh, Ryleigh, Rylie, Rillie

Ryley 🅱 (Irish) a form of Riley.
Ryely

Ryman (English) rye seller.

Ryne (Irish) a form of Ryan.
Rynn

Ryohei (Japanese) splendidly peaceful helper.

Ryoichi (Japanese) first son of Ryo.

Ryoji (Japanese) refreshingly splendid governor.

Ryoma (Japanese) dragon; horse.

Ryon (Irish) a form of Ryan.

Ryosuke (Japanese) cool; mediation.

Ryota (Japanese) very splendid.

Ryozo (Japanese) third son of Ryo.

Ryu (Japanese) dragon.

Ryuhei (Japanese) prosperous and peaceful.

Ryuichi (Japanese) first son of Ryu.

Ryuji (Japanese) dragon man.

Ryunosuke (Japanese) peaceful dragon.

S 🅖 (American) an initial used as a first name.

Saabir (Indian) patient.

Saahil (Indian) seashore.

Saahir (Indian) wakeful.

Saajid (Indian) he who worships God.

Saalih (Indian) good; righteous.

Saariyah (Indian) clouds at night.

Sabastian (Greek) a form of Sebastian.
Sabastain, Sabastiano, Sabastien, Sabastin, Sabastion, Sabaston, Sabbastiun, Sabestian

Sabeeh (Indian) beautiful.

Sabelio (Spanish) a form of Sabino.

Saber (French) sword.
Sabir, Sabre

Sabin (Basque) ancient tribe of central Italy.
Saban, Saben, Sabian, Sabien, Sabino

Sabino (Basque) a form of Sabin.

Sabiti (Rutooro) born on Sunday.

Sabola (Nguni) pepper.

Sabrang (Indian) rainbow.

Sabrina 🅖 (Latin) boundary line. (English) child of royalty. (Hebrew) a familiar form of Sabra (see Girls' Names).

Saburo (Japanese) third-born son.

Sacha 🅱🅖 (Russian) a form of Sasha.
Sascha

Sachar (Russian) a form of Zachary.

Sachidanandha (Indian) total bliss.

Sachio (Japanese) fortunately born.

Saddam (Arabic) powerful ruler.

Sade 🅖 (Hebrew) a form of Sarah.

Sadeeq (Indian) trustworthy.

Sadgun (Indian) virtues.

Sadiki (Swahili) faithful.
Saadiq, Sadeek, Sadek, Sadik, Sadiq, Sadique

Sadiva (Indian) eternal.

Sadler (English) saddle maker.
Saddler

Sadoc (Hebrew) just one.

Safari (Swahili) born while traveling.
Safa, Safarian

Safford (English) willow river crossing.

Safiy (Indian) best friend.

Safwan (Indian) rocks.

Sagardutt (Indian) gift of the ocean.

Sage 🅱🅖 (English) wise. Botany: an herb.
Sagen, Sager, Saige, Saje

Sahale (Native American) falcon.
Sael, Sahal, Sahel, Sahil

Sahar (Indian) sun; dawn.

Sahastrabahu (Indian) one with a thousand arms.

Sahastrajit (Indian) a thousand times victorious in battle.

Sahen (Hindi) above.
Sahan

Sahil (Native American) a form of Sahale.
Saheel, Sahel

Sahir (Hindi) friend.

Sai (Indian) flower; everywhere.

Saiasi (Fijian) a form of Isaias.

Sa'id (Arabic) happy.
Sa'ad, Saaid, Saed, Sa'eed, Saeed, Sahid, Saide, Sa'ied, Saied, Saiyed, Saiyeed, Sajid, Sajjid, Sayed, Sayeed, Sayid, Seyed, Shahid

Sairos (Pohnpeian) a form of Cyress.

Sairusi (Fijian) a form of Cyress.

Sajag (Hindi) watchful.

Saka (Swahili) hunter.

Sakeri (Danish) a form of Zachary.
Sakarai, Sakari

Sakima (Native American) king.

Saksham (Indian) capable.

Sakshik (Indian) witness.

Saku (Japanese) remembrance of the Lord.

Sakuruta (Pawnee) coming sun.

Sal (Italian) a short form of Salvatore.

Salah Udeen (Indian) the righteousness of the faith.

Salaj (Indian) water that flows from melted ice.

Salam (Arabic) lamb.
Salaam

Salamon (Spanish) a form of Solomon.
Saloman, Salomón

Salaun (French) a form of Solomon.

Sálih (Arabic) right, good.
Saleeh, Saleh, Salehe

Salim (Swahili) peaceful.

Salím (Arabic) peaceful, safe.
Saleem, Salem, Saliym, Salman

Sally **G** (Italian) a familiar form of Salvatore.

Salmalin (Hindi) taloned.

Salman (Czech) a form of Salím, Solomon.
Salmaan, Salmaine, Salmon

Salomon (French) a form of Solomon.
Salomone

Salton (English) manor town; willow town.

Salustio (Latin) he who offers salvation.

Salvador (Spanish) savior.
Salvadore

Salvatore (Italian) savior. See also Xavier.
Sal, Salbatore, Sallie, Sally, Salvator, Salvattore, Salvidor, Sauveur

Salviano (Spanish) a form of Salvo.

Salvio (Latin) cured, healthy; upright.

Salvo (Latin) healthy one.

Sam **B** (Hebrew) a short form of Samuel.
Samm, Sammy, Sem, Shem, Shmuel

Samantha **G** (Aramaic) listener. (Hebrew) told by God.

Samarjeet (Indian) winner of the battle.

Sambaran (Indian) restraint; name of an ancient king.

Sambathkrishna (Indian) a gift from Lord Krishna.

Sambha (Indian) shining.

Sambhav (Indian) born; manifested.

Sambhddha (Indian) wise.

Sambit (Indian) consciousness.

Sambo (American) a familiar form of Samuel.
Sambou

Sambodh (Indian) complete knowledge.

Sameen (Indian) valuable.

Sameer (Arabic) a form of Samír.

Samendra (Indian) winner of a war.

Sami, Samy **B** (Hebrew) forms of Sammy.
Sameeh, Sameh, Samie, Samih, Sammi

Samik (Indian) peaceful.

Samín (Quechua) fortunate, lucky; adventurous; successful; happy.

Samír (Arabic) entertaining companion.
Sameer

Samiran (Indian) breeze.

Samit (Indian) always making friends.

Sammad (Indian) joy.

Samman (Arabic) grocer.
Saman, Sammon

Sammy 🅱 (Hebrew) a familiar form of Samuel.
Saamy, Samey, Sami, Sammee, Sammey, Sammie, Samy

Samo (Czech) a form of Samuel.
Samho, Samko

Sampat (Indian) well to do.

Samrat (Indian) emperor.

Samrudh (Indian) the enriched one.

Samson (Hebrew) like the sun. Bible: a judge and powerful warrior betrayed by Delilah.
Sampson, Sansao, Sansom, Sansón, Shem, Shimshon

Samual (Hebrew) a form of Samuel.
Samuael, Samuail

Samudra (Indian) sea.

Samudragupta (Indian) a famous Gupta king.

Samuel 🐦 🅱 (Hebrew) heard God; asked of God. Bible: a famous Old Testament prophet and judge. See also Kamuela, Zamiel, Zanvil.
Sam, Samael, Samaru, Samauel, Samaul, Sambo, Sameul, Samiel, Sammail, Sammel, Sammuel, Sammy, Samo, Samouel, Samu, Samual, Samuele, Samuelis, Samuell, Samuello, Samuil, Samuka, Samule, Samuru,

Samvel, Sanko, Saumel, Schmuel, Shem, Shmuel, Simão, Simuel, Somhairle, Zamuel

Samuele (Italian) a form of Samuel.
Samulle

Samuelle 🅶 (Hebrew) a form of Samuela (see Girls' Names).

Samuru (Japanese) a form of Samuel.

Samvar (Indian) content.

Samyak (Indian) enough.

San (Chinese) three.

Sanabhi (Indian) related.

Sanam (Indian) beloved.

Sanat (Hindi) ancient.

Sanatan (Indian) eternal.

Sanborn (English) sandy brook.
Sanborne, Sanbourn, Sanbourne, Sanburn, Sanburne, Sandborn, Sandbourne

Sanchez (Latin) a form of Sancho.
Sanchaz, Sancheze

Sanchit (Indian) collection.

Sancho (Latin) sanctified; sincere. Literature: Sancho Panza was Don Quixote's squire.
Sanchez, Sauncho

Sandananda (Indian) eternal bliss.

Sandeep 🅱 (Punjabi) enlightened.
Sandip

Sandeepen (Indian) a sage.

Sander (English) a short form of Alexander, Lysander.
Sandor, Sándor, Saunder

Sanders (English) son of Sander.
Sanderson, Saunders, Saunderson

Sandesh (Indian) message.

Sándor (Hungarian) a short form of Alexander.
Sanyi

Sandro (Greek, Italian) a short form of Alexander.
Sandero, Sandor, Sandre, Saundro, Shandro

Sandy 🅶 (English) a familiar form of Alexander.
Sande, Sandey, Sandi, Sandie

Sanford (English) sandy river crossing.
Sandford

Sang (Vietnamese) looking or behaving like people of upper classes.

Sani (Hindi) the planet Saturn. (Navajo) old.

Saniiro (Japanese) praise; admirable.

Sanil (Indian) gifted, bestowed.

Sanjay (Sanskrit) triumphant. (American) a combination of Sanford + Jay.
Sanjaya, Sanje, Sanjey, Sanjo

Sanjiv (Hindi) long lived.
Sanjeev

Sanjivan (Indian) immortality.

Sanjog (Indian) coincidence.

Sankalp (Indian) aim.

Sankalpa (Indian) resolve.

Sankar (Hindi) a form of Shankara, another name for the Hindu god Shiva.

Sankarshan (Indian) a name of Balaram, brother of Lord Krishna.

Sanket (Indian) signal.

Sannath (Indian) accompanied by a protector.

Sanobar (Indian) palm tree.

Sansón (Spanish) a form of Samson.
Sanson, Sansone, Sansun

Santana **G** (Spanish) Saint Anne. History: Antonio López de Santa Anna was a Mexican general and political leader.
Santanna

Santiago (Spanish) Saint James.

Santino (Spanish) a form of Santonio.
Santion

Santo (Italian, Spanish) holy.
Santos

Santon (English) sandy town.

Santonio (Spanish) a short form of San Antonio or Saint Anthony.
Santino, Santon, Santoni

Santos (Spanish) saint.
Santo

Santosh (Hindi) satisfied.

Sanurag (Indian) affectionate.

Sanyam (Indian) to have control.

Sanyu **BG** (Luganda) happy.

Sapan (Indian) dream.

Sapay (Quechua) unique; main.

Saqr (Arabic) falcon.

Saquan (American) a combination of the prefix Sa + Quan.
Saquané, Saquin, Saquon, Saqwan, Saqwone

Sara **G** (Hebrew) a form of Sarah.

Sarad (Hindi) born in the autumn.

Sarah **G** (Hebrew) child of royalty.

Sarang (Indian) musical instrument.

Saras, Sashank, Sasi (Indian) the moon.

Sarasvat (Indian) learned.

Sargam (Indian) musical notes.

Sargent (French) army officer.
Sargant, Sarge, Sarjant, Sergeant, Sergent, Serjeant

Sarin (Indian) helpful.

Sarito (Spanish) a form of Caesar.
Sarit

Saritupac (Quechua) glorious prince.

Sariyah (Arabic) clouds at night.

Sarngin (Hindi) archer; protector.

Sarojin (Hindi) like a lotus.
Sarojun

Sarthak (Indian) to have its own importance.

Sarvbhanu (Indian) name of the sun.

Sarvendra, Sarvesh (Indian) god of all.

Sasha **G** (Russian) a short form of Alexander.
Sacha, Sash, Sashenka, Sashka, Sashok, Sausha

Sashang (Indian) connected.

Sashwat (Indian) eternal.

Sasmit (Indian) ever smiling.

Sasson (Hebrew) joyful.
Sason

Satadev (Indian) God.

Satchel (French) small bag.
Satch

Sathi (Indian) partner.

Satin (Indian) real.

Satordi (French) Saturn.
Satori

Satoru (Japanese) to enlighten; complete.

Satpal (Indian) protector.

Satu (Japanese) fairy tale.

Saturio (Latin) protector of the sown fields.

Saturnín (Spanish) gift of Saturn.

Saturnino (Spanish) a form of Saturno.

Saturno (Latin) he who is living an abundant life.

Satvik (Indian) virtuous.

Satwaki (Indian) fighter.

Satya (Indian) truth.

Satya Pramod (Indian) the true person.

Satyadarshi (Indian) one who can see the truth.

Satyamurty (Indian) statue of truth.

Satyaprakash (Indian) light of truth.

Satyavan (Indian) one who speaks truth.

Satyavrat (Indian) one who has taken the vow of truth.

Saul B (Hebrew) asked for, borrowed. Bible: in the Old Testament, a king of Israel and the father of Jonathan; in the New Testament, Saint Paul's original name was Saul.
Saül, Shaul, Sol, Solly

Saúl (Hebrew) a form of Saul.

Saulo (Greek) he who is tender and delicate.

Saumit (Indian) easy to get.

Saumya (Indian) handsome.

Saurabh (Indian) fragrant.

Saurav (Indian) melodious.

Saurjyesh (Indian) Kartikeya, the lord of valor.

Savannah G (Spanish) treeless plain.

Saverio (Italian) a form of Xavier.

Saville (French) willow town.
Savelle, Savil, Savile, Savill, Savylle, Seville, Siville

Savio (Indian) saint's name.

Savitendra (Indian) the sun.

Savon B (Spanish) a treeless plain.
Savan, Savaughn, Saveion, Saveon, Savhon, Saviahn, Savian, Savino, Savion, Savo, Savone, Sayvon, Sayvone

Saw (Burmese) early.

Sawyer B (English) wood worker.
Sawyere

Sax (English) a short form of Saxon.
Saxe

Saxon (English) swordsman. History: the Roman name for the Teutonic raiders who ravaged the Roman British coasts.
Sax, Saxen, Saxsin, Saxxon

Sayani (Quechua) I stay on foot.

Sayarumi (Quechua) erect and strong as stone.

Sayer (Welsh) carpenter.
Say, Saye, Sayers, Sayr, Sayre, Sayres

Sayf Udeen (Indian) sword of the faith.

Sayri (Quechua) prince; he who is always helping those who ask for it.

Sayyid (Arabic) master.
Sayed, Sayid, Sayyad, Sayyed

Scanlon (Irish) little trapper.
Scanlan, Scanlen

Schafer (German) shepherd.
Schaefer, Schaffer, Schiffer, Shaffar, Shäffer

Schmidt (German) blacksmith.
Schmid, Schmit, Schmitt, Schmydt

Schneider (German) tailor.
Schnieder, Snider, Snyder

Schön (German) handsome.
Schoen, Schönn, Shon

Schuyler (Dutch) sheltering.
Schuylar, Schyler, Scoy, Scy, Skuyler, Sky, Skylar, Skyler, Skylor

Schyler G (Dutch) a form of Schuyler.
Schylar, Schylre, Schylur

Scorpio (Latin) dangerous, deadly. Astronomy: a southern constellation near Libra and Sagittarius. Astrology: the eighth sign of the zodiac.
Scorpeo

Scott B (English) from Scotland. A familiar form of Prescott.
Scot, Scottie, Scotto, Scotty

Scottie (English) a familiar form of Scott.
Scotie, Scotti

Scotty (English) a familiar form of Scott.
Scottey

Scoville (French) Scott's town.

Scully (Irish) town crier.

Seabert (English) shining sea.
Seabright, Sebert, Seibert

Seabrook (English) brook near the sea.

Seamus (Irish) a form of James.
Seamas, Seumas, Shamus

Sean ₩ B (Irish) a form of John.
Seaghan, Séan, Seán, Seanán, Seane, Seann, Shaan, Shaine, Shane, Shaun, Shawn, Shayne, Shon, Siôn

Searlas (Irish, French) a form of Charles.
Séarlas, Searles, Searlus

Searle (English) armor.

Seasar (Latin) a form of Caesar.
Seasare, Seazar, Sesar, Sesear, Sezar

Seaton (English) town near the sea.
Seeton, Seton

Sebastian ☀ **B** (Greek) venerable. (Latin) revered.
Bastian, Sabastian, Sabastien, Sebashtian, Sebastain, Sebastiane, Sebastiano, Sebastien, Sébastien, Sebastin, Sebastine, Sebastion, Sebbie, Sebestyén, Sebo, Sepasetiano

Sebastián (Greek) a form of Sebastian.

Sebastien, Sébastien B (French) forms of Sebastian.
Sebasten, Sebastyen

Sebastion (Greek) a form of Sebastian.

Sedgely (English) sword meadow.
Sedgeley, Sedgly

Sedric (Irish) a form of Cedric.
Seddrick, Sederick, Sedrick, Sedrik, Sedriq

Seeley (English) blessed.
Sealey, Seely, Selig

Sef (Egyptian) yesterday. Mythology: one of the two lions that make up the Akeru, guardian of the gates of morning and night.

Sefton (English) village of rushes.

Sefu (Swahili) sword.

Seger (English) sea spear; sea warrior.
Seager, Seeger, Segar

Segismundo (Germanic) victorious protector.

Segun (Yoruba) conqueror.

Segundino (Latin) family's second son.

Segundo (Spanish) second.

Sehej (Indian) calm.

Seibert (English) bright sea.
Seabert, Sebert

Seif (Arabic) religion's sword.

Seifert (German) a form of Siegfried.

Seiichi (Japanese) first son of Sei.

Seiji (Japanese) lawful.

Seiko (Japanese) force; truth.

Sein (Basque) innocent.

Seito (Japanese) star.

Seiya (Japanese) he who is like a star.

Sekaye (Shona) laughter.

Sekove (Fijian) a form of Jacob.

Selby (English) village by the mansion.
Selbey, Shelby

Seldon (English) willow tree valley.
Selden, Sellden

Selemías (Hebrew) God rewards.

Selena G (Greek) moon.

Selig (German) a form of Seeley.
Seligman, Seligmann, Zelig

Selwyn (English) friend from the palace.
Selvin, Selwin, Selwinn, Selwynn, Selwynne, Wyn

Semanda (Luganda) cow clan.

Semarias (Hebrew) God guarded him.

Semer (Ethiopian) a form of George.
Semere, Semier

Semes (Chuukese) a form of James.

Semesa, Semisi (Fijian) forms of James.

Semon (Greek) a form of Simon.
Semion

Sempala (Luganda) born in prosperous times.

Sempronio (Latin) name of a Roman family based on male descent.

Sen BG (Japanese) wood fairy.
Senh

Senajit (Indian) conqueror of an army.

Séneca (Latin) venerable elderly man.

Sener (Turkish) bringer of joy.

Senichi (Japanese) first son of Sen.

Senín (Grego) god Jupiter.

Senior (French) lord.

Sennett (French) elderly.
Sennet

Senon (Spanish) living.

Senwe (African) dry as a grain stalk.

Sepp (German) a form of Joseph.
Seppi

Septimio (Latin) seventh child.

Séptimo (Latin) family's seventh son.

Septimus (Latin) seventh.

Serafín (Hebrew) a form of Seraphim.

Serafino (Portuguese) a form of Seraphim.

Seraphim (Hebrew) fiery, burning. Bible: the highest order of angels, known for their zeal and love.
Saraf, Saraph, Serafim, Serafin, Serafino, Seraphimus, Seraphin

Serapio (Latin) consecrated to Serapes, an Egyptian divinity.

Seremaia (Fijian) a form of Jeremy.

Seremesa (Chuukese) a form of Jeremy.

Sereno (Latin) calm, tranquil.

Serge (Latin) attendant.
Seargeoh, Serg, Sergei, Sergio, Sergios, Sergius, Sergiusz, Serguel, Sirgio, Sirgios

Sergei (Russian) a form of Serge.
Sergey, Sergeyuk, Serghey, Sergi, Sergie, Sergo, Sergunya, Serhiy, Serhiyko, Serjiro, Serzh

Sergio (Italian) a form of Serge.
Serginio, Serigo, Serjio

Servando (Spanish) to serve.
Servan, Servio

Sesario (Pohnpeian) a form of Cesar.

Sese (Kosraean) a form of Jesse.

Sesko (Pohnpeian) a form of Francisco.

Setefano (Fijian) a form of Esteban.

Seth ♥ **B** (Hebrew) appointed. Bible: the third son of Adam.
Set, Sethan, Sethe, Shet

Setimba (Luganda) river dweller. Geography: a river in Uganda.

Setu (Indian) sacred symbol.

Seumas (Scottish) a form of James.
Seaumus

Seung (Korean) successor.

Severiano (Italian) a form of Séverin.

Séverin (French) severe.
Seve, Sevé, Severan, Severian, Severiano, Severo, Sevien, Sevrin, Sevryn

Severino (Spanish) a form of Severo.

Severn (English) boundary.
Sevearn, Sevren, Sevrnn

Severo (French) a form of Severin.

Sevilen (Turkish) beloved.

Seward (English) sea guardian.
Sewerd, Siward

Sewati (Moquelumnan) curved bear claws.

Sexton (English) church official; sexton.

Sextus (Latin) sixth.
Sixtus

Seymour (French) prayer. Religion: name honoring Saint Maur. See also Maurice.
Seamor, Seamore, Seamour, See

Shaady (Indian) singer.

Shabar (Indian) nectar.

Shabouh (Armenian) king, noble. History: a fourth-century Persian king.

Shad (Punjabi) happy-go-lucky.
Shadd

Shadi (Arabic) singer.
Shadde, Shaddi, Shaddy, Shade, Shadee,

Shadeed, Shadey, Shadie, Shady, Shydee, Shydi

Shadrach (Babylonian) god; godlike. Bible: one of three companions who emerged unharmed from the fiery furnace of Babylon.
Shad, Shadrack, Shadrick, Sheddrach, Shedrach, Shedrick

Shadwell (English) shed by a well.

Shae **G** (Irish) a form of Shay.

Shafeeq (Indian) compassionate, tender.

Shah (Persian) king. History: a title for rulers of Iran.

Shaheem (American) a combination of Shah + Raheem.
Shaheim, Shahiem, Shahm

Shahid (Arabic) a form of Sa'id.
Shahed, Shaheed

Shahnaaz (Indian) pride of a king.

Shai (Hebrew) a short form of Yeshaya.
Shaie

Shail, Sheil (Indian) mountain.

Shaildhar (Indian) he who holds mountains.

Shaiming (Chinese) life; sunshine.

Shaina **G** (Yiddish) beautiful.

Shaine (Irish) a form of Sean.
Shain

Shaka **B** (Zulu) founder, first. History: Shaka Zulu was the founder of the Zulu empire.

Shaka-Nyorai (Chinese) historic Buddha.

Shakeel (Arabic) a form of Shaquille.
Shakeil, Shakel, Shakell, Shakiel, Shakil, Shakille, Shakyle

Shakir (Arabic) thankful.
Shaakir, Shakeer, Shakeir, Shakur

Shakti (Indian) power.

Shaktidhar (Indian) powerful one.

Shakunt (Indian) blue jay.

Shakur (Arabic) a form of Shakir.
Shakuur

Shalang (Indian) emperor.

Shalik (Indian) a sage.

Shalin (Indian) good manners.

Shalina (Indian) courteous.

Shaline (Indian) praiseworthy.

Shalmali (Indian) Lord Vishnu's power.

Shalom (Hebrew) peace.
Shalum, Shlomo, Sholem, Sholom

Shalya (Hindi) throne.

Shama (Indian) the sun.

Shaman (Sanskrit) holy man, mystic, medicine man.
Shamaine, Shamaun, Shamin, Shamine, Shammon, Shamon, Shamone

Shamar (Hebrew) a form of Shamir.
Shamaar, Shamare, Shamari

Shami (Indian) fire; name of a tree.

Shamir (Hebrew) precious stone.
Shahmeer, Shahmir, Shamar, Shameer, Shamyr

Shamun (Indian) name of a prophet.

Shamus (American) slang for detective.
Shamas, Shames, Shamos, Shemus

Shan (Irish) a form of Shane.
Shann, Shanne

Shanahan (Irish) wise, clever.

Shandy (English) rambunctious.
Shandey, Shandie

Shane **B** (Irish) a form of Sean.
Shan, Shayn, Shayne

Shang (Chinese) to forge ahead.

Shangobunni (Yoruba) gift from Shango.

Shang-Ti (Chinese) the supreme God.

Shankhdhar (Indian) one who carries a conch shell.

Shankhi (Indian) the ocean; Lord Vishnu.

Shanley **G** (Irish) small; ancient.
Shaneley, Shannley

Shannon **G** (Irish) small and wise.
Shanan, Shannan, Shannen, Shannin, Shannone, Shanon

Shantae **G** (French) a form of Chante.
Shant, Shanta, Shantai, Shante, Shantell, Shantelle, Shanti, Shantia, Shantie, Shanton, Shanty

Shante **G** (French) a form of Shantae.

Shantell **G** (American) song.

Shao (Chinese) glorious youth.

Shap (English) a form of Shep.

Shaquan (American) a combination of the prefix Sha + Quan.
Shaqaun, Shaquand, Shaquane, Shaquann, Shaquaunn, Shaquawn, Shaquen, Shaquian, Shaquin, Shaqwan

Shaquell (American) a form of Shaquille.
Shaqueal, Shaqueil, Shaquel, Shaquelle, Shaquiel, Shaquiell, Shaquielle

Shaquille **B** (Arabic) handsome.
Shakeel, Shaquell, Shaquil, Shaquile, Shaquill, Shaqul

Shaquon (American) a combination of the prefix Sha + Quon.
Shaikwon, Shaqon, Shaquoin, Shaquoné

Sharad (Pakistani) autumn.
Sharod

Sharíf (Arabic) honest; noble.
Shareef, Sharef, Shareff, Shareif, Sharief, Sharife, Shariff, Shariyf, Sharrif, Sharyif

Sharod (Pakistani) a form of Sharad.
Sharrod

Sharon **G** (Hebrew) a form of Sharron.

Sharron (Hebrew) flat area, plain.
Sharon, Sharone, Sharonn, Sharonne

Sharvarish, Shashank, Shashee, Shashi, Shashin (Indian) moon.

Shashibhushan (Indian) one who wears the moon as an ornament.

Shashidhar (Indian) one who carries the moon.

Shashikant (Indian) moon stone.

Shashikar (Indian) moon ray.

Shashipushpa (Indian) lotus.

Shashishekhar (Indian) the one with the moon at the top of his head.

Shashvat (Indian) eternal, constant.

Shashwat (Indian) permanent; one who never dies; always present.

Shatrughna (Indian) destroyer of enemies; Lord Rama's brother.

Shatrunjay (Indian) he who defeats enemies.

Shattuck (English) little shad fish.

Shaun B (Irish) a form of Sean.
Shaughan, Shaughn, Shaugn, Shauna, Shaunahan, Shaune, Shaunn, Shaunne

Shavar (Hebrew) comet.
Shavit

Shavon G (American) a combination of the prefix Sha + Yvon.
Shauvan, Shauvon, Shavan, Shavaughn, Shaven, Shavin, Shavone, Shawan, Shawon, Shawun

Shaw (English) grove.

Shawn B (Irish) a form of Sean.
Shawen, Shawne, Shawnee, Shawnn, Shawon

Shawnta G (American) a combination of Shawn + the suffix Ta.
Shawntae, Shawntel, Shawnti

Shay BG (Irish) a form of Shea.
Shae, Shai, Shaya, Shaye, Shey

Shayan (Cheyenne) a form of Cheyenne.
Shayaan, Shayann, Shayon

Shayne B (Hebrew) a form of Sean.
Shayn, Shaynne, Shean

Shazad (Indian) prince.

Shea G (Irish) courteous.
Shay

Shedrick (Babylonian) a form of Shadrach.
Shadriq, Shederick, Shedric, Shedrique

Sheece (Indian) prophet's name.

Sheehan (Irish) little; peaceful.
Shean

Sheffield (English) crooked field.
Field, Shef, Sheff, Sheffie, Sheffy

Shel (English) a short form of Shelby, Sheldon, Shelton.

Shelby G (English) ledge estate.
Shel, Shelbe, Shelbey, Shelbie, Shell, Shellby, Shelley, Shelly

Sheldon B (English) farm on the ledge.
Shel, Sheldan, Shelden, Sheldin, Sheldyn, Shell, Shelley, Shelly, Shelton

Shelley G (English) a familiar form of Shelby, Sheldon, Shelton. Literature: Percy Bysshe Shelley was a nineteenth-century British poet.
Shell, Shelly

Shelly G (English) a form of Shelby, Sheldon, Shelley.

Shelton B (English) town on a ledge.
Shel, Shelley, Shelten

Shem (Hebrew) name; reputation. (English) a short form of Samuel. Bible: Noah's oldest son.

Shen (Egyptian) sacred amulet. (Chinese) meditation.

Sheng (Chinese) winning.

Shen-Nung (Chinese) god of medicine, pharmacy, agriculture.

Shep (English) a short form of Shepherd.
Shap, Ship, Shipp

Shepherd (English) shepherd.
Shep, Shepard, Shephard, Shepp, Sheppard, Shepperd

Shepley (English) sheep meadow.
Sheplea, Sheplee, Shepply, Shipley

Sherborn (English) clear brook.
Sherborne, Sherbourn, Sherburn, Sherburne

Sheridan G (Irish) wild.
Dan, Sheredan, Sheriden, Sheridon, Sherridan

Sherill (English) shire on a hill.
Sheril, Sherril, Sherrill

Sherlock (English) light haired. Literature: Sherlock Holmes is a famous British detective character, created by Sir Arthur Conan Doyle.
Sherlocke, Shurlock, Shurlocke

Sherman (English) sheep shearer; resident of a shire.
Scherman, Schermann, Sherm, Shermain, Shermaine, Shermann, Shermie, Shermon, Shermy

Sherrod (English) clearer of the land.
Sherod, Sherrad, Sherrard, Sherrodd

Sherry **G** (French) beloved, dearest. A familiar form of Sheryl (see Girls' Names).

Sherwin (English) swift runner, one who cuts the wind.
Sherveen, Shervin, Sherwan, Sherwind, Sherwinn, Sherwyn, Sherwynd, Sherwynne, Win

Sherwood (English) bright forest.
Sherwoode, Shurwood, Woody

Sheshdhar (Indian) one who holds Shesha.

Shigekazu (Japanese) first son of Shige.

Shigeo (Japanese) luxuriant husband.

Shigeru (Japanese) luxuriant.

Shigeto (Japanese) luxuriant person.

Shihab (Arabic) blaze.

Shikhar (Indian) mountain; top of the mountain.

Shilang (Indian) virtuous.

Shilín (Chinese) intellectual.
Shilan

Shiloh (Hebrew) God's gift.
Shi, Shile, Shiley, Shilo, Shiloe, Shy, Shyle, Shylo, Shyloh

Shimon (Hebrew) a form of Simon.
Shymon

Shimshon (Hebrew) a form of Samson.
Shimson

Shin (Japanese) faithful.

Shinakio (Japanese) faithful boy.

Shing (Chinese) victory.
Shingae, Shingo

Shinichi (Japanese) first son of Shin.

Shinjiro (Japanese) faithful second son.

Shino (Japanese) stem of bamboo.

Shinshiro (Japanese) faithful fourth-born son.

Shipton (English) sheep village; ship village.

Shiquan (American) a combination of the prefix Shi + Quan.
Shiquane, Shiquann, Shiqawn, Shiquoin, Shiqwan

Shirish (Indian) name of a tree.

Shiro (Japanese) fourth-born son.

Shishul (Indian) baby.

Shiva (Hindi) life and death. Religion: the most common name for the Hindu god of destruction and reproduction.
Shiv, Shivan, Siva

Shivam (Indian) auspicious.

Shivanand (Indian) one who is happy in Lord Shiva's thoughts.

Shivang (Indian) part of Lord Shiva.

Shivank (Indian) mark of the Lord.

Shivendu (Indian) moon.

Shiveshvar (Indian) god of welfare.

Shivkumar (Indian) son of Lord Shiva.

Shivshekhar (Indian) one at the top of Shiva; moon.

Shlesh (Indian) physical bonding.

Shlomo (Hebrew) a form of Solomon.
Shelmu, Shelomo, Shelomoh, Shlomi, Shlomot

Shmuel (Hebrew) a form of Samuel.
Shem, Shemuel, Shmelke, Shmiel, Shmulka

Shneur (Yiddish) senior.
Shneiur

Sho (Japanese) commander; prosper; happiness.

Shoda (Japanese) a flat and level field.

Shogo (Japanese) a perceptive and prosperous person.

Shoichi (Japanese) first son of Sho.

Shoji (Japanese) he who governs properly.

Shon (German) a form of Schön. (American) a form of Sean.
Shoan, Shoen, Shondae, Shondale, Shondel, Shone, Shonn, Shonntay, Shontae, Shontarious, Shouan, Shoun

Shota (Japanese) great commander.

Shou (Chinese) leader.

Shou-Hsing (Chinese) god of longevity and old people.

Shravan (Indian) a Hindu month; the devoted son.

Shree (Indian) God.

Shreedhar (Indian) husband of Lakshmi.

Shreekant (Indian) husband of Shree; beautiful.

Shreekumar (Indian) beautiful.

Shreenivas (Indian) abode of Lakshmi.

Shrestajna (Indian) top knowledge.

Shresth, Shresthi (Indian) the best of all.

Shreyas (Indian) the best.

Shrikanth (Indian) Shiva.

Shrikrishna (Indian) Krishna.

Shrikumar (Indian) beautiful.

Shrinivas (Indian) abode of Lakshmi.

Shuang (Chinese) bright, clear; openhearted.

Shubh (Indian) fortunate.

Shubhankar (Indian) virtuous.

Shubhashis (Indian) blessings.

Shubhay (Indian) blessing.

Shubhojit (Indian) handsome.

Shubhranshu (Indian) moon; camphor.

Shu-Fang (Chinese) kind; gentle; sweet.

Shui (Chinese) water.

Shuichi (Japanese) first son of Shu.

Shui-Khan (Chinese) god who defends men against all evil and forgives.

Shulabh (Indian) easy.

Shun (Chinese) unhindered.

Shunichi (Japanese) first son of Shun.

Shunnar (Arabic) pheasant.

Shunsuke (Japanese) excellent mediator.

Shunya (Japanese) spring.

Shuo (Chinese) great achievements.

Shushil (Indian) pleasant.

Shusuke (Japanese) he who strives to help.

Shvant (Indian) placid.

Shvetang (Indian) fair complexion.

Shvetank (Indian) has a white mark.

Shvetanshu, Shwetanshu, Shwetbhanu (Indian) moon.

Shwetambar (Indian) one who wears white clothes.

Shyam (Indian) dark.

Shyamsundar (Indian) dark and handsome.

Shyla 🄶 (English) a form of Sheila (see Girls' Names).

Si (Hebrew) a short form of Silas, Simon.
Sy

Siañu (Quechua) brown like the color of coffee.

Sid (French) a short form of Sidney.
Cyd, Siddie, Siddy, Sidey, Syd

Siddel (English) wide valley.
Siddell

Siddhanth (Indian) principle.

Siddhartha (Hindi) History: Siddhartha Gautama was the original name of Buddha, the founder of Buddhism.
Sida, Siddartha, Siddhaarth, Siddhart,

Siddharth, Sidh, Sidharth, Sidhartha, Sidhdharth

Sidney 🄶 (French) from Saint-Denis, France.
Cydney, Sid, Sidnee, Sidny, Sidon, Sidonio, Sydney, Sydny

Sidonio (Spanish) a form of Sidney.

Sidwell (English) wide stream.

Siegfried (German) victorious peace. See also Zigfrid, Ziggy.
Seifert, Seifried, Siegfred, Siffre, Sig, Sigfrid, Sigfried, Sigfroi, Sigfryd, Siggy, Sigifredo, Sigvard, Singefrid, Sygfried, Szygfrid

Sierra 🄶 (Irish) black. (Spanish) sawtoothed.
Siera

Sig (German) a short form of Siegfried, Sigmund.

Siggy (German) a familiar form of Siegfried, Sigmund.

Sigifredo (German) a form of Siegfried.
Sigefriedo, Sigfrido, Siguefredo

Sigmund (German) victorious protector. See also Ziggy, Zsigmond, Zygmunt.
Siegmund, Sig, Siggy, Sigismond, Sigismondo, Sigismund, Sigismundo, Sigismundus, Sigmond, Sigsmond, Szygmond

Sigurd (German, Scandinavian) victorious guardian.
Sigord, Sjure, Syver

Sigwald (German) victorious leader.

Sikander (Persian) a form of Alejandro.

Silas **B** (Latin) a short form of Silvan.
Si, Sias, Sylas

Silence (Japanese) thoughtful.

Silvan (Latin) forest dweller.
Silas, Silvain, Silvano, Silvaon, Silvie, Silvio, Sylvain, Sylvan, Sylvanus, Sylvio

Silvano (Italian) a form of Silvan.
Silvanos, Silvanus, Silvino

Silverio (Spanish, Greek) god of trees.

Silvester (Latin) a form of Sylvester.
Silvestr, Silvestre, Silvestro, Silvy

Silvestro (Italian) a form of Sylvester.

Silvio (Italian) a form of Silvan.

Simão (Portuguese) a form of Samuel.

Simba (Swahili) lion. (Yao) a short form of Lisimba.
Sim

Simcha **B** (Hebrew) joyful.
Simmy

Simeon (French) a form of Simon.
Simione, Simone

Simeón (Spanish) a form of Simón.

Simms (Hebrew) son of Simon.
Simm, Sims

Simmy (Hebrew) a familiar form of Simcha, Simon.
Simmey, Simmi, Simmie, Symmy

Simon **B** (Hebrew) he heard. Bible: one of the Twelve Disciples. See also Symington, Ximenes.
Saimon, Samien, Semon, Shimon, Si, Sim, Simao, Simen, Simeon, Simion, Simm,

Simmon, Simmonds, Simmons, Simms, Simmy, Simonas, Simone, Simson, Simyon, Síomón, Symon, Szymon

Simón (Hebrew) a form of Simon.

Simone **G** (French) a form of Simeon.

Simplicio (Latin) simple.

Simpson (Hebrew) son of Simon.
Simonson, Simson

Simran **G** (Sikh) absorbed in God.

Sinche, Sinchi (Quechua) boss, leader; strong, valorous, hard working.

Sinchipuma (Quechua) strong leader and as valuable as a puma.

Sinchiroca (Quechua) strongest prince amongst the strong ones.

Sinclair (French) prayer. Religion: name honoring Saint Clair.
Sinclare, Synclair

Sinesio (Greek) intelligent one, the shrewd one.

Sinforiano (Spanish) a form of Sinforoso.

Sinforoso (Greek) he who is full of misfortune.

Singh (Hindi) lion.
Sing

Sinh (Vietnamese) birth; life.

Sinha (Hindi) hero.

Sinjon (English) saint, holy man. Religion: name honoring Saint John.
Sinjin, Sinjun, Sjohn, Syngen, Synjen, Synjon

Siobhan **G** (Irish) a form of Joan (see Girls' Names).

Sipatu (Moquelumnan) pulled out.

Sipho (Zulu) present.

Siraaj (Indian) lamp, light.

Siraj (Arabic) lamp, light.

Sirio (Latin) native of Syria; brilliant like the Syrian sun.

Siro (Latin) native of Syria.

Siseal (Irish) a form of Cecil.

Sisebuto (Teutonic) he who fulfills his leadership role whole-heartedly.

Sisi (Fante) born on Sunday.

Sitanshu (Indian) moon.

Siuca (Quechua) youngest son.

Siva (Hindi) a form of Shiva.
Siv

Sivan (Hebrew) ninth month of the Jewish year.

Siwatu (Swahili) born during a time of conflict.
Siwazuri

Siwili (Native American) long fox's tail.

Sixto (Greek) courteous one; he who has been treated well.

Skah (Lakota) white.
Skai

Skee (Scandinavian) projectile.
Ski, Skie

Skeeter (English) swift.
Skeat, Skeet, Skeets

Skelly (Irish) storyteller.
Shell, Skelley, Skellie

Skelton (Dutch) shell town.

Skerry (Scandinavian) stony island.

Skip (Scandinavian) a short form of Skipper.

Skipper (Scandinavian) shipmaster.
Skip, Skipp, Skippie, Skipton

Skiriki (Pawnee) coyote.

Skule (Norwegian) hidden.

Skye 🄶 (Dutch) a short form of Skylar,
Skyler, Skylor.
Sky

Skylar 🄱🄶 (Dutch) a form of Schuyler.
*Skilar, Skkylar, Skye, Skyelar, Skylaar, Skylare,
Skylarr, Skylayr*

Skyler 🄱 (Dutch) a form of Schuyler.
Skieler, Skiler, Skye, Skyeler, Skylee, Skyller

Skylor (Dutch) a form of Schuyler.
*Skye, Skyelor, Skyloer, Skylore, Skylour,
Skylur, Skylyr*

Slade (English) child of the valley.
Slaide, Slayde

Slane (Czech) salty.
Slan

Slater (English) roof slater.
Slader, Slate, Slayter

Slava (Russian) a short form of Stanislav,
Vladislav, Vyacheslav.
Slavik, Slavoshka

Slawek (Polish) a short form of Radoslaw.

Slevin (Irish) mountaineer.
Slaven, Slavin, Slawin

Sloan (Irish) warrior.
Sloane, Slone

Smaran (Indian) meditation.

Smedley (English) flat meadow.
Smedleigh, Smedly

Smith (English) blacksmith.
*Schmidt, Smid, Smidt, Smitt, Smitty, Smyth,
Smythe*

Snehakant (Indian) the lord of love.

Snehal (Indian) friendly.

Snowden (English) snowy hill.
Snowdon

So (Vietnamese) smart.

Soas, Sos (Chuukese) forms of George.

Socorro (Spanish) helper.

Socrates (Greek) wise, learned. History: a
famous ancient Greek philosopher.
Socratis, Sokrates, Sokratis

Sócrates (Greek) a form of Socrates.

Socso (Quechua) blackbird.

Sofanor (Greek) wise man.

Sofia 🄶 (Greek) a form of Sophia.

Sofian (Arabic) devoted.

Sofoclés, Sófocles (Greek) famous for his
wisdom.

Soham (Indian) I am.

Sohan (Hindi) handsome.

Sohil (Indian) beautiful.

Sohrab (Persian) ancient hero.

Sohse (Pohnpeian) a form of George.

Soja (Yoruba) soldier.

Soji (Japanese) he who loves to rule.

Sol (Hebrew) a short form of Saul, Solomon.
Soll, Sollie, Solly

Solano (Latin) like the eastern wind.

Solly (Hebrew) a familiar form of Saul,
Solomon.
Sollie, Zollie, Zolly

Solomon 🄱 (Hebrew) peaceful. Bible: a
king of Israel famous for his wisdom. See
also Zalman.
*Salamen, Salamon, Salamun, Salaun,
Salman, Salomo, Salomon, Selim, Shelomah,
Shlomo, Sol, Solamh, Solaman, Solly,
Solmon, Soloman, Solomonas, Sulaiman*

Solon (Greek) wise. History: a noted ancient
Athenian lawmaker.

Solón (Greek) a form of Solon.

Somac (Quechua) beautiful.

Somali (Indian) moon's love.

Somanshu (Indian) moonbeam.

Somerset (English) place of the summer
settlers. Literature: William Somerset
Maugham was a well-known British writer.
Sommerset, Sumerset, Summerset

Somerville (English) summer village.
Somerton, Summerton, Summerville

Somesh (Indian) moon.

Somkar, Somprakash (Indian) moonlight.

Son (Vietnamese) mountain. (Native American) star. (English) son, boy. A short form of Madison, Orson.
Sonny

Sonco, Sonjoc, Suncu (Quechua) heart; he who has a good and noble heart.

Soncoyoc, Sonjoyoc (Quechua) he who has a good heart.

Songan (Native American) strong.
Song

Sonis (Pohnpeian) a form of Jona.

Sonny **B** (English) a familiar form of Grayson, Madison, Orson, Son.
Soni, Sonnie, Sony

Sono (Akan) elephant.

Sonya **G** (Greek) wise. (Russian, Slavic) a form of Sophia.

Sophia **G** (Greek) wise.

Sophie **G** (Greek) a familiar form of Sophia.

Sora (Japanese) sky.

Sören (Danish) thunder; war.
Sorren

Soroush (Persian) happy.

Sorrel **G** (French) reddish brown.
Sorel, Sorell, Sorrell

Sosay (Pohnpeian) a form of Jose.

Sosef, Soses (Chuukese) forms of Jose.

Sota (Japanese) very gallant.

Soterios (Greek) savior.
Soteris, Sotero

Soumil (Hindi) friend.

Southwell (English) south well.

Sovann (Cambodian) gold.

Sowande (Yoruba) wise healer sought me out.

Spalding (English) divided field.
Spaulding

Spangler (German) tinsmith.
Spengler

Spark (English) happy.
Sparke, Sparkie, Sparky

Spear (English) spear carrier.
Speare, Spears, Speer, Speers, Spiers

Speedy (English) quick; successful.
Speed

Spence (English) a short form of Spencer.
Spense

Spencer **B** (English) dispenser of provisions.
Spence, Spencre, Spenser

Spenser (English) a form of Spencer. Literature: Edmund Spenser was the British poet who wrote *The Faerie Queene*.
Spanser, Spense

Spike (English) ear of grain; long nail.
Spyke

Spiro (Greek) round basket; breath.
Spiridion, Spiridon, Spiros, Spyridon, Spyros

Spoor (English) spur maker.
Spoors

Sproule (English) energetic.
Sprowle

Spurgeon (English) shrub.

Spyros (Greek) a form of Spiro.

Squire (English) knight's assistant; large landholder.

Sravan (Indian) the devoted son.

Sridatta (Hindi) given by God.

Srikant (Indian) lover of wealth.

Stacey, Stacy **G** (English) familiar forms of Eustace.
Stace, Stacee

Stafford (English) riverbank landing.
Staffard, Stafforde, Staford

Stamford (English) a form of Stanford.

Stamos (Greek) a form of Stephen.
Stamatis, Stamatos

Stan (Latin, English) a short form of Stanley.

Stanbury (English) stone fortification.
Stanberry, Stanbery, Stanburghe, Stansbury

Stancio (Spanish) a form of Constantine.
Stancy

Stancliff (English) stony cliff.
Stanclife, Stancliffe

Standish (English) stony parkland. History: Miles Standish was a leader in colonial America.

Stane (Slavic) a short form of Stanislaus.

Stanfield (English) stony field.
Stansfield

Stanford (English) rocky ford.
Sandy, Stamford, Stan, Standford, Stanfield

Stanislaus (Latin) stand of glory. See also
Lao, Tano.
*Slavik, Stana, Standa, Stane, Stanislao,
Stanislas, Stanislau, Stanislav, Stanislus,
Stannes, Stano, Stasik, Stasio*

Stanislav (Slavic) a form of Stanislaus. See
also Slava.
Stanislaw

Stanley ☒ (English) stony meadow.
*Stan, Stanely, Stanlea, Stanlee, Stanleigh,
Stanly*

Stanmore (English) stony lake.

Stannard (English) hard as stone.

Stanton (English) stony farm.
Stan, Stanten, Staunton

Stanway (English) stony road.

Stanwick (English) stony village.
Stanwicke, Stanwyck

Stanwood (English) stony woods.

Starbuck (English) challenger of fate.
Literature: a character in Herman Melville's
novel *Moby-Dick.*

Stark (German) strong, vigorous.
Starke, Stärke, Starkie

Starling ☒☐ (English) bird.
Sterling

Starr ☐ (English) star.
Star, Staret, Starlight, Starlon, Starwin

Stasik (Russian) a familiar form of
Stanislaus.
Stas, Stash, Stashka, Stashko, Stasiek

Stasio (Polish) a form of Stanislaus.
Stas, Stasiek, Stasiu, Staska, Stasko

Stavros (Greek) a form of Stephen.

Steadman (English) owner of a farmstead.
Steadmann, Stedman, Stedmen, Steed

Steel (English) like steel.
Steele

Steen (German, Danish) stone.
Steenn, Stein

Steeve (Greek) a short form of Steeven.

Steeven (Greek) a form of Steven.
*Steaven, Steavin, Steavon, Steevan, Steeve,
Steevn*

Stefan (German, Polish, Swedish) a form of
Stephen.
*Steafan, Steafeán, Stefaan, Stefane,
Stefanson, Stefaun, Stefawn, Steffan*

Stefano (Italian) a form of Stephen.
Stefanos, Steffano

Stefanos (Greek) a form of Stephen.
Stefans, Stefos, Stephano, Stephanos

Stefen (Norwegian) a form of Stephen.
Steffen, Steffin, Stefin

Steffan (Swedish) a form of Stefan.
Staffan

Stefon (Polish) a form of Stephon.
Staffon, Steffon, Steffone, Stefone, Stefonne

Stein (German) a form of Steen.
Steine, Steiner

Steinar (Norwegian) rock warrior.

Stella ☐ (Latin) star. (French) a familiar
form of Estelle (see Girls' Names).

Stepan (Russian) a form of Stephen.
Stepa, Stepane, Stepanya, Stepka, Stipan

Steph (English) a short form of Stephen.

Stephan (Greek) a form of Stephen.
*Stepfan, Stephanas, Stephano, Stephanos,
Stephanus, Stephaun*

Stephane ☒ (Greek) a form of Stephanie.

Stéphane (French) a form of Stephen.
Stefane, Stepháne, Stephanne

Stephanie ☐ (Greek) crowned.

Stephany ☐ (Greek) a form of Stephanie.

Stephen ☒ (Greek) crowned. See also
Estéban, Estebe, Estevan, Estevao, Étienne,
István, Szczepan, Tapani, Teb, Teppo,
Tiennot.
*Stamos, Stavros, Stefan, Stefano, Stefanos,
Stefen, Stenya, Stepan, Stepanos, Steph,
Stephan, Stephanas, Stéphane, Stephens,
Stephenson, Stephfan, Stephin, Stephon,
Stepven, Steve, Steven, Stevie*

Stephon (Greek) a form of Stephen.
*Stefon, Stepfon, Stepfone, Stephfon,
Stephion, Stephone, Stephonne*

Sterling ☒ (English) valuable; silver penny.
A form of Starling.
Sterlen, Sterlin, Stirling

Stern (German) star.

Sterne (English) austere.
Stearn, Stearne, Stearns

Stetson **B** (Danish) stepson.
Steston, Steton, Stetsen, Stetzon

Stevan (Greek) a form of Steven.
Stevano, Stevanoe, Stevaughn, Stevean

Steve (Greek) a short form of Stephen, Steven.
Steave, Stevie, Stevy

Steven ♛ **B** (Greek) a form of Stephen.
Steeven, Steiven, Stevan, Steve, Stevens, Stevie, Stevin, Stevon, Stiven

Stevens (English) son of Steven.
Stevenson, Stevinson

Stevie **G** (English) a familiar form of Stephen, Steven.
Stevey, Stevy

Stevin, Stevon (Greek) forms of Steven.
Stevieon, Stevion, Stevyn

Stewart **B** (English) a form of Stuart.
Steward, Stu

Sthir (Hindi) focused.

Stian (Norwegian) quick on his feet.

Stig (Swedish) mount.

Stiggur (Gypsy) gate.

Stillman (English) quiet.
Stillmann, Stillmon

Stimit (Indian) astonishing.

Sting (English) spike of grain.

Stockman (English) tree-stump remover.

Stockton (English) tree-stump town.

Stockwell (English) tree-stump well.

Stoddard (English) horse keeper.

Stoffel (German) a short form of Christopher.

Stoker (English) furnace tender.
Stoke, Stokes, Stroker

Stone (English) stone.
Stoen, Stoner, Stoney, Stonie, Stonie, Stoniy, Stony

Storm **B** (English) tempest, storm.
Storme, Stormey, Stormi, Stormmie, Stormy

Stormy **G** (English) a form of Storm.

Storr (Norwegian) great.
Story

Stover (English) stove tender.

Stowe (English) hidden; packed away.

Strahan (Irish) minstrel.
Strachan

Stratford (English) bridge over the river.
Literature: Stratford-upon-Avon was Shakespeare's birthplace.
Stradford

Stratton (Scottish) river valley town.
Straten, Straton

Strephon (Greek) one who turns.

Strom (Greek) bed, mattress. (German) stream.

Strong (English) powerful.

Stroud (English) thicket.

Struthers (Irish) brook.

Stu (English) a short form of Stewart, Stuart.
Stew

Stuart **B** (English) caretaker, steward.
History: a Scottish and English royal family.
Stewart, Stu, Stuarrt

Studs (English) rounded nail heads; shirt ornaments; male horses used for breeding.
History: Louis "Studs" Terkel is a famous American journalist.
Stud, Studd

Styles (English) stairs put over a wall to help cross it.
Stiles, Style, Stylz

Su (Chinese) respectful.

Subali (Indian) strong.

Subaru (Japanese) rise.

Subeer (Indian) courageous.

Subhadr (Indian) gentleman.

Subhas (Indian) shining.

Subhash (Hindi) he who speaks good words.

Subhi (Arabic) early morning.

Subhy (Indian) early morning.

Subodh (Hindi) good lesson.

Suchet (Indian) attentive, alert.

Suchir (Indian) eternity.

Suck Chin (Korean) unshakable rock.

Sucsu (Quechua) blackbird.

Sudarsh (Indian) good-looking.

Sudarshan (Indian) good-looking.

Suday (Hindi) gift.

Sudeep (Indian) illuminated.

Sudeepta (Indian) bright.

Sudesh (Indian) strong; wise; skilled.

Sudesha (Indian) son of Lord Krishna.

Sudhakar (Indian) mine of nectar; moon.

Sudhang, Sudhanshu, Sudhanssu (Indian) moon.

Sudhir, Sumay, Sumed, Sunay (Hindi) wise.

Sudhit (Hindi) kind.

Sudi (Swahili) lucky.
Su'ud

Sudip, Sudir (Indian) bright.

Sued (Arabic) master, chief.
Suede

Suelita (Spanish) little lily.

Suffield (English) southern field.

Sugden (English) valley of sows.

Sughosh (Indian) one with a melodious voice.

Sugriva (Indian) one with a graceful neck; king of monkeys.

Suguru (Japanese) superiority; gentleness.

Suhail (Arabic) gentle.
Sohail, Sohayl, Souhail, Suhael, Sujal

Suhas (Indian) laughter.

Suhay (Quechua) he who is like yellow corn, fine and abundant; rock.

Suhayb (Indian) reddish hair or complexion.

Suhuba (Swahili) friend.

Sui (Chinese) peaceful.

Sujan (Indian) a good person.

Sujat (Indian) belonging to a good clan.

Sujit (Indian) great conqueror.

Suka (Indian) wind.

Sukanth (Indian) one with a sweet voice; one with a graceful neck.

Sukarma (Indian) one who does good deeds.

Sukhdeep ☞ (Sikh) light of peace and bliss.

Sukhen (Indian) happy boy.

Sukhwant (Indian) full of happiness; pleasant.

Sukrant (Indian) extremely beautiful.

Sukru (Turkish) grateful.

Sukumar (Indian) very sensitive.

Sulabh (Indian) easy to get.

Sulaiman (Arabic) a form of Solomon.
Sulaman, Sulay, Sulaymaan, Sulayman, Suleiman, Suleman, Suleyman, Sulieman, Sulman, Solomon, Sulyman

Sulalit (Indian) graceful.

Sulek (Hindi) sun.

Sullivan (Irish) black eyed.
Sullavan, Sullevan, Sully

Sully (Irish) a familiar form of Sullivan. (French) stain, tarnish. (English) south.
Sulleigh, Sulley

Sulochna (Indian) beautiful eyes.

Sultan (Swahili) ruler.
Sultaan

Sum (Tai) appropriate.

Sumainca (Quechua) beautiful Inca.

Sumant (Hindi) friendly.

Sumanyu (Indian) heaven.

Sumitr (Indian) good friend.

Sumitranandan (Indian) son of Sumitra.

Summer ☞ (English) a form of Sumner.

Summit (English) peak, top.
Sumeet, Sumit, Summet, Summitt

Sumner (English) church officer; summoner.
Summer

Sunam (Indian) good name; fame.

Sunandan (Indian) happy.

Sunar (Hindi) happy.

Suncuyuc (Quechua) he who has a good heart.

Sundar (Indian) beautiful; pleasant to the eyes and ears.

Sundaravathana (Indian) smart; handsome.

Sundeep (Punjabi) light; enlightened.
Sundip

Sunder (Indian) handsome.

Suneet (Indian) righteous.

Sunny BG (English) sunny, sunshine.
Sun, Sunni

Sunreep (Hindi) pure.
Sunrip

Suoud (Indian) good luck.

Suraj (Hindi) sun.

Suram (Indian) beautiful.

Suran (Indian) pleasant sound.

Suri (Quechua) fast like an ostrich.

Surjeet (Indian) conqueror of the suras.

Surush (Hindi) shining.

Suryabhan (Indian) sun.

Suryadev (Indian) sun god.

Suryakant (Indian) loved by the sun; a
shining crystal.

Suryanshu (Hindi) sunbeam.

Suryaprakash (Indian) sunlight.

Suryesh (Indian) the sun is God.

Susan G (Hebrew) lily.

Susana G (Hebrew) a form of Susan.

Sushant (Hindi) quiet.

Susher (Indian) kind.

Sushil (Indian) a man of good character.

Sushim (Hindi) moonstone.

Sutcliff (English) southern cliff.
Sutcliffe

Sutherland (Scandinavian) southern land.
Southerland, Sutherlan

Sutosh (Indian) one who becomes happy
easily.

Sutoya (Indian) a river.

Sutton (English) southern town.

Suvel (Indian) placid.

Suvidh (Indian) kind.

Suvit (Indian) good; wealth.

Suvrata (Indian) strict in religious vows.

Suyai, Suyay (Quechua) hope.

Suyash (Indian) good result, victory.

Suycauaman (Quechua) youngest son of the
falcons.

Suzanne G (English) a form of Susan.

Suzu (Japanese) crane.

Svang (Indian) good looks.

Svanik (Indian) handsome.

Svarg (Indian) heaven.

Sven (Scandinavian) youth.
Svein, Svend, Svenn, Swen, Swenson

Swagat (Indian) welcome.

Swaggart (English) one who sways and
staggers.
Swaggert

Swain (English) herdsman; knight's
attendant.
Swaine, Swane, Swanson, Swayne

Swaley (English) winding stream.
Swail, Swailey, Swale, Swales

Swami (Hindi) a lord.

Swapnesh (Indian) king of dreams.

Swapnil (Indian) dreamy.

Swaraj (Indian) liberty, freedom.

Swarit (Hindi) toward heaven.

Swarup (Indian) figure.

Swastik (Indian) auspicious.

Sweeney (Irish) small hero.
Sweeny

Swinbourne (English) stream used by swine.
*Swinborn, Swinborne, Swinburn, Swinburne,
Swinbyrn, Swynborn*

Swindel (English) valley of the swine.
Swindell

Swinfen (English) swine's mud.

Swinford (English) swine's crossing.
Swynford

Swinton (English) swine town.

Sy (Latin) a short form of Sylas, Symon.
Si

Sydnee G (French) a form of Sydney.

Sydney G (French) a form of Sidney.
Syd, Sydne, Sydnee, Syndey

Syed B (Arabic) happy.
Syeed, Syid

Sying BG (Chinese) star.

Sylas (Latin) a form of Silas.
Sy, Syles, Sylus

Sylvain (French) a form of Silvan, Sylvester.
Sylvan, Sylvian

Sylvester (Latin) forest dweller.
Silvester, Silvestro, Sly, Syl, Sylvain, Sylverster, Sylvestre

Symington (English) Simon's town, Simon's estate.

Symon (Greek) a form of Simon.
Sy, Syman, Symeon, Symion, Symms, Symon, Symone

Syon (Hindi) gentle.

Syum, Syun (Hindi) a ray.

Syuto (Japanese) holly.

Szczepan (Polish) a form of Stephen.

Szygfrid (Hungarian) a form of Siegfried.
Szigfrid

Szymon (Polish) a form of Simon.

T

T BG (American) an initial used as a first name.

Taahir (Indian) chaste, modest.

Taamir (Indian) one who knows dates.

Taaveti (Finnish) a form of David.
Taavi, Taavo

Tab (German) shining, brilliant. (English) drummer.
Tabb, Tabbie, Tabby

Tabaré (Tupi) man of the village.

Tabari (Arabic) he remembers.
Tabahri, Tabares, Tabarious, Tabarius, Tabarus, Tabur

Tabatha G (Greek, Aramaic) a form of Tabitha (see Girls' Names).

Tabib (Turkish) physician.
Tabeeb

Tabo (Spanish) a short form of Gustave.

Tabor (Persian) drummer. (Hungarian) encampment.
Tabber, Taber, Taboras, Taibor, Tayber, Taybor, Taver

Taciano, Tácito (Spanish) forms of Tacio.

Tacio (Latin) he who is quiet.

Tad (Welsh) father. (Greek, Latin) a short form of Thaddeus.
Tadd, Taddy, Tade, Tadek, Tadey

Tadaaki (Japanese) faithful; bright.

Tadahiro (Japanese) very loyal.

Tadan (Native American) plentiful.
Taden

Tadanori (Japanese) loyal ruler.

Tadao (Japanese) complacent, satisfied.

Tadarius (American) a combination of the prefix Ta + Darius.
Tadar, Tadarious, Tadaris, Tadarrius

Taddeo (Italian) a form of Thaddeus.
Tadeo

Taddeus (Greek, Latin) a form of Thaddeus.
Taddeous, Taddeusz, Taddius, Tadeas, Tades, Tadesz, Tadio, Tadious

Tadi (Omaha) wind.

Tadzi (Carrier) loon.

Tadzio (Polish, Spanish) a form of Thaddeus.
Taddeusz

Taffy G (Welsh) a form of David. (English) a familiar form of Taft.

Taft (English) river.
Taffy, Tafton

Tage (Danish) day.
Tag

Taggart (Irish) son of the priest.
Tagart, Taggert

Tahír (Arabic) innocent, pure.
Taheer

Tai (Vietnamese) weather; prosperous; talented.

Taichi (Japanese) large first son.

Taiga (Japanese) big river.

Taiki (Japanese) big; noble; brilliant.

Taima G (Native American) born during a storm.

Taimu (Japanese) big dream.

Taishawn (American) a combination of Tai + Shawn.
Taisen, Taishaun, Taishon

Tait (Scandinavian) a form of Tate.
Taite, Taitt

Taiwan (Chinese) island; island dweller.
Geography: a country off the coast of China.
*Taewon, Tahwan, Taivon, Taiwain, Tawain,
Tawan, Tawann, Tawaun, Tawon, Taywan,
Tywan*

Taiwo (Yoruba) first-born of twins.

Taiyo (Japanese) big sun.

Taj (Urdu) crown.
Taje, Tajee, Tajeh, Tajh, Taji

Tajo (Spanish) day.
Taio

Tajuan (American) a combination of the
prefix Ta + Juan.
*Taijuan, Taijun, Taijuon, Tájuan, Tajwan,
Taquan, Tyjuan*

Takahiro (Japanese) roof; heaven; air; space.

Takashi (Japanese) he who has dutiful
ambitions.

Takayoshi (Japanese) obedient;
righteousness.

Takeo (Japanese) strong as bamboo.
Takeyo

Takis (Greek) a familiar form of Peter.
Takias, Takius

Takoda (Lakota) friend to everyone.

Taksha (Indian) King Bharat's son.

Taksheel (Hindi) someone with a strong
character.

Takuma (Japanese) the clear truth.

Takumi (Japanese) open; clear; truth; fruit.

Tal (Hebrew) dew; rain.
Tali, Talia, Talley, Talor, Talya

Talal (Indian) nice; admirable.

Talbert (German) bright valley.

Talbot (French) boot maker.
Talbott, Tallbot, Tallbott, Tallie, Tally

Talcott (English) cottage near the lake.

Tale (Tswana) green.

Talen (English) a form of Talon.
Talin, Tallen

Talha (Indian) a kind of tree.

Talib (Arabic) seeker.

Taliesin (Welsh) radiant brow.
Tallas, Tallis

Taliki (Hausa) fellow.

Talli (Delaware) legendary hero.

Talmadge (English) lake between two towns.
Talmage

Talmai (Aramaic) mound; furrow.
Telem

Talman (Aramaic) injured; oppressed.
Talmon

Talon **B** (French, English) claw, nail.
Taelon, Taelyn, Talen, Tallin, Tallon, Talyn

Talor (English) a form of Tal, Taylor.
Taelor, Taelur

Tam **B** (Vietnamese) number eight.
(Hebrew) honest. (English) a short form of
Thomas.
*Tama, Tamas, Tamás, Tameas, Tamlane,
Tammany, Tammas, Tammen, Tammy*

Tamam (Indian) generous.

Taman (Slavic) dark, black.
Tama, Tamann, Tamin, Tamon, Tamone

Tamar **G** (Hebrew) date; palm tree.
Tamarie, Tamario, Tamarr, Timur

Tamasine (Japanese) twin.

Tambo (Swahili) vigorous.

Tamer (Arabic) he who makes way.

Tamir (Arabic) tall as a palm tree.
Tameer

Tamish (Indian) god of darkness.

Tammy **G** (English) a familiar form of
Thomas.
Tammie

Tamson (Scandinavian) son of Thomas.
Tamsen

Tan (Burmese) million. (Vietnamese) new.
Than

Tanak (Hindi) prize.

Tanav (Hindi) flute.

Tancredo (Germanic) he who shrewdly gives
advice.

Tanek (Greek) immortal. See also Atek.

Taneli (Finnish) God is my judge.
Taneil, Tanell, Tanella

Taner (English) a form of Tanner.
Tanar

Tanesha G (American) a combination of the prefix Ta + Nesha (see Girls' Names).

Tang (Chinese) dignified.

Tanguy (French) warrior.

Tanh (Vietnamese) having his way.

Tani G (Japanese) valley.

Tanis G (Slavic) a form of Tania (see Girls' Names).

Tanish (Hindi) ambition.

Tanjiro (Japanese) highly valued second son.

Tanmay (Sanskrit) engrossed.

Tanner B (English) leather worker; tanner.
Tan, Taner, Tanery, Tann, Tannar, Tannir, Tannor, Tanny

Tannin (English) tan colored; dark.
Tanin, Tannen, Tannon, Tanyen, Tanyon

Tanny (English) a familiar form of Tanner.
Tana, Tannee, Tanney, Tannie, Tany

Tano (Spanish) camp glory. (Ghanaian) Geography: a river in Ghana. (Russian) a short form of Stanislaus.
Tanno

Tanoj (Indian) son.

Tanton (English) town by the still river.

Tanvir (Hindi) strong.

Tao (Chinese) long life.

Tapan (Sanskrit) sun; summer.

Tapani (Finnish) a form of Stephen.
Tapamn, Teppo

Tapesh (Indian) the Holy Trinity.

Täpko (Kiowa) antelope.

Taporaj (Indian) moon.

Taquan (American) a combination of the prefix Ta + Quan.
Taquann, Taquawn, Taquon, Taqwan

Taquiri (Quechua) he who creates much music and dance.

Tara G (Aramaic) throw; carry. (Irish) rocky hill. (Arabic) a measurement.

Tarachandra (Indian) star; moon.

Tarak (Sanskrit) star; protector.

Taraksh (Hindi) mountain.

Taran (Sanskrit) heaven.
Tarran

Tarang (Hindi) wave.

Tarani (Indian) boat; sun.

Tarek (Arabic) a form of Táriq.
Tareek, Tareke

Tarell (German) a form of Terrell.
Tarelle, Tarrel, Tarrell, Taryl

Taren (American) a form of Taron.
Tarren, Tarrin

Tarendra (Hindi) prince of stars.

Taresh, Tarkesh (Indian) god of the stars.

Tarfah (Indian) a type of tree.

Tarif (Arabic) uncommon.
Tareef

Tarik (Arabic) a form of Táriq.
Taric, Tarick, Tariek, Tarikh, Tarrick, Tarrik, Taryk

Táriq (Arabic) conqueror. History: Tariq bin Ziyad was the Muslim general who conquered Spain.
Tareck, Tarek, Tarik, Tarique, Tarreq, Tereik

Tarius (Chuukese) a form of Dario.

Tarleton (English) Thor's settlement.
Tarlton

Taro (Japanese) first-born male.

Taron (American) a combination of Tad + Ron.
Taeron, Tahron, Taren, Tarone, Tarrion, Tarron, Taryn

Tarquino (Latin) he who was born in Tarquinia, an ancient Italian city.

Tarrant (Welsh) thunder.
Terrant

Tarsicio (Greek) valiant.

Taru (Hindi) small plant.

Tarun (Sanskrit) young, youth.
Taran

Tarver (English) tower; hill; leader.
Terver

Taryn G (American) a form of Taron.
Tarryn, Taryon

Tas (Gypsy) bird's nest.

Tasha G (Greek) born on Christmas day. (Russian) a short form of Natasha.

Tashawn (American) a combination of the prefix Ta + Shawn.
Tashaan, Tashan, Tashaun, Tashon, Tashun

Tass (Hungarian) ancient mythology name.

Tasunke (Dakota) horse.

Tate **B** (Scandinavian, English) cheerful. (Native American) long-winded talker.
Tait, Tayte

Tatharaj (Indian) Buddha.

Tatiano (Latin) he who is quiet.

Tatius (Latin) king, ruler. History: a Sabine king.
Tatianus, Tazio, Titus

Tatsuya (Japanese) like a dragon.

Tatum **G** (English) cheerful.

Tau (Tswana) lion.

Taua (Quechua) fourth child.

Tauacapac (Quechua) fourth lord; lord of the four regions.

Tauheed (Indian) victorious.

Tauno (Finnish) a form of Donald.

Taurean (Latin) strong; forceful. Astrology: born under the sign of Taurus.
Tauraun, Taurein, Taurin, Taurion, Taurone, Taurus

Taurino (Spanish) bull-like.

Tauro (Spanish) a form of Toro.

Taurus (Latin) Astrology: the second sign of the zodiac.
Taurice, Tauris

Tautik (Indian) pearl.

Tavares (Aramaic) a form of Tavor.
Tarvarres, Tavarres, Taveress

Tavaris (Aramaic) a form of Tavor.
Tarvaris, Tavar, Tavaras, Tavari, Tavarian, Tavarious, Tavarius, Tavarous, Tavarri, Tavarris, Tavars, Tavarse, Tavarus, Tevaris, Tevarius, Tevarus

Tavey (Latin) a familiar form of Octavio.

Tavi (Aramaic) good.

Tavian (Latin) a form of Octavio.
Taveon, Taviann, Tavien, Tavieon, Tavin, Tavio, Tavion, Tavionne, Tavon, Tayvon

Tavish (Scottish) a form of Thomas.
Tav, Tavi, Tavis

Tavo (Slavic) a short form of Gustave.

Tavon (American) a form of Tavian.
Tavonn, Tavonne, Tavonni

Tavor (Aramaic) misfortune.
Tarvoris, Tavares, Tavaris, Tavores, Tavorious, Tavoris, Tavorise, Tavorres, Tavorris, Tavuris

Tawfeeq (Indian) success; reconciliation.

Tawno (Gypsy) little one.
Tawn

Tayib (Hindi) good; delicate.

Tayler **G** (English) a form of Taylor.
Tailer, Taylar, Tayller, Teyler

Taylor **G** (English) tailor.
Tailor, Talor, Tayler, Tayllor, Taylour, Taylr, Teylor

Tayseer (Indian) facilitation.

Tayshawn (American) a combination of Taylor + Shawn.
Taysean, Tayshan, Tayshun, Tayson

Tayvon (American) a form of Tavian.
Tayvan, Tayvaughn, Tayven, Tayveon, Tayvin, Tayvohn, Taywon

Taz (Arabic) shallow ornamental cup.
Tazz

Tazio (Italian) a form of Tatius.

Te (Chinese) special.

Teagan **G** (Irish) a form of Teague.
Teagen, Teagun, Teegan

Teague (Irish) bard, poet.
Teag, Teagan, Teage, Teak, Tegan, Teige

Tearence (Latin) a form of Terrence.
Tearance, Tearnce, Tearrance

Tearlach (Scottish) a form of Charles.

Tearle (English) stern, severe.

Teasdale (English) river dweller. Geography: a river in England.

Teb (Spanish) a short form of Stephen.

Ted (English) a short form of Edward, Edwin, Theodore.
Tedd, Tedek, Tedik, Tedson

Teddy (English) a familiar form of Edward, Theodore.
Teddey, Teddie, Tedy

Tedmund (English) protector of the land.
Tedman, Tedmond

Tedorik (Polish) a form of Theodore.
Teodoor, Teodor, Teodorek

Tedrick (American) a combination of Ted + Rick.
Teddrick, Tederick, Tedric

Teerth (Indian) holy place; sacred water.

Teetonka (Lakota) big lodge.

Tefere (Ethiopian) seed.

Tegan ☒ (Irish) a form of Teague.
Teghan, Teigan, Tiegan

Teiji, Teijo (Japanese) righteous; well governed.

Teiljo (Japanese) established, regulated.

Tej (Sanskrit) light; lustrous.

Tejas (Sanskrit) sharp.

Tejeshwar (Indian) sun.

Tejomay (Indian) glorious.

Tekle (Ethiopian) plant.

Telek (Polish) a form of Telford.

Telem (Hebrew) mound; furrow.
Talmai, Tel

Telémaco (Greek) he who prepares for battle.

Telford (French) iron cutter.
Telek, Telfer, Telfor, Telfour

Teller (English) storyteller.
Tell, Telly

Telly (Greek) a familiar form of Teller, Theodore.

Telmo (English) tiller, cultivator.

Telutci (Moquelumnan) bear making dust as it runs.

Telvin (American) a combination of the prefix Te + Melvin.
Tellvin, Telvan

Tem (Gypsy) country.

Teman (Hebrew) on the right side; southward.

Tembo (Swahili) elephant.

Tempest ☒ (French) storm.

Temple (Latin) sanctuary.

Templeton (English) town near the temple.
Temp, Templeten

Teng (Chinese) gallop; prance.

Tenma (Japanese) sky; horse.

Tennant (English) tenant, renter.
Tenant, Tennent

Tennessee (Cherokee) mighty warrior. Geography: a southern U.S. state.
Tennessee, Tennesy, Tennysee

Tennyson (English) a form of Dennison. Literature: Alfred, Lord Tennyson was a nineteenth-century British poet.
Tenney, Tenneyson, Tennie, Tennis, Tennison, Tenny, Tenson

Teo (Vietnamese) a form of Tom.

Teobaldo (Italian, Spanish) a form of Theobald.

Teócrito (Greek) God's chosen one.

Teodoro (Italian, Spanish) a form of Theodore.
Teodore, Teodorico

Teodosio (Greek) he who gives to God.

Teófano (Greek) friend of God; loved by God.

Teófilo (Greek) loved by God.

Teppo (French) a familiar form of Stephen.

Tequan (American) a combination of the prefix Te + Quan.
Tequinn, Tequon

Terance (Latin) a form of Terrence.
Terriance

Tercio, Tertulio (Greek) third child of the family.

Terell (German) a form of Terrell.
Tarell, Tereall, Terel, Terelle, Tyrel

Teremun (Tiv) father's acceptance.

Terence ☒ (Latin) a form of Terrence.
Teren, Teryn

Terencio (Spanish) a form of Terrence.

Tereshan (Indian) solid redemption.

Teri ☒ (Greek) reaper. A familiar form of Theresa.

Terra ☒ (Latin) earth. (Japanese) swift arrow. (American) forms of Tara.

Terran (Latin) a short form of Terrance.
Teran, Teren, Terran, Terren

Terrance ☒ (Latin) a form of Terrence.
Tarrance, Terran

Terrell ☒ (German) thunder ruler.
Terell, Terrail, Terral, Terrale, Terrall, Terreal, Terrel, Terrelle, Terrill, Terryal, Terryel, Tirel, Tirrel, Tirrell, Turrell, Tyrel, Tyrell

Terrence (Latin) smooth.
Tarrance, Tearence, Terance, Terence,
Terencio, Terrance, Terren, Terrin, Terry,
Torrence, Tyreese

Terri **G** (English) a form of Terry.

Terrick (American) a combination of the
prefix Te + Derrick.
Teric, Terick, Terik, Teriq, Terric, Terrik, Tirek,
Tirik

Terrill (German) a form of Terrell.
Teriel, Teriell, Terril, Terryl, Terryll, Teryll,
Teryl, Tyrill

Terrin (Latin) a short form of Terrence.
Terin, Terrien, Terryn, Teryn, Tiren

Terris (Latin) son of Terry.

Terron (American) a form of Tyrone.
Tereon, Terion, Terione, Teron, Terone,
Terrion, Terrione, Terriyon, Terrone, Terronn,
Terryon, Tiron

Terry **B** (English) a familiar form of
Terrence. See also Keli.
Tarry, Terrey, Terri, Terrie, Tery

Tertius (Latin) third.

Teru (Japanese) brilliant shine.

Teruaki (Japanese) brilliant autumn.

Teruyoshi (Japanese) brilliant justice.

Teseo (Greek) founder.

Teshawn (American) a combination of the
prefix Te + Shawn.
Tesean, Teshaun, Teshon

Tess **G** (Greek) a short form of Theresa.

Tessa **G** (Greek) reaper.

Tet (Vietnamese) Vietnamese.

Tetsuo (Japanese) philosophical husband.

Teva (Hebrew) nature.

Tevan (American) a form of Tevin.
Tevaughan, Tevaughn, Teven, Tevvan

Tevel (Yiddish) a form of David.

Tevin **B** (American) a combination of the
prefix Te + Kevin.
Teavin, Teivon, Tevan, Tevien, Tevinn, Tevon,
Tevvin, Tevyn

Tevis (Scottish) a form of Thomas.
Tevish

Tevon (American) a form of Tevin.
Tevion, Tevohn, Tevone, Tevonne, Tevoun,
Teyvon

Tewdor (German) a form of Theodore.

Tex (American) from Texas.
Tejas

Thaabit (Indian) firm.

Thabit (Arabic) firm, strong.

Thad (Greek, Latin) a short form of
Thaddeus.
Thadd, Thade, Thadee, Thady

Thaddeus (Greek) courageous. (Latin)
praiser. Bible: one of the Twelve Apostles. See
also Fadey.
Tad, Taddeo, Taddeus, Thaddis, Thadeaus,
Tadzio, Thad, Thaddaeus, Thaddaus,
Thaddeau, Thaddeaus, Thaddeo, Thaddeous,
Thaddiaus, Thaddius, Thadeaou, Thadeous,
Thadeus, Thadieus, Thadious, Thadius,
Thadus

Thady (Irish) praise.
Thaddy

Thai (Vietnamese) many, multiple.

Thakur (Indian) leader; God.

Thaman (Hindi) god; godlike.

Than (Burma) million.
Tan, Thanh

Thane (English) attendant warrior.
Thain, Thaine, Thayne

Thang (Vietnamese) victorious.

Thanh (Vietnamese) finished.

Thaniel (Hebrew) a short form of Nathaniel.

Thanos (Greek) nobleman; bear-man.
Athanasios, Thanasis

Thao (Vietnamese) courtesy.

Thaqib (Indian) shooting star.

Thatcher (English) roof thatcher, repairer of
roofs.
Thacher, Thatch, Thaxter

Thaw (English) melting ice.

Thayer (French) nation's army.
Thay

Thel (English) upper story.

Thenga (Yao) bring him.

Theo (English) a short form of Theodore.

Theobald (German) people's prince; bold
people. See also Dietbald.
Teobaldo, Thebault, Theòbault, Thibault,
Tibalt, Tibold, Tiebold, Tiebout, Toiboid,
Tybald, Tybalt, Tybault

Theodore 🄱 (Greek) gift of God. See also Feodor, Fyodor.
Téadóir, Teador, Ted, Teddy, Tedor, Tedorek, Tedorik, Telly, Teodomiro, Teodoro, Teodus, Teos, Tewdor, Theo, Theodor, Theódor, Theodors, Theodorus, Theodosios, Theodrekr, Tivadar, Todor, Tolek, Tudor

Theodoric (German) ruler of the people. See also Dedrick, Derek, Dirk.
Teodorico, Thedric, Thedrick, Thierry, Till

Theophilus (Greek) loved by God.
Teofil, Théophile, Theophlous, Theopolis

Theresa 🄶 (Greek) reaper.

Theron (Greek) hunter.
Theran, Theren, Thereon, Therin, Therion, Therrin, Therron, Theryn, Theryon

Thian (Vietnamese) smooth.
Thien

Thibault (French) a form of Theobald.
Thibaud, Thibaut

Thierry (French) a form of Theodoric.
Theirry, Theory

Thinh (Vietnamese) prosperity.

Tho (Vietnamese) longevity.

Thom (English) a short form of Thomas.
Thomy

Thoma (German) a form of Thomas.

Thomas ☙ 🄱 (Greek, Aramaic) twin. Bible: one of the Twelve Apostles. See also Chuma, Foma, Maslin.
Tam, Tammy, Tavish, Tevis, Thom, Thoma, Thomason, Thomaz, Thomeson, Thomison, Thommas, Thompson, Thomson, Tom, Toma,

Tomas, Tomás, Tomasso, Tomcy, Tomey, Tomey, Tomi, Tommy, Toomas

Thompson (English) son of Thomas.
Thomason, Thomison, Thomsen, Thomson

Thor (Scandinavian) thunder. Mythology: the Norse god of thunder.
Thorin, Tor, Tyrus

Thorald (Scandinavian) Thor's follower.
Terrell, Terrill, Thorold, Torald

Thorbert (Scandinavian) Thor's brightness.
Torbert

Thorbjorn (Scandinavian) Thor's bear.
Thorburn, Thurborn, Thurburn

Thorgood (English) Thor is good.

Thorleif (Scandinavian) Thor's beloved.
Thorlief

Thorley (English) Thor's meadow.
Thorlea, Thorlee, Thorleigh, Thorly, Torley

Thorndike (English) thorny embankment.
Thorn, Thorndyck, Thorndyke, Thorne

Thorne (English) a short form of names beginning with "Thorn."
Thorn, Thornie, Thorny

Thornley (English) thorny meadow.
Thorley, Thorne, Thornlea, Thornleigh, Thornly

Thornton (English) thorny town.
Thorne

Thorpe (English) village.
Thorp

Thorwald (Scandinavian) Thor's forest.
Thorvald

Thu (Vietnamese) autumn.

Thuan (Vietnamese) tamed, conforming.

Thuc (Vietnamese) aware.

Thuong (Vietnamese) to love tenderly; in pursuit.

Thurlow (English) Thor's hill.
Thurlo

Thurmond (English) defended by Thor.
Thormond, Thurmund

Thurston (Scandinavian) Thor's stone.
Thorstan, Thorstein, Thorsten, Thurstain, Thurstan, Thursten, Torsten, Torston

Thuyet (Vietnamese) theory.

Tiago (Spanish) a form of Jacob.

Tian (Chinese) heaven.

Tiarra 🄶 (Latin) a form of Tiara (see Girls' Names).

Tiberio (Italian) from the Tiber River region.
Tiberias, Tiberious, Tiberiu, Tiberius, Tibius, Tyberious, Tyberius, Tyberrius

Tibor (Hungarian) holy place.
Tiburcio

Tiburón (Spanish) shark.

Tichawanna (Shona) we shall see.

Ticho (Spanish) a short form of Patrick.

Ticiano (Spanish) a form of Tito.

Tico (Greek) adventurous one; happy, fortunate.

Tieler (English) a form of Tyler.
Tielar, Tielor, Tielyr

T'ien-Khuan (Chinese) god who bestows happiness.

Tiennot (French) a form of Stephen.
Tien

Tiernan (Irish) lord.

Tierney **G** (Irish) lordly.
Tiarnach, Tiernan

Tiffany **G** (Latin) trinity. (Greek) a short form of Theophania (see Girls' Names).

Tige (English) a short form of Tiger.
Ti, Tig, Tighe, Ty, Tyg, Tyge, Tygh, Tyghe

Tiger (American) tiger; powerful and energetic.
Tige, Tigger, Tyger

Tiimu (Moquelumnan) caterpillar coming out of the ground.

Tijil (Indian) moon.

Ti-Khuan (Chinese) god who grants remission of sins.

Tiktu (Moquelumnan) bird digging up potatoes.

Tilak (Indian) spot of vermillion or sandalwood paste on the forehead.

Tilden (English) tilled valley.
Tildon

Tilford (English) prosperous ford.

Till (German) a short form of Theodoric.
Thilo, Til, Tillman, Tilman, Tillmann, Tilson

Tilo (Teutonic) skillful and praises God.

Tilton (English) prosperous town.

Tim (Greek) a short form of Timothy.
Timmie, Timmy

Timin (Arabic) born near the sea.

Timirbaran (Indian) dark.

Timmothy (Greek) a form of Timothy.
Timmathy, Timmithy, Timmoty, Timmthy

Timmy (Greek) a familiar form of Timothy.
Timmie

Timo (Finnish) a form of Timothy.
Timio

Timofey (Russian) a form of Timothy.
Timofei, Timofej, Timofeo

Timon (Greek) honorable.

Timoteo (Portuguese, Spanish) a form of Timothy.

Timothy ☸ **B** (Greek) honoring God. See also Kimokeo.
Tadhg, Taidgh, Tiege, Tim, Tima, Timithy, Timka, Timkin, Timmothy, Timmy, Timo, Timofey, Timok, Timon, Timontheo, Timonthy, Timót, Timote, Timotei, Timoteo, Timoteus, Timothé, Timothée, Timotheo, Timotheos, Timotheus, Timothey, Timothie, Timthie, Tiomóid, Tisha, Tomothy, Tymon, Tymothy

Timur (Hebrew) a form of Tamar. (Russian) conqueror.
Timour

Tin (Vietnamese) thinker.

Tina **G** (Spanish, American) a short form of Augustine.

Tincupuma, Tinquipoma (Quechua) he who creates much music and dance.

Ting (Chinese) palace; pavilion.

Tinh (Vietnamese) mindful, aware.

Tino (Spanish) venerable, majestic. (Italian) small. A familiar form of Antonio. (Greek) a short form of Augustine.
Tion

Tinsley (English) fortified field.

Tiquan (American) a combination of the prefix Ti + Quan.
Tiquawn, Tiquine, Tiquon, Tiquwan, Tiqwan

Tíquico (Greek) very fortunate person.

Tirishaanth (Indian) king of the Surya dynasty.

Tirso (Greek) crowned with fig leaves.

Tirth (Indian) pilgrim.

Tirtha (Indian) holy place.

Tisha **G** (Russian) a form of Timothy.
Tishka

Tishawn (American) a combination of the prefix Ti + Shawn.
Tishaan, Tishaun, Tishean, Tishon, Tishun

Titir (Indian) a bird.

Tito (Italian) a form of Titus.
Titas, Titis, Titos

Titoatauchi, Tituatauchi (Quechua) he who brings luck in trying times.

Titu (Quechua) difficult, complicated.

Titus (Greek) giant. (Latin) hero. A form of Tatius. History: a Roman emperor.
Tite, Titek, Tito, Tytus

Tivon (Hebrew) nature lover.

Boys S–Z

TJ (American) a combination of the initials T. + J.
Teejay, Tj, T.J., T Jae, Tjayda

Toai (Vietnamese) satisfied.

Tobal (Spanish) a short form of Christopher.
Tabalito

Tobar (Gypsy) road.

Tobi 🄶 (Yoruba) great.

Tobias (Hebrew) God is good.
Tobia, Tobiah, Tobiás, Tobiath, Tobin, Tobit, Toby, Tobyas, Tuvya

Tobías (Hebrew) a form of Tobias.

Tobikuma (Japanese) cloud; misty.

Tobin (Hebrew) a form of Tobias.
Toben, Tobian, Tobyn, Tovin

Toby 🄱 (Hebrew) a familiar form of Tobias.
Tobbie, Tobby, Tobe, Tobee, Tobey, Tobie

Todd 🄱 (English) fox.
Tod, Toddie, Toddy

Todor (Basque, Russian) a form of Theodore.
Teodor, Todar, Todas, Todos

Toft (English) small farm.

Tohon (Native American) cougar.

Tokala (Dakota) fox.

Tokujiro (Japanese) virtuous second son.

Tokutaro (Japanese) virtuous son.

Toland (English) owner of taxed land.
Tolan

Tolbert (English) bright tax collector.

Toller (English) tax collector.

Tolomeo (Greek) powerful in battle.

Tom (English) a short form of Tomas, Thomas.
Teo, Thom, Tommey, Tommie, Tommy

Toma (Romanian) a form of Thomas.
Tomah

Tomas (German) a form of Thomas.
Tom, Tomaisin, Tomaz, Tomcio, Tome, Tomek, Tomelis, Tomico, Tomik, Tomislaw, Tommas, Tomo, Tomson

Tomás (Irish, Spanish) a form of Thomas.
Tomas, Tómas, Tomasz

Tomasso (Italian) a form of Thomas.
Tomaso, Tommaso

Tombe (Kakwa) northerners.

Tomé (Hebrew) identical twin brother.

Tomeo (Japanese) cautious man.

Tomey (Irish) a familiar form of Thomas.
Tome, Tomi, Tomie, Tomy

Tomi 🄶 (Japanese) rich. (Hungarian) a form of Thomas.

Tomlin (English) little Tom.
Tomkin, Tomlinson

Tommie 🄱 (Hebrew) a form of Tommy.
Tommi

Tommy 🄱 (Hebrew) a familiar form of Thomas.
Tommie, Tomy

Tomofumi (Japanese) wise writer.

Tomohiro (Japanese) very wise.

Tomoya (Japanese) he who is wise.

Tonda (Czech) a form of Tony.
Tonek

Tong (Vietnamese) fragrant.

Toni 🄶 (Greek, German, Slavic) a form of Tony.
Tonee, Tonie, Tonio, Tonis, Tonnie

Tonio (Portuguese) a form of Tony. (Italian) a short form of Antonio.
Tono, Tonyo

Tonto (Indian) indulgence; devotion.

Tony 🄱 (Greek) flourishing. (Latin) praiseworthy. (English) a short form of Anthony. A familiar form of Remington.
Tonda, Tonek, Toney, Toni, Tonik, Tonio, Tonny

Tooantuh (Cherokee) spring frog.

Toomas (Estonian) a form of Thomas.
Toomis, Tuomas, Tuomo

Topa, Tupa (Quechua) honorific title; royal, majestic, glorious, noble, honorable.

Topher (Greek) a short form of Christopher, Kristopher.
Tofer, Tophor

Topo (Spanish) gopher.

Topper (English) hill.

Tor (Norwegian) thunder. (Tiv) royalty, king.
Thor

Torao (Japanese) tiger; wild.

Torcuato (Latin) adorned with a collar or garland.

Tori 🄶 (English) a form of Tory.

Torian (Irish) a form of Torin.
Toran, Torean, Toriano, Toriaun, Torien,
Torrian, Torrien, Torryan

Toribio (Greek) he who makes bows.

Torin (Irish) chief.
Thorfin, Thorstein, Torian, Torion, Torrin, Toryn

Torkel (Swedish) Thor's cauldron.

Tormey (Irish) thunder spirit.
Tormé, Tormee

Tormod (Scottish) north.

Torn (Irish) a short form of Torrence.
Toran

Toro (Spanish) bull.

Torquil (Danish) Thor's kettle.
Torkel

Torr (English) tower.
Tory

Torrance (Irish) a form of Torrence.
Torance

Torren (Irish) a short form of Torrence.
Torehn, Toren

Torrence (Irish) knolls. (Latin) a form of
Terrence.
Tawrence, Toreence, Torence, Torenze, Torey,
Torin, Torn, Torr, Torrance, Torren, Torreon,
Torrin, Torry, Tory, Torynce, Tuarence, Turance

Torrey (English) a form of Tory.
Toreey, Torie, Torre, Torri, Torrie, Torry

Toru (Japanese) sea.

Tory **G** (English) familiar form of Torr,
Torrence.
Torey, Tori, Torrey

Toshan (Indian) satisfaction.

Toshi (Japanese) mirror image.

Toshiharu (Japanese) excellent governor.

Toshihiro (Japanese) wise.

Toshiro (Japanese) talented; intelligent.

Toshi-Shita (Japanese) junior.

Toshiyuki (Japanese) excellent; auspicious;
fortunate.

Tovi (Hebrew) good.
Tov

Townley (English) town meadow.
Townlea, Townlee, Townleigh, Townlie,
Townly

Townsend (English) town's end.
Town, Townes, Towney, Townie, Townsen,
Townshend, Towny

Toyo (Japanese) plentiful.

Trabunco (Mapuche) meeting at the marsh.

Trace (Irish) a form of Tracy.
Trayce

Tracey **G** (Irish) a form of Tracy.

Traci **G** (Irish) a form of Tracy.

Tracy **G** (Greek) harvester. (Latin)
courageous. (Irish) battler.
Trace, Tracey, Tracie, Treacy

Trader (English) well-trodden path; skilled
worker.

Trae (English) a form of Trey.
Trai, Traie, Tre, Trea

Traful (Araucanian) union.

Trahern (Welsh) strong as iron.
Traherne, Tray

Trailokva, Tribhuvan, Trilok (Indian) the
three worlds (heaven, earth, hell).

Tramaine (Scottish) a form of Tremaine,
Tremayne.
Tramain, Traman, Tramane, Tramayne,
Traymain, Traymon

Tranamil (Mapuche) low, scattered light.

Trang (Vietnamese) decorated, honored.

Traquan (American) a combination of Travis
+ Quan.
Traequan, Traqon, Traquon, Traqwan,
Traqwaun, Trayquan, Trayquane, Trayqwon

Trashawn **B** (American) a combination of
Travis + Shawn.
Trasen, Trashaun, Trasean, Trashon, Trashone,
Trashun, Trayshaun, Trayshawn

Traugott (German) God's truth.

Travaris (French) a form of Travers.
Travares, Travaress, Travarious, Travarius,
Travarous, Travarus, Travauris, Traveress,
Traverez, Traverus, Travoris, Travorus

Travell (English) traveler.
Travail, Travale, Travel, Travelis, Travelle,
Trevel, Trevell, Trevelle

Traven (American) a form of Trevon.
Travin, Travine, Trayven

Travers (French) crossroads.
Travaris, Traver, Travis

Travion (American) a form of Trevon.
Traveon, Travian, Travien, Travione, Travioun

Travis ⬛ (English) a form of Travers.
Travais, Travees, Traves, Traveus, Travious, Traviss, Travius, Travous, Travus, Travys, Trayvis, Trevais, Trevis

Travon ⬛ (American) a form of Trevon.
Traevon, Traivon, Travone, Travonn, Travonne

Tray (English) a form of Trey.
Traye

Trayton (English) town full of trees.
Trayten

Trayvon (American) a combination of Tray + Von.
Trayveon, Trayvin, Trayvion, Trayvond, Trayvone, Trayvonne, Trayvyon

Treavon (American) a form of Trevon.
Treavan, Treavin, Treavion

Trecaman (Mapuche) majestic steps of the condor.

Tredway (English) well-worn road.
Treadway

Tremaine, Tremayne ⬛ (Scottish) house of stone.
Tramaine, Tremain, Tremane, Treymaine, Trimaine

Trent ⬛ (Latin) torrent, rapid stream. (French) thirty. Geography: a city in northern Italy.
Trente, Trentino, Trento, Trentonio

Trenton (Latin) town by the rapid stream. Geography: the capital of New Jersey.
Trendon, Trendun, Trenten, Trentin, Trentton, Trentyn, Trinten, Trintin, Trinton

Trequan (American) a combination of Trey + Quan.
Trequanne, Trequaun, Trequian, Trequon, Treqwon, Treyquane

Treshawn (American) a combination of Trey + Shawn.
Treshaun, Treshon, Treshun, Treysean, Treyshawn, Treyshon

Treston (Welsh) a form of Tristan.
Trestan, Trestin, Trestton, Trestyn

Trev (Irish, Welsh) a short form of Trevor.

Trevaughn (American) a combination of Trey + Vaughn.
Trevaughan, Trevaugn, Trevaun, Trevaune, Trevaunn, Treyvaughn

Trevelyan (English) Elian's homestead.

Trevin (American) a form of Trevon.
Trevian, Trevien, Trevine, Trevinne, Trevyn, Treyvin

Trevion (American) a form of Trevon.
Trevione, Trevionne, Trevyon, Treyveon, Treyvion

Trevis (English) a form of Travis.
Treves, Trevez, Treveze, Trevius

Trevon ⬛ (American) a combination of Trey + Von.
Traven, Travion, Travon, Tre, Treavon, Trévan, Treveyon, Trevin, Trevion, Trevohn, Trevoine, Trévon, Trevone, Trevonn, Trevonne, Treyvon

Trevor ⬛ (Irish) prudent. (Welsh) homestead.
Travor, Treavor, Trebor, Trefor, Trev, Trevar, Trevares, Trevarious, Trevaris, Trevarius, Trevaros, Trevarus, Trever, Trevore, Trevores, Trevoris, Trevorus, Trevour, Trevyr, Treyvor

Trey (English) three; third.
Trae, Trai, Tray, Treye, Tri, Trie

Treyvon (American) a form of Trevon.
Treyvan, Treyven, Treyvenn, Treyvone, Treyvonn, Treyvun

Tridev (Indian) the Hindu trinity (Brahma, Vishnu, and Mahesh).

Tridhaman, Trimurti (Indian) the Holy Trinity.

Tridib (Indian) heaven.

Trieu (Vietnamese) tide.

Trigg (Scandinavian) trusty.

Trigun (Indian) the three dimensions.

Trilokchand (Indian) moon of the three worlds.

Triman (Indian) ruler of three worlds; worshipped in three worlds.

Trina 🄶 (Greek) pure.

Trini (Latin) a short form of Trinity.

Trinity 🄶 (Latin) holy trinity.
Trenedy, Trini, Trinidy

Trip, Tripp (English) traveler.

Trishanku (Indian) a king of the Surya dynasty.

Trishar (Indian) pearl necklace.

Tristan ⬛ (Welsh) bold. Literature: a knight in the Arthurian legends who fell in love with his uncle's wife.
Treston, Tris, Trisan, Tristain, Tristán, Tristano, Tristen, Tristian, Tristin, Triston, Tristyn, Trystan

Tristano (Italian) a form of Tristan.

Tristen **B** (Welsh) a form of Tristan.
Trisden, Trissten

Tristin **B** (Welsh) a form of Tristan.
Tristian, Tristinn

Triston **B** (Welsh) a form of Tristan.

Tristram (Welsh) sorrowful. Literature: the title character in Laurence Sterne's eighteenth-century novel *Tristram Shandy*.
Tristam

Tristyn (Welsh) a form of Tristan.
Tristynne

Trivikram (Indian) a name of Vishnu.

Troilo (Egyptian) he who was born in Troy.

Trong (Vietnamese) respected.

Trong Tri (Vietnamese) not of small mind.

Trot (English) trickling stream.

Trowbridge (English) bridge by the tree.

Troy **B** (Irish) foot soldier. (French) curly haired. (English) water. See also Koi.
Troi, Troye, Troyton

Truc (Vietnamese) bamboo; wish.

True (English) faithful, loyal.
Tru

Truesdale (English) faithful one's homestead.

Truitt (English) little and honest.
Truett

Truman (English) honest. History: Harry S. Truman was the thirty-third U.S. president.
Trueman, Trumain, Trumaine, Trumann

Trumble (English) strong; bold.
Trumball, Trumbell, Trumbull

Trustin (English) trustworthy.
Trustan, Trusten, Truston

Trygve (Norwegian) brave victor.

Trystan (Welsh) a form of Tristan.
Tryistan, Trysten, Trystian, Trystin, Trystn, Tryston, Trystyn

Tsai-Shen (Chinese) god of wealth; most popular god.

Tsalani (Nguni) good-bye.

Tse (Ewe) younger of twins.

Tsubasa (Japanese) wing.

Tsukasa (Japanese) administrator.

Tsukiya (Japanese) he who is like the moon.

Tsutomu (Japanese) hard worker; diligent.

Tsuyoshi (Japanese) strong gentleman.

Tu **B** (Vietnamese) tree.

Tuaco (Ghanaian) eleventh-born.

Tuan (Vietnamese) goes smoothly.

Tubal (Hebrew) he who tills the soil.

Tucker **B** (English) fuller, tucker of cloth.
Tuck, Tuckie, Tucky, Tuckyr

Tudor (Welsh) a form of Theodore. History: an English ruling dynasty.
Todor

Tufan (Indian) storm.

Tug (Scandinavian) draw, pull.
Tugg

Tuhin (Indian) snow.

Tuhinsurra, Tusharsuvra (Indian) white as snow.

Tuka (Indian) young boy.

Tukaram (Indian) a poet saint.

Tuketu (Moquelumnan) bear making dust as it runs.

Tukuli (Moquelumnan) caterpillar crawling down a tree.

Tulasidas (Indian) servant of Tulsi.

Tulio (Italian, Spanish) lively.
Tullio

Tullis (Latin) title, rank.
Tullius, Tullos, Tully

Tully (Irish) at peace with God. (Latin) a familiar form of Tullis.
Tull, Tulley, Tullie, Tullio

Tulsidas (Indian) a famous saint.

Tumaini (Mwera) hope.

Tumu (Moquelumnan) deer thinking about eating wild onions.

Tung (Vietnamese) stately, dignified. (Chinese) everyone.

Tungar (Sanskrit) high; lofty.

Tungesh (Indian) moon.

Tuo (Chinese) appropriate.

Tuong (Vietnamese) everything.

Tupac (Quechua) Lord.

Tupacamaru (Quechua) glorious Amaru, an Incan lord.

Tupacapac (Quechua) glorious and kindhearted lord.

Tupacusi (Quechua) happy and majestic.

Tupaquiupanqui, Tupayupanqui (Quechua) memorable and glorious lord.

Tupi (Moquelumnan) pulled up.

Tupper (English) ram raiser.

Turag (Hindi) a thought.

Turi (Spanish) a short form of Arthur.
Ture

Turk (English) from Turkey.

Turner B (Latin) lathe worker; wood worker.

Turpin (Scandinavian) Finn named after Thor.

Tushar (Hindi) winter.

Tut (Arabic) strong and courageous. History: a short form of Tutankhamen, an Egyptian king.
Tutt

Tutu (Spanish) a familiar form of Justin.

Tuvya (Hebrew) a form of Tobias.
Tevya, Tuvia, Tuviah

Tuwile (Mwera) death is inevitable.

Tuyen (Vietnamese) angel.

Twain (English) divided in two. Literature: Mark Twain (whose real name was Samuel Langhorne Clemens) was one of the most prominent nineteenth-century American writers.
Tawine, Twaine, Twan, Twane, Tway, Twayn, Twayne

Twen-Ch'ang (Chinese) god of literature and poetry.

Twia (Fante) born after twins.

Twitchell (English) narrow passage.
Twytchell

Twyford (English) double river crossing.

Txomin (Basque) like the Lord.

Ty B (English) a short form of Tyler, Tyrone, Tyrus.
Tye

Tyagraja (Indian) a famous poet.

Tyee (Native American) chief.

Tyger (English) a form of Tiger.
Tige, Tyg, Tygar

Tylar (English) a form of Tyler.
Tyelar, Tylarr

Tyler · B (English) tile maker.
Tieler, Tiler, Ty, Tyel, Tyeler, Tyelor, Tyhler, Tylar, Tyle, Tylee, Tylere, Tyller, Tylor, Tylyr

Tylor B (English) a form of Tyler.
Tylour

Tymon (Polish) a form of Timothy. (Greek) a form of Timon.
Tymain, Tymaine, Tymane, Tymeik, Tymek, Tymen

Tymothy (English) a form of Timothy.
Tymithy, Tymmothy, Tymoteusz, Tymothee, Timothi

Tynan (Irish) dark.
Ty

Tynek (Czech) a form of Martin.
Tynko

Tyquan (American) a combination of Ty + Quan.
Tykwan, Tykwane, Tykwon, Tyquaan, Tyquane, Tyquann, Tyquine, Tyquinn, Tyquon, Tyquone, Tyquwon, Tyqwan

Tyra G (Scottish) a form of Tyree.

Tyran (American) a form of Tyrone.
Tyraine, Tyrane

Tyree B (Scottish) island dweller. Geography: Tiree is an island off the west coast of Scotland.
Tyra, Tyrae, Tyrai, Tyray, Tyre, Tyrea, Tyrée

Tyreese (American) a form of Terrence.
Tyreas, Tyrease, Tyrece, Tyreece, Tyreice, Tyres, Tyrese, Tyresse, Tyrez, Tyreze, Tyrice, Tyriece, Tyriese

Tyrel, Tyrell B (American) forms of Terrell.
Tyrelle, Tyrrel, Tyrrell

Tyrick (American) a combination of Ty + Rick.
Tyreck, Tyreek, Tyreik, Tyrek, Tyreke, Tyric, Tyriek, Tyrik, Tyriq, Tyrique

Tyrin (American) a form of Tyrone.
Tyrinn, Tyrion, Tyrrin, Tyryn

Tyron (American) a form of Tyrone.
Tyrohn, Tyronn, Tyronna, Tyronne

Tyrone (Greek) sovereign. (Irish) land of Owen.
Tayron, Tayrone, Teirone, Terron, Ty, Tyerone, Tyhrone, Tyran, Tyrin, Tyron, Tyroney, Tyronne, Tyroon, Tyroun

Tyrus (English) a form of Thor.
Ty, Tyruss, Tyryss

Tyshawn (American) a combination of Ty + Shawn.
Tyshan, Tyshaun; Tyshauwn, Tyshian, Tyshinn, Tyshion, Tyshon, Tyshone, Tyshonne, Tyshun, Tyshunn, Tyshyn

Tyson **B** (French) son of Ty.
Tison, Tiszon, Tyce, Tycen, Tyesn, Tyeson, Tysen, Tysie, Tysin, Tysne, Tysone

Tytus (Polish) a form of Titus.
Tyus

Tyvon (American) a combination of Ty + Von.
Tyvan, Tyvin, Tyvinn, Tyvone, Tyvonne

Tywan (Chinese) a form of Taiwan.
Tywain, Tywaine, Tywane, Tywann, Tywaun, Tywen, Tywon, Tywone, Tywonne

Tzadok (Hebrew) righteous.
Tzadik, Zadok

Tzion (Hebrew) sign from God.
Zion

Tzuriel (Hebrew) God is my rock.
Tzuriya

Tzvi (Hebrew) deer.
Tzevi, Zevi

Uaine (Irish) a form of Owen.

Ubadah (Arabic) serves God.

Ubaid (Arabic) faithful.

Ubaidah (Indian) servant of God.

Ubaldo (Germanic) he of daring thoughts.

Uberto (Italian) a form of Hubert.

Uche (Ibo) thought.

Uchit (Indian) correct.

Uchu (Quechua) hot like pepper.

Ucumari (Quechua) he who has the strength of a bear.

Udant (Hindi) correct message.

Udarsh (Hindi) brimming.

Uday (Sanskrit) to rise.

Udbal (Hindi) mighty.

Udbhav (Indian) creation; to arise from.

Uddip (Indian) giving light.

Uddiyan (Indian) flying speed.

Udeep (Indian) flood.

Udell (English) yew-tree valley.
Dell, Eudel, Udale, Udall, Yudell

Udit (Sanskrit) grown; shining.

Udo (Japanese) ginseng plant. (German) a short form of Udolf.

Udolf (English) prosperous wolf.
Udo, Udolfo, Udolph

Udu (Hindi) water.

Ugo (Italian) a form of Hugh, Hugo.

Ugutz (Basque) a form of John.

Uilliam (Irish) a form of William.
Uileog, Uilleam, Ulick

Uinseann (Irish) a form of Vincent.

Uistean (Irish) intelligent.
Uisdean

Uja (Sanskrit) growing.

Ujas (Indian) first light.

Ujendra (Indian) conqueror.

Ujesh (Indian) one who bestows light.

Ujjay (Indian) victorious.

Ujjwal, Ujval (Indian) splendorous.

Uku (Hawaiian) flea, insect; skilled ukulele player.

Ulan (African) first-born twin.

Ulbrecht (German) a form of Albert.

Ulf (German) wolf.

Ulfred (German) peaceful wolf.

Ulfrido (Teutonic) he imposes peace through force.

Ulger (German) warring wolf.

Boys S–Z

Ulises (Latin) a form of Ulysses.
Ulishes, Ulisse, Ulisses

Ullanta (Aymara) warrior who sees everything from his watchtower.

Ullantay (Quechua) lord Ollanta.

Ullas (Indian) light.

Ullock (German) sporting wolf.

Ulmer (English) famous wolf.
Ullmar, Ulmar

Ulmo (German) from Ulm, Germany.

Ulpiano, Ulpio (Latin) sly as a fox.

Ulric (German) a form of Ulrich.
Ullric

Ulrich (German) wolf ruler; ruler of all. See also Alaric.
Uli, Ull, Ulric, Ulrick, Ulrik, Ulrike, Ulu, Ulz, Uwe

Ulrico (Germanic) noble as a king.

Ultman (Hindi) god; godlike.

Ulyses (Latin) a form of Ulysses.
Ulysee, Ulysees

Ulysses (Latin) wrathful. A form of Odysseus.
Eulises, Ulick, Ulises, Ulyses, Ulysse, Ulysees, Ulyses, Ulyssius

Umang (Sanskrit) enthusiastic.
Umanga

Umar (Arabic) a form of Omar.
Umair, Umarr, Umayr, Umer

Umberto (Italian) a form of Humbert.
Uberto

Umi (Yao) life.

Umio (Japanese) sea hero.

Umit (Turkish) hope.

Unai (Basque) shepherd.
Una

Unay (Quechua) previous; remote, underlying.

Uner (Turkish) famous.

Unika 🄶 (Lomwe) brighten.

Unique 🄶 (Latin) only, unique.
Uneek, Unek, Unikque, Uniqué, Unyque

Unnabh (Hindi) highest.

Unwin (English) nonfriend.
Unwinn, Unwyn

Upanshu (Indian) chanting of hymns or mantras in a low tone.

Uppas (Indian) gem.

Upshaw (English) upper wooded area.

Upton (English) upper town.

Upwood (English) upper forest.

Uqbah (Indian) the end of everything.

Urav (Indian) excitement.

Urban (Latin) city dweller; courteous.
Urbain, Urbaine, Urbane, Urbano, Urbanus, Urvan, Urvane

Urbane (English) a form of Urban.

Urbano (Italian) a form of Urban.

Urcucolla (Quechua) hill; the god Colla.

Uri (Hebrew) a short form of Uriah.
Urie

Uriah (Hebrew) my light. Bible: a soldier and the husband of Bathsheba. See also Yuri.
Uri, Uria, Urias, Urijah

Urian (Greek) heaven.
Urihaan

Urías (Greek) light of the lord.

Uriel 🄱 (Hebrew) God is my light.
Urie

Urso (Latin) bear.

Urson (French) a form of Orson.
Ursan, Ursus

Urtzi (Basque) sky.

Urvang (Indian) mountain.

Usaamah (Indian) description of a lion.

Usaku (Japanese) moonlit.

Usamah (Arabic) like a lion.
Usama

Usco, Uscu (Quechua) wild cat.

Uscouiyca, Uscuiyca (Quechua) sacred; wild cat.

Useni (Yao) tell me.
Usene, Usenet

Ushakanta (Indian) sun.

Ushapati (Indian) husband of dawn.

Ushi (Chinese) ox.

Usi (Yao) smoke.

Ustin (Russian) a form of Justin.

V

Usuy (Quechua) he who brings abundances.

Utanka (Indian) a disciple of the sage Veda.

Utatci (Moquelumnan) bear scratching itself.

Uthman (Arabic) companion of the Prophet.
Usman, Uthmaan

Utkarsh (Hindi) high quality.

Utkarsha (Indian) advancement.

Utpal (Indian) burst open.

Utsav (Indian) festival.

Uttam (Sanskrit) best.

Uttiya (Indian) a name in Buddhist literature.

Uturuncu (Quechua) jaguar; tiger; the bravest.

Uturuncu Achachi (Quechua) he who has brave ancestors, jaguar ancestors.

Uwe (German) a familiar form of Ulrich.

Uzi (Hebrew) my strength.
Uzzia

Uziel (Hebrew) God is my strength; mighty force.
Uzie, Uzziah, Uzziel

Uzoma (Nigerian) born during a journey.

Uzumati (Moquelumnan) grizzly bear.

V G (American) an initial used as a first name.

Vachel (French) small cow.
Vache, Vachell

Vaclav (Czech) wreath of glory.
Vasek

Vadin (Hindi) speaker.
Vaden

Vaijayi (Indian) victor.

Vaikartan (Indian) name of Karna.

Vaikunth (Indian) abode of Vishnu.

Vail B (English) valley.
Vaile, Vaill, Vale, Valle

Vairaj (Indian) spiritual glory.

Vairat (Indian) gem.

Vaishvik (Indian) belonging to the world.

Vajramani (Indian) diamond.

Val B (Latin) a short form of Valentin.

Valborg (Swedish) mighty mountain.

Valdemar (Swedish) famous ruler.

Valdo (Teutonic) he who governs, the monarch.

Valentin (Latin) strong; healthy.
Val, Valencio, Valenté, Valentijn, Valentine, Valentino, Valenton, Valentyn, Velentino

Valentín (Latin) a form of Valentin.

Valentino (Italian) a form of Valentin.

Valerian (Latin) strong; healthy.
Valeriano, Valerii, Valerio, Valeryn

Valerie G (Russian) a form of Valerii.

Valerii (Russian) a form of Valerian.
Valera, Valerie, Valerij, Valerik, Valeriy, Valery

Valfredo (Germanic) peaceful king.

Valfrid (Swedish) strong peace.

Valin (Hindi) a form of Balin. Mythology: a tyrannical monkey king.

Vallis (French) from Wales.
Valis

Valter (Lithuanian, Swedish) a form of Walter.
Valters, Valther, Valtr, Vanda

Van (Dutch) a short form of Vandyke.
Vander, Vane, Vann, Vanno

Vanad (Hindi) cloud.

Vance B (English) thresher.

Vanda G (Lithuanian) a form of Walter.
Vander

Vandyke (Dutch) dyke.
Van

Vanessa G (Greek) butterfly.

Vaninath (Indian) husband of goddess Saraswati.

Vansh (Indian) the coming generation.

Vanya (Russian) a familiar form of Ivan.
Vanechka, Vanek, Vanja, Vanka, Vanusha, Wanya

Varana (Indian) holy river.

Vardon (French) green knoll.
Vardaan, Varden, Verdan, Verdon, Verdun

Varian (Latin) variable.

Varick (German) protecting ruler.
Varak, Varek, Warrick

Vartan (Armenian) rose producer; rose giver.

Varun (Hindi) rain god.
Varron

Vasant (Sanskrit) spring.
Vasanth

Vasavaj, Vasavi (Indian) son of Indra.

Vashawn (American) a combination of the prefix Va + Shawn.
Vashae, Vashan, Vashann, Vashaun, Vashawnn, Vashon, Vashun, Vishon

Vashita (Indian) one who hypnotizes by her virtues.

Vasilis (Greek) a form of Basil.
Vas, Vasaya, Vaselios, Vashon, Vasil, Vasile, Vasileior, Vasileios, Vasilios, Vasilius, Vasilos, Vasilus, Vasily, Vassilios, Vasylko, Vasyltso, Vazul

Vasily (Russian) a form of Vasilis.
Vasilek, Vasili, Vasilii, Vasilije, Vasilik, Vasiliy, Vassili, Vassilij, Vasya, Vasyenka

Vasin (Hindi) ruler, lord.

Vasu (Sanskrit) wealth.

Vasuman (Indian) born of fire.

Vasur (Hindi) precious.

Vasyl (German, Slavic) a form of William.
Vasos, Vassily, Vassos, Vasya, Vasyuta, VaVaska, Wassily

Vatsa (Hindi) son.

Vaughn ☒ (Welsh) small.
Vaughan, Vaughen, Vaun, Vaune, Von, Voughn

Vayun (Hindi) lively.

Vayya (Indian) friend.

Veasna (Cambodian) lucky.

Ved (Sanskrit) sacred knowledge.

Vedaant (Indian) the scriptures.

Vedang (Indian) from the Vedas.

Vedant (Indian) Hindu philosophy.

Vedbhushan (Indian) one adorned with knowledge of the Vedas.

Vedie (Latin) sight.

Veer (Sanskrit) brave.

Veerbhadra (Indian) the Ashwamedha horse.

Vegard (Norwegian) sanctuary; protection.

Velvel (Yiddish) wolf.

Venancio (Latin) a fan of hunting.

Vencel (Hungarian) a short form of Wenceslaus.
Venci, Vencie

Venceslao (Slavic) crowned with glory.

Venedictos (Greek) a form of Benedict.
Venedict, Venediktos, Venka, Venya

Veniamin (Bulgarian) a form of Benjamin.
Venyamin, Verniamin

Venkat (Hindi) god; godlike. Religion: another name for the Hindu god Vishnu.

Ventura (Latin) he who will be happy.

Venturo (Spanish) food fortune.

Venya (Russian) a familiar form of Benedict.
Venedict, Venka

Vere (Latin, French) true.

Vered (Hebrew) rose.

Vergil (Latin) a form of Virgil. Literature: a Roman poet best known for his epic poem *Aenid*.
Verge

Vern (Latin) a short form of Vernon.
Verna, Vernal, Verne, Verneal, Vernel, Vernell, Vernelle, Vernial, Vernine, Vernis, Vernol

Vernados (German) courage of the bear.

Verner (German) defending army.
Varner

Verney (French) alder grove.
Vernie

Vernon (Latin) springlike; youthful.
Vern, Varnan, Vernen, Verney, Vernin

Vero (Latin) truthful, sincere, credible.

Verrill (German) masculine. (French) loyal.
Verill, Verrall, Verrell, Verroll, Veryl

Vespasiano (Latin) name of the Roman emperor from the first century.

Vian (English) full of life.

Vibhaas (Indian) shining.

Vibhakar (Indian) one emitting light.

Vibhas (Indian) luminous.

Vibhat (Indian) dawn.

Vibhishan (Indian) a character from the epic Ramayana.

Vibhor (Indian) ecstatic.

Vibhu (Indian) all-pervading.

Vibhut (Indian) strong.

Vibodh (Hindi) wise.

Vic (Latin) a short form of Victor.
Vick, Vicken, Vickenson

Vicente **B** (Spanish) a form of Vincent.
Vicent, Visente

Vicenzo (Italian) a form of Vincent.

Vicky **G** (Latin) a familiar form of Victoria.

Victoir (French) a form of Victor.

Victor (Latin) victor, conqueror.
Vic, Victa, Victer, Victoir, Victoriano, Victorien, Victorin, Victorio, Viktor, Vitin, Vittorio, Vitya, Wikoli, Wiktor, Witek

Víctor (Spanish) a form of Victor.

Victoria **G** (Latin) a form of Victor.

Victorio (Spanish) a form of Victor.
Victorino

Victoro (Latin) victor.

Vidal (Spanish) a form of Vitas.
Vida, Vidale, Vidall, Videll

Vidar (Norwegian) tree warrior.

Videl (Spanish) life.

Vidip (Indian) bright.

Vidor (Hungarian) cheerful.

Vidur (Hindi) wise.

Vidyacharan (Indian) learned.

Vidyadhar (Indian) demigod.

Vidyanand (Indian) one who enjoys learning.

Vidyaranya (Indian) forest of knowledge.

Vidyasagar (Indian) ocean of knowledge.

Vidyut (Hindi) brilliant.

Vien (Vietnamese) completion, accomplishment; satisfaction.

Vihaan (Hindi) morning, dawn.

Vihang, Vihanga (Indian) a bird.

Viho (Cheyenne) chief.

Vijanyendra, Vijendra (Indian) victorious.

Vijay (Hindi) victorious.

Vijayendra (Indian) the god of victory.

Vijayketu (Indian) the flag of victory.

Vijval (Hindi) intelligent.

Vikas (Hindi) growing.
Vikash, Vikesh

Vikhyath (Indian) fame.

Vikram (Hindi) valorous.
Vikrum

Vikramaditya, Vikramajit (Indian) a famous king.

Vikramendra (Indian) king of prowess.

Vikrant (Hindi) powerful.
Vikran

Vikranta (Indian) brave.

Viktor (German, Hungarian, Russian) a form of Victor.
Viktoras, Viktors

Vilas (Hindi) coolness.

Vilfredo (Germanic) peaceful king.

Vilhelm (German) a form of William.
Vilhelms, Vilho, Vilis, Viljo, Villem

Vili (Hungarian) a short form of William.
Villy, Vilmos

Viliam (Czech) a form of William.
Vila, Vilek, Vilém, Viliami, Viliamu, Vilko, Vilous

Viljo (Finnish) a form of William.

Ville (Swedish) a short form of William.

Vilok (Indian) to see.

Vilokan (Indian) gaze.

Vimal (Hindi) pure.

Vimaladitya (Indian) clean sun.

Vimalmani (Indian) pure jewel.

Vin (Latin) a short form of Vincent.
Vinn

Vinay (Hindi) polite.

Vince (English) a short form of Vincent.
Vence, Vint

Vincent ☒ (Latin) victor, conqueror. See
also Binkentios, Binky.
*Uinseann, Vencent, Vicente, Vicenzo, Vikent,
Vikenti, Vikesha, Vin, Vince, Vincence,
Vincens, Vincente, Vincentius, Vincents,
Vincenty, Vincenzo, Vinci, Vincien, Vincient,
Vinciente, Vincint, Vinny, Vinsent, Vinsint,
Wincent*

Vincente (Spanish) a form of Vincent.
Vencente

Vincenzo (Italian) a form of Vincent.
*Vincenz, Vincenza, Vincenzio, Vinchenzo,
Vinzenz*

Vinci (Hungarian, Italian) a familiar form of
Vincent.
Vinci, Vinco, Vincze

Vineet (Hindi) knowledgeable.

Vinesh (Hindi) godly.

Vinh (Vietnamese) bay, gulf.

Vinil (Indian) blue.

Vinny (English) a familiar form of Calvin,
Melvin, Vincent.
Vinnee, Vinney, Vinni, Vinnie

Vinod (Hindi) happy, joyful.
Vinodh, Vinood

Vinoth (Indian) pleasing.

Vinson (English) son of Vincent.
Vinnis

Vipan (Indian) sail; small trade.

Vipin (Indian) forest.

Vipinbehari (Indian) forest wanderer.

Viplab (Indian) floating; revolution.

Viplav (Indian) drifting about; revolution.

Vipra (Indian) a priest.

Vipul (Hindi) plentiful.

Viraaj (Indian) king.

Viraj (Hindi) resplendent.

Viral (Hindi) precious.

Virat (Hindi) very big.

Virgil (Latin) rod bearer, staff bearer.
Vergil, Virge, Virgial, Virgie, Virgilio

Virgilio (Spanish) a form of Virgil.
Virjilio

Virginio (Latin) he is pure and simple.

Virote (Tai) strong, powerful.

Virurch, Vishresh (Indian) the Holy Trinity.

Vishal (Hindi) huge; great.
Vishaal

Vishesh (Hindi) special.

Vishnu (Hindi) protector.

Vishnudev (Indian) God.

Vishnudutt (Indian) gift of Vishnu.

Vishva (Indian) the universe.

Vishvajit (Indian) conqueror of the world.

Vishvakarma (Indian) architect of the
universe.

Vishvamitra (Indian) a sage.

Vishvas (Indian) faith.

Vishvatma, Vishwatma (Indian) universal
soul.

Vishwa (Indian) earth; universe.

Vishwajit (Indian) one who conquers the
universe.

Vishwakarma (Indian) architect of the
universe.

Vishwalochan (Indian) eyes of the universe.

Vishwambhar (Indian) the all-pervading
one.

Vishwamitra (Indian) friend of the universe.

Vishwanath, Viswanath (Indian) god of
the universe.

Vishwankar (Indian) creator of the universe.

Vishwas (Indian) faith; trust.

Vitaliano, Vitalicio (Latin) young and
strong.

Vitas (Latin) alive, vital.
Vidal, Vitus

Vito (Latin) a short form of Vittorio.
*Veit, Vidal, Vital, Vitale, Vitalis, Vitas, Vitin,
Vitis, Vitus, Vitya, Vytas*

Vitola (Indian) peaceful.

Vítor (Latin) victor.

Vittanath (Indian) owner of money.

Vittorio (Italian) a form of Victor.
Vito, Vitor, Vitorio, Vittore, Vittorios

Vitya (Russian) a form of Victor.
Vitenka, Vitka

Vivash (Hindi) bright.

Vivek (Hindi) wisdom.
Vivekinan

Vivekanand (Indian) joy of discrimination.

Vivian **G** (Latin) full of life.

Viviano (Spanish) small man.

Vladimir (Russian) famous prince. See also
Dima, Waldemar, Walter.
*Bladimir, Vimka, Vlad, Vladamir, Vladik,
Vladimar, Vladimeer, Vladimer, Vladimere,
Vladimire, Vladimyr, Vladjimir, Vladka, Vladko,
Vladlen, Vladmir, Volodimir, Volodya, Volya,
Vova, Wladimir*

Vladimiro (Spanish) a form of Vladimir.

Vladislav (Slavic) glorious ruler. See also
Slava.
*Vladik, Vladya, Vlas, Vlasislava, Vyacheslav,
Wladislav*

Vlas (Russian) a short form of Vladislav.

Volker (German) people's guard.
Folke

Volney (German) national spirit.

Von (German) a short form of many German
names.

Vova (Russian) a form of Walter.
Vovka

Vrishab (Hindi) excellent.

Vrishin (Indian) peacock.

Vrushket (Indian) son of Karna.

Vuai (Swahili) savior.

Vulpiano (Latin) sly as a fox.

Vuong (Vietnamese) prosperous, developed.

Vyacheslav (Russian) a form of Vladislav.
See also Slava.

Vyan (Indian) air.

Vyas (Indian) sage who wrote *Mahabharat*.

Vyoman (Indian) sky.

W **B** (American) an initial used as a first
name.

Waahid (Indian) single; exclusively;
unequaled.

Waa'il (Indian) coming back for shelter.

Waban (Ojibwa) white.
Wabon

Wade (English) ford; river crossing.
*Wad, Wadesworth, Wadi, Wadie, Waed,
Waid, Waide, Wayde, Waydell, Whaid*

Wadee' (Indian) calm, peaceful.

Wadley (English) ford meadow.
Wadleigh, Wadly

Wadsworth (English) village near the ford.
Waddsworth

Wafeeq (Indian) successful.

Wagner (German) wagoner, wagon maker.
Music: Richard Wagner was a famous
nineteenth-century German composer.
Waggoner

Wahid (Arabic) single; exclusively
unequaled.
Waheed

Wahkan (Lakota) sacred.

Wahkoowah (Lakota) charging.

Wain (English) a short form of Wainwright.
A form of Wayne.

Wainwright (English) wagon maker.
*Wain, Wainright, Wayne, Wayneright,
Waynewright, Waynright, Wright*

Waite (English) watchman.
Waitman, Waiton, Waits, Wayte

Wajeeh (Indian) noble.

Wakaki (Japanese) young; life; brilliant.

Wakato (Japanese) youthful person.

Wakefield (English) wet field.
Field, Wake

Wakely (English) wet meadow.

Wakeman (English) watchman.
Wake

Wakin (Chuukese) a form of Joaquin.

Wakiza (Native American) determined
warrior.

Walcott (English) cottage by the wall.
Wallcot, Wallcott, Wolcott

Boys S–Z

Waldemar (German) powerful; famous. See also Vladimir.
Valdemar, Waldermar, Waldo

Walden (English) wooded valley. Literature: Henry David Thoreau made Walden Pond famous with his book *Walden*.
Waldi, Waldo, Waldon, Welti

Waldino (Teutonic) having an open and bold spirit.

Waldo (German) a familiar form of Oswald, Waldemar, Walden.
Wald, Waldy

Waldron (English) ruler.

Waleed (Arabic) newborn.
Waled, Walid

Walerian (Polish) strong; brave.

Wales (English) from Wales.
Wael, Wail, Wali, Walie, Waly

Walford (English) Welshman's ford.

Walfred (German) peaceful ruler.
Walfredo, Walfried

Wali (Arabic) all-governing.

Waliyudeen (Indian) supporter of the faith.

Waliyullah (Indian) supporter of God.

Walker ☙ (English) cloth walker; cloth cleaner.
Wallie, Wally

Wallace (English) from Wales.
Wallach, Wallas, Wallie, Wallis, Wally, Walsh, Welsh

Wallach (German) a form of Wallace.
Wallache

Waller (German) powerful. (English) wall maker.

Wally (English) a familiar form of Walter.
Walli, Wallie

Walmond (German) mighty ruler.

Walsh (English) a form of Wallace.
Welch, Welsh

Walt (English) a short form of Walter, Walton.
Waltey, Waltli, Walty

Walter (German) army ruler, general. (English) woodsman. See also Gautier, Gualberto, Gualtiero, Gutierre, Ladislav, Vladimir.
Valter, Vanda, Vova, Walder, Wally, Walt, Waltli, Walther, Waltr, Wat, Waterio, Watkins, Watson, Wualter

Walther (German) a form of Walter.

Walton (English) walled town.
Walt

Waltr (Czech) a form of Walter.

Walworth (English) fenced-in farm.

Walwyn (English) Welsh friend.
Walwin, Walwinn, Walwynn, Walwynne, Welwyn

Wamblee (Lakota) eagle.

Wan (Chinese) ten thousand.

Wang (Chinese) hope; wish.

Wanikiya (Lakota) savior.

Wanya ☙ (Russian) a form of Vanya.
Wanyai

Wapi (Native American) lucky.

Warburton (English) fortified town.

Ward (English) watchman, guardian.
Warde, Warden, Worden

Wardell (English) watchman's hill.

Wardley (English) watchman's meadow.
Wardlea, Wardleigh

Ware (English) wary, cautious.

Warfield (English) field near the weir or fish trap.

Warford (English) ford near the weir or fish trap.

Warley (English) meadow near the weir or fish trap.

Warner (German) armed defender. (French) park keeper.
Werner

Warren (German) general; warden; rabbit hutch.
Ware, Waring, Warrenson, Warrin, Warriner, Worrin

Warton (English) town near the weir or fish trap.

Warwick (English) buildings near the weir or fish trap.
Warick, Warrick

Washburn (English) overflowing river.

Washi (Japanese) eagle.

Washington (English) town near water. History: George Washington was the first U.S. president.
Wash

Wasili (Russian) a form of Basil.
Wasyl

Wasim (Arabic) graceful; good-looking.
Waseem, Wasseem, Wassim

Wataru (Japanese) he who reaches out to others.

Watende (Nyakyusa) there will be revenge.

Waterio (Spanish) a form of Walter.
Gualtiero

Watford (English) wattle ford; dam made of twigs and sticks.

Watkins (English) son of Walter.
Watkin

Watson (English) son of Walter.
Wathson, Whatson

Waverly **G** (English) quaking aspen-tree meadow.
Waverlee, Waverley

Wayland (English) a form of Waylon.
Weiland, Weyland

Waylon (English) land by the road.
Wallen, Walon, Way, Waylan, Wayland, Waylen, Waylin, Weylin

Wayman (English) road man; traveler.
Waymon

Wayne (English) wagon maker. A short form of Wainwright.
Wain, Wanye, Wayn, Waynell, Waynne, Wene, Whayne

Wazir (Arabic) minister.

Webb (English) weaver.
Web, Weeb

Weber (German) weaver.
Webber, Webner

Webley (English) weaver's meadow.
Webbley, Webbly, Webly

Webster (English) weaver.

Weddel (English) valley near the ford.

Wei-Quo (Chinese) ruler of the country.
Wei

Welborne (English) spring-fed stream.
Welborn, Welbourne, Welburn, Wellborn, Wellborne, Wellbourn, Wellburn

Welby (German) farm near the well.
Welbey, Welbie, Wellbey, Wellby

Weldon (English) hill near the well.
Weldan

Welfel (Yiddish) a form of William.
Welvel

Welford (English) ford near the well.

Wells (English) springs.
Welles

Welsh (English) a form of Wallace, Walsh.
Welch

Welton (English) town near the well.

Wemilat (Native American) all give to him.

Wemilo (Native American) all speak to him.

Wen (Gypsy) born in winter.

Wenceslaus (Slavic) wreath of honor.
Vencel, Wenceslao, Wenceslas, Wenzel, Wenzell, Wiencyslaw

Wendell (German) wanderer. (English) good dale, good valley.
Wandale, Wendall, Wendel, Wendle, Wendy

Wene (Hawaiian) a form of Wayne.

Wenford (English) white ford.
Wynford

Wentworth (English) pale man's settlement.

Wenutu (Native American) clear sky.

Werner (English) a form of Warner.
Wernhar, Wernher

Wes (English) a short form of Wesley.
Wess

Wesh (Gypsy) woods.

Wesley **B** (English) western meadow.
Wes, Weseley, Wesle, Weslee, Wesleyan, Weslie, Wesly, Wessley, Westleigh, Westley, Wezley

West (English) west.

Westbrook (English) western brook.
Brook, West, Westbrooke

Westby (English) western farmstead.

Westcott (English) western cottage.
Wescot, Wescott, Westcot

Westley (English) a form of Wesley.
Westlee, Westly

Weston **B** (English) western town.
West, Westen, Westin

Wetherby (English) wether-sheep farm.
Weatherbey, Weatherbie, Weatherby, Wetherbey, Wetherbie

Wetherell (English) wether-sheep corner.

Wetherly (English) wether-sheep meadow.

Weylin (English) a form of Waylon.
Weylan, Weylyn

Whalley (English) woods near a hill.
Whaley

Wharton (English) town on the bank of a lake.
Warton

Wheatley (English) wheat field.
Whatley, Wheatlea, Wheatleigh, Wheatly

Wheaton (English) wheat town.

Wheeler (English) wheel maker; wagon driver.

Whistler (English) whistler, piper.

Whit (English) a short form of Whitman, Whitney.
Whitt, Whyt, Whyte, Wit, Witt

Whitby (English) white house.

Whitcomb (English) white valley.
Whitcombe, Whitcumb

Whitelaw (English) small hill.
Whitlaw

Whitey (English) white skinned; white haired.

Whitfield (English) white field.

Whitford (English) white ford.

Whitley ☙ (English) white meadow.
Whitlea, Whitlee, Whitleigh

Whitman (English) white-haired man.
Whit

Whitmore (English) white moor.
Whitmoor, Whittemore, Witmore, Wittemore

Whitney ☙ (English) white island; white water.
Whit, Whittney, Widney, Widny

Whittaker (English) white field.
Whitacker, Whitaker, Whitmaker

Wicasa (Dakota) man.

Wicent (Polish) a form of Vincent.
Wicek, Wicus

Wichado (Native American) willing.

Wickham (English) village enclosure.
Wick

Wickley (English) village meadow.
Wilcley

Wid (English) wide.

Wies (German) renowned warrior.

Wikoli (Hawaiian) a form of Victor.

Wiktor (Polish) a form of Victor.

Wilanu (Moquelumnan) pouring water on flour.

Wilbert (German) brilliant; resolute.
Wilberto, Wilburt

Wilbur (English) wall fortification; bright willows.
Wilber, Wilburn, Wilburt, Willbur, Wilver

Wilder (English) wilderness, wild.
Wylder

Wildon (English) wooded hill.
Wilden, Willdon

Wile (Hawaiian) a form of Willie.

Wiley (English) willow meadow; Will's meadow.
Whiley, Wildy, Willey, Wylie

Wilford (English) willow-tree ford.
Wilferd

Wilfred (German) determined peacemaker.
Wilferd, Wilfredo, Wilfrid, Wilfride, Wilfried, Wilfryd, Will, Willfred, Willfried, Willie, Willy

Wilfredo (Spanish) a form of Wilfred.
Fredo, Wifredo, Wilfrido, Willfredo

Wilhelm (German) determined guardian.
Wilhelmus, Willem

Wiliama (Hawaiian) a form of William.
Pila, Wile

Wilkie (English) a familiar form of Wilkins.
Wikie, Wilke

Wilkins (English) William's kin.
Wilkens, Wilkes, Wilkie, Wilkin, Wilks, Willkes, Willkins

Wilkinson (English) son of little William.
Wilkenson, Willkinson

Will (English) a short form of William.
Wil, Wilm, Wim

Willard (German) determined and brave.
Williard

Willem (German) a form of William.
Willim

William 🖐 **B** (English) a form of Wilhelm. See also Gilamu, Guglielmo, Guilherme, Guillaume, Guillermo, Gwilym, Liam, Uilliam, Wilhelm.
Bill, Billy, Vasyl, Vilhelm, Vili, Viliam, Viljo, Ville, Villiam, Welfel, Wilek, Wiliam, Wiliama, Wiliame, Will, Willaim, Willam, Willeam, Willem, Williams, Willie, Willil, Willis, Willium, Williw, Willyam, Wim

Williams (German) son of William.
Wilams, Willaims, Williamson, Wuliams

Willie **B** (German) a familiar form of William.
Wile, Wille, Willi, Willia, Willy

Willis (German) son of Willie.
Willice, Wills, Willus, Wyllis

Willoughby (English) willow farm.
Willoughbey, Willoughbie

Wills (English) son of Will.

Willy (German) a form of Willie.
Willey, Wily

Wilmer (German) determined and famous.
Willimar, Willmer, Wilm, Wilmar, Wylmar, Wylmer

Wilmot (Teutonic) resolute spirit.
Willmont, Willmot, Wilm, Wilmont

Wilny (Native American) eagle singing while flying.

Wilson **B** (English) son of Will.
Wilkinson, Willson, Wilsen, Wolson

Wilt (English) a short form of Wilton.

Wilton (English) farm by the spring.
Will, Wilt

Wilu (Moquelumnan) chicken hawk squawking.

Win **B** (Cambodian) bright. (English) a short form of Winston and names ending in "win."
Winn, Winnie, Winny

Wincent (Polish) a form of Vincent.
Wicek, Wicenty, Wicus, Wince, Wincenty

Winchell (English) bend in the road; bend in the land.

Windsor (English) riverbank with a winch. History: the surname of the British royal family.
Wincer, Winsor, Wyndsor

Winfield (English) friendly field.
Field, Winfred, Winfrey, Winifield, Winnfield, Wynfield, Wynnfield

Winfried (German) friend of peace.

Wing (Chinese) glory.
Wing-Chiu, Wing-Kit

Wingate (English) winding gate.

Wingi (Native American) willing.

Winslow (English) friend's hill.

Winston (English) friendly town; victory town.
Win, Winsten, Winstin, Winstonn, Winton, Wynstan, Wynston

Winter **G** (English) born in winter.
Winterford, Wynter

Winthrop (English) victory at the crossroads.

Winton (English) a form of Winston.
Wynten, Wynton

Winward (English) friend's guardian; friend's forest.

Wit (Polish) life. (English) a form of Whit. (Flemish) a short form of DeWitt.
Witt, Wittie, Witty

Witek (Polish) a form of Victor.

Witha (Arabic) handsome.

Witter (English) wise warrior.

Witton (English) wise man's estate.

Wladislav (Polish) a form of Vladislav.
Wladislaw

Wo (Chinese) fertile.

Wolcott (English) cottage in the woods.

Wolf (German, English) a short form of Wolfe, Wolfgang.
Wolff, Wolfie, Wolfy

Wolfe (English) wolf.
Wolf, Woolf

Wolfgang (German) wolf quarrel. Music: Wolfgang Amadeus Mozart was a famous eighteenth-century Austrian composer.
Wolf, Wolfegang, Wolfgans

Wood (English) a short form of Elwood, Garwood, Woodrow.
Woody

Woodfield (English) forest meadow.

Woodford (English) ford through the forest.

Woodrow (English) passage in the woods. History: Thomas Woodrow Wilson was the twenty-eighth U.S. president.
Wood, Woodman, Woodroe, Woody

Boys

Woodruff (English) forest ranger.

Woodson (English) son of Wood.
Woods, Woodsen

Woodville (English) town at the edge of the woods.

Woodward (English) forest warden.
Woodard

Woody (American) a familiar form of Elwood, Garwood, Woodrow.
Wooddy, Woodie

Woolsey (English) victorious wolf.

Worcester (English) forest army camp.

Wordsworth (English) wolf-guardian's farm. Literature: William Wordsworth was a famous British poet.
Worth

Worie (Ibo) born on market day.

Worth (English) a short form of Wordsworth.
Worthey, Worthington, Worthy

Worton (English) farm town.

Wouter (German) powerful warrior.

Wrangle (American) a form of Rangle.
Wrangler

Wray (Scandinavian) corner property. (English) crooked.
Wreh

Wren (Welsh) chief, ruler. (English) wren.

Wright (English) a short form of Wainwright.

Wrisley (English) a form of Risley.
Wrisee, Wrislie, Wrisly

Wriston (English) a form of Riston.
Wryston

Wu (Chinese) army squad; crow; sorcerer.

Wuliton (Native American) will do well.

Wunand (Native American) God is good.

Wuyi (Moquelumnan) turkey vulture flying.

Wyatt ♛ **B** (French) little warrior.
Wiatt, Wyat, Wyatte, Wye, Wyeth, Wyett, Wyitt, Wytt

Wybert (English) battle bright.

Wyborn (Scandinavian) war bear.

Wyck (Scandinavian) village.

Wycliff (English) white cliff; village near the cliff.
Wyckliffe, Wycliffe

Wylie (English) charming.
Wiley, Wye, Wyley, Wyllie, Wyly

Wyman (English) fighter, warrior.

Wymer (English) famous in battle.

Wyn (Welsh) light skinned; white. (English) friend. A short form of Selwyn.
Win, Wyne, Wynn, Wynne

Wyndham (Scottish) village near the winding road.
Windham, Wynndham

Wynono (Native American) first-born son.

Wythe (English) willow tree.

X

Xabat (Basque) savior.

Xaiver (Basque) a form of Xavier.
Xajavier, Xzaiver

Xan (Greek) a short form of Alexander.
Xane

Xander (Greek) a short form of Alexander.
Xande, Xzander

Xanthus (Latin) golden haired.
Xanthos

Xarles (Basque) a form of Charles.

Xavier ♛ **B** (Arabic) bright. (Basque) owner of the new house. See also Exavier, Javier, Salvatore, Saverio.
Xabier, Xaiver, Xavaeir, Xaver, Xavian, Xaviar, Xavior, Xavon, Xavyer, Xever, Xizavier, Xxavier, Xzavier, Zavier

Xenophon (Greek) strange voice.
Xeno, Zennie

Xenos (Greek) stranger; guest.
Zenos

Xerxes (Persian) ruler. History: a king of Persia.
Zerk

Xi (Chinese) uncommon.

Xia (Chinese) the glow of sunrise or sunset.

Xiang (Chinese) to soar; auspicious; fragrant.

Xiao-Chen (Chinese) early morning.

Xiaoping (Chinese) brightest star.

Xie (Chinese) harmonious.

Ximenes (Spanish) a form of Simon.
Ximenez, Ximon, Ximun, Xymenes

Xing (Chinese) to rise, spring up.

Xing-Fu (Chinese) happy.

Xiong (Chinese) mighty; hero.

Xiu (Chinese) mastery.

Xi-Wang (Chinese) optimistic.

Xochiel, Xochtiel (Nahuatl) flower.

Xu (Chinese) open minded.

Xuan (Vietnamese) spring.

Xue (Chinese) snow; studious.

Xue-Fang (Chinese) snow; fragrant.

Xun (Chinese) fast.

Xylon (Greek) forest.

Xzavier (Basque) a form of Xavier.
Xzavaier, Xzaver, Xzavion, Xzavior, Xzvaier

Ya (Chinese) refined; correct.

Yacu (Quechua) water.

Yadid (Hebrew) friend; beloved.
Yedid

Yadira **G** (Hebrew) friend.

Yadon (Hebrew) he will judge.
Yadean, Yadin, Yadun

Yael **G** (Hebrew) a form of Jael.

Yafeu (Ibo) bold.

Yagil (Hebrew) he will rejoice.

Yago (Spanish) a form of James.

Yaguatí (Guarani) leopard.

Yahto (Lakota) blue.

Yahya (Arabic) living.
Yahye

Yair (Hebrew) he will enlighten.
Yahir

Yajas (Indian) fame.

Yakecen (Dene) sky song.

Yakez (Carrier) heaven.

Yakov (Russian) a form of Jacob.
Yaacob, Yaacov, Yaakov, Yachov, Yacoub, Yacov, Yakob, Yashko

Yale (German) productive. (English) old.

Yamato (Japanese) mountain; scaling heights.

Yamqui (Aymara) title of nobility, master.

Yan, Yann **B** (Russian) forms of John.
Yanichek, Yanick, Yanka, Yannick

Yana (Native American) bear.

Yanamayu (Quechua) black river.

Yancy (Native American) Englishman, Yankee.
Yan, Yance, Yancey, Yanci, Yansey, Yansy, Yantsey, Yauncey, Yauncy, Yency

Yanick, Yannick (Russian) familiar forms of Yan.
Yanic, Yanik, Yannic, Yannik, Yonic, Yonnik

Yanka (Russian) a familiar form of John.
Yanikm

Yanni (Greek) a form of John.
Ioannis, Yani, Yannakis, Yannis, Yanny, Yiannis, Yoni

Yanton (Hebrew) a form of Johnathon, Jonathon.

Yan-Yan (Chinese) swallow; elegant.

Yao (Ewe) born on Thursday.

Yao-Shih (Chinese) master of healing.

Yaphet (Hebrew) a form of Japheth.
Yapheth, Yefat, Yephat

Yarb (Gypsy) herb.

Yardan (Arabic) king.

Yarden (Hebrew) a form of Jordan.

Yardley (English) enclosed meadow.
Lee, Yard, Yardlea, Yardlee, Yardleigh, Yardly

Yarom (Hebrew) he will raise up.
Yarum

Yaron (Hebrew) he will sing; he will cry out.
Jaron, Yairon

Yasashiku (Japanese) gentle; polite.

Yash (Hindi) victorious; glory.

Yasha (Russian) a form of Jacob, James.
Yascha, Yashka, Yashko

Yashneil (Indian) famous; glorious; successful.

Yashodhar (Indian) one who has gained fame.

Yashwant (Hindi) glorious.

Yashwanth (Indian) always famous.

Yasin (Arabic) prophet.
Yasine, Yasseen, Yassin, Yassine, Yazen

Yasir (Afghan) humble; takes it easy. (Arabic) wealthy.
Yasar, Yaser, Yashar, Yasser

Yasuo (Japanese) restful.

Yasushi (Japanese) peace; historian.

Yasutaro (Japanese) peaceful.

Yates (English) gates.
Yeats

Yatin (Hindi) ascetic.

Yauar (Quechua) blood.

Yauarguacac (Quechua) he sheds tears of blood.

Yauarpuma (Quechua) puma blood.

Yauri (Quechua) lance, needle; copper.

Yavin (Hebrew) he will understand.
Jabin

Yawo (Akan) born on Thursday.

Yazid (Arabic) his power will increase.
Yazeed, Yazide

Ye (Chinese) professional work.

Yechiel (Hebrew) God lives.

Yedidya (Hebrew) a form of Jedidiah. See also Didi.
Yadai, Yedidia, Yedidiah, Yido

Yegor (Russian) a form of George. See also Egor, Igor.
Ygor

Yehoshua (Hebrew) a form of Joshua.
Yeshua, Yeshuah, Yoshua, Y'shua, Yushua

Yehoyakem (Hebrew) a form of Joachim, Joaquín.
Yakim, Yehayakim, Yokim, Yoyakim

Yehudi (Hebrew) a form of Judah.
Yechudi, Yechudit, Yehuda, Yehudah, Yehudit

Yelutci (Moquelumnan) bear walking silently.

Yemon (Japanese) guarding the palace.

Yen (Chinese) calming; capable.

Yeng-Wang-Yeh (Chinese) ruler of hell.

Yens (Vietnamese) calm.

Yeoman (English) attendant; retainer.
Yoeman, Youman

Yeremey (Russian) a form of Jeremiah.
Yarema, Yaremka, Yeremy, Yerik

Yervant (Armenian) king, ruler. History: an Armenian king.

Yeshaya (Hebrew) gift. See also Shai.

Yeshurun (Hebrew) right way.

Yeshwant (Indian) success

Yeshwanth (Indian) a person who attains fame and glory.

Yeska (Russian) a form of Joseph.
Yesya

Yestin (Welsh) just.

Yevgenyi (Russian) a form of Eugene.
Gena, Yevgeni, Yevgenij, Yevgeniy

Yigal (Hebrew) he will redeem.
Yagel, Yigael

Yi-Jie (Chinese) happy; pure.

Yi-Min (Chinese) happy; smart.

Yin (Chinese) flourishing.

Ying (Chinese) hawk, eagle.

Yirmaya (Hebrew) a form of Jeremiah.
Yirmayahu

Yishai (Hebrew) a form of Jesse.

Yisrael (Hebrew) a form of Israel.
Yesarel, Yisroel

Yitro (Hebrew) a form of Jethro.

Yitzchak (Hebrew) a form of Isaac. See also Itzak.
Yitzak, Yitzchok, Yitzhak

Ynaganta (Chamorro) a form of Inagangta.

Yngve (Swedish) ancestor; lord, master.

Yo (Cambodian) honest.

Yoakim (Slavic) a form of Jacob.
Yoackim

Yoan (German) a form of Johan, Johann.
Yoann

Yoav (Hebrew) a form of Joab.

Yochanan (Hebrew) a form of John.
  Yohanan

Yoel (Hebrew) a form of Joel.

Yog (Japanese) yoga practitioner.

Yoga (Japanese) he who makes things grow.

Yogendra (Indian) again; god of yoga.

Yogesh (Hindi) ascetic. Religion: another name for the Hindu god Shiva.

Yohan, Yohann (German) forms of Johan, Johann.
  Yohane, Yohanes, Yohanne, Yohannes, Yohans, Yohn

Yohance (Hausa) a form of John.

Yohei (Japanese) calm ocean.

Yojiro (Japanese) hopes.

Yokuto (Japanese) wing.

Yonah (Hebrew) a form of Jonah.
  Yona, Yonas

Yonatan (Hebrew) a form of Jonathan.
  Yonathan, Yonathon, Yonaton, Yonattan

Yong (Chinese) courageous.
  Yonge

Yong-Sun (Korean) dragon in the first position; courageous.

Yoni (Greek) a form of Yanni.
  Yonis, Yonnas, Yonny, Yony

Yoofi (Akan) born on Friday.

Yooku (Fante) born on Wednesday.

Yoonus (Indian) a prophet's name.

Yoram (Hebrew) God is high.
  Joram

Yorgos (Greek) a form of George.
  Yiorgos, Yorgo

Yori (Japanese) dependence.

York (English) boar estate; yew-tree estate.
  Yorick, Yorke, Yorker, Yorkie, Yorrick

Yorkoo (Fante) born on Thursday.

Yosef (Hebrew) a form of Joseph. See also Osip.
  Yoceph, Yoosuf, Yoseff, Yoseph, Yosief, Yosif, Yosuf, Yosyf, Yousef, Yusif

Yoselin **G** (Latin) a form of Jocelyn.

Yoshi (Japanese) good; respectful.

Yóshi (Japanese) adopted son.
  Yoshiki, Yoshiuki

Yoshiaki (Japanese) attractive.

Yoshihiro (Japanese) very good and righteous.

Yoshikatsu (Japanese) good.

Yoshikazu (Japanese) joyous; harmonious.

Yoshinobu (Japanese) goodness.

Yoshio (Japanese) giving.

Yoshiro (Japanese) good son.

Yoshiyahu (Hebrew) a form of Josiah.
  Yoshia, Yoshiah, Yoshiya, Yoshiyah, Yosiah

Yoskolo (Moquelumnan) breaking off pine cones.

Yosu (Hebrew) a form of Jesus.

Yosuke (Japanese) helper.

Yota (Japanese) big sun.

Yotimo (Moquelumnan) yellow jacket carrying food to its hive.

Yottoko (Native American) mud at the water's edge.

You (Chinese) first-rate.

Young (English) young.
  Yung

Young-Jae (Korean) pile of prosperity.

Young-Soo (Korean) keeping the prosperity.

Youri (Russian) a form of Yuri.

Yousef (Yiddish) a form of Joseph.
  Yousaf, Youseef, Youset, Youseph, Yousif, Youssef, Yousseff, Yousuf

Youssel (Yiddish) a familiar form of Joseph.
  Yussel

Yov (Russian) a short form of Yoakim.

Yovani (Slavic) a form of Jovan.
  Yovan, Yovanni, Yovanny, Yovany, Yovni

Yoyi (Hebrew) a form of George.

Yrjo (Finnish) a form of George.

Ysaoahy (Chuukese) a form of Isaoshi.

Ysidro (Greek) a short form of Isidore.

Yu (Chinese) universe.
  Yue

Yuan (Chinese) the original.

Yudell (English) a form of Udell.
 Yudale, Yudel

Yudhajit (Indian) victor in war.

Yudhishthir (Indian) eldest Pandava brother.

Yudhisthir, Yudishtra (Indian) firm in battle.

Yue-Wan (Chinese) happy; gentle.

Yue-Yan (Chinese) happy; beautiful.

Yue-Ying (Chinese) happy; smart; kind.

Yue-You (Chinese) happy; friendly.

Yuga (Japanese) distant; long time; river.

Yugandhar (Indian) celestial god.

Yuji (Japanese) snow.

Yu-Jie (Chinese) jade; pure.

Yuki 🄱🄶 (Japanese) snow.
 Yukiko, Yukio, Yuuki

Yukichi (Japanese) lucky snow.

Yukio (Japanese) gets what he wants.

Yul (Mongolian) beyond the horizon.

Yule (English) born at Christmas.

Yuli (Basque) youthful.

Yuma (Native American) son of a chief.

Yun (Chinese) fair, just.

Yunus (Turkish) a form of Jonah.

Yupanqui (Quechua) he who honors his ancestors.

Yurac (Quechua) white.

Yurcel (Turkish) sublime.

Yuri 🄶 (Russian, Ukrainian) a form of George. (Hebrew) a familiar form of Uriah.
 Yehor, Youri, Yura, Yure, Yuric, Yurii, Yurij, Yurik, Yurko, Yurri, Yury, Yusha

Yursa (Japanese) lily; delicate.

Yusif (Russian) a form of Joseph.
 Yuseph, Yusof, Yussof, Yusup, Yuzef, Yuzep

Yustyn (Russian) a form of Justin.
 Yusts

Yusuf (Arabic, Swahili) a form of Joseph.
 Yusef, Yusuff

Yuta (Japanese) very gentle; a great leader.

Yutaka (Japanese) abundant; prosperity.

Yuto (Japanese) he who travels a lot.

Yutu (Moquelumnan) coyote out hunting.

Yuval (Hebrew) rejoicing.

Yuvaraj, Yuvraj (Indian) prince, heir apparent.

Yuya (Japanese) he who is superior and gentle.

Yuyutsu (Indian) eager to fight.

Yuzuru (Japanese) he who is humble and modest.

Yves (French) a form of Ivar, Ives.
 Yvens, Yvon, Yyves

Yvon (French) a form of Ivar, Yves.
 Ivon, Yuvon, Yvan, Yvonne

Yvonne 🄶 (French) a form of Yvon.

Z

Z 🄱 (American) an initial used as a first name.

Zaafir (Indian) victorious.

Zaahid (Indian) abstemious; ascetic.

Zaahir (Indian) bright; shining.

Zac (Hebrew) a short form of Zachariah, Zachary.
 Zacc

Zacarias (Portuguese, Spanish) a form of Zachariah.
 Zacaria, Zacariah

Zacary (Hebrew) a form of Zachary.
 Zac, Zacaras, Zacari, Zacariah, Zacarias, Zacarie, Zacarious, Zacery, Zacory, Zacrye

Zaccary (Hebrew) a form of Zachary.
 Zac, Zaccaeus, Zaccari, Zaccaria, Zaccariah, Zaccary, Zaccea, Zaccharie, Zacchary, Zacchery, Zaccury

Zaccheus (Hebrew) innocent, pure.
 Zacceus, Zacchaeus, Zacchious

Zach (Hebrew) a short form of Zachariah, Zachary.

Zachari (Hebrew) a form of Zachary.
 Zacheri

Zacharia (Hebrew) a form of Zachary.
 Zacharya

Zachariah **B** (Hebrew) God remembered.
Zac, Zacarias, Zacarius, Zacary, Zaccary, Zach, Zacharias, Zachary, Zacharyah, Zachory, Zachury, Zack, Zakaria, Zako, Zaquero, Zecharia, Zechariah, Zecharya, Zeggery, Zeke, Zhachory

Zacharias (German) a form of Zachariah.
Zacarías, Zacharais, Zachariaus, Zacharius, Zackarias, Zakarias, Zecharias, Zekarias

Zacharie **B** (Hebrew) a form of Zachary.
Zachare, Zacharee, Zachurie, Zecharie

Zachary 🦆 **B** (Hebrew) a familiar form of Zachariah. History: Zachary Taylor was the twelfth U.S. president. See also Sachar, Sakeri.
Xachary, Zac, Zacary, Zaccary, Zach, Zacha, Zachaery, Zachaios, Zacharay, Zacharey, Zachari, Zacharia, Zacharias, Zacharie, Zacharry, Zachaury, Zachery, Zachory, Zachrey, Zachry, Zachuery, Zachury, Zack, Zackary, Zackery, Zackory, Zakaria, Zakary, Zakery, Zakkary, Zechary, Zechery, Zeke

Zachery (Hebrew) a form of Zachary.
Zacheray, Zacherey, Zacheria, Zacherias, Zacheriah, Zacherie, Zacherius, Zackery

Zachory (Hebrew) a form of Zachary.

Zachry (Hebrew) a form of Zachary.
Zachre, Zachrey, Zachri

Zack (Hebrew) a short form of Zachariah, Zachary.
Zach, Zak, Zaks

Zackary (Hebrew) a form of Zachary.
Zack, Zackari, Zacharia, Zackare, Zackaree, Zackariah, Zackarie, Zackery, Zackhary, Zackie, Zackree, Zackrey, Zackry

Zackery (Hebrew) a form of Zachery.
Zackere, Zackeree, Zackerey, Zackeri, Zackeria, Zackeriah, Zackerie, Zackerry

Zackory (Hebrew) a form of Zachary.
Zackoriah, Zackorie, Zacorey, Zacori, Zacory, Zacry, Zakory

Zadok (Hebrew) a short form of Tzadok.
Zaddik, Zadik, Zadoc, Zaydok

Zadornin (Basque) Saturn.

Zafir (Arabic) victorious.
Zafar, Zafeer, Zafer, Zaffar

Zahid (Arabic) self-denying, ascetic.
Zaheed

Zahir (Arabic) shining, bright.
Zahair, Zahar, Zaheer, Zahi, Zair, Zaire, Zayyir

Zahur (Swahili) flower.

Zaid (Arabic) increase, growth.
Zaied, Zaiid, Zayd

Zaide (Hebrew) older.

Zaim (Arabic) brigadier general.

Zain (English) a form of Zane.
Zaine

Zakaria (Hebrew) a form of Zachariah.
Zakaraiya, Zakareeya, Zakareeyah, Zakariah, Zakariya, Zakeria, Zakeriah

Zakariyya (Arabic) prophet. Religion: an Islamic prophet.

Zakary (Hebrew) a form of Zachery.
Zak, Zakarai, Zakare, Zakaree, Zakari, Zakarias, Zakarie, Zakarius, Zakariye, Zake, Zakhar, Zaki, Zakir, Zakkai, Zako, Zakqary, Zakree, Zakri, Zakris, Zakry

Zakery (Hebrew) a form of Zachary.
Zakeri, Zakerie, Zakiry

Zaki (Arabic) bright; pure. (Hausa) lion.
Zakee, Zakia, Zakie, Zakiy, Zakki

Zakia **BG** (Swahili) intelligent.

Zakkary (Hebrew) a form of Zachary.
Zakk, Zakkari, Zakkery, Zakkyre

Zako (Hungarian) a form of Zachariah.

Zale (Greek) sea strength.
Zayle

Zalmai (Afghan) young.

Zalman (Yiddish) a form of Solomon.
Zaloman

Zamiel (German) a form of Samuel.
Zamal, Zamuel

Zamir (Hebrew) song; bird.
Zameer

Zan (Italian) clown.
Zann, Zanni, Zannie, Zanny, Zhan

Zana **G** (Spanish) a form of Zanna (see Girls' Names).

Zander (Greek) a short form of Alexander.
Zandore, Zandra, Zandrae, Zandy

Zane **B** (English) a form of John.
Zain, Zayne, Zhane

Zanis (Latvian) a form of Janis.
Zannis

Zanvil (Hebrew) a form of Samuel.
Zanwill

Zapriel (Pohnpeian) a form of Gabriel.

Zaquan (American) a combination of the prefix Za + Quan.
Zaquain, Zaquon, Zaqwan

Zaqueo (Hebrew) pure, innocent.

Zareb (African) protector.

Zared (Hebrew) ambush.
Zaryd

Zarek (Polish) may God protect the king.
Zarik, Zarrick, Zerek, Zerick, Zerric, Zerrick

Zavier (Arabic) a form of Xavier.
Zavair, Zaverie, Zavery, Zavierre, Zavior, Zavyr, Zayvius, Zxavian

Zayit ☙ (Hebrew) olive.

Zayne (English) a form of Zane.
Zayan, Zayin, Zayn

Zdenek (Czech) follower of Saint Denis.

Ze (Chinese) duty.

Zeb (Hebrew) a short form of Zebediah, Zebulon.
Zev

Zebedee (Hebrew) a familiar form of Zebediah.
Zebadee

Zebediah (Hebrew) God's gift.
Zeb, Zebadia, Zebadiah, Zebedee, Zebedia, Zebidiah, Zedidiah

Zebulon (Hebrew) exalted, honored; lofty house.
Zabulan, Zeb, Zebulan, Zebulen, Zebulin, Zebulun, Zebulyn, Zev, Zevulon, Zevulun, Zhebulen, Zubin

Zechariah ☒ (Hebrew) a form of Zachariah.
Zecharia, Zecharian, Zecheriah, Zechuriah, Zekariah, Zekarias, Zeke, Zekeria, Zekeriah, Zekerya

Zed (Hebrew) a short form of Zedekiah.

Zedekiah (Hebrew) God is mighty and just.
Zed, Zedechiah, Zedekias, Zedikiah

Zedidiah (Hebrew) a form of Zebediah.

Zeeman (Dutch) seaman.

Zeév (Hebrew) wolf.
Zeévi, Zeff, Zif

Zeheb (Turkish) gold.

Zeke (Hebrew) a short form of Ezekiel, Zachariah, Zachary, Zechariah.

Zeki (Turkish) clever, intelligent.
Zeky

Zelgai (Afghan) heart.

Zelig (Yiddish) a form of Selig.
Zeligman, Zelik

Zelimir (Slavic) wishes for peace.

Zemar (Afghan) lion.

Zen (Japanese) religious. Religion: a form of Buddhism.

Zenda ⚥ (Czech) a form of Eugene.
Zhek

Zeng (Chinese) increase.

Zenjiro (Japanese) just second son.

Zeno (Greek) cart; harness. History: a Greek philosopher.
Zenan, Zenas, Zenon, Zino, Zinon

Zenón (Greek) he who lives.

Zenshiro (Japanese) just fourth-born son.

Zentaro (Japanese) just first-born son.

Zenzo (Italian) a form of Lorenzo.

Zephaniah (Hebrew) treasured by God.
Zaph, Zaphania, Zeph, Zephan

Zephyr ⚥☙ (Greek) west wind.
Zeferino, Zeffrey, Zephery, Zephire, Zephram, Zephran, Zephrin

Zero (Arabic) empty, void.

Zeroun (Armenian) wise and respected.

Zeshawn (American) a combination of the prefix Ze + Shawn.
Zeshan, Zeshaun, Zeshon, Zishaan, Zishan, Zshawn

Zesiro (Luganda) older of twins.

Zeus (Greek) living. Mythology: chief god of the Greek pantheon.

Zeusef (Portuguese) a form of Joseph.

Zev (Hebrew) a short form of Zebulon.

Zevi (Hebrew) a form of Tzvi.
Zhvie, Zhvy, Zvi

Zhane ⚥ (English) a form of Zane.

Zhang (Chinese) jade tablet.

Zhao (Chinese) vigorous.

Zhe (Chinese) philosopher.

Zhek (Russian) a short form of Evgeny.
Zhenechka, Zhenka, Zhenya

Zhen (Chinese) genuine.

Zheng (Chinese) honest.

Zhen-Juan (Chinese) precious; beautiful.

Zhìxin (Chinese) ambitious.
Zhi, Zhìhuán, Zhipeng, Zhi-yang, Zhìyuan

Zhong (Chinese) middle brother; loyal.

Zhora (Russian) a form of George.
Zhorik, Zhorka, Zhorz, Zhurka

Zhou (Chinese) to help.

Zhuàng (Chinese) strong.

Zia **G** (Hebrew) trembling; moving. (Arabic) light.
Ziah

Zigfrid (Latvian, Russian) a form of Siegfried.
Zegfrido, Zigfrids, Ziggy, Zygfryd, Zygi

Ziggy (American) a familiar form of Siegfried, Sigmund.
Ziggie

Zigor (Basque) punishment.

Zikomo (Nguni) thank-you.

Zilaba (Luganda) born while sick.
Zilabamuzale

Zimra (Hebrew) song of praise.
Zemora, Zimrat, Zimri, Zimria, Zimriah, Zimriya

Zimraan (Arabic) praise.

Zinan (Japanese) second son.

Zindel (Yiddish) a form of Alexander.
Zindil, Zunde

Zion (Hebrew) sign, omen; excellent. Bible: the name used to refer to Israel and to the Jewish people.
Tzion, Zyon

Ziskind (Yiddish) sweet child.

Ziv (Hebrew) shining brightly. (Slavic) a short form of Ziven.

Ziven (Slavic) vigorous, lively.
Zev, Ziv, Zivka, Zivon

Ziyad (Arabic) increase.
Zayd, Ziyaad

Zlatan (Czech) gold.
Zlatek, Zlatko

Zoami (Japanese) artistic figure.

Zoe **G** (Greek) life.

Zoé (Hindu) life.

Zoey **G** (Greek) a form of Zoe.

Zohar **B** (Hebrew) bright light.
Zohair

Zoki (Japanese) literary figure.

Zollie, Zolly (Hebrew) forms of Solly.
Zoilo

Zoltán (Hungarian) life.

Zorba (Greek) live each day.

Zorion (Basque) a form of Orion.
Zoran, Zoren, Zorian, Zoron, Zorrine, Zorrion

Zorya (Slavic) star; dawn.

Zosime (French) a form of Zosimus.
Zosyme

Zósimo (Greek) he who fights.

Zosimus (Greek) full of life.
Zosimos, Zosymos, Zosymus

Zótico (Greek) of a long life.

Zotikos (Greek) saintly, holy. Religion: a saint in the Eastern Orthodox Church.

Zotom (Kiowa) a biter.

Zsigmond (Hungarian) a form of Sigmund.
Ziggy, Zigmund, Zsiga

Zuberi (Swahili) strong.

Zubin (Hebrew) a short form of Zebulon.
Zuban, Zubeen, Zuben, Zubon, Zubyn

Zuhayr (Arabic) brilliant, shining.
Zyhair, Zuheer

Zuisho (Japanese) literary figure.

Zuka (Shona) sixpence.

Zuriel (Hebrew) God is my rock.
Zurial, Zuryal, Zuryel

Zygmunt (Polish) a form of Sigmund.
Zygismon, Zygismond, Zygismondo, Zygismun, Zygismund, Zygismundo, Zygysmon, Zygysmond, Zygysmondo, Zygysmun, Zygysmund, Zygysmundo

Also from Meadowbrook Press

✦ *The Official Lamaze Guide*
The first official guide to pregnancy and childbirth presenting the Lamaze philosophy of natural childbirth, this book gives expectant mothers confidence in their ability to give birth free of unnecessary medical intervention, and provides detailed information couples can use to deal with whatever issues arise.

✦ *Pregnancy, Childbirth, and the Newborn*
More complete and up-to-date than any other pregnancy guide, this remarkable book is the "bible" for childbirth educators. Now revised with a greatly expanded treatment of pregnancy tests, complications, and infections; an expanded list of drugs and medications (plus advice for uses); and a brand-new chapter on creating a detailed birth plan.

✦ *The Simple Guide to Having a Baby*
All the basic knowledge first-time parents need for a successful pregnancy and childbirth. This is a simple, just-the-facts guide for expectant parents who want only the most important, down-to-earth how-to information covering health during pregnancy, labor and delivery, and care for a new baby.

✦ *First-Year Baby Care*
This is one of the leading baby-care books to guide you through your baby's first year. Newly revised, it contains the latest, greatest information on the basics of baby care, including bathing, diapering, medical facts, and feeding your baby.

We offer many more titles written to delight, inform, and entertain.
To order books with a credit card or browse our full
selection of titles, visit our website at:

www.meadowbrookpress.com

or call toll-free to place an order, request a free catalog, or ask a question:

1-800-338-2232

Meadowbrook Press • 5451 Smetana Drive • Minnetonka, MN • 55343